STO

Y0-ACG-132

Information Please business almanac & sourcebook

Praise for
The Information Please®
Business Almanac

"As thorough an information compendium as can be found in one
volume." — *The Orange County Register*

"An indispensable resource."
— Jay Conrad Levinson, author of *Guerrilla Marketing*

"Highly recommended." — *The Library Journal*

"An excellent addition to the business bookshelf."
— *The Internet Business Journal*

"These facts could make you filthy rich." — *The Wall Street Journal*

"The Business Bible." — CBS Radio

"The best book I have seen since I have opened my store."
— President of Office Max

"It will get much use." — Faith Popcorn

"Wonderful to leaf through but pointedly relevant time and again…
Will become a valued time-saving resource."
— Mitchell T. Rabkin, M.D., President,
Beth Israel Hospital, Boston

"A wonderful book full of great information."
— Small Business Crain's Detroit

"Filled with interesting information."
— Paul Edwards, author of *Working from Home*

"This is an amazingly varied compendium of business information."
— Michael Perish, Business Librarian, University of Indiana

"A must have!" — Tim Collins, WBCK–AM, Battle Creek, MI

"A bargain." — Bob Kwesell and Ken Sterling,
    WIBC–AM, Indianapolis, IN

"Phenomenal!" — Duke Brooks, WETT–AM, Ocean City, MD

"A great reference! I love having it on my desk!"
    — Evelyn Nuessenbaum, CNN, "Your Money"

"The *Almanac*'s layout facilitates quick and easy lookups."
    — Peter Latusek, Jackson Library,
        Stanford Business School

"Invaluable... Easy to access and understand." — Zig Ziglar

"It is something we use all the time. We are delighted to have it."
    — Jill Parchuck, Columbia Business School Library

"Concise, with a great deal of information."
    — Rose Marie Lorenze, Head Librarian, IBM Corporation

"Worthwhile!"
    — Betty Schneider, Feldberg Library,
        Tuck Business School, Dartmouth College

"An amazingly varied compendium of business information."
    — Michael Perish, Capital Spea Library, University of Indiana

"A great product!" — Thom Hartman, The Newsletter Factory

"A blockbuster! Contains everything you never knew could be so
    invaluable." — Sid Cato, President, Cato Communications, Inc.

"I think every business teacher should have one in his/her
    classroom."— Laurie Hansen, business teacher

"Indispensable information... Essential... High quality... Great buy."
    — *Success* magazine

THE 1996
INFORMATION PLEASE®
BUSINESS ALMANAC &
SOURCEBOOK

THE 1996 INFORMATION PLEASE®
BUSINESS ALMANAC &
SOURCEBOOK

Seth Godin, Editor

HOUGHTON MIFFLIN COMPANY
Boston • New York

Copyright ©1995 by Seth Godin Productions, Inc.

For information about permission to reproduce selections from this book in print form write to Permissions, Houghton Mifflin Company, 215 Park Avenue South, New York, New York 10003. For information about permission to reproduce selections from this book in non-print form write to Permissions, Inso Corporation, 31 St. James Avenue, Boston, Massachusetts, 02116-4101.

INFORMATION PLEASE and INFORMATION PLEASE ALMANAC are registered trademarks of Inso Corporation.

ISBN: 0-395-75450-3 (Sourcebook version)
       0-395-75451-1 (Software version)

ISSN: 1070-4639

Printed in the United States of America

DOW 10 9 8 7 6 5 4 3 2 1

CONTENTS

E-Mail on Demand

The Information Please Business Almanac offers a variety of resources for free via e-mail. Simply send a message to one of the addresses listed below, and you will receive the desired document within minutes.

How to Receive a Document by E-Mail

1. Compose a message with one of the addresses listed below as the destination, depending on which document you wish to receive. You can also send mail to info@almanac.yoyo.com for an index of all available items. The *Business Almanac* may add new documents periodically.

2. You can put anything into the subject line and the body, as long as the address is correct.

3. Send the message.

4. You should receive your document within a few seconds or minutes depending on the type of service you are using.

5. If you have any questions or comments, send mail to almanac@sgp.com. You can also write to the *Business Almanac* at Box 321, Dobbs Ferry, NY 10522.

E-Mail on Demand Items

- Index of Available Documents. A list of all documents available for free via e-mail, including all items listed here as well as new items. Send mail to info@almanac.yoyo.com

- *Auto Theft and Damage*. Tables of auto registrations and thefts, average lost payment, and claim frequency, from the FBI and the Highway Loss Data Institute. Send mail to theft@almanac.yoyo.com

- *Causes of Business Failures*. Seven primary reasons for business failure and incidence of failure in nine sectors of business. Send mail to failures@almanac.yoyo.com

- *Consumer Price Indexes*. Table of consumer price indexes by major groups. Send mail to consumer@almanac.yoyo.com

- *Domestic Airline Hubs*. The top domestic airlines and their major hubs, from *Business Travel News*. Send mail to hubs@almanac.yoyo.com

- *eMarketing*. A book from the editor of the *Information Please Business Almanac* on high-technology methods of marketing products, from the Internet to database marketing to multimedia. The entire text of this book is available for free. Send mail to emarketing@almanac.yoyo.com

- *Employer Costs*. Tables of employer costs for employee compensation and employees with pension plans or group health plans. Send mail to employer@almanac.yoyo.com

- *Executive's Yellow Pages*. Business service phone numbers, from the first coat-pocket-sized nationwide book of important phone numbers for the executive. Send mail to yellow@almanac.yoyo.com

- *Free Government Resources*. List of subject bibliographies available from the Government Printing Office. Send mail to resource@almanac.yoyo.com

- *Government Spending*. Tables of federal budget outlays, gross federal debt, and federal receipts by source, from the 1994 *Statistical Abstract of the United States*. Send mail to spending@almanac.yoyo.com

- *Government Publications*. A list of the most popular government publications and how many copies have sold to date. Send mail to publications@almanac.yoyo.com

- *Guerrilla Marketing Book*. The advertising section from *The Guerrilla Marketing Handbook*, written by Guerrilla Marketing guru Jay Conrad Levinson and *Information Please Business Almanac* editor Seth Godin. Send mail to guerrilla@almanac.yoyo.com

- *Labor Force*. Tables of civilian labor force by educational attainment, self-employed workers and employed workers by selected characteristics. Send mail to labor@almanac.yoyo.com

- *Law Firm Fees*. A description of types of fees and suggestions for negotiating a billing method. Send mail to lawfees@almanac.yoyo.com

- *Manhattan Address Locator*. A chart that makes it easy to find a location in Manhattan if you know the address. Send mail to nyc@almanac.yoyo.com

- *Money-Saving Tips*. Report by Kimberly Stanséll, named one of "America's Best Penny-Pinchers" by *Home Office Computing* magazine. Cost-cutting strategies businesses can use to boost their profits. Send mail to money@almanac.yoyo.com

- *Newsletters*. "Balancing Promotional Content with News" from the book *Marketing with Newsletters* by Elaine Floyd, owner of Newsletter Resources and author of the newsletter *Newsletter News & Resources*. Send mail to newsletter@almanac.yoyo.com

- *NLRB Field Offices*. Names, addresses, and phone numbers of the field offices of the National Labor Relations Board. Send mail to nlrb@almanac.yoyo.com

E-Mail on Demand (cont'd)

- *Paris Anglophone.* One hundred important phone numbers from *Paris Anglophone*, the most up-to-date, comprehensive directory of American, British, Irish, Canadian, and Australian businesses, organizations, services, and activities in France. Send mail to paris@almanac.yoyo.com

- *Producer Price Indexes.* A detailed table of producer price indexes for selected commodities. Send mail to producer@almanac.yoyo.com

- *Publicity.* "66 Ways to Make Your Business Newsworthy." Dozens of creative ideas for becoming worthy of media coverage and then getting into print or on the air, from Marcia Yudkin, Ph.D., author of *Six Steps to Free Publicity.* Send mail to publicity@almanac.yoyo.com

- *Time Spent at Work.* Tables of gross average weekly earnings and hours worked for selected non-manufacturing and manufacturing industries. Send mail to time@almanac.yoyo.com

- *Transportation from Airport.* Tables of taxi fares from major domestic and international airports to the cities they serve. Send mail to transport@almanac.yoyo.com

- *U.S. Investment Abroad.* Tables of U.S. direct investment abroad, historical cost basis, from *Survey of Current Business.* Send mail to invest@almanac.yoyo.com

- *U.S. Exports and Imports.* A table of U.S. exports and imports for six major countries. Send mail to exports@almanac.yoyo.com

- *World Gross Domestic Product.* A table of the gross domestic product for 24 major countries, from the OECD. Send mail to product@almanac.yoyo.com

How to Use This Book

There are three easy ways to access the *Almanac*:

Chapter by Chapter

The front and back inside covers give a map of the organization of the *Almanac*, together with page numbers for each chapter. At the start of each chapter you'll find a listing of every article contained in the chapter.

The Table of Contents

The *Almanac* is organized in much the same way a company is. Information about doing business abroad is in the International section, while data on brand names and ad agencies are listed under Marketing. The Table of Contents lists each chapter, together with the name of each article in that chapter.

The Index

A comprehensive index of companies, reference sources, and basic concepts is located at the back of the book, in the Reference section.

Feedback

The editors of the *Almanac* would like to hear from you. Tell us your likes and dislikes, and let us know what information you'd like to see included in future volumes. While we can't answer every letter, we promise that each suggestion will be carefully reviewed and included wherever possible.

To reach the editorial staff:

Internet: almanac@sgp.com
Fax: (914) 693-8132
Mail: Box 321, Dobbs Ferry, NY 10522

Editorial and Production Staff

Editor in Chief:	Seth Godin
Senior Editor:	Carol Markowitz
Acquisition Editor:	Steve Lewers
Research:	David Bloom Gwen Helene Bronson Lauren Fox Vic Lapuzynski Anne Shepherd
Technical Layout:	Martin Erb Julie Maner
Consulting Editor:	Michael Cader
Editorial Assistance:	Robin Dellabough Lisa DiMona Nicole Goldstein Wendy Hall Ellen Kenny Cynthia Liu Megan O'Connor Anthony Schneider Karen Watts Lucy Wood
Additional Research:	José Arroyo Kate Grossman Marcia Layton Margery Mandell
Data Entry:	Louise Anderson Becky McPeters Mark Underwager
Copyediting:	Jolanta Benal
Proofreading:	Phyllis Kosminsky
Design:	Charles Kreloff
Template Design:	Lisa Jahred
Troubleshooting:	Steve Ketchum
Houghton Mifflin:	Doug Eisenhart Tom Endyke Bob Enos Dorothy Henderson Chris Leonesio Elizabeth Mosimann Marnie Patterson Bill Trippe Steve Vana-Paxhia
Output:	R.R. Donnelley & Sons
Maps:	MicroMaps

ACKNOWLEDGMENTS

More than 500 people and organizations contributed valuable insights, information, and advice to the creation of this *Almanac*. This is a partial list of those who were so gracious in their help.

Individuals:

Kathleen Antonini, United Parcel Service
Talie Bar-Nadav, Organization Resources Counselors
Tom Barrett, Touch Tone Services
Tracy Bell, *American Banker*
Dr. Beverly Berger, Federal Laboratory Consortium
Jody Beutler, *Mergerstat*^{SM} *Review*, Merrill Lynch & Co.
Rick Boyle, Center for Advanced Purchasing Studies
Shelly Burton, *North American Office Market Review*, Building Owners and Managers Association
Peggy Castillo, *Entrepreneur Magazine*
Paul Clolery, *NonProfit Times*
David Cudaback, *Institutional Investor*
Kathleen Dempsey, *Corporate Real Estate Executive*, NACORE
Lisa Kay Dowd, Sprint
Steven Dworman, *Infomercial Marketing Report*
John Gawalt , National Science Foundation
Tom Gibson, *Financial World*
Cindy Giglio, Standard & Poor's
Stephen Gold, Tax Foundation
Riana Goodstein, *Accounting Today*
Jill Hancock, Wells Fargo
Herschell Gordon Lewis
Dianna Losey, *Interior Design*
Tom Mariam, American Stock Exchange
Alice Teppler Marlin, Council on Economic Priorities
John McIlquham, *NonProfit Times*
Charlie McKuen, GPO Marketing
Meara McLaughlin, *Air Charter Guide*, Boston Aviation Services
Jonathan Meigs, *Frequent Flyer*
Ira Mayer, *The Licensing Letter*, EPM Communications
Terry Murphy, National Business Incubation Association
Rebecca Oakes, National Foundation for Women Business Owners
Jack O'Dwyer, J.R. O'Dwyer
Marian Nelson, *Guide to Worldwide Postal Code & Address Formats*
Peter Packer, Runzheimer
Karen Pratt, Kinder, Lydenberg, Domini & Co.
Sandee Richardson, *Infomercial Marketing Report*
Allan Ripp, The Zagat Survey
Abigail Roeder-Johnson
Art Samansky, Securities Industry Association
Susan Scott, *Upside*
Stan Simon, Simmons Market Research Bureau

Art Spinella, CNW Marketing Research
Laura Stepanek, *Security Distributing & Marketing*
Judith Sussman, Pezzano & Co.
Toby Taylor, Futures Industry Association
Ed Welch
Barbara Zimmerman, B Z Rights and Permissions

Steve Lewers, Kristin Robbins, Andy Roberts, Debbie Applefield, Alan Andrés, Steve Vana-Paxhia, Marty Grief, Joe Kanon, Bob Moses, and Bob Enos were responsible for much of the vision that helped us refine the *Almanac* and bring it to its present form.

Finally, thanks to all the spouses and family members who were so patient, insightful, and supportive.

Organizations:

9 to 5, Working Women Education Fund; A.M. Best; Abelow Response; Addison-Wesley; ADP; Adweek Directories; Affiliated Warehouse Companies; AFL-CIO; Air & Waste Management Association; Alternative Press Center; AMACOM; American Academy of Actuaries; American Arbitration Association; American Association of Advertising Agencies; American Association of Port Authorities; American Bankers Association; American Bar Association; American Institute of Architects; American League of Lobbyists; American Management Association; American Marketing Association; American Productivity and Quality Center; American Red Cross; American Society for Interior Designers; American Society for Quality Control; American Society for Training and Development; American Society of Journalists and Authors; American Stock Exchange; American Translators Association; Amusement Business; Andrews & McMeel; Art Directors Club; Association of Alternative Newsweeklies; Association of Independent Colleges and Schools; Association of Management Consulting Firms; Association of National Advertisers; Association of Shareware Professionals; Association of Small Business Development Centers; Association of Venture Clubs; AT&T; Avon Books; Axiom Information Resources; B Z Rights and Permissions; B. Klein Publications; Bacon's Information; BBP/Prentice-Hall Newsletters; Bergano Books; Bill Communications; Blenheim Franchise Shows; Blumberg's Law Products; Bob Adams; Boston Aviation Services; Boston Stock Exchange; Buck Consultants; Building Owners and Managers Association; Bureau of Economic Analysis; Bureau of National Affairs; Business Council for International Understanding; Business Information Service for the Newly Independent States; Business One Irwin; Business Research Publications; Business Research Services;

Business Trend Analysts; Buyers Laboratory; Cass Communications; CDA Investment Technologies; CDC National AIDS Clearinghouse; CEEM Information Services; Celebrity Service; Center for Advanced Purchasing Studies; Chambers of Commerce; Chicago Board of Trade; Chicago Board Options Exchange; Chicago Mercantile Exchange; Chicago Stock Exchange; Child and Waters; Cincinnati Stock Exchange; Citadel Press; Citibank; Clio Awards; CNW Marketing Research; Color Marketing Group; Columbia Books; Commerce Clearing House; The Conference Board; Congressional Quarterly; Conney Safety Products; Consulting Psychologists Press; Consumers Union; Contemporary Books; Cooperative Education Association; Corporate Agents; Council of State Governments; Council on Economic Priorities; The Dartnell Corporation; Datapro Research; Dearborn Financial Publishing; Demand Research; Direct Marketing Association; Doubleday; Dow Jones-Irwin; Du Pont Quality Management & Technology Center; Dun & Bradstreet Receivable Management Services; Dun's Marketing Services; "E" Awards Program, International Trade Administration; Earth Share; Earthworks Press; Elsevier-Dutton; Employee Benefit Research Institute; Environmental Action Coalition; Environmental Federation of New York; EPM Communications; Equal Employment Opportunity Commission; Executive Enterprises Publications; Export-Import Bank; Facts on File; Families and Work Institute; Federal Express; Find/SVP; The Foundation Center; Frank Russell; Freedom of Information Clearinghouse; Frost & Sullivan; Futures Industry Association; Gale Research; Grant Thornton; Greenwood Publishing Group; Greeting Card Association; Grey House Publishing; HarperCollins; Harvard Business Services; Hay/Huggins; Health Insurance Association of America; Henry Holt; Hewitt Associates; Houghton Mifflin; Industrial Designers Society of America; Information USA; Institute for Personality Ability Testing; Institute of Clean Air Companies; Institute of International Education; Institute of Outdoor Advertising; Institute of Packaging Professionals; Institute of Real Estate Management; Institute of Scrap Recycling Industries; Insurance Fund Foundation; Insurance Information Institute; Intercultural Press; Internal Revenue Service; International Advertising Association; International Association of Convention and Visitors Bureaus; International Business Brokers Association; International Currency Analysis; International Franchise Association; International Licensing and Industry Merchandisers Association; International Quality and Productivity Center; International Society for Intercultural Education, Training and Research; Investment Company Institute; Irwin Professional Publishing; J. R. O'Dwyer; Jobs for the Future; John Wiley & Sons; Johnson and Johnson; Jossey-Bass; Journal of Commerce; Judicial Arbitration and Mediation Services; Kemper National Insurance; Kinder, Lydenberg, Domini & Co.; Landauer Real Estate Counselors; Leon Henry; Liberty Press, McGraw-Hill; Libraries Unlimited; Lipper Analytical Services; LNA/Arbitron Multimedia Services; London Stock Exchange; Luce Press Clippings; Macmillan; Magazine Publishers of America; Manufacturers' Agents National Association; Manufacturers' Alliance for Productivity and Innovation; McCann Erickson; McGraw-Hill; MCI Communications; Merrill Lynch & Co.; Midwest Stock Exchange; Minerva Books; Moody's Investor Services; Morningstar; Multiprint; NACORE International; National AIDS Clearing House; National Alliance for Choice in Giving; National Association of Broadcasters; National Association of Manufacturers; National Association of Securities Dealers; National Association of Small Business Investment Companies; National Association of Television Program Executives; National Association of Temporary Services; National Automated Clearing House Association; National Business Education Association; National Business Incubation Association; National Career Network; National Center for Standards and Certification Information; National Coalition for Advanced Manufacturing; National Coalition for Advanced Technology; National Commercial Finance Association; National Commission for Cooperative Education; National Committee for Responsive Philanthropy; National Federation of Export Associations; National Foreign Trade Council; National Foreman's Institute; National Foundation for Women Business Owners; National Home Study Council; National Institute for Aviation Research; National Institute of Standards and Technology; National Insurance Association; National Labor Relations Board; National Leadership Coalition on AIDS; National Materials Exchange Network; National Occupational Information Coordinating Committee; National Organization for Women; National Real Estate Index; National Recycling Coalition; National Register Publishing; National Safety Council; National Science Foundation; National Small Business United; National Society for Experiential Education; National Solid Wastes Management Association; National Speakers Association; New York Department of Health; New York Mercantile Exchange; New York State Department of Economic Development; New York State Division of Alcoholism and Alcohol Abuse; New York Stock Exchange; Nielsen Media Research; Nikkei America; Nolo Press; North American Publishing; Northwestern National Life; NYNEX Information Resources; The Oasis Press/PSI Research; Occupational Safety and Health Administration; Office Planners and Users Group; Omnigraphics; On Location Publishing; The One Club; Organization for Economic Cooperation and Development; Organization Resources Counselors; Outdoor Advertising Association of America; Overseas Private Investment; Pacific Stock Exchange; Package Design Council; PC Data; Pezzano & Co.; Philadelphia Stock Exchange; Plume; Post Import Export Reporting Service; Praeger Publishers; Prentice-Hall Information Services; Printbooks; Professional Dynametric

Programs; Professional Lobbying Consulting Center; Promotional Products Association; Public Relations Society of America; Publishers Information Bureau; QCI Training & Educational Materials & Services; Quigley Publishing; R.R. Bowker; Radio Advertising Bureau; Radio Network Association; Rand McNally; Reed Publishing; The Reference Press; Research Institute of America; Roper Starch; Royal Wholesale Banner; Runzheimer; Sales & Marketing Executives of Greater New York; Salomon Brothers; Scangrafics; Securities Data; Securities Industry Association; Self Counsel Press; Sheshunoff Information Services; Simmons Market Research Bureau; Simon & Schuster; Small Business Administration; Small Business Foundation of America; Society of Actuaries; Society of Industrial and Office Realtors; Society of the Plastics Industry; Solid Waste Assistance Program; Southern Waste Information Exchange; Specialty Advertising Association of Greater New York; Sprint; The Spy Store; SQAD; St. Martin's Press; Standard & Poor's; Statistical Research/RADAR; Suburban Publishing of Connecticut; Tax Foundation; Thomas International Publishing; Thomson & Thomson; Time; Todd Publications; Tokyo Stock Exchange; Tompkins Associates; Trade Information Center; Trademark Research; Travel Industry Association of America; U.S. and Foreign Commercial Service; U.S. Chamber of Commerce; U.S. Conference of Mayors; U.S. Congress; U.S. Deparment of Transportation, Office of the Secretary of Transportation; U.S. Department of Commerce; U.S. Department of Commerce, Advanced Technology Program; U.S. Department of Commerce, Bureau of Economic Analysis; U.S. Department of Commerce, Economics and Statistics Administration, Office of Business Analysis; U.S.

Department of Justice, Internal Security Division; U.S. Department of Labor, Bureau of Labor Statistics; U.S. Department of Labor, Bureau of Labor Statistics, Office of Compensation and Working Conditions; U.S. Department of Labor, Bureau of Labor Statistics, Office of International Prices; U.S. Department of Labor, Bureau of Labor Statistics, Office of Productivity and Technology; U.S. Department of Labor, Ergonomics Division; U.S. Department of State; U.S. Environmental Protection Agency; U.S. Environmental Protection Agency, Control Technology Center; U.S. Environmental Protection Agency, Office of Solid Waste; U.S. Federal Information Center; U.S. Federal Laboratory Consortium; U.S. Federal Reserve Board; U.S. Federal Trade Commission; U.S. General Services Administration; U.S. Government Printing Office; U.S. International Trade Administration; U.S. International Trade Administration, Office of Public Affairs; U.S. International Trade Commission; U.S. Postal Service; U.S. Securities and Exchange Commission; U.S. Small Business Administration; U.S. Tradmark Association; U.S. Travel and Tourism Administration; U.S. Travel Data Center; UNIPUB; United Parcel Service; Upstart Publishing; Urban Land Institute; Van Nostrand Reinhold; Vance Bibliographies; Ventana Press; Venture Economics; Video Storyboard Tests; VR Business Brokers; W. Foulsham & Co.; Walters International Speakers Bureau; Warner Books; Warren, Gorham & Lamont; Washington Speakers Bureasu; Wells Fargo; West Publishing; William M. Mercer; Wilshire Associates; Women's Bureau, U.S. Dept. of Labor; Women's Legal Defense Fund; The World Bank; World Trade Centers Association; The Zagat Survey

Reference Sources

The *Information Please Business Almanac* would also like to mention the following invaluable reference sources:

43 Proven Ways to Raise Capital for Your Small Business, Dearborn Financial Publishing
50 Simple Things You Can Do to Save the Earth, Earthworks Press
The 90-Minute Hour, Plume
The 100 Best Companies to Work For in America, Doubleday
Access EPA, Environmental Protection Agency
Accounting Desk Book, Prentice-Hall
Accounting Today
Advanced Selling Power
Advertising Age
Adweek
Adweek Agency Directory, Adweek
Air Charter Guide, Boston Aviation Services
Air Traveler's Handbook, St. Martin's Press
Almanac of Business and Industrial Financial Ratios, Prentice-Hall
AMA Guide for Meeting and Event Planners, Gale Research
AMA Managament Handbook, American Management Association
America's Best Restaurants, The Zagat Survey
American Academy of Actuaries Yearbook, American Acedemy of Actuaries
American Almanac of Jobs and Salaries, Avon Books
The American Almanac, The Reference Press
American Banker
American Demographics

American Export Register, Thomas International Publishing
American Lobbyists Directory, Gale Research
Annual of Advertising, Editorial and Television Art and Design, Art Directors Club
ASTD Buyer's Guide & Consultant Directory, American Society for Training and Development
Auto Rental News
Bacon's Newspaper/Magazine Directory, Bacon's Information
Barron's: The Dow Jones Business and Financial Weekly
A Basic Guide to Exporting, U.S. Department of Commerce
Before & After
Bergano's Register of Interntional Importers
Best's Insurance Reports
Best's Review
The Better World Investment Guide, Prentice-Hall
Beyond Race and Gender, American Management Association
Boardwatch
Bond Guide, Standard and Poor's
The Bordwin Letter: Preventive Law for Business
Bulletin to Management
Business America
Business Forms on File, Facts on File
Business Franchise Guide, Commerce Clearing House
Business History of the World: A Chronology, Greenwood Publishing Group
Business Information Alert
Business One Irwin Business & Investment Almanac, Business One Irwin
Business Protocol, John Wiley & Sons
Business Rankings and Salaries Index, Gale Research
Business Statistics, Bureau of Economic Analysis
Business Travel News
Business Week
Buyers Laboratory Test Reports: Reports on Office Products, Buyers Laboratory
C.Q. Almanac, Congressional Quarterly
Celebrity Directory, Axiom Information Resources
Census of Manufacturers, U.S. Government Printing Office
Chronicle of Philanthropy
Co-op Source Directory, National Register Publishing
College Blue Book: Occupational Education, Macmillan
Commerce Business Daily
Common Market Reports, Commerce Clearing House
Compensation and Benefits Manager's Report, BBP/Prentice-Hall Newsletters
Competitive Edge
Computer Industry Almanac
Computers and Computing Information Resources, Gale Research
Consultants and Consulting Organizations, Gale Research
Consumer Reports Travel Buying Guide, Consumers Union
Consumer Reports Travel Letter
Consumer Sourcebook, Gale Research
Copyright Basics, U.S. Government Printing Office
Copyrights, Patents, and Trademarks, Liberty Press, McGraw-Hill
Corporate 500: The Directory of Corporate Philanthropy, Gale Research
Corporate ARTnews
The Corporate Finance Sourcebook, National Register Publishing Company
Corporate Real Estate Executive, NACORE International
Corporate Travel
Corporation Forms, Prentice-Hall Information Services
Crain's New York Business
The Crystal Report
Datapro Office Products Evaluation Service, Datapro Research Corporation
Deadlines
Design Access
Design and Drafting News
Design for a Livable Planet, HarperCollins
Directory of Accredited Home Study Schools, National Home Study Council
Directory of Accredited Institutions, Association of Independent Colleges and Schools
Directory of Conventions, Bill Communications

Directory of Leading U.S. Export Management Companies, Bergano Books
The Directory of Mail Order Catalogs, Grey House Publishing
Directory of Mailing List Companies, Todd Publications
Directory of Manufacturers' Sales Agencies, Manufacturers' Agents National Association
Directory of U.S. Importers/Exporters, Journal of Commerce
Directory of United States Importers, Journal of Commerce
The Directory to Industrial Design in the United States, Van Nostrand Reinhold
Discount Store News
Do's and Taboos Around the World, John Wiley & Sons
Dun's Employment Opportunites Directory, Dun's Marketing Services
Economic Indicators
The Economist
Effective Business Communication, Houghton Mifflin
Employment Coordinator, Research Institute of America
Engineering News Record, McGraw-Hill
Entertainment Weekly
Entrepreneur Magazine
The Entrepreneur and Small Business Problem Solver, Dow Jones-Irwin
The Europa World Year Book, Gale Research
Every Manager's Guide to Firing, Irwin Professional Publishing
The Excutive Desk Register of Publicly Held Companies, Demand Research
Executive Compensation Alert
Export Profits: A Guide for Small Business, Upstart Publishing
Exportise, Small Business Foundation of America
FAA Statistical Handbook of Aviation, U.S. Government Printing Office
The Fact Book, Insurance Information Institute
Federal Regulatory Directory, Congressional Quarterly
Financial World
The Five Minute Interview, John Wiley & Sons
Forbes
Foreign Trade Barriers
Fortune
Franchise Bible: A Comprehensive Guide, The Oasis Press/PSI Research
Franchise Opportunities Guide, International Franchise Association
Franchising World
Frequent Flyer
Fundamentals of Business Law, Prentice-Hall
Fundamentals of Employee Benefit Programs, Employee Benefit Research Institute
Global Investor
Grant Thornton Survey of American Manufacturers
Graphic Arts Monthly
Graphics Arts Monthly Printing Industry Sourcebook
Green MarketAlert
Greetings Magazine - Buyers Guide Directory
Guerrilla Financing, Houghton Mifflin
Guerrilla Marketing, Houghton Mifflin
Guide to Worldwide Postal Code & Address Formats
Guidebook to Fair Employment Practices, Commerce Clearing House
Handbook of Business Information, Libraries Unlimited
Harvard Business Review
Hiring the Best, Bob Adams
How to Buy Foreign Stocks and Bonds: A Guide, HarperCollins
How to Cut Your Company's Health Care Costs, Prentice-Hall Press
How to Develop an Employee Handbook, The Dartnell Corporation
How to Fire an Employee, Facts on File
How to Form Your Own Corporation Without a Lawyer for Under $75.00, Dearborn Financial Publishing
The Hulbert Financial Digest
The Human Resources Yearbook, Prentice-Hall
I.D. Magazine
Inc.
Inc. Yourself, Warner Books
Incorporating Your Business, Contemporary Books
Infomercial Marketing Report
The Information Please Almanac, Houghton Mifflin

InsideFlyer
The Insider's Guide to Franchising, AMACOM
Institutional Investor
Interior Design
International Business Practices, U.S. Department of Commerce
The International Businesswoman of the 1990s: A Guide to Success in the Global Marketplace, Praeger Publishers
International Directory of Corporate Affiliations, Reed Publishing
International Marketing Handbook, Gale Research
International Price Indexes: Export and Import, U.S. Department of Labor, Bureau of Labor Statistics, Office of International Prices
Investing in Employee Health, Jossey-Bass
Investment Dealers' Digest
The Investor's Dictionary, John Wiley & Sons
Investors Business Daily
Journal of Commerce
The Journal of the Small Business Forum
Law and Legal Information Directory, Gale Research
Law Dictionary for Non-Lawyers, West Publishing
The Legal Guide for Starting and Running a Small Business, Nolo Press
Legal Research: How to Find and Understand the Law, Nolo Press
Legal Thesaurus, Macmillan
Lesko's Info-Power, Information USA
The Licensing Journal
The Licensing Letter
The Lobbying Handbook, Professional Lobbying Consulting Center
London Stock Exchange Fact Book, London Stock Exchange
Louis Rukeyser's Business Almanac, Simon & Schuster
MacUser
Macweek
Mail Order Business Directory, B. Klein Publications
Mail Order Product Guide, Todd Publications
Marketer's Guide to Media, Adweek Directories
Marketing Made Easier, Todd Publications
Meetings and Conventions, Reed Travel Group
Mergerstat^{SM} Review, Merrill Lynch & Co.
Money
Moody's Bank and Finance Manual, Moody's Investors Service
Moody's Bond Record, Moody's Investors Service
Moody's Handbook of OTC Stocks, Moody's Investors Service
Moody's International Manual, Moody's Investors Service
Motion Picture Almanac, Quigley Publishing
Multinational Executive Travel Companion, Suburban Publishing of Connecticut
Mutual Fund Fact Book, Investment Company Institute
NASDAQ Fact Book and Company Directory, National Association of Securities Dealers
Nation's Business
National Business Education Yearbook, National Business Education Association
The National Directory of Addresses and Telephone Numbers, Omnigraphics
National Directory of Corporate Giving, The Foundation Center
National Directory of Women-Owned Business, Business Research Services
The National Law Journal
National Real Estate Index Market Monitor, National Real Estate Index
National Real Estate Investor
National Trade Data Bank, U.S. Department of Commerce
New York Public Library Desk Reference, Webster's New World
New York Stock Exchange Fact Book, New York Stock Exchange
The New York Times
The Newsletter on Newsletters
The NonProfit Times
North American International Business
North American Office Market Review, Building Owners and Managers Association
O'Dwyer's Directory of Public Relations Firms, J. R. O'Dwyer
Occupational Outlook Handbook, U.S. Government Printing Office
OEL Insider
Office Adminstration Handbook, The Dartnell Corporation

Official U.S. Custom House Guide, North American Publishing
On Location National Film and Videotape Production Directory, On Location Publishing
The Partnership Book: How to Write a Partnership Agreement, Nolo Press
Patent It Yourself, Nolo Press
PC Computing
PC World
Pensions & Investments
Pensions and Other Retirement BenefitsPlans, Bureau of National Affairs
Personal Selling Power
Personnel and Human Relations Management, West Publishing
Personnel Management Abstracts
Personnel Management Guide, Prentice-Hall Information Services
Perspectives, American Productivity and Quality Center
Pocket Station Listing Guide, National Association of Television Program Executives
Political Finance and Lobby Reporter
PR/Media Connection
Practical Guide to Credit and Collection, AMACOM
Pratt's Guide to Venture Capital Sources, Venture Economics
Productivity and the Economy: A Chartbook, U.S. Department of Labor, Bureau of Labor Statistics
Protect Your Company from A to Z, Business Research Publications
Public Relations Journal
Publishers Weekly
Radio and Records Magazine
Rand McNally Bankers Directory: United States, Rand McNally
Rand McNally Bankers Directory: International, Rand McNally
Rating Guide to Franchises, Facts on File
Real Estate Market Forecast, Landauer Real Estate Counselors
Robert Half on Hiring, Plume
Safety Management: Office and Branch Manager's Bulletin, National Foreman's Institute
Science & Engineering Indicators, National Science Foundation
The Second Hulbert Financial Digest Almanac and Newsletter, Minerva Books
A Secretary's Handbook: Addressing Overseas Letters, W. Foulsham & Co.
Security Distributing & Marketing
Sid Cato's Newsletter on Annual Reports
The Small Business Advocate
Small Business Handbook, Prentice-Hall
The Small Business Legal Guide, Dearborn Financial Publishing
Small Business Reports
Small Business Resource Guide, Chamber of Commerce
Small Business Sourcebook, Gale Research
Society of Actuaries Yearbook, Society of Actuaries
Software Reviews on File, Facts on File
Standard and Poor's Creditweek
Standard Directory of Advertising Agencies: The Agency Red Book, National Register Publishing Company
Standard Legal Forms and Agreements for Small Businesses, Self Counsel Press
State and Metropolitan Area Databook, U.S. Government Printing Office
State Tax Guide, Commerce Clearing House
Statistical Abstract of the United States, U.S. Government Printing Office
Success Magazine
Superbrands
Survey of Current Business
Telemarketing Buyer's Guide
The Teleommuting Resource Guide
Ten-Second Business Forms, Bob Adams
Thomas Register of American Manufacturers, Thomas Publishing
Thorndyke Encyclopedia of Banking and Financial Tables, Warren, Gorham & Lamont
Tokyo Stock Exchange Fact Book, Tokyo Stock Exchange
Trade Show and Convention Guide, Amusement Business
Traders' Catalog & Resource Guide
Trading Company Sourcebook, National Federation of Export Associations
Travel Industry World Yearbook, Child and Waters
U.S. News & World Report
The Ultimate College Shopper's Guide, Addison-Wesley
Understanding Wall Street, TAB Books, Liberty House Division

UNESCO Statistical Yearbook, UNIPUB
The Universal Almanac, Andrews & McMeel
Upside
USA Today
Vest Pocket CEO, Prentice-Hall
Vest Pocket Marketer, Prentice Hall
Vest Pocket MBA, Prentice-Hall
The Wall Street Journal
Wall Street Words, Houghton Mifflin
Washington Information Directory, Congressional Quarterly
Washington Representatives, Columbia Books
Waste Age, National Solid Wastes Management Association
What Every Executive Better Know About the Law, Simon & Schuster
Who Knows What, Henry Holt
Who Owns What Is in Your Head?, Elsevier-Dutton
Who's Who in Entertainment, R.R. Bowker
Who's Who in Professional Speaking, National Speakers Association
Who's Who of Customs Brokers and Forwarding Agents
Windows
Workers' Relocation: A Bibliography, Vance Bibliographies
Working Mother
Working Woman
Worksite Wellness, Prentice-Hall
The World Almanac
The World Bank Atlas, The World Bank
World Currency Yearbook, International Currency Analysis
World Technology/Patent Licensing Gazette
World Trade
Your Rights in the Workplace, Nolo Press
The Zen of Media Hype, Citadel Press

The Business Almanac 2,000 list in the Reference Section is based upon information compiled from sources including *Hoover's MasterList of Major U.S. Companies*. Copyright © 1995, The Reference Press, Inc. Reprinted with permission. Book and disk versions of this product are available from The Reference Press, 6448 Highway 290 East, E-104, Austin, TX 78723; Phone (800) 486-8666; Fax (512) 454-9401; email refpress6@aol.com. For more information see Hoover's Online on the Internet (http://www.hoovers.com).

THE 1996
INFORMATION PLEASE®
BUSINESS ALMANAC &
SOURCEBOOK

BUSINESS LAW & GOVERNMENT

Legal Issues in Hiring and Firing

ACCORDING TO THE Equal Employment Opportunity Commission, the most frequently cited employment bias charges in 1994 were related to hiring and firing practices. Hiring and firing procedures should be carefully reviewed to assess the potential liability hidden within established practices.

Hiring

Hiring, in many cases, begins with a job application. Many of the questions found on traditional applications for employment have become sources of discrimination suits. A non-discriminatory job application should not contain questions about the following:

- Race, age, sex, religion, and national origin. An employer may ask if an applicant is 18 years of age or older and has a legal right to work in this country either through citizenship or status as a resident alien.

- Marital status, maiden name, and number, names, and ages of children or other dependents.

- Employment of the spouse and child-care arrangements unless such queries are made of both male and female applicants.

- A woman's pregnancy or related condition.

- Arrest records that did not result in convictions. It is permissible to inquire about convictions or pending felony charges.

- The existence, nature, or severity of a disability. An employer may ask about an applicant's ability to perform specific job functions.

- An applicant's height and weight, except in specific professions such as law enforcement, when valid guidelines have been established for various national organizations.

- Organizational affiliations except those pertaining to professional memberships related to the specific job.

- Military history unless the job requires such a background.

- Status as a high school graduate. It is permissible to request the applicant to supply the details of his or her educational history.

- Lowest salary acceptable for a specific position.

An interview can often be more litigiously threatening than the employment application, because uninformed interviewers often ask seemingly harmless questions that may, in fact, be discriminatory. An interviewer may casually ask a 32-year-old female applicant if she anticipates having a family. If she responds affirmatively and subsequently is not hired, she could file suit for discriminatory hiring practices. Experts say the general rule of thumb is: if a question does not have anything to do with the job, or is not vital to determining the applicant's ability to perform the responsibilities associated with the job, do not ask it.

Firing

Improperly handled employee terminations generate a significant number of lawsuits against corporations. Complete and accurate records of such actions protect the interests of both the employer and the former employee.

Firing generates stress for the employee being discharged, the individual who does the terminating, and the employees who remain with the company. There are several concepts to consider before, during, and after the discharge is completed that can significantly affect the attitudes and reactions of all involved as well as the vulnerability of the employer.

Before Firing an Employee

- Be sure the action is approved by top management and conforms to written company policy. Corporate legal advice may be sought regarding severance conditions for higher-level employees.

- Except in a for-cause dismissal, an employee is entitled to a documented, concise explanation of the reasons for his or her dismissal. Plan the interview carefully to anticipate responses and defuse reactions.

- Federal law requires 60-day advance notification of employees affected by layoffs and plant or office closings. Prematurely early notification may significantly affect production and possibly invite undesirable reactions.

- Consider the possibility of an irrational response by a dismissed employee. Take the necessary precautions to change security codes, access codes to computers, and entry to the corporate premises.

Handling a Termination

- Be honest and completely clear about the reasons for discharge. Avoid personal statements that might degrade or humiliate the individual, or vague statements which might suggest that the situation is reversible.

- It is sometimes helpful to have another individual, such as a professional from human resources,

Legal Issues in Hiring and Firing (cont'd)

present as a witness and a support for the employee, particularly if emotional reactions are anticipated.

- Present a precise explanation of severance pay procedures, benefits continuation forms, pension or profit-sharing payouts, and other available assistance, such as outplacement counseling. In larger corporations, the human resources department handles the filling out of the necessary forms and documents.

- Allow the individual to remove personal belongings at a low-visibility time, after hours or on a weekend. Prepare a checklist of company property that should be accounted for, including keys, credit cards, ID cards, and computer disks.

- Respond to all questions and discuss the cover story to be presented when future employers inquire about the individual. Be prepared with a version that is supportive of the employee but does not threaten the company's credibility.

After Firing an Employee

- Document the termination in writing immediately, detailing conversation, reactions, and emotional tone of both parties. This is essential for a response to any future challenge to the termination.

- Inform the staff or co-workers of the termination by word of mouth or by memo. In the case of for-cause termination, the incident should be mentioned only briefly, in a non-defamatory manner. If performance is the reason, experts suggest that simply stating that the employee and the organization have agreed to part company should suffice.

- In the case of staff reduction or layoffs, the remaining staff should be assured that downsizing was warranted and that no additional layoffs are anticipated at this time. (If additional reductions are expected, employees should be informed that such an action may be required, and that they will be informed on or before a specific date.)

- Invite employees who have additional questions and concerns to meet with specified representatives of the company privately.

- Inform clients or customers who deal with the discharged individual that the company will continue to serve their needs. When necessary, name a specific individual who will replace the terminated employee.

Recommended Resources

The Human Resources Yearbook
Prentice-Hall, $79.95
(800) 223-1360

Every Manager's Guide to Firing
Irwin Professional Publishing, $45
(708) 789-4000

Non-Compete Agreements

LOSING A VALUED EMPLOYEE is disconcerting. Discovering that the individual has defected to a competitor and has taken proprietary information with him or her is shocking and infuriating. Considerable damage can result when an employee takes invaluable company information, such as proposed new product lines or strategic planning, and ultimately gives the competition an unfair advantage. Small and large businesses alike are faced with the problem of reducing the risk of losing more than an employee.

One commonly adopted solution is requiring a new employee to sign a non-compete agreement. Such a document is an agreement between the employer and employee stating that, should the employee choose to leave the company, he or she will not go to work for a competitor for a specified period of time, frequently two years.

A non-compete document is particularly useful for employees who have access to critical information, either through job responsibility or through social interactions with owners or high-level executives. While the signed agreement does not provide foolproof protection against such disruption, it deters this type of action by forcing the employee to reconsider the temptations. A signed document is an excellent reminder of one's responsibility.

A standard non-compete agreement might read this way:

Employee agrees as a condition of employment that, in the event of termination for any reason, he/she will not engage in a similar or competitive business for a period of two years, nor will he/she contact or solicit any customer with whom Employer conducted business during his/her employment. This restrictive covenant shall be for a term of two years from termination, and shall encompass an area within a 50-mile radius of Employer's place of business.

Additional clauses might specify the protections desired by an individual business.

Non-Compete Agreements (cont'd)

Employee agrees that Employer's customer lists, processes, manufacturing techniques, sales materials, and pricing information constitute the sole and exclusive property of Employer, and that the same are "trade secrets" under the law. Employee promises that under no circumstances shall he/she disclose same, during or after the term hereof, and upon violation of this provision Employee agrees that Employer shall be entitled to an injunction, compensatory and punitive damages, and reimbursement for its counsel fee.

Source: What Every Executive Better Know About the Law

It is important to note that non-compete agreements may be illegal in Montana, Nevada, North Dakota, and Oklahoma. Such agreements may be invalid or limited in Colorado, Florida, Hawaii, Louisiana, Oregon, South Dakota, and Wisconsin. While there is no federal law regarding non-compete agreements, employers should consult state regulations before using such a document.

Employment Contracts

AN EMPLOYMENT CONTRACT spells out the conditions of employment including wages, hours, and type of work.

Depending upon the level of employment, the responsibility of the new employee, and the nature of the business, the conditions of employment should be detailed regarding the following elements:

* Term of employment.

* Duties of the employee including general and specific responsibilities and performance of duties.

* Compensation including monthly salary, automobile expenses, relocation and moving expenses, and a one-time bonus inducement if used. Details such as bonus or incentive plans, stock options, salary deferment plans, disability benefits, and health and retirement plans may or may not be spelled out.

* Confidentiality required of the employee regarding employer's operating expenses, pricing formulas, procedures, trade secrets, and proprietary information. This confidentiality extends to employee lists, customer lists, or prospective customers who become clients of the organization during the individual's term.

* A non-compete clause as described above.

* Provisions for termination including a violation of responsibility, an inability to perform duties, reorganization, or low company profits. Higher-level employees frequently have a clause included in the contract to state a certain amount of money, often from six to twelve months' salary, that will be paid to the employee in the event of termination by disagreement or dispute.

It is important to remember that any item not covered in the original employment contract falls under common-law rights. Therefore, an employee owns the rights to all ideas, inventions, or discoveries unless he or she was specifically hired to develop those ideas or inventions. If the idea or invention is the incidental result of employment, then the rights belong to the employee unless otherwise specified in the employment contract.

The Top Reference Sources

Copyright Clearance Center
222 Rosewood Dr.
Danvers, MA 01923
(508) 750-8400

The Copyright Clearance Center is a non-profit organization created to ease the process of securing copyright permission and collecting fees. Thousands of publishers and users of business magazines, newsletters, books, technical and trade journals, and other publications register with the CCC and allow it to grant permission and collect fees for the right to reproduce copyrighted materials.

Contracts

JUST AS A BUSINESSPERSON scans the corporate environment for potential legal pitfalls within the organization, so, too, he or she must similarly judge potential liability for decisions involving outside individuals or businesses. While a written contract is not necessary for every action and decision taken by a businessperson, it can prove invaluable when:

• Disputes arise over delivery dates or option terms;

• Clear, precise written proof is required to resolve litigation;

• Complex details are anticipated and dealt with on paper instead of in the courtroom.

There are several instances when it is in an executive's own best interests to have a simple written agreement on file. First, a boilerplate model of a basic agreement should be kept on file and used when a company hires a consultant or independent contractor. Second, a letter of agreement should be used when an executive wants to create a "written handshake" that states the essentials of the agreement without becoming mired in details. Such an agreement states the simple facts in writing, and is confirmed and accepted when signed and returned to the sender.

This simple document should:

• Identify both parties and the role of each in the agreement;

• Describe the nature of the agreement;

• State payment terms, time expectations, and other contingencies of the agreement.

In the case of independent contractors, the document should include a clause prohibiting the disclosure to a competitor of any work created for this employer.

An early-warning system of liability sensitivity requires prudence rather than panic. It isn't necessary to call an attorney before making every decision. Such hesitation affects the spontaneity of business agreements. Yet it is wise to have boilerplate documents reviewed by counsel before they are used for the first time. When in doubt regarding a simple agreement, it is worth the peace of mind to consult an attorney. Counsel should be sought when complex situations are involved, such as incorporation, partnership, lease agreements real estate agreements, debt collection, litigation, and labor/management relations.

The Small Business Administration (SBA) has business development specialists who can provide useful information and direction in response to telephone queries. To find a nearby regional office, call the SBA Answer Desk at (800) 827-5722. (*See also* "*Small Business Administration Regional Offices*" on page 385.)

Recommended Resource

Small Business Legal Handbook
by Robert Friedman
Dearborn Financial Publishing, $69.95
(800) 533-2665

Intellectual Property Protection

IF AN INTRUDER STEALS a word processor or piece of equipment from a factory, the owner becomes acutely aware of the loss. Yet the daily misuse of a company's intellectual property, including its logo or trademark, constitutes theft as well and can be far more damaging. An organization's intellectual property is protected by trademarks (on the company name or logo), patents (on its inventions or product designs), and copyrights (on the literary, musical, or photographic products) generated by or for the company.

Trademarks

A trademark is potentially the most valuable asset of an organization. It is a word, symbol, design, or combination of these elements which identifies one's products and services and distinguishes them from others in the marketplace. The identity created by a distinct trademark is priceless in the customer loyalty and product awareness it generates. Trademarks extend the company's public image not only through the product or service, but also through printed material, packaging, and advertising which bear that mark.

An owner can protect a trademark by common law or by federal registration. Common-law protection begins with the first use of a mark and is indicated by ™, while federal registration requires a more complicated procedure.

Why Register a Trademark?

An unregistered trademark (™) is protected by common law only within states where it is used. When a trademark is used in interstate commerce, experts suggest that it is in the owner's best interests to register the trademark (®) with the Federal Patent and Trademark Office (PTO). Such registration guarantees ownership of the mark and entitlement to its

Intellectual Property Protection (cont'd)

use throughout the nation. It can be devastating to a corporation to establish a product name and trademark recognition only to find that its use is challenged by a previously unknown owner. Imagine the effect on Apple Computer if they suddenly discovered, six months after the first computer rolled off the assembly line, that their trademark rainbow apple with one bite missing was legally in use by an obscure organic fruit grower in California. Registration protects against litigation and liability as well as costly damages. When a trademark is to be used in a complicated manner, it is wise to consult a lawyer regarding the value of federally registering the mark.

Once a trademark is registered, ownership continues for a renewable period of ten years. Midway through the first decade, however, the owner must file an affidavit of intent to continue use of the trademark. In the absence of such documentation, the registration is canceled.

Life Cycle of a Trademark

Whenever a new business is begun or a new product line is established in an existing company, a unique name, trademark, or logo is created. A corporate trademark, name, or symbol evolves out of the following process:

- Possible names are suggested in brainstorming sessions, by use of software designed to generate names, or by name-creation consultants.

- Suggestions are screened via trademark directories or on-line research systems to determine the existence of conflicting U.S. federal, state, or international trademark registrations or applications. (See below.)

- Candidates that survive the initial screening are subjected to professional trademark searches and reports on the availability of use of the desired trademark.

- An application and filing fee are presented to the Patent and Trademark Office (PTO) of the U.S. Department of Commerce and the application is reviewed by its federal staff.

- If no opposition or conflict is found in the application review process, the trademark is presented in the PTO's official gazette for opposition or challenge.

- Having survived this last hurdle, the owner of the proposed trademark is permitted to register the trademark. All subsequent use of the trademark should include the symbol ® as notification that

the trademark is protected under federal trademark law. It is important to note, however, that a mark may be challenged for up to five years under federal law.

How to File an Application for Registration

The trademark owner can apply for registration independently or may be represented by an attorney. The risks associated with the financial advantages of self-representation include the possibility of having the application rejected and forfeiting the application fee if the PTO attorney discovers a conflicting mark. However, with some reasonable preparation, an enterprising individual can complete the application form and proceed through at least the initial stages of the procedure.

If a reasonably thorough search is conducted and no conflicting marks are uncovered, the application may be completed and submitted with the fee to the PTO for review.

Application for registration requires:

- A completed application form;

- A drawing of the mark to be used;

- Specimens showing intended use of the mark;

- Filing fee ($210 or more; check with the PTO).

The PTO has documented all the pertinent information about trademark registration applications and filing requirements in a useful booklet called *Basic Facts About Trademarks*.

All correspondence with the PTO, as well as requests for this booklet, can be addressed to:

The Commissioner of Patents and Trademarks
Washington, DC 20231

Contact Options

Information Hotlines:

General Trademark or Patent Information
(703) 308-4357

Automated (Recorded) General Trademark or Patent Information
(800) 557-4636

Automated Line for Status Information on Trademark Applications
(703) 305-8747

Copyright Information (Library of Congress)
(202) 707-3000

America Online offers the Microsoft Small Business Center, an amalgam of information and articles from the American Management Association, Dun & Bradstreet, Nation's Business, the SBA, and others. KEYWORD MSBC.

Intellectual Property Protection (cont'd)

TRADEMARK/SERVICE MARK APPLICATION, PRINCIPAL REGISTER, WITH DECLARATION	MARK (Word(s) and/or Design)	CLASS NO. (If known)

TO THE ASSISTANT SECRETARY AND COMMISSIONER OF PATENTS AND TRADEMARKS:

APPLICANT'S NAME:

APPLICANT'S BUSINESS ADDRESS:
(Display address exactly as it should appear on registration) _____

_____

_____

_____

APPLICANT'S ENTITY TYPE: (**Check one** and supply requested information)

Individual - Citizen of (Country):

Partnership - State where organized (Country, if appropriate): _____
Names and Citizenship (Country) of General Partners: _____

_____

_____

Corporation - State (Country, if appropriate) of Incorporation: _____

Other (Specify Nature of Entity and Domicile): _____

GOODS AND/OR SERVICES:

Applicant requests registration of the trademark/service mark shown in the accompanying drawing in the United States Patent and Trademark Office on the Principal Register established by the Act of July 5, 1946 (15 U.S.C. 1051 et. seq., as amended) for the following goods/services (**SPECIFIC GOODS AND/OR SERVICES MUST BE INSERTED HERE**):

_____

_____

_____

_____

BASIS FOR APPLICATION: (Check boxes which apply, **but never both the first AND second boxes**, and supply requested information related to each box checked.)

[ ]	Applicant is using the mark in commerce on or in connection with the above identified goods/services. (15 U.S.C. 1051(a), as amended.) Three specimens showing the mark as used in commerce are submitted with this application. •Date of first use of the mark in commerce which the U.S. Congress may regulate (for example, interstate or between the U.S. and a foreign country): _____ •Specify the type of commerce: _____ (for example, interstate or between the U.S. and a specified foreign country) •Date of first use anywhere (the same as or before use in commerce date): _____ •Specify manner or mode of use of mark on or in connection with the goods/services: _____ (for example, trademark is applied to labels, service mark is used in advertisements)
[ ]	Applicant has a bona fide intention to use the mark in commerce on or in connection with the above identified goods/services. (15 U.S.C. 1051(b), as amended.) •Specify intended manner or mode of use of mark on or in connection with the goods/services: _____ (for example, trademark will be applied to labels, service mark will be used in advertisements)
[ ]	Applicant has a bona fide intention to use the mark in commerce on or in connection with the above identified goods/services, and asserts a claim of priority based upon a foreign application in accordance with 15 U.S.C. 1126(d), as amended. • Country of foreign filing: _____ • Date of foreign filing: _____
[ ]	Applicant has a bona fide intention to use the mark in commerce on or in connection with the above identified goods/services and, accompanying this application, submits a certification or certified copy of a foreign registration in accordance with 15 U.S.C. 1126(e), as amended. • Country of registration: _____ • Registration number: _____

NOTE: Declaration, on Reverse Side, MUST be Signed

PTO Form 1478 (REV. 8/92)
OMB No. 0651-0009 (Exp. 6/30/95)

U.S. DEPARTMENT OF COMMERCE/Patent and Trademark Office

Intellectual Property Protection (cont'd)

DECLARATION

The undersigned being hereby warned that willful false statements and the like so made are punishable by fine or imprisonment, or both, under 18 U.S.C. 1001, and that such willful false statements may jeopardize the validity of the application or any resulting registration, declares that he/she is properly authorized to execute this application on behalf of the applicant; he/she believes the applicant to be the owner of the trademark/service mark sought to be registered, or, if the application is being filed under 15 U.S.C. 1051(b), he/she believes applicant to be entitled to use such mark in commerce; to the best of his/her knowledge and belief no other person, firm, corporation, or association has the right to use the above identified mark in commerce, either in the identical form thereof or in such near resemblance thereto as to be likely, when used on or in connection with the goods/services of such other person, to cause confusion, or to cause mistake, or to deceive; and that all statements made of his/her own knowledge are true and that all statements made on information and belief are believed to be true.

_____
DATE

_____
SIGNATURE

_____
TELEPHONE NUMBER

_____
PRINT OR TYPE NAME AND POSITION

INSTRUCTIONS AND INFORMATION FOR APPLICANT

TO RECEIVE A FILING DATE, THE APPLICATION <u>MUST</u> BE COMPLETED AND SIGNED BY THE APPLICANT AND SUBMITTED ALONG WITH:

1. The prescribed **FEE ($210.00)** for each class of goods/services listed in the application;
2. A **DRAWING PAGE** displaying the mark in conformance with 37 CFR 2.52;
3. If the application is based on use of the mark in commerce, **THREE (3) SPECIMENS** (evidence) of the mark as used in commerce for each class of goods/services listed in the application. All three specimens may be in the nature of: (a) labels showing the mark which are placed on the goods; (b) photographs of the mark as it appears on the goods, (c) brochures or advertisements showing the mark as used in connection with the services.
4. An **APPLICATION WITH DECLARATION** (this form) - The application must be signed in order for the application to receive a filing date. Only the following person may sign the declaration, depending on the applicant's legal entity: (a) the individual applicant; (b) an officer of the corporate applicant; (c) one general partner of a partnership applicant; (d) all joint applicants.

SEND APPLICATION FORM, DRAWING PAGE, FEE, AND SPECIMENS (IF APPROPRIATE) TO:

U.S. DEPARTMENT OF COMMERCE
Patent and Trademark Office, Box TRADEMARK
Washington, D.C. 20231

Additional information concerning the requirements for filing an application is available in a booklet entitled **Basic Facts About Trademarks**, which may be obtained by writing to the above address or by calling: (703) 308-HELP.

This form is estimated to take an average of 1 hour to complete, including time required for reading and understanding instructions, gathering necessary information, recordkeeping, and acutally providing the information. Any comments on this form, including the amount of time required to complete this form, should be sent to the Office of Management and Organization, U.S. Patent and Trademark Office, U.S. Department of Commerce, Washington, D.C. 20231, and to Paperwork Reduction Project 0651-0009, Office of Information and Regulatory Affairs, Office of Management and Budget, Washington, D.C. 20503. Do NOT send completed forms to either of these addresses.

Trademark Protection

"ASPIRIN," "THERMOS," "CELLOPHANE," "shredded wheat," "nylon," and "zipper" are examples of the greatest danger facing a trademark holder. Each was once a registered but, unfortunately, poorly protected trademark. Public misuse caused the trademark name to degenerate into a generic term describing the class or nature of an article. Subsequently, the holder was denied the renewal of trademark rights, and the product name became simply a generic term for competitors' products.

A company or individual holding trademark rights should take the following precautions:

- Make sure the mark being used isn't already in use. Protect interests through a trademark search by a professional search organization.

- Use the trademark symbol ™ to indicate that it is the company's selected mark.

- Once registration is complete, use the ® symbol to indicate that the trademark is officially registered.

- Consider the services of a trademark-search firm to monitor the valid and unscrupulous use of the mark.

- Notify in writing anyone who is misusing a trademark.

- In all advertising, use the trademark as an adjective modifier, rather than as a noun or a verb. Xerox®, for example, is careful to remind the public that Xerox® is a type of photocopier, rather than a process of duplicating a document.

Properly protected, a trademark can last indefinitely.

Contact Option

Patent and Trademark Office
(703) 308-4357, or (703) 557-4636 for recorded information

Trademark Searches

THE KEY TO THE SUCCESSFUL adoption of a trademark lies in the trademark search. This process ensures that a desired trademark does not infringe on another existing mark. An informal search can be performed independently and is particularly useful when screening suggestions for trademarks. Searches are generally conducted through computer subscriber databases such as Compu-Mark, Dialog, or IntelliGate, using a computer, modem, and printer.

At a cost of between $5 and $10 per search, an individual may uncover duplicate, conflicting trademarks. A search may also be conducted in a state patent and trademark depository library using Cassis, the free government on-line system. Finally, a search may be made in the library used by the PTO. This facility is located on the second floor of the South Tower Building, 2900 Crystal Dr., Arlington, VA 22202. Note: while these libraries have CD-ROMs containing a database of both registered and pending trademarks in written descriptions, they do not contain the graphics of the actual design marks.

While the informal, independent search described above is a sound preliminary step, it is critical to ensure that the search process has been comprehensive. A successful challenge to the use of a trademark can result in staggering damages, legal costs, and loss of profits by the party found guilty of infringement. This financial devastation could be compounded by the expense of removing the offending trademark from all advertising materials, labels and packaging, printed corporate stationery, checks, price lists, catalogues, and any other place in which the mark is displayed.

The wise alternative to an informal search is the use of professional trademark-search services, such as those listed below. These organizations serve a wide range of functions designed to determine the availability of a trademark or trade name for use. Such services also monitor the marketplace for infringement of trademark use, supervise the maintenance of an existing trademark, and advise a client regarding the possible acquisition of a specific mark. The value of such a service lies in the thoroughness with which trademark candidates are investigated from among common-law sources, pending applications, and actual registrations. Investigations can extend to the state, national, or international marketplace, and can be performed in the preliminary screening stage as well as during the critical pre-filing period. Using such a service in the preliminary design stages of trademark development can save dollars in a costly design budget.

Once a trademark is secured, these agencies can provide additional services such as monitoring the activity of competitors, including the application for new marks from within a specific industry.

Trademark Searches (cont'd)

Contact Options

Trademark-Search Services:

Thomson & Thomson
500 Victory Rd.
North Quincy, MA 02171
(800) 692-8833 or (617) 479-1600

Trademark Research
300 Park Ave. S., 8th floor
New York, NY 10010
(800) 872-6275 or (212) 228-4084

Additional organizations may be listed in the business pages of the local telephone directory.

Filing for a Copyright

THE COPYRIGHT LAW is important to business individuals from two perspectives: as an owner and as a potential user of registered material. A copyright is used to protect the rights of the author of published or unpublished literature, music and lyrics, drama, choreography, graphics and other art forms, motion pictures, and sound recording.

A revision in the copyright law no longer requires copyright owners to mark their works in a special way to qualify for protection. However, many copyright owners continue to indicate their ownership in the work by using a © to indicate copyright protection.

The copyright registration process originates with an application form obtained from the U.S. Copyright Office. Form TX is the most commonly used application for most business uses and covers non-dramatic literary works such as fiction, nonfiction, textbooks, reference works, directories, catalogues, advertising copy, and computer programs.

Other Common Forms and Their Uses

- Form PA: Material to be performed, including music (with accompanying lyrics), choreography, motion pictures, audio-visuals.

- Form VA: Visual arts. "Pictorial, graphic, or sculptural works," graphic arts, photographs, prints and art reproductions, maps, globes, charts, technical drawings, diagrams, and models.

- Form SR: Sound recordings.

Once the application is completed, it should be sent with the $20.00 application fee, payable to the Register of Copyrights, Copyright Office, Library of Congress, Washington, DC 20559. After the copyright has been issued, the owner has three months to supply two copies of the registered work, one for registration and one for the Library of Congress, to the Copyright Office.

Confusion arises concerning what can and cannot be copyrighted. Phrases, slogans, ideas, and mottoes cannot be copyrighted. Neither can blank forms, methods, systems, concepts, and names of products. Occasionally, a business owner will attempt to copyright a product or service name, only to be informed that such registration is covered under trademark law rather than copyright law.

Fair Use

The general rule of thumb is that up to 250 words of text from a book or long article may be used without securing permission for such use. Be very careful of poetry, songs, famous individuals, and endorsements, however. Recent case law has made some works (like directories) more open to fair use, and others (like a star's singing style) less open.

Contact Options

Copyright Office
Public Information Office
(202) 707-3000
To obtain specific copyright forms, call the Forms Hotline (202) 707-9100.

Software Publishers Association Piracy Hotline
(800) 388-7478

3 1833 02719 9238

The Top Reference Sources

Your Rights in the Workplace
Nolo Press, $15.95
(800) 992-6656 or (510) 549-1976

Written by Dan Lacey, a workplace consultant, this book is an employee's guide to firing and layoffs, wages and overtime, maternal and parental leave, unemployment and disability insurance, workers' compensation, job safety, and sex, race, and age discrimination. It also explains the latest changes in laws passed to protect workers.

While written from an employee's point of view, this book is also an excellent resource for ensuring that an employer doesn't violate the law.

Filing for a Copyright (cont'd)

FORM TX
For a Literary Work
UNITED STATES COPYRIGHT OFFICE

REGISTRATION NUMBER

TX   TXU

EFFECTIVE DATE OF REGISTRATION

Month   Day   Year

DO NOT WRITE ABOVE THIS LINE. IF YOU NEED MORE SPACE, USE A SEPARATE CONTINUATION SHEET.

1

TITLE OF THIS WORK ▼

PREVIOUS OR ALTERNATIVE TITLES ▼

PUBLICATION AS A CONTRIBUTION If this work was published as a contribution to a periodical, serial, or collection, give information about the collective work in which the contribution appeared. **Title of Collective Work ▼**

If published in a periodical or serial give: **Volume ▼**   **Number ▼**   **Issue Date ▼**   **On Pages ▼**

2

a

NAME OF AUTHOR ▼

DATES OF BIRTH AND DEATH
Year Born ▼   Year Died ▼

Was this contribution to the work a "work made for hire"?
☐ Yes
☐ No

AUTHOR'S NATIONALITY OR DOMICILE
Name of Country
OR { Citizen of ▶
Domiciled in ▶

WAS THIS AUTHOR'S CONTRIBUTION TO THE WORK
Anonymous? ☐ Yes ☐ No
Pseudonymous? ☐ Yes ☐ No

If the answer to either of these questions is "Yes," see detailed instructions.

NATURE OF AUTHORSHIP Briefly describe nature of material created by this author in which copyright is claimed. ▼

NOTE

Under the law, the "author" of a "work made for hire" is generally the employer, not the employee (see instructions). For any part of this work that was "made for hire" check "Yes" in the space provided, give the employer (or other person for whom the work was prepared) as "Author" of that part, and leave the space for dates of birth and death blank.

b

NAME OF AUTHOR ▼

DATES OF BIRTH AND DEATH
Year Born ▼   Year Died ▼

Was this contribution to the work a "work made for hire"?
☐ Yes
☐ No

AUTHOR'S NATIONALITY OR DOMICILE
Name of Country
OR { Citizen of ▶
Domiciled in ▶

WAS THIS AUTHOR'S CONTRIBUTION TO THE WORK
Anonymous? ☐ Yes ☐ No
Pseudonymous? ☐ Yes ☐ No

If the answer to either of these questions is "Yes," see detailed instructions.

NATURE OF AUTHORSHIP Briefly describe nature of material created by this author in which copyright is claimed. ▼

c

NAME OF AUTHOR ▼

DATES OF BIRTH AND DEATH
Year Born ▼   Year Died ▼

Was this contribution to the work a "work made for hire"?
☐ Yes
☐ No

AUTHOR'S NATIONALITY OR DOMICILE
Name of Country
OR { Citizen of ▶
Domiciled in ▶

WAS THIS AUTHOR'S CONTRIBUTION TO THE WORK
Anonymous? ☐ Yes ☐ No
Pseudonymous? ☐ Yes ☐ No

If the answer to either of these questions is "Yes," see detailed instructions.

NATURE OF AUTHORSHIP Briefly describe nature of material created by this author in which copyright is claimed. ▼

3

a **YEAR IN WHICH CREATION OF THIS WORK WAS COMPLETED** This information must be given in all cases.
◀Year

b **DATE AND NATION OF FIRST PUBLICATION OF THIS PARTICULAR WORK** Complete this information ONLY if this work has been published.
Month ▶ Day ▶ Year ▶ ◀ Nation

4

See instructions before completing this space.

COPYRIGHT CLAIMANT(S) Name and address must be given even if the claimant is the same as the author given in space 2. ▼

TRANSFER If the claimant(s) named here in space 4 is (are) different from the author(s) named in space 2, give a brief statement of how the claimant(s) obtained ownership of the copyright. ▼

DO NOT WRITE HERE / OFFICE USE ONLY

APPLICATION RECEIVED

ONE DEPOSIT RECEIVED

TWO DEPOSITS RECEIVED

FUNDS RECEIVED

MORE ON BACK ▶ • Complete all applicable spaces (numbers 5-11) on the reverse side of this page.
• See detailed instructions. • Sign the form at line 10.

DO NOT WRITE HERE
Page 1 of _____ pages

Filing for a Copyright (cont'd)

EXAMINED BY	FORM TX
CHECKED BY	
☐ CORRESPONDENCE Yes	FOR COPYRIGHT OFFICE USE ONLY

DO NOT WRITE ABOVE THIS LINE. IF YOU NEED MORE SPACE, USE A SEPARATE CONTINUATION SHEET.

PREVIOUS REGISTRATION Has registration for this work, or for an earlier version of this work, already been made in the Copyright Office?

☐ Yes ☐ No If your answer is "Yes," why is another registration being sought? (Check appropriate box) ▼

a. ☐ This is the first published edition of a work previously registered in unpublished form.

b. ☐ This is the first application submitted by this author as copyright claimant.

c. ☐ This is a changed version of the work, as shown by space 6 on this application.

If your answer is "Yes," give: **Previous Registration Number** ▼   **Year of Registration** ▼

5

DERIVATIVE WORK OR COMPILATION   Complete both space 6a and 6b for a derivative work; complete only 6b for a compilation.
a. Preexisting Material Identify any preexisting work or works that this work is based on or incorporates. ▼

b. Material Added to This Work Give a brief, general statement of the material that has been added to this work and in which copyright is claimed. ▼

6

See instructions before completing this space.

—space deleted—

7

REPRODUCTION FOR USE OF BLIND OR PHYSICALLY HANDICAPPED INDIVIDUALS A signature on this form at space 10 and a check in one of the boxes here in space 8 constitutes a non-exclusive grant of permission to the Library of Congress to reproduce and distribute solely for the blind and physically handicapped and under the conditions and limitations prescribed by the regulations of the Copyright Office: (1) copies of the work identified in space 1 of this application in Braille (or similar tactile symbols); or (2) phonorecords embodying a fixation of a reading of that work; or (3) both.

       a ☐ Copies and Phonorecords   **b** ☐ Copies Only   **c** ☐ Phonorecords Only

8

See instructions.

DEPOSIT ACCOUNT If the registration fee is to be charged to a Deposit Account established in the Copyright Office, give name and number of Account.
Name ▼   **Account Number** ▼

9

CORRESPONDENCE Give name and address to which correspondence about this application should be sent.   Name/Address/Apt/City/State/ZIP ▼

Area Code and Telephone Number ▶

Be sure to give your daytime phone number ◀

CERTIFICATION*   I, the undersigned, hereby certify that I am the

Check only one ▶

☐ author
☐ other copyright claimant
☐ owner of exclusive right(s)
☐ authorized agent of _____

of the work identified in this application and that the statements made by me in this application are correct to the best of my knowledge.

Name of author or other copyright claimant, or owner of exclusive right(s) ▲

10

Typed or printed name and date ▼ If this application gives a date of publication in space 3, do not sign and submit it before that date.

date ▶

Handwritten signature (X) ▼

MAIL CERTIFICATE TO

Certificate will be mailed in window envelope

Name ▼

Number/Street/Apartment Number ▼

City/State/ZIP ▼

YOU MUST:
• Complete all necessary spaces
• Sign your application in space 10

SEND ALL 3 ELEMENTS IN THE SAME PACKAGE:
1. Application form
2. Nonrefundable $20 filing fee in check or money order payable to *Register of Copyrights*
3. Deposit material

MAIL TO:
Register of Copyrights
Library of Congress
Washington, D.C. 20559-6000

The Copyright Office has the authority to adjust fees at 5-year intervals, based on changes in the Consumer Price Index. The next adjustment is due in 1996. Please contact the Copyright Office after July 1995 to determine the actual fee schedule.

11

*17 U.S.C. § 506(e): Any person who knowingly makes a false representation of a material fact in the application for copyright registration provided for by section 409, or in any written statement filed in connection with the application, shall be fined not more than $2,500.

July 1993—400,000   ♻ PRINTED ON RECYCLED PAPER   ☆U.S. GOVERNMENT PRINTING OFFICE: 1993-342-582/80,020

Patents

A PATENT IS A GOVERNMENT-GRANTED right that allows the holder to exclude all others from making, using, or selling the registered inventions. Patents are issued to the original inventor, joint inventors, legal representatives, or guardians for a non-renewable period of 17 years. The patent grant allows the owner to pursue litigation against anyone who makes, uses, or sells the patented invention without the written permission of the patent holder. However, patents also lend prestige to a product and are sometimes secured to impress financial investors or consumers of the product.

Three Types of Patents

- Utility patents cover new inventions that serve a particular useful function, such as Velcro fasteners, paper clips, and automatic transmissions.

- Design patents protect the unique design or shape of an object which is used for an ornamental or aesthetic purpose, such as a computer icon or the shape of a desk lamp. Design patents are granted for only 14 years.

- Plant patents are issued to an individual who has invented or discovered and produced asexually (from a seed) a new variety of plant, such as a flower. This patent type has been extended to include living cells or cell combinations as produced in biochemical research facilities.

The formula for determining the appropriate patent type—design or utility—is simple. Can the invention function without this feature? If the answer is yes, then a design patent is the appropriate protection.

Seven Important Points about Patents

- Patents are issued for objects or inventions, not ideas. Mental concepts and abstract ideas are not patentable. Protection for written materials and ideas is covered under copyright law while company logos and corporate marks are protected under trademark laws.

- A patent is not necessary to market an invention commercially. An inventor may make, use, or sell an invention without the benefit of a patent, provided it is not covered by an existing patent currently held by another individual.

- It is a criminal offense to use the words "patent pending" in advertising if the patent application is not active.

- If a patent is desired, an application must be made within one year from the time the invention is first commercialized, or the right to patent is lost.

- Patented products are not superior products. A patent only guarantees that the product is significantly different from others similar to it. Superiority is determined by the user rather than by the inventor.

- Until the invention is commercialized and in widespread use, the patent has little value. However, consider where Polaroid would be today if Dr. Edwin Land had not patented the company's products.

- Patent protection is only as good as the vigilance one maintains against infringers. The value of a patent lies in its offensive power, which becomes apparent when a patent holder warns a violator to discontinue the unauthorized use of the invention or risk litigation. (Unfortunately, all too often the party with the most money prevails.) In court proceedings, patent holders are certainly looked upon more favorably than violators. However, the burden of vigilance falls upon the patent holder.

Obtaining a Patent

It is safest to file a patent application before an invention is commercialized. Applications are filed with the Patent and Trademark Office (PTO) and include drawings of the invention, specifications, description, explanation of use, and a sworn declaration of origin.

Determining the patentability of the invention and meeting the requirements for application are complex processes that experts believe warrant the assistance of a patent attorney, a lawyer who has a degree in physical science or engineering. A list of attorneys and patent agents (qualified experts in patent applications and procedures who can practice before the Patent and Trademark Office but do not possess a law degree) is available in the following government publication:

Patent Attorneys and Agents Registered to Practice Before the U.S. Patent and Trademark Office
#003-004-00667-6, $30
U.S. Government Printing Office
Washington, DC 20402
(202) 512-1800

The explicit directions for filing application materials and the required fees are available from:

Commissioner of Patents and Trademarks
Washington, DC 20231
(703) 308-4357, or (703) 557-4636 for recorded information

Recommended Resource

Patent It Yourself
by David Pressman
Nolo Press, $39.95
(800) 992-6656

Patents (cont'd)

Companies with the Most U.S. Patents

Rank	Company	Number of U.S. Patents, 1993
1	IBM	1,085
2	Toshiba	1,040
3	Canon	1,038
4	Eastman Kodak	1,007
5	General Electric	932
6	Mitsubishi Denki	926
7	Hitachi	912
8	Motorola	729
9	Matsushita Electric Industrial	713
10	Fuji Photo Film	632
11	NEC	594
12	DuPont	568
13	Sony	565
14	Xerox	561
15	Fujitsu	452
16	AT&T	448
17	Bayer	443
18	U.S. Philips	441
19	General Motors	438
20	3M	413
21	Sharp	373
22	Siemens	371
23	Texas Instruments	369
24	Robert Bosch	363
25	BASF	360
26	Hoechst	356
27	Samsung Electronics	346
28	United States of America, Navy	344
29	Hewlett-Packard	338
30	Ciba-Geigy	332

Source: Technology Assessment & Forecast Report, U.S. Department of Commerce, Patent & Trademark Office, Aug., 1994

 E-MAIL

Government Spending. Send e-mail to spending@almanac.yoyo.com. See p. xi for instructions.

Tables of federal budget outlays, gross federal debt, and federal receipts by source, from the 1994 Statistical Abstract of the United States.

Work for Hire

IF EXECUTIVE RALPH HIRES engineer Susan to create a super gizmo, who owns the rights to the super gizmo? If Susan tinkers in the company laboratory and develops a super widget, who owns the rights to her invention? Suppose, however, that Susan develops the super widget at home using all her own materials. Does Ralph have any rights or ownership in the super widget?

Law journals are full of cases in which employees and employers waged legal battles about the rights to inventions developed by the employee. According to experts, common law provides that the employer may assume title for those inventions developed within the scope of the individual's employment, particularly if "inventing" was included in the job description. In the absence of a contract, ownership of an invention that is outside the scope of the inventor's employment belongs to the inventor, but the employer is given "shop right," or the license to use the invention without paying royalties. If the invention was developed without the employer's resources and is outside the realm of the employer's business, the employer has no rights whatsoever to the employee's invention.

To avoid such disputes and the resulting litigation, the "work for hire" clause was introduced into employment contracts. Such agreements supersede the common law and clear up the misunderstandings regarding the exact nature of the employee's work responsibilities.

A "work for hire" clause entitles the employer to take ownership of all ideas, inventions, and discoveries made by the employee as a condition of employment. It is not uncommon to include a clause in the contract that states that employees agree to sell for the sum of $1.00 any inventions, ideas, and/or improvements developed during the term of employment which relate to products, methods, designs, and equipment used by the company or any of its subsidiaries. The following is an example of a "work for hire" clause.

_____ hereby certifies that (the "Work") was specially commissioned by and is to be considered a "work made for hire" under the Copyright Act of 1976, as amended, for _____ ("Company"), and that Company is entitled to the copyright thereto.

Without limiting the foregoing, for good and valuable consideration, receipt of which is hereby acknowledged, the undersigned hereby assigns and transfers to the Company, its successors and assigns, absolutely and forever, all right, title, and interest, throughout the world in and to the Work and each element thereof, including but not limited to the copyright therein, for the full term of such copyright, and any and all renewals or extensions thereof, in each country of the world, together with any and all present or future claims and causes of action against third parties arising from or related to the Work and the copyrights therein, and the right to use and retain the proceeds relating to such claims and causes of action.

Rights in the Workplace

TREATING EMPLOYEES WITH respect and fairness is critical for two reasons. First, it establishes a company's reputation for fairness and impartiality. This reputation is carefully scrutinized by individuals both within and outside the organization and is a vital factor in keeping and attracting desirable employees. The second, equally important reason is that identifying and safeguarding employee rights reduces the possibility that the company will be embroiled in charges of discrimination, lengthy litigation, and costly settlements. Employee rights fall into three categories: the right to job security, the right to fair treatment by the employer, and the right to fair treatment in the workplace.

Right to Job Security

This right protects the employee from "termination at will" or the previously popular employer practice of discharging an individual for virtually any reason. Legislation including Title VII of the Civil Rights Act of 1964 and more recent anti-discrimination laws is being cited in courts around the country in disputes about employee rights.

Court rulings have determined that an employee cannot be fired for:

- Whistle-blowing regarding employer policies or violations of laws;

- Complaints or testimony regarding violations of employee rights;

- Lawful union activities;

- Filing claims for workers' compensation;

- Filing charges of unfair labor practices;

- Reporting OSHA violations;

- Garnishment for indebtedness.

Justifiable terminations should be spelled out in an employee handbook or personnel manual. Some of these reasons include:

- Incompetence or failure to respond to training;

- Gross insubordination;

Rights in the Workplace (cont'd)

- Repeated unexcused absences or lateness;
- Sexual harassment;
- Verbal abuse;
- Physical violence;
- Falsification of records;
- Theft;
- Intoxication on the job.

Right to Fair Treatment by Employer

Fair treatment of employees includes honoring their rights to privacy and providing feedback regarding their performance in order to enable them to successfully meet job requirements. Employee privacy issues include:

- The right to refuse a polygraph or drug test as a condition for employment;
- The right to access employment records. Although federal agencies and only six states have laws regarding this right, over 50 percent of major companies now have written guidelines for allowing employees access to their personnel files;
- The right to prohibit release of information regarding the employee to other organizations without the employee's consent.

Fair treatment of the employee is guaranteed by:

- The right to specific information regarding company expectations and prohibitions as stated in an employee manual;
- The right to due process procedures including consistent rules and protocol for grievances;
- The right to a progressive system of discipline including an oral warning, a written warning, suspension, transfer or demotion, and, as a last resort, discharge.

Right to Fair Treatment Within the Workplace

Executives often forget that their employees are entitled to an environment in which they are treated with fairness and respect by their fellow workers. Among these workplace rights are:

- The right to equal and impartial treatment by other employees regardless of race, sex, age, national origin, disability, religion;
- The right to be free from sexual harassment;
- The right to information about a plant or office closing. The Plant Closing Act of 1988 requires employers to provide affected employees with 60 days' notification of a plant closing;
- The right to knowledge about workplace hazards, ranging from warnings about chemicals used in the company to necessary safety precautions and simple guidelines for avoiding accidents.

Federal legislation protects employee rights, and it is the responsibility of the employer to be informed regarding the interpretation of these laws. Violations of workplace rights make the employer liable to charges of discriminatory practices.

Recommended Resources

Beyond Race and Gender
R. Roosevelt Thomas, Jr., $15.95
AMACOM (American Management Association)
(212) 586-8100

Guidebook to Fair Employment Practices
Commerce Clearing House, $21
(800) 835-5224, Dept. 3376

Sexual Harassment

ALTHOUGH NOT A NEW WORKPLACE problem, the most frequently discussed current employment issue is sexual harassment. Studies over the last ten years indicate that 40 to 70 percent of women interviewed have been exposed to inappropriate sexual behavior on the job. The 1991 Justice Clarence Thomas confirmation hearings raised American consciousness about the issue while the publicity regarding the litigation between Dr. Frances Cooney, an esteemed brain surgeon, and her employer, Stanford University Medical School, demonstrated the presence of harassment at all levels in the workplace. Consequently, every employer must develop an awareness of situations that constitute sexual harassment, and an understanding of accountability and liability.

Sexual harassment is defined in one of two ways: (1) quid pro quo situations; and (2) circumstances that create a "hostile environment." In the first category, employment, advancement, or benefits are dependent upon the employee's submission to unwelcome sexual advances or behavior, including demands for sexual favors, unwanted touching, leering, and sexually suggestive gestures.

The second category, a hostile environment, is created when the victim is subjected to offensive behavior that consistently affects his/her work performance. Such behavior includes sexually explicit graffiti, offensive sexual epithets, abusive language, or vulgarities. The differences between incidents of bad taste and those of sexual harassment are based upon the frequency of behavior, the severity of the incident, the reaction of the victim, and the harasser's recognition of the victim's response.

Sexual Harassment (cont'd)

According to the Civil Rights Act of 1991, the potential for employer liability may be unlimited. Employers are liable for the sexual harassment actions of their supervisors, and their liability may extend to the behavior of other employees. Legal experts point out that employers are held responsible if the employer knows or should have been aware of the harassment and took no steps to correct the situation.

In order to avoid liability, an employer should take the following preventive steps:

• Adopt and implement a company policy against sexual harassment;

• Inform all employees about that policy;

• Train all supervisory staff to recognize a hostile environment and to respond sensitively to a complaint of harassment;

• Establish procedures for handling sexual harassment complaints;

• Take investigative and corrective action in response to any complaints, including discharge of the offender, when warranted.

How to Handle a Sexual Harassment Complaint

1. The charge should be reported immediately to the company official designated by corporate policy.

2. The designated official should conduct a thorough, documented, but confidential investigation, in-forming only those individuals considered essential to the investigatory process. Subsequent interviews should be conducted with witnesses or others with knowledge of the incident(s).

3. All information regarding the investigation should be documented and kept in a separate file.

4. Once the investigation is complete, the victim should be informed that appropriate disciplinary action has been taken. The victim does not need to be informed of the exact nature of the discipline.

5. The victim should be reassured that he or she will not be subject to retaliation and that he or she has legitimately pursued employee rights.

Contact Options

Equal Employment Opportunity Commission
Office of Communications and Legislative Affairs
1801 L St., NW
Washington, DC 20507
(202) 663-4900, or (800) 669-4000 (to contact local EEOC office)

9 to 5, Working Women Education Fund
614 Superior Ave., NW, Room 852
Cleveland, OH 44113
(216) 566-9308
Offers training programs for management and non-management employees.

Discrimination

TITLE VII OF THE CIVIL RIGHTS ACT OF 1964 prohibits discrimination based on race, color, religion, sex, or national origin. Under this law, companies employing 15 or more individuals are prevented from discriminating in the areas of:

• Hiring and firing;

• Compensation and promotion;

• Transfer or layoff;

• Job advertisements and recruitment;

• Testing;

• Training and apprenticeship programs;

• Use of company facilities;

• Fringe benefits, retirement plans, and disability leave.

Amendments to the Civil Rights Act of 1964

Illegal discrimination is further prohibited by the following amendments to Title VII, which are monitored by the Equal Employment Opportunity Commission (EEOC):

• The Equal Pay Act (EPA) requires that an employer pay all employees equally for equal work, regardless of gender. The law covers situations where men and women perform jobs that require equal skill, effort, and responsibility. The exception to this law is a pay system which is based on a factor other than gender, such as seniority, or the quantity or quality of items produced or processed. Thus, Jessica cannot be hired as a reservations agent at a base rate lower or higher than that of Randy who was hired 2 months earlier. However, Jessica can be hired at a base rate lower than that of Tom, who has been a reservations agent for five years and has received annual salary increases in return for five years of service to the company.

• The Age Discrimination in Employment Act (ADEA) of 1967 protects persons 40 years of age or older from discriminatory practices in hiring, firing, promotions, pay, and reduction in pension benefits.

• The Older Workers Benefit Protection Act of 1990 was established to discourage employers from targeting older workers for staff-cutting programs. It

Discrimination (cont'd)

prohibits employers from requiring employees who accept a severance pay package, or an early retirement plan, to sign away their rights to pursue legal action against age-based discrimination.

- The Pregnancy Discrimination Act prohibits employers from refusing to hire a pregnant woman, terminating her employment on the basis of her pregnancy, or forcing her to take a maternity leave. The law also requires that a pregnant woman be allowed the same medical leave rights available to other employees for medical conditions. An employer may not refuse to provide health care insurance benefits for pregnancy, if such insurance is provided for other medical conditions.

While Title VII forbids an employer from refusing to grant men the same child-care leave rights as women, experts report that only 8% of U.S. companies offer the same option to male employees. Individual states, however, have specific laws regarding parental rights for childbirth, adoption, and parental-responsibility leaves. The prudent employer will investigate such specific state laws either through the local library or in recommended resources.

The Americans with Disabilities Act (ADA) enacted on July 26, 1992, prohibits discrimination against qualified individuals who are defined as persons "with a physical or mental impairment that substantially limits one or more major life activities." While job applicants may not be questioned about the existence, nature, or severity of a disability, they may be asked about their ability to perform specific job functions.

Medical examinations may be a condition of employment, but only if all entering employees in the same category are requested to submit to the same exams. Likewise, medical examinations of current employees must be job related and consistent with the employer's business needs. The ADA does not cover employees or applicants who are currently using illegal drugs. Tests for illegal use of drugs are not subject to the ADA's restrictions on medical examinations.

Often Overlooked Applications of Title VII

There are several other applications of Title VII that may be unknown to employers:

- An employer is required to reasonably accommodate the religious practices of an employee or prospective employee through flexible scheduling, voluntary substitutions or swaps, job reassignments, and lateral transfers, unless to do so would create undue hardship(s) on the employer.

- An employee whose religious practices prohibit payment of union dues to a labor organization cannot be required to pay the dues, but may pay an equal sum to a charitable organization.

- Pregnant employees must be permitted to work as long as they are able to perform their jobs. They may not be prohibited from returning to work for a predetermined length of time after childbirth.

- Leave for childcare must be granted on the same basis as leave granted to employees for other non-medical reasons, such as non-job-related travel or education.

- English-only rules in the workplace may constitute illegal discrimination unless an employer can demonstrate that such a practice is necessary for conducting business. In such a situation, employees have to be told when they must speak English and the consequences for violating the rule.

- An "eligible small business" can receive a 50% tax credit for expenditures exceeding $250, but not in excess of $10,250, if those expenses are incurred in order to modify existing environments to comply with the requirements of the Americans with Disabilities Act.

Informing Employees of EEOC Regulations

An employer is expected to post notices describing the federal laws prohibiting job discrimination based on race, color, sex, national origin, religion, age, and disability, and describing the provisions of the Equal Pay Act. The EEOC provides a poster summarizing the laws and procedures for filing a complaint.

Contact Option

Equal Employment Opportunity Commission
Office of Communications and Legislative Affairs
1801 L St., NW
Washington, DC 20507
(800) 669-3362 or (202) 663-4900
Provides posters and fact sheets on discrimination law.

Recommended Resource

Your Rights in the Workplace
by Dan Lacey
Nolo Press, $15.95
(800) 992-6656

TIP: *According to the Family Support Act, an employer must withhold child support money from a deadbeat dad's paycheck and pass it along to the authorities. Any employer who fails to do so may be held responsible for the payments.*

AIDS

THE 1990s BROUGHT THE BUSINESS world a startling realization of the presence of AIDS in the workplace. The Centers for Disease Control (CDC) reports that more than a million people in the United States are infected with HIV. While 243,423 people have died from AIDS in this country as of June 1994, many more are living with both diagnosed and undiagnosed infection with the human immunodefieciency virus (HIV), which causes AIDS. The impact on business is staggering in terms of both direct costs (increased costs in medical benefits, short-term and long-term disability coverage, and increased Medicaid costs), as well as indirect costs (lost productivity, lost talent, and increased recruitment and training expenses).

Individuals living with HIV/AIDS are protected under the Americans with Disabilities Act of 1992 and consequently it is illegal for businesses with 15 or more employees to discriminate against applicants or workers because they are infected with HIV or suffering from AIDS. Companies covered by ADA are expected to make reasonable accommodations in order to permit affected employees to continue working. These accommodations include extended leave policies, reassignment to available positions within the company, and flexible work schedules.

Understanding the responsibilities required by law and responding to the very human needs of those employees living with HIV and those who work alongside these individuals is a daunting task. There are three organizations dedicated to assisting large and small businesses in formulating policy, providing education and planning, and responding to the immediate concerns of companies that suddenly find themselves face to face with this situation. (*See also "Facts about AIDS" on page 325.*)

The American Red Cross

The American Red Cross will provide facilitators/instructors or train staff members of an individual company to provide a company training program on HIV/AIDS. This consists of a minimum one-hour presentation on the facts of HIV/AIDS infection and transmission. In addition, the Red Cross offers expanded presentations on the rights and responsibilities of businesses, the facts of disclosure, and a particularly useful training program for managers and supervisors. The Red Cross provides assistance to companies in policy planning.

The National Headquarters of the American Red Cross advises that interested individuals should first contact the local chapter of the American Red Cross to obtain advice and plan a program suited to the needs of the specific organization. If there is no local branch of the ARC, the AIDS Education staff at the National Headquarters of the American Red Cross will provide assistance.

American Red Cross National Headquarters
AIDS Education Division
8111 Gatehouse Rd.
Falls Church, VA 22042
(703) 206-7457

The CDC's National AIDS Clearing House

The CDC's National AIDS Clearing House is a new referral service established under the National AIDS Information and Education Program. This service has divisions for information, education, and experimental drug programs as well as a new division called Business Response to AIDS Resource Service. This division will provide information and local non–health care referrals to individuals in the business community anywhere in the nation. Their referrals regarding business policy and programs, training programs, legal questions, and insurance issues are made on the local, state, and national levels. In addition, they will refer inquiries to the appropriate state HIV coordinator.

The CDC National AIDS Clearing House
P.O. Box 6003
Rockville, MD 20849
(800) 458-5231

The National Leadership Coalition on AIDS

The National Leadership Coalition on AIDS offers businesses technical assistance and guidance in establishing policies and programs tailored to the individual needs of companies ranging from IBM to small businesses. They will send free literature to companies and individuals seeking to be proactive rather than reactive in the face of increasing HIV throughout the workplace. This particular organization is most useful in determining the specific needs of the company seeking to assist its employees. Its information agents offer clear, supportive direction to any and all inquiries regarding people living with HIV/AIDS. They are equipped to meet the immediate and long-term needs of any organization and are most interested in doing so. The Coalition will also provide one free copy in response to a first request for any printed materials they publish on the topic of HIV/AIDS.

The National Leadership Coalition on AIDS
1730 M St., NW, Suite 905
Washington, DC 20036
(202) 429-0930

Acting as Your Own Lawyer

A MAN WHO ACTS AS HIS OWN ATTORNEY has a fool for a client. Obviously, the originator of this quote never had to pay a sizable fee in return for a simple, routine legal procedure.

Armed with general interest, the time to conduct preliminary research, and a desire to save corporate funds, an ambitious business owner can conduct many of his or her own legal matters. The prudent business owner, however, should be aware of the times when one does and does not require the services of an attorney. The key lies in realizing that the most basic business situation can become complicated and require the guidance of an attorney. The following are some examples of such legal situations:

- Choosing among sole proprietorship, partnership, or corporation;
- Structuring a partnership agreement;
- Establishing a corporation;
- Dealing with stock and security laws;
- Registering trademarks, copyrights, and patents;
- Filing for licenses or permits on federal, state, and local levels;
- Fulfilling the basic tax requirements for small businesses;
- Purchasing real estate or a business;
- Leasing real estate or equipment;
- Negotiating a lease;
- Insuring a business;
- Hiring employees and independent contractors;
- Handling labor disagreements;
- Dealing with customer litigation;
- Extending credit and collecting debts;
- Planning for an estate;
- Dealing with criminal proceedings;
- Handling bankruptcy and reorganization proceedings.

In order to determine the extent to which an individual can handle any one of the above situations, he or she should:

- Understand the basic issues;

- Have a clear understanding of the forms and procedures involved in completing the legal transaction;
- Determine which, if any, aspects of the process can be handled by the individual without legal help;
- Evaluate the complexities and honestly assess the need for legal assistance;
- Decide if it is worthwhile in terms of time and savings to proceed independently.

Contact Option

Small Business Administration Answer Desk
(202) 205-7717, or (800) 827-5722 or
(202) 205-7701 for recorded information
    Offers low-cost publications on a variety of topics.

Recommended Resources

Complete Small Business Legal Guide
by Robert Friedman
Dearborn Financial Publishing, $69.95
(800) 533-2665

The Partnership Book: How to Write a Partnership Agreement
by Denise Clifford and Ralph Warner
Nolo Press, $24.95
(800) 992-6656 or (510) 549-1976

Legal Research: How to Find and Understand the Law
by Stephen Elias and Susan Levinkind
Nolo Press, $19.95
(800) 992-6656 or (510) 549-1976

The Bordwin Letter: Preventive Law for Business
by Milton Bordwin
Ounce of Prevention, $65/year
(617) 330-7033
A Newsletter for the Layperson

Incorporation

Total Number of Incorporated Businesses (thousands)

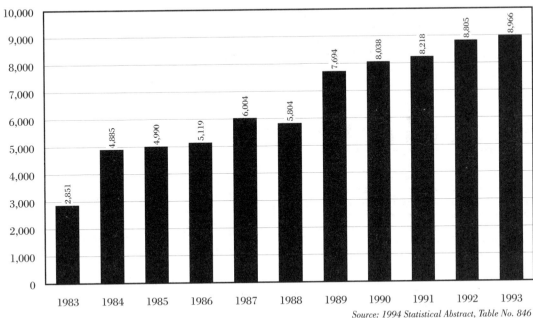

Source: 1994 Statistical Abstract, Table No. 846

SINCE ITS INCEPTION IN THE UNITED STATES more than 300 years ago, the corporation has continued to grow and flourish as a legal entity. Experts note that in North America more than 50,000 new corporations are formed each month, a fact that testifies to sustained commercial growth.

A business owner must choose from among the three types of legal structures (sole proprietorship, partnership, and corporation) when establishing a new firm. The table above demonstrates the growth of business corporations as a popular choice in the U.S. during the last decade.

Forming a corporation can appear to be a formidable task requiring quantities of legal assistance, but there are many resources available to those seeking such a legal structure for their businesses. The primary step is to recognize the basic procedure of incorporating. The basic steps are the following:

- Select and reserve a corporate name;
- Prepare and file articles of incorporation;
- Select the board of directors;
- Establish corporate bylaws;
- Record the minutes of the first meeting of the board of directors;
- Establish a corporate bank account;
- Issue stock certificates to shareholders;
- Create a corporate record book;
- Conform to individual state requirements on incorporation;
- Review bulk sales laws that pertain to the corporation.

The business owner who possesses neither the time nor the inclination to perform these procedures independently can either enlist the services of a lawyer or utilize the services of organizations that deal directly with the individual owner in the incorporation process. Such specialists in incorporation can answer a business owner's questions over the telephone and can act as an agent for the company. For nominal fees advertised at $75 to $300, based on required services, these groups will help the organization choose from among the general, the closed, and the non-stock corporation, and will guide the owner through the procedures to incorporation.

Contact Options

Incorporation Consultants:

Corporate Agents
P.O. Box 1281
Wilmington, DE 19899
(800) 877-4224 or (302) 998-0598

Incorporation (cont'd)

Harvard Business Services
25 Greystone Manor
Lewes, DE 19958
(800) 345-2677

   The more adventurous individual can secure the guidance of several good publications and perform the process on his or her own. These and other self-help books contain step-by-step descriptions of the procedures and, in some cases, provide specimens of the required forms.

Recommended Resources

How to Form Your Own Corporation without a Lawyer for under $75.00
by Ted Nicholas
Dearborn Financial Publishing, $19.95
(800) 533-2665

The Legal Guide for Starting and Running a Small Business
by Fred S. Steingold
Nolo Press, $22.95
(800) 992-6656 or (510) 549-1976

Prepared Legal Forms

THE PHOTOCOPIER as well as the personal computer and its powerful software have threatened the survival of all but the hardiest of suppliers of legal forms and documents. The enterprising business owner can produce the most commonly used documents through a combination of a reasonably powerful PC, a hard disk, and a laser printer. There is software available that allows the user to produce blank electronic forms.

   The business owner who infrequently uses legal forms can select either local stationers dealing with legal documents or one of the well-known suppliers of legal forms. Upon request they will send a catalogue and order form.

Recommended Resources

Blumberg's Law Products (Excelsior Legal)
62 White St.
New York, NY 10013
(800) 221-2972 or (212) 431-5000
Legal Supply Source

Standard Legal Forms and Agreements for Small Businesses
Self-Counsel Press, $14.95
1704 N. State St.
Bellingham, WA 98225
(800) 663-3007 or (206) 676-4530

Important Documents for All Firms

CORPORATE RECORDS ARE A VITAL component in an organization's self-defense program. Such documents can ensure that the protective umbrella of the corporation will serve the officers, the employees, the board of directors, and the stockholders.

   All businesses should have the following documents in a corporate kit. This is merely a collection of documents held together in a loose-leaf notebook or in a more formal corporate document holder, available from a supplier of law products.

   The following should be included in the corporate kit:

- Articles of incorporation;

- Amendments to the articles of incorporation;

- Minutes of the stockholders' and board of directors' meetings;

- Bylaws of the corporation;

- List of the corporation's shareholders;

- Corporate secretary's affidavit of verification of corporate shares of stock;

- All directors' resolutions;

- All stockholders' resolutions;

- Record of dividends;

- Outstanding loans;

- Contracts;

- Ledgers including accounts receivable, accounts payable, and general inventory;

- Insurance policies;

- Resolutions regarding salaries and bonuses of top executives;

- Employment contracts and agreements;

- Stock option plans;

- Medical-dental expense plans;

- Verification of citizenship or right to work according to the Immigration and Reform Control Act (IRCA) of 1986.

Employee Handbook

WHILE MOST EMPLOYERS ARE AWARE of the importance of adhering to the law when hiring, firing, and paying employees, few recognize the legal value of the employee handbook. This document outlines the company's expectations of all employees and, when signed by the employee, acknowledges agreement to conform to those policies and practices.

A prudent employer will carefully prepare the employee handbook to present specific company policy on the following important topics:

- Administrative policies such as hours, security, and safety procedures;

- Wage and salary information regarding salary increases, shift differential, non-scheduled work reimbursement, pay periods and checks, overtime, deduction types, annual evaluation policy;

- Benefits including parking, paid holidays, vacation policy, sick leave and personal leave policy, workers' compensation, and details of the health care and insurance plans;

- Personnel policies including hiring, performance appraisal, disciplinary procedures, resignation, severance pay, and grievance procedures;

- Causes for immediate dismissal including:
  Falsification of records, particularly application for employment;
  Incompetence in performance despite additional training;
  Repeated or gross insubordination;

A pattern of unexcused absence or lateness;
Abusive or threatening language to supervisors or other employees;
Sexual harassment;
Unauthorized possession of firearms on the company premises;
Physical violence or attempted injury to another employee or visitor;
Intoxication on the job;
Theft of company property or property of another employee;
Receiving three notices of reprimand during any one-year period.

Recommended Resources

Complete Small Business Legal Guide
by Robert Friedman
Dearborn Financial Publishing, $69.95
(800) 533-2665

How to Develop an Employee Handbook
by Joseph W. R. Lawson
The Dartnell Corporation, $91.50
(800) 621-5463 or (312) 561-4000

Dartnell also publishes *How to Develop a Personnel Policy Manual* (also $91.50). In their terminology, an "employee handbook" as described above is a "personnel policy manual" whereas an "employee handbook" is a more informal summary of company policy written for employees and their families. For more information, consult these books.

The Top Reference Sources

The Copyright Handbook
Nolo Press, $24.95
(800) 992-6656 or (510) 549-1976

This is a very thorough guide to copyright procedures that includes a good summation of copyright laws and requirements. Chapters are included on registration, completing all the nec-

essary forms, what copyright protects, what copyright does not protect, works made for hire, jointly authored works, compilations, automated databases, fair use privilege, uses that are less likely to be deemed fair, fair use and the photocopy machine, obtaining permission to use copyrighted material, and much more.

TIP: *The SBA offers special assistance to help minority-owned small businesses grow and thrive. The agency acts as the prime contractor for a share of all awards made by federal agencies, and subcontracts to firms owned by socially and economically disadvantaged Americans. Call the SBA at (800) 827-5722 for more information.*

Biggest Verdicts of 1994

Amount ($)	Plaintiff v. Defendant	State
5.287 billion	The Exxon Valdez	AK
1.47 billion	Schoen v. Schoen	AZ
1.2 billion	Ferdinand E. Marcos Human Rights Litigation	HI
253 million	Alpex Computer v. Nintendo	NY
221 million	Remington Rand v. Amsterdam-Rotterdam Bank N.V.	NY
219.88 million	Dominguez Energy v. Shell Oil	CA
96 million	LMP v. Universal Manufacturing	CA
85.8 million	Apex Municipal Fund v. N-Group Securities	TX
84 million	Maglica v. Maglica	CA
67 million	Bocci and Edwards v. Key Pharmaceutical	OR
60.58 million	Gayle v. City of New York	NY
59.2 million	Morse/Diesel v. Trinity Industries	NY
50.09 million	Johnson v. Mercury Finance	AL
47.30 million	Depradine v. New York City Health and Hospitals	NY
43.7 million	IT v. Motco Site Trust Fund	TX
42.64 million	Ford v. Uniroyal Goodrich Tire	GA
42 million	Mattco Forge v. Arthur Young & Co.	CA
38.5 million	Bennett v. Farmers Insurance Co. of Oregon	OR
35.7 million	Moran v. Vinson & Elkins	TX
31.6 million	Haft v. Dart Group	DE

Source: Reprinted with permission of The National Law Journal, © Feb. 6, 1995, The New York Law Publishing Company

Alternate Dispute Resolution

WHILE MOST COURT CASES are settled before, during, or after trial, alternate dispute resolution (ADR) can be a faster and less expensive means of reaching a settlement. ADR has been utilized in construction contract disputes, labor-management disagreements, international commerce, insurance claims, and securities cases, to name a few.

Parties involved in dispute or negotiation may be referred to a neutral third party by a court, or one or both parties may use the assistance of an ADR organization. The organization will also assist the parties in choosing an ADR procedure according to the nature of the dispute. The neutral party may be an ex-judge, attorney, or other expert.

The main ADR procedures are as follows:

- Arbitration: The third party hears both sides and gives a specific decision, which is either binding or non-binding (decided in advance).

- Mediation: The third party negotiates a voluntary, non-binding settlement between the two parties.

- Mini-trial: The two parties each have an attorney make a brief presentation of their cases to a panel of representatives from each side of the dispute with a neutral third party. The neutral party then mediates a non-binding settlement.

- Summary jury trial: Similar to a standard jury trial, except the jury delivers a non-binding verdict, and the attorneys can question the jurors after the trial and use their findings in their settlement negotiations.

Contact Options

Both of these organizations have offices throughout the United States:

American Arbitration Association
140 W. 51st St.
New York, NY 10020
(212) 484-4000

Judicial Arbitration and Mediation Services
345 Park Ave., 8th Floor
New York, NY 10154
(212) 751-2700

Finding a Lawyer

WHILE LARGE CORPORATIONS have equally large law firms on retainer to answer legal questions and monitor all legal transactions, the small business owner frequently cannot afford this luxury. He or she must analyze the specific needs of the company and carefully enlist the services of a legal professional. Selecting a good lawyer whose skills, experience, and rapport match the needs of the business should begin with a recognition of the legal matters that may require an attorney's assistance.

Services Provided by a Business Lawyer

- Review partnership agreements or incorporation documents;

- Review proposed leases;

- Interpret zoning ordinances regarding land use;

- Evaluate employment agreements or advise regarding difficult terminations;

- Assist in patent, copyright, trademark, and business name proceedings;

- Represent the company interests in lawsuits or arbitrations;

- Review documents regarding business or real estate sale or purchase;

- Draft or evaluate estate planning documents such as wills and trusts;

- Advise on public offerings of corporate stock.

How to Select the Right Lawyer

Selecting a lawyer to represent business interests is no casual task, but a business owner should not be intimidated by the process. By following some basic steps, an individual can accumulate a list of prospective attorneys.

- Talk to people in the business community and ask whose legal services they've used and, more important, why they've made those selections.

- Ask a trusted banker, accountant, insurance agent, or real estate broker for a recommendation.

- Inquire among friends, relatives, and business associates for candidate suggestions.

- Solicit the advice of the director of the local chamber of commerce.

- Visit a law librarian to ascertain the names of authors of business law books who may practice in the area. Their recommendations, while potentially more difficult to obtain, may be particularly useful for unusual, specialized businesses.

- If a continuing legal education program (CLE) is available in the area, ask the director to suggest the names of well-qualified individuals.

- In many states, the bar association will provide a Lawyer Referral and Information Service. Where available, the service offers the caller a referral to a local lawyer who provides the type of legal services needed by the caller. Participating lawyers will usually agree to provide an initial consultation for a nominal fee. The rest is up to the individual and the attorney. It is important to note that the state bar associations can provide names of attorneys, but they cannot provide evaluations of these individuals.

Checking Out the Suggestions

After compiling a list of candidates, it is wise to seek additional information from the Martindale-Hubbell Law Directory, available at most law libraries and some local public libraries. This directory offers a compilation of biographical information, education, professional organizations, and the specialties of all listed lawyers. Each individual is also given a confidential rating solicited from lawyers and judges. While some ratings are not published at the behest of a lawyer or because one is not available, the information and rating system can serve to narrow the list considerably.

Interview Prospective Candidates

The final step in the selection process is to request interviews from several good prospects, making clear the purpose of the interview and thus avoiding consultation fees. It is important to look for experience, rapport, accessibility, and value by assessing the interview in terms of the following criteria:

- Does the candidate understand your field and the needs of your business?

- How accessible is this attorney to client phone calls, questions, document review?

- Is this attorney willing to assist in your business legal education, or is he or she proprietary and secretive about legal matters?

- Is this candidate willing to allow you to defray some legal costs by performing negotiations and preparing preliminary drafts of documents, and willing to advise, review, and fine tune transactions when necessary?

- Is the candidate a practical problem solver or likely to become mired in legalistic technicalities?

Finding a Lawyer (cont'd)

- Is the prospective attorney willing to leave the control of the business to you, as owner, and serve as advisor in legal matters?

- Which services are billed by flat fees, contingency fees, annual fees, and hourly charges? Is the billing method clear and concise?

- Are all your questions answered?

- Is the individual clear and understandable in his or her answers?

- Do you feel comfortable and compatible with this individual?

Recommended Resource

The Legal Guide for Starting and Running a Small Business
by Fred S. Steingold
Nolo Press, $22.95
(800) 992-6656 or (510) 549-1976

State Bar Association Directory

State	Bar Association Telephone
Alabama	(205) 269-1515
Alaska	(907) 272-7469
Arizona	(602) 252-4804
Arkansas	(501) 375-4605
California	(415) 561-8200
Colorado	(303) 860-1115
Connecticut	(203) 721-0025
Delaware	(302) 658-5279
District of Columbia	(202) 223-6600
	(202) 737-4700
Florida	(904) 561-5600
Georgia	(404) 527-8755
Hawaii	(808) 537-1868
Idaho	(208) 334-4500
Illinois	(217) 525-1760
Indiana	(317) 639-5465
Iowa	(515) 243-3179
Kansas	(913) 234-5696
Kentucky	(502) 564-3795
Louisiana	(504) 566-1600
Maine	(207) 622-7523
Maryland	(410) 685-7878
Massachusetts	(617) 542-3602
Michigan	(517) 372-9030
Minnesota	(612) 333-1183
Mississippi	(601) 948-4471
Missouri	(314) 635-4128
Montana	(406) 442-7660
Nebraska	(402) 475-7091
Nevada	(702) 382-2200

State	Bar Association Telephone
New Hampshire	(603) 224-6942
New Jersey	(908) 249-5000
New Mexico	(505) 842-6132
New York	(518) 463-3200
North Carolina	(919) 677-0561
	(919) 828-4620
North Dakota	(701) 255-1404
Ohio	(614) 487-2050
Oklahoma	(405) 524-2365
Oregon	(503) 620-0222
Pennsylvania	(717) 238-6715
Puerto Rico	(809) 721-3358
Rhode Island	(401) 421-5740
South Carolina	(803) 799-6653
South Dakota	(605) 224-7554
Tennessee	(615) 383-7421
Texas	(512) 463-1400
Utah	(801) 531-9077
Vermont	(802) 223-2020
Virginia	(804) 775-0500
	(804) 644-0041
Virgin Islands	(809) 778-7497
Washington	(206) 727-8200
West Virginia	(304) 558-2456
	(304) 342-1474
Wisconsin	(608) 257-3838
Wyoming	(307) 632-9061

Source: 1994/95 ABA Directory

E-MAIL   **Law Firm Fees.** Send e-mail to lawfees@almanac.yoyo.com. See p. xi for instructions.
A description of types of fees and suggestions for negotiating a billing method.

Law Firm Billing

Largest Law Firms in the U.S. by Partners and Associates

Firm	Headquarters	Partners	Associates
Baker & McKenzie	Chicago	608	1,011
Jones, Day, Reavis & Pogue	Cleveland	385	580
Skadden, Arps, Slate, Meagher & Flom	New York	247	808
Morgan, Lewis & Bockius	Philadelphia	305	396
Gibson, Dunn & Crutcher	Los Angeles	229	362
Sidley & Austin	Chicago	304	320
Weil, Gotshal & Manges	New York	161	482
Fulbright & Jaworski	Houston	272	304
Latham & Watkins	Los Angeles	231	350
Mayer, Brown & Platt	Chicago	259	320
Shearman & Sterling	New York	132	407
O'Melveny & Myers	Los Angeles	185	317
White & Case	New York	135	399
Morrison & Foerster	San Francisco	202	295
Pillsbury Madison & Sutro	San Francisco	234	278

Source: Reprinted with permission of The National Law Journal, © Oct. 6, 1994, The New York Law Publishing Company

Cities with at least ten law firms in the top 250 where the firms had the largest average increase in number of attorneys:

- Austin
- Boston
- Chicago
- Dallas
- Denver
- Harrisburg, PA
- Miami
- Newark, NJ
- Palo Alto
- Pittsburgh
- Sacramento
- San Diego
- Washington, DC

Cities with at least ten law firms in the top 250 where the firms had the largest average decrease in number of attorneys:

- Atlanta
- Baltimore
- Columbus, OH
- Houston
- Los Angeles
- New York
- Philadelphia
- Phoenix
- San Francisco
- Seattle

Source: National Law Journal, October 3, 1994

Specialty Law Firms

FINDING A LAW FIRM that deals with the specific needs of a company can appear to be a formidable process. A simple way to accomplish this process is to call the county or state bar association. Ask if they have a lawyer referral system. If it is available, ask for a list of attorneys or firms which handle the particular specialty you need.

Frequently these services will provide a printed listing of attorneys by specialty. The referrals include attorneys who have agreed to offer an initial consultation for a nominal fee to the prospective client.

U.S. Law Firms with Foreign Offices

THE FOLLOWING DATA WERE COMPILED from *National Law Journal*'s top 100 law firms by size.

	Argentina	Australia	Belgium	Brazil	Canada	China	Czech Republic	Egypt	England	France	Germany	Hong Kong	Hungary	Indonesia	Italy	Japan	Mexico	Netherlands	Poland	Russia	Saudi Arabia	Singapore	Spain	Sweden	Switzerland	Taiwan	Thailand	Vietnam
Altheimer & Gray							•												•									
Baker & McKenzie	•	•	•	•	•	•	•	•	•	•	•	•	•	•	•	•	•	•	•	•	•	•	•	•	•	•	•	•
Bryan, Cave									•		•	•									•							
Cleary, Gottlieb			•						•	•	•	•				•												
Coudert Brothers		•	•			•			•	•		•				•						•	•				•	
Cravath, Swaine & Moore									•				•															
Davis Polk & Wardwell									•	•	•	•				•												
Debevoise & Plimpton									•	•		•	•															
Dechert Price & Rhoads			•						•																			
Dewey Ballantine							•		•			•	•						•									
Dorsey & Whitney			•						•																			
Fulbright & Jaworski									•			•																
Gibson, Dunn & Crutcher			•						•	•		•				•					•							
Graham & James						•			•		•	•		•	•	•					•					•	•	
Hogan & Hartson			•			•	•		•	•									•									
Hunton & Williams			•																•									
Jones, Day			•						•	•	•	•				•					•				•	•		
Kaye, Scholer												•																
Kelley Drye & Warren			•													•												
Latham & Watkins									•			•							•	•								
LeBoeuf, Lamb			•						•											•								
Mayer, Brown & Platt			•						•		•					•												
Milbank, Tweed									•			•		•		•					•	•						
Morgan, Lewis & Bockius			•						•		•					•												
Morrison & Foerster			•						•			•				•												
O'Melveny & Myers									•			•				•												
Paul, Weiss, Rifkind						•				•	•					•												
Rogers & Wells									•	•	•																	
Shearman & Sterling					•	•			•	•	•	•		•		•										•		
Sidley & Austin									•																			
Simpson, Thacher									•			•				•												
Skadden, Arps		•	•		•	•	•		•	•	•	•				•						•						
Squire, Sanders			•			•			•				•															
Stroock & Stroock													•															
Sullivan & Cromwell		•							•	•		•				•												
Vinson & Elkins									•									•		•								
Weil, Gotshal & Manges			•				•						•						•									
White & Case			•			•	•		•	•	•	•		•			•		•	•	•	•		•			•	•
Wilmer, Cutler			•						•		•																	

Source: Reprinted with permission of The National Law Journal, © Oct. 6, 1994, The New York Law Publishing Company

Federal Information Center

KNOWING EXACTLY WHOM TO CALL is the first step in obtaining information. When an individual is searching for information from the federal government, the task of finding the appropriate office can be overwhelming. The General Services Administration has set up a clearinghouse for such needs. The Federal Information Center is a telephone service that is staffed with individuals who can direct a caller to the appropriate federal agency.

The attractive feature of this service is the availability of regional offices serving the larger metropolitan areas of over 35 states. The following numbers all connect the caller to the same office, but they also offer recorded information about local services. If there is no number for a certain location, an individual can call the main FIC center at (301) 722-9000.

U.S. Federal Information Center

State	Telephone	Metropolitan Area Served
AK	(800) 729-8003	Anchorage
AL	(800) 366-2998	Birmingham, Mobile
AR	(800) 366-2998	Little Rock
AZ	(800) 359-3997	Phoenix
CA	(800) 726-4995	Los Angeles, Sacramento, San Diego, San Francisco, Santa Ana
CO	(800) 359-3997	Colorado Springs, Denver, Pueblo
CT	(800) 347-1997	Hartford, New Haven
DC	(800) 347-1997	Washington metropolitan area
FL	(800) 347-1997	Fort Lauderdale, Jacksonville, Miami, Orlando, St. Petersburg, Tampa, W. Palm Beach
GA	(800) 347-1997	Atlanta
HI	(800) 733-5996	Honolulu
IA	(800) 735-8004	All points in Iowa
IL	(800) 366-2998	Chicago
IN	(800) 366-2998	Gary
IN	(800) 347-1997	Indianapolis
KS	(800) 735-8004	All points in Kansas
KY	(800) 347-1997	Louisville
LA	(800) 366-2998	New Orleans
MA	(800) 347-1997	Boston
MD	(800) 347-1997	Baltimore
MI	(800) 347-1997	Detroit, Grand Rapids
MN	(800) 366-2998	Minneapolis
MO	(800) 366-2998	St. Louis
MO	(800) 735-8004	Other points in Missouri
NC	(800) 347-1997	Charlotte
NE	(800) 366-2998	Omaha
NE	(800) 735-8004	Other points in Nebraska
NJ	(800) 347-1997	Newark, Trenton
NM	(800) 359-3997	Albuquerque
NY	(800) 347-1997	Albany, Buffalo, New York City, Rochester, Syracuse
OH	(800) 347-1997	Akron, Cincinnati, Cleveland, Columbus, Dayton, Toledo
OK	(800) 366-2998	Oklahoma City, Tulsa
OR	(800) 726-4995	Portland
PA	(800) 347-1997	Philadelphia, Pittsburgh
RI	(800) 347-1997	Providence
TN	(800) 347-1997	Chattanooga
TN	(800) 366-2998	Memphis, Nashville
TX	(800) 366-2998	Austin, Dallas, Fort Worth, Houston, San Antonio
UT	(800) 359-3997	Salt Lake City
VA	(800) 347-1997	Norfolk, Richmond, Roanoke
WA	(800) 726-4995	Seattle, Tacoma
WI	(800) 366-2998	Milwaukee

Regulatory Agencies

Consumer Product Safety Commission
Washington, DC 20207
(301) 504-0580

Environmental Protection Agency
401 M St., SW
Washington, DC 20460
(202) 260-4454

Equal Employment Opportunity Commission
Office of Communications and Legislative Affairs
1801 L St., NW
Washington, DC 20507
(202) 663-4900, or (800) 669-4000 (to contact local EEOC office)

Federal Communications Commission
1919 M St., NW
Washington, DC 20554
(202) 418-0200

Federal Deposit Insurance Corporation
550 17th St., NW
Washington, DC 20429
(202) 393-8400

Federal Energy Regulatory Commission
941 N. Capitol St., NE
Washington, DC 20426
(202) 208-1371

Federal Reserve System
20th and C Sts., NW
Washington, DC 20551
(202) 452-3215

Federal Trade Commission
6th St. and Pennsylvania Ave., NW
Washington, DC 20580
(202) 326-2222

Food and Drug Administration
5600 Fishers Ln.
Rockville, MD 20857
(301) 443-3170

Immigration and Naturalization Service
U.S. Dept. of Justice
425 I St., NW, Room 7116
Washington, DC 20536
(800) 755-0777

Interstate Commerce Commission
12th St. and Constitution Ave., NW
Washington, DC 20423
(202) 927-7600

National Credit Union Administration
1775 Duke St.
Alexandria, VA 22314
(703) 518-6300

National Labor Relations Board
1099 14th St., NW
Washington, DC 20570
(202) 273-1000

National Transportation Safety Board
490 L'Enfant Plaza, SW
Washington, DC 20594
(202) 382-6600

Occupational Safety and Health Administration
200 Constitution Ave., NW
Washington, DC 20210
(202) 219-8148

Pension Benefit Guaranty Corporation
Office of Coverage and Inquiries
1200 K St., NW
Washington, DC 20005
(202) 326-4000

Resolution Trust Corporation
801 17th St., NW
Washington, DC 20434
(202) 416-6900

Securities and Exchange Commission
450 5th St., NW
Washington, DC 20549
(202) 942-8088

Small Business Administration
409 3rd St., SW
Washington, DC 20416
(202) 205-7717, or (800) 827-5722 or
(202) 205-7701 for recorded information

United States International Trade Commission
500 E St., SW
Washington, DC 20436
(202) 205-2000

U.S. Postal Service
(Current Rates, Fees, and Services)
475 L'Enfant Plaza, SW
Washington, DC 20260
(202) 268-2000

Regulatory Agencies (cont'd)

Other Useful Federal Offices:

Bureau of Export Administration (Commerce Dept.)
P. O. Box 273
Washington, DC 20044
(202) 482-4811

Economic Development Administration
(Commerce Dept.)
14th St. and Constitution Ave., NW
Washington, DC 20230
(202) 482-2000

Patent and Trademark Office (Commerce Dept.)
Washington, DC 20231
(703) 308-4357, or (703) 557-4636 for
recorded information

Trade Regulation Enforcement (Federal Trade
Commission)
Enforcement Division
6th St. & Pennsylvania Ave., NW
Washington, DC 20580
(202) 326-2000

Office for Civil Rights (Health and Human
Services Dept.)
330 Independence Ave., SW
Washington, DC 20201
(202) 619-0585

Public Health Service (Health and Human
Services Dept.)
5600 Fishers Ln.
Rockville, MD 20857
(301) 443-2403

Social Security Administration (Health and
Human Services Dept.)
6401 Security Blvd.
Baltimore, MD 21235
(410) 965-7700 or (800) 772-1213

Government National Mortgage Association
(Housing and Urban Development Dept.)
451 7th St., SW
Washington, DC 20410
(202) 708-0980

Employment Standards Administration
(Labor Dept.)
200 Constitution Ave., NW
Washington, DC 20210
(202) 219-8743

Employment and Training Administration
(Labor Dept.)
200 Constitution Ave., NW
Washington, DC 20210
(202) 219-6871

Pension and Welfare Benefits Administration
(Labor Dept.)
200 Constitution Ave., NW
Washington, DC 20210
(202) 219-8776

Veterans' Employment and Training Services
(Labor Dept.)
200 Constitution Ave., NW
Washington, DC 20210
(202) 219-9116

Internal Revenue Service (Treasury Dept.)
1111 Constitution Ave., NW
Washington, DC 20224
(800) 829-1040

United States Customs Service (Treasury Dept.)
1301 Constitution Ave., NW
Washington, DC 20229
(202) 927-2095

Hotlines:

Small Business Administration Answer Desk
(202) 205-7717, or (800) 827-5722 or
(202) 205-7701 for recorded information

Small Business Export/Import Advisory Service
(800) 565-3946

The Top Reference Sources

*Congressional Quarterly's Washington
Information Directory*
Congressional Quarterly, $99.95
(202) 887-8500

This directory lists the departments and agencies
of the federal government, congressional committees, and private, nonprofit organizations in the

nation's capital. Each chapter covers a broad
subject area, such as health, energy, or science.
Entries include the name, address, and telephone number of the organization; the name and
title of the best person to contact for information;
and a brief description of the work performed by
the organization.

OSHA

THE OCCUPATIONAL SAFETY AND Health Administration (OSHA) is the arm of the U.S. Department of Labor which deals with maintaining health and safety in the workplace. Established under the OSHA Act of 1970, this agency was set up to:

• Reduce workplace hazards.

• Establish minimum standards for health and safety for industries.

• Regularly inspect workplace sites to ensure compliance with standards. Note: Any business with ten or fewer employees is not subject to these inspections. However, OSHA produces a checklist for self-inspections of premises which can assist the small business owner in maintaining a hazard-free workplace.

• Maintain a systematic method of reporting incidents of on-the-job or work-related illnesses or injuries, including those which entitle an individual to compensation.

In order to provide businesses with information about OSHA requirements, free consultation assistance is available to employers. Representatives of OSHA will assist in identifying specific and potential hazards which may exist in the workplace. They will also assist in implementing health and safety programs, particularly concerning issues such as maintaining a smoke-free environment. To obtain a list of free OSHA publications as well as information regarding on-site consultation, interested individuals should contact:

OSHA Publications
Occupational Safety and Health Administration
Department of Labor
200 Constitution Ave., NW, Room N3101
Washington, DC 20210
(202) 219-4667

To obtain information regarding OSHA programs, and to be referred to the appropriate department of OSHA, the interested individual should call the Information Office at OSHA at (202) 219-8148.

The upside of the OSHA safety regulations is a program called Voluntary Protection Program (VPP) which rewards companies for maintaining safer workplace environments. Those companies which have effective health and safety programs and a lower-than-average injury and illness rate may be eligible for the program. The benefits for participants in the program are reduced worker compensation costs, a reduction in workday injuries with potential for reduced insurance rates, and possible automatic exemption from OSHA's programmed inspections.

To find out about the program write or call:

Occupational Safety and Health Administration
Department of Labor
200 Constitution Ave., NW, Room N3700
Washington, DC 20210
(202) 219-7266

Accidental Deaths in the U.S.

	1993	1992
All Accidents	90,000	83,000
Motor Vehicles	42,000	40,300
Home	22,500	19,500
Work	9,100	8,500
Public	20,000	18,000

Source: National Safety Council

The Top Reference Sources

Access EPA
National Technical Information Service, $24
(703) 487-4650
Stock #TB93-170-041

First published in 1991, this annual directory of U.S. Environmental Protection Agency (EPA) and other public sector environmental information

resources contains information for everyone interested in the environment.

Chapters include major EPA dockets, clearinghouses and hotlines, major EPA environmental databases, library and information services, state environmental libraries, alternate state environmental contacts, and EPA scientific models.

Governors, Mayors, Congress

U.S. Governors

State	Governor	Phone
Alabama	Fob James (R)	(205) 242-7100
Alaska	Tony Knowles (D)	(907) 465-3500
Arizona	Fife Symington (R)	(602) 542-4331
Arkansas	Jim Guy Tucker (D)	(501) 682-2345
California	Pete Wilson (R)	(916) 445-2841
Colorado	Roy R. Romer (D)	(303) 866-2471
Connecticut	John Rowland (R)	(203) 566-4840
Delaware	Thomas Carper (D)	(302) 577-3210
Florida	Lawton Chiles (D)	(904) 488-4441
Georgia	Zell Miller (D)	(404) 656-1776
Hawaii	Ben Cayetano (D)	(808) 586-0034
Idaho	Phil Batt (R)	(208) 334-2100
Illinois	Jim Edgar (R)	(217) 782-6830
Indiana	Evan Bayh(D)	(317) 232-4567
Iowa	Terry E. Branstad (R)	(515) 281-5211
Kansas	Bill Graves (R)	(913) 296-3232
Kentucky	Brereton Jones (D)	(502) 564-2611
Louisiana	Edwin W. Edwards (D)	(504) 342-7015
Maine	Angus King (I)	(207) 287-3531
Maryland	Parris Glendening (D)	(410) 974-3901
Massachusetts	William F. Weld (R)	(617) 727-3600
Michigan	John Engler (R)	(517) 373-3400
Minnesota	Arne Carlson (R)	(612) 296-3391
Mississippi	Kirk Fordice (R)	(601) 359-3100
Missouri	Mel Carnahan (D)	(314) 751-3222
Montana	Marc Racicot (R)	(406) 444-3111
Nebraska	E. Benjamin Nelson (D)	(402) 471-2244
Nevada	Bob Miller (D)	(702) 687-5670
New Hampshire	Stephen Merrill (R)	(603) 271-2121
New Jersey	Christine Todd Whitman (R)	(609) 292-6000
New Mexico	Gary Johnson (R)	(505) 827-3000
New York	George Pataki (R)	(518) 474-8390
North Carolina	James B. Hunt, Jr. (D)	(919) 733-4240
North Dakota	Edward T. Schafer (R)	(701) 328-2200
Ohio	George V. Voinovich(R)	(614) 644-0813
Oklahoma	Frank Keating (R)	(405) 521-2342
Oregon	John Kitzhaber (D)	(503) 378-3111
Pennsylvania	Tom Ridge (R)	(717) 787-2500
Rhode Island	Lincoln Almond (R)	(401) 277-2080, ext. 227
South Carolina	David Beasley (R)	(803) 734-9818
South Dakota	Bill Janklow (R)	(605) 773-3212
Tennessee	Don Sundquist (R)	(615) 741-2001
Texas	George Bush (R)	(512) 463-1762
Utah	Mike Leavitt (R)	(801) 538-1000
Vermont	Howard Dean (D)	(802) 828-3333
Virginia	George Allen (R)	(804) 786-2211
Washington	Mike Lowry (D)	(206) 753-6780
West Virginia	Gaston Caperton (D)	(304) 558-2000
Wisconsin	Tommy G. Thompson (R)	(608) 266-1212
Wyoming	Jim Geringer (R)	(307) 777-7435

BUSINESS LAW & GOVERNMENT

Governors, Mayors, Congress (cont'd)

Mayors of Major U.S. Cities

City	Mayor	Phone
Atlanta	Bill Campbell	(404) 330-6100
Baltimore	Kurt Schmoke	(410) 396-3100
Boston	Thomas M. Menino	(617) 635-4500
Buffalo	Anthony Masiello	(716) 851-4841
Chicago	Richard M. Daley	(312) 744-3300
Cincinnati	Roxanne Qualls	(513) 352-3637
Cleveland	Michael R. White	(216) 664-3990
Columbus	Greg Lashutka	(614) 645-7671
Dallas	Steve Bartlett	(214) 670-0773
Denver	Wellington E. Webb	(303) 640-2721
Detroit	Dennis Archer	(313) 224-3400
Hartford	Mike Peters	(203) 543-8500
Honolulu	Frank F. Fasi	(808) 523-4141
Houston	Bob Lanier	(713) 247-2200
Indianapolis	Stephen Goldsmith	(317) 327-3601
Jacksonville	Edward Austin	(904) 630-1776
Los Angeles	Richard Riordan	(213) 847-2489
Memphis	Willie W. Herenton	(901) 576-6000
Miami	Steve Clark	(305) 250-5300
Milwaukee	John O. Norquist	(414) 286-2200
Minneapolis	Sharon Sayles Belton	(612) 673-2100
Nashville	Philip N. Bredesen	(615) 862-6000
New Orleans	Mark Morial	(504) 565-6400
New York	Rudolph Giuliani	(212) 788-3000
Norfolk	Paul D. Fraim	(804) 441-5126
Orlando	Glenda Hood	(407) 246-2221
Philadelphia	Edward Rendell	(215) 686-2181
Phoenix	Skip Rimsza	(602) 262-7111
Pittsburgh	Tom Murphy	(412) 255-2626
Portland, OR	Vera Katz	(503) 823-4120
Sacramento	Joseph Serna, Jr.	(916) 264-5300
St. Louis	Freeman R. Bosley, Jr.	(314) 622-3201
Salt Lake City	Deedee Corradini	(801) 535-7704
San Antonio	Nelson W. Wolff	(210) 299-7060
San Diego	Susan Golding	(619) 236-6330
San Francisco	Frank Jordan	(415) 554-6141
Seattle	Norman Rice	(206) 684-4000
Tampa	Sandra W. Freedman	(813) 223-8251
Washington, DC	Marion S. Barry	(202) 727-2980

Source: U.S. Conference of Mayors

CompuServe offers access to Findex, McGraw-Hill, PTS Mars, and other business-related databases. GO MGMTRC.

Governors, Mayors, Congress (cont'd)

U.S. Senators

Senator	State	Party	Phone
Murkowski, Frank H.	AK	R	(202) 224-6665
Stevens, Ted	AK	R	(202) 224-3004
Heflin, Howell T.	AL	D	(202) 224-4124
Shelby, Richard C.	AL	R	(202) 224-5744
Bumpers, Dale	AR	D	(202) 224-4843
Pryor, David	AR	D	(202) 224-2353
Kyl, Jon	AZ	R	(202) 224-4521
McCain, John	AZ	R	(202) 224-2235
Boxer, Barbara	CA	D	(202) 225-5161
Feinstein, Dianne	CA	D	(202) 224-3841
Brown, Mark	CO	R	(202) 224-5941
Campbell, Ben N.	CO	R	(202) 224-5852
Dodd, Christopher J.	CT	D	(202) 224-2823
Lieberman, Joseph I.	CT	D	(202) 224-4041
Biden, Jr., Joseph R.	DE	D	(202) 224-5042
Roth, Jr., William V.	DE	R	(202) 224-2441
Graham, Robert	FL	D	(202) 224-3041
Mack, Connie	FL	R	(202) 224-5274
Coverdell, Paul	GA	R	(202) 224-3643
Nunn, Samuel	GA	D	(202) 224-3521
Akaka, Daniel K.	HI	D	(202) 224-6361
Inouye, Daniel K.	HI	D	(202) 224-3934
Grassley, Charles E.	IA	R	(202) 224-3744
Harkin, Thomas	IA	D	(202) 224-3254
Craig, Larry E.	ID	R	(202) 224-2752
Kempthorne, Dirk	ID	R	(202) 224-6142
Moseley-Braun, Carol	IL	D	(202) 224-2854
Simon, Paul	IL	D	(202) 224-2152
Coats, Daniel R.	IN	R	(202) 224-5623
Lugar, Richard G.	IN	R	(202) 224-4814
Dole, Robert	KS	R	(202) 224-6521
Kassebaum, Nancy L.	KS	R	(202) 224-4774
Ford, Wendell H.	KY	D	(202) 224-4343
McConnell, Mitch	KY	R	(202) 224-2541
Breaux, John B.	LA	D	(202) 224-4623
Johnston, J. Bennett	LA	D	(202) 224-5824
Kennedy, Edward M.	MA	D	(202) 224-4543
Kerry, John F.	MA	D	(202) 224-2742
Mikulski, Barbara A.	MD	D	(202) 224-4654
Sarbanes, Paul S.	MD	D	(202) 224-4524
Cohen, William S.	ME	R	(202) 224-2523
Snowe, Olympia	ME	R	(202) 224-5344
Abraham, Spencer	MI	R	(202) 224-4822
Levin, Carl	MI	D	(202) 224-6221
Grams, Rod	MN	R	(202) 224-3244
Wellstone, Paul	MN	D	(202) 224-5641
Ashcroft, John	MO	R	(202) 224-6154
Bond, Christopher S.	MO	R	(202) 224-5721
Cochran, Thad	MS	R	(202) 224-5054
Lott, Trent	MS	R	(202) 224-6253

Senator	State	Party	Phone
Baucus, Max	MT	D	(202) 224-2651
Burns, Conrad R.	MT	R	(202) 224-2644
Faircloth, D. M.	NC	R	(202) 224-3154
Helms, Jesse	NC	R	(202) 224-6342
Conrad, Kent	ND	D	(202) 224-2043
Dorgan, Byron L.	ND	D	(202) 224-2551
Exon, J. J.	NE	D	(202) 224-4224
Kerrey, Bob	NE	D	(202) 224-6551
Gregg, Judd	NH	R	(202) 224-3324
Smith, Robert	NH	R	(202) 224-2841
Bradley, William	NJ	D	(202) 224-3224
Lautenberg, Frank R.	NJ	D	(202) 224-4744
Bingaman, Jeff	NM	D	(202) 224-5521
Domenici, Pete V.	NM	R	(202) 224-6621
Bryan, Richard H.	NV	D	(202) 224-6244
Reid, Harry	NV	D	(202) 224-3542
D'Amato, Alfonse M.	NY	R	(202) 224-6542
Moynihan, Daniel P.	NY	D	(202) 224-4451
DeWine, Michael	OH	R	(202) 224-2315
Glenn, John	OH	D	(202) 224-3353
Inhofe, James	OK	R	(202) 224-4721
Nickles, Donald	OK	R	(202) 224-5754
Hatfield, Mark O.	OR	R	(202) 224-3753
Packwood, Robert	OR	R	(202) 224-5244
Santorum, Rick	PA	R	(202) 224-6324
Specter, Arlen	PA	R	(202) 224-4254
Chafee, John H.	RI	R	(202) 224-2921
Pell, Claiborne	RI	D	(202) 224-4642
Hollings, Ernest F.	SC	D	(202) 224-6121
Thurmond, Strom	SC	R	(202) 224-5972
Daschle, Thomas A.	SD	D	(202) 224-2321
Pressler, Larry	SD	R	(202) 224-5842
Frist, Bill	TN	R	(202) 224-3344
Thompson, Fred	TN	R	(202) 224-4944
Gramm, Phil	TX	R	(202) 224-2934
Hutchison, Kay Bailey	TX	R	(202) 224-5922
Bennett, Robert	UT	R	(202) 224-5444
Hatch, Orrin G.	UT	R	(202) 224-5251
Robb, Charles S.	VA	D	(202) 224-4024
Warner, John W.	VA	R	(202) 224-2023
Leahy, Patrick J.	VT	D	(202) 224-4242
Jeffords, James M.	VT	R	(202) 224-5141
Gorton, Slade	WA	R	(202) 224-3441
Murray, Patty	WA	D	(202) 224-2621
Feingold, Russell	WI	D	(202) 224-5323
Kohl, Herbert H.	WI	D	(202) 224-5653
Byrd, Robert C.	WV	D	(202) 224-3954
Rockefeller IV, John D.	WV	D	(202) 224-6472
Simpson, Alan K.	WY	R	(202) 224-3424
Thomas, Craig	WY	R	(202) 224-6441

Governors, Mayors, Congress (cont'd)

U.S. Representatives

Representative	State	Party	Phone	Representative	State	Party	Phone
Young, Don	AK	R	(202) 225-5765	Packard, Ronald	CA	R	(202) 225-3906
Bachus, Spencer	AL	R	(202) 225-4921	Pelosi, Nancy	CA	D	(202) 225-4965
Bevill, Thomas	AL	D	(202) 225-4876	Pombo, Richard	CA	R	(202) 225-1947
Browder, Glen	AL	D	(202) 225-3261	Radanovich, George	CA	R	(202) 225-4540
Callahan, Sonny	AL	R	(202) 225-4931	Riggs, Frank	CA	R	(202) 225-3311
Cramer, Jr., Robert E.	AL	D	(202) 225-4801	Rohrabacher, Dana	CA	R	(202) 225-2415
Everett, Terry	AL	R	(202) 225-2901	Roybal-Allard, Lucille	CA	D	(202) 225-1766
Hilliard, Earl F.	AL	D	(202) 225-2665	Royce, Ed	CA	R	(202) 225-4111
Dickey, Jay	AR	R	(202) 225-3772	Seastrand, Andrea	CA	R	(202) 225-3601
Hutchinson, Tim	AR	R	(202) 225-4301	Stark, Fortney Pete	CA	D	(202) 225-5065
Lambert-Lincoln, Blanche	AR	D	(202) 225-4076	Thomas, Bill	CA	R	(202) 225-2915
Thornton, Raymond	AR	D	(202) 225-2506	Torres, Esteban E.	CA	D	(202) 225-5256
Faleomavaega, Eni F. H.	AS	D	(202) 225-8577	Tucker III, Walter R.	CA	D	(202) 225-7924
Hayworth, John	AZ	R	(202) 225-2190	Waters, Maxine	CA	D	(202) 225-2201
Kolbe, James T.	AZ	R	(202) 225-2542	Waxman, Henry A.	CA	D	(202) 225-3976
Pastor, Ed	AZ	D	(202) 225-4065	Woolsey, Lynn	CA	D	(202) 225-5161
Salmon, Matthew	AZ	R	(202) 225-4065	Allard, Wayne	CO	R	(202) 225-4676
Shadegg, John	AZ	R	(202) 225-3361	Hefley, Joel	CO	R	(202) 225-4422
Stump, Robert	AZ	R	(202) 225-4576	McInnis, Scott	CO	R	(202) 225-4761
Baker, Bill	CA	R	(202) 225-1880	Schaefer, Daniel	CO	R	(202) 225-7882
Becerra, Xavier	CA	D	(202) 225-6235	Schroeder, Patricia	CO	D	(202) 225-4431
Beilenson, Anthony	CA	D	(202) 225-5911	Skaggs, David E.	CO	D	(202) 225-2161
Berman, Howard L.	CA	D	(202) 225-4695	DeLauro, Rosa	CT	D	(202) 225-3661
Bilbray, Brian	CA	R	(202) 225-2040	Franks, Gary	CT	R	(202) 225-3822
Bono, Sonny	CA	R	(202) 225-5330	Gejdenson, Samuel	CT	D	(202) 225-2076
Brown, Jr., George E.	CA	D	(202) 225-6161	Johnson, Nancy L.	CT	R	(202) 225-4476
Calvert, Ken	CA	R	(202) 225-1986	Kennelly, Barbara B.	CT	D	(202) 225-2265
Condit, Gary	CA	D	(202) 225-6131	Shays, Christopher	CT	R	(202) 225-5541
Cox, Christopher	CA	R	(202) 225-5611	Norton, Eleanor Holmes	DC	D	(202) 225-8050
Cunningham, Randy	CA	R	(202) 225-5452	Castle, Michael N.	DE	R	(202) 225-4165
Dellums, Ronald V.	CA	D	(202) 225-2661	Bilirakis, Michael	FL	R	(202) 225-5755
Dixon, Julian C.	CA	D	(202) 225-7084	Brown, Corrine	FL	D	(202) 225-0123
Dooley, Calvin M.	CA	D	(202) 225-3341	Canady, Charles T.	FL	R	(202) 225-1252
Doolittle, John T.	CA	R	(202) 225-2511	Deutsch, Peter	FL	D	(202) 225-7931
Dornan, Robert K.	CA	R	(202) 225-2965	Diaz-Balart, Lincoln	FL	R	(202) 225-4211
Dreier, David	CA	R	(202) 225-2305	Foley, Mark	FL	R	(202) 225-5792
Eshoo, Anna G.	CA	D	(202) 225-8104	Fowler, Tillie	FL	R	(202) 225-2501
Farr, Sam	CA	D	(202) 225-2861	Gibbons, Samuel M.	FL	D	(202) 225-3376
Fazio, Vic	CA	D	(202) 225-5716	Goss, Porter J.	FL	R	(202) 225-2536
Filner, Bob	CA	D	(202) 225-8045	Hastings, Alcee L.	FL	D	(202) 225-1313
Gallegly, Elton	CA	R	(202) 225-5811	Johnston, Harry	FL	D	(202) 225-3001
Harman, Jane	CA	D	(202) 225-8220	McCollum, William	FL	R	(202) 225-2176
Herger, Walter W.	CA	R	(202) 225-3076	Meek, Carrie	FL	D	(202) 225-4506
Horn, Steve	CA	R	(202) 225-6676	Mica, John L.	FL	R	(202) 225-4035
Hunter, Duncan L.	CA	R	(202) 225-5672	Miller, Dan	FL	R	(202) 225-5015
Kim, Jay C.	CA	R	(202) 225-3201	Peterson, Douglas (Pete)	FL	D	(202) 225-5235
Lantos, Thomas	CA	D	(202) 225-3531	Ros-Lehtinen, Ileana	FL	R	(202) 225-3931
Lewis, Jerry	CA	R	(202) 225-5861	Scarborough, Joe	FL	R	(202) 225-4136
Lofgren, Zoe	CA	D	(202) 225-3071	Shaw, Jr., E. C.	FL	R	(202) 225-3026
Martinez, Matthew G.	CA	D	(202) 225-5464	Stearns, Clifford B.	FL	R	(202) 225-5744
Matsui, Robert T.	CA	D	(202) 225-7163	Thurman, Karen	FL	D	(202) 225-1002
McKeon, Howard P.	CA	R	(202) 225-1956	Weldon, Dave	FL	R	(202) 225-3671
Miller, George	CA	D	(202) 225-2095	Young, C. W.	FL	R	(202) 225-5961
Mineta, Norman Y.	CA	D	(202) 225-2631	Barr, Bob	GA	R	(202) 225-2931
Moorhead, Carlos J.	CA	R	(202) 225-4176	Bishop, Jr., Sanford	GA	D	(202) 225-3631

Governors, Mayors, Congress (cont'd)

U.S. Representatives

Representative	State	Party	Phone
Chambliss, Saxby	GA	R	(202) 225-6531
Collins, Mac	GA	R	(202) 225-5901
Deal, Nathan	GA	R	(202) 225-5211
Gingrich, Newt	GA	R	(202) 225-4501
Kingston, Jack	GA	R	(202) 225-5831
Lewis, John	GA	D	(202) 225-3801
Linder, John	GA	R	(202) 225-4272
McKinney, Cynthia	GA	D	(202) 225-1605
Norwood, Jr., Charles	GA	R	(202) 225-4101
Underwood, Robert A.	GU	D	(202) 225-1188
Abercrombie, Neil	HI	D	(202) 225-2726
Mink, Patsy T.	HI	D	(202) 225-4906
Ganske, Greg	IA	R	(202) 225-4426
Latham, Tom	IA	R	(202) 225-5476
Leach, James	IA	R	(202) 225-6576
Lightfoot, James R.	IA	R	(202) 225-3806
Nussle, James Allen	IA	R	(202) 225-2911
Chenoweth, Helen	ID	R	(202) 225-6611
Crapo, Michael D.	ID	R	(202) 225-5531
Collins, Cardiss	IL	D	(202) 225-5006
Costello, Jerry F.	IL	D	(202) 225-5661
Crane, Philip M.	IL	R	(202) 225-3711
Durbin, Richard J.	IL	D	(202) 225-5271
Evans, Lane	IL	D	(202) 225-5905
Ewing, Thomas	IL	R	(202) 225-2371
Fawell, Harris W.	IL	R	(202) 225-3515
Flanagan, Michael	IL	R	(202) 225-4061
Gutierrez, Luis V.	IL	D	(202) 225-8203
Hastert, J. D.	IL	R	(202) 225-2976
Hyde, Henry J.	IL	R	(202) 225-4561
LaHood, Ray	IL	R	(202) 225-6201
Lipinski, William O.	IL	D	(202) 225-5701
Manzullo, Donald	IL	R	(202) 225-5676
Porter, John E.	IL	R	(202) 225-4835
Poshard, Glenn	IL	D	(202) 225-5201
Reynolds, Mel	IL	D	(202) 225-0773
Rush, Bobby L.	IL	D	(202) 225-4372
Weller, Gerald	IL	R	(202) 225-3635
Yates, Sidney R.	IL	D	(202) 225-2111
Burton, Daniel	IN	R	(202) 225-2276
Buyer, Steve	IN	D	(202) 225-5037
Hamilton, Lee H.	IN	D	(202) 225-5315
Hostettler, John	IN	R	(202) 225-4636
Jacobs, Jr., Andrew	IN	D	(202) 225-4011
McIntosh, David	IN	R	(202) 225-3021
Myers, John T.	IN	R	(202) 225-5805
Roemer, Timothy	IN	D	(202) 225-3915
Souder, Mark	IN	R	(202) 225-4436
Visclosky, Peter J.	IN	D	(202) 225-2461
Brownback, Sam	KS	R	(202) 225-6601
Meyers, Jan	KS	R	(202) 225-2865
Roberts, Pat	KS	R	(202) 225-2715
Tiahrt, Todd	KS	R	(202) 225-6216
Baesler, Scotty	KY	D	(202) 225-4706
Bunning, James	KY	R	(202) 225-3465

Representative	State	Party	Phone
Lewis, Ron	KY	R	(202) 225-3501
Rogers, Harold	KY	R	(202) 225-4601
Ward, Michael	KY	D	(202) 225-5401
Whitfield, Edward	KY	R	(202) 225-3115
Baker, Richard H.	LA	R	(202) 225-3901
Fields, Cleo	LA	D	(202) 225-8490
Hayes, James A.	LA	D	(202) 225-2031
Jefferson, William	LA	D	(202) 225-6636
Livingston, Robert	LA	R	(202) 225-3015
McCrery, James	LA	R	(202) 225-2777
Tauzin, W. J.	LA	D	(202) 225-4031
Blute, Peter I.	MA	R	(202) 225-6101
Frank, Barney	MA	D	(202) 225-5931
Kennedy II, Joseph P.	MA	D	(202) 225-5111
Markey, Edward J.	MA	D	(202) 225-2836
Meehan, Martin T.	MA	D	(202) 225-3411
Moakley, John Joseph	MA	D	(202) 225-8273
Neal, Richard E.	MA	D	(202) 225-5601
Olver, John W.	MA	D	(202) 225-5335
Studds, Gerry E.	MA	D	(202) 225-3111
Torkildsen, Peter G.	MA	R	(202) 225-8020
Bartlett, Roscoe G.	MD	R	(202) 225-2721
Cardin, Benjamin L.	MD	D	(202) 225-4016
Ehrlich, Jr., Robert	MD	R	(202) 225-3061
Gilchrest, Wayne T.	MD	R	(202) 225-5311
Hoyer, Steny H.	MD	D	(202) 225-4131
Mfume, Kweisi	MD	D	(202) 225-4741
Morella, Constance	MD	R	(202) 225-5341
Wynn, Albert R.	MD	D	(202) 225-8699
Baldacci, John	ME	D	(202) 225-6306
Longley, James	ME	R	(202) 225-6116
Barcia, James A.	MI	D	(202) 225-8171
Bonior, David E.	MI	D	(202) 225-2106
Camp, David Lee	MI	R	(202) 225-3561
Chrysler, Dick	MI	R	(202) 225-4872
Collins, Barbara Rose	MI	D	(202) 225-2261
Conyers, Jr., John	MI	D	(202) 225-5126
Dingell, John D.	MI	D	(202) 225-4071
Ehlers, Vern	MI	R	(202) 225-3831
Hoekstra, Peter	MI	R	(202) 225-4401
Kildee, Dale E.	MI	D	(202) 225-3611
Knollenberg, Joe	MI	R	(202) 225-5802
Levin, Sander M.	MI	D	(202) 225-4961
Rivers, Lynn	MI	D	(202) 225-6261
Smith, Nick	MI	R	(202) 225-6276
Stupak, Bart	MI	D	(202) 225-4735
Upton, Frederick S.	MI	R	(202) 225-3761
Gutknecht, Gilbert	MN	R	(202) 225-2472
Luther, William	MN	D	(202) 225-2271
Minge, David	MN	D	(202) 225-2331
Oberstar, James L.	MN	D	(202) 225-6211
Peterson, Collin C.	MN	D	(202) 225-2165
Ramstad, James M.	MN	D	(202) 225-2871
Sabo, Martin O.	MN	D	(202) 225-4755
Vento, Bruce F.	MN	D	(202) 225-6631

Governors, Mayors, Congress (cont'd)

U.S. Representatives

Representative	State	Party	Phone
Clay, William L.	MO	D	(202) 225-2406
Danner, Pat	MO	D	(202) 225-7041
Emerson, Bill	MO	R	(202) 225-4404
Gephardt, Richard A.	MO	D	(202) 225-2671
Hancock, Melton D.	MO	R	(202) 225-6536
McCarthy, Karen	MO	D	(202) 225-4535
Skelton, Ike	MO	D	(202) 225-2876
Talent, James M.	MO	R	(202) 225-2561
Volkmer, Harold L.	MO	D	(202) 225-2956
Montgomery, G. V.	MS	D	(202) 225-5031
Parker, Paul M.	MS	D	(202) 225-5865
Taylor, Gene	MS	D	(202) 225-5772
Thompson, Bennie G.	MS	D	(202) 225-5876
Wicker, Roger	MS	R	(202) 225-4306
Williams, Pat	MT	D	(202) 225-3211
Ballenger, Thomas C.	NC	R	(202) 225-2576
Burr, Richard	NC	R	(202) 225-2071
Clayton, Eva	NC	D	(202) 225-3101
Coble, Howard	NC	R	(202) 225-3065
Funderburk, David	NC	R	(202) 225-4531
Hefner, W. G.	NC	D	(202) 225-3715
Heineman, Frederick	NC	R	(202) 225-1784
Jones, Jr., Walter	NC	R	(202) 225-3415
Myrick, Sue	NC	R	(202) 225-1976
Rose, Charles	NC	D	(202) 225-2731
Taylor, Charles Hart	NC	R	(202) 225-6401
Watt, Melvin	NC	D	(202) 225-1510
Pomeroy, Earl	ND	D	(202) 225-2611
Barrett, William E.	NE	R	(202) 225-6435
Bereuter, Douglas	NE	R	(202) 225-4806
Christensen, Jon	NE	R	(202) 225-4155
Bass, Charles	NH	R	(202) 225-5206
Zeliff, Jr., William	NH	R	(202) 225-5456
Andrews, Robert E.	NJ	D	(202) 225-6501
Franks, Bob	NJ	R	(202) 225-5361
Frelinghuysen, Rodney	NJ	R	(202) 225-5034
LoBiondo, Frank	NJ	R	(202) 225-6572
Martini, Bill	NJ	R	(202) 225-5751
Menendez, Robert	NJ	D	(202) 225-7919
Pallone, Jr., Frank	NJ	D	(202) 225-4671
Payne, Donald M.	NJ	D	(202) 225-3436
Roukema, Marge	NJ	R	(202) 225-4465
Saxton, H. James	NJ	R	(202) 225-4765
Smith, Christopher	NJ	R	(202) 225-3765
Torricelli, Robert	NJ	D	(202) 225-5061
Zimmer, Richard A.	NJ	R	(202) 225-5801
Richardson, William	NM	D	(202) 225-6190
Schiff, Steven H.	NM	R	(202) 225-6316
Skeen, Joseph	NM	R	(202) 225-2365
Ensign, John	NV	R	(202) 225-5965
Vucanovich, Barbara	NV	R	(202) 225-6155
Ackerman, Gary L.	NY	D	(202) 225-2601
Boehlert, Sherwood	NY	R	(202) 225-3665
Engel, Eliot L.	NY	D	(202) 225-2464
Flake, Floyd H.	NY	D	(202) 225-3461

Representative	State	Party	Phone
Forbes, Michael	NY	R	(202) 225-3826
Frisa, Daniel	NY	R	(202) 225-5516
Gilman, Benjamin A.	NY	R	(202) 225-3776
Hinchey, Maurice D.	NY	D	(202) 225-6335
Houghton, Amory	NY	R	(202) 225-3161
Kelly, Sue	NY	R	(202) 225-5441
King, Peter T.	NY	R	(202) 225-7896
LaFalce, John J.	NY	D	(202) 225-3231
Lazio, Rick A.	NY	R	(202) 225-3335
Lowey, Nita M.	NY	D	(202) 225-6506
Maloney, Carolyn B.	NY	D	(202) 225-7944
Manton, Thomas J.	NY	D	(202) 225-3965
McHugh, John M.	NY	R	(202) 225-4611
McNulty, Michael R.	NY	D	(202) 225-5076
Molinari, Susan	NY	D	(202) 225-3371
Nadler, Jerrold	NY	D	(202) 225-5635
Owens, Major R.	NY	D	(202) 225-6231
Paxon, Bill	NY	R	(202) 225-5265
Quinn, Jack	NY	R	(202) 225-3306
Rangel, Charles B.	NY	D	(202) 225-4365
Schumer, Charles E.	NY	D	(202) 225-6616
Serrano, Jose E.	NY	D	(202) 225-4361
Slaughter, Louise M.	NY	D	(202) 225-3615
Solomon, Gerald B.	NY	R	(202) 225-5614
Towns, Edolphus	NY	D	(202) 225-5936
Velazquez, Nydia M.	NY	D	(202) 225-2361
Walsh, James T.	NY	R	(202) 225-3701
Boehner, John Andrew	OH	R	(202) 225-6205
Brown, Sherrod	OH	D	(202) 225-3401
Chabot, Steve	OH	R	(202) 225-2216
Cremeans, Frank	OH	R	(202) 225-5705
Gillmor, Paul E.	OH	R	(202) 225-6405
Hall, Tony P.	OH	D	(202) 225-6465
Hobson, David L.	OH	R	(202) 225-4324
Hoke, Martin R.	OH	R	(202) 225-5871
Kaptur, Marcy	OH	D	(202) 225-4146
Kasich, John R.	OH	R	(202) 225-5355
LaTourette, Steven	OH	R	(202) 225-5731
Ney, Bob	OH	R	(202) 225-6265
Oxley, Michael G.	OH	R	(202) 225-2676
Portman, Rob	OH	R	(202) 225-3164
Pryce, Deborah	OH	R	(202) 225-2015
Regula, Ralph	OH	R	(202) 225-3876
Sawyer, Thomas C.	OH	D	(202) 225-5231
Stokes, Louis	OH	D	(202) 225-7032
Traficant, Jr., James	OH	D	(202) 225-5261
Brewster, Bill Kent	OK	D	(202) 225-4565
Coburn, Tom	OK	R	(202) 225-2701
Istook, Jr., Ernest Jim	OK	R	(202) 225-2132
Largent, Steve	OK	R	(202) 225-2211
Lucas, Frank	OK	R	(202) 225-5565
Watts, Jr., J. C.	OK	R	(202) 225-6165
Bunn, Jim	OR	R	(202) 225-5711
Cooley, Wes	OR	R	(202) 225-6730
DeFazio, Peter A.	OR	D	(202) 225-6416

Governors, Mayors, Congress (cont'd)

U.S. Representatives

Representative	State	Party	Phone
Furse, Elizabeth	OR	D	(202) 225-0855
Wyden, Ronald	OR	D	(202) 225-4811
Borski, Robert A.	PA	D	(202) 225-8251
Clinger, Jr., William	PA	R	(202) 225-5121
Coyne, William J.	PA	D	(202) 225-2301
Doyle, Mike	PA	D	(202) 225-2135
English, Phil	PA	R	(202) 225-5406
Fattah, Chaka	PA	D	(202) 225-4001
Foglietta, Thomas M.	PA	D	(202) 225-4731
Fox, Jon	PA	R	(202) 225-6111
Gekas, George W.	PA	R	(202) 225-4315
Goodling, William F.	PA	R	(202) 225-5836
Greenwood, Jim	PA	R	(202) 225-4276
Holden, Tim	PA	D	(202) 225-5546
Kanjorski, Paul E.	PA	D	(202) 225-6511
Klink, Ron	PA	D	(202) 225-2565
Mascara, Frank	PA	D	(202) 225-4665
McDade, Joseph M.	PA	R	(202) 225-3731
McHale, Paul	PA	D	(202) 225-6411
Murtha, John P.	PA	D	(202) 225-2065
Shuster, Bud	PA	R	(202) 225-2431
Walker, Robert S.	PA	R	(202) 225-2411
Weldon, Curt	PA	R	(202) 225-2011
Romero-Barcelo, Carlos	PR	D	(202) 225-2615
Kennedy, Patrick	RI	D	(202) 225-4911
Reed, John F.	RI	D	(202) 225-2735
Clyburn, James E.	SC	D	(202) 225-3315
Graham, Lindsey	SC	R	(202) 225-5301
Inglis, Bob	SC	R	(202) 225-6030
Sanford, Mark	SC	R	(202) 225-3176
Spence, Floyd	SC	R	(202) 225-2452
Spratt, Jr., John M.	SC	D	(202) 225-5501
Johnson, Timothy P.	SD	D	(202) 225-2801
Bryant, Ed	TN	R	(202) 225-2811
Clement, Robert	TN	D	(202) 225-4311
Duncan, Jr., John J.	TN	R	(202) 225-5435
Ford, Harold E.	TN	D	(202) 225-3265
Gordon, Bart	TN	D	(202) 225-4231
Hilleary, Van	TN	R	(202) 225-6831
Quillen, James H.	TN	R	(202) 225-6356
Tanner, John S.	TN	D	(202) 225-4714
Wamp, Zach	TN	R	(202) 225-3271
Archer, William	TX	R	(202) 225-2571
Armey, Richard K.	TX	R	(202) 225-7772
Barton, Joseph	TX	R	(202) 225-2002
Bentsen, Ken	TX	D	(202) 225-7508
Bonilla, Henry	TX	R	(202) 225-4511
Bryant, John	TX	D	(202) 225-2231
Chapman, Jim	TX	D	(202) 225-3035
Coleman, Ronald D.	TX	D	(202) 225-4831
Combest, Larry	TX	R	(202) 225-4005
de la Garza, E.	TX	D	(202) 225-2531
DeLay, Thomas	TX	R	(202) 225-5951
Doggett, Lloyd	TX	D	(202) 225-4865
Edwards, Chet	TX	D	(202) 225-6105

Representative	State	Party	Phone
Fields, Jack	TX	R	(202) 225-4901
Frost, Martin	TX	D	(202) 225-3605
Geren, Peter	TX	D	(202) 225-5071
Gonzalez, Henry B.	TX	D	(202) 225-3236
Green, Gene	TX	D	(202) 225-1688
Hall, Ralph M.	TX	D	(202) 225-6673
Jackson-Lee, Sheila	TX	D	(202) 225-3816
Johnson, Eddie Bernice	TX	D	(202) 225-8885
Johnson, Sam	TX	R	(202) 225-4201
Laughlin, Gregory H.	TX	D	(202) 225-2831
Ortiz, Solomon P.	TX	D	(202) 225-7742
Smith, Lamar S.	TX	R	(202) 225-4236
Stenholm, Charles W.	TX	D	(202) 225-6605
Stockman, Steve	TX	R	(202) 225-6565
Tejeda, Frank	TX	D	(202) 225-1640
Thornberry, William	TX	R	(202) 225-3706
Wilson, Charles	TX	D	(202) 225-2401
Hansen, James V.	UT	R	(202) 225-0453
Orton, William H.	UT	D	(202) 225-7751
Waldholtz, Enid	UT	R	(202) 225-3011
Bateman, Herbert H.	VA	R	(202) 225-4261
Bliley, Jr., Thomas J.	VA	R	(202) 225-2815
Boucher, Rick	VA	D	(202) 225-3861
Davis, Thomas	VA	R	(202) 225-1492
Goodlatte, Robert W.	VA	R	(202) 225-5431
Moran, Jr., James P.	VA	D	(202) 225-4376
Payne, Jr., Lewis F.	VA	D	(202) 225-4711
Pickett, Owen B.	VA	D	(202) 225-4215
Scott, Robert C.	VA	D	(202) 225-8351
Sisisky, Norman	VA	D	(202) 225-6365
Wolf, Frank R.	VA	R	(202) 225-5136
Frazer, Victor	VI	C	(202) 225-1790
Sanders, Bernard	VT	I	(202) 225-4115
Dicks, Norman D.	WA	D	(202) 225-5916
Dunn, Jennifer	WA	R	(202) 225-7761
Hastings, Doc	WA	R	(202) 225-5816
McDermott, James A.	WA	D	(202) 225-3106
Metcalf, Jack	WA	R	(202) 225-2605
Nethercutt, George	WA	R	(202) 225-2006
Smith, Linda	WA	R	(202) 225-3536
Tate, Randy	WA	R	(202) 225-8901
White, Rick	WA	R	(202) 225-6311
Barrett, Thomas M.	WI	D	(202) 225-3571
Gunderson, Steve	WI	R	(202) 225-5506
Kleczka, Gerald D.	WI	D	(202) 225-4572
Klug, Scott	WI	R	(202) 225-2906
Neumann, Mark	WI	R	(202) 225-3031
Obey, David R.	WI	D	(202) 225-3365
Petri, Thomas E.	WI	R	(202) 225-2476
Roth, Toby	WI	R	(202) 225-5665
Sensenbrenner, Jr., F. J.	WI	R	(202) 225-5101
Mollohan, Alan B.	WV	D	(202) 225-4172
Rahall II, Nick Joe	WV	D	(202) 225-3452
Wise, Jr., Robert E.	WV	D	(202) 225-2711
Cubin, Barbara	WY	R	(202) 225-2311

C: Resident Commissioner; I: Independent

Congressional Chairs

Senate Committees

Committee	Chair
Agriculture, Nutrition, and Forestry	Richard G. Lugar, R-IN
Appropriations	Mark O. Hatfield, R-OR
Armed Services	Strom Thurmond, R-SC
Banking, Housing, and Urban Affairs	Alfonse D'Amato, R-NY
Budget	Pete V. Domenici, R-NM
Commerce, Science, and Transportation	Larry Pressler, R-SD
Energy and Natural Resources	Frank H. Murkowski, R-AK
Environment and Public Works	John H. Chafee, R-RI
Finance	Bob Packwood, R-OR
Foreign Relations	Jesse Helms, R-NC
Government Affairs	William V. Roth, Jr., R-DE
Judiciary	Orrin G. Hatch, R-UT
Labor and Human Resources	Nancy L. Kassebaum, R-KS
Rules and Administration	Ted Stevens, R-AK
Select Ethics	Mitch McConnell, R-KY
Select Indian Affairs	John McCain, R-AZ
Select Intelligence	Arlen Specter, R-PA
Small Business	Christopher S. Bond, R-MO
Special Aging	William S. Cohen, R-ME
Veterans' Affairs	Alan K. Simpson, R-WY

House Committees

Committee	Chair
Agriculture	Pat Roberts, R-KS
Appropriations	Bob Livingston, R-LA
Banking and Financial Services	James A. Leach, R-LA
Budget	John R. Kasich, R-OH
Commerce	Thomas J. Bliley, Jr., R-VA
Economic and Educational Opportunities	William F. Goodling, R-PA
Government Reform and Oversight	William F. Clinger, Jr., R-PA
House Oversight	William M. Thomas, R-CA
Intelligence	Robert K. Dornan, R-CA
International Relations	Benjamin A. Gilman, R-NY
Judiciary	Henry J. Hyde, R-IL
National Security	Floyd Spence, R-SC
Resources	Don Young, R-AK
Rules	Gerald B. Solomon, R-NY
Science	Robert S. Walker, R-PA
Small Business	Jan Meyers, R-KS
Standards of Official Conduct	Nancy L. Johnson, R-CT
Transportation and Infrastructure	Bud Shuster, R-PA
Veterans' Affairs	Bob Stump, R-AZ
Ways and Means	Bill Archer, R-TX

Joint Committees of Congress

Committee	Senate Chair	House Chair
Economic	Connie Mack, R-FL	Tim Saxton, R-NJ
Library	Mark O. Hatfield, R-OR	William M. Thomas, R-CA
Printing	Ted Stevens, R-AK	William M. Thomas, R-CA
Taxation	Bob Packwood, R-OR	Bill Archer, R-TX

Congressional E-Mail Addresses

U.S. Senators

State	Name	E-mail Address
ID	Craig, Larry	larry_craig@craig.senate.gov
ID	Kempthorne, Dirk	dirk_kempthorne@kempthorne.senate.gov
IL	Simon, Paul	senator@simon.senate.gov
MA	Kennedy, Ted	senator@kennedy.senate.gov
NM	Bingaman, Jeff	Senator_Bingaman@bingaman.senate.gov
TX	Hutchison, Kay B.	senator@hutchison.senate.gov
VA	Robb, Charles	senator_robb@robb.senate.gov
VT	Jeffords, Jim	vermont@jeffords.senate.gov
VT	Leahy, Patrick	senator_leahy@leahy.senate.gov

Congressional E-Mail Addresses (cont'd)

U.S. Representatives

State	Name	E-Mail Address
AR	Dickey, Jay	jdickey@hr.house.gov
AZ	Pastor, Ed	edpastor@hr.house.gov
CA	Eshoo, Anna	annagram@hr.house.gov
CA	Harman, Jane	jharman@hr.house.gov
CA	Lantos, Tom	talk2tom@hr.house.gov
CA	Miller, George	fgeorgem@hr.house.gov
CA	Mineta, Norman Y.	tellnorm@hr.house.gov
CA	Stark, Pete	petemail@hr.house.gov
CA	Tucker III, Walter	tucker96@hr.house.gov
CO	Skaggs, David	skaggs@hr.house.gov
CT	Gejdenson, Sam	bozrah@hr.house.gov
CT	Shays, Christopher	cshays@hr.house.gov
FL	Canady, Charles	canady@hr.house.gov
FL	Deutsch, Peter	pdeutsch@hr.house.gov
FL	Stearns, Cliff	cstearns@hr.house.gov
GA	Gingrich, Newton	georgia6@hr.house.gov
IL	Fawell, Harris	hfawell@hr.house.gov
IL	Hastert, Dennis	dhastert@hr.house.gov
KS	Roberts, Pat	emailpat@hr.house.gov
MI	Camp, Dave	davecamp@hr.house.gov
MI	Conyers, John	jconyers@hr.house.gov
MI	Ehlers, Vernon	congehlr@hr.house.gov
MN	Ramstad, Jim	mn03@hr.house.gov
NC	Rose, Charlie	crose@hr.house.gov
NC	Taylor, Charles	chtaylor@hr.house.gov
NC	Watt, Mel	melmail@hr.house.gov
ND	Pomeroy, Earl	epomeroy@hr.house.gov
NJ	Zimmer, Dick	dzimmer@hr.house.gov
NY	Boehlert, Sherwood	boehlert@hr.house.gov
NY	Manton, Thomas	tmanton@hr.house.gov

State	Name	E-Mail Address
NY	Paxon, Bill	bpaxon@hr.house.gov
OH	Hoke, Martin	hokemail@hr.house.gov
OH	Portman, Rob	portmail@hr.house.gov
OK	Istook, Jr. Ernest	istook@hr.house.gov
OR	DeFazio, Pete	pdefazio@hr.house.gov
OR	Furse, Elizabeth	furseor1@hr.house.gov
PA	Walker, Robert	pa16@hr.house.gov
TX	Barton, Joe	barton06@hr.house.gov
TX	Johnson, Sam	samtx03@hr.house.gov
TX	Wilson, Charles	cwilson@hr.house.gov
VA	Boucher, Rick	jshoumak@hr.house.gov
VA	Goodlatte, Bob	talk2bob@hr.house.gov
VA	Pickett, Owen	opickett@hr.house.gov
VT	Sanders, Bernie	bsanders@igc.apc.org

House Committees

Committee	E-Mail Address
Subcommittee on Labor Management Relations	slabmgnt@hr.house.gov
Resources	resource@hr.house.gov
Science	housesst@hr.house.gov

White House Conference

THE WHITE HOUSE HAS established its Conference on Small Business in order to provide businesspeople with the opportunity to give their input and ideas on business-related topics. Through regional conferences, small business owners and entrepreneurs develop ideas to promote small business success as well as electing delegates who will present these ideas to the President and Congress at the National Conference.

Recommendations from two previous national conferences, held in 1980 and 1986, led to the Regulatory Flexibility, Equal Access to Justice, and Minority Business Opportunity Reform acts. About half of the recommendations produced at these conferences have been acted upon by the legislative or executive branches of government.

To be eligible, an individual must be an owner, corporate officer, or employee of a for-profit business employing fewer than 500 people and must personally reside in the state in which the conference is being held. If an individual does not meet these qualifications, then he or she may attend the conference as a non-participating observer.

Contact Option

The White House Conference on Small Business
1800 G St., NW, Suite 250
Washington, DC 20006
(202) 724-0891

Small Business Administration

THE U.S. SMALL BUSINESS Administration (SBA) is an independent government agency created by Congress to help small businesses grow and prosper. The SBA has more than 100 offices that offer small firms financial assistance through guaranteed loans, management assistance, help in obtaining government contracts, counseling services, and many low-cost publications.

The SBA offers assistance to small businesses and pays particular attention to those owned by ethnic minorities, women, veterans, and others with special needs and circumstances. There are fact sheets available covering each of these and many more categories.

The SBA publishes over 100 business booklets that sell for modest fees (usually under $2.00). They address issues which concern prospective and exist-

ing small business owners. A free directory of Small Business Administration publications may be obtained from the SBA Answer Desk or from any regional SBA office. *(See also "Small Business Administration Regional Offices" on page 385.)*

Contact Option

Small Business Answer Desk
(202) 205-7717, or (800) 827-5722 or (202) 205-7701 for recorded information

This hotline provides the caller with an automated menu of topics on relevant small business issues. Informative brochures will be sent upon request.

Getting an SBA Loan

SBA LOANS ARE AVAILABLE to small companies that have sought and been refused financing from other lending institutions prior to applying to the SBA for assistance. Most of the SBA loans are made through the guaranteed loan program, in which the private lender agrees to loan funds to the small business and the SBA agrees to guarantee 90% of a loan under $155,000 and up to 85% of a loan greater than that figure, up to a maximum of $750,000.

Although the interest rates on SBA guaranteed loans are negotiated between the borrower and lender, they are subject to SBA maximums and generally cannot exceed 2.75% over the New York prime rate.

The SBA also provides specialized loan guarantee programs which include:

- Export revolving lines of credit

- International trade loans

- Seasonal lines of credit

- Small general contractor financing

- Lender incentives for small loans of less than $50,000

- Pollution control loans

- Community development loans.

Direct loans of up to $150,000 by the SBA are very limited in number and are available only to applicants unable to secure an SBA-guaranteed loan. Before applying, a small business owner must seek financing from his or her bank of account and, in cit-

ies of over 200,000, from at least one other lender. Direct loan funds are available to businesses located in high-unemployment areas, or owned by low-income or handicapped individuals, Vietnam veterans or disabled veterans. Interest on direct loans is calculated quarterly.

Eligibility Requirements

To be eligible for SBA loan assistance, a company must be operated for profit and fall within size standards. It cannot be a business involved in the creation or distribution of ideas or opinions such as newspapers, magazines, and academic schools. It cannot be engaged in speculation or investment in rental real estate.

The SBA has other eligibility requirements that qualify a business as a small business:

- Manufacturing: the maximum number of employees may range from 500 to 1,500 depending on the type of product manufactured.

- Wholesaling: the maximum number of employees may not exceed 100.

- Services: the average annual receipts may not exceed $3.5 to $14.5 million depending on the industry.

- Retailing: the average annual receipts may not exceed $3.5 to $13.5 million, depending on the industry.

- Construction: general construction average annual receipts may not exceed $9.5 to $17 million depending on the industry.

Getting an SBA Loan (cont'd)

- Special trade construction: average annual receipts may not exceed $7 million.

- Agriculture: average annual receipts range from $1 million to $3.5 million, depending on the industry.

Applying for an SBA Loan

To apply for a loan, a small business owner must do the following:

- Prepare a current business balance sheet listing all assets, liabilities, and net worth. Start-up businesses should prepare an estimated balance sheet including the amount invested by the owner and others.

- Prepare a profit-and-loss statement for the current period and the most recent three fiscal years. Start-up businesses should prepare a detailed projection of earnings and expenses for at least the first year of operation.

- Prepare a personal financial statement of the proprietor and each partner or stockholder owning 20% or more of the business.

- List collateral to be offered as security for the loan.

- List any existing liens.

- State the amount of the requested loan and the purposes for which it is intended.

- Present the above items to a selected lender. If the loan request is refused, the business owner should contact the local SBA office regarding the guaranteed-loan program.

- If the guaranteed loan is not possible, other loans may be available from the SBA.

Alternatives to an SBA Loan

ALTHOUGH THE SBA is perhaps the best-known "friend" to the small business owner, there are several other governmental and private sector organizations which can offer financial assistance and guidance to individuals requiring it.

SBIC (Small Business Investment Companies) are privately organized and managed firms which make equity capital and long-term credit available to small, independent businesses. SBICs are licensed by the SBA but set their own policies and investment decisions. SSBICs (Special Small Business Investment Companies) invest specifically in socially and economically disadvantaged entrepreneurs. The SBIC can borrow up to four times its private capital through a federally guaranteed funding system, at an interest rate slightly above the cost of money to the U.S., making it an attractive and powerful source of capital for new and growing businesses.

The National Association of Small Business Investment Companies (NASBIC) is the national trade association for the 215 SBICs and 127 SSBICs. It publishes a directory of members, broken down by state, size of financing, industry preference, and geographical preference. The NASBIC directory is entitled *Venture Capital: Where to Find It*. Phone and credit card orders are not accepted.

To obtain the directory, send a check for $10, payable to NASBIC, to:

NASBIC Directory
P.O. Box 2039
Merrifield, VA 22116

For other questions or information, call or write:

National Association of Small Business
Investment Companies
1199 N. Fairfax St., Suite 200
Alexandria, VA 22314
(703) 683-1601

BDCs (Business Development Corporations) are groups affiliated with 30 various state governments and they differ from SBAs. BDCs agree to accept riskier loans, for longer terms. They frequently sell parts of these loans to others on the secondary loan market to offset the risk. Interest rates usually average 2% to 4% above the prime lending rate and some BDCs charge a flat fee.

To locate the BDC within a state, or to obtain assistance in locating other funding sources, an individual should write or call a specific state Small Business Development Center. The national organization will direct the caller to one of 750 state or regional centers. These centers provide assistance in the form of training, counseling, and research assistance in start-up, operation, and expansion of business in all 50 states. While the centers do not provide funding, they do refer individuals to the organizations that can offer the greatest assistance. *(See also "Small Business Development Centers" on page 385.)*

Association of Small Business Development Centers
1313 Farnum, Suite 132
Omaha, NE 68182
(402) 595-2387

Small Business Support

EACH STATE HAS offices that provide assistance for prospective or existing small business owners. These agencies help businesses to prosper and create and retain jobs. They also increase economic opportunities for communities and populations in need.

The following phone numbers connect to the main business support office in each state. These offices in turn can direct the caller to an appropriate regional or local office, if necessary.

State-by-State Support

State	Department of Economic Development
AK	(907) 465-2500
AL	(205) 242-0400
AR	(501) 682-2052
AZ	(602) 280-1306
CA	(916) 322-3982
CO	(303) 892-3840
CT	(203) 258-4202
DC	(202) 727-6600
DE	(302) 739-4271
FL	(904) 488-6300
GA	(404) 656-3556
HI	(808) 586-2355
IA	(515) 242-4814
ID	(208) 334-2470
IL	(217) 782-7500
IN	(317) 232-8894
KS	(913) 296-3480
KY	(502) 564-7670
LA	(504) 342-5388
MA	(617) 727-8380
MD	(410) 333-6901
ME	(207) 287-2656
MI	(517) 373-0347
MN	(612) 296-6424
MO	(314) 751-3946
MS	(601) 359-3449
MT	(406) 444-3814
NC	(919) 733-4151

State	Department of Economic Development
ND	(701) 221-5300
NE	(402) 471-3747
NH	(603) 271-2411
NJ	(609) 292-2444
NM	(505) 827-0305
NV	(702) 687-4325
NY	(518) 474-4100
OH	(614) 466-2317
OK	(405) 843-9770
OR	(503) 373-1205
PA	(717) 787-3003
RI	(401) 277-2601
SC	(803) 737-0400
SD	(605) 773-5032
TN	(615) 741-1888
TX	(512) 472-5059
UT	(801) 538-8700
VA	(804) 371-8106
VT	(802) 828-3221
WA	(206) 753-7426
WI	(608) 266-7884
WV	(304) 558-3650
WY	(307) 777-7284

The Top Reference Sources

The Legal Guide for Starting and Running a Small Business
Nolo Press, $22.95
(800) 992-6656 or (510) 549-1976

This book contains legal information the small business owner needs to know about partnerships, cor-

porations, buying businesses, franchises, licenses, permits, leases, contracts, hiring and firing, customer relations, independent contractors, insurance, and taxes.

Useful sample forms and letters are also included throughout.

Winning Government Contracts

IN ONE RECENT YEAR, the federal government and its purchasing agents and departments contracted for $184.2 billion worth of goods and services from the private sector. This represents 16% of the total federal outlay. Of that total, $31.6 billion, or 17.2%, was purchased directly from small businesses. The SBA reports that another $27.2 billion reached small businesses through subcontracts to large prime contractors to the federal government.

The SBA Answer Desk Hotline can provide prerecorded messages regarding business opportunities in the federal government sector. The regional offices of the SBA can also provide such information. *(See also "Small Business Administration Regional Offices" on page 385.)*

Small Business Answer Desk
(800) 827-5722 or (202) 205-7701

The Small Business Innovation Research Program administers a program among government agencies that provides grants to small businesses for innovation research and development. The Pre-Solicitation Announcement, published by the SBIR in March, June, September, and December, lists the needs of 11 federal agencies for R&D activities.

For more information, contact:

Small Business Innovation Research Program
U.S. Small Business Administration
Office of Innovation, Research & Technology
409 Third St., Mail Code 6470
Washington, DC 20416
(202) 205-6450

Each business day, the GPO releases the *Commerce Business Daily* ($275/year), a publication that provides a daily list of U.S. government procurement invitations, contract awards, subcontracting leads, sales of surplus property, and foreign business opportunities. Each edition contains 500 to 1,000 such notices and each notice appears in the CBD only once. Back issues are available in the public library, and a subscription may be obtained for six-month or one-year time periods.

Information about the rates and service may be obtained from:

Superintendent of Documents
Government Printing Office
Washington, DC 20402
(202) 512-1800

A useful document that is available from the GPO is the *U.S. Government Purchasing and Sales Directory.*

Another helpful source is the General Services Administration. It handles the government's purchases, sales, and services. GSA Business Service Centers provide small businesses with information about contracting opportunities. Call the GSA for the phone number of the nearest Business Service Center:

General Services Administration
18th and F Sts., NW
Washington, DC 20405
(202) 708-5804

Procurement Automated Source System

The SBA designed the Procurement Automated Source System (PASS) to establish a centralized, computer-based inventory and referral system of small businesses interested in being a prime or subcontractor for federal requirements. Using computers and remote video terminals, PASS furnishes sources by matching keywords which small firms have used to describe their capabilities. When procurement agencies or prime contractors request small business sources, the SBA furnishes the names and capabilities of those firms meeting the buyers specifications. Also, a profile of the firm can be made available giving information as to minority status, quality assurance programs, and other useful information.

Since 1978, the system has grown to an "inventory" of more than 230,000 firms. A firm that provides goods or services purchased by the federal government may register with PASS. PASS registration is not intended to guarantee contracting opportunities, but small firms registered with the system will have their capabilities available if requests are made by the Federal Procuring Offices or purchasing agents of prime contractors. Interested individuals may contact an SBA office for an application form.

> *The SBIR Pre-Solicitation Announcement is available on a free BBS that can be accessed by dialing (800) 697-4636. Go to menu "Quick Search," then to "Search by Topic," and finally to "Government Contracting Opportunities."*

GPO Electronic Bulletin Board

DURING 1993, THE GOVERNMENT Printing Office (GPO) established an electronic bulletin board as an efficient way to retrieve government information. Armed with a PC and a modem, the interested user can access information from participating federal agencies. The Federal Bulletin Board (BBS) is available 22 hours each day, seven days a week. It is not available from 3:00 A.M. to 5:00 A.M., EST. Users are allowed to browse complementary files, review product announcements through README.doc files, and receive a free user's manual, all without a time-based charge. E-mail allows users to place electronic orders for all GPO products using VISA, MasterCard, or GPO account numbers.

Some of the information available to users includes:

* Daily press briefings from the State Department;

* Background information on 170 countries;

* Congressional policy statements, fact sheets, and testimony;

* Clearinghouses and hotlines for EPA information resources.

To use the system call (202) 512-1387; for user assistance, call (202) 512-1524. A 2400 bps or 9600 bps modem should be set to 8-N-1. The system will adjust to the rate of the incoming modem and allow the user to enter the system. A menu-driven program permits the user to log on and enter information for billing purposes (if billable data is accessed), and browse through a bulletin board of serviceable items.

CD-ROMs Available from the GPO

THE GPO HAS BEGUN TO MAKE information available on CD-ROM at prices from approximately $13 to $40. Generally, these CD-ROM disks are in ISO 9660 format and will run on any IBM-compatible PC with 640K RAM, a minimum of 12 megabytes of free hard disk space, and a CD-ROM reader with MS-DOS extensions. Additional requirements are provided with individual title listings.

While there are a limited number of publications available on CD-ROM at this time, many are timely and pertinent to specific industries. People in the food industry, for instance, may find the latest in food labeling regulations on CD-ROM.

The Federal Acquisition Regulation (FAR) and Federal Information Resources Management Regulation (FIRMR) from the General Services Administration are now available quarterly on one compact disc for easy access to information needed to sell goods and services to the federal government.

The SIGCAT (Special Interest Group) CD-ROM Compendium (1994) is a useful reference that gives

an annotated index of approximately 300 CD-ROM products containing information supplied by federal, state, and other non-profit agencies. The index includes source and vendor information and technical requirements and is available from the GPO for $13.

To get more information about the current and upcoming CD-ROMs, call the GPO Office of Electronic Information Dissemination Services between 8:00 A.M. and 4:00 P.M.

Recommended Resource

GPO Office of Electronic Information
Dissemination Services
732 N. Capitol St., NW
Mail Stop: SDE
Washington, DC 20401
Information: (202) 512-1265
Order assistance: (202) 512-1526

The Top Reference Sources

1995 Washington Representatives
Columbia Books, $80
(202) 898-0662

This essential reference book is a compilation of names of representatives of the major national

associations, labor unions, and U.S. companies, registered foreign agents, lobbyists, lawyers, law firms, and special interest groups, together with their clients and areas of legislative and regulatory concern.

U.S. Government Subscriptions

SMALL AND LARGE CORPORATIONS alike rely on magazines and periodical publications for the most up-to-date information on the changing climate of the business community. The federal government maintains access to such information and offers it to the general public in periodic publications. The U.S. Government Printing Office offers a quarterly catalogue of periodical and subscription services. The catalogue is available from:

Superintendent of Documents
U.S. Government Printing Office
Washington, DC 20402
(202) 512-1800

Several noteworthy publications of interest to the business community include:

Business America: The Magazine of
International Trade
A biweekly publication providing American exporters with information on trade opportunities and methods of doing business in foreign countries. A typical issue includes an analytical piece on current U.S. trade policy, a how-to article for the novice exporter, a picture of the nation's economic health, and news of congressional and government actions affecting trade. Subscriptions can be obtained for $32 per year; issues can be ordered on an individual basis for $3 each.

Census and You
Monthly newsletter for users of the Census Bureau statistics. A free sample copy is available from DUSD, Bureau of the Census, Washington, DC 20233. Subscriptions cost $21 per year.

Department of Defense Telephone Directory
An alphabetical directory of Departments of Army, Navy, and Air Force personnel, and a classified section by agency for the Washington, DC, metropolitan area. The directory costs $24 per year.

Foreign Labor Trends
American Embassy reports describing labor developments, labor-management relations, trade unions, employment, wages and working conditions, labor and government, training, and a list of key labor indicators for some of the most important foreign countries. The reports cost $33 per year.

Survey of Current Business
Monthly report on general trends in industry, the business situation, future outlook, and other points pertinent to the business world. Subscriptions to the monthly report cost $34 per year, or $9 per copy.

Federal Acquisition Regulation (FAR) and the
Federal Information Resources Management
Regulation
Quarterly listing of primary regulations used by federal executive agencies requesting supplies and services. The listings cost $33 per copy or $160 per year.

GPO Business Publications

INSTEAD OF BROWSING THROUGH a general catalogue of GPO publications, request the *Catalog of Publications and Subscriptions for Business*. This includes titles on general business reference, publications on import/export, patents and trademarks, selling to the government, employment, health and safety, labor law and statistics, accounting and auditing, as well as regulatory information. The catalogue is available from:

Superintendent of Documents
U.S. Government Printing Office
Washington, DC 20402
(202) 512-1800

Government Publications. Send e-mail to publications@almanac.yoyo.com. See p. xi for instructions.
A list of the most popular government publications and how many copies have sold to date.

Assistance from the Government

The Service Corps of Retired Executives (SCORE)

SCORE is a volunteer program of the SBA. The organization matches the skills and experience of the volunteers with a business that needs expert advice. Approximately 14,000 men and women business executives participate in the program and share their management and technical expertise with present and prospective owners and managers of small businesses.

Volunteers are members of 390 locally organized, self-administered chapters offering services in more than 700 locations throughout the U.S. There is no charge for the counseling, but there may be a nominal fee for the training programs. Volunteers offer counseling in distribution channels, expansion potential, and product changes. They offer workshops to present and prospective small business entrepreneurs within the local community. An individual currently operating a small business or contemplating a business start-up is eligible for help from SCORE. The service is not tied to any SBA loan. Any local office of the SBA can advise a caller of the availability of a SCORE program.

Small Business Development Centers (SBDCs)

This branch of the SBA sponsors 57 SBDCs in 50 states as well as the District of Columbia, Puerto Rico, and the Virgin Islands. Through a network of subcenters located at educational institutions, chambers of commerce, economic development corporations, and downtown storefronts, the state SBDCs provide up-to-date counseling and training, and deal with financing, marketing, production, organization, engineering, technical problems, and feasibility studies.

More specialized programs include services to inventors with patentable products, international trade centers for how-to export and import advice, business law information and guidance, procurement matching, venture capital formation, and small business incubators.

The location of a local SBDC can be found by calling the Association of Small Business Development Centers at (402) 595-2387. *(See also "Small Business Development Centers" on page 385.)*

Small Business Institute (SBI)

The SBA sponsors more than 500 SBIs in all states and territories in order to offer small business owners an opportunity to receive intensive management counseling from qualified college level business students working under expert faculty guidance. The studies focus on market studies, accounting systems, personnel policies, production design, product line diversification, exporting, expansion feasibility, and strategy. A local office of the SBA can advise the caller of the availability of an SBI in the area.

The Top Reference Sources

How to Form Your Own Corporation without a Lawyer for under $75.00
Dearborn Financial Publishing, $19.95
(800) 533-2665

The kind of information provided in this book previously had to be bought from an attorney.

Author Ted Nicholas explains how to avoid the hassle of lawyers and how to save hundreds or even thousands of dollars by following simple instructions. The book includes a complete set of forms, a certificate of incorporation, minutes, by-laws, and more.

Lobbying

THERE ARE APPROXIMATELY 14,000 individuals in the nation's capital whose profession might be listed as "advocacy." They include persons who work to influence government policies and actions by advocating for their own or their client's interests. They work in government affairs or in public relations departments for trade associations, professional societies, labor unions, corporations, and a wide variety of special interest and public interest groups. Some are registered as lobbyists on Capitol Hill. Others, who represent foreign industry or governments, are registered with the Justice Department as foreign agents. Still others are part of the executive branch of the federal government and act as liaisons between that office and Congress.

The Justice Department requires agents representing foreign countries and organizations to file forms in their Foreign Agents Registration Unit: (202) 514-1216. These files are open for public inspection at the Justice Department.

Lobbyists also register with the Clerk of the House of Representatives and Secretary of the Senate, indicating the party or individuals in whose interest they work, the length of employment, amount of reimbursement received by the lobbyist, and what expenses are covered by this reimbursement. Furthermore, lobbyists must file quarterly financial reports stating the name and address of each individual who has made a contribution of $500 or more, and the total contributions made during the calendar year.

Recommended Resources

National Association of Registered Lobbyists
1111 14th St., NW, Suite 1001
Washington, DC 20005
(202) 898-0084

Washington Representatives (1995)
Columbia Books, $80
(202) 898-0662

Directory of Washington Lobbyists, Lawyers, and Interest Groups
Amward Publications, $97.50
(703) 525-7227

Political Finance and Lobby Reporter
Amward Publications, $287/year
2030 Clarendon Blvd., Suite 401
Arlington, VA 22201
(703) 525-7227
A Semimonthly Newsletter

The Lobbying Handbook
by John Zorak
Professional Lobbying Consulting Center, $125
1111 14th St., NW, Suite 1001
Washington, DC 20005
(202) 898-0084

 Free Government Resources. Send e-mail to resource@almanac.yoyo.com. See p. xi for instructions. A list of subject bibliographies available from the Government Printing Office.

Political Action Committees

POLITICAL ACTION COMMITTEES are groups devoted to special interests. These groups raise and distribute funds for political candidates who support their specific concerns, as well as for lobbyists who represent their interests to legislators. PACs can be sponsored by a trade association, a union, a special interest group, or a company.

Contact Options

Business-Associated PACs:

AFL-CIO Committee on Political Education
(202) 637-5102

Americans for Free International Trade
(202) 659-8545

Business and Industry
(202) 833-1880

Political Interest Groups:

American Conservative Union
(202) 546-6555
   Focuses on defense, foreign policy, economics, and legal issues.

U.S. Chamber of Commerce
(202) 463-5604
   Promotes the enaction of pro-business legislation.

Congressional Economic Leadership Institute
(202) 546-5007
   Nonpartisan group, promotes discussion between Congress and private sector.

Family Research Council
(202) 393-2100
   Advocates the interests of the family in public policy formulation.

Foundation for Public Affairs
(202) 872-1750
   Disseminates information on corporate public affairs programs.

Several organizations monitor the voting records of members of Congress on particular issues and publish the results periodically. Some of those organizations which might be of interest to the business community include:

American Federation of Labor
Congress of Industrial Organizations
(202) 637-5000

Common Cause
(202) 833-1200

National Federation of Independent Business
(202) 554-9000

National Taxpayers Union
(202) 543-1300

National Women's Political Caucus
(202) 785-1100

Recommended Resource

Almanac of Federal PACs
Amward Publications, $97.50
(703) 525-7227

The Top Reference Sources

Leadership Directories
Monitor Leadership Directories, $125–$185
(212) 627-4140

These books provide easy access to decision-makers in business, government, and professional organizations. The books are updated quarterly or semiannually.

Titles include *Corporate Yellow Book, Financial Yellow Book, NASDAQ Yellow Book, International Corporate Yellow Book, Congressional Yellow Book, Federal Yellow Book, Federal Regional Yellow Book, State Yellow Book, Municipal Yellow Book, Law Firms Yellow Book, Associations Yellow Book,* and *News Media Yellow Book.*

Major Trade Associations

Selected Associations and Telephone Numbers

Trade Association	Telephone Number
American Advertising Federation	(202) 898-0089
American Bankers Association	(202) 663-5000
American Council of Life Insurance	(202) 624-2000
American Electronics Association	(408) 987-4200
American Farm Bureau Federation	(312) 399-5700
American Financial Services Association	(202) 296-5544
American Health Care Association	(202) 842-4444
American Hotel and Motel Association	(202) 289-3100
American Institute of Certified Public Accountants	(212) 596-6200
American Petroleum Institute	(202) 682-8000
American Society of Association Executives	(202) 626-2723
American Society of Travel Agents	(703) 739-2782
American Trucking Association	(202) 544-6245
American Wholesale Marketers Association	(202) 463-2124
Associated General Contractors of America	(202) 393-2040
Association of American Publishers	(212) 255-0200
Automotive Service Association	(202) 543-1440
Direct Marketing Association	(202) 347-1222
Electronic Industries Association	(202) 457-4900
Food Marketing Institute	(202) 452-8444
Grocery Manufacturers Association	(202) 337-9400
Health Industry Manufacturers Association	(202) 783-8700
Independent Petroleum Association of America	(202) 857-4722
Information Industry Association	(202) 639-8260
Information Technology Association of America	(703) 522-5055
Information Technology Industry Council	(202) 737-8888
International Association for Financial Planning	(404) 395-1605
International Communications Industries Association	(703) 273-7200
National Association of Broadcasters	(202) 429-5300
National Association of Chain Drug Stores	(703) 549-3001
National Association of Convenience Stores	(703) 684-3600
National Association of Home Builders	(202) 822-0200
National Association of Realtors	(312) 329-8200
National Association of Wholesalers-Distributors	(202) 872-0885
National Automobile Dealers Association	(703) 821-7000
National Forest and Paper Association	(202) 463-2700
National Home Furnishing Association	(910) 883-1650
National Industrial Transportation League	(703) 524-5011
National Restaurant Association	(202) 331-5900
National Retail Federation	(202) 783-7971
Printing Industries of America	(703) 519-8100
Travel Industry Association of America	(202) 408-8422

Government Bookstores

Branch Bookstores of the U.S. Government Printing Office

Address	City, State, Zip	Telephone
2021 3rd Ave., N	Birmingham, AL 35203	(205) 731-1056
505 S. Flower St.	Los Angeles, CA 90071	(213) 239-9844
303 2nd St.	San Francisco, CA 94107	(415) 512-2270
1961 Stout St.	Denver, CO 80294	(303) 844-3964
201 W. 8th St.	Pueblo, CO 81003	(719) 544-3142
710 N. Capitol St., NW	Washington, DC 20401	(202) 512-0132
1510 H St., NW	Washington, DC 20005	(202) 653-5075
100 W. Bay St.	Jacksonville, FL 32202	(904) 353-0569
999 Peachtree St., NE	Atlanta, GA 30309	(404) 347-1900
401 S. State St.	Chicago, IL 60605	(312) 353-5133
10 Causeway St.	Boston, MA 02222	(617) 720-4180
8660 Cherry Ln.	Laurel, MD 20707	(301) 953-7974
477 Michigan Ave.	Detroit, MI 48226	(313) 226-7816
5600 E. Bannister Rd.	Kansas City, MO 64137	(816) 765-2256
26 Federal Plaza	New York, NY 10278	(212) 264-3825
1240 E. 9th St.	Cleveland, OH 44199	(216) 522-4922
200 N. High St.	Columbus, OH 43215	(614) 469-6956
1305 S.W. 1st Ave.	Portland, OR 97201	(503) 221-6217
100 N. 17th St.	Philadelphia, PA 19103	(215) 636-1900
1000 Liberty Ave.	Pittsburgh, PA 15222	(412) 644-2721
1100 Commerce St.	Dallas, TX 75242	(214) 767-0076
801 Travis St.	Houston, TX 77002	(713) 228-1187
915 2nd Ave.	Seattle, WA 98174	(206) 553-4270
310 W. Wisconsin Ave.	Milwaukee, WI 53203	(414) 297-1304

Freedom of Information Act

THE FREEDOM OF INFORMATION Act (FOIA) became law in 1966 and guaranteed the public the right of access to information held by the federal government. According to the act, any individual may request and receive a document, file, or other record held by any agency of the federal government. The burden of proof has shifted from the individual to the government, and the law requires that the government justify the need for secrecy regarding a document. However, there are nine specific exemptions to the access rule, including national defense, foreign policy, trade secrets, and criminal investigations.

The Privacy Act of 1974 enhances the FOIA by permitting individuals access to records about themselves, which are held by federal agencies. Such information must be complete, accurate, and relevant; the law requires that each agency publish a description of its record system and forbids the agency from disclosing personal information except to the individual who is the subject of such informa-tion. Both laws permit the individual to request access to federal records regarding himself or herself and allows the individual to appeal a denial of that request.

The FOIA sets a deadline of ten working days for replying to the information request and a 20-day deadline on responding to the appeal. The initial request letter and the appeals letter, if necessary, should be clearly and simply written. The Freedom of Information Clearinghouse will provide a brochure detailing how to write a request as well as an appeals letter.

Recommended Resource

A User's Guide to the Freedom of Information Act
Freedom of Information Clearinghouse
P.O. Box 19367
Washington, DC 20036
(202) 833-3000

COMMUNICATIONS

Area Codes

U.S. Area Codes by State

State	City	Code
AL	All points	205
AK	All points	907
AZ	All points	602
AR	All points	501
CA	Alameda	510
	Alhambra	818
	Altadena	818
	Anaheim	909
	Arcadia	818
	Azusa	818
	Bakersfield	805
	Baldwin Park	818
	Bell Gardens	213
	Bellflower	310
	Belmont	415
	Berkeley	510
	Beverly Hills	310
	Buena Park	714
	Burbank	818
	Burlingame	415
	Campbell	408
	Carmichael	916
	Carson	310
	Castro Valley	510
	Chula Vista	619
	Claremont	909
	Compton	310
	Concord	510
	Corona	909
	Costa Mesa	714
	Covina	818
	Culver City	310
	Cypress	714
	Daly City	415
	Davis	916
	Downey	310
	East Los Angeles	213
	El Cerrito	510
	El Monte	818
	Escondido	619
	Eureka	707
	Fairfield	707
	Fountain Valley	714
	Fremont	510
	Fresno	209
	Fullerton	714
	Gardena	310
	Garden Grove	714
	Glendale	818
	Hawthorne	310
	Hollywood	213
	Huntington Beach	714
	Huntington Park	213
	Inglewood	310
	La Habra	310

State	City	Code
CA	Lakewood	310
	La Mesa	619
	La Mirada	714
	Lancaster	805
	La Puente	818
	Lawndale	310
	Livermore	510
	Lodi	209
	Lompoc	805
	Long Beach	310
	Los Altos	415
	Los Angeles	213
	Los Gatos	408
	Lynwood	310
	Malibu	310
	Manhattan Beach	310
	Menlo Park	415
	Merced	209
	Milpitas	408
	Modesto	209
	Monrovia	818
	Montclair	909
	Montebello	213
	Monterey	408
	Monterey Park	818
	Mountain View	415
	Napa	707
	National City	619
	Newark	510
	Newport Beach	714
	North Highlands	916
	Norwalk	310
	Novato	415
	Oakland	510
	Oceanside	619
	Ontario	909
	Orange	714
	Oxnard	805
	Pacifica	415
	Palm Springs	619
	Palo Alto	415
	Palos Verde	310
	Paramount	310
	Pasadena	818
	Petaluma	707
	Pico Rivera	310
	Pleasant Hill	510
	Rancho Cordova	916
	Redlands	909
	Redondo Beach	310
	Redwood City	415
	Rialto	909
	Richmond	510
	Riverside	909
	Rosemead	818

State	City	Code
CA	Sacramento	916
	Salinas	408
	San Bernardino	909
	San Bruno	415
	San Carlos	415
	San Diego	619
	San Francisco	415
	San Gabriel	818
	San Jose	408
	San Leandro	510
	San Lorenzo	510
	San Luis Obispo	805
	San Rafael	415
	Santa Ana	714
	Santa Barbara	805
	Santa Clara	408
	Santa Cruz	408
	Santa Maria	805
	Santa Monica	310
	Santa Rosa	707
	Seal Beach	310
	Seaside	408
	Simi Valley	805
	South Gate	213
	South Pasadena	818
	S. San Francisco	510
	Spring Valley	619
	Stockton	209
	Sunnyvale	408
	Temple City	818
	Thousand Oaks	805
	Torrance	310
	Upland	909
	Vallejo	707
	Ventura	805
	Visalia	209
	Vista	619
	Walnut Creek	510
	West Covina	818
	West Hollywood	213
	Westminster	714
	Whittier	310
CO	Aspen	303
	Colorado Springs	719
	Denver	303
	Grand Junction	303
	Pueblo	719
	Vail	303
	Woodland Park	719
CT	All points	203
DE	All points	302
DC	All points	202
FL	Boca Raton	407
	Carol City	305
	Clearwater	813

Area Codes (cont'd)

State	Location	Code	State	Location	Code	State	Location	Code
FL	Coral Gables	305	IL	Champaign	217	IN	Columbus	812
	Daytona Beach	904		Chicago	312		East Chicago	219
	Fort Lauderdale	305		Chicago Heights	708		Elkhart	219
	Fort Myers	813		Cicero	708		Evansville	812
	Fort Pierce	407		Danville	217		Fort Wayne	219
	Gainesville	904		Decatur	217		Gary	219
	Hallandale	305		De Kalb	815		Hammond	219
	Hialeah	305		Des Plaines	708		Highland	219
	Jacksonville	904		Dolton	708		Indianapolis	317
	Kendall	305		Downers Grove	708		Kokomo	317
	Key West	305		East St. Louis	618		Lafayette	317
	Lake Worth	407		Elgin	708		Marion	317
	Lakeland	813		Elk Grove Village	708		Merrillville	219
	Melbourne	407		Elmhurst	708		Michigan City	219
	Merritt Island	407		Elmwood Park	708		Mishawaka	219
	Miami	305		Evanston	708		Muncie	317
	Miami Beach	305		Evergreen Park	708		New Albany	812
	Miramar	305		Freeport	815		Richmond	317
	North Miami	305		Galesburg	309		South Bend	219
	N. Miami Beach	305		Granite City	618		Terre Haute	812
	Ocala	904		Harvey	708	IA	Ames	515
	Orlando	407		Highland Park	708		Burlington	319
	Panama City	904		Hinsdale	708		Cedar Falls	319
	Pensacola	904		Hoffman Estates	708		Cedar Rapids	319
	Plantation	305		Joliet	815		Clinton	319
	Pompano Beach	305		Kankakee	815		Council Bluffs	712
	St. Petersburg	813		La Grange	708		Davenport	319
	Sarasota	813		Lansing	708		Des Moines	515
	Tallahassee	904		Lombard	708		Dubuque	319
	Tampa	813		Maywood	708		Fort Dodge	515
	Titusville	407		Melrose Park	708		Iowa City	319
	W. Palm Beach	407		Moline	309		Marshalltown	515
GA	Albany	912		Morton Grove	708		Ottumwa	515
	Athens	706		Mount Prospect	708		Sioux City	712
	Atlanta	404		Naperville	708		Waterloo	319
	Augusta	706		Niles	708	KS	Emporia	316
	Columbus	706		Normal	309		Hutchinson	316
	East Point	404		Northbrook	708		Kansas City	913
	Gainesvillle	404		North Chicago	708		Lawrence	913
	Griffin	404		Oak Lawn	708		Leavenworth	913
	La Grange	706		Oak Park	708		Manhattan	913
	Macon	912		Palatine	708		Overland Park	913
	Marietta	404		Park Forest	708		Salina	913
	Rome	706		Park Ridge	708		Topeka	913
	Savannah	912		Pekin	309		Wichita	316
	Valdosta	912		Peoria	309	KY	Ashland	606
	Warner Robins	912		Rantoul	217		Bowling Green	502
HI	All points	808		Rockford	815		Covington	606
ID	All points	208		Rock Island	309		Fort Knox	502
IL	Addison	708		Schaumburg	708		Frankfort	502
	Alton	618		Skokie	708		Henderson	502
	Arlington Hts.	708		South Holland	708		Lexington	606
	Aurora	708		Springfield	217		Louisville	502
	Belleville	618		Urbana	217		Newport	606
	Berwyn	708		Villa Park	708		Owensboro	502
	Bloomington	309		Waukegan	708		Paducah	502
	Blue Island	708		Wheaton	708		Pleasure Ridge Pk.	502
	Calumet City	708		Wilmette	708		Valley Station	502
	Carbondale	618	IN	Anderson	317	LA	Alexandria	318
	Carpentersville	708		Bloomington	812		Baton Rouge	504

Area Codes (cont'd)

State	City	Code	State	City	Code	State	City	Code
LA	Bossier City	318	MA	Milton	617	MI	Oak Park	810
	Gretna	504		Nantucket	508		Pontiac	810
	Houma	504		Needham	617		Portage	616
	Kenner	504		New Bedford	508		Port Huron	810
	Lafayette	318		Newton	617		Roseville	810
	Lake Charles	318		North Adams	413		Royal Oak	810
	Marrero	504		Northampton	413		Saginaw	517
	Metairie	504		Norwood	617		St. Clair Shores	313
	Monroe	318		Paxton	508		St. Joseph	616
	New Iberia	318		Pittsfield	413		Southfield	810
	New Orleans	504		Quincy	617		Southgate	313
	Scotlandville	504		Randolph	617		Sterling Heights	810
	Shreveport	318		Reading	617		Taylor	313
ME	All points	207		Revere	617		Trenton	313
MD	Annapolis	410		Roxbury	617		Troy	810
	Baltimore	410		Sandwich	508		Warren	313
	Cumberland	301		Saugus	617		Westland	313
	Frederick	301		Somerville	617		Wyandotte	313
	Hagerstown	301		Springfield	413		Wyoming	616
	Ocean City	410		Stoughton	617		Ypsilanti	313
	Rockville	301		Taunton	508	MN	Austin	507
	Salisbury	410		Tewksbury	508		Bloomington	612
	Towson	410		Wakefield	617		Brooklyn Center	612
MA	Amherst	413		Waltham	617		Columbia Hts.	612
	Andover	508		Watertown	617		Coon Rapids	612
	Arlington	617		Wellesley	617		Crystal	612
	Attleboro	508		West Springfield	413		Duluth	218
	Barnstable	508		Westfield	413		Edina	612
	Belmont	617		Weymouth	617		Fridley	612
	Beverly	508		Woburn	617		Mankato	507
	Boston	617		Worcester	508		Minneapolis	612
	Braintree	617	MI	Allen Park	313		Minnetonka	612
	Brookline	617		Ann Arbor	313		Moorhead	218
	Cambridge	617		Battle Creek	616		Rochester	507
	Chelmsford	508		Bay City	517		Roseville	612
	Chelsea	617		Benton Harbor	616		St. Cloud	612
	Chicopee	413		Birmingham	810		St. Louis Park	612
	Danvers	508		Dearborn	313		St. Paul	612
	Dedham	617		Detroit	313		White Bear Lake	612
	Everett	617		East Detroit	810		Winona	507
	Fall River	508		East Lansing	517	MS	All points	601
	Fitchburg	508		Ferndale	810	MO	Afton	314
	Framingham	508		Flint	810		Cape Girardeau	314
	Gardner	508		Garden City	313		Columbia	314
	Gloucester	508		Grand Rapids	616		Ferguson	314
	Greenfield	413		Hamtramck	313		Florissant	314
	Haverhill	508		Hazel Park	810		Ft. Leonard Wood	314
	Holyoke	413		Highland Park	313		Gladstone	816
	Lawrence	508		Holland	616		Independence	816
	Leominster	508		Inkster	313		Jefferson City	314
	Lexington	617		Jackson	517		Joplin	417
	Longmeadow	413		Kalamazoo	616		Kansas City	816
	Lowell	508		Lansing	517		Kirkwood	314
	Lynn	617		Livonia	313		Lemay	314
	Malden	617		Madison Heights	810		Overland	314
	Marblehead	617		Marquette	906		Raytown	816
	Marlborough	508		Midland	517		St. Charles	314
	Medford	617		Monroe	313		St. Joseph	816
	Melrose	617		Muskegon	616		St. Louis	314
	Methuen	508		Niles	616		Sedalia	816

Area Codes (cont'd)

State	Location	Code	State	Location	Code	State	Location	Code
MO	Springfield	417	NJ	Montclair	201	NY	Bethpage	516
	University City	314		Morristown	201		Binghamton	607
	Webster Groves	314		Mount Holly	609		Brentwood	516
MT	All points	406		Newark	201		Brewster	914
NE	Fremont	402		Newark Airport	201		Bridgehampton	516
	Grand Island	308		New Brunswick	908		Bronx	718
	Hastings	402		New Milford	201		Bronxville	914
	Lincoln	402		North Arlington	201		Brooklyn	718
	North Platte	308		North Plainfield	908		Brookville	516
	Omaha	402		Nutley	201		Buffalo	716
NV	All points	702		Old Bridge	908		Callicoon	914
NH	All points	603		Orange	201		Carmel	914
NJ	Asbury Park	908		Paramus	201		Center Moriches	516
	Atlantic City	609		Passaic	201		Central Islip	516
	Bayonne	201		Paterson	201		Chappaqua	914
	Belleville	201		Perth Amboy	908		Cohoes	518
	Bellmawr	609		Phillipsburg	908		Cold Spring	914
	Bergenfield	201		Plainfield	908		Commack	516
	Bloomfield	201		Pleasantville	609		Congers	914
	Bound Brook	908		Point Pleasant	908		Copiague	516
	Bridgeton	609		Pompton Lakes	201		Corning	607
	Burlington	609		Princeton	609		Cortland	607
	Camden	609		Rahway	908		Croton	914
	Carteret	908		Red Bank	908		Deer Park	516
	Cliffside Park	201		Ridgefield	201		Depew	716
	Clifton	201		Ridgewood	201		Dobbs Ferry	914
	Collingswood	609		Roselle	908		Dunkirk	716
	Dover	201		Rutherford	201		East Hampton	516
	Dumont	201		Sayreville	908		East Massapequa	516
	East Orange	201		Somerville	908		East Meadow	516
	East Paterson	201		South Amboy	908		Eastchester	914
	Eatontown	908		South Orange	201		Eastport	516
	Elizabeth	908		South Plainfield	908		Ellenville	914
	Englewood	201		South River	908		Elmira	607
	Fair Lawn	201		Summit	908		Elmsford	914
	Flemington	908		Teaneck	201		Elwood	516
	Fort Dix	609		Trenton	609		Endicott	607
	Fort Lee	201		Union City	201		Endwell	607
	Garfield	201		Verona	201		Fairmount	315
	Glassboro	609		Vineland	609		Fallsburg	914
	Glen Ridge	201		Weehawken	201		Farmingdale	516
	Gloucester	609		Westfield	908		Fire Island	516
	Hackensack	201		West New York	201		Fishers Island	516
	Haddonfield	609		West Orange	201		Floral Park	516
	Hasbrouck Hts.	201		Wildwood	609		Franklin Square	516
	Hawthorne	201		Woodbridge	908		Freeport	516
	Hoboken	201		Woodbury	609		Fulton	315
	Irvington	201		Wyckoff	201		Garden City	516
	Jersey City	201	NM	All points	505		Garrison	914
	Kearny	201	NY	Albany	518		Geneva	315
	Lakewood	908		Amityville	516		Glen Cove	516
	Linden	908		Amsterdam	518		Glens Falls	518
	Long Branch	908		Armonk Village	914		Gloversville	518
	Madison	201		Auburn	315		Grahamsville	914
	Maplewood	201		Babylon	516		Great Neck	516
	Mendham	201		Baldwin	516		Grossinger	914
	Metuchen	908		Batavia	716		Hamilton	315
	Middlesex	908		Bay Shore	516		Hampton Bays	516
	Millburn	201		Bedford Village	914		Harrison	914
	Millville	609		Bellmore	516		Hastings	914

COMMUNICATIONS

Area Codes (cont'd)

State	City	Code	State	City	Code	State	City	Code
NY	Haverstraw	914	NY	Oceanside	516	NY	Westchester Co.	914
	Hempstead	516		Olean	716		Westhampton	516
	Hicksville	516		Oneida	315		Wheatley Hills	516
	Hudson	518		Oneonta	607		White Lake	914
	Huntington	516		Ossining	914		White Plains	914
	Huntington Sta.	516		Oswego	315		Williamsville	716
	Hurleyville	914		Oyster Bay	516		Woodbourne	914
	Irvington	914		Patchogue	516		Woodmere	516
	Islip	516		Pearl River	914		Woodridge	914
	Ithaca	607		Peekskill	914		Woodstock	914
	Jamestown	716		Pelham	914		Wyandanch	516
	Jeffersonville	914		Penn Station	212		Yonkers	914
	Johnson City	607		Picrmont	914		Yorktown Hts.	914
	Kenmore	716		Plainview	516	NC	Asheville	704
	Kennedy Airport	718		Plattsburgh	518		Burlington	910
	Kerhonkson	914		Pleasantville	914		Camp Le Jeune	919
	Kiamesha	914		Port Chester	914		Chapel Hill	919
	Kingston	914		Port Jefferson	516		Charlotte	704
	Lackawanna	716		Port Washington	516		Durham	919
	LaGuardia Airport	718		Potsdam	315		Fayetteville	910
	Lake Huntington	914		Poughkeepsie	914		Gastonia	704
	Lakeland	914		Queens	718		Goldsboro	919
	Lake Success	516		Riverhead	516		Greensboro	910
	Larchmont	914		Rochester	716		Greenville	919
	Levittown	516		Rockville Centre	516		High Point	910
	Liberty	914		Rome	315		Kannapolis	704
	Lindenhurst	516		Ronkonkoma	516		Kinston	919
	Livingston Manor	914		Roosevelt	516		Lexington	704
	Lockport	716		Roscoe	607		Raleigh	919
	Long Beach	516		Roslyn	516		Rocky Mount	919
	Long Island	516		Rye	914		Salisbury	704
	Lynbrook	516		Sag Harbor	516		Wilmington	910
	Mahopac	914		Saratoga Springs	518		Wilson	919
	Mamaroneck	914		Sayville	516		Winston-Salem	910
	Manhasset	516		Scarsdale	914	ND	All points	701
	Manhattan	212		Schenectady	518	OH	Akron	216
	Massapequa	516		Seaford	516		Alliance	216
	Massapequa Park	516		Shelter Island	516		Ashtabula	216
	Massena	315		Sloatsburg	914		Athens	614
	Merrick	516		Smithtown	516		Austintown	216
	Middletown	914		Southampton	516		Barberton	216
	Mineola	516		Spring Valley	914		Boardman	216
	Montauk Point	516		Staten Island	718		Brook Park	216
	Monticello	914		Stony Point	914		Canton	216
	Mount Kisco	914		Suffern	914		Chillicothe	614
	Mount Vernon	914		Suffolk County	516		Cincinnati	513
	Nanuet	914		Syracuse	315		Cleveland	216
	Narrowsburg	914		Tarrytown	914		Columbus	614
	Nassau County	516		Ticonderoga	518		Cuyahoga Falls	216
	Newark	315		Tonawanda	716		Dayton	513
	Newburgh	914		Troy	518		East Cleveland	216
	New City	914		Tuckahoe	914		East Liverpool	216
	New Rochelle	914		Uniondale	516		Elyria	216
	Niagara Falls	716		Utica	315		Euclid	216
	North Babylon	516		Valley Stream	516		Fairborn	513
	North Bellmore	516		Wantagh	516		Findlay	419
	N. Massapequa	516		Watertown	315		Garfield Heights	216
	N. Tonawanda	716		W. Hempstead	516		Hamilton	513
	Norwich	607		West Islip	516		Kent	216
	Nyack	914		Westbury	516		Kettering	513

Area Codes (cont'd)

State	City	Code
OH	Lakewood	216
	Lancaster	614
	Lima	419
	Lorain	216
	Mansfield	419
	Maple Heights	216
	Marion	614
	Massillon	216
	Mentor	216
	Middletown	513
	Newark	614
	North Olmsted	216
	Norwood	513
	Parma	216
	Parma Heights	216
	Portsmouth	614
	Rocky River	216
	Sandusky	419
	Shaker Heights	216
	South Euclid	216
	Springfield	513
	Steubenville	614
	Toledo	419
	Upper Arlington	614
	Warren	216
	Whitehall	614
	Xenia	513
	Youngstown	216
	Zanesville	614
OK	Altus	405
	Bartlesville	918
	Bethany	405
	Del City	405
	Enid	405
	Lawton	405
	Midwest City	405
	Muskogee	918
	Oklahoma City	405
	Ponca City	405
	Shawnee	405
	Stillwater	405
	Tulsa	918
OR	All points	503
PA	Allentown	215
	Altoona	814
	Beaver Falls	412
	Bellefonte	814
	Bethel Park	412
	Bethlehem	610
	Bloomsburg	717
	Bradford	814
	Chambersburg	717
	Chester	610
	Columbia	717
	DuBois	814
	Easton	610
	Erie	814
	Greensburg	412
	Harrisburg	717
	Hazelton	717

State	City	Code
	Indiana	412
	Johnstown	814
	Lancaster	717
	Lebanon	717
	Levittown	215
	Lock Haven	717
	McKeesport	412
	Monroeville	412
	New Castle	412
	Norristown	610
	Philadelphia	215
	Pittsburgh	412
	Pottstown	610
	Reading	610
	Scranton	717
	Sharon	412
	State College	814
	Stroudsburg	717
	Sunbury	717
	Uniontown	814
	Warren	814
	Washington	412
	Wayne	610
	West Chester	610
	West Mifflin	412
	Wilkes-Barre	717
	Wilkinsburg	412
	Williamsport	717
	York	717
PR	All points	809
RI	All points	401
SC	All points	803
SD	All points	605
TN	Chattanooga	615
	Clarksville	615
	Jackson	901
	Johnson City	615
	Kingsport	615
	Knoxville	615
	Memphis	901
	Murfreesboro	615
	Nashville	615
	Oak Ridge	615
TX	Abilene	915
	Amarillo	806
	Arlington	817
	Austin	512
	Baytown	713
	Beaumont	409
	Big Spring	915
	Brownsville	210
	Bryan	409
	Corpus Christi	512
	Dallas	214
	Denison	903
	Denton	817
	El Paso	915
	Farmers Branch	214
	Fort Hood	817
	Fort Worth	817

State	City	Code
TX	Galveston	409
	Garland	214
	Grand Prairie	214
	Harlingen	210
	Houston	713
	Hurst	817
	Irving	214
	Killeen	817
	Kingsville	512
	Laredo	210
	Longview	903
	Lubbock	806
	Lufkin	409
	Marshall	903
	McAllen	210
	Mesquite	214
	Midland	915
	Nacogdoches	409
	Odessa	915
	Orange	409
	Paris	903
	Pasadena	713
	Port Arthur	409
	Richardson	214
	San Angelo	915
	San Antonio	210
	Sherman	903
	Temple	817
	Texarkana	903
	Texas City	409
	Tyler	903
	Victoria	512
	Waco	817
	Wharton	409
	Wichita Falls	817
UT	All points	801
VT	All points	802
VI	All points	809
VA	Alexandria	703
	Annandale	703
	Arlington	703
	Charlottesville	804
	Chesapeake	804
	Covington	703
	Danville	804
	Hampton	804
	Hopewell	804
	Jefferson	804
	Lynchburg	804
	Newport News	804
	Norfolk	804
	Petersburg	804
	Portsmouth	804
	Richmond	804
	Roanoke	703
	Staunton	703
	Virginia Beach	804
	Woodbridge	703
WA	Bellevue	206
	Bellingham	206

Area Codes (cont'd)

State	City	Code
WA	Bremerton	206
	Edmonds	206
	Everett	206
	Longview	206
	Olympia	206
	Renton	206
	Richland	509
	Seattle	206
	Spokane	509
	Tacoma	206
	Vancouver	206
	Walla Walla	509
	Yakima	509
WV	All points	304
WI	Appleton	414
	Beloit	608
	Brookfield	414
	Eau Claire	715
	Fond Du Lac	414
	Green Bay	414

State	City	Code
	Greenfield	414
	Janesville	608
	Kenosha	414
	La Crosse	608
	Madison	608
	Manitowoc	414
	Menomonee Falls	414
	Milwaukee	414
	Neenah	414
	New Berlin	414
	Oshkosh	414
	Racine	414
	Sheboygan	414
	South Milwaukee	414
	Stevens Point	715
	Superior	715
	Waukesha	414
	Wausau	715
	Wauwatosa	414
	West Allis	414
WY	All points	307

Canadian Area Codes

Province	City	Code
AB	All points	403
BC	All points	604
MA	All points	204
NB	All points	506
NF	All points	709
NS	All points	902
ON	Ft. William	807
	London	519
	North Bay	705
	Ottawa	613
	Thunder Bay	807
	Toronto	416, 905
PEI	All points	902
PQ	Montreal	514
	Quebec	418
	Sherbrooke	819
SK	All points	306

The Top Reference Sources

Small Business Success
Pacific Bell Directory, free
(800) 848-8000

This magazine, published every year in April, is replete with information and resources for the small business. Articles in the 1993 edition included "Buying Insurance for Your Small Busi-ness," "Boosting Employee Morale," "Marketing to Minorities," "The Wide World of International Trade," and more. Each issue also contains a directory of organizations, publications, and computer resources for the businessperson.

Small Business Success is also sponsored by the U.S. Small Business Administration.

Area Codes (cont'd)

Area Codes by Code

Code	Location
201	New Jersey (Newark)
202	Washington, DC
203	Connecticut
205	Alabama
206	Washington (Seattle)
207	Maine
208	Idaho
209	California (Fresno)
210	Texas (San Antonio)
212	New York (Manhattan)
213	California (Los Angeles)
214	Texas (Dallas)
215	Pennsylvania (Phila.)
216	Ohio (Cleveland)
217	Illinois (Springfield)
218	Minnesota (Duluth)
219	Indiana (South Bend)
301	Maryland (Bethesda)
302	Delaware
303	Colorado (Denver)
304	West Virginia
305	Florida (Miami)
307	Wyoming
308	Nebraska (North Platte)
309	Illinois (Peoria)
310	California (Los Angeles)
312	Illinois (Chicago)
313	Michigan (Detroit)
314	Missouri (St. Louis)
315	New York (Syracuse)
316	Kansas (Wichita)
317	Indiana (Indianapolis)
318	Louisiana (Shreveport)
319	Iowa (Dubuque)
401	Rhode Island
402	Nebraska (Omaha)
403	Alberta, Northwest Territories, and Yukon
404	Georgia (Atlanta)
405	Oklahoma (Oklahoma City)
406	Montana
407	Florida (Orlando)
408	California (San Jose)
409	Texas (Galveston)
410	Maryland (Baltimore)
412	Pennsylvania (Pittsburgh)
413	Massachusetts (Springfield)
414	Wisconsin (Milwaukee)
415	California (San Francisco)
416	Ontario (Toronto)
417	Missouri (Springfield)

Code	Location
418	Quebec (Quebec)
419	Ohio (Toledo)
501	Arkansas
502	Kentucky (Louisville)
503	Oregon
504	Louisiana (New Orleans)
505	New Mexico
506	New Brunswick
507	Minnesota (Rochester)
508	Massachusetts (Worcester)
509	Washington (Spokane)
510	California (Oakland)
512	Texas (Austin)
513	Ohio (Cincinnati)
514	Quebec (Montreal)
515	Iowa (Des Moines)
516	New York (Long Island)
517	Michigan (Lansing)
518	New York (Albany)
519	Ontario (London)
601	Mississippi
602	Arizona
603	New Hampshire
604	British Columbia
605	South Dakota
606	Kentucky (Newport)
607	New York (Ithaca)
608	Wisconsin (Madison)
609	New Jersey (Trenton)
610	Pennsylvania (Reading)
612	Minnesota (Minneapolis)
614	Ohio (Columbus)
615	Tennessee (Nashville)
616	Michigan (Grand Rapids)
617	Massachusetts (Boston)
618	Illinois (Centralia)
619	California (San Diego)
701	North Dakota
702	Nevada
703	Virginia (Arlington)
704	North Carolina (Charlotte)
705	Ontario (North Bay)
706	Georgia
707	California (Santa Rosa)
708	Illinois (Des Plaines)
712	Iowa (Council Bluffs)
713	Texas (Houston)
714	California (Orange County)
715	Wisconsin (Eau Clair)
716	New York (Buffalo)

Code	Location
717	Pennsylvania (Harrisburg)
718	New York (Brooklyn)
719	Colorado (Colorado Spr.)
801	Utah
802	Vermont
803	South Carolina
804	Virginia (Richmond)
805	California (Bakersfield)
806	Texas (Amarillo)
807	Ontario (Ft. William)
808	Hawaii
810	Michigan (Pontiac)
812	Indiana (Evansville)
813	Florida (Fort Myers)
814	Pennsylvania (Erie)
815	Illinois (Rockford)
816	Missouri (Kansas City)
817	Texas (Fort Worth)
818	California (Los Angeles)
819	Quebec and Northwest Territories
901	Tennessee (Memphis)
902	Nova Scotia
903	Texas (Dallas)
904	Florida (Jacksonville)
905	Ontario (Toronto)
906	Michigan (Marquette)
907	Alaska
908	New Jersey (Elizabeth)
909	California (San Bernardino)
910	North Carolina (Winston-Salem)
912	Georgia (Savannah)
913	Kansas (Topeka)
914	New York (White Plains)
915	Texas (El Paso)
916	California (Sacramento)
917	New York (cellular)
918	Oklahoma (Tulsa)
919	North Carolina

International Dialing to the U.S.

TRAVELERS CAN SAVE MONEY by using a calling card when making calls from foreign countries to the United States. To reach an operator, an access code must be dialed.

AT&T Access Codes

Country	Code
American Samoa	633-2-872
Anguilla	1-800-872-2881
Antigua	#1
Argentina	001-800-200-1111
Armenia	8†14111
Australia	1-800-881-011
Austria	022-903-011
Bahamas	1-800-872-2881
Bahrain	800-001
Barbados	1-800-872-2881
Belgium	0-800-100-10
Bermuda	1-800-872-2881
Bolivia	0-800-1112
Brazil	000-8010
British Virgin Islands	1-800-872-2881
Cayman Islands	1-800-872-2881
Chile	00 † 0312
China, PRC	10811
Colombia	980-11-0010
Cook Islands	09-111
Costa Rica	114
Croatia	99-38-0011
Cuba (Guantanamo Bay)	935
Cyprus	080-90010
Czech Republic	00-420-00101
Denmark	8001-0010
Dominica	1-800-872-2881
Dominican Rep.	1-800-872-2881
Egypt (Cairo)	510-0200
Egypt	02-510-0020
El Salvador	190
Fiji	004-890-1001
Finland	9800-100-10
France	19 † 0011
Gabon	00 † 001
Gambia	00111
Germany	0130-0010
Ghana	0191
Gibraltar	8800
Greece	00-800-1311
Grenada	1-800-872-2883
Guam	018-872
Guatemala	190
Guyana	165
Haiti	001-800-872-2881

Country	Code
Honduras	123
Hong Kong	800-1111
Hungary	00 † 800-01111
India	000-117
Indonesia	00-801-10
Ireland	1-800-550-000
Israel	177-100-2727
Italy	172-1011
Ivory Coast	00-111-11
Jamaica	0-800-872-2881
Japan	0039-111
Kenya	0800-10
Korea	009-11
Kuwait	800-288
Lebanon (Beirut)	426-801
Lebanon	01-426-801
Liberia	797-797
Liechtenstein	155-00-11
Lithuania	8 † 196
Luxembourg	0-800-0111
Macao	0800-0111
Macedonia	99-800-4288
Malaysia	800-0011
Malta	0800-890-110
Mexico	95-800-462-4240
Monaco	19 † 0011
Montserrat	1-800-872-2881
Monaco	002-11-0011
Netherlands	06-022-9111
Netherlands Antilles	001-800-872-2881
New Zealand	000-911
Nicaragua	174
Norway	800-190-11
Panama	109
Paraguay (Asuncion City)	0081-800
Peru	191
Philippines	105-11
Poland	0-010-480-0111
Portugal	05017-1-288
Qatar	0800-011-77
Romania	01-800-4288
Russia (Moscow)	155-5042
St. Kitts	1-800-872-2881
St. Vincent	1-800-872-2881
Saipan	235-2872

International Dialing to the U.S. (cont'd)

Country	Code
San Marino	172-1011
Saudi Arabia	1-800-10
Sierra Leone	1100
Singapore	800-0111-111
Slovakia	00-420-00101
South Africa	0-800-99-0123
Spain	900-9900-11
Sri Lanka	430-430
Suriname	156
Sweden	020-795-611
Switzerland	155-00-11
Syria	0-801
Taiwan	0080-102880
Thailand	001-999-11111
Turkey	00-800-12277
Ukraine	8 † 100-11
United Arab Emirates	800-121
United Kingdom	0800-89-0011
Uruguay	000410
Venezuela	00-0410
Zambia	80-011-120
Zimbabwe	110899

† wait for second dial tone

MCI Access Codes

Country	Code
American Samoa	633-2624
Antigua	#2
Argentina	001-800-333-1111
Australia	1-800-881-100
Austria	022-903-012
Bahamas	1-800-624-1000
Bahrain	800-002
Belgium	0800-10012
Bermuda	1-800-623-0484
Bolivia	0800-2222
Brazil	000-8012
Cayman Islands	1-800-624-1000
Chile (ENTEL)	12300316
Chile (CTC)	800-207-300
China	108-12
Colombia	980-16-0001
Costa Rica	162
Cyprus	080-9000
Denmark	8001-0022
Dominican Rep.	1-800-751-6624
Ecuador	170
El Salvador	195
Finland	9800-102-80
France	19 † 00-19
Gambia	00-1-99

Country	Code
Germany	0130-0012
Greece	00-800-1211
Grenada	1-800-624-8721
Guam	950-1022
Guatemala	189
Haiti	011-800-444-1234
Honduras	122
Hong Kong	800-1121
Hungary	00 † 800-01411
Iceland	800-9002
India	000-127
Indonesia	00-801-11
Ireland	1-800-551-1001
Israel	177-150-2727
Italy	172-1022
Japan (KDD)	0039-121
Japan (IDC)	0066-55-121
Kenya	0800-11
Korea	009-14
Korea (U.S. bases)	550-2255
Kuwait	800-624
Lebanon (Beirut)	600-624
Lebanon	01-425-036
Liechtenstein	155-0222
Luxembourg	0800-0112
Macau	0800-131
Malaysia	800-0012
Mexico	95-800-674-7000
Monaco	19 † 00-19
Netherlands	06-022-91-22
New Zealand	000-912
Nicaragua (Managua)	166
Nicaragua	02-166
Norway	800-19912
Panama	108
Peru (CPT-Lima)	001-190
Peru (ENTEL)	190
Philippines	10514
Poland	0 † 01-04-800-222
Portugal	05-017-1234
Qatar	0800-012-77
Saipan	950-1022
San Marino	172-1022
Singapore	8000-112-112
Slovakia	00-42-000112
South Africa	0800-99-0011
Spain	900-99-0014
Sweden	020-795-922
Switzerland	155-0222
Syria	0800

† wait for second dial tone

International Dialing to the U.S. (cont'd)

Country	Code
Taiwan	00801-34567
Thailand	001-999-1-2001
Turkey	00-8001-1177
United Arab Emirates	800-111
United Kingdom (BT)	0800-89-0222
United Kingdom (Mercury)	0500-89-0222
Uruguay	000-412
Vatican City	172-1022
Venezuela	800-1114-0

† *wait for second dial tone*

Note: Call WorldPhone Hotline at (800) 444-4141 from the U.S. for new countries that may have been added.

Sprint Access Codes

Country	Code
Antigua	#0
Argentina	001-800-777-1111
Australia	0014-881-877
Australia (Optus)	008-5511-10
Australia (Telstra)	1-800-881-877
Austria	022-903-014
Bahamas	1-800-389-2111
Barbados	1-800-877-8000
Belgium	0800-10014
Belize (hotels)	556
Belize	*4 (star key + 4)
Bermuda	1-800-623-0877
Bolivia	0800-3333
Brazil	000-8016
British Virgin Islands	1-800-877-8000
Canada	1-800-877-8000
Chile	00 † 0317
China	108-13
Colombia	980-13-0010
Costa Rica	163
Cyprus	080-900-01
Denmark	800-1-0877
Dominican Rep.	1-800-751-7877
Ecuador	171
El Salvador	191
Finland	9800-1-0284
France	19 † 0087
Germany	0130-0013
Greece	008-001-411
Guatemala	195
Honduras	001-800-1212000
Hong Kong	011
Hungary	00 † 800-01-877
India	000-137
Indonesia	00-801-15

Country	Code
Ireland	1-800-55-2001
Israel	177-102-2727
Italy	172-1877
Japan (KDD)	0039-131
Japan (IDC)	0066 † 55-877
Kenya	0800-12
Korea	009-16
Korea (U.S. bases)	550-3663
Kuwait	800-777
Liechtenstein	155-9777
Luxembourg	0800-0115
Macao	0800-121
Malaysia	800-0016
Monaco	19 † 0087
Netherlands	06 † 022-9119
New Zealand	000-999
Nicaragua (Managua)	171
Nicaragua	02-161
Norway	800-19877
Panama	115
Peru	196
Philippines (ETP)	105-01
Philippines (PhilCom)	102-611
Poland	00104-800-115
Portugal	05017-1-877
Puerto Rico	1-800-877-8000
Saint Lucia	187
San Marino	172-1877
Singapore	8000-177-177
South Africa	0-800-99-0001
Spain	900-99-0013
Sweden	020-799-011
Switzerland	155-9777
Taiwan	0080-14-0877
Thailand	001-999-13-877
Trinidad & Tobago	23
Turkey	00-800-1-4477
United Arab Emirates	800-131
United Kingdom (BT)	0800-89-0877
United Kingdom (MER)	0500-89-0877
United States	1-800-877-8000
Uruguay	000417
U.S. Virgin Islands	1-800-877-8000
Vatican City	172-1877
Venezuela	800-1111-0

† *wait for second dial tone*

Note: For any countries not listed, call (913) 624-5336 collect from any country.

Country Codes

Selected Country and City Codes

Location	Country Code	City Code
Albania	355	
Algeria	213	
American Samoa	684	
Andorra	33	
Angola	244	
Anguilla	809	
Antigua	809	
Argentina	54	
Buenos Aires		1
Aruba	297	
Ascension Island	247	
Australia	61	
Melbourne		3
Perth		9
Sydney		2
Austria	43	
Vienna		1
Bahamas	809	
Bahrain	973	
Bangladesh	880	
Barbados	809	
Belgium	32	
Antwerp		3
Brussels		2
Belize	501	
Benin	229	
Bermuda	809	
Bhutan	975	
Bolivia	591	
Botswana	267	
Brazil	55	
Rio de Janeiro		21
British Virgin Islands	809	
Brunei	673	
Bulgaria	359	
Cameroon	237	
Cape Verde Islands	238	
Cayman Islands	809	
Chad Republic	235	
Chile	56	
Santiago		2
China	86	
Peking		1
Shanghai		21
Columbia	57	
Congo	242	
Cook Islands	682	
Costa Rica	506	
Cyprus	357	
Czech Republic	42	
Prague		2
Denmark	45	
Copenhagen		3
Dominican Republic	809	
Ecuador	593	
Egypt	20	
Cairo		2
El Salvador	503	
Equatorial Guinea	240	
Ethiopia	251	
Falkland Islands	500	
Fiji Islands	679	
Finland	358	
Helsinki		0
France	33	
Paris		1
French Antilles	596	
French Guiana	594	
French Polynesia	689	
Gabon Republic	241	
Gambia	220	
Germany	49	
Berlin		30
Munich		89
Ghana	233	
Gibraltar	350	
Greece	30	
Athens		1
Greenland	299	
Grenada	809	
Guadeloupe	590	
Guam	671	
Guantanamo Bay	53	
Guatemala	502	
Guinea	224	
Guyana	592	
Haiti	509	
Honduras	504	
Hong Kong	852	
Hungary	36	

Country Codes (cont'd)

Location	Country Code	City Code
Budapest		1
Iceland	354	
Reykjavik		1
India	91	
Bombay		22
Calcutta		33
New Delhi		11
Indonesia	62	
Jakarta		21
Iran	98	
Tehran		21
Iraq	964	
Baghdad		1
Ireland	353	
Dublin		1
Israel	972	
Jerusalem		2
Tel Aviv		3
Italy	39	
Florence		55
Rome		6
Venice		41
Ivory Coast	225	
Jamaica	809	
Japan	81	
Osaka		6
Tokyo		33
Jordan	962	
Kenya	254	
Korea	82	
Seoul		2
Kuwait	965	
Lesotho	266	
Liberia	231	
Libya	218	
Liechtenstein	41	
Luxembourg	352	
Macao	853	
Madagascar	261	
Malawi	265	
Malaysia	60	
Kuala Lumpur		3
Mali Republic	223	
Malta	356	
Mauritania	222	
Mauritius	230	
Mexico	52	
Mexico City		5
Monaco	33	
Montserrat	809	

Location	Country Code	City Code
Morocco	212	
Mozambique	258	
Namibia	264	
Nepal	977	
Netherlands	31	
Amsterdam		20
Netherlands Antilles	599	
New Caledonia	687	
New Zealand	64	
Auckland		9
Nicaragua	505	
Niger	227	
Nigeria	234	
Norway	47	
Oslo		2
Oman	968	
Pakistan	92	
Panama	507	
Papua New Guinea	675	
Paraguay	595	
Peru	51	
Lima		14
Philippines	63	
Manila		2
Poland	48	
Warsaw		22
Portugal	351	
Lisbon		1
Qatar	974	
Reunion Island	262	
Romania	40	
Russia	7	
Moscow		95
Rwanda	250	
St. Kitts	809	
St. Lucia	809	
San Marino	39	
Saudi Arabia	966	
Riyadh		1
Senegal Republic	221	
Sierra Leone	232	
Singapore	65	
Slovakia	42	
Solomon Islands	677	
South Africa	27	
Cape Town		21
Johannesburg		11
Spain	34	
Barcelona		3
Madrid		1

Country Codes (cont'd)

Location	Country Code	City Code
Sri Lanka	94	
Suriname	597	
Sweden	46	
Stockholm		8
Switzerland	41	
Zurich		1
Syria	963	
Damascus		11
Taiwan	886	
Taipei		2
Tanzania	255	
Thailand	66	
Bangkok		2
Trinidad & Tobago	809	
Tunisia	216	
Turkey	90	
Istanbul		1
Uganda	256	
United Arab Emirates	971	
United Kingdom	44	

Location	Country Code	City Code
Belfast		232
Glasgow		41
Liverpool		51
London (inner)		71
London (outer)		81
Manchester		61
Uruguay	598	
Vatican City	39	
Venezuela	58	
Western Samoa	685	
Yugoslavia	38	
Belgrade		11
Sarajevo		71
Zaire	243	
Zambia	260	
Zimbabwe	263	

NOTE: Dial 011 before dialing a country code. For most telephone numbers that start with a zero, the zero should not be dialed when calling from abroad. Check with an international operator.

Source: AT&T

Phone Cards on Other Systems

AT&T

Dial (800) 225-5288 (CALL-ATT) and follow the instructions (for calling card, credit card, or customer service).

MCI

Dial (800) 674-7000. (WorldPhone card customers should dial (800) 888-8000.) Enter MCI card number and then the party's area code and phone number.

For international calls, dial (800) 674-7000. Enter MCI card number, then 011, and then the party's country code and number.

Sprint

Dial 1-0-333-0 and then the party's area code and number. You should hear "Welcome to Sprint." Then enter Sprint card number. If not, dial (800) 877-8000. At the tone, dial 0 and then the party's area code and number. Then enter Sprint card number.

For international calls, dial 1-0-333-0-1 and then the party's country code and number. Then press the # button. If there is a problem, dial (800) 877-8000 and repeat.

To make another call, do not hang up. Hold down the # key for two seconds. At the tone, dial 0 and then the party's area code and number. This applies to both domestic and international calls.

The Top Reference Sources

AT&T Toll-Free 800 Directory
AT&T, business edition $24.99,
consumer edition $14.99, both $34.95
(800) 426-8686

These are essential references for businesses and consumers. The business edition is a business-to-business directory, with over 150,000 numbers. The consumer edition lets the average person comparison-shop from coast to coast. It contains over 120,000 numbers.

Listings are alphabetical by company name in the white pages, and by classified headings in the yellow pages.

Zip Codes

Manhattan Zip Codes

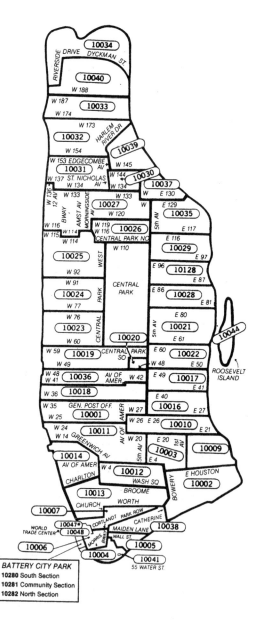

BATTERY CITY PARK
10280 South Section
10281 Community Section
10282 North Section

For fastest service, use the exact zip code for the destination address. The zip codes in this table will bring mail to the main post office in each city, which is faster than no zip code at all.

This table can also be used to send a batch of letters to a central zip code by Express Mail. The local postmaster will then deliver the individual letters locally, saving time and money.

To obtain a zip code for any location, call the U.S. Postal Service at (202) 682-9595 from 8:00 A.M. to 8:00 P.M., Monday through Friday and 8:00 A.M. to 5:00 P.M. on Saturday. After hours, call the Honolulu Post Office at (808) 423-3930.

Main Post Office Zip Codes

City	Zip Code
Atlanta	30301
Baltimore	21233
Boston	02101
Chicago	60601
Cincinnati	45202
Cleveland	44101
Columbus	43216
Dallas	75201
Denver	80201
Detroit	48231
Houston	77052
Indianapolis	46206
Los Angeles	90086
Miami	33101
Milwaukee	53201
Minneapolis	55401
New York	10001
Norfolk	23503
Philadelphia	19104
Phoenix	85201
Pittsburgh	15233
Portland	97208
Sacramento	95814
St. Louis	63166
San Antonio	78265
San Diego	92183
San Francisco	94142
Seattle	98101
Tampa	33602
Washington, DC (federal)	20500
Washington, DC (other)	20090

E-MAIL **Manhattan Address Locator.** Send e-mail to nyc@almanac.yoyo.com. See p. xi for instructions.
A chart that makes it easy to find a location in Manhattan if you know the address.

Postal Service

FOR MOST USERS, the United States Postal Service offers five classes of mail. From most expensive to least expensive, they are:

- *Express Mail:* overnight, seven days a week
- *Priority Mail:* two-day service to most locations
- *First Class:* quick and relatively inexpensive
- *Third Class:* bulk mail–permit required
- *Fourth Class:* parcel post and books.

In addition to these services, the Postal Service offers insurance, registration, certification, and (though rarely used) Special Delivery.

First Class Mail (single-piece letter rates)

Weight in oz.	Postage ($)
Postcard	0.20
1	0.32
2	0.55
3	0.78
4	1.01
5	1.24
6	1.47
7	1.70
8	1.93
9	2.16
10	2.39
11*	2.62

* For pieces weighing more than 11 oz., use priority mail service

Priority Mail

Weight in lb.	Postage ($)
1	3.00
2	3.00
3	4.00
4	5.00
5	6.00

Size Requirements

Pieces must meet the following minimum size requirements to be mailable in any class:

- All pieces must be at least .007 inch thick
- Pieces (except keys and identification devices) that are 1/4 inch or less thick must be:
  - rectangular in shape
  - at least 3 1/2 inches high
  - at least 5 inches long.

Pieces greater than 1/4 inch thick can be mailed even if they measure less than 3 1/2 by 5 inches.

Non-Standard Mail

Mail that doesn't meet the above requirements is subject to a ten-cent surcharge in addition to the applicable postage. For Presort First Class and carrier route First Class, the surcharge is five cents in addition to applicable postage.

Mail is characterized as non-standard First Class mail or single-piece Third Class mail if it weighs one ounce and:

- Any of the following dimensions are exceeded:

  Length: 11 1/2 inches

  Height: 6 1/8 inches

  Thickness: 1/4 inch, or

- The length divided by the height (aspect ratio) is less than 1.3 or more than 2.5.

Second Class Mail

Second Class mail is only available to newspapers and periodicals that have qualified for Second-Class mail privileges.

Third Class Mail

Third Class mail is restricted to specific types of matter–circulars, books, catalogues, and other printed materials–weighing less than 16 ounces. A permit is required, and the rules governing this class of service are numerous. Contact your postmaster for details.

Single-Piece Third Class Rates*

Weight Not Exceeding (oz.)	Postage ($)
1	0.32
2	0.55
3	0.78
4	1.01
5	1.24
6	1.47
7	1.70
8	1.93
9	2.16
10	2.39

* For pieces up to six pounds, the rate is the same as that of first class mail.

Fourth Class Mail

To the general public, Fourth Class is the cheapest postal rate available for anything weighing over one pound.

Postal Service (cont'd)

For authorized bulk users, there are subrates available for printed matter. This is a single rate charged to the company regardless of the zone.

The Fourth Class rates are based on the distance sent. There are some discounts available.

Special Services (domestic mail only)

* *Certified Mail* allows the sender to receive evidence of delivery for an extra fee. A mailing receipt and delivery record are sent from the destination post office. Available at a rate of $1 in addition to the applicable postage.

* *COD* (collect on delivery): The maximum value for COD service is $600. Consult postmaster for fees and conditions of mailing.

Insurance

Liability ($)	Fee in Addition to Postage ($)
.01 to 50.00	0.75
50.01 to 100.00	1.60
100.01 to 200.00	2.50
200.01 to 300.00	3.40
300.01 to 400.00	4.30
400.01 to 500.00	5.20
500.01 to 600.00	6.20

* *Registered Mail* allows the sender maximum protection and security. The letter is signed for at every step of the mailing process to insure that it has been delivered properly. The sender also receives a return receipt upon completion of delivery. There is an additional fee for registered mail.

Registered Mail Additional Fees

Value ($)	Insured ($)	Uninsured ($)
1 to 100.00	4.95	4.85
100.01 to 500.00	5.40	5.20

Note: For higher values, consult postmaster.

* *Special Delivery* provides expedited delivery to specified zones. First-Class packages up to 2 pounds are $7.65, between 2 and 10 pounds are $7.95, and more than 10 pounds are $8.55.

* *Special Handling* gives preferential handling to Third- and Fourth-Class packages. Packages less than 10 pounds are $1.80 extra. Those over 10 pounds are $2.50 more.

Additional Services

* *Certificate of Mailing* (for bulk mailing and firm mailing books, see the postmaster). Fifty cents per certificate.

* *Return Receipt* (available for COD, Express Mail, certified, insured for over $50, and registered mail). There are two levels of service: requested at time of mailing, showing to whom (signature) and date delivered, $1; and showing to whom (signature), date, and address where delivered, $1.35.

* *Restricted Delivery* (not available for Express Mail). $2.50.

* *Return Receipt for Merchandise* (provides proof of delivery for merchandise shipments only. Cheaper but less secure than certified or registered mail). There are two levels of service: showing to whom (signature) and date delivered, $1.10; and showing to whom (signature), date, and address delivered, $1.50.

Express Mail

Express Mail is available seven days a week, 365 days a year, for mailable items up to 70 pounds in weight and 108 inches in combined length and width. Features include noon delivery between major business markets; merchandise and document reconstruction insurance; Express Mail shipping containers; shipping receipts; special collection boxes; and such options as return receipt service, COD service, waiver of signature, and pickup service. Call (800) 222-1811 for pickup service for a flat fee of $4.50, no matter how many pieces.

Rates:
Up to 8 ounces, $9.95
Up to 2 pounds, $13.95
Over 2 pounds, consult your local postmaster.

Contact Option

U.S. Postal Service
(800) 222-1811

All rates included here are as of May 1995. Call the Postal Service to confirm prices.

Postal Service (cont'd)

International Air Mail—Small Packets and Printed Matter

Weight Not Over	Canada	Mexico	Western Hemisphere (except Canada & Mexico)	Europe	Asia/Africa	Pacific Rim
1 oz	0.38	0.40	0.70	0.85	0.93	0.95
2 oz	0.60	0.63	1.07	1.35	1.57	1.61
3 oz	0.82	0.85	1.44	1.85	2.21	2.27
4 oz	1.04	1.07	1.81	2.35	2.85	2.93
6 oz	1.48	1.51	2.18	3.01	3.76	3.85
8 oz	1.92	1.95	2.55	3.67	4.67	4.77
10 oz	2.36	2.39	2.92	4.33	5.58	5.69
12 oz	2.80	2.83	3.29	4.99	6.49	6.61
1 lb	3.12	3.55	4.03	6.31	8.31	8.45
1.5 lb	3.72	4.40	5.51	8.95	11.95	12.13
2 lb	4.32	5.25	6.99	11.59	15.59	15.81
2.5 lb	5.12	6.10	8.39	14.09	19.14	19.41
3 lb	5.92	6.95	9.79	16.59	22.69	23.01
3.5 lb	6.72	7.80	11.19	19.09	26.24	26.61
4 lb	7.52	8.65	12.59	21.59	29.79	30.21
Each additional 1/2 lb over 4 lb	.80	.85	1.40	2.50	3.55	3.60

Postal Business Centers

The U.S. Postal Service maintains Business Centers around the country. The sole function of these offices is to provide businesses with help and support in sending bulk mail.

State	City	Phone	Zip Codes Served
Alabama	Birmingham	(205) 323-6510	350-368
Alaska	Anchorage	(907) 564-2823	995-999
Arizona	Phoenix	(602) 225-5454	850, 852-853, 855-857, 859-860, 863-864
	Tucson	(602) 620-5108	856-857
Arkansas	Little Rock	(501) 228-4300	716-729
California	Long Beach	(310) 494-2301	902-908
	Los Angeles	(213) 586-1843	900
	Oakland	(510) 874-8600	945-948
	Sacramento	(916)923-4357	942, 952-953, 956-960
	San Diego	(619) 674-0400	919-925
	San Francisco	(415) 550-6565	940-941, 943-944, 949, 954-955, 962-966
	San Jose	(408) 723-6262	932-933, 936-939, 950-951
	Santa Ana	(714) 662-6213	917-918, 926-928
	Van Nuys	(818) 374-4943	910-916, 930-931, 934-935
Colorado	Denver	(303) 297-6118	967-969
Connecticut	Hartford	(203) 524-6494	060-069
	Grand Rapids	(616) 776-6161	484-497
District of Columbia	Washington, DC	(301) 565-2177	200, 202-209
Florida	Fort Lauderdale	(305) 527-6981	333
	Jacksonville	(904) 260-8101	320-326, 344
	Miami	(305) 470-0803	330-332, 340
	Orlando	(407) 826-5602	327-329, 347
	Tampa	(813) 871-6245	335-339, 342, 346
	W. Palm Beach	(407) 697-2180	334, 349
Georgia	Macon	(912) 784-3917	310, 312, 316-319
	North Metro	(404) 717-3440	300-303, 305-306, 311
	Savannah	(912) 235-4591	298-299, 304, 308-309, 313-315
Hawaii	Honolulu	(808) 423-3761	832-838, 990-994
Illinois	Aurora	(708) 978-4455	604-605, 609, 613-619, 625-627
	Carol Stream	(708) 260-5511	600-603, 610-611

Postal Service (cont'd)

State	City	Phone	Zip Codes Served
Illinois	Chicago	(312) 765-4215	606-607
Indiana	Indianapolis	(317) 464-6010	460-469, 472-475, 478-479
Iowa	Des Moines	(515) 251-2336	500-514, 520-528, 612
Kentucky	Louisville	(502) 473-4200	400-418, 420-427, 471, 476-477
Louisiana	New Orleans	(504) 589-1366	700-701, 703-708, 710-714
Maine	Portland	(207) 871-8567	039-049
Maryland	Baltimore	(410) 347-4358	210-212, 214-219
Massachusetts	Boston	(617) 654-5725	021-022
	Springfield	(413) 731-0306	010-013, 050-059
	Woburn	(617) 938-1450	018-019, 01730, 01741-01742
	Worcester	(508) 795-3608	014-017
Michigan	Birmingham	(810) 546-1321	480, 483
	Detroit	(313) 225-5445	481-482
Minnesota	Minneapolis	(612) 349-6360	540, 546-548, 550-551, 553-564, 566
Mississippi	Jackson	(601) 360-2700	369, 386-397
Missouri	Kansas City	(816) 374-9513	636-641, 644-649, 654-658, 660-662, 667
	St. Louis	(314) 534-2678	620, 622-624, 628-631, 633-635, 650-653
Montana	Billings	(406) 255-6432	590-595, 59715
	Missoula	(406) 329-2231	596-599
Nebraska	Omaha	(402) 573-2100	515-516, 664-666, 668-681, 683-693
Nevada	Las Vegas	(702) 361-9318	889-891, 893-895, 897-898, 961
New Hampshire	Manchester	(603) 644-3838	030-038
New Jersey	Bellmawr	(609) 933-6000	080-084, 197-199
	Edison	(908) 777-0565	077-079, 085-089
	West Orange	(201) 731-4866	070-076
New Mexico	Albuquerque	(505) 245-9480	865, 870-875, 877-884
New York	Albany	(518) 869-6526	120-123, 128-139
	Buffalo	(716) 846-2581	140-143, 147
	Elmsford	(914) 345-1237	105-109, 124-127
	Flushing	(718) 321-5700	103, 110-114, 116
	Hauppauge	(516) 582-7600	115, 117-119
	New York	(212) 330-3809	100-102, 104
	Rochester	(716) 272-7220	144-146, 148-149
North Carolina	Charlotte	(704) 393-4427	280-285, 287-289, 297
	Greensboro	(910) 665-9740	270-279, 286
Ohio	Akron	(216) 996-9721	434-436, 439, 442-449
	Cincinnati	(513) 723-9900	410, 450-455, 458, 470
	Cleveland	(216) 443-4401	440-441
	Columbus	(614) 469-4336	430-433, 437-438, 456-457
Oklahoma	Oklahoma City	(405) 720-2675	730-731, 734-741, 743-749
Oregon	Portland	(503) 294-2306	970-979, 986
Pennsylvania	Erie	(814) 878-0002	155, 157-168
	Harrisburg	(717) 257-2108	169-172, 177-178, 180-188
	Lancaster	(717) 396-6994	173-176, 179, 195-196
	Philadelphia	(215) 895-8046	190-192
	Pittsburgh	(412) 359-7601	150-154, 156, 260
	Southeastern	(215) 964-6441	189, 193-194
Puerto Rico	San Juan	(809) 782-3929	006-009
Rhode Island	Providence	(401) 276-5038	020, 023-029
South Carolina	Columbia	(803) 926-6200	290-296

Postal Service (cont'd)

State	City	Phone	Zip Codes Served
South Dakota	Sioux Falls	(605) 339-8854	565, 567, 570-577, 580-588
Tennessee	Memphis	(901) 576-2035	380-383
	Nashville	(615) 885-9399	307, 370-374, 376-379, 384-385
Texas	Dallas	(214) 393-6701	750-759
	Fort Worth	(817) 625-3600	739, 760-764, 768-769, 790-796
	Houston	(713) 226-3349	770-778
	North Houston	(713) 985-4108	770-778
	San Antonio	(210) 657-8578	733, 765-767, 779-789, 797-799
Utah	Salt Lake City	(801) 974-2503	840-841, 843-847
Vermont		(800) 230-2370	All locations
Virginia	Merrifield	(703) 207-6800	201, 220-223, 226-227
	Richmond	(804) 775-6224	224-225, 228-239, 244
Washington	Seattle	(206) 625-7016	980-985, 988-989
West Virginia	Charleston	(304) 340-4233	240-243, 245-259, 261-268
Wisconsin	Madison	(608) 246-1245	535-539, 549
	Milwaukee	(414) 287-2522	498-499, 530-532, 534-535, 537-539, 541-545, 549

Postal Abbreviations

State	Abbr.	State	Abbr.	State	Abbr.
Alabama	AL	Maine	ME	Pennsylvania	PA
Alaska	AK	Marshall Islands	TT	Puerto Rico	PR
American Samoa	AS	Maryland	MD	Rhode Island	RI
Arizona	AZ	Massachusetts	MA	South Carolina	SC
Arkansas	AR	Michigan	MI	South Dakota	SD
California	CA	Minnesota	MN	Tennessee	TN
Colorado	CO	Mississippi	MS	Texas	TX
Connecticut	CT	Missouri	MO	Utah	UT
Delaware	DE	Montana	MT	Vermont	VT
District of Columbia	DC	Nebraska	NE	Virginia	VA
Florida	FL	Nevada	NV	Virgin Islands	VI
Georgia	GA	New Hampshire	NH	Washington	WA
Hawaii	HI	New Jersey	NJ	West Virginia	WV
Idaho	ID	New Mexico	NM	Wisconsin	WI
Illinois	IL	New York	NY	Wyoming	WY
Indiana	IN	North Carolina	NC		
Iowa	IA	North Dakota	ND		
Kansas	KS	Ohio	OH		
Kentucky	KY	Oklahoma	OK		
Louisiana	LA	Oregon	OR		

United Parcel Service

UNITED PARCEL SERVICE (UPS) is one of the most cost-effective ways to move packages across the country. They offer four levels of service:

• Ground

• 3 Day Select

• 2nd Day Air

• Next Day Air

In all instances, the maximum weight of the package is 70 pounds. The maximum size of 130 inches is figured out by a formula: [(longest side) + (next longest side x 2)] + (shortest side x 2).

Ground Service

Pricing on UPS ground service, the most inexpensive means of shipping most packages, is based on zones. The price of a given shipment changes depending on the origin and destination zip codes. The zone map used by UPS is different in every part of the country.

The charts on the next two pages give the price of sending one-pound and five-pound packages to and from major cities. These numbers are only a guideline—contact UPS for precise figures.

3 Day Select

This new service provides guaranteed three-day service throughout the country. Rates are based on the origin and destination zip codes. Call (800) 742-5877 for pricing.

2nd Day Air (Blue)

All packages sent by this service within the 48 contiguous states are charged a flat rate.

Next Day Air (Red)

All packages sent by this service within the 48 contiguous states are charged a flat rate.

UPS Air Pricing

Weight (lb.)	Next Day Air ($)	Second Day Air ($)
Letter	11.25	6.00
1	16.00	6.25
2	16.75	7.25
3	18.00	8.00
4	19.25	8.50
5	21.00	9.25
6	23.00	10.50
7	25.00	12.00
8	27.00	13.25
9	29.00	14.50
10	31.00	15.50

Note: All rates as of February 1995

The costs above do not reflect pickup charges. With 24 hours' notice, UPS will pick up any number of packages for a flat fee of $5.00. For air packages, UPS will pick up on the same day for a charge of $3.25 per package.

Contact Option

United Parcel Service
(800) 742-5877

The Top Reference Sources

Bacon's Newspaper/Magazine Directory
Bacon's Information, $250
(312) 922-2400

This annual directory of magazines and newspapers offers descriptive editorial profiles of leading consumer magazines and prominent trade publications.

The reference also contains a listing of Hispanic newspapers, a schedule of ad rates, and an index of multiple publishers for daily newspaper chains

United Parcel Service (cont'd)

UPS Rates, One-Pound Package, Ground Service ($)

		Atlanta, 30301	Baltimore, 21233	Boston, 02101	Chicago, 60601	Cincinnati, 45202	Cleveland, 44101	Columbus, 43216	Dallas, 75201	Denver, 80201	Detroit, 48231	Houston, 77052	Indianapolis, 46206	Los Angeles, 90806	Miami, 33101	Milwaukee, 53201
Atlanta	30301	2.71	3.13	3.22	3.13	3.13	3.13	3.13	3.22	3.30	3.13	3.22	3.13	3.46	3.13	3.22
Baltimore	21233	3.13	2.71	3.13	3.13	3.13	2.88	3.13	3.30	3.40	3.13	3.30	3.13	3.46	3.22	3.22
Boston	02101	3.22	3.13	2.71	3.22	3.22	3.13	3.22	3.40	3.40	3.22	3.40	3.22	3.46	3.30	3.22
Chicago	60601	3.13	3.13	3.22	2.71	2.88	2.88	2.88	3.22	3.22	2.88	3.22	2.71	3.40	3.30	2.71
Cincinnati	45202	3.13	3.13	3.22	2.88	2.71	2.88	2.71	3.22	3.30	2.88	3.22	2.71	3.46	3.22	2.88
Cleveland	44101	3.13	2.88	3.13	2.88	2.88	2.71	2.71	3.22	3.30	2.71	3.30	2.88	3.46	3.30	3.13
Columbus	43216	3.13	3.13	3.22	2.88	2.71	2.71	2.71	3.22	3.30	2.88	3.22	2.71	3.46	3.22	3.13
Dallas	75201	3.22	3.30	3.40	3.22	3.22	3.22	3.22	2.71	3.22	3.22	2.88	3.22	3.30	3.30	3.22
Denver	80201	3.30	3.40	3.40	3.22	3.30	3.30	3.30	3.22	2.71	3.30	3.22	3.22	3.22	3.40	3.22
Detroit	48231	3.13	3.13	3.22	2.88	2.88	2.71	2.88	3.22	3.30	2.71	3.30	2.88	3.46	3.30	2.88
Houston	77052	3.22	3.30	3.40	3.22	3.22	3.30	3.22	2.88	3.22	3.30	2.71	3.22	3.30	3.22	3.22
Indianapolis	46206	3.13	3.13	3.22	2.71	2.71	2.88	2.71	3.22	3.22	2.88	3.22	2.71	3.40	3.30	2.71
Los Angeles	90086	3.46	3.46	3.46	3.40	3.46	3.46	3.46	3.30	3.22	3.46	3.30	3.40	2.71	3.46	3.40
Miami	33101	3.13	3.22	3.30	3.30	3.22	3.30	3.22	3.30	3.40	3.30	3.22	3.30	3.46	2.71	3.30
Milwaukee	53201	3.22	3.22	3.22	2.71	2.88	3.13	3.13	3.22	3.22	2.88	3.22	2.71	3.40	3.30	2.71
Minneapolis	55401	3.22	3.22	3.30	3.13	3.13	3.22	3.13	3.22	3.22	3.13	3.30	3.13	3.40	3.40	2.88
New York	10001	2.71	2.71	2.88	3.22	3.13	3.13	3.13	3.30	3.40	3.13	3.30	3.22	3.46	3.30	3.22
Norfolk	23503	3.13	2.88	3.13	3.22	3.13	3.13	3.13	3.30	3.40	3.13	3.30	3.13	3.46	3.22	3.22
Philadelphia	19104	3.22	2.71	2.88	3.22	3.13	3.13	3.13	3.30	3.40	3.13	3.30	3.13	3.46	3.22	3.22
Phoenix	85201	3.40	3.46	3.46	3.40	3.40	3.40	3.40	3.22	3.13	3.40	3.22	3.40	3.13	3.46	3.40
Pittsburgh	15233	3.13	2.88	3.13	3.13	2.88	2.71	2.71	3.30	3.30	2.88	3.30	3.13	3.46	3.22	3.13
Portland, OR	97208	3.46	3.46	3.46	3.40	3.46	3.46	3.46	3.40	3.22	3.46	3.46	3.46	3.22	3.46	3.40
Sacramento	95814	3.46	3.46	3.46	3.40	3.46	3.46	3.46	3.40	3.22	3.46	3.40	3.46	3.13	3.46	3.40
St. Louis	63166	3.13	3.22	3.30	2.88	2.88	3.13	3.13	3.13	3.22	3.13	3.13	3.22	3.40	3.30	3.13
San Antonio	78265	3.22	3.30	3.40	3.30	3.30	3.30	3.30	2.88	3.22	3.30	2.88	3.22	3.30	3.30	3.30
San Diego	92183	3.46	3.46	3.46	3.40	3.46	3.46	3.46	3.30	3.22	3.46	3.30	3.40	2.71	3.46	3.40
San Fran.	94142	3.46	3.46	3.46	3.46	3.46	3.46	3.46	3.40	3.22	3.46	3.40	3.46	3.13	3.46	3.46
Seattle	98101	3.46	3.46	3.46	3.40	3.46	3.46	3.46	3.40	3.30	3.46	3.46	3.46	3.22	3.46	3.40
Tampa	33602	3.13	3.22	3.30	3.22	3.22	3.22	3.22	3.22	3.40	3.22	3.22	3.22	3.46	2.88	3.30
DC	20090	3.13	2.71	3.13	3.13	3.13	2.88	3.13	3.30	3.40	3.13	3.30	3.13	3.46	3.22	3.22

		Minneapolis, 55401	New York, 10001	Norfolk, 23503	Philadelphia, 19104	Phoenix, 85201	Pittsburgh, 15233	Portland, OR, 97208	Sacramento, 95814	St. Louis, 63166	San Antonio, 78265	San Diego, 92183	San Francisco, 94142	Seattle, 98101	Tampa, 33602	DC, 20900
Minneapolis	55401	2.71	3.22	3.30	3.22	3.30	3.22	3.40	3.40	3.13	3.30	3.40	3.40	3.30	3.30	3.22
New York	10001	3.22	2.71	2.88	3.22	3.46	3.13	3.46	3.46	3.22	3.40	3.46	3.46	3.46	3.22	2.88
Norfolk	23503	3.30	2.88	2.71	2.88	3.46	3.13	3.46	3.46	3.22	3.30	3.46	3.46	3.46	3.22	2.71
Philadelphia	19104	3.22	3.22	2.88	2.71	3.46	2.88	3.46	3.46	3.22	3.40	3.46	3.46	3.46	3.22	2.71
Phoenix	85201	3.30	3.46	3.46	3.46	2.71	3.46	3.30	3.22	3.30	3.22	3.13	3.22	3.30	3.40	3.46
Pittsburgh	15233	3.22	3.13	3.13	2.88	3.46	2.71	3.46	3.46	3.13	3.30	3.46	3.46	3.46	3.22	2.88
Portland, OR	97208	3.40	3.46	3.46	3.46	3.30	3.46	2.71	2.71	3.40	3.40	3.22	2.71	2.71	3.46	3.46
Sacramento	95814	3.40	3.46	3.46	3.46	3.22	3.46	2.71	2.71	3.40	3.40	3.13	2.71	3.22	3.46	3.46
St. Louis	63166	3.13	3.22	3.22	3.22	3.30	3.13	3.40	3.40	2.71	3.22	3.40	3.40	3.40	3.22	3.22
San Antonio	78265	3.30	3.40	3.30	3.40	3.22	3.30	3.40	3.40	3.22	2.71	3.30	3.40	3.40	3.22	3.30
San Diego	92183	3.40	3.46	3.46	3.46	3.13	3.46	3.22	3.13	3.40	3.30	2.71	3.13	3.30	3.46	3.46
San Fran.	94142	3.40	3.46	3.46	3.46	3.22	3.46	2.71	2.71	3.40	3.40	3.13	2.71	3.22	3.46	3.46
Seattle	98101	3.30	3.46	3.46	3.46	3.30	3.46	2.71	3.22	3.40	3.40	3.30	3.22	2.71	3.46	3.46
Tampa	33602	3.30	3.22	3.22	3.22	3.40	3.22	3.46	3.46	3.22	3.22	3.46	3.46	3.46	2.71	3.22
DC	20090	3.22	2.88	2.71	2.71	3.46	2.88	3.46	3.46	3.22	3.30	3.46	3.46	3.46	3.22	2.71

United Parcel Service (cont'd)

UPS Rates, Five-Pound Package, Ground Service ($)

		Atlanta, 30301	Baltimore, 21233	Boston, 02101	Chicago, 60601	Cincinnati, 45202	Cleveland, 44101	Columbus, 43216	Dallas, 75201	Denver, 80201	Detroit, 48231	Houston, 77052	Indianapolis, 46206	Los Angeles, 90806	Miami, 33101	Milwaukee, 53201
Atlanta	30301	3.11	3.89	4.13	3.89	3.89	3.89	3.89	4.13	4.49	3.89	4.13	3.89	5.19	3.89	4.13
Baltimore	21233	3.89	3.11	3.89	3.89	3.89	3.00	3.89	4.49	4.74	3.89	4.49	3.89	5.19	4.13	4.13
Boston	02101	4.13	3.89	3.11	4.13	4.13	3.89	4.13	4.74	4.74	4.13	4.74	4.13	5.19	4.49	4.13
Chicago	60601	3.89	3.89	4.13	3.11	3.00	3.00	3.00	4.13	4.13	3.00	4.13	3.11	4.74	4.49	3.11
Cincinnati	45202	3.89	3.89	4.13	3.00	3.11	3.00	3.11	4.13	4.49	3.00	4.13	3.11	5.19	4.49	3.00
Cleveland	44101	3.89	3.00	3.89	3.00	3.00	3.11	3.11	4.13	4.49	3.11	4.49	3.00	5.19	4.13	3.89
Columbus	43216	3.89	3.89	4.13	3.00	3.11	3.11	3.11	4.13	4.49	3.00	4.13	3.11	5.19	4.13	3.89
Dallas	75201	4.13	4.49	4.74	4.13	4.13	4.13	4.13	3.11	4.13	4.13	3.00	4.13	4.49	4.49	4.13
Denver	80201	4.49	4.74	4.74	4.13	4.49	4.49	4.49	4.13	3.11	4.49	4.13	4.13	4.13	4.74	4.13
Detroit	48231	3.89	3.89	4.13	3.00	3.00	3.11	3.00	4.13	4.49	3.11	4.49	3.00	5.19	4.49	3.00
Houston	77052	4.13	4.49	4.74	4.13	4.13	4.49	4.13	3.00	4.13	4.49	3.11	4.13	4.49	4.13	4.13
Indianapolis	46206	3.89	3.89	4.13	3.11	3.11	3.00	3.11	4.13	4.13	3.00	4.13	3.11	4.74	4.49	3.11
Los Angeles	90086	5.19	5.19	5.19	4.74	5.19	5.19	5.19	4.49	4.13	5.19	4.49	4.74	3.11	5.19	4.74
Miami	33101	3.89	4.13	4.49	4.49	4.49	4.13	4.13	4.49	4.74	4.49	4.13	4.49	5.19	3.11	4.49
Milwaukee	53201	4.13	4.13	4.13	3.11	3.00	3.89	3.89	4.13	4.13	3.00	4.13	3.11	4.74	4.49	3.11
Minneapolis	55401	4.13	4.13	4.49	3.89	3.89	4.13	3.89	4.13	4.13	3.89	4.49	3.89	4.74	4.74	3.00
New York	10001	3.11	3.11	3.00	4.13	3.89	3.89	3.89	4.49	4.74	3.89	4.49	4.13	5.19	4.49	4.13
Norfolk	23503	3.89	3.00	3.89	4.13	3.89	3.89	3.89	4.49	4.74	3.89	4.49	3.89	5.19	4.13	4.13
Philadelphia	19104	4.13	3.11	3.00	4.13	3.89	3.89	3.89	4.49	4.74	3.89	4.49	3.89	5.19	4.13	4.13
Phoenix	85201	4.74	5.19	5.19	4.74	4.74	4.74	4.74	4.13	3.89	4.74	4.49	4.74	3.89	5.19	4.74
Pittsburgh	15233	3.89	3.00	3.89	3.89	3.00	3.11	3.11	4.49	4.49	3.00	4.49	3.89	5.19	4.13	3.89
Portland, OR	97208	5.19	5.19	5.19	4.74	5.19	5.19	5.19	4.74	4.13	5.19	5.19	5.19	4.13	5.19	4.74
Sacramento	95814	5.19	5.19	5.19	4.74	5.19	5.19	5.19	4.74	4.13	5.19	4.74	5.19	3.89	5.19	4.74
St. Louis	63166	3.89	4.13	4.49	3.00	3.00	3.89	3.89	3.89	4.13	3.89	3.89	4.13	4.74	4.49	3.89
San Antonio	78265	4.13	4.49	4.74	4.49	4.49	4.49	4.49	3.00	4.13	4.49	3.00	4.13	4.49	4.49	4.49
San Diego	92183	5.19	5.19	5.19	4.74	5.19	5.19	5.19	4.49	4.13	5.19	4.49	4.74	3.11	5.19	4.74
San Fran.	94142	5.19	5.19	5.19	5.19	5.19	5.19	5.19	4.74	4.13	5.19	4.74	5.19	3.89	5.19	5.19
Seattle	98101	5.19	5.19	5.19	4.74	5.19	5.19	5.19	4.74	4.49	5.19	5.19	5.19	4.13	5.19	4.74
Tampa	33602	3.89	4.13	4.49	4.13	4.13	4.13	4.13	4.13	4.74	4.13	4.13	4.13	5.19	3.00	4.49
DC	20090	3.89	3.11	3.89	3.89	3.89	3.00	3.89	4.49	4.74	3.89	4.49	3.89	5.19	4.13	4.13

		Minneapolis, 55401	New York, 10001	Norfolk, 23503	Philadelphia, 19104	Phoenix, 85201	Pittsburgh, 15233	Portland, OR, 97208	Sacramento, 95814	St. Louis, 63166	San Antonio, 78265	San Diego, 92183	San Francisco, 94142	Seattle, 98101	Tampa, 33602	DC, 20900
Minneapolis	55401	3.11	4.13	4.49	4.13	4.49	4.13	4.74	4.74	3.89	4.49	4.74	4.74	4.49	4.49	4.13
New York	10001	4.13	3.11	3.00	3.11	5.19	3.89	5.19	5.19	4.13	4.74	5.19	5.19	5.19	4.13	3.00
Norfolk	23503	4.49	3.00	3.11	3.00	5.19	3.89	5.19	5.19	4.13	4.49	5.19	5.19	5.19	4.13	3.11
Philadelphia	19104	4.13	3.11	3.00	3.11	5.19	3.00	5.19	5.19	4.13	4.74	5.19	5.19	5.19	4.13	3.11
Phoenix	85201	4.49	5.19	5.19	5.19	3.11	5.19	4.49	4.13	4.49	4.13	3.89	4.13	4.49	4.74	5.19
Pittsburgh	15233	4.13	3.89	3.89	3.00	5.19	3.11	5.19	5.19	3.89	4.49	5.19	5.19	5.19	4.13	3.00
Portland, OR	97208	4.74	5.19	5.19	5.19	4.49	5.19	3.11	3.11	4.74	4.74	4.13	3.11	3.11	5.19	5.19
Sacramento	95814	4.74	5.19	5.19	5.19	4.13	5.19	3.11	3.11	4.74	4.74	3.89	3.11	4.13	5.19	5.19
St. Louis	63166	3.89	4.13	4.13	4.13	4.49	3.89	4.74	4.74	3.11	4.13	4.74	4.74	4.74	4.13	4.13
San Antonio	78265	4.49	4.74	4.49	4.74	4.13	4.49	4.74	4.74	4.13	3.11	4.49	4.74	4.74	4.13	4.49
San Diego	92183	4.74	5.19	5.19	5.19	3.89	5.19	4.13	3.89	4.74	4.49	3.11	3.89	4.49	5.19	5.19
San Fran.	94142	4.74	5.19	5.19	5.19	4.13	5.19	3.11	3.11	4.74	4.74	3.89	3.11	4.13	5.19	5.19
Seattle	98101	4.49	5.19	5.19	5.19	4.49	5.19	3.11	4.13	4.74	4.74	4.49	4.13	3.11	5.19	5.19
Tampa	33602	4.49	4.13	4.13	4.13	4.74	4.13	5.19	5.19	4.13	4.13	5.19	5.19	5.19	3.11	4.13
DC	20090	4.13	3.00	3.11	3.11	5.19	3.00	5.19	5.19	4.13	4.49	5.19	5.19	5.19	4.13	3.11

Federal Express

FEDERAL EXPRESS INVENTED the mass-market overnight delivery business in 1973. They now serve 185 countries and deliver to virtually every location in America. There are three basic classes of service:

- *Priority Overnight Service*: delivered the next business day by 10:30 A.M.

- *Standard Overnight Service*: delivered by 3:00 P.M. the next business day.

- *Economy Two-Day Service*: second business afternoon delivery by 4:30 P.M.

The maximum weight for all three classes of service is 150 pounds per package. The maximum size of 165 inches must be figured out by a formula: (longest side) + (next longest x 2) + (shortest side x 2). Other services offered include:

- *Overnight Freight Service:* Either by noon or 4:30 P.M. the next business day. For packages weighing more than 150 pounds up to 750 pounds or more, with advance approval. A confirmed flight reservation is required in advance.

- *Two-Day Freight Service:* Second business day delivery by 4:30 P.M. Each piece may weigh more than 150 pounds and up to 1,500 pounds or more, with advance approval. For delivery commitment to Hawaii call in advance.

Federal Express Standard Rates

Weight	Priority Overnight ($)	Standard Overnight ($)	Economy Two-Day ($)
<8 oz.	15.50	11.50	NA
1 lb.	22.50	15.50	13.00
2 lb.	24.25	16.50	14.00
3 lb.	27.00	17.50	15.00
4 lb.	29.75	18.50	16.00
5 lb.	32.50	19.50	17.00
6 lb.	35.25	21.25	18.00
7 lb.	38.00	23.00	19.00
8 lb.	40.75	24.75	20.00
9 lb.	43.50	26.50	21.00
10 lb.	46.25	28.25	22.00

Note: All prices $2.50 less if dropped off at a service center. Rates as of April 1995

Special services in addition to the regular service charge:

- *Saturday Delivery:* Priority Overnight shipments dropped off on Friday (call for the latest drop-off time) can be delivered on Saturday. Saturday de-livery is available for two-day service and must be dropped off by Thursday. (There is an extra charge of $10 per package.)

- *Saturday Pickup:* Priority and Standard packages can be picked up on Saturdays. There is a $10 charge per package. There is no additional charge if the package is dropped off at a Service Center.

- *COD:* available to destinations in the U.S. including Hawaii and Alaska. A check or money order is collected on delivery. (Charge is $5 per destination.)

- *Dangerous Goods Service:* $10 per package

- *Address Correction:* $5

- *Billing Special Handling Fee:* $5

- *Air Charter Services*: (800) 238-0181

- *Telecommunications for the Deaf:* (800) 238-4461

- *Transportation of Animals:* (800) 238-5355

- *International Service:* Federal Express serves more than 185 countries. It offers a variety of services. For more information, call (800) 247-4747.

Saving Money on Federal Express

- Drop off packages instead of requesting pickup. If your business ships ten packages a day, you're currently paying as much as $25 per day for pickups.

- Negotiate a discount. Call (800) 238-5355 and ask for the number of your sales rep. Request a face-to-face meeting, and feel free to talk about your other delivery options. There is flexibility built in to the rates.

- Use Standard Overnight instead of Priority.

- Routinely request verbal proof of delivery on all packages, and ask for a refund for all packages delivered late.

Contact Option

Federal Express
General information: (800) 238-5355
Billing and pricing inquiries: (800) 622-1147

Small Package Rates

8-oz. Package

	Next day A.M. ($)	Next day P.M. ($)	2-day ($)
UPS*	16.00	NA	6.25
Federal Express*	13.00	9.00	NA
Post Office	10.75	NA	3.00
DHL*	12.50	NA	NA

1-lb. Package

	Next day A.M. ($)	Next day P.M. ($)	2-day ($)
UPS*	16.00	NA	6.25
Federal Express*	20.00	13.00	10.50
Post Office	10.75	NA	3.00
DHL*	19.50	NA	NA

5-lb. Package

	Next day A.M. ($)	Next day P.M. ($)	2-day ($)
UPS*	21.00	NA	9.25
Federal Express*	30.00	17.00	14.50
Post Office	21.55	NA	6.00
DHL*	29.50	NA	NA

* Rates listed are for drop-off at designated centers. Consult representative for pick-up surcharge.

Postal Answer Line

THE UNITED STATES POSTAL SERVICE has set up an automated telephone system to provide recorded messages regarding the most frequently needed information. The local PAL number is available from your local post office or you may use the number for Manhattan, (212) 330-4000, or Los Angeles, (213) 587-6142. The recorded instructions will tell the caller when to push the buttons that correspond with the desired message number. The following are some useful messages.

Message	No.
Which class of mail should I use?	333
First Class Mail and Priority Mail rates	323
Second Class (newspapers and magazines)	336
Third Class and Bulk Business Mail	322
Fourth Class Parcel Post rates (packages)	122
Express Mail–P. O. to Addressee–up to 5 lb.	154
Express Mail–P. O. to P. O.–up to 5 lb.	354
Express Mail Same-Day Airport Svc.–up to 5 lb.	302

Message	No.
INTERNATIONAL MAIL/SENDING PACKAGES	
Rates for First-Class surface mail	319
Air Mail rates and information	134
Express Mail International Service	318
Parcel Post rates and information	317
Customs	308
Special services available	142
International Reply Coupons	302
Which mail option should I select?	310
Special services available for packages	143
Removing your name from mailing lists	140
Mailroom security (business)	303
Postage meter security (business)	151
Self-service postal centers	321
Express Mail Next-Day Service	332
Express Mail Same-Day Airport Service	110
Where to deposit Express Mail items	138

The Top Reference Sources

The Elements of Style
Macmillan, $5.95
(212) 702-2000

This classic reference by William Strunk, Jr., and E. B. White is a required text in most high school and college English classes.

In six brief chapters, the book explains the basic rules of grammar and punctuation, plus principles of composition, matters of form, and words and expressions commonly misused. A valuable book for anyone who writes.

Mailroom Phone Directory

FREIGHT & PACKAGE SERVICES	
A.A. Freight Forwarding	(800) 922-2017
Airborne Express	(800) 247-2676
Airgroup Express	(800) 843-4784
America West Airlines	(800) 228-7862
American Airlines Cargo	(800) 638-7320
American Vanpac Carriers	(800) 877-0444
Amtrak	(800) 368-8725
ATMC	(800) 822-2215
Austrian Airlines Cargo Service	(800) 637-2957
Cannonball Air Couriers	(800) 323-6850
Challenger Freight Systems	(800) 225-2836
Coman Courier Service	(800) 824-6420
Consolidated Air Service	(800) 362-1906
Continental Airlines Cargo Center	(800) 421-2456
Delta Airlines	(800) 638-7333
DeSantis Despatch	(800) 962-7260
DHL Worldwide Express	(800) 225-5345
Emery Worldwide ACF	(800) 443-6379
Fast Air Carrier	(800) 327-2578
Federal Express	(800) 238-5355
Global Mail	(800) 426-7478
Griffin Express	(800) 648-2310
Hawaii Air Cargo	(800) 227-3540
International Bonded Couriers	(800) 322-3067
J & B Fast Freight	(800) 841-8029
Jack Rabbit Delivery Service	(800) 782-8149
KLM Royal Dutch Airlines Cargo	(800) 556-9000
Kuwait Airway Cargo Sales	(800) 221-6727
Moonlite Courier	(800) 872-4113
Nippon Cargo Airlines	(800) 622-2746
Northwest Airlines Cargo	(800) 692-2746
Philippine Airlines	(800) 227-6144
Primac Courier	(800) 232-6245
Priority Courier Group	(800) 433-4675

Qantas Airways	(800) 227-0290
Sabena Airlines Cargo	(800) 955-0770
Service by Air	(800) 662-0160
Sky Cab	(800) 631-5488
Sky & Highway Transportation	(800) 328-1972
Southern Air Transport	(800) 327-6456
United Airlines	(800) 631-1500
United Parcel Service	(800) 742-5877
U.S. Express	(800) 468-1012
FACSIMILE COMMUNICATIONS	
Mita Copystar America	(800) 222-6482
Omnifax Facsimile	(800) 221-8330
Panafax Fax Machines	(800) 843-0080
Pitney Bowes Facsimile Systems	(800) 672-6937
Sharp	(800) 237-4277
Toshiba Facsimile Systems	(800) 468-6744
FACSIMILE TRANSMISSION SERVICES	
Facsimile Services	(800) 621-8201
Swift Global Communications	(800) 722-9119
PAGING SYSTEMS	
Infopage	(800) 365-2337
Mobile Media	(800) 437-2337
U.S. Paging	(800) 473-0846
TELEPHONE CONFERENCE SYSTEMS	
AT&T Alliance Teleconference	(800) 544-6363
AT&T Classic Teleconference	(800) 232-1234
American Conferencing	(800) 852-8852
Conference Call Service	(800) 272-5663
Conference Call USA	(800) 654-0455
Darome Teleconferencing	(800) 922-1124
MCI Forum	(800) 475-4700
Sprint Conference Line	(800) 366-2663
CELLULAR PHONE SERVICES	
Nationwide Cellular Service	(800) 627-2355

Note: For guidelines on choosing a telecommunications service, see "Telecommunications Services" on page 533.

E-MAIL

Executive's Yellow Pages. Send e-mail to yellow@almanac.yoyo.com. See p. xi for instructions.

Business service phone numbers, from the first coat-pocket-sized nationwide book of important phone numbers for the executive.

World Time Chart

Place	If it is 11:00 A.M. EST	Time +/- Hrs.
Afghanistan	8:30 P.M.	9.5
Albania ‡	5:00 P.M.	6
Algeria	5:00 P.M.	6
American Samoa	5:00 A.M.	-6
Andorra ‡	5:00 P.M.	6
Angola	5:00 P.M.	6
Anguilla	NOON	1
Antigua	NOON	1
Argentina ◊	1:00 P.M.	2
Aruba	NOON	1
Australia ◊		
Northern Territories	1:30 A.M.*	14.5
Western Australia	MIDNIGHT*	13
Other	2:00 A.M.*	15
Austria ‡	5:00 P.M.	6
Baffin Island	11:00 A.M.	0
Bahamas †	11:00 A.M.	0
Bahrain	7:00 P.M.	8
Baja California	8:00 A.M.	-3
Bangladesh	10:00 P.M.	11
Barbados	NOON	1
Barbuda	NOON	1
Belgium ‡	5:00 P.M.	6
Belize	10:00 A.M.	-1
Benin	5:00 P.M.	6
Bermuda †	NOON	1
Bhutan	10:00 P.M.	11
Bikini Island	4:00 A.M.*	17
Bolivia	NOON	1
Bophuthatswana	6:00 P.M.	7
Borneo	MIDNIGHT*	13
Botswana	6:00 P.M.	7
Brazil ◊		
Fernando de Noronha	2:00 P.M.	3
East	1:00 P.M.	2
West	NOON	1
Territory of Acre	11:00 A.M.	0
British Virgin Islands	NOON	1
Bulgaria ‡	6:00 P.M.	7
Burkina Faso	4:00 P.M.	5
Burma	10:30 P.M.	11.5
Burundi	6:00 P.M.	7
Cameroon	5:00 P.M.	6
Canada †		
Atlantic Time	NOON	1

Place	If it is 11:00 A.M. EST	Time +/- Hrs.
Eastern Time	11:00 A.M.	0
Central Time	10:00 A.M.	-1
Mountain Time	9:00 A.M.	-2
Pacific Time	8:00 A.M.	-3
Canary Islands ‡	4:00 P.M.	5
Cape Verde Islands	3:00 P.M.	4
Cayman Islands	11:00 A.M.	0
Central African Republic	5:00 P.M.	6
Chad	5:00 P.M.	6
Chile ◊	NOON	1
China ◊	MIDNIGHT*	13
Colombia	11:00 A.M.	0
Congo	5:00 P.M.	6
Cook Islands ◊	6:00 A.M.	-5
Costa Rica	10:00 A.M.	-1
Crete	6:00 P.M.	7
Cuba ◊	11:00 A.M.	0
Cyprus ‡	6:00 P.M.	7
Czech Republic	5:00 P.M.	6
Denmark ‡	5:00 P.M.	6
Djibouti	7:00 P.M.	8
Dominica	NOON	1
Dominican Republic	NOON	1
Ecuador	11:00 A.M.	0
Egypt ◊	6:00 P.M.	7
El Salvador	10:00 A.M.	-1
Equatorial Guinea	5:00 P.M.	6
Ethiopia	7:00 P.M.	8
Falkland Islands ◊	NOON	1
Fiji	4:00 A.M.*	17
Finland ‡	6:00 P.M.	7
France ‡	5:00 P.M.	6
French Antilles	NOON	1
French Guiana	1:00 P.M.	2
French Polynesia		
Gambier Island	7:00 A.M.*	-4
Marquesa Island	6:30 A.M.	-4.5
Society Island	6:00 A.M.	-5
Galapagos Islands	10:00 A.M.	-1
Germany ‡	5:00 P.M.	6
Ghana	4:00 P.M.	5
Gibraltar ‡	5:00 P.M.	6
Great Britain ‡	4:00 P.M.	5
Greece ‡	6:00 P.M.	7
Greenland	1:00 P.M.	2

*Based on Eastern Standard Time. *Indicates time on the following day.*
NOTE: Countries around the world shift to daylight savings time on different schedules.
† Add one hour to time shown from April 1 to October 27. ‡ Add one hour to time shown from March 25 to September 22.
◊ See "Non-Standard Daylight Savings" on page 82 for details for this country.

World Time Chart (cont'd)

Place	If it is 11:00 A.M. EST	Time +/- Hrs.
Mesters Vig	4:00 P.M.	5
Scoresby Sound	3:00 P.M.	4
Thule	NOON	1
Grenada	NOON	1
Guadeloupe	NOON	1
Guam	2:00 A.M.*	15
Guatemala	10:00 A.M.	-1
Guinea-Bissau	4:00 P.M.	5
Guyana	11:00 A.M..	0
Haiti †	11:00 A.M.	0
Hawaii †	6:00 A.M.	-5
Hebrides Islands, U.K.	4:00 P.M.	5
Honduras	10:00 A.M.	-1
Hong Kong	MIDNIGHT*	13
Hungary ‡	5:00 P.M.	6
Iceland	4:00 P.M.	5
India	9:30 P.M.	10.5
Indonesia		
Jakarta	11:00 P.M.	12
Central	MIDNIGHT*	13
East	1:00 A.M.*	14
Iran	7:30 P.M.	8.5
Iraq ◊	7:00 P.M.	8
Ireland ‡	4:00 P.M.	5
Isle of Man, U.K.	4:00 P.M.	5
Isle of Wight, U.K.	4:00 P.M.	5
Israel ◊	6:00 P.M.	7
Italy ‡	5:00 P.M.	6
Ivory Coast	4:00 P.M.	5
Jamaica †	11:00 A.M.	0
Japan	1:00 A.M.*	14
Jordan ◊	6:00 P.M.	7
Kamaran Island	7:00 P.M.	8
Kenya	7:00 P.M.	8
Korea	1:00 A.M.*	14
Kuwait	7:00 P.M.	8
Laos	11:00 P.M.	12
Lebanon ◊	6:00 P.M.	7
Liberia	4:00 P.M.	5
Libya ◊	5:00 P.M.	6
Liechtenstein ‡	5:00 P.M.	6
Luxembourg ‡	5:00 P.M.	6
Madagascar	7:00 P.M.	8
Malawi	6:00 P.M.	7
Malaysia	MIDNIGHT*	13

Place	If it is 11:00 A.M. EST	Time +/- Hrs.
Mali	4:00 P.M.	5
Malta ‡	5:00 P.M.	6
Marshall Islands	4:00 A.M.*	17
Martinique	NOON	1
Mauritius	8:00 P.M.	9
Mexico †		
Mexico City, Yucatan	10:00 A.M.	-1
Baja S., N. Pacific coasts	9:00 A.M.	-2
Baja N. above 28th parallel	8:00 A.M.	-3
Micronesia		
Kosrae, Ponape Islands	3:00 A.M.	16
Truk, Yap Islands	1:00 A.M.*	14
Monaco ‡	5:00 P.M.	6
Mongolia ‡	MIDNIGHT*	13
Morocco	5:00 P.M.	6
Mozambique	6:00 P.M.	7
Mustique, St. Vincent	NOON	1
Namibia	6:00 P.M.	7
Nepal	9:30 P.M.	10.5
Netherlands ‡	5:00 P.M.	6
Netherlands Antilles	NOON	1
New Britain (Papua N.G.)	2:00 A.M.*	15
New Caledonia	3:00 A.M.*	16
Newfoundland, Canada	1:30 P.M.	2.5
New Zealand ◊	4:00 A.M.*	17
Nicaragua	10:00 A.M.	-1
Nigeria	5:00 P.M.	6
Norfolk Island	3:30 A.M.*	16.5
N. Sound Island, British V.I.	NOON	1
Northern Ireland, U.K.	4:00 P.M.	5
Norway ‡	5:00 P.M.	6
Pakistan	9:00 P.M.	10
Panama	11:00 A.M.	0
Papua New Guinea	2:00 A.M.*	15
Paraguay ◊	NOON	1
Peru ◊	11:00 A.M.	0
Philippines	MIDNIGHT*	13
Pitcairn Island	8:00 A.M.	-3
Poland ‡	5:00 P.M.	6
Portugal ‡		
Azores	3:00 P.M.	4
Madeira	4:00 P.M.	5
Pr. Edward I., Canada	NOON	1
Pr. Edward I., Indian Ocean	7:00 P.M.	8
Puerto Rico	NOON	1

Based on Eastern Standard Time. *Indicates time on the following day.
NOTE: Countries around the world shift to daylight savings time on different schedules.
† Add one hour to time shown from April 1 to October 27. ‡ Add one hour to time shown from March 25 to September 22.
◊ See "Non-Standard Daylight Savings" on page 82 for details for this country.

World Time Chart (cont'd)

Place	If it is 11:00 A.M. EST	Time +/- Hrs.
Qatar	7:00 P.M.	8
Romania ‡	6:00 P.M.	7
Russia		
Moscow, European part	7:00 P.M.	8
Baku, Gorki, Arkhangelsk	8:00 P.M.	9
Sverdlovsk	9:00 P.M.	10
Tashkent	10:00 P.M.	11
Novosibirsk	11:00 P.M.	12
Taymyr Pen.	MIDNIGHT*	13
Vladivostok	2:00 A.M.*	15
Magadan, Sakhalin	3:00 A.M.*	16
Kamchatka Pen.	4:00 A.M.*	17
St. Barthelemy	NOON	1
St. Croix, U.S.V.I.	NOON	1
St. Helena Island	4:00 P.M.	5
St. John, U.S.V.I.	NOON	1
St. Kitts	NOON	1
St. Lucia	NOON	1
St. Thomas, U.S.V.I.	NOON	1
St. Vincent, Grenadines	NOON	1
Saudi Arabia	7:00 P.M.	8
Scotland, U.K.	4:00 P.M.	5
Senegal	4:00 P.M.	5
Seychelles	8:00 P.M.	9
Shetland Islands, U.K.	4:00 P.M.	5
Sicily, Italy	5:00 P.M.	6
Sierra Leone	4:00 P.M.	5
Singapore	MIDNIGHT*	13
Somalia	7:00 P.M.	8
South Africa	6:00 P.M.	7
Spain ‡	5:00 P.M.	6
Sri Lanka	9:30 P.M.	10.5
Sudan	6:00 P.M.	7
Swaziland	6:00 P.M.	7
Sweden ‡	5:00 P.M.	6
Switzerland ‡	5:00 P.M.	6
Syria ◊	6:00 P.M.	7
Tahiti	6:00 A.M.	-5
Taiwan	MIDNIGHT*	13
Tanzania	7:00 P.M.	8
Thailand	11:00 P.M.	12
Tibet	10:00 P.M.	11
Tierra del Fuego	1:00 P.M.	2
Trinidad & Tobago	NOON	1
Tunisia	5:00 P.M.	6
Turkey ‡	6:00 P.M.	7
Turks & Caicos Islands †	4:00 A.M.*	17
Uganda	7:00 P.M.	8
United Arab Emirates	8:00 P.M.	9
United Kingdom	4:00 P.M.	5

Place	If it is 11:00 A.M. EST	Time +/- Hrs.
Uruguay	1:00 P.M.	2
U.S.A. †		
Eastern Time	11:00 A.M.	0
Central Time	10:00 A.M.	-1
Mountain Time	9:00 A.M.	-2
Pacific Time	8:00 A.M.	-3
Alaska Time	7:00 A.M.	-4
Hawaii Time	6:00 A.M.	-5
Vancouver Island	8:00 A.M.	-3
Venezuela	NOON	1
Vietnam	11:00 P.M.	12
Virgin Gorda, B.V.I.	NOON	1
Virgin Islands	NOON	1
Wales	4:00 P.M.	5
West Indies	NOON	1
Zaire	5:00 P.M.	6
Zambia	6:00 P.M.	7
Zanzibar	7:00 P.M.	8
Zimbabwe	6:00 P.M.	7

Based on Eastern Standard Time.

*Indicates time on the following day.

Non-Standard Daylight Savings

Country	Daylight Savings Time
Argentina	December 1–March 3
Australia	October 8–March 17
Brazil	December 1–March 3
Chile	October 8–March 10
China	April 15–September 15
Cook Islands	October 8–March 17
Cuba	March 18–October 6
Egypt	May 4–September 29
Falkland Islands	September 10–April 14
Iraq	May 4–September 29
Israel	April 29–September 1
Jordan	May 4–September 29
Lebanon	May 1–October 14
Libya	May 1–October 14
New Zealand	October 8–March 17
Paraguay	December 1–March 3
Peru	January 1–March 31
Syria	May 4–September 19

Note: Countries around the world shift to daylight savings time on different schedules. † Add one hour to time shown from April 1 to October 27. ‡ Add one hour to time shown from March 25 to September 22.

CORPORATE ADMINISTRATION

Charity and the Corporation

IN RECENT YEARS, U.S. corporations have continued to make increasingly larger contributions to non-profit charitable organizations. Studies indicate that during the 20 years from 1970 to 1991, contributions rose from $797 million to $6 billion.

Experts point out that the reasons for this largesse range from altruism to practical self-interest and include the following:

• To seek to improve the quality of life in a specific geographic region;

• To ensure a steady supply of future employees from within the community;

• To maintain a favorable corporate perception in the eyes of both employees and customers;

• To qualify for tax advantages by contributing to organizations that are registered with the IRS;

• To enhance a corporate image and influence the opinions of legislators.

Those who assess these trends predict that corporate contributions, which have maintained a level of 1.7–1.9 percent of pre-tax income over the last ten years, will continue at this rate.

Recommended Resource

The Foundation Directory
The Foundation Center, $175
79 Fifth Ave.
New York, NY 10003
(212) 620-4230

Supporters of the Arts & Charities

WHAT TYPES OF CHARITIES have been the recipients of corporate contributions? Research indicates that education has been the main focus of corporate charity. Thirty-five percent of corporate giving has been directed to public education through programs directed at elementary through post-secondary education programs, with a major focus given to the pre-college level. Many of these contributions are in the form of human resources such as business/education partnerships. These projects provide personal involvement through programs designed to expand the horizons of the nation's youth in preparation for their participation in the work force.

Health and human services have received 26 percent of the corporate dollar while culture and the arts have accounted for 11 percent. Civic and community activities have received 14 percent of the contributions, with a major focus being on the environment.

Contact Options

Council on Foundations
1828 L St., NW, Suite 300
Washington, DC 20036
(202) 466-6512
Provides information on starting a philanthropic program.

The Foundation Center
79 Fifth Ave.
New York, NY 10003
(212) 620-4230
Provides information on foundations and corporate-giving programs.

Corporate Philanthropy: Where Are the Dollars Going?

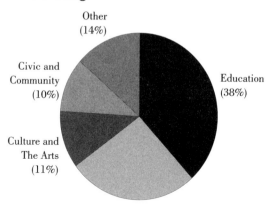

Other (14%)

Civic and Community (10%)

Culture and The Arts (11%)

Education (38%)

Health and Human Services (27%)

Source: The Conference Board, Corporate Contributions, 1993

The United Way and Alternatives

THE UNITED WAY'S ANNUAL fund-raising totals more than $3 billion. With 2,100 autonomous local agencies and a host of more than 44,000 public service groups supported, the United Way continues to be a significant element in corporate philanthropy.

Less than 16 percent of the money raised by the United Way goes to cover overhead. Because of the large number of volunteers—many of them on loan from corporations—the United Way is able to keep costs low.

In an increasingly aware labor force, employees have expressed concern that the corporate-giving program selected for their company did not represent their charitable interests. As a result, alternative funds have been established. These are umbrella organizations that represent multiple charities with the same focus. Such programs offer an alternative for the donor who prefers to contribute to a specific type of cause not encompassed in another fund.

Contact Options

The United Way of America
(703) 836-7100
For the local agency in your area, check the white pages of your phone book.

Earth Share
(800) 875-3863
Represents 43 environmental organizations including the American Farmland Trust, the National Audubon Society, the Rainforest Alliance, the Sierra Club Foundation, and the Wilderness Society.

Independent Charities of America
(800) 477-0733
Represents 407 organizations including Disabled American Veterans Charitable Service Trust, Toys for Tots, and Ronald McDonald House.

International Service Agencies
(800) 638-8079
Represents 55 groups including CARE, the U.S. Committee of UNICEF, Save the Children, Project Hope, Catholic Relief Services, and Oxfam.

America's Charities
(800) 458-9505
Represents 82 organizations including the Make-a-Wish Foundation, the Children's Defense Fund, Farm Aid, Covenant House, the NAACP Legal Defense and Education Fund, and Phyllis Schlafly's Eagle Forum.

National Voluntary Health Agencies
(202) 467-5913
Represents the Alzheimer's Association, the American Cancer Society, the Muscular Dystrophy Association, and the National Kidney and Myasthenia Gravis foundations.

United Negro College Fund
(703) 205-3400
Represents 41 primarily African-American colleges and universities.

National Coalition of United Arts Funds
(212) 223-2787, ext. 231
Represents 60 funds which support symphonies, the ballet, zoos, museums, the theater, and historical societies.

Selecting an Alternative Fund

The National Committee for Responsive Philanthropy (NCRP) was organized in 1976 to make more information about philanthropic funds available to the public. As a watchdog group, the NCRP pressed for disclosure of foundation funds available and sought to create alternatives to the corporate charity fund-raising efforts of the United Way. As a result of the organization's efforts, alternative funds were established to organize charities not covered under the United Way. Employees are frequently offered a choice of target funds for their contributions, both through payroll deductions and from direct fund-raisers.

Apple Computer was one of the first Fortune 500 companies to offer employees the opportunity to contribute through their company to alternatives to the United Way. Other companies have followed suit as increasing awareness of employee preferences has occurred.

In order to find alternative funds in a particular area, interested individuals should contact the NCRP, which assists in establishing such funds and provides a booklet describing each of the alternative funds.

Contact Options

National Committee for Responsive Philanthropy
2001 S St., NW, Suite 620
Washington, DC 20009
(202) 387-9177

National Alliance for Choice in Giving
2001 O St., NW
Washington, DC 20036
(202) 296-8470

The Top Charities

Top 20 Charities by Income

Rank	Organization	Location	Year Founded	Income ($ mil.)
1	Catholic Charities U.S.A.	Alexandria, VA	1910	1,934
2	American Red Cross	Washington, DC	1881	1,796
3	YMCA of the U.S.A.	Chicago, IL	1851	1,763
4	Salvation Army	Alexandria, VA	1865	1,297
5	Goodwill Industries International	Bethesda, MD	1902	849
6	Shriners Hospital for Crippled Children	Tampa, FL	1922	601
7	Boy Scouts of America	Irving, TX	1910	504
8	Association for Retarded Citizens	Arlington, TX	1950	478
9	United Cerebral Palsy Associations	Washington, DC	1948	462
10	Girl Scouts of the U.S.A.	New York, NY	1912	457
11	CARE	Atlanta, GA	1945	451
12	Planned Parenthood Federation	New York, NY	1916	446
13	Second Harvest	Chicago, IL	1979	439
14	United Jewish Appeal	New York, NY	1938	408
15	YWCA of the U.S.A.	New York, NY	1906	408
16	American Cancer Society	Atlanta, GA	1913	388
17	National Easter Seal Society	Chicago, IL	1919	352
18	Metropolitan Museum of Art	New York, NY	1870	339
19	Boys & Girls Clubs of America	Atlanta, GA	1906	302
20	Catholic Relief Services	Baltimore, MD	1943	296

Source: The NonProfit Times, Nov. 1994

Top Ten Charities Ranked by Contributions

Total income for these charities may come from public support, government support, investment, or member dues. The *Chronicle of Philanthropy* lists the top ten charities in 1994 based on contributions alone:

Rank	Organization	Contributions ($ mil.)
1	Salvation Army	682.9
2	American Red Cross	535.7
3	Second Harvest	430.6
4	United Jewish Appeal	408.2
5	YMCA of the U.S.A.	361.2
6	American Cancer Society	359.1
7	Catholic Charities U.S.A.	344.1
8	American Heart Association	239.9
9	YWCA of the U.S.A.	239.6
10	Public Broadcasting Service	229.9

Source: Chronicle of Philanthropy, Nov. 1, 1994. Reprinted with permission

The Top Charities (cont'd)

Some Leaders by Category

Category	Name	Donations ($ mil.)
Human Services	Salvation Army	682.9
Health Charities	American Cancer Society	359.1
Public Broadcasting	Public Broadcasting Service	229.9
Colleges and Universities	Harvard University	221.8
Youth	Boys & Girls Clubs of America	220.9
International Relief and Development	World Vision	209.0
Museums	Metropolitan Museum of Art	185.6
Environment	Nature Conservancy	143.6
United Way	United Way/Crusade of Mercy (Chicago)	86.0
Community Foundations	Hawaii Community Foundation	63.6
Performing Arts	Metropolitan Opera Association	48.3

Source: Chronicle of Philanthropy, Nov. 1, 1994. Reprinted with permission

Recommended Resources

NonProfit Times, $59/year
190 Tamarack Circle
Skillman, NJ 08558
(609) 921-1251

Chronicle of Philanthropy, $67.50/year
1255 23rd St., NW
Washington, DC 20037
(202) 466-1200

The Top Reference Sources

National Directory of Corporate Giving
The Foundation Center, $195
(212) 620-4230

This directory profiles 1,791 companies making contributions to non-profit organizations. It is intended for use by grant seekers in locating potential support, grant makers in learning more about other grant seekers, scholars researching the field, journalists reporting on contributions activities of the corporate world, and everyone generally interested in philanthropy.

It lists company, address, contacts, financial data, types of philanthropic support, geographic limitations, and application information.

Foundations and Grants

THERE ARE FOUR MAJOR types of foundations in operation throughout the country today.

Independent Foundations

These foundations are frequently funded through the gift of an individual or a family. The foundations provide grants to individuals or institutions that meet the specific criteria for proposed application of philanthropic funds. The ten largest independent foundations and the total grant amounts are:

Foundation	Total Grants ($)
Ford Foundation	263,620,911
W. K. Kellogg Foundation	173,158,573
Pew Charitable Trusts	143,537,605
J. D. and C. T. MacArthur Foundation	137,000,000
Lilly Endowment	118,907,952
Robert Wood Johnson Foundation	103,124,020
Andrew W. Mellon Foundation	95,865,156
Rockefeller Foundation	93,070,397
DeWitt Wallace-Reader's Digest Fund	72,324,761
Kresge Foundation	67,678,493

Source: Foundation Giving, The Foundation Center, 1994

Company-Sponsored Foundations

Company-sponsored foundations are funded by endowments and annual contributions of a profit-making corporation. These foundations are generally independent of the corporation. However, the grants awarded by the groups frequently reflect the interests of the corporation and are often made in the community in which the corporation is located.

The largest company-sponsored foundations, based on amount of gifts received, include:

Foundation	Gifts Received ($)
AT&T Foundation	50,000,000
Amoco Foundation	27,047,546
US West Foundation	24,000,000
GTE Foundation	19,558,767
Levi Strauss Foundation	15,500,000
Johnson & Johnson Family of Companies	14,888,250
Mobil Foundation	14,800,000
General Mills Foundation	14,700,000
General Electric Foundation	14,696,262
Wal-Mart Foundation	14,500,000

Source: Foundation Giving, The Foundation Center, 1994

Community Foundations

Community foundations usually appeal to the general public for contributions that are used annually in support of ongoing local services. Their funds come from many sources rather than a single donor, and they are usually classified as public charities under tax law.

The top ten community foundations or public charities, based on total grants and total assets, are as follows:

Community Foundation	Total Grants ($ thou.)	Total Assets ($ thou.)
New York Community Trust	100,843	1,060,055
Chicago Community Trust	41,028	369,839
Cleveland Foundation	32,761	710,277
Communities Foundation of Texas	26,201	219,635
Marin Community Foundation	25,627	590,055
San Francisco Foundation	25,580	286,508
Boston Foundation	18,510	276,609
Columbus Foundation	15,202	200,101
Greater Kansas City Community Foundation	13,699	59,107
Hartford Foundation for Public Giving	11,832	228,933

Source: Foundation Giving, The Foundation Center, 1994

Operating Foundations

Operating foundations are organizations that use their resources to counduct research or provide a direct service. Funding usually comes from an endowment from a specific source; however, the foundation is eligible for tax-deductible contributions from the public. These groups provide few grants since the contributions are earmarked for specific purposes.

Recommended Resource

Foundation Giving
The Foundation Center, $24.95
(212) 620-4230
Provides a comprehensive overview of the latest trends in foundation grantmaking.

Environmental Awareness

THE AVERAGE WORKER IN AN American office is responsible for discarding 180 pounds of high-grade recyclable paper every year.

While federal laws are designed to protect the environment against unscrupulous industrial pollution, the corporate citizen can take steps to promote environmental awareness both within and outside of the company through the education of its employees.

Six Simple Projects for Office Conservation

The following are some simple suggestions from conservation specialists regarding ways in which the corporate citizen can protect the environment:

- Ask employees to bring a coffee cup to work instead of using foam or other disposable cups.

- Set up glass and aluminum recycling programs with containers in lunchrooms or next to beverage machines.

- Set up a paper recycling program with containers at each employee's desk or in central locations. The recyclable papers can be collected and placed in outdoor containers by the custodial staff.

- Investigate a two-sided copy machine to reduce the amount of paper used in copying reports.

- Investigate conducting an energy audit to determine what minor changes can result in significant savings in energy and dollars.

- Investigate water-saving measures such as installing faucet aerators and toilet water displacement devices.

Recommended Resources

50 Simple Things You Can Do to Save the Earth
by The Earthworks Group
Earthworks Press, $4.95
(510) 841-5866

Design for a Livable Planet
by Jon Naar
HarperCollins Publishing, $15
(212) 207-7000

30 Ways to Use Less Paper
3M, Commerical Office Supply Division, free
(800) 395-1223

Directing Corporate Dollars

National organizations will make presentations to companies to promote environmental programs that seek corporate funding. They will readily explain organized programs that can be set up to direct corporate dollars to preserving and enhancing the environment on a national and global level.

Contact Options

Earth Share
(800) 875-3863
Umbrella Organization for 43 Environmental Groups

Independent regional organizations will provide information sessions to corporate employees regarding opportunities to extend their support throughout and beyond the workplace environment.

Environmental Action Coalition
625 Broadway, 2nd Floor
New York, NY 10012
(212) 677-1601

Environmental Federations

Individuals interested in directing their contributions and efforts to local environmental needs may contact one of several federations that operate in a variety of states. These environmental federations raise funds for regional conservation organizations and will frequently make presentations to corporate gatherings regarding such programs. The following is a list of environmental federations by state.

Name	Phone
Environmental Fund for Arizona	(602) 254-9330
Earth Share of California	(415) 882-9330
Nature Conservancy of Florida	(407) 628-5887
Environmental Fund for Georgia	(404) 873-3173
Environmental Fund for Illinois	(708) 615-8905
Environmental Fund for Indiana	(317) 349-1062
Environmental Fund for Michigan	(517) 332-3800
Minnesota Environmental Fund	(612) 379-3850
Missouri Coal. for the Environment	(314) 727-0600
Environmental Fed. of New England	(617) 542-3363
Environmental Fed. of New York	(518) 436-0421
Environmental Fed. of North Carolina	(919) 687-4840
Environmental Federation of Oregon	(503) 223-9015
Rails and Trails Conservancy (PA)	(717) 238-1717
Environmental Fund for Texas	(512) 472-5518
Nature Conservancy of Virginia	(804) 295-6106
Earth Share of Washington	(206) 622-9840

Corporate Responsibility

CORPORATE RESPONSIBILITY CAN BE expressed in a full range of business responses to the needs of society. It can be in the form of direct giving of funds to a targeted non-profit organization. In addition, a corporation may elect to become directly involved in a project such as the Adopt-a-School Program in which corporations provide services rather than direct dollars to the target school or school district. The participating company supplies mentors, tutors, facilities, equipment, and technology in order to have a positive impact on the educational progress, and consequently exercises considerable control over its own benevolence.

Still other corporations establish company foundations that direct contributions to worthwhile programs or projects. This option offers companies more control over their contribution dollars and permits direction of these funds to specific areas or needs. The largest company-based foundations are listed in "Foundations and Grants" on page 90. Advice on establishing a corporate foundation may be obtained from organizations that monitor and counsel foundations.

Contact Option

The Foundation Center
79 Fifth Ave., 8th Floor
New York, NY 10003
(212) 620-4230

Socially Conscious Investments

A HEIGHTENED SENSE OF CIVIC responsibility is being expressed in the types of investments selected by individual and corporate investors. Frequently investors will seek not only a return on their expenditure, but also a vehicle to express their concerns regarding corporate and public policies.

There are several investment funds that deal with socially and environmentally responsible companies.

Contact Options

Affirmative Investments Group
33 Union St., 2nd Floor
Boston, MA 02108
(617) 367-4300

Calvert Social Investment Fund
c/o Calvert Group
4550 Montgomery Ave., Suite 1000
Bethesda, MD 20814
(800) 368-2750 or (301) 951-4800

Dreyfus Third Century Fund
200 Park Ave.
New York, NY 10166
(212) 922-6000

Parnassus Fund
244 California St.
San Francisco, CA 94111
(800) 999-3505 or (415) 362-3505

Social Investment Forum
430 First Ave., N
Minneapolis, MN 55401
(612) 333-8338

Socially Responsible Banking Fund
Vermont National Bank
P.O. Box 804
Brattleboro, VT 05301
(800) 544-7108

Working Assets Common Holdings
111 Pine St.
San Francisco, CA 94111
(800) 533-3863 or (415) 989-3200

Recommended Resource

Design for a Livable Planet
by Jon Naar
HarperCollins Publishing, $15
(212) 207-7000

Corporate Conscience

THE COUNCIL ON ECONOMIC Priorities (CEP) is an independent public interest organization dedicated to researching and reporting on, among other issues, corporate social responsibility. Each year the CEP reviews hundreds of U.S. corporations and selects winners that meet standard criteria for excellence, improvement, and innovation in the areas of charitable contributions, environmental concern, responsiveness to employees, equal opportunity, and community outreach.

Contact Option

Council on Economic Priorities
30 Irving Pl.
New York, NY 10003
(212) 420-1133

CEP Corporate Conscience Awards

1991 Category	1991 Winner
Charitable Contrib., Large Co.	H. B. Fuller
Charitable Contrib., Small Co.	Foldcraft
Community Involvement	Time Warner
Responsiveness to Employees	Kellogg
Equal Opportunity	Hallmark Cards
Environment, Large Co.	Herman Miller
Environment, Small Co.	Smith & Hawken

1992 Category	1992 Winner
Charitable Contrib., Large Co.	US West
Charitable Contrib., Small Co.	Tom's of Maine
Community Outreach	Supermarkets General Holdings
	Prudential Insurance
Responsiveness to Employees	Donnelley
Equal Opportunity	General Mills
Environment, Large Co.	Church & Dwight
Environment, Small Co.	Conservatree Paper
Special Recognition for Innovative Benefit	Lotus Development

1993 Category	1993 Winner
Community Involvement	Clorox
Equal Opportunity	Pitney Bowes
Responsiveness to Employees	Merck
	Quad/Graphics
Environment, Large Co.	Digital Equipment
Environment, Small Co.	Aveda
Special Recognition for Defense Conversion	Galileo Electro-Optics
	Kaman Aircraft
	Kavlico
	Science Applications International

1994 Category	1994 Winner
Community Involvement, Large Co.	Brooklyn Union Gas
Responsiveness to Employees	SAS Institute
Environment, Large Co.	S. C. Johnson & Son
Environment, Small Co.	Stonyfield Farm
International Commitment	Levi Strauss

1995 Category	1995 Winner
Community Involvement	Colgate-Palmolive
	Timberland
Equal Employment Opportunity	Coca-Cola
Employer Responsiveness	Polaroid
Environmental Stewardship	New England Electric System
Global Ethics	Merck

Source: Council on Economic Priorities

Labor Force

Civilian Labor Force (millions) by Race, Hispanic Origin, Sex, and Age

Race, Sex, Age	1970	1980	1985	1990	1992	1993	2000 (est.)	2005 (est.)
TOTAL	82.8	106.9	115.5	124.8	127.0	128.0	141.8	150.5
White	73.6	93.6	99.9	107.2	108.5	109.4	118.8	124.8
Male	46.0	54.5	56.5	59.3	59.8	60.2	63.8	66.0
Female	27.5	39.1	43.5	47.9	48.7	49.2	55.1	58.8
Black	9.2	10.9	12.4	13.5	13.9	13.9	16.0	17.4
Male	5.2	5.6	6.2	6.7	6.9	6.9	7.8	8.3
Female	4.0	5.3	6.1	6.8	7.0	7.0	8.2	9.0
Hispanic	NA	6.1	7.7	9.6	10.1	10.4	14.3	16.6
Male	NA	3.8	4.7	5.8	6.1	6.3	8.7	9.6
Female	NA	2.3	3.0	3.8	4.0	4.1	5.8	7.0
Male	51.2	61.5	64.4	68.2	69.2	69.6	75.3	78.7
16 to 19 years	4.0	5.0	4.1	3.9	3.5	3.6	4.4	4.6
20 to 24 years	5.7	8.6	8.3	7.3	7.2	7.2	7.2	8.1
25 to 34 years	11.3	17.0	18.8	19.8	19.4	19.1	17.2	16.5
35 to 44 years	10.5	11.8	14.5	17.3	18.2	18.5	20.7	19.6
45 to 54 years	10.4	9.9	9.9	11.2	12.2	12.6	15.8	18.1
55 to 64 years	7.1	7.2	7.1	6.8	6.7	6.6	7.7	9.6
65 years and over	2.2	1.9	1.8	2.0	2.1	2.0	2.1	2.2
Female	31.5	45.5	51.1	56.6	57.8	58.4	66.6	71.8
16 to 19 years	3.2	4.4	3.8	3.5	3.2	3.3	4.0	4.2
20 to 24 years	4.9	7.3	7.4	6.6	6.5	6.4	6.4	7.2
25 to 34 years	5.7	12.3	14.7	16.0	15.7	15.4	14.9	14.8
35 to 44 years	6.0	8.6	11.6	14.6	15.4	15.7	18.8	18.6
45 to 54 years	6.5	7.0	7.5	9.3	10.3	10.9	14.7	17.4
55 to 64 years	4.2	4.7	4.9	5.1	5.2	5.2	6.2	7.8
65 years and over	1.1	1.2	1.2	1.5	1.6	1.5	1.6	1.7

Source: 1994 Statistical Abstract, Table No. 615

E-MAIL — **Labor Force.** Send e-mail to labor@almanac.yoyo.com. See p. xi for instructions.

Tables of civilian labor force by educational attainment, self-employed workers, and employed workers by selected characteristics.

The Top Reference Sources

Commerce Business Daily
U.S. Government Printing Office, $324 /year
(202) 783-3238

This extremely useful publication contains a daily list of U.S. government procurement invitations, contract awards, subcontracting leads, surplus property, and foreign business opportunities. It is essential reading for anyone who wants to obtain business from the government.

Labor Force (cont'd)

Labor Force Participation Rates (%) by Race, Sex, and Age

Race, Sex, Age	1970	1980	1985	1990	1992	1993	2000 (est.)	2005 (est.)
TOTAL	60.4	63.8	64.8	66.4	66.3	66.2	68.2	68.8
White	60.2	64.1	65.0	66.8	66.7	66.7	68.7	69.3
Male	80.0	78.2	77.0	76.9	76.4	76.1	76.0	75.3
Female	42.6	51.2	54.1	57.5	57.8	58.0	61.8	63.6
Black	61.8	61.0	62.9	63.3	63.3	62.4	65.5	66.2
Male	76.5	70.3	70.8	70.1	69.7	68.6	70.8	70.5
Female	49.5	53.1	56.5	57.8	58.0	57.4	61.2	62.6
Hispanic	NA	64.0	64.6	67.0	66.5	65.9	68.0	68.4
Male	NA	81.4	80.3	81.2	80.5	80.0	80.2	79.5
Female	NA	47.4	49.3	53.0	52.6	52.0	55.8	57.3
Male	79.7	77.4	76.3	76.1	75.6	75.2	75.3	74.7
16 to 19 years	56.1	60.5	56.8	55.7	53.3	53.1	55.4	55.5
20 to 24 years	83.3	85.9	85.0	84.3	83.3	83.1	84.0	84.4
25 to 34 years	96.4	95.2	94.7	94.2	93.8	93.5	73.1	93.5
35 to 44 years	96.9	95.5	95.0	94.4	93.8	93.5	93.7	93.5
45 to 54 years	94.3	91.2	91.0	90.7	90.8	90.1	90.4	90.2
55 to 64 years	83.0	72.1	67.9	67.7	67.0	66.5	69.1	69.7
65 years and over	26.8	19.0	15.8	16.4	16.1	15.6	15.0	14.7
Female	43.3	51.5	54.5	57.5	57.8	57.9	61.6	63.2
16 to 19 years	44.0	52.9	52.1	51.8	49.2	49.9	52.0	52.4
20 to 24 years	57.7	68.9	71.8	71.6	71.2	71.3	72.5	73.6
25 to 34 years	45.0	65.5	70.9	73.6	74.1	73.6	78.1	80.7
35 to 44 years	51.1	65.5	71.8	76.5	76.8	76.7	83.0	86.2
45 to 54 years	54.4	59.9	64.4	71.2	72.7	73.5	79.7	82.8
55 to 64 years	43.0	41.3	42.0	45.3	46.6	47.3	50.3	52.4
65 years and over	9.7	8.1	7.3	8.7	8.3	8.2	8.5	8.8

Source: 1994 Statistical Abstract, Table No. 615

Labor Force Participation Rates (%) for Wives, Husband Present, by Age of Youngest Child

Presence, Age of Child	Total 1975	Total 1985	Total 1990	Total 1993	White 1975	White 1985	White 1990	White 1993	Black 1975	Black 1985	Black 1990	Black 1993
WIVES, TOTAL	44.4	54.2	58.2	59.4	43.6	53.3	57.6	58.9	54.1	63.8	64.7	64.8
0 under 18	43.8	48.2	51.1	52.4	43.6	47.5	50.8	52.2	47.6	55.2	52.9	53.8
All under 18	44.9	60.8	66.3	67.5	43.6	59.9	65.6	66.9	58.4	71.7	75.6	75.3
Under 6	36.7	53.4	58.9	59.6	34.7	52.1	57.8	58.6	54.9	69.6	73.1	70.9
Under 3	32.7	50.5	55.5	57.3	30.7	49.4	54.9	56.7	50.1	66.2	67.5	65.6
1 yr., under	30.8	49.4	53.9	57.5	29.2	48.6	53.3	56.8	50.0	63.7	64.4	64.8
2 yrs.	37.1	54.0	60.9	58.1	35.1	52.7	60.3	56.5	56.4	69.9	75.4	74.5
3 to 5 yrs.	42.2	58.4	64.1	63.1	40.1	56.6	62.5	61.6	61.2	73.8	80.4	78.1
3 yrs.	41.2	55.1	63.1	61.6	39.0	52.7	62.3	60.2	62.7	72.3	74.5	79.4
4 yrs.	41.2	59.7	65.1	65.7	38.7	58.4	63.2	64.3	64.9	70.6	80.6	79.3
5 yrs.	44.4	62.1	64.5	63.1	43.8	59.9	62.0	61.4	56.3	79.1	86.2	77.5
6 to 13 yrs.	51.8	68.2	73.0	74.7	50.7	67.7	72.6	74.5	65.7	73.3	77.6	80.6
14 to 17 yrs.	53.5	67.0	75.1	75.6	53.4	66.6	74.9	75.6	52.3	74.4	78.8	75.7

Source: 1994 Statistical Abstract, Table No. 627

Labor Force (cont'd)

Unemployed Workers (thousands) by Work Schedules, Sex, and Age

Characteristic	1980	1985	1990	1993
TOTAL	7,637	8,312	6,874	8,734
LOOKING FOR FULL-TIME WORK	6,269	6,793	5,541	7,146
Male	3,703	3,925	3,264	4,277
16 to 19 years old	537	446	328	343
20 to 24 years old	994	857	582	704
25 to 54 years old	1,923	2,329	2,098	2,884
55 years and over	250	292	255	346
Female	2,564	2,868	2,277	2,869
16 to 19 years old	430	331	233	246
20 to 24 years old	636	636	439	476
25 to 54 years old	1,363	1,727	1,491	1,968
55 years and over	135	173	115	179
LOOKING FOR PART-TIME WORK	1,369	1,519	1,332	1,588
Male	563	596	535	655
16 to 19 years old	377	360	301	385
20 to 24 years old	81	87	84	103
25 to 54 years old	54	79	89	102
55 years and over	52	70	61	64
Female	806	923	797	933
16 to 19 years old	326	330	286	322
20 to 24 years old	124	158	116	137
25 to 54 years old	299	359	323	396
55 years and over	57	75	72	78

Source: 1994 Statistical Abstract, Table No. 632

Selected Labor Force Characteristics

Item	Number (thou.)
OCCUPATION	
Executive, administrative, & managerial	15,376
Professional specialty	16,904
Technicians & related support	4,014
Sales	14,245
Administrative support, including clerical	18,555
Private household	912
Protective service	2,152
Service, except professional & household	13,457
Farming, forestry, & fishing	3,326
Precision production, craft, & repair	13,326
Machine oper., assemblers, & inspect.	7,415
Transportation & material moving	5,004
Handlers, equipment cleaners, laborers	4,619

Item	Number (thou.)
INDUSTRY	
Agriculture, forestry, and fisheries	3,074
Mining	669
Construction	7,220
Manufacturing	19,557
Trans., communs., other public utilities	8,481
Wholesale trade	4,606
Retail trade	20,163
Finance, insurance, and real estate	7,962
Business and repair services	6,838
Personal services	4,443
Entertainment and recreation	2,060
Health services, except hospitals	5,521
Public administration	5,756

Source: 1994 Statistical Abstract, Table Nos. 637, 641

Demographics

Civilian Employment Estimates (thousands)

Occupation	1992 Employment	2005 Low Growth Employment	2005 Moderate Growth Employment	2005 High Growth Employment
TOTAL	121,099	139,007	147,482	154,430
LARGEST JOB GROWTH				
Salespersons, retail	3,660	4,137	4,446	4,611
Registered nurses	1,835	2,479	2,601	2,637
Cashiers	2,747	3,201	3,417	3,520
General office clerks	2,688	3,143	3,342	3,489
Truck drivers, light and heavy	2,391	2,836	3,039	3,235
Waiters and waitresses	1,756	2,280	2,394	2,415
Nursing aides, orderlies, and attendants	1,308	1,824	1,903	1,937
Janitors and cleaners	2,862	3,246	3,410	3,519
Food preparation workers	1,223	1,661	1,748	1,775
Systems analysts	455	891	956	1,001
Home health aides	347	794	827	835
Teachers, secondary school	1,263	1,640	1,724	1,789
Child care workers	684	1,100	1,135	1,183
Guards	803	1,138	1,211	1,255
Marketing and sales worker supervisors	2,036	2,303	2,443	2,565
Teacher aides and educational assistants	885	1,209	1,266	1,308
General managers and top executives	2,871	3,050	3,251	3,418
Maintenance repairers, general utility	1,145	1,388	1,464	1,542
Gardeners and groundskeepers, except farm	884	1,152	1,195	1,261
Teachers, elementary	1,456	1,683	1,767	1,830
Food counter, fountain, and related workers	1,564	1,776	1,872	1,895
Receptionists and information clerks	904	1,149	1,210	1,245
Accountants and auditors	939	1,167	1,243	1,301
Clerical supervisors and managers	1,267	1,473	1,568	1,622
Cooks, restaurant	602	837	879	889
Teachers, special education	358	594	625	648
Licensed practical nurses	659	879	920	933
Cooks, short order and fast food	714	921	971	978
Human services workers	189	429	445	451
Computer engineers and scientists	211	409	447	484
Teachers, preschool and kindergarten	434	646	669	682
Food service and lodging managers	532	732	764	787
Hairdressers, hairstylists, and cosmetologists	628	824	846	876
Blue-collar worker supervisors	1,757	1,844	1,974	2,131
College and university faculty	812	976	1,026	1,064
Carpenters	978	1,131	1,176	1,317
Corrections officers	282	452	479	503
Physicians	556	720	751	769
Lawyers	626	781	821	850
Social workers	484	645	676	693
Financial managers	701	828	875	917
Computer programmers	555	673	723	759
Automotive mechanics	739	857	907	960
Personal and home care aides	127	283	293	296
Legal secretaries	280	415	439	447
Stock clerks	1,782	1,801	1,940	2,024

Source: 1994 Statistical Abstract, Table Nos. 638, 639

Demographics (cont'd)

Civilian Labor Force Status by Selected Metropolitan Area

Metropolitan Areas Ranked by Labor Force Size, 1993	Total Employed (thou.)	Total Unemployed (thou.)	Unemployment Rate (%)
U.S. TOTAL	128,040.0	8,743.0	6.8
Los Angeles-Long Beach, CA	4,411.0	427.0	9.7
Chicago, IL	3,951.9	281.6	7.1
New York, NY	3,901.6	367.0	9.4
Washington, DC-MD-VA-WV	2,550.3	115.9	4.5
Philadelphia, PA-NJ	2,452.4	165.7	6.8
Detroit, MI	2,114.8	150.7	7.1
Houston, TX	1,923.4	138.5	7.2
Atlanta, GA	1,773.1	91.8	5.2
Boston, MA-NH	1,745.4	104.0	6.0
Dallas, TX	1,617.4	97.1	6.0
Minneapolis-St. Paul, MI-WI	1,509.9	65.2	4.3
Nassau-Suffolk, NY	1,359.1	86.4	6.4
Orange County, CA	1,315.5	88.3	6.7
St. Louis, MO-IL	1,270.3	82.5	6.5
Riverside-San Bernardino, CA	1,245.2	131.0	10.5
Baltimore, MD	1,215.0	89.2	7.3
San Diego, CA	1,208.8	94.1	7.8
Seattle-Bellevue-Everett, WA	1,194.7	76.1	6.4
Phoenix-Mesa, AZ	1,165.6	60.0	5.1
Pittsburgh, PA	1,153.8	79.0	6.8
Oakland, CA	1,109.9	73.7	6.6
Cleveland-Lorain-Elyria, OH	1,082.1	72.7	6.7
Tampa-St. Petersburg-Clearwater, FL	1,031.9	66.9	6.5
Miami, FL	1,019.8	78.7	7.7
Newark, NJ	994.3	75.9	7.6
Denver, CO	974.3	46.0	4.7
Portland-Vancouver, OR-WA	915.8	55.9	6.1
San Francisco, CA	899.5	54.6	6.1
Kansas City, MO-KS	873.9	46.8	5.4
San Jose, CA	838.8	56.7	6.8
Cincinnati, OH-KY-IN	797.6	44.7	5.6
Fort Worth-Arlington, TX	789.3	50.7	6.4
Indianapolis, IN	757.4	33.3	4.4
Columbus, OH	756.7	37.3	4.9
Milwaukee-Waukesha, WI	755.5	32.9	4.4
Orlando, FL	719.7	44.6	6.2
Fort Lauderdale, FL	693.9	47.0	6.8
Norfolk-Virginia Beach-Newport News, VA-NC	692.0	37.1	5.4
Sacramento, CA	684.6	56.8	8.3
San Antonio, TX	681.6	38.4	5.6
Charlotte-Gastonia-Rock Hill, NC-SC	673.2	31.2	4.6
Bergen-Passaic-NJ	655.0	50.3	7.7
Hartford, CT	627.6	41.7	6.6
Greensboro-Winston-Salem-High Point, NC	599.6	24.4	4.1
Providence-Fall River-Warwick, RI-MA	588.1	49.1	8.4
Salt Lake City-Ogden, UT	587.8	21.3	3.6
New Orleans, LA	585.6	40.0	6.8
Middlesex-Somerset-Hunterdon, NJ	581.1	34.7	6.0
Buffalo-Niagara Falls, NY	577.2	38.1	6.6
Rochester, NY	568.2	27.9	4.9

Source: 1994 Statistical Abstract, Table No. 620

Demographics (cont'd)

Average Hourly and Weekly Earnings in Current Dollars by Private Industry Group

Private Industry Group	1970	1980	1985	1989	1990	1993
AVERAGE HOURLY EARNINGS	3.23	6.66	8.57	9.66	10.02	10.83
Manufacturing	3.35	7.27	9.54	10.48	10.83	11.76
Mining	3.85	9.17	11.98	13.26	13.69	14.60
Construction	5.24	9.94	12.32	13.54	13.78	14.35
Transportation, public utilities	3.85	8.87	11.40	12.60	12.96	13.64
Wholesale trade	3.43	6.95	9.15	10.39	10.79	11.71
Retail trade	2.44	4.88	5.94	6.53	6.76	7.29
Finance, insurance, real estate	3.07	5.79	7.94	9.53	9.97	11.32
Services	2.81	5.85	7.90	9.38	9.83	10.81
AVERAGE WEEKLY EARNINGS	120.00	235.00	299.00	334.00	346.00	374.00
Manufacturing	133.00	289.00	386.00	430.00	442.00	487.00
Mining	164.00	397.00	520.00	570.00	604.00	645.00
Construction	195.00	368.00	464.00	513.00	526.00	551.00
Transportation, public utilities	156.00	351.00	450.00	490.00	504.00	542.00
Wholesale trade	137.00	267.00	351.00	395.00	411.00	447.00
Retail trade	82.00	147.00	175.00	189.00	195.00	210.00
Finance, insurance, real estate	113.00	210.00	289.00	341.00	357.00	404.00
Services	97.00	191.00	257.00	306.00	320.00	351.00

Source: 1994 Statistical Abstract, Table No. 661

The Top Reference Sources

Martindale-Hubbell Law Directory
Reed, $600
(800) 521-8110, Ext. 5001

More than 800,000 lawyers are profiled in this 27-volume set.

In addition to providing valuable information on the background of all lawyers, it provides extensive cross-referencing to make it easier to find specialists in almost any area of the law.

Martindale-Hubbell is updated annually. The hardcover version is available in most libraries.

E-MAIL

Time Spent at Work. Send e-mail to time@almanac.yoyo.com. See p. xi for instructions.

Tables of gross average weekly earnings and hours worked for selected non-manufacturing and manufacturing industries.

Unemployment

Unemployed Persons by Sex and Reason (thousands)

Sex & Reason Unemployed	1984	1985	1986	1987	1988	1989	1990	1992	1993
MALE	4,744	4,521	4,530	4,101	3,655	3,525	3,799	5,380	4,932
Job losers	2,976	2,749	2,725	2,432	2,078	1,975	2,208	3,518	3,091
Job leavers	375	409	520	494	503	495	511	479	490
Re-entrants	867	876	805	761	697	726	782	950	914
New entrants	526	487	480	413	376	328	298	433	437
FEMALE	3,794	3,791	3,707	3,324	3,046	3,003	3,075	4,005	3,801
Job losers	1,445	1,390	1,308	1,134	1,014	1,008	1,114	1,773	1,677
Job leavers	449	468	494	471	480	529	503	496	456
Re-entrants	1,317	1,380	1,355	1,213	1,112	1,117	1,101	1,278	1,230
New entrants	584	552	549	506	440	349	357	457	438

Unemployment Rates by Industry (%)

Industry	1975	1980	1985	1988	1989	1990	1993
ALL UNEMPLOYED	8.5	7.1	7.2	5.5	5.3	5.5	6.8
Agriculture	10.4	11.0	13.2	10.6	9.6	9.7	11.6
Mining	4.1	6.4	9.5	7.9	5.8	4.8	7.3
Construction	18.0	14.1	13.1	10.6	10.0	11.1	14.3
Manufacturing	10.9	8.5	7.7	5.3	5.1	5.8	7.2
Transportation and public utilities	5.6	4.9	5.1	3.9	3.9	3.8	5.1
Wholesale and retail trade	8.7	7.4	7.6	6.2	6.0	6.4	7.8
Finance, insurance, and real estate	4.9	3.4	3.5	3.0	3.1	3.0	4.1
Services	7.1	5.9	6.2	4.9	4.8	5.0	6.1
Government	4.1	4.1	3.9	2.8	2.7	2.6	3.3

Unemployment Rates by Sex

Industry	Male 1980	Male 1993	Female 1980	Female 1993
ALL UNEMPLOYED	6.9	7.1	7.4	6.5
Agriculture	9.7	11.2	15.1	12.8
Mining	6.7	7.6	4.5	5.6
Construction	14.6	14.8	8.9	9.9
Manufacturing	7.4	6.5	10.8	8.4
Transportation and public utilities	5.1	5.4	4.4	4.3
Wholesale and retail trade	6.6	7.3	8.3	8.3
Finance, insurance, and real estate	3.2	3.8	3.5	4.2
Services	6.3	6.6	5.8	5.7
Government	3.9	3.6	4.3	3.0

Source: 1994 Statistical Abstract, Table Nos. 647, 648

Consumer Trends

Average Annual Consumer Expenditures by Household ($)

Item	1984	1985	1988	1989	1992
TOTAL EXPENDITURES	21,975	23,490	25,892	27,810	29,846
Food, total	3,290	3,477	3,748	4,152	4,273
Food at home, total	1,970	2,037	2,136	2,390	2,643
Cereal and bakery products	262	283	312	359	411
Meats, poultry, fish, and eggs	586	579	551	611	687
Dairy products	253	266	274	304	302
Fruits and vegetables	313	322	373	408	428
Other food at home	556	585	625	708	814
Food away from home	1,320	1,441	1,612	1,762	1,631
Alcoholic beverages	275	306	269	284	301
Tobacco products and smoking supplies	228	219	242	261	275
Housing, total	6,674	7,087	8,079	8,609	9,477
Shelter	3,489	3,833	4,493	4,835	5,411
Fuels, utilities, and public services	1,638	1,648	1,747	1,835	1,984
Household operations and furnishings	1,241	1,282	1,477	1,546	433
Housekeeping supplies	307	325	361	394	1,710
Apparel and services	1,319	1,420	1,489	1,582	5,228
Transportation, total	4,304	4,587	5,093	5,187	2,189
Vehicles	1,813	2,043	2,361	2,291	973
Gasoline and motor oil	1,058	1,035	932	985	1,634
Other transportation	1,433	1,509	1,800	1,911	353
Health care	1,049	1,108	1,298	1,407	2,397
Life insurance	300	278	314	346	29,846
Pensions and Social Security	1,598	1,738	1,935	2,125	4,273
Other expenditures	2,936	3,269	3,426	3,857	2,643

Source: 1994 Statistical Abstract, Table No. 703

The Top Reference Sources

Fortune
Time, $57/year
(800) 621-8000

Fortune is a biweekly magazine for decision-makers in the business world. Each issue contains a variety of articles, from ways to avoid employee burnout to the state of the global marketplace.

Fortune is also the definitive source of a number of famous rankings, including the Fortune 500 largest publicly-owned companies in the United States as well as the Global 500 largest companies worldwide, the most-admired corporations, the largest transportation companies, and the oldest companies.

Consumer Trends (cont'd)

Average Annual Consumer Expenditures for Metropolitan Statistical Areas, 1992 ($)

Metropolitan Statistical Area	Total Expenditures	Food	Total Housing	Shelter	Apparel & Services	Total Transportation
Anchorage, AK	42,331	5,213	13,800	8,675	2,135	6,684
Atlanta, GA	36,774	4,236	12,409	6,913	2,398	6,167
Baltimore, MD	32,746	4,655	11,362	7,193	1,969	5,050
Boston-Lawrence-Salem, MA-NH	31,824	4,371	11,296	7,356	1,957	5,147
Buffalo-Niagara Falls, NY	24,709	4,537	8,062	4,766	1,905	4,373
Chicago-Gary-Lake County, IL-IN-WI	34,105	4,867	11,160	6,649	2,143	5,751
Cincinnati-Hamilton, OH-KY-IN	29,769	4,662	9,137	5,081	1,967	5,307
Cleveland-Akron-Lorain, OH	27,751	4,353	8,364	4,234	1,972	4,754
Dallas Fort Worth, TX	35,190	4,869	10,825	6,094	2,238	6,962
Detroit-Ann Arbor, MI	30,442	4,331	10,156	5,859	2,092	5,838
Honolulu, HI	37,273	6,333	11,863	8,080	1,448	5,628
Houston-Galveston-Brazoria, TX	32,823	4,887	9,377	4,911	2,312	6,455
Kansas City, MO-Kansas City, KS	31,218	4,482	9,013	4,958	2,169	5,816
Los Angeles-Long Beach, CA	35,034	4,808	12,932	8,403	1,873	5,453
Miami-Fort Lauderdale, FL	30,002	4,941	9,862	6,107	1,962	5,047
Milwaukee, WI	30,296	4,268	9,535	5,734	1,725	5,702
Minneapolis-St. Paul, MN-WI	38,887	4,837	12,047	6,967	1,836	6,153
New York-Northern New Jersey-Long Island, NY-NJ-CT	35,807	5,011	13,193	8,724	2,283	4,672
Philadelphia-Wilmington-Trenton, PA-NJ-DE-MD	31,985	4,596	10,705	6,285	2,183	4,252
Pittsburgh-Beaver Valley, PA	28,177	4,374	8,412	4,392	2,113	4,808
Portland-Vancouver, OR-WA	30,649	4,497	9,368	5,705	1,662	5,667
San Diego, CA	35,670	4,587	12,518	8,536	1,623	7,164
San Francisco-Oakland-San Jose, CA	39,584	5,212	14,019	9,402	1,731	6,680
Seattle-Tacoma, WA	35,785	4,490	11,911	7,745	1,641	6,328
St. Louis-East St. Louis-Alton, MO-IL	28,341	3,993	8,347	4,403	2,249	5,086
Washington, DC-MD-VA	39,745	4,713	13,609	8,682	2,016	5,868

Source: 1994 Statistical Abstract, Table No. 705

America Online's Macintosh Business Forum features information, advice, conferences, and shareware for all Macintosh users. KEYWORD MBS.

Per Capita Personal Income

Average Annual Pay by State

State	1990 Avg. Annual Pay ($)	1991 Avg. Annual Pay ($)	1992 Avg. Annual Pay ($)	% Change 1990-91	% Change 1991-92
U.S. TOTAL	23,602	24,578	25,903	4.1	5.4
AK	29,946	30,830	31,825	2.9	3.2
AL	20,468	21,287	22,340	4.0	4.9
AR	18,204	19,008	20,108	4.4	5.8
AZ	21,443	22,207	23,161	3.6	4.3
CA	26,180	27,513	28,934	5.0	5.2
CO	22,908	23,981	25,040	4.7	4.4
CT	28,995	30,689	32,587	5.8	6.2
DC	33,717	35,570	37,971	5.5	6.7
DE	24,423	25,647	26,596	5.0	3.7
FL	21,032	21,992	23,144	4.6	5.2
GA	22,114	23,165	24,373	4.7	5.2
HI	23,167	24,104	25,613	4.0	6.3
IA	19,224	19,810	20,937	3.0	5.7
ID	18,991	19,688	20,649	3.7	4.9
IL	25,312	26,317	27,910	3.9	6.1
IN	21,699	22,522	23,570	3.8	4.7
KS	20,238	21,002	21,982	3.8	4.7
KY	19,947	20,730	21,858	3.9	5.4
LA	20,646	21,503	22,340	4.1	3.9
MA	26,689	28,041	29,664	5.0	5.8
MD	24,730	25,962	27,145	5.0	4.6
ME	20,154	20,870	21,808	3.6	4.5
MI	25,376	26,125	27,463	3.0	5.1
MN	23,126	23,962	25,315	3.6	5.6
MO	21,716	22,574	23,550	3.9	4.3
MS	17,718	18,411	19,237	3.9	4.5
MT	17,895	18,648	19,378	4.2	3.9
NC	20,220	21,095	22,248	4.3	5.5
ND	17,626	18,132	18,945	2.9	4.5
NE	18,577	19,372	20,355	4.3	5.1
NH	22,609	23,600	24,925	4.4	5.6
NJ	28,449	29,991	32,125	5.4	7.1
NM	19,347	20,272	21,051	4.8	3.8
NV	22,358	23,083	24,743	3.2	7.2
NY	28,873	30,011	32,399	3.9	8.0
OH	22,843	23,602	24,846	3.3	5.3
OK	20,288	20,968	21,699	3.3	3.5
OR	21,332	22,338	23,514	4.8	5.3
PA	23,457	24,393	25,785	4.0	5.7
RI	22,388	23,082	24,315	3.1	5.3
SC	19,669	20,439	21,423	3.9	4.8
SD	16,430	17,143	18,016	4.3	5.1
TN	20,611	21,541	22,807	4.5	5.9
TX	22,700	23,760	25,080	4.7	5.6
UT	20,074	20,874	21,976	4.0	5.3
VA	22,750	23,805	24,937	4.6	4.8
VT	20,532	21,355	22,347	4.0	4.6
WA	22,646	23,942	25,553	5.7	6.7
WI	21,101	21,838	23,022	3.5	5.4
WV	20,715	21,356	22,169	3.1	3.8
WY	20,049	20,591	21,215	2.7	3.0

Source: 1994 Statistical Abstract, Table No. 663

Taxes

Real Median Family Income After Taxes, 1981 to 1994 ($)

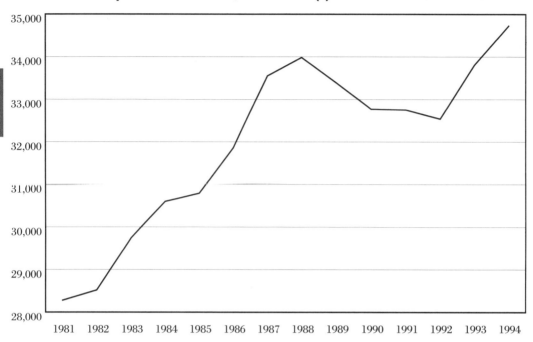

Typical American Family Budget, 1994

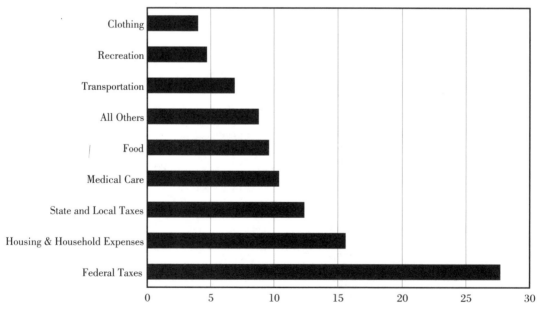

Source: Tax Foundation, Special Report, Nov., 1994, No. 43

State Taxes

Major State Taxes and Rates as of January, 1994

State	Corporate (%)	Individual (%)	General Sales and Use Tax (%)	Gasoline Tax (cents per gallon)	Cigarette Tax (cents per pack of 20)
Alabama	5.0	2 to 5	4	16	16.5
Alaska	1 to 9.4	none	none	8	29
Arizona	9.3	3.8 to 7	5	18	18
Arkansas	1 to 6.5	1 to 7	4.5	18.5	31.5
California	9.3	1 to 11	6	17	37
Colorado	5.0	5	3	22	20
Connecticut	11.5	4.5	6	29	47
Delaware	8.7	3.2 to 7.7	none	22	24
DC	10.0	6 to 9.5	6	20	65
Florida	5.5	none	6	12.1 to 16.6	33.9
Georgia	6.0	1 to 6	5 to 6	7.5	12
Hawaii	4.4 to 6.4	2 to 10	4	16	60
Idaho	8.0	2 to 8.2	5	22	18
Illinois	4.8	3	6.25	19	44
Indiana	3.4	3.4	5	15	15.5
Iowa	6 to 12	.4 to 9.98	5	20	36
Kansas	4.0	4.4 to 7.75	4.9	18	24
Kentucky	4 to 8.25	2 to 6	6	15	3
Louisiana	4 to 8	2 to 6	4	20	20
Maine	3.5 to 8.93	2 to 8.5	6	19	37
Maryland	7.0	2 to 6	5	23.5	36
Massachusetts	9.5	5.95	5	21	51
Michigan	0.0 to 2.35	4.6	4	15	25
Minnesota	9.8	6 to 8.5	6.5	20	48
Mississippi	3 to 5	3 to 5	7	18	18
Missouri	6.25	1.5 to 6	4.225	13	17
Montana	6.75	2 to 11	none	24	18
Nebraska	5.58 to 7.81	2.62 to 6.99	5	26	37
Nevada	none	none	6.5 to 7	23	35
New Hampshire	0.0 to 7.5	5	none	18	25
New Jersey	9.0	2 to 7	6	10.5	40
New Mexico	4.8 to 7.6	1.8 to 8.5	5	22	21
New York	9.0	4 to 7.875	4	8	56
North Carolina	7.75	6 to 7.75	4	22	5
North Dakota	3 to 10.5	14.70*	5	18	44
Ohio	5.1 to 8.9	.743 to 7.5	5	22	24
Oklahoma	6.0	.5 to 7	4.5	17	23
Oregon	6.6	5 to 9	none	24	38
Pennsylvania	12.25	2.95	6	12	31
Rhode Island	9.0	27.5*	7	28	44
South Carolina	5.0	2.5 to 7	5	16	7
South Dakota	none	none	4	18	23
Tennessee	6.0	6	6	22.4	13
Texas	none	none	6.25	20	41
Utah	5.0	2.55 to 7.2	6	19.5	26.5
Vermont	5.5 to 8.25	25*	5	15	20
Virginia	6.0	2 to 5.75	3.5	17.5	2.5
Washington	none	none	6.5	23	54
West Virginia	9.08	3 to 6.5	6	15.5	17
Wisconsin	7.9	4.9 to 6.93	5	23.2	38
Wyoming	none	none	4	9	12

*of federal income tax liability

Source: Tax Foundation, Special Report, Jan. 1994

State Taxes (cont'd)

Per Capita Federal Tax Burden by State, 1993

State	Per Capita Burden ($)	Per Capita Federal Spending	Per Capita State Rank
U.S. TOTAL	4,360	NA	NA
Alabama	3,348	14	41
Alaska	5,502	1	3
Arizona	3,488	31	37
Arkansas	3,189	34	46
California	4,698	21	11
Colorado	4,272	13	19
Connecticut	6,647	15	1
Delaware	5,463	42	4
DC	5,826	NA	3
Florida	4,245	18	20
Georgia	3,795	33	32
Hawaii	4,880	5	9
Idaho	3,249	27	45
Illinois	5,018	44	8
Indiana	3,868	50	30
Iowa	3,868	36	31
Kansas	4,198	26	21
Kentucky	3,316	35	43
Louisiana	3,325	30	42
Maine	3,593	8	35
Maryland	5,120	2	7
Massachusetts	5,316	6	5
Michigan	4,388	46	18
Minnesota	4,458	48	16
Mississippi	2,703	9	50
Missouri	3,984	11	27
Montana	3,413	12	40
Nebraska	4,016	32	26
Nevada	4,519	37	13
New Hampshire	4,757	43	10
New Jersey	6,302	29	2
New Mexico	3,153	3	47
New York	5,290	20	6
North Carolina	3,618	47	34
North Dakota	3,516	7	36
Ohio	4,138	39	22
Oklahoma	3,462	25	38
Oregon	4,036	40	25
Pennsylvania	4,479	19	14
Rhode Island	4,464	10	15
South Carolina	3,288	28	44
South Dakota	3,457	16	39
Tennessee	3,655	23	33
Texas	3,926	38	28
Utah	3,080	41	48
Vermont	3,911	45	29
Virginia	4,413	4	17
Washington	4,666	17	12
West Virginia	3,078	24	49
Wisconsin	4,103	49	24
Wyoming	4,112	22	23

Source: Tax Foundation, Special Report, May 1993

Gross National Product

THE GROSS NATIONAL PRODUCT (GNP) is the total dollar value of all final goods and services produced for consumption in society during a particular time period. Its rise or fall thus measures economic activity based on the labor and production output within a country. The figures used to assemble data include the manufacture of tangible goods such as cars, furniture, and bread, and the provision of services used in daily living such as education, health care, and auto repair. Intermediate services used in the production of the final product are not separated since they are reflected in the final price of the goods or service. The GNP does include allowances for depreciation and indirect business taxes such as those on sales and property.

The Gross Domestic Product (GDP) measures output generated through production by labor and property which is physically located within the confines of a country. It excludes such factors as income earned by U.S. citizens working abroad, but does include factors such as the rental value of owner-occupied housing. In December 1991, the Bureau of Economic Analysis began using the GDP rather than the GNP as the primary measure of United States production. This figure facilitates comparisons between the United States and other countries, since it is the standard used in international guidelines for economic accounting.

Money Supply, Yield Curve

PAPER MONEY AND COINS WERE originally used as the only mediums of exchange, but the sophistication of financial needs has expanded the types of financial instruments used today. In order to monitor the money supply, the Federal Reserve System, the nation's central bank and controller of the monetary policy of the country, uses four measures:

• M1 is the base measurement of the money supply and includes currency, coins, demand deposits, traveler's checks from non-bank issuers, and other checkable deposits.

• M2 is equal to M1 plus overnight repurchase agreements issued by commercial banks, overnight Eurodollars, money market mutual funds, money market deposit accounts, savings accounts, time deposits less than $100,000.

• M3 is M2 plus institutionally held money market funds, term repurchase agreements, term Eurodollars, and large timedeposits.

• L, the fourth measure, is equal to M3 plus Treasury bills, commercial paper, bankers, acceptances, and very liquid assets such as savings bonds.

Recommended Resource

Irwin Business & Investment Almanac
Irwin Professional Publishing, $75
(800) 634-3966

The Top Reference Sources

The Vest-Pocket MBA
Prentice Hall, $12.95
(800) 223-1360

This handy reference contains all the formulas, guidelines, ratios, and rules of thumb needed to evaluate and solve dozens of business problems. The book contains scores of tables, graphs, and charts.

Topics include balance sheet analysis, statistics, break even, working capital, budgeting techniques, margin analysis, and more.

E-MAIL **World Gross Domestic Product.** Send e-mail to product@almanac.yoyo.com. See p. xi for instructions.
A table of the gross domestic product for 24 major countries, from the OECD.

Economic Indicators

ECONOMIC INDICATORS ARE FIGURES used by forecasters to predict changes in market economies. There are eleven leading economic indicators used to track developments in areas which together predict changes in the overall level of the economy. These indicators are:

* The length of the average work week of production workers in manufacturing settings;

* The average weekly state unemployment insurance claims;

* New orders for consumer goods and materials based on 1982 dollars;

* Vendor performance or percentage of companies receiving slower deliveries from suppliers;

* Contracts and orders for equipment;

* Index of new private housing units;

* Changes in unfulfilled orders by manufacturers of durable goods;

* Changes in sensitive materials prices;

* Index of S&P 500 common stock prices;

* Money supply;

* Index of consumer expectations.

Producer Price Index

The Producer Price Index (PPI) measures prices at the wholesale level only. The PPI is viewed as a leading indicator of inflation.

Consumer Price Index

The Consumer Price Index (CPI) is also a leading economic indicator. Although changes are reported from month to month, the more meaningful analysis is found in charting the percent change from the same month in the prior year.

Other economic indicators include the index of industrial materials prices, the Dow Jones Commodity Spot Price Index, the Futures Price Index, the Employment Cost Index, and the Hourly Compensation Index or the Unit Labor Cost Index as a measure of the change in cost of the labor factor of production. Long-term interest rates are also used to measure changes in the cost of the capital factor of production.

The Conference Board

Noted for its carefully managed research program, the Conference Board generates the monthly "Consumer Confidence Survey" designated by the Department of Commerce as a leading economic indicator and predictor of recessions and recovery.

Other services offered consist of timely publications, data collection services for marketing executives, demographic information services, periodic consumer surveys, and over 100 annual conferences and seminars.

Recommended Resources

The Conference Board
845 Third Ave.
New York, NY 10022
(212) 759-0900 or (800) 872-6273

Economic Indicators
Council of Economic Advisors, $33/year
Superintendent of Documents
Government Printing Office
Washington, DC 20402
(202) 512-1800
Monthly Publication of National and International Economic Statistics

The Top Reference Sources

The Conference Board
845 Third Ave.
New York, NY 10022
(212) 759-0900 or (800) 872-6273

The Conference Board is a non-partisan, non-advocacy organization which publishes 20 special reports and more than 50 surveys a year. The Con-

ference Board is supported by a membership of more than 2,000 organizations.

The Board offers monthly and quarterly surveys on consumer confidence and other macro-economic topics, as well as special reports that discuss these topics in depth.

The Board also sponsors conferences and seminars of interest to executives and economists.

Consumer Price Index

THE CONSUMER PRICE INDEX (CPI) is a way of tracking the cost of living. It is computed based on prices for the "market basket" of necessities including housing, food and beverages, transportation, apparel, entertainment, medical care, and other goods and services. The CPI is updated monthly based on the Department of Labor surveys.

To track the effects of price increases, the years 1982 to 1984 are set as a basis (equal to 100). A price index of 33, therefore, indicates that the price was one-third that of the average in 1982–1984.

Consumer Price Index for All Urban Consumers

Average Annual Group	1993	1994
ALL ITEMS	144.5	148.2
Food	140.9	144.3
Alcoholic beverages	149.6	151.5
Housing	141.2	144.8
Renters' costs	165.0	169.4
Fuel oil and other household fuel commodities	90.3	88.8
Gas (piped) and electricity (energy services)	118.5	119.2
Household furnishings and operations	119.3	121.0
Apparel and upkeep	133.7	133.4
Men's and boys' apparel	127.5	126.4
Women's and girls' apparel	132.6	130.9
Footwear	125.9	126.0
Transportation	130.4	134.3
Medical care	201.4	211.0
Entertainment	145.8	150.1
Tobacco and smoking products	228.4	220.0
Personal care	141.5	144.6
Personal and educational expenses	210.7	223.2

Source: Bureau of the Census, U.S. Department of Labor

Oldest Companies

The Ten Oldest Companies in the U.S.

Rank	Company	Year Founded
1	J. E. Rhoads & Sons (conveyor belts)	1702
2	Covenant Life Insurance	1717
3	Philadelphia Contributionship (insurance)	1752
4	Dexter (adhesives and coatings)	1767
5	D. Landreth Seed	1784
6	Bank of New York	1784
7	Mutual Assurance	1784
8	Bank of Boston	1784
9	George R. Ruhl & Sons (bakery supplies)	1789
10	Burns & Russell (building materials)	1790

Source: Fortune, July 26, 1993, © Time, Inc. All rights reserved

Inc. 500 Fastest-Growing Companies

Rank	Company	1993 Sales ($ thousands)	1993 Profit Range	No. of Employees 1993	% Sales Growth 1989-93
1	Object Design, Burlington, MA	24,650	D	196	23,376
2	Card Member Publishing, Stamford, CT	25,029	D	148	21,111
3	Rasna, San Jose, CA	16,200	C	134	15,628
4	Furst Group, Shamong, NJ	42,555	B	117	15,545
5	Micro Voice Applications, Minneapolis, MN	25,726	D	62	15,213
6	Access America Tele., Chesterfield, MO	26,154	F	165	14,511
7	Travelpro Luggage, Deerfield Beach, FL	27,553	A	40	13,275
8	Tivoli Systems, Austin, TX	12,771	E	170	12,545
9	Duracom Computer Systems, Irving, TX	15,090	D	24	11,876
10	PC & More, Fremont, CA	12,866	D	35	11,388
11	Mid-Com Communications, Seattle, WA	56,623	D	236	11,385
12	Vektron International, Grand Prairie, TX	11,828	D	35	11,273
13	United Vision Group, Ossining, NY	21,000	F	250	10,725
14	Quik-Pak, Lafayette, IN	25,625	D	50	9,462
15	Oasis Imaging Products, Hudson, NH	11,100	E	51	9,307
16	Payroll Transfers, Tampa, FL	174,665	D	140	8,950
17	America II Electronics, St. Petersburg, FL	75,906	A	360	8,615
18	Diamond Multimedia Systems, Sunnyvale, CA	75,906	C	125	8,499
19	Spectrum Astro, Gilbert, AZ	17,273	D	52	8,048
20	Washing Systems, Cincinnati, OH	8,367	D	30	7,176
21	Tectrix Fitness Equipment, Irvine, CA	19,073	D	43	6,811
22	MA Laboratories, San Jose, CA	248,785	D	120	6,771
23	Premier Ambulatory Systems, Pasadena, CA	18,055	F	200	6,637
24	XcelleNet, Atlanta, GA	14,212	B	138	6,419
25	Shamrock Computer Resources, Moline, IL	8,045	C	126	6,285
26	American Magnetite, St. Louis, MO	10,568	D	215	6,080
27	CME Conference Video, Mt. Laurel, NJ	6,087	C	27	5,868
28	ERM EnviroClean-West, Walnut Creek, CA	6,449	B	32	5,710
29	American Laser Games, Albuquerque, NM	16,621	B	67	5,671
30	Flood Data Services, Austin, TX	7,002	B	121	5,639
31	Clam Associates, Cambridge, MA	5,973	C	88	5,330
32	SkillPath, Mission, KS	36,691	C	130	5,312
33	Chatham Village, Wareham, MA	6,166	F	100	5,125
34	Bluestone, Mt. Laurel, NJ	7,748	D	60	5,065
35	Labor World America, Boca Raton, FL	8,665	D	45	4,938
36	Legal Information Technology, New York, NY	6,018	B	28	4,915
37	Intcomex, Miami, FL	40,792	D	32	4,693
38	Hot Topic, Montclair, CA	9,849	E	75	4,568
39	Levenger, Delray Beach, FL	28,824	C	143	4,170
40	TGV, Santa Cruz, CA	14,720	A	37	4,023
41	Typed Letters, Wichita, KS	4,392	D	53	4,005
42	Pinnacle Group, Athens, AL	4,003	C	25	3,903
43	Mevatec, Huntsville, AL	17,156	D	225	3,844
44	Flagship Converters, Danbury, CT	8,769	D	37	3,780
45	Zeitech, New York, NY	14,511	C	153	3,650
46	Universal Tax Systems, Rome, GA	3,766	F	49	3,629
47	Everyday Learning, Evanston, IL	3,949	B	14	3,625
48	ADNET Telemanagement, La Mirada, CA	8,006	F	22	3,624
49	AGF Direct Gas Sales, Manchester, NH	29,377	D	6	3,509
50	PCs Plus Computer Center, Kettering, OH	3,707	D	18	3,499

Profit Range: A-16% or more; B-11% to 15%; C-6% to 10%; D-1% to 5%; E-break-even; F-loss

Inc. 500 Fastest-Growing Companies (cont'd)

Rank	Company	1993 Sales ($ thousands)	1993 Profit Range	No. of Employees 1993	% Sales Growth 1989-93
51	Quantum Security Service, Norcross, GA	4,351	D	72	3,466
52	SBA, Boca Raton, FL	5,292	D	36	3,405
53	Transworld Services Group, Winter Park, FL	24,305	D	33	3,362
54	Indus Group, San Francisco, CA	27,492	B	250	3,328
55	MicroTac Software, San Diego, CA	4,746	A	20	3,196
56	Micro Design International, Winter Park, FL	28,387	B	97	3,186
57	Maier Group, New York, NY	36,832	D	30	3,183
58	Contract Manufacturer, Madill, OK	12,390	D	190	3,178
59	Encore Productions, Las Vegas, NV	8,431	D	54	3,155
60	Tomkats, Nashville, TN	3,437	E	35	3,082
61	Shoe Doctor, Dover, NH	3,273	E	67	3,017
62	SETA, McLean, VA	10,740	C	150	2,969
63	Advantage Computing, Salt Lake City, UT	3,105	C	12	2,944
64	Diversified Data Products, Ann Arbor, MI	12,200	D	12	2,883
65	Friendship Manor Homes, Madison, WI	7,884	D	625	2,875
66	Resolute Systems, Brookfield, WI	3,383	D	47	2,842
67	Nationwide Remittance Centers, McLean, VA	16,973	D	500	2,831
68	Magellan Systems, San Dimas, CA	29,557	E	144	2,829
69	Select Comfort, Minneapolis, MN	9,274	F	115	2,816
70	AEM, San Diego, CA	3,508	D	12	2,799
71	Digital Systems Research, Arlington, VA	28,978	C	262	2,778
72	XVT Software, Boulder, CO	11,418	F	130	2,769
73	Health-Drive, Newton, MA	4,738	E	90	2,704
74	Office Stop, Butte, MT	6,203	D	66	2,657
75	Legalgard, Philadelphia, PA	4,544	F	53	2,654
76	Spectrum Associates, Woburn, MA	25,716	C	161	2,610
77	Princeton Softech, Princeton, NJ	2,951	B	29	2,583
78	Kellaway Transportation, Braintree, MA	7,668	F	150	2,572
79	Pete's Brewing, Palo Alto, CA	11,800	D	25	2,558
80	PharMingen, San Diego, CA	6,791	B	77	2,542
81	Co-Mack Technology, Carlsbad, CA	7,263	D	59	2,532
82	Geerlings & Wade, Canton, MA	12,608	D	37	2,489
83	Dodson Group, Indianapolis, IN	6,238	D	20	2,478
84	Graphics Express, Boston, MA	5,660	C	98	2,461
85	Alantec, San Jose, CA	13,639	C	70	2,445
86	One Step Ahead, Lake Bluff, IL	23,872	D	125	2,421
87	McCue, Salem, MA	5,260	D	32	2,417
88	WinterBrook Beverage Group, Bellevue, WA	34,500	F	35	2,382
89	Davis Cos., Marlborough, MA	8,893	D	23	2,377
90	Ocean Isle Software, Vero Beach, FL	2,793	C	37	2,372
91	Parts Now, Madison, WI	7,407	B	35	2,329
92	Enrich International, Orem, UT	67,621	C	145	2,318
93	American Messenger Service, Harrisburg, NC	7,070	F	218	2,313
94	UniSource Energy, West Chicago, IL	11,892	C	3	2,274
95	AnTel, Plano, TX	4,105	F	24	2,259
96	Linderlake, Alsip, IL	2,369	F	60	2,223
97	Facilities Plus, Rockville, MD	7,838	D	200	2,212
98	Floor Coverings International, Forest Park, GA	5,787	A	42	2,206
99	Staffing, Grand Rapids, MI	11,587	D	65	2,163
100	Q&E Software, Raleigh, NC	13,563	C	155	2,161

Profit Range: A-16% or more; B-11% to 15%; C-6% to 10%; D-1% to 5%; E-break-even; F-loss

Inc. 500 Fastest-Growing Companies (cont'd)

Rank	Company	1993 Sales ($ thousands)	1993 Profit Range	No. of Employees 1993	% Sales Growth 1989-93
101	Prodea Software, Eden Prairie, MN	4,446	F	60	2,157
102	Medical Equipment Repair Services, Sarasota, FL	2,053	D	24	2,135
103	CMX Systems, Wallingford, CT	8,616	B	37	2,126
104	Advanced Hardware Architectures, Pullman, WA	8,922	C	52	2,071
105	Strategic Technologies, Cary, NC	8,682	D	30	2,071
106	Ni-Med, Arnold, MO	7,255	D	70	2,066
107	Cedar Computer Center, West Des Moines, IA	198,915	C	180	2,057
108	Advanced Laser Graphics, Washington, DC	10,800	E	56	2,047
109	Easy Returns Midwest, Chesterfield, MO	2,137	C	48	2,037
110	Gale Force Compression Service, Enid, OK	2,175	A	7	2,012
111	Campbell Services, Southfield, MI	7,419	D	83	2,008
112	Banyan Construction & Development, Clermont, FL	6,029	B	5	2,001
113	Abide International, Kirkland, WA	5,136	B	38	1,971
114	Superior Pharmaceutical, Cincinnati, OH	20,434	A	42	1,952
115	MC2 Microsystems, Warren, NJ	2,056	C	18	1,916
116	Triumph Technologies, Burlington, MA	5,152	D	8	1,913
117	Wisconsin Technicolor, Pewaukee, WI	2,791	A	35	1,908
118	Kestrel Associates, Arlington, VA	4,401	D	58	1,891
119	Tower Cleaning Systems, Wayne, PA	11,756	D	75	1,886
120	Combined Resource Technology, Baton Rouge, LA	1,997	A	14	1,858
121	Capital Cleaning Services, Lake Bluff, IL	2,035	D	175	1,857
122	Jelyn Associates/Old Glory, West Point, PA	24,645	B	50	1,854
123	Main Street Computer, Sarasota, FL	11,720	D	25	1,847
124	Larkin Industries, Birmingham, AL	2,082	D	21	1,846
125	Simsim, Natick, MA	6,296	D	6	1,814
126	Viking Components, Laguna Hills, CA	110,061	C	80	1,813
127	Sports Endeavors, Hillsborough, NC	17,631	D	125	1,810
128	Clubsource, San Francisco, CA	2,865	E	80	1,810
129	CARL, Denver, CO	10,218	D	115	1,803
130	Max Distribution, Dallas, TX	2,376	D	42	1,771
131	Pampered Chef, Addison, IL	65,310	A	228	1,760
132	Futron, Bethesda, MD	7,675	D	105	1,758
133	Ace Personnel, Overland Park, KS	2,384	D	15	1,748
134	R&R Recreation Products, Englewood Cliffs, NJ	7,392	A	5	1,748
135	Intellisel, Omaha, NE	10,923	C	71	1,745
136	Morningstar, Chicago, IL	21,233	F	280	1,745
137	Cedar Cliff Systems, Springfield, VA	8,765	D	24	1,734
138	Half Off Card Shop, Southfield, MI	23,346	D	200	1,722
139	Digicon, Bethesda, MD	19,361	C	265	1,718
140	Alternative Resources, Lincolnshire, IL	53,061	C	205	1,715
141	Ready International, Keyport, NJ	1,869	D	5	1,715
142	Triangle Technologies, Downers Grove, IL	5,380	E	17	1,711
143	Coda, Chesterfield, MO	2,221	B	22	1,706
144	Dowden Publishing, Montvale, NJ	4,142	F	28	1,701
145	FUNacho, Cincinnati, OH	3,069	D	9	1,695
146	Datasys, Dallas, TX	6,266	D	35	1,680
147	Spirit Rent-A-Car, Cleveland, OH	14,853	C	180	1,679
148	Metro Services Group, New York, NY	5,315	E	38	1,678
149	Capitol Environmental Services, Vienna, VA	5,436	D	12	1,676
150	American Harvest, Chaska, MN	72,047	D	143	1,674

Profit Range: A-16% or more; B-11% to 15%; C-6% to 10%; D-1% to 5%; E-break-even; F-loss

Inc. 500 Fastest-Growing Companies (cont'd)

Rank	Company	1993 Sales ($ thousands)	1993 Profit Range	No. of Employees 1993	% Sales Growth 1989-93
151	Anadigics, Warren, NJ	29,024	C	208	1,667
152	MicroBiz, Spring Valley, NY	8,660	D	72	1,664
153	Sprint Staffing, Tampa, FL	13,893	D	52	1,650
154	Information Systems & Services, Silver Springs, MD	5,339	C	55	1,645
155	Embroidery Services, Erlanger, KY	10,163	C	89	1,634
156	Network U.S., Pensacola, FL	17,994	D	310	1,630
157	Teltrust, Salt Lake City, UT	47,699	D	90	1,600
158	Interplay Productions, Irvine, CA	25,445	B	139	1,576
159	Pen-Group, Springfield, MO	14,121	D	38	1,569
160	Patterson Fan, Columbia, SC	2,130	A	16	1,564
161	LTL Home Products, Schuylkill Haven, PA	8,696	D	24	1,563
162	Computer Professionals, Lake Wylie, SC	14,744	D	350	1,557
163	Novare Services, Cincinnati, OH	16,050	D	180	1,553
164	Vanguard Automation, Tuscon, AZ	17,139	F	150	1,515
165	Small Systems Management, New Castle, DE	10,489	D	17	1,504
166	Promark One Marketing Services, Phoenix, AZ	10,081	A	525	1,500
167	CottageCare, Overland Park, KS	1,585	F	15	1,469
168	Alpine Computer System, Holliston, MA	4,438	C	25	1,446
169	Tekno, Cave City , KY	5,467	D	32	1,444
170	Integrated Environmental Solutions, Jacksonville, FL	2,648	A	12	1,440
171	Grand Aire Express, Monroe, MI	10,659	D	57	1,436
172	General Scientific, Arlington, VA	7,803	C	150	1,418
173	Broadband Communications Products, Melbourne, FL	1,986	A	18	1,416
174	Axiom, San Francisco, CA	11,986	E	98	1,413
175	Foster, Dayville, CT	1,740	E	16	1,413
176	Topique Associates, Houston, TX	3,915	C	14	1,406
177	TeleMark, Wilsonville, OR	7,904	B	450	1,403
178	CKS Partners, Cupertino, CA	12,224	B	30	1,394
179	Ralph Marlin & Co., Hartland, WI	12,971	C	60	1,394
180	Flexible Plan Investments, Bloomfield, MI	3,242	C	24	1,394
181	Working Assets Funding Service, San Francisco, CA	35,857	D	43	1,393
182	Snappy Lube, Monterey, CA	5,687	D	100	1,393
183	Advanced Engineering & Research Associates, Arlington , VA	8,120	D	105	1,379
184	CD ROM, Golden, CO·	1,500	D	8	1,356
185	CD Technology, Sunnyvale, CA	4,552	D	20	1,350
186	Maryland Screen Printers, Baltimore, MD	12,296	A	65	1,348
187	Aegis Research, Huntsville, AL	1,836	C	20	1,346
188	Daryan International, Montebello, CA	10,664	E	26	1,343
189	LBS Capital Management, Clearwater, FL	4,371	A	21	1,343
190	Dantz Development, Orinda, CA	9,080	B	42	1,341
191	Summit Technical Services, Warwick, RI	7,066	D	17	1,316
192	Project, Los Angeles, CA	2,303	C	2	1,313
193	OccuSystems, Dallas, TX	47,038	D	750	1,311
194	Flap Happy, Santa Monica, CA	3,031	D	25	1,310
195	Airs International, Watsonville, CA	1,432	C	17	1,304
196	Computer Corner, Albuquerque, NM	4,985	D	18	1,300
197	Sound Choice Accompaniment Tracks, Pineville, NC	4,430	B	25	1,297
198	Alfrebro, Monroe, OH	3,506	B	8	1,280
199	Mobius Group, Research Triangle Park, NC	2,191	B	18	1,278
200	Allen-Culton, Birmingham, AL	4,037	C	60	1,273

Profit Range: A-16% or more; B-11% to 15%; C-6% to 10%; D-1% to 5%; E-break-even; F-loss

Inc. 500 Fastest-Growing Companies (cont'd)

Rank	Company	1993 Sales ($ thousands)	1993 Profit Range	No. of Employees 1993	% Sales Growth 1989-93
201	Florida Infusion Services, Palm Harbor, FL	62,809	C	30	1,271
202	Collins/Reisenbichler Architects, Dallas, TX	2,747	A	27	1,253
203	Anstec, Fairfax, VA	30,402	D	470	1,232
204	Corporate Child Care Management Services, Nashville, TN	16,967	F	700	1,220
205	Aegis Associates, Watertown, MA	3,920	D	22	1,220
206	HCFS, Dallas, TX	2,534	A	75	1,220
207	Resident Publishing, New York, NY	2,528	E	80	1,217
208	Chiptec, Decatur, AL	3,785	A	58	1,210
209	ConQuest Telecommunication, Dublin, OH	23,187	D	95	1,207
210	Starr Industries, Camden, MI	1,318	D	18	1,205
211	Executive Mortgage Bankers, Melville, NY	2,125	B	45	1,204
212	Nest Entertainment, Irving, TX	55,130	B	347	1,197
213	Country Peddlers & Co. of America, Alsip, IL	7,826	D	60	1,191
214	SOTAS, Rockville, MD	5,784	C	33	1,188
215	Isyx LAN Systems, Rockville, MD	9,259	D	16	1,188
216	All Exim, Miami, FL	38,322	D	40	1,183
217	Delphi Consulting Group, Boston, MA	1,997	C	15	1,180
218	Daydots Label, Fort Worth, TX	4,512	C	40	1,171
219	Cherry Creek Mortgage, Denver, CO	9,442	A	131	1,171
220	ComPro Systems, Baltimore , MD	6,990	D	35	1,162
221	Cutchall Management, Omaha, NE	4,403	D	100	1,158
222	Whitlock Group-Hampton Roads, Norfolk, VA	7,591	F	33	1,157
223	M2, San Francisco, CA	2,120	E	5	1,154
224	Implant Innovations, West Palm Beach, FL	19,115	D	74	1,149
225	CMT, Colorado Springs, CO	2,593	C	65	1,147
226	Acucobol, San Diego, CA	8,000	B	57	1,144
227	Vail Research & Technology, Alexandria, VA	6,256	D	67	1,144
228	Trandes, Lanham, MD	14,360	D	265	1,142
229	Payroll 1 Group SE/SW, Tampa, FL	1,946	C	42	1,139
230	Eagle Point, Dubuque, IA	9,436	D	150	1,137
231	City Express, Boston, MA	1,271	C	39	1,134
232	Melaleuca, Idaho Falls, ID	206,828	A	953	1,121
233	Special Teams, Brookings, SD	3,475	D	53	1,115
234	Dunn Computer, Sterling, VA	5,804	D	25	1,114
235	Hamlin, Power & Reaves, Springfield, IL	5,347	C	30	1,110
236	FACT, Clifton Park, NY	2,757	D	22	1,109
237	Support Services Alliance, Schoharie, NY	3,542	D	62	1,109
238	OSC Consulting Services, Orlando, FL	2,424	C	40	1,106
239	Cavanaugh Gallery, Half Moon Bay, CA	2,551	C	32	1,103
240	Computers Etc. of New Hampshire, Manchester, NH	4,252	D	24	1,101
241	APPtitude Seminars, Pittsburg, PA	1,224	A	11	1,088
242	Computer Trend Systems, City of Industry, CA	67,881	D	75	1,088
243	Fiber Options, Bohemia, NY	7,373	C	63	1,087
244	CytoDiagnostics, Oaklahoma City, OK	9,348	F	137	1,086
245	Sytel, Bethesda, MD	1,884	C	40	1,085
246	Corporate Health Dimensions, Troy, NY	25,222	D	230	1,085
247	Sounds True, Boulder, CO	3,006	B	20	1,083
248	Winner International, Sharon, PA	118,565	A	200	1,082
249	Barclays Law Publishers, South San Francisco, CA	8,952	C	70	1,079
250	Venture VI, Walled Lake, MI	1,177	C	7	1,077

Profit Range: A-16% or more; B-11% to 15%; C-6% to 10%; D-1% to 5%; E-break-even; F-loss

Inc. 500 Fastest-Growing Companies (cont'd)

Rank	Company	1993 Sales ($ thousands)	1993 Profit Range	No. of Employees 1993	% Sales Growth 1989-93
251	Windmill International, Nashua, NH	1,377	D	13	1,077
252	Raytel Medical, San Mateo, CA	47,144	C	500	1,076
253	Wastren, Idaho Falls, ID	9,604	D	125	1,073
254	Prosperity Sciences Group, Walnut Creek, CA	6,361	D	125	1,069
255	Healthcare Automation, Warwick, RI	2,287	B	38	1,055
256	Accurate Automation, Chattanooga, TN	1,527	D	21	1,048
257	FWB, San Francisco, CA	16,232	C	44	1,048
258	Universal Rewards, Pine Brook, NJ	1,640	F	32	1,039
259	Atlanta Legal Copies, Atlanta, GA	33,917	D	1,200	1,034
260	Value Added Distribution, Gaithersburg, MD	8,947	E	20	1,032
261	Access Conference Call Service, Washington, DC	3,714	B	41	1,025
262	NatureForm, Jacksonville, FL	14,181	A	122	1,022
263	FASTech Integration, Lincoln, MA	8,669	F	67	1,021
264	Sweetwater Sound, Fort Wayne, IN	11,349	D	48	1,021
265	Rock Financial, Bingham Farms, MI	22,269	A	300	1,017
266	Atlantic Network Systems, Cary, NC	9,361	D	21	1,008
267	Custom Camera Design, Lakebay, WA	3,945	C	48	1,005
268	Insight Direct, Tempe, AZ	131,633	D	350	997
269	Dominion Capital, Dallas, TX	4,328	F	14	996
270	Keys Fitness Products, Dallax, TX	15,159	D	32	994
271	Impact Telecommunications, Spokane, WA	34,406	F	219	989
272	Fidelity Technologies, Reading, PA	9,992	C	175	988
273	HydroLogic, Asheville, NC	14,676	F	255	987
274	MuniFinancial Services, Temecula, CA	3,041	A	37	986
275	Flash Creative Management, River Edge, NJ	1,776	B	20	983
276	Practice Management Information, Los Angeles, CA	12,686	B	43	982
277	GET Travel Services, Walnut Creek, CA	6,130	D	27	981
278	Lokring, Foster City, CA	8,117	F	71	978
279	Coldwater Creek, Sandpoint, ID	29,253	B	84	967
280	Quick Start Technologies, Newport Beach, CA	4,099	D	42	956
281	Saturn Electronics & Engineering, Rochester Hills, MI	40,338	B	350	950
282	Engineered Endeavors, Mentor, OH	4,533	C	12	947
283	MDIgrafx, Buffalo Grove, IL	4,152	C	42	946
284	Lens Express, Deerfield Beach, FL	34,659	D	254	942
285	HazWaste Industries, Richmond, VA	50,455	D	281	939
286	PCBM Management, Ishpeming, MI	3,140	C	81	936
287	Capital Data, Milwaukee, WI	9,390	D	7	931
288	Victorian Papers, Kansas City, MO	3,879	B	69	921
289	One Stop, Grand Rapids, MI	20,342	D	51	921
290	Dapru, San Francisco, CA	4,867	D	67	918
291	Data Systems & Management, St. Paul, MN	7,579	C	147	917
292	Digital Network Associates, New York, NY	11,733	C	32	917
293	Hot Box-NFE, Jacksonville, FL	1,098	D	20	917
294	MFI Investments, Byron, OH	5,010	E	20	914
295	Stormfront Studios, San Rafael, CA	1,748	C	29	910
296	Roll Systems, Burlington, VT	23,697	D	104	905
297	Telamon, Indianapolis, IN	18,942	D	90	896
298	Waldec Group, Tampa, FL	38,011	D	120	896
299	Alpha & Omega Integrated Control Systems, Pittsburgh, PA	2,794	C	22	894
300	Zedco, Kirkland, WA	5,317	D	16	894

Profit Range: A-16% or more; B-11% to 15%; C-6% to 10%; D-1% to 5%; E-break-even; F-loss

Inc. 500 Fastest-Growing Companies (cont'd)

Rank	Company	1993 Sales ($ thousands)	1993 Profit Range	No. of Employees 1993	% Sales Growth 1989-93
301	Automated Systems Design, Roswell, GA	7,516	D	75	893
302	Personal Workstations, Kirkland, WA	9,458	D	23	888
303	Zeftek, Batavia, IL	8,403	A	8	887
304	R&D Laboratories, Marina Del Ray, CA	1,902	F	14	885
305	Factura Composites, Rochester, NY	2,728	D	40	885
306	Select Design, Burlington, VT	1,206	B	15	880
307	Technautics, Alexandria, VA	4,713	D	86	870
308	BOWA Builders, Arlington, VA	1,629	D	22	870
309	Lite-Form, Sioux City, IA	3,210	C	10	861
310	MultiLink, Andover, MA	12,086	A	72	858
311	Ultimate Prospecting Services, Marlborough, MA	1,225	D	10	857
312	Master Translating Services, Miami, FL	1,003	D	10	855
313	Property Tax Specialists, Silver Springs , MD	1,020	A	6	853
314	Response Technologies, East Greenwich, RI	1,624	A	22	850
315	Compatible Systems, Boulder, CO	3,670	C	22	843
316	Blackhawk Furniture, Riverside, CA	9,965	D	130	838
317	MicroFridge, Sharon, MA	12,257	D	40	838
318	Hi-Tech Engineering, Hot Springs, AR	8,855	D	92	836
319	Calais Home Corp. of Texas, Houston, TX	24,292	D	60	829
320	Metamor Technologies, Chicago, IL	5,783	C	96	819
321	Corporate Environments, Atlanta, GA	21,524	D	75	815
322	Blue Moving, Austin, TX	1,665	F	49	815
323	Compusist, Dryden, NY	4,003	F	74	810
324	CompuSense, Nashua, NH	2,828	C	25	806
325	Operator Service, Lubbock, TX	22,393	C	47	804
326	SCC Communication, Boulder, CO	15,268	C	133	803
327	EcoChem, Seattle, WA	1,209	D	20	802
328	R. J. Gordon & Co., Los Angeles, CA	3,973	D	50	801
329	Troy Systems, Alexandria, VA	10,918	C	160	790
330	Saber Software, Dallas , TX	13,128	B	85	788
331	Original American Scones, Oak Park, IL	3,001	C	40	775
332	Digital Data Voice, Eagan, MN	1,430	A	12	772
333	J&M Laboratories, Dawsonville, GA	7,598	C	54	769
334	Evinco, Alcoa, TN	894	D	40	768
335	Fetpak, Islandia, NY	988	D	6	767
336	Sherwood Promotions, Aurora, OH	5,628	A	12	766
337	Mortgage Choice, Durham, NC	5,596	A	35	765
338	DataOK, Los Angeles, CA	5,551	B	110	763
339	Peregrine Outfitters, Wilson, VT	3,890	D	15	761
340	Voice-Tel Enterprises, Cleveland, OH	18,558	D	93	760
341	Gemini Industries, Burlington , MA	2,224	D	53	759
342	PID , Phoenix, AZ	3,425	D	49	756
343	Interbio, Baton Rouge, LA	5,229	B	50	752
344	Zitter Group, San Francisco, CA	1,347	D	11	747
345	Sullivan & Co., New York, NY	4,048	A	18	747
346	Summit Medical Systems, Minneapolis, MN	3,966	D	55	746
347	Environmental & Foundation Drilling, Waunakee, WI	3,441	D	29	745
348	Campus Concepts, Baltimore, MD	1,818	F	9	742
349	Powerhouse Carpet Systems, Tampa, FL	2,915	D	20	740
350	QCC, Dedham, MA	3,028	A	30	739

Profit Range: A-16% or more; B-11% to 15%; C-6% to 10%; D-1% to 5%; E-break-even; F-loss

Inc. 500 Fastest-Growing Companies (cont'd)

Rank	Company	1993 Sales ($ thousands)	1993 Profit Range	No. of Employees 1993	% Sales Growth 1989-93
351	Galaxy Scientific, Pleasantville, NJ	22,914	C	212	738
352	RWD Technologies, Columbia, MD	18,418	C	222	736
353	ExecuTrain of Texas, Dallas, TX	5,877	B	85	736
354	Botec Analysis, Cambridge, MA	911	D	9	736
355	Flamers Charburgers, Jacksonville, FL	1,779	C	20	727
356	Boxes, New Haven, CT	7,867	C	33	724
357	Van Wyk Enterprises, Martinsburg, WV	8,801	D	15	723
358	Concord Service & Affiliates, Williamsport, PA	16,962	E	500	721
359	POS Systems, Phoenix, AZ	11,162	C	332	721
360	International Marketing Specialists, St. Louis, MO	2,988	D	6	721
361	Xymox Systems, Van Nuys, CA	1,270	B	11	719
362	Red Rose Collection, Burlingame, CA	12,588	F	100	717
363	Computer One, Albuquerque, NM	11,819	D	24	717
364	Teubner & Associates, Stillwater, OK	4,098	C	38	716
365	Compliance Services International, Tacoma, WA	3,344	C	25	716
366	Protech Communications, Burlington, NC	3,736	E	59	714
367	Pro Mark Technologies, River Forest, IL	5,365	C	36	710
368	Sterling National Mortgage, Clark, NJ	10,955	A	52	710
369	Fulton Computer Products Programming, Rockville Centre, NY	31,888	F	34	709
370	American Courier Express, Edison, NJ	2,363	D	30	706
371	A&L Shatto, Bel Air, MD	1,289	E	20	706
372	Gould-Kreutzer Associates, Cambridge, MA	1,253	D	12	703
373	Computer Generated Solutions, New York, NY	26,003	D	120	703
374	Cybex, Huntsville, AL	12,812	B	88	701
375	Richards & Richards, Nashville, TN	1,031	C	18	699
376	Correspondence Management, Marlton, NJ	2,884	C	46	697
377	Tova Industries, Louisville, KY	5,924	B	42	692
378	Automation Group, Redwood City, CA	4,173	C	27	689
379	System Connection, Provo, UT	22,047	C	130	689
380	Sherpa, San Jose, CA	23,787	C	167	687
381	Kitty Hawk Group, DFW Airport, TX	65,779	C	109	687
382	Potomac Group, Nashville, TN	6,326	D	61	685
383	I-Net, Bethesda, MD	147,982	D	1,800	681
384	Business Media, Lincoln, NE	2,044	D	6	680
385	Oread Laboratories, Lawrence, KS	7,584	E	101	672
386	K&M Engineering & Consulting, Washington, DC	13,548	D	105	670
387	Softsense Computer Products, Atlanta, GA	6,111	B	41	670
388	Inside Communications, Boulder, CO	5,087	D	39	670
389	OCS Group, Pittsford, NY	9,192	C	146	669
390	DAZSER Corps, Clearwater, FL	7,009	D	20	668
391	Hub City Terminals NY-NJ, Englewood, NJ	15,449	D	16	666
392	Softub, Chatsworth, CA	13,357	D	120	665
393	AmChex Collection Services, Birmingham, AL	1,286	D	24	661
394	Collectech Systems, Calabasas, CA	3,669	D	44	658
395	Energy Consortium, Iselin, NJ	3,893	D	22	656
396	Binary Arts, Alexandria, VA	4,086	C	12	655
397	Action Temporary Service, Evansville, IN	9,258	D	12	653
398	Whitacre Trucking, Portage, OH	7,155	D	98	652
399	Ethix, Portland, OR	43,769	D	605	650
400	Custom Transportation Service, Braintree, MA	1,183	C	16	649

Profit Range: A-16% or more; B-11% to 15%; C-6% to 10%; D-1% to 5%; E-break-even; F-loss

Inc. 500 Fastest-Growing Companies (cont'd)

Rank	Company	1993 Sales ($ thousands)	1993 Profit Range	No. of Employees 1993	% Sales Growth 1989-93
401	Diamond Flower Southeast, Miami, FL	9,925	D	34	647
402	Fugazy Executive Travel, Boston, MA	5,861	D	65	647
403	Travel Store, Los Angeles, CA	4,374	D	86	645
404	Covey Leadership Center, Provo, UT	48,516	C	430	645
405	Pencils, New Bedford, MA	2,011	D	12	645
406	Preferred Staffing, Rolling Meadows, IL	5,044	C	34	644
407	JMR Electronics, Chatsworth, CA	25,814	C	323	643
408	Boxlight, Poulsbo, WA	6,607	D	16	642
409	AJT & Associates, Cape Canaveral, FL	4,653	D	115	640
410	Timecorp Systems, Atlanta, GA	3,306	B	40	640
411	U.S. Personnel, Columbia, SC	12,767	D	47	638
412	Motherwear, Northampton, MA	2,439	B	12	637
413	Aspen Health Services, Huntington Beach, CA	3,389	A	60	634
414	Donovan Group, Worcester, MA	2,887	C	16	633
415	User Technology Associates, Arlington, VA	26,395	B	396	631
416	Nguyen Electronics, Minneapolis, MN	4,755	A	168	629
417	Fisher Industrial Service, Glencoe, AL	10,550	C	145	627
418	PMT Services, Nashville, TN	31,313	D	105	627
419	Hobby Town Unlimited, Lincoln, NE	2,461	C	25	622
420	Bock Pharmacal, St. Louis, MO	58,468	B	333	621
421	Priority Group, Louisville, KY	1,238	A	15	620
422	Augustine Medical, Eden Prairie, MN	19,227	C	146	612
423	JVC Technologies, Wayne, PA	6,530	D	16	611
424	Pet Ventures, Arlington, VA	14,210	D	168	611
425	DXI, Pittsburgh, PA	2,520	F	48	608
426	Southern Financial Network, Stone Mountain, GA	2,860	C	47	604
427	Whitlock Group, Glen Allen, VA	20,985	D	87	604
428	Sunrise Terrace, Fairfax, VA	28,732	F	1,250	603
429	Registry, Newton, MA	39,787	D	148	600
430	Melmedica Children's Healthcare, Country Club Hills, IL	4,829	D	106	600
431	First Commonwealth, Chicago, IL	17,337	C	80	597
432	U.S. Computer Maintenance, Farmingdale, NY	10,109	C	114	597
433	Nature's Recipe Pet Foods, Corona, CA	36,243	C	58	596
434	Impact Telemarketing, Woodbury, NJ	3,000	D	510	596
435	Roach Air, Fort Worth, TX	4,899	E	60	596
436	SabreData, Austin, TX	27,531	D	103	595
437	Buschman, Cleveland, OH	2,737	A	18	595
438	Maria Elena Torano & Associates, Miami, FL	18,244	C	240	590
439	ExecuTrain, Overland Park, KS	2,158	C	26	589
440	Link Computer, Placentia, CA	22,597	D	22	587
441	Telecommunication Systems Management, Sterling, VA	5,298	D	54	584
442	Tower Commercial Cleaning, Columbus, OH	833	D	16	583
443	Continental Business Service, San Bernardino, CA	857	D	10	580
444	Coverall of Virginia, Richmond, VA	3,256	D	13	580
445	Learnsoft, San Diego, CA	3,443	E	57	579
446	Applied Computer Technology, Fort Collins, CO	13,405	E	45	579
447	TarHeel Roofing, St. Petersburg, FL	7,653	D	100	577
448	Yield Techniglobal, Staten Island, NY	6,025	C	8	576
449	Adaptive Technologies, Frederick, MD	1,785	F	18	576
450	Maximum Strategy, Milpitas, CA	11,098	A	27	575

Profit Range: A-16% or more; B-11% to 15%; C-6% to 10%; D-1% to 5%; E-break-even; F-loss

Inc. 500 Fastest-Growing Companies (cont'd)

Rank	Company	1993 Sales ($ thousands)	1993 Profit Range	No. of Employees 1993	% Sales Growth 1989-93
451	Univenture, Columbus, OH	2,403	D	26	575
452	Micro Information Services, Mequon, WI	6,911	D	31	575
453	ProForma Watsonrise Business Systems, Arlington, TX	1,902	D	9	574
454	Kalow Controls, North Clarendon, VT	4,082	B	25	574
455	Knowledge Systems, Cary, NC	5,797	F	41	573
456	Audio Partners, Auburn, CA	2,813	D	22	573
457	Kiber Environmental Services, Atlanta, GA	2,537	D	27	573
458	BDR Executive Custom Homes, Grand Rapids, MI	3,367	B	11	572
459	Oakville Forest Products, Oakville, WA	7,296	D	23	571
460	EKS, Naperville, IL	11,902	D	10	571
461	Lai, Venuti & Lai, Santa Clara, CA	3,969	C	35	570
462	United Personnel Services, Springfield, MA	3,484	D	9	569
463	Smithton Sanitation Service, Washington, NC	1,792	C	35	569
464	Village Homes of Colorado, Littleton, CO	87,037	C	130	567
465	Dunsirn Industries, Neenah, WI	23,194	C	147	566
466	Cadapult Graphic Systems, Allendale, NJ	5,500	D	14	565
467	Abundant Life Childcare Centers, Kirkland, WA	2,515	F	76	564
468	Allwest Systems, Denver, CO	12,550	D	71	563
469	Mustang Software, Bakersfield, CA	2,797	C	33	563
470	HVJ Associates, Houston, TX	1,881	E	28	562
471	Concept Automation, Sterling, VA	69,500	D	130	561
472	Gap International, Springfield, PA	3,651	A	21	560
473	Abacus Technology, Chevy Chase, MD	24,141	D	189	559
474	Fortitech, Schenectady, NY	13,195	C	35	558
475	Capitol Concierge, Washington, DC	3,812	D	70	557
476	Innosoft International, West Covina, CA	1,472	C	14	557
477	Beechwood Data Systems, Clark, NJ	7,012	A	81	556
478	State of the Art Computing, San Diego, CA	7,755	E	87	556
479	Maxis, Orinda, CA	23,509	C	71	553
480	North Central Gaming, Great Falls, MT	809	D	7	552
481	Multi-Bank Services, Southfield, MI	3,592	A	82	551
482	OmniTech Corporate Solutions, Teaneck, NJ	10,085	D	37	550
483	Gardner Fox Associates, Bryn Mawr, PA	8,319	D	45	548
484	Campus Creations, Urbana, IL	1,130	C	24	546
485	Scottsdale Securities, St. Louis, MO	13,977	A	86	544
486	Wild Oats Market, Boulder, CO	47,266	D	500	544
487	Financial Independence Network, Crystal Lake, IL	1,261	F	6	543
488	Engineering Services & Products, South Windsor, CT	14,891	E	70	542
489	Copithorne & Bellows Public Relations, San Francisco, CA	5,450	A	53	541
490	KRA, Silver Spring, MD	2,875	D	120	540
491	Advanced Systems Technology, Atlanta, GA	12,754	D	169	539
492	Camelot Systems, Haverhill, MA	9,476	C	78	537
493	Wasser, Seattle, WA	6,244	D	14	532
494	SolarCare Technologies, Bethlehem, PA	4,503	A	29	532
495	Grafton, Kansas City, MO	2,977	D	10	529
496	Integrated Quality Solutions, Framington Hills, MI	679	D	8	529
497	Dine-A-Mate, Binghamton, NY	1,886	D	32	529
498	AmerInd, Alexandria, VA	20,893	D	82	527
499	Buckeye Beans & Herbs, Spokane, WA	4,137	D	42	524
500	Manufacturing Modes, Danville, CA	6,577	D	17	523

Profit Range: A-16% or more; B-11% to 15%; C-6% to 10%; D-1% to 5%; E-break-even; F-loss   *Source: Inc. magazine, 1994*

Most-Admired Corporations

Rank	Company
1	Rubbermaid
2	Home Depot
3	Coca-Cola
4	Microsoft
5	3M
6	Walt Disney
7	Motorola
8	J. P. Morgan
9	Procter & Gamble
10	UPS
11	Merck
12	Levi Strauss
13	Corning
14	Banc One
14	Johnson & Johnson
16	AT&T
17	Pfizer
18	Boeing
19	General Electric
19	Hewlett-Packard
21	Kimberly-Clark
22	Toys 'R' Us
23	General Mills
24	Roadway Services
25	Gillette

Rank	Company
26	PepsiCo
27	Shaw Industries
28	Southwest Airlines
29	Publix Super Markets
30	Berkshire Hathaway
31	Norfolk Southern
32	Albertson's
33	Golden West Financial
34	Goodyear Tire
35	Sara Lee
36	Union Pacific
37	Herman Miller
37	Wal-Mart Stores
39	Enron
40	Nike
41	Bankers Trust
41	Fluor
41	V. F.
44	Morgan Stanley Group
45	Harley-Davidson
45	Unifi
47	U.S. Healthcare
48	Du Pont
49	Time Warner
50	Cooper Tire & Rubber

Source: Fortune, Feb. 7, 1994, © Time, Inc. All rights reserved

---

E-MAIL **Consumer Price Indexes.** Send e-mail to consumer@almanac.yoyo.com. See p. xi for instructions.
Table of consumer price indexes by major groups.

The Domini 400 Social Index

THE DOMINI 400 SOCIAL INDEX (DSI) monitors the performance of 400 corporations that pass multiple broad-based social screens. It was created to fill two primary needs: to give social investors more information on the broad market available to them, and to provide a resource for social investors who want a broad index of companies in many different industries that pass these social screens.

The DSI eliminates companies using the following social screens:

- Eliminate companies that derive 2 percent or more of current sales from weapons-related products, or the manufacture of alcohol, tobacco, or gambling products;

- Eliminate electric companies that own interests in nuclear power plants or companies that derive 4 percent or more of current sales from the nuclear power industry;

- Eliminate companies facing substantial environmental controversies; and

- Eliminate companies experiencing a recent history of notably unstable employee relations.

Kinder, Lydenberg, Domini & Co. (KLD) provides social research on U.S. and foreign corporations to the investment community. KLD makes a particular effort to include companies that have a positive record in the environment, employee relations, and community relations, or that make products of particular social usefulness.

Contact Option

Kinder, Lydenberg, Domini & Co.
129 Mt. Auburn St.
Cambridge, MA 02138
(617) 547-7479

The DSI 400, Alphabetically by Name

Company	Type
AMR	Air transport
ARCO Chemical	Chemicals
Acuson	Medical equipment
Advanced Micro Devices	Semiconductors
Aetna Life & Casualty	Multi-line insurance
Ahmanson, A. H.	Savings & loan
Air Products & Chemicals	Chemicals
Airborne Freight	Transport
Alaska Air Group	Air transport
Alberto-Culver	Home
Albertson's	Food retail
Alco Standard	Miscellaneous
Alexander & Alexander Services	Insurance brokers
Allergan	Medical equipment
Allwaste	Pollution abatement
Aluminum Co. of America	Metals
ALZA	Pharmaceuticals
Amdahl	Computers
American Express	Financial
American General	Multi-line insurance
American Greetings	Miscellaneous
American International Group	Multi-line insurance
American Power Conversion	Electrical components
American Stores	Food retail
American Water Works	Utility
Ameritech	Telephone
AMP	Electrical components
Amoco	Petroleum
Anadarko Petroleum	Natural gas
Analog Devices	Semiconductors

Company	Type
Angelica	Medical equipment
Apache	Natural gas
Apogee Enterprises	Construction materials
Apple Computer	Computers
Applied Materials	Manufacturing
Archer Daniels Midland	Packaged food
Atlanta Gas	Natural gas
Atlantic Richfield	Petroleum
Autodesk	Software & services
Automatic Data Processing	Software & services
Avery Dennison	Office furniture
Avnet	Miscellaneous
Avon Products	Home
Baldor Electric	Electrical components
Banc One	Banks/major regional
Bank of Boston	Banks/other major
BankAmerica	Banks/other major
Bankers Trust New York	Banks/money center
Barnett Banks	Banks/major regional
Bassett Furniture	Furniture & appliances
Battle Mountain Gold	Mining
Becton, Dickinson & Co.	Medical equipment
Bell Atlantic	Telephone
BellSouth	Telephone
Bemis	Miscellaneous
Ben & Jerry's	Packaged food
Beneficial	Financial
Bergen Brunswig	Health care
BET Holdings	Entertainment
Betz Laboratories	Chemicals

The Domini 400 Social Index (cont'd)

Company	Type
Biomet	Medical equipment
Block, H & R	Financial
Bob Evans	Restaurants
Borland	Software & services
Briggs & Stratton	Manufacturing
Brooklyn Union Gas	Natural gas
Brown Group	Footwear
CBS	Broadcasting
CCH	Publishers
CIGNA	Multli-line insurance
CPI	Miscellaneous
CPC	Packaged food
CSX	Rail transport
Cabot	Chemicals
Calgon Carbon	Chemicals
California Energy	Utility
Campbell Soup	Packaged food
Capital Cities/ABC	Broadcasting
Carolina Freight	Truck transport
Centex	Housing construction
Charming Shoppes	Specialty retail
Chubb	Insurance
Church & Dwight	Home
Cincinnati Financial	Multi-line insurance
Cincinnati Milacron	Machine tools
Circuit City Stores	Specialty retail
Cisco Systems	Computers
Cintas	Commerical services
Citizens Utilities	Electric companies
Claire's Stores	Specialty retail
CLARCOR	Manufacturing
Clark Equipment	Manufacturing
Clorox	Home
Coca-Cola	Beverages
Colgate-Palmolive	Home
Comcast	Broadcasting
Community Psychiatric Centers	Health facility mgmt.
Compaq Computer	Computers
Computer Associates Int'l	Software & services
Connecticut Energy	Natural gas
Conrail	Rail transport
Consolidated Freightways	Truck transport
Consolidated Natural Gas	Natural gas
Consolidated Papers	Forest & paper
Continental	Insurance
Cooper Industries	Electrical components
Cooper Tire & Rubber	Vehicle components
CoreStates Financial	Banks/major regional
Cross, A. T.	Miscellaneous
Cummins Engine	Vehicle components
Cyprus-Amax Minerals	Mining
DSC Communications	Telecommunications
Dana	Vehicle components
Dayton Hudson	Department stores
Delta Airlines	Air transport

Company	Type
Deluxe	Printing
DeVRY	Commercial services
Digital Equipment	Computers
Dillard Department Stores	Department stores
Dime Bancorp	Savings & loan
Dionex	Pollution abatement
Disney, Walt	Entertainment
Dollar General	General retail
Donnelley, R. R., & Sons	Printing
Dow Jones	Newspapers
Eastern Enterprises	Natural gas
Echo Bay Mines	Mining
Edwards, A. G.	Financial
Egghead	Specialty retail
El Paso Natural Gas	Natural gas
Energen	Natural gas
Enron	Oil & gas drilling
Equitable Resources	Natural gas
Fastenal	Manufacturing
Fedders	Furniture & appliances
Federal Express	Transport
Federal Home Loan Mortgage	Financial
Federal-Mogul	Vehicle components
Federal Nat'l Mortgage Ass'n	Financial
Fifth Third Bancorp	Banks/major regional
First Chicago	Banks/money center
First Fidelity Bancorp	Banks/major regional
FirstFed Financial	Savings & loan
Fleetwood Enterprises	Housing construction
Fleming	Wholesale food
Forest Laboratories	Pharmaceuticals
Frontier	Telephone
Fuller, H. B.	Chemicals
GATX	Transport
GEICO	Insurance
Gannett	Newspapers
Gap	Specialty retail
General Mills	Packaged food
General Re	Insurance
General Signal	Miscellaneous
Genuine Parts	Vehicle components
Giant Food	Food retail
Gibson Greetings	Miscellaneous
Golden West Financial	Savings & loan
Goulds Pump	Manufacturing
Graco	Manufacturing
Grainger, W. W.	Electrical components
Great Atlantic & Pacific Tea	Food retail
Great Western Financial	Savings & loan
Groundwater Technology	Pollution abatement
Handleman	Leisure
Hannaford Brothers	Food retail
Harcourt General	Miscellaneous
Harland, John H.	Printing
Harman	Leisure

The Domini 400 Social Index (cont'd)

Company	Type
Hartford Steam Boiler Insurance	Insurance
Hartmarx	Textiles
Hasbro	Leisure
Hechinger	Specialty retail
Heinz, H. J.	Packaged food
Helmerich & Payne	Oil & gas drilling
Hershey Foods	Packaged food
Hewlett-Packard	Computers
Hillenbrand Industries	Miscellaneous
Home Depot	Specialty retail
HON Industries	Office furniture
Household	Financial
Hubbell	Electrical components
Huffy	Leisure
Humana	Health facility mgmt.
Hunt Manufacturing	Miscellaneous
Idaho Power	Electric companies
Illinois Tool Works	Machine tools
Inland Steel Industries	Metals
Intel	Semiconductors
International Dairy Queen	Restaurants
Ionics	Miscellaneous
Isco	Pollution abatement
James River of Virginia	Forest & paper
Jefferson-Pilot	Life insurance
Johnson & Johnson	Medical equipment
Jostens	Miscellaneous
K Mart	General retail
Kaufman & Broad Home	Housing construction
Kellogg's	Packaged food
Kelly Services	Commercial services
Kenetech	Utility
King World Productions	Entertainment
Knight-Ridder	Newspapers
Kroger	Food retail
LG&E Energy	Electric companies
Lands' End	Specialty retail
Lawson Products	Manufacturing
Lee Enterprises	Newspapers
Leggett & Platt	Furniture & appliances
Lillian Vernon	Specialty retail
Limited, The	Specialty retail
Lincoln National	Life insurance
Liz Claiborne	Textiles
Longs Drug Stores	Specialty retail
Lotus Development	Software & services
Louisiana Land & Exploration	Natural gas
Lowe's Companies	Specialty retail
Luby's Cafeterias	Restaurants
MCI Communications	Telecommunications
MCN	Natural gas
Manor Care	Health care
Marsh & McLennan	Insurance brokers
Marriott	Miscellaneous
Mattel	Leisure

Company	Type
May Department Stores	Department stores
Maytag	Furniture & appliances
McDonald's	Restaurants
McGraw-Hill	Publishers
Mead	Forest & paper
Media General	Newspapers
Medtronic	Medical equipment
Mellon Bank	Banks/other major
Melville	Specialty retail
Mercantile Stores	Department stores
Merck	Pharmaceuticals
Meredith	Publishers
Merrill Lynch	Financial
Micron Technology	Semiconductors
Miller, Herman	Office furniture
Millipore	Manufacturing
Modine Manufacturing	Vehicle components
Moore	Office furniture
Morgan, J. P.	Banks/money center
Morrison Restaurants	Restaurants
Morton	Chemicals
Mylan Laboratories	Pharmaceuticals
NBD Bancorp	Banks/major regional
NWNL	Life insurance
Nalco Chemical	Chemicals
National Education	Commercial services
National Service Industries	Commercial services
New England Business Service	Office furniture
New York Times	Newspapers
Newell	Housewares
Nicor	Natural gas
Nike	Footwear
Noram Energy	Natural gas
Nordson	Manufacturing
Nordstrom	Department stores
Norfolk Southern	Rail transport
Northwestern Public Service	Electric companies
Norwest	Banks/major regional
Novell	Software & services
Nucor	Metals
NYNEX	Telephone
Oklahoma Gas & Electric	Electric
Omnicom Group	Miscellaneous
Oneida	Housewares
Oneok	Natural gas
Oryx Energy	Natural gas
Oshkosh B'Gosh	Textiles
PNC Bank	Banks/major regional
Pacific Enterprises	Natural gas
Pacific Telesis Group	Telephone
Penney, JC	General retail
Pennzoil	Petroleum
Peoples Energy	Natural gas
Pep Boys, The	Specialty retail
Pepsico	Beverages

The Domini 400 Social Index (cont'd)

Company	Type
Perkin-Elmer	Electrical components
Petrie Stores	Specialty retail
Phillips–Van Heusen	Textiles
Piper, Jaffray & Hopwood	Financial
Pitney Bowes	Office equipment
Polaroid	Miscellaneous
Potomac Electric Power	Electric companies
Praxair	Chemicals
Premier Industrial	Miscellaneous
Price/CostCo	Specialty retail
Procter & Gamble	Home
Providian	Life insurance
Public Service of Colorado	Electric
Quaker Oats	Packaged food
Quarterdeck Office Systems	Software & services
Ralston Purina	Packaged food
Raychem	Electrical components
Reebok	Footwear
Roadway Services	Truck transport
Rouse	Housing construction
Rowan	Oil & gas drilling
Rubbermaid	Housewares
Russell	Textiles
Ryan's Family Steakhouse	Restaurants
Ryder Systems	Transport
SPX	Vehicle components
SAFECO	Insurance
St. Jude Medical	Medical equipment
St. Paul Companies	Insurance
Santa Fe Energy Resources	Natural gas
Santa Fe Pacific	Rail transport
Schering-Plough	Pharmaceuticals
Scott Paper	Forest & paper
Sealed Air	Miscellaneous
Sears, Roebuck	General retail
Service	Miscellaneous
Shared Medical Systems	Software & services
Shaw Industries	Furniture & appliances
Shawmut National	Banks/major regional
Sherwin-Williams	Construction materials
Sigma-Aldrich	Chemicals
Skyline	Housing construction
Smith, A. O.	Vehicle components
Smucker, J. M.	Packaged food
Snap-On Tools	Tools
Sonoco Products	Miscellaneous
Southern New England Telecom	Telephone
Southwest Airlines	Air transport
Southwestern Bell	Telephone
Spartan Motors	Vehicle components
Spec's Music	Specialty retail
Springs Industries	Textiles
Sprint	Telecommunications
Standard Register	Office furniture
Stanhome	Home

Company	Type
Stanley Works	Tools
Status Computer	Computers
Stride-Rite	Footwear
Stryker	Medical equipment
Student Loan Marketing	Financial
Sun	Petroleum
Sun Microsystems	Computers
Sunrise Medical	Medical equipment
SunTrust Banks	Banks/major regional
Super Valu Stores	Wholesale food
SYSCO	Wholesale food
TCBY	Restaurants
TJ	Construction materials
TJX Companies	Specialty retail
Tandem Computers	Computers
Tandy	Specialty retail
Tektronix	Electric components
Tele-Communications	Broadcasting
Telephone & Data Systems	Telephone
Tellabs	Telecommunications
Tennant	Commercial services
Thermo Electron	Pollution abatement
Thomas & Betts	Electrical components
Thomas Industries	Furniture & appliances
Times Mirror	Newspapers
Tootsie Roll	Packaged food
Torchmark	Life insurance
Toro	Miscellaneous
Toys 'R' Us	Specialty retail
TransAmerica	Financial
Travelers	Multi-line insurance
Turner Broadcasting Systems	Broadcasting
UAL	Air transport
UNUM	Multi-line insurance
USF&G	Insurance
U.S. Healthcare	Health facility mgmt.
US West	Telephone
USlife	Life insurance
V. F.	Textiles
Value Line	Financial
Vermont Financial Services	Banks/major regional
Viacom	Entertainment
Wachovia	Banks/major regional
Wal-Mart	General retail
Walgreen	Specialty retail
Wallace Computer Services	Office furniture
Washington Gas Light	Natural gas
Washington Post	Newspapers
Watts Industries	Manufacturing
Wellman	Pollution abatement
Wells Fargo	Banks/major regional
Wesco Financial	Savings & loan
Westvaco	Forest & paper
Whirlpool	Furniture & appliances
Whitman	Miscellaneous

The Domini 400 Social Index (cont'd)

Company	Type
Whole Foods Market	Food retail
Williams Companies	Natural gas
Woolworth, F. W.	General retail
Worthington Industries	Metals
Wrigley, Wm.	Packaged food

Company	Type
Xilinx	Semiconductors
Xerox	Office equipment
Yellow	Truck transport
Zenith Electronics	Furniture & appliances
Zurn Industries	Pollution abatement

Source: Kinder, Lydenberg, Domini & Co., Feb. 1995

Minority and Women Owners

ACCORDING TO STATISTICS generated by the National Foundation for Women Business Owners, women own at least 5.4 million businesses. *Working Woman* in conjunction with NFWBO ranked the top 25 women-owned businesses in the first annual salute to women business owners. To be considered, candidates had to own at least 20 percent of the stock in private companies and 10 percent in public ones, and the women had to be top executives running the day-to-day operations.

Recommended Resource

National Foundation for Women Business Owners
1377 K St., NW, Suite 637
Washington, DC 20005
(301) 495-4975

The Top 25 Women-Owned Businesses

Rank	Owner(s)	Business	Employees	% of Ownership
1	Marian Ilitch	Little Caesar Enterprises	27,000	50
2	Joyce Raley Teel	Raley's	11,000	100
3	Lynda Resnick	Roll International	7,500	50
4	Antonia Axson Johnson	Axel Johnson	2,000	100
5	Liz Minyard/Gretchen Minyard Williams	Minyard Food Stores	6,200	67
6	Linda Wachner	Warnaco Group	11,800	12
7	Jenny Craig	Jenny Craig	4,910	>30
8	Donna Wolf Steigerwaldt	Jockey International	5,000	100
9	Donna Karan	Donna Karan	1,088	50
10	Helen Copley	Copley Press	3,500	100
11	Barbara Levy Kipper	Chas. Levy	1,800	100
12	Bettye Martin Marsham	Gear Holdings	30	20
13	Susie Tompkins	Esprit De Corp	1,250	67
14	Annabelle Lundy Fetterman	Lundy Packaging	900	>20
15	Dian Graves Owen	Owen Healthcare	2,250	38
16	Carole Little	Carole Little	850	50
17	Ellen Gordon	Tootsie Roll Industries	1,400	>20
18	Josephine Chaus	Bernard Chaus	750	63
19	Christel DeHaan	Resort Condominiums International	2,300	100
20	Linda Paresky	Thomas Cook Travel	3,500	50
21	Patricia Gallup	PC Connection	450	50
22	Ebba Hoffman/Sharon Hoffman Avent	Smead Manufacturing	2,600	100
23	Sydell Miller	Matrix Essentials	900	>50
24	Gertrude Boyle	Columbia Sportswear	700	>50
25	Rachelle Friedman	J&R Music World	600	51

Source: Working Woman magazine (May 1994) and
National Foundation for Women Business Owners. Reprinted with permission.

Minority and Women Owners (cont'd)

Top 25 Hispanic-Owned Businesses

Rank	Company	1993 Revenue ($ mil.)
1	Burt on Broadway/Arapahoe	529.12
2	Goya Foods	480.00
3	Troy Ford	260.41
4	Sedano's Supermarkets	236.52
5	Galeana's Van Dyke Dodge	188.89
6	Ancira Enterprises	181.10
7	Cal-State Lumber Sales	168.40
8	International Bancshares	160.46
9	Normac Foods	160.38
10	CareFlorida	151.60
11	Infotec Development	135.00
12	The Vincam Group	134.50
13	CTA	133.00
14	Capital Bancorp	117.47
15	Lloyd A. Wise	116.89
16	COLSA	112.00
17	Gaseteria Oil	106.00
18	Avanti Press	105.00
19	Eagle Brands	102.23
20	Private Jet Expeditions	100.00
21	TELACU Industries	100.00
22	Mexican Industries in Michigan	100.00
23	Miami Honda/Central Hyundai/Sunshine Ford	98.91
24	United Poultry/Belca Foodservice	96.63
25	Precision Trading	96.00

Source: Hispanic Business, June 1994, Santa Barbara, CA

The Top Reference Sources

Working Woman, $11.97/year
(800) 234-9675

This monthly magazine is focused on women and their careers. Features provide guidelines on women's legal rights, management skills, career tactics and developments, plus how to maintain fitness and a positive self-image.

Regular surveys and statistical features, including an annual salary survey, make this an excellent resource.

The Forbes 400 Wealthiest Ranking

Name	Worth ($ mil.)	Primary Sources
du Pont (F)	10,000	Du Pont (I)
Gates, William III	9,350	Microsoft
Buffett, Warren	9,200	Stock market
Rockefeller (F)	6,000	Oil (I)
Kluge, John Werner	5,900	Metromedia
Johnson, Edward III	5,100	Fidelity Investments
Mellon (F)	5,000	(I)
DeVos, Richard M.	4,500	Amway
Perelman, Ronald	4,500	LBOs
Van Andel, Jay	4,500	Amway
Walton, Alice L.	4,340	Wal-Mart (I)
Walton, Helen	4,340	Wal-Mart (I)
Walton, Jim C.	4,340	Wal-Mart (I)
Walton, John T.	4,340	Wal-Mart (I)
Walton, S. Robson	4,340	Wal-Mart (I)
Murdoch, Keith	4,000	Publishing
Newhouse, Donald	4,000	Publishing
Newhouse, Samuel Jr.	4,000	Publishing
Redstone, Sumner	4,000	Viacom
Allen, Paul G.	3,910	Microsoft
Anthony, Barbara Cox	2,900	Cox (I)
Chambers, Anne Cox	2,900	Cox (I)
Ellison, Lawrence J.	2,900	Oracle
Annenberg, Walter	2,800	Publishing
Bronfman, Edgar Sr.	2,500	Seagram
Kerkorian, Kirk	2,500	Investments
Mars, Forrest Jr.	2,500	Candy (I)
Mars, Forrest Sr.	2,500	Candy (I)
Mars, John Franklyn	2,500	Candy (I)
Perot, Henry Ross	2,500	Computer services
Vogel, Jacqueline	2,500	Candy (I)
Crown, Lester	2,400	(I)
Hillman, Henry	2,200	Industralist
Packard, David	2,200	Hewlett-Packard
Pritzker, Jay & Robert	2,200	Finance, etc.
Bass, Robert	2,000	Oil, investments
Bren, Donald	2,000	Real estate
Davis, Marvin Harold	2,000	Oil
Phipps (F)	2,000	Bessemer Trust (I)
Anschutz, Philip	1,900	Oil
Ballmer, Steven	1,750	Microsoft
Bass, Lee Marshall	1,750	Oil, investments
Hewlett, William	1,750	Hewlett-Packard
Johnson, Samuel	1,750	Johnson Wax
Davis (F)	1,700	Winn-Dixie Stores
Knight, Philip	1,700	Nike
Scripps, E. W. (F)	1,700	Newspapers (I)
Smith (F)	1,700	Illinois Tool (I)
Hunt, Ray Lee	1,600	Oil (I)
Turner, Robert	1,600	Turner Broad.
Bacardi (F)	1,500	Liquor
Bass, Sid	1,500	Oil, investments
Getty, Gordon	1,500	Oil (I)
Moore, Gordon	1,500	Intel
Nordstrom (F)	1,500	Retailing
Bancroft (F)	1,400	Dow-Jones (I)
Bechtel, Riley P.	1,400	Eng., construc.
Bechtel, Stephen Jr.	1,400	Eng., construc.
Hillenbrand (F)	1,400	Caskets
Kroc, Joan Beverly	1,400	McDonald's (I)
Simplot, John	1,400	Potatoes
Wexner, Leslie	1,400	The Limited
Wrigley, William	1,360	Chewing gum
Busch (F)	1,300	Anheuser-Busch
Chandler (F)	1,300	Times Mirror
Collier (F)	1,300	Real estate
Haas, Peter Sr.	1,300	Levi Strauss
Helmsley, Harry O.	1,300	Real estate
Ingram, Erskine	1,300	Distribution
Weyerhaeuser (F)	1,300	Timber (I)
Blaustein (F)	1,200	Oil (I)
Clapp (F)	1,200	Weyerhaeuser (I)
Donnelley (F)	1,200	R. R. Donnelley
Dorrance, Bennett	1,200	Campbell Soup (I)
Dorrance, John III	1,200	Campbell Soup (I)
Johnson (F)	1,200	Johnson & Johnson
Koch, Charles	1,200	Oil services (I)
Koch, David	1,200	Oil services (I)
Lilly (F)	1,200	Pharmaceuticals
Magness, Bob	1,200	TCI
Malone, Mary	1,200	Campbell Soup (I)
Meijer (F)	1,200	Retailing
Rockefeller, David Sr.	1,200	Oil (I)
Soros, George	1,200	Money manager
Tisch, Laurence	1,135	Loews
Tisch, Preston	1,135	Loews
Albertson, Kathryn	1,100	Albertson's
Brown (F)	1,100	Whiskey
Galvin, Robert	1,100	Motorola
Gund (F)	1,100	Sanka, banking (I)

(I) = inheritance; (F) = family

The Forbes 400 Wealthiest Ranking (cont'd)

Name	Worth ($ mil.)	Primary Sources
Hill, Margaret Hunt	1,100	Oil (I)
LeFrak, Samuel	1,100	Real estate
Pitcairn (F)	1,100	PPG Industries (I)
Rockefeller, Laurance	1,100	Oil (I)
Carlson, Curtis	1,000	Radisson
Fribourg, Michel	1,000	Grain trader
Geffen, David	1,000	Recording
Hall, Donald Joyce	1,000	Hallmark (I)
Hixon (F)	1,000	Connectors
Hughes (F)	1,000	Hughes Aircraft
Huntsman, Jon	1,000	Plastics, chemicals
Jenkins (F)	1,000	Publix
Lauder, Estée	1,000	Cosmetics
Lauder, Leonard	1,000	Cosmetics
Lauder, Ronald	1,000	Cosmetics
Lennon, Fred A.	1,000	Valves, pipe fittings
Mellon, Paul	1,000	(I)
Reed (F)	1,000	Lumber, paper
Rockefeller, Winthrop	1,000	Oil (I)
Schwan (F)	1,000	(I)
Walton, James	1,000	Wal-Mart
Upjohn (F)	985	Upjohn (I)
Idema (F)	945	Steelcase
Petrie, Milton	940	Petrie Stores
Jordan (F)	925	Media, retailing (I)
Tyson, Donald John	925	Tyson Foods
Davidson, William	900	Guardian Industries
Dayton (F)	900	Dayton Hudson
Feeney, Charles	900	Duty Free Shoppers
Hearst, Randolph	900	(I)
Horvitz (F)	900	Media (I)
Johnson, Barbara	900	Johnson & Johnson (I)
Louis, John Jeffrey	900	Johnson Wax (I)
Lykes (F)	900	Shipping
Scripps, J. E. (F)	900	Newspapers (I)
Searle (F)	900	(I)
Weber, Charlotte	900	Campbell Soup (I)
Richardson (F)	885	Richardson-Vicks (I)
Zell, Samuel	880	Real estate
Temple (F)	870	Timber (I)
Cargill, James R.	860	Cargill
Cargill, Margaret	860	Cargill
DeBartolo, Edward	860	Shopping centers
Greenberg, Maurice	855	American Int'l
Murdock, David	855	Real estate
Sorenson, James	855	Medical devices
Lerner, Alfred	850	Banking
Haebler (F)	830	Int'l Flavors
Stern, Leonard N.	825	Pet supplies
Batten, Frank Sr.	820	Media

Name	Worth ($ mil.)	Primary Sources
Frist, Thomas F. Jr.	810	Columbia/HCA
Campbell (F)	800	Real estate
Green, Pincus	800	Commodities
Hamilton, Dorrance	800	Campbell Soup (I)
Hostetter, Amos Jr.	800	Continental Cable
McCaw, Craig O.	800	McCaw Cellular
Mennen (F)	800	The Mennen Co.
Norris (F)	800	Lennox
Rich, Marc	800	Commodities
Taylor, Jack Crawford	800	Auto rentals
Mead (F)	790	Consolidated Papers
Ford, William Clay	785	Ford Motor (I)
Abramson, Leonard	780	U.S. Healthcare
Kravis, Henry R.	780	LBOs
Roberts, George R.	780	LBOs
Pigott (F)	775	Paccar (I)
Buffett, Susan	765	Berkshire Hathaway
Dedman, Robert Sr.	750	Country clubs
Scaife, Richard	750	(I)
Whittier (F)	750	Oil (I)
Hess, Leon	745	Amerada Hess
Tyson, Barbara	745	Tyson Foods
van Beuren, Hope	740	Campbell Soup (I)
Gaylord, Edward	735	Broadcasting, pub.
Sammons (F)	735	(I)
Pulitzer (F)	725	Publishing (I)
Dolan, Charles	715	Cable TV
Pohlad, Carl Ray	710	Banking
Cook, William A.	700	Medical supplies
Cooke, Jack Kent	700	Real estate
Fisher, Donald	700	The Gap
Fisher, Doris F.	700	The Gap
Gore (F)	700	Gore-Tex
Huizenga, Harry	700	Blockbuster Ent.
Jamail, Joseph Jr.	700	Lawsuits
Kleberg (F)	700	(I)
Koch, William	700	Oil services (I)
Marcus, Bernard	700	Home Depot
Pamplin, Robert Jr.	700	Textiles
Rainwater, Richard	700	Investments
Rowling, Reese	700	Oil and gas
Stanley, John R.	700	Gas
Stuart (F)	700	Carnation (I)
Washington, Dennis	700	Mining
Broad, Eli	690	Home building
McGraw (F)	690	McGraw-Hill
Naify, Robert Allen	690	Movie theaters
Miner, Robert N.	685	Oracle
Haas, John C.	680	Rohm & Haas
Demoulas (F)	675	Supermarkets

(I) = inheritance; (F) = family

The Forbes 400 Wealthiest Ranking (cont'd)

Name	Worth ($ mil.)	Primary Sources
Fireman, Paul	670	Reebok
Lindner, Carl Jr.	660	Insurance
Terra, Daniel James	660	Lawter
Wilmot (F)	660	Shopping centers
Heinz, Teresa F.	655	H. J. Heinz (I)
Kohlberg, Jerome Jr.	650	LBOs
Moran, James	650	Toyota
Gates, Charles Jr.	645	Gates
Haas, Josephine B.	640	Levi Strauss
Johnson, Charles B.	640	Franklin Resources
Singleton, Henry Earl	630	Teledyne
Skaggs, Leonard Jr.	630	American Stores
McClatchy (F)	620	Newspapers
Spangler, Clemmie Jr.	615	Investments
McCaw, Bruce R.	610	McCaw Cellular
Allen, Herbert	600	Stock market
Allen, Herbert A.	600	Stock market
Barbey (F)	600	V. F. (I)
Bean (F)	600	L. L. Bean
Cafaro, William	600	Shopping malls
Cullen (F)	600	Oil
Durst (F)	600	Real estate
Edson, John Orin	600	Boats
Field, Frederick W.	600	Marshall Field (I)
Gerry, Alan	600	Cable TV
Goldman (F)	600	Real estate (I)
Holding, Robert Earl	600	Oil refining
Landegger (F)	600	Paper mills
May, Cordelia Scaife	600	(I)
O'Connor (F)	600	(I)
Peltz, Nelson	600	LBOs
Perdue, Franklin	600	Chickens
Rollins (F)	600	(I)
Sarofim, Fayez	600	Money manager
Spielberg, Steven	600	Movies
Stephens, Jackson	600	Investment banking
Taylor (F)	600	Publishing (I)
Waitt, Theodore W.	600	Gateway 2000
Whitney, Betsey	600	(I)
Wirtz (F)	600	Real estate
Yates (F)	600	Oil
Simmons, Harold	595	Investments
Bass, Edward Perry	590	Oil, investments
Harbert, John III	590	Construction
Lindemann, George	590	Cable, cellular
McCaw, Keith W.	590	McCaw Cellular
Ford, Josephine	585	Ford Motor (I)
Graham (F)	580	Washington Post
Krehbiel, John Jr.	580	Molex
Levine, Stuart	580	Cabletron Systems

Name	Worth ($ mil.)	Primary Sources
Simon, Melvin	580	Shopping centers
Copley, Helen	575	Publishing
Mitchell, George	575	Oil and gas
Watson (F)	575	Real estate
Gottwald (F)	570	Ethyl
Keinath, Pauline	570	Cargill
MacMillan, Cargill Jr.	570	Cargill
MacMillan, John III	570	Cargill
MacMillan, W.	570	Cargill
MacMillan, Whitney	570	Cargill
Pictet, Marion	570	Cargill
Rich, Robert Sr.	570	Food products
Malone, John C.	565	Cable TV
McCaw, John Jr.	560	McCaw Cellular
Smith, Charles (F)	560	Real estate
Nicholas, Peter M.	555	Medical devices
Anderson, John	550	Beverages
Earhart, Anne	550	Oil (I)
Getty, Caroline	550	Oil (I)
Kohler (F)	550	Plumbing fixtures
Litwin, Leonard	550	Real estate
Milliken, Roger	550	Textiles
Perry, Claire	550	Oil (I)
Schneider, Donald J.	550	Trucking
Abele, John E.	545	Medical devices
Kelly, William	545	Kelly Services
Berry, John Sr.	535	Yellow Pages
Getty, Eugene	530	Oil (I)
Ellis, Alpheus Lee	525	Banking
Close (F)	520	Textiles
Cowles (F)	520	Newspapers
Bennett, William	515	Circus Circus
Lewis, Peter	515	Progressive
Stempel, Ernest E.	515	American Int'l
Anderson (F)	500	Windows
Arrillaga, John	500	Real estate
Bloomberg, Michael	500	Financial News
Brittingham (F)	500	Dal-Tile Group
Davenport, Elizabeth	500	Coca-Cola
Fisher, Lawrence	500	Real estate
Fisher, Zachary	500	Real estate
Flagler (F)	500	Standard Oil (I)
Hollingsworth, John	500	Textile machinery
Huber (F)	500	J. M. Huber
Ilitch, Michael	500	Pizza
Johnson, Rupert Jr.	500	Franklin Resources
Kauffman, Muriel	500	(I)
Koch, Frederick	500	Oil services (I)
Lauren, Ralph	500	Apparel
Lupton, John	500	Coca-Cola Bottling

(I) = inheritance; (F) = family

The Forbes 400 Wealthiest Ranking (cont'd)

Name	Worth ($ mil.)	Primary Sources
Marshall, Barbara	500	Hallmark (I)
McGoven, Patrick	500	Publishing
Monaghan, Thomas	500	Domino's Pizza
Noorda, Raymond J.	500	Novell
O'Neill (F)	500	Real estate
Peery, Richard	500	Real estate
Pennington, Claude	500	Oil and gas
Reid, Elizabeth Ann	500	Hallmark (I)
Ward, Louis Larrick	500	Russell Stover
Ziff, Daniel Morton	500	Publishing (I)
Ziff, Dirk Edward	500	Publishing (I)
Ziff, Robert David	500	Publishing (I)
Benson, Craig Robert	490	Cabletron Systems
Haas, Walter A. Jr.	490	Levi Strauss
Ryan, Patrick George	490	Insurance
Schottenstein (F)	490	Discount chain
Breed, Allen Kent	485	Air bags
Haas, Peter E. Jr.	485	Levi Strauss
Milstein, Monroe	485	Burlington Coat
Swig (F)	485	Real estate
Alfond (F)	480	Shoes
Clark (F)	480	Singer
Pennington, William	480	Circus Circus
Wolfe (F)	480	Media
Krehbiel, Frederick	475	Molex
Bass, Perry	470	Oil, investments
Haas, Robert D.	470	Levi Strauss
Houghton (F)	470	Corning Glass
Sulzberger (F)	470	New York Times
Comer, Gary	460	Lands' End
Manoogian, Richard	460	Masco
Unanue (F)	460	Goya Foods
Bose, Amar G.	450	Loudspeakers
Boudjakdji, Millicent	450	Hearst (I)
Butt, Charles C.	450	Supermarkets
Cooke, Phoebe	450	Hearst (I)
Hearst, Austin	450	(I)
Hearst, David Jr.	450	(I)
Hearst, George Jr.	450	(I)
Hearst, William III	450	(I)
Hunt, Caroline	450	Oil (I)
Hyde, Joseph III	450	Auto parts
Jacobs, Jeremy	450	Sports concessions
Kovner, Bruce	450	Trading
Milken, Michael	450	Junk bonds
Pew (F)	450	Sun Oil (I)
Reinhart, Dewayne	450	Wholesale foods
Rosenwald (F)	450	Sears, Roebuck (I)
Stryker (F)	450	Stryker (I)
Ueltschi, Albert	450	FlightSafety

Name	Worth ($ mil.)	Primary Sources
Wasserman, Lewis	450	MCA
Marshall, James II	445	Oil
Ashton, Alan C.	440	WordPerfect
Bastian, Bruce W.	440	WordPerfect
de Menil (F)	440	Schlumberger (I)
du Pont, Alexis Jr.	440	Du Pont (I)
Kelley (F)	440	Hotels
Marriott, Richard	440	Hotels
Mills, Alice du Pont	440	Du Pont (I)
Farmer, Richard T.	435	Cintas
Block (F)	430	Block Drug
Posner, Victor	425	Investments
Sommer, Viola	425	Real estate (I)
Disney (F)	420	(I)
Disney, Roy	420	Dillion, Read (I)
Goldman, Rhoda	420	Levi Strauss
Lee, Thomas	420	LBOs
Mandel, Morton L.	420	Premier Industrial
Sandler (F)	420	Banking
Coulter, Wallace	415	Medical technology
Frost, Phillip	415	Medicine
Marriott, John Jr.	415	Hotels
Schwab, Charles R.	415	Charles Schwab
Mandel, Jack N.	410	Premier Industrial
Waitt, Norman W.	410	Gateway 2000
Carver, Lucille	405	Bandag (I)
Dell, Michael	405	Dell Computer
Taubman, A. Alfred	405	Shopping centers
Bredin, Octavia	400	Du Pont (I)
Carter (F)	400	Direct selling
Connell, Grover	400	Equipment leasing
Coors (F)	400	Beer
Coulter, Joseph	400	Medical technology
Darden, Constance	400	Du Pont (I)
du Pont, Irénée Jr.	400	Du Pont (I)
Engelhard, Jane	400	(I)
Engelstad, Ralph	400	Casino
Farish (F)	400	Standard Oil (I)
Fisher, Max Martin	400	Oil
Flint, Lucile du Pont	400	Du Pont (I)
Glazer, Guilford	400	Real estate
Herb, Marvin	400	Bottling
Hobby, Oveta Culp	400	Media
Huffington (F)	400	Oil
Icahn, Carl Celian	400	Financier
Kaiser, George B.	400	Oil and gas
Mandel, Joseph C.	400	Premier Industrial
Mathile, Clayton	400	Pet food
May, Irene	400	Du Pont (I)
Menard, John R. Jr.	400	Home improve.

(I) = inheritance; (F) = family

The Forbes 400 Wealthiest Ranking (cont'd)

Name	Worth ($ mil.)	Primary Sources
Naify, Marshall	400	Movie theaters
Perenchio, Andrew	400	Television
Shorenstein, Walter	400	Real estate
Solheim, Karsten	400	Golf clubs
Solomon, Russell	400	Tower Records
Stowers, James Jr.	400	Mutual funds
Cook, Jane Bancroft	395	Dow Jones (I)
Smith, Frederick	395	Federal Express
Strawbridge, George Jr.	395	Campbell Soup (I)
Brennan, Bernard F.	390	Montgomery Ward
Kimmel, Sidney	390	Jones Apparel
Norris, Diana	390	Campbell Soup (I)
Dixon, Fitz Eugene Jr.	385	(I)
Hardie, Mary Jane	385	Publishing
Hoiles, Harry	385	Publishing
Keck, Howard	385	Superior Oil (I)
Murphy, Charles Jr.	385	Murphy Oil
Robinson, Jesse	385	Banking
Blank, Arthur	380	Home Depot
Jacobs, Richard E.	380	Shopping centers
Munger, Charles	380	Berkshire Hathaway
Binger, Virginia	375	3M (I)
Block, Henry W.	375	H&R Block
Day, Robert Jr.	375	Money management
Marks, Nancy	375	Harcourt General
Petersen, Robert	375	Publishing
Smith, Richard	375	Harcourt General
Weis, Sigfried	375	Weis Markets
McEvoy, Nan Tucker	370	Publishing
Dyson, Charles	360	Conglomerator
Goizueta, Roberto	360	Coca-Cola
Littlefield, Edmund	360	Utah International
Milken, Lowell Jay	360	Junk bonds
Teel, Joyce Raley	360	Supermarkets
Getty, Mark	355	Oil (I)
Getty, Tara	355	Oil (I)
Heyman, Samuel J.	355	GAF
Williams, Ariadne	355	Oil (I)
Ackerman, Peter	350	Junk bonds
Clayton, James	350	Mobile homes
Cohn, Seymour	350	Real estate
du Pont, Willis	350	Du Pont (I)
Feld, Kenneth	350	Circus
Kennedy (F)	350	(I)
Pearson, Edith	350	Du Pont (I)
Roberts, Ralph J.	350	Comcast
Sakioka, Katsumasa	350	Real estate
Scharbauer, Clarence Jr.	350	Oil, land (I)
Smith, Athalie	350	(I)
Taper, Sydney	350	First Charter

Name	Worth ($ mil.)	Primary Sources
Hilton, William	345	Hilton Hotels
Pasculano, Lynne	345	UIS
Saul, B. Francis II	345	(I)
Simon, Herbert	345	Shopping centers
Udvar-Hazy, Steven	345	International leases
Abraham, S. Daniel	340	Slim-Fast Foods
Autry, Orvon Gene	340	Broadcasting
Behring, Kenneth	340	Real estate
Egan, Richard J.	340	EMC
Eisner, Michael D.	340	The Walt Disney Co.
Gonda, Leslie & Louis	340	International leases
Grainger, David	340	Electrical equipment
Jones, Glenn	340	Cable TV
Primm, Gary	340	Casinos
Hunt, Johnnie	335	Trucking
Kamins, Philip	335	Plastics, chemicals
Lyon, Frank Jr.	335	Bottling
McGlothlin, James	335	Coal
Speer, Roy M.	335	Home shopping
Brown, Jack	330	Oil
Daniels, Robert Jr.	330	Cable TV
Dart, Robert & William	330	Dart Container
Hascoe, Norman	330	Semiconductors
Marion, Anne	330	(I)
McLane, Robert Jr.	330	Grocery distribution
Moncrief, William Jr.	330	Oil and gas
Riggio, Leonard	330	Bookstores
Solow, Sheldon	330	Real estate
Wagner, Cyril Jr.	330	Oil
Wexner, Bella	330	The Limited
Boyd, William	325	Casinos
Cosby, William Jr.	325	Entertainment
Ebrahimi, Farhad	325	Quark
Gallo, Ernest	325	Wine
Gill, Timothy E.	325	Quark
Howard, Robert	325	Publishing
Sharp, Bayard & Hugh	325	Du Pont (I)
Simmons, Richard	325	Allegheny Ludlum
Spanos, Alexander	325	Construction
Steinberg, Saul	325	Financier
Weis, Robert	325	Weis Markets
Franchetti, Anne	320	Textiles
Jones, Jerral Wayne	320	Oil and gas
Milliken, Gerrish	320	Textiles
Guccione, Robert	315	Publishing
Stein, Jay	315	Stein Mart
Bass, Anne	310	Divorce
Butler, Sarah	310	Coca-Cola stock (I)
Corn, Elizabeth	310	Coca-Cola stock (I)
Egan, Michael S.	310	Rental cars

The Forbes 400 Wealthiest Ranking (cont'd)

Name	Worth ($ mil.)	Primary Sources
Geballe, Frances K.	310	Levi Strauss
Koshland, Daniel Jr.	310	Levi Strauss
Levy, Leon	310	Money manager
Rinker, Marshall Sr.	310	Concrete
Spelling, Aaron	310	TV
Turner, William B.	310	Coca-Cola stock (I)
Thorne, Oakleigh	305	Commerce Clearing
Ansin, Edmund	300	TV stations
Block, William	300	Media
Cantor, Barnard	300	Bond trading

Name	Worth ($ mil.)	Primary Sources
Hillblom, Larry L.	300	DHL
Maglica, Anthony	285	Flashlights
Penske, Roger	285	Cars and engines

Source: Forbes Magazine, Oct. 17, 1994, © Forbes, Inc.
Reprinted with permission

(I) = inheritance; (F) = family

*Note: Due to multiple entries, rankings have been omitted and more than 400 names appear.

Business Plan Outline

THE BUSINESS PLAN IS a critical element in planning, growing, and financing a business. Here is a sample outline created by Jan W. Zupnick, president of the Entrepreneurship Institute:

I. Overview
  A. Summary of Fundamental Elements upon Which the Venture Is Built
  B. Background and Critical Success Factors
    1. Introduction
      a. Purpose
      b. History of company
      c. General description of products or services
      d. Benefits
      e. Objectives
      f. Critical success factors
    2. Business Environment
      a. Industry description
      b. Regulatory climate
      c. Market description
      d. Competition
      e. Barriers to achieving objectives
    3. Alternatives (existing businesses)
      a. Business as usual
      b. Growth through expansion
      c. Growth through merger, acquisition, etc.
      d. Contraction
      e. Sell out
    4. Risks and Opportunities
      a. Strengths
      b. Weaknesses
  C. Description of Products and Services
    1. Description of Each Product or Service
    2. Uniqueness and Special Aspects
      a. Features, advantages, benefits
      b. Strengths and weaknesses
      c. Patents, licenses, royalties

    3. Anticipated Changes (existing businesses)
      a. Planned products and services
      b. Discontinued products and services
      c. Life cycles
      d. Environment
    4. Product Strategy
      a. Buy for resale
      b. Make
        – R & D
        – Engineering
      c. Unique or similar
      d. Narrow or broad market
      e. Quality
II. Marketing
  A. Critical Success Factors
  B. Strategy
  C. Market Analysis
    1. Economic Environment
    2. Industry Environment
    3. Customer Base
    4. Market Size, Geography
    5. Market Share
    6. Market Segment and Target Market
    7. Market Needs Analysis
    8. Market Opportunity Trend Analysis
    9. Technological Trends
    10. Growth Trends
    11. Government Regulations
  D. Competition
  E. Sales Tactics
  F. Pricing
  G. Promotion
  H. Packaging
    1. Physical Package for Products
    2. Product and Service Philosophy (Maintenance)
    3. Product or System Philosophy

Business Plan Outline (cont'd)

III. Management and Operational Plan
  A. Management Team
    1. Organization Chart
    2. Key Management Personnel Descriptions
    3. Management Compensation & Ownership
    4. Board of Directors
    5. Supporting Professional Services
  B. Human Resources
    1. Number
    2. Recruitment
    3. Selection
    4. Skills
    5. Training
  C. Facilities and Equipment
    1. Plant, Offices, Warehouse
    2. Capacity, Percent Utilized
    3. Location
    4. Strategy & Plans
    5. Equipment
      a. Production tools and machinery
      b. Inspection equipment
      c. Vendor quality assurance inspection
IV. Financial Plan
  A. Financial Situation
    1. Financial History Highlights
    2. Present Financial Condition
    3. Credit Arrangements and Sources
    4. Revenue Projections
    5. Ratios and Comparative Analyses
      a. Internal ratio analysis
      b. External ratio analysis
      c. Budget analysis
    6. Contingent Liabilities
    7. Insurance

    8. Tax Considerations
    9. Review and Control
  B. Financing Requirements
    1. Equity Policy Statement
    2. Capital Requirements
      a. Amount
      b. Purpose
    3. Funding Sources
      a. Internal
      b. External
      c. List of potential sources
    4. Financing Proposal
V. Appendices
  A. Schedule of Major Events
  B. Personnel Resources, Key-Person Resumes
  C. Facilities and Equipment Data
  D. Financial History
  E. Revenue Forecast
  F. Product or Service Cost Analysis
  G. Expense Budgets
  H. Income Statement Projection
  I. Cash Flow Projection
  J. Balance Sheet Projection
  K. Financial Ratios
  L. Collateral
  M. Organization Chart
  N. Major Customers
  O. Principal Suppliers
  P. Insurance Coverages
  Q. Formats
  R. Other Supporting Documents and Data

Source: © The Entrepreneurship Institute

The Top Reference Sources

Corporate 500: The Directory of Corporate Philanthropy
Gale Research, $375.00
(800) 877-4253

Compiled by the research staff of the Public Management Institute, this reference is a good source of factual information on the funding programs of the 500 American corporations with the most active philanthropic programs.

Entries include the address and phone number of each corporation, plus contact person, eligibility, number of grants made, application process, sample grants, and more.

Business Failures

Number of Business Failures by Industry

Industry	1987	1989	1990	1991	1992	1993*
TOTAL	61,111	50,361	60,432	81,672	97,069	85,982
Agriculture, forestry, fishing	3,766	1,540	1,727	2,256	2,871	2,282
Mining	627	351	381	411	430	307
Construction	6,735	7,120	8,072	11,963	12,452	10,496
Manufacturing	4,273	3,933	4,709	6,595	7,120	6,142
Food and kindred products	191	216	226	305	350	299
Textile mill products	73	75	101	143	171	148
Apparel, other textile products	265	204	318	505	566	566
Lumber and wood products	374	368	417	576	554	437
Furniture and fixtures	200	253	257	383	398	303
Paper and allied products	60	46	66	86	88	85
Printing and publishing	633	679	728	1,062	1,245	1,054
Chemicals and allied products	116	102	134	207	219	171
Petroleum refining	21	21	21	33	35	17
Primary metal products	107	71	114	145	141	97
Transportation equipment	175	190	240	318	263	229
Instruments and related products	112	108	119	192	175	153
Miscellaneous	241	206	269	375	446	413
Transportation, public utilities	2,236	2,115	2,610	3,891	3,922	3,089
Wholesale trade	4,336	3,687	4,376	6,170	6,744	5,975
Retail trade	12,240	11,120	12,826	17,242	19,084	15,600
Finance, insurance, real estate	2,550	2,932	3,881	5,962	6,260	4,923
Services	23,802	13,679	17,673	22,852	26,871	24,311

* preliminary   *Source: Business Failure Record, Dun and Bradstreet*

The Top Reference Sources

Corporate Meeting Planners
Reed Publishing, $345
(908) 464-6800

This directory of corporate meeting planners lists approximately 18,090 meeting planners, together with their titles, for over 11,686 top companies in the U.S. Also included are the complete address, telephone number, and type of business for each firm.

Listings also include the number of meetings held during the calendar year, the months and seasons these meetings are held, the number of days, the number of attendees, and the location.

Causes of Business Failures. Send e-mail to failures@almanac.yoyo.com. See p. xi for instructions.

Seven primary reasons for business failure and incidence of failure in nine sectors of business.

50 Largest Companies Worldwide

Rank	Company	Country	Sales ($ millions)	Profits ($ millions)	No. of Employees
1	General Motors	U.S.	133,621.9	2,465.8	710,800
2	Ford Motor	U.S.	108,521.0	2,529.0	322,200
3	Exxon	U.S.	97,825.0	5,280.0	91,000
4	Royal Dutch/Shell Group	Brit./Neth.	94,134.4	4,505.2	117,000
5	Toyota Motor	Japan	85,283.2	1,473.9	109,279
6	Hitachi	Japan	68,581.8	605.0	330,637
7	IBM	U.S.	67,716.0	-8,101.0	267,196
8	Matsushita Electric Industrial	Japan	61,384.5	227.0	254,059
9	General Electric	U.S.	60,823.0	4,315.0	222,000
10	Daimler-Benz	Germany	59,102.0	364.0	366,736
11	Mobil	U.S.	56,576.0	2,084.0	61,900
12	Nissan Motor	Japan	53,759.8	-805.5	143,310
13	British Petroleum	Britain	52,485.4	923.6	72,600
14	Samsung	South Korea	51,345.2	519.7	191,303
15	Philip Morris	U.S.	50,621.0	3,091.0	173,000
16	IRI	Italy	50,488.1	NA	366,471
17	Siemens	Germany	50,381.3	1,112.6	391,000
18	Volkswagen	Germany	46,311.9	-1,232.4	251,643
19	Chrysler	U.S.	43,600.0	-2,551.0	128,000
20	Toshiba	Japan	42,917.2	112.5	175,000
21	Unilever	Brit./Neth.	41,842.6	1,946.2	302,000
22	Nestle	Switzerland	38,894.5	1,953.3	209,755
23	Elf Aquitane	France	37,016.3	188.9	94,000
24	Honda Motor	Japan	35,797.9	219.6	91,300
25	ENI	Italy	34,791.3	266.6	106,391
26	Fiat	Italy	34,706.7	1,134.3	260,351
27	Sony	Japan	34,602.5	141.8	130,000
28	Texaco	U.S.	34,359.0	1,068.0	32,514
29	NEC	Japan	33,175.9	61.2	147,910
30	E. I. du Pont de Nemours	U.S.	32,621.0	555.0	114,000
31	Chevron	U.S.	32,123.0	1,265.0	47,576
32	Philips Electronics	Netherlands	31,665.5	1,057.8	238,500
33	Daewoo	South Korea	30,893.4	482.6	76,986
34	Procter & Gamble	U.S.	30,433.0	-656.0	103,500
35	Renault	France	29,974.8	189.1	139,733
36	Fujitsu	Japan	29,093.9	-349.1	163,990
37	Mitsubishi Electric	Japan	28,779.8	191.8	111,053
38	ABB Asea Brown Boveri	Switzerland	28,315.0	68.0	206,490
39	Hoechst	Germany	27,844.8	281.8	170,161
40	Alcatel Alsthom	France	27,599.4	1,246.7	196,500
41	Mitsubishi Motors	Japan	27,310.9	51.8	46,000
42	PEMEX (Petroleos Mexicanos)	Mexico	26,572.9	970.8	106,951
43	Mitsubishi Heavy Industries	Japan	25,804.0	740.1	68,057
44	Peugeot	France	25,669.1	-249.5	143,700
45	Nippon Steel	Japan	25,480.5	-501.3	50,458
46	Amoco	U.S.	25,336.0	1,820.0	46,317
47	Boeing	U.S.	25,285.0	1,244.0	134,400
48	PepsiCo	U.S.	25,020.7	1,587.9	423,000
49	Bayer	Germany	24,797.1	802.4	151,900
50	BASF	Germany	24,531.9	518.7	112,020

50 Largest Companies Worldwide (cont'd)

Largest Companies in the World by Industry

Industry	Company	Country	Sales ($ millions)
Aerospace	Boeing	U.S.	25,285
Apparel	Levi Strauss	U.S.	5,892
Beverages	PepsiCo	U.S.	25,021
Building materials, glass	Saint-Gobain	France	12,630
Chemicals	Du Pont	U.S.	32,621
Computers, office equipment	IBM	U.S.	62,716
Electronics, electrical equipment	Hitachi	Japan	68,582
Food	Philip Morris	U.S.	50,621
Forest and paper products	International Paper	U.S.	13,685
Industrial and farm equipment	Mitsubishi Heavy Industries	Japan	25,804
Jewelry, silverware	Citizen Watch	Japan	3,501
Metal products	Pechiney	France	11,127
Metals	IRI	Italy	50,488
Mining, crude-oil production	Ruhrkohle	Germany	14,155
Motor vehicles and parts	General Motors	U.S.	133,622
Petroleum refining	Exxon	U.S.	97,825
Pharmaceuticals	Johnson & Johnson	U.S.	14,138
Publishing, printing	Bertelsmann	Germany	10,957
Rubber and plastic products	Bridgestone	Japan	14,377
Scientific, photog., control equipment	Eastman Kodak	U.S.	20,059
Soaps, cosmetics	Procter & Gamble	U.S.	30,433
Textiles	Toray Industries	Japan	8,193
Tobacco	RJR Nabisco Holdings	U.S.	15,104
Toys, sporting goods	Nintendo	Japan	4,500
Transportation equipment	Hyundai Heavy Industries	South Korea	6,735

Source: Fortune, July 25, 1994, "The Global 500," © *1994 Time, Inc. All rights reserved*

Worldwide Taxes

Range of Personal Tax Brackets in the Seven Industrialized Nations (%)

Country	Lowest	Highest
Canada	17	29
France	5	57
Germany	17	55
Italy	10	50
Japan	10	50
United Kingdom	25	40
United States	15	31

Percent of GDP Collected as National Taxes

Country	Percentage
France	44.2
Italy	39.7
Germany	39.2
Canada	37.3
United Kingdom	36.0
Japan	30.9
United States	29.8

Source: "OECD in Figures," 1994 Edition, supplement to
The OECD Observer, No. 188, June/July 1994

Balance of Trade with the World

National Trade Balances, 1992

Country	Goods and Services, Imports ($ bil.)	Goods and Services, Exports ($ bil.)
Australia	53.6	52.9
Austria	70.9	73.3
Belgium	146.6	153.5
Canada	153.7	150.5
Denmark	41.9	52.7
Finland	27.3	28.6
France	288.3	304.3
Germany	474.0	598.6
Greece	25.7	18.0
Iceland	2.1	2.1
Ireland	25.4	31.3
Italy	240.9	243.3

Country	Goods and Services, Imports ($ bil.)	Goods and Services, Exports ($ bil.)
Japan	285.4	374.3
Luxembourg	9.8	9.4
Netherlands	153.1	167.4
New Zealand	12.2	12.7
Norway	40.5	48.8
Portugal	32.6	24.5
Spain	117.5	101.2
Sweden	64.7	68.9
Switzerland	78.4	86.9
Turkey	24.6	23.4
United Kingdom	263.2	246.8
United States	668.9	627.6

Source: "OECD in Figures," 1994 Edition, supplement to the OECD Observer, No. 188, June/July 1994

U.S. Merchandise Trade ($ billions)

Commodities	Exports	Imports	Balance
TOTAL TRADE			
1990 annual	393.6	495.3	-101.7
1991 annual	421.9	488.1	-66.2
1992 annual	448.2	532.7	-84.5
1993			
First Quarter	453.3	557.4	-104.1
Second Quarter	460.2	582.7	-122.5
Third Quarter	456.5	573.9	-117.3
MANUFACTURES TRADE			
1990 annual	315.4	388.8	-73.5
1991 annual	345.4	393.1	-47.7
1992 annual	368.6	434.3	-65.7
1993			
First Quarter	376.9	739.3	-62.4
Second Quarter	395.9	473.4	-77.5
Third Quarter	370.1	491.0	-120.9
AGRICULTURAL TRADE			
1990 annual	39.6	22.3	17.3
1991 annual	39.3	22.2	17.1
1992 annual	43.1	23.4	19.7
1993			
First Quarter	45.7	24.5	21.2
Second Quarter	40.7	23.9	16.8
Third Quarter	37.0	22.1	14.9

Source: U.S. Department of Commerce, International Trade Administration

Balance of Trade with the World (cont'd)

U.S Merchandise Trade with Japan ($ billions)

Commodities	Exports	Imports	Balance
Total merchandise trade			
1991	48.1	91.6	-43.5
1992	47.8	97.2	-49.4
Food and beverages			
1991	8.6	0.3	8.3
1992	8.2	0.3	7.9
Capital goods			
1991	15.1	36.1	-21.0
1992	15.1	39.3	-24.2
Automobile vehicles and parts			
1991	1.5	32.8	-31.3
1992	1.8	33.5	-31.7
Consumer goods			
1991	6.1	12.5	-6.4
1992	5.9	13.1	-7.2
Industrial supplies			
1991	15.3	8.5	6.8
1992	13.4	9.3	4.1
Other products			
1991	1.9	1.3	0.6
1992	1.9	1.7	0.2

Source: U.S. Department of Commerce, International Trade Administration

The Top Reference Sources

Co-op Source Directory
National Register Publishing, $399
(800) 323-6772

The *Co-op Source Directory* provides a comprehensive quick reference guide to manufacturers' cooperative advertising programs. It is divided into 52 product classifications under which co-op summaries appear alphabetically by manufacturer.

The summaries are detailed and include eligible media, regional variations, reimbursement methods, accrual, timing, international availability, media requirements, advertising aids, etc.

America Online's Business News area features up-to-the-minute reports on the business world, including U.S. business, world business, news by industry, and market indicators and indexes. KEYWORD NEWS.

Balance of Trade with the World (cont'd)

Composition of U.S. Merchandise Trade ($ billions, annual rates)

Commodities	Exports	Imports	Balance
CAPITAL GOODS			
1990 annual	152.7	116.4	36.3
1991 annual	166.8	121.4	45.4
1992 annual	176.7	134.2	42.5
1993			
First Quarter	177.2	143.1	34.1
Second Quarter	183.0	151.3	31.7
Third Quarter	178.6	153.2	25.4
CONSUMER GOODS			
1990 annual	43.3	105.7	-62.4
1991 annual	46.2	107.9	-61.7
1992 annual	50.4	123.0	-72.6
1993			
First Quarter	51.4	128.4	-77.0
Second Quarter	52.1	132.3	-80.2
Third Quarter	54.2	137.8	-83.6
AUTOMOTIVE VEHICLES AND PARTS			
1990 annual	37.4	87.3	-49.9
1991 annual	40.2	85.3	-45.1
1992 annual	47.1	91.8	-44.7
1993			
First Quarter	51.4	100.4	-49.0
Second Quarter	51.3	102.1	-50.8
Third Quarter	48.4	100.1	-51.7
FOOD AND BEVERAGES			
1990 annual	35.1	26.7	8.4
1991 annual	36.3	26.5	9.8
1992 annual	40.2	27.9	12.3
1993			
First Quarter	40.8	27.4	13.4
Second Quarter	39.5	27.5	12.0
Third Quarter	38.8	28.4	10.4
PETROLEUM AND PRODUCTS			
1990 annual	7.7	62.2	-54.5
1991 annual	7.6	51.5	-43.9
1992 annual	6.9	51.5	-44.6
1993			
First Quarter	6.6	51.1	-44.5
Second Quarter	7.2	57.3	-50.1
Third Quarter	6.1	50.4	-44.3
OTHER INDUSTRIAL SUPPLIES			
1990 annual	96.8	81.0	15.8
1991 annual	101.6	80.1	21.5
1992 annual	102.4	86.8	15.6
1993			
First Quarter	102.8	90.0	12.8
Second Quarter	103.3	93.3	10.0
Third Quarter	105.5	93.9	11.6

Source: U.S. Department of Commerce, International Trade Administration

Balance of Trade with the World (cont'd)

U.S. Merchandise Trade by Area ($ billions, annual rates)

Area	Exports	Imports	Balance
WESTERN EUROPE			
1990 annual	113.1	109.0	4.1
1991 annual	118.7	102.6	16.1
1992 annual	117.1	110.7	6.4
1993			
First Quarter	121.0	106.7	14.3
Second Quarter	112.2	115.9	-3.7
Third Quarter	101.7	113.6	-11.9
JAPAN			
1990 annual	48.6	89.7	-41.1
1991 annual	48.1	91.6	-43.4
1992 annual	47.8	97.4	-49.6
1993			
First Quarter	48.0	101.0	-53.0
Second Quarter	48.2	102.5	-54.3
Third Quarter	47.5	108.8	-61.3
CANADA			
1990 annual	83.7	91.4	-7.7
1991 annual	85.1	91.1	-6.0
1992 annual	90.6	98.6	-8.0
1993			
First Quarter	95.6	102.9	-7.3
Second Quarter	106.2	117.3	-11.1
Third Quarter	95.5	104.9	-9.4
OPEC			
1990 annual	13.7	38.1	-24.4
1991 annual	19.1	33.0	-13.9
1992 annual	22.0	33.2	-11.2
1993			
First Quarter	20.7	31.8	-11.1
Second Quarter	19.0	34.4	-15.4
Third Quarter	16.7	31.1	-14.4
OTHER DEVELOPING COUNTRIES			
1990 annual	113.6	142.4	-28.8
1991 annual	127.7	142.1	-14.4
1992 annual	145.1	158.3	-13.2
1993			
First Quarter	148.5	159.1	-10.6
Second Quarter	157.4	169.2	-11.8
Third Quarter	152.7	182.3	-29.6
EASTERN EUROPE/FORMER U.S.S.R./COMMUNIST ASIA			
1990 annual	9.0	17.4	-8.4
1991 annual	11.1	20.8	-9.7
1992 annual	13.0	27.7	-14.7
1993			
First Quarter	12.3	26.9	-14.6
Second Quarter	15.3	33.0	-17.7
Third Quarter	14.5	41.6	-27.1

Source: U.S. Department of Commerce, International Trade Administration

World Unemployment

World Unemployment Rates (%, 1992 and 1982)

Country	1992 Both Sexes	1982 Both Sexes	1992 Women	1982 Women	1992 Men	1982 Men	1992, 12 or More Months Unemployed	1982, 12 or More Months Unemployed
Australia	10.8	6.7	10.0	7.5	11.3	6.2	34.6	19.0
Austria	3.6	3.5	3.8	4.8	3.5	2.8	NA	NA
Belgium	9.3	11.9	13.2	17.0	6.5	8.7	61.6	66.3
Canada	11.2	10.9	10.4	10.9	11.9	10.9	13.1	5.4
Denmark	9.1	11.0	10.0	11.2	8.3	10.7	31.2	33.0
Finland	13.0	5.3	10.5	5.2	15.1	5.4	9.1	22.3
France	10.2	8.1	12.7	11.2	8.2	6.0	36.1	42.1
Germany	5.8	6.4	6.4	7.3	5.4	5.9	45.5	39.3
Greece	7.0	5.8	11.7	8.0	4.3	4.7	47.0	35.0
Iceland	2.1	0.7	1.5	NA	2.6	NA	NA	NA
Ireland	15.7	11.4	12.1	9.7	17.3	12.1	60.3	36.9
Italy	11.4	8.4	17.2	13.9	7.9	5.6	67.1	57.7
Japan	2.1	2.4	2.0	2.3	2.2	2.4	15.3	14.8
Luxembourg	1.2	1.2	2.0	1.7	1.1	1.0	NA	NA
Netherlands	7.0	11.3	9.5	11.3	5.3	11.4	43.0	50.5
New Zealand	10.3	3.5	9.5	4.6	11.0	3.0	31.9	7.0
Norway	5.9	2.6	5.2	3.0	6.5	2.3	22.6	2.0
Portugal	4.1	7.3	4.9	12.1	3.5	4.0	38.3	56.0
Spain	18.1	15.6	25.3	18.5	14.0	14.4	47.4	48.5
Sweden	5.3	3.1	4.1	3.4	6.3	2.9	8.1	8.4
Switzerland	2.6	0.4	2.7	0.5	2.5	0.4	NA	NA
Turkey	7.7	6.8	7.4	NA	7.8	NA	NA	NA
United Kingdom	9.5	10.4	5.1	7.0	12.9	12.6	28.1	47.0
United States	7.3	9.5	6.9	9.4	7.6	9.6	11.2	7.7

Source: "OECD in Figures," 1994 Edition, supplement to The OECD Observer, No. 188, June/July 1994

The Top Reference Sources

Statistical Forecasts of the United States
Gale Research, 1993, $95.00
(800) 877-4253

This reference covers population, employment, labor, crime, education, health care, and other key areas. Statistics are compiled from a diverse range of sources, and data are presented in hundreds of charts, graphs, tables, and other statistical illustrations portraying both long- and short-term forecasts of future developments in the United States.

TIP: *The 1994 Statistical Abstract of the United States is now available on CD-ROM for $50 from the Bureau of the Census, U.S. Department of Commerce. To order, call Customer Services at (301) 457-4100.*

Vacancy Rates and Rental Costs

City	Total Office Inventory Surveyed	Office Occupancy Rate (%)	Rental Range ($ per sq. ft.)
Akron	1,519,605	13.5	11.50-18.50
Albuquerque Downtown	3,082,923	18.2	12.00-17.50
Albuquerque Suburban	7,481,302	7.8	11.25-17.50
Anchorage	6,423,636	6.9	15.60-20.40
Atlanta Downtown	15,464,366	21.4	11.20-18.51
Atlanta Suburban	71,275,879	11.8	13.08-19.59
Baltimore Downtown	13,892,017	18.1	13.00-18.00
Baltimore Suburban	22,510,174	13.4	15.00-18.00
Birmingham Downtown	5,362,185	19.2	6.00-19.00
Birmingham Suburban	9,780,869	9.4	7.50-17.00
Boise Downtown	1,386,878	4.9	14.92
Boise Suburban	3,882,789	6.6	12.42
Boston City	58,369,052	12.9	6.68-27.22
Boston Suburban	80,110,948	15.1	11.77-18.25
Buffalo	7,548,339	19.2	8.00-24.00
Calgary	31,492,505	13.0	6.00-18.00
Charlotte Downtown	9,574,914	7.5	11.07-20.40
Charlotte Suburban	11,764,774	14.6	10.22-16.60
Chicago Downtown	100,098,172	23.2	NA
Chicago Suburban	104,381,283	19.5	NA
Cincinnati Downtown	13,805,104	14.8	19.01
Cincinnati Suburban	8,088,254	16.2	13.25
Cleveland	16,983,367	21.2	20.35
Columbus Downtown	8,533,613	12.0	8.50-20.00
Columbus Suburban	15,234,612	11.6	NA
Dallas Downtown	31,934,169	32.3	9.80-15.70
Dallas Suburban	87,664,321	18.4	10.92-15.52
Denver Downtown	23,320,575	12.5	8.97-15.76
Denver Suburban	45,277,669	12.9	9.65-14.94
Detroit Downtown	13,118,019	21.0	10.00-19.97
Detroit Suburban	35,450,160	17.6	10.00-19.97
Fairfield County, CT - Stamford	13,869,000	18.3	15.69-20.85
Fairfield County, CT - Suburban	23,270,000	16.9	13.53-24.72
Fort Worth Downtown	7,964,657	20.8	9.50-15.34
Fort Worth Suburban	13,863,313	19.8	10.10-12.49
Hartford Downtown	11,161,786	24.1	17.76-20.71
Hartford Suburban	12,868,642	20.8	13.00-16.81
Houston Downtown	41,094,590	25.7	9.54-14.73
Houston Suburban	177,018,719	20.8	9.62-14.48
Indianapolis Downtown	9,329,743	22.4	10.00-22.00
Indianapolis Suburban	11,413,563	15.7	9.00-20.00
Kansas City, MO/KS - Downtown	12,330,712	16.1	10.00-20.00
Kansas City, MO/KS - Suburban	21,883,804	9.5	10.00-20.00
Knoxville Downtown	4,499,428	8.8	9.68
Knoxville Suburban	5,985,912	9.7	10.21
Los Angeles Downtown	48,244,499	22.9	15.72
Los Angeles Suburban	111,188,146	18.6	17.88
Memphis Downtown	7,081,000	24.4	8.80-15.74
Memphis Suburban	12,717,000	12.2	7.62-14.68
Miami Downtown	12,008,289	25.6	14.00-24.00

Vacancy Rates and Rental Costs (cont'd)

City	Total Office Inventory Surveyed	Office Occupancy Rate (%)	Rental Range ($ per sq. ft.)
Miami Suburban	19,440,696	12.0	12.00-19.50
Milwaukee Downtown	11,648,800	19.9	NA
Milwaukee Suburban	10,473,301	9.6	NA
Minneapolis Downtown	21,338,017	12.9	10.29-20.09
Minneapolis Suburban	18,546,141	10.3	15.00-19.88
Norfolk Downtown	3,452,475	26.1	8.50-15.64
Norfolk/Hampton Roads	12,318,529	13.3	8.50-13.75
Orange County, CA–Airport Area	24,492,967	18.2	19.08
Orange County, CA–Suburban	27,094,656	21.2	17.03
Orlando Downtown	5,540,229	11.4	17.93
Orlando Suburban	16,493,196	12.4	14.19
Philadelphia Downtown	34,219,908	17.3	16.50-20.50
Philadelphia Suburban	36,232,985	17.7	16.00-18.00
Phoenix Downtown	20,133,557	18.0	11.08-15.69
Phoenix Suburban	21,504,136	14.1	10.03-14.87
Pittsburgh Downtown	18,728,031	14.5	12.51-21.75
Pittsburgh Suburban	11,563,892	10.9	NA
Portland Downtown	13,706,037	10.1	10.98-18.39
Portland Suburban	6,053,299	7.3	NA

Source: 1994 North American Office Market Review, BOMA

Contact Options

Building Owners and Managers Assn. (BOMA)
1201 New York Ave., NW, Suite 300
Washington, DC 20005
(202) 408-2662

Society for Industrial and Office Realtors
700 11th St., NW, Suite 510
Washington, DC 20001
(202) 737-1150

Recommended Resource

ULI Market Profiles: 1994
Urban Land Institute, $329.95/2 volumes
Washington, DC 20005
(800) 321-5011
　　Urban Land Institute economic report on 35 major locations plus 13 international markets for real estate development in residential, retail, hotel, office, and industrial sectors.

The Top Reference Sources

Comparative Statistics of Industrial and Office Real Estate Markets, 1994
Society of Industrial and Office Realtors, $70
(202) 737-1150

This publication includes a detailed review and forecast of both industrial and office real estate markets, as well as an analysis of economic trends and their effect on industrial and office markets.
　　The book is compiled by a select group of SIOR members in major metropolitan areas in the U.S., Canada, and abroad. The book includes many charts and graphs.

Construction Starts

Housing Starts (thousands of units)

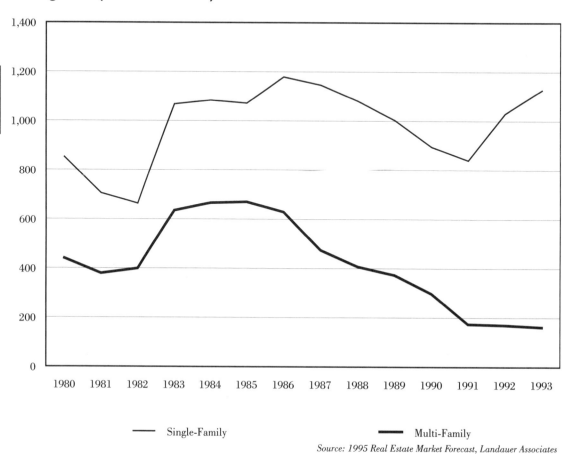

Source: 1995 Real Estate Market Forecast, Landauer Associates

---

The Top Reference Sources

Construction Review
U.S. Government Printing Office, $17/year
(202) 512-1800

This quarterly publication of the International Trade Administration canvasses the major construction series published by the Census Bureau and Bureau of Labor Statistics. It includes about 50 pages of statistics, from building permits to housing starts, construction materials to price indexes, plus one or two brief articles per issue.

Features include articles on world trade in building materials and non-residential building improvements in the United States.

Landauer Momentum Index

LANDAUER ASSOCIATES HAS RANKED 24 major metropolitan areas by their real estate momentum. This is computed as the prospective change in supply and demand balance for office space. The median value is set to 100.

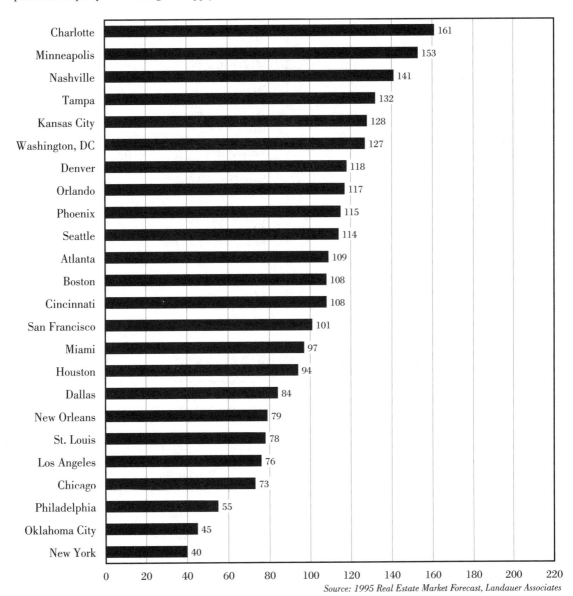

Charlotte	161
Minneapolis	153
Nashville	141
Tampa	132
Kansas City	128
Washington, DC	127
Denver	118
Orlando	117
Phoenix	115
Seattle	114
Atlanta	109
Boston	108
Cincinnati	108
San Francisco	101
Miami	97
Houston	94
Dallas	84
New Orleans	79
St. Louis	78
Los Angeles	76
Chicago	73
Philadelphia	55
Oklahoma City	45
New York	40

Source: 1995 Real Estate Market Forecast, Landauer Associates

Major Real Estate Developers

NATIONAL REAL ESTATE INVESTOR conducts an annual survey of real estate developers and ranks the respondents based on the total square feet under development in North America. The top ten listings from the 1994 survey are:

Homart
55 W. Monroe, Suite 3100
Chicago, IL 60603
(312) 551-5000

Hines Interests
2800 Post Oak Blvd.
Houston, TX 77056
(713) 621-8000

Opus Group of Cos.
9900 Brcn Rd. E., Suite 800
Minnetonka, MN 55343
(612) 936-4444

Zeckendorf Realty
55 E. 59th St.
New York, NY 10022
(212) 826-2900

The Hahn Co.
4350 La Jolla Village Dr., Suite 700
San Diego, CA 92122
(619) 546-1001

Simon Property Group
P.O. Box 7033
Indianapolis, IN 46207
(317) 636-1600

Westcor Partners
11411 N. Tatum Blvd.
Phoenix, AZ 85028
(602) 953-6200

Edward Rose Building Enterprise
23999 W. Ten Mile Rd.
Southfield, MI 48307
(810) 352-0952

Park Tower Realty
499 Park Ave.
New York, NY 10022
(212) 355-7570

Carter-Oncor International
1275 Peachtree St., NE
Atlanta, GA 30367
(404) 888-3000

Major Property Managers

NATIONAL REAL ESTATE INVESTOR conducts an annual survey of property managers ranking the respondents based on the amount of space in their management portfolios. The top ten listings from the 1994 survey are:

Trammell Crow
2001 Ross Ave., Suite 3500
Dallas, TX 75201
(214) 979-5100

LaSalle Partners
11 S. LaSalle St.
Chicago, IL 60603
(312) 782-5800

Lincoln Property
500 N. Akard, Suite 3300
Dallas, TX 75201
(214) 740-3300

Insignia Financial Group
1 Insignia Financial Plaza
Greenville, SC 29602
(803) 239-1518

Koll
4343 Von Karman Ave.
Newport Beach, CA 92660
(714) 833-9360

Cushman & Wakefield
51 W. 52nd St.
New York, NY 10019
(212) 841-7500

CB Commercial Real Estate Group
533 S. Fremont Ave.
Los Angeles, CA 90071
(213) 613-3442

PM Realty Group
1177 W. Loop S., Suite 1200
Houston, TX 77027
(713) 966-3600

NHP Management
12355 Sunrise Valley Dr.
Reston, VA 22091
(703) 716-2000

Axiom Real Estate Management
5 High Ridge Park
Stamford, CT 06905
(203) 321-3300

Major Real Estate Lenders

Top 50 Commercial Banks in Deposits

Rank	Name	Location	Deposits ($ thou.)*
1	Citibank, NA	New York	136,108,000
2	Bank of America NT&SA	San Francisco	109,150,000
3	Chemical Bank	New York	73,234,000
4	Chase Manhattan Bank, NA	New York	63,834,000
5	Morgan Guaranty Trust	New York	45,405,110
6	Wells Fargo Bank, NA	San Francisco	41,641,379
7	Bank of New York	New York	30,208,816
8	NationsBank of Texas, NA	Dallas	24,304,984
9	First National Bank	Chicago	23,852,516
10	First Fidelity Bank, NA	Salem, NJ	23,401,643
11	PNC Bank, NA	Pittsburgh	23,015,853
12	First National Bank	Boston	22,933,949
13	Bankers Trust	New York	22,283,000
14	Mellon Bank, NA	Pittsburgh	22,255,031
15	First Union National Bank of Florida	Jacksonville	22,224,387
16	First Interstate Bank of California	Los Angeles	19,655,698
17	Republic National Bank of New York	New York	19,417,949
18	NBD Bank, NA	Detroit	18,400,211
19	First Union National Bank of North Carolina	Charlotte	17,023,371
20	Society National Bank	Cleveland	16,731,452
21	Texas Commerce Bank, NA	Houston	15,984,599
22	Comerica Bank	Detroit	15,826,834
23	State Street Bank & Trust	Boston	14,845,238
24	Bank One, Texas, NA	Dallas	14,483,601
25	NationsBank of Florida, NA	Tampa	14,411,000
26	NationsBank of North Carolina, NA	Charlotte	13,986,000
27	Marine Midland Bank	Buffalo, NY	13,271,236
28	Bank of America, Illinois	Chicago	13,179,000
29	CoreStates Bank, NA	Philadelphia	12,757,158
30	Union Bank	San Francisco	12,592,678
31	NationsBank, NA	Bethesda, MD	12,483,000
32	Seattle-First National Bank	Seattle	11,796,000
33	National Westminster Bank USA	New York	11,493,982
34	Key Bank of New York	Albany	11,436,195
35	Wachovia Bank of North Carolina, NA	Winston-Salem	10,916,056
36	Bank One, Arizona, NA	Phoenix	10,860,489
37	First Bank, NA	Minneapolis	10,350,945
38	Shawmut Bank Connecticut, NA	Hartford	9,960,433
39	Meridian Bank	Reading, PA	9,858,515
40	NationsBank of Virgina, NA	Richmond	9,270,000
41	Crestar Bank	Richmond	9,217,441
42	Banco Popular de Puerto Rico	San Juan	8,883,516
43	Northern Trust	Chicago	8,686,720
44	NationsBank of Georgia, NA	Atlanta	8,648,513
45	Shawmut Bank, NA	Boston	8,394,534
46	Norwest Bank Minnesota, NA	Minneapolis	8,253,071
47	Midlantic National Bank	Newark, NJ	8,163,534
48	Fleet Bank of New York	Albany	8,036,129
49	BayBank	Burlington, MA	7,978,559
50	NBD Bank, NA	Indianapolis	7,577,259

*as of June 30, 1994

Source: American Banker

Lease Negotiation Tips

ACCORDING TO *Corporate Real Estate Executive*, techniques used during negotiations depend on whether you are in the "early," "middle," or "ending" phase of the process.

In the early phase of negotiations, it is important to develop basic trust, spell out realistic objectives, learn relevant facts, and establish procedural guidelines. Careful preparation will set the stage for this process. The one who is best prepared and who has anticipated objections generally has the advantage right to the end.

There are certain tactics that help. For example, meeting at your place, if possible, or at a neutral location may eliminate distractions or interruptions, and may allow you to plan seating or even lighting to your advantage. Because important decisions are best made at midday, scheduling the meeting over lunch would enable you to start with some small talk that may reveal more about the other person's needs and personality. Above all, schedule enough time.

The early phase is the time to ask a lot of questions, probe for information, and concentrate on what the other party is saying and how it is being said. Establish reasonable expectations. This is also the time to show how much both sides have in common, as well as learn about related problems. During this phase, listen carefully and attempt to get the other side to talk and make commitments. Save most of your talking for the middle phase, when you will concentrate on problem solving.

During the middle phase of negotiations, explore alternatives to show you understand the other party's position. At this point, you can start to narrow down the issues and establish a positive tone and a sense of coming to an agreement. Keep asking the other party to explain the reasoning behind every demand and be ready to explain your own. Observe his eyes and body language carefully when he is making an important point. Try trading small compromises in return for larger ones.

Never concede anything too quickly; be sure each concession is fully appreciated and always made for something in return. Save your energy for what is important—which is usually the price.

Throughout negotiations, it is important to avoid common pitfalls. Don't ask for too little. If you don't ask, you don't get. Don't make excessive demands that destroy your credibility. Know exactly what you will settle for, or you will transfer control of negotiations to the other side. Be prepared to break a stalemate with new information or by changing the subject or by asking questions. Have a deadline to work against. If you are negotiating with more than one principal, leave something for the other principals to negotiate just prior to closing.

When it is time to wrap up the agreement, the parties should review together what is agreed upon and confirm that all the problems are resolved. This is not the time for you to bring up new issues. If you have everything you want, stop negotiating. As you get into the document stage, be prepared to illustrate to the party's lawyer how and why they have a good deal.

In working out the documents, ask the other party's lawyer to note any questions or give you any comments before changing the language. Once the other party is committed to its own language, it is more difficult to reverse direction.

Finally, be available in person when the documents are prepared to answer any last-minute questions or to resolve any remaining matters.

When the deal is done, analyze your approach. Remember that hard work, practice, and experience are essential for consistent success. And do not underestimate your ability to earn a reputation as an excellent negotiator.

Source: NACORE International, reprinted by permission

Recommended Resources

Corporate Real Estate Executive
NACORE International, $65/year
440 Columbia Dr., Suite 100
West Palm Beach, FL 33409
(407) 683-8111

Negotiating Commercial Real Estate Leases
by Martin Zankel
Dearborn Financial Publishing, $34.95
(800) 982-2850
Provides nontechnical guidance to elements in leases and other related topics.

Tenant's Handbook of Office Leasing
by Stanley Wolfson
McGraw-Hill, $49.50
(800) 262-4729
Features negotiating tips for leasing contracts enhanced by tables, charts, graphs, and forms.

Total Personal Income

Percent Growth, 1993-1994

	14 fastest growing		all other states		14 slowest growing

Source: Survey of Current Business

The Top Reference Sources

State and Metropolitan Area Data Book
U.S. Government Printing Office, $26
(202) 512-1800

A supplement to the *Statistical Abstract*, this publication is compiled by the Economics and Statistics Administration, Bureau of the Census. The data presented come from over fifty federal and private agencies and represent some of the most up-to-date statistics available.

The statistics included cover a range of topics: commercial office space, manufacturers, personal income, housing, civilian labor force, farms, and retail trade.

The book is updated on a five-year cycle. The next expected update should be available in 1996.

BOMA Standards

THE BUILDING OWNERS AND MANAGERS Association International (BOMA) is an organization whose purpose is to establish standards through which building owners, managers, tenants, appraisers, architects, lending institutions, and others can communicate and compute on a clear and understandable basis. To achieve that objective, BOMA publishes standards for measuring floor area, calculating and analyzing expenses and income for office buildings, and other related tasks. In addition, BOMA provides annual surveys of office space utilization, rental prices/square foot, vacancy rates, and the general rental market in major downtown and suburban locations throughout the nation as well as in Canada.

Contact Option

Building Owners and Managers Association International (BOMA)
1201 New York Ave., NW, Suite 300
Washington, DC 20005
(202) 408-2662

Management Consulting Firms

Major Management Consulting Firms in the U.S.

Firm	Telephone
A. Foster Higgins	(212) 574-9000
Alexander Consulting Group	(201) 460-6700
Alexander Proudfoot	(407) 697-9600
Andersen Consulting	(312) 580-0069
Arthur D. Little	(617) 498-5000
Bain & Co.	(617) 572-2000
Booz, Allen & Hamilton	(212) 697-1900
Boston Consulting Group	(617) 973-1200
Coopers & Lybrand	(212) 536-3306
CSC Consulting	(617) 661-0900
Deloitte & Touche	(212) 489-1600
Ernst & Young	(216) 861-5000
Hay Group	(215) 875-2300
Hewitt Associates	(312) 295-5000
KPMG Peat Marwick	(212) 909-5000
McKinsey & Co.	(212) 446-7000
Mercer Consulting Group	(212) 345-4500
Milliman & Robertson	(206) 624-7940
Towers Perrin	(212) 309-3400

Business Brokers

THE TREND TOWARD INDEPENDENTLY owned and operated small- and medium-sized businesses is increasing dramatically. In fact, small companies created more than 13 million jobs in the last decade.

Business brokers bring the buyers and sellers of these businesses together. When the companies that are for sale exceed $1 million in value, the negotiations are usually handled by mergers and acquisitions specialists. Smaller business deals—sales below $1 million—are handled by business brokers.

For sellers, business brokers:

- Advise on how to prepare a business for sale;
- Advise on pricing the business;
- Market the business to potential buyers;
- Keep the sale confidential to protect business standing;
- Pre-qualify prospects to find the right match;
- Negotiate the transaction;
- Manage the close.

For buyers, business brokers:

- Provide access to an inventory of businesses for sale;
- Answer questions about buying a business;
- Match buyer's interests, goals, and desires with the right business;
- Prepare buyers to act quickly when the right opportunity is uncovered;
- Identify financing options;
- Manage the close;
- Support the transition.

Contact Options

International Business Brokers Association
P.O. Box 704
Concord, MA 01742
(508) 369-2490
The IBBA is a trade association that has a directory of its members arranged alphabetically and by location.

International Association of Merger and Acquisition Consultants
60 Revere Dr., Suite 500
Northbrook, IL 60062
(708) 480-9037

Business Brokers:

New England Business Advisors
196 Danbury Rd., P.O. Box 786
Wilton, CT 06897
(203) 834-0070

Corporate Investment International
101 Wymore Rd., Suite 225
Altamonte Springs, FL 32714
(407) 682-9600

Georgia Business Associates
2401 Lake Park Dr., Suite 350
Smyrna, GA 30080
(404) 319-6500

Hoganson Venture Group
15 Salt Creek Ln., Suite 217
Hinsdale, IL 60521
(708) 887-4788

Finn & Associates
545 North Woodlawn
Wichita, KS 67208
(316) 683-3466

UBI of Louisiana
4205 Canal St.
New Orleans, LA 70119
(504) 486-5375

Vernon A. Martin
1 Corporate Pl., 55 Ferncroft Rd.
Danvers, MA 01923
(508) 774-0160

Inexco Business Brokerage & Development
800 Monroe, NW, Suite 100
Grand Rapids, MI 49503
(616) 774-8080

Calhoun Companies
4930 W. 77th St., Suite 100
Minneapolis, MN 55435
(612) 831-3300

Opportunities in Business
1097 Tenth Ave., SE
Minneapolis, MN 55414
(612) 331-8392

Siegel Business Services
1 Bala Plaza, Suite 621
Bala-Cynwyd, PA 19004
(610) 668-9780

Business Brokers (cont'd)

Landmark Business Brokers
600 W. Park Row Dr.
Arlington, TX 76010
(817) 265-9188

Certified Business Brokers
10301 N.W. Freeway, Suite 200
Houston, TX 77092
(713) 680-1200

Country Business
Box 1071
Manchester Center, VT 05255
(802) 362-4710

J. S. Keate & Co.
Croger Bldg., 1014 Vine St., Suite 1600
Cincinnati, OH 45202
(513) 241-3700

Bluestem Resources Group
1427 E. 41st St.
Tulsa, OK 74105
(918) 749-4315

The Hughes Group & Associates
621 N. Robinson
Oklahoma City, OK 73102
(405) 848-1866

Probus/MBI Business Brokers & Consultants
307 Orchard City Dr., Suite 100
Campbell, CA 95008
(408) 370-9500

Geneva Business Services
5 Park Plaza
Irvine, CA 92714
(714) 756-2200

Business Team
3031 Tisch Way, Suite 400
San Jose, CA 95128
(408) 246-1102

VR Business Brokers
11314 South St.
Cerritos, CA 90703
(310) 402-2686

Colorado Business Consultants
899 Logan St., Suite 309
Denver, CO 80203
(303) 832-2020

Corporate Finance Associates
1801 Broadway, Suite 1200
Denver, CO 80202
(303) 296-6300

VR Business Brokers
1151 Dove St., Suite 100
Newport Beach, CA 92660
(800) 377-8722
    VR has 82 franchises around the country, each independently owned and operated. It is the only national company of business brokers in the United States.

Corporate Art

ESTABLISHING A CORPORATE ART collection is no longer the privilege of Fortune 500 companies alone. In recent years, more and more small- and mid-sized firms have begun to collect art, not only to create ambiance in their office space but because of its potential investment value.
    As a result, an entire industry has developed to serve the needs of corporate art collections. The following directories provide information on what other companies are collecting as well as complete listings of the agents, dealers, and consultants who help companies choose their collections.

Recommended Resources

ARTnews International Directory of Corporate Art Collections
ARTnews & International Art Alliance, $109.95
P.O. Box 1608
Largo, FL 34649
(813) 581-7328

    This annual directory provides an alphabetical listing by company of major national and international corporate art collections. Each listing includes a brief description of the corporation as well as information pertinent to the collection, including size, year begun, location, source of artwork, loan policy, and selection process.

Encyclopedia of Living Artists
ArtNetwork, $15.95
18757 Wildflower Dr.
Penn Valley, CA 95946
(916) 432-7630
    This annual book is a full-color catalogue of the work of American artists, complete with personal profiles, names and addresses of the artists and their agents. It is used as a resource for galleries, publishers, private and corporate collectors, and consultants.

Choosing an Architect

THERE ARE MANY METHODS of selecting an architect, ranging from formal design competitions to negotiated procurement to competitive bidding. You need to determine which approach fits your requirements and designate an individual or group to manage your selection process. To begin the selection process:

- Make a list of potential architects by asking colleagues for referrals.

- Contact your local chapter of the American Institute of Architects.

- Discover who designed projects similar to yours that appeal to you.

You may want to ask for qualifications and references at this stage. If the scope of the project is still indefinite, narrow the field based on what you learn.

You may want the architect to prepare a preliminary or full proposal explaining how he or she would approach your project. In that case, you may wish to send a written project description to the most promising firms; sending the same information to each architecture firm will make it easier to compare responses.

Decide how much cost information to request and when you want to request it; you may want to know only how the architect will charge for services, or you may need more—such as preliminary estimates or even a detailed proposal. The choice is yours to make based on your needs and the nature of your project.

With your in-house team, or whichever staff you delegate to manage the project, review the information you have collected. Useful factors to consider include:

- The size of the firm and the amount of time it has been in practice;

- Experience and past projects;

- Their ability to work within budget/time schedules;

- Cost of services;

- Special expertise including experience in your project type, management ability, and knowledge of building codes/zoning regulations.

Beyond review of the proposal, you may also wish to:

- Visit at least one finished project of each architect under consideration;

- Call client references.

An interview can give you important information on how well you will be able to work with a potential architect. If the written material you have received doesn't tell you all you need to know to select a firm, here is one way to pursue the process further:

- Create a short list of perhaps three to five firms to interview.

- Decide who from your firm will be responsible for the interviewing and final selection.

- Allow at least an hour for the interview.

- Decide on location of interview. At your office the architect can gain a better understanding of you and your project; at the architect's office you can see how the architect and staff work.

- Make sure that the people you interview are the people who will actually be working on your project.

In making your final determination, look at:

- Design quality

- Technical competence

- Experience

- Cost

- Organization.

You will need to evaluate for yourself the weight to give each of the factors.

You will also be looking for an architect who:

- Is responsive to your needs

- Listens carefully

- Seems to understand your company

- Makes you feel comfortable.

You will be working with the architect for a long time and may work with him or her on future projects. It is important that you trust the architect's judgment and ability.

Contact Option

The American Institute of Architects
1735 New York Ave., NW
Washington, DC 20006
(202) 626-7300

In addition to its role as the national organization of architects, the AIA maintains local and regional offices that will work with a company to help it find an architect. To reach a local office, contact the national headquarters above.

Interior Design

EVERY JANUARY AND JULY, *Interior Design* ranks the country's top design firms.

Interior Design's Top 25 Design Firms

Name	Location	Interior Design Fees ($ millions)	No. of Employees
Gensler and Associates/Architects	San Francisco, CA	44.37	490
ISI (Interior Space International)	Chicago, IL	30.00	240
HNTB	Kansas City, MO	22.12	35
NBBJ	Seattle, WA	20.43	66
R. J. Pavlik (The Pavlik Design Team)	Ft. Lauderdale, FL	20.24	87
HOK (Hellmuth, Obata & Kassabaum)	St. Louis, MO	19.01	144
Leo A. Daly	Omaha, NE	18.81	56
Sverdrup	St. Louis, MO	15.82	91
Retail Planning Associates (RPA)	Columbus, OH	15.56	81
HLW (Haines Lundberg Waehler)	New York, NY	15.08	68
Smith, Hinchman & Grylls Associates	Detroit, MI	13.37	47
SDI/HTI	Cincinnati, OH	12.91	160
Skidmore, Owings & Merrill	Chicago, IL	12.35	83
The Phillips Janson Group Architects	New York, NY	12.20	148
Swanke Hayden Connell Architects	New York, NY	11.92	65
Perkins & Will	Chicago, IL	11.32	52
Walker Group/CNI	New York, NY	10.94	101
IA Interior Architects	San Francisco, CA	10.07	93
Interprise	Chicago, IL	9.61	95
SCR Design Organization	New York, NY	9.50	71
STUDIOS Architecture	San Francisco, CA	9.18	119
RTKL Associates	Baltimore, MD	8.80	113
Griswold, Heckel & Kelly Associates	Chicago, IL	8.33	100
3D/International	Houston, TX	7.84	44
AI/Boggs	Washington, DC	7.57	70

Source: Interior Design, Jan. 1995

Contact Options

American Society of Interior Designers
608 Massachusetts Ave., NE
Washington, DC 20002
(202) 546-3480
   Provides referrals for interior designers in its local offices around the country.

Office Planners and Users Group
Box 11182
Philadelphia, PA 19136
(215) 335-9400
   Plans and manages office facilities.

Recommended Resource

Interior Design
249 W. 17th St.
New York, NY 10011
(212) 463-6675

Architects/Designers

Award Winners

Almost every year since 1907, the American Institute of Architects has awarded a gold medal to one architect for outstanding design work.

Year	Architect
1981	Josep Liuis Sert
1982	Romaldo Giurgola
1983	Nathaniel A. Owings
1985	William Wayne Caudill (posthumously)
1986	Arthur Erickson
1989	Joseph Esherick
1990	E. Fay Jones
1991	Charles W. Moore

Year	Architect
1992	Benjamin Thompson
1993	Kevin Roche
1994	Sir Norman Foster
1995	César Pelli

Contact Option

The American Institute of Architects
1735 New York Ave., NW
Washington, DC 20006
(202) 626-7300

Annual Reports

Sid Cato's Standards for the Best Annual Report

- Does the front cover demand readership? Has the report utilized readership-enhancing devices, including an intriguing cover statement, textual call-outs, boldface lead-ins, action subheads, bulleted paragraphs, and the like? Does it contain an open, inviting layout, solicit readership on every page, and have an action-filled index–that is, a "talking table of contents"?

- Is the writing sprightly and efficient? How does the text score on readability? Has use of complex words been avoided?

- Does it truly aim to inform fully, presenting items such as a special editorial section, glossary of terms, a mission statement?

- Does it truly shed light on the competition, market position and market share? Also, does it provide a breakdown of operations, results, and prospects?

- Is a photo of the organization's head person used, and does it lead off the shareholder letter?

- Has management wholeheartedly assumed responsibility, alongside the auditors, for the financials?

- Does the report contain biographical data on officers and directors–more than simply age and year of affiliation?

- Has it broken any new ground–in other words, is the report unquestionably other than run-of-the-mill? Does the board include women and/or minorities?

- Does it have a discernible point of view–a theme clearly thought out, delineated, and woven throughout?

- Does it communicate a favorable image–or identity–of the company, through its stature, articulation, point of view, and furtherance of understanding of the entity's business and performance?

- Is financial disclosure extensive–more than the minimum five-year-data required by the SEC? Are graphs fully explained?

- Does honesty exist throughout, starting with the letter to shareholders? Is bad news delivered without

The Top Reference Sources

Directory of Industrial Designers
Industrial Designers Society of America, $85
(703) 759-0100

This annual directory lists 2,200 industrial designers by their specialty. It includes consumer products, appliances, heavy equipment, computers, toys, furniture, and medical instrument designers, as well as listings by geographical location and by employer.

Annual Reports (cont'd)

subterfuge or delay? Is the report forthright to the ultimate—without conflicts between its parts, for example?

- Is CEO involvement (whether actual or perceived) displayed in the shareholder letter?

- Is the CEO unequivocally (a) presenting a revelatory view of the company as well as (b) providing substantive insight into where it's headed?

Copyright © 1984-1993, Cato Communications, Inc. Reprinted by permission.

Every year, *Institutional Investor* magazine picks what it considers to be the best annual reports. Besides the best annual reports, 22 others were singled out for excellence.

Best Annual Reports

Union Pacific
Philip Morris
Quaker Oats
Hewlett-Packard
Whirlpool
J. P. Morgan

The Runners-up

AMP
AMR
Capital Cities/ABC
Cummins Engine
DSC Communications
Duracell
Enron
Federal National Mortgage Association
Fluor
General Electric
IBM
Lowes
Masco
Mobil
Northrop
Owens-Illinois
Pfizer
Phelps Dodge
Salomon
Sybase
Time Warner

Source: Institutional Investor, Sept. 1994

Annual Report Designers

Contact Options

Graphic design firms specializing in annual reports:

The Conceptual Communications Group
41 E. 11th St., 2nd Floor
New York, NY 10003
(212) 505-1607

Addison Corporate Annual Reports
79 Fifth Ave., 6th Floor
New York, NY 10003
(212) 229-5000

WYD
61 Wilton Rd.
Westport, CT 06880
(203) 227-2627

Little & Co.
1010 S. 7th St., Suite 550
Minneapolis, MN 55415
(612) 375-0077

Gunn Associates
275 Newbury St.
Boston, MA 02116
(617) 267-0618

Boller Coates Spadaro
900 N. Franklin St., Suite 800
Chicago, IL 60139
(312) 787-2783

Curran & Connors
333 Marcus Blvd.
Happauge, NY 11788
(516) 435-0400

Recommended Resource

Graphic Arts Monthly Printing Industry Sourcebook
Cahners Publishing, $50
(800) 637-6089

FINANCE

The Stock Market

AT THE EXPLOSIVE PEAK of the '80s bull market, U.S. stock-trading volume reached a record high of 2.25 trillion (1987). For a time after this period, the stock outlook for the '90s appeared bleak, but it seems that the early years of the decade have taken investors by surprise. The markets have done more than rebound from that temporary and terrifying 508-point correction of October 19, 1987, the biggest drop ever. With indexes soaring, the 1991 and 1992 markets set new records, demonstrating the astonishing strength and sustained power of America's financial system and corporations.

Market Value of Stocks on U.S. Exchanges

Year	Value of Stocks ($ thousands)
1986	1,705,123,953
1987	2,284,165,520
1988	1,587,011,727
1989	1,844,768,135
1990	1,611,667,363
1991	1,776,275,383
1992	2,033,199,819

Source: U.S. Securities and Exchange Commission
Annual Report, 1993

Volume of Stock Sales on U.S. Exchanges

Year	Stocks (shares in thousands)
1986	48,337,694
1987	63,770,625
1988	52,533,283
1989	54,238,571
1990	53,337,731
1991	58,031,077
1992	65,500,684

Volume of Stock Sales by Exchange: 1992

Exchange	Stocks (shares in thousands)
AMEX	3,630,733
BSE	1,033,357
CSE	1,203,874
CHX	3,035,435
NYSE	53,343,563
PSE	2,087,257
PHLX	1,128,439
ARIZ	38,027
CBOE	0

Source: U.S. Securities and Exchange Commission
Annual Report, 1993

Stock Sales on all U.S. Exchanges (total dollar volume in millions)

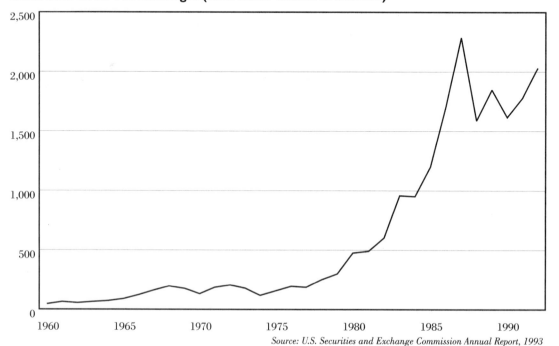

Source: U.S. Securities and Exchange Commission Annual Report, 1993

The Stock Market (cont'd)

Share Volume (%) by Exchange, 1945 to 1991

Year	NYSE	AMEX	MSE	PSE	PHLX	BSE	CSE	Others
1945	65.87	21.31	1.77	2.98	1.06	0.66	0.05	6.30
1950	73.32	13.54	2.16	3.11	0.97	0.65	0.09	3.16
1955	68.85	19.19	2.09	3.08	0.85	0.48	0.05	5.41
1960	68.47	22.27	2.20	3.11	0.88	0.38	0.04	2.65
1965	69.90	22.53	2.63	2.33	0.81	0.26	0.05	1.49
1970	71.28	19.03	3.16	3.68	1.63	0.51	0.02	0.69
1975	80.99	8.97	3.97	3.26	1.54	0.85	0.13	0.29
1980	79.94	10.78	3.84	2.80	1.54	0.57	0.32	0.21
1985	81.52	5.78	6.12	3.66	1.47	1.27	0.15	0.03
1986	81.12	6.28	5.73	3.68	1.53	1.33	0.30	0.02
1987	83.09	5.57	5.19	3.23	1.30	1.28	0.30	0.04
1988	83.74	4.95	5.26	3.03	1.29	1.32	0.39	0.02
1989	81.33	6.02	5.44	3.34	1.80	1.64	0.41	0.02
1990	81.86	6.23	4.68	3.16	1.82	1.71	0.53	0.01
1991	82.00	5.52	4.66	3.58	1.60	1.77	0.86	0.01
1992	81.29	5.73	4.62	3.18	1.72	1.57	1.83	0.06

Source: U.S. Securities and Exchange Commission Annual Report, 1993

New York Stock Exchange (NYSE)

OVER 80 PERCENT OF American securities are traded on the NYSE, the United States' oldest and largest exchange. In 1991, over 10,000 institutions managing $3.5 trillion in securities had access to and used the NYSE market.

New York Stock Exchange (NYSE)
11 Wall St.
New York, NY 10005
(212) 656-3000
Founded: 1792
Members/Seats: 1,420 members; 1,366 seats
Companies/Issues listed: 1,885 companies; 2,426 issues

NYSE Record Reported Trades

Record	Date	No. of Trades
Week ending	2/5/93	1,069,920
Month	3/93	4,251,147
Year	1993	46,431,825

NYSE Record Volume

Record	Date	Volume (shares)
First hour	9/17/93	184,300,000
Day	10/20/87	608,148,710
Year	1993	66,923,276,708

NYSE Record Value of Trading

Record	Date	Value of Trading ($ millions)
Day	10/19/87	20,993.0
Year	1993	2,283,389.6

Source: New York Stock Exchange Fact Book, 1993

Delphi offers access to continuous 30-minute updates on the Dow Jones Averages. GO BUS DOW.

New York Stock Exchange (cont'd)

NYSE Average Share Prices

End of Year	Average Price ($)
1924	62.45
1950	39.86
1960	47.53
1970	39.61
1975	30.48
1976	35.03
1977	30.53
1978	29.84
1979	31.99
1980	36.87
1981	29.87
1982	33.03
1983	35.11
1984	32.31
1985	37.20
1986	36.89
1987	30.87
1988	32.26
1989	36.51
1990	31.08
1991	37.27
1992	34.83
1993	34.65

Source: New York Stock Exchange Fact Book, 1993

NYSE Seat Sales

Year	High ($)	Low ($)
1970	320,000	130000
1971	300,000	145,000
1972	250,000	150,000
1973	190,000	72,000
1974	105,000	65,000
1975	138,000	55,000
1976	104,000	40,000
1977	95,000	35,000
1978	105,000	46,000
1979	210,000	82,000
1980	275,000	175,000
1981	285,000	220,000
1982	340,000	190,000
1983	425,000	310,000
1984	400,000	290,000
1985	480,000	310,000
1986	600,000	455,000
1987	1,150,000	605,000
1988	820,000	580,000
1989	675,000	420,000
1990	430,000	250,000
1991	440,000	345,000
1992	600,000	410,000
1993	775,000	500,000

Source: New York Stock Exchange Fact Book, 1993

NYSE Reported Share Volume, 1960–1992

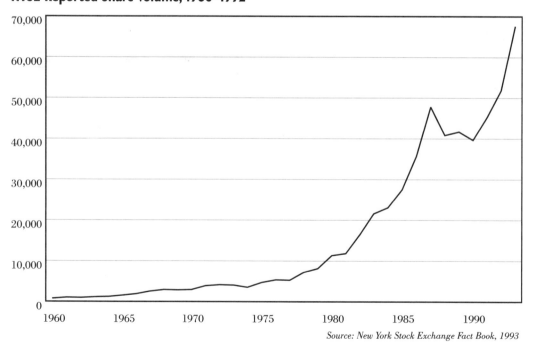

Source: New York Stock Exchange Fact Book, 1993

NYSE Stocks Ranked

Ten Most Active NYSE Stocks, 1994

Stock	Share Volume
Teléfonos de Mexico	1,048,700,000
General Motors	685,900,000
Merck & Company	680,400,000
Wal-Mart Stores	648,400,000
IBM	593,600,000
General Electric	570,300,000
Philip Morris	566,500,000
Chrysler	565,500,000
AT&T	507,400,000
Compaq Computer	503,000,000

Source: The New York Times, Jan. 2, 1995

Ten Most Active NYSE Stocks, 1993

Stock	Share Volume
Merck & Company	728,600,000
RJR Nabisco	685,300,000
Philip Morris	642,900,000
Wal-Mart Stores	600,400,000
Teléfonos de Mexico	584,100,000
General Motors	578,600,000
IBM	566,900,000
Chrysler	542,400,000
Citicorp	523,900,000
Glaxo Holdings	480,500,000

Source: The New York Times, Jan. 3, 1994

Ten Best Performers on the NYSE, 1994

Common Stock	Closing Price ($)	% Change from 1992
United Inns	24.75	214.3
General Datacomm Industries	32.38	212.0
Cytec Industries	39.00	194.3
Network Equipment Tech.	24.00	170.4
LSI Logic	40.38	154.3
Micron Technology	44.13	137.2
Borden Chemicals & Plastics	23.00	130.0
Hudson Foods class "A"	25.13	125.8
Three-Five Systems	36.38	106.4
Barrett Resources	20.50	97.6

Source: The New York Times, Jan. 2, 1995

Ten Worst Performers on the NYSE, 1994

Common Stock	Closing Price ($)	% Change from 1992
House of Fabrics	1.25	-84.4
UDC Homes	1.13	-83.6
Grupo Financiero Serfin	7.50	-74.6
Huntington Int'l Holdings	2.63	-71.2
Datapoint	1.75	-70.2
Gr. Mexicano Desarrollo "B"	7.63	-68.2
USAir Group	4.25	-67.0
Bombay Company	10.00	-66.7
Grupo Dina	9.50	-65.9
Washington Homes	3.38	-65.8

Source: The New York Times, Jan. 2, 1995

Transactions (%) in NYSE-Listed Stock on Participating Markets

Year	NYSE	AMEX	PSE	CHX*	PHLX	BSE	CSE	NASD	INST	Total
1982	78.61	0.00	8.27	5.89	3.92	1.00	0.84	1.44	0.04	100.00
1983	77.68	0.00	8.58	6.81	3.88	1.25	0.49	1.28	0.04	100.00
1984	75.40	0.00	8.93	7.95	4.10	1.78	0.34	1.41	0.09	100.00
1985	74.24	0.00	9.51	8.16	3.82	2.17	0.32	1.70	0.10	100.00
1986	72.68	0.00	10.57	8.52	3.65	2.25	0.29	2.00	0.03	100.00
1987	73.60	0.00	9.31	8.94	3.50	2.32	0.26	2.05	0.02	100.00
1988	72.99	0.00	8.44	9.74	3.22	2.33	0.35	2.91	0.03	100.00
1989	69.23	0.00	8.35	10.43	3.39	3.16	0.44	4.98	0.03	100.00
1990	66.17	0.00	8.14	9.71	3.02	3.77	0.63	8.53	0.03	100.00
1991	67.33	0.00	8.12	8.03	2.84	3.37	0.74	9.53	0.03	100.00
1992	65.17	0.00	7.55	8.34	3.31	3.17	1.85	10.57	0.03	100.00
1993	70.49	0.00	5.77	6.14	2.81	2.56	2.59	9.63	0.00	100.00

MSE changed its name to CHX on July 8, 1993.

Source: New York Stock Exchange Fact Book, 1993

American Stock Exchange (Amex)

The American Stock Exchange (Amex)
86 Trinity Pl.
New York, NY 10006
(212) 306-1000
Members/Seats: 661 regular members;
203 options principal members
Companies/Issues listed: 824 companies;
981 issues

The Amex list includes many younger, smaller firms and mid-size growth companies, oil, and high-technology issues.

Typical Amex Company, 1994 ($ millions)

	Average	Median
Total assets ($ mil.)	378.6	54.6
Shareholders' equity ($ mil.)	106.3	25.3
Sales ($ mil.)	243.5	40.7
Market value ($ mil.)	177.8	31.5
Long-term debt ($ mil.)	83.4	6.2
Shares outstanding ($ mil.)	13.3	4.5
Pre-tax income ($ mil.)	10.2	1.6

Amex Volume Since 1970

Year	Volume ($)
1970	14,266,040,599
1975	5,678,028,284
1980	35,788,327,624
1981	24,520,205,419
1982	21,056,649,904
1983	31,237,023,941
1984	21,376,098,408
1985	27,838,566,791
1986	45,356,898,691
1987	50,469,993,686
1988	30,921,806,605
1989	44,401,174,619

Year	Volume ($)
1990	37,714,827,819
1991	40,919,297,189
1992	42,238,331,156
1993	56,736,606,769
1994	58,511,170,791

Amex Record Volume

Record	Date	Volume
Daily	10/20/87	43,432,760
Weekly	10/19/87	158,680,590
Monthly	Jan. 1992	450,182,190
Yearly	1993	4,582,013,270

Prices Paid for Amex Seats Since 1970

Year	High ($)	Low ($)
1970	185,000	70,000
1975	72,000	34,000
1980	252,000	95,000
1981	275,000	200,000
1982	285,000	180,000
1983	325,000	261,000
1984	255,000	160,000
1985	160,000	115,000
1986	285,000	145,000
1987	420,000	265,000
1988	280,000	180,000
1989	215,000	155,000
1990	170,000	83,500
1991	120,000	80,000
1992	110,000	76,000
1993	163,000	92,000
1994	205,000	155,000

Source: American Stock Exchange Fact Book, 1995

The Top Reference Sources

The Business One Irwin Business and Investment Almanac
Irwin Professional Publishing, $75
(800) 634-3966

Edited by Sumner N. Levine, this annual publication is a standard reference for the business and investment community. It includes major and group stock market averages, reviews of the major futures markets, charts for futures-traded commodities, the performance of mutual funds, and the performance of leading economies.

The book also contains data on future employment opportunities, U.S. demographics, international stock price indexes, and consumer price indexes.

Amex Stocks Ranked

Ten Most Active Amex Stocks, 1994

Stock	Share Volume
Cheyenne Software	176,600,000
Echo Bay Mines	165,300,000
Viacom class "B"	159,000,000
Royal Oak Mines	114,200,000
Ivax	107,200,000
Amdahl	80,000,000
Hasbro	68,900,000
Interdigital Communications	61,200,000
U.S. Bioscience	54,600,000
Top Source Technologies	52,000,000

Source: The New York Times, Jan. 2, 1995

Ten Most Active Amex Stocks, 1993

Stock	Share Volume
Echo Bay Mines	265,900,000
Royal Oak Mines	234,600,000
Energy Services	181,400,000
Amdahl	83,700,000
Cheyenne Software	69,500,000
Atari	66,800,000
Interdigital Communications	60,300,000
Hasbro	59,900,000
Nabors Industries	58,200,000
NTN Communications	57,300,000

Source: The New York Times, Jan. 3, 1994

Best Performers on the Amex, 1994

Common Stock	Closing Price ($)	% Change from 1993
Simula	22.50	318.6
Bio-Rad Labs class "A"	27.75	177.5
Organogenesis	19.88	120.8
Hondo Oil & Gas	11.75	104.3
Anuhco	10.36	102.4
Cagle's class "A"	44.00	96.4
Circa Pharmaceutical	17.88	90.7
Rogers	49.75	90.4
Globalink	14.88	86.0
Amdahl	11.00	83.3

Source: The New York Times, Jan. 2, 1995

Worst Performers on the Amex, 1994

Common Stock	Closing Price ($)	% Change from 1993
Spectravision	0.25	-97.2
Conversion Industries	0.50	-96.4
Wilshire Technologies	1.38	-90.3
Beta Well Service	1.63	-88.4
Quality Products	6.38	-87.7
Diversified Communications	0.75	-86.0
Trans World Airlines	0.81	-85.6
Styles on Video	2.81	-83.8
Greyhound Lines	2.31	-79.9
Citadel Holdings	2.50	-78.7

Source: The New York Times, Jan. 2, 1995

Stocks Outstanding on the Amex, 1980–1994 (billions)

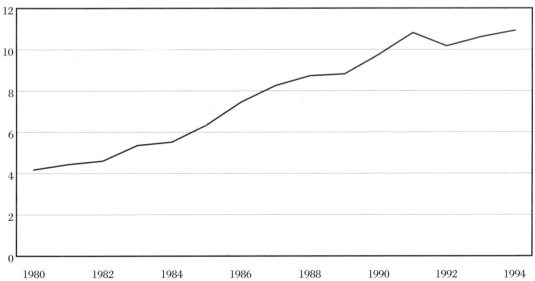

Source: American Stock Exchange Fact Book, 1995

Amex Stocks Ranked (cont'd)

Amex Seat Sales, 1980 to 1994

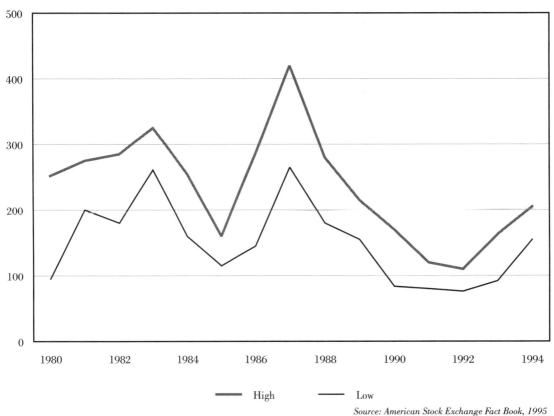

Source: American Stock Exchange Fact Book, 1995

The Top Reference Sources

Causes of Business Failures. Send e-mail to failures@almanac.yoyo.com. See p. xi for instructions.

Seven primary reasons for business failure and incidence of failure in nine sectors of business.

The OTC Market: NASDAQ

SHARES OF SMALL AND relatively new companies are traded over-the-counter, in the OTC market. This market has no location: transactions are executed over telephones, private wires, and computers by a vast network of brokers and dealers. Sales and trading information on most (but not all) OTC transactions is received and stored by the National Association of Securities Dealers (NASD). The NASD transmits price and volume data on its computerized quote system, the National Association of Securities Dealers Automated Quotations System (NASDAQ).

National Association of Securities Dealers (NASD)
1735 K St., NW, Eighth Floor
Washington, DC 20006
(202) 728-8000
Members: 6,000

NASD is a not-for-profit association of brokers and dealers founded in 1939. A self-regulating organization, the NASD establishes standards of conduct for members trading through NASDAQ and other over-the-counter securities markets. Members of NASD may sell securities to each other at wholesale prices while selling retail to non-members.

NASDAQ is the third-largest market in the world, after the New York and Tokyo exchanges, and handles over 45 percent of all shares traded in the major U.S. markets. More than 4,900 companies have their stocks traded in the NASDAQ; statistics on over 5,700 domestic and foreign securities are transmitted through NASDAQ.

NASDAQ Single-Day Trading Records

Date	Share Volume
Mar. 31, 1994	413,951,000
Mar. 30, 1994	398,194,000
Oct. 28, 1994	378,495,800
Feb. 4, 1994	376,034,700
Mar. 24, 1994	373,500,100

Profile of Typical NASDAQ Company

Total assets ($ mil.)	626.7
Shareholders' equity ($ mil.)	109.2
Total revenues ($ mil.)	295.8
P/E ratio	28.0

Profile of Typical NASDAQ Security

Share price ($)	17.4
Number of market makers	11.9
Total shares outstanding ($ mil.)	12.2
Public float (shares, $ mil.)	8.8
Market value of shares outstanding ($ mil.)	212.2

Source: NASDAQ Fact Book & Company Directory, 1995

NASDAQ Volume Since 1981 ($ billions)

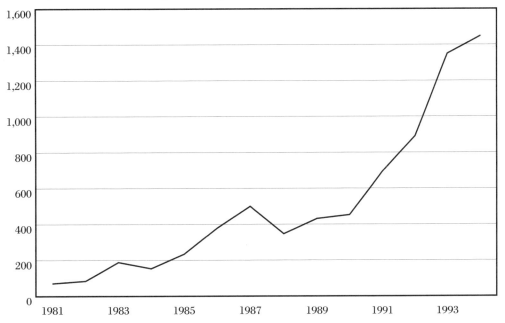

Source: NASDAQ Fact Book & Company Directory, 1995

The OTC Market: NASDAQ (cont'd)

Ten Most Active NASDAQ Stocks, 1994

Stock	Share Volume
Intel	1,183,200,000
Cisco Systems	1,035,500,000
Microsoft	793,700,000
MCI Communications	745,900,000
Novell	741,500,000
Oracle Systems	565,900,000
Apple Computer	511,500,000
Bay Networks	475,800,000
DSC Communications	459,600,000
Lotus Development	422,900,000

Source: The New York Times, Jan. 2, 1995

Ten Most Active NASDAQ Stocks, 1993

Stock	Share Volume
Intel	894,100,000
Novell	735,800,000
Tele-Comm. class "A"	620,300,000
SynOptics Comm.	571,000,000
Cisco Systems	554,900,000
MCI Communications	549,900,000
Microsoft	503,500,000
Apple Computer	494,100,000
Amgen	459,600,000
Oracle Systems	448,900,000

Source: The New York Times, Jan. 3, 1994

Ten Best-Performing NASDAQ Stocks, 1994

Common Stock	Closing Price ($)	% Change from 1993
Microtouch Systems	45.00	554.5
Tekelec	32.88	471.7
Printronix	24.75	336.8
Stratacom	35.00	317.9
Proxima	28.88	260.9
C-Cor Electronics	31.00	244.4
Educational Development	16.00	212.2
Tencor Instruments	38.50	208.0
Xylogics	25.25	206.1
Alliance Semiconductor	31.25	204.9

Source: The New York Times, Jan. 2, 1995

Ten Worst-Performing NASDAQ Stocks, 1994

Common Stock	Closing Price ($)	% Change from 1993
Water Point Systems	0.09	-98.2
Florida West Airlines	0.25	-98.1
Community Health Computing	0.13	-97.8
Tellos Pharmaceuticals	0.25	-95.2
American Complex Care	0.34	-95.0
New Day Beverage	0.28	-94.7
Alpha 1 Biomedicals	0.78	-94.6
Zam's	0.38	-93.8
Golden Systems	0.63	-92.7
Sapien's	1.78	-90.6

Source: The New York Times, Jan. 2, 1995

The Top Reference Sources

The NASDAQ Fact Book & Company Directory
National Association of Securities Dealers, $20
(301) 590-6578

Published annually, this book provides extensive data on the performance of NASDAQ securities and statistics on the NASDAQ market as a whole, as well as information to assist in contacting each company directly.

It is used as a resource by shareholders, corporations, investment analysts, brokerage firms, financial media, government, and educational institutions.

U.S. Stock Exchanges

Pacific Stock Exchange (PSE)

618 S. Spring St.
Los Angeles, CA 90014
(213) 977-4500

- Members listed: 551;

- Hours: The PSE is the last full-auction U.S. market to close, at 1:50 P.M. Pacific Time, 50 minutes past the New York close;

- Volume: 2.0 billion shares (1994);

- Options: 20.9 million contracts (1994).

Boston Stock Exchange (BSE)

1 Boston Pl.
Boston, MA 02108
(617) 723-9500

- Founded: 1834; the third-oldest stock exchange in the United States;

- Members/seats: 204 seats held by 145 member firms;

- Companies/issues listed: 190 exclusive listings; over 2,300 issues total;

- Volume: 5.2 million shares traded daily.

The Cincinnati Stock Exchange (CSE)

205 Dixie Terminal Bldg.
Cincinnati, OH 45202
(312) 786-8803

- Founded: 1885; the youngest regional exchange in the country;

- Seats: 275;

- Volume: 1.496 billion shares traded in 1994; 2.901 million trades daily.

Chicago Stock Exchange (CHX)

440 LaSalle St.
Chicago, IL 60605
(312) 663-2980

- Founded: 1882, as the Chicago Stock Exchange. In 1949 the St. Louis, Cleveland, and Minneapolis–St. Paul exchanges merged with the Chicago exchange to form the Midwest Stock Exchange. The New Orleans Stock Exchange joined in 1959. In 1993, the name changed back to Chicago Stock Exchange;

- Members/seats: 445 (including specialists, floor brokers, and off-floor members);

- Companies/issues listed: 3,289.

Philadelphia Stock Exchange (PHLX)

1900 Market St.
Philadelphia, PA 19103
(215) 496-5000

- Founded: 1790; the oldest security exchange in the United States;

- Volume: 1,347,339,898 shares traded in 1994;

- Companies/issues traded: 2,500.

Note: The above information was submitted by the public relations departments of the individual exchanges.

The Top Reference Sources

The Corporate Finance Sourcebook
Reed Publishing, $479
(800) 521-8110

This annual directory catalogues 19 sources of capital funding and management, including venture capital firms, private lenders, banks, trusts, commercial financing and factoring firms, pension managers, and accounting firms. Listings include the names and numbers of investment officers, industry preference, minimum to maximum investment limits, and lending criteria.

Over 3,600 firms and 20,000 key executives are included in this highly recommended publication.

U.S. Exchange Markets

Foreign Securities Listed on U.S. Exchanges (as of Dec. 31, 1992)

Exchange	No. Common Stocks	Value ($ millions)	No. Preferred Stocks	Value ($ millions)
American	85	21,971	3	292
Boston	2	54	0	0
New York	121	153,800	21	3,400
Pacific	2	38	0	0
Philadelphia	NA	NA	NA	NA
TOTAL	210	175,863	24	3,692

Source: U.S. Securities and Exchange Commission Annual Report, 1993

Recommended Resources

New York Stock Exchange Fact Book
New York Stock Exchange, $10
11 Wall St.
New York, NY 10005
(212) 656-3000

American Stock Exchange Fact Book
American Stock Exchange, $15
86 Trinity Pl.
New York, NY 10006
(212) 306-1000

NASDAQ Fact Book & Company Directory
National Association of Securities Dealers, $20
1735 K St., NW, Eighth Floor
Washington, DC 20006
(301) 590-6578

The Top Reference Sources

The Directory of Corporate Affiliations
Reed Publishing, $950/five volumes
(800) 551-8110

Published annually, this directory gives a view-at-a-glance of the corporate structure of more than 5,000 major U.S companies and their 50,000 subsidiaries, divisions, and affiliates.

Parent company listings contain address, numbers, ticker symbols, stock markets, financial data, number of employees, sales, balance sheet data, SIC codes, a description of the company's line of business, key personnel, and members of the board. Also included are summaries of mergers and acquisitions and name changes.

Dividends and Splits

A COMPANY'S DIVIDEND PAYMENT to stockholders represents the stockholder's share of the company's net profits. The dividend amount is decided by the company's directors; it is fixed per share and typically paid quarterly in cash (mailed checks). A split is a commensurate increase in the number of shares of outstanding stock without increasing the shareholder's equity. A firm's stock will split to reduce the market price and increase the stock's attractiveness to investors.

Cash Dividends on NYSE-Listed Common Stocks

Year	Number of Issues Listed at Year End	Number Paying Cash Dividends During Year	Estimated Aggregate Cash Payments ($ millions)
1970	1,330	1,120	19,781
1971	1,399	1,132	20,256
1972	1,478	1,195	21,490
1973	1,536	1,276	23,627
1974	1,543	1,308	25,662
1975	1,531	1,273	26,901
1976	1,550	1,304	30,608
1977	1,549	1,360	36,270
1978	1,552	1,373	41,151
1979	1,536	1,359	46,937
1980	1,540	1,361	53,072
1981	1,534	1,337	60,628
1982	1,499	1,287	62,224
1983	1,518	1,259	67,102
1984	1,511	1,243	68,215
1985	1,503	1,206	74,237
1986	1,536	1,180	76,161
1987	1,606	1,219	84,377
1988	1,643	1,270	102,190
1989	1,683	1,303	101,778
1990	1,741	NA	103,150*
1991	1,860	NA	123,385*
1992	2,068	NA	109,696*
1993	2,331	NA	120,206*

* Estimate based on average annual yield of the NYSE Composite Index

Source: New York Stock Exchange Fact Book, 1993

Annual Number of Stock Splits on the NYSE

Year	Total
1983	300
1984	178
1985	166
1986	272
1987	244
1988	104
1989	142
1990	105

Year	Total
1991	107
1992	182
1993	181

Source: New York Stock Exchange Fact Book, 1993

Block Trading

BLOCKS ARE LARGE HOLDINGS OF STOCK, usually 10,000 shares or more. Blocks are most likely owned by institutions; block trades usually occur between institutions.

Block Trading on the NYSE

Year	Total Transactions	% of Reported Volume
1965	2,171	3.1
1970	17,217	15.4
1975	34,420	16.6
1976	47,632	18.7
1977	54,27	22.4
1978	75,036	22.9
1979	97,509	26.5
1980	133,597	29.2
1981	145,564	31.8
1982	254,707	41.0
1983	363,415	45.6
1984	433,427	49.8
1985	539,039	51.7
1986	665,587	49.9
1987	920,679	51.2
1988	768,419	54.5
1989	872,811	51.1
1990	843,365	49.6
1991	981,077	49.6
1992	1,134,832	50.7
1993	1,477,859	53.7

Source: New York Stock Exchange Fact Book, 1993

Block Trading on the Amex

Year	Number of Blocks	% of Total Dollar Volume
1970	2,260	6.9
1975	1,803	7.6
1980	9,895	11.5
1981	10,463	16.2
1982	12,330	17.9
1983	20,629	21.4
1984	18,820	29.2
1985	29,094	34.0
1986	44,421	35.4
1987	53,814	36.0
1988	39,865	36.7
1989	51,907	33.4
1990	60,830	37.7
1991	52,678	34.8
1992	54,345	31.8
1993	75,754	38.1
1994	79,645	45.5

Source: American Stock Exchange Fact Book, 1995

The Top Reference Sources

S&P 500 Directory
Standard & Poor's, $39.95
(212) 208-1649

This annual fact book provides a good overview of the S&P 500 index, including background infor-

mation and methodology. It includes a "year in review" section, plus a directory of S&P index products and an A–Z listing of the S&P 500 companies.

S&P 500 company reports and statistical tables are also provided.

Initial Public Offerings

WHEN A COMPANY FIRST OFFERS ITS STOCK for sale to potential investors it conducts what is known as an initial public offering (IPO).

Total IPO Issuance on NASDAQ*

Year	Proceeds ($ mil.)	Market Share	No. of Issues
1976	79.7	0.2	3
1977	47.7	0.1	2
1981	25.0	0.1	1
1982	12.1	0.0	2
1983	80.3	0.2	2
1984	167.0	0.4	4
1985	31.7	0.1	4
1986	197.2	0.4	8
1987	278.1	0.6	8
1988	300.0	0.6	24
1989	1,014.2	2.1	47
1990	1,736.8	3.7	84
1991	6,972.4	14.7	244
1992	9,265.0	19.5	280
1993	14,193.3	29.9	405
1994	10,081.6	21.3	341
1995	2,950.5	6.2	71
TOTAL	47,432.8	100.0	1,530

Total IPO Issuance on Amex*

Year	Proceeds ($ mil.)	Market Share	No. of Issues
1976	9.9	0.1	2
1979	20.4	0.2	2
1980	9.6	0.1	1
1981	61.9	0.6	5
1983	129.8	1.2	7
1984	113.6	1.0	9
1985	520.4	4.8	17
1986	2,316.9	21.3	53
1987	2,008.8	18.5	52
1988	2,226.3	20.5	36
1989	346.2	3.2	10
1990	344.3	3.2	9
1991	191.3	1.8	11
1992	428.5	3.9	12
1993	1,661.7	15.3	45
1994	401.7	3.7	16
1995	91.2	0.8	2
TOTAL	10,882.4	100.0	289

Total IPO Issuance on NYSE*

Year	Proceeds ($ mil.)	Market Share	No. of Issues
1976	73.4	0.0	2
1977	63.2	0.0	2
1980	101.6	0.1	2
1981	60.0	0.0	1
1982	154.0	0.1	2
1983	1,141.7	0.6	14
1984	901.7	0.0	13
1985	3,994.4	2.2	25
1986	9,692.8	5.3	67
1987	17,983.0	9.8	72
1988	19,501.3	10.7	72
1989	10,816.1	5.9	64
1990	7,380.5	4.0	57
1991	17,406.1	9.5	87
1992	28,539.0	15.6	168
1993	40,048.3	21.9	212
1994	21,863.0	12.0	146
1995	2,863.9	1.6	13
TOTAL	182,584.0	100.0	1,019

*1995 figures are correct as of May 1995

Total IPO Issuances*

Year	Proceeds ($ mil.)	Market Share	No. of Issues
1976	337.2	0.1	40
1977	221.6	0.1	32
1978	225.4	0.1	38
1979	398.4	0.1	62
1980	1,387.1	0.5	149
1981	3,114.7	1.1	348
1982	1,339.1	0.5	122
1983	12,466.4	4.3	686
1984	3,868.9	1.3	357
1985	8,497.6	2.9	355
1986	22,251.8	7.6	728
1987	26,847.3	9.2	556
1988	23,807.5	8.2	291
1989	13,706.1	4.7	254
1990	10,117.4	3.5	213
1991	25,147.7	8.6	403
1992	39,947.1	13.7	605
1993	57,517.1	19.7	819
1994	34,003.8	11.7	647
1995	6,240.6	2.1	121
TOTAL	291,442.6	99.9	6,826

Source: Securities Data Company

Initial Public Offerings (cont'd)

20 Largest Domestic IPOs, 1985–1994 (Excluding Closed-End Funds)

Date	Issuer	Offering Amount ($ mil.)	No. of Shares Offered (mil.)	Offering Price ($)	Book Manager
10/30/87	British Petroleum	2,864.1	42,150,000	67.95	Goldman, Sachs
06/02/93	Allstate	1,849.5	68,500,000	27.00	Goldman, Sachs
03/26/87	Consolidated Rail	1,456.0	52,000,000	28.00	Goldman, Sachs
06/28/93	YPF Sociedad Anónima	1,235.0	65,000,000	19.00	CS First Bos./Merrill Lynch
04/27/94	TeleDanmark	1,219.6	51,839,540	23.53	Goldman, Sachs
05/20/86	Henley Group	1,190.0	56,000,000	21.25	Lazard Frères & Co.
07/27/92	Wellcome	1,067.5	70,000,000	15.25	Morgan Stanley
11/21/86	Coca-Cola	1,001.4	60,690,000	16.50	Allen & Co.
12/02/93	PacTel	966.0	42,000,000	23.00	Salomon Bros./Lehman Bros.
01/18/89	Lyondell Petrochemical	960.0	32,000,000	30.00	Goldman, Sachs
10/23/85	Fireman's Fund	824.0	32,000,000	25.75	Salomon Bros.
04/20/93	TIG Holdings	800.5	35,380,000	22.63	Morgan Stanley
04/09/92	First Data	770.0	35,000,000	22.00	Lehman Bros.
09/12/85	Rockefeller Center Properties	750.0	37,500,000	20.00	Goldman, Sachs
12/13/93	Simon Property Group	713.9	32,087,500	22.25	Merrill Lynch
02/22/93	Dean Witter Discover	695.3	25,750,000	27.00	Dean Witter Reynolds
01/22/91	MBNA	689.3	30,636,000	22.50	Goldman, Sachs
10/29/86	Commercial Credit	662.2	32,300,000	20.50	CS First Boston
12/13/93	Grupo Televisa	640.0	10,000,000	64.00	Goldman, Sachs
02/26/92	HCA–Hospital Corp. of America	584.8	27,200,000	21.50	Goldman, Sachs

Source: Securities Data Company

The Top Reference Sources

Securities Data
1180 Raymond Blvd.
Newark, NJ 07102
(201) 622-3100

Securities Data, a member of the Boston-based Thomson Financial Services family, is the leading provider of merger and financing data worldwide. Its products include online databases, publications, and research services covering mergers and acquisitions, corporate and municipal financing, venture capital, restructurings, and corporate governance.

The World's Stock Exchanges

Stock Exchange	Tokyo	New York	Toronto	London	Germany	Paris	Zurich
No. stock-listed companies (D)	1,651	1,969	1,049	1,816	410	515	180
No. stock-listed companies (F)	119	120	70	576	356	217	240
No. listed issues, stocks (D)	1,652	2,516	1,418	1,902	496	835	303
No. listed issues, stocks (F)	119	142	74	781	379	234	247
No. listed issues, bonds (D)	1,196	2,190	NA	2,631	5,918	2,918	1,508
No. listed issues, bonds (F)	134	164	NA	1,957	1,259	344	897
Total mkt. value, stocks ($ mil.)	2,320,509	3,877,905	242,997	933,452	321,375	328,460	195,284
Total mkt. value, bonds ($ mil.)	1,277,889	2,044,122	NA	608,189	992,999	578,491	186,731
Trading value, stocks ($ mil.)	475,858	1,745,466	63,002	673,861	300,028	121,344	88,011
Trading value, bonds ($ mil.)	116,635	11,629	NA	1,170,618	699,906	816,592	NA
NO. OF MEMBER FIRMS	124	503	79	414	227	46	25

Stock Exchange	Amsterdam	Milan	Australia	Hong Kong	Singapore	Taiwan	Korea
No. stock-listed companies (D)	251	225	1,038	386	188	256	688
No. stock-listed companies (F)	244	3	35	27	25	NA	NA
No. listed issues, stocks (D)	310	341	1,286	395	193	286	1,014
No. listed issues, stocks (F)	295	3	46	30	25	NA	NA
No. listed issues, bonds (D)	829	974	1,592	6	38	62	9,439
No. listed issues, bonds (F)	173	19	NA	9	134	2	NA
Total mkt. value, stocks ($ mil.)	171,262	115,258	135,339	172,184	50,096	100,217	107,661
Total mkt. value, bonds ($ mil.)	198,123	641,697	48,979	489	101,453	20,876	82,791
Trading value, stocks ($ mil.)	44,401	28,129	45,660	78,663	13,930	235,178	116,007
Trading value, bonds ($ mil.)	93,375	40,506	4,544	36	65	152	774
NO. OF MEMBER FIRMS	137	108	99	620	26	277	32

D=Domestic, F=Foreign

Source: Tokyo Stock Exchange Fact Book, 1994

Dollar Volume of Equity Trading in Major World Markets (U.S. $ billions)

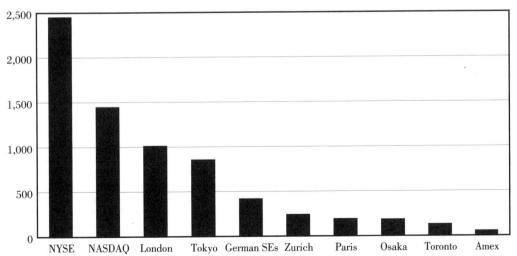

Source: NASDAQ Fact Book & Company Directory, 1995

Major Foreign Exchanges

London Stock Exchange

Old Broad St.
London EC2N 1HP
[44] (71) 797-1000

Ten Most Active UK Companies

Company	Value of Turnover (£ mil.)	Shares Traded (mil.)
HSBC Holdings	19,210.8	2,425.2
British Telecommun.	16,025.0	4,191.2
British Petroleum	15,687.3	3,285.0
Glaxo	14,792.4	2,150.2
Shell Transport & Trading	12,102.6	1,530.6
Hanson	9,876.5	4,019.1
Barclays	9,614.9	1,689.0
British Gas	9,609.3	3,023.8
BTR	8,919.0	3,195.7
National Westminster Bank	8,576.3	1,723.6

Source: London Stock Exchange Fact Book, 1995

Tokyo Stock Exchange

2-1 Nihombashi-Kabuto-Cho
Chuo-ku, Tokyo 103
[81] (3) 3666-0141

New York Research Office
44 Broadway, 12th Floor
New York, NY 10006
(212) 363-2350

The Tokyo Stock Exchange is divided into two sections. Approximately 1,220 companies are listed in the first section, the marketplace for stocks of larger companies. In the second section, the marketplace for smaller and newly listed companies, approximately 420 companies are listed.

Tokyo Stock Price Index (TOPIX) measures the performance of all stocks listed on the first section of the Tokyo Stock Exchange. The TOPIX is separated into 28 sub-indexes by industry groups and size.

The Nikkei Stock Average is the Dow Jones Industrial Average of the Tokyo stock market, tracking the price movements of 225 large, well-known issues in the first section of the Tokyo Stock Exchange. The stocks included represent a broad range of industries including foods, textiles, pulp and paper, chemicals, drugs, petroleum, rubber, glass and ceramics, iron and steel, non-ferrous metals, machinery, electrial equipment, shipbuilding, motor vehicles, transportation equipment, precision instruments, marine products, mining, construction, trade, retail stores, banks, securities, insurance, real estate, railroad and bus transportation, trucking, sea transportation, air transportation, warehousing, communications, electric power, gas, and services.

Ten Most Active Tokyo Stock Exchange Issues by Number of Shares

Company	Reported Share Volume
Nippon Steel	1,514,000,000
NEC	979,000,000
Sumitomo Metal Mining	922,000,000
Mitsubishi Heavy Industries	904,000,000
Fujitsu	903,000,000
Nikkatsu	903,000,000
Isuzu Motors	827,000,000
Hitachi	789,000,000
NKK	681,000,000
Toshiba	651,000,000

Source: Tokyo Stock Exchange Fact Book, 1994

The Top Reference Sources

Tokyo Stock Exchange Fact Book
Tokyo Stock Exchange, free
(800) 829-5916

This is a useful annual reference for anyone interested in following the Tokyo Stock Exchange.

It is made available in English by the New York Research Office of the Exchange.

Statistical data are provided, along with explanatory comments. The book also includes stock price trends, companies listed, commission rates, investors, and other topics.

Major Foreign Exchanges (cont'd)

Just as the Dow Jones Industrial Average is used as a barometer of stock market performance in the U.S., the FT-SE tracks the London Stock Exchange, and the Topix and the Nikkei track the Tokyo Stock Exchange.

FT-SE Financial Times Index, 1984–1994

Source: London Stock Exchange Fact Book, 1995

Topix Performance, 1950–1993

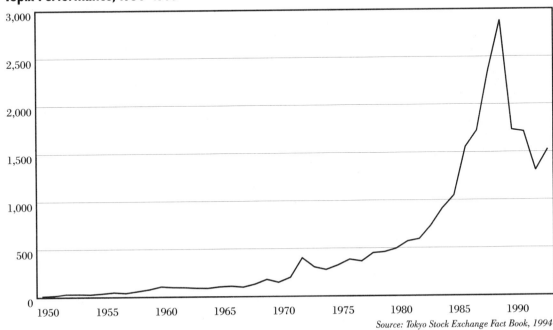

Source: Tokyo Stock Exchange Fact Book, 1994

Major Foreign Exchanges (cont'd)

Largest Nikkei Average Advances (as of November 1994)

Date	% Advanced	Index
10/02/90	13.24	22,898.41
12/15/49	11.29	109.62
10/21/87	9.30	23,947.40
01/31/94	7.84	20,229.12
04/10/92	7.55	17,850.66
04/16/53	6.41	355.03
03/06/53	6.31	361.88
08/21/92	6.22	16,216.88
08/27/92	6.13	17,555.00
01/06/88	5.63	22,790.50

Largest Nikkei Average Declines (as of November 1994)

Date	% Declined	Index
10/20/87	-14.90	21,910.08
03/05/53	-10.00	340.41
04/30/70	-8.69	2,114.32
08/16/71	-7.68	2,530.48
12/14/49	-6.97	98.50
03/30/53	-6.73	318.96
06/24/72	-6.61	3,421.02
04/02/90	-6.60	28,002.07
08/19/91	-5.95	21,456.76
08/19/71	-5.93	2,190.16

Source: Nikkei

The Top Reference Sources

The Nikkei Stock Average Data Book
Nihon Keizai Shimbun, free
(212) 261-6240

This is a very useful reference for anyone interested in following the Nikkei Stock Average. Periodically updated, it provides a thorough overview of the Stock Average, with performance charts, comparisons with other indexes, stock price rankings, lists of the most advanced and declined stocks, annual quotations, long-term trends, average daily closing prices, largest losses and gains, and other relevant facts.

Major Foreign Exchanges (cont'd)

Foreign Purchases of Japanese Stocks (billions of yen)

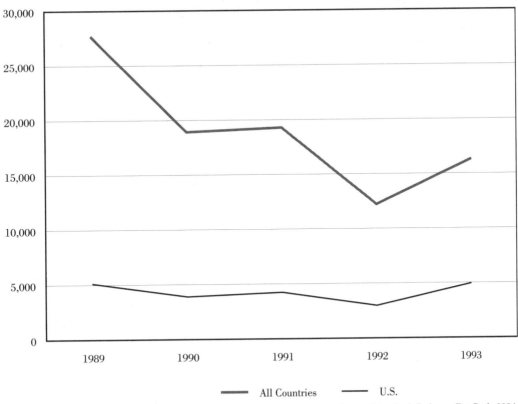

All Countries — U.S.

Source: Tokyo Stock Exchange Fact Book, 1994

The Top Reference Sources

Financial World
Financial World Partners, $36/year
(212) 594-5030

This monthly magazine concentrates on business, economic, and financial topics. It includes a focus on the national economy and effects of Washington policy upon it, statistical analysis of stock, bond, and mutual fund activity, and the international industrial and financial arena. Highlights include the list of America's 200 Best Growth Companies.

TIP: *It may be important for an individual to collect comprehensive data on a company. Lexis-Nexis Express will search through newspapers and periodicals for all references to and mention of a particular company. They will provide a list of all citations and/or the text of the actual article for the client. Fees for this service include $6 per minute search time (the average search ranges from five to 15 minutes) and $2.50 per page of printouts. Additional information is available at (800) 843-6476.*

The Dow Jones Averages

The Dow Jones Industrial Average

The Dow Jones Industrial Average ("the Dow") tracks price movements in 30 of the largest blue-chip issues traded on the NYSE, including:

3M
AlliedSignal
Alcoa
American Express
AT&T
Bethlehem Steel
Boeing
Caterpillar
Chevron
Coca-Cola
Walt Disney
DuPont
Eastman Kodak
Exxon
General Electric
General Motors
Goodyear
IBM
International Paper
McDonald's
Merck
J. P. Morgan
Philip Morris
Procter & Gamble
Sears, Roebuck
Texaco
Union Carbide
United Technologies
Westinghouse
Woolworth

The Dow Jones Transportation Average

The Dow Jones Transportation Average was originally of railroads alone. The current index also reflects developments in the airline and trucking business in this mix of twenty transport companies:

AMR
Airborne Freight
Alaska Air
American President
Burlington Northern
Carolina Freight
Consolidated Freightways
Consolidated Rail
CSX
Delta Air Lines
Federal Express
Norfolk Southern
Roadway Services
Ryder Systems
Santa Fe Pacific
Southwest Airlines
UAL
Union Pacific
USAir
XTRA

The Dow Jones Utility Average

The Dow Jones Utility Average tracks the following 15 large electricity and natural gas utilities:

American Electric Power
Arkla
Centerior
Commonwealth Edison
Consolidated Edison
Consolidated Natural Gas
Detroit Edison
Houston Industries
Niagara Mohawk Power
Pacific Gas & Electric
Panhandle Eastern
Peoples Energy
Philadelphia Electric
Public Service Enterprises
SCE

Performance of Dow Jones Industrials, 1994

Company	1994 Close ($)	% Change from 1993
Union Carbide	29.38	31.28
IBM	73.50	30.09
Alcoa	86.63	24.86
Caterpillar	55.13	23.88
DuPont	56.13	16.32
Coca-Cola	51.50	15.41
Int'l Paper	75.38	11.25
Merck	38.13	10.91
American Express	29.50	8.87
Procter & Gamble	62.00	8.77
Boeing	47.00	8.67
Walt Disney	46.00	7.92

Company	1994 Close ($)	% Change from 1993
Eastman Kodak	47.75	7.35
Philip Morris	57.50	3.37
McDonald's	29.25	2.63
Chevron	44.63	2.44
United Technologies	62.88	1.41
3M	53.38	1.84
General Electric	51.00	-2.74
Exxon	60.75	-3.76
AT&T	50.25	-4.29
Texaco	59.88	-7.53
Bethlehem Steel	18.00	-11.66
Sears, Roebuck	46.00	-13.00

The Dow Jones Averages (cont'd)

Company	1994 Close ($)	% Change from 1993
Westinghouse	12.25	-13.27
AlliedSignal	34.00	-13.92
J. P. Morgan	56.13	-19.10
General Motors	42.13	-23.23

Company	1994 Close ($)	% Change from 1993
Goodyear	33.63	-26.50
Woolworth	15.00	-40.89

Source: The Wall Street Journal, Jan. 2, 1995

Dow Jones Industrial Average Performance Since 1900

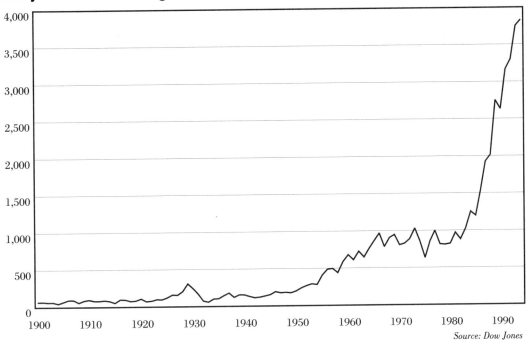

Source: Dow Jones

S&P 500 Index Performance, Yearly Close

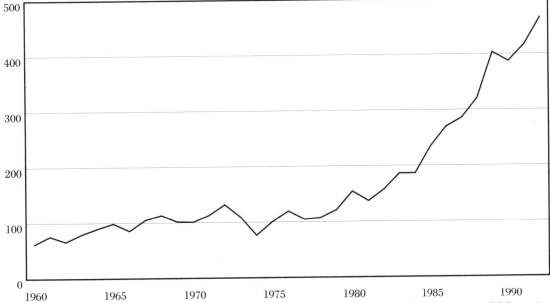

Source: S&P 500 Directory, 1994. Reprinted by permission of Standard & Poor's, a division of The McGraw-Hill Companies

Standard & Poor's 500

STANDARD & POOR'S 500 Index (S&P 500) represents approximately 80 percent of the value of all issues traded on the NYSE, reflecting the performance of 500 stocks including industrials, public utilities, transportation companies, and financial companies. Movement within each of these industry categories is tracked in sub-indexes.

The S&P 500 Index is currently one of the 12 leading economic indicators cited by the U.S. Commerce Department.

S&P 500 Composite Stock Price Index

Ticker Symbol	Company Name
MMM	3M
AMP	AMP
AMR	AMR
T	AT&T
ABT	Abbott Laboratories
AMD	Advanced Micro Devices
AET	Aetna Life & Casualty
AHM	Ahmanson (H.F.) & Co.
APD	Air Products and Chemicals
ACV	Alberto-Culver
ABS	Albertson's
AL	Alcan Aluminum
ASN	Alco Standard
AAL	Alexander & Alexander Services
AGN	Allergan
ALD	AlliedSignal
AA	Alcoa
AZA	ALZA
AMH	Amdahl
AHC	Amerada Hess
ABX	American Barrick Resources
AMB	American Brands
ACY	American Cyanamid
AEP	American Electric Power
AXP	American Express
AGC	American General
AGREA	American Greetings
AHP	American Home Products
AIG	American International Group
ASC	American Stores
AIT	Ameritech
AMEN	Amgen
AN	Amoco
ANDW	Andrew
BUD	Anheuser-Busch Companies
AAPL	Apple Computer
ADM	Archer-Daniels-Midland
ALG	Arkla
AS	Armco
ACK	Armstrong World Industries
AR	Asarco
ASH	Ashland Oil
ARC	Atlantic Richfield
ACAD	Autodesk
AUD	Automatic Data Processing

Ticker Symbol	Company Name
AVY	Avery Dennison
AVP	Avon Products
BHI	Baker Hughes
BLL	Ball
BLY	Bally Manufacturing
BGE	Baltimore Gas & Electric
ONE	Banc One
BKB	Bank of Boston
BAC	BankAmerica
BT	Bankers Trust New York
BCR	Bard (C.R.)
BBI	Barnett Banks
BSET	Bassett Furniture Industries
BOL	Bausch & Lomb
BAX	Baxter International
BDX	Becton, Dickinson & Co.
BEL	Bell Atlantic
BLS	BellSouth
BMS	Bemis
BNL	Beneficial
BS	Bethlehem Steel
BEV	Beverly Enterprises
BMET	Biomet
BDK	Black & Decker
HRB	Block (H&R)
BV	Blockbuster Entertainment
BOAT	Boatmen's Bancshares
BA	Boeing
BCC	Boise Cascade
BN	Borden
BGG	Briggs & Stratton
BMY	Bristol-Myers Squibb
BFD	Brown-Forman
BG	Brown Group
BFI	Browning-Ferris Industries
BRNO	Bruno's
BC	Brunswick
BNI	Burlington Northern
BR	Burlington Resources
CBS	CBS
CNA	CNA Financial
CPC	CPC
CSX	CSX
CPB	Campbell Soup
CCB	Capital Cities/ABC

Standard & Poor's 500 (cont'd)

Ticker Symbol	Company Name
CPH	Capital Holding
CPL	Carolina Power & Light
CAT	Caterpillar
CTX	Centex
CSR	Central & Southwest
CEN	Ceridian
CHA	Champion
CHRS	Charming Shoppes
CMB	Chase Manhattan
CHL	Chemical Banking
CHV	Chevron
C	Chrysler
CB	Chubb
CSCO	Cisco Systems
CI	Cigna
CMZ	Cincinnati Milacron
CC	Circuit City Stores
CCI	Citicorp
CKL	Clark Equipment
CLX	Clorox
CGP	Coastal
KO	Coca-Cola
CL	Colgate-Palmolive
CG	Columbia Gas System
COL	Columbia Healthcare
CMCSK	Comcast Class A Special
CWE	Commonwealth Edison
CMY	Community Psychiatric Centers
CPQ	Compaq Computer
CA	Computer Associates
CSC	Computer Sciences
CAG	Conagra
CRR	Conrail
ED	Consolidated Edison Co. of New York
CNF	Consolidated Freightways
CNG	Consolidated Natural Gas
CIC	Continental
CBE	Cooper Industries
CTB	Cooper Tire & Rubber
ACCOB	Coors (Adolph)
CFL	CoreStates Financial
GLW	Corning
CR	Crane
CYR	Cray Research
CCK	Crown Cork & Seal
CUM	Cummins Engine
CYM	Cyprus-Amax Minerals
DIGI	DSC Communications
DCN	Dana
DGN	Data General

Ticker Symbol	Company Name
DH	Dayton Hudson
DWD	Dean Witter, Discover & Co.
DE	Deere & Company
DAL	Delta Air Lines
DLX	Deluxe
DTE	Detroit Edison
DL	Dial
DEC	Digital Equipment
DDS	Dillard Department Stores
DIS	Disney (Walt)
D	Dominion Resources
DNY	Donnelley (R.R.) & Sons
DOV	Dover
DOW	Dow Chemical
DJ	Dow Jones & Co.
DI	Dresser Industries
DUK	Duke Power
DNB	Dun & Bradstreet
DD	DuPont (E.I.) De Nemours
EGG	EG & G
ESY	E-Systems
EFU	Eastern Enterprises
EK	Eastman Kodak
ETN	Eaton
ECH	Echlin
ECO	Echo Bay Mines
ECL	Ecolab
EMR	Emerson Electric
EC	Engelhard
ENE	Enron
ENS	Enserch
ETR	Entergy
EY	Ethyl
XON	Exxon
FMC	FMC
FPL	FPL Group
FJQ	Fedders
FDX	Federal Express
FRE	Federal Home Loan Mortgage
FNM	Federal National Mortgage Assn.
FBO	Federal Paper Board
FNB	First Chicago
FFB	First Fidelity Bancorp
I	First Interstate Bancorp
FRM	First Mississippi
FTU	First Union
FLT	Fleet Financial Group
FLE	Fleetwood Enterprises
FLM	Fleming Companies
FLR	Fluor

Standard & Poor's 500 (cont'd)

Ticker Symbol	Company Name
F	Ford Motor
FWC	Foster Wheeler
GTE	GTE
GCI	Gannett
GPS	Gap (The)
GCN	General Cinema
GD	General Dynamics
GE	General Electric
GIS	General Mills
GM	General Motors
GRN	General Re
GSX	General Signal
GCO	Genesco
GPC	Genuine Parts
GP	Georgia-Pacific
GEB	Gerber Products
GFSA	Giant Food
GIDL	Giddings & Lewis
GS	Gillette
GDW	Golden West Financial
GR	Goodrich (B. F.)
GT	Goodyear Tire & Rubber
GRA	Grace (W. R.) & Co.
GWW	Grainger (W. W.)
GAP	Great Atlantic & Pacific Tea
GLK	Great Lakes Chemical
GWF	Great Western Financial
GQ	Grumman
HAL	Halliburton
HDL	Handleman
H	Harcourt General
JH	Harland (John H.)
HPH	Harnischfeger Industries
HRS	Harris
HMX	Hartmarx
HAS	Hasbro
HNZ	Heinz (H. J.)
HP	Helmerich & Payne
HPC	Hercules
HSY	Hershey Foods
HWP	Hewlett-Packard
HLT	Hilton Hotels
HD	Home Depot
HM	Homestake Mining
HON	Honeywell
HI	Household
HOU	Houston Industries
IBM	IBM
ITT	ITT
ITW	Illinois Tool Works
IMA	Imcera Group
N	Inco
IR	Ingersoll-Rand
IAD	Inland Steel Industries
INTC	Intel

Ticker Symbol	Company Name
INGR	Intergraph
IFF	International Flavors & Fragrances
IP	International Paper
IPG	Interpublic Group
JR	James River
JP	Jefferson-Pilot
JCI	Johnson Controls
JNJ	Johnson & Johnson
JOS	Jostens
KBH	Kaufman & Broad Home
K	Kellogg
KMG	Kerr-McGee
KMB	Kimberly-Clark
KWP	King World Productions
KM	K Mart
KRI	Knight-Ridder
KR	The Kroger Co.
LLY	Lilly (Eli) & Co.
LTD	Limited (The)
LNC	Lincoln National
LIT	Litton Industries
LIZC	Liz Claiborne
LK	Lockheed
LDG	Longs Drug Stores
LOR	Loral
LOTS	Lotus Development
LLX	Louisiana Land & Exploration
LPX	Louisiana-Pacific
LOW	Lowe's Companies
LUB	Luby's Cafeterias
MAI	M/A-Com
KRB	MBNA
MCIC	MCI Communications
MNR	Manor Care
MAR	Marriott
MMC	Marsh & McLennan
ML	Martin Marietta
MAS	Masco
MAT	Mattel
MXS	Maxus Energy
MA	May Department Stores
MYG	Maytag
MCAWA	McCaw Cellular
MDR	McDermott
MCD	McDonald's
MD	McDonnell Douglas
MHP	McGraw-Hill
MCK	McKesson
MEA	Mead
MDT	Medtronic
MEL	Mellon Bank
MES	Melville
MST	Mercantile Stores
MRK	Merck & Co.
MDP	Meredith

Standard & Poor's 500 (cont'd)

Ticker Symbol	Company Name
MER	Merrill Lynch & Co.
MIL	Millipore
MOB	Mobil
MTC	Monsanto
MCL	Moore
JPM	Morgan (J. P.) & Co.
MRN	Morrison Knudsen
MII	Morton
MOT	Motorola
NBD	NBD Bancorp
NL	NL Industries
NC	NACCO Industries
NLC	Nalco Chemical
NEC	National Education
NII	National Intergroup
NME	National Medical Enterprises
NSM	National Semiconductor
NSI	National Service Industries
NB	NationsBank
NAV	Navistar International
NYTA	New York Times (The)
NWL	Newell
NEM	Newmont Mining
NMK	Niagara Mohawk Power
GAS	Nicor
NIKE	Nike
NOBE	Nordstrom
NSC	Norfolk Southern
NSP	Northern States Power
NT	Northern Telecom
NOC	Northrop
NOB	Norwest
NOVL	Novell
NUE	Nucor
NYN	NYNEX
OXY	Occidental Petroleum
OG	Ogden
OEC	Ohio Edison
OKE	Oneok
ORCL	Oracle Systems
ORX	Oryx Energy
GOSHA	Oshkosh B'Gosh
OM	Outboard Marine
OCF	Owens-Corning Fiberglas
PT	PET
PNC	PNC Bank
PPG	PPG Industries
PIN	PSI Resources
PCAR	Paccar
PET	Pacific Enterprises
PCG	Pacific Gas & Electric
PAC	Pacific Telesis Group
PPW	Pacificorp
PLL	Pall
PEL	Panhandle Eastern

Ticker Symbol	Company Name
PH	Parker Hannifin
JCP	Penney (J. C.)
PZL	Pennzoil
PGL	Peoples Energy
PBY	Pep Boys (Manny, Moe & Jack)
PEP	PepsiCo
PKN	Perkin-Elmer
PFE	Pfizer
PD	Phelps Dodge
PE	Philadelphia Electric
MO	Philip Morris
P	Phillips Petroleum
PHYB	Pioneer Hi-Bred
PBI	Pitney Bowes
PZS	Pittston Services Group
PDG	Placer Dome
PRD	Polaroid
PCH	Potlatch
PX	Praxair
PMI	Premark International
PCCW	Price/CostCo
PA	Primerica
PG	Procter & Gamble
PRI	Promus
PEG	Public Service Enterprises
PHM	Putte
OAT	Quaker Oats
RAL	Ralston–Ralston Purina Group
RYC	Raychem
RTN	Raytheon
RBK	Reebok
RLM	Reynolds Metals
RAD	Rite Aid
ROAD	Roadway Services
ROK	Rockwell
ROH	Rohm & Haas
REN	Rollins Environmental Services
RDC	Rowan
RD	Royal Dutch Petroleum
RBD	Rubbermaid
RML	Russell
RYAN	Ryan's Family Steak Houses
R	Ryder Systems
SAFC	SAFECO
SCE	SCE
SPW	SPX
SK	Safety-Kleen
STJM	St. Jude Medical
STPL	St. Paul Companies
SB	Salomon
SFR	Santa Fe Energy Resources
SFX	Santa Fe Pacific
SLE	Sara Lee
SGP	Schering-Plough
SLB	Schlumberger

Standard & Poor's 500 (cont'd)

Ticker Symbol	Company Name
SFA	Scientific-Atlanta
SPP	Scott Paper
VO	Seagram Company (The)
S	Sears, Roebuck & Co.
SRV	Service International
SMED	Shared Medical Systems
SNC	Shawmut National
SHW	Sherwin-Williams
SHN	Shoney's
SKY	Skyline
SNA	Snap-On Tools
SNT	Sonat
SO	Southern
SBC	Southwestern Bell
SMI	Springs Industries
FON	Sprint
SWK	Stanley Works
STO	Stone Container
SRR	Stride-Rite
SUN	Sun
SUNW	Sun Microsystems
STI	Suntrust Banks
SVU	Supervalu
SYN	Syntex
SYY	SYSCO
TJX	TJX Companies
TRW	TRW
TDM	Tandem Computers
TAN	Tandy
TEK	Tektronix
TCOMA	Tele-Communications
TDY	Teledyne
TIN	Temple-Inland
TGT	Tenneco
TX	Texaco
TXN	Texas Instruments
TXU	Texas Utilities
TXT	Textron
TNB	Thomas & Betts
TWX	Time Warner
TMC	Times Mirror
TKR	Timken
TMK	Torchmark
TOY	Toys 'R' Us
TA	TransAmerica
E	Transco Energy
TIC	Travelers
TRB	Tribune
TNV	Trinova
TYC	Tyco

Ticker Symbol	Company Name
UAL	UAL
FG	USF & G
UST	UST
MRO	USX-Marathon Group
X	USX-U.S. Steel Group
UN	Unilever
UCC	Union Camp
UK	Union Carbide
UEP	Union Electric
UNP	Union Pacific
UIS	Unisys
USBC	U.S. Bancorp
USS	U.S. Surgical
USW	US West
UTX	United Technologies
UCL	Unocal
UPJ	Upjohn
U	USAir
USH	USLife
VAT	Varity
VFC	V. F.
WMX	WMX Technologies
WB	Wachovia
WMT	Wal-Mart Stores
WAG	Walgreen
WLA	Warner-Lambert
WFC	Wells Fargo & Co.
WEN	Wendy's
WX	Westinghouse Electric
W	Westvaco
WY	Weyerhaeuser
WHR	Whirlpool
WH	Whitman
WMB	Williams Companies (The)
WIN	Winn-Dixie Stores
Z	Woolworth
WTHG	Worthington Industries
WWY	Wm. Wrigley Jr.
XRX	Xerox
YELL	Yellow
ZE	Zenith Electronics
ZRN	Zurn Industries

Source: S&P 500 Directory, 1994. Reprinted by permission of Standard & Poor's, a division of The McGraw-Hill Companies

Standard & Poor's 500 (cont'd)

Representation of Industry Groups in the S&P 500, 1993 (%)

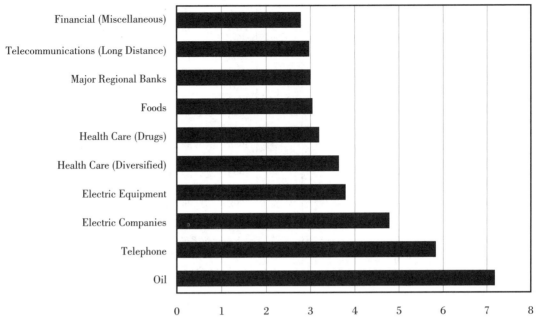

Source: S&P 500 Directory, 1994. Reprinted by permission of Standard & Poor's, a division of The McGraw-Hill Companies

Most Widely Held S&P Companies, 1993

Rank	Company	Number of Shareholders
1	AT&T (T)	2,344,160
2	BellSouth (BLS)	1,387,800
3	NYNEX (NYN)	1,093,200
4	Bell Atlantic (BEL)	1,064,792
5	Ameritech (AIT)	1,042,400
6	Southwestern Bell (SBC)	973,600
7	Pacific Telesis (PAC)	933,400
8	General Motors (GM)	891,600
9	US West (USW)	867,800
10	IBM (IBM)	764,600
11	Exxon (XON)	620,500
12	GTE (GTE)	504,000
13	Royal Dutch Petroleum (RD)	500,000
14	General Electric (GE)	475,000
15	Occidental Petroleum (OXY)	463,000
16	McDonald's (MCD)	378,000
17	Sears, Roebuck (S)	331,800
18	Mobil (MOB)	286,600
19	Ford Motor (F)	282,600
20	Pacific Gas & Electric (PCG)	261,000

Source: S&P 500 Directory, 1994. Reprinted by permission of Standard & Poor's, a division of The McGraw-Hill Companies

Standard & Poor's 500 (cont'd)

S&P 500 Index Performance, Yearly Close, P/E Ratio

Year	Close	Close P/E Ratio
1960	61.49	18.14
1961	75.72	22.47
1962	66.00	17.05
1963	79.25	18.69
1964	89.62	18.55
1965	98.47	17.87
1966	85.24	14.47
1967	105.11	18.57
1968	113.02	18.38
1969	101.49	16.45
1970	100.90	18.58
1971	112.72	18.72
1972	131.87	19.31
1973	109.14	12.32
1974	76.47	7.89
1975	100.88	11.80
1976	119.46	11.19
1977	104.71	9.01
1978	107.21	8.17
1979	121.02	7.47

Year	Close	Close P/E Ratio
1980	154.45	9.58
1981	137.12	8.29
1982	157.62	11.92
1983	186.24	12.64
1984	186.36	10.36
1985	234.56	15.39
1986	269.93	18.73
1987	285.86	14.09
1988	321.26	12.35
1989	403.49	15.31
1990	387.42	15.90
1991	417.09	26.12
1992	435.71	22.82
1993	466.45	21.31

Source: S&P 500 Directory, 1994. Reprinted by permission of Standard & Poor's, a division of The McGraw-Hill Companies

The Top Reference Sources

S&P MidCap 400 Directory
Standard & Poor's, $39.95
(212) 208-1649

Published for the first time in 1992, this annual directory is designed to provide money managers, analysts, institutional and individual investors, corporative executives, journalists, and observers of financial markets and the overall economy with a comprehensive and authoritative analysis of the growing middle-capitalization sector of the U.S. equities market.

The book includes a complete listing of the MidCap 400 companies, company reports, and statistical tables.

Money-Saving Tips. Send e-mail to money@almanac.yoyo.com. See p. xi for instructions.

Report by Kimberly Stanséll, named one of "America's Best Penny-Pinchers" by Home Office Computing magazine. Cost-cutting strategies businesses can use to boost their profits.

Composite Indexes

The Amex Market Value Index

The Amex Market Value Index is composed of all common stocks listed on the American Stock Exchange.

Amex Market Value Index Performance, Yearly Highs

Year	Index
1976	54.92
1977	63.95
1978	88.44
1979	123.54
1980	185.38
1981	190.18
1982	170.93
1983	249.03
1984	227.73
1985	246.13
1986	285.19
1987	365.01
1988	309.59
1989	397.03
1990	382.45
1991	395.05
1992	418.99
1993	484.28
1994	487.89

Source: American Stock Exchange Fact Book, 1995

The Value Line Composite Index

The Value Line Composite Index tracks the performance of 1,700 stocks listed on the New York Stock Exchange, the American Stock Exchange, the Regional and Canadian exchanges, and the over-the-counter market.

The New York Stock Exchange Composite Index

The New York Stock Exchange Composite Index measures price movement of all NYSE-listed common stocks as well as performance in four subgroups: Industrial, Transportation, Utility, and Finance.

NASDAQ Composite Index

The NASDAQ Composite Index indicates price movements of all domestic OTC common stocks listed on the NASDAQ system. The composite is broken down into six specialized industry indexes.

NASDAQ Composite Index Market Value, 1981 to 1994

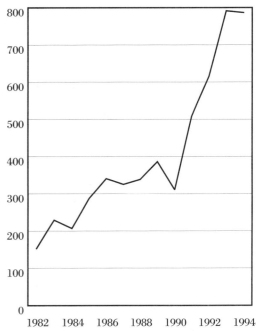

Source: NASDAQ Fact Book & Company Directory, 1995

The Amex Market Value Index

Index Performance

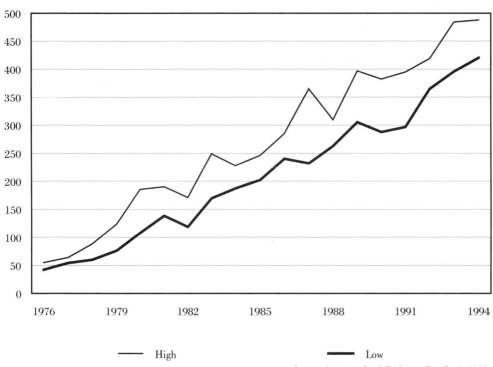

Source: American Stock Exchange Fact Book, 1995

The Top Reference Sources

Pensions & Investments
Crain Communications, $180/year
(800) 678-9595

This newspaper of corporate and institutional
investing includes informative articles on a range
of investment topics.

Regular features track the changes in the S&P
500, Russell 3000 Stock Index, Morgan Stanley
Capital Internationals, and other stock indexes.

P&I also sponsors a number of surveys
throughout the year, on topics as varied as the
largest real estate investors and the popularity of
Ross Perot.

The Wilshire 5000 Equity Index

THE WILSHIRE 5000 EQUITY INDEX measures price movements of all stocks listed on the New York Stock Exchange (85%) and American Stock Exchange (3%) and of most active over-the-counter stocks (12%), or all common equity securities for which pricing is available. December 31, 1980, is the base, at 1,404.596.

The Wilshire 5000 Equity Index

Source: Wilshire Associates

The Top Reference Sources

Hulbert Financial Digest
Hulbert, $135
(703) 683-5905

There are literally hundreds of newsletters written for investors. In most cases, the primary source of income for the editor is not the stock market, but the revenue from the newsletter. In order to separate the pros from the pretenders, the monthly *Hulbert Financial Digest* keeps track of each newsletter's performance. Hulbert's compilations give the regular investor the data needed to choose the best advice available.

The Russell 2000 Index

THE RUSSELL 2000 INDEX TRACKS the stock prices of 2,000 small-capitalization companies (average market capitalization $155 million).

The Russell 2000 Index Performance

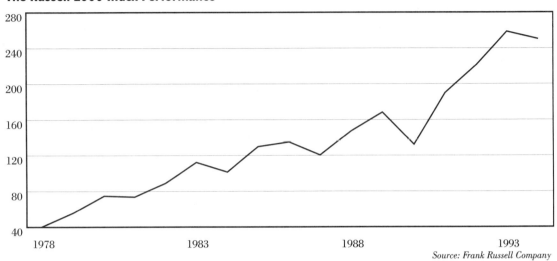

Source: Frank Russell Company

Stock Indexes Performance

Performance of Stock Indexes, Year-End

Year	Dow Jones Industrial Average	S&P 500	NYSE Composite	Amex Market Value	NASDAQ Composite	Value Line
1981	875.00	122.55	71.11	160.32	195.84	137.81
1982	1,046.54	140.64	81.03	170.30	232.41	158.94
1983	1,258.64	164.93	95.18	223.01	278.60	194.35
1984	1,211.57	167.24	96.38	204.26	247.35	177.98
1985	1,546.67	211.28	121.58	246.13	324.93	214.86
1986	1,895.95	242.17	138.58	263.27	348.83	225.62
1987	1,938.83	247.08	138.23	260.35	330.47	201.62
1988	2,168.57	277.72	156.26	306.01	381.38	232.68
1989	2,753.20	353.40	195.04	378.00	454.82	258.78
1990	2,633.66	330.22	180.49	308.11	373.84	195.99
1991	3,168.83	417.09	229.44	395.05	586.34	249.34
1992	3,301.11	435.71	240.21	399.23	676.95	266.68
1993	3,754.09	466.45	252.08	477.15	776.80	295.28

Source: Securities Industry Association Fact Book, 1994

Stock Indexes Performance (cont'd)

Performance of Stock Indexes, Annual Percent Change

Year	Dow Jones Industrial Average	S&P 500	NYSE Composite	Amex Market Value	NASDAQ Composite	Value Line
1981	-9.2	-9.7	-8.7	-8.1	-3.2	-4.4
1982	19.6	14.8	14.0	6.2	18.7	15.3
1983	20.3	17.3	17.5	31.0	19.9	22.3
1984	-3.7	1.4	1.3	8.4	-11.2	-8.4
1985	27.7	26.3	26.1	20.5	31.4	20.7
1986	22.6	14.6	14.0	7.0	7.4	5.0
1987	2.3	2.0	-0.3	-1.1	-5.3	-10.6
1988	11.8	12.4	13.0	17.5	15.4	15.4
1989	27.0	27.3	24.8	23.5	19.3	11.2
1990	-4.3	-6.6	-7.5	-18.5	-17.8	-24.3
1991	20.3	26.3	27.1	28.2	56.8	27.2
1992	4.2	4.5	4.7	1.1	15.5	7.0
1993	13.7	7.1	7.9	19.5	14.7	10.7

Source: Securities Industry Association Fact Book, 1994

The Top Reference Sources

The Ernst & Young Tax Guide
John Wiley & Sons, $14.95
(212) 850-6000

This comprehensive, readable guide is really two books in one. It is the official, annually published IRS tax guide. More important, it is a taxpayer guide that offers explanations, comments, and tax-saving tips. In addition to official tax forms, this very readable book contains pointers and strategies called TaxSavers, TaxPlanners, TaxOrganizers, and TaxAlerts, all of which offer advice to the individual, the corporate or stock market investor, the real estate investor, the self-employed entrepreneur, and the senior citizen.

Prodigy offers access to current benchmark credit ratings, such as rates for T-bills, U.S. Treasury notes and bonds, and the prime rate. JUMP CREDIT RATES.

Financial Ratios by Industry

Five-Year Average Financial Ratios for Selected Industries (1989–1993)

Financial Ratios	Food, Tobacco	Textile Mill Products	Paper, Allied Products	Printing, Publishing	Chemicals, Allied Products
Current ratio	1.2	2.1	1.5	1.6	1.3
Quick ratio	0.7	1.2	0.9	1.3	0.9
Long-term debt to equity (%)	94.6	90.5	99.2	77.6	56.6
Total liabilities to total assets (%)	66.1	62.7	63.9	60.2	60.6
Total liabilities to equity (%)	195.1	172.0	179.4	151.7	154.4
Fixed assets to equity (%)	85.7	93.8	165.5	60.5	90.2
Current to total liabilities (%)	34.4	37.3	25.7	32.2	38.7
Cash flow to total assets (%)	8.8	8.0	7.2	7.3	9.6
Short-term debt to total assets (%)	7.2	8.1	4.4	3.9	6.9
Long-term debt to total assets (%)	32.0	32.9	35.3	30.8	22.3
Equity to total assets (%)	33.9	37.3	36.0	39.8	39.4
Average collection period (days)	26.5	49.6	35.1	54.0	50.4
Inventory turnover (times)	9.8	6.5	9.9	15.1	8.0
Fixed assets turnover (times)	4.3	4.1	1.6	3.9	2.4
Total assets turnover (times)	1.3	1.4	1.0	0.9	0.9
Profit margin before taxes (%)	6.6	3.4	3.5	6.3	8.8
Return on assets before taxes (%)	8.4	4.9	3.5	5.9	7.7
Return on assets after taxes (%)	5.5	2.9	2.1	3.6	5.6
Return on equity before taxes (%)	24.6	12.8	9.1	15.0	18.9
Return on equity after taxes (%)	16.3	7.5	5.4	9.0	13.8

Financial Ratios	Industrial Chemicals, Synthetics	Drugs	Petroleum, Coal Products	Rubber, Plastic Products	Stone, Clay, Glass Products
Current ratio	1.3	1.2	1.0	1.3	1.4
Quick ratio	0.8	0.8	0.7	0.8	0.9
Long-term debt to equity (%)	70.3	26.8	53.1	71.5	107.2
Total liabilities to total assets (%)	63.9	52.4	59.4	66.5	68.6
Total liabilities to equity (%)	180.6	110.6	146.1	199.0	221.2
Fixed assets to equity (%)	118.3	59.9	136.7	112.4	135.0
Current to total liabilities (%)	32.0	55.8	30.8	48.8	31.8
Cash flow to total assets (%)	7.9	14.9	9.3	8.0	4.9
Short-term debt to total assets (%)	6.0	9.8	4.6	11.7	7.8
Long-term debt to total assets (%)	24.9	12.7	21.6	23.9	33.3
Equity to total assets (%)	35.7	47.6	40.6	33.5	31.3
Average collection period (days)	56.4	46.0	34.0	49.1	51.7
Inventory turnover (times)	7.9	7.9	15.6	8.3	8.6
Fixed assets turnover (times)	1.8	3.0	1.6	3.7	2.1
Total assets turnover (times)	0.8	0.9	0.9	1.4	0.9
Profit margin before taxes (%)	5.2	18.8	4.8	2.9	0.6
Return on assets before taxes (%)	4.3	15.9	4.3	4.2	1.0
Return on assets after taxes (%)	3.1	11.9	3.7	3.0	0.6
Return on equity before taxes (%)	10.4	33.0	10.2	11.8	2.4
Return on equity after taxes (%)	7.6	24.8	8.9	8.4	1.2

Financial Ratios by Industry (cont'd)

Financial Ratios	Primary Metal Industries	Iron, Steel	Non-ferrous Metals	Fabricated Metal Products	Machinery, Except Electrical
Current ratio	1.7	1.7	1.6	1.9	1.6
Quick ratio	1.0	1.0	1.0	1.1	1.0
Long-term debt to equity (%)	87.5	159.3	66.2	61.3	42.6
Total liabilities to total assets (%)	70.8	82.2	61.6	59.2	54.7
Total liabilities to equity (%)	244.7	509.2	163.0	144.9	122.6
Fixed assets to equity (%)	148.8	271.8	110.7	70.7	52.2
Current to total liabilities (%)	32.4	30.1	34.9	45.7	49.0
Cash flow to total assets (%)	5.2	4.2	6.0	8.3	5.0
Short-term debt to total assets (%)	4.9	4.2	5.6	7.2	6.0
Long-term debt to total assets (%)	25.3	25.6	25.1	25.0	19.1
Equity to total assets (%)	29.1	17.5	38.1	40.8	45.2
Average collection period (days)	46.8	45.4	48.0	51.4	61.6
Inventory turnover (times)	7.0	6.3	7.7	6.8	6.3
Fixed assets turnover (times)	2.6	2.6	2.6	4.8	4.3
Total assets turnover (times)	1.1	1.2	1.1	1.4	1.0
Profit margin before taxes (%)	0.8	0.0	1.5	4.3	0.6
Return on assets before taxes (%)	1.2	0.2	1.9	6.1	0.7
Return on assets after taxes (%)	0.8	-0.2	1.6	4.2	0.3
Return on equity before taxes (%)	2.8	-3.5	3.9	14.9	1.1
Return on equity after taxes (%)	2.1	-4.4	3.4	10.3	0.3

Financial Ratios	Electrical, Electronic Equipment	Transportation Equipment	Motor Vehicles, Equipment	Aircraft, Guided Missiles, Parts	Instruments, Related Products
Current ratio	1.4	1.3	1.3	1.2	1.7
Quick ratio	0.9	0.7	1.0	0.5	1.0
Long-term debt to equity (%)	35.7	59.9	61.8	56.5	47.4
Total liabilities to total assets (%)	56.2	74.8	75.6	73.1	55.2
Total liabilities to equity (%)	128.3	310.9	353.8	273.2	123.1
Fixed assets to equity (%)	50.1	100.4	121.7	75.6	54.2
Current to total liabilities (%)	58.3	46.6	35.7	63.3	42.5
Cash flow to total assets (%)	8.1	3.5	1.9	5.5	9.0
Short-term debt to total assets (%)	9.3	3.3	3.0	3.4	5.8
Long-term debt to total assets (%)	15.6	14.6	13.8	15.1	21.2
Equity to total assets (%)	43.8	24.6	22.8	26.8	44.9
Average collection period (days)	56.2	49.2	47.4	49.8	60.0
Inventory turnover (times)	5.9	5.7	13.7	2.8	6.0
Fixed assets turnover (times)	4.9	4.4	4.1	4.9	3.6
Total assets turnover (times)	1.1	1.1	1.1	1.0	0.9
Profit margin before taxes (%)	5.8	-1.4	-4.9	3.4	7.6
Return on assets before taxes (%)	6.2	-1.2	-4.6	3.4	6.7
Return on assets after taxes (%)	4.1	-0.6	-2.7	2.2	5.2
Return on equity before taxes (%)	14.0	-5.6	-20.0	11.6	14.6
Return on equity after taxes (%)	9.3	-3.1	-12.0	7.6	11.3

The financial ratios presented here are based on consistent, seasonally adjusted time series. Source data for the series are published in the Census Bureau's Quarterly Financial Report. Corporations are classified in accordance with the Standard Industrial Classification Manual, 1987. All corporations included in the report receive a greater portion of gross receipts from manufacturing than from other activities; final industry classification is determined by the major source of receipts within the manufacturing sector.

Financial Ratios by Industry (cont'd)

In the calculations on the preceding pages, the federal government uses the following formulas. These formulas are valuable in evaluating the financial reports of any business.

Formulas for Financial Ratios

Current Ratio
Current assets/current liabilities. Measures short-term solvency.

Quick Ratio
Current assets less inventories/current liabilities. Measures short-term solvency.

Long-term Debt to Equity
Long-term debt/stockholders' equity. Measures the relationship of long-term debt to equity financing.

Liabilities to Assets
Total liabilities/total assets. Measures the proportion of assets provided by creditors, or the extent of leverage.

Liabilities to Equity
Total liabilities/stockholders' equity. Measures the relationship of debt to equity financing.

Fixed Assets to Equity
Net property, plant, and equipment/stockholders' equity. Indicates the relative investment in operational assets.

Current to Total Liabilities
Current liabilities/total liabilities. Indicates reliance on short-term as opposed to long-term debt.

Cash Flow to Total Assets
Net income after tax plus depreciation/total assets. Measures cash flow relative to assets.

Short-term Debt to Total Assets
Short-term debt/total assets. Indicates the reliance on short-term debt to support the asset structure.

Long-term Debt to Total Assets
Long-term debt/total assets. Indicates the reliance on long-term debt to support the asset structure.

Equity to Total Assets
Stockholders' equity/total assets. Measures the stockholders' share of total assets.

Average Collection Period
Accounts receivable/sales per day. Indicates the relative level and quality of accounts receivable.

Inventory Turnover
Net sales/inventory. Measures the relative efficiency of the use of inventory investment.

Fixed Assets Turnover
Net sales/net property, plant, and equipment. Measures the relative efficiency of the use of property, plant, and equipment.

Total Assets Turnover
Net sales/total assets. Measures the relative efficiency of the use of all assets.

Profit Margin
Net income/net sales. Measures the percent of profit per sales dollar.

Return on Assets
Net income/total assets. Measures the return on total investment.

Return on Equity
Net income/stockholders' equity. Measures the return on stockholders' share of total investment.

Source: U.S. Department of Commerce, Office of Business Analysis

The Top Reference Sources

The American Almanac
The Reference Press, $17.95
(800) 486-8666

This reference book is based on the *Statistical Abstract of the United States*, which is compiled annually by the Bureau of the Census and published by the U.S. Government Printing Office.

The American Almanac contains standard summary statistics on the social, political, and economic organization of the United States, from college enrollment to crop production to population growth rates. This handsome paperback volume is perhaps more reader-friendly than the *Statistical Abstract* and is also available in trade-book stores.

Flow of Funds

Total Net Borrowing in Domestic Credit Markets, 1982–1993 ($ billions)

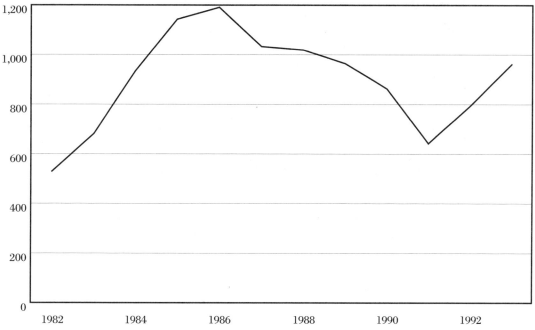

Source: Board of Governors, Federal Reserve System Flow of Funds

---

The Top Reference Sources

Institutional Investor, $375/year
88 Madison Ave.
New York, NY 10022
(212) 303-3300

Published monthly, this magazine is edited for the investor and consumer interested in the current state of the national and international investment world. The magazine focuses on the role of major corporations in high finance through analysis of international banking and business deals. It also features corporate profiles and commentaries on general market trends.

Institutional Investor is well known for its annual rankings issues, which include the largest employee benefit pension funds, the top money managers, and the well-known "*Institutional Investor*'s All-Star Stock Analyst Team."

TIP: *To check on a prospective stockbroker's reputation, anyone can call (800) 289-9999 weekdays between 9:00 A.M. and 5:00 P.M. (EST). This puts the caller in contact with an operator at the National Association of Securities Dealers, the self-regulatory organization for the over-the-counter market. The caller will be told if the broker has a "clean record," but if that is not the case, a free report will be mailed out. For additional information, investors can call their state regulator. To locate the state regulator in a particular state, call the North American Securities Administrators Association at (202) 737-0900.*

The Top Stock Analysts

Stock Research Departments Ranked

Rank	Stock Analyst
1	Goldman, Sachs
2	Merrill Lynch
3	Donaldson, Lufkin & Jenrette
4	Salomon Brothers
5	Smith Barney

Rank	Stock Analyst
6	Morgan Stanley
7	CS First Boston
8	PaineWebber
9	Lehman Brothers
10	Prudential Securities

The Best Analysts: Stock Pickers

Name	Industry	Firm
Todd Baker	PC hardware & peripherals	Hambrecht & Quist
Michael Blumstein	Insurance/life	Morgan Stanley
Thomas Brown	Banks/regional	Donaldson, Lufkin & Jenrette
Bruce Harting	Gov't-sponsored enterprises	Salomon Brothers
David Korus	PC hardware & peripherals, service & enterprise hardware	Kidder Peabody
Anthony Langham	Telcom. equip. & networking	NatWest Securities
Tobias Levkovich	Engineering & construction	Smith Barney
Gerry Paul	Autos & auto parts	Sanford C. Bernstein
Jessica Reif	Broadcasting, entertainment	Merrill Lynch
Gary Yablon	Railroads	Wertheim Schroder

The Best Analysts: Written Reports

Name	Industry	Firm
Kenneth Abramowitz	Healthcare services	Sanford C. Bernstein
Gary Black	Tobacco	Sanford C. Bernstein
Jerome Brimeyer	Pharmaceuticals	Lehman Brothers
Michael Goldstein	Portfolio strategy	Sanford C. Bernstein
Weston Hicks	Life insurance	Sanford C. Bernstein
Edward Hyman Jr.	Economics	ISI Group
David Korus	PC hardware & peripherals	Kidder Peabody
Carl Seiden	Pharmaceuticals	Sanford C. Bernstein
Nicholas Spencer	Major chemicals	Sanford C. Bernstein
W. Bruce Turner	Gaming & lodging	Salomon Brothers

Source: Institutional Investor, 1994 All-American Research Team

The Top Reference Sources

Standard & Poor's Register of Corporations, Directors and Executives
Standard & Poor's, $595/year
(212) 208-8702

Published since 1928, this annual, three-volume reference provides information on the nation's major corporations and their key staff.

Volume 1 profiles more than 55,000 corporations in alphabetical order. Volume 2 gives brief biographies of directors and executives. Volume 3 contains indexes by geography and industry, among other categories. Supplements are published in April, July, and October.

The Top Stock Analysts (cont'd)

The Best Analysts: Overall Service

Name	Industry	Firm
Michael Blumstein	Insurance/life	Morgan Stanley
Andrew Conway	Beverages	Salomon Brothers
Thomas Facciola	Specialty finance companies	Salomon Brothers
Gary Gordon	Gov't-sponsored enterprises	PaineWebber
Bruce Harting	Gov't-sponsored enterprises	Salomon Brothers
Daniel Khoshaba	Packaging	Salomon Brothers
Richard Rippe	Economics	Prudential Securities
Stanley Rubin	Electrical equipment	Merrill Lynch
Carl Seiden	Pharmaceuticals	Sanford C. Bernstein
Nicholas Spencer	Chemicals	Sanford C. Bernstein

Source: Institutional Investor, 1994 All-American Research Team

The All-Star Research Team

Industry	Name	Firm
Accounting	Patricia McConnell	Bear, Stearns
Advertising agencies	Susan Decker	Donaldson, Lufkin & Jenrette
Aerospace	George Shapiro	Salomon Brothers
Airlines	Paul Karos	CS First Boston
Appliances	Robert Cornell	Lehman Brothers
Autos & auto parts	Steven Girsky	PaineWebber
Banks/money center	Thomas Hanley	CS First Boston
Banks/regional	Thomas Brown	Donaldson, Lufkin & Jenrette
Beverages	Emanuel Goldman	PaineWebber
Biotechnology	Teena Lerner	Lehman Brothers
Broadcasting	Jessica Reif	Merrill Lynch
Brokers & asset managers	Dean Eberling	Prudential Securities
Building	David Dwyer	Kidder Peabody
Cable	Dennis Leibowitz	Donaldson, Lufkin & Jenrette
Cellular	Linda Runyon	Merrill Lynch
Chemicals/fertilizers	Charles LoCastro	Donaldson, Lufkin & Jenrette
Chemicals/major	William Young	Donaldson, Lufkin & Jenrette
Chemicals/specialty	Katharine Plourde	Donaldson, Lufkin & Jenrette
Computer services	Stephen McClellan	Merrill Lynch
Connectors	Mark Hassenberg	Donaldson, Lufkin & Jenrette
Convertibles	Mark Hunt	Smith Barney
Cosmetics	Jack Salzman	Goldman, Sachs
Defense electronics	Elliott Rogers	Cowen & Co.
Economics	Edward Hyman Jr.	ISI Group
Electrical equipment	Robert Cornell	Lehman Brothers
Electrical utilities	Barry Abramson	Prudential Securities
Engineering & construction	Jeanne Gallagher Terrile	Merrill Lynch
Entertainment	Harold Vogel	Merrill Lynch
Equity derivatives	Mark Zurack	Goldman, Sachs
Food	John McMillin	Prudential Securities
Gaming & lodging	W. Bruce Turner	Salomon Brothers
Gas distribution	Daniel Tulis	Smith Barney
Gas transmission	Curt Launer	Donaldson, Lufkin & Jenrette
Gold mining	John Tumazos	Donaldson, Lufkin & Jenrette
Government-sponsored enterprises	Jonathan Gray	Sanford C. Bernstein

The Top Stock Analysts (cont'd)

Industry	Name	Firm
Healthcare services	Kenneth Abramowitz	Sanford C. Bernstein
Household products	Jack Salzman	Goldman, Sachs
Insurance/life	Margaret Alexandre	Salomon Brothers
Insurance/non-life	Weston Hicks	Sanford C. Bernstein
Machinery	Mitchell Quain	Wertheim Schroder
Medical supplies & technology	Daniel Lemaitre	Cowen & Co.
Multi-industry	Jack Kelly	Goldman, Sachs
Non-ferrous metals	Robert Hageman	Kidder Peabody
Oil & gas exploration & production	Thomas Driscoll	Salomon Brothers
Oil services & equipment	Gordon Hall	CS First Boston
Oil/domestic	Frank Knuettel	Prudential Securities
Oil/international	William Randol	Salomon Brothers
Packaging	Daniel Khoshaba	Salomon Brothers
Paper & forest products	John Chrysikopoulos	Goldman, Sachs
PC hardware & peripherals	David Korus	Kidder Peabody
PC software	Richard Sherlund	Goldman, Sachs
Pharmaceuticals	Jerome Brimeyer	Lehman Brothers
Photography & electronic imaging	B. Alexander Henderson	Prudential Securities
Pollution control	Marc Sulam	Kidder Peabody
Portfolio strategy	Greg Smith	Prudential Securities
Publishing	Kevin Gruneich	CS First Boston
Quantitative research	Elaine Garzarelli	Lehman Brothers
Railroads	Gary Yablon	Wertheim Schroder
Real estate investment trusts	Eric Hemel	Morgan Stanley
Restaurants	John Rohs	Wertheim Schroder
Retailing/broadlines	Joseph Ellis	Goldman, Sachs
Retailing/food & drug chains	Gary Giblen	PaineWebber
Retailing/hardlines	David Bolotsky	Goldman, Sachs
Retailing/softlines	Richard Baum	Goldman, Sachs
Savings & loans	Jerry Gitt	Merrill Lynch
Semiconductors	James Barlage	Smith Barney
Server & enterprise hardware	Steven Milunovich	Morgan Stanley
Server & enterprise software	Charles Phillips Jr.	Kidder Peabody
Small companies	Claudia Mott	Prudential Securities
Specialty finance companies	Guy Moszkowski	Sanford C. Bernstein
Steel	Michelle Galanter Applebaum	Salomon Brothers
Technical analysis	Alan Shaw	Smith Barney
Telecommunications equipment & networking	Danielle Danse	Salomon Brothers
Telecommunications services	Jack Grubman	Salomon Brothers
Textiles & apparel	Josephine Esquivel	Lehman Brothers
Tire & rubber	Steven Girsky	PaineWebber
Tobacco	Gary Black	Sanford C. Bernstein
Trucking & air freight	Paul Schlesinger	Donaldson, Lufkin & Jenrette
Washington research	Mark Melcher	Prudential Securities

Source: Institutional Investor, 1994 All-American Research Team

Corporate Activity

Announced U.S. Mergers and Acquisitions

Announcement Date	Value ($ mil.)	Market Share	No. of Deals
1982	56,035.1	2.0	1,932
1983	96,185.0	3.5	3,385
1984	169,138.9	6.2	3,619
1985	187,013.3	6.8	2,259
1986	212,911.1	7.8	3,149
1987	208,425.3	7.6	3,317
1988	334,869.9	12.2	3,920
1989	292,710.8	10.7	5,464
1990	176,479.0	6.4	5,670
1991	136,540.1	5.0	5,295
1992	149,148.7	5.4	5,547
1993	240,216.9	8.8	6,358
1994	343,694.2	12.5	7,511
TOTAL	2,603,368.3	94.9	57,426

Ten Largest Completed U.S. Merger and Acquisition Deals, 1984–1994

Date Effective	Acquirer Name	Target Name	Attitude	Value ($ mil.)
04/28/89	Kohlberg Kravis Roberts & Co.	RJR Nabisco	Hostile	30,598.8
09/19/94	AT&T	McCaw Cellular Commun.	Friendly	18,923.4
01/10/90	Time	Warner Communications	Friendly	14,110.0
12/07/88	Philip Morris	Kraft	Hostile	13,444.0
06/15/84	Standard Oil Co. of California	Gulf Oil	Friendly	13,400.0
10/04/89	Bristol-Myers	Squibb	Friendly	12,094.0
02/17/84	Texaco	Getty Oil	Friendly	10,120.0
07/07/94	Viacom (Nat'l Amusements)	Paramount Communications	Friendly	9,600.0
12/21/94	American Home Products	American Cyanamid	Hostile	9,560.9
04/04/94	Shareholders	PacTel (Pacific Telesis)	NA	8,639.0

Ten Largest U.S. Merger and Acquisition Deals Completed in 1994

Date Effective	Acquirer Name	Target Name	Attitude	Value ($ mil.)
09/19/94	AT&T	McCaw Cellular Commun.	Friendly	18,923.4
07/07/94	Viacom (Nat'l Amusements)	Paramount Communications	Friendly	9,600.0
12/21/94	American Home Products	American Cyanamid	Hostile	9,560.9
04/04/94	Shareholders	PacTel (Pacific Telesis)	NA	8,639.0
09/29/94	Viacom (Nat'l Amusements)	Blockbuster Entertainment	Friendly	7,971.1
02/10/94	Columbia Healthcare	HCA–Hospital Corp. of America	Friendly	5,605.0
11/03/94	Roche Holding	Syntex	Friendly	5,307.2
01/03/94	Shareholders	Eastman Chemical	NA	4,038.0
11/21/94	Eli Lilly & Co.	PCS Health Systems (McKesson)	Friendly	4,000.0
03/01/94	Society	KeyCorp	Friendly	3,923.9

Source: Securities Data Company

198   FINANCE

Corporate Activity (cont'd)

Announced U.S. LBOs

Announcement Date	Value ($ mil.)	Market Share	No. of Deals
1982	2,343.8	0.7	22
1983	9,191.9	2.7	63
1984	13,505.4	4.0	121
1985	28,081.9	8.3	169
1986	39,211.1	11.6	254
1987	48,489.2	14.3	245
1988	93,893.6	27.7	326
1989	35,486.5	10.5	341
1990	12,357.7	3.6	213
1991	6,007.9	1.8	227
1992	9,650.1	2.8	251
1993	9,506.8	2.8	209
1994	5,919.1	1.7	188
TOTAL	313,645.0	92.5	2,629

Announced U.S. Divestitures

Announcement Date	Value ($ mil.)	Market Share	No. of Deals
1982	11,622.2	1.1	442
1983	33,508.5	3.3	1,037
1984	49,378.6	4.8	1,138
1985	57,580.2	5.6	930
1986	79,701.0	7.8	1,218
1987	83,317.7	8.2	1,141
1988	120,779.6	11.8	1,453
1989	101,611.6	10.0	2,086
1990	79,102.6	7.8	2,263
1991	56,583.3	5.5	2,205
1992	76,488.0	7.5	2,121
1993	86,303.9	8.5	2,439
1994	143,358.1	14.0	2,621
TOTAL	979,335.3	95.9	21,094

Source: Securities Data Company

S&P 500 Company Activity

Activity	1989	1990	1991	1992	1993
Mergers and acquisitions among companies in the index	10	8	6	2	2
Acquisition by company outside the index	15	2	2	0	4
Restructurings	4	2	1	3	3
Bankruptcies	0	2	3	1	1
TOTAL NUMBER OF COMPANY CHANGES	29	14	12	6	10

Source: S&P 500 Directory, 1994. Reprinted by permission of Standard & Poor's, a division of The McGraw-Hill Companies

Securities and Exchange Commission

THE SECURITIES AND EXCHANGE Commission is the independent, non-partisan, federal agency that administers U.S. laws that provide protection for investors. The SEC was created under the Securities Exchange Act of 1934 to ensure that securities markets are fair and honest. In addition, the SEC acts as an advisor to federal courts in corporate reorganization proceedings under Chapter 11 of the Bankruptcy Reform Act of 1978. The Commission is composed of five members: a chairman and four commissioners. Commission members are appointed by the President, with the advice and consent of the Senate, for five-year terms, and the chairman is designated by the President. Terms are staggered; one expires on June 5 of every year. Not more than three members may be of the same political party.

The Commission meets to deliberate on and resolve issues such as interpretations of federal securities laws, amendments to existing rules under the laws, new rules (often to reflect changed conditions in the marketplace), actions to enforce the laws or to discipline those subject to direct regulation, legislation to be proposed by the Commission, and matters concerning administration of the Commission itself. The Commission staff is organized into divisions including the following:

- The Division of Corporation Finance, which ensures that disclosure requirements are met by publicly held companies registered with the Commission.

- The Division of Market Regulation, which is responsible for overseeing the activity of the secondary markets, for registration and regulation of broker-dealers, and for supervising self-regulating organizations (such as the nation's stock exchanges). In addition, the division monitors the activities, including trading and sales practices, of other participants in the secondary market, and examines policies that affect the operation of the securities markets.

- The Division of Investment Management, which ensures compliance with regulations regarding the registration, financial responsibility, sales practices, and advertising of mutual funds and of investment advisers. The division's Office of Public Utility Regulation oversees the activities of the 12 active registered holding-company systems.

- The Division of Enforcement, which supervises the enforcement of federal securities laws, investigates possible violations of these laws, and recommends appropriate remedies for consideration by the Commission.

For public information on the U.S. Securities and Exchange Commission the interested individual can write to:

U.S. Securities and Exchange Commission
450 Fifth St., NW
Washington, DC 20549
(202) 272-3100 (information line)
(202) 272-7460 (publications of SEC educational and informational materials)

U.S. Government Printing Office (to order the SEC Annual Report, $5)
(202) 512-1800

Regional Offices of the SEC

Atlanta District Office
3475 Lenox Rd., NE, Suite 1000
Atlanta, GA 30326
(404) 842-7600

Boston District Office
73 Tremont St., Suite 600
Boston, MA 02108
(617) 424-5900

Midwest Regional Office
Northwestern Atrium Center
500 W. Madison St., Suite 1400
Chicago, IL 60661
(312) 353-7390

Central Regional Office
1801 California St., Suite 4800
Denver, CO 80202
(303) 391-6800

Fort Worth District Office
801 Cherry St., 19th Floor
Fort Worth, TX 76102
(817) 334-3821

Pacific Regional Office
5760 Wilshire Blvd., 11th Floor
Los Angeles, CA 90036
(213) 965-3998

Southeast Regional Office
1401 Brickell Ave., Suite 200
Miami, FL 33131
(305) 536-5765

Northeast Regional Office
7 World Trade Center, Suite 1300
New York, NY 10048
(212) 748-8000

Philadelphia District Office
The Curtis Center, Suite 1005 E
601 Walnut St.
Philadelphia, PA 19106
(215) 597-3100

Securities and Exchange Commission (cont'd)

Salt Lake District Office
500 Key Bank Tower
50 S. Main St., Suite 500
Salt Lake City, UT 84144
(801) 524-5796

San Francisco District Office
44 Montgomery St., 11th Floor
San Francisco, CA 94104
(415) 705-2500

Seattle District Office
3040 Jackson Federal Bldg.
915 Second Ave.
Seattle, WA 98174
(206) 220-7500

Full Disclosure Reviews: Corporate Filings

Major Filing Review	1988	1989	1990	1991	1992	1993
SECURITIES ACT REGISTRATIONS						
New issuers	1,444	1,177	895	630	831	863
Repeat issuers	640	604	635	776	970	967
Post-effective amendments*	NA	320	203	308	210	251
ANNUAL REPORTS						
Full reviews	2,166	1,949	1,129	1,557	1,450	1,826
Full financial reviews	567	388	292	712	1,126	1,153
Tender offers (14D-1)	254	188	95	37	27	56
Going-private schedules	276	176	108	68	61	61
Contested proxy solicitations	93	84	75	65	58	35
MERGER/GOING PRIVATE						
Proxy statements	314	291	240	188	141	149
Other	790	428	351	374	395	1,292

*P/E amendments with new financial statements only.

SEC Total Enforcement Actions Initiated

Type of Action	1988	1989	1990	1991	1992	1993
TOTAL	252	310	304	320	394	416
Civil injunctive actions	125	140	186	171	156	172
Administrative proceedings	109	155	111	138	226	229
Civil and criminal contempt proceedings	17	15	7	10	11	15
Reports of investigation	1	0	0	1	1	0

SEC Litigation and Legal Activities: Increase in Matters Handled, 1991 to 1993

Action Taken	1991	1992	1993
Litigation matters opened	263	264	262
Litigation matters closed	247	267	NA
Adjudication			
Cases received	30	56	65
Cases completed	39	52	64
Legislation			
Testimony	29	16	NA
Comments to Congress and others	29	64	NA
Ethics matters	249	247	NA

Source: U.S. Securities and Exchange Commission Annual Report, 1993

Bonds

BONDS ARE LONG-TERM debt obligations issued typically in $1,000 or $5,000 denominations by companies, governments (including the U.S. Treasury), municipalities, or federal agencies. The interest paid on these loans–the coupon or coupon rate–depends upon the amount of risk assumed by the buyer, the loan's backing, and the overall economic climate at the time of issuance. The range of rates offered at any given time is determined in relation to benchmark interest rates set by the U.S. Federal

Reserve. But from the date of issuance, a bond's rate of interest remains fixed until maturity. While the prime interest rate may greatly fluctuate over the term of the bond, the rate of interest on the bond remains the same, providing a sure, steady source of income.

The term, repayment schedule, and security of bonds vary widely depending upon the financial needs of the issuer and the bond's intended use, as well as by the type of issuance.

Interest and Bond Yields, 1981–1994

Period	U.S. Treasury 3-Month Bills	U.S. Treasury 3-yr. Maturity	U.S. Treasury 10-yr. Maturity	High-Grade Muni Bonds	Corp. AAA Bonds	Prime Comm'l Paper	Discount Rate	Prime Rate	New-Home Mortge. Yields
1981	14.03	14.44	13.91	11.23	14.17	14.76	13.42	18.87	14.70
1982	10.69	12.92	13.00	11.57	13.79	11.89	11.02	14.86	15.14
1983	8.63	10.45	11.10	9.47	12.04	8.89	8.50	10.79	12.57
1984	9.58	11.89	12.44	10.15	12.71	10.16	8.80	12.04	12.38
1985	7.48	9.64	10.62	9.18	11.37	8.01	7.69	9.93	11.55
1986	5.98	7.06	7.68	7.38	9.02	6.39	6.33	8.33	10.17
1987	5.82	7.68	8.39	7.73	9.38	6.85	5.66	8.21	9.31
1988	6.69	8.26	8.85	7.76	9.71	7.68	6.20	9.32	9.19
1989	8.12	8.55	8.49	7.24	9.26	8.80	6.93	10.87	10.13
1990	7.51	8.26	8.55	7.25	9.32	7.95	6.98	10.01	10.05
1991	5.42	6.82	7.86	6.89	8.77	5.85	5.45	8.46	9.32
1992	3.45	5.80	7.01	6.41	8.14	3.80	3.25	6.25	8.24
1993	3.02	4.44	5.87	5.63	7.22	3.30	3.00	6.00	7.20
1994	4.29	6.27	7.09	6.19	7.97	4.93	3.60	7.15	7.49
Jan.	3.02	4.48	5.75	5.30	6.92	3.30	3.00	6.00	6.95
Feb.	3.21	4.83	5.97	5.44	7.08	3.62	3.00	6.00	6.85
Mar.	3.52	5.40	6.48	5.93	7.48	4.08	3.00	6.20	6.99
Apr.	3.74	5.99	6.97	6.28	7.88	4.40	3.00	6.50	7.31
May	4.19	6.34	7.18	6.26	7.99	4.92	3.25	7.00	7.43
June	4.18	6.27	7.1	6.14	7.97	4.86	3.50	7.25	7.62
July	4.39	6.48	7.3	6.19	8.11	5.13	3.50	7.25	7.71
Aug.	4.50	6.50	7.24	6.19	8.07	5.19	3.75	7.50	7.67
Sept.	4.64	6.69	7.46	6.33	8.34	5.32	4.00	7.75	7.70
Oct.	4.96	7.04	7.74	6.50	8.57	5.70	4.00	7.75	7.76
Nov.	5.25	7.44	7.96	6.96	8.68	6.01	4.40	8.25	7.81
Dec.	5.64	7.71	7.81	6.76	8.46	6.62	4.75	8.50	7.83
1995									
Jan.	5.81	7.66	7.78	6.53	8.46	6.63	4.75	8.50	NA

Source: Economic Indicators, Council of Economic Advisers

Corporate and Taxable Bonds

CORPORATIONS ISSUE VARIOUS types of debt securities to fund their operations and investments. Their short-term needs are filled by the issuance of commercial paper, which can be bought only in $100,000 denominations with a maturity of 90 to 180 days. For the longer term of 20 to 30 years, companies issue bonds in denominations of $1,000, which can be classified by length of time until maturity and by the type of security put up to secure the bond.

Debenture Bonds
A loan not secured by any particular asset but by the company's unpledged assets. The most common type of taxable bond, backed only by the company's word and financial capacity to meet regular principal and interest payments. High-yield and convertible bonds are examples of debentures.

High-Yield (Junk) Bonds
An unsecured loan rated higher in risk because of the uncertain financial strength of the issuing company; graded lower than BBB.

Convertible Bond
A loan that can be converted at the owner's discretion from company debt into a designated amount of equity, e.g. from bonds into stock shareholdings.

Collateral Trust Bond
A loan backed by securities–other companies' stocks and bonds–held by the issuing company.

Mortgage Bond
A loan secured by a piece of real estate or fixed property, such as a factory, warehouse, or laboratory.

Equipment Trust Certificate
A loan secured by movable equipment, such as a fleet of trucks or a locomotive.

Income Bond
A loan that is repaid only when the company operates at a profit.

Senior and Junior or Subordinated Bonds
Loans that are classified by the issuer according to seniority. Repayment to senior debt holders takes priority if the company develops financial trouble.

Sinking Fund Bond
A loan that is retired through partial payments over time until final maturity. Repayment usually commences five to ten years after the date of issue.

Zero Coupon Bonds
A corporate, municipal, or treasury bond that is sold at a deeply discounted price, a fraction of its par value, but pays no interest until final maturity, typically decades from the date of issue.

Secondary markets for corporate bonds are made by investors trading primarily on the New York Stock Exchange and on the American Stock Exchange.

U.S. Domestic Corporate Investment-Grade Debt, Sales Volume

Date	Proceeds ($ mil.)	Market Share	No. of Issues
1977	25,175.7	1.2	340
1978	19,939.2	0.9	231
1979	24,369.3	1.1	232
1980	35,373.7	1.6	373
1981	33,864.4	1.6	346
1982	37,685.2	1.8	449
1983	30,031.5	1.4	334
1984	39,125.3	1.8	328
1985	62,013.0	2.9	517
1986	117,925.4	5.5	879
1987	90,005.1	4.2	696
1988	92,673.8	4.3	586
1989	109,550.0	5.1	652
1990	104,779.2	4.9	710
1991	190,455.3	8.9	1,562
1992	274,735.7	12.8	1,899
1993	377,981.0	17.6	2,895
1994	335,769.8	15.6	3,249
TOTAL	2,001,452.6	93.2	16,278

Source: Securities Data Company

Corporate and Taxable Bonds (cont'd)

U.S. Non-Investment-Grade Debt, Sales Volume

Date	Proceeds ($ mil.)	Market Share	No. of Issues
1977	1,030.8	0.3	61
1978	1,583.2	0.5	82
1979	1,390.8	0.5	56
1980	1,374.2	0.5	45
1981	1,247.2	0.4	34
1982	2,433.7	0.8	51
1983	7,406.4	2.5	95
1984	14,002.7	4.7	131
1985	14,175.8	4.7	174
1986	31,901.2	10.6	225
1987	28,095.8	9.4	187
1988	27,718.8	9.3	160
1989	25,236.8	8.4	129
1990	1,394.9	0.5	10
1991	9,971.0	3.3	48
1992	38,185.7	12.7	236
1993	54,505.9	18.2	345
1994	31,583.8	10.5	192
TOTAL	293,238.7	97.8	2,261

Source: Securities Data Company

Mortgage-Backed Bonds

Mortgage-Backed Securities, Sales Volume

Date	Proceeds ($ mil.)	Market Share	No. of Issues
1977	1,338.9	0.1	13
1978	1,251.7	0.1	19
1979	1,476.8	0.1	24
1980	500.2	0.0	8
1981	512.6	0.0	12
1982	1,076.8	0.1	36
1983	8,566.9	0.5	66
1984	12,069.2	0.7	117
1985	19,581.3	1.1	212
1986	57,827.0	3.3	372
1987	82,321.7	4.7	469
1988	98,365.1	5.6	620
1989	110,701.7	6.3	464
1990	133,996.5	7.6	474
1991	249,877.7	14.2	724
1992	376,887.7	21.4	984
1993	415,439.4	23.6	1,088
1994	178,152.2	10.1	742
TOTAL	1,749,943.4	99.5	6,444

Source: Securities Data Company

Convertible Bonds

U.S. Convertible Bonds, Sales Volume

Date	Proceeds ($ mil.)	Market Share	No. of Issues
1977	495.7	0.5	17
1978	393.4	0.4	19
1979	724.1	0.8	31
1980	4,359.6	4.6	98
1981	4,652.9	4.9	92
1982	3,201.0	3.4	67
1983	6,120.3	6.5	113
1984	4,093.7	4.3	66
1985	7,484.6	7.9	139
1986	10,115.9	10.7	207
1987	9,863.6	10.4	148
1988	3,136.1	3.3	36
1989	5,519.9	5.8	63
1990	4,756.5	5.0	34
1991	7,478.6	7.9	49
1992	7,036.2	7.4	65
1993	9,303.0	9.8	90
1994	4,674.7	4.9	35
TOTAL	93,409.8	98.5	1,369

Source: Securities Data Company

U.S. Government Securities

GUARANTEED BY THE U.S. government and exempt from state and local income taxes, these securities are some of the safest you can purchase. But because of the near absence of default risk they offer lower interest rates than do corporate issues. Government issues are actively traded on the over-the-counter market after their initial sale to large investors through an auction conducted by the Treasury.

Treasury Bills
Issued at a discount and repaid at face value at final maturity, T-bills pay no interest. They have the shortest maturation of all government securities: 91, 182, or 364 days. $10,000 minimum face value investment.

Treasury Notes
Maturing in the range of two to ten years, T-notes yield a steady stream of interest. $1,000 minimum purchase; most notes are sold in $5,000 denominations.

Treasury Bonds
Long-term government debt that bears interest, T-bonds generally mature in ten years or longer. Like T-notes, they come in denominations of $1,000, $5,000, $10,000, $100,000, and $1,000,000 and are popular with traders and institutional investors. They are highly sensitive to interest-rate movements.

Zero Coupon Government Bonds
Long-term government debt that bears interest, which is all paid in a lump sum at the end of the term. Similar to other zero coupon bonds but tax free.

Flower Bonds
This limited series of bonds (the last issue was in 1971) can be redeemed at the time of the holder's death for the payment of estate taxes.

U.S. Savings Bonds
Unlike Treasury bills, notes, and bonds, U.S. Savings Bonds cannot be traded in a secondary market. They are sold mostly to individual investors who buy them directly from the Treasury. The most popular variety of U.S. Savings Bond sells at a 50 percent discount from its face value and is entirely free of commissions.

U.S. Government Securities (cont'd)

Through the sale of securities, the U.S. government has created more than $200 billion in debt yearly since 1985. Daily volume in U.S. Treasury securities is up to $100 billion.

Federal Agency Issues

While the federal government does not back all these issues, it authorizes a variety of its agencies to issue debentures and notes to finance their operations. Among these agencies are:

- U.S. Postal Service
- Tennessee Valley Authority
- Export-Import Bank

- Federal Home Loan Mortgage (FHLMC or Freddie Mac)
- Federal Intermediate Credit Bank (FICB)
- Federal National Mortgage Association (FNMA or Fannie Mae)
- Government National Mortgage Association (GNMA or Ginnie Mae).

As a group, these securities offer a higher rate of interest than direct U.S. Treasury obligations, even though the majority are backed by the full faith and credit of the U.S. government. Certain issues are also exempt from state and local taxes.

Non-Convertible Debt Issued by Federal Agencies

Date	Proceeds	Market Share	No. of Issues
1982	4,974.1	0.9	29
1983	2,957.9	0.5	19
1984	5,394.2	1.0	21
1985	4,814.0	0.9	23
1986	8,656.5	1.6	48
1987	7,192.2	1.3	47
1988	15,333.6	2.8	68
1989	27,317.1	4.9	107
1990	27,741.1	5.0	169
1991	44,657.2	8.1	265
1992	91,233.8	16.5	567
1993	146,291.3	26.5	1,186
1994	165,449.4	30.0	1,625
TOTAL	552,012.4	100.0	4,174

Source: Securities Data Company

Municipal Bonds

ISSUED BY STATES, CITIES, towns, counties, and their agencies, municipal bonds (often called munis or tax-exempts) are free of federal tax and often from state and local tax in their state of issuance. A new municipal issue subject to federal tax was created by the Tax Reform Act of 1986. Like corporate issues, municipal bonds are categorized by the form of collateral used to back them and to raise their revenue.

General Obligation Bonds (GO Bonds)
GO Bonds represent the largest group of municipal issues. Paid back by general revenues–secured by the government's tax revenue and its ability to impose new taxes–these bonds are only slightly less secure than similar government issues. By law, the government is required to levy taxes in order to pay its bondholders.

Revenue Bonds
Used in the development of toll roads, bridges, or tunnels, or any revenue-producing projects, these bonds are paid off by the revenues generated from the specific development. They typically offer a higher rate of interest than GO Bonds, as payment is more narrowly backed.

Industrial Development Bonds
These specific bonds are issued by state and local governnments to fund the construction of new industrial parks or plants, or any development that might attract businesses and increase leasing revenue for the state. The financial strength of the private businesses involved in the project generally determines the quality of the bond. Most are now taxable under the Tax Reform Act of 1986.

Municipal Bonds (cont'd)

Redevelopment Agency Bonds
Used for the construction of commercial projects, these bonds are secured by part of the property taxes levied on the development.

Airport Bonds
One type of airport bond is used toward, and secured by, general operations and usage. Another, much riskier, bond is tied specifically to facilities leased by individual airlines and is secured by the leasing contract itself.

Bond ratings are listed in *Moody's Bond Record* and *Standard & Poor's Bond Guide*. Weekly newsletters, *Moody's Bond Survey*, and *CreditWeek* (a publication of Standard & Poor's) offer more detailed information on select issues.

As newspapers and financial journals do not carry complete information on municipal bonds, current prices, and trading data, investors must turn to specific bond publications to track these issues.

The bible of bond issuance, pricing, and trading is the annual publication *Moody's Municipal & Government Manual*. Organized by state, city, town, and political subdivision, the compendium lists all bond issues (including, as well, information on federal agency issues) and offers information critical to bond buyers, from state tax revenues and census fig-

ures to statistics on attendance at local schools. Updates to *Moody's Municipal* are published in a semi-weekly newsletter that lists new and changed issues as well as call notices.

Recommended Resources

The Blue List
Standard & Poor's, $270/year
65 Broadway
New York, NY 10004
(212) 770-4300

The Daily Bond Buyer, $1,897/year
1 State St. Plaza
New York, NY 10004
(212) 803-8200

Bond Week, $1,395/year
488 Madison Ave.
New York, NY 10022
(212) 303-3300

Moody's Municipal & Government Manual, $2,095
99 Church St.
New York, NY 10007
(800) 342-5647, ext. 0546

The Top Reference Sources

Moody's Industrial Manual
Moody's Investors Service, $1,550/year
(800) 342-5647, ext. 0546

Moody's annual bound volume of its twice-weekly publication covers U.S., Canadian, and foreign companies listed on U.S. exchanges.

The listings include corporate history, subsidiaries, principal facilities, products, and financial data.

An excellent resource for broad background data on a wide array of companies.

Bond Performance

Merrill Lynch High-Yield Master Index

Year	Return (%)
1985	24.61
1986	16.35
1987	4.69
1988	13.47
1989	4.23
1990	-4.38
1991	34.58
1992	18.16
1993	17.18
1994	-1.17

Merrill Lynch Mortgage Master Index

Year	Return (%)
1985	25.45
1986	13.14
1987	3.53
1988	9.15
1989	14.60
1990	10.84
1991	15.78
1992	7.33
1993	7.29
1994	-1.60

Merrill Lynch Agency Master Index

Year	Return (%)
1985	17.79
1986	13.87
1987	3.42
1988	4.47
1989	12.93
1990	9.90
1991	15.21
1992	7.27
1993	10.44
1994	-2.72

Note: Includes government, U.S. agencies (all maturities)

Merrill Lynch Corporate Master Index

Year	Return (%)
1985	25.38
1986	16.30
1987	1.84
1988	9.76
1989	14.12
1990	7.37
1991	18.24
1992	9.12
1993	12.43
1994	-3.34

Merrill Lynch Domestic Master Index

Year	Return (%)
1985	22.40
1986	15.22
1987	2.40
1988	8.04
1989	14.18
1990	9.10
1991	15.85
1992	7.58
1993	10.02
1994	-2.82

Merrill Lynch 1–10 Year Treasury Index

Year	Return (%)
1985	18.36
1986	13.20
1987	3.63
1988	6.33
1989	12.60
1990	9.50
1991	13.99
1992	6.94
1993	8.18
1994	-1.71

Note: Includes Corporate-Government-Mortgage-Bond Index

Source: Reprinted by permission of Merrill Lynch, Pierce, Fenner & Smith Incorporated. Copyright 1995

Bond Performance (cont'd)

Merrill Lynch 10+ Treasury Index

Year	Return (%)
1985	31.53
1986	23.99
1987	-2.66
1988	9.20
1989	18.90
1990	6.46
1991	18.43
1992	7.94
1993	17.23
1994	-7.44

Government, U.S. Treasury, intermediate-term, 1-9.99 years

Merrill Lynch 30-Year Treasury Strip

Year	Return (%)
1988	-5.76
1989	28.41
1990	-4.02
1991	15.36
1992	5.67
1993	36.80
1994	-19.60

Government, U.S. Treasury, intermediate-term, 10 years and over

Merrill Lynch Convertible Securities Index

Year	Return (%)
1990	-6.99
1991	31.96
1992	22.41
1993	18.91
1994	-7.68

Convertible securities (bonds and preferreds), all qualities

Merrill Lynch Eurodollar Index

Year	Return (%)
1985	18.12
1986	13.89
1987	2.63
1988	8.90
1989	12.67
1990	9.37
1991	15.84
1992	8.04
1993	8.87
1994	-1.21

Eurodollar straight bonds

Merrill Lynch 1–10-Year Treasury Index (% return)

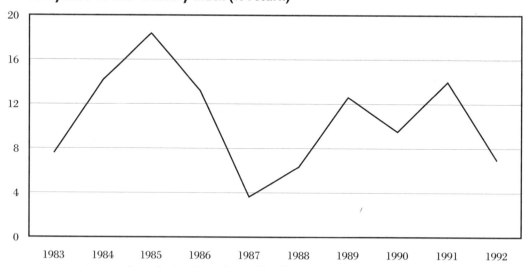

Source: Reprinted by permission of Merrill Lynch, Pierce, Fenner & Smith Incorporated. Copyright 1995

Bond Performance (cont'd)

New Security Issues of Corporations: By Type of Offering

Type of Bond Offering	1988	1989	1990	1991	1992
TOTAL	353.1	320.0	298.8	390.0	471.1
Public, domestic	202.0	179.7	188.8	287.1	377.7
Private placement, domestic	127.7	117.4	87.0	74.9	65.9
Sold abroad	23.1	22.9	23.1	28.0	27.6

New Security Issues of Corporations: By Industry Group

Industry Group	1988	1989	1990	1991	1992
Manufacturing	70.1	74.7	51.8	86.6	82.0
Commercial and miscellaneous	61.9	50.3	40.7	37.6	42.9
Transportation	10.9	10.2	12.8	13.6	10.0
Public utility	21.1	18.6	17.6	23.9	48.0
Communication	6.0	9.3	6.7	9.4	15.4
Real estate and financial	182.0	156.9	169.2	219.7	272.8

Bonds Listed on the New York Stock Exchange

	1985	1986	1987	1988	1989	1990	1991	1992
No. of issuers	1,010.0	951.0	885.0	846.0	794.0	743.0	706.0	589.0
No. of issues	3,856.0	3,611.0	3,346.0	3,106.0	2,961.0	2,912.0	2,727.0	1,462.0
Face value ($ bil.)	1,327.0	1,380.0	1,651.0	1,610.0	1,435.0	1,689.0	2,219.0	2,009.0
Market value ($ bil.)	1,339.0	1,458.0	1,621.0	1,561.0	1,412.0	1,610.0	2,227.0	2,044.0
Average price ($)	100.9	105.7	98.2	97.0	98.4	95.3	100.3	101.8

Source: 1994 Statistical Abstract, Table No. 815

U.S. Exchanges Listing Bonds

Exchange	No. of Listed Bonds	Market Value ($ millions)
American	174	16,431
Arizona	0	0
Boston	1	15
Cincinnati	NA	NA
Midwest	0	0
New York	2,190	2,019,100
Pacific	54	1,476
Philadelphia	15	NA
TOTAL	2,434	2,037,022

Source: U.S. Securities and Exchange Commission Annual Report, 1993

Bond Performance (cont'd)

Foreign Purchases and Sales of U.S. Securities

Year and Country	Total	Treasury Bonds and Notes	U.S. Government Corporations Bonds	Corporate Bonds	Corporate Stocks
1980	15.8	4.9	2.6	2.9	5.4
1985	78.3	29.2	4.3	39.8	4.9
1987	69.4	25.6	5.0	22.5	16.3
1988	74.8	48.8	6.7	21.2	-2.0
1989	96.6	54.2	15.1	17.4	9.9
1990	19.4	17.9	6.3	10.4	-15.1
1991	61.1	22.5	9.8	17.7	11.1
1992 TOTAL	73.2	39.3	18.3	20.8	-5.1
United Kingdom	33.9	24.2	3.8	9.1	-3.3
Japan	5.6	9.5	1.5	-1.7	-3.6
Canada	2.2	0.6	0.1	0.1	1.4
Bermuda	-2.2	-5.8	1.1	1.9	-1.3
Netherlands Antilles	-1.0	-1.8	0.2	0.4	0.3
France	-0.3	-0.2	0.4	0.8	0.8
1993 TOTAL	111.6	24.2	36.1	29.8	21.5
United Kingdom	29.7	6.3	7.1	11.8	4.5
Japan	32.5	17.1	6.8	4.8	3.8
Canada	9.7	11.3	0.4	1.3	-3.2
Bermuda	-0.2	-5.1	2.8	2.0	0.1
Netherlands Antilles	4.4	0.8	0.3	1.9	1.4
France	1.9	-0.3	0.4	1.9	-0.1

Source: 1994 Statistical Abstract, Table No. 817

TIP: *Dun & Bradstreet will prepare a report on any company's history and background, its payment record and finances, and a record of lawsuits, liens, and judgments. The fee for this service is $75. Call (800) 362-2255.*

Bonds on the NYSE

THE NYSE'S BOND MARKET IS the largest of all the U.S. exchanges, offering investors a selection of nearly 2,800 bonds issued by the U.S. government, U.S. corporations, foreign governments, foreign cor- porations, and international banks. In 1991, bond trading on the exchange reached a record $12.7 bil- lion. About 90 percent of the NYSE bond volume is in straight or non-convertible debt.

Groups Listing Bonds on the New York Stock Exchange

Major Group	Number of Issuers	Number of Issues	Par Value ($ mil.)	Market Value ($ mil.)
U.S. companies	529	1168	240,176	215,142
Foreign companies	20	24	7,682	7,917
U.S. government	1	724	2,065,924	2,280,780
International banks	5	155	26,236	22,585
Foreign governments	19	32	1,935	2,013
TOTAL	574	2,103	2,341,953	2,528,437

Source: New York Stock Exchange Fact Book, 1993

Most Active Bonds on the New York Stock Exchange, 1993

Issue	Par Value of Reported Volume ($ thousands)
General Motors Acceptance	285,460
General Motors Acceptance	262,210
Stone Container	243,056
Stone Container	220,121
RJR Nabisco	213,766
DuPont	171,476
RJR Nabisco	168,539
Stone Container	162,549
Stone Container	149,564
Stone Container	114,324
MGM/UA Communications	113,912
RJR Nabisco	111,487
Time Warner	110,708
McDonnell Douglas	105,751
Chrysler	103,326
RJR Nabisco	80,390
AT&T	75,736
Republic Steel	75,349
Chrysler	74,267
USG	73,286
Time Warner	72,414
Eastman Kodak	72,232

Source: New York Stock Exchange Fact Book, 1993

Volume of Bond Trading on the NYSE

Year	Volume ($ millions)
1984	6,982
1985	9,046
1986	10,464
1987	9,727
1988	7,702
1989	8,836
1990	10,892
1991	12,698
1992	11,629
1993	9,743

NYSE Bond Trading Activity Records

Most Active	Volume ($ millions)
DAYS	TOTAL VOLUME
February 6, 1991	158.4
February 7, 1991	128.1
February 5, 1991	124.3
July 17, 1990	113.9
January 29, 1990	111.8
January 30, 1991	108.3
July 16, 1990	105.2
February 8, 1991	102.0
February 11, 1991	99.1
February 13, 1990	98.7
MONTHS	AVG. DAILY VOLUME
February 1991	88.9
February 1992	65.9
March 1991	62.4
YEARS	AVG. DAILY VOLUME
1991	50.2
1992	45.8
1990	43.1

Source: New York Stock Exchange Fact Book, 1993

Bonds on the NYSE (cont'd)

Volume of Bond Trading on the NYSE ($ millions)

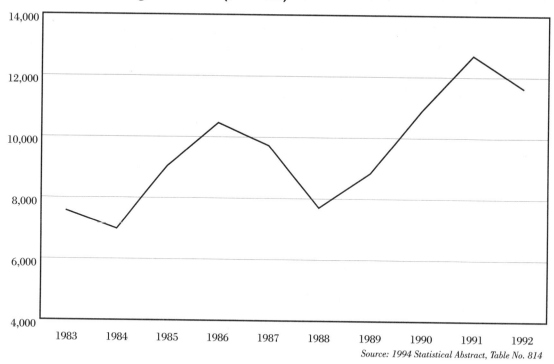

Source: 1994 Statistical Abstract, Table No. 814

The Top Reference Sources

The Corporate Directory of U.S. Public Companies
Gale/Walker's Western Research, $360
(800) 877-4253

This mammoth two-volume set lists the essential facts on every U.S. public company (more than 10,000 in all) with sales greater than $5 million.
Entries include contact data, legal counsel, stock price range, SIC codes, and major subsidiaries.

Bonds on the NYSE (cont'd)

Largest Corporate Bond Listings on the New York Stock Exchange, 1993

Issue	Principal Amount ($ thousands)	Listing Date
Time Warner (convertible)	3,200,000	Apr. 1
Time Warner	2,415,000	June 22
International Bank for Reconstruction & Development	2,150,000	July 12
International Bank for Reconstruction & Development	1,823,000	Nov. 10
International Bank for Reconstruction & Development	1,250,000	Sep. 20
International Bank for Reconstruction & Development	1,250,000	Jan. 20
IBM	1,250,000	June 15
Time Warner	1,000,000	Jan. 19
Time Warner	1,000,000	Feb. 4
RJR Nabisco	750,000	Jan. 14
Pacific Bell Telephone	625,000	Apr. 5
IBM	550,000	June 15
Pacific Bell Telephone	550,000	Oct. 29
Coleman Worldwide	500,000	May 21
General Instruments	500,000	June 18
PVD America	500,000	Aug. 3
Pennzoil (convertible)	500,000	Oct. 25
RJR Nabisco	500,000	Aug. 19
RJR Nabisco	500,000	Aug. 19
Time Warner	500,000	Jan. 28
Time Warner	500,000	Jan. 28
TransTexas Gas	500,000	Aug. 20
BellSouth Telecommunications	450,000	May 18
New York Telephone	450,000	May 17
New York Telephone	450,000	May 17

Source: New York Stock Exchange Fact Book, 1993

Bonds on the Amex

THE AMEX OPENED TRADING of U.S. government securities, Treasury Notes, and Treasury Bonds, in 1975. As of December 31, 1991, 236 corporate and 744 government issues were listed, including U.S. government securities in odd-lot denominations, Treasury Notes (2 to 10 years' maturity), Treasury Bonds (20 years' or more maturity), federal agency securities (Federal Home Loan Banks, Federal National Mortgage Association, Federal Farm Credits, and Federal Land Banks), one-year U.S. Treasury Bills, and three- and six-month Treasury Bills.

Corporate Bond Trading on the Amex

Year	Principal Amount ($)
1983	395,089,000
1984	371,857,000
1985	644,882,000
1986	810,151,000
1987	686,922,000
1988	603,882,000
1989	708,836,000
1990	767,118,000

Year	Principal Amount ($)
1991	952,477,000
1992	894,210,000
1993	785,623,000
1994	1,019,404,000

Government Bond Trading on the Amex

Year	Principal Amount ($)
1983	1,808,921,000
1984	2,086,817,000
1985	2,117,007,000
1986	2,421,255,000
1987	3,016,038,000
1988	3,691,901,000
1989	3,518,454,000
1990	2,719,710,000
1991	2,770,900,000
1992	3,681,143,000
1993	3,430,042,000
1994	3,508,993,000

Source: American Stock Exchange Fact Book, 1995

Bonds on the Amex (cont'd)

Corporate Bond Listings on the Amex

Year	No. of Issues	Principal Amount Outstanding ($)	Total Market Value ($)	Average Price ($)
1970	169	3,178,354,510	2,044,735,556	64.34
1975	197	4,421,821,224	2,998,605,993	67.82
1980	225	6,195,258,443	4,853,002,615	78.34
1981	237	6,863,444,443	4,894,243,593	71.31
1982	244	7,419,099,691	6,213,798,988	83.75
1983	262	8,764,565,391	7,443,389,349	84.93
1984	290	12,670,599,101	9,646,216,836	76.13
1985	347	22,853,452,911	17,655,245,818	77.25
1986	341	24,118,069,806	19,845,653,627	82.28
1987	324	25,461,827,026	19,069,341,030	74.89
1988	309	25,557,448,968	20,993,531,457	82.14
1989	279	27,279,065,889	21,443,266,531	78.61
1990	260	27,195,333,970	29,458,671,424	108.32
1991	236	25,415,012,661	18,859,931,447	74.21
1992	183	23,289,522,693	16,862,072,362	72.40
1993	125	15,341,122,198	12,435,401,236	81.06
1994	103	13,679,226,838	8,705,295,421	63.64

Source: American Stock Exchange Fact Book, 1995

Bond Ratings

WHILE BOND PRICES AND interest rates are broadly determined by bond categories (zero-coupon, convertible, income, for example), an issue's exact pricing and coupon are determined by a credit rating. Standard & Poor's and Moody's are the best-known and most influential credit rating agencies. Their role as raters is to assess the risk of certain bonds through the study of all information provided to the public, and to assign to the issue and issuing company grades that accurately reflect the company's ability to meet the promised principal and interest payments.

While S&P warns investors that a credit rating is not a recommendation to purchase, sell, or hold a particular security, their initial ratings, and revised downgrades and upgrades, greatly affect the attractiveness of the issuance in the eyes of both issuers and holders. Bonds with higher ratings offer lower yields and easier money for the issuer. A lower rating usually results in a lower price on the bond–a less expensive purchase for the investor, but a riskier investment. In 1991, those who gambled on lower-rated bonds (junk bonds) reaped the highest total returns: an average 34.5 percent. One year later, in a less outstanding year for bonds, junk debt took second place in the race for high returns, 18.2 percent compared to a 22.4 percent return on convertible debt.

Although somewhat different in their letter usage, Standard & Poor's and Moody's both rate bonds in descending alphabetical order from A to C.

Standard & Poor's rates some 2,000 domestic and foreign companies; 8,000 munipical, state, and supranational entities; and 1,300 commercial-paper-issuing entities. Moody's rates 19,000 long-term debt issues; 28,000 municipals; and 2,000 commercial paper issuers.

Bond Rating Codes

Rating	S&P	Moody's
Highest quality	AAA	Aaa
High quality	AA	Aa
Upper medium grade	A	A
Medium grade	BBB	Baa
Somewhat speculative	BB	Ba
Low grade, speculative	B	B
Low grade, default possible	CCC	Caa
Low grade, partial recovery possible	CC	Ca
Default, recovery unlikely	C	C

Recommended Resources

Moody's Investors Service
99 Church St.
New York, NY 10007
(212) 553-0376

Standard & Poor's Credit Week, $2,400/year
25 Broadway
New York, NY 10004
(212) 208-1842

Futures

A COMMODITY IS a generic good such as grains, metals, and minerals, which is traded in large amounts in financial markets. Futures contracts are agreements between traders that establish a price level at the current time for commodities to be delivered later. These contracts are bought and sold frequently by speculators seeking profit from active, liquid, and competitive markets.

Major Commodities Futures Traded on the U.S. Exchanges

- Grains and oilseeds (barley, corn, flaxseed, oats, rapeseed, rye, sorghum, soybean meal, soybean oil, soybeans, wheat)
- Wood (lumber, plywood)
- Metals and petroleum (aluminum, copper, crude oil, gold, heating oil, palladium, petroleum, platinum, propane, silver, unleaded gas)
- Livestock and meat (broilers, feeder cattle, pork bellies, hogs, live cattle)

- Food and fiber (cocoa, coffee, cotton, eggs, orange juice, potatoes, rice, sugar).

Major Financial Futures Traded on the U.S. Exchanges

- Interest rates (certificates of deposit, commercial paper, GNMA certificates, T-Bills, T-Bonds, T-Notes)
- Foreign currencies (British pound, Canadian dollar, deutsche mark, Dutch guilder, French franc, Japanese yen, Mexican peso, Swiss franc)
- Indexes (Consumer Price Index [CPI-W], CRB Futures Index, Municipal Bond Index, NYSE Index, NYSE Beta Index, Standard & Poor's 500 Index, Standard & Poor's 100 Index, Standard & Poor's OTC Index, U.S. Dollar Index).

Market Volume of Futures Trading (millions)

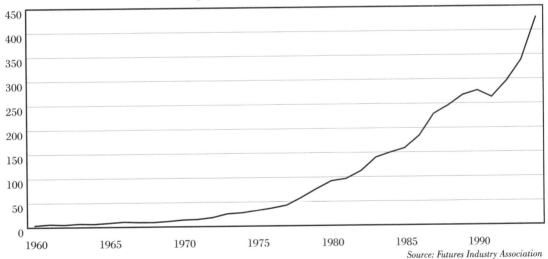

Source: Futures Industry Association

CompuServe's Current Market Snapshot presents hot key data, including highs and lows of the Dow Jones 30, the NASDAQ composite indexes, and the S&P 500. GO SNAPSHOT.

Futures (cont'd)

U.S. Futures Contracts Traded by Commodity Group

Rank	Commodity Group	Contracts	Percent
1990			
1	Interest rate	123,419,532	44.63
2	Agricultural commodities	57,088,348	20.64
3	Energy products	35,441,295	12.82
4	Foreign currency/index	28,880,894	10.44
5	Precious metals	14,812,847	5.36
6	Equity indexes	14,767,090	5.34
7	Non-precious metals	1,853,281	0.67
8	Other	272,217	0.10
	TOTAL	276,535,504	100.00
1991			
1	Interest rate	119,764,959	45.56
2	Agricultural commodities	52,229,512	19.87
3	Energy products	33,670,228	12.81
4	Foreign currency/index	28,715,961	10.92
5	Equity indexes	14,861,067	5.65
6	Precious metals	11,791,525	4.49
7	Non-precious metals	1,640,065	0.62
8	Other	221,706	0.08
	TOTAL	262,895,023	100.00
1992			
1	Interest rate	153,335,831	51.93
2	Agricultural commodities	51,207,959	17.34
3	Energy products	37,776,601	12.79
4	Foreign currency/index	26,594,835	9.01
5	Equity indexes	14,685,096	4.97
6	Precious metals	9,754,216	3.30
7	Non-precious metals	1,674,163	0.57
8	Other	263,341	0.09
	TOTAL	295,292,042	100.00
1993			
1	Interest rate	173,768,387	51.25
2	Agricultural commodities	56,724,601	16.73
3	Energy products	45,618,438	13.45
4	Foreign currency/index	30,816,446	9.09
5	Equity indexes	14,996,787	4.42
6	Precious metals	14,683,066	4.33
7	Non-precious metals	2,064,629	0.61
8	Other	403,272	0.12
	TOTAL	339,075,626	100.00
1994			
1	Interest rate	248,743,673	58.35
2	Agricultural commodities	58,703,203	13.77
3	Energy products	49,672,893	11.65
4	Foreign currency/index	29,676,899	6.96
5	Equity indexes	20,622,974	4.84
6	Precious metals	15,704,863	3.68
7	Non-precious metals	2,737,967	0.64
8	Other	445,470	0.10
	TOTAL	426,307,942	100.00

Source: Futures Industry Association

Futures (cont'd)

U.S. Futures: Top 50 Contracts with Volume over 100,000

1994 Rank	Contracts	1994 Contracts	Percent	1993 Contracts	Percent	1993 Rank
1	Eurodollar, CME	104,823,245	24.59	64,411,394	19.00	2
2	T-Bonds, CBOT	99,959,881	23.45	79,428,474	23.43	1
3	Crude oil, NYMEX	26,812,262	6.29	24,868,602	7.33	3
4	T-Notes (10-Year), CBOT	24,077,828	5.65	16,601,258	4.90	4
5	S&P 500 Index, CME	18,708,599	4.39	13,204,413	3.89	5
6	T-Notes (5-Year), CBOT	12,462,838	2.92	8,123,939	2.40	11
7	Corn, CBOT	11,529,884	2.70	11,462,618	3.38	8
8	Deutsche mark, CME	10,956,479	2.57	12,866,451	3.79	6
9	Soybeans, CBOT	10,749,109	2.52	11,649,333	3.44	7
10	#2 heating oil, NYMEX	8,986,835	2.11	8,625,061	2.54	10
11	Gold (100 oz.), COMEX Div. of NYMEX	8,503,366	1.99	8,916,195	2.63	9
12	Unleaded regular gas, NYMEX	7,470,836	1.75	7,407,809	2.18	12
13	Japanese yen, CME	6,612,993	1.55	6,023,132	1.78	13
14	Natural gas, NYMEX	6,357,560	1.49	4,671,533	1.38	17
15	Silver (5,000 oz.), COMEX Div. of NYMEX	5,994,345	1.41	4,855,924	1.43	15
16	Swiss franc, CME	5,217,236	1.22	5,604,841	1.65	14
17	Soybean oil, CBOT	5,063,188	1.19	4,612,229	1.36	18
18	Sugar #11, CSC	4,719,218	1.11	4,285,945	1.26	19
19	Soybean meal, CBOT	4,593,814	1.08	4,718,095	1.39	16
20	Wheat, CBOT	3,620,631	0.85	3,019,629	0.89	22
21	Live cattle, CME	3,580,896	0.84	3,306,952	0.98	21
22	British pound, CME	3,562,865	0.84	3,701,427	1.09	20
23	High-grade copper, COMEX Div. of NYMEX	2,737,967	0.64	2,064,629	0.61	25
24	Coffee C, CSC	2,658,073	0.62	2,489,223	0.73	23
25	Cocoa, CSC	2,417,006	0.57	2,128,384	0.63	24
26	Cotton, NYCE	2,289,998	0.54	1,603,027	0.47	26
27	1-month LIBOR, CME	1,911,184	0.45	1,128,321	0.33	30
28	Canadian dollar, CME	1,740,205	0.41	1,410,818	0.42	27
29	Municipal bond index, CBOT	1,600,533	0.38	1,120,510	0.33	32
30	Live hogs, CME	1,554,022	0.36	1,401,754	0.41	28
31	Wheat, KCBT	1,502,348	0.35	1,348,500	0.40	29
32	T-Bonds, MIDAM	1,385,904	0.33	1,125,645	0.33	31
33	T-Bills (90-Day), CME	1,020,491	0.24	1,017,350	0.30	33
34	T-Notes (2-year), CBOT	939,043	0.22	532,293	0.16	41
35	Platinum, NYMEX	895,805	0.21	651,222	0.19	38
36	Soybeans, MIDAM	797,803	0.19	966,244	0.28	34
37	Wheat, MGE	737,089	0.17	822,898	0.24	36
38	NYSE Composite Index, NYFE	729,231	0.17	848,522	0.25	35
39	Orange juice (frozen conc.), NYCE	653,824	0.15	640,131	0.19	39
40	Pork bellies, CME	633,646	0.15	698,799	0.21	37
41	U.S. Dollar Index, NYCE	558,439	0.13	599,112	0.18	40
42	Nikkei 225, CME	548,233	0.13	356,523	0.11	44
43	Oats, CBOT	492,504	0.12	455,335	0.13	42
44	Feeder cattle, CME	446,639	0.10	419,888	0.12	43
45	30-day federal funds, CBOT	416,200	0.10	182,319	0.05	48
46	Australian dollar, CME	355,183	0.08	198,954	0.05	47
47	S&P MidCap 400 Index, CME	285,962	0.07	218,531	0.06	46
48	Corn, MIDAM	232,855	0.05	276,502	0.08	45
49	Lumber, CME	172,963	0.04	178,184	0.05	49
50	Goldman, Sachs Commodity Index, CME	154,511	0.04	122,281	0.04	53

Source: Futures Industry Association

Options

AN OPTION IS A CONTRACT that permits the holder to buy an asset (a *call*) or sell an asset (a *put*) at a set price for a specified period of time. Before 1973, options were traded on an unregulated basis through a limited number of firms. Now options are listed and traded on five major U.S. exchanges, including the world's largest, the Chicago Board of Exchange.

Market Value of Options Sales on U.S. Exchanges: Non-Equity Options

Calendar Year	Non-Equity Options Traded
1986	47,887,805
1987	65,748,621
1988	35,455,956
1989	36,351,306
1990	51,793,712
1991	49,012,406
1992	45,590,003

Market Value of Options Sales on U.S. Exchanges: Equity Options

Calendar Year	Equity Options Traded
1986	40,054,282
1987	53,123,325
1988	27,163,915
1989	40,423,407
1990	27,218,738
1991	27,104,021
1992	26,585,937

Source: U.S. Securities and Exchange Commission

U.S. Options Contracts Traded by Commodity Group

Rank	Commodities Group	Contracts	Percent
1990			
1	Interest rate	35,336,832	55.13
2	Agricultural commodities	9,580,512	14.95
3	Foreign currency/index	8,588,796	13.40
4	Energy products	6,097,107	9.51
5	Precious metals	2,686,774	4.19
6	Equity indexes	1,672,425	2.61
7	Non-precious metals	107,387	0.17
8	Other	33,261	0.05
	TOTAL	64,103,094	100.00
1991			
1	Interest rate	31,015,006	49.86
2	Agricultural commodities	11,486,318	18.47
3	Foreign currency/index	8,860,003	14.24
4	Energy products	6,405,652	10.30
5	Precious metals	2,462,854	3.96
6	Equity indexes	1,863,125	3.00
7	Non-precious metals	97,163	0.16
8	Other	11,784	0.02
	TOTAL	62,201,905	100.00
1992			
1	Interest rate	37,428,654	54.05
2	Agricultural commodities	10,320,550	14.90
3	Foreign currency/index	8,750,896	12.64
4	Energy products	8,450,869	12.20
5	Precious metals	2,273,025	3.28
6	Equity indexes	1,916,447	2.77
7	Non-precious metals	87,324	0.13
8	Other	17,010	0.02
	TOTAL	69,244,775	100.00

Options (cont'd)

Rank	Commodities Group	Contracts	Percent
1993			
1	Interest rate	47,458,153	57.98
2	Agricultural commodities	9,766,714	11.93
3	Foreign currency/index	9,588,967	11.71
4	Energy products	8,966,434	10.95
5	Precious metals	2,965,862	3.62
6	Equity indexes	2,888,520	3.53
7	Non-precious metals	146,594	0.18
8	Other	77,391	0.09
	TOTAL	81,858,635	100.00
1994			
1	Interest rate	65,767,610	65.19
2	Agricultural commodities	10,857,240	10.76
3	Foreign currency/index	9,664,547	9.58
4	Energy products	7,469,287	7.40
5	Precious metals	3,866,134	3.83
6	Equity indexes	3,003,919	2.98
7	Non-precious metals	184,166	0.18
8	Other	68,597	0.07
	TOTAL	100,881,500	100.00

Source: Futures Industry Association

U.S. Options: Top 50 Contracts with Volume over 100,000

1994 Rank	Contracts	1994 Contracts	Percent	1993 Contracts	Percent	1993 Rank
1	S&P 100 Index, CBOE	81,824,650	35.24	64,031,944	35.21	1
2	Eurodollar, CME	28,145,929	12.12	17,008,764	9.33	3
3	T-Bonds, CBOT	28,142,549	12.12	23,435,164	12.85	2
4	S&P 500 Index, CBOE	28,016,776	12.07	16,454,282	9.02	4
5	T-Notes (10-year), CBOT	6,437,215	2.77	4,844,272	2.66	8
6	Crude oil, NYMEX	5,675,072	2.44	7,156,518	3.93	5
7	Deutschemark, CME	4,793,639	2.06	5,916,463	3.24	7
8	French franc, PSE	4,507,655	1.94	3,978,929	2.18	9
9	S&P 500 Index, CME	3,820,893	1.65	2,916,047	1.60	11
10	Deutschemark, PHLX	3,445,024	1.48	6,217,792	3.41	6
11	Japanese yen, CME	2,946,432	1.27	2,261,977	1.24	12
12	Soybeans, CBOT	2,710,656	1.17	2,927,072	1.61	10
13	T-Notes (5-year), CBOT	2,675,097	1.15	1,976,924	1.08	14
14	Corn, CBOT	2,144,461	0.92	2,031,284	1.11	13
15	Gold (1,000 oz.), COMDEX Div. of NYMEX	1,589,065	0.68	1,717,015	0.94	16
16	NASDAQ 100, CBOE	1,358,930	0.59	NA	NA	NA
17	Silver (5,000 oz.), COMDEX Div. of NYMEX	1,316,650	0.57	1,094,702	0.60	18
18	Stock Index Flex, CBOE	1,262,336	0.54	NA	NA	NA
19	Coffee, CSC	1,208,925	0.52	1,022,017	0.56	19
20	Sugar, CSC	1,166,748	0.50	916,170	0.50	20
21	Major Market Index, AMEX	1,125,678	0.48	1,737,250	0.95	15
22	Japanese yen, PHLX	998,660	0.43	1,302,396	0.71	17
23	British pound, CME	920,109	0.40	528,239	0.29	29
24	Wheat, CBOT	827,930	0.36	713,670	0.39	24
25	Bank Index, PHLX	816,442	0.35	236,122	0.13	41

Options (cont'd)

1994 Rank	Contracts	1994 Contracts	Percent	1993 Contracts	Percent	1993 Rank
26	Cottton #2, NYCE	816,031	0.35	372,074	0.20	34
27	Swiss franc, CME	767,583	0.33	627,923	0.34	27
28	OEX Leaps, CBOE	732,797	0.32	289,424	0.16	39
29	Heating oil, NYMEX	699,325	0.30	803,216	0.44	21
30	Japan Index, AMEX	677,024	0.29	758,969	0.42	22
31	Russell 2000, CBOE	651,009	0.28	494,980	0.27	31
32	S&P MidCap Index, AMEX	579,450	0.25	720,553	0.40	23
33	Unleaded regular gas, NYMEX	573,502	0.25	660,886	0.36	26
34	Utility Index, PHLX	540,086	0.23	124,050	0.07	50
35	Gold/Silver Index, PHLX	529,421	0.23	298,221	0.16	38
36	Live cattle, CME	519,813	0.22	500,664	0.27	30
37	Natural gas, NYMEX	493,491	0.21	345,814	0.19	35
38	Institutional Index, AMEX	492,365	0.21	696,894	0.38	25
39	Swiss franc, PHLX	428,360	0.18	450,105	0.25	32
40	British pound, PHLX	410,981	0.18	528,957	0.29	28
41	SPX Leaps, CBOE	369,149	0.16	146,451	0.08	48
42	OTC Index, PHLX	361,282	0.16	392,330	0.22	33
43	Cocoa (10 metric tons), CSC	341,131	0.15	326,760	0.18	36
44	Soybean oil, CBOT	287,905	0.12	181,938	0.10	43
45	Soybean meal, CBOT	263,734	0.11	306,523	0.17	37
46	Interest Rate Comp., CBOE	216,592	0.09	NA	NA	NA
47	Canadian dollar, CME	185,652	0.08	176,930	0.10	44
48	High-grade copper, COMEX Div. of NYMEX	184,125	0.08	146,060	0.08	49
49	Mexico Index, CBOE	176,947	0.08	NA	NA	NA
50	Flexible U.S. T-Bonds, CBOT	174,295	0.08	NA	NA	NA

Source: Futures Industry Association

U.S. Futures and Options Exchanges

Options Traded on U.S. Futures Exchanges: Volume and Market Share, 1994 and 1993

1994 Rank	Exchange	1994 Contracts	Percent	1993 Contracts	Percent	1993 Rank
1	Chicago Board of Trade	43,806,394	43.42	36,531,698	44.63	1
2	Chicago Mercantile Exchange	42,489,574	42.12	30,331,877	37.05	2
3	New York Mercantile Exchange	10,651,003	10.56	11,989,619	14.65	3
4	Coffee, Sugar & Cocoa Exchange	2,717,012	2.69	2,265,417	2.77	5
5	New York Cotton Exchange	1,017,664	1.01	541,097	0.66	6
6	Kansas City Board of Trade	93,358	0.09	89,011	0.11	7
7	Minneapolis Grain Exchange	40,411	0.04	37,521	0.05	8
8	New York Futures Exchange	34,131	0.03	36,389	0.04	9
9	MidAmerica Commodity Exchange	31,953	0.03	36,006	0.04	10
	TOTAL	100,881,500	100.00	81,858,635	100.00	

Source: Futures Industry Association

U.S. Futures and Options Exchanges (cont'd)

Options Traded on U.S. Securities Exchanges: Volume and Market Share, 1994 and 1993*

1994 Rank	Exchange	1994 Contracts	Percent	1993 Contracts	Percent	1993 Rank
1	Chicago Board Options Exchange	114,952,472	87.56	81,640,387	81.27	1
2	Philadelphia Stock Exchange	12,612,020	9.61	14,246,794	14.18	2
3	American Stock Exchange	3,613,651	2.75	4,365,512	4.35	3
4	Pacific Stock Exchange	73,678	0.06	155,959	0.16	4
5	New York Stock Exchange	31,004	0.02	41,745	0.04	5
	TOTAL	131,282,825	100.00	100,450,397	100.00	

Options Volume on U.S. Futures and U.S. Securities Exchanges 1989–1994*

Year	Total Options on Futures Exchanges	Percent Change	Total Options on Securities Exchanges	Percent Change	Grand Total	Percent Change
1989	55,446,130	12.84	84,910,688	2.77	140,356,818	6.52
1990	64,103,094	15.61	98,371,455	15.85	162,474,549	15.76
1991	62,201,905	-2.97	93,336,788	-5.12	155,538,693	-4.27
1992	69,244,775	11.32	95,989,877	2.84	165,234,652	6.23
1993	81,858,635	18.22	100,468,129	4.67	182,326,764	10.34
1994	100,881,500	23.24	131,282,825	30.67	232,164,325	27.33

* Does not include options on individual equities traded on U.S. securities exchanges.   *Source: Futures Industry Association*

Contact Options

American Stock Exchange (Amex)
86 Trinity Pl.
New York, NY 10006
(212) 306-1000

Chicago Board of Trade (CBOT)
141 W. Jackson Blvd.
Chicago, IL 60604
(312) 435-3500

Chicago Board Options Exchange (CBOE)
400 S. LaSalle St.
Chicago, IL 60605
(312) 786-5600

Chicago Cotton and Rice Exchange (CRCE)
141 W. Jackson Blvd.
Chicago, IL 60604
(312) 341-3078

Chicago Mercantile Exchange (CME), International
Monetary Fund, and Index and Option Market
30 S. Wacker Dr.
Chicago, IL 60606
(312) 930-1000

Citrus Associates of the New York Cotton Exchange
4 World Trade Center
New York, NY 10048
(212) 938-2702

Coffee, Sugar and Cocoa Exchange (CSCE)
4 World Trade Center
New York, NY 10048
(212) 938-2800

Commodity Exchange (COMEX)
4 World Trade Center
New York, NY 10048
(212) 938-2900

Financial Instrument Exchange (FINEX)
4 World Trade Center
New York, NY 10048
(212) 938-2629

Kansas City Board of Trade (KCBT)
4800 Main St.
Kansas City, MO 64112
(816) 753-7500 or (816) 753-1101 (hotline)

MidAmerica Commodity Exchange (MidAm)
141 W. Jackson Blvd.
Chicago, IL 60604
(312) 341-3000

Minneapolis Grain Exchange (MGE)
400 S. Fourth St.
Minneapolis, MN 55415
(612) 338-6212

New York Cotton Exchange (NYCE)
4 World Trade Center
New York, NY 10048
(212) 938-2650

New York Futures Exchange (NYFE)
4 World Trade Center
New York, NY 10048
(212) 938-4940 or (800) 843-6933

U.S. Futures and Options Exchanges (cont'd)

New York Mercantile Exchange (NYMEX)
4 World Trade Center
New York, NY 10048
(212) 938-2222

New York Stock Exchange (NYSE)
11 Wall St.
New York, NY 10005
(212) 656-3000 or (800) 692-6973

Pacific Stock Exchange (PSE)
301 Pine St.
San Francisco, CA 94104
(415) 393-4000

Philadelphia Board of Trade (PBOT)
1900 Market St.
Philadelphia, PA 19103
(215) 496-5000

Mutual Fund Rankings and Data

A MUTUAL FUND IS A POOL OF MONEY professionally invested by a money manager. Group performance is measured by one-year, three-year, five-year, and ten-year performance of the following fund categories:

General Equity Funds

CA–Capital appreciation fund
G–Growth fund
SG–Small company growth fund
GI–Growth and income fund
EI–Equity income fund

Specialty Equity-Oriented Funds

H–Health/biotechnology fund
NR–Natural resources fund
EN–Environmental fund
TK–Science and technology fund
UT–Utility fund
FS–Financial services fund
RE–Real estate fund
OI–Option income fund
AU–Gold-oriented fund
GL–Global fund
IF–International fund
EU–European region fund
PC–Pacific region fund
JA–Japanese fund
LT–Latin America fund
CN–Canadian fund

Other Funds

B–Balanced fund
CV–Convertible securities fund
I–Income fund
FI–Fixed income fund

Money Market Funds (Taxable)

UST–U.S. Treasury money market funds
USS–U.S. Government money market funds

Money Market Funds (Municipal)

TEM–Tax-exempt money market funds

General Domestic Taxable Fixed-Income Funds

GUT–General U.S. Treasury
GUS–General U.S. government funds
GNM–GNMA funds
USM–U.S. mortgage funds
A–Corporate debt funds, A rated
BBB–Corporate debt funds, BBB rated
GB–General bond funds
HY–High current yield funds

World Taxable Fixed-Income Funds

GWI–General world income funds

General Municipal Debt Funds

GM–General municipal debt funds

Single-State Municipal Debt Funds

AZ, CA, CO, CT, FL, GA, KY, LA, MA, MD, MI, MN, MO, NC, NJ, NY, OH, OR, PA, SC, TX, and VA

Mutual Fund Rankings and Data (cont'd)

Percent Distribution of Funds by Total Net Assets

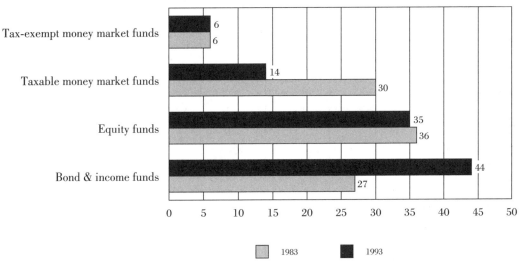

Fund Assets: Equity, Income, and Bond Funds ($ billions)

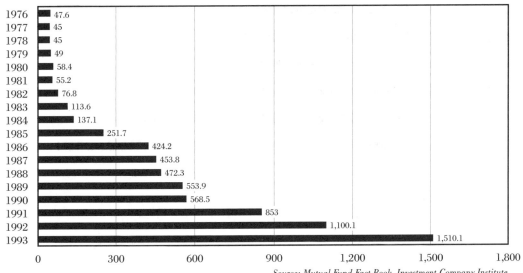

Source: Mutual Fund Fact Book, Investment Company Institute,
Washington, DC, 1994. Reprinted with permission.

Mutual Fund Rankings and Data (cont'd)

Number of Mutual Funds by Type of Fund

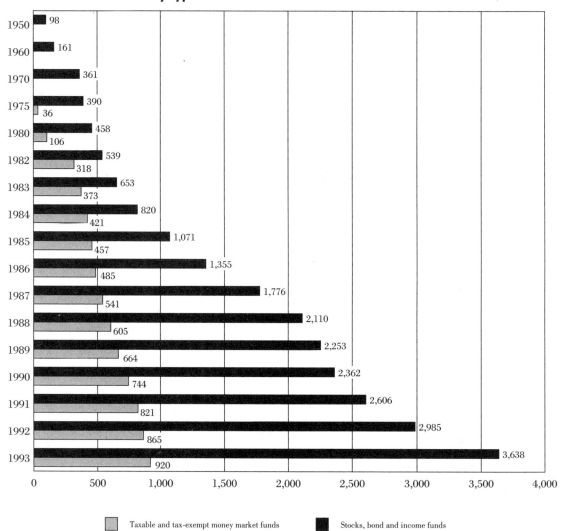

| Taxable and tax-exempt money market funds | Stocks, bond and income funds |

*Source: Mutual Fund Fact Book, Investment Company Institute,
Washington, DC, 1994. Reprinted with permission.*

Mutual Fund Rankings and Data (cont'd)

Fund Assets: Taxable Money Market Funds ($ billions)

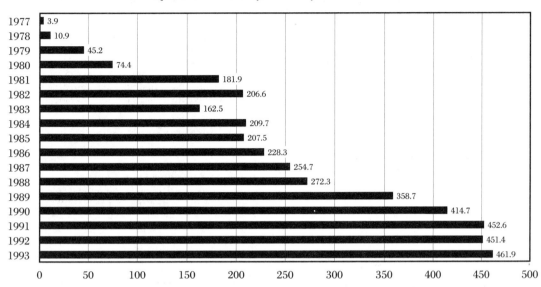

Fund Assets: Tax-Exempt Money Market Funds ($ billions)

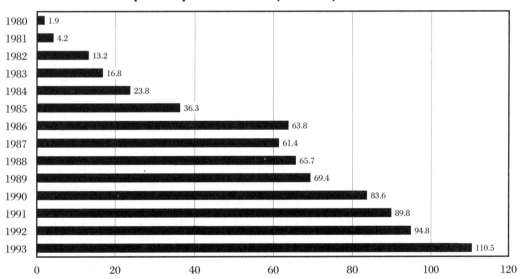

Source: Mutual Fund Fact Book, Investment Company Institute,
Washington, DC, 1994. Reprinted with permission.

Eight Types of Mutual Funds

Aggressive Growth Funds

Aggressive growth funds strive to maximize capital gains (they aim to buy low and sell high). These funds may leverage their assets by borrowing funds, and may trade in stock options.

These funds often have low current yields. Because they don't invest for dividend income, and often have little cash in interest-bearing accounts, short-term yield is not optimized.

If the market is going up, these are the funds that will benefit the most. Conversely, aggressive growth funds are the ones hardest hit in bear markets. The volatility of these funds makes them inappropriate for risk-averse investors.

Growth Funds

Growth funds are similar to aggressive growth funds, but do not usually trade stock options or borrow money with which to trade. Most growth funds surpass the S&P 500 during bull markets, but do a little worse than average during bear markets.

Just as in aggressive growth funds, growth funds are not aimed at the short-term market timer. The aggressive investor may find that they are an ideal complement for aggressive growth funds, as the differing investment strategies used by the two types of funds can produce maximum gains.

The volatility of these funds makes them inappropriate as the sole investment vehicle for risk-averse investors.

Growth-Income Funds

Growth-income funds are specialists in blue-chip stocks. These funds invest in utilities, Dow industrials, and other seasoned stocks. They work to maximize dividend income while also generating capital gains.

These funds are appropriate as a substitute for conservative investment in the stock market.

Income Funds

Income funds focus on dividend income, while also enjoying the capital gains that usually accompany investment in common and preferred stocks. These funds are particularly favored by conservative investors.

International Funds

International funds hold primarily foreign securities. There are two elements of risk in this invest-

ment: the normal economic risk of holding stocks, as well as the currency risk associated with repatriating money after taking the investment profits.

These funds are an important part of many portfolios, but any individual fund may prove too volatile for the average investor as the sole investment.

Asset Allocation Funds

Asset allocation funds don't invest in just stocks. Instead, they focus on stocks, bonds, gold, real estate, and money market funds. This portfolio approach greatly decreases the reliance on any one segment of the marketplace, easing any declines. The upside is limited by this strategy as well.

Precious Metal Funds

Precious metal funds invest in gold, silver, and platinum. Gold and (to a lesser degree) silver often move in the opposite direction from the stock market, and thus these funds can provide a hedge against investments in common stocks.

Bond Funds

Bond funds invest in corporate and government bonds. A common misunderstanding among investors is that the return on a bond fund is similar to the returns of the bonds purchased. One might expect that a fund that owns primarily 8 percent-yielding bonds would return 8 percent to investors. In fact, the yield from the fund is based primarily on the trading of bonds, which are extraordinarily sensitive to interest rates. Thus, one could find a bond fund that was earning double-digit returns as the prime rate climbed from 4 percent to 6 percent.

In addition to mutual funds, there are money market funds, which are essentially mutual funds that invest solely in government-insured short-term instruments. These funds nearly always reflect the current interest rates, and rarely engage in interest-rate speculation.

Recommended Resource

The Mutual Fund Encyclopedia
by Gerald W. Perritt
Dearborn Financial Publishing, $35.95
(800) 533-2665

Equity Funds

20 Largest Equity Funds

Fund Name	Objective	1994 Assets ($ millions)
Fidelity Magellan Fund	Growth	36,441.5
Investment Co. of America	Growth and income	19,279.6
Washington Mutual Investment	Growth and income	12,668.3
Fidelity Puritan	Equity income	11,769.4
Fidelity Asset Manager	Flexible	11,075.6
Vanguard Windsor	Growth and income	10,672.9
Income Fund of America	Equity income	10,502.7
Twentieth Century: Ultra Investment	Mid-cap	9,850.8
Janus Fund	Capital appreciation	9,400.6
Vanguard Index: 500 Portfolio	S&P 500 Index objective	9,356.3
Fidelity Growth & Income	Growth and income	9,344.9
Vanguard Wellington Fund	Balanced	8,809.4
Fidelity Contrafund	Growth	8,682.4
Europacific Growth	International	8,269.5
Vanguard Windsor II	Growth and income	7,959.0
Fidelity Equity-Income II	Equity income	7,697.5
Fidelity Equity-Income	Equity income	7,412.8
Dean Witter Dividend Growth	Growth and income	6,696.0
New Prospective Fund	Global	6,540.2
Merritt Global Allocation; B	Global flexible	6,155.3

20 Best-Performing Equity Funds, 1994

Fund Name	Objective	1994 Return (%)	Five-Year Return (%)
Seligman Communications: A	Science and technology	35.30	200.07
Seligman Communications: D	Science and technology	33.94	NA
DFA Group: Japan Small Companies	Japanese	29.49	-22.04
Govett: Smaller Companies	Small company growth	28.74	NA
Alliance Technology: A	Science and technology	28.51	169.88
Alliance Technology: C	Science and technology	27.70	NA
Alliance Technology: B	Science and technology	27.65	NA
Merrill Technology: A	Science and technology	26.63	NA
Merrill Technology: B	Science and technology	25.50	NA
Capstone Nikko Japan	Japanese	24.27	-30.45
PBHG Emerging Growth	Small company growth	23.78	NA
Robertson Stephenson: Value and Growth	Small company growth	23.11	NA
Fidelity Select Health	Health/biotechnology	21.43	134.03
Montgomery: Growth	Growth	20.91	NA
Fidelity Select Computer	Science and technology	20.45	193.20
Fidelity Select Medical	Health/biotechnology	19.82	126.94
BT Investment: Small Cap	Small company growth	19.31	NA
Amelia Earhart: Eagle Equity	Growth	17.72	NA
Strong Growth	Growth	17.27	NA
AIM Equity: Aggressive Growth	Small company growth	17.18	187.69

Source: Lipper Analytical Services, Inc.

Equity Funds (cont'd)

Ten Best-Performing Equity Funds: Five-Year

Fund Name	Objective	1994 Return (%)	Five-Year Return (%)
Seligman Communications: A	Science and technology	35.30	200.07
Fidelity Select Computer	Science and technology	20.45	193.20
Fidelity Select Home Financial	Financial services	2.64	188.15
AIM Equity: Aggressive Growth	Small company growth	17.18	187.69
Fidelity Select Electronic	Science and technology	17.17	182.48
Invesco Strategic: Technology	Science and technology	5.27	176.33
Oppenheimer Main: Income and Growth; A	Growth and income	-1.53	174.93
Fidelity Select Technology	Science and technology	11.14	173.13
Twentieth Century: Giftrust	Small company growth	13.49	170.21
T. Rowe Price Science & Technology	Science and technology	15.79	169.99
Alliance Technology; A	Science and technology	28.51	169.88
PBHG Growth Fund	California	4.75	169.35
J. Hancock Special Equity; A	Small company growth	13.49	170.21
Fidelity Select Software	Science and technology	0.39	165.19
MFS Emerging Growth; B	Mid-cap	4.00	163.49
PIMCO Advantage: Opportunity; C	California	-4.73	159.51
United New Concepts	Small company growth	11.32	147.35
Crabbe Huson Special	Mid-cap	11.72	143.67
Twentieth Century: Ultra Investment	Mid-cap	-3.62	142.43
Kaufmann Fund	Small company growth	8.99	141.14

Source: Lipper Analytical Services, Inc.

Taxable Bond Funds

20 Largest Taxable Bond Funds

Fund Name	Objective	1994 Assets ($ millions)
CMA Money Fund	Money market	26,474.0
Smith Barney Money: Cash; A	Money market	17,589.9
Vanguard Money Market Reserves: Prime	Money market	15,321.2
Fidelity Cash Reserves	Money market	15,077.5
Charles Schwab: Money Market	Money market	11,227.2
Franklin Custodian: U.S. Government	GNMA	10,984.6
Dean Witter Liquid Asset	Money market	8,906.6
Dean Witter U.S. Government	General U.S. government	8,199.9
Fidelity Spartan Money Market	Money market	7,489.3
Merrill Retirement: Reserves	Money market	7,373.2
Prudential Money Market	Money market	6,594.5
PIMCO Total Return; Institutional	Intermediate investment grade debt	6,554.8
Merrill Ready Assets	Money market	6,241.0
Vanguard Fixed: GNMA Port	GNMA	5,777.8
AARP GNMA	GNMA	5,248.9
Temporary Investment Fund: Temporary fund; Shares	Institutional money market	5,160.2
Bond Fund of America	Corporate debt–A rated	4,941.2
Dreyfus Liquid Assets	Money market	4,894.3
Active Assets Money Tree	Money market	4,759.6
Fidelity Institutional: Money Market; A	Institutional money market	4,748.1

Source: Lipper Analytical Services, Inc.

Taxable Bond Funds (cont'd)

20 Best-Performing Taxable Bond Funds, 1994

Fund Name	Objective	1994 Return (%)	Five-Year Return (%)
Fidelity D-Mark Performance	Short world single market	16.39	49.27
Franklin/Temp Hard Currency	Short world multi-market	15.10	61.17
Fidelity Yen Performance	Short world single market	12.64	68.29
Franklin/Temp High Income	Short world multi-market	10.19	39.18
Fidelity Sterling Performance	Short world single market	9.88	43.31
Franklin/Temp German Government	General world income	9.62	NA
Franklin/Temp GL Currency	Short world multi-market	8.08	47.20
Glenmede: International Fixed Income	General world income	7.42	NA
Hotchkis & Wiley: Low Duration	Short-term institutional debt	5.18	NA
GMO: International Bond	General world income	5.16	NA
Hotchkis & Wiley: Short-Term Investment	Ultra-short obligation	4.42	NA
SS Research: International Fixed Income; C	General world income	4.26	NA
Lazard: International Fixed Income	General world income	4.22	NA
Dekalb: Short Duration Government	U.S. mortgage	4.18	NA
Smith Breeden: Short Government	Adjustable rate mortgage	4.14	NA
Seven Seas: Yield Plus	Short-term institutional debt	4.10	NA
Benchmark: Short Duration	Ultra-short obligation	3.84	NA
FFTW: U.S. Short-Term Fixed Income	Short world single market	3.75	27.45
Regis: Sirach Short-Term Reserves	Short-term institutional debt	3.75	NA
Dreyfus Institutional Short Treasury; A	Short U.S. treasury	3.58	NA

20 Best-Performing Taxable Bond Funds: Five-Year

Name	Objective	1994 Return (%)	Five-Year Return (%)
Fidelity Advantage High Yield; A	High yield	-1.49	111.35
Fidelity Capitol & Income	High yield	-4.61	90.32
Liberty High Income; A	High yield	-1.68	89.30
Oppenheimer Champion High Yield; A	High yield	-0.12	87.70
Advantage: High Yield	High yield	-2.18	85.23
Merrill Corp: High Income; A	High yield	-2.68	83.64
Mainstay: High Yield Corporate; B	High yield	1.50	83.05
Putnam High Yield Advantage; A	High yield	-5.15	82.37
Kemper Diversified Income; A	High yield	-3.83	81.55
PaineWebber High Income; A	High yield	-11.71	80.22
AIM: High Yield; A	High yield	-1.68	78.03
Colonial High Yield Security; A	High yield	-0.36	76.93
Kemper High Yield; A	High yield	-1.72	76.89
Merrill Corporate: High Income; B	High yield	-3.53	76.83
Putnam High Yield; A	High yield	-4.72	76.67
HAS Funds: High Yield	High yield	-7.06	76.20
Federated High Yield Treasury	High yield	-2.41	75.54
Seligman High Income: Bond; A	High yield	0.80	75.33
Lutheran Brothers High Yield	High yield	-5.29	73.22
Fortis Advantage: High Yield	High yield	-3.46	72.20

Source: Lipper Analytical Services, Inc.

Tax-Exempt Funds

20 Largest Tax-Exempt Funds

Fund Name	Objective	1994 Assets ($)
Franklin Custodian: U.S. Government	GNMA	10,984.6
Dean Witter U.S. Government	General U.S. government	8,199.9
CMA Tax-Exempt Fund	Tax-exempt money market	6,610.5
PIMCO Total Return; Institutional	Intermediate investment grade debt	6,554.8
Vanguard Fixed: GNMA Portfolio	GNMA	5,777.8
AARP GNMA	GNMA	5,248.9
Bond Fund of America	Corporate debt–A rated	4,941.2
Kemper U.S. Government Security; A	GNMA	4,746.0
Smith Barney Municipal: Money Market	Tax-exempt money market	4,412.5
Vanguard Municipal: Money Market	Tax-exempt money market	4,248.2
Fidelity Tax-Exempt Money Market	Tax-exempt money market	3,584.4
Prudential High Yield; B	High yield	3,337.0
Lord Abbett U.S. Government	General U.S. government	3,219.6
Charles Schwab: Tax-Exempt	Tax-exempt money market	3,015.9
Putnam U.S. Government Income; A	GNMA	2,987.4
Oppenheimer Strategic Income; A	General	2,986.9
Vankamp Fixed: Short Term Corporate	U.S. mortgage	2,917.4
Vanguard Fixed: Short Term Corporate	Short-term investment grade debt	2,905.8
GE S&S Program: Long Term Institutional	Intermediate investment grade debt	2,741.4
Putnam High Yield; A	High yield	2,715.0

20 Best-Performing Tax-Exempt Funds, 1994

Fund Name	Objective	1994 Return (%)	Five-Year Return (%)
Hanifen, Imhoff CO Bond Share: Tax-Exempt; A	Colorado	6.17	37.35
Twentieth Century: Tax-Exempt Short Term	Short-term municipal debt	2.47	NA
Calvert Tax-Free Reserves: Limited; A	Short-term municipal debt	2.42	26.84
Venture Municipal Plus; B	High-yield municipal	2.29	38.03
Vanguard Municipal: Short Term	Short-term municipal debt	1.70	26.23
Merrill Municipal: Limited Maturity; A	Short-term municipal debt	1.33	27.18
Colonial Short-Term Tax-Exempt; A	Short-term municipal debt	1.23	NA
Pacifica: Short-Term California Tax-Free	California short municipal	1.12	NA
Merrill Municipal: Limited Maturity; B	Short-term municipal debt	1.02	NA
USAA Tax-Exempt: Short-Term	Short-term municipal debt	0.83	28.56
SIT Minnesota Tax-Free Income	Minnesota	0.62	NA
Nations: Short-Term Municipal Trust; A	Short-term municipal debt	0.45	NA
Kent Funds: Michigan Municipal; Institutional	Michigan intermed. muni. debt	0.36	NA
Managers: Short Municipal	Short-term municipal debt	0.36	21.05
59 Wall Street: Tax-Free Short/Intermediate	Short-term municipal debt	0.33	NA
T. Rowe Price Tax-Free Short/Intermediate	Short-term municipal debt	0.33	29.37
Nations: Short-Term Municipal; Investment A	Short-term municipal debt	0.28	NA
Lipper Short Municipal Debt Fund IX	Short-term municipal debt	0.21	29.05
American Cap Texas Municipal; C	Texas	0.20	NA
American Cap Tax-Exempt: High Yield; A	High-yield municipal	0.19	41.14

Source: Lipper Analytical Services, Inc.

Tax-Exempt Funds (cont'd)

20 Best-Performing Tax-Exempt Funds: Five-Year

Fund Name	Objective	1994 Return (%)	Five-Year Return (%)
Vista: Tax-Free Income; A	General municipal debt	-7.64	46.58
Smith Barney Managed Municipal; A	General municipal debt	-4.53	45.54
United Municipal High Income	High yield municipal	-3.11	45.01
UST Master Tax-Exempt Long Term	General municipal debt	-5.76	44.43
Flagship Tax-Exempt: American; A	General municipal debt	-5.89	44.03
Dreyfus Premium Municipal: Texas; A	Texas	-4.87	43.90
Dreyfus Premium Municipal Bond; A	General municipal debt	-6.43	43.87
Fidelity Advantage High Income Municipal; A	High yield municipal	-8.05	43.83
Putnam Pennsylvania Tax-Exempt; A	Pennsylvania	-4.82	43.69
Prairie: Municipal Bond; A	General	-2.00	43.18
Dreyfus Premium Municipal: Pennsylvania; A	Pennsylvania	-5.30	42.89
Vanguard Municipal: Intermediate Term	Intermediate municipal debt	-2.12	42.76
Vanguard Municipal: High Yield	High yield municipal	-5.06	42.75
Franklin New York Tax-Free Income	New York	-3.58	42.66
Smith Barney Municipal: National; A	General municipal debt	-5.83	42.44
Dreyfus General Municipal Bond	General municipal debt	-7.32	42.39
Dreyfus Premium Municipal: Michigan; A	Michigan	-4.59	42.24
Putnam Massachusetts Tax-Exempt II; A	Massachusetts	-6.09	42.11
Vanguard Pennsylvania Tax-Free: Insured Long-Term	Pennsylvania	-4.54	42.10
Dupree: Kentucky Tax-Free Income	Kentucky	-2.93	42.01

Source: Lipper Analytical Services, Inc.

Performance of Equity Fund Groups

Overall Performance of Equity Fund Groups, 1994: Ten-Year, Five-Year, One-Year

Type of Fund	Dec. 1994 Assets ($ mil.)	No. of Funds	Ten-Year Return (%)	Five-Year Return (%)	One-Year Return (%)
General equity funds average	585,222.5	1,673	234.89	55.51	-1.68
Capital appreciation funds	40,991.8	155	227.19	54.54	-3.43
Growth funds	196,181.4	564	239.11	53.01	-2.15
Midcap funds	32,005.4	99	270.08	78.14	-2.05
Small company growth funds	36,824.5	283	270.59	76.56	-0.72
Growth & income funds	190,435.7	412	224.93	49.48	-0.94
S&P 500 objective funds	19,639.8	40	253.86	47.64	0.91
Equity income funds	69,143.8	120	197.77	42.97	-2.41
Health/biotechnology funds	4,283.5	18	512.63	98.62	4.26
Natural resources funds	3,065.0	36	137.69	13.56	-4.20
Environmental funds	120.6	6	176.89	6.79	-10.50
Science & technology funds	5,186.4	37	303.40	123.87	10.59
Specialty/miscellaneous funds	2,236.9	27	248.95	66.26	-2.29
Utility funds	22,172.1	86	174.35	37.53	-8.99
Financial services funds	2,321.1	16	250.86	105.72	-2.69
Real estate funds	1,445.4	21	NA	41.51	-2.84
World equity funds average	162,474.9	614	253.43	24.95	-3.66
Gold-oriented funds	6,772.6	38	96.90	1.34	-12.23
Global funds	42,221.0	123	286.80	34.17	-3.03
Global small company funds	6,612.9	23	175.86	44.85	-2.86

Performance of Equity Fund Groups (cont'd)

Type of Fund	Dec. 1994 Assets ($ mil.)	No. of Funds	Ten-Year Return (%)	Five-Year Return (%)	One-Year Return (%)
International funds	67,470.6	223	328.06	31.14	-0.70
International small co. funds	2,726.4	11	NA	22.61	-4.09
Pacific region funds	13,158.4	69	365.79	38.42	-12.07
Emerging markets funds	10,308.4	47	236.52	66.21	-9.57
Japanese funds	1,886.6	12	304.84	-19.37	15.39
Latin american funds	4,373.1	19	NA	NA	-14.24
Canadian funds	410.0	2	NA	5.92	-12.90
ALL EQUITY FUNDS AVERAGE	768,526.4	2,534	236.54	51.65	-2.25
Flexible portfolio funds	29,588.2	149	162.53	49.20	-2.64
Global flexible portfolio funds	11,005.7	45	129.61	35.17	-4.68
Balanced funds	51,441.9	196	202.40	46.03	-2.52
Balanced target maturity funds	962.6	13	NA	40.97	-4.99
Convertible securities funds	3,809.8	31	181.45	57.09	-3.79
Income funds	14,317.1	22	181.87	47.06	-2.92
World income funds	28,444.2	197	161.40	45.15	-5.52
Fixed-income funds	304,518.7	1,375	138.94	42.69	-3.28
AVERAGE			197.25	44.14	-2.58

Top-Performing Funds: Science & Technology

Fund Name	1994 Return (%)	Five-Year Return (%)	Ten-Year Return (%)
Seligman Communications; A	35.30	200.07	674.13
Seligman Communications; B	33.94	NA	NA
Alliance Technology; A	28.51	169.88	385.25
Alliance Technology; C	27.70	NA	NA
Alliance Technology; B	27.65	NA	NA
Merrill Technology; A	26.63	NA	NA
Merrill Technology; B	25.50	NA	NA
Fidelity Select Computer	20.45	193.20	NA
Fidelity Select Electronic	17.17	182.48	NA
T. Rowe Price Science & Technology	15.79	169.99	NA

Top Performing Funds: Health & Biotechnology

Fund Name	1994 Return (%)	Five-Year Return (%)	Ten-Year Return (%)
Fidelity Select Health	21.43	134.03	601.44
Fidelity Select Medical	19.82	126.94	NA
Putnam Health Sciences; A	15.16	77.00	381.08
Putnam Health Sciences; B	14.30	NA	NA
Franklin Strategic:Global Health	10.43	NA	NA
Vanguard Special: Health	9.54	106.02	519.35
J. Hancock Global Rx; A	8.85	NA	NA
Invesco Strategic: Health	0.94	92.41	548.66
GI Global Health Care; A	0.29	58.96	NA
GI Global Health Care; B	-0.19	NA	NA

Source: Lipper Analytical Services, Inc.

Performance of Equity Fund Groups (cont'd)

Top-Performing Funds: Financial Services

Fund Name	1994 Return (%)	Five-Year Return (%)	Ten-Year Return (%)
Fidelity Select Home Financial	2.64	188.15	NA
J. Hancock Regional Bank; A	0.55	NA	NA
Fidelity Select Regional Banks	0.23	117.41	NA
J. Hancock Regional Bank; B	-0.20	130.64	NA
Fidelity Select Insurance	-0.35	62.80	NA
PaineWebber Regional Financial Group; A	-0.75	120.30	NA
PaineWebber Regional Financial Group; D	-1.50	NA	NA
Sife Trust Fund	-1.52	65.88	244.72
PaineWebber Regional Financial Group; B	-1.53	NA	NA
Fidelity Select Financial	-3.65	97.93	258.74

Source: Lipper Analytical Services, Inc.

Total Institutional Assets in Mutual Funds ($ billions)

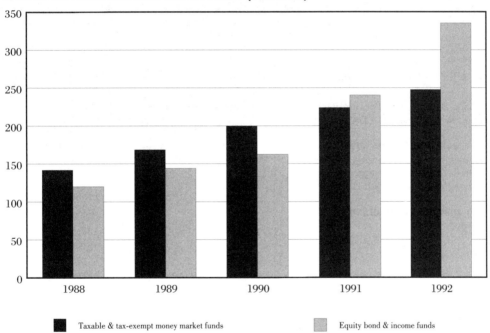

■ Taxable & tax-exempt money market funds   ▨ Equity bond & income funds

Source: Mutual Fund Fact Book, Investment Company Institute,
Washington, DC, 1994. Reprinted with permission.

Delphi offers current commodities quotes from exchanges around the world. GO BUS COM.

Choosing a Mutual Fund

Ten Questions to Ask about a Mutual Fund

1. Does this fund match my investment objectives?

Spend some time to determine your investment goals, then find a fund or funds that match them.

2. What is the load (fee) for purchasing shares?

Some funds charge an upfront fee (a load) for buying into a fund, while others don't. This can dramatically affect your real return.

3. Is there a redemption fee or a management fee?

Some funds charge you to redeem your shares. You should also check to see if the fund is liquid—making it easy to redeem your shares.

4. How often, and in what form, are reports generated?

If you're concerned about keeping very close tabs on your investment, ask to see sample reports.

5. Can I write checks against the fund?

This convenient feature makes it easy to remove money from a fund. Some funds charge a per-check fee, and others don't permit this at all.

6. Can I switch among a family of funds? Is there a charge?

Major fund providers give you the flexibility of switching from one fund to another by phone. This is convenient for those interested in short-range management of their money, and is less important to those seeking a long-term home for their cash.

7. Is the fund registered with the SEC?

While overseas funds may occasionally post tremendous profits, in the long run the oversight provided by the SEC provides an important safety net.

8. Is the fund leveraged?

Funds that borrow money to invest can post spectacular gains during bull markets. On the other hand, this strategy can virtually wipe out an investment if the market reacts poorly. Be aware of the risk to your principal as well as your interest.

9. What are the fund's philosophy and current holdings?

Closely examine a fund's approach to the market. You may be concerned about investments in certain industries or countries, or you may find the management of the fund too conservative or aggressive for your comfort.

10. What is the fund's long-term track record?

While there is little correlation between immediate past performance and future performance, there is some. Look for a fund that has consistently ranked in the top third or quarter of its category. This consistency makes it more likely that the firm will continue the policies that attracted you to it in the first place.

The Top Reference Sources

Morningstar Mutual Funds, $395/year
225 W. Wacker Dr.
Chicago, IL 60606
(800) 876-5005

Morningstar is considered to be a watchdog organization for information on mutual funds. Its 32-page, biweekly updates cover more than 1,200 mutual funds. The analysis provided includes a history of the fund's performance, information on fund managers, ranking against other funds, top holdings, and quarterly returns. Morningstar also adds its own rating of risk and return so that the reader can analyze potential investments.

Non-Stock Investments

IN ADDITION TO INVESTING IN STOCKS and bonds, commodities, futures, options, and all types of funds, people over time have invested their money in the pursuit of comfort and culture–in real estate, diamonds, paintings, and ceramics. While these investments can bring great personal and aesthetic pleasure, they are known to be notoriously volatile. Experts advise that you purchase only what you love. Here's how real estate and collectibles compare to more traditional investments:

Compound Rates of Return on Various Investments, 1994

Asset	20 Years		10 Years		5 Years		1 Year	
	Return (%)	Rank	Return (%)	Rank	Return (%)	Rank	Return (%)	Rank
Stocks	13.1	1	15.5	1	10.4	2	2.6	6
Foreign exchange	11.9	2	13.0	3	10.6	1	3.3	5
Bonds	10.2	3	14.1	2	9.9	3	0.7	10
Stamps	9.1	4	-0.9	10	1.1	11	1.9	8
3-month Treasury bills	8.3	5	6.7	4	5.6	4	4.3	4
Diamonds	7.9	6	5.9	5	1.4	9	0.0	11
Housing	6.3	7	4.1	6	2.9	6	1.8	9
Consumer Price Index	5.7	8	3.6	7	3.5	5	2.1	7
Farmland	4.6	9	-0.7	9	2.4	7	6.4	2
Gold	4.5	10	-0.2	8	1.3	10	4.7	3
Oil	2.9	11	-5.2	12	-1.9	12	-9.8	12
Silver	1.0	12	-4.9	11	1.9	8	31.1	1
Sotheby's common	NA		NA		-3.3	13	-11.4	13

Source: STI Management

The Top Reference Sources

Lipper Analytical Services
74 Trinity Pl.
New York, NY 10006
(212) 393-1300

Lipper Analytical Services is a publisher of statistical data covering the investment company industry in the U.S. and overseas. Lipper currently tracks the performance of more than 8,600 investment companies, including those invested in by variable annuity and variable life contracts with assets in excess of $1.8 trillion.

The company also publishes specialized reports intended for investment managers. These include reports on fund performance, portfolio analysis, and fee and expense breakdown. Analysis of the brokerage firm industry is another specialized service.

Retirement

FEDERAL INCOME TAX LAWS permit the establishment of a number of types of retirement plans, each of which may be funded with mutual fund shares.

Individual Retirement Accounts

All wage-earners under the age of 70 1/2 may set up an Individual Retirement Account (IRA). The individual may contribute as much as 100 percent of his or her compensation each year, up to $2,000. Earnings are tax-deferred until withdrawal. The amount contributed each year may be wholly or partially tax-deductible. Under the Tax Reform Act of 1986, all taxpayers not covered by employer-sponsored retirement plans can continue to take the full deduction for IRA contributions. Those who are covered, or who are married to someone who is covered, must have an adjusted gross income of no more than $25,000 (single) or $40,000 (married, filing jointly) to take the full deduction. The deduction is phased out for incomes between $25,000 and $35,000 (single) and $40,000 and $50,000 (married, filing jointly). An individual who qualifies for an IRA and has a spouse who either has no earnings or elects to be treated as having no earnings, may contribute up to 100 percent of his or her income or $2,250, whichever is less.

Simplified Employee Pensions (SEPs)

SEPs are employer-sponsored plans that may be viewed as an aggregation of separate IRAs. In an SEP, the employer contributes up to $30,000 or 15 percent of compensation, whichever is less, to an Individual Retirement Account maintained for the employee. SEPs established for employers with 25 or fewer employees may contain a "cash or deferred" arrangement allowing employees to make additional elective salary deferrals to the SEP. The cash-or-deferred arrangement for smaller employers is called a SARSEP, for "salary reduction SEP."

Corporate and Self-Employed Retirement Plans

Tax-qualified pension and profit-sharing plans may be established by corporations or self-employed individuals. Changes in the tax laws have made retirement plans for employees of corporations and those for self-employed individuals essentially comparable. Contributions to a plan are tax-deductible

and earnings accumulate on a tax-sheltered basis.

The maximum annual amount which may be contributed to a defined contribution plan on behalf of an individual is limited to the lesser of 13 percent of the individual's compensation or $30,000.

Section 403(b)of the Internal Revenue Code permits employees of certain charitable organizations and public school systems to establish tax-sheltered retirement programs. These plans may be invested in either annuity contracts or mutual fund shares.

Section 401(k) Plans

One particularly popular type of tax-qualified retirement plan which may be offered by either corporate or non-corporate entities is the 401(k) plan. A 401(k) plan is usually a profit-sharing plan that includes a "cash or deferred" arrangement. The cash-or-deferred arrangement permits employees to have a portion of their compensation contributed to a tax-sheltered plan on their behalf, or paid to them directly as additional taxable compensation. Thus, an employee may elect to reduce his or her taxable compensation with contributions to a 401(k) plan where those amounts will accumulate tax free. Employers often "match" these amounts with employer contributions. The Tax Reform Act of 1986 established new, tighter anti-discrimination requirements for 401(k) plans and curtailed the amount of elective deferrals which may be made by all employees. Nevertheless, 401(k) plans remain excellent and popular retirement savings vehicles.

Section 403(b) Plans

Section 403(b) of the Internal Revenue Code permits employees of certain charitable organizations and public school systems to establish tax-sheltered retirement programs. These plans may be invested in either annuity contracts or mutual fund shares.

Source: Mutual Fund Fact Book, Investment Company Institute, Washington, DC, 1993. Reprinted with permission.

Recommended Resource

Mutual Fund Fact Book
Investment Company Institute, $25
P.O. Box 66140
Washington, DC 20035
(202) 326-5872

Retirement (cont'd)

Growth in Mutual Fund IRA Plans ($ billions)

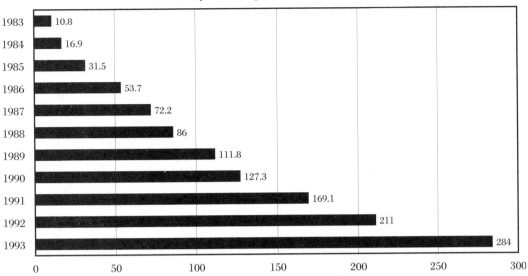

Year	Value
1983	10.8
1984	16.9
1985	31.5
1986	53.7
1987	72.2
1988	86
1989	111.8
1990	127.3
1991	169.1
1992	211
1993	284

Growth in Mutual Fund Self-Employed Retirement Plans ($ billions)

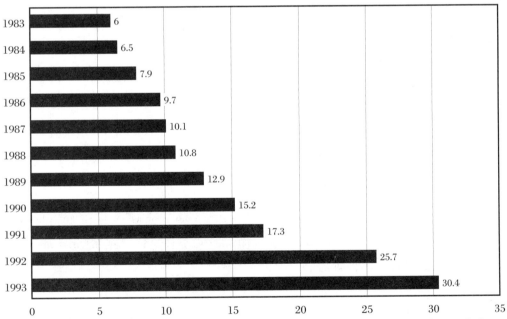

Year	Value
1983	6
1984	6.5
1985	7.9
1986	9.7
1987	10.1
1988	10.8
1989	12.9
1990	15.2
1991	17.3
1992	25.7
1993	30.4

Source: Mutual Fund Fact Book, Investment Company Institute,
Washington, DC, 1994. Reprinted with permission.

Actuaries

ACTUARIES USE MATHEMATICAL probability to
project the financial effects that various events–
birth, marriage, sickness, accident, fire, liability,
retirement, death–have on insurance, benefit plans,
and other financial security systems.

The American Academy of Actuaries is the best
source of information on the actuarial profession.
The Academy's *Fact Book* provides the most general
information on the field, including assessments of
the industry's past and future, and information about
academy programs and publications for people both
inside and outside the field. The Academy's bimonthly magazine, *Contingencies*, its monthly newsletter, *The Actuarial Update*, and the *Enrolled Actuaries Report* (published five to six times yearly)
explore current actuarial issues in depth. Another
publication, *The Issues Digest*, summarizes recent
Washington legislative activities as they relate to the
actuarial profession.

The *Directory of Actuarial Memberships*, published jointly by the two largest actuarial societies,
the Academy and the Society of Actuaries (see
below) lists all actuaries in North America, their professional affiliations, and their qualifications.

Recommended Resources

The American Academy of Actuaries
1100 17th St., NW, Seventh Floor
Washington, DC 20036
(202) 223-8196
Represents actuaries in all practice specialties.

Society of Actuaries
475 N. Martingale Rd., Suite 800
Schaumburg, IL 60173
(708) 706-3500
Represents actuaries working in the fields of life
and health insurance, employee benefits, and pensions.

Casualty Actuarial Society
1100 N. Glebe Rd., Suite 600
Arlington, VA 22201
(703) 276-3100
Represents actuaries specializing in property
and liability insurance, workers' compensation, and
liability coverage fields.

Conference of Consulting Actuaries
1110 W. Lake Cook Rd., Suite 235
Buffalo Grove, IL 60089
(708) 419-9090
Represents consulting actuaries in all fields of
the practice.

American Society of Pension Actuaries
4350 N. Fairfax Dr., Suite 820
Arlington, VA 22203
(703) 516-9300
Provides membership services to pension plan
consultants and administrators.

Financing a Business

INSTITUTIONS THAT OFFER VENTURE capital vary in
size, scope of interest, and qualification requirements. Although banking institutions do offer venture capital, much of this money is available
through non-bank-related venture capital firms.
Some offer start-up loans, while others lend money
to established businesses. Some of these organizations have a minimum as low as $5,000, while oth-
ers have a much larger minimum requirement. The
following is a list of venture capital firms around the
country:

Venture Capital Firms

Company	Location	Phone
ABS Ventures Limited Partnership	Baltimore, MD	(410) 783-3263
Advanced Technology Ventures	Boston, MA	(617) 423-4050
Allsop Venture Partners	Cedar Rapids, IA	(319) 363-8971
Applied Technology	Lexington, MA	(617) 862-8622
Arete Ventures	Rockville, MD	(301) 881-2555
Asset Management	Palo Alto, CA	(415) 494-7400
Austin Ventures	Austin, TX	(512) 479-0055
BT Capital	New York, NY	(212) 454-1903
Bradford Ventures	New York, NY	(212) 221-4620
Capital Health Venture Partners	Chicago, IL	(312) 427-1227

Financing a Business (cont'd)

Company	Location	Phone
Capital Southwest	Dallas, TX	(214) 233-8242
The Centennial Funds	Denver, CO	(303) 298-9066
Charter Venture Capital	Palo Alto, CA	(415) 325-6953
Cherry Tree Ventures	Bloomington, MN	(612) 893-9012
Cureton & Co.	Houston, TX	(713) 658-9806
DSV Partners	Princeton, NJ	(609) 924-6420
Edelson Technology Partners	Woodcliff Lake, NJ	(201) 930-9898
First Analysis	Chicago, IL	(312) 258-1400
Frontenac	Chicago, IL	(312) 368-0044
Grace/Horn Ventures	Cupertino, CA	(408) 725-0774
Hickory Venture Capital	Huntsville, AL	(205) 539-1931
Horizon Partners	Milwaukee, WI	(414) 271-2200
Houston Partners	Houston, TX	(713) 222-8600
IEG Venture Management	Chicago, IL	(312) 993-7500
Johnston Associates	Princeton, NJ	(609) 924-3131
Key Equity Capital	Cleveland, OH	(216) 689-5776
Lubar & Co.	Milwaukee, WI	(414) 291-9000
M&I Ventures	Milwaukee, WI	(414) 765-7910
Marquette Venture Partners	Deerfield, IL	(708) 940-1700
Medical Innovation Partners	Minnetonka, MN	(612) 931-0154
Meridian Venture Partners	Radnor, PA	(610) 254-2999
Mesirow Private Equity Investments	Chicago, IL	(312) 595-6099
Northwood Ventures	Syosset, NY	(516) 364-5544
O'Donnell & Masur	Dallas, TX	(214) 692-8177
P.R. Venture Partners	Boston, MA	(617) 357-9600
Palmer Partners	Woburn, MA	(617) 933-5445
Paragon Venture Partners	Menlo Park, CA	(415) 854-8000
Philadelphia Ventures	Philadelphia, PA	(215) 732-4445
Phoenix Partners	Seattle, WA	(206) 624-8968
Point Venture Partners	Pittsburgh, PA	(412) 261-1966
Primus Venture Partners	Cleveland, OH	(216) 621-2185
S.R. One	Wayne, PA	(610) 293-3400
Saugatuck Capital	Stamford, CT	(203) 348-6669
Senmed Medical Ventures	Cincinnati, OH	(513) 563-3240
Sierra Ventures	Menlo Park, CA	(415) 854-1000
South Atlantic Venture Fund	Tampa, FL	(813) 253-2500
Technology Partners	Belvedere, CA	(415) 435-1935
Technology Venture Investors	Menlo Park, CA	(415) 854-7472
Utah Ventures	Salt Lake City, UT	(801) 583-5922
Venture Capital Fund of America	New York, NY	(212) 838-5577
Venture Capital Fund of New England	Boston, MA	(617) 439-4646
VIMAC	Boston, MA	(617) 227-1300
Wind Point Partners	Chicago, IL	(312) 649-4000
Wolfensohn	New York, NY	(212) 909-8100

Financing a Business (cont'd)

Looking for Investors Online

Finding interested and appropriate investors for your company can be the greatest of all start-up challenges. Now a number of computer-based services are making the process of meeting and matching much easier by sharing financial and investment information online. Subscribers to these services, both the company and the investor, pay a fee for listing their investment needs and criteria.

Sources for Investors Online

Network	Area Served	Phone
Kentucky Investment Capital	National	(502) 564-4252
Mid-Atlantic Investment Network	Mostly Mid-Atlantic	(301) 405-2149
Northwest Capital	Oregon	(503) 282-6273
Pacific Venture Capital Network	California	(714) 509-2990
Private Investor	South Carolina	(803) 648-6851
Texas Capital Network	National	(512) 794-9398
Technology Capital Network	Mostly Northeast	(617) 253-7163

Investment Banks/Brokerage Houses

Top Ten Underwriters of U.S. Debt and Equity, 1994

Managers	Proceeds ($ mil.)	Market Share	No. of Issues
Merrill Lynch	116,953.0	16.4	690
Lehman Brothers	79,021.9	11.1	577
CS First Boston	73,001.0	10.2	517
Goldman, Sachs	65,216.7	9.2	399
Morgan Stanley	58,860.9	8.3	435
PaineWebber	58,199.5	8.2	309
Salomon Brothers	57,238.0	8.0	482
Bear, Stearns	34,885.0	4.9	202
J. P. Morgan	26,524.5	3.7	181
Donaldson, Lufkin & Jenrette	23,534.2	3.3	224

Top Ten Underwriters of U.S. Debt and Equity (U.S. Issuers), 1994

Managers	Proceeds ($ mil.)	Market Share	No. of Issues
Merrill Lynch	106,499.0	16.0	644
Lehman Brothers	75,720.4	11.4	555
CS First Boston	69,266.0	10.4	496
Goldman, Sachs	58,713.1	8.8	362
PaineWebber	57,859.1	8.7	306
Salomon Brothers	54,630.5	8.2	464
Morgan Stanley	53,882.0	8.1	407
Bear, Stearns	32,903.4	4.9	188
J. P. Morgan	23,887.9	3.6	163
Donaldson, Lufkin & Jenrette	23,114.4	3.5	221

Source: Securities Data Company

Top Ten Underwriters of International Debt and Equity, 1994

Managers	Proceeds ($ mil.)	Market Share	No. of Issues
Nomura Securities	29,593.5	7.0	213
CS First Boston/Crédit Suisse	26,109.0	6.1	155
Merrill Lynch	23,459.4	5.5	200
Goldman, Sachs	22,199.1	5.2	119
Swiss Bank	18,549.7	4.4	135
Daiwa Securities	17,034.6	4.0	120
Morgan Stanley	16,713.3	3.9	136
UBS	16,272.5	3.8	87
J. P. Morgan	14,901.6	3.5	95
Banque Paribas	13,477.1	3.2	103

Top Ten Underwriters of International Debt and Equity (U.S. Issuers), 1994

Managers	Proceeds ($ mil.)	Market Share	No. of Issues
Morgan Stanley	5,351.6	10.7	53
Merrill Lynch	5,140.3	10.2	62
Goldman, Sachs	5,115.9	10.2	36
CS First Boston/Crédit Suisse	4,196.1	8.4	31
J. P. Morgan	3,107.3	6.2	23
Lehman Brothers	2,586.6	5.2	31
Deutsche Bank	2,283.0	4.6	13
Swiss Bank	2,131.1	4.2	11
PaineWebber	1,704.6	3.4	18
Salomon Brothers	1,581.3	3.2	13

Source: Securities Data Company

The Top Reference Sources

Commodity Prices
Gale Research, $75
(800) 877-4253

Encompassing 14,000 listings for 10,000 products and 200 sources, this book gives you specific information to lead you to the periodicals, yearbooks, and other sources that list commodity prices. The entries are arranged by commodity, and there is an extensive index.

Wells Fargo on Business Loans

Five Simple Steps to a Successful Business Loan

1. Choose a Lender
It's best to set up a banking relationship when you don't really need the money. When talking with prospective bankers, explain your business and its cash needs, then find out if the bank provides an easy-to-understand loan documentation process, responds quickly to loan requests, and has small-business-loan specialists.

2. Be Prepared
An established banking relationship can help speed up the loan approval process, but when it comes time to actually borrow, the byword is "Be prepared." You should be able to clearly outline your company's history, products, and services; explain what the money will be used for; and show how it will be repaid.

3. Submit Complete Documentation
Incomplete documentation is the most frequent cause of approval delays. At most banks, the following will be needed to support your loan request:

- CPA-prepared business financial statements or business tax returns for the last three years;

- Current interim business financial statements, if over six months has elapsed since your fiscal year end;

- Owner's personal financial statement and personal tax returns for the last three years;

- Business principals' tax returns and personal financial statements for the past two years;

- Secondary source of repayment. (Sole proprietors and corporate principals are usually asked to secure loans with personal assets. If you're in a partnership, a personal guarantee must often be signed by all principals.)

4. Provide "Intangibles"
Numbers on loan documents don't always tell the whole story. There are intangible assets some banks will consider, such as how much experience you have, whom you're competing against, whether you're in a growing market, and whether your product or service is unique. Making sure your banker is aware of such information can increase the probability of approval.

5. Enlist Your Banker's Help
It takes bankers just as much time to review an incomplete loan application as it does a complete one, so it's to the bank's advantage to have a professionally trained representative to help guide you through the process and ensure that all necessary documentation is correctly completed. Never hesitate to ask questions. Your bank representative's expertise can help you avoid common pitfalls and ensure that you get an answer as quickly as possible.

Source: Wells Fargo, 1991

Contact Option
Wells Fargo
(800) 359-3557

The Top Reference Sources

Traders' Catalog & Resource Guide
Crawford Associates, $39.50/year
(619) 736-0366

This monthly 160-page publication is a combination of information about product and service vendors and a series of commentaries, reviews, and opinions all directed toward individual and institutional investors and traders. The magazine combines yellow- and white-pages-style listings of tools for all kinds of market analysis, software for trading and system development, newsletters, rating services, hotlines, market timers, and brokerage services.

Alternative Financing

IN ADDITION TO BANKS, SBA loans, and traditional venture capital firms, there is a range of other, less traditional financing alternatives available to entrepreneurs.

Here is a checklist of five alternatives, as assembled by Jay Levinson and Bruce Blechman, authors of *Guerrilla Financing*.

Receivable Financing

Extending credit to your customers is similar to lending them money. You are essentially loaning them cash while they have your product or service.

Short-term revolving financing is provided by factors or receivable lenders. These firms recognize your receivables as a valuable asset, and are usually willing to lend against it, regardless of your company's financial position.

Factors will purchase your receivables (at a discount) and collect the money from your customers directly. For example, if a company sells $1 million in clothing to Macy's, a factor might pay $900,000 for the receivable. It is then up to the factor to collect the entire invoice directly from Macy's.

A receivables lender will loan money against the invoice and hold it as collateral. Once the invoice is paid, your company repays the lender.

This is a common form of lending. Check your local yellow pages under "Factors," or the *Corporate Finance Sourcebook* for firms that offer this service.

Customer Financing

No one knows your business better than your customers. If your product or service is valuable and difficult to replace, many of your customers may be interested in financing your growth.

This is obviously a risky, time-consuming method of finding financing, but if the proper match is made, both parties can benefit.

Equipment Financing

When purchasing expensive capital equipment, a company often has the opportunity to finance the purchase, or enter into a lease. In both cases, money is freed up, and the company gains the ability to use the machinery without sacrificing its cash position.

Many banks and manufacturers are willing to finance the purchase of capital equipment. They will lend your company money against the value of the equipment purchased, holding the equipment as collateral. The downside of this approach is that the loan appears on your balance sheet, affecting your company's leverage and your ability to borrow against the value of the company.

Leasing is an increasingly common method of financing. In this situation, the company never takes title to the equipment. Instead, the leasing company purchases the equipment and leases it to the com-

pany for a monthly fee. There are two significant advantages to this arrangement: the company doesn't need to dispose of the equipment at the end of the lease, and the lease is off balance sheet, meaning that since there is no loan, a company's debt load is not affected.

Real Estate Financing

Many companies don't realize that their real estate is not fully leveraged. Banks prefer to make loans against land because they are more comfortable placing a value on it. Check the real estate section of the Sunday paper to find mortgage brokers in your area.

Venture Capital Clubs

These clubs seek to eliminate the middleman by bringing small investors together with entrepreneurs in search of capital. These small organizations make it easy for a company to speak directly to a motivated lender. The downside is that these are people lending their own money, so there is often an emotional side to the process.

Alabama
Birmingham Venture Club
P.O. Box 10127
Birmingham, AL 35202
(205) 323-5461

California
Orange Coast Venture Group
c/o American Accounting
23011 Moulton Pkwy., F2
Laguna Hills, CA 92653
(714) 859-3646

Orange County Venture Forum
P.O. Box 2011
Laguna Hills, CA 92654
(714) 855-0652

Community Entrepreneurs Organization
P.O. Box 2781
San Rafael, CA 94912
(415) 435-4461

Connecticut
Connecticut Venture Capital Fund
200 Fisher Dr.
Avon, CT 06001
(203) 677-0183

Florida
Gold Coast Venture Capital Club
5820 N. Federal, Suite 4
Boca Raton, FL 33478
(407) 997-6594

Alternative Financing (cont'd)

Florida Venture Group
2838 Kansas St.
Oviedo, FL 32765
(407) 365-5374

Iowa
Venture Club of Iowa City
First Capital Development
325 E. Washington
Iowa City, IA 52240
(319) 354-3939

Louisiana
Louisiana Seed Capital
339 Florida St., Suite 525
Baton Rouge, LA 70801
(504) 383-1508

Greater New Orleans Venture Capital Club
301 Camp St.
New Orleans, LA 70130
(800) 949-7890 (voice mail for information on meetings)

Michigan
Southeastern Venture Capital
The Meyering Corporation
20630 Harper Ave., Suite 103
Harper Woods, MI 48225
(313) 886-23331

New Enterprise Forum
211 E. Hebron, Suite 1
Ann Arbor, MI 48104
(313) 665-4433

Montana
Montana Private Capital Network
7783 Valley View Rd.
Poulson, MT 59860
(406) 883-5470

Nebraska
Grand Island Industrial Foundation
309 W. Second St.
P.O. Box 1486
Grand Island, NE 68802
(308) 382-9210

New Jersey
Venture Association of New Jersey
177 Madison Ave., CN 1982
Morristown, NJ 07960
(201) 267-4200, ext. 193

New York
Long Island Venture Group
C.W. Post Campus
Long Island University
College of Management, Dean's Office
Worth Hall, Room 309
North Blvd.
Brookville, NY 11548
(516) 299-3017

New York Venture Group
605 Madison Ave., Suite 300
New York, NY 10022
(212) 832-7300

Westchester Venture Capital Network
c/o Chamber of Commerce
222 Mamaroneck Ave.
White Plains, NY 10605
(914) 948-2110

Ohio
Greater Columbus Chamber of Commerce
Columbus Investment Interest Group
37 N. High St.
Columbus, OH 43215
(614) 255-6087

Ohio Venture Association
1127 Euclid Ave., Suite 343
Cleveland, OH 44125
(216) 566-8884

Pennsylvania
Delaware Valley Venture Group
1234 Market St., Suite 1800
Philadelphia, PA 19107
(215) 972-3960

Tennessee
Mid-South Venture Group
5180 Park Ave., Suite 310
Memphis, TN 38119
(901) 761-3084

Texas
Houston Venture Capital Association
1221 McKinney, Suite 2400
Houston, TX 77010
(713) 750-1500

Utah
Mountainwest Venture Group
c/o Bonneville Research
48 Market St., #200
Salt Lake City, UT 84101
(801) 364-5300

Washington
Northwest Venture Group
P.O. Box 21693
Seattle, WA 98111
(206) 746-1973

Alternative Financing (cont'd)

Contact Option

For a complete list of venture capital clubs, contact (by mail if possible):
Lisa Jones
Association of Venture Clubs
265 E. 100th S., #300
P.O. Box 3358
Salt Lake City, UT 84110
(801) 364-1100

Recommended Resource

Guerrilla Financing
by Bruce Blechman and Jay Conrad Levinson
Houghton Mifflin, $19.95
(800) 225-3362

Insurance Companies

Aetna Life & Casualty
151 Farmington Ave.
Hartford, CT 06156
(203) 273-0123

Allstate Life
2775 Sanders Rd.
Northbrook, IL 60062
(708) 402-5000

Cigna
900 Cottage Grove Rd.
Hartford, CT 06152
(203) 726-6000

Equitable Life Assurance
787 Seventh Ave.
New York, NY 10019
(212) 554-1234

IDS Life
American Express Financial Advisers
733 Marquette Ave.
Minneapolis, MN 55402
(612) 671-3131

Jackson National Life
5901 Executive Dr.
Lansing, MI 48911
(517) 394-3400

John Hancock Mutual Life
101 Huntington Ave.
Boston, MA 02199
(617) 572-6000

Lincoln National Life
1300 S. Clinton St.
Fort Wayne, IN 46802
(219) 455-2000

Massachusetts Mutual Life
1295 State St.
Springfield, MA 01111
(413) 788-8411

Metropolitan Life Insurance
1 Madison Ave.
New York, NY 10010
(212) 578-2211

Mutual of New York
1740 Broadway
New York, NY 10019
(212) 708-2000

Nationwide Life
1 Nationwide Plaza
Columbus, OH 43215
(614) 249-7111

The New England
501 Boylston St.
Boston, MA 02116
(617) 578-2000

New York Life Insurance
51 Madison Ave.
New York, NY 10010
(212) 576-7000

Northwestern Mutual Life
720 E. Wisconsin Ave.
Milwaukee, WI 53202
(414) 271-1444

Pacific Mutual Life
700 Newport Center Dr.
Newport Beach, CA 92660
(714) 640-3011

Principal Mutual Life
711 High St.
Des Moines, IA 50392
(515) 247-5111

Prudential of America
751 Broad St.
Newark, NJ 07107
(201) 802-6000

Insurance Companies (cont'd)

State Farm Life
1 State Farm Plaza
Bloomington, IL 61710
(309) 766-2311

Teachers Insurance & Annuity
730 Third Ave.
New York, NY 10017
(212) 675-7000

Travelers
1 Tower Square
Hartford, CT 06183
(203) 277-0111

Variable Annuity Life
2919 Allen Pkwy.
Houston, TX 77019
(713) 526-5251

Real Estate Advisers

Real Estate Investment Advisers Ranked by Assets

Rank	Company	Tax-Exempt Assets* ($ millions)	Total Assets ($ millions)*
1	Equitable Real Estate	11,410	37,820
2	Prudential Real Estate	6,722	6,722
3	Heitman Advisory	6,618	6,774
4	O'Connor Group	5,800	5,900
5	Copley Real Estate	5,421	8,013
6	J. P. Morgan	5,401	5,443
7	Yarmouth Group	5,130	6,954
8	RREEF Funds	4,885	5,298
9	LaSalle Advisors	4,532	6,800
10	GE Investment	4,483	4,483
11	JMB Institutional Realty	4,172	4,236
12	Aetna Realty Investors	3,644	3,644
13	Alex Brown Kleinwort Benson	3,553	3,553
14	Aldrich, Eastman & Waltch	3,450	4,430
15	Jones Lang Wootton	3,373	4,746
16	TCW Realty Advisors	3,012	3,012
17	Corporate Property	2,420	4,400
18	Hancock Timber Resource	2,193	2,248
19	L&B Real Estate Counsel	2,173	2,236
20	Phoenix Realty Advisors	2,060	2,626
21	MacFarlane Partners	2,046	2,086
22	Sentinel Real Estate	1,844	2,279
23	McMorgan	1,693	1,693
24	MIG Realty Advisors	1,680	3,340
25	Trammell Crow Realty	1,571	1,571

As of June 30, 1994

Accounting Firms

Accounting Firms Ranked by Revenue, 1993

Rank	Name	Location	Revenue ($ mil.)	No. of Professionals
1	Arthur Andersen & Co.	New York, NY	3,317.2	21,715
2	Ernst & Young	New York, NY	2,543.0	13,030
3	Deloitte & Touche	Wilton, CT	2,230.0	11,350
4	KPMG Peat Marwick	New York, NY	1,907.0	12,321
5	Coopers & Lybrand	New York, NY	1,783.0	11,185
6	Price Waterhouse	New York, NY	1,570.0	9,369
7	H&R Block Tax Services	Kansas City, MO	970.0	125,708
8	Grant Thornton	Chicago, IL	229.0	1,548
9	McGladrey & Pullen	Davenport, IA	208.9	1,512
10	BDO Seidman	New York, NY	201.0	1,069
11	Kenneth Leventhal & Co.	Los Angeles, CA	195.0	763
12	Baird Kurtz & Dobson	Springfield, MO	67.8	442
13	Crowe, Chizek & Co.	South Bend, IN	65.3	579
14	Plante & Moran	Southfield, MI	58.3	410
15	Moss Adams	Seattle, WA	54.0	406
16	Clifton Gunderson & Co.	Peoria, IL	51.6	370
17	American Express Tax & Business Services	Minneapolis, MN	40.4	341
18	Altschuler, Melvoin & Glasser	Chicago, IL	40.2	250
19	Comprehensive Business Services	Carlsbad, CA	40.0	244
20	Jackson Hewitt	Virginia Beach, VA	39.7	1,200
21	Geo. S. Olive & Co.	Indianapolis, IN	39.0	265
22	Richard A. Eisner & Co.	New York, NY	38.2	273
23	Friedman, Eisenstein, Raemer & Schwartz	Chicago, IL	38.0	192
24	Goldstein Golub Kessler & Co.	New York, NY	36.2	235
25	General Business Svc. & E. K. Williams & Co.	Waco, TX	35.0	650
26	Larson, Allen, Weishair & Co.	Minneapolis, MN	29.8	203
27	Triple Check	Burbank, CA	25.6	900
28	David Bardon & Co.	New York, NY	24.0	165
29	Campos & Stratis	Teaneck, NJ	23.7	189
30	Checkers Simon & Rosner	Chicago, IL	23.3	178
31	Parente, Randolph, Orlando, Carey & Associates	Wilkes-Barre, PA	23.0	190
32	Reznick Fedder & Silverman	Bethesda, MD	22.8	222
33	Wipfli Ullrich Bertelson	Wausau, WI	22.7	190
34	M. R. Weiser & Co.	New York, NY	22.5	164
35	J. H. Cohn & Co.	Roseland, NJ	22.0	150
36	Mitchell, Titus & Co.	New York, NY	22.0	344
37	Thomas Harvey & Co.	Chicago, IL	21.5	166
38	Anchin, Block & Anchin	New York, NY	20.0	97
39	Cherry Bekaert & Holland	Richmond, VA	19.8	190
40	Hausser & Taylor	Cleveland, OH	17.9	99
41	Zelenkofske Axelrod & Co.	Jenkintown, PA	17.9	138
42	Urbach, Kahn & Werlin	Albany, NY	16.8	150
43	Virchow Krause & Co.	Madison, WI	16.7	181
44	Schenck & Associates	Appleton, WI	16.2	155
45	Padgett Business Services	Athens, GA	15.7	388
46	Margolin Winer Evens	Garden City, NY	15.0	110
47	Rehmann Robson & Co.	Saginaw, MI	14.8	105
48	Mahoney Cohen & Co.	New York, NY	14.6	85
49	Eide Helmeke & Co.	Fargo, ND	14.4	147
50	Kennedy & Co.	Salina, KS	14.4	126

Accounting Firms (cont'd)

Rank	Name	Location	Revenue ($ mil.)	No. of Professionals
51	Edward Isaacs & Co.	New York, NY	14.1	94
52	Charles Bailly & Co.	Fargo, ND	14.0	126
53	Blackman Kallick Bartlestein	Chicago, IL	14.0	118
54	Dixon Odom & Co.	High Point, NC	13.9	109
55	Follmer, Rudzewicz & Co.	Southfield, MI	13.9	132
56	Blum Shapiro & Co.	West Hartford, CT	13.5	102
57	Kemper CPA Group	Robinson, IL	13.4	106
58	Mayer Hoffman McCann	Kansas City, MO	13.2	115
59	Tofias, Fleishman, Shapiro & Co.	Cambridge, MA	13.2	104
60	Rubin, Brown, Gornstein & Co.	St. Louis, MO	13.1	126
61	LeMaster & Daniels	Spokane, WA	12.8	125
62	Rothstein, Kass & Co.	Roseland, NJ	12.7	95
63	Blue & Co.	Indianapolis, IN	12.6	126
64	Katz, Sapper & Miller	Indianapolis, IN	12.5	71
65	Joseph Decosimo & Co.	Chattanooga, TN	12.1	95
66	Hill Barth & King	Youngstown, OH	11.8	75
67	Lopez, Edwards, Frank & Co.	Valley Stream, NY	11.6	85
68	C.W. Amos & Co.	Baltimore, MD	11.4	76
69	Clark, Schaefer, Hackett & Co.	Middletown, OH	11.4	82
70	Amper Politziner & Mattia	Edison, NJ	11.2	82
71	Elliott Davis & Co.	Greenville, SC	10.8	84
72	Habif, Arogeti & Wynne	Atlanta, GA	10.8	88
73	Doeren Mayhew & Co	Troy, MI	10.8	50
74	Mauldin & Jenkins	Albany, GA	10.6	89
75	Goodman & Co.	Norfolk, VA	10.3	60
76	Berry, Dunn, McNeil & Parker	Portland, ME	10.0	72
77	Lurie Besikof Lapidus & Co.	Minneapolis, MN	10.0	60
78	Wolpoff & Co.	Baltimore, MD	10.0	88
79	Mortenson & Associates	Cranford, NJ	10.0	70
80	Philip Rootberg & Co.	Chicago, IL	9.9	62
81	Meaden & Moore	Cleveland, OH	9.9	74
82	Kaufman Rossin & Co.	Miami, FL	9.8	51
83	Keller Brunner & Co.	Frederick, MD	9.6	68
84	Kafoury, Armstrong & Co.	Reno, NV	9.5	70
85	Yergen & Meyer	Portland, OR	9.5	55
86	Buchbinder Tunick	New York, NY	9.5	60
87	Kerber Eck & Braeckel	Springfield, IL	9.2	104
88	S. R. Snodgrass	Wexford, PA	9.2	75
89	Suby, von Haden & Associates	Madison, WI	9.1	35
90	Morrison, Brown, Argiz & Co.	Miami, FL	9.1	63
91	Brady Martz & Associates	Grand Forks, ND	9.0	63
92	Hemming Morse	San Mateo, CA	8.9	55
93	Walpert, Smullian & Blumenthal	Baltimore, MD	8.7	65
94	Hood & Strong	San Francisco, CA	8.5	65
95	Aronson Fetridge Weigle & Stern	Rockville, MD	8.5	57
96	Rachlin Cohen & Holtz	Coral Gables, FL	8.5	38
97	Windes & McClaughry	Long Beach, CA	8.4	41
98	Schumaker, Romenesko & Associates	Appleton, WI	8.0	60
99	Cohen & Co.	Cleveland, OH	8.0	56
100	Konigsberg, Wolf & Co.	New York, NY	8.0	32

Source: Accounting Today, Special Report, Dec., 12, 1994

Influential Accountants

The 100 Most Influential People in Accounting

Name	Position	Firm
J. Mason Andres	Chairman, private co. practice section	AICPA
James F. Antonio	Chairman	Governmental Accounting Standards Board
Jerrell A. Atkinson	Managing director	Atkinson & Co.
Andrew D. Bailey Jr.	President	American Accounting Association
Dennis R. Beresford	Chairman	Financial Accounting Standards Board
William T. Bishop	President	Institute of Internal Auditors
Thomas M. Bloch	President, chief executive	H&R Block
L. Gary Boomer	Partner	Varney Mills Rogers Burnett & Associates
Michele R. Bourgerie	Chairwoman	New York State Board for Public Accountancy
Charles A. Bowsher	Comptroller general	U. S. Government Accounting Office
Abe Briloff	Partner	A. J. and L. A. Briloff, CPAs
Milton Brown	First vice president	National Society of Public Accountants
Robert Bunting	President	Moss Adams
John C. Burton	Ernst & Young professor of accounting	Columbia University
Jean Marie Caragher	President	Association for Accounting Marketing
Philip B. Chenok	President	AICPA
Shirley J. Cheramy	Chair, Women and Family Issues Committee	AICPA
Ronald S. Cohen	Managing partner	Crowe, Chizek & Co.
Allison Conte	Executive director	American Society of Women Accountants
J. Michael Cook	Chairman and chief executive	Deloitte & Touche
Scott D. Cook	President	Intuit
Beryl Davis	Member and former chairwoman	Florida Board of Accountancy
Stephen W. DeFilippis	Owner	West Suburban Income Tax Service
James Don Edwards	Professor of accounting	J. M. Tull School of Accounting, Univ. of Georgia
Richard Eisner	Managing partner	Richard A. Eisner & Co.
Robert K. Elliott	Assistant to the chairman	KPMG Peat Marwick
Mark Ernst	Vice president, general manager	IDS Financial Services
Richard E. Flaherty	Executive director	Accounting Education Change Commission
Eugene Freedman	Chairman and chief executive	Coopers & Lybrand
Welling W. Fruehauf	President-elect	National Ass'n of State Boards of Accountancy
Carl George	Managing partner	Clifton Gunderson & Co.
James Glauser	Managing partner	Baird Kurtz & Dobson
Dan L. Goldwasser	Partner	Vedder Price Kaufman Kammholz & Day
Gerald L. Golub	Managing partner	Goldstein Golub Kessler & Co.
John W. Goodhew III	President	Peachtree Software
Robert L. Gray	Executive director	New York State Society of CPAs
John D. Harris	Managing partner	George S. Olive
Nancy Marie Heimer	President	American Women's Society of CPAs
John E. Hunnicutt	Group vice president of government affairs	AICPA
Robert L. Israeloff	Vice chairman	AICPA
Donald F. Istvan	President	D. F. Istvan Associates
Martin Ives	Vice chairman and director of research	Governmental Accounting Standards Board
Edmund L. Jenkins	Managing director, accounting principles	Arthur Andersen & Co.
Thomas P. Kelley	Vice president–professional	AICPA
Sidney Kess	Educator	–
Stuart Kessler	Partner	Goldstein Golub Kessler & Co.
Noel Kirch	President	National Ass'n of State Boards of Accountancy
James Kurtz	Executive director	California Society of CPAs
Joseph LaGambina	Executive V.P. and chief administrative officer	Financial Accounting Foundation
Charles Larson	Managing director	Larson Consulting

Influential Accountants (cont'd)

Name	Position	Firm
Philip A. Laskawy	Deputy chairman	Ernst & Young
James Leisenring	Vice chairman	Financial Accounting Standards Board
Norman W. Lipshie	Senior partner	Weber Lipshie & Co.
Jon Madonna	Chairman	KPMG Peat Marwick
LeRoy E. Martin	Managing partner	McGladrey & Pullen
Eli Mason	Senior partner	Mason & Co.
Edward L. Massie	President and chief executive	CCH
William Matthews	Managing partner	Plante & Moran
Patricia McConnell	Managing director	Bear, Stearns
Robert Mednick	Managing partner, prof. and regulatory matters	Arthur Andersen & Co.
James C. Metzler	Partner	Gaines Emhof Metzler & Kriner
Bert Mitchell	Chairman and chief executive	Mitchell, Titus & Co.
Robert Nason	Executive partner	Grant Thornton
Jay Nisberg	Management consultant	Jay Nisberg & Assoc.
Shaun O'Malley	Chairman and chief executive	Price Waterhouse
Thomas Ochsenschlager	Partner	Grant Thornton
Alan Prahl	Executive director	National Association of Tax Practitioners
William L. Raby	Tax advisor	–
Margaret Milner Richardson	Commissioner	Internal Revenue Service
Gary C. Rohrs	President	National Society of Public Accountants
Martin Rosenberg	Executive director	Illinois CPA Society
Stan Ross	Managing partner	Kenneth Leventhal & Co.
P. Norman Roy	President	Financial Executives Institute
Ronnie Rudd	Chairman	Texas State Board of Public Accountancy
Eric Schindler	Vice president, finance & administration	Columbia Paint & Coatings
Donald B. Scholl	Consultant	D. B. Scholl
Walter Paul Schuetze	Chief accountant	Securities and Exchange Commission
Abram Serotta	President	Serotta, Maddocks, Evans & Co.
Jerome P. Solomon	Director, past president	National Ass'n of State Boards of Accountancy
Stanley H. Stearman	Executive vice president	National Society of Public Accountants
Irwin Steinberg	Managing partner	Friedman, Eisenstein, Raemer & Schwartz
Howard Stone	Managing partner, chairman	Altschuler, Melvoin & Glasser
A. Marvin Strait	Partner	Baird Kurtz & Dobson
Norman N. Strauss	Chairman, accounting standards committee	AICPA
John B. Sullivan	Director of auditing services	Deloitte & Touche
Dominic Tarantino	Chairman	AICPA
W. J. Tauzin	U.S. congressman	–
Lloyd Turman	Executive director	Florida Institute of CPAs
Bernie Valek	President	Alliance of Practicing CPAs
Herb D. Vest	Chairman and chief executive	H. D. Vest
Charles B. Wang	Chairman and chief executive	Computer Associates International
Lawrence Weinbach	Managing partner, chief executive	Arthur Andersen & Co.
Melvyn I. Weiss	Senior partner	Milberg Weiss Bershad Hynes & Lerach
Don Weldon	Executive director	Texas Society of CPAs
Alan D. Westheimer	Adviser	Alan D. Westheimer CPA
Gary Wetstein	Chairman	BDO Seidman
Janice Wilson	President	California State Board of Accountancy
Stephen T. Winn	President and chief executive	Computer Language Research
Ronald T. Wyden	U.S. congressman	–
Richard Ziegler	Chairman	Illinois Committee on Accountancy

Source: Accounting Today, Mar. 14, 1994

Tax Freedom Day

IN 1993, THE AVERAGE AMERICAN worker worked 123 days–from January 1 to May 3–to satisfy all federal, state, and local tax obligations for the year. Tax Freedom Day is that day on which taxpayers stop working to earn the tax money they owe and start working for themselves–taking home their own paycheck for real. Over time, this day of freedom has fallen later and later in the year.

Recommended Resource

Public Accounting Report
Strafford Publications, $247/year (24 issues)
590 Dutch Valley Rd.
P.O. Drawer 13729
Atlanta, GA 30324
(404) 881-1141

Tax Freedom Day

Year	Day
1960	April 16
1965	April 14
1970	April 26
1975	April 27
1980	May 1
1985	April 30
1990	May 3
1991	May 2
1992	May 5
1993	May 3
1994	May 5

Source: The 1995 Information Please Almanac

The Top Reference Sources

Accounting Today
Faulkner & Gray, $69/year
(212) 967-7000
This semi-monthly publication offers the inside scoop on the accounting field. Lively articles, news, and in-depth surveys offer the reader insight into the rules affecting accounting, and, more important, the intricacies of running a successful accounting practice.

Choosing an Accountant

THE TERM "ACCOUNTANT" CAN MEAN many different things, depending on a company's size and needs. A huge company like IBM thinks of an accountant not just as one person but rather as a professional team of consultants. The team may consist of specialists who audit financial statements, prepare tax returns, and give tax advice, or who analyze computer and information systems.

A smaller company might need just one individual, probably a tax expert who periodically reviews the company's financial statements.

Finding an accountant whose specialties and interests match your needs is a critical step in setting up a long-term financial structure.

Here are 13 questions you can ask when interviewing a prospective accountant:

I. Have you helped a client in a similar situation?

It saves time to work with an accountant who has already dealt with similar situations. Probe to discover exactly how he has dealt with problems similar to yours.

2. Will our firm be serviced by a partner or by junior accountants?

Many firms train new associates at the client's expense. Be sure that you get what you pay for.

3. What is the nature, scope, and timing of your work, and what will it cost me?

Often, an accountant's work plan can be more extensive and more expensive than you might expect. Get the accountant to be specific about what he or she will do, and get a detailed written engagement letter and cost estimate.

4. Can you give me two or three quick ideas on how you might be able to save our company money?

A good accountant should have sharp business acumen and be willing to be creative. A question like this can show whether the accountant can call on his or her many skills to truly help you increase profits, improve productivity, trim costs, enhance returns, and lower taxes.

5. Can you tell me a little about your practice, and your successes and failures?

Open-ended questions can elicit a wealth of information. Let the accountant talk. You will also learn a lot about the accountant's priorities, risk-tolerance levels, and various personality characteristics, all of which can be helpful in gauging compatibility.

6. How are your fees calculated? Will you be charging me for every phone discussion?

To avoid friction later, it is essential to discuss the accountant's fee structure, including the hourly rate of the accountant and staff, overhead expense reimbursement (how much should you pay for a fax?), and whether certain time is not billed.

7. What can I do to help you with your work and keep your fees to a minimum?

A great deal of your accountant's time can be saved by preparing information beforehand. Find out if your accountant is willing to work with you to offload this work to your firm.

8. How will you be communicating the results of your work to me?

The results of an audit usually take the form of an audit report, and tax return preparation yields tax returns. But this work also can lead to many suggestions by the accountant on how to cut taxes, increase income, restructure investments, build business, and improve information flow. Some accountants are more comfortable with interactive discussions and others prefer written action reports.

9. Do you perceive any conflicts of interest?

Accountants work for dozens of firms, and you should probe to see if any of your direct competition is represented by the firm. If so, inquire as to how this conflict is handled.

10. Are you a certified public accountant, and what other licenses do you hold?

If the accountant is certified, you should inquire at the state CPA organization to discover if there have been any disciplinary actions entered. Some accountants also have credentials as financial planners, securities representatives, even lawyers.

II. How well have you integrated computers into your practice, and have they enabled you to do more for clients at less cost?

Integrating your computer files with those of your accountant's can save time and money, and increase accuracy.

12. Will you need to overhaul our current system?

Your internal bookkeeping and cost-accounting systems are expensive to alter. Find out up front whether you can integrate with the firm's systems.

13. Are you conservative or aggressive in interpreting tax laws and regulations, and accounting and auditing standards?

Save yourself the hassle and be certain that your accountant approaches your books in the same way you would.

Source: Frank Sisco

Mortgage Tables

TO COMPUTE A MORTGAGE PAYMENT, divide the amount borrowed by $100,000, then multiply that number by the number in the table.

Rate (%)	Length of Mortgage (years)					
	5	10	15	20	25	30
5.0	1,887.12	1,060.66	790.79	659.96	584.59	536.82
5.5	1,910.12	1,085.26	817.08	687.89	614.09	567.79
6.0	1,933.28	1,110.21	843.86	716.43	644.30	599.55
6.5	1,956.61	1,135.48	871.11	745.57	675.21	632.07
7.0	1,980.12	1,161.08	898.83	775.30	706.78	665.30
7.5	2,003.79	1,187.02	927.01	805.59	738.99	699.21
8.0	2,027.64	1,213.28	955.65	836.44	771.82	733.76
8.5	2,051.65	1,239.86	984.74	867.82	805.23	768.91
9.0	2,075.84	1,266.76	1,014.27	899.73	839.20	804.62
9.5	2,100.19	1,293.98	1,044.22	932.13	873.70	840.85
10.0	2,124.70	1,321.51	1,074.61	965.02	908.70	877.57
10.5	2,149.39	1,349.35	1,105.40	998.38	944.18	914.74
11.0	2,174.24	1,377.50	1,136.60	1,032.19	980.11	952.32
11.5	2,199.26	1,405.95	1,168.19	1,066.43	1,016.47	990.29
12.0	2,224.44	1,434.71	1,200.17	1,101.09	1,053.22	1,028.61
12.5	2,249.79	1,463.76	1,232.52	1,136.14	1,090.35	1,067.26
13.0	2,275.31	1,493.11	1,265.24	1,171.58	1,127.84	1,106.20
13.5	2,300.98	1,522.74	1,298.32	1,207.37	1,165.64	1,145.41
14.0	2,326.83	1,552.66	1,331.74	1,243.52	1,203.76	1,184.87
14.5	2,352.83	1,582.87	1,365.50	1,280.00	1,242.16	1,224.56
15.0	2,378.99	1,613.35	1,399.59	1,316.79	1,280.83	1,264.44
15.5	2,405.32	1,644.11	1,433.99	1,353.88	1,319.75	1,304.52
16.0	2,431.81	1,675.13	1,468.70	1,391.26	1,358.89	1,344.76
16.5	2,458.45	1,706.42	1,503.71	1,428.90	1,398.24	1,385.15
17.0	2,485.26	1,737.98	1,539.00	1,466.80	1,437.80	1,425.68
17.5	2,512.22	1,769.79	1,574.58	1,504.94	1,477.53	1,466.33
18.0	2,539.34	1,801.85	1,610.42	1,543.31	1,517.43	1,507.09
18.5	2,566.62	1,834.17	1,646.52	1,581.90	1,557.48	1,547.94
19.0	2,594.06	1,866.72	1,682.88	1,620.68	1,597.68	1,588.89
19.5	2,621.64	1,899.52	1,719.47	1,659.66	1,638.01	1,629.92
20.0	2,649.39	1,932.56	1,756.30	1,698.82	1,678.45	1,671.02
20.5	2,677.29	1,965.82	1,793.35	1,738.15	1,719.01	1,712.18
21.0	2,705.34	1,999.32	1,830.61	1,777.64	1,759.66	1,753.40
21.5	2,733.54	2,033.03	1,868.08	1,817.28	1,800.41	1,794.67
22.0	2,761.89	2,066.97	1,905.76	1,857.06	1,841.24	1,835.98

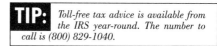

TIP: *Toll-free tax advice is available from the IRS year-round. The number to call is (800) 829-1040.*

Business Incubators

BUSINESS INCUBATORS ARE FACILITIES that provide start-up and fledgling firms with business and management assistance, affordable space, and shared support services. They are an alternative to the office at home or the long-term lease.

A business incubator's services may include the following:

- Flexible space and flexible leases, often at below-market rates;

- Shared basic business services such as telephone answering, bookkeeping, word-processing and other secretarial help, receptionist services, and access to fax and copy machines, computers, and business libraries;

- Business and technical assistance through a combination of in-house expertise and a network of community support;

- Financing assistance, such as help in obtaining a bank loan or assistance in gaining access to federal and state R&D funds;

- A network of relationships with other business owners who provide support for each other and who may become customers or suppliers.

There are now about 500 business incubators in North America, up from about 15 in 1980. They are commonly operated by universities, colleges and community colleges, for-profit businesses and economic development agencies, local governments, or consortia of all of these organizations. They are often targeted to serve the needs of light manufacturing and service firms and those developing new products or engaged in research and development. Incubator tenants may also include construction-related, sales and marketing, or wholesale and distribution firms.

Incubators vary in the services they offer and in the charges to their tenants. Some items to consider when looking at a business incubator are:

- What are the charges for space and services? How do they compare to market rates in the area? What

are the lease requirements? Is there room for business growth?

- What services does the incubator provide? Can the management offer on-site assistance and access to contacts and community business services? Does it provide seminar or training programs? Are some services provided free of charge?

- What is the experience of "incubator graduates," firms who have made use of the incubator for one to three years and then moved to their own space in the community? How about current tenants of the facility?

- What are the policies and procedures of the incubator? How long can a business remain a tenant? Is there a graduated structure as the business matures, or does the incubator take royalties or ownership right in its tenants in return for reduced charges? How simple is it to leave if the business fails?

- Does the incubator appear to be managed well? Does it have support from sponsoring organizations? Who are these sponsors and what are their goals and reasons for supporting the incubator?

Source: National Business Incubation Association

Contact Options

National Business Incubation Association
20 E. Circle Dr., Suite 190
Athens, OH 45701
(614) 593-4331

Small Business Administration
Business Initiative, Education, and Training
409 Third St., SW, Sixth Floor
Washington, DC 20416
(202) 205-6665
Contact the above office or a local SBA office.

Payroll Efficiency

Direct Deposit

Experts estimate that the annual cost for generating payroll checks is about $200 per year for each employee. Direct deposit is a convenient way to reduce payroll time and expense. While larger companies with many employees experience a greater reduction in payroll processing expenses, even the smaller company will experience proportionate savings.

A secondary benefit is the reduction in lost time and productivity. Employees no longer have to leave work to deposit checks since funds are instantly available in the checking or savings accounts that are targeted to receive these deposits. Morale and productivity show improvement, particularly on paydays, since employees do not have to make time to personally deposit or cash payroll checks.

Additional cost-cutting strategies include reconsidering the company's payroll schedule. Corporate

Payroll Efficiency (cont'd)

studies show that companies can reduce payroll expenses by 20-40% by changing payroll schedules from weekly to bimonthly.

Information on direct deposit is available from the bank that handles a company's payroll account or from an organization that specializes in this service.

Contact Option

National Automated Clearing House
Association (NACHA)
607 Herndon Pkwy., Suite 200
Herndon, VA 22070
(703) 742-9190

Payroll Processing

Processing a payroll for a large or small company can be time-consuming and requires careful attention to government regulations. Payroll efficiency can be affected by IRS requirements about depositing payroll taxes. Untimely payment errors can result in penalties and undesired attention from government taxation officials. One way to avoid such problems is to hire the services of specialists to process the corporation's payroll.

Automatic Data Processing (ADP), the largest of these payroll processing companies, offers a free, annually updated booklet on payroll information and IRS regulations. To obtain the booklet, call (800) 225-5237.

Contact Options

ADP Response Center
(800) 225-5237

Paychex
911 Panorama Trail
Rochester, NY 14625
(800) 322-7292

There are 90 local Paychex offices nationwide. The main office will provide information and convenient locations for callers.

Low-Cost Labor Alternatives

Temporary Help

More and more corporations are finding that their workforce needs change with marketplace fluctuations and business cycles, special projects and vacation periods. During these times, employers need individuals with skills ranging from professional/technical to industrial and office/clerical skills, but do not want to increase their basic core of workers. Temporary service firms have changed to meet more specialized corporate needs. They provide the necessary screening, interviewing, and training needed to fulfill the wide variety of expertise requirements of the corporate community. The employer is relieved of these responsibilities as well as the expense of hiring, paying benefits, payroll taxes, and other related bookkeeping.

For a free copy of *How to Buy Temporary Services*, which explains how to evaluate, select, and use temporary services, the interested individual should write to:

The National Association of Temporary Services
119 S. St. Asaph St.
Alexandria, VA 22314
(703) 549-6287

While the yellow pages of the local telephone book will list temporary employment services, the following is a list of temporary help companies that have at least 20 offices in ten different states in the U.S.

Ablest Service
810 N. Belcher Rd.
Clearwater, FL 34625
(813) 461-5656
26 offices; industrial, office/clerical

Accountemps
(Service of Robert Half)
2884 Sand Hill Rd.
Menlo Park, CA 94025
(415) 854-9700
150 offices; technical/professional

AccuStaff
2600 Potters Rd., P.O. Box 2218
Virginia Beach, VA 23452
(804) 431-2004
60 offices; industrial, office/clerical, technical/professional

Adia Services
64 Willow Pl., P.O. Box 3044
Menlo Park, CA 94026
(415) 324-0696
582 offices; industrial, medical, office/clerical, technical/professional

Alternative Resources
300 Tri-State International, Suite 270
Lincolnshire, IL 60069
(708) 317-1000
28 offices; technical/professional

Low-Cost Labor Alternatives (cont'd)

Career Horizons
177 Crossways Park Dr.
Woodbury, NY 11797
(516) 496-2300
153 offices; industrial, office/clerical, technical/professional

Claims Overload Systems
11900 Olympic Blvd., Suite 720
Los Angeles, CA 90064
(310) 447-7144
29 offices; office/clerical, technical/professional

DayStar Temporary Services
1127 Euclid Ave., #910
Cleveland, OH 44115
(216) 696-1122
26 offices; office/clerical

Dunhill Temporary Systems
1000 Woodbury Rd.
Woodbury, NY 11797
(516) 364-8800
38 offices; industrial, office/clerical

Express Personnel Services
6300 Northwest Expwy.
Oklahoma City, OK 73132
(800) 652-6400
194 offices; industrial, medical, office/clerical, technical/professional

Hooper Holmes
170 Mount Airy Rd.
Basking Ridge, NJ 07920
(908) 953-6250
41 offices; medical, office/clerical

Interim Services
2050 Spectrum Blvd.
Ft. Lauderdale, FL 33309
(305) 938-7600
700 offices; industrial, medical, office/clerical, technical/professional

Kelly Services
999 W. Big Beaver Rd.
Troy, MI 48084
(313) 362-4444
850 offices; industrial, office/clerical, technical/professional

Labor World of America
8000 N. Federal Hwy.
Boca Raton, FL 34487
(407) 997-5000
40 offices; industrial

MacTemps
66 Church St.
Cambridge, MA 02138
(617) 868-6800
21 offices; office/clerical, technical/professional

Manpower
5301 N. Ironwood Rd., P.O. Box 2053
Milwaukee, WI 53201
(414) 961-1000
902 offices; industrial, office/clerical, technical/professional

Norrell
3535 Piedmont Rd., NE
Atlanta, GA 30305
(404) 240-3000
250 offices; industrial, medical, office/clerical

Office Specialists
Corporate Pl., 128 Audubon Rd.
Wakefield, MA 01880
(617) 246-4900
50 offices; office/clerical, technical/professional

The Olsten Corporation
1 Merrick Ave.
Westbury, NY 11590
(516) 832-8200
1200 offices; industrial, medical, office/clerical

Pro Staff Personnel Services
920 Second Ave. S., Suite 920
Minneapolis, MN 55402
(612) 339-2221
60 offices; industrial, office/clerical, technical/professional

Remedy Temporary Services
32122 Camino Capistrano
San Juan Capistrano, CA 92675
(714) 661-1211
86 offices; industrial, office/clerical, technical/professional

Snelling and Snelling
12801 N. Central Expwy., Suite 700
Dallas, TX 75243
(214) 239-7575
200 offices; industrial, medical, office/clerical, technical/professional

Stivers Temporary Personnel
200 W. Monroe St., Suite 1100
Chicago, IL 60606
(312) 558-3550
30 offices; office/clerical

TAC/TEMPS
109 Oak St., P.O. Box 9110
Newton Upper Falls, MA 02164
(617) 969-3100
49 offices; office/clerical

TAD Temporaries
158 Monroe Ave.
Rochester, NY 14607
(716) 546-1660
31 offices; industrial, office/clerical

Low-Cost Labor Alternatives (cont'd)

Today's Temporary
18111 Preston Rd., #700
Dallas, TX 75252
(214) 380-9380
68 offices; office/clerical

TRC Staffing Services
100 Ashford Center N., Suite 500
Atlanta, GA 30338
(404) 392-1411
40 offices; industrial, office/clerical

Talent Tree
9703 Richmond Ave.
Houston, TX 77042
(713) 789-1818
140 offices; industrial, medical, office/clerical, technical/professional

Triad Personnel
1 Tower Ln., Suite 2100
Oakbrook Terrace, IL 60181
(708) 954-0455
23 offices; office/clerical

Uniforce Services
1335 Jericho Tpke.
New Hyde Park, NY 11040
(516) 437-3300
56 offices; industrial, office/clerical, technical/professional

Volt Temporary Services
2401 N. Glassell St., P.O. Box 13500
Orange, CA 92665
(714) 921-8800
95 offices; industrial, office/clerical

Western Temporary Services
301 Lennon Ln.
Walnut Creek, CA 94598
(510) 930-5300
350 offices; industrial, medical, office/clerical, technical/professional

Telecommuting Employees

Companies are frequently in search of ways to offer a flexible work environment to their employees. Telecommuting is becoming more and more popular among large and small companies alike. No longer limited to high-powered executives, telecommuting is now well-used in a variety of employment situations, where the employee can perform work functions at home using a PC, modem, and telephone line to connect to a host computer in the workplace. To investigate the process of setting up and evaluating a program, several contact options are available.

Recommended Resources

Telecommuting Resource Guide
Pacific Bell Telecommunications, free
(510) 901-6418

Telecommuting Review
Gil Gordon Associates, $157/year
(908) 329-2266
Monthly Newsletter

Creating a Flexible Workplace
by Barney Olmsted and Suzanne Smith
American Management Association
(AMACOM), $59.95
(800) 262-9699

Cost Accounting Tips

Telephone Accounting Codes

Cost accounting has always presented a challenge to companies. Tracking reimbursable expenses such as photocopies, mileage, postage, and food continues to be a challenge. Telephone companies now provide services that track and list the costs of calls made to predetermined numbers. An accounting code number, dialed with the telephone number called, enables the phone company to flag that call so that the user can quickly and easily identify the telephone expenses associated with a specific account. Call-accounting code service information is available from the major companies.

Contact Options

AT&T Call Manager
(800) 222-0400

Sprint Business Services
(800) 877-4020 or (800) 788-8981

MCI Business Services
(800) 950-5555

Credit and Collection

All businesses have to deal with collection of payments from debtors. Finding creative and effective ways to collect on invoices can be a challenge to anyone responsible for a company's finances. There are organizations of experts available who produce publications and standard credit forms as well as offering assistance and advice.

Cost Accounting Tips (cont'd)

Contact Options

National Association of Credit Management
8815 Centre Park Dr., Suite 200
Columbia, MD 21045
(410) 740-5560

Dun & Bradstreet
Receivable Management Services
(800) 234-3867
For international collections:
(800) 274-6454

Dun & Bradstreet
Small Business Services
(800) 544-3867

TRW Business Credit Services National Hotline
(800) 344-0603

Tax Deductions

Business tax deductions are available to organizations with excess inventory: new products which are not being used and, in some cases, older or surplus equipment such as computers. Several non-profit organizations distribute these corporate donations to other non-profit establishments such as schools, colleges, universities, and groups serving disabled people or special needs students. These organizations are most willing to supply donation guidelines and information packets.

Contact Options

National Exchange of Industrial
Resources (NAEIR)
P.O. Box 8076
560 McClure St.
Galesburg, IL 61402
(800) 562-0955
   Accepts office supplies, computer accessories, tools and hardware, lab equipment, maintenance supplies, electrical and plumbing fixtures, appliances, paper products, books, and other items for distribution to schools and charities around the country.

National Cristina Foundation
591 W. Putnam Ave.
Greenwich, CT 06830
(800) 274-7846
   Accepts surplus personal computers, software, and related technology for distribution to disabled individuals, at-risk students, and the disadvantaged.

Free Government Help

Updating Mailing Lists

Mailing lists must continually be updated in order to ensure efficiency. Inaccurate address labels result in incomplete delivery, lost business, and increased mailing expenses. Companies are faced with the dual task of weeding out bad addresses and updating zip codes to include the additional four digits now used by the U.S. Postal Service. The USPS now offers a one-time Diskette Coding Service which corrects most faulty street and city names and adds the four-digit extension to the existing zip codes. By submitting a computer disk containing the mailing list, the interested user can obtain a one-time clean-up/update. Call the National Customer Support Center of the USPS at (800) 238-3150 for information and computer disk requirements for this useful service.

Free Government Marketing Data

While marketing information companies provide vital demographics for corporate marketing needs, much of this information comes from agencies of the federal government, which collects such data. By calling the appropriate department in several government agencies, the interested user can speak directly to an expert who knows and collects this information. Often these experts can direct the caller through the maze of government offices to locate an appropriate source for the precise information being sought.

Contact Options

Economic and Demographic Statistics
Bureau of the Census
U.S. Dept. of Commerce
Data User Service Division
Customer Service
Washington, DC 20233
(301) 763-4100

Food and Agriculture Statistics
National Agriculture Statistics Service
Estimates Division, U.S. Dept. of Agriculture
Washington, DC 20250
(202) 720-3896

National, Regional, and International Economics
Bureau of Economic Analysis
U.S. Dept. of Commerce
Washington, DC 20230
(202) 606-9900

Employment, Prices, Living Conditions,
Productivity, and Occupational Health and Safety
Bureau of Labor Statistics, U.S. Dept. of Labor
Washington, DC 20212
(202) 606-7828

Free Government Help (cont'd)

Import and Export Statistics
World Trade Reference Room
U.S. Dept. of Commerce
Washington, DC 20230
(202) 482-2185

The following are phone numbers of government hotlines that provide the latest economic statistics on topics ranging from selected interest rates to advance reports of retail trade.

Government Hotlines

Topic	Department	Phone
News highlights	Federal Reserve Board	(202) 452-3206
News highlights	Department of Commerce	(202) 393-1847
Consumer Price Index	Bureau of Labor Statistics	(202) 606-7828
Employment Cost Index	Bureau of Labor Statistics	(202) 606-7828
Foreign trade	Bureau of the Census	(301) 457-3041
GNP	Bureau of Economic Analysis	(202) 606-5306
Inventories	Bureau of the Census	(900) 555-2329
Leading Economic Indicators	Bureau of Economic Analysis	(202) 606-5361
Mortgage rates	Federal National Mortgage Ass'n	(800) 752-7020
Producer Price Index	Bureau of Labor Statistics	(202) 606-7828
Retail trade	Bureau of the Census	(900) 555-2329
Treasury Bills, Notes, bonds, and securities	Department of the Treasury	(202) 874-4000

The Government's Kimberly bulletin board is a terrific source of financial forecasts and data, Federal Reserve information, securities-auction results, and consumer-finance statistics. Modem (612) 340-2489.

HUMAN RESOURCES

Business School Placement Offices

Carnegie-Mellon University
Career Opportunities Center
Graduate School of Industrial Administration
Schenley Park
Pittsburgh, PA 15213
(412) 268-2277

Columbia University
Columbia Business School
MBA Career Services, 206 Uris Hall
New York, NY 10027
(212) 854-5471

Cornell University
Johnson Graduate School of Management
Placement Office
217 Malott Hall
Ithaca, NY 14853
(607) 255-4888

Dartmouth University
Amos Tuck School of Business Administration
Placement Office
100 Tuck Hall
Hanover, NH 03755
(603) 646-3820

Duke University
The Fuqua School of Business
Placement Office, Box 90112
Durham, NC 27708
(919) 660-7810

Harvard University
Graduate School of Business Administration
Placement Office
Soldiers Field
Boston, MA 02163
(617) 495-6232

Indiana University at Bloomington
Graduate School of Business
Business Placement Office
Tenth St. and Fee Ln.
Bloomington, IN 47405
(812) 855-5317

Massachusetts Institute of Technology
Sloan School of Management
Placement Office
50 Memorial Dr., E52-111
Cambridge, MA 02142
(617) 253-6149

New York University
Graduate School of Business Administration
Office of Career Development
44 W. Fourth St., Suite 10-77
New York, NY 10012
(212) 998-0623

Northwestern University
Kellogg Graduate School of Management
Placement Office
2001 Sheridan Rd., Leverone Hall
Evanston, IL 60208
(708) 491-3168

Purdue University
Krannert Graduate School of Management
Placement Office
1310 Krannert Bldg., #160
W. Lafayette, IN 47907
(317) 494-4377

Stanford University
Graduate School of Business
Career Management Center
Stanford, CA 94305
(415) 723-2151

University of California at Berkeley (Haas)
Graduate School of Business Administration
Placement Center
350 Barrows Hall
Berkeley, CA 94720
(510) 642-8124

University of California at Los Angeles
John E. Anderson Graduate School of Management
Career Management Services
405 Hilgard Ave., Suite 1349
Los Angeles, CA 90024
(310) 825-3325

University of Chicago
Graduate School of Business
Office of Career Services
1101 E. 58th St.
Chicago, IL 60637
(312) 702-7405

University of Michigan
School of Business Administration
Placement Office
701 Tappan
Ann Arbor, MI 48109
(313) 764-1372

University of North Carolina-Chapel Hill
Graduate School of Business Administration
Career Services
CB #3490 Carroll Hall
Chapel Hill, NC 27599
(919) 962-2360

Business School Placement Offices (cont'd)

University of Pennsylvania
The Wharton School, Graduate Division
Career Development and Placement
McNeil Building
3718 Locust Walk, Suite 50
Philadelphia, PA 19104
(215) 898-4383

University of Pittsburgh
Joseph M. Katz Graduate School of Business
Placement and Career Services
201 Mervis Hall
Pittsburgh, PA 15260
(412) 648-1510

University of Rochester
William E. Simon Graduate School of Business
Career Services
Schlegel Hall
Rochester, NY 14627
(716) 275-4881

University of Southern California
MBA School of Business Administration
Career Services
Bridge Hall, #204
Los Angeles, CA 90089
(213) 740-0156

University of Texas at Austin
Graduate School of Business
Career Services Office
CBA 2.202
Austin, TX 78712
(512) 471-7748

University of Virginia
Darden Graduate School of Business Administration
Career Services and Placement Office
Box 6550
Charlottesville, VA 22906
(804) 924-7283

Vanderbilt University
Owen Graduate School of Management
Career Planning and Placement Office
401 21st Ave. S.
Nashville, TN 37203
(615) 322-4069

Yale University
Yale School of Management
Career Development Office
Box 208200
New Haven, CT 06520
(203) 432-5900

Law School Placement Offices

Boston College
Law School
Placement Office
885 Centre St.
Newton, MA 02159
(617) 552-4345

Columbia University
School of Law
Career Services
435 W. 116th St.
New York, NY 10027
(212) 854-2683

Cornell University
Cornell Law School
Career Services
Myron Taylor Hall
Ithaca, NY 14853
(607) 255-5252

Duke University
School of Law
Career Services
P.O. Box 90367
Durham, NC 27708
(919) 684-5429

Georgetown University
Law Center
Career Services
600 New Jersey Ave., NW
Washington, DC 20008
(202) 662-9300

George Washington University
The National Law Center
Career Services
2000 G St., NW
Washington, DC 20052
(202) 994-7340

Harvard University
Harvard Law School
Career Services
Cambridge, MA 02138
(617) 495-3119

New York University
School of Law
Office of Placement Services
110 W. Third St.
New York, NY 10012
(212) 998-6090

Law School Placement Offices (cont'd)

Northwestern University
School of Law
Placement Office
357 E. Chicago Ave.
Chicago, IL 60611
(312) 503-8438

Stanford University
Stanford Law School
Career Services and Placement
Crown Quadrangle
Stanford, CA 94305
(415) 723-3924

University of California at Berkeley
School of Law
Office of Career Services
291 Boalt Hall
Berkeley, CA 94720
(510) 642-4567

University of California at Hastings
College of Law
Career Services
200 MacAllister St., Suite 211
San Francisco, CA 94102
(415) 565-4619

University of California at Los Angeles
School of Law
Placement Office
405 Hilgard Ave.
Los Angeles, CA 90095
(310) 206-1117

University of Chicago
Law School
Placement Office
1111 E. 60th St.
Chicago, IL 60637
(312) 702-9625

University of Iowa
College of Law
Placement Office
Boyd Law Building
Melrose and Byington Sts.
Iowa City, IA 52242
(319) 335-9011

University of Michigan
Law School
Office of Career Services
210 Hutchins Hall
625 S. State St.
Ann Arbor, MI 48109
(313) 764-0546

University of Minnesota
Law School
Career Services
229 19th Ave. S.
Minneapolis, MN 55455
(612) 625-1866

University of Notre Dame
Notre Dame Law School
Placement Office
Law Building, Room 118
Notre Dame, IN 46556
(219) 631-7542

University of Pennsylvania
Law School
Career Planning and Placement
3400 Chestnut St.
Philadelphia, PA 19104
(215) 898-7493

University of Southern California
Law Center
Career Services
University Park
Los Angeles, CA 90089
(213) 740-7397

University of Texas at Austin
School of Law
Career Services
727 E. 26th St.
Austin, TX 78705
(512) 471-4768

University of Virginia
School of Law
Placement Office
North Grounds
580 Massie Rd.
Charlottesville, VA 22903
(804) 924-7349

Vanderbilt University
School of Law
Career Services
Law Building, Room 127
Nashville, TN 37240
(615) 322-6192

Yale University
Law School
Career Development
P.O. Box 208330
New Haven, CT 06520
(203) 432-1676

Business Co-Op Programs

COOPERATIVE EDUCATION BEGAN in 1906 at the University of Cincinnati in Ohio. The purpose then, as now, was to strengthen classroom learning with periods of study-related employment in companies outside the academic environment. Cooperative students take part in a college program that alternates periods of study with periods of work, either on a full-time or a part-time basis.

The goal of businesses that participate in co-operative learning programs is to enhance the education of college and university students through integrated, structured programs which combine academic study with paid, productive work experience. Co-op education can provide a cost-effective means of meeting recruiting goals and training potential career employees, as well as providing an opportunity to influence the education process.

Co-op education is practiced in over 1,000 colleges and universities in the U.S., as well as in various countries around the world. It is found mostly in two- and four-year college programs but is also in a limited number of five-year programs. Co-op is available in virtually every college curriculum and is offered at all levels, from the associate to the doctoral degree. Age is no factor for participation. Co-op is open to both traditional and non-traditional college students. In most programs, students receive academic credit for work experience and are charged comparable tuition rates. In other programs, no academic credit is awarded and no tuition is charged.

Over 275,000 students are enrolled in co-op programs each year with over 50,000 employers. Although student earnings vary with college major, years in school, and geographic location, co-op students earn a national average of $7,000 per year.

Recommended Resources

Cooperative Education Association
11710 Beltsville Dr., Suite 520
Beltsville, MD 20705
(301) 572-2329

This organization provides services for professionals who either hire or place cooperative education students. They publish *The Journal of Cooperative Education*, a research journal for educators; *Co-Op Experience* magazine for an audience of businesses and co-op students; and a newsletter and annual directory for educator and business members.

National Commission for Cooperative Education
360 Huntington Ave.
Boston, MA 02115
(617) 373-3778

Provides information on setting up co-op programs for businesses and educational institutions.

ESL Programs

TO FIND THE LOCATION of an English as a Second Language program, contact:

The National Literacy Hotline
(800) 228-8813

This hotline has a listing of available ESL programs in high schools, colleges, and universities throughout the United States and Canada.

Contact Option

Institute of International Education
Information Center
809 United Nations Plaza
New York, NY 10017
(212) 883-8200

Provides information about English language and orientation programs in the United States.

The Top Reference Sources

The Idea-a-Day Guide to Super Selling and Customer Service
Dartnell, $19.95
(800) 621-5463

This excellent reference includes a self-diagnostic test to identify special selling needs; sections devoted to specific sales skills, techniques, and strategies; more than 100 tips, ideas, and information sources; worksheets and 250 practical money-making ideas for each working day of the year. The oversized format and easy-to-use design make it an excellent workbook.

Correspondence Courses

THE FOLLOWING IS A LIST of selected programs that provide accredited home study programs. Most of them offer financial assistance through the G.I. Bill or through employee assistance programs.

Accounting/Secretarial/Computer
North American Correspondence Schools
925 Oak St.
Scranton, PA 18515
(717) 342-7701

Business/Engineering
International Correspondence Schools
925 Oak St.
Scranton, PA 18515
(717) 342-7701

Electronics/Computers
McGraw-Hill Continuing Education Center
4401 Connecticut Ave., NW
Washington, DC 20008
(202) 244-1600

Electronics/Computers
People's College of Independent Studies
233 Academy Dr.
P.O. Box 421768
Kissimmee, FL 34742
(407) 847-4444

English Usage
English Language Institute
925 Oak St.
Scranton, PA 18515
(717) 342-7701

High School Diploma
American School
850 E. 58th St.
Chicago, IL 60637
(312) 947-3300

High School Diploma
Cambridge Academy
1111 S.W. 17th St.
Ocala, FL 34474
(904) 620-2717

High School Diploma
Citizens' High School
188 College Dr.
P.O. Box 1929
Orange Park, FL 32067
(904) 276-1700

High School Diploma
ICS-Newport/Pacific High School
Scranton, PA 18515
(717) 342-7701

Paralegal
Paralegal Institute
3602 W. Thomas Rd., Suite 9
Drawer 11408
Phoenix, AZ 85061-1408
(602) 272-1855

Paralegal
Southern Career Institute
164 W. Royal Palm Rd.
Boca Raton, FL 33432
(800) 669-2555

Secretarial Training
Laurel School
2538 N. Eighth St.
P.O. Box 5338
Phoenix, AZ 85010
(602) 994-3460

Tax Training
National Tax Training School
4 Melnick Dr.
P.O. Box 382
Monsey, NY 10952
(914) 352-3634

Contact Option

Distance Education and Training Council
1601 18th St., NW
Washington DC 20009
(202) 234-5100
   Produces listing of fully accredited home study programs.

Executive Education

EXECUTIVE EDUCATION IS undergoing a series of changes as companies reconsider the most effective way to improve executive performance and make corporations more competitive. The biggest changes can be seen the the shift from traditional forms of educational programs to brief, expensive, but more needs-directed pragmatic courses offered by specialist consultants.

Contact Options

Amos Tuck School of Business Administration
Dartmouth College
Attn: Executive Education Department
Hanover, NH 03755
(603) 646-2839

Babson College
1 Woodland Hill Dr.
Babson Park
Wellesley, MA 02157
(617) 235-1200

Boston University
Leadership Institute
621 Commonwealth Ave.
Boston, MA 02215
(617) 353-4217

Carnegie-Mellon Program for Executives
C-MU
GSIA
Posner Hall 150
5000 Forbes Ave.
Pittsburgh, PA 15213
(412) 268-2305

Center for Creative Leadership
Client Relations
P.O. Box 26301
Greensboro, NC 27410
(910) 545-2810

Columbia University
Executive Programs
2880 Broadway, Fourth Floor
New York, NY 10025

Darden Executive Education
University of Virginia
P.O. Box 6550
Charlottesville, VA 22903
(804) 924-3000

Duke University
Department of Executive Education
R. David Thomas Ctr.
Durham, NC 27708
(919) 660-8011

Harvard Business School
Executive Education Programs
Soldiers Field–Gladd Hall
Boston, MA 02163
(617) 495-6000

Kellogg Graduate School of Management
Northwestern University
James L. Allen Center
Evanston, IL 60208
(708) 467-7000

Office of Executive Education
Graduate School of Business
Stanford University
Stanford, CA 94305
(415) 723-3341

Penn State
Executive Education
309 Business Administration Building
University Park, PA 16802
(814) 863-1224

Sloan School of Management
Massachusetts Institute of Technology
50 Memorial Dr., E-52-126
Cambridge, MA 02139
(617) 253-2659

UCLA
AGSM Office of Executive Education
405 Hilgard Ave., Suite 2381
Los Angeles, CA 90024
(310) 825-2001

University of California at Berkeley (Haas)
Executive Program
350 Barrows Hall, #1906
Berkeley, CA 94720
(510) 642-1406

University of Michigan
Executive Education Center
700 E. University, Room E-2540
Ann Arbor, MI 48109
(810) 763-1003

Executive Education (cont'd)

University of North Carolina
Kenan Center
Campus Box 3445
Chapel Hill, NC 27599
(919) 962-3123

University of Pennsylvania
Executive Education
Steinberg Conference Ctr.
255 S. 38th St.
Philadelphia, PA 19104
(215) 898-4560

University of Southern California
Office of Executive Education
School of Business Administration, DCC 107
Los Angeles, CA 90089
(213) 740-8990

Trainers and Seminars

ON-SITE PERSONNEL TRAINING, whether in the form of books, audio cassettes, films, videotapes, software, or live seminars, is available through a wide range of human resources companies and consultants.

One of the most extensive sources for finding the right training program is published by the American Society for Training and Development. Their book offers a listing of companies and consultants that provide hardware, training facilities, and other training and equipment supplies. Also included is an alphabetized listing of companies and consultants and a listing of specialists who cater to industry-specific audiences. The directory features a subject index of companies and consultants who provide human resources development in areas as specific as AIDS in the workplace, ergonomics, quality control, and time management skills.

Recommended Resource

American Society for Training and Development Buyer's Guide and Consultant Directory, $75
1640 King St., Box 1443
Alexandria, VA 22313
(703) 683-8100

Contact Options

Personal Progress Library
7657 Winnetka Ave., #331
Winnetka, CA 91306
(800) 748-6245
America's largest cassette-lending library in the field.

Training and Development Resource Catalogues:

Blanchard Training and Development
125 State Pl.
Escondido, CA 92029
(800) 728-6000

CareerTrack
3085 Center Green Dr.
Boulder, CO 80301
(800) 423-3001

The Myers Method
P.O. Box 1526
Princeton, NJ 08542
(609) 737-6832

Nightingale-Conant
7300 N. Lehigh Ave.
Niles, IL 60714
(800) 323-5552

QCI International
P.O. Box 1503
1350 Vista Way
Red Bluff, CA 96080
(800) 527-6970

Sybervision Systems
1 Sansome St., #810
San Francisco, CA 94104
(800) 888-9980

The Zig Ziglar Company
3330 Earhart #204
Carrollton, TX 75006
(800) 527-0306

Executive Training

AUDIO RECORDINGS, VIDEOCASSETTES, training programs, and seminars designed to expand the skills of the corporate executive are a multibillion-dollar industry in this country.

There are several companies that design and present executive training programs that run anywhere from one day to several weeks. Seminars are offered in a wide array of topics ranging from quality control to stress reduction and from business writing to budget planning.

Contact Options

Executive Training Firms:

CareerTrack
3085 Center Green Dr.
Boulder, CO 80301
(800) 423-3001

Fred Pryor Seminars
Pryor Resources
2000 Shawnee Mission Pkwy.
Shawnee Mission, KS 66205
(800) 255-6139

National Seminars Group
6901 W. 63rd St.
Shawnee Mission, KS 66202
(800) 258-7246

First Seminar Service
600 Suffolk St.
Lowell, MA 01854
(800) 321-1990

For a fee, First Seminar will do a search and find all of the available seminars on a particular topic anywhere in the country over the course of the year.

Recommended Resources

The Corporate University Guide to Management Seminars
The Corporate University Press, $129

A thorough listing of seminars available by topic, training organization, date, and location.

Evaluation Guide to Executive Programs
The Corporate University Press, $189

An in-depth evaluation of 170 of the best short programs available.

The Corporate University Press
124 Washington Ave.
Suite B2
Point Richard, CA 94801
(510) 236-9400

Speakers Bureaus

COMPANIES OFTEN NEED SPEAKERS, either to motivate a sales force or to entertain at a company event. For the right price, it's possible to hire anyone, from Henry Kissinger to a foreign expert on quality control, to lecture an audience of company personnel. A number of agencies exist whose sole function is to book speakers for corporate events.

Contact Options

Lecture Agents:

Walters International Speakers Bureau
P.O. Box 1120
Glendora, CA 91740
(818) 335-8069

Washington Speakers Bureau
310 S. Henry St.
Alexandria, VA 22314
(703) 684-0555

The Harry Walker Agency
1 Penn Plaza, Suite 2400
New York, NY 10119
(212) 563-0700

National Speakers Bureau
222 Wisconsin Ave.
Lake Forest, IL 60045
(708) 295-1122

Keppler Associates
4350 N. Fairfax Dr., Suite 700
Arlington, VA 22203
(703) 516-4000

Recommended Resource

Who's Who in Professional Speaking
National Speakers Association, $25
(602) 968-2552

This directory lists names, addresses, and phone numbers of members alphabetically, geographically, and by specialty.

Speech and Image Consultants

SEMINARS THAT ASSIST EXECUTIVES and managers in developing a solid professional image and effective presentation skills are available from a number of human resources consultants. These programs focus on effective communication styles for public speaking engagements.

Contact Options

Human Resource Consultants:

Achievement Concepts
1963 Cynthia Ln.
P.O. Box 430
Merrick, NY 11566
(516) 868-5100

Anderson Management Group
413 Victoria Court, NW
Box 1745-A
Vienna, VA 22183
(703) 938-9672

Commocore
156 Fifth Ave., #701
New York, NY 10010
(212) 206-1003

Communication Resources
Harvard Sq.
P.O. Box 537
Cambridge, MA 02238
(617) 332-4334

Conrad Communications
6 Black Birch Ln.
Scarsdale, NY 10583
(914) 725-2360

Dale Carnegie & Associates
1475 Franklin Ave.
Garden City, NY 11530
(800) 231-5800

Decker Communications
44 Montgomery St., Suite 1700
San Francisco, CA 94104
(415) 391-5544

Kaufman Professional Image Consultants
233 S. Sixth St., Suite 702
Philadelphia, PA 19106
(215) 592-9709

Parkhurst Communications
311 W. 75th St.
New York, NY 10023
(212) 580-9390

Tracy Presentation Skills
2414 Londonderry Rd., Suite 767
Alexandria, VA 22308
(703) 360-3222

Top Business Speakers

Cavett Award Winners

THE CAVETT AWARD is the top speaker's award given annually by the National Speakers Association:

Year	Recipient
1979	Robert Cavett
1980	Bill Gove
1981	Dave Yoho
1982	Ty Boyd
1983	Joe Larson
1984	Ira M. Hayes
1985	Nido R. Qubein
1986	Don Hutson
1987	James "Doc" Blakely
1988	Robert H. Henry
1989	Jeanne Robertson
1990	D. Michael Frank

Year	Recipient
1991	Rosita Perez
1992	D. John Hammond
1993	Jim Cathcart
1994	George Morrissey

Contact Option

National Speakers Association
1500 S. Priest Dr.
Tempe, AZ 85281
(602) 968-2552

Coping with Illiteracy

Percentage of Companies That Provide Remedial Training Programs

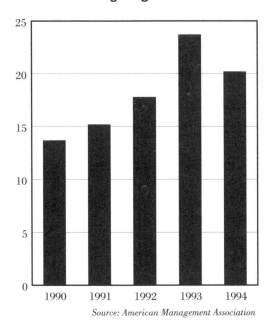

Source: American Management Association

Percentage of Companies That Conduct Literacy and Math Testing

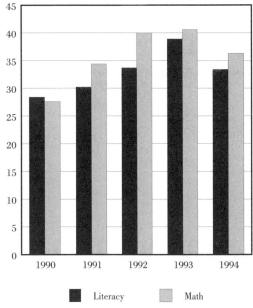

■ Literacy   ▢ Math

Source: American Management Association

Action on Skills-Deficient Employees, 1994

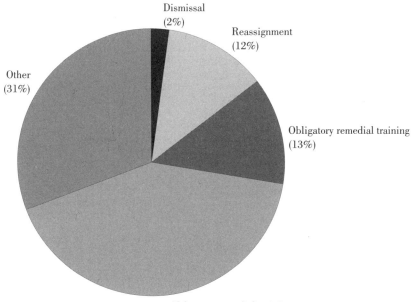

Dismissal (2%)

Reassignment (12%)

Other (31%)

Obligatory remedial training (13%)

Voluntary remedial training (42%)

Source: American Management Association

Skills Training

A NUMBER OF COMPANIES specialize in training programs to improve the reading and writing speeds and the efficiency of company personnel. These companies will conduct on-site seminars or provide materials for corporations to conduct their own courses.

Contact Options

Companies Specializing in Literacy Training:

Aztec Software Associates
24 Tulip St., Box 863
Summit, NJ 07901
(908) 273-7443

Conover
P.O. Box 155
Omro, WI 54963
(800) 933-1933

Reading Development Resources
7201 S. Broadway, Suite 11
Littleton, CO 80122
(800) 328-5099

Writing Development Associates
254-39 Bates Rd.
Little Neck, NY 11363
(718) 279-3143

Recommended Resource

National Literacy Hotline
P.O. Box 81826
Lincoln, NE 68501
(800) 228-8813

Compensation and Benefits

A COMPANY NEEDING TO DESIGN a benefits package for its employees can contact a consulting firm that specializes in this field.

The following is a list of some of the largest U.S.-based consultants:

A. Foster Higgins & Co.
125 Broad St.
New York, NY 10004
(212) 574-9000

Alexander Consulting Group
125 Chubb Ave.
Lyndhurst, NJ 07071
(201) 460-6600

Buck Consultants
2 Penn Plaza, 23rd Floor
New York, NY 10121
(212) 330-1000

Hewitt Associates
100 Half Day Rd.
Lincolnshire, IL 60069
(708) 295-5000

KPMG Peat Marwick
345 Park Ave.
New York, NY 10154
(212) 758-9700

Mercer Consulting Group
1166 Ave. of the Americas
New York, NY 10036
(212) 345-4500

Segal
1 Park Ave.
New York, NY 10016
(212) 251-5000

Towers Perrin
245 Park Ave.
New York, NY 10167
(212) 309-3400

Wyatt
601 13th St., NW
Washington, DC 20005
(202) 624-0600

Compensation and Benefits (cont'd)

A survey of more than 1,400 organizations produced this summary of plans offered by medium to large employers.

Compensation and Benefits Offered

Benefits Program	Total % With	Total % Without	Do Not Have But Are Considering
BASIC HEALTH CARE PLANS			
Medical Insurance Coverage (excluding dental)	97.6	2.4	0.0
Health Maintenance Organization (HMO)	76.6	21.1	2.3
Preferred Provider Organization (PPO)	66.2	27.2	6.6
SPECIAL HEALTH CARE PLANS (not included under Basic Health Care)			
Dental Coverage	94.2	5.0	0.8
Vision Coverage	48.5	47.7	3.8
Alcohol/Drug Program	65.3	32.4	2.3
Physical Fitness Program	33.9	60.0	6.1
Prescription Drug Coverage	80.8	17.7	1.6
Hearing Examination Coverage	24.2	74.0	1.8
OTHER EMPLOYEE BENEFITS			
Formal Training/Professional Development Program	73.1	19.6	7.3
Flextime (employee chooses alternative work schedules)	48.6	43.5	7.9
Group Term Life Insurance	98.3	1.5	0.1
Educational Assistance	93.3	5.7	1.0
Pre-Retirement Counseling	47.1	42.4	10.5
Accidental Death and Dismemberment Insurance	96.2	3.5	0.2
Short-Term Disability Insurance	85.3	12.7	2.0
Long-Term Disability Insurance	98.4	1.3	0.2
Annual Computerized Benefits Statement	62.9	24.8	12.2
Group Personal Insurance (payroll deduction auto or homeowners insurance)	12.4	84.1	3.6
Flexible Benefits	47.2	42.1	10.7
Flexible Spending Account (Section 125)	72.3	23.3	4.4
RETIREMENT INCOME			
Pension Plan	75.9	23.5	0.7
Profit Sharing Plan	28.1	70.2	1.7
Thrift Plan	19.6	79.4	1.0
401(k) Salary Reduction Plan	86.2	12.9	0.9
ESOP (Employee Stock Ownership Plan)	23.7	73.8	2.5
EXECUTIVE STOCK PLANS			
Incentive Stock Options	33.5	64.3	2.2
Non-Qualified Stock Options	38.7	59.8	1.5
Stock Appreciation Rights	11.6	85.9	2.6
Restricted Stock Award	26.5	71.1	2.4
Performance Share Plan	12.0	85.6	2.4
EXECUTIVE INCENTIVE PLANS			
Performance Unit Plan	26.4	71.9	1.7
Annual Cash Incentive	67.0	31.3	1.7
Medium-Term Cash Incentive (2-3 yrs.)	5.1	92.1	2.8
Long-Term Cash Incentive (3 yrs. or longer)	19.8	77.9	2.3
SPECIAL EXECUTIVE BENEFIT PROGRAMS			
Low/No Interest Loan Program	7.6	91.9	0.5
Executive Physical Examination	65.2	34.0	0.8
Executive Medical Reimbursement	16.7	81.7	1.7
Executive Supplemental Disability	23.8	73.8	2.4
Executive Supplemental Retirement	41.5	56.0	2.5
Executive Supplemental Survivor Income	17.1	81.8	1.1
Voluntary Deferred Compensation	37.5	59.1	3.4
Executive Employment Contracts	36.3	62.9	0.8
Financial Counseling/Tax Planning	37.4	60.1	2.5

Compensation and Benefits (cont'd)

Benefits Program	Total % With	Total % Without	Do Not Have But Are Considering
COMPENSATION PROGRAMS			
Formal Point-Factor Job Evaluation System	53.6	41.6	4.8
Formal Performance Appraisal	93.1	5.6	1.2
Special Project-Oriented Incentive for Engineers, Programmers, or Inventors	6.8	90.2	3.0
Other Group Incentives	29.8	63.2	6.9
Lump Sum Merit Increase	35.1	59.4	5.5
Gainsharing	9.3	83.5	7.1
Specialized Compensation Software	25.4	63.1	11.5

Source: 1994 Human Resources Management Survey by William M. Mercer, Inc.

Job Eliminations

Largest Job Eliminations Announced by American Companies (January 1993 - March 1994)

Company	Jobs to Be Eliminated
General Motors	69,650
Sears, Roebuck	50,000
IBM	38,500
AT&T	33,525
Boeing	31,000
GTE	27,975
NYNEX	22,000
Philip Morris	14,000

Company	Jobs to Be Eliminated
Procter & Gamble	13,000
Woolworth	13,000
Martin Marietta	12,060
Eastman Kodak	12,000
Xerox	11,200
McDonnell Douglas	10,966
Raytheon	10,624
Pacific Telesis	10,000

Source: New York Times, Mar. 22, 1994

The Top Reference Sources

Fundamentals of Employee Benefit Programs
Employee Benefit and Research Institute, $24.95
(202) 775-6341

A comprehensive and accessible primer on the whole range of employee benefits, including pension and retirement programs, profit-sharing plans, savings plans, life insurance plans, education assistance and legal services programs, dependent care benefits, and all manner of healthcare benefits. This guide is a must for any employer creating or changing a company benefit program.

Social Security

Covered Employment, Earnings, and Contribution Rates

Item	1980	1984	1985	1986	1987
WORKERS WITH INSURED STATUS (millions)	137.4	147.0	148.7	150.6	152.7
Male (millions)	75.4	78.8	79.7	80.7	81.5
Female (millions)	62.0	68.2	69.0	69.9	71.2
Under 25 years old (millions)	25.5	23.1	22.3	21.9	21.3
25 to 34 years old (millions)	34.9	39.7	39.9	40.0	40.6
35 to 44 years old (millions)	22.4	27.2	28.5	29.8	31.2
45 to 54 years old (millions)	18.6	18.8	19.0	19.3	19.8
55 to 59 years old (millions)	9.2	9.1	9.1	9.0	8.9
60 to 64 years old (millions)	7.9	8.6	8.7	8.8	8.7
65 to 69 years old (millions)	6.7	7.1	7.3	7.5	7.6
70 years old and older (millions)	12.1	13.4	13.9	14.3	14.7
WORKERS REPORTED WITH					
Taxable earnings (millions)	112.0	116.0	120.0	123.0	125.0
Maximum earnings (millions)	10.0	7.0	7.0	7.0	8.0
Earnings in covered employment ($ billions)	1,326.0	1,772.0	1,912.0	2,035.0	2,198.0
Reported taxable ($ billions)	1,176.0	1,609.0	1,724.0	1,844.0	1,960.0
Percent of total (%)	88.7	90.8	90.2	90.6	89.2
AVERAGE PER WORKER					
Total earnings ($)	11,817.0	15,260.0	15,955.0	16,587.0	17,584.0
Taxable earnings ($)	10,500.0	13,871.0	14,367.0	14,992.0	15,680.0
Annual maximum taxable earnings ($)	25,900.0	37,800.0	39,600.0	42,000.0	43,800.0
Maximum tax ($)	1,588.0	2,533.0	2,792.0	3,003.0	3,132.0

Item	1988	1989	1990	1991	1992
WORKERS WITH INSURED STATUS (millions)	155.4	158.0	161.1	163.6	166.0
Male (millions)	82.6	83.7	85.1	86.1	87.2
Female (millions)	72.8	74.3	76.0	77.4	78.8
Under 25 years old (millions)	21.3	21.1	21.3	21.2	21.0
25 to 34 years old (millions)	41.0	41.3	41.6	41.5	41.2
35 to 44 years old (millions)	32.3	33.5	34.8	36.3	37.2
45 to 54 years old (millions)	20.5	21.4	22.2	22.8	23.9
55 to 59 years old (millions)	8.8	8.7	8.7	8.7	8.8
60 to 64 years old (millions)	8.7	8.7	8.6	8.7	8.7
65 to 69 years old (millions)	7.7	7.9	8.0	8.1	8.2
70 years old and older (millions)	15.0	15.4	15.8	16.3	16.8
WORKERS REPORTED WITH					
Taxable earnings (millions)	130.0	133.0	133.0	132.0	132.0
Maximum earnings (millions)	8.0	8.0	8.0	8.0	8.0
Earnings in covered employment ($ billions)	2,411.0	2,593.0	2,720.0	2,796.0	2,960.0
Reported taxable ($ billions)	2,101.0	2,243.0	2,363.0	2,428.0	2,541.0
Percent of total (%)	87.1	86.5	86.9	86.8	85.8
AVERAGE PER WORKER					
Total earnings ($)	18,610.0	19,494.0	20,442.0	21,131.0	22,342.0
Taxable earnings ($)	16,215.0	16,863.0	17,759.0	18,350.0	19,182.0
Annual maximum taxable earnings ($)	45,000.0	48,000.0	51,300.0	53,400.0	55,500.0
Maximum tax ($)	3,380.0	3,605.0	3,924.0	4,085.0	5,329.0

Source: 1994 Statistical Abstract, Table No. 580

Social Security (cont'd)

Social Security: Beneficiaries, Annual Payments, and Average Monthly Benefit

Year	Total Number of Beneficiaries (thousands)	Total Annual Payments ($ millions)	Average Monthly Benefit ($)
1970	26,229	31,863	118
1980	35,585	120,472	341
1985	37,058	186,195	479
1986	37,703	196,692	489
1987	38,190	204,156	513
1988	38,627	217,214	537
1989	39,151	230,850	567
1990	39,832	247,796	603
1991	40,592	268,098	629
1992	41,497	285,980	653

Social Security: Beneficiaries, Annual Payments, and Average Monthly Benefit, by State

Division, State, Other Area	Total Number of Beneficiaries (thousands)	Total Annual Payments ($ millions)	Average Monthly Benefits ($)
UNITED STATES	40,524	281,673	NA
New England	2,231	15,913	NA
Maine	224	1,436	601
New Hampshire	172	1,210	655
Vermont	92	624	640
Massachusetts	1,011	7,144	655
Rhode Island	186	1,314	652
Connecticut	546	4,185	718
Middle Atlantic	6,470	48,001	NA
New York	2,910	21,642	698
New Jersey	1,267	9,720	716
Pennsylvania	2,293	16,639	672
East North Central	7,006	50,976	NA
Ohio	1,859	13,259	669
Indiana	938	6,799	679
Illinois	1,800	13,267	692
Michigan	1,546	11,478	697
Wisconsin	863	6,173	669
West North Central	3,105	21,263	NA
Minnesota	689	4,706	637
Iowa	532	3,706	653
Missouri	941	6,402	638
North Dakota	114	736	615
South Dakota	132	836	602
Nebraska	276	1,891	643
Kansas	421	2,986	669
South Atlantic	7,548	50,714	NA
Delaware	112	813	680
Maryland	641	4,501	652
District of Columbia	79	477	556
Virginia	883	5,810	619
West Virginia	376	2,542	644
North Carolina	1,143	7,394	612
South Carolina	575	3,686	611
Georgia	937	6,010	610
Florida	2,802	19,481	651

Social Security (cont'd)

Social Security: Beneficiaries, Annual Payments, and Average Monthly Benefit, by State

Division, State, Other Area	Total Number of Beneficiaries (thousands)	Total Annual Payments ($ millions)	Average Monthly Benefits ($)
East South Central	2,752	17,253	NA
Kentucky	674	4,238	602
Tennessee	870	5,581	611
Alabama	739	4,674	604
Mississippi	469	2,760	569
West South Central	4,032	26,151	NA
Arkansas	482	2,975	588
Louisiana	679	4,263	607
Oklahoma	552	3,636	622
Texas	2,319	15,277	633
Mountain	2,098	14,207	NA
Montana	146	974	633
Idaho	166	1,113	634
Wyoming	66	455	651
Colorado	453	3,045	635
New Mexico	235	1,468	612
Arizona	635	4,416	660
Utah	205	1,392	658
Nevada	192	1,344	658
Pacific	5,279	37,195	NA
Washington	747	5,377	677
Oregon	521	3,675	663
California	3,819	26,852	667
Alaska	37	250	653
Hawaii	155	1,041	643
Puerto Rico	581	2,504	418
Guam	6	25	459
American Samoa	4	14	388
Virgin Islands	11	59	548
Abroad	350	1,705	452

Source: 1994 Statistical Abstract, Table No. 583

The Top Reference Sources

Companies and Their Brands, 1995
Gale, $425
(800) 877-4253

This valuable resource alphabetically lists the manufacturers, distributors, marketers, and im-

porters of 250,000 consumer products.
     Complete addresses, phone numbers, and fax numbers are provided for the 47,000 companies listed. The book is updated annually.

Personnel Testing

Physical Examinations

Physical examinations can be used to screen out applicants when the results indicate that job performance would be adversely affected. For example, jobs that require a great deal of physical force may require job applicants to receive back X-rays, while desk jobs may not.

Drug Testing

Drug testing for employees and job applicants has increased 250 percent since 1987. Perhaps as a result of increased testing and related educational programs, drug use among workers and job seekers has declined in recent years.

Only a handful of states presently outlaw drug testing for private sector businesses. Many government workers, on the other hand, are required to submit to random or periodic drug testing as mandated by the Federal Workplace Drug Testing Regulations.

Just about all drug testing is done by urinalysis which, when performed under the guidelines established by the Federal Workplace Drug Testing Regulations, offers a 99.9 percent accuracy rate.

Polygraph Tests

With the passage of the Employee Polygraph Protection Act of 1988, employers are restricting their use of polygraph or lie detector tests. The law virtually outlaws the use of lie detectors in connection with employment, and covers all private employers in interstate commerce. Supporters of the law claim that the tests are accurate only two-thirds of the time and are far more likely to be inaccurate for honest employees. The new law restricts pre-employment screening and random use of the device.

The Employee Polygraph Protection Act allows polygraph tests to be used in connection with jobs in security or that involve handling drugs, or in investigating a theft or other suspected crime. Before an employee can be required to take such a test as part of an investigation of an employment-related crime, however, the employee must be given a written notice stating that he or she is a suspect.

AIDS

Employees with disabilities, including AIDS and HIV infection, are protected by law from discrimination in employment. In most cases, HIV testing of new or present employees for employment is prohibited by human rights laws. In the very few areas of employment where testing may be allowed, an employee may never be singled out for testing; tests must be required of all employees or none.

Because of the many sensitive legal issues involving privacy and discrimination, it is advised that employers develop a comprehensive "AIDS in the Workplace" policy, and should not require HIV screening as part of pre-employment or general workplace physical examination.

Contact Options

Drug Testing and Program Management Firms:

Drug Intervention Services of America
11200 Westheimer, Suite 630
Houston, Texas 77042
(713) 972-3472

National MRO
P.O. Box 261426
Lakewood, CO 80226
(303) 238-2000

Substance Abuse Management
2 Plaza E.
330 E. Kilbourn Ave., Suite 1075
Milwaukee, WI 53202
(414) 273-7264

University Services
Arsenal Business Center
5301 Tacony St., Bldg. 4
Philadelphia, PA 19137
(215) 743-4200

Weber Consultants Unlimited
2331-D2 E. Ave. S., Suite 198
Palmdale, CA 93550
(805) 294-5033

Recommended Resources

CDC Business Responds to AIDS Manager's Kit
CDC National AIDS Clearinghouse, $25
(800) 458-5231

A terrific source for the straight scoop on developing a sensitive, effective policy on AIDS in the workplace.

Sample Policies
National Leadership Coalition on AIDS, $15
(202) 452-8845

This booklet offers a sampling of real company policies on AIDS in the workplace, and is a great place to start in determining your company's approach to AIDS.

Personnel Testing (cont'd)

Corporate Methods for Combating Drug Abuse

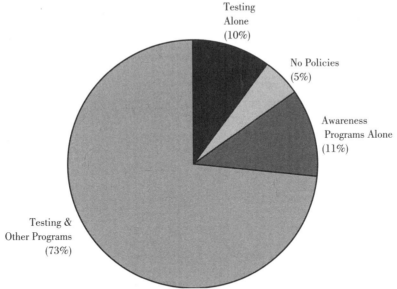

Testing
Alone
(10%)

No Policies
(5%)

Awareness
Programs Alone
(11%)

Testing &
Other Programs
(73%)

Source: American Management Association

Percentage of Workplace Drug Testing 1990-1994

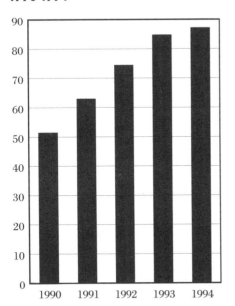

Source: American Management Association

Percentage of Executives Who Say Drug Testing Is Effective

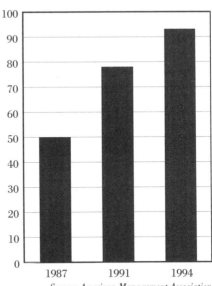

Source: American Management Association

Best Companies to Work For

ROBERT LEVERING AND Milton Moskowitz did a study of companies in America and ranked them according to a variety of factors, including pay, benefits, job security, chances of advancement, and work pride. Their aim was to look at companies through the eyes of their employees. The following is the list of 100 companies that they felt were the best to work for according to these criteria.

The 100 Best Companies to Work For

Company	City
3M	St. Paul, MN
Acipco	Birmingham, AL
Advanced Micro Devices	Sunnyvale, CA
Alagasco	Birmingham, AL
Anheuser-Busch	St. Louis, MO
Apogee Enterprises	Minneapolis, MN
Armstrong	Lancaster, PA
Avis	Garden City, NY
Baptist Hospital of Miami	Miami, FL
BE&K	Birmingham, AL
Ben & Jerry's Homemade	Waterbury, VT
Beth Israel Hospital Boston*	Boston, MA
Leo Burnett	Chicago, IL
Chaparral Steel	Midlothian, TX
Compaq Computer	Houston, TX
Cooper Tire	Findlay, OH
Corning	Corning, NY
Cray Research	Eagan, MN
Cummins Engine	Columbus, IN
Dayton Hudson	Minneapolis, MN
John Deere	Moline, IL
Delta Air Lines*	Atlanta, GA
Donnelly*	Holland, MI
Du Pont	Wilmington, DE
A. G. Edwards	St. Louis, MO
Erie Insurance	Erie, PA
Federal Express*	Memphis, TN
Fel-Pro*	Skokie, IL
First Federal Bank of California	Santa Monica, CA
H. B. Fuller	St. Paul, MN
General Mills	Minneapolis, MN
Goldman, Sachs	New York, NY
W. L. Gore & Associates	Newark, DE
Great Plains Software	Fargo, ND
Hallmark Cards*	Kansas City, MO
Haworth	Holland, MI
Hershey Foods	Hershey, PA
Hewitt Associates	Lincolnshire, IL
Hewlett-Packard	Palo Alto, CA
Honda of America Manufacturing	Marysville, OH

Company	City
IBM	Armonk, NY
Inland Steel	Chicago, IL
Intel	Santa Clara, CA
Johnson & Johnson	New Brunswick, NJ
SC Johnson Wax	Racine, WI
Kellogg	Battle Creek, MI
Knight-Ridder	Miami
Lands' End	Dodgeville, WI
Lincoln Electric	Cleveland, OH
Los Angeles Dodgers	Los Angeles, CA
Lotus Development	Cambridge, MA
Lowe's	North Wilkesboro, NC
Lyondell Petrochemical	Houston, TX
Marquette Electronics	Milwaukee, WI
Mary Kay Cosmetics	Dallas, TX
McCormick	Hunt Valley, MD
Merck	Whitehouse Sta., NJ
Methodist Hospital	Houston, TX
Microsoft	Redmond, WA
Herman Miller	Zeeland, MI
Moog	E. Aurora, NY
J. P. Morgan	New York, NY
Morrison & Foerster	San Francisco, CA
Motorola	Schaumburg, IL
Nissan Motor Manufacturing	Smyrna, TN
Nordstrom	Seattle, WA
Northwestern Mutual Life	Milwaukee, WI
Odetics	Anaheim, CA
Patagonia	Ventura, CA
J. C. Penney	Plano, TX
Physio-Control	Redmond, WA
Pitney Bowes	Stamford, CT
Polaroid	Cambridge, MA
Preston Trucking	Preston, MD
Procter & Gamble	Cincinnati, OH
Publix Super Markets*	Lakeland, FL
Quad/Graphics	Pewaukee, WI
Reader's Digest	Pleasantville, NY
REI	Seattle, WA
Rosenbluth*	Philadelphia, PA

Indicates one of top ten

Best Companies to Work For (cont'd)

Company	City
SAS Institute	Cary, NC
J. M. Smucker	Orrville, OH
Southwest Airlines*	Dallas, TX
Springfield ReManufacturing	Springfield, MO
Springs	Fort Mill, SC
Steelcase	Grand Rapids, MI
Syntex	Palo Alto, CA
Tandem	Cupertino, CA
TDIndustries	Dallas, TX
Tennant	Minneapolis, MN
UNUM	Portland, ME
USAA*	San Antonio, TX
US West	Englewood, CO
Valassis Communications	Livonia, MI
Viking Freight System	San Jose, CA

Company	City
Wal-Mart	Bentonville, AR
Wegmans	Rochester, NY
Weyerhaeuser	Tacoma, WA
Worthington Industries	Columbus, OH
Xerox	Stamford, CT

*Indicates one of top ten

Source: Robert Levering and Milton Moskowitz, The 100 Best Companies to Work For in America, Doubleday, 1993

Family and Medical Leave

MORE THAN 70 PERCENT of all American women between the ages of 20 and 54 now work outside the home. The Family and Medical Leave Act of 1993 guarantees family leave for employees under certain circumstances. The FMLA requires private sector employers of 50 or more employees and public agencies to provide up to 12 weeks of unpaid, job-protected leave to "eligible" employees for certain family and medical reasons. Employees are "eligible" if they have worked for a covered employer for at least one year, and for 1,250 hours over the previous 12 months, and if there are at least 50 employees within 75 miles. Similar provisions may apply to federal and congressional employees. For more information on the new federal regulations, contact the nearest office of the Wage and Hour Division, listed in most telephone directories under U.S. Government, Department of Labor, Employment Standards Administration.

The following state regulations augment and supersede the federal requirements for employers:

Alaska

Alaska's family leave law provides state and other public employees with up to 18 weeks of leave every 24 months to care for the serious health condition of a child, spouse, or parent, or for the worker's own serious health condition. Additionally, the law provides 18 weeks of leave per year to care for a newborn or newly adopted child. It covers the state and political subdivisions of the state with at least 21 employees. Workers must work at least 35 hours per week for six consecutive months or 17.5 hours per week for 12 consecutive months to be eligible.

California

California's family leave law provides up to 16 weeks of leave over two years for birth or adoption, or for the serious health condition of a child, spouse, or parent. It applies to employers of 50 or more; employees must be employed for 12 months to be eligible.

Colorado

Colorado provides employees guarantees of a "reasonable period" of leave for pregnancy, child-birth, and adoption.

Connecticut

Connecticut provides 16 weeks of family and medical leave every two years for employers of 75 or more.

Employees must be employed for 1,000 hours in the 12-month period preceding the first day of leave to be eligible. Connecticut also provides state employees with a total of 24 weeks over two years for family or medical leave.

Connecticut's pregnancy disability law provides job-guaranteed leave for the period that a worker is physically disabled due to pregnancy, childbirth, and related medical conditions. The law covers employers with three or more employees; certain family businesses are exempted.

Delaware

Delaware provides state employees who have had one year of continuous employment with six weeks of family leave for adoption or birth of a child.

District of Columbia

The District of Columbia's family and medical leave law provides up to 16 weeks of unpaid leave every two years to care for a newborn or newly adopted child or for a seriously ill family member. "Family member" is defined broadly to include a

Family and Medical Leave (cont'd)

person related by blood, legal custody, or marriage, or a person with whom an employee shares a residence in the context of a committed relationship. Sixteen weeks of medical leave every two years is separately available for the employee's own serious health condition. Covers employers of 50 or more for the first three years after enactment; covers employers of 20 or more thereafter. Employees must have worked for the employer for at least 1,000 hours during the last 12 months to be eligible.

Florida

Florida law grants up to six months of family leave per year to state employees for birth or adoption, or for the serious illness of a worker's spouse, child, or parent.

Georgia

Georgia provides up to 12 weeks of family and medical leave per year for state employees. Employees must be employed for at least 12 months and 1,040 hours to be eligible.

Hawaii

For state employees, and for private sector employers of 100 or more, Hawaii law provides employees four weeks of family leave for birth, adoption, or the serious health condition of a child, spouse, or parent.

Hawaii also provides pregnancy disability leave to all employees for the period that a worker is physically disabled by pregnancy, childbirth, or related medical conditions.

Illinois

Illinois provides certain permanent, full-time state employees with family leave of up to one year for "bona fide family responsibilities" (including birth or adoption, or care of a seriously ill family member).

Iowa

Iowa provides up to eight weeks' pregnancy disability leave. Employers with four or more employees are covered.

Kansas

Kansas provides pregnancy disability leave for the period that a worker is physically disabled by pregnancy, childbirth, or related medical conditions. Employers with four or more employees are covered.

Kentucky

Kentucky provides all employees with six weeks' leave for adopting a child under age seven.

Louisiana

Louisiana provides up to four months of leave to employees who are temporarily disabled because of pregnancy, childbirth, or related medical conditions. Only six weeks of disability leave is generally avail-

able for normal pregnancy or childbirth. Employers with 26 or more employees are covered.

Maine

Maine provides ten weeks of family and medical leave over a two-year period. Employers with 25 or more employees are covered. Employees must work for the same employer for 12 consecutive months to be eligible.

Maryland

Maryland provides 12 weeks of leave for birth, adoption, or family illness for state employees.

Massachusetts

Female employees in Massachusetts are eligible for eight weeks of leave for birth or adoption of a child under age three. Employees are eligible after completing employer's initial probationary period or three consecutive months as a full-time employee. Covers employers of six or more employees.

Minnesota

Minnesota employers with 21 or more employees must provide their employees with six weeks of leave for the birth or adoption of a child. Employees must work 12 months at 20 or more hours per week to be eligible.

Missouri

Missouri provides equal leave for childbirth and adoption for state employees.

Montana

Montana provides pregnancy disability leave for workers when temporarily disabled by pregnancy, childbirth, or related medical conditions. Covers employers with one or more employees.

New Hampshire

New Hampshire provides pregnancy disability leave for workers when temporarily disabled by pregnancy, childbirth, or related medical conditions. Covers employers of six or more.

New Jersey

New Jersey provides 12 weeks of leave over a 24-month period for birth, adoption, or the serious health condition of a child, parent, or spouse. Employers of 50 or more are covered. Employee must have been employed at least 1,000 hours in the 12 months before the leave to be eligible.

New York

New York provides equal leave for childbirth and adoption.

North Carolina

North Carolina provides all state employees with pregnancy disability leave when temporarily dis-

Family and Medical Leave (cont'd)

abled by pregnancy, childbirth, or related medical conditions.

North Dakota

North Dakota provides state employees (with one-year minimum employment at an average of 20 hours per week) four months of leave per year for birth, adoption, or serious health condition of spouse, child, or parent.

Oklahoma

Oklahoma provides state employees with 12 weeks of family leave per year for birth or adoption, or for the care of a critically ill child or dependent adult. Employees must work six months to be eligible.

Oregon

Oregon's family leave law provides employees with 12 weeks of leave every two years for the illness of a child requiring "home care," or to care for a child, spouse, or parent suffering from "any mental or physical condition requiring constant care." Covers employers with 50 or more employees.

Oregon's parental leave law provides 12 weeks of leave for the birth of a child or for adopting a child up to age 12. This law covers employers of 25 or more employees; employees are eligible after 90 days of employment. Employees hired on a seasonal or temporary basis are not covered.

Oregon provides pregnancy disability leave for the period of physical disability if such leave can be reasonably accommodated.

Rhode Island

Rhode Island provides up to 13 weeks of family medical leave over a two-year period. Covers private employers with 50 or more employees; city, town, or municipal agencies with 30 or more employees; and all state agencies. Employee must be employed for an average of 30 or more hours per week by same employer for 12 consecutive months to be eligible.

Tennessee

Tennessee provides up to four months of leave for pregnancy disability and childbirth. Covers employees who have worked full-time for 12 consecutive months at companies with 100 or more employees.

Texas

Texas provides state employees six weeks' leave for childbirth or adoption.

Vermont

Vermont provides 12 weeks of family and medical leave per year. Employers of ten or more must provide leave to care for a newborn or newly adopted child; employers of 15 or more must also provide leave to care for the serious health condition of a child, spouse, or parent, or for the worker's own serious health condition. Employees must work for at least one year for an average of 30 hours per week to be eligible.

Virginia

Virginia provides state employees with six weeks of parental leave per year for birth or adoption.

Washington

Washington's parental leave law provides 12 weeks of leave over a two-year period for the birth, adoption, or serious illness of a child. Employees must be employed 52 weeks at 35 or more hours per week to be eligible. Covers employers of 100 or more employees.

Effective October 28, 1973, Washington also provides pregnancy disability leave for the period of physical disability. Covers employees of eight or more.

West Virginia

West Virginia provides state and school employees with 12 weeks of leave per year for the birth or adoption of a child, or for the serious health condition of a spouse, child, or parent. Employees must have 12 consecutive weeks of employment to be eligible.

Wisconsin

Wisconsin provides six weeks of leave for birth or adoption of a child; two weeks of leave for serious health condition of a child, spouse, or parent; and two weeks of medical leave for a worker's own serious health condition (including pregnancy disability). No more than ten weeks may be taken in a 12-month period for any combination of these reasons. Law covers employers with 50 or more employees; an employee must be employed for 52 consecutive weeks and have worked 1,000 hours to be eligible.

Family and Medical Leave (cont'd)

Mothers Participating in Labor Force (%)

Year	With Children Under 18 Years	With Children 6-17 Years	With Children Under 6 Years
1955	27.0	38.4	18.2
1965	35.0	45.7	25.3
1975	47.4	54.8	38.9
1980	56.6	64.4	46.6
1985	62.1	69.9	53.5
1986	62.8	70.4	54.4
1987	64.7	72.0	56.7
1988	65.0	73.3	56.1
1989	NA	NA	NA
1990	66.7	74.7	58.2
1991	66.6	74.4	58.4
1992	67.2	75.9	58.0
1993	66.9	75.4	57.9

Source: 1995 Information Please Almanac

Family-Friendly Companies

The Families and Work Institute (FWI) rigorously researched work-family problems and evaluated a range of work-family solutions.

The index measures the overall responsiveness to employees' family and personal needs in light of business objectives. It covers seven primary categories: flexible work arrangements, leaves, financial assistance, corporate giving/community service, dependent-care services, management change, and work-family management.

The score for each work-family initiative is based on six criteria that the Families and Work Institute consider important:

• Impact: the program's capacity to reduce work-family conflicts.

• Coverage: the more widely available a program or services, the higher the score.

• Institutionalization: a policy that is formally written, thus sanctioning usage, will score higher.

• Commitment: a program that requires a great investment of resources in terms of money, people, time, or leadership will receive more points.

• Level of effort: the higher the complexity that the implementation of a program requires, the higher the score.

• Innovativeness: a program that is uniquely responsive scores higher.

The rankings are arranged in stages and are listed in descending order with the highest score (245) signifying the most family-friendly company in the study. Note: Only companies that participated in the study are included. The top two stages of companies are listed here.

Rankings of companies within each stage of development are based on FWI Family-Friendly Index Scores.

Most Friendly (Scores of 179+)

Aetna Life & Casualty
Corning
IBM
Johnson & Johnson

Friendly (Scores of 100-178)

3M
AlliedSignal
Allstate Insurance
American Express
AT&T
Bank of America N.T. & S.A.
Campbell Soup
Champion International
Chase Manhattan
Citicorp
Coors Brewing
Digital Equipment
Dow Chemical U.S.A.
E. I. Du Pont de Nemours
Eastman Kodak
Equitable Life Assurance Society of the U.S.
Gannett
General Dynamics
Hewlett-Packard
Hoffmann-LaRoche
Honeywell
Household
John Hancock Mutual Life Insurance
McDonnell Douglas
Merck
Metropolitan Life Insurance
Mobil
Norton
Polaroid
Procter & Gamble
Time
Travelers Insurance
US West
Warner-Lambert
Wells Fargo Bank

Companies for Working Mothers

Working Mother Ten Best for 1994

- AT&T (2)
- Barnett Banks (2)
- Fel-Pro (6)
- Glaxo (2)
- John Hancock (1)
- IBM (7)
- Johnson & Johnson (3)
- Lancaster Laboratories (1)
- NationsBank (2)
- Xerox (3)

Number in parentheses=Number of years in Top Five or Top Ten

Working Mother 100

Company	Location
3M	St. Paul, MN
Aetna Life & Casualty	Hartford, CT
Allstate Insurance	Northbrook, IL
American Airlines	Dallas/Fort Worth Airport, TX
American Express	New York, NY
American Management Systems*	Fairfax, VA
Amoco	Chicago, IL
Arthur Andersen & Co.	New York, NY
AT&T	New York, NY
Avon Products	New York, NY
Baptist Hospital of Miami	Miami, FL
Barnett Banks	Jacksonville, FL
Bausch & Lomb	Rochester, NY
Baxter International	Deerfield, IL
Bayfront Medical Center*	St. Petersburg, FL
BE&K Engineering and Construction	Birmingham, AL
Ben & Jerry's Homemade	Waterbury, VT
Boston's Beth Israel Hospital	Boston, MA
Bright Horizons Children's Centers	Cambridge, MA
The Bureau of National Affairs	Washington, DC
Leo Burnett U.S.A.	Chicago, IL
Calvert Group	Bethesda, MD
Campbell Soup	Camden, NJ
CIGNA	Philadelphia, PA
Citibank	New York, NY
CMP Publications	Manhasset, NY
The Condé Nast Publications*	New York, NY
CoreStates Financial*	Philadelphia, PA
Corning	Corning, NY
Deloitte & Touche*	Wilton, CT

Company	Location
Dow Chemical	Midland, MI
Dow Jones & Company*	New York, NY
DuPont	Wilmington, DE
Ernst & Young*	New York, NY
Exxon	Irving, TX
Federal National Mortgage Association	Washington, DC
Fel-Pro	Skokie, IL
First Chicago*	Chicago, IL
Frontier Cooperative Herbs	Norway, IA
Gannett	Arlington, VA
Genentech	S. San Francisco, CA
General Motors	Detroit, MI
Glaxco	Research Triangle Park, NC
G.T. Water Products	Moorpark, CA
Hallmark Cards	Kansas City, MO
John Hancock Mutual Life Insurance	Boston, MA
Hanna Andersson	Portland, OR
Home Box Office	New York, NY
Hewitt Associates	Lincolnshire, IL
Hill Holliday Connors Cosmopulos	Boston, MA
Hoechst Celanese	Somerville, NJ
Household	Prospect Heights, IL
IBM	Armonk, NY
Johnson & Johnson	New Brunswick, NJ
SC Johnson Wax	Racine, WI
Lancaster Laboratories	Lancaster, PA
Lincoln National	Fort Wayne, IN
Lotus Development	Cambridge, MA
Lucasfilm	San Rafael, CA
Lutheran General HealthSystem	Park Ridge, IL
Marquette Electronics	Milwaukee, WI
Marriott	Washington, DC
Massachusetts Mutual Life Insurance	Springfield, MA
Mattel	El Segundo, CA
MBNA America Bank, N.A.	Newark, DE
Mentor Graphics	Wilsonville, OR
Merck & Co.	Whitehouse Sta., NJ
The Miami Herald*	Miami, FL
Morrison & Foerster	San Francisco, CA
Motorola	Schaumburg, IL
Mutual of New York (MONY)	New York, NY
NationsBank	Charlotte, NC
Neuville Industries	Hildebran, NC
Nike	Beaverton, OR
Northern Trust	Chicago, IL

Companies for Working Mothers (cont'd)

Company	Location
NYNEX	New York, NY
Pacific Gas & Electric	San Francisco, CA
The Partnership Group*	Lansdale, PA
Patagonia	Ventura, CA
Phoenix Home Life Mutual Insurance	Hartford, CT
Pitney Bowes	Stamford, CT
Procter & Gamble	Cincinnati, OH
The Prudential Insurance Company of America	Newark, NJ
Quad/Graphics	Pewaukee, WI
Riverside Methodist Hospitals	Columbus, OH
The St. Paul Companies	St. Paul, MN
St. Petersburg Times	St. Petersburg, FL
Salt River Project*	Phoenix, AZ
SAS Institute	Cary, NC
Schering-Plough	Madison, NJ

Company	Location
The Seattle Times	Seattle, WA
Silicon Graphics	Mountain View, CA
Tom's of Maine	Kennebunk, ME
United States Hosiery	Lincolnton, NC
UNUM Life Insurance Company of America	Portland, ME
USA GROUP	Fishers, IN
WearGuard*	Norwell, MA
Wegmans Food Markets	Rochester, NY
Work/Family Directions	Boston, MA
Xerox	Stamford, CT

New to list

Source: Working Mother, Oct. 1994

Ethnicity and Bias

Race, Ethnicity, and Sex of Executives, Managers, and Administrators in Private-Industry Fields, 1994

Employment Category	Total (%)	Men (%)	Women (%)
U.S. Population, Total			
White	75.3		
Hispanic	9.0		
Black	12.0		
Asian/Pacific Islander	2.9		
Native American	0.8		
Business Services			
White	84.4	51.6	32.8
Hispanic	8.4	5.2	3.2
Black	4.0	3.5	0.5
Asian	2.9	1.7	1.2
Finance			
White	82.4	44.8	37.6
Hispanic	8.4	3.4	5.0
Black	5.2	2.6	2.6
Asian	4.4	1.8	2.6
Insurance			
White	82.4	44.0	40.7
Hispanic	8.4	2.0	4.2
Black	6.2	3.2	3.0
Asian	4.4	0.5	1.7
Communications			
White	84.0	58.4	25.6
Hispanic	9.5	6.1	3.4
Black	3.4	2.4	1.0
Asian	2.0	1.7	0.3

Ethnicity and Bias (cont'd)

Employment Category	Total (%)	Men (%)	Women (%)
Retail Trade			
White	80.8	41.7	39.1
Hispanic	4.8	2.8	2.0
Black	4.9	2.3	2.6
Asian	5.2	3.5	1.7
Transportation			
White	85.0	58.4	25.6
Hispanic	9.5	6.1	3.4
Black	3.4	2.4	1.0
Asian	2.0	1.7	0.3
Utilities			
White	89.1	71.9	17.2
Hispanic	3.9	3.1	0.7
Black	3.9	3.1	0.8
Asian	0.8	0.0	0.8
Wholesale Trade			
White	89.6	53.4	36.2
Hispanic	4.8	2.7	2.1
Black	1.5	1.2	0.3
Asian	4.2	2.4	1.8

Source: Glass Ceiling Commission, U.S. Department of Labor

According to a study by the Equal Employment Opportunity Commission, firing was the most common employment bias issue in 1994 as well as 1993. However, sexual harassment issues showed the largest increase between 1993 and 1994.

Top Employment Bias Issues, 1994

Issue	Complaints in 1994	Change from 1993 (%)
Firing	42,756	-1.9
Working conditions	15,029	10.4
Non-sexual harassment	11,657	12.5
Sexual harassment	8,234	13.2
Promotion	8,060	4.5
Hiring	7,252	-8.2
Wages	6,482	2.9
Layoff	5,382	-2.3

Source: U.S. Equal Employment Opportunity Commission

Affirmative Action

EMPLOYERS ALL OVER THE COUNTRY sign contracts with the federal government guaranteeing nondiscrimination and equal opportunity in all their employment practices. In these contracts, employers also agree to take affirmative action to hire and promote workers who traditionally have been discriminated against in the job market.

Each year, the U.S. government awards hundreds of thousands of these contracts for supplies, services, use of property, and construction work, totaling over $200 billion. Construction contractors, banks, utilities, insurance and real estate companies, manufacturers, producers, builders, and universities are among those who do federal contract and subcontract work.

Under two statutes and one executive order, minorities, women, members of religious and ethnic groups, handicapped persons, and Vietnam and disabled veterans of all wars are protected by the Equal Employment Opportunity Commission (EEOC) and affirmative action requirements. These state that special efforts must be made by employers in outreach, recruitment, training, and other areas to help members of protected groups compete for jobs and promotions on an equal footing with other applicants and employees. Affirmative action is not preferential treatment. Nor does it mean that unqualified persons should be promoted over other people. What affirmative action does mean is that positive steps must be taken to provide equal employment opportunity.

Enforcement of these contracts is carried out by the Office of Federal Contract Compliance Programs (OFCCP), a division of the U.S. Department of Labor's Employment Standards Administration. OFCCP's compliance officers regularly review the employment practices of federal contractors, subcontractors, and federally assisted construction contractors to determine whether or not they are fulfilling their EEOC and affirmative action obligations.

Complaints of Discrimination

Individuals who are protected by the contract compliance programs may file complaints if they believe that they have been discriminated against by federal contractors, subcontractors, or federally assisted construction contractors or subcontractors. Complaints may also be filed by organizations or other individuals on behalf of the person or persons affected.

If a complaint filed under the Executive Order involves discrimination against only one person, OFCCP will refer it to the EEOC, an independent agency. Cases that involve groups of people or indicate patterns of discrimination are generally investigated by the OFCCP.

Complaints must be filed within 180 days from the date of the alleged discrimination, unless the time for filing is extended because of a good reason, which requires approval by the OFCCP director.

Persons filing complaints should include a description of the discrimination involved and any other related information which would assist in an investigation.

Complaints may be filed directly with the OFCCP in Washington, DC, or with any of the program's regional offices throughout the country.

Enforcing Contract Compliance

When a complaint is filed, or a compliance review turns up problems, the OFCCP attempts to enter into a conciliation agreement with the contractor.

A conciliation agreement may include back pay, seniority credit, promotions, or other forms of relief for the victims of discrimination. It may also involve new training programs, special recruitment efforts, or other affirmative action measures.

The conciliation agreement allows the contractor to continue doing government business, and guarantees that employees' rights are protected.

When conciliation efforts are unsuccessful, the OFCCP moves to enforcement. Federal rules and regulations set forth administrative and judicial procedures to be followed when enforcement actions are necessary.

Contractors or subcontractors cited for violating their EEO and affirmative action requirements may have a formal hearing before an administrative law judge. If conciliation is not reached before or after the hearing, sanctions may be imposed. For example, contractors or subcontractors could lose their government contracts or subcontracts; they could have payments withheld by the government; or they could be declared ineligible for any federal contract work.

In some cases the Department of Justice, on behalf of the Department of Labor, may file suit in federal court against a contractor for violation of the contract requirements.

For more information about contract compliance, filing complaints, or special assistance, contact any of the OFCCP's ten regional offices, or get in touch with a program area office, listed in the telephone directory under U.S. Department of Labor, Employment Standards Administration, Office of Federal Contract Compliance Programs.

Contact Option

The Office of Federal Contract
Compliance Programs
U.S. Department of Labor
200 Constitution Ave., NW, Room C-3325
Washington, DC 20210
(202) 219-9430

Unemployment Benefits

Unemployment Insurance by State, 1992

State	Beneficiaries' First Payments ($ thousands)	Benefits Paid ($ millions)	Average Weekly Unemployment Benefits ($)
TOTAL	9,243	25,153	174
Alabama	157	209	121
Alaska	44	117	170
Arizona	90	211	147
Arkansas	100	185	151
California	1,444	3,852	152
Colorado	79	179	178
Connecticut	157	587	211
Delaware	29	72	181
District of Columbia	27	128	228
Florida	339	861	158
Georgia	232	381	148
Hawaii	39	138	240
Idaho	46	84	156
Illinois	391	1,339	183
Indiana	150	217	126
Iowa	89	195	170
Kansas	71	189	179
Kentucky	127	228	144
Louisiana	110	210	118
Maine	59	146	167
Maryland	145	461	180
Massachusetts	249	1,036	226
Michigan	487	1,288	211
Minnesota	134	409	198
Mississippi	79	129	123
Missouri	184	380	146
Montana	25	45	135
Nebraska	33	50	133
Nevada	60	155	168
New Hampshire	40	61	136
New Jersey	340	1,429	225
New Mexico	32	73	138
New York	673	2,635	197
North Carolina	244	378	158
North Dakota	15	30	146
Ohio	357	972	180
Oklahoma	66	148	159
Oregon	142	382	172
Pennsylvania	518	1,751	201
Rhode Island	61	196	206
South Carolina	125	215	143
South Dakota	9	12	128
Tennessee	190	289	124
Texas	430	1,181	176
Utah	38	82	174
Vermont	26	66	155
Virginia	138	288	164
Washington	219	661	176
West Virginia	61	148	163
Wisconsin	216	463	175
Wyoming	12	29	163

Source: 1994 Statistical Abstract, Table No. 591

Benefits Checklist

Percent of Full-Time Employees Participating in Selected Employee Benefit Programs

Employee Benefit Program	All Employees	Professional & Technical	Clerical & Sales	Production & Service
PAID				
Vacations	96	97	98	95
Holidays	92	93	94	90
Jury duty leave	86	92	88	82
Funeral leave	80	84	82	77
Rest time	67	58	67	71
Military leave	54	63	56	48
Sick leave	67	87	82	48
Personal leave	21	29	26	13
Lunch time	8	5	4	11
Maternity leave	2	3	2	1
Paternity leave	1	1	1	NA
UNPAID				
Maternity leave	37	43	38	33
Paternity leave	26	31	26	23
INSURANCE PLANS				
Medical care	83	85	81	84
Noncontributory	41	38	35	46
Hospital/room and board	83	85	81	84
Inpatient surgery	83	85	81	84
Mental health care	81	83	79	82
Dental	60	67	60	57
Extended-care facility	66	70	66	66
Home health care	67	71	66	66
Hospice care	46	48	45	45
Vision*	23	21	21	25
In HMOs	14	15	15	12
Alcohol abuse treatment	82	83	80	82
Inpatient detoxification	81	82	79	81
Inpatient rehabilitation	64	63	63	66
Outpatient	64	66	63	64
Drug abuse treatment	81	83	79	80
Inpatient detoxification	80	82	79	80
Inpatient rehabilitation	63	62	62	65
Outpatient	62	65	62	61
Life	94	98	95	92
Noncontributory	80	83	82	77
Accident/sickness	45	32	35	57
Noncontributory	33	19	23	46
Long-term disability	40	61	49	24
Noncontributory	31	46	38	20
RETIREMENT AND SAVINGS PLANS				
Defined-benefit pension	59	60	56	59
Earnings-based formula	41	52	46	32
Defined contribution	48	57	53	39
Savings and thrift	29	38	35	20
EMPLOYEE STOCK OWNERSHIP				
Deferred profit-sharing	3	4	4	2
Money purchase pension	16	13	16	18

Benefits Checklist (cont'd)

Percent of Full-Time Employees Participating in Selected Employee Benefit Programs

Employee Benefit Program	All Employees	Professional & Technical	Clerical & Sales	Production & Service
ADDITIONAL BENEFITS				
Parking	7	11	7	5
Educational assistance	88	86	85	92
Travel accident insurance	72	87	73	64
Severance pay	42	55	47	32
Relocation allowance	41	55	48	30
Recreation facilities	31	50	30	21
Nonproduction bonuses, cash	26	34	25	23
Child care	35	33	36	35
Flexible benefits plans	8	11	9	5
Reimbursement accounts	10	16	10	6
Elder care	36	48	40	26
Long-term care insurance	9	11	12	6
Wellness programs	4	6	5	2
Employee assistance programs	35	47	34	28

Source: 1994 Statistical Abstract, Table No. 673

Sampling of Benefit Plans and Programs Offered by Employers

Accidental death and dismemberment insurance
Adoption benefits
Birthdays (time off)
Business and professional memberships
Cash profit-sharing
Civic activities (time off)
Club memberships
Company medical assistance
Company-provided or subsidized automobiles
Company-provided housing
Company-provided or subsidized travel
Credit unions
Day-care centers
Death leave
Deferred bonus
Deferred compensation plan
Deferred profit-sharing
Dental and eye-care insurance
Discount on company products
Discount on other products
Educational activities (time off)
Education costs
Employment contract
Executive dining room
Financial counseling
Free or subsidized lunches
Group automobile insurance
Group homeowners insurance
Group legal insurance
Group life insurance

Health maintenance organization fees
Holidays
Home health care
Hospital-surgical-medical insurance
Interest-free loans
Layoff pay
Legal, estate planning, and other professional
  assistance
Loans of company equipment
Long-term disability benefits
Matching educational, charitable contributions
Nurseries
Nursing home care
Outside medical services
Paid attendance at business, professional, and
  other outside meetings
Parking facilities
Pension
Personal accident insurance
Personal counseling
Personal credit cards
Personal liability insurance
Physical examinations
Physical fitness programs
Political activities (time off)
Pre-retirement counseling
Price discount plan
Professional activities
Psychiatric services
Recreation facilities, sports activities
Resort facilities
Retirement gratuity

Benefits Checklist (cont'd)

Sabbatical leave
Salary continuation
Savings plan
Scholarships for dependents
Severance pay
Sickness and accident insurance
Social Security
Social service sabbaticals
Split-dollar insurance
State disability plans

Stock appreciation rights
Stock bonus plans
Stock option plans (qualified, nonqualified, tandem)
Stock purchase plans
Survivors' benefits
Tax assistance
Training program
Travel accident insurance
Vacations
Weekly indemnity insurance

Source: Buck Consultants

Choosing a Benefits Program

The SBA's Tips for Choosing a Benefits Program

1. What do you want to offer your employees?

What are the specific needs of your employees, such as child care, health and dental coverage, or a pension plan? How extensive will coverage be and what eligibility requirements will apply? Will employees contribute to the plan or will you pay for the entire package?

2. How much can you afford to spend on employee benefits?

In addition to the price of the benefit package, you must estimate:

- Start-up costs

- Implementation costs

- Ongoing administrative expenses

- Additional bookkeeping and tax preparation expenses

- Fees for professional tax and legal counsel.

These costs will be affected by plan design, management, and the business's administrative practices.

3. Does the plan provide tax advantages?

Will you or your employees benefit from any tax advantages? Are there similar plans with greater tax advantages you should consider? Will you be able to adapt to future changes in the tax code?

4. Is the plan legal?

In 1974, the Employee Retirement Security Act (ERISA) required employers who provide pension plans to meet certain minimum standards. From 1981 to 1986, five major tax laws further specified the legal requirements for providing retirement benefits to employees. The Tax Reform Act of 1986 included new "non-discrimination" rules on health and life insurance plans governed by Section 89 of the IRS Code. In November 1989, these changes to Section 89 were repealed because of the great burden it would have placed on employers to prove their benefit plans did not discriminate.

> **TIP:** *Every May brings a new edition of Job Hotlines USA, which features over 800 job hotlines operated by businesses nationwide. Call (800) 829-5220 to order. It costs $24.95. Another item available is Government Job Finder, which costs $16.95.*

Child Care and Elder Care Services

ONE OF THE MOST IMPORTANT issues facing employers today involves "family-responsive policies" in the workplace. Programs and policies are being established in many businesses as employers try to assist their employees in balancing the responsibilities of work and family. Under the auspices of the Women's Bureau of the U.S. Department of Labor, the Work and Family Clearinghouse was established to help employers identify the most appropriate policies for responding to the needs of employees and their dependents.

The Clearinghouse offers technical assistance to individualize the employees' needs, and guidance to both national and state information sources, bibliographic references, conference information, research, and statistics in five areas relating to child care and/or elder care:

- Direct services such as onsite/offsite centers, consortium centers, after school/summer camps, family day care networks, emergency/sick-child care, "warmline" phones for school-age children;

- Information services such as resource and referral, parenting seminars, caregiver fairs, publications;

- Financial assistance such as vouchers/reimbursement, purchase of space discounts, flexible spending accounts, salary reduction plans, contributions to community resources;

- Cooperative policies such as flextime, job sharing, flexiplace, telecommuting, part-time work, cafeteria-style benefits, maternity/parental leave;

- Public-private partnerships such as projects which address child care and elder care needs within communities.

Among the specific materials now available to employers are individual company "Program Profiles" which describe 100 employer-sponsored child care and/or elder care programs in operation around the nation. "How-to" guides address 26 work/family options, including onsite and offsite child care centers, family day care networks, flexible leave policies, resource and referral services, and the Dependent Care Assistance Program (DCAP).

The Clearinghouse responds to written or telephone inquiries from employers, unions, and other interested organizations.

Another valuable resource is the Families and Work Institute, a non-profit research and planning organization committed to developing new approaches to balancing the needs of families with workplace productivity. The Institute deals with all issues from prenatal care to elder care, and management from the perspective of worker as well as manager.

This organization covers four areas of interest:

- Policy research;

- Dissemination of information through conferences, seminars, publications, and public speaking;

- Strategic planning by advising government, business, and community organizations on the design, implementation, and evaluation of work-family solutions;

- Management training for corporations wishing to respond to work-family needs.

Contact Options

Women's Bureau Work and Family Clearinghouse
U.S. Department of Labor
200 Constitution Ave., NW
Washington, DC 20210
(800) 827-5335 or (202) 219-4486

Telephone hours are from 11:00 A.M. to 4:00 P.M. (EST) Monday through Thursday and from 11:00 A.M. to 3:00 P.M. on Friday.

Eldercare Locator
(800) 677-1116

Run by the National Association of Area Agencies on Aging, the Eldercare Locator provides information on services for older people specific to the caller's location.

Recommended Resource

Families and Work Institute
330 Seventh Ave., 14th Floor
New York, NY 10001
(212) 465-2044

Father-Friendly Companies

Child Magazine and the Families and Work Institute have identified ten companies who have made a real effort to support paternity leave, training on childbirth and child-development issues for dads, flexible and comprehensive on-site day care, and other father-friendly policies. The ten best are:

Apple Computer
AT&T
Ben & Jerry's
DuPont
Eastman Kodak
John Hancock Financial Services
Los Angeles Department of Water and Power
Peabody and Arnold
Sacramento County Sheriff's Department
Tom's of Maine

Source: Child Magazine and the Fatherhood Project, Families and Work Institute

Outplacement Firms & Headhunters

Major Search Firms in the U.S.

Firm	Headquarters	Telephone Number
A. T. Kearney	Chicago	(312) 648-0111
Battalia Winston	New York	(212) 308-8080
D. E. Foster Partners	New York	(212) 872-6232
DHR	Chicago	(312) 782-1581
Diversified Search Companies	Philadelphia	(215) 732-6666
Egon Zehnder	New York	(212) 838-9199
Gilbert Tweed Associates	New York	(212) 758-3000
Goodrich & Sherwood	New York	(212) 697-4131
Gould & McCoy	New York	(212) 688-8671
Handy HRM	New York	(212) 557-0400
Heidrick & Struggles	Chicago	(312) 372-8811
Howe-Lewis	New York	(212) 697-5000
Korn/Ferry	New York	(212) 687-1834
Lamalie Amrop	New York	(212) 953-7900
Norman Broadbent	New York	(212) 953-6990
Paul Ray Berndtson	Fort Worth	(817) 334-0500
Russell Reynolds	New York	(212) 351-2000
Sampson, Neill & Wilkins	Upper Montclair, NJ	(201) 783-9600
Ward Howell	New York	(212) 697-3730
Witt, Keiffer, Ford, Hadelman, Lloyd	Oakbrook, IL	(708) 990-1370

Human Resource Software Systems

A NUMBER OF FIRMS MANUFACTURE low-cost management-software systems designed to assist corporations in employee selection, motivation, evaluation, and integration. Using a brief questionnaire, the software can create a comprehensive profile. The computer program is designed to analyze the individual's behavioral traits, stress and energy styles, and organizational skills.

Contact Options

Consulting Psychologists Press
3803 E. Bayshore Rd.
Palo Alto, CA 94303
(415) 969-8901
    This company has an extensive catalogue of management software systems and training programs.

Professional Dynametric Programs
400 W. Highway 24, Suite 201
Woodland Park, CO 80866
(719) 687-6074
    This software manufacturer will also provide training in how to use and interpret the test results.

Job Interview Tips

Preparation

- Learn about the organization;
- Have a specific job or jobs in mind;
- Review your qualifications for the job;
- Prepare answers to broad questions about yourself;
- Review your résumé;
- Practice an interview with a friend or relative;
- Arrive before the scheduled time of your interview.

Personal Appearance

- Be well groomed;
- Dress appropriately;
- Do not chew gum or smoke.

The Interview

- Answer each question concisely;
- Respond promptly;
- Use good manners. Learn the name of your interviewer and shake hands as you meet;
- Use proper English and avoid slang;
- Be cooperative and enthusiastic;
- Ask questions about the position and the organization;
- Thank the interviewer and follow up with a letter.

Test (if given)

- Listen closely to instructions;
- Read each question carefully;
- Write legibly and clearly;
- Budget your time wisely and don't dwell on one question.

Information to Bring to an Interview

- Social Security number;
- Driver's license number;
- Résumé. Although not all employers require applicants to bring a résumé, you should be able to furnish the interviewer with information about your education, training, and previous employment;
- References. Usually an employer requires three references. Get permission from people before using their names, and make sure they will give you a good reference. Avoid using relatives. For each reference, provide the following information: name, address, telephone number, and job title.

Source: U.S. Department of Labor, Bureau of Labor Statistics

Job Interview Questions

MANY MANAGERS ENCOUNTER a mental block when facing an interview. A checklist of questions makes it easier to elicit revealing answers from a job candidate.

Martin Yate, an employment analyst and best-selling author, has collected more than twenty questions that are of use in most interview settings.

According to Yate, some of the most important skill sets we can have for employees in the coming years are:

- analytical skills
- speed and mental processing
- ability to work with others
- understanding of the necessity of taking direction.

The following questions will help you explore these areas with a job candidate:

- How would you describe the ideal job for you?
- What kind of work interests you most?
- How many levels of management did you interact with?
- What was the job's biggest challenge?
- If you were hiring for this position, what would you be looking for?
- What have you done that shows initiative and willingness to work?
- Why are you interviewing with us?
- What special characteristics should I consider about you?
- How do you plan your day?
- How do you plan your week?
- How do you determine your priorities?

Job Interview Questions (cont'd)

- What happens when two priorities compete for your time?
- What's the toughest communication problem you faced?
- When have your verbal communications been important enough to follow up in writing?
- Tell me about the time when someone has lost his/her temper at you in a business environment.
- Have you ever worked in a place where it seemed to be just one crisis after another?
- How did you handle it? How did you feel?
- What do you see as some of your most pressing developmental needs?

- Define cooperation.
- What quality should a successful manager possess?
- How have past managers gotten the best out of you?
- A two-part question. Describe the best manager you've ever had. Describe the toughest manager you've ever had.
- And last, for what have you been most frequently criticized?

Sources for Interns

SEVERAL COMPANIES PUBLISH directories with extensive listings of internships available in a wide range of industries. Prospective interns may contact corporations listed therein. A few of these companies also provide access to data bases with listings of interns and internships, and will do an executive search for a small fee. Subscribing to one of these services may provide an inexpensive alternative to hiring a search firm or placing classified ads.

Recommended Resources

National Society for Experiential Education
3509 Haworth Dr., Suite 207
Raleigh, NC 27609
(919) 787-3263
   This professional association of educators, career counselors, and employers who sponsor interns is the best place to start if you want to explore

incorporating an internship into your business. This organization promotes internships by providing information, referrals, publications, and consulting services to businesses and educational institutions. NSEE also publishes a directory of internships available across the country.

Internships, 1995
Peterson's, $29.95
202 Carnegie Center
P.O. Box 2123
Princeton, NJ 08543
(609) 243-9111

The Top Reference Sources

Hiring the Best
Bob Adams Publishers, $9.95
(800) 872-5627

This fourth edition of Martin Yate's indispensable book includes more than 400 interview questions. The book also includes a chapter on what consti-

tutes a discriminatory, or perhaps illegal, interviewing question, an in-depth review of what it will take to recruit the best in the '90s, information on drug testing, plus four ready-to-use outlines for use as a starting point in critical interview areas: management, sales, recent graduates, and clerical.

Employee Relocation Firms

MORE THAN HALF THE COMPANIES that relocate employees on a regular basis contract with a relocation firm that will help in the purchasing, managing, and disposing of the former homes of relocated employees. In general, the client company retains full ownership responsibilities for the homes during the time the employee agrees to accept the company's offer until the time of closing the sale. Home purchase firms charge a fee for their role in establishing a fair market value for the home, maintaining it after the employee has relocated, and managing the sale. The following relocation firms are among the largest in the country:

Contact Options

Associates Relocation Management
250 E. Carpenter Freeway
Irving, TX 75062
(800) 241-6529 or (214) 541-6700

Coldwell Banker Relocation Services
27271 Las Ramblas
Mission Viejo, CA 92691
(714) 367-2500

PHH Homequity
249 Danbury Rd.
Wilton, CT 06897
(203) 834-8500

Prudential Relocation Management
200 Summit Lake Dr.
Valhalla, NY 10595
(914) 741-6111

Relocation Resources
(Eastern Operations Center)
120 Longwater Dr.
Norwell, MA 02061
(617) 871-4500

Relocation Resources
(Western Operations Center)
1099 18th St.,#1900
Denver, CO 80202
(303) 297-0500

Cost-of-Living Values in Selected Locations

The following table is based on a family of four with a $60,000 annual income, residing in a 2,200-square-foot home that carries a current mortgage, and incurring all normal home ownership and maintenance costs. They own two cars: a late-model car driven 14,000 miles per year and a four-year-old model driven 6,000 miles yearly. Car expenses include both fixed and operating costs. They pay federal, state, and local income taxes. They also pay sales taxes and purchase goods and services typical for a family in their income bracket at their location. This family has also set aside a certain amount for investments and savings. Costing is based on representative communities surrounding the core city in which families earning $60,000 yearly are most likely to reside.

Location	Total Annual Costs ($)	Index
Los Angeles, CA	72,943	121.6
Washington, DC	71,314	118.9
Chicago, IL	66,176	110.3
Atlanta, GA	62,935	104.9
Seattle, WA	62,184	103.6
Miami, FL	61,281	102.1
STANDARD CITY, USA	60,000	100.0
Denver, CO	59, 451	99.1
Salt Lake City, UT	58,757	97.9
Albuquerque, NM	58,692	97.8
Louisville, KY	58,443	97.4
San Antonio, TX	55,713	92.9

Average Annual Home Rental Costs in Ten Expensive Locations Nationwide

The annual rental values shown in the table below are based on an 800-square-foot, three-room, one-bedroom, one-bath rental unit. This accommodation is typical for a single renter earning $25,000 in annual income in Standard City, USA. Rental units are typically located in communities surrounding the core city. The ranking is based on an analysis of nearly 300 population centers nationwide.

Location	Annual Rental Costs ($)	Index
Honolulu, HI	12,480	244.7
San Francisco, CA	9,270	181.8
Washington, DC	8,980	176.1
San Jose, CA	8,820	172.9
Boston, MA	8,740	171.4
New York, NY	8,720	171.0
Los Angeles, CA	7,880	154.5
Princeton, NJ	7,680	150.6
Chicago, IL	7,440	145.9
Philadelphia, PA	7,050	138.2
STANDARD CITY, USA	5,100	100.0

Source: Runzheimer International, 1994

Employee Relocation Firms (cont'd)

Average Annual Rental Costs in Ten Inexpensive Locations Nationwide

Location	Annual Rental Costs ($)	Index
Corbin, KY	2,400	47.1
Newport, TN	3,060	60.0
Scottsboro, AL	3,060	60.0
Hennessey, OK	3,180	62.4
Casper, WY	3,180	62.4
Roanoke Rapids, NC	3,540	69.4
Midland, TX	3,600	70.6
Austin, MN	3,660	71.8
Hobbs, NM	3,660	71.8
Lafayette, LA	3,720	72.9
STANDARD CITY, USA	5,100	100.0

Average Cost to Relocate Employees ($)

Year	Homeowners	Renters	New Hires
1986	34,984	9,218	NA
1987	36,253	10,503	12,847
1988	36,891	9,924	13,192
1989	40,939	10,666	13,937
1990	45,620	13,139	15,955
1991	44,804	13,358	17,903
1992	48,426	14,272	28,900
1993	49,601	14,405	20,494
1994	50,101	15,826	20,789

Source: Runzheimer International, 1994

Total Annual Vehicle Costs in Five Expensive U.S. Locations

The total annual vehicle costs shown above are based on a 1995 Ford Taurus GL, 6-cylinder, 4-door sedan driven 15,000 miles per year with a 4-year, 60,000-mile retention cycle. Costs include both ownership expenses of insurance, depreciation, license and registration fees, and miscellaneous taxes; and operating expenses of fuel, oil, tires, and maintenance. The table above is based on an analysis of 90 locations nationwide, and the vehicle costed is driven within a 50-mile radius of the central city.

Location	Total Annual Cost ($)	Cost per Mile (cents)
Los Angeles, CA	8,375	55.8
Boston, MA	7,476	49.8
Philadelphia, PA	7,344	49.0
Providence, RI	7,277	48.5
Hartford, CT	7,195	48.0

Total Annual Vehicle Costs in Five Inexpensive U.S. Locations

Location	Total Annual Cost ($)	Cost per Mile (cents)
Sioux Falls, SD	5,368	35.8
Bismarck, ND	5,445	36.3
Burlington, VT	5,459	36.4
Boise, ID	5,509	36.7
Nashville, TN	5,564	37.1

Source: Runzheimer International, 1994

Labor Union Directory

Actors' Equity Association
165 W. 46th St.
New York, NY 10036
(212) 869-8530

Amalgamated Clothing and Textile Workers Union
15 Union Sq.
New York, NY 10003
(212) 242-0700

Amalgamated Transit Union
5025 Wisconsin Ave., NW
Washington, DC 20016
(202) 537-1645

American Association of University Professors
1012 14th St., NW, Suite 500
Washington, DC 20005
(202) 737-5900

American Federation of Government Employees
80 F St., NW
Washington, DC 20001
(202) 737-8700

American Federation of Grain Millers
4949 Olson Memorial Hwy.
Minneapolis, MN 55422
(612) 545-0211

Labor Union Directory (cont'd)

American Federation of Musicians of the United
States and Canada
1501 Broadway, Suite 600
New York, NY 10036
(212) 869-1330

American Federation of State, County and
Municipal Employees
1625 L St., NW
Washington, DC 20036
(202) 429-1000

American Federation of Teachers
555 New Jersey Ave., NW
Washington, DC 20001
(202) 879-4400

American Federation of Television and Radio Artists
260 Madison Ave., Seventh Floor
New York, NY 10016

American Nurses' Association
600 Maryland Ave., SW, Suite 100 West
Washington, DC 20024
(202) 651-7000

American Postal Workers Union
1300 L St., NW
Washington, DC 20005
(202) 842-4200

Associated Actors and Artistes of America
165 W. 46th St.
New York, NY 10036
(212) 869-0358

Association of Flight Attendants
1625 Massachusetts Ave., NW
Washington, DC 20036
(202) 328-5400

Brotherhood of Locomotive Engineers
Standard Building
1370 Ontario St.
Cleveland, OH 44113
(216) 241-2630

Brotherhood of Maintenance of Way Employees
12050 Woodward Ave.
Detroit, MI 48203
(313) 868-0490

California School Employees Association
2045 Lundy Ave.
P.O. Box 640
San Jose, CA 95106
(408) 263-8000

Civil Service Employees Association
143 Washington Ave.
Albany, NY 12210
(518) 434-0191

Communications Workers of America
501 Third St., NW
Washington, DC 20001
(202) 434-1100

Federation of Nurses and Health Professionals
555 New Jersey Ave., NW
Washington, DC 20001
(202) 879-4491

Graphic Communications International Union
1900 L St., NW
Washington, DC 20036
(202) 462-1400

International Air Line Pilots Association
1625 Massachusetts Ave., NW
Washington, DC 20036
(202) 797-4010

International Alliance of Theatrical Stage
Employees and Moving Picture Machine
Operators of the United States and Canada
1515 Broadway, Suite 601
New York, NY 10036
(212) 730-1770

International Association of Bridge, Structural and
Ornamental Iron Workers
1750 New York Ave., NW, Suite 400
Washington, DC 20006
(202) 383-4800

International Association of Fire Fighters
1750 New York Ave., NW
Washington, DC 20006
(202) 737-8484

International Association of Machinists and
Aerospace Workers
9000 Machinists Pl.
Upper Marlboro, MD 20772
(301) 967-4500

International Brotherhood of Boilermakers, Iron
Ship Builders, Blacksmiths,
Forgers and Helpers
753 State Ave.
Kansas City, KS 66101
(913) 371-2640

International Brotherhood of Electrical Workers
1125 15th St., NW
Washington, DC 20005
(202) 833-7000

Labor Union Directory (cont'd)

International Brotherhood of Firemen and Oilers
1100 Circle 75 Pkwy., Suite 350
Atlanta, GA 30339
(404) 933-9104

International Brotherhood of Painters and Allied
Trades of the United States and Canada
1750 New York Ave., NW
Washington, DC 20006
(202) 637-0700

International Brotherhood of Teamsters
25 Louisiana Ave., NW
Washington, DC 20001
(202) 624-6800

International Chemical Workers Union
1655 W. Market St.
Akron, OH 44313
(216) 867-2444

International Ladies' Garment Workers' Union
1710 Broadway
New York, NY 10019
(212) 265-7000

International Longshoremen's Association
17 Battery Pl., Suite 1530
New York, NY 10004
(212) 425-1200

International Longshoremen's and Warehousemen's
Union
1188 Franklin St.
San Francisco, CA 94109
(415) 775-0533

International Union of Allied Industrial Workers of
America
3520 W. Oklahoma Ave.
P.O. Box 343913
Milwaukee, WI 53215
(414) 645-9500

International Union of Aluminum, Brick and Glass
Workers
3362 Hollenberg Dr.
Bridgeton, MO 63044
(314) 739-6142

International Union of Bakery, Confectionery and
Tobacco Workers
10401 Connecticut Ave.
Kensington, MD 20895
(301) 933-8600

International Union of Bricklayers and Allied
Craftsmen
815 15th St., NW
Washington, DC 20005
(202) 783-3788

International Union of Electronic, Electrical,
Salaried, Machine and Furniture Workers
1126 16th St., NW
Washington, DC 20036
(202) 296-1201

International Union of Glass, Molders, Pottery,
Plastics and Allied Workers
608 E. Baltimore Pike
P.O. Box 607
Media, PA 19063
(610) 565-5051

International Union of Hotel Employees and
Restaurant Employees
1219 28th St., NW
Washington, DC 20007
(202) 393-4373

International Union of Operating Engineers
1125 17th St., NW
Washington, DC 20036
(202) 429-9100

International Union of Police Associations
1016 Duke St.
Alexandria, VA 22314
(703) 549-7473

International Union of United Automobile,
Aerospace and Agricultural Implement Workers of
America
8000 E. Jefferson Ave.
Detroit, MI 48214
(313) 926-5000

International Woodworkers of America
25 Cornell Ave.
Gladstone, OR 97027
(503) 656-1475

Laborers' International Union of North America
905 16th St., NW
Washington, DC 20006
(202) 737-8320

National Association of Letter Carriers
100 Indiana Ave., NW
Washington, DC 20001
(202) 393-4695

National Education Association
1201 16th St., NW
Washington, DC 20036
(202) 833-4000

National Federation of Federal Employees
1016 16th St., NW
Washington, DC 20036
(202) 862-4400

Labor Union Directory (cont'd)

National Fraternal Order of Police
1410 Donelson Pike, Suite A-17
Nashville, TN 37217
(615) 399-0900

National Marine Engineers' Beneficial Association
444 N. Capitol St., NW, Suite 800
Washington, DC 20001
(202) 638-5355

National Rural Letter Carriers' Association
1448 Duke St.
Alexandria, VA 22314
(703) 684-5545

National Treasury Employees Union
901 E St. NW
Washington, DC 20004
(202) 783-4444

National Union of Hospital and Health Care
Employees
505 Eighth Ave.
New York, NY 10018
(212) 239-3590

The Newspaper Guild
8611 Second Ave.
Silver Spring, MD 20910
(301) 585-2990

Office and Professional Employees International
Union
265 W. 14th St., Suite 610
New York, NY 10011
(212) 675-3210

Oil, Chemical and Atomic Workers International
Union
P.O. Box 281200
Denver, CO 80228
(303) 987-2229

Operative Plasterers' and Cement Masons' International Association of the United States and Canada
1125 17th St., NW
Washington, DC 20036
(202) 393-6569

Retail, Wholesale and Department Store Union
30 E. 29th St.
New York, NY 10016
(212) 684-5300

Screen Actors Guild
7065 Hollywood Blvd.
Hollywood, CA 90028
(213) 465-4600

Service Employees' International Union
1313 L St., NW
Washington, DC 20005
(202) 898-3200

Sheet Metal Workers' International Association
1750 New York Ave., NW
Washington, DC 20006
(202) 783-5880

State Employees Association of North Carolina
P.O. Drawer 27727
Raleigh, NC 27611
(919) 833-6436

Transport Workers Union of America
80 West End Ave.
New York, NY 10023
(212) 873-6000

Transportation Communications International Union
3 Research Pl.
Rockville, MD 20850
(301) 948-4910

United Brotherhood of Carpenters and Joiners of
America
101 Constitution Ave., NW
Washington, DC 20001
(202) 546-6206

United Electrical, Radio and Machine Workers of
America
2400 Oliver Bldg.
535 Smithfield St.
Pittsburgh, PA 15222
(412) 471-8919

United Food and Commercial Workers International
Union
1775 K St., NW
Washington, DC 20006
(202) 223-3111

United Mine Workers of America
900 15th St., NW
Washington, DC 20005
(202) 842-7200

United Paperworkers International Union
3340 Perimeter Hill Dr.
Nashville, TN 37211
(615) 834-8590

United Rubber, Cork, Linoleum and Plastic Workers
of America
570 White Pond Dr.
Akron, OH 44320
(216) 869-0320

Labor Union Directory (cont'd)

United Steelworkers of America
5 Gateway Center
Pittsburgh, PA 15222
(412) 562-2400

United Transportation Union
14600 Detroit Ave.
Cleveland, OH 44107
(216) 228-9400

Utility Workers Union of America
815 16th St., NW, Room 605
Washington, DC 20006
(202) 347-8105

Note: Unions listed here have 25,000 or more members

Source: 1994/1995 Directory of U.S. Labor Organizations

Collective Bargaining

Major Collective Bargaining Agreements: Wage Rate Changes (%)

Changes	1980	1985	1990	1991	1992	1993
AVERAGE WAGE RATE CHANGE (pro-rated over all workers)	9.9	3.3	3.5	3.6	3.1	3.0
Source						
Current settlements	3.6	0.7	1.3	1.1	0.8	0.9
Prior settlements	3.5	1.8	1.5	1.9	1.9	1.9
COLA provisions	2.8	0.7	0.7	0.5	0.4	0.2
Industry						
Manufacturing	10.2	2.8	4.4	3.7	3.1	3.3
Non-manufacturing	9.7	3.6	3.0	3.5	3.1	2.8
Construction	9.9	3.0	3.4	3.4	3.4	2.7
Transportation and public utilities	10.8	3.6	2.2	3.3	2.7	3.0
Wholesale and retail trade	7.6	3.3	3.6	3.5	3.5	2.3
Services	8.1	5.1	4.3	4.9	3.7	3.4
Nonmanufacturing, excluding construction	9.6	3.7	2.9	3.6	3.0	2.8
AVERAGE WAGE RATE INCREASE (for workers receiving an increase)	10.1	4.2	4.2	4.0	3.7	3.5
Source						
Current settlements	9.4	4.1	4.1	4.2	3.6	3.2
Prior settlements	5.6	3.7	3.3	3.7	3.8	3.4
COLA provisions	7.7	2.2	2.7	2.0	2.0	1.3
TOTAL NO. OF WORKERS RECEIVING A WAGE RATE INCREASE (millions)	8.9	5.5	4.9	5.1	4.7	4.8
Source (mil.)						
Current settlements	3.5	1.4	1.9	1.5	1.3	1.7
Prior settlements	5.6	3.4	2.7	3.0	2.8	3.0
COLA provisions	3.4	2.3	1.4	1.3	1.0	0.9
NO. OF WORKERS NOT RECEIVING A WAGE RATE INCREASE (millions)	0.2	1.5	1.0	0.5	0.9	0.7

Source: 1994 Statistical Abstract, Table No. 674

Labor Unions Ranked

Unions Ranked by Membership, 1994

Union	Membership
National Education Association	2,000,000
International Brotherhood of Teamsters, Chauffeurs, Warehousemen and Helpers of America	1,400,000
United Food and Commercial Workers, International Union	1,400,000
American Federation of State, County and Municipal Employees	1,300,000
Service Employees' International Union	1,030,000
American Federation of Teachers	850,000
International Brotherhood of Electrical Workers	800,000
International Union, United Automobile, Aerospace and Agricultural Implement Workers of America	796,729
Laborers' International Union of North America	700,000
Communications Workers of America	650,000
United Steelworkers of America	600,000
International Association of Machinists and Aerospace Workers	550,000
United Brotherhood of Carpenters and Joiners of America	510,000
International Union of Operating Engineers	375,000
American Postal Workers Union	365,000
National Association of Letter Carriers	310,000
United Association of Journeymen and Apprentices of the Plumbing and Pipe Fitting Industry	300,000
International Union, Hotel Employees and Restaurant Employees	300,000
United Paper Workers International Union	290,000
Amalgamated Clothing and Textile Workers Union	234,000
American Federation of Government Employees	210,000
American Nurses' Association	209,000
United Mine Workers of America	200,000
International Association of Fire Fighters	195,000
Graphic Communications International Union	175,000

Source: The 1995 Information Please Almanac

Executive Perks

Percent of Companies Offering Perquisites, by Category, 1985–1994*

Perquisite	1994	1993	1991	1989	1987	1985
Executive dining rooms	19	20	26	30	34	35
Company plane	52	53	56	63	67	66
Reserved parking	27	29	29	32	37	36
Airline VIP clubs	29	30	32	34	38	37
Chauffeur service	34	35	36	40	42	43
Loans	7	6	7	9	8	7
First-class air travel	56	57	60	62	66	66
Club memberships	58	62	63	71	73	70
Company car	61	63	63	68	70	71
Physical exams	83	85	89	91	93	94
Financial counseling	70	70	70	74	73	68
Personal liability insurance	45	47	46	50	48	42
Home security system	26	26	27	25	28	22
Home computer	11	9	7	6	5	6
Cellular telephone	49	45	37	22	NA	NA

* Results of a survey of over 700 companies   *Source: Hewitt Associates*

Highly Compensated Executives

THANKS TO RISING profits, directors' pursuit of outside talent, and reduced public criticism, CEO pay is soaring again. The following is a survey of the five highest-paid executives in America in several categories, compiled by the Securities and Exchange Commission and reported by William M. Mercer.

The Highest-Paid Executives, by Category

Category and Company	Executive	1994 Salary ($ thou.)	1994 Bonus ($ thou.)	1994 Salary + Bonus ($ thou.)
BASIC MATERIALS				
Scott Paper	Albert J. Dunlap	705.8	2,500.0	3,205.8
Monsanto	Richard J. Mahoney	933.3	680.0	2,613.3
International Paper	John A. Georges	953.8	1,115.0	2,068.8
DuPont	Edgar S. Woolard Jr.	840.0	1,185.0	2,025.0
Nucor	F. Kenneth Iverson	312.2	1,467.4	1,779.7
ENERGY				
Occidental	Ray R. Irani	1,900.0	872.0	2,772.0
USX	Charles A. Corry	977.5	1,200.0	2,177.5
Exxon	Lee R. Raymond	1,300.0	550.0	1,850.0
Dresser Industries	John J. Murphy	961.5	787.2	1,748.7
Chevron	Kenneth T. Derr	1,000.0	700.0	1,700.0
INDUSTRIAL				
AlliedSignal	Lawrence A. Bossidy	1,625.0	2,000.0	3,625.0
WMX Technologies	Dean L. Buntrock	1,400.0	1,120.0	2,520.0
Union Pacific	Drew Lewis	880.0	1,500.0	2,380.0
Eaton	William E. Butler	694.2	1,308.4	2,002.6
PPG Industries	Jerry E. Dempsey	616.7	1,360.0	1,976.7
CYCLICAL				
Disney (Walt)	Michael D. Eisner	750.0	9,907.2	10,657.2
Time Warner	Gerald M. Levin	1,050.0	4,000.0	5,050.0
Kodak	George M. C. Fisher	2,000.0	1,816.4	3,816.4
Chrysler	Robert J. Eaton	1,063.8	2,200.0	3,263.8
Harcourt General	Robert J. Tarr Jr.	1,400.0	1,050.0	2,450.0
NON-CYCLICAL				
IBP	Robert L. Peterson	1,000.0	3,873.0	4,873.0
Coca-Cola	Roberto D. Goizueta	1,548.2	2,823.0	4,371.2
RJR Nabisco	Charles M. Harper	600.0	2,410.0	3,010.0
Archer-Daniels-Midland	D. O. Andreas	2,972.6	0.0	2,972.6
PepsiCo	D. Wayne Calloway	968.3	1,975.0	2,943.3
TECHNOLOGY				
IBM	Louis V. Gerstner Jr.	2,000.0	2,600.0	4,600.0
General Electric	John F. Welch Jr.	1,850.0	2,500.0	4,350.0
Compaq Computer	Eckhard Pfeiffer	1,050.0	2,500.0	3,550.0
AT&T	Robert E. Allen	1,109.0	2,253.6	3,362.6
General Dynamics	James R. Mellor	670.0	1,600.0	2,270.0
FINANCIAL				
Bear, Stearns	James E. Cayne	200.0	14,372.0	14,572.0
Merrill Lynch	Daniel P. Tully	500.0	4,340.0	4,840.0
Citicorp	John S. Reed	1,275.0	3,000.0	4,275.0
Morgan (J. P.)	Dennis Weatherstone	700.0	3,569.0	4,269.0
ITT	Rand V. Araskog	1,625.0	2,405.0	4,030.0

Highly Compensated Executives (cont'd)

Category and Company	Executive	1994 Salary ($ thou.)	1994 Bonus ($ thou.)	1994 Salary + Bonus ($ thou.)
UTILITIES				
GTE	Charles R. Lee	784.6	1,219.5	2,004.1
Southwestern Bell	Edward E. Whitacre Jr.	762.0	1,190.0	1,952.0
Sprint	William T. Esrey	863.9	1,085.6	1,949.5
MCI Communications	Bert C. Roberts Jr.	850.0	900.0	1,750.0
NYNEX	William C. Ferguson	800.0	885.0	1,685.0

Source: William M. Mercer, Inc.

Wage Data

Percent Job Distribution of Non-farm Establishments and Employees

Year	Total Goods Prod.	Mining	Const.	Mfg.	Total Service Prod.	Trans. & Utilities	Wholesale Trade	Retail Trade	Finance	Svcs.	Gov't.
1960	37.7	1.3	5.4	31.0	62.3	7.4	5.8	15.2	4.8	13.6	15.4
1965	36.1	1.0	5.3	29.7	63.9	6.6	5.7	15.2	4.9	14.9	16.6
1970	33.3	0.9	5.1	27.3	66.7	6.4	5.7	15.6	5.1	16.3	17.7
1975	29.4	1.0	4.6	23.8	70.6	5.9	5.8	16.4	5.4	18.1	19.1
1980	28.4	1.1	4.8	22.4	71.6	5.7	5.9	16.6	5.7	19.8	18.0
1985	25.5	1.0	4.8	19.7	74.5	5.4	5.9	17.8	6.1	22.6	16.8
1986	24.7	0.8	4.8	19.1	75.3	5.3	5.8	18.0	6.3	23.2	16.8
1987	24.2	0.7	4.9	18.6	75.8	5.3	5.7	18.1	6.4	23.7	16.6
1988	23.9	0.7	4.8	18.3	76.1	5.2	5.7	18.1	6.3	24.3	16.5
1989	23.4	0.6	4.8	17.9	76.6	5.2	5.7	18.0	6.2	25.0	16.4
1990	22.7	0.6	4.7	17.4	77.3	5.3	5.6	17.9	6.1	25.7	16.7
1991	22.0	0.6	4.3	17.0	78.0	5.3	5.6	17.8	6.2	26.1	17.0
1992	21.3	0.6	4.1	16.7	78.7	5.3	5.6	17.8	6.1	26.8	17.2
1993	20.9	0.5	4.2	16.2	79.1	5.2	5.5	17.9	6.0	27.4	17.1

Weekly Earnings of Non-farm Employees ($)

Year	Total Goods, Svcs.	Total Goods Prod.	Mining	Const.	Mfg.	Total Svc. Prod.	Trans. & Utilities	Whsl. Trade	Retail Trade	Finance	Svcs.	Gov't.
1960	81	NA	105	113	90	NA	NA	91	58	75	NA	NA
1965	95	NA	124	138	108	NA	125	106	67	89	74	NA
1970	120	NA	164	195	133	NA	156	137	82	113	97	NA
1975	164	NA	249	266	191	NA	233	182	109	148	135	NA
1980	235	NA	397	368	289	NA	351	267	147	210	191	NA
1985	299	NA	520	464	386	NA	450	351	175	289	256	NA
1986	305	NA	526	467	396	NA	459	358	176	304	266	NA
1987	313	NA	532	480	406	NA	472	365	179	317	276	NA
1988	322	NA	541	496	419	NA	476	380	184	325	289	NA
1989	334	NA	570	513	430	NA	490	395	189	341	306	NA
1990	345	NA	603	526	442	NA	505	411	194	357	319	NA
1991	354	NA	630	533	455	NA	512	425	199	371	331	NA
1992	364	NA	638	536	470	NA	524	435	205	387	343	NA
1993	374	NA	645	551	487	NA	542	447	210	404	351	NA

Source: 1994 Statistical Abstract, Table No. 654

Wage Data (cont'd)

Selected Occupations and Median Weekly Earnings

Occupation (Male and Female)	1993 Median Weekly Earnings ($)	% Change 1983–1993
Accountants and auditors	612	49.5
Administrators and officials, public administration	724	54.4
Advertising and related sales	590	64.8
Airplane pilots and navigators	1,086	76.6
Architects	694	39.4
Bank tellers	350	71.6
Bookkeepers, accounting and auditing clerks	375	49.4
Chemical engineers	996	58.1
Clergy	499	57.9
Computer programmers	747	58.0
Computer systems analysts and scientists	821	56.7
Economists	793	31.7
Editors and reporters	574	49.9
Electricians	549	30.1
Engineers	911	51.8
Financial managers	776	57.7
Firefighters and fire prevention workers	614	54.7
Insurance salespeople	565	48.3
Lawyers	1,164	86.2
Librarians, archivists, curators	577	54.3
Managers in marketing, advertising, public relations	851	49.3
Managers of properties and real estate	511	52.1
Mechanical engineers	895	50.2
Personnel and labor relations managers	723	47.6
Personnel, training, and labor relations specialists	598	44.4
Pharmacists	913	81.9
Physicians	1,019	102.9
Police and detectives, public service	632	56.0
Public relations specialists	613	37.8
Purchasing managers	773	36.3
Real estate sales	610	58.9
Receptionists	316	49.8
Secretaries	386	53.2
Securities and financial services salespeople	783	50.9
Social scientists and urban planners	670	44.7
Supervisors, general office	548	55.2
Supervisors, police and detectives	750	49.1
Teachers, secondary school	625	60.7
Telephone line installers and repairers	664	37.2
Telephone operators	386	37.9
Truck drivers, heavy	445	36.5
Waiters and waitresses	230	42.0

Source: Bureau of Labor Statistics

Job Outlook Data

Change in Age Distribution (%) of the Labor Force, 1975 to Projected 2005

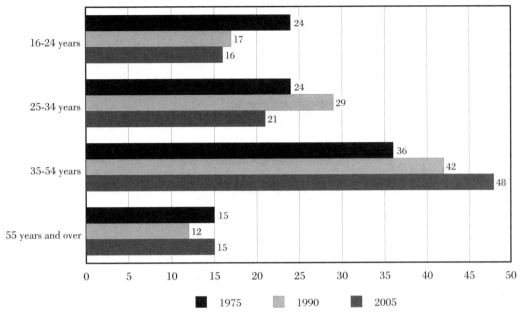

Source: U.S. Dept. of Labor, Bureau of Labor Statistics

Proportion of Workers 25 and 64 Years Old with a College Background, 1975 vs. 1990

1975

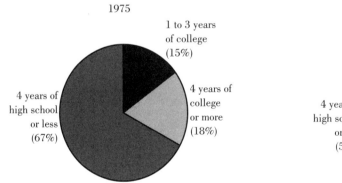

1990

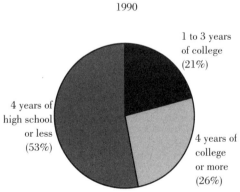

Source: U.S. Dept. of Labor, Bureau of Labor Statistics

Job Outlook Data (cont'd)

Projected Percent Change in Employment by Industry, 1990 to 2005

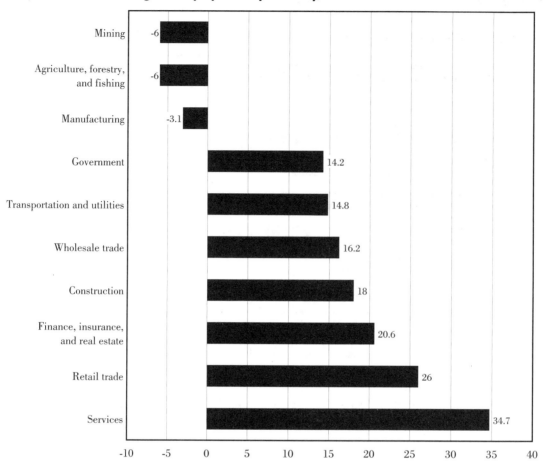

Source: U.S. Dept. of Labor, Bureau of Labor Statistics

Job Outlook Data (cont'd)

Projected Percent Change in Employment by Broad Occupational Group, 1990 to 2005

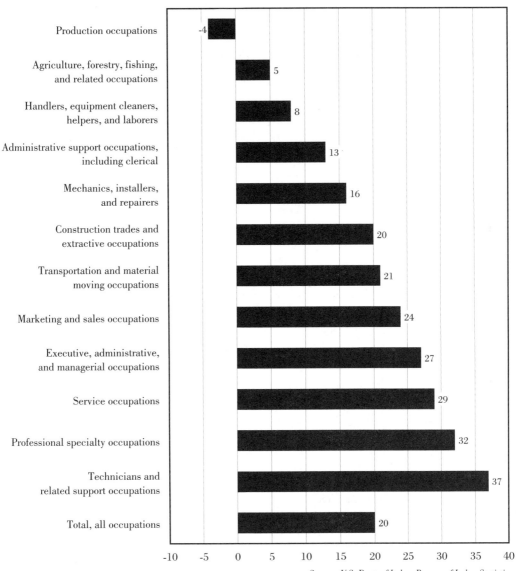

Source: U.S. Dept. of Labor, Bureau of Labor Statistics

State Job Market Information

STATE AND LOCAL JOB MARKET and career information is available from State Occupational Information Coordinating Committees (SOICCs). They provide or help locate labor market and career information.

Contact Options

Alabama
Alabama OICC
Alabama Center for Commerce, Room 364
401 Adams Ave - P. O. Box 5690
Montgomery, AL 36103
(205) 242-2990

Alaska
Alaska Department of Labor
Research and Analysis Section
P. O. Box 25501
Juneau, AK 99802
(907) 465-4518

American Samoa
American Samoa OICC and Research
Department of Human Resources
American Samoa Government
Pago Pago, AS 96799
(684) 633-4485

Arizona
Arizona State OICC
P. O. Box 6123, Site Code 8971
1789 W. Jefferson St. First Floor N.
Phoenix, AZ 85005
(602) 542-3871

Arkansas
Arkansas OICC/Employment Security Division
Employment and Training Services
P. O. Box 2981
Little Rock, AR 72203
(501) 682-3159

California
California OICC
1116 Ninth Street, Lower Level
P. O. Box 944222
Sacramento, CA 94244
(916) 323-6544

Colorado
Colorado OICC
State Board Community College
1391 Speer Blvd., Suite 600
Denver, CO 80204
(303) 866-4488

Connecticut
Connecticut OICC
Connecticut Department of Education
25 Industrial Park Rd.
Middletown, CT 06457
(203) 638-4042

Delaware
Office of Occupational and LMI/DOL
University Office Plaza
P. O. Box 9029
Newark, DE 19714
(302) 368-6963

District of Columbia
District of Columbia OICC
Department of Employment Services
500 C St. NW, Room 215
Washington, DC 20001
(202) 724-7237

Florida
Bureau of LMI/DOL and ES
Suite 200, Harman Bldg.
2012 Capitol Circle, SE
Tallahassee, FL 32399
(904) 438-1048

Georgia
Georgia OICC/Department of Labor
148 International Boulevard
Sussex Pl.
Atlanta, GA 30303
(404) 656-9639

Guam
Guam OICC/Human Resources
Development Agency
Jay Ease Bldg., Third Floor
P. O. Box 2817
Agana, GU 96910
(671) 646-9341

Hawaii
Hawaii State OICC
830 Punchbowl St.
Room 315
Honolulu, HI 96813
(808) 586-8750

Idaho
Idaho OICC
Lee B. Jordan Bldg., Room 301
P.O. Box 83720
650 W. State St.
Boise, ID
(208) 334-3705

State Job Market Information (cont'd)

Illinois
Illinois OICC
217 E. Monroe, Suite 203
Springfield, IL 62706
(217) 785-0789

Indiana
Indiana OICC
Indiana Government Center, S.
10 N. Senate, Second Floor
Indianapolis, IN 46204
(317) 232-8528

Iowa
Iowa OICC
Iowa Department of Economic Development
200 E. Grand Ave.
Des Moines, IA 50309
(515) 242-4889

Kansas
Kansas OICC
401 Topeka Ave.
Topeka, KS 66603
(913) 296-2387

Kentucky
Kentucky OICC
2031 Capital Plaza Tower
Frankfort, KY 40601
(502) 564-4258

Louisiana
Louisiana OICC
P. O. Box 94094
Baton Rouge, LA 70804
(504) 342-5149

Maine
Maine OICC
State House Stn. 71
Augusta, ME 04333
(207) 624-6200

Maryland
Maryland SOICC
State Department of Employment and Training
1100 N. Entaw St., Room 103
Baltimore, MD 21201
(410) 767-2953

Massachusetts
Massachusetts OICC/MA Division of Employment
Security
C. F. Hurley Bldg., Second Floor
Government Center
Boston, MA 02114
(617) 626-5718

Michigan
Michigan OICC
Victor Office Center, Third Floor
201 N. Washington Sq.
Box 30015
Lansing, MI 48909
(517) 373-0363

Minnesota
Minnesota OICC/Department of Jobs and Training
390 N. Robert St.
St. Paul, MN 55101
(612) 296-2072

Mississippi
Mississippi SOICC
301 W. Pearl St.
Jackson, MS 39203
(601) 949-2240

Missouri
Missouri OICC
400 Dix Rd.
Jefferson City, MO 65109
(314) 751-3800

Montana
Montana OICC
1327 Lockey St., Second Floor
P. O. Box 1728
Helena, MT 59624
(406) 444-2741

Nebraska
Nebraska OICC
P. O. Box 94600
State House Stn.
Lincoln, NE 68509
(402) 471-9953

Nevada
Nevada OICC/DETR
500 E. Third St.
Carson City, NV 89713
(702) 687-4550

New Hampshire
New Hampshire State OICC
64 Old Soncook Rd.
Concord, NH 03301
(603) 228-3349

New Jersey
New Jersey OICC
609 Labor & Industry Bldg.
CN 056
Trenton, NJ 08625
(609) 292-2682

State Job Market Information (cont'd)

New Mexico
New Mexico OICC
401 Broadway, NE
Tiwa Bldg.
P. O. Box 1928
Albuquerque, NM 87103
(505) 841-8455

New York
New York State OICC/DOL
Research & Statistics Division
State Campus Bldg. 12 - Room 488
Albany, NY 12240
(518) 457-3806

North Carolina
North Carolina OICC
700 Wade Ave.
P. O. Box 25903
Raleigh, NC 27611
(919) 733-6700

North Dakota
North Dakota SOICC
1720 Burnt Boat Dr.
P. O. Box 5507
Bismarck, ND 58502
(701) 328-2733

N. Mariana Isl.
Northern Mariana Islands OKCC
P. O. Box 149, Room N-1, Bldg. N
Northern Mariana College
Saipan, CM 96950
(670) 234-1457

Ohio
Ohio OICC/Division of LMI
Ohio Bureau of Employment Services
145 S. Front St.
Columbus, OH 43215
(614) 466-1109

Oklahoma
Oklahoma OICC
Department of Voc/Tech Education
1500 W. Seventh Ave.
Stillwater, OK 74074
(405) 743-5198

Oregon
Oregon OICC
875 Union St., NE
Salem, OR 97311
(503) 378-5747

Pennsylvania
Pennsylvania OICC
Pennsylvania Department of Labor and Industry
300 Capital Associate
901 N. Seventh St.
Harrisburg, PA 17120
(717) 787-8545

Puerto Rico
Puerto Rico OICC
P. O. Box 366212
San Juan, PR 00936
(809) 723-7110

Rhode Island
Rhode Island OICC
22 Hayes St., Room 133
Providence, RI 02908
(401) 272-0830

South Carolina
South Carolina OICC
1550 Gadedeo St.
P. O. Box 995
Columbia, SC 29202
(803) 737-2733

South Dakota
South Dakota OICC
South Dakota Department of Labor
420 S. Roosevelt St.
P. O. Box 4730
Aberdeen, SD 57402
(605) 626-2314

Tennessee
Tennessee OICC
11th Floor, Volunteer Plaza
500 James Robertson Pkwy.
Nashville, TN 37219
(615) 741-6451

Texas
Texas OICC
Texas Employment Commission Bldg.
3520 Executive Center Dr., Suite 205
Austin, TX 78731
(512) 502-3750

Utah
Utah OICC
c/o Utah Department of Employment Security
P. O. Box 11249
140 East 300 South
Salt Lake City, UT 84147
(801) 536-7806

State Job Market Information (cont'd)

Vermont
Vermont OICC
5 Green Mountain Dr.
P. O. Box 488
Montpelier, VT 05601
(802) 229-0311

Virginia
Virginia OICC/VA Employment Commission
703 E. Main St.
P. O. Box 1358
Richmond, VA 23211
(804) 786-7496

Virgin Islands
Virgin Islands OICC
P. O. Box 3159
St. Thomas, US VI 00803
(809) 776-3700

Washington
Washington OICC
c/o Employment Security Department
P. O. Box 9046
Olympia, WA 98507
(206) 438-4803

West Virginia
West Virginia OICC
5088 Washington St. West
Cross Lanes, WV 25313
(304) 759-0724

Wisconsin
The Wisconsin OIC Council
201 E. Washington Ave.
P. O. Box 7944
Madison, WI 53707
(608) 266-8012

Wyoming
Wyoming OICC
P. O. Box 2760
100 W. Midwest
Casper, WY 82602
(307) 265-6715

National Labor Relations Board

What Is the NLRB?

The National Labor Relations Board is an independent federal agency created in 1935 by Congress to administer the National Labor Relations Act, the basic law governing relations between labor unions and the employers whose operations affect interstate commerce.

The statute guarantees the right of employees to organize and to bargain collectively with their employers or to refrain from all such activity. Generally applying to all employers involved in interstate commerce—other than airlines, railroads, agriculture, and government—the Act implements the national labor policy of assuring free choice and encouraging collective bargaining as a means of maintaining industrial peace.

Through the years, Congress has amended the Act, and the Board and courts have developed a body of law drawn from the statute. This section is intended to give a brief explanation of the Act to employees, employers, unions, and the public.

What Does It Do?

In its statutory assignment, the NLRB has two principal functions: (1) to determine, through secret ballot elections, the free democratic choice by employees as to whether or not they wish to be represented by a union in dealing with their employers and, if so, by which union; and (2) to prevent and remedy unlawful acts, called unfair labor practices, by either employers or unions.

The Act's election provisions provide the authority for conducting representation elections, which determine the views of the employees regarding representation by a labor union. Its unfair labor practice provisions place certain restrictions on actions of both employers and labor organizations in their relations with employees, as well as with each other.

The agency does not act on its own initiative in either function. It processes only those charges of unfair labor practices and petitions for employee elections which are filed with the NLRB in one of its Regional, Subregional, or Resident Offices.

The staff in each office is available to assist the public with inquiries concerning the Act and to provide appropriate forms and other technical assistance to those who wish to file charges or petitions.

What Does the Act Provide?

The Act sets forth the basic rights of employees as follows:

- To self-organize;
- To form, join, or assist labor organizations;
- To bargain collectively about wages and working conditions through representatives of their own choosing;
- To engage in other protected "concerted activities," that is, to act together for purposes of collective bargaining, or other mutual aid or protection;
- To refrain from any of these activities. (However, a union and employer may, in a state where such agreements are permitted, enter into a lawful union security clause.)

The Act prohibits both employers and unions from violating these employee rights. As an example, an employer may not discriminate against employees with regard to hiring, discharge, or working conditions because of their union activities. A union may not engage in acts of violence against employees who refrain from union activity. These examples are for illustration only.

For further information about employer and union unfair labor practices, refer to *The National Labor Relations Board and You: Unfair Labor Practices*, available from your nearest NLRB office. A related publication, *The National Labor Relations Board and You: Representation Cases*, describes the election process in more detail.

What Is the NLRB's Structure?

The agency has two separate components. The Board itself has five members and primarily acts as a quasi-judicial body in deciding cases on the basis of formal records in administrative proceedings. Board members are appointed by the President to five-year terms, with Senate consent, the term of one member expiring each year. The general counsel, appointed by the President to a four-year term with Senate consent, is independent from the Board and is responsible for the investigation and prosecution of unfair labor practice cases and for the general supervision of the NLRB field offices in the processing of unfair labor practice and representation cases.

Each Regional Office is headed by a Regional Director who is responsible for making the initial determination in unfair labor practice and representation cases arising within the geographical area served by the Region (including any Resident or Subregional Offices within the Region).

What Are the NLRB's Procedures?

Representation Cases

In a typical representation election case, a union employer or individual files a petition with the field office requesting that an election be held among a particular group of employees (referred to as a "bargaining unit") to determine whether the group wishes to be represented, or wishes to continue to be represented, by a union. A petition filed by a union or an individual must be supported by showing that at least 30 percent of affected employees desire an election.

If the Region's investigation reveals that the

National Labor Relations Board (cont'd)

petition should be processed, attempts are made to secure agreement of the parties on the issues involved, including the appropriate unit and the time and place of the election. Over 80 percent of meritorious election petitions result in such agreements. If an agreement cannot be reached, the Region conducts a hearing. On the basis of the record of the hearing, the Regional Director issues a decision disposing of the issues. The Regional Director's decision may be appealed to the Board.

When an unfair labor practice charge is filed, the appropriate field office conducts an investigation to determine whether there is reasonable cause to believe the Act has been violated. If the Regional Director determines that the charge lacks merit, it will be dismissed, unless the charging party decides to withdraw the charge. A dismissal may be appealed to the General Counsel's office in Washington, DC.

If the Regional Director finds reasonable cause to believe a violation of the law has been committed, the Region seeks a voluntary settlement to remedy the alleged violations. If these settlement efforts fail, a formal complaint is issued, and the case goes to a hearing before an NLRB administrative law judge.

The judge issues a written decision which may be appealed to the Board for a final Agency determination. That final determination is subject to review in the federal courts. More than 90 percent of the unfair labor practice cases filed with the NLRB are disposed of in an average of 45 days without the necessity of formal litigation before the Board. Only about 4 percent of the cases proceed to Board decision.

Since its establishment, the NLRB has processed more than 900,000 unfair labor practice charges and conducted in excess of 360,000 secret ballot elections. The Agency handles approximately 40,000 cases each year, including more than 7,000 representation petitions.

For Additional Information

For further information, to find the NLRB field office nearest to you, or to receive copies of the publications referred to here, contact the headquarters of the NLRB.

Contact Option

The National Labor Relations Board
Office of Information
1099 14th St., NW, Room 9400
Washington, DC 20570
(202) 273-1991

Recommended Resources

The National Labor Relations Board and You: Unfair Labor Practices
National Labor Relations Board, free
(202) 273-1991
Provides information about employer and union unfair labor practices.

The National Labor Relations Board and You: Representation Cases
National Labor Relations Board, free
(202) 273-1992
Describes the union election process in detail.

A Guide to Basic Law and Procedures Under the National Labor Relations Act
U.S. Government Printing Office, $2.75
(202) 512-1800

The Top Reference Sources

The Evaluation Guide to Corporate Wellness Programs
The Corporate University Press, $99
(510) 236-9400

This looseleaf binder features more than 400 pages of in-depth evaluations of hundreds of corporate wellness seminars given around the country. These seminars offer executives an opportunity to learn how to control health costs through preventive techniques.

This book is the preeminent resource on the topic.

E-MAIL **NLRB Field Offices.** Send e-mail to nlrb@almanac.yoyo.com. See p. xi for instructions.
Names, addresses, and phone numbers of the field offices of the National Labor Relations Board.

Time Management Techniques

Ten Tips for Better Time Management

I. Anytime you handle any piece of paper, limit your contact with it to one time.

If it requires a response, respond now–not later. If it must be filed, file it now. If it might be better off in the wastebasket, toss it now.

2. Learn how to say no.

This is not an easy word to say, and you'll have to say it to some of the nicest people in the world. Be nice, direct, and compassionate, but say it immediately. Don't leave people hanging and waste their time.

3. Respect your instincts and your mood.

If you're not in the mood to do something, do something else, saving the original task for a time when you are more likely to tackle it efficiently.

4. Make a public commitment.

If you want to complete a task by a certain hour, go public with your pronouncement. "I'll have that report to you by three o'clock" leaves you with little choice.

5. Take breaks.

If you work straight through without any break at all, chances are your work will suffer. If you take brief breaks, you'll be better able to keep an attentive pace and your work will be more accurate.

6. Learn to tolerate your faults in an effort to overcome perfectionism.

You'll have a far better time of almost anything in life if you strive for excellence rather than perfection.

7. Get things done right now.

It is estimated that a minimum of 80 percent of the business coming across the desk of an efficient executive gets handled immediately, through either personal action or delegation.

8. Force yourself to be neat.

Neatness leads to organization, and organization leads to time efficiency.

9. Do things one at a time.

This simple mindset can keep you well organized, because the main reason some people can't seem to organize anything is that they fear having to organize everything.

I0. When negotiating, realize that the shortest route to an agreement isn't necessarily the straightest.

It takes 90 percent of the total discussion time to resolve 10 percent of the issues, and the final 10 percent of the time to resolve the other 90 percent. By recognizing this fact of negotiation, you can save a great deal of valuable time.

Source: Adapted from Jay Conrad Levinson's The 90-Minute Hour

Recommended Resources

How to Get Organized When You Don't Have the Time
by Stephanie Culp
Writer's Digest Books, $10.99
(800) 289-0963

The Effective Executive
by Peter Drucker
HarperCollins, $12
(800) 242-7737

Working Smart
by Michael Leboeuf
Warner Books, $5.50
(800) 222-6747

The Top Reference Sources

Business Rankings Annual
Gale, $170
(800) 877-4253

This mammoth book (800+ pages) lists more than 4,000 top-ten lists–from largest public compa-

nies to highest-paid CEOs.
   Covering more than 1,500 different topics, this volume is an excellent place to look for a wide breadth of information.

First Aid

The Information Please Business Almanac & Sourcebook *is not responsible and assumes no responsibility for any action undertaken by anyone utilizing the first aid procedures which follow.*

The Heimlich Maneuver for Choking

What to look for: Victim cannot speak or breathe, turns blue, collapses.

To perform the Heimlich Maneuver when the victim is standing or sitting:

1. Stand behind the victim and wrap your arms around his or her waist.

2. Place the thumb side of your fist against the victim's abdomen, slightly above the navel and below the rib cage.

3. Grasp your fist with the other hand and press your fist into the victim's abdomen with a quick upward thrust. Repeat as often as necessary.

4. If the victim is sitting, stand behind the victim's chair and perform the maneuver in the same manner.

5. After the food is dislodged, have the victim see a doctor.

When the victim has collapsed and cannot be lifted:

1. Lay the victim on his or her back.

2. Face the victim and kneel astride his or her hips.

3. With one hand on top of the other, place the heel of your bottom hand on the abdomen slightly above the navel and below the rib cage.

4. Press into the victim's abdomen with a quick upward thrust. Repeat as often as necessary.

5. Should the victim vomit, quickly roll on his or her side and wipe out the mouth to prevent aspiration (drawing of vomit into the throat).

6. After the food is dislodged, have the victim see a doctor.

NOTE: If you start to choke when alone, and help is not available, you should attempt to self-administer this maneuver.

Burns

First Degree:

Signs/Symptoms: reddened skin.

Treatment: Immerse quickly in cold water or apply ice until pain stops.

Second Degree:

Signs/Symptoms: reddened skin, blisters.

Treatment: (1) Cut away loose clothing; (2) cover with several layers of cold, moist dressings or, if limb is involved, immerse in cold water for relief of pain; (3) treat for shock.

Third Degree:

Signs/Symptoms: skin destroyed, tissues damaged, charring.

Treatment: (1) Cut away loose clothing (do not remove clothing adhered to skin); (2) cover with several layers of sterile, cold, moist dressings for relief of pain and to stop burning action; (3) treat for shock.

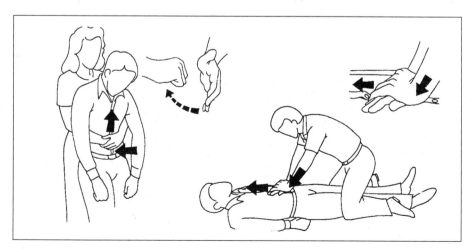

Source: New York City Department of Health

First Aid (cont'd)

Poisons

Treatment: (1) Dilute by drinking large quantities of water; (2) induce vomiting except when poison is corrosive or a petroleum product; (3) call a Poison Control center or a doctor.

Poison Control Center: (800) 336-6997

Shock

Shock may accompany any serious injury: blood loss, breathing impairment, heart failure, burns. Shock can kill, so treat as soon as possible and continue until medical aid is available.

Signs/Symptoms: (1) shallow breathing; (2) rapid and weak pulse; (3) nausea, collapse, vomiting; (4) shivering; (5) pale, moist skin; (6) mental confusion; (7) drooping eyelids, dilated pupils.

Treatment: (1) Establish and maintain an open airway; (2) control bleeding; (3) keep victim lying down. Exception: head and chest injuries, heart attack, stroke, sunstroke. If no spine injury, victim may be more comfortable and breathe better in a semi-reclining position. If in doubt, keep the victim flat. Elevate the feet unless injury would be aggravated. Maintain normal body temperature. Place blankets under and over victim.

Heat Cramps

Heat cramps affect people who work or do strenuous exercises in a hot environment. To prevent them, drink large amounts of cool water and add a pinch of salt to each glass of water.

Signs/Symptoms: (1) painful muscle cramps in legs and abdomen; (2) faintness; (3) profuse perspiration.

Treatment: (1) Move victim to a cool place; (2) give him or her sips of salted drinking water (one teaspoon of salt to one quart of water); (3) apply manual pressure to the cramped muscle.

Heat Exhaustion

Signs/Symptoms: (1) pale and clammy skin; (2) profuse perspiration; (3) rapid and shallow breathing; (4) weakness, dizziness, and headache.

Treatment: (1) Care for victim as if he or she were in shock; (2) move victim to a cool area, do not allow chilling; (3) if body gets too cold, cover victim.

Heat Stroke

Signs/Symptoms: (1) Face is red and flushed; (2) victim rapidly loses consciousness; (3) skin is hot and dry with no perspiration.

Treatment: (1) Lay victim down with head and shoulders raised; (2) apply cold packs to the body and head; (3) use ice and fan if available; (4) watch for signs of shock and treat accordingly; (5) get medical aid as soon as possible.

Artificial Respiration

Artificial respiration is mouth-to-mouth breathing, used in cases such as drowning, electric shock, or smoke inhalation.

There is need for help when breathing movements stop or lips, tongue, and fingernails become blue. When in doubt, apply artificial respiration until you get medical help. No harm can result from its use, and delay may cost the patient his or her life. Start immediately. Seconds count. Clear mouth and throat of any obstructions with your fingers.

For adults: Place patient on back with face up. Lift the chin and tilt the head back. If air passage is still closed, pull chin up by placing fingers behind the angles of the lower jaw and pushing forward. Take a deep breath; place your mouth over patient's mouth, making leak-proof seal. Pinch patient's nostrils closed. Blow into patient's mouth until you see his or her chest rise.

Repeat about 12 times a minute. (If the patient's stomach rises markedly, exert moderate hand pressure on the stomach just below the rib cage to keep it from inflating.)

For infants and small children: Place your mouth over patient's mouth and nose. Blow into mouth and nose until you see patient's chest rise normally.

Repeat 20 to 30 times per minute. (Don't exaggerate the tilted position of an infant's head.)

NOTE: *For emergency treatment of heart attack, cardiopulmonary resuscitation (CPR) is recommended. Instruction in CPR can be obtained through local health organizations or schools.*

Source: The Information Please Almanac

First-Aid Kit Contents

THE FEDERAL GOVERNMENT has no prescribed standard for the contents of an office first-aid kit. But Johnson & Johnson, the leading manufacturer of first-aid kits, suggests that the following be included in a first-aid kit for an office:

- 150 or more mixed-size bandages, plastic and/or flexible fabric;
- Sterile sponges, gauze, and eyepads;
- Hypo-allergenic adhesive tape and an elastic bandage;
- Antiseptic wipes, burn cream, and first-aid cream;
- Instant cold packs;
- Ophthalmic irrigating solution;

- Acetaminophen;
- Scissors, tweezers, and disposable gloves;
- A first-aid guide.

Recommended Resource

Conney Safety Products
3202 Latham Dr.
P.O. Box 44190
Madison, WI 53744
(800) 356-9100

Conney Safety Products, one of the country's largest suppliers of first-aid, medical, and work safety products, is a one-stop source for custom-assembled or standard first-aid kits for any size shop or office. Call for the catalogue.

Dealing with Stress

ACCORDING TO *PERSONNEL* MAGAZINE, the cost of stress-related illnesses to American business is approximately $90 billion a year. Being able to identify serious signs of stress and/or burnout in employees and co-workers and alleviating the causes of stress where possible will increase productivity. In the long run, stress reduction can save millions of dollars in stress-related workers' compensation claims.

Stress is generally defined as any outside stimulus that disrupts the body's mental, physical, or chemical functioning.

Studies indicate that extreme forms of stress are characterized by restlessness, impatience, extreme competitiveness, and feelings of being under pressure. Furthermore, extreme stress can, over time, lead to deteriorating performance in the workplace, as well as to health problems such as migraines, high blood pressure, arthritis, eczema, gastric and/or peptic ulcers, asthma, heart disease, and stroke.

The most common forms of workplace-related stress arise from one of the following conditions:

- Job changes that place new demands on a worker's time and personal or family relationships;
- Poor organizational climate and insufficient social support from friends or co-workers;
- Conflicts between workers' personal values and the values of the company;
- Frustrated career plans;
- Bad lighting, uncomfortable temperatures, noise, or other environmental factors.

An employee's ability to cope with stress is affected by the intensity and duration of one or more of the conditions listed above.

Strategies Designed to Cope with Stress

- Physical maintenance
  Diet
  Sleep
  Exercise
- Internal assistance
  Relaxation response
  Biofeedback
  Autogenic training
- Personal organization
  Stress plan
  Delegation of responsibility
  Ability to choose or alternate environments
  Creative problem solving and decision making
  Goal setting
  Time management
  Conflict management
  Ability to restructure job
  Self-assessment measures
- Outside assistance
  Psychotherapy
  Stress counseling
  Development program
  Behavior change techniques
- Stress-directed strategies
  Systematic desensitization
  Dynamic psychotherapy
- Situational and support group
  Assertiveness training and role-playing
  Development of supportive relationships
- Negative strategies
  Avoidance of substance abuse (alcohol, cigarettes, drugs)

Dealing with Stress (cont'd)

45 Elements of the Stress-Free Workplace

Northwestern National Life has created a simple evaluation that allows workers to judge the level of stress they face at work. Some of the items on the evaluation (with which the individual must decide if he or she agrees or disagrees) are:

1. Management is supportive of employees' efforts.

2. Management encourages work and personal support groups.

3. Management and employees talk openly.

4. Employees receive training when assigned new tasks.

5. Employees are recognized and rewarded for their contributions.

6. Work rules are published and are the same for everyone.

7. Employees have current and understandable job descriptions.

8. Management appreciates humor in the workplace.

9. Employees and management are trained in how to resolve conflicts.

10. Employees are free to talk with one another.

11. Workloads do not vary greatly for individuals or between individuals.

12. Employees have work spaces that are not crowded.

13. Employees have access to technology they need.

14. Opportunities for advancement are available.

15. Employees are given some control in how they do their work.

16. Employees generally are not physically isolated.

17. Mandatory overtime is seldom required.

18. Employees have some privacy.

19. Performance of work units is above average.

20. Personal conflicts on the job are not common.

21. Consequences of making a mistake on the job are not extremely severe.

22. Employees do not expect the organization will be sold or relocated.

23. There has been no major reorganization in the past 12 months.

24. Meal breaks are predictable.

25. Medical and mental health benefits are provided by the employer.

26. Employees are given information regularly on how to cope with stress.

27. Sick and vacation benefits are above those of similar organizations.

28. Employee benefits were not significantly cut in the past 12 months.

29. An employee assistance program (EAP) is offered.

30. Pay is above the going rate.

31. Employees can work flexible hours.

32. Employees have a place and time to relax during the workday.

33. Employer has a formal employee communications program.

34. Child care programs or referral services are available.

35. Referral programs or day care for elderly relatives are offered.

36. Special privileges are granted fairly based on an employee's level.

37. New machines or ways of working were introduced in the past year.

38. Employer offers exercise or other stress-reduction programs.

39. Work is neither sedentary nor physically exhausting.

40. Not all work is machine-paced or fast-paced.

41. Staffing and expense budgets are adequate.

42. Noise or vibration is low, and temperatures are not extreme or fluctuating.

43. Employees do not deal with a lot of red tape to get things done.

44. Downsizing or layoffs have not occurred in the past 12 months

45. Employees can put up personal items in their work area.

Contact Option

Northwestern National Life
20 Washington Ave. S.
Minneapolis, MN 55401
(612) 372-5432

Employee Burnout

STRESS AND BURNOUT are increasingly common in the workplace. Nearly half of all American workers say their jobs are very or extremely stressful. Job expectations that suddenly change, demands for greater productivity, and fear of losing one's job during a period of recession are adding to these already high stress levels. Though not a precisely defined medical condition, burnout has recognizable symptoms and is a result of prolonged stress.

Workers report feeling lethargic, empty, and no longer able to take satisfaction in what they once enjoyed. They also have a deep questioning of the value of the tasks they perform. In everyday parlance, they hate to go to work, not just on an occasional morning but on most mornings. This can only hurt business. In fact, 50 percent of employees said job stress reduces their productivity, and those who report high stress are three times more likely to suffer from frequent illness.

Reducing stress in the workplace takes a committed management and may take a financial investment. Spending money up front, however, is likely to save money in the long run.

Ways to Reduce Burnout

- Allow employees to talk freely with one another.
- Reduce personal conflicts on the job.
- Give employees adequate control over how they do their work.
- Ensure that staffing and expense budgets are adequate.
- Talk openly with employees.
- Support employees' efforts.
- Provide competitive personal leave and vacation benefits.
- Maintain current levels of employee benefits.
- Reduce the amount of red tape for employees.
- Recognize and reward employees for their accomplishments and contributions.

Source: Northwestern National Life

Contact Option

American Society of Training and Development (ASTD)
1640 King St.
Alexandria, VA 22313
(703) 683-8100

Change Management

THE AMERICAN MANAGEMENT Association and Deloitte & Touche Management Consulting conduct an annual survey that documents corporate and business leaders' actions in the area of change management. This survey notes that approximately 84 percent of American companies are undergoing at least one major business transformation. Their findings state that as companies respond to a rapidly evolving marketplace, their single greatest challenge is corporate culture and resistance to change.

Changes Implemented, 1994

Category	In Process (%)	Complete (%)
Information technology	84.2	6.6
Business strategy development	65.6	25.9
Business process reengineering	80.3	5.0
Organizational flattening	53.3	20.1
Total quality management	52.5	11.2
Telecommunicating	51.4	6.9
External alliances	50.6	4.2
Downsizing	38.6	22.0
Diversity programs	48.3	4.6
Globalization	46.3	6.6
Merger integration	35.5	11.6
Learning organization	42.9	2.7
Divestiture	21.2	15.4

Source: American Management Association

Computer-Related Illnesses

THE APPLICATIONS OF COMPUTER technology and the use of video display terminals are revolutionizing the workplace. Along with their growing use, however, have come reports about adverse health effects for VDT operators.

For every potential hazard, health specialists recommend interventions that can be used by employers and computer operators alike. Here is a list of the most commonly recognized harmful effects of frequent computer use and some suggested means of alleviating potential problems.

Eyestrain

Visual problems such as eyestrain and irritation are among the most frequently reported complaints by VDT operators. These visual problems can result from improper lighting, glare from the screen, poor positioning of the screen itself, or copy that is difficult to read. These problems can usually be corrected by arranging workstations and lighting to avoid direct or reflected glare. VDT operators can also reduce eyestrain by taking vision breaks and by doing exercises that relax eye muscles.

Radiation

Some workers, including pregnant women, are concerned that their health could be affected by X-rays or electromagnetic fields emitted from VDTs. To date, however, there is no conclusive evidence that the low levels of radiation emitted from VDTs pose a health risk. The issue is still being researched and studied. In the meantime, some workplace designs have incorporated changes such as increasing the distance between workstations and between the operator and the terminal, to reduce potential exposures to electromagnetic fields.

Fatigue and Musculoskeletal Problems

Work performed at VDTs may require sitting still for considerable amounts of time and usually involves small, frequent movements of the eyes, head, arms, and fingers. Retaining a fixed posture over long periods of time requires a significant static holding force, which causes fatigue. Proper workstation design is very important in eliminating these types of problems. An individual workstation should provide the operator with a comfortable sitting position sufficiently flexible to reach, use, and observe the display screen, keyboard, and document. Proper chair height and support to the lower region of the back are critical factors in reducing fatigue and related musculoskeletal complaints. Document holders also allow the operator to position and view material without straining the eyes or the muscles in the neck, shoulder, and back.

Repetitive Stress Syndrome

VDT operators are also subject to a potential risk of developing various nerve or cumulative trauma disorders. Carpal tunnel syndrome (CTS), a commonly recognized cumulative trauma disorder, is caused by repetitive wrist-hand movement and exertion. CTS is the compression and entrapment of the median nerve where it passes through the wrist into the hand. When irritated, the tendons and their sheaths, housed inside the narrow carpal tunnel in the wrist, swell and press against the median nerve. The pressure causes tingling, numbness, or severe pain in the wrist and hand. CTS usually can be reduced by maintaining correct posture and by limiting the activity that aggravates the tendon and the median nerve. For correct posture, VDT operators should sit in an upright position at the keyboard, with arms parallel to the floor and wrists and forearms supported where possible. Additional exercises may help eliminate the problem. In extreme cases, surgery may be required.

Ways to Help VDT Users Reduce Job-Related Stress

- Maintain a well-designed work area. (*See next page.*)

- Limit continuous hours. The longer the time spent at a VDT, the higher the rate of health problems reported. Users should spend no more than four hours at one time doing demanding work.

- Allow frequent breaks. Give workers the opportunity to get up and move about and give their eyes a chance to rest. A 15-minute break every two hours is recommended.

- Train workers thoroughly.

- Maintain variety. Limit the time workers spend on VDTs by giving staffers varied duties.

- Provide interaction or privacy as needed.

Source: Office and Branch Managers Bulletin

Computer-Related Illnesses (cont'd)

VDT Workstation Checklist

- Does the workstation lend itself to proper posture considerations such as:
  thighs horizontal;
  lower legs vertical;
  feet flat on floor or footrest;
  wrists neutral or slightly extended?

- Does the chair in use:
  adjust easily;
  have a padded seat with a rounded front;
  have a backrest that is adjustable;
  provide lumbar support;
  have casters?

- Is the keyboard worksurface:
  height adjustable;
  tilt adjustable?

- Is the keyboard detachable?

- Does keying require minimal force?

- Does the thickness of the keyboard affect wrist posture?

- Is there an adjustable document holder?

- Are armrests provided where needed?

- Are glare and reflections avoided?

- Do the VDTs have brightness and contrast controls?

- Is there proper distance between eyes and work?

- Is there sufficient space for knees and feet?

- Is the workstation biased toward right- or left-handed activity?

- Are adequate rest breaks provided for task demand?

- Are employees measured or rewarded by the number of keystrokes they type per minute?

- Is the employee's ability to maintain typing speed assisted by:
  job rotation;
  proper work methods;
  when and how to adjust workstations;
  how to get questions answered quickly?

Source: OSHA: Ergonomic Program Management Recommendations for General Industry

Contact Options

Occupational Safety and Health Administration (OSHA)
U.S. Department of Labor
Technical Data Center, Room N2625
200 Constitution Ave., NW
Washington DC 20210
(202) 219-7500

U.S. Department of Health and Human Services
Public Health Service, Centers for Disease Control
National Institute for Occupational Safety and Health (NIOSH)
Robert A. Taft Laboratories
4676 Columbia Pkwy.
Cincinnati, OH 45226
(513) 533-8236

Proper VDT Posture

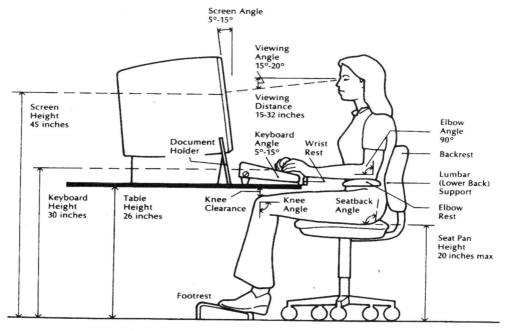

Illustration courtesy of the Kemper National Insurance Companies

Accessibility for the Handicapped

THE AMERICANS WITH DISABILITIES ACT covers a broad range of topics relating to the working conditions of the disabled. All qualified handicapped workers are covered. An employer is not required to hire or retain an individual who is not qualified to perform a job. The regulations define a qualified individual with a disability as a person with a disability who "satisfies the requisite skills, experience, education, and other job-related requirements of the employment position such individual holds or desires, and who, with or without a reasonable accommodation, can perform the essential functions of such a position."

It is important that employers be familiar with the issues covered by ADA and with those discussed in Title I and Title III in particular.

Title I

Employment deals specifically with employment. It prohibits discrimination against a qualified individual with a disability in regard to:

- Applications
- Testing
- Hiring
- Assignments
- Evaluation
- Disciplinary actions
- Training
- Promotion
- Medical examinations
- Layoff/recall
- Termination
- Compensation
- Leave
- Benefits.

Title III

Public Accommodations and Services Operated by Private Entities prohibits discrimination in public accommodations and services operated by private entities. The term "public accommodation" means any business that provides goods or services to the general public. In general, persons with disabilities must be accorded the full and equal enjoyment of the goods, services, facilities, privileges, advantages, and accommodations by any person who owns, leases, or operates a place of public accommodation. To accomplish this end, this title requires:

- Provision of auxiliary aids and services;
- Removal of architectural and communications barriers in existing vehicles;
- Removal of transportation barriers in existing vehicles;
- Modifications in policies, practices, and procedures.

Many areas and items must be addressed in an accessibility audit of public accommodations. The following is a sample accessibility checklist:

- Accessible routes (paths or walks) at least 3 feet wide and with at least 80 inches of headroom;
- Ramps that are at least 3 feet wide and with a maximum slope equal to 1 inch in 12 and maximum rise equal to 30 inches;
- Stairs with treads at least 11 inches wide and having a tactile warning at the top of the stairs;
- Parking facilities with spaces at least 8 feet wide and having special reserved spaces for the handicapped;
- Passenger loading zone that is at least 4 feet wide and 20 feet long;
- Drinking fountain: spout 3 feet high or less;
- Public telephones that are controlled by push button;
- Seating and tables that are 27 to 34 inches wide and 19 inches deep;
- Corridors with carpet pile one half inch or less;
- Door openings at least 32 inches wide.

Employers with questions on how to accommodate applicants and employees with disabilities may contact the Job Accommodation Network (JAN). This free service, located at West Virginia University, may be reached at (800) 526-7234.

Recommended Resources

The Employer's Guide to Understanding and Complying with the Americans with Disabilities Act
Dartnell Publishing, $129
(800) 441-7878

Americans with Disabilities Act Handbook, 2nd Edition
John Wiley & Sons, $125
(800) 225-5945, ext. 2497

Facts about AIDS

APPROXIMATELY ONE IN EVERY 250 Americans— most of whom are of working age—is living with HIV. What's more, nearly one in ten small employers already have employees who are living and working with HIV infection, including AIDS.

According to the American Red Cross, there is no danger in working with someone who is HIV-positive or who has AIDS. An individual cannot become infected through everyday work activities that do not involve contact with blood, semen, or vaginal fluids. Scientific studies from around the world have shown that HIV is not spread through ordinary employee, client, or public contact; nor through a handshake, a hug, or a social kiss.

For most workers, there is no need for special precautions. Scientific studies do not indicate any risk of HIV infection from contact with body fluids or waste—feces, nasal fluid, saliva, sweat, tears, urine, or vomit—unless these contain visible blood. Workers (such as sanitation workers) who may handle fluids and waste that sometimes contain blood should wear rubber or vinyl gloves. Furthermore, hairstylists, cosmetologists, electrologists, or any workers who use instruments that can penetrate the skin or become contaminated with blood should sterilize those instruments or throw them away after one use.

It is important that employees and employers alike be educated about HIV/AIDS and how to help support co-workers infected with the virus. An effective HIV/AIDS policy should address such issues as:

- Insurance and health-care costs
- Productivity
- Work disruption
- Employee benefits
- Customer concern
- Employee morale
- Legal considerations
- Confidentiality and privacy
- Discrimination concerns
- Disability requirements
- Job accommodation.

Reducing the Risk of Infection

- Avoid direct contact with blood. Use a barrier such as a clean cloth or wear disposable latex or vinyl gloves to protect yourself from any blood.
- Wash your hands with soap and water as soon as you can after giving first aid, whether or not you have worn gloves.
- If you perform rescue breathing, avoid contact with any blood.

- When cleaning someone's blood from surfaces, always wear rubber gloves and use a disinfectant solution. If a disinfectant is not available, you can make one by mixing 1/4 cup of liquid household chlorine bleach with one gallon of water. (This solution must be made fresh just prior to use and discarded each day.)

Source: The American Red Cross

Responding to AIDS: Ten Principles for the Workplace

The Citizens Commission on AIDS of New York City and New Jersey suggests the following policies be adopted:

- People with HIV infection or AIDS are entitled to the same rights and opportunities as people with other serious or life-threatening illnesses.
- Employment policies must, at a minimum, comply with federal, state, and local laws and regulations.
- Employment policies should be based on the scientific and epidemiological evidence that people with HIV infection or AIDS do not pose a risk of transmission of the virus to co-workers through ordinary workplace contact.
- The highest levels of management and union leadership should unequivocally endorse nondiscriminatory employment policies and education programs about HIV/AIDS.
- Employers and unions should communicate their support of these policies clearly, simply, and unambiguously.
- Employers should provide employees with sensitive, accurate, and up-to-date education about risk reduction in their personal lives.
- Employers have a duty to protect the confidentiality of employees' medical information.
- To prevent work disruption and rejection by co-workers of employees with HIV infection or AIDS, employers and unions should undertake education for all employees before incidents occur and as needed thereafter.
- Employers should not require HIV screening as part of pre-employment or general workplace physical examinations.
- In those special occupational settings where there may be a potential risk of exposure to HIV, employers should provide specific ongoing education and training, as well as necessary equipment, to reinforce appropriate infection-control procedures and ensure that they are implemented.

Alcohol and Substance Abuse

ALL ALCOHOL AND SUBSTANCE ABUSE programs in work settings are called Employee Assistance Programs or EAPs. According to the U.S. Department of Labor, the use of EAPs has grown dramatically over the last decade. Although there is no standardized EAP, most are based on the assumption that helping employees with alcohol and substance abuse problems will reduce employee turnover as well as reducing absenteeism, tardiness, accidents, and other problems that affect productivity. Many of these programs are also concerned with ensuring efficient healthcare cost containment and providing a new benefit to enhance employee morale and company commitment. Most companies employ one of the following four types of EAP:

- Internal company programs staffed by a company employee who accepts referrals from supervisors as well as self-referrals, conducts initial assessments, and refers employees to community resources for professional counseling or treatment.

- External company programs in which companies contract with outside agencies to provide most services. These are more common in small- and medium-sized firms.

- Labor union programs which usually revolve around a peer referral process that encourages union members with substance-abuse problems to seek help.

- Professional association programs which are usually aimed at maintaining standards of professional conduct. Threats to withdraw licensure are frequently used to pressure members into seeking assistance.

In most EAPs, alcohol and substance abuse problems are defined by poor job performance. Supervisors should confront employees constructively, demanding improved job performance as a condition of continued employment. Studies reveal that constructive confrontation rather than more severe forms of discipline leads to improvement in employee work performance.

In the last few years, more and more small- and medium-sized companies have begun investing their own resources in EAPs without any outside regulatory pressure from the government. This suggests the growing recognition among employers of the value of these efforts. The average annual cost for an EAP ranges from $12 to $20 per employee. Statistics from the National Council on Alcoholism and Drug Dependence indicate that an employer saves anywhere from $5 to $16 for every dollar invested in an EAP.

Establishing an EAP, however, is only one part of the way that a company can deal with substance abuse in the workplace.

Five Steps to a Workplace Substance Abuse Program

1. Write a clear and comprehensive policy

- Let employees and applicants know that drug and alcohol use on the job, or any use that affects job performance, is not permitted.

- Explain that you are establishing the policy for workplace safety, worker health, product quality, and productivity, and to avoid public liability.

- Tell employees what will happen if they violate the policy.

2. Train your supervisors. Supervisors should be responsible for:

- Observing and documenting unsatisfactory work performance or behavior;

- Talking to employees about work problems and what needs to be done about them.

Supervisors are *not* responsible for diagnosing or treating substance abuse problems.

3. Educate your employees. An employee education and awareness program:

- Explains your workplace substance abuse policy and the consequences of using drugs and alcohol on or off the job.

- Tells your employees how to get help with their drug and alcohol problems, including a description of services available to help employees by a representative of the EAP, if the company has one, or by a community resource.

- Informs employees on how drugs and alcohol actually affect the company's productivity, product quality, absenteeism, healthcare costs, and accident rates.

- Explains testing procedures—if drug testing is part of the program—with special attention to the consequences of testing positive, and procedures for ensuring accuracy and confidentiality.

4. Provide an employee assistance program

5. Start a drug testing program

Some companies must set up a drug testing program because of the kind of work they do. The Drug-Free Workplace Act of 1988 is a federal statute requiring certain federal contractors and grantees to maintain a drug-free workplace. Companies covered by the act must have a single contract with the federal government of $25,000 or more, or must receive a grant

Alcohol and Substance Abuse (cont'd)

from the federal government. Any company that sets up a drug testing program must make sure that the program explains:

- Statutory or regulatory requirements;
- Disability discrimination provisions;
- Collective bargaining agreements;
- Any other requirements in effect.

Source: An Employer's Guide to Dealing with Substance Abuse, U.S. Dept. of Labor, October, 1990

Alternative or Complementary Strategies to EAPs

- Alcohol education in the workplace, directed both toward information about the effects of drinking and identification of problem drinking and alcoholism;
- Alcohol control policies associated with work, such as prohibited lunchtime drinking, limiting availability of alcohol in executive dining rooms, excluding alcohol at company-sponsored functions, and prohibiting reimbursement of employee expenses for the purchase of alcohol for themselves and their clients;
- Wellness programs, including health risk appraisals, blood pressure screening, and counseling of employees regarding health risks associated with different drinking lifestyles.

Source: Alcohol Health & Research World, Vol. 13

Ten Facts about Alcohol and Substance Abuse in the Workplace

- 12 percent of the American workforce reports heavy drinking, defined as drinking five or more drinks per occasion on five or more days in the past 30 days.
- Up to 40 percent of industrial fatalities and 47 percent of industrial injuries can be linked to alcohol consumption and alcoholism.
- 70 percent of all current adult illegal drug users are employed.
- 63 percent of firms responding to a 1991 survey were engaged in some sort of drug testing, a 200 percent increase since 1987.
- Absenteeism among alcoholics or problem drinkers is 3.8 to 8.3 times greater than normal and up to 16 times greater among all employees with alcohol and other drug-related problems. Drug-using employees use three times as many sick benefits as other workers. They are five times more likely to file a workers' compensation claim.

- Non-alcoholic members of alcoholic families use ten times as much sick leave as members of families in which alcoholism is not present.
- 43 percent of CEOs responding to one survey estimate that use of alcohol and other drugs cost them 1 percent to 10 percent of their payroll.
- For every dollar they invest in an Employee Assistance Program, employers generally save anywhere from $5 to $16. The average annual cost for an EAP ranges from $12 to $20 per employee.
- While roughly 90 percent of the Fortune 500 companies have established EAPs, this percentage is much lower among smaller companies. Only 9 percent of businesses with fewer than 50 employees have EAP programs. Fully 90 percent of U.S. businesses fall into this category.
- A recent survey reports that nearly nine out of ten employers limit benefits for alcoholism, other drug dependence, and mental disorders despite the fact that 52 percent of the survey participants could not say how much it cost them to provide treatment for these conditions.

Source: National Council on Alcoholism and Drug Dependence

Contact Options

Dr. Richard K. Fuller
Division of Clinical and Prevention Research
National Institute on Alcohol Abuse and Alcoholism
Willco Bldg., #505
6000 Executive Blvd.
Rockville, MD 20892
(301) 443-1206

Center for Substance Abuse Prevention
Workplace Helpline
(800) 843-4971
Provides information and publications that will help companies research and develop drug-free workplace programs.

The National Association of State Alcohol and Drug Abuse Directors (NASADAD)
Drug-Free Workplace Project
444 N. Capitol St., NW, Suite 642
Washington DC 20001
(202) 783-6868

Center for Substance Abuse Treatment
National Treatment Referral Hotline
(800) 662-HELP
Refers callers to treatment programs locally and nationwide.

Workers' Compensation

IF A WORKER IS INJURED ON THE JOB, he or she cannot sue the employer for negligence. The exclusive remedy is workers' compensation. The worker gets no more if the employer is to blame and no less if he or she is at fault. Instead, the worker is entitled to medical care, certain wage replacement or indemnity benefits, and, often, vocational rehabilitation, regardless of fault.

This is a state program, and laws vary greatly from one state to another. All states except New Jersey, South Carolina, and Texas require that every employer provide workers' compensation coverage. Very large employers usually choose to be self-insured, while others purchase insurance from insurance companies or, in some states, from funds sponsored by the state or trade associations. In most states the price of workers' compensation insurance is set by the state, but an increasing number of states are allowing varying forms of price competition.

Workers receive a portion of their wages (usually two thirds) while they are recovering from an injury. These are called temporary total benefits. Very often the employee returns to work and there is no further problem. If that does not happen, temporary total benefits continue until maximum medical improvement occurs, or until the worker is medically stable. At that point most states make an assessment of whether the worker has a permanent impairment, and award additional benefits based on its severity. About ten states, however, base continuing benefits on the amount of the worker's wage loss rather than his or her degree of impairment.

Originally this was intended to be a simple system in which there would be no need for lawyers or formal litigation. Recently, however, workers have come to rely more and more on attorneys and employers have found the system increasingly more costly. It has become very popular for politicians to attempt to "reform" state workers' compensation laws. In some cases these changes have been successful and in others they have not.

Research in Michigan has shown that there is much employers can do to control their workers' compensation expenses regardless of the laws. A study conducted by the Upjohn Institute examined 5,000 employers in 29 different industries. It found that in each of the 29 industries some employers had ten times as many claims as others. What made the difference? Three things seemed to stand out: safety, disability management, and the corporate culture.

Ed Welch's Suggestions for Controlling Costs

- Safety is the first and most important approach. Nothing reduces costs more than preventing injuries from occurring.

- Create an atmosphere in which safety is important. Du Pont has 100,000 employees in the United States and it averages 30 lost claims per year. Safety has always been the most important aspect of its corporate culture.

- Return workers to the job as quickly as possible. Most workers want to go back during the first few weeks or months after an injury but if they are allowed to sit idle for several months their attitude changes. They begin to view themselves as disabled people who can never return to work.

- Most successful employers have very aggressive return-to-work programs which are designed to keep the worker in the habit of "getting up and brushing his teeth every morning."

- Larger employers often find it best to become self-insured and to take more control over their workers' compensation program.

- Smaller employers need to demand more service from their insurance companies. This might include help with safety and return-to-work programs and more active claims management.

- Employers should find out if price competition is allowed in their state and shop for the best deal. Note, however, that good service may be more important than a small difference in price.

- Employers and insurers should work together. If you have more than a few open claims you should expect your insurance company to meet with you a few times each year to discuss those claims and to plan what should be done about them.

Ed Welch teaches continuing education courses and publishes a newsletter on workers' compensation. For more information, he can be contacted at:

Ed Welch on Workers' Compensation
2875 Northwind Dr., Suite 210-A
East Lansing, MI 48823
(517) 332-5266

Employer Costs. Send e-mail to employer@almanac.yoyo.com. See p. xi for instructions.

Tables of employer costs for employee compensation and employees with pension plans or group health plans.

Insurance

Work Fatalities and Injuries

Year	Employed Labor Force (millions)	Fatalities	Fatalities per 100,000 Workers	Injuries (millions)	Injuries per 100,000 Workers
1960	65.8	13,800	21.0	1,950	2,964
1970	78.7	13,800	17.5	2,200	2,795
1980	99.3	13,200	13.3	2,200	2,216
1983	100.8	11,700	11.6	1,900	1,885
1984	105.0	11,500	11.0	1,900	1,810
1985	107.2	11,500	10.7	2,000	1,866
1986	109.6	11,100	10.1	1,800	1,642
1987	112.4	11,300	10.1	1,800	1,601
1988	114.3	11,000	10.0	1,800	1,565
1989	116.7	10,700	9.0	1,700	1,449
1990	117.4	10,500	9.0	1,800	1,527
1991	116.4	9,300	8.0	NA	NA
1992	117.0	8,500	7.0	NA	NA
1993	118.7	9,100	8.0	NA	NA

Source: National Safety Council

Economic Losses from Work Accidents

Year	Loss ($ millions)	Loss in 1993 Dollars ($ millions)	Cost per Worker in 1993 Dollars ($)
1960	4,400	21,480	327
1970	8,000	29,794	379
1980	28,000	49,102	494
1984	30,800	42,835	408
1985	35,000	47,003	439
1986	32,800	43,245	395
1987	39,800	50,626	450
1988	44,500	54,355	473
1989	48,500	56,508	482
1990*	63,800	70,536	598
1991	63,300	67,157	575
1992**	111,700	115,044	978
1993	111,900	111,900	940

*Data include an estimate of the replacement cost of household services of injured workers and are not comparable to prior years. **Loss figures have been revised by adding new components, benchmarks, and inflation factors and are not comparable to prior years.*

Sources: National Safety Council; Bureau of Labor Statistics; Consumer Prices; Insurance Information Institute estimates

Contact Options

Providers of Information, Support, and/or Educational Materials:

Insurance Information Institute
110 William St.
New York, NY 10038
(212) 669-9200

Insurance Fund Foundation
13555 S.E. 36th St., Suite 105
Bellevue, WA 98006
(206) 747-6631

National Insurance Consumer Helpline
(800) 942-4242

National Safety Council
1121 Spring Lake Dr.
Itasca, IL 60143
(708) 285-1121

Risk and Insurance Management Society
205 E. 42nd St.
New York, NY 10017
(212) 286-9292

Insurance Rating Agencies

THERE ARE FOUR NATIONAL RATING agencies that monitor the status of the country's insurance companies. The ratings are no guarantee of an insurer's strength. Most experts agree, however, that if an insurance company receives either the highest or the second highest grade from two or more of the major rating companies and receives no grade below the fourth level from any of the raters, the insurance policy or annuity is relatively secure.

A company can call A. M. Best and Standard & Poor's to order their reports or can find the Moody's and Duff & Phelps reports in some public libraries.

Recommended Resources

The Insurance Forum
P.O. Box 245
Ellettsville, IN 47429
(812) 876-6502

This monthly newsletter costs $60 and reports thoroughly on the insurance industry. Each year *The Insurance Forum* publishes a special ratings issue, containing listings of hundreds of life insurance companies and how they are rated by A.M. Best, Standard & Poor's, Moody's, and Duff & Phelps. *The Insurance Forum* special issue can be purchased for $10.

A. M. Best
Ambest Rd.
Old Wick, NJ 08858
(908) 439-2200

A custom-generated report of all insurance companies in a particular category for a fee dependent on the breadth of the report.

Duff & Phelps
Rating Hotline
55 E. Monroe St., 35th Floor
Chicago, IL 60603
(312) 629-3833

Besides the quick information available via the hotline, an annual subscription to the Duff & Phelps insurance company/claims paying ability report is available for $795 per year.

Moody's Investors Service
Corporate Ratings Desk
99 Church St.
New York, NY 10007
(212) 553-0377

A caller can inquire about a maximum of three insurance company ratings per call, but is invited to call as many times as desired.

Standard & Poor's
Ratings Information Department
25 Broadway
New York, NY 10004
(212) 208-1527

In addition to their ratings information telephone service, Standard & Poor's publishes the *S&P Insurer Solvency Review*, which gives the annual ratings of several hundred insurance companies and costs $145.

The Top Reference Sources

Insuring Your Business
Insurance Information Institute, $22.50
(212) 669-9200

This is an essential reference for anyone who is planning to open and insure a business. There are, among others, chapters on property insur-

ance, liability insurance, workers' compensation, insuring key employees, and employee benefits insurance. There are also sections on specific types of businesses, such as restaurants, manufacturers, construction firms, and trading companies.

Health Insurance Coverage

EVERY SMALL BUSINESS owner has unique needs when it comes to selecting a health insurance policy for employees. That is why it is so important for you to make an informed decision about the health insurance coverage you choose for yourself and your employees.

This section discusses the small group market, defines the basic choices, and provides a checklist to help you compare policies you consider. A glossary is included as an easy reference to health insurance terms and common benefits.

If you come across terms not defined, call the National Insurance Consumer Helpline at (800) 942-4242. The Helpline staff will try to explain them, and answer any other questions you may have about health insurance.

Small Group Health Insurance

"Small group" refers to the number of employees (sometimes 1 or 2, but most often between 3 and 25) covered under a company's group insurance plan.

In the small group market, health insurance prices are based mainly upon two factors. The first is the expected cost of medical services in a given geographic area; the second is the projected utilization of services. Usually, insurers estimate the probability of an insured person using medical services based upon factors such as age, sex, and medical history. These factors influence an insurer's charges to you and your employees. Often, those individuals who are considered a greater risk due to age or other factors will pay a higher premium for insurance. Of course, the type of benefit plan chosen also affects the premium.

Most small group health insurance companies use a process known as medical underwriting, which enables them to better predict claims. An underwriter analyzes a number of risk factors, including the medical history of each individual, to determine the group's insurability.

The insurer's goal is to offer coverage at a price that is fair to the insured group and to assure adequate income to pay future claims and other expenses.

Private Commercial Insurance Options

Today, there are many options for the small group employer. It is important to be aware of the pros and cons of each choice when selecting a plan. While premiums can vary among different carriers, recognize that there can be substantial differences in the covered benefits and in what your employees must pay out-of-pocket for medical services.

1. Fee-for-service plans

Fee-for-service is the traditional form of commercial health insurance. Fee-for-service plans enable you to choose your own physicians and hospitals. Most of these plans require deductible and co-insurance payments.

Simply put, coverage results from your insurer's paying "reasonable and customary" or usual charges (i.e., reasonable compared with other providers in the same geographic area) for physician and hospital services. Typically, fee-for-service coverage for employer-sponsored health insurance has been characterized by three major features:

- Employers and employees share the premiums in most cases;

- Employees have complete freedom to select any medical care provider;

- The insurance company pays the allowable claim.

Fee-for-service coverage has dominated employee benefits packages for many years. In the past, fee-for-service coverage often did not include cost containment provisions, and the major advantage of these plans was the freedom for the consumer to choose providers.

Today, however, many fee-for-service plans also offer a wide variety of cost containment features. These plans can hold down costs for both the insurance company and the business owner, as well as encourage consumers to be efficient users of medical services.

2. Managed care options

A managed care health insurance plan integrates both the financing and the delivery of appropriate health care services to covered individuals. Managed health care plans are becoming more common among small groups. Today, more than 70 percent of Americans who obtain health insurance through their employers are enrolled in some type of managed care plan. Most managed care plans have the following basic characteristics:

- Arrangements with selected doctors, hospitals, and other providers to furnish a comprehensive set of health care services to members;

- Explicit standards for the selection of health care providers;

- Formal programs for quality assurance and utilization review;

- Significant financial incentives when using the specific providers and procedures associated with the plan.

Health Insurance Coverage (cont'd)

3. Fee-for-service with managed care features

These plans combine some of the features of managed care plans with traditional fee-for-service insurance arrangements. They hold down costs and discourage unnecessary use of services. Examples of managed care features that may appear in a fee-for-service plan include:

- Case management
- Centers of excellence
- Employee assistance plans
- Pre-admission certification
- Second surgical opinion
- Special benefit networks
- Utilization review.

Preferred Provider Organizations (PPOs)

A PPO typically consists of groups of hospitals and providers that contract with employers, insurers, third-party administrators, or other sponsoring groups to provide health care services to covered persons and accept negotiated fees as payment for services rendered.

There are different sponsoring arrangements:

- Hospital-sponsored PPOs, which often include a network of institutions in order to cover a wider geographic area, as well as many of the physicians on their medical staffs;
- Physician-sponsored PPOs, which are developed by local medical societies, local professional associations or clinics, or groups of physicians;
- Third-party payer-sponsored PPOs, which include those initiated by commercial insurers and Blue Cross and Blue Shield plans;
- Entrepreneur-sponsored PPOs, which create a broker relationship, with the entrepreneur acting as an intermediary between the provider of service and the payer;
- Employer- or labor-sponsored PPOs, which contract directly with providers on behalf of their employees or members;
- Other provider-sponsored PPOs, which are developed by non-hospital and non-physician providers, such as dentists, optometrists, pharmacists, chiropractors, and podiatrists, through their professional associations, local groups, or clinics.

Health Maintenance Organizations (HMOs)

These were the original managed care arrangements, first emerging as prepaid group practices in the 1930s. The name "health maintenance organization" was coined in the early 1970s, and was given to 1973 federal legislation promoting their development. HMOs constitute an organized system for providing, or assuring delivery of, health care in a certain geographic area; they provide an agreed-on set of basic and supplemental health-maintenance and treatment services to a voluntarily enrolled group of people.

In exchange for a set amount of premium or dues, HMOs provide all the agreed-on health services to their enrollees; there are generally no deductibles and no, or minimal, co-payments. The HMO bears the risk if the cost of providing the care exceeds the premium received. There are now several types of HMOs:

- The staff model, where providers are directly employed by the HMO;
- The group model, where medical groups contract with the HMO (Kaiser plans are the best-known example of this type);
- The independent practice association (IPA), where the HMO contracts with physicians in independent practice, or with associations of independent physicians. IPA physicians frequently have arrangements with more than one HMO;
- The network model, which contracts to cover two or more independent practices.

Choosing Quality Coverage

Choosing health insurance can be confusing because the healthcare marketplace constantly changes. Finding a policy that provides quality coverage for you and your employees and stays within your budget can seem impossible. It doesn't have to be—you simply need to find an agent with whom you are comfortable, and a plan that is backed by a reputable insurance company.

I. Choosing an insurance agent or broker

Agents and brokers are licensed by the state to solicit and negotiate contracts of insurance and serve policyholders. Agents may represent one company or several companies. They earn commissions based on the policies they sell.

When choosing an agent you should:

- Consult relatives, friends, and business associates for referrals;
- Make sure the agent has been licensed by your state insurance department and is a full-time agent;
- Look for an agent with special professional qualifications or many years' experience. The best agents have specialized training in health insurance and other related subjects.

Health insurance agents do more than just sell policies; they are paid to provide service to their clients. Services you should expect from your agent include:

- Advising you on the right insurance policy to fit your special needs. The agent should ask enough questions to understand your entire insurance picture before advising you;

Health Insurance Coverage (cont'd)

- Explaining the cost and coverage of a policy you are considering;

- Keeping you informed about the new insurance plans that may be of interest to you;

- Reviewing your insurance every year to consider changes in your employees' financial or family status which may change your insurance requirements;

- Helping you handle claims, answering your questions, and helping you resolve any other insurance problems.

2. Choosing an insurance company

When you purchase insurance, you are buying the insurer's promise to make the payments as specified in the policy if you incur covered medical expenses.

In order to satisfy this promise, the company must be able and willing to pay the claim. The best way to investigate a company's ability to pay the claim is to check on its financial stability. (See Company Reliability/Rating below).

Checking the company's willingness to pay claims can be more difficult. The best source for this kind of information is your agent or a personal referral from someone who has had a policy with the company for some time and has filed several claims. Either can give you a sense of the "friendliness" of the company, its willingness to answer questions and resolve complaints or problems.

Another good source of information is your state insurance department. The state insurance department regulates insurers and collects information about the number of complaints received about a particular company. Local consumer groups, newspaper columnists, and Better Business Bureaus may have additional information specific to your area.

3. Company reliability/rating

The financial stability of your insurance company is an important indicator of its ability to pay your future claims. A number of financial publishing firms investigate the financial standing of specific insurance companies and report their findings. Some of these firms are A. M. Best Company, Moody's Investor Service, Duff & Phelps, and Standard & Poor's Corporation. These reports are expensive but often are available in the reference sections of business and public libraries.

If you have trouble finding published information about an insurance company, ask your agent for information or call or write the company home office and ask for a copy of its most recent annual report or report from a rating firm. The company's earnings or losses will be reported, along with information about its cash reserves and liabilities.

It is important to find out if the company and agent are licensed to do business in your state. Your state insurance department is the source for this information. It requires the companies it licenses to file yearly financial reports, maintain legally required reserve funds, undergo periodic inspection audits, and comply with state laws regarding fairness.

A Final Note

Remember that price alone is not the sole factor in good insurance protection. The service provided by the company and agent you select is important, too. Therefore, in making your choice, personal knowledge of both the company's and agent's reputation for good service is a significant consideration.

Be aware, also, that quite a few small employer health benefit plans are sold through a multiple-employer trust (MET) or a multiple employer welfare association (MEWA). Care should be exercised with such programs, as many are uninsured, i.e., don't have the backing of a financially sound life and health insurance company. Such plans present a high risk to employers as there may be no assurance that adequate funds will be set aside to pay future claims.

Source: Health Insurance Association of America

Glossary of Health Insurance Terms

Case Management
This is a process for directing the ongoing course of treatment to be sure that it occurs in the most appropriate setting and that the best form of service is selected. Case management often can produce alternatives to institutional care that result in better patient outcomes as well as lower costs.

Centers of Excellence
These are hospitals that specialize in treating particular illnesses, such as cancer, or performing particular treatments, such as organ transplants.

Co-insurance
Sometimes called "co-payment," it is the portion of covered healthcare expenses an insured must pay in addition to a deductible. Co-insurance is usually described as a percentage. For example, on a standard 80/20 co-insurance plan, the insurance company will pay 80 percent of covered expenses and the insured employee will pay 20 percent.

Concurrent Review
See Utilization Review.

Glossary of Health Insurance Terms (cont'd)

Deductible
A deductible is the amount of covered expenses that the insured must pay in each benefit period before the insurer pays for allowable claims. A higher deductible will usually result in a lower premium.

Employee Assistance Program (EAP)
"EAP" is a generic term for the variety of counseling services made available to employees (and frequently their families) through an employer-sponsored program. These programs often refer employees to appropriate treatment.

Fee-for-Service
Fee-for-service is a method of charging, whereby a physician or other practitioner bills for each visit or service. Premium costs for fee-for-service agreements can increase if physicians or other providers increase their fees, increase the number of visits, or substitute more costly services for less expensive ones.

Health Maintenance Organization (HMO)
HMOs constitute an organized system for providing, or assuring delivery of, health care in a certain geographic area; they provide an agreed-on set of basic and supplemental health-maintenance and treatment services to a voluntarily enrolled group of people. In exchange for a set amount of premium or dues, HMOs provide all the agreed-on health services to their enrollees; there are generally no deductibles and no, or minimal, co-payments. The HMO bears the risk if the cost of providing the care exceeds the premium received.

Indemnity
An indemnity is a benefit paid by an insurance policy for an insured loss. Often it is used to refer to benefits paid directly to the insured.

Insurance Department
Each state has an insurance department that is responsible for implementing state insurance laws and regulations.

Limitations
Limitations describe conditions or circumstances under which the insurer will not pay or will limit payments. Detailed information about limitations and exclusions is found in the certificate of insurance. An employer gets a group policy, with all details of the contract. An employee gets a booklet on the insurance, which is a more concise presentation of the insurance contract.

Major Medical
Major medical insurance plans provide broad coverage and substantial protection from large, unpredictable medical care expenses. They cover a wide range of medical care charges with few internal limits and a high overall maximum benefit.

Maximum Out-of-Pocket
The maximum amount of money an insured will pay in a benefit period, in addition to regular premium payments, is called the maximum out-of-pocket. The out-of-pocket payment is usually the sum of the deductible and co-insurance payments. Non-covered expenses are the employee's responsibility in addition to out-of-pocket amounts.

National Association of Insurance Commissioners (NAIC)
This national organization of state insurance commissioners promotes national uniformity in the regulation of insurance. Each state has an appointed or elected commissioner.

Pre-Admission Certification
See Utilization Review.

Pre-Admission Testing
Tests taken prior to a hospital admission are called pre-admission tests.

Pre-Existing Condition
A medical condition that existed before obtaining insurance coverage and for which a reasonably prudent person would seek medical treatment is called a pre-existing condition. Examples of pre-existing conditions include a sickness, injury, or complication of pregnancy for which an insured person received medical advice, consultation, prescription drugs, or treatment during a specified time period before the effective date of coverage.

Preferred Provider Organization (PPO)
A PPO consists of hospitals and providers that contract with employers, insurers, third-party administrators, or other sponsoring groups to provide healthcare services to covered persons and accept negotiated fee schedules as payment for services rendered.

Premium
A premium is a periodic payment made by a policyholder (employer, individual) for the cost of insurance.

Reasonable and/or Customary Charge
A charge for health care that is consistent with the going rate or charge in a certain geographical area for the same or similar services is called a reasonable and/or customary charge.

Retrospective Review
See Utilization Review.

Second Surgical Opinion
See Utilization Review.

Special Benefit Networks
Special networks of providers for a particular service, such as mental health, substance abuse, or prescription drugs, are known as special benefit networks.

Glossary of Health Insurance Terms (cont'd)

State-Mandated Benefits

Each state requires insurance policies sold in that state to include benefits for a variety of medical conditions or providers. These mandated benefits can add to costs greatly. For example, an insurance policy may have to cover mental health or podiatry services.

Third-Party Administrator (TPA)

A TPA is a company or broker that handles the administration of an insurance plan. Depending on the terms of its agreement with an insurance plan, a TPA may collect premiums, pay claims, and handle routine underwriting and administrative functions. The TPA typically acts on guidelines that the insurance plan establishes.

Underwriting

The process by which an insurer determines whether and on what basis it will accept an application for insurance is called underwriting.

Utilization Review (UR)

UR is a process that assesses the delivery of medical services to determine if the care provided is appropriate, medically necessary, and of high quality. Utilization review may include review of appropriateness of admissions, services ordered and provided, length of stay and discharge practices, both on a concurrent and retrospective basis. For example:

- Pre-Admission Certification: determines whether a hospital should admit a patient and whether services can be provided on an outpatient basis; its goal is eliminating unnecessary non-emergency procedures.

- Concurrent Review: includes continued-stay review of hospital cases, discharge-planning efforts to include proper and efficient placement of the hospital patient on discharge, and case management.

- Retrospective Review: follow-up analysis that ensures medical care services were necessary and appropriate (to detect and reduce the incidence of fraud and unnecessary services).

- Second Surgical Opinion: a process that requires patients to obtain an opinion from a second doctor before certain elective surgeries. Insurers rely on second surgical opinions to eliminate unnecessary surgical procedures.

Explanation of Common Benefits

Ambulatory Care

Also known as outpatient care, ambulatory care is medical, surgical, or diagnostic services provided in a non-hospital setting, not requiring an overnight stay.

Dental Care

This coverage provides reimbursement of dental services and supplies, including preventive care. Benefits may be provided through a plan integrated with other medical insurance coverage, or a plan may be written separately from other coverage (non-integrated).

Diagnostic X-Ray and Laboratory Examinations

This coverage provides reimbursement for outpatient diagnostic and laboratory examinations.

Home Health Care

Home Health Care services are given at home to aged, disabled, sick, or convalescent individuals who do not need institutional care. The most common types of home care are visiting nurse services and speech, physical, occupational, and rehabilitation therapy. Home health agencies, hospitals, or other community organizations provide these services.

Hospice Care

Hospices care for the terminally ill and their families, in the home or a non-hospital setting, emphasizing alleviation of pain rather than medical cure.

Hospital Care

Both in-patient medical care expenses and outpatient medical care expenses incurred in a hospital are reimbursed under this coverage.

Inpatient Benefits

- Charges for room and board

- Charges for necessary services and supplies, sometimes referred to as "hospital extras," "miscellaneous charges," and "ancillary charges."

Outpatient Benefits

- Surgical procedures

- Rehabilitation therapy

- Physical therapy.

Physician Visits

This coverage provides reimbursement for physician's fees for visits in cases of injury or sickness. The two types of plans commonly offered are one covering in-hospital visits only and another that covers doctor visits both in and out of the hospital.

Pregnancy Care

Federal maternity legislation, enacted in 1978, requires that employers with 15 or more employees who are engaged in interstate commerce provide the same benefits for pregnancy, childbirth, and related medical conditions as for any other sickness or injury. This includes all employers who are, or become, subject to Title VII of the Civil Rights Act of 1964.

Glossary of Health Insurance Terms (cont'd)

Prescription Drug Plan
Some prescription drug expense insurance plans are subject to the same deductible and co-payments as are other covered medical expenses. Other plans use a prescription drug card and cover these expenses with very little, if any, cost to the insured.

Rehabilitation Care
A program of care that provides physical and mental restoration of disabled insured individuals to maximum independence and productivity.

Skilled Nursing Facility
A licensed institution engaged in providing regular medical care and treatment to sick and injured persons is known as a skilled nursing facility. The institution maintains a daily medical record and requires that each patient be under the care of a licensed physician.

Supplemental Accident
Many plans contain supplemental accident insurance that provides first-dollar coverage (no deductible or co-payments) when an injury is due to an accident. Another type of accident plan pays a fixed dollar amount–$5,000 or $10,000, for example–if a serious accidental injury occurs.

Vision Care
This coverage is designed to provide benefits for preventive and corrective eye care. Insurers usually offer vision care with basic coverage such as hospital, surgical, medical, or X-ray and laboratory benefits.

Checklist for Comparing Plans

THIS CHECKLIST CAN GUIDE your discussions with your broker or agent.

I. Evaluating your company's needs

- Number of employees
- Number of dependents
- Sex of employees
- Age of employees
- Employees and dependents of childbearing age
- Employees/dependents with pre-existing medical conditions
- Employees with health problems making them high-risk
- Employees insured elsewhere.

2. Covered medical services

- Inpatient hospital services
- Outpatient surgery
- Psychiatric and mental health care
- Drug and alcohol abuse treatment
- Skilled nursing care
- Home healthcare visits
- Rehabilitation facility care
- Hospice care
- Dental care
- Maternity care
- Supplemental accident accident

- Prescription drugs
- Vision care
- Preventive care and checkups
- Chiropractic care
- Physician visits
- Medical tests and X-rays
- Mammograms.

3. Are there medical service limits, exclusions, or pre-existing conditions that will affect employees?

4. What cost containment and quality assurance procedures are included? (i.e., utilization review, pre-certification, second surgical opinions)

5. What is the total cost of the policy?

- Cost for the employer
- Cost for employees
- Single deductible
- Family deductible
- Co-insurance
- Single out-of-pocket maximum per year
- Family out-of-pocket maximum per year
- Share of premium.

6. Is the rate guaranteed? For how long?

7. What is the policy's lifetime maximum amount of coverage?

Checklist for Comparing Plans (cont'd)

8. What has the rate history been for comparable groups over the past five years and how is it calculated?

9. What will happen to premiums if one of the employees has a major claim?

10. How will service needs be handled?

11. Will the agent/broker or a customer service representative be available to meet with employees and dependents?

12. How long will it take to process a claim?

13. How often will the employer be billed?

14. Is the agent or broker qualified in the small group market? Does the agent or broker know about small group insurance?

- Good references
- Licensed in my state
- Professional qualifications
- Experience in the small group market
- Doing business for at least three years
- Member of recognized professional organization.

The Top Reference Sources

Infolink
(914) 736-1565

This group of researchers uses databases, computers, and libraries to track down obscure information on almost any topic.

For a rate of about $150 an hour, they will research any question you need answered, from competitive pricing and market share to the best ways to design a playground. Their specialties are advertising and marketing.

INTERNATIONAL

Foreign Investors in the U.S.

THE MAJOR FOREIGN INVESTOR IN THE UNITED STATES is Japan, followed by the United Kingdom and the Netherlands. The United Kingdom and the Netherlands concentrate on manufacturing and petroleum, while Japan is focused on trade, real estate, and financial services.

Foreign Direct Investment Position in the United States, Historical-Cost Basis by Account

Location	1993 Total ($ mil.)	1992 Total ($ mil.)
WORLD	445,268	425,636
Petroleum	32,647	34,347
Manufacturing	166,698	163,354
Wholesale trade	59,290	59,024
Other	186,633	168,911
Canada	39,408	37,845
Petroleum	1,991	1,649
Manufacturing	16,600	17,005
Wholesale trade	1,101	1,506
Other	19,716	17,686
Europe	270,767	251,206
Petroleum	24,979	26,006
Manufacturing	122,590	117,617
Wholesale trade	21,776	21,811
Other	101,422	85,772
Netherlands	68,477	65,323
Petroleum	12,424	11,783
Manufacturing	22,856	22,994
Wholesale trade	6,253	5,724
Other	26,944	24,822

Location	1993 Total ($ mil.)	1992 Total ($ mil.)
United Kingdom	95,415	89,073
Petroleum	9,367	10,901
Manufacturing	42,543	40,777
Wholesale trade	4,908	5,096
Other	38,598	32,299
Japan	96,213	97,537
Petroleum	254	140
Manufacturing	17,746	18,321
Wholesale trade	33,910	32,841
Other	44,303	46,235
Other areas	38,879	39,047
Petroleum	5,423	6,552
Manufacturing	9,762	10,411
Wholesale trade	2,504	2,866
Other	21,190	19,218

Source: Survey of Current Business, Aug. 1994

Foreign Direct Investment in the United States, Historical-Cost Basis ($ millions)

The foreign direct investment position is calculated from the equity in, and net outstanding loans to, subsidiaries in the United States owned by foreign corporations. This is the foreign corporation's contribution to subsidiary assets.

Country	1989	1990	1991	1992	1993
ALL COUNTRIES	368,924	394,911	418,780	425,636	445,268
CANADA	30,370	29,544	36,341	37,845	39,408
EUROPE	239,190	247,320	252,692	251,206	270,767
Austria	386	625	520	518	557
Belgium	3,799	3,900	3,204	4,288	4,589
Denmark	656	819	1,426	1,508	833
Finland	1,297	1,504	1,508	1,416	1,500
France	15,365	18,650	25,359	25,459	28,470
Germany	28,386	28,232	28,602	29,603	34,667
Ireland	1,416	1,340	2,232	2,750	2,593
Italy	1,436	1,524	2,749	274	1,229
Liechtenstein	177	167	110	40	-15
Luxembourg	407	2,195	1,054	730	990
Netherlands	56,734	64,671	59,776	65,323	68,477
Norway	576	773	620	709	844

Foreign Investors in the U.S. (cont'd)

Country	1989	1990	1991	1992	1993
Spain	601	792	1,406	1,546	623
Sweden	5,435	5,484	5,322	6,850	8,077
Switzerland	18,746	17,674	20,155	20,635	21,384
United Kingdom	103,458	98,676	98,236	89,073	95,415
Other	316	295	413	485	537
LATIN AMERICA AND WESTERN HEMISPHERE	16,218	20,168	18,907	21,098	20,342
SOUTH AND CENTRAL AMERICA	5,819	6,140	7,096	7,790	6,604
Brazil	428	377	539	574	714
Mexico	350	575	759	1,230	1,039
Panama	3,392	4,188	4,818	5,040	4,754
Venezuela	1,163	496	476	440	-398
Other	486	504	505	507	494
OTHER WESTERN HEMISPHERE	10,399	14,028	11,810	13,308	13,739
AFRICA	505	505	756	723	805
MIDDLE EAST	7,588	4,425	4,725	4,786	5,027
Israel	630	640	1,295	1,284	1,712
Kuwait	4,280	1,805	1,662	1,643	1,555
Lebanon	-9	-16	-23	-29	-35
Saudi Arabia	2,455	1,811	1,606	1,688	1,591
United Arab Emirates	112	99	68	93	107
Other	119	86	116	106	98
ASIA AND PACIFIC	75,053	92,948	105,359	109,978	108,918
Australia	4,962	6,542	6,364	7,069	7,278
Hong Kong	1,124	1,511	1,859	1,842	2,015
Japan	67,268	83,091	93,787	97,537	96,213
Korea, Republic of	-307	-1,009	661	823	795
Malaysia	29	56	52	73	250
New Zealand	166	157	92	69	104
Philippines	82	77	63	68	67
Singapore	934	1,289	923	873	228
Taiwan	476	836	1,109	1,117	1,272
Other	318	398	450	506	694

Note: Values for 1991 and 1992 are restated.   *Source: Survey of Current Business, Aug. 1994*

The Top Reference Sources

Business America
U.S. Government Printing Office, $32/year
(202) 512-1800

Published monthly by the U.S. Department of Commerce, this informative magazine is focused on international trade issues. Features include articles on the U.S. trade balance, exporting to Japan, economic reforms in Africa, and the outlook for stronger commercial ties with North Africa and the Near East.

The many contact names and numbers for government support throughout each issue are extremely valuable.

Foreign Investors in the U.S. (cont'd)

Sales of U.S. Companies to Foreign Buyers: By Industry ($ millions)

Industry Classification of Seller	1990	1991	1992	1993	1994
Drugs, medical supplies, & equipment	3,844.0	1,309.7	118.9	766.5	9,976.9
Computer software, supplies, & services	197.7	52.5	35.0	297.9	5,063.2
Food processing	1,052.6	440.0	445.9	285.0	4,248.1
Retail	701.6	125.0	275.0	14.0	2,014.0
Household goods	1,250.0	0.0	0.0	0.0	1,550.0
Paper	275.5	0.0	41.0	0.0	1,480.0
Industrial & farm equipment & machinery	254.1	225.7	79.0	154.8	1,433.7
Agricultural production	131.7	0.0	0.0	0.0	1,300.0
Banking & finance	150.0	767.9	207.0	817.1	1,215.6
Printing & publishing	285.0	32.0	1,059.5	76.6	1,014.9
Broadcasting	0.0	0.0	77.0	462.0	989.0
Brokerage, investment, & mgmt. consulting	11.0	357.7	0.0	23.6	853.2
Mining & minerals	1,489.0	218.8	413.0	722.4	794.2
Insurance	4,688.1	1,251.5	20.0	5.0	561.4
Office equipment & computer hardware	362.6	10.0	8.0	237.4	372.6
Instruments & photography equipment	100.0	180.0	8.0	4.1	352.1
Wholesale & distribution	280.0	314.0	59.8	323.4	325.2
Electronics	221.5	114.9	3.7	2.4	321.1
Electric, gas, water, & sanitary services	0.0	643.2	95.0	150.0	291.5
Miscellaneous services	622.1	122.6	16.5	23.0	290.6
Chemicals, paints, & coatings	1,060.4	388.2	901.7	376.5	213.9
Valves, pumps, & hydraulics	640.2	0.0	0.0	207.0	210.0
Health services	293.0	257.0	118.1	0.0	195.0
Primary metal processing	785.5	0.0	203.7	15.0	152.8
Aerospace, aircraft, & defense	103.0	0.0	115.6	0.0	111.0
Packaging & containers	0.0	0.0	0.0	0.0	100.0
Auto products & accessories	380.0	0.0	170.0	216.3	87.0
Fabricated metal products	567.5	1,226.5	43.6	139.5	80.0
Leisure & entertainment	8,029.5	204.9	35.0	109.1	41.6
Energy services	193.0	0.0	0.0	0.0	39.7
Toys & recreational products	20.0	0.0	0.0	314.2	38.5
Autos & trucks	340.1	99.8	0.0	337.0	33.0
Transportation	234.8	96.7	30.4	27.4	27.8
Plastics & rubber	76.8	12.9	95.0	720.0	14.3
Electrical equipment	26.5	2,828.2	146.2	301.3	11.6
Real estate	2.0	0.0	2.0	0.0	9.8
Textiles	0.0	0.0	0.0	310.5	5.5
Apparel	125.0	0.0	61.5	0.0	0.0
Beverages	21.0	103.0	0.0	645.3	0.0
Building products & materials	40.0	0.0	0.0	0.0	0.0
Communications	217.8	266.0	3,604.0	3,407.3	0.0
Conglomerate	0.0	0.0	0.0	0.0	0.0
Construction contractors & eng. svcs.	7.6	10.7	64.7	16.3	0.0
Construction, mining & oil equip., & mach.	21.1	0.0	0.0	60.0	0.0
Furniture	0.0	0.0	0.0	0.0	0.0
Miscellaneous manufacturing	5.5	0.0	4.0	6.5	0.0
Oil & gas	1,522.0	558.8	261.9	589.4	0.0
Stone, clay, & glass	2,323.3	0.0	38.0	133.6	0.0
Timber & forest products	0.0	0.0	0.0	54.0	0.0
Toiletries & cosmetics	107.0	43.0	445.3	0.0	0.0

Source: Mergerstat[SM] Review

Foreign Investors in the U.S. (cont'd)

Industries Attracting Foreign Buyers: By Number of Transactions

Industry Classification of Seller	1990	1991	1992	1993	1994	Five-Year Cumulative
Computer software, supplies, & service	13	4	6	15	15	53
Drugs, medical supplies, & equipment	18	9	13	11	14	65
Printing & publishing	4	7	6	4	13	34
Food processing	13	6	7	3	12	41
Wholesale & distribution	4	6	4	15	11	40
Retail	8	1	2	8	9	28
Industrial & farm equipment & machinery	8	7	6	5	8	34
Miscellaneous services	17	12	9	7	8	53
Banking & finance	4	11	3	6	7	31
Broadcasting	1	0	3	4	7	15
Brokerage, investment, & mgmt. consulting	10	10	1	6	7	34
Chemicals, paints, & coatings	17	14	6	5	7	49
Insurance	10	14	5	2	7	38
Office equipment & computer hardware	8	5	4	8	7	32
Primary metal processing	7	1	6	4	7	25
Electrical equipment	6	9	11	4	6	36
Mining & minerals	6	5	5	12	6	34
Toys & recreational products	2	0	0	3	6	11
Instruments & photographic equipment	6	7	3	2	5	23
Plastics & rubber	6	3	4	5	5	23
Communications	4	6	3	6	4	23
Electric, gas, water, & sanitary services	0	3	4	4	4	15
Electronics	13	9	3	3	4	32
Fabricated metal products	7	5	3	2	4	21
Leisure & entertainment	11	7	4	4	4	30
Construction, mining, & oil equip. & mach.	1	1	1	1	3	7
Textiles	2	1	0	3	3	9
Agricultural production	5	0	0	0	2	7
Automotive products & accessories	5	0	5	2	2	14
Autos & trucks	3	2	0	6	2	13
Energy services	2	0	0	0	2	4
Oil & gas	4	3	9	9	2	27
Packaging & containers	0	0	0	0	2	2
Paper	4	0	2	0	2	8
Stone, clay, & glass	6	1	3	5	2	17
Toiletries & cosmetics	3	1	4	0	2	10
Aerospace, aircraft, & defense	4	1	3	0	1	9
Beverages	2	2	1	3	1	9
Construction contractors & eng. svcs.	5	5	5	4	1	20
Health services	5	7	3	1	1	17
Household goods	1	0	0	0	1	2
Real estate	1	0	2	0	1	4
Transportation	5	2	1	3	1	12
Valves, pumps, & hydraulics	1	0	0	1	1	3
Apparel	1	0	5	1	0	7
Building products & materials	1	0	0	0	0	1
Conglomerate	0	0	0	0	0	0
Furniture	0	0	0	0	0	0
Miscellaneous manufacturing	2	1	2	1	0	6
Timber & forest products	0	0	0	2	0	2
TOTAL	266	188	167	190	219	1,030

Source: Mergerstat[SM] Review

Foreign Investors in the U.S. (cont'd)

Largest Foreign Acquisitions of U.S. Companies, Jan. 1987-Dec. 1994*

Date	Acquirer Name	Target Name	Value of Deal ($ mil.)
03/31/89	Beecham Group	SmithKline Beckman	7,922.0
09/24/90	Matsushita Electric Industrial	MCA	7,406.0
01/24/88	Campeau	Federated Department Stores	6,511.9
10/04/88	Grand Metropolitan	Pillsbury	5,757.9
05/02/94	Roche Holding	Syntex	5,307.2
05/23/94	Sandoz	Gerber Products	3,685.7
11/21/88	Pechiney (France)	Triangle Industries	3,658.0
01/18/90	Rhone-Poulenc (France)	Rorer Group	3,476.0
06/02/93	British Telecommunications	MCI Communications	3,465.2
08/07/91	Altus Finance	Executive Life Insurance—Junk Bond	3,250.0

* excludes spin-offs   *Source: Securities Data Company*

Trade-Weighted Dollar Exchange Rate

THE TRADE-WEIGHTED DOLLAR represents the foreign currency price of the U.S. dollar or the export value of the U.S. dollar. When these index numbers increase, the value of the dollar increases, making it easier for Americans to afford imports, but making American exports more expensive to those in other countries.

Trade-Weighted Dollar Index

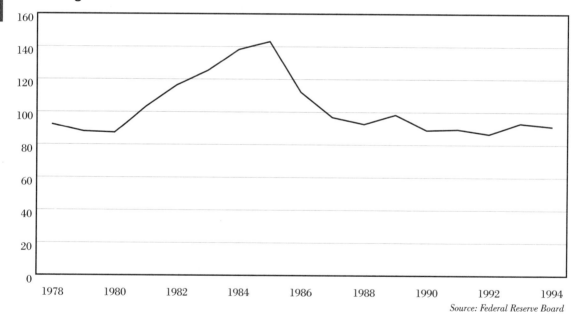

Source: Federal Reserve Board

E-MAIL **World Gross Domestic Product.** Send e-mail to product@almanac.yoyo.com. See p. xi for instructions.
Table of the gross domestic product for 24 major countries, from the OECD.

The Top Exporters

1993 Rank	Name	Major Exports	Exports ($ mil.)	% of Sales	Sales ($ mil.)
1	General Motors, Detroit	Motor vehicles and parts	14,913.1	11.2	133,621.9
2	Boeing, Seattle	Commercial aircraft	14,616.0	57.8	25,285.0
3	Ford Motor, Dearborn, MI	Motor vehicles and parts	9,483.0	8.7	108,521.0
4	General Electric, Fairfield, CT	Jet engines, turbines, plastics, med. sys.	8,498.0	14.0	60,823.0
5	Chrysler, Highland Park, MI	Motor vehicles and parts	8,397.0	19.3	43,600.0
6	IBM, Armonk, NY	Computers and related equipment	7,297.0	11.6	62,716.0
7	Motorola, Schaumburg, IL	Communications equipment	4,990.0	29.4	16,963.0
8	Hewlett-Packard, Palo Alto	Measurement, computation products	4,738.0	23.3	20,317.0
9	Philip Morris, New York	Tobacco, beer, food products	4,105.0	8.1	50,621.0
10	Caterpillar, Peoria, IL	Heavy machinery, engines, turbines	3,743.0	32.2	11,615.0
11	United Technologies, Hartford	Jet engines, helicopters	3,503.0	16.9	20,736.0
12	E. I. Du Pont, Wilmington, DE	Specialty chemicals	3,500.0	10.7	32,621.0
13	Intel, Santa Clara, CA	Microcomputer components, modules	3,406.0	38.8	8,782.0
14	McDonnell Douglas, St. Louis	Aerospace prod., electronic systems	3,405.0	23.5·	14,487.0
15	Archer Daniels Midland, Decatur, IL	Computers and related equipment	2,900.0	29.6	9,811.4
16	Eastman Kodak, Rochester, NY	Cameras and related equipment	2,242.0	11.2	20,059.0
17	Raytheon, Lexington, MA	Electronic systems, engineering projects	2,063.0	22.4	9,201.2
18	Compaq Computer, Houston	Computers and related equipment	1,922.0	26.7	7,191.0
19	Digital Equipment, Maynard, MA	Computers and related equipment	1,800.0	12.5	14,371.4
20	Lockheed, Calabasas, CA	Aerospace products, electronics	1,743.0	13.3	13,071.0
21	AlliedSignal, Morristown, NJ	Aircraft and automotive parts, chemicals	1,699.0	14.4	11,827.0
22	Textron, Providence	Aerospace and commercial products	1,589.0	18.3	8,668.5
23	3M, St. Paul	Ind., elec., health care, imaging prod.	1,491.7	10.6	14,020.0
24	Weyerhaeuser, Tacoma	Pulp, newsprint, paperboard, lumber	1,445.0	15.1	9,544.8
25	Dow Chemical, Midland, MI	Chemicals, plastics	1,442.0	8.0	18,060.0
26	IBP, Dakota City, NB	Computers and related equipment	1,392.0	11.9	11,671.4
27	Westinghouse Electric, Pittsburgh	Electronic products, electronic systems	1,338.0	11.6	11,564.0
28	Unisys, Blue Bell, PA	Computers and related equipment	1,335.4	17.2	7,742.5
29	Sun Microsystems, Mountain View, CA	Computers and related equipment	1,270.4	29.5	4,308.6
30	Union Carbide, Danbury, CT	Chemicals, plastics	1,154.0	24.9	4,640.0
31	Xerox, Stamford, CT	Copiers, printers, processing services	1,104.0	62.0	17,790.0
32	International Paper, Purchase, NY	Pulp, paperboard, wood products	1,100.0	8.0	13,685.0
33	Miles, Pittsburgh	Chemicals, healthcare products	1,057.7	16.1	6,586.0
34	Hoechst Celanese, Somerville, NJ	Chemicals, plastics, fibers	1,043.0	15.1	6,899.0
35	Abbott Laboratories, Abbott Park, IL	Drugs, diagnostic equipment	1,008.0	12.0	8,407.8
36	Merck, Whitehouse Station, NJ	Health products, specialty chemicals	1,003.5	9.6	10,498.2
37	Deere, Moline, IL	Farm and industrial equipment	961.0	12.5	7,693.8
38	Monsanto, St. Louis	Food ingredients, herbicides, chemicals	932.0	11.8	7,902.0
39	Bristol-Myers Squibb, New York	Pharmaceuticals, healthcare products	918.0	8.0	11,413.0
40	Cummins Engine, Columbus, IN	Diesel engines, diesel engine parts	906.0	21.3	4,247.9
41	Cooper Industries, Houston	Industrial and petroleum equipment	897.7	14.3	6,273.8
42	Alcoa, Pittsburgh	Aluminum products	896.0	9.9	9,055.9
43	FMC, Chicago	Armored military vehicles, chemicals	886.8	23.6	3,753.9
44	RJR Nabisco Holdings, New York	Food, tobacco	882.0	5.8	15,104.0
45	General Dynamics, Falls Church, VA	Battle tanks, related support services	836.0	17.9	4,661.0
46	Georgia Pacific, Atlanta	Pulp, building products, paper	825.0	6.7	12,330.0
47	Rockwell, Seal Beach, CA	Auto parts, high-speed printing presses	787.0	7.3	10,840.0
48	Honeywell, Minneapolis	Building, industrial systems	769.0	12.9	5,963.0
49	Tenneco, Houston	Farm, construction, and auto equipment	745.0	5.6	13,255.0
50	Exxon, Irving, TX	Petroleum chemicals	741.0	0.8	97,825.0

Exporting

GREAT POTENTIAL EXISTS for businesses in the United States to become more active in exporting. Only 15 percent of U.S. exporters account for 85 percent of the value of U.S.-manufactured exports. One-half of all exporters sell in only one foreign market. Fewer than 20 percent of exporters (less than 3 percent of U.S. companies) export to more than five markets.

Competing effectively abroad helps companies keep the edge they need at home. However, because there are real costs and risks associated with exporting, it is up to each company to weigh the necessary commitment against the potential benefit.

Ten Recommendations for Successful Exporting

- Obtain qualified export counseling and develop a master international marketing plan before starting an export business. The plan should clearly define goals, objectives, and problems that may be encountered.

- Secure a commitment from top management to overcome the initial difficulties and financial requirements of exporting. Take a long-range view of this process.

- Select overseas distributors carefully. International communication and transportation require international distributors to act more independently than their domestic counterparts.

- Establish a basis for profitable operations and orderly growth. Unsolicited trade leads should not be ignored, but the successful exporter will not rely solely on these inquiries.

- Continue to pursue export business even when the U.S. market is healthy.

- Treat international distributors on an equal basis with domestic counterparts, offering similar advertising, special discounts, sales incentive programs, special credit terms, warranty offers, etc.

- Do not assume that a marketing technique that works in Japan will be equally successful in France. Treat each market individually to ensure maximum success.

- Be willing to adapt products to meet regulations or cultural preferences of other countries.

- Print service, sale, and warranty messages in local languages.

- Provide readily available servicing for the product.

Source: A Basic Guide to Exporting

 E-MAIL

U.S. Investment Abroad. Send e-mail to invest@almanac.yoyo.com. See p. xi for instructions.

Tables of U.S. direct investment abroad, historical-cost basis, from Survey of Current Business.

The Top Reference Sources

A Basic Guide to Exporting
U.S. Government Printing Office, $9.50
(202) 512-1800

This excellent publication of the U.S. Department of Commerce is designed to help companies learn the costs and risks associated with exporting and develop a successful strategy. Reference appendi-

ces include an export glossary, directory of federal export assistance, state and local sources of assistance, and U.S. and foreign contacts for major overseas markets. Topics discussed include preparing products for export, service exports, business travel, pricing, regulations, tax incentives, customs benefits, and financing.

NAFTA

THE NORTH AMERICAN FREE TRADE Agreement was passed in November 1993. Its objectives are:

* to eliminate barriers to trade in, and facilitate the cross-border movement of, goods and services between the territories of the parties (Canada, the United States, Mexico);

* to promote conditions of fair competition in the free trade area;

* to increase substantially investment opportunities in their territories;

* to provide adequate and effective protection and enforcement of intellectual property rights in each party's territory;

* to create effective procedures for the implementation application of the agreement, and for its joint administration and the resolution of disputes;

* to establish a framework for further trilateral, regional, and multilateral cooperation to expand and enhance the benefits of the agreement.

Source: Article 102, Objectives, North American Free Trade Agreement

NAFTA and Small Business

NAFTA provides the following for small businesses:

Tariff reduction
NAFTA removes Mexican tariffs on U.S. goods by the year 2009 (56 percent immediately and 98 percent by the year 2004) and Mexican customs users' fees by 1999, allowing U.S. small businesses to export to Mexico more cheaply than before.

Deregulation
NAFTA removes regulations, such as licensing requirements, that hinder small businesses trying to enter the Mexican market.

Intellectual property rights
NAFTA enacts protection for intellectual property rights. The enforcement of these rights will help small business owners who are dependent on copyrights and patents.

Customs regulations
Under NAFTA, the United States, Canada, and Mexico will all institute the same requirements for customs regulations, documentation, record keeping, and origin verification. This will make it easier and less expensive to export to Mexico and Canada.

Service industries
NAFTA will provide access to Mexico's $146 billion services market, including its financial, telecommunications, and land transport sectors. The United States is the world's leading services provider–

exporting $164 billion worth of services in 1991– and reducing trade barriers and modernizing the Mexican economy will accelerate Mexican consumer and business users' needs for services.

Government procurement
NAFTA preserves U.S. minority and small business government procurement preferences and creates a trilateral commission to educate small and medium-sized businesses about the government procurement process and notify them of openings in each nation's market.

Jobs
NAFTA will remove trade barriers, allowing export-dependent jobs to grow. The Institute for International Economics predicts that by 1995, 1 million U.S. workers will owe their jobs to U.S. exports to Mexico.

Latin America
U.S. firms expanding into Mexico may increase their access to Central and South America as well through Mexico's existing linkages to Latin America.

Source: The Small Business Advocate, Dec. 1993

Contact Options

Americafax (24-hour automated information line) (202) 482-4464

NAFTA Implementation Line (202) 482-0305

Key NAFTA Contacts

Agency	Office	Telephone
Agriculture	Mexico Desk	(202) 720-1340
Commerce	Office of Mexico	(202) 482-4464
Defense	Mexico Desk	(703) 697-9301
Energy	Mexico Desk	(202) 586-5902
EPA	Mexico Desk	(202) 260-4890
Eximbank	Loan Office, Mexico	(202) 566-8234
Interior	Mexico Desk	(202) 501-9688
Labor	Latin America	(202) 219-7631
OPIC	Latin America	(202) 336-8488
State	Mexico Desk	(202) 647-9292
TDP	Latin America	(703) 875-4357
Transportation	Mexico Desk	(202) 366-2892
Treasury	Trade Mexico	(202) 622-1539
Treasury	Mexico Desk	(202) 622-1276
Treasury	Invest-Mexico	(202) 622-1860
USIA	Mexico Desk	(202) 619-6835
USTR	Mexico Desk	(202) 395-5663

NAFTA (cont'd)

Top 50 U.S. Imports from Mexico

Commodity	1992 ($ thou.)	1993 ($ thou.)	1994 ($ thou.)	% Change 1993-1994
Crude oil from petroleum or bituminous minerals	4,362,020	4,244,566	4,652,882	9.62
Motorcars & other motor vehicles	2,591,051	3,083,997	3,944,328	27.90
Equipment for distributing electricity	2,009,567	2,287,095	2,972,707	29.98
Parts and accessories of motor vehicles, etc.	1,965,187	2,350,738	2,384,851	1.45
Television receivers	1,280,839	1,589,330	2,264,606	42.49
Telecommunications equipment & parts	1,228,480	1,351,047	2,016,043	49.22
Apparatus for switching or protecting electrical circuits	1,080,783	1,348,912	1,729,461	28.21
Special transactions & commod not classif by kind	1,165,646	1,334,827	1,599,148	19.80
Internal combustion pistons, engines, & parts	886,956	1,011,026	1,568,154	55.11
Electrical machinery and apparatus	897,799	970,401	1,274,790	31.37
Furniture & parts; bedding, mattresses, etc.	781,288	882,181	1,107,233	25.51
Vegetables, roots, tubers	715,324	943,468	1,002,031	6.21
Automatic data process machinery & parts	456,487	482,798	931,642	92.97
Radio broadcast receivers	630,700	651,243	915,024	40.50
Thermionic, cold cathode, photocathode valves, etc.	472,286	602,297	780,113	29.52
Rotating electric plant and parts thereof	483,277	558,113	725,577	30.01
Articles of apparel of textile fabrics	409,976	516,708	712,729	37.94
Electric power machinery and parts thereof	531,004	684,188	705,431	3.10
Measuring/checking/analyzing & constr. inst. & appt.	488,493	575,075	650,287	13.08
Goods-transporting & special-purpose motor vehicles	442,309	542,956	643,141	18.45
Parts, office & auto data processing machinery	446,612	513,917	628,919	22.38
Household elec & non-elec equipment	476,623	558,172	582,413	4.34
Pumps, air or other gas compressors, and fans	136,404	175,623	529,407	201.45
Meters and counters	39,645	219,862	528,774	140.50
Manufactures of base metal	337,188	387,251	494,894	27.80
Men's, boy's coats, jackets, non-knit textiles	316,276	391,979	491,753	25.45
Baby carriages, toys, games, and sporting goods	285,702	356,161	465,487	30.70
Heating & cooling equipment and parts	277,458	320,299	442,127	38.04
Fruit, nuts (except oil nuts) fresh or dried	451,479	403,061	403,924	0.21
Taps, cocks, valves, & similar appliances	237,386	320,338	390,859	22.01
Women's/girls' coats, capes, non-knit textiles	265,087	275,193	388,648	41.23
Live animals other than animals of division 03	343,335	432,366	352,802	-18.40
Medical, dental, instruments, appliances, etc.	293,018	304,696	348,766	14.46
Estimate of low values import transactions	319,669	358,776	343,085	-4.37
Coffee and coffee substitutes	251,853	251,048	332,672	32.51
Oil (not crude) from petrol & bitum minerals etc	284,260	552,897	325,850	-41.06
Musical instruments & parts; records, tapes, etc.	224,273	251,305	321,464	27.92
Alcoholic beverages	239,725	268,501	300,678	11.98
Crustaceans–shellfish, fresh/processed	166,964	234,141	288,883	23.38
Iron steel primary forms & semifinished products	24,220	87,135	288,823	231.47
Sound & TV recorders, recording media units	420,231	368,262	277,456	-24.66
Household equipment of base metal	206,719	227,284	266,613	17.30
Made-up articles of textile materials	205,720	237,572	254,596	7.17
Glass	136,209	151,866	251,637	65.70
Articles of plastic	188,961	204,040	250,168	22.61
Copper	142,773	205,177	229,830	12.02
Office machines	50,574	91,246	219,484	140.54
Footwear	212,107	215,784	206,141	-4.47
Lighting fixtures and fittings	134,119	168,914	193,130	14.34
Mechanical handling equipment & parts	153,489	140,837	184,069	30.70

Source: U.S. Bureau of the Census

NAFTA (cont'd)

Top 50 U.S. Exports to Mexico

Commodity	1992 ($ thou.)	1993 ($ thou.)	1994 ($ thou.)	% Change 1993-1994
Motor vehicle parts and accessories	3,897,196	4,269,425	4,641,466	8.71
Thermionic, cold cathode, photocathode valves, etc.	872,948	1,103,861	1,916,253	73.60
Est. low value shipments; Canadian low value	1,375,287	1,411,996	1,756,361	24.39
Telecommunications equipment & parts	1,529,478	1,592,876	1,731,648	8.71
Apparatus for switching or protecting electrical circuits	1,040,492	1,120,391	1,609,665	43.67
Equipment for distributing electricity	1,263,941	1,376,525	1,401,236	1.80
Electrical machinery and apparatus	1,173,136	1,342,633	1,362,872	1.51
Articles of plastic	758,102	818,329	1,162,727	42.09
Manufactures of base metal	774,584	840,109	1,131,766	34.72
Internal combustion/piston engines, parts	978,597	892,665	1,100,943	23.33
Measuring/checking/analysing & contr inst. & appt.	921,541	1,000,062	1,086,372	8.63
Automatic data process machinery, parts	666,302	693,610	967,576	39.50
Parts, office & auto data processing machinery	574,599	830,799	943,957	13.62
Paper & paperboard, cut to size or shape, articles	629,728	662,467	776,214	17.17
Furniture & parts; bedding, mattresses, etc.	629,052	479,727	707,313	4.06
Oil (not crude) from petrol & bitum minerals etc	812,661	717,945	691,032	-3.75
Electric power machinery and parts thereof	466,149	554,712	658,891	18.78
Motorcars, other motor vehicles	121,248	125,504	606,496	383.25
Oil seeds/oleaginous fruit	496,144	454,462	591,618	30.18
Specialized industrial machinery, etc.	451,321	431,840	581,225	34.59
Plates, sheets, film, foil, & strips of plastics	379,375	407,559	561,883	37.87
Aircraft, associated equipment; spacecraft; parts	885,038	501,740	553,783	10.37
Paper and paperboard	356,351	400,949	539,473	34.55
Heating & cooling equipment, parts	383,185	420,842	503,860	19.73
Rotating electric plant and parts thereof	384,877	480,485	497,714	3.59
Civil engineering & contractors' plant & equipment	422,357	331,756	478,813	44.33
Pumps, air or other gas compressors, and fans	355,537	258,019	446,274	24.65
Household elec. & non-elec. equipment	362,672	426,239	432,805	1.54
Aluminum	353,785	339,103	432,407	27.51
Cereals, unmilled except wheat, rice, barley, corn	580,775	392,230	406,375	3.61
Pulp and waste paper	297,464	283,187	388,625	37.23
Maize (not including sweet corn), unmilled	163,776	75,697	373,136	392.93
Meat, edible offal, fish; chilled, frozen	303,064	318,153	372,488	17.08
Musical instruments, parts; records, tapes, etc.	283,206	272,401	371,885	36.52
Baby carriages, toys, games, and sporting goods	266,291	239,316	368,192	53.85
Plastics, in primary forms	302,781	307,685	367,800	19.54
Articles of apparel made of textile fabrics	145,570	214,185	351,043	63.90
Printed matter	217,202	263,953	340,029	28.82
Taps, cocks, valves, & similar appliances	183,989	246,568	332,547	34.87
Mechanical handling equipment & parts	339,554	279,151	331,582	18.78
Nonelectrical machry, tools, app & pts	216,281	241,147	319,440	32.47
Hydrocarbons & specified derivatives	228,919	262,496	313,229	19.33
Polymers of ethylene, in primary forms	162,635	209,357	297,216	41.97
Miscellaneous chemical products	152,477	187,008	290,169	55.16
Special yarns, special textile fabrics, etc.	229,676	250,070	283,346	13.31
Men's/boy's coats, jackets, of non-knit textiles	250,406	271,757	282,738	4.04
Copper	189,142	230,207	277,277	20.45
Nails, screws, nuts, etc., iron, steel, copp, alumin	128,268	155,375	274,143	75.44
Animal feedstuffs, not including unmilled cereal	264,083	215,429	270,822	25.71
Meat of bovine animals, fresh, chilled, frozen	208,115	113,062	227,558	101.27

Source: U.S. Bureau of the Census

GATT

THE GENERAL AGREEMENT on Tariffs and Trade (GATT) was passed recently. Its objectives are:

- to build an international trading system that will ensure the orderly and equitable expansion of world trade and contribute to the prosperity of the United States;

- to reduce foreign export subsidies, tariffs and non-tariff barriers, and internal supports;

- to obtain commercially meaningful increases in access to markets of developing countries;

- to cut costs by 50 to 100 percent on important electronics items sold by major U.S. trading partners;

- to significantly increase access to markets that represent approximately 85 percent of world trade in terms of reduced tariffs on specific items of key interest to U.S. exporters;

- to strengthen and clarify rules for agricultural trade;

- to reduce or eliminate the subsidization of agricultural production.

GATT and Small Business

For the United States, GATT represents the most monumental change ever in U.S. trade laws. One hundred twenty-four countries around the globe are participating in the GATT agreement. With tariffs and duties reduced by up to 38 percent on many goods and services, U.S. exports become significantly less expensive for foreigners to buy. With worldwide customers eager for American products and services and increasing competition for American consumers on the home front, in a short time most American businesses will find that they can no longer ignore the vast potential of selling in foreign markets. According to the Small Business Administration, over 90 percent of small businesses that have not exported could do so profitably today.

Contact Options

Small Business Answer Desk
(202) 205-7717, or (800) 827-5722 or
(202) 205-7701 for recorded information

The Top Reference Sources

Guide to Worldwide Postal-Code
& Address Formats
Marian Nelson, $99.50
(212) 362-9855

This postal guide is an extremely useful reference for anyone using the mail to do business with a foreign country, from executives to data managers to mailroom personnel.

The book includes practical tips for standardizing foreign addresses, including city and county names, postal-code formats, abbreviations, sample addresses, information sources, and more. It is updated annually.

Small Business and Trade

NATIONAL SMALL BUSINESS UNITED and Arthur Andersen Enterprises Group conducted a survey of small and mid-sized businesses in June 1994. The study focused in part on the businesses' position in the international market. The following graphs contain their findings:

Scope of Marketplace

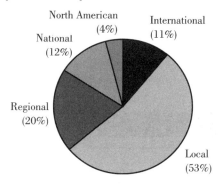

Businesses That Export

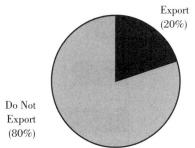

Source: National Small Business United and Arthur Andersen Enterprises, June 1994

Businesses That Import

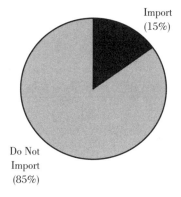

U.S. Exports and Imports. Send e-mail to exports@almanac.yoyo.com. See p. xi for instructions.

A table of U.S. exports and imports for six major countries.

Small Business and Trade (cont'd)

Top Five Export Markets

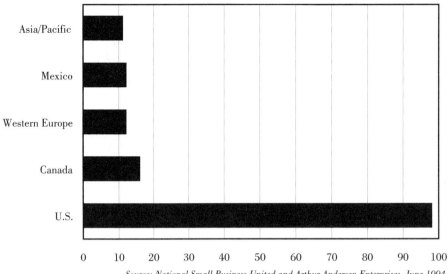

Source: National Small Business United and Arthur Andersen Enterprises, June 1994

Top Trading Partners

The United States' Top Ten Trading Partners

Country	1994 Exports ($ bil.)	1994 Imports ($ bil.)	% of Trade
Canada	114.4	128.9	20.7
Japan	53.5	119.1	14.7
Mexico	50.8	49.5	8.5
United Kingdom	26.8	25.1	4.4
Germany	19.2	31.7	4.3
China	9.3	38.8	4.1
Taiwan	17.1	26.7	3.7
Korea	18.0	19.7	3.2
France	13.6	16.8	2.6
Singapore	13.0	15.4	2.4
Italy	7.2	14.7	1.9
Hong Kong	11.4	9.7	1.8
Malaysia	7.0	14.0	1.8
Netherlands	13.6	6.0	1.7
Belgium	10.9	6.3	1.5

Source: U.S. Bureau of the Census, Foreign Trade Division, Dec. 1994

Methods of Payment Abroad

Letters of Credit

The most secure and most often used method of payment in export/import transactions is the documentary letter of credit. A letter of credit is a document issued by a bank on the instruction of a buyer of goods (importer), authorizing the seller (exporter) to draw a specified sum of money under specified terms, usually the receipt by the bank of certain documents within a given time.

Before payment, the bank responsible for making payment on behalf of the buyer verifies that all documents are exactly as required by the letter of credit.

If a U.S. exporter is unfamiliar with the credit risk of the foreign bank, or if there is concern about the political or economic risk associated with the country in which the bank is located, it is advised that a letter of credit issued by a foreign bank be *confirmed* by a U.S. bank. This means that the U.S. bank adds its pledge to pay to that of the foreign bank. Letters of credit that are not confirmed are called *advised* letters of credit. The local Department of Commerce district office or an international banker will help exporters determine whether a confirmed or advised letter of credit is appropriate for a particular transaction.

Letters of credit may be irrevocable (cannot be changed unless both the buyer and seller agree) or revocable (either party can make changes). An *at sight* letter of credit means that payment is made immediately upon presentation of documents. *Time* or *date* letters of credit specify when payment is to be made in the future.

Changes made to a letter of credit are called amendments. The fees charged by the banks involved in amending the letter of credit may be paid either by the buyer or the seller, but the letter of credit should specify which party is responsible. Since changes are costly and time-consuming, every effort should be made to get the letter of credit right the first time.

An exporter is usually not paid until the advising or confirming bank receives the funds from the issuing bank. To expedite the receipt of funds, wire transfers may be used. Bank practices vary, however, and the exporter may be able to receive funds by discounting the letter of credit at the bank, which involves paying a fee to the bank for this service. Exporters should consult with their international bankers about bank policy on these issues.

Other Methods of Payment for International Transactions

Cash in Advance (CIA)
Usually used only for small purchases and when the goods are built to order.

Draft (or Bill of Exchange)
An unconditional order in writing from one person (the drawer) to another (the drawee), directing the drawee to pay a specified amount to a named drawer at a fixed or determinable future date. May be date, sight, or time draft.

Credit cards
Used mainly in transactions where the dollar value of the items sold is low and shipment is to be made directly to the end user.

Open Account
The exporter bills the customer, who is expected to pay under agreed terms at a future date. Some of the largest firms abroad make purchases only on an open account, which is a convenient method of payment if the buyer is well established and has demonstrated a long and favorable payment record.

Consignment Sales
Exporter delivers goods to an agent under agreement that the agent sell the merchandise for the account of the exporter. The agent sells the goods for commission and remits the net proceeds to the exporter.

Countertrade/barter
Sale of goods or services that are paid for in whole or in part by the transfer of goods or services from a foreign country.

Payment Problems

The best solution to a payment problem is to negotiate directly with the customer. If negotiations fail and the sum involved is large enough to warrant the effort, obtain the assistance of your bank, legal counsel, and other qualified experts. If both parties can agree to take their dispute to an arbitration agency, this step is faster and less costly than legal action. The International Chamber of Commerce handles the majority of international arbitrations and is usually acceptable to foreign companies because it is not affiliated with any single country.

Source: A Basic Guide to Exporting

Contact Options

U.S. Council for International Business, American National Committee of the ICC
(212) 354-4480

American Arbitration Association
(212) 484-4000

Trade Remedy Assistance Office
International Trade Commission
(202) 205-2200

U.S. Exports by State

Origin of Movement of U.S. Exports of Merchandise by State, 1994 ($ millions)

Item	Manufactured Commodities	Non-Manufactured Commodities	Total Cumulative to Date
U.S. TOTAL	468,894.2	43,775.5	512,669.7
Alabama	3,527.0	367.7	3,894.7
Alaska	1,020.2	1,435.7	2,455.9
Arizona	6,150.7	315.8	6,466.5
Arkansas	1,576.1	95.8	1,671.9
California	61,408.5	4,883.1	66,291.6
Colorado	3,699.5	102.0	3,801.5
Connecticut	5,300.8	363.1	5,663.9
Delaware	1,479.0	18.5	1,497.5
Florida	15,464.1	822.7	16,286.8
Georgia	7,566.4	670.7	8,237.1
Hawaii	222.9	73.6	296.5
Idaho	1,374.3	91.3	1,465.6
Illinois	18,517.2	579.7	19,096.9
Indiana	8,092.0	163.5	8,255.5
Iowa	3,023.6	190.2	3,213.8
Kansas	2,702.0	326.4	3,028.4
Kentucky	4,515.1	287.7	4,802.8
Louisiana	6,994.1	7,555.2	14,549.3
Maine	956.6	132.9	1,089.5
Maryland	4,773.1	100.8	4,873.9
Massachusetts	10,728.8	470.3	11,199.1
Michigan	25,342.8	487.2	25,830.0
Minnesota	6,135.8	484.8	6,620.6
Mississippi	1,785.7	60.7	1,846.4
Missouri	3,350.5	190.1	3,540.6
Montana	164.1	163.7	327.8
Nebraska	1,406.2	166.6	1,572.8
Nevada	567.7	52.8	620.5
New Hampshire	933.8	66.1	999.9
New Jersey	9,710.1	808.5	10,518.6
New Mexico	478.3	47.8	526.1
New York	23,996.7	1,915.7	25,912.4
North Carolina	10,845.3	1,018.0	11,863.3
North Dakota	382.1	75.4	457.5
Ohio	18,290.5	716.4	19,006.9
Oklahoma	2,037.8	72.3	2,110.1
Oregon	4,503.9	1,599.2	6,103.1
Pennsylvania	11,094.0	556.3	11,650.3
Rhode Island	793.1	129.4	922.5
South Carolina	5,101.3	134.6	5,235.9
South Dakota	279.4	15.7	295.1
Tennessee	6,298.9	450.1	6,749.0
Texas	48,689.7	3,128.7	51,818.4
Utah	1,964.5	390.1	2,354.6
Vermont	1,335.4	35.1	1,370.5
Virginia	8,029.6	1,542.9	9,572.5
Washington	21,222.9	2,406.2	23,629.1
West Virginia	1,092.6	493.1	1,585.7
Wisconsin	7,152.5	569.9	7,722.4
Wyoming	344.3	15.8	360.1
Dist. of Columbia	519.7	26.4	546.1
Puerto Rico	4,402.8	69.7	4,472.5
U.S. Virgin Islands	138.7	0.3	139.0

Source: U.S. Bureau of the Census

Global High-Tech Markets

THE NATION'S COMPETITIVENESS in the global marketplace depends on its ability to sell products abroad and to compete against imports in the home market. According to studies by the National Science Foundation, the international market for high-tech goods is growing faster than that for other manufactured goods. The following charts provide a comparison of the leading three exporters.

Global Market Share: Leading Exporters, by Industry (%), 1993

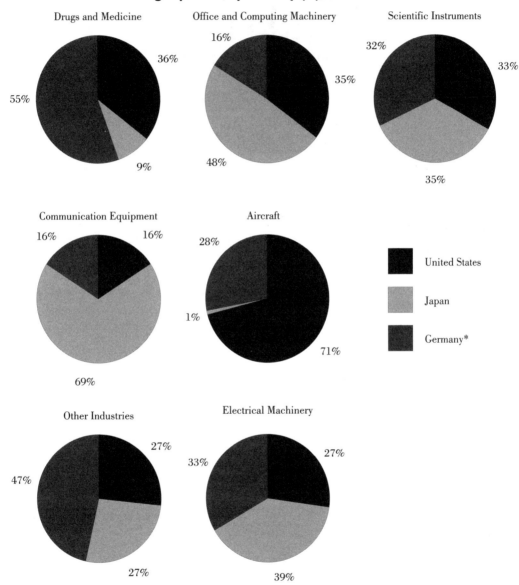

*Germany refers to the former West Germany.

Note: Some figures do not add up to 100 due to rounding.

Source: National Science Board, Science & Engineering Indicators, 1994

Global High-Tech Markets (cont'd)

Country Share of Global High-Tech Markets (%)

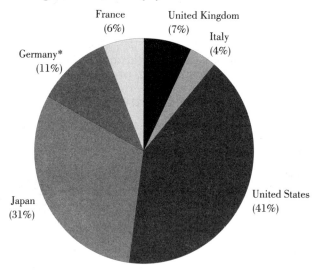

*Germany refers to the former West Germany.   *Source: National Science Board, Science & Engineering Indicators, 1994*

The Top Reference Sources

Journal of Commerce, $349/year
(212) 837-7000

This daily magazine provides information on the conditions and influences affecting national and international commerce.

It covers a variety of topics, including manufacturing, world trade, processing, shipping, foreign exchange, energy, and commodities. It also reports on trade and investment studies within and outside the U.S.

Intellectual Property Protection

WHILE THE UNITED STATES HAS a long-standing tradition of protecting the intellectual property of its citizens, such protection is not offered by all foreign countries. The patents, trademarks, and copyrights of U.S. citizens are, at times, ignored in other countries, and piracy and product counterfeiting result in a considerable loss of revenue for American companies.

Despite the efforts of the General Agreement on Tariffs and Trade (GATT), the Paris Convention for the Protection of Industrial Property (trademarks and patents), and the Berne Convention for the Protection of Literary and Artistic Works (copyrights), there is no uniform protection available to an individual whose invention, mark, literary works, or computer software might be used in foreign countries.

Property protection in a foreign country frequently is dependent upon the owner meeting the registration requirements of the individual country. Individual applications for patent protection, for example, must be filed in each country in which the patent owner desires protection, unless the country conforms to an international agreement. Usually a foreign patent agent or attorney is needed to execute the filing of the application in another country. The Patent Trade Office (PTO) will provide a list of individuals who are qualified to practice before the U.S. PTO and knowledgeable about foreign registration requirements.

More recent treaties, such as the Patent Cooperation Treaty, allow applicants from member countries to file one standardized international application to use in member countries in which intellectual property protection is desired.

Despite these strides in international cooperation, a number of countries are frequently cited as locations where property rights protection is often inadequate:

- Copyrights are inadequately protected in Brazil, China, India, Korea, Indonesia, Malaysia, Singapore, and Saudi Arabia.

- Patents are unprotected or inadequately protected in Indonesia, Mexico, Thailand, Brazil, India, Korea, Philippines, Singapore, Saudi Arabia, Taiwan, the United Arab Emirates, and China.

- Trademarks are inadequately protected in Brazil, India, Indonesia, Philippines, and Thailand.

- Product piracy and counterfeiting are a recurring problem in Taiwan, particularly with audiovisual materials.

A good source of information about protecting a business against foreign infringement of property rights is the U.S. and Foreign Commercial Service (US&FCS), which maintains 47 district offices and 20 branches in 67 cities around the United States. These offices are staffed by trade specialists and maintain business libraries of the latest reports of the Department of Commerce. For assistance, call the nearest Department of Commerce district office (see list this chapter) or call (800) 872-8723. The United States Patent Trademark Office will also provide additional information.

Recommended Resources

Copyrights, Patents and Trademarks
by Hoyt L. Barber
Liberty Press, McGraw-Hill, $16.95
(800) 262-4729

*Exportise: An International Trade Source Book
for Smaller Company Executives*
The Small Business Foundation of America, $19.95
(202) 223-1103

The Top Reference Sources

The Multinational Executive Travel Companion
Suburban Publishing, $60
(203) 324-6439

This is an indispensable resource for executives traveling overseas. Published annually, it includes 160 country profiles, with information on population, GNP, imports and exports, country affiliations, and trade groups.

The business traveler will also find listings of major companies' performance, weather conditions, time differences, passport and visa requirements, postage, English-speaking physicians, embassies and consulates, tipping guidelines, travel and transportation tips, and more. Particularly useful are the listings of important addresses and phone numbers.

Export Intermediaries

EXPORT MANAGEMENT COMPANIES and export trading companies are firms that market American products and services abroad on behalf of manufacturers, farm groups, and distributors. These export intermediaries may handle products in a single sector, such as automotive equipment or clothing, or they may handle a variety of items from a number of different sectors. Intermediaries may service markets worldwide, or they may specialize in certain countries or regions.

Export management companies (EMCs) help U.S. manufacturers establish an overseas market for their products, usually on an exclusive basis. The management company maintains a close relationship with its clients as well as with overseas distributors. Its business is supply-driven.

Management companies may take title to the products they sell, making a profit on the markup, or they may charge a commission, depending on the type of products being sold, the overseas market, or the manufacturer-client's needs. Export management companies may also work on a retainer basis.

In contrast, export trading companies (ETCs) most often act as independent distributors, bringing buyers and sellers together for a transaction. Business for ETCs is demand-driven and transaction-oriented. Most export trading companies take title to the products involved, but others may work on commission.

There are more than 1,500 ETCs and EMCs in the United States. Potential exporters should develop a list of those ETCs and EMCs which specialize in exporting the types of products proposed to be sold overseas.

For assistance in locating and selecting the proper ETC/EMC, contact the Commerce Department's Office of Export Trading Company Affairs, International Trade Administration, Washington, DC 20230, (202) 482-5131. Or, call a local office of the Small Business Administration or local world trade center (see pages 385 and 388).

Source: Business America

Recommended Resources

The Export Yellow Pages
Office of Export Trading Company Affairs, free
International Trade Administration
Washington, DC 20230

This directory of more than 15,000 firms involved in foreign trade is designed to facilitate contact between producers of goods and services and firms providing export trade services. The directory is available free of charge from an ITA district office (see page 383). Call the nearest Commerce Department district office to list your company in the next edition. For advertising information, call (800) 288-2582.

Directory of Leading U.S. Export Management Companies
Bergano Books, $49.50
P.O. Box 190
Fairfield, CT 06430
(203) 254-2054
Provides contacts, names, and addresses for 400 EMCs and 41 product categories. Geographic specialties and language capacities are also included. Lists export consultants. Cross-referenced by company name, state, and product category.

Export Profits
Upstart Publishing, $19.95
Dover, NH 03820
(603) 749-5071

Trading Company Sourcebook
International Business Affairs, $22
4938 Hampden Ln., Suite 346
Bethesda, MD 20814
(301) 907-8650

Brokers and Forwarders

EVERY SHIPMENT ENTERING THE United States is subject to more than 500 pages of customs and tariff regulations. Customs brokers are import professionals, licensed by the U.S. Department of the Treasury, who have a thorough knowledge of these regulations, and who help clients choose the best modes of transportation, types of carriers, and shipping routes. Brokers also assist with exchange rates, appraisal, and determining proper classifications and duties. The broker's job often transcends the customs bureau, and involves contact with other government agencies such as the USDA (for meat import questions), EPA (for vehicle emissions standards), or the FDA (product safety).

Ocean freight forwarders are licensed by the Federal Maritime Commission. Air cargo or air transport agents are accredited by the International Air Transportation Association. These freight forwarding professionals advise clients of the best rates, routings, and modes of transporting goods to or from any area in the world. Freight forwarders are experts on such items as foreign documentation requirements, hazardous materials regulations, special packaging or handling requirements, licensing provisions, etc.

The following licensed customs brokers and freight forwarders have been selected on the basis of range of services and the number of branch offices. The job titles provided include four or more of the following: customs broker (CB), ocean freight forwarder (OFF), international air freight forwarder (AFF), international air transport agent (IATA), container station (CS), drawback specialist (DS), steamship agent (SA), motor property broker (MPB), non-vessel operating common carrier (NVO), warehouseman (WH).

Source: National Customs Brokers and Forwarders Association

Customs Brokers and Freight Forwarders in the United States

Air Express
P.O. Box 1231
120 Tokeneke Rd.
Darien, CT 06820
AFF, CB, CS, IATA, OFF, WH
(203) 655-7900

Amerford
8010 Roswell Rd., Suite 300
Atlanta, GA 30350
AFF, CB, IATA, NVO, OFF
(404) 353-4200

Burlington Air Express
5149 S. Ridge Pkwy.
Atlanta, GA 30349
AFF, CB, DB, IATA, NVO, OFF, WH
(404) 997-9447

John V. Carr & Son
P.O. Box 33479
Detroit, MI 48232
AFF, CB, DB, IATA, MPB, NVO, OFF, WH
(313) 222-1121

Danzas
3650 131st Ave., SE
Newport Towers, Suite 700
Bellevue, WA 98015
AFF, CB, IATA, MPB, NVO, OFF, WH
(206) 649-9339

A. N. Deringer
P.O. Box 1309
St. Albans, VT 05478
AFF, CB, CS, DB, IATA, MPB, NVO, OFF, WH
(802) 524-8110

Expeditors International of Washington
P.O. Box 69620
Seattle, WA 98168
AFF, CB, DB, IATA, MPB, NVO, OFF
(206) 246-3711

Fritz Companies
P.O. Box 7221
San Francisco, CA 94120
AFF, CB, DB, IATA, MPB, NVO, OFF, SA, WH
(415) 904-8360

The Harper Group
260 Townsend St.
San Francisco, CA 94107
AFF, CB, CS, DB, IATA, MPB, NVO, OFF, WH
(415) 978-0600

Intertrans
125 E. John Carpenter Freeway
Irving, TX 75062
AFF, CB, DB, IATA, MPB, NVO, OFF
(214) 830-8888

Norman G. Jensen
3050 Metro Dr., Suite 300
Minneapolis, MN 55425
AFF, CB, IATA, MPB, OFF
(612) 854-7363

F. W. Myers and Co.
Myers Bldg.
Rouses Point, NY 12979
AFF, CB, CS, DB, IATA, MPB, NVO, OFF, WH
(518) 297-2222

Brokers and Forwarders (cont'd)

Panalpina
Harborside Financial Center
Plaza Two, 34 Exchange Pl.
Jersey City, NJ 07311
AFF, CB, CS, DB, IATA, MP, NVO, OFF
(201) 451-4000

Schenkers International Forwarders
Exchange Place Center
10 Exchange Pl., Suite 1500
Jersey City, NJ 07302
AFF, CB, IATA, MPB, NVO, OFF
(201) 434-5500

Tower Group International
128 Dearborn St.
Buffalo, NY 14207
AFF, CB, CS, DB, IATA, MPB, NVO, OFF, WH
(716) 874-1300

Yusen Air & Sea Service USA
60 E. 42nd St., Room 1915
New York, NY 10165
AFF, CB, IATA, OFF
(212) 983-1170

Customs Brokers and Freight Forwarders Outside the United States

Affiliated Customs Brokers
411 Des Recollets
Montreal, PQ, Canada H2Y 1W3
AFF, CB, DB, IATA, OFF, WH
(514) 288-1211

Constantine Shipping and
International Services
10 Grafton St.
London, England W1X 3LA
AFF, OFF, SA
(01) 493-9484

Footwork-Hamacher GmbH
Martinistr. 24
P.O. Box 10 51 05
Bremen, Germany 1 2800
AFF, CB, CS, IATA, NVO, OFF, WH
421-33-77-60

A. Hartrodt GmbH & Co.
P.O. Box 10 29
Hamburg, Germany 1 0-200
AFF, CB, IATA, NVO, OFF
(040) 239-0383

Livingston Group
405 The West Mall, Suite 600
Toronto, ON, Canada M9C 5K7
AFF, CB, DB, IATA, MPB, NVO, OFF, WH
(416) 626-2828

Malenstein Rotterdam B.V.
Bergambachstraat 10
Rotterdam, Netherlands 3079 DA
AFF, CB, CS, DB, IATA, NVO, OFF, WH
010-492-8700

Naigai Nitto
38-8 Higashi-Shinagawa 1-Chome
Shinagawa-ku
Tokyo, Japan 140
AFF, CB, CS, IATA, MPB, NVO, OFF, SA, WH
(03) 3450-7400

Starber International
410 St. Nicholas St.
Montreal, PQ, Canada H2Y 2P5
AFF, CB, DB, IATA, NVO, OFF, WH
(514) 285-1500

Swift Freight
Carrera (Bin Hendi Building)
Zabeel Road-Karama
P.O. Box 50177
Dubai, United Arab Emirates
AFF, CB, CS, IATA, NVO, OFF, WH
457 325

Recommended Resource

*The Who's Who of Customs Brokers and
International Freight Forwarders*
National Customs Brokers & Forwarders
Association of America, $20
One World Trade Center, Suite 1153
New York, NY 10048
(212) 432-0050

Contact Options

U.S. Customs Service
1301 Constitution Ave., NW
Washington, DC 20229
(202) 927-2095

Federal Maritime Commission
800 N. Capitol St.
Washington, DC 20573
(202) 523-5725

International Air Transportation Association (IATA)
1001 Pennsylvania Ave., Suite 285N
Washington, DC 20004
(202) 624-2977

TIP: *The U.S. Department of Commerce has specialists from over 100 different industries who work with manufacturing and service industry associations and firms to identify trade opportunities and obstacles by product or service, industry sector, and market. Call (800) 872-8723 to contact a specialist.*

Government Resources for Exporters

Trade Information Center

Trade Information Center
Department of Commerce
Washington, DC 20230
(800) 872-8723

Established in the Department of Commerce, the Trade Information Center is the first point of contact for information on U.S. government programs and activities that support exporting, including:

- Export counseling

- Seminars and conferences

- Overseas buyers and representatives

- Export financing

- Technical assistance.

National Trade Data Bank

Department of Commerce
Washington, DC 20230
(202) 482-1986

Established by the Omnibus Trade and Competitiveness Act of 1988, the NTDB collects in one place the federal government's offerings of information on international trade, export promotion, trade contracts, country profiles, and other international economic data.

Each monthly NTDB disk sells for $35, and a 12-month subscription is available for $360.

Trade with Eastern Europe and Selected Areas

The following offices have been established within the International Trade Administration to respond to the greatly expanded need for business information on new opportunities for trade and investment in selected parts of the world.

Eastern Europe Business Information Center
(202) 482-2645

The Baltics (Latvia, Lithuania, and Estonia) are now considered part of Eastern Europe.

Japan Export Information Center
(202) 482-2425

Latin America/Caribbean Business Dev. Center
(202) 482-0841

Office of European Union and Regional Affairs
(202) 482-5276

The key Department of Commerce sources for information on trade potential for U.S. products in specific countries are the international economic policy country desk officers (listed below). These specialists can identify the needs of an individual firm wishing to sell in a particular country in the full context of that country's economy, trade policies, and political situation, as well as U.S. policies toward that country.

Country Desk Officers

Country	Desk Officer	Phone
Afghanistan	Timothy Gilman	(202) 482-2954
Albania	EEBIC	(202) 482-2645
Algeria	Christopher Cerone	(202) 482-1860
	Claude Clement	(202) 482-5545
Angola	Finn Holm-Olsen	(202) 482-4228
Anguilla	Michelle Brooks	(202) 482-2527
Argentina	Randy Mye	(202) 482-1548
Aruba	Michelle Brooks	(202) 482-2527
Antigua/Barbuda	Michelle Brooks	(202) 482-2527
Armenia	BISNIS	(202) 482-4655
ASEAN	Karen Goddin	(202) 482-3877
Austria	Philip Combs	(202) 482-2920
Azerbaijan	BISNIS	(202) 482-4655
Bahamas	Mark Siegelman	(202) 482-5680
Bahrain	Christopher Cerone	(202) 482-1860
	Claude Clement	(202) 482-5545
Balkan States (former Yugoslav Republics)	EEBIC	(202) 482-2645
Bangladesh	John Simmons	(202) 482-2954
Barbados	Michelle Brooks	(202) 482-2527
Belarus	BISNIS	(202) 482-4655

Government Resources for Exporters (cont'd)

Country	Desk Officer	Phone
Belgium	Simon Bensimon	(202) 482-5401
Belize	Michelle Brooks	(202) 482-2527
Benin	Debra Henke	(202) 482-5149
Bhutan	Timothy Gilman	(202) 482-2954
Bolivia	Rebecca Hunt	(202) 482-2521
Botswana	Finn Holm-Olsen	(202) 482-4228
Brazil	Horace Jennings	(202) 482-3871
Brunei	Edward Oliver; Raphael Cung	(202) 482-4958
Bulgaria	EEBIC	(202) 482-2645
Burkina Faso	Philip Michelini	(202) 482-4388
Burma (Myanmar)	Gary Bouck; Raphael Cung	(202) 482-4958
Burundi	Philip Michelini	(202) 482-4388
Cambodia	Gary Bouck	(202) 482-4958
Cameroon	Debra Henke	(202) 482-5149
Canada	Kathy Keim	(202) 482-3103
Cape Verde	Philip Michelini	(202) 482-4388
Cayman Islands	Mark Siegelman	(202) 482-5680
Central African Republic	Philip Michelini	(202) 482-4388
Chad	Philip Michelini	(202) 482-4388
Chile	Roger Turner	(202) 482-1495
Colombia	Paul Moore	(202) 482-1659
Comoros	Chandra Watkins	(202) 482-4564
Congo	Debra Henke	(202) 482-5149
Costa Rica	Mark Siegelman	(202) 482-5680
Cuba	Mark Siegelman	(202) 482-5680
Cyprus	Ann Corro	(202) 482-3945
Czech Republic	EEBIC	(202) 482-2645
Denmark	James Devlin	(202) 482-3254
DJibouti	Chandra Watkins	(202) 482-4564
Dominica	Michelle Brooks	(202) 482-2527
Dominican Republic	Mark Siegelman	(202) 482-5680
Ecuador	Paul Moore	(202) 482-1659
Egypt	Thomas Sams; Corey Wright	(202) 482-5506
El Salvador	Helen Lee	(202) 482-2528
Equatorial Guinea	Philip Michelini	(202) 482-4388
Estonia	EEBIC	(202) 482-2645
Eritrea	Chandra Watkins	(202) 482-4564
Ethiopia	Chandra Watkins	(202) 482-4564
European Community	Charles Ludolph	(202) 482-5276
Finland	James Devlin	(202) 482-3254
France	Elena Mikalis	(202) 482-6008
Gabon	Debra Henke	(202) 482-5149
Gambia	Philip Michelini	(202) 482-4388
Georgia	BISNIS	(202) 482-4655
Germany	Brenda Fisher; John Larsen	(202) 482-2435
Ghana	Debra Henke	(202) 482-5149
Greece	Ann Corro	(202) 482-3945
Grenada	Michelle Brooks	(202) 482-2527
Guatemala	Helen Lee	(202) 482-2528
Guinea	Philip Michelini	(202) 482-4388
Guinea-Bissau	Philip Michelini	(202) 482-4388
Guyana	Michelle Brooks	(202) 482-2527
Haiti	Mark Siegelman	(202) 482-5680
Honduras	Helen Lee	(202) 482-2528
Hong Kong	Sheila Baker	(202) 482-3932

Government Resources for Exporters (cont'd)

Country	Desk Officer	Phone
Hungary	EEBIC	(202) 482-2645
Iceland	James Devlin	(202) 482-3254
India	John Crown; John Simmons	(202) 482-2954
	Timothy Gilman	(202) 482-2954
Indonesia	Edward Oliver; Karen Goddin	(202) 482-3877
Iran	Paul Thanos	(202) 482-1860
Iraq	Thomas Sams; Corey Wright	(202) 482-1860
Ireland	Boyce Fitzpatrick	(202) 482-2177
Israel	Paul Thanos	(202) 482-1860
Italy	Boyce Fitzpatrick	(202) 482-2177
Ivory Coast	Philip Michelini	(202) 482-4388
Jamaica	Mark Siegelman	(202) 482-5680
Japan	Ed Leslie	(202) 482-2425
	Cynthia Campbell; Eric Kennedy	(202) 482-2425
	Allan Christian	(202) 482-2425
Jordan	Paul Thanos	(202) 482-1860
Kazakhstan	BISNIS	(202) 482-4655
Kenya	Chandra Watkins	(202) 482-4564
Korea	William Golike	(202) 482-4390
	Dan Duvall	(202) 482-4390
	Jeffrey Donius	(202) 482-4390
Kuwait	Corey Wright; Thomas Sams	(202) 482-5506
Kyrgyz Republic	BISNIS	(202) 482-4655
Laos	Gary Bouck	(202) 482-4958
	Hong-Phon B. Pho	(202) 482-4958
Latvia	EEBIC	(202) 482-2645
Lebanon	Corey Wright	(202) 482-5506
	Thomas Sams	(202) 482-1860
Lesotho	Finn Holm-Olsen	(202) 482-4228
Lithuania	EEBIC	(202) 482-2645
Luxembourg	Simon Bensimon	(202) 482-5401
Liberia	Philip Michelini	(202) 482-4388
Libya	Claude Clement	(202) 482-5545
	Christopher Cerone	(202) 482-1860
Macau	Sheila Baker	(202) 482-3932
Madagascar	Chandra Watkins	(202) 482-4564
Malawi	Finn Holm-Olsen	(202) 482-4228
Malaysia	Edward Oliver	(202) 482-4958
	Raphael Cung	
Maldives	John Simmons	(202) 482-2954
Mali	Philip Michelini	(202) 482-4388
Malta	Robert McLaughlin	(202) 482-3748
Mauritania	Philip Michelini	(202) 482-4388
Mauritius	Chandra Watkins	(202) 482-4564
Mexico	Shawn Ricks	(202) 482-0300
Moldova	BISNIS	(202) 482-4655
Mongolia	Sheila Baker	(202) 482-3932
Montserrat	Michelle Brooks	(202) 482-2527
Morocco	Claude Clement	(202) 482-5545
	Christopher Cerone	(202) 482-1860
Mozambique	Finn Holm-Olsen	(202) 482-4228
Namibia	Finn Holm-Olsen	(202) 482-4228
Nepal	Timothy Gilman	(202) 482-2954
Netherlands	Simon Bensimon	(202) 482-5401
Netherlands Antilles	Michelle Brooks	(202) 482-2527

Government Resources for Exporters (cont'd)

Country	Desk Officer	Phone
New Zealand	Gary Bouck; George Paine	(202) 482-4958
Nicaragua	Mark Siegelman	(202) 482-5680
Niger	Philip Michelini	(202) 482-4388
Nigeria	Debra Henke	(202) 482-5149
Norway	James Devlin	(202) 482-4414
Oman	Paul Thanos	(202) 482-1860
Pacific Islands	Gary Bouck; George Paine	(202) 482-4958
Pakistan	Timothy Gilman	(202) 482-2954
Panama	Helen Lee	(202) 482-2528
Paraguay	Randolph Mye	(202) 482-1548
People's Republic of China	Cheryl McQueen; Laura McCall	(202) 482-3932
Peru	Rebecca Hunt	(202) 482-2521
Philippines	Edward Oliver; Jean Kelly	(202) 482-4958
Poland	EEBIC	(202) 482-2645
Portugal	Mary Beth Double	(202) 482-4508
Puerto Rico	Mark Siegelman	(202) 482-5680
Qatar	Paul Thanos	(202) 482-1860
Romania	EEBIC	(202) 482-2645
Russia	BISNIS	(202) 482-4655
Rwanda	Philip Michelini	(202) 482-4388
St. Barthélemy	Michelle Brooks	(202) 482-2527
St. Kitts - Nevis	Michelle Brooks	(202) 482-2527
St. Lucia	Michelle Brooks	(202) 482-2527
St. Martin	Michelle Brooks	(202) 482-2527
St. Vincent - Grenadines	Michelle Brooks	(202) 482-2527
São Tomé & Principe	Philip Michelini	(202) 482-4388
Saudi Arabia	Christopher Cerone; Claude Clement	(202) 482-1860
Senegal	Philip Michelini	(202) 482-4388
Seychelles	Chandra Watkins	(202) 482-4564
Sierra Leone	Philip Michelini	(202) 482-4388
Singapore	Edward Oliver; Raphael Cung	(202) 482-4958
Slovakia	EEBIC	(202) 482-2645
Somalia	Chandra Watkins	(202) 482-4564
South Africa	Emily Solomon	(202) 482-5148
Spain	Mary Beth Double	(202) 482-4508
Sri Lanka	John Simmons	(202) 482-2954
Sudan	Chandra Watkins	(202) 482-4564
Suriname	Michelle Brooks	(202) 482-2527
Swaziland	Finn Holm-Olsen	(202) 482-4228
Sweden	James Devlin	(202) 482-4414
Switzerland	Philip Combs	(202) 482-2920
Syria	Corey Wright; Thomas Sams	(202) 482-5506
Taiwan	Robert Chu; Dan Duvall	(202) 482-4390
Tajikistan	BISNIS	(202) 482-4655
Tanzania	Finn Holm-Olsen	(202) 482-4228
Thailand	Edward Oliver; Jean Kelly	(202) 482-4958
Togo	Debra Henke	(202) 482-5149
Trinidad & Tobago	Michelle Brooks	(202) 482-2527
Tunisia	Corey Wright; Thomas Sams	(202) 482-5506
Turkey	Anne Corro	(202) 482-3945
Turkmenistan	BISNIS	(202) 482-4655
Turks & Caicos Islands	Mark Siegelman	(202) 482-5680
Uganda	Chandra Watkins	(202) 482-4564
Ukraine	BISNIS	(202) 482-4655
United Arab Emirates	Claude Clement; Christopher Cerone	(202) 482-5545

Government Resources for Exporters (cont'd)

Country	Desk Officer	Phone
United Kingdom	Robert McLaughlin	(202) 482-3748
Uruguay	Roger Turner	(202) 482-1495
Uzbekistan	BISNIS	(202) 482-4655
Venezuela	Laura Zeiger-Hatfield	(202) 482-4303
Vietnam	Gary Bouck; Hong-Phong B. Pho	(202) 482-4958
Virgin Islands (U.K.)	Michelle Brooks	(202) 482-2527
Yemen, Republic of	Paul Thanos	(202) 482-1860
Zaire	Philip Michelini	(202) 482-4388
Zambia	Finn Holm-Olsen	(202) 482-4228
Zimbabwe	Finn Holm-Olsen	(202) 482-4228

U.S. and Foreign Commercial Service

The US&FCS, a division of the U.S. Department of Commerce, maintains a network of locations throughout the world. Services for U.S. exporters include the following:

- Free general export support services: includes product and/or country information, private counseling by appointment, trade statistics;

- Custom support services: may include surveys of potential sales representatives; interpreting and secretarial services; office space; market research; single-company promotional events; arranging appointments with local contacts;

- Product promotion (US&FCS will mail company brochures to potential clients and key industry associations);

- Customized sales survey (sales potential, competitors, normal sales channels, comparable product prices are all provided in a report on a particular product);

- Foreign market research (in-depth market data on selected products and industries, focusing on the best opportunities for U.S. goods);

- Agent/distributor service includes contacting potential agents and finally providing a list of six most interested and best-suited contacts for a specific product;

- Export contact list service (company profiles).

Contact Options

U.S. and Foreign Commercial Service
Office of Domestic Operations
(202) 482-4767

U.S. and Foreign Commercial Service
Office of International Operations
(202) 482-6228

US&FCS Overseas Posts

The following addresses are a combination of domestic and international information. Here are examples of ways to address an envelope depending on its origin and destination:

Posts with APO/FPO Numbers:

APO/FPO Address*
Organization
PSC or Unit number, Box number
APO AE 09080 or APO AA 34038 or
APO AP 96337

International Address**
American Embassy
P.O. Box 26431***
Manama, Bahrain

Posts without APO/FPO Numbers:

Diplomatic Pouch Address*
Name of Post
Department of State
Washington, DC 20521

International Address**
American Embassy
Jubilaeumstrasse 93***
3005 Bern, Switzerland

NOTE: Do not combine any of the above forms (e.g., international plus APO/FPO addresses). This will result in confusion and possible delays in delivery. Mail sent to the department for delivery through its pouch system for posts with APO/FPO addresses cannot be accepted and will be returned to the sender.

* Use domestic postage.

** Use international postage.

*** Use street address only when P.O. box is not supplied.

Albania
(Tirane)
American Embassy Tirana Rruga
E. Elbansanit 103
PSC 59, Box 100 (A)
APO AE 09624
[355] (42) 32875

Government Resources for Exporters (cont'd)

Algeria
(Algiers)
4 Chemin Cheikh Bachir El-Ibrahimi
B.P. Box 549
Alger-Gare 16000
[213] (2) 601-69-11-86

Angola
(Luanda)
Rua Major Kanhangulo
CP 6484
Pouch: American Embassy Luanda
Dept. of State, Washington, DC, 20521
[244] (2) 345-481

Antigua and Barbuda
(St. John's)
FPO AA34054 0001
(809) 462-3505/06

Argentina
(Buenos Aires)
4300 Colombia 1425
Unit 4334
APO AA 34034
[54] (1) 777-4533/4

Armenia
(Yerevan)
18 Gen Bagramian
[7] 8852-151-144

Australia
(Brisbane)
Fourth Floor
383 Wickham Terrace
Brisbane, Queensland 4000
Unit 11018
[61] (7) 831-3330

(Canberra)
Moonah Pl.
Canberra, A.C.T. 2600
APO AP 96549
[61] (6) 270-5000

(Melbourne)
553 St. Kilda Rd.
P.O. Box 6722
Melbourne, Victoria 3004
Unit 11011
APO AP 96551-0002
[61] (3) 526-5900

(Perth)
13th Floor
16 St. Georges Terrace
Perth, WA 6000
[61] (9) 231-9400

(Sydney)
59th Floor, MLE Centre
19-29 Martin Pl.
Sydney, N.S.W. 2000
Unit 11026
APO AP 96554-0002
[61] (2) 373-9200

Austria
(Vienna)
Boltzmanngasse 16
1-1091
[43] (1) 313-39

U.S. Delegation to the Conference on Security
and Cooperation in Europe (CSCE)
Obersteinergasse 11
A-1190
[43] (1) 36-31-52

U.S. Mission to International
Organizations in Vienna (UNVIE)
Obersteinergasse 11
A-1190
[43] (1) 36-31-52

Azerbaijan
(Baku)
Azadliq Prospect 83
[7] 8922-96-00-19

Bahamas
(Nassau)
Queen St.
P.O. Box N-8197
(809) 322-1181

Bahrain
(Manama)
Bldg. No. 979
Rd. 3119 (next to Al-Ahli Sports Club)
Zinj District
FPO AE 09834-5100
International Mail
P.O. Box 26431
[973] 273-300

Bangladesh
(Dhaka)
Diplomatic Enclave
Madani Ave.
Baridhara
G.P.O. Box 323
Dhaka 1212
[880] (2) 884700-22

Barbados
(Bridgetown)
P.O. Box 302
FPO AA 34055
(809) 436-4950

Government Resources for Exporters (cont'd)

Belarus
(Minsk)
Starovilenskaya #46
[7] (172) 34-65-37

Belgium
(Antwerp)
European Logistical Support Office
(ELSO)
Noorderlann 147
Bus 12A
B-2030
APO AE 09724
[32] (3) 542-4775

(Brussels)
27 Blvd. du Régent
B-1000
APO AE 09724
[32] (2) 513-3830

U.S. Mission to the North Atlantic Treaty
Organization (USNATO)
Autoroute de Zaventem
B-1110
APO AE 09724
[32] (2) 726-4580

(Lummen)
EURMAC
15 Klaverbladstraat
B-3560 Lummen
APO AE 09724
[32] (013) 531-071

(Shape)
POLAD
B-7010
APO AE 09705
[32] (65) 445-000

Belize
(Belize City)
Gabourel Land and Hutson St.
P.O. Box 286
APO Belize, Unit 7401
APO AA 34025
[501] (2) 77161

Benin
(Cotonou)
Rue Caporal Bernard Anani
B.P. 2012
[229] 30-06-50

Bermuda
(Hamilton)
Crown Hill, 16 Middle Rd., Devonshire
P.O. Box HM325
Hamilton, HMBX
PSC 1002
FPO AE 09727-1002
(809) 295-1342

Bolivia
(La Paz)
Banco Popular del Peru Bldg.
Corner of Calles Mercado and Colón
P.O. Box 425
La Paz
APO AA 34032
[591] (2) 350251

Bosnia-Herzegovina
(Sarajevo)
AmEmbassy Bosnia
c/o AmEmbassy Vienna
Boltzmanngasse 16, A-1091
Vienna, Department of State
Washington, DC 20521
[43] (1) 31-399

Botswana
(Gaborone)
P.O. Box 90
[267] 356-947

Brazil
(Belém [CA and FCS Branch])
Rua Osvaldo Cruz
165, 66017-090 Belém, Pará
[55] (91) 223-0800

(Belo Horizonte [USIS and FCS Branch, AV])
Alvares Cabral
1600 3 Andar–Belo Horizonte
MG CEP 30170
[55] (31) 335-3555

(Brasília)
Avenida das Nacoes
Lote 3
Unite 3500
APO AA 34030
[55] (61) 321-7272

(Fortaleza)
[55] (85) 252-1539

(Manaus)
Rua Recife 1010
Adrianopolois
CEP 69057-001
Manaus, Amazonas
[55] (92) 234-4546

(Commercial Office)
Rua Estados Unidos
1812 São Paulo
[55] (11) 853-2011; 2411; 2778

(Pôrto Alegre)
Rua Coronel Genuíno
421 (Ninth Floor)
Unit 3504
APO AA 34030
[55] (51) 226-4288

Government Resources for Exporters (cont'd)

(Recife)
Rua Goncalves Maia 163
APO AA 34030
[55] (81) 221-1412

(Rio de Janeiro)
Avendia Presidente Wilson 147
APO AA 34030
[55] (21) 297-7117

(Salvador da Bahia)
Avenida Antonio Carlos Magalhaes
S/N –Ed. Cidadella Center 1
Sala 410
40275-440 Salvador, Bahia, Brazil
[55] (71) 358-9166

(Sao Paulo)
Rua Padre João Manoel, 933, 01411
P.O. Box 8063
APO AA 34030
[55] (11) 881-6511

Brunei
(Bandar Seri Begawan)
Third Floor-Teck Guan Plaza
Jalan Sultan
AMEMB Box B
APO AP 96440
[673] (2) 229-670

Bulgaria
(Sofia) 1 Saborna St., Unit 1335
APO AE 09213-1335
[359] (2) 88-48-01

Burkina Faso
(Ouagadougou)
01 B.P. 35
[226] 30-67-23

Burma (Myammar)
(Rangoon)
581 Merchant St.
(GPO521)
AMEMB Box B
APO AP 96546
[95] (1) 82055

Burundi
(Bujumbura) B.P. 1720
Ave. des Etats-Unis
[257] 223-454

Cambodia
(Phnom Penh)
27 EO St. 240
Mail:
Box P
APO AP 96546
(855) 23-26436

Cameroon
(Yaoundé)
Re Nachtigal
B.P. 817
[237] 23-40-14

Canada
(Calgary, Alberta)
Suite 1050
615 Macleod Trail, SE
T2G 4T8
(403) 266-8962

(Halifax, Nova Scotia)
Suite 910
Cogswell Tower, Scotia Sq.
B3J 3K1
(902) 429-2480

(Montreal, Quebec)
P.O. Box 65
Postal Station Desjardins
H5B 1G1
P.O. Box 847
Champlain, NY 12919
(514) 398-0711

U.S. Mission to the International Civil Aviation
Organization (ICAO)
1000 Sherbrooke St.
W. Room 753
Montréal, Quebec
P.O. Box 847
Champlain, NY 12919
(514) 285-8304

(Ottawa, Ontario)
100 Wellington St.
K1P 5T1
P.O. BOX 5000
Ogdensburg, NY 13669
(613) 238-5335

(Quebec City, Quebec)
2 Place Terrasse Dufferin
C. P. 939
G1R 4T9
P.O. Box 1547
Champlain, NY 12919
(418) 692-2095

(Toronto, Ontario)
360 University Ave.
M5G 1S4
P.O. Box 135
Lewiston, NY 14092
(416) 595-1700

Government Resources for Exporters (cont'd)

(Vancouver, British Columbia)
1095 W. Pender St.
V6E 2M6
P.O. Box 5002
Point Roberts, WA 98281
(604) 685-4311

Republic of Cape Verde
(Praia)
Rua Abilio Macedo 81
C.P. 201
[238] 61-56-16

Central African Republic
(Bangui)
Ave. David Dacko
B.P. 924
[236] 61-02-00

Chad
(N'Djamena)
Ave. Félix Eboue
B.P. 413
[235] 51-62-18

Chile
(Santiago)
Codina Bldg.
Agustians 1343
Unit 4127
APO AA 34033
[56] (2) 232-2600

China
(Beijing)
Xiu Shui Bei Jie 3
100600
PSC 461, Box 50
FPO AP 96521-0002
[86] (1) 532-3831

(Chengdu)
4 Lingshiquan Lu
Renmin Nan Lu Si
Duan Chengdu 610041
PSC 461, Box 85
FPO AP 96521-0002
[86] (28) 558-3992

(Guangzhou)
No. 1 S. Shamian St.
Shamian Island
Guangzhou 510133
PSC 461, Box 100
FPO AP 96521-0002
[86] (20) 888-8911

(Shanghai)
1469 Huai Hai Middle Rd.
Shanghai 200031
PSC 461, Box 200
FPO AP 96521-0002
[86] (21) 433-6880

(Shenyang)
52 14th Wei Rd.
Heping District 110003
PSC 461, Box 45
FPO AP 96521-0002
[86] (24) 282-0068

Colombia
(Barranquilla)
Calle 77, Carrera 68
Centro Comercial Mayorista
Apartado Aereo 51565
APO AA 34038
[57] (58) 45-8480

(Bogotá)
Calle 38, No. 8-61
Apartado Aereo 3831
APO AA 34038
[57] (1) 320 1300

Republic of the Congo
(Brazzaville)
Ave. Amilcar Cabral
B.P. 1015
[242] 83-20-70

Costa Rica
(San José)
Pavas, San José
APO AA 34020
[506] 220-3939

Croatia
(Zagreb)
Andrije Hebranga 2
Unit 1345
APO AE 09213
[385] (41) 45600

Cuba
(Havana)
Swiss Embassy
Calzada Entre
LYM, Vedado
33-3551/9

Cyprus
(Nicosia)
Metochiou and Ploutarchou Sts.
Engomi Nicosia, Cyprus
APO AE 09836
[357] (2) 476100

Czech Republic
(Prague)
(Int'l) Trziste 15
11801 Prague 1
Unit 1330
APO AE 09213
[42] (2) 2451-0847

Government Resources for Exporters (cont'd)

Denmark
(Copenhagen)
Dag Hammarskjölds
Alle 24
2100 Copenhagen O or
APO AE 09716
[45] (31) 42-31-44

Republic of Djibouti
(Djibouti)
Plateau du Serpent
Blvd. Marechal Joffré
B.P. 185
[253] 35-39-95

Dominican Republic
(Santo Domingo)
Corner of Calle César Nicolás
Penson & Calle Leopoldo Navarro
Unit 5500
APO AA 34041
(809) 5412171

Ecuador
(Guayaquil)
9 de Octubre y García Moreno
APO AA 34039
[593] (4) 323-570

(Quito)
Avenida 12 de Octubre y Avenida Patria
P.O. Box 358
Unit 5309
APO AA 34039-3420
[593] (2) 562-890

Egypt
(Cairo)
(North Gate)
8, Kamal El-Din Salah St.
Garden City
APO AE 09839-4900
[20] (2) 355-7371

El Salvador
(San Salvador)
Final Blvd.
Antiguo Cuscatlán
Unit 3116
APO AA 34023
(503) 78-4444

Equatorial Guinea
(Malabo)
Calle de Los Ministros
P.O. Box 597
[240] (9) 2185

Eritrea
(Asmara)
34 Zera Yacob St.
P.O. Box 211
[291] (1) 12-00-04

Estonia
(Tallinn)
Kentamanni 20
EE 0001
[372] (6) 312-021

Ethiopia
(Addis Ababa)
Entoto St.
P.O. Box 1014
[251] (1) 550-666

Fiji
(Suva)
31 Loftus St.
P.O. Box 218
[679] 314-466

Finland
(Helsinki)
Itainen Puistotie 14A
SF-00140
APO AE 09723
[358] (0) 171931

France
(Bordeaux)
22 Cours du Maréchal Foch
33080 Bordeaux Cedex
Unit 21551
APO AE 09777
[33] (56) 52-65-95

(Lyon)
U.S. Commercial Office
45 Rue de la Bourse
Unit 21551
APO AE 09777
[33] (16) 72-40-58

(Marseille)
12 Blvd. Paul Peytral
13286 Marseille Cedex
Paris Embassy (MAR)
PSC 116
APO AE 09777
[33] (91) 549-200

(Nice)
U.S. Commercial Office
Rue du Maréchal Joffre
c/o AMEMB Paris
Unit 21551
APO AE 09777
[33] (16) 93-88-89-55

(Paris)
2 Ave. Gabriel
75382 Paris Cedex 08
Unit 21551
APO AE 09777
[33] (1) 4296-12-02

Government Resources for Exporters (cont'd)

U.S. Mission to the Organization for Economic
Cooperation and Development (USOECD)
19 Rue de Franqueville
75016
Unit 21551
APO AE 09777
[33] (1) 45-24-74-77

U.S. Observer Mission to the United Nations
Educational, Scientific, and Cultural Organization
(UNESCO)
2 Ave. Gabriel, 75382
Cedex 08
Unit 21551
APO AE 09777
[33] (1) 42-96-12-02

(Strasbourg)
15 Ave. d'Alsace
67082 Strasbourg Cedex or
Unit 21551
APO AE 09777
[33] (88) 35-31-04

Gabon
(Libreville)
Blvd. de la Mer
B.P. 4000
[241] 762003/4

Gambia
(Banjul)
Fajara
Kairaba Ave.
P.M.B. 19
Banjul
[220] 392-856

Georgia
(Tbilisi)
#25 Antoneli
[7] (8832) 989-967; 933-803

Federal Republic of Germany
(Berlin)
Neustaedtische Kirchstrasse 4-5
10117 Berlin or
Unit 26738
APO AE 09235-5500
[49] 30-238-5174

(Bonn)
Deichmanns Aue 29
53170 Bonn
Unit 21701
PSC 117
APO AE 09080
[49] (228) 3391

(Düsseldorf)
U.S. Commercial Office
Emanuel-Leutz Str.
1B 40547 Düsseldorf
c/o AMEMB Bonn
Unit 21701, Box 30
APO AE 09080
[49] (211) 596-798

(Frankfurt Am Main)
Siesmayerstrasse 21
60323 Frankfurt
Unit 115
APO AE 09213-0115
[49] (69) 7535-0

(Hamburg)
Alsterufer 27/28
20354 Hamburg
[49] (40) 411710

(Leipzig)
Wilhelm Seyfferth Str. 4
04107 Leipzig
USEMB Berlin
Unit 26738
APO AE 09235-5500
[49] (341) 213-840

(Munich)
Koeniginstrasse 5
80539 Muenchen
Unit 24718
APO AE 09178
[49] (89) 28880

(Stuttgart)
Urbanstrasse 7
70182 Stuttgart
Unit 30607
APO AE 09154-0001
[49] (711) 21008-11

Ghana
(Accra)
Ring Rd. E.
P.O. Box 194
Chancery
[233] (21) 775348/9

Greece
(Athens)
91 Vasilissis Sophias Blvd.
10160 Athens or
PSC 108
APO AE 09842
[30] (1) 721-2951

Government Resources for Exporters (cont'd)

(Thessaloniki)
59 Leoforos Nikis
GR-546-22
PSC 108, Box 37
APO AE 09842
[30] (31) 242905

Grenada
(St. George's)
P.O. Box 54
St. George's
Grenada, W.I.
(809) 444-1173/8

Guatemala
(Guatemala City)
7-01 Avenida de la Reforma
Zone 10
APO AA 34024
[502] (2) 31-15-41

Guinea
(Conakry)
Second Blvd. and Ninth Ave.
B.P. 603
[224] 41-15-20

Guinea-Bissau
(Bissau)
Bairro de Penha
C.P. 297
1067 Codex
[245] 25-2273/6

Guyana
(Georgetown)
99-100 Young and Duke Sts.
Kingston, Georgetown, Guyana
P.O. Box 10507
[592] (2) 54900-9 or 57960-9

Haiti
(Port-au-Prince)
Harry Truman Blvd.
P.O. Box 1761
[509] 22-0354

The Holy See
(Vatican City)
Via Delle Terme Deciane 26
Rome 00153
PSC 59
APO AE 09624
[396] 46741

Honduras
(Tegucigalpa)
Avenida La Paz
Apartado Postal No. 3453
AMEMB Honduras
APO AA 34022
[504] 36-9320

Hong Kong
(Hong Kong)
26 Garden Rd.
PSC 464 Box 30
FPO AP 96522-0002
[852] 523-9011

Hungary
(Budapest)
V. Szabadsag Terrace 12
Am Embassy
Unit 1320
APO AE 09213-1320
[36] (1) 112-6450

Iceland
(Reykjavík)
Laufasvegur 21, Box 40
USEMB
PSC 1003, Box 40
FPO AE 09728-0340
[354] (1) 629100

India
(Bombay)
Lincoln House
78 Bhulabhai Desai Rd.
400026
[91] (22) 363-3611

(Calcutta)
5/1 Ho Chi Minh Sarani
700071
[91] (33) 242-3611

(Madras)
220 Mount Rd.
600006
[91] (44) 827-3040

(New Delhi)
Shanti Path
Chanakyapuri 110021
[91] (11) 600651

Indonesia
(Jakarta)
Medan Merdeka Selatan 5, Box 1
APO AP 96520
[62] (21) 360-360

(Medan)
Jalan Imam Bonjol 13
APO AP 96520
[62] (61) 322200

(Surabaya)
Jalal Raya Dr. Sutomo 33
AMCONGEN, Box 1, Unit 8131
APO AP 96520-0002
[62] (31) 582287/8

Government Resources for Exporters (cont'd)

Iraq
(Baghdad)
Opp. For. Ministry Club (Masbah Quarter)
P.O. Box 2447
Alwiyah, Baghdad
[964] (1) 719-6138/9

Ireland
(Dublin)
42 Elgin Rd.
Ballsbridge
[353] (1) 6687122

Israel
(Jerusalem)
18 Agron Rd.
Jerusalem 94190
P.O. Box 290
PSC 98, Box 100
APO AE 09830
[972] (2) 253288

(Tel Aviv)
71 Hayarkon St.
PSC 98, Box 100
APO AE 09830
[972] (3) 517-4338

Italy
(Florence)
Lungarno Amerigo Vespucci, 38
50123 Firenze
APO AE 09613
[39] (55) 239-8276/7/8/9

(Milan)
Via Principe Amedo, 2/10
20121 Milano
c/o U.S. Embassy, Box M
PSC 59
APO AE 09624
[39] (2) 290-351

U.S. Information Service
Via Bigli 11/A
20121
[39] (2) 795051/2/3/4/5

(Naples)
Piazza della Repubblica
80122 Napoli
Box 18, PSC 810
FPO AE 09619-0002
[39] (81) 583-8111

(Rome)
Via Veneto 119/A
00187-Roma
PSC 59, Box 100
APO AE 09624
[39] (6) 46741

U.S. Mission to the United Nations Agencies for
Food and Agriculture (FODAG)
Annex, Via Sardegna 49
00187 Rome;
or c/o U.S. Embassy Rome
PSC 59, Box 100
APO AE 09624
[39] (6) 4674-4260

Ivory Coast
(Abidjan)
5 Rue Jesse Owens
01 B.P. 1712
[225] 21-09-79

(African Development Bank/Fund)
Ave. Joseph Anoma
01 B.P. 1387
Agidjan 01
[225] 20-40-15

Jamaica
(Kingston)
Jamaica Mutual Life Center
2 Oxford Rd., Third Floor
(809) 929-4850

Japan
(Fukuoka)
5-26 Ohori 2-chome
Chuo-ku
Fukuoka-810 or
Unit 45004, Box 242
APO AP 96337-0001
[81] (92) 751-9331/4

(Nagoya)
Nishiki SIS Building 6F 10-33
Nishiki 3-chome Naka-ku
Nagoya 460
c/o AMEMB Tokyo
Unit 45004, Box 280
APO AP 96337-0001
[81] (52) 203-4011

(Naha, Okinawa)
2564 Nishihara
Urasoe City
Okinawa 90121
PSC 556, Box 840
Unit 45
FPO AP 96372-0840
[81] (98) 876-4211

(Osaka-Kobe)
11-5 Nishitenma 2-chome
Kita-Ku, Osaka 530
Unit 45004, Box 239
APO AP 96337-0002
[81] (6) 315-5900

Government Resources for Exporters (cont'd)

(Sapporo)
Kita 1-Jo Nishi 28-chome
Chuo-ku
Sapporo 064
Unit 45004, Box 276
APO AP 96337-0003
[81] (11) 641-1115/7

(Tokyo)
10-5 Akasaka 1-chome
Minato-ku (107)
Unit 45004, Box 258
APO AP 96337-0001
[81] (3) 3224-5000

U.S. Trade Center
Seventh Floor, World Import Mart, 1-3
Higashi Ikebukuro 3-chome
Toshima-ku
Tokyo 170
[81] (3) 3987-2441

Jordan
(Amman)
P.O. Box 354
Amman 11118 or
APO AE 09892-0200
[962] (6) 820-101

Kazakhstan
(Almaty)
99/97 Furmanova St.
Almaty
Republic of Kazakhstan 480012
[7] (3272) 63-24-26

Kenya
(Nairobi)
Moi/Haile Selassie Ave.
P.O. Box 30137
Unit 64100
APO AE 09831
[254] (2) 334141

Korea
(Pusan)
24 2-Ka
Daechung-Dong
Chunk-ku
[82] (51) 246-7791

(Seoul)
82 Sejong-Ro
Chongro-ku
AMEMB, Unit 15550
APO AP 96205-0001
[82] (2) 397-4114

U.S. Export Development Office/
U.S. Trade Center
c/o U.S. Embassy
[82] (2) 397-4212

Kuwait
(Kuwait)
P.O. Box 77 SAFAT
13001 SAFAT
Unit 69000
APO AE 09880-9000
[965] 242-4151

Kyrgystan
(Bishkek)
Erkindik Propssekt #66
720002
[7] (3312)22-29-20

Laos
(Vientiane)
Rue Bartholonie
B.P. 114
Mail to AMEMB Vientiane Box V
APO AP 96546
[856] (21) 212581

Latvia
(Riga)
Raina Blvd. 7
226050
[371] (2) 213-962

Lebanon
(Beirut)
Antelias
P.O. Box 70-840 or
PSC 815, Box 2
FPO AE 09836-0002
[961] (1) 402-200

Lesotho
(Maseru)
P.O. Box 333
Maseru 100 Lesotho
[266] 312-666

Liberia
(Monrovia)
111 United Nations Dr.
P.O. Box 10-0098
Mamba Point
[231] 222-991/2/3/4

Lithuania
(Vilnius)
Akmenu 6
APO AE 09723
[370] (2) 223-031

Luxembourg
(Luxembourg)
22 Blvd. Emmanuel-Servais
2535 Luxembourg
PSC 11
APO AE 09132-5380
[352] 460123

Government Resources for Exporters (cont'd)

Macedonia
(Skopje)
ul. 27 Mart No. 5
9100 Skopje
APO USLO Skopje
c/o Embassy Sofia
APO AE 09213-5740
[389] (91) 117-2121

Madagascar
(Antananarivo)
14-16 Rue Rainitovo
Antsahavola
B.P. 620
[261] (2) 212-57

Malawi
(Lilongwe)
P.O. Box 30016
Lilongwe 3
[265] 783-166

Malaysia
(Kuala Lumpur)
376 Jalan Tun Razak
50400 Kuala Lumpur
P.O. Box No. 10035
50700 Kuala Lumpur
APO AP 96535-8152
[60] (3) 248-9011

Mali
(Bamako)
Rue Rochester, New York, and
Rue Mohamed V
B.P. 34
[223] 225470

Malta
(Valetta)
Second Floor
Development House
St. Anne
St. Floriana, Malta
P.O. Box 535
[356] 235960

Republic of the Marshall Islands
(Majuro)
P.O. Box 1379
[692] 247-4011

Mauritania
(Nouakchott)
B.P. 222
[222] (2) 526-60; 526-63

Mauritius
(Port Louis)
Rogers House
(Fourth Floor)
John Kennedy St.
[230] 208-9763

Mexico
(Ciudad Juárez)
Chihuahua Avenida Lopez
Mateos 924N
32000 Ciudad Juárez
Mail:
Box 10545
El Paso, TX 79995
[52] (16) 113000

(Guadalajara)
JAL
Progreso 175
44100 Guadalajara, Jalisco
Mail:
Box 3088
Laredo, TX 78044
[52] (3) 625-2998

(Hermosillo)
Sonora
Monterrey 141
83260 Hermosillo
Mail:
Box 3598
Laredo, TX 78044
[52] (62) 17-2375

(Matamoros)
Tamaulipas
Calle Primera 2002
Mail:
Box 633
Brownsville, TX 78522
[52] (88) 12-44-02

(Mérida)
Yucatán
Paseo Montejo 453
97000 Merida
Mail:
Box 3087
Laredo, TX 78044
[52] (99) 25-5011

(Mexico City)
Paseo de la Reforma 305
06500 D.F.
Mail:
P.O. Box 3087
Laredo, TX 78044
[52] (5) 211-0042

U.S. Export Development Office
Liverpool 31
06600 D.F.
[52] (5) 591-0155

U.S. Travel and Tourism Office
Plaza Comermex
M. Avila Camacho 1-402
11560 D.F.
[52] (5) 520-2101

Government Resources for Exporters (cont'd)

(Monterrey)
Nuevo León
Avenida Constitución 411 Poniente
64000 Monterrey, N.L.
Mail:
Box 3098
Laredo, TX 78044
[52] (83) 45-2120

(Nuevo Laredo)
Tamaulipas
Calle Allende 3330
Colonia Jardin
88260 Nuevo Laredo, Tamaulipas
Mail:
Drawer 3089
Laredo, TX 78044
[52] (871) 4-0512

(Tijuana)
Tapachula 96
22420 Tijuana
Baja California Norte
Mail:
P.O. Box 439039
San Diego, CA 92143
[52] (66) 81-7400

Micronesia
(Kolonia)
P.O. Box 1286
Pohnpei
Federated States of Micronesia 96941
[691] 320-2187

Moldova
(Chisçinau)
Strada Alexei Mateevici #103
[373] (2) 23-37-72

Mongolia
(Ulaanbaatar)
c/o American Embassy, Beijing
Micro Region 11
Big Ring Rd.
PSC 461, Box 300
FPO AP 96521-0002
[976] (1) 329095

Morocco
(Casablanca)
8 Blvd. Moulay Youssef
APO AE 09718
[212] (2) 26-45-50

(Rabat)
2 Ave. de Marrakech
PSC 74, Box 003
APO AE 09718
[212] (7) 76 22 65

Mozambique
(Maputo)
Avenida Kenneth Kaunda 193
P.O. Box 783
[258] (1) 49-27-97

Namibia
(Windhoek)
Ausplan Bldg.
14 Lossen St.
Private Bag 12029
Ausspannplatz, Windhoek, Namibia
[264] (61) 221-601

Nepal
(Kathmandu)
Pani Pokhari
[977] (1) 411179

Netherlands
(Amsterdam)
Museumplein 19
1071 DJ Amsterdam
PSC 71, Box 1000
APO AE 09715
[31] (20) 5755 309

(The Hague)
Lange Voorhout 102
2514 EJ The Hague
PSC 71 Box 1000
APO AE 09715
[31] (70) 310-9209

Netherlands Antilles
(Curaçao)
St. Anna Blvd. 19
P.O. Box 158
Willemstad
[599] (9) 613066

New Zealand
(Auckland)
Fourth Floor
Yorkshire General Building
Corner of Shortland and O'Connell Sts.
Auckland
Private Bag, 92022
PSC 467, Box 99
FPO AP 96531-1099
[64] (9) 303-2724

(Wellington)
29 Fitzherbert Terrace
Thorndon, Wellington
P.O. Box 1190
PSC 467, Box 1
FPO AP 96531-1001
[64] (4) 472-2068

Government Resources for Exporters (cont'd)

Nicaragua
(Managua)
Km 4-1/2 Carretera Sur
APO AA 34021
[505] (2) 663861

Niger
(Niamey)
Rue des Ambassades
B.P. 11201
[227] 72-26-61/2/3/4

Nigeria
(Abuja [Branch Office])
11 Mambilla, Maitama District
P.O. Box 5760
Garki District
[234] (9) 523-0960

(Ibadan [USIS])
Bodija Estate
(022) 410-775

(Kaduna)
9 Maska Rd.
P.O. Box 170
[234] (62) 235990

(Lagos)
2 Eleke Crescent
P.O. Box 554
[234] (1) 261-0097

Norway
(Oslo)
Drammensveien 18
0244 Oslo or
PSC 69, Box 1000
APO AE 09707
[47] 22-44-85-50

Oman
(Muscat)
P.O. Box 202
Code No. 115
[968] 698-989

(Ruwi)
U.S. Delegation to the Oman/American Joint
Commission for Economic and
Technical Cooperation
P.O. Box 3001
Code No. 112
[968] 703-000

Pakistan
(Islamabad)
Diplomatic Enclave, Ramna 5
P.O. Box 1048
PSC 1212, Box 2000
Unit 6220
APO AE 09812-2000
[92] (51) 86161

(Karachi)
8 Abdullah Haroon Rd.
PSC 1214, Box 2000
Unit 62400
APO AE 09814-6150
[92] (21) 5685170

(Lahore)
50 Sharah E-Bin Badees (50 Empress Rd.)
Simla Hills, Lahore K
Unit 62216
APO AE 09812-2216
[92] 6365530

(Peshawar)
11 Hospital Rd.
Peshawar Cantt
AC Peshawar
Unit 62217
APO AE 09812-2217
[92] (521) 279801

Republic of Palau
(Koror)
P.O. Box 6028
96940
[680] 488-2920

Panama
(Panama City)
Apartado 6959
Panamá 5
AMEMB
Unit 0945
APO AA 34002
[507] 27-1777

Papua New Guinea
(Port Moresby)
Armit St.
P.O. Box 1492
APO AE 96533
[675] 211-455; 594; 654

Paraguay
(Asunción)
1776 Mariscal Lopez Ave.
Casilla Postal 402
Unit 4711
APO AA 34036-0001
[595] (21) 213-715

Peru
(Lima)
Corner Avenidas Inca Garcilaso de la
Vega and España
P.O. Box 1995
Lima 1 or
American Embassy (Lima)
APO AA 34031
[51] (41) 33-8000

Government Resources for Exporters (cont'd)

Philippines
(Cebu)
Third Floor
PCI Bank Bldg.
Gorordo Ave.
Lahug Cebu City 6000
APO AP 96440
[63] (32) 311-261

(Manila)
1201 Roxas Blvd.
Ermita Manila 1000
APO AP 96440
[63] (2) 521-7116

Asian Development Bank
#6 ADB Ave. Mandaluyong
Metro Manila
P.O. Box 789
APO AP 96440
[63] (2) 632-6050

Poland
(Kraków)
Ulica Stolarska 9
31043 Kraków
Unit 25402
APO AE 09213
[48] (12) 229764

(Poznán)
Ulica Chopina 4
61708 Poznán
Unit 25402
APO AE 09213
[48] (61) 551088

(Warsaw)
Aleja Ujazdowskie 29/31
AmEmbassy Warsaw
Box 5010, Unit 1340
APO AE 09213-1340
[48] (2) 628-3041

U.S. Trade Center
Aleja Jerozolimskia 56C
IKEA Bldg., Second Floor
00-803 Warszawa
AmEmbassy Warsaw
Unit 1340
APO AE 09213
[48] (22) 21-45-15

Portugal
(American Business Center [Oporto])
Praça Conde de Samodaes 65
4000 Pôrto
APO AE 09726
[351] (2) 606-30-94

(Lisbon)
Avenida das Forças Armadas
1600 Lisboa
PSC 83
APO AE 09726
[351] (1) 726-6600

(Ponta Delgada São Miguel Azores)
Avenida D. Henrique
PSC 76
APO AE 09720-0002
[351] (96) 22216/7/8/9

Qatar
(Doha)
149 Ali Bin Ahmed St.
Farig Bin Omran
P.O. Box 2399
[0974] 864701/2/3

Romania
(Bucharest)
Strada Tudor Arghezi 7-9 or
AmConGen (Buch)
Unit 1315
APO AE 09213
[40] (1) 210-4042

(Cluj-Napoca)
U.S. Branch Office
Universitatii 7-9
Etage 1
Cluj-Napoca 3400
c/o American Embassy Bucharest
Unit 1315
APO AE 09213-1315
[40] (95) 19-38-15

Russia
(Moscow)
Novinskiy Bul'var 19/23 or
APO AE 09721
[7] (095) 252-2451

U.S. Commercial Office
Novinskiy Bul'var 15
[7] (095) 956-4255

(St. Petersburg)
FurshtadtskayaUlitsa 15
St. Petersburg 191028
PSC 78 Box L
APO AE 09723
[7] (812) 275-1701

(Vladivostok)
Ulitsa Mordovtseva 12
[7] (4232) 268-458; 554

Government Resources for Exporters (cont'd)

(Yekaterinburg)
P.O. Box 400
620151 Yekaterinburg
AmConGen Yekaterinburg
Dept. of State
Washington, DC 20521
[7] (3432) 601-143

Rwanda
(Kigali)
Blvd. de la Révolution
B.P. 28
[250] 75601/2/3

Saudi Arabia
(Dhahran)
Between Aramco Hdqrs. and Dhahran Int'l Airport
P.O. Box 81
Dhahran Airport, 31932 or
Unit 66803
APO AE 09858-6803
[966] (3) 891-3200

(Jeddah)
Palestine Rd.
Ruwais
P.O. Box 149
Jeddah 21411 or
Unit 6112
APO AE 09811-2112
[966] (2) 667-0080

(Riyadh)
Collector Road M.
Riyadh Diplomatic Quarter
AMEMB
Unit 61307
APO AE 09803-1307
International Mail:
P.O. Box 94309
Riyadh, 11693
[966] (1) 488-3800

U.S. Rep. to the Saudi Arabian – U.S. Joint
Commission on Economic Cooperation
(USREP/JECOR)
P.O. Box 5927
[966] (1) 464-0433

Senegal
(Dakar)
B.P. 49
Ave. Jean XXIII
[221] 23-42-96

Serbia-Montenegro
(Belgrade)
AmEmbassy
Unit 13180
APO AE 09213-1310
[381] (11) 645-655

Seychelles
(Victoria)
Box 148
Unit 62501
APO AE 09815-2501 or
Victoria House
Box 251
Victoria, Mahé, Seychelles
[248] 225256

Sierra Leone
(Freetown)
Corner of Walpole and Siaka Stevens Sts.
[232] (22) 226-481

Singapore
(AGR/ATO OFF)
541 Orchard Rd.
Unit 08-04
Liat Towers Bldg.
0923
[65] 737-1233

(FAA)
Changi Airport Terminal 2
South Finger, Fourth Floor
Security Unit 048-002
International Area Office
Director and Field Office Unit 048-006
1781
[65] 543-1466

30 Hill St.
0617
FPO AP 96534
(65) 338-0251

(USAID/RIG/A)
111 No. Bridge Rd.
No. 17-03
Peninsula Plaza
0617
[65] 334-2766

(USIS/American Center MPH Building)
Level 4
71-77 Stamford Rd.
0617
[65] 334-0910

Slovak Republic
(Bratislava)
(Int'l) Hviezdoslavovo Namestie 4
81102 Bratislava
[42] (7) 330861

Slovenia
(Ljubljana)
Box 254
Prazakova 4
61000 Ljubljana
[386] (61) 301-427/472/485

Government Resources for Exporters (cont'd)

Somalia
(Mogadishu)
USLO Unit 64105
APO AE 09831-4105

South Africa
(Cape Town)
Broadway Industries Centre
Heerengracht, Foreshore
[27] (21) 214-280

(Durban)
Durban Bay House, 29th Floor
333 Smith St.
[27] (31) 304-4737

(Johannesburg)
11th Floor
Kine Center
Commissioner and Kruis Sts.
P.O. Box 2155
[27] (11) 331-1681

(Pretoria)
877 Pretorius St.
Arcadia 0083
P.O. Box 9536
Pretoria 0001
[27] (12) 342-1048

Spain
(Barcelona)
Reina Elisenda 23
08034 Barcelona or
PSC 61, Box 0005
APO AE 09642
[34] (3) 280-2227

(Bilbao)
Lehendakari Agirre 11-3
48014 Bilbao
PSC 61
Box 0006
APO AE 09642
[34] (4) 475-8300

(Madrid)
Serrano 75
28006 Madrid or
APO AE 09642
[34] (1) 577-4000

Sri Lanka
(Colombo)
210 Galle Rd.
Colombo 3
P.O. Box 106
[94] (1) 448007

Sudan
(Khartoum)
Sharia Ali Abdul Latif
P.O. Box 699
APO AE 09829
[249] 74700

Suriname
(Paramaribo)
Dr. Sophie Redmondstraat 129
P.O. Box 1821
[597] 472900

Swaziland
(Mbabane)
Central Bank Bldg.
Warner St.
P.O. Box 199
[268] 46441/5

Sweden
(Stockholm)
Strandvagen 101
S-115 89
[46] (8) 783-5300

Switzerland
(Bern)
Jubilaeumstrasse 93
3005 Bern
[41] (31) 357-7011

(Geneva)
U.S. Delegation to the Conference on
Disarmament
Botanic Bldg.
1-3 Ave. de la Paix
1202 Geneva
[41] (22) 749-5355

U.S. Mission to the European Office of the UN
and Other International Organizations
Mission Permanente des Etats-Unis
Route de Pregny 11
1292 Chambesy-Genève
[41] (22) 749-4111

U.S. Trade Representative (USTR)
Botanic Bldg.
1-3 Ave. de la Paix
1202
[41] (22) 749-4111

(Zurich)
Zollikerstrasse 141
8008 Zurich
[41] (1) 422-25-66

Government Resources for Exporters (cont'd)

Syria
(Damascus)
Abou Roumeneh
Al-Mansur St. No. 2
P.O. Box 29
[963] (11) 332-814

Tajikistan
(Dushanbe)
Interim Chancery
#39 Ainii St.
Residences: Oktyabrskaya Hotel
[7] (3772) 21-03-56

Tanzania
(Dar es Salaam)
36 Laibon Rd.
(off Bagamoyo Rd.)
P.O. Box 9123
[255] (51) 66010/1/2/3/4/5

Thailand
(Bangkok)
95 Wireless Rd.
APO AP 96546
[66] (2) 252-5040

(Chiang Mai)
Vidhayanond Rd.
Box C
APO AP 96546
[66] (53) 252-629

(Udorn)
35/6 Supakitjanya Rd.
Box UD
APO AP 96546
[66] (42) 244-270

Togo
(Lomé)
Rue Pelletier Caventou and Rue Vauban
B.P. 852
[228] 21-77-17

Trinidad and Tobago
(Port of Spain)
15 Queen's Park W.
P.O. Box 752
(809) 622-6372/6

Tunisia
(Tunis)
144 Ave. de la Liberté
1002 Tunis-Belvedere
[216] (1) 782-566

Turkey
(Adana)
Atatürk Caddesi
PSC 94
APO AE 09824
[90] (322) 453-9106

(Ankara)
110 Atatürk Blvd.
PSC 93, Box 5000
APO AE 09823
[90] (312) 468-6110

(Istanbul)
104-108 Mesrutiyet Caddesi, Tepebasi
PSC 97, Box 0002
APO AE 09827-0002
[90] (212) 251 36 02

Turkmenistan
(Ashgabat)
6 Teheran St.
Yubilenaya Hotel
[7] (3632) 24-49-25

Uganda
(Kampala)
Parliament Ave.
P.O. Box 7007
[256] (41) 259792/3/5

Ukraine
(Kiev)
10 Yuria Kotsyubinskovo
252053 Kiev 53
[7] (044) 244-7349

United Arab Emirates
(Abu Dhabi)
Al-Sudan St.
P.O. Box 4009
Pouch: AmEmbassy Abu Dhabi
Department of State
Washington, DC 20521
[971] (2) 436-691

(Dubai)
Dubai International Trade Center, 21st Floor
P.O. Box 9343
[971] (4) 313-115

United Kingdom
(Belfast, Northern Ireland)
Queen's House
14 Queen St.
BT1 6EQ
PSC 801, Box 40
APO AE 09498-4040
[44] (232) 328239

(Edinburgh, Scotland)
3 Regent Terrace
EH7 5BW
PSC 801, Box 40
FPO AE 09498-4040
[44] (31) 556-8315

Government Resources for Exporters (cont'd)

(London, England)
24/31 Grosvenor Sq.
W.1A 1AE
PSC 801, Box 40
FPO AE 09498-4040
[44] (71) 499-9000

European Bank for Reconstruction
and Development
1 Exchange Sq.
EC2A 2EH
[44] (71) 338-6502

United States
(New York, NY)
U.S. Mission to the United Nations
(USUN)
799 United Nations Plaza
10017
(212) 415-4050

(Washington, DC)
U.S. Mission to the Organization of American States
(USOAS)
Department of State
20520
(202) 647-9376

Uruguay
(Montevideo)
Lauro Muller 1776
APO AA 34035
[598] (2) 23-60-61

Uzbekistan
(Tashkent)
82 Chilanzarskaya
[7] (3712) 77-14-07; 11-32

Venezuela
(Caracas)
Avenida Francisco de Miranda and
Avenida Principal de la Floresta
P.O. Box 62291
Caracas 1060-A or
APO AA 34037
[58] (2) 285-2222

Western Samoa
(Apia)
Fifth Floor, Beach Rd.
P.O. Box 3430
[685] 21-631

Republic of Yemen
(Sanaa)
Dhahr Himyar Zone
Sheraton Hotel District
P.O. Box 22347
Sanaa, Republic of Yemen or
Sanaa–Department of State
Washington, DC 20521
[967] (1) 238-843/52

Zaire
(Kinshasa)
310 Ave. des Aviateurs
Unit 31550
APO AE 09828
[243] (12) 21532; 21628

Zambia
(Lusaka)
Corner of Independence and United Nations Aves.
P.O. Box 31617
[260] (1) 228-595

Zimbabwe
(Harare)
172 Herbert Chitepo Ave.
P.O. Box 3340
[263] (4) 794-521

The Top Reference Sources

*Exportise: An International Trade Source Book
for Smaller Company Executives*
Small Business Foundation of America, $19.95
(202) 223-1103

This is a comprehensive sourcebook on international trade for small business managers. It focuses primarily on exporting, but includes an expanded chapter on importing and foreign com-petition at home.

Topics covered include foreign markets, overseas marketing, channels of distribution, international finance, methods of payment, legal issues, regulations, taxation, and international communications. Also helpful are the country-by-country overviews that describe the potential for exports and list vital statistics.

International Trade Administration

THE INTERNATIONAL TRADE Administration (ITA) is a branch of the Department of Commerce that deals with increasing international trade opportunities for U.S. businesses, both large and small. The district offices are particularly useful because they are staffed by individuals who can advise the caller about national programs and assistance. In addition, they can direct the individual to state and local groups that may meet his or her needs more directly.

ITA District Offices

State	City	Telephone
AK	Anchorage	(907) 271-6237
AL	Birmingham	(205) 731-1331
AR	Little Rock	(501) 324-5794
AZ	Phoenix	(602) 640-2513
CA	Los Angeles	(310) 235-7104
	Long Beach	(310) 980-4551
	Newport Beach	(714) 660-1688
	Ontario	(909) 380-5650
	San Diego	(619) 557-5395
	San Francisco	(415) 705-2300
	Santa Clara	(408) 970-4610
CO	Denver	(303) 844-6622
CT	Hartford	(203) 240-3530
DC	Call Baltimore	(410) 962-4539
DE	Call Philadelphia	(215) 962-4980
FL	Miami	(305) 526-7425
	Clearwater	(813) 461-0011
	Orlando	(407) 648-6235
	Tallahassee	(904) 488-6469
GA	Atlanta	(404) 452-9101
HI	Honolulu	(808) 541-1782
IA	Des Moines	(515) 284-4222
ID	Boise	(208) 334-3857
IL	Chicago	(312) 353-8040
	Wheaton	(312) 353-4332
	Rockford	(815) 987-8123
IN	Indianapolis	(317) 582-2300
KS	Wichita	(316) 269-6160
KY	Louisville	(502) 582-5066
LA	New Orleans	(504) 589-6546
MA	Boston	(617) 565-8563
MD	Baltimore	(410) 962-4539
ME	Augusta	(207) 622-8249
MI	Detroit	(313) 226-3650
	Grand Rapids	(616) 456-2411
MN	Minneapolis	(612) 348-1638
MO	St. Louis	(314) 425-3302
	Kansas City	(816) 426-3141
MS	Jackson	(601) 965-4388
MT	Call Boise	(208) 334-3857
NC	Greensboro	(919) 333-5345
ND	Call Minneapolis	(612) 348-1638
NE	Omaha	(402) 221-3664
NH	Nashua	(603) 598-4315
	Portsmouth	(603) 334-6074

State	City	Telephone
NJ	Trenton	(609) 989-2100
NM	Santa Fe	(505) 827-0350
NV	Reno	(702) 784-5203
NY	Buffalo	(716) 846-4191
	Rochester	(716) 263-6480
	New York	(212) 264-0634
OH	Cincinnati	(513) 684-2944
	Cleveland	(216) 522-4750
OK	Oklahoma City	(405) 231-5302
	Tulsa	(918) 581-7650
OR	Portland	(503) 326-3001
PA	Philadelphia	(610) 962-4980
	Pittsburgh	(412) 644-2850
PR	San Juan	(809) 766-5555
RI	Providence	(401) 528-5104
SC	Columbia	(803) 765-5345
	Charleston	(803) 727-4051
SD	Sioux Falls	(606) 330-4264
TN	Nashville	(615) 736-5161
	Knoxville	(615) 545-4637
	Memphis	(901) 544-4137
TX	Dallas	(214) 767-0542
	Austin	(512) 482-5939
	Houston	(713) 229-2578
UT	Salt Lake City	(801) 524-5116
VA	Richmond	(804) 771-2246
VT	Montpelier	(802) 828-4508
WA	Seattle	(206) 553-5615
	Tri-Cities	(509) 735-2751
WI	Milwaukee	(414) 297-3473
WV	Charleston	(304) 347-5123
WY	Call Denver	(303) 844-6622

TIP: *An ITA District Office may be able to provide information on publications that are available in that particular state. For instance, the New York District Office has information on a free booklet produced by the state government called* Global New York, *which is a listing of useful numbers and services for businesses doing international trade from New York.*

Export Financing Assistance

Export-Import Bank of the United States

The Export-Import Bank, known as Eximbank, is an independent U.S. government agency with the primary purpose of facilitating the export of U.S. goods and services. Eximbank meets this objective by providing loans, guarantees, and insurance coverage to U.S. exporters and foreign buyers, normally on market-related credit terms.

Eximbank's insurance and guarantee programs encourage private financial institutions to fund U.S. exports by reducing the commercial and political risks exporters face. The financing made available under Eximbank's guarantees and insurance is generally on market terms, and most of the commercial and political risks are borne by Eximbank.

Eximbank's loan program is structured to neutralize interest rate subsidies offered by foreign governments. By responding with its own subsidized loan assistance, Eximbank enables U.S. financing to be competitive with that offered by foreign exporters.

Contact Option

Export-Import Bank
Marketing and Program Division
811 Vermont Ave., NW
Washington, DC 20571
(800) 565-3946

The Overseas Private Investment Corporation

The Overseas Private Investment Corporation (OPIC) is a U.S. government agency that provides project financing, investment insurance, and a variety of investor services in more than 130 developing nations and emerging economies throughout the world. OPIC assists U.S. investors through three principal programs:

• Financing of investments through direct loans and loan guarantees;

• Insuring investment projects against a broad range of political risks;

• Providing investor services, including advisory services, country and regional information, computer-assisted project/investor matching, investment missions, and outreach.

Contact Option

Overseas Private Investment Corporation
1100 New York Ave., NW
Washington, DC 20537
(202) 336-8799

Department of Agriculture

The Foreign Agriculture Service of the Department of Agriculture administers several programs to make U.S. exporters competitive in international markets and make U.S. products affordable to countries that have greater need than they have ability to pay. The Export Credit Guarantee program offers risk protection for U.S. exporters against non-payment by foreign banks.

Contact Option

Foreign Agricultural Service
Export Credits
14th St. and Independence Ave., SW
A.G. Box 1030
Washington, DC 20250
(202) 720-6301

State and Local Export Finance Programs

Several states and cities have export financing programs. To be eligible for assistance, an export sale must generally be made under a letter of credit or with credit insurance coverage. A certain percentage of state or local content may also be required. Some programs may require only that certain facilities, such as a state or local port, be used. Exporters should contact a Department of Commerce district office or state economic development agency for more information.

Private Export Funding Corporation

The Private Export Funding Corporation (PEFCO) is owned by more than five-dozen investors, primarily commercial banks. PEFCO supplements the financing activities of commercial banks and Eximbank, lending only to finance the export of goods and services of U.S. manufacture and origin. PEFCO loans normally mature in the medium- term (181 days to five years), and all are unconditionally guaranteed by Eximbank with regard to payment of interest and repayment of principal.

Contact Option

PEFCO
280 Park Ave.
New York, NY 10017
(212) 916-0300

Export Assistance from the SBA

U.S. Small Business Administration

The Small Business Administration is also involved in encouraging and supporting export activities of small businesses. Companies eligible for SBA programs include manufacturers with a maximum of 1,500 employees; wholesalers with maximum annual sales of $9.5 million; and service companies with maximum average annual sales for the past three years of $2 million.

Specific Programs

Management:

- Counseling by volunteers with international trade experience;
- Counseling through Small Business Development Center programs;
- Referral to other public-or private-sector organizations offering more in-depth international trade programs and services;
- International trade and export marketing publications;
- Business management training.

Financial:

- Pre-export financing of supply purchases, inventories, materials, and working capital needed for manufacture of export goods and for financing shipping costs, and receivable collection on exports;
- Activities to develop foreign markets, professional marketing advisors and services, foreign business travel, participation in trade shows, and other promotions overseas.

Other:

- Joint programs with the Commerce Department's International Trade Administration, the National Oceanic and Atmospheric Administration, and the Department of Agriculture.

Contact Option

Small Business Administration
(800) 827-5722

Small Business Administration Regional Offices

155 Federal St., Ninth Floor
Boston, MA 02110
(617) 451-2023

26 Federal Plaza, Suite 31-08
New York, NY 10007
(212) 264-1450

475 Allendale Rd., Suite 201
King of Prussia, PA 19406
(215) 962-3700

1375 Peachtree St., NE, Fifth Floor
Atlanta, GA 30367
(404) 347-2797

300 S. Riverside Plaza, Suite 1975S
Chicago, IL 60606
(312) 353-5000

8625 King George Dr., Bldg. C
Dallas, TX 75235
(214) 767-7633

911 Walnut St., 13th Floor
Kansas City, MO 64106
(816) 426-3608

999 18th St., Suite 701
Denver, CO 80202
(303) 294-7186

71 Stevenson St., 20th Floor
San Francisco, CA 94105
(415) 744-6402

2615 4th Ave., Suite 440
Seattle, WA 98121
(206) 553-5676

Small Business Development Centers

Funded jointly by the Small Business Administration and private agencies, SBDCs also provide assistance in the area of international trade, including:

- Joint ventures/license programs;
- Assistance with overseas trade shows;
- Packaging international trade finance loans;
- Language training and translation services.

Contact one of the following state SBDCs, or:

Association of Small Business Development Centers
1313 Farnam St., Suite 132
Omaha, NE 68182
(402) 595-2387

Export Assistance from the SBA (cont'd)

Alabama
University of Alabama at Birmingham
Medical Towers Bldg.
1717 11th Ave., Suite 419
Birmingham, AL 35294
(205) 934-7260

Alaska
University of Alaska at Anchorage
430 W. Seventh Ave., Suite 110
Anchorage, AK 99501
(907) 274-7232

Arizona
Arizona SBDC Network
2411 W. 14th St., Suite 132
Tempe, AZ 85281
(602) 731-8720

Arkansas
University of Arkansas at Little Rock
100 S. Main, Suite 401
Little Rock, AR 72201
(501) 324-9043

California
California SBDC Program
801 K St., Suite 1700
Sacramento, CA 95814
(916) 324-5068

Colorado
Colorado Office of Business Development
1625 Broadway, Suite 1710
Denver, CO 80202
(303) 892-3809

Connecticut
University of Connecticut
368 Fairfield Rd., Box U-41, Room 422
Storrs, CT 06269
(203) 486-4135

Delaware
University of Delaware
Purnell Hall, Suite 005
Newark, DE 19716
(302) 831-2747

District of Columbia
Howard University
Sixth and Fairmont St., NW, Room 128
Washington, DC 20059
(202) 806-1550

Florida
University of West Florida
19 W. Garden St.
Pensacola, FL 32501
(904) 444-2060

Georgia
University of Georgia
Chicopee Complex
1180 E. Broad St.
Athens, GA 30602
(706) 542-5760

Hawaii
University of Hawaii at Hilo
200 W. Kiwili St.
Hilo, HI 96720
(808) 933-3515

Idaho
Boise State University
1910 University Dr.
Boise, ID 83725
(208) 385-1640

Illinois
Department of Commerce and Community Affairs
620 E. Adams St., Sixth Floor
Springfield, IL 62701
(217) 524-5856

Indiana
Economic Development Council
1 N. Capitol, Suite 420
Indianapolis, IN 46204
(317) 264-6871

Iowa
Iowa State University
137 Lynn Ave.
Ames, IA 50014
(515) 292-6351

Kentucky
University of Kentucky
Center for Business Development
225 Business and Economics Bldg.
Lexington, KY 40506
(606) 257-7668

Louisiana
Northeast Louisiana University
College of Business Administration
700 University Ave., Adm. 2-57
Monroe, LA 71209
(318) 342-5506

Maine
University of Southern Maine
96 Falmouth St.
Portland, ME 04103
(207) 780-4420

Export Assistance from the SBA (cont'd)

Maryland
Department of Economic and
Employment Development
217 E. Redwood St., 10th Floor
Baltimore, MD 21202
(410) 333-6995

Massachusetts
University of Massachusetts at Amherst
School of Management, Room 205
Amherst, MA 01003
(413) 545-6301

Michigan
Michigan Small Business Development Center
2727 Second Ave.
Detroit, MI 48201
(313) 964-1798

Mississippi
University of Mississippi
Old Chemistry Bldg., Suite 216
University, MS 38677
(601) 232-5001

Missouri
University of Missouri
300 University Pl.
Columbia, MO 65211
(314) 882-0344

Montana
Montana Department of Commerce
1424 Ninth Ave.
Helena, MT 59620
(406) 444-4780

Nebraska
University of Nebraska at Omaha
60th and Dodge Sts., CBA Room 407
Omaha, NE 68182
(402) 554-2521

Nevada
University of Nevada at Reno
College of Business Adminstration–032, Room 411
Reno, NV 89557
(702) 784-1717

New Hampshire
University of New Hampshire
15 College Rd., 108 McConnell Hall
Durham, NH 03824
(603) 862-2200

New Jersey
Rutgers University Graduate School of Management
180 University Ave., Ackerson Hall, Third Floor
Newark, NJ 07102
(201) 648-5950

New Mexico
Santa Fe Community College
P.O. Box 4187
Santa Fe, NM 87502
(505) 438-1362

New York
State University of New York
SUNY Central Plaza, S-523
Albany, NY 12246
(518) 443-5398

North Carolina
University of North Carolina at Chapel Hill
4509 Creedmoor Rd., Suite 201
Raleigh, NC 27612
(919) 571-4154

North Dakota
University of North Dakota
118 Gamble Hall, Box 7308
Grand Forks, ND 58202
(701) 777-3700

Ohio
Ohio Small Business Development Center
77 S. High St., 28th Floor
P.O. Box 1001
Columbus, OH 43226
(614) 466-2711

Oklahoma
Southeastern Oklahoma State University
P.O. Box 2584, Sta. A
Durant, OK 74701
(405) 924-0277

Oregon
Lane Community College
44 W. Broadway, Suite 501
Eugene, OR 97401
(503) 726-2250

Pennsylvania
Wharton School of Business
University of Pennsylvania
444 Vance Hall
3733 Spruce St.
Philadelphia, PA 19104
(215) 898-1219

Rhode Island
Bryant College
1150 Douglas Pike
Smithfield, RI 02917
(401) 232-6111

South Carolina
University of South Carolina
College of Business Administration
Columbia, SC 29201
(803) 777-4907

Export Assistance from the SBA (cont'd)

South Dakota
University of South Dakota
414 E. Clark
Vermillion, SD 57069
(605) 677-5279

Tennessee
Memphis State University
Bldg. 1, South Campus
Memphis, TN 38152
(901) 678-2500

Texas
Bill J. Priest Institute for Economic Development
1402 Corinth St.
Dallas, TX 75215
(214) 565-5833

University of Houston
1100 Louisiana, Suite 500
Houston, TX 77002
(713) 752-8444

Texas Tech University
2579 S. Loop 289, Suite 114
Lubbock, TX 79423
(806) 745-3973

University of Texas at San Antonio
1222 Main St., Suite 450
San Antonio, TX 78212
(210) 558-0791

Utah
University of Utah
102 W. 500 S., Suite 315
Salt Lake City, UT 84101
(801) 581-7905

Vermont
Vermont Technical College
P. O. Box 422
Randolph, VT 05060
(802) 728-9101

Virginia
Virginia Small Business Development Center
901 E. Byrd St., Suite 1800
Richmond, VA 23219
(804) 371-8253

Washington
Washington State University
Kruegel Hall, Suite 135
Pullman, WA 99164
(509) 335-1576

West Virginia
West Virginia Small Business Development Center
1115 Virginia St., E.
Charleston, WV 25301
(304) 558-2960

Wisconsin
University of Wisconsin
432 N. Lake St., Room 423
Madison, WI 53706
(608) 263-7794

World Trade Centers

HEADQUARTERED IN NEW YORK, the World Trade Centers Association includes 241 affiliated organizations in 60 countries with a total membership of over 400,000 companies worldwide. World Trade Centers provide one-stop shopping in a region for international trade. The World Trade buildings usually house freight forwarders, customs brokers, international companies, and government agencies. Additional services include:

- Office space for the international trading community;

- Information and trade research services;

- Consumer/business services (hotels, restaurants, banks);

- Educational services (seminars, language training).

Contact Option

World Trade Centers Association
1 World Trade Center, Suite 7701
New York, NY 10048
(212) 432-2626

World Trade Centers

Alaska
World Trade Center –Anchorage
University of Alaska, Anchorage
421 W. First Ave., Suite 300
Anchorage, AK 99501
(907) 278-7233

Arizona
World Trade Center–Phoenix
201 N. Central Ave., Suite 2700
Phoenix, AZ 85073
(602) 495-6480

World Trade Centers (cont'd)

California
Greater Los Angeles World Trade Center
1 World Trade Center, Suite 295
Long Beach, CA 90831
(310) 495-7070

World Trade Center–San Diego
1250 Sixth Ave., Suite 100
San Diego, CA 92101
(619) 685-1453

World Trade Center–San Francisco
345 California St., Seventh Floor
San Francisco, CA 94104
(415) 392-2705

Los Angeles World Trade Center
350 S. Figueroa St., Suite 172
Los Angeles, CA 90071
(213) 680-1888

World Trade Center–Irvine
1 Park Plaza, Suite 150
Irvine, CA 92714
(714) 724-9822

Colorado
World Trade Center–Denver
1625 Broadway, Suite 680
Denver, CO 80202
(303) 592-5760

Connecticut
Connecticut World Trade Association
177 State St., Fourth Floor
Bridgeport, CT 06604
(203) 336-5353

Delaware
World Trade Center–Delaware
1207 King St.
P.O. Box 709
Wilmington, DE 19899
(302) 656-7905

Florida
World Trade Center–Orlando
105 E. Robinson St., Suite 200
Orlando, FL 32801
(407) 649-1899

World Trade Center–Tampa Bay
800 Second Ave. S., Suite 340
St. Petersburg, FL 33701
(813) 822-2492

Jacksonville World Trade Center
3 Independent Dr.
Jacksonville, FL 32202
(904) 366-6658

World Trade Center–Miami
1 World Trade Plaza
80 S.W. Eighth St., Suite 1800
Miami, FL 33130
(305) 579-0064

World Trade Center–Fort Lauderdale
200 E. Las Olas Blvd., Suite 100
Fort Lauderdale, FL 33301
(305) 761-9797

World Trade Center–Asuncion
c/o Royal Hotels International
1001 S. Bayshore Dr., Suite 2210
Miami, FL 33131
(305) 377-0304

World Trade Center–Barranquilla
c/o Royal Hotels International
1001 S. Bayshore Dr., Suite 2210
Miami, FL 33131
(305) 377-0304

Georgia
World Trade Center–Atlanta
303 Peachtree St., NE
Lower Lobby 100
Atlanta, GA 30308
(404) 880-1550

Hawaii
State of Hawaii World Trade Center–Honolulu
201 Merchant St., Suite 1510
P.O. Box 2359
Honolulu, HI 96804
(808) 587-2797

Illinois
World Trade Center–Chicago
The Merchandise Mart
200 World Trade Center, Suite 929
Chicago, IL 60654
(312) 467-0550

Indiana
World Trade Center–Indianapolis
54 Monument Circle, Suite 600
Indianapolis, IN 46204
(317) 269-2032

Iowa
Iowa World Trade Center–Des Moines
3200 Ruan Center
666 Grand Ave.
Des Moines, IA 50309
(515) 245-2555

Kansas
World Trade Center–Wichita
350 W. Douglas Ave.
Wichita, KS 67202
(316) 262-3232

World Trade Centers (cont'd)

Kentucky
Kentucky World Trade Center–Lexington
410 W. Vine, Suite 290
Lexington, KY 40507
(606) 258-3139

Louisiana
World Trade Center–New Orleans
2 Canal St., Suite 2900
New Orleans, LA 70130
(504) 529-1601

Maryland
World Trade Center–Baltimore
World Trade Center, Suite 1355
Baltimore, MD 21202
(410) 576-0022

Massachusetts
World Trade Center–Boston
Executive Offices, Suite 50
Boston, MA 02210
(617) 439-5001

Michigan
World Trade Center–Detroit/Windsor
1251 Fort St.
Trenton, MI 48183
(313) 965-6500

Minnesota
Minnesota World Trade Center–St. Paul
30 E. Seventh St., Suite 400
St. Paul, MN 55101
(612) 297-1580

Missouri
World Trade Center–St. Louis
121 S. Meramec, Suite 1111
St. Louis, MO 63105
(314) 854-6141

Greater Kansas City World Trade Center
2600 Commerce Tower
911 Main St.
Kansas City, MO 64105
(816) 221-2424

Nevada
Nevada World Trade Center–Las Vegas
P.O. Box 71961
Las Vegas, NV 89170
(702) 387-5581

New York
World Trade Center–Schenectady/Capital District
1 Broadway Center, Suite 750
Schenectady, NY 12305
(518) 393-7252

World Trade Center–New York
The Port Authority of New York & New Jersey
1 World Trade Center, Suite 35 E.
New York, NY 10048
(212) 435-8385

North Carolina
Research Triangle World Trade Center
P.O. Box 13487
Research Triangle Park, NC 27709
(919) 544-8969

World Trade Center–Wilmington
Greater Wilmington Chamber of Commerce
P.O. Box 330
Wilmington, NC 28402
(910) 762-2611

Ohio
World Trade Center–Cleveland
200 Tower City Center
50 Public Sq.
Cleveland, OH 44113-2291
(216) 621-3300

World Trade Center–Columbus
Greater Columbus Chamber of Commerce
37 N. High St.
Columbus, OH 43215
(614) 225-6907

Oregon
World Trade Center–Portland
1 World Trade Center
121 S.W. Salmon St., Suite 250
Portland, OR 97204
(503) 464-8888

Pennsylvania
Greater Philadelphia World Trade Center
Carl Marks & Co.
135 E. 57th St.
New York, NY 10022
(212) 909-8400

World Trade Center–Pittsburgh
Koppers Bldg., Suite 2312
436 Seventh Ave.
Pittsburgh, PA 15219
(412) 227-3180

Rhode Island
World Trade Center–Rhode Island
1 W. Exchange St.
Providence, RI 02903
(401) 351-2701

South Carolina
The Greenville-Spartanburg World Trade Center
315 Old Boiling Springs Rd.
Greer, SC 29650
(803) 297-8600

World Trade Centers (cont'd)

South Carolina World Trade Center–Charleston
P.O. Box 975
Charleston, SC 29402
(803) 577-2510

Tennessee
World Trade Center–Memphis
67 Madison Ave., Suite 1004
Memphis, TN 38103
(901) 521-0142

World Trade Center–Chattanooga
1001 Market St.
Chattanooga, TN 37327
(615) 752-4316

Texas
The Alliance World Trade Center
Hillwood Development
12377 Merit Dr., Suite 1700
Dallas, TX 75251
(214) 788-3050

World Trade Center–El Paso/Juarez
851 Broadmoor Dr.
El Paso, TX 79912
(915) 581-8683

Houston World Trade Association
1200 Smith, Suite 700
Houston, TX 77002
(713) 651-2229

World Trade Center–San Antonio
118 Broadway
San Antonio, TX 78205
(210) 978-7600

World Trade Center–Rio Grande Valley
Neuhaus Tower, Suite 510
200 South Tenth St.
McAllen, TX 78501
(210) 686-1982

Virginia
World Trade Center–Norfolk
Virginia Port Authority
600 World Trade Center
Norfolk, VA 23510
(804) 683-8000

Washington
World Trade Center–Seattle
1301 Fifth Ave., Suite 2400
Seattle, WA 98101
(206) 389-7301

World Trade Center–Tacoma
3600 Port of Tacoma Rd., Suite 309
Tacoma, WA 98424
(206) 383-9474

Washington, DC
World Trade Center–Washington, D.C.
6801 Oxon Hill Rd. at PortAmerica
Oxon Hill, MD 20745
(301) 839-2477

Wisconsin
Wisconsin World Trade Center–Madison
8401 Greenway Blvd.
Middleton, WI 53562
(608) 831-0666

Wisconsin World Trade Center–Milwaukee
Pfister Hotel
424 E. Wisconsin Ave.
Milwaukee, WI 53202
(414) 274-3840

The Top Reference Sources

Nation's Business
Chamber of Commerce of the United States,
$22/year
(202) 463-5650

This monthly publication is written for members
of the national business community concerned

with regional and national business and fractional
trends.
    Sample features include tax planning ideas,
key professional investment opportunities, corporate shifts and/or mergers, and association meetings coverage.

Organizations Focusing on Trade

THE FOLLOWING PRIVATE ORGANIZATIONS and associations are useful contacts for trade and export issues:

United States Council for International Business
1212 Ave. of the Americas
New York, NY 10036
(212) 354-4480
  The Council is the official U.S. affiliate of the International Chamber of Commerce. In addition to addressing policy issues, the Council and the ICC provide a number of programs available for members:

• Court of Arbitration

• International Environmental Bureau

• Counterfeiting Intelligence Bureau

• Institute of International Business Law and Practice.

American Association for Exporters and Importers
11 W. 42nd St., 30th Floor
New York, NY 10036
(212) 944-2230

Committee for Small Business Exports
P.O. Box 6
Aspen, CO 81612
(303) 925-7567

Federation of International Trade Associations
1851 Alexander Bell Dr.
Reston, VA 22091
(703) 620-1588

International Trade Facilitation Council
818 Connecticut Ave., NW, 12th Floor
Washington, DC 20006
(202) 331-4328
  Helps importers and exporters simplify the procedures and paperwork associated with world trade.

International Trade Council
3114 Circle Hill Rd.
Alexandria, VA 22305
(703) 548-1234
  Conducts research and offers educational programs on topics such as market conditions abroad, transportation costs, and trade regulations.

National Foreign Trade Council
1625 K St., NW
Washington, DC 20006
(202) 887-0278
  Trade association that deals exclusively with U.S. public policy affecting international trade and investment. Members are companies with substantial international operations or interests.

Small Business Foundation of America
1155 15th St., NW
Washington, DC 20005
(202) 223-1103
Export Opportunity Hotline: (800) 243-7232

American Chambers of Commerce

THE AMERICAN CHAMBERS of Commerce Abroad are voluntary associations of American business enterprises and individuals doing business in a given country, as well as firms of that country operating in the United States. American Chambers of Commerce Abroad will usually handle inquiries from any U.S. business. Detailed service, however, may be provided free of charge only for members of affiliated organizations. Some chambers have a set schedule of charges for services for non-members. Services available to U.S. companies may include:

• Briefings on market conditions;

• Export-import trade leads, business and government contacts;

• Periodic news bulletins and other publications on living and trading abroad;

• Information on customs duties, tariffs, and regulations;

• Clearinghouse of information on trade, investment, and commerce;

• Information on the host country business environment.

American Chambers of Commerce Abroad

Argentina
Leandro N. Alem 1110, Piso 13
1001 Buenos Aires
[54] (1) 331-5420 5126

Australia
Level 1, 300 Flinders St.
Adelaide, S. A. 5000
[61] (8) 224-0761

American Chambers of Commerce (cont'd)

Level 2, 41 Lower Fort Street
Sydney, N. S. W. 2000
[61] (2) 241-1907

Level 1, 123 Lonsdale St.
Melbourne, Victoria 3000
[61] (3) 663-2644

Level 23, 68 Queen St.
Brisbane, Queensland 4000
[61] (7) 221-8542

Level 6, 231 Adelaide Terrace
Perth, W. A. 6000
[61] (9) 325-9540

Austria
Porzellangasse 35
1090 Vienna
[43] (1) 319-5751

Belgium
Ave. des Arts 50, Boíte 5
1040, Brussels
[32] (2) 513-6770/9

Bolivia
Casilla 8268, Avda. Area No. 20171, Oficina 3
La Paz
[591] (2) 342-523

Brazil
C.P. 916, Praça Pio X-15, Fifth Floor
20040 Rio de Janeiro, RJ
[55] (21) 203-2477

Rua da Espanha 2, Salas 604-606
40000 Salvador, Bahia
[55] (71) 242-0077; 5606

Rua Alexandre Dumas 1976
04717 São Paulo, SP
[55] (11) 246-9199

Chile
Av. Amerigo Vespucio Sur 80, 9 Pisco
82 Correo 34, Santiago
[56] (2) 208-4140; 3451

China (PRC)
Great Wall Sheraton Hotel, Room 301
N. Donghuan Ave.
Beijing 100026
[86] (1) 500-5566 ext. 2271

Shanghai Centre, Room 435
1376 Nanjing Rd., W
Shanghai 200040
[86] (21) 279-7119

Colombia
Apdo. Aereo 8008, Transversal 19, #12263
Bogotá
[57] (1) 215-8859

Avenida 1N, No. 3N-97
Cali
[57] (23) 610-162; 572-993

Centro Comercial Bocagrande
Avda. San Martín, Of. 309
P.O. Box 15555
Cartagena
[57] (53) 657-724

Centro Colombo Americano
Apdo. Aereo 734
Medellin
[57] (4) 513-4444

Costa Rica
c/o Aerocasillas
P.O. Box 025216, Dept. # 1526
Miami, FL 33102
[506] 220-2200

Czech Republic
Karlovo námestí: 24
110 00 Prague 1
[42] (2) 299-887; 296-778

Dominican Republic
American Chamber EPS #A-528
P.O. Box 02-5256
Miami, FL 33102
(809) 544-2222

Ecuador
Av. Cevallos y Montalvo
3er. Piso, Oficína 301
Ambato
[593] (2) 821-073

Avda. Octavio Chacon 1-55
Centro Comercial de Parque Industrial
2do Piso, Oficina 303
Casilla 01.01.0534
Cuenca
[593] (7) 861-873

Edificio Banco del Pichincha
Manta
[593] (4) 621-699

Edificio Multicentro, 4P
La Nina y Avda. 6 de Diciembre
Quito
[593] (2) 507-450

American Chambers of Commerce (cont'd)

Egypt
Cairo Marriott Hotel, Suite 1541
P.O. Box 33
Zamalek, Cairo
[20] (2) 340-8888

El Salvador
87 Avenida Norte, No. 720, Apt. A
Col. Escalon
San Salvador
(503) 223-3292

Germany
Rossmarkt 12, Postfach 100 162
60311 Frankfurt am Main 1
[49] (69) 28-34-01

Budapesterstrasse 29
W-1000 Berlin 30
[49] (30) 261-55-86

Greece
16 Kanari St., Third Floor
Athens 106 74
[30] (1) 36-18-385; 36-36-407

Guam
102 Ada Plaza Center
P.O. Box 283
Agana, Guam 96910
[671] 472-6311; 8001

Guatemala
6a Avenida 14-77, Zona 10
Guatemala 01010
[502] (2) 374-489; 683-106

Honduras
Hotel Honduras Maya, Ap. Pos. 1838
Tegucigalpa
[504] 32-70-43

Centro Bella Aurora
6 Avenida, 13-14 Calles, N.O.
San Pedro Sula
[504] 58-0164

Hong Kong
1030 Swire House, Chater Rd.
[852] 526-0165

Hungary
Dozsa Gyorgy ut. 84/A, Room 222
1068 Budapest
[36] (1) 142-7518

India
Mohan Development Bldg., 11th Floor
13, Tolstoy Marg
New Delhi 110 001
[91] (11) 332-2723

Indonesia
The Landmark Centre
22nd Floor, Suite 2204
Jl. Jendral Sudirman, Jakarta
[62] (21) 571-0800 ext. 2222

Ireland
20 College Green
Dublin 2
[353] (1) 679-3733

Israel
35 Shaul Hamelech Blvd.
64927 Tel Aviv
[972] (3) 695-2341

Italy
Via Cantu 1
20123 Milano
[39] (2) 86-90-661

Ivory Coast
01 BP 3394
Abidjan 01
[225] 21-46-16

Jamaica
The Wyndham Hotel
77 Knutsford Blvd.
Kingston 5
(809) 926-7866

Japan
Bridgestone Toranomon Bldg., Fifth Floor
3-25-2 Toranomon, Minato-ku
Tokyo 105
[81] (3) 3433-5381

P.O. Box 235
Okinawa City 904
[81] (9) 889-8935-2684

Korea
Room 307, Chosun Hotel
Seoul
[82] (2) 753-6471; 6516

Latvia
Jauniela 24, Room 205
Riga
[371] (2) 215-205

Malaysia
15.01 Lev 15th Fl., Amoda
22 Jalan Imbi
55100 Kuala Lumpur
[60] (3) 248-2407; 2540

Mexico
P.O. Box 60326, Apdo. 113
Houston, TX 77205
[52] (57) 24-3800

American Chambers of Commerce (cont'd)

Avda. Moctezuma #442
Col. Jardines del Sol
45050 Zapopan, Jalisco
[52] (36) 34-6606

Rio Orinoco 307 Ote.
Col. del Valle
San Pedro Garza García, Nuevo León
[52] (8) 335-6210

Morocco
18, Rue Colbert
Casablanca 01
[212] (2) 31-14-48

Netherlands
Carnegieplein 5
2517 KJ
The Hague
[31] (70) 3-65-98-08

New Zealand
P.O. Box 106-002 Downtown
Auckland 1001
[64] (9) 309-9140

Nicaragua
Apdo. 202
Managua
[505] (2) 67-30-99

Pakistan
NIC Building, Sixth Floor
Abbasi Shaheed Rd.
G.P.O. Box 1322
Karachi 74000
[92] (21) 526-436

Panama
Apdo. 168, Estafeta Balboa
Panamá
[507] 69-3881

Paraguay
Edif. El Faro International Piso 4
Asunción
[595] (21) 442-135/6

Peru
Av. Ricardo Palma 836, Miraflores
Lima 18
[51] (14) 47-9349

Philippines
P.O. Box 1578, MCC
Manila
[63] (2) 818-7911

Poland
Swietokrzyska 36 m 6, Entrance I
00-116 Warsaw
[48] (22) 209-867 ext. 222

Portugal
Rua de D. Estefania, 155, 5 Esq.
Lisbon P-1000
[351] (1) 57 25 61

Romania
Str. Gh. Manu nr. 9
71-106 Bucharest 1
[40] (1) 659-3600 ext. 127

Saudi Arabia
P.O. Box 88
Dhahran Airport 31932
[966] (3) 857-6464

Hyatt Regency–Jeddah
P.O. Box 8483
Jeddah 21482
[966] (2) 652-1234 ext. 1759

P.O. Box 3050
Riyadh 11471, 07045
[966] (1) 477-7341

Singapore
1 Scotts Rd., 16-07 Shaw Center, 0922
[65] 235-0077

South Africa
P. O. Box 1132
60 Fifth St., Lower Houghton
2196 Johannesburg
[27] (11) 788-0265/6

Spain
Avda. Diagonal 477
08036 Barcelona
[34] (3) 405-1266

Hotel EuroBuilding
Padre Damian 23
28036 Madrid
[34] (1) 458-6559

Sri Lanka
P.O. Box 1000, Lotus Rd.
Colombo Hilton, Third Floor
Colombo 1
[94] (1) 54-4644 ext. 2318

Sweden
Box 5512
114 85 Stockholm
[46] (8) 666-11-00

Switzerland
Talacker 41
8001 Zürich
[41] (1) 211-24-54

American Chambers of Commerce (cont'd)

Taiwan
123-3, Ta-Pei Rd., First Floor, #1-1
Niao Sung Hsiang
Kaohsiung County 83305
[886] (7) 731-3712

Room 1012, Chia Hsin Bldg. Annex
96 Chung Shan N. Rd., Section 2
Taipei
[886] (2) 581-7089

Thailand
P.O. Box 1095
140 Wireless Rd., Seventh Floor
Kian Gwan Building, Bangkok
[66] (2) 251-9266

Trinidad & Tobago
Hilton International, Upper Arcade
Lady Young Rd.
Port of Spain
(809) 627-8570

Turkey
Altay Is Merkezi 601
Sair Esref Bulvari No. 18
Izmir 35250
[90] (51) 41-40-68/70

Fahri Gizdem Sokak 22/5
80280 Gayrettepe, Istanbul
[90] (1) 274-2824; 288-6212

Ukraine
7 Kudriavsky Uzviv, Second Floor
Kiev 252053
[7] (044) 417-1015

United Arab Emirates
International Trade Center, Suite 1610
P.O. Box 9281, Dubai
[971] (4) 314-735

United Kingdom
75 Brook St.
London WIY 2EB
[44] (71) 493-03-81

Uruguay
Calle Bartolomé Mitre 1337
Cassilla de Correo 809
Montevideo
[598] (2) 9-590-59/48

Venezuela
Torre Credival, Piso 10
2da. Avenida de Campo Alegre
Campo Alegre, Apdo. 5181
Campo
Caracas 1010-A
[582] 267-3348

Trade Assistance

Trade Adjustment Assistance

Trade adjustment assistance, part of the Commerce Department's Economic Development Administration, helps firms that have been harmed by imported products to adjust to international competition. Companies eligible for trade adjustment assistance may receive technical consulting to upgrade operations such as product engineering, marketing, information systems, export promotion, and energy management. The federal government may assume up to 75 percent of the cost of these services.

Contact Option

Trade Adjustment Assistance Division
U.S. Department of Commerce
14th St. and Constitution Ave., Room 7023
Washington, DC 20230
(202) 482-3373

Trade Remedy Assistance

The Trade Remedy Assistance Office, part of the U.S. International Trade Commission, will provide continuing technical assistance and legal support to certified small businesses pursuing remedies under the international trade laws.

For example, selling merchandise in another country at a price below the price at which the same merchandise is sold in the home market, or selling such merchandise below the costs incurred in production and shipment, is known as *dumping*. If a U.S. firm is adversely affected by a competitor's practices, a complaint may be filed with the Trade Remedy Assistance Office. In addition to information and assistance on anti-dumping laws, this office also provides remedies on countervailing duty laws (where subsidized foreign goods are sold in the U.S.); intellectual property laws (where articles imported into the U.S. infringe valid patents, trademarks, or copyrights); and investigations of situations where U.S. exports are subject to unfair restrictions in overseas markets.

Trade Assistance (cont'd)

Contact Option

Trade Remedy Assistance Office
U.S. International Trade Commission
500 E St., SW
Washington, DC 20436
(800) 343-9822

Port Import Export Reporting Service

Companies interested in finding out about their own market share, a competitor's exports and practices, who's dumping in which ports and cities, or where to find a new source of supply, can request such information from Port Import Export Reporting Service. For a fee, PIERS generates computer reports from original ships' manifests customized to meet an individual company's requirements.

PIERS reports provide product data, name and location of U.S. consignee/exporter, overseas shipper, country of origin or destination, quantities, weights, and other information. PIERS is a division of Journal of Commerce.

Contact Option

Ed Dear
PIERS
2 World Trade Center, Suite 2750
New York, NY 10048
(800) 223-0243 or (212) 837-7051

The President's "E" Award

ESTABLISHED BY AN EXECUTIVE order of the President in 1961, the "E" Certificate of Service is awarded to persons, firms, and organizations that may or may not export directly, but assist or facilitate export efforts through financing, transportation, market promotion, or other export-related services. In addition to manufacturers, other firms such as banks, utilities, chambers of commerce, trade associations, and individuals that promote and assist exporting may receive this award.

Applications must be submitted through the nearest Commerce Department district office. Award ceremonies may be held in conjunction with trade events, such as conventions, trade shows, conferences, and seminars. "E Star" Awards are presented to "E" Award winners to recognize continued superior performance in increasing or promoting exports.

Contact Option

"E" Awards Program
Office of Domestic Operations
International Trade Administration
Room 3810
U.S. Department of Commerce
Washington, DC 20230
(202) 482-1289

Recent "E Star" Award Recipients

Name	Location	Type
Besser	Alpena, MI	Concrete-block-making machinery
Crestar Bank	Richmond, VA	Commercial bank
Energy Absorption Systems	Chicago, IL	Highway safety products
First American National Bank Intl. Division	Nashville, TN	Commercial bank
Mateer-Burt	Wayne, PA	Packaging machinery
Porex Technologies	Fairburn, GA	Porous plastic components; chemical and industrial products
Rich Lumber	Beardstown, IL	Hardwood dimension products
Unz & Company	Jersey City, NJ	Business forms
Wahl Clipper	Sterling, IL	Corded and cordless hair clippers, other appliances

The President's "E" Award (cont'd)

Recent "E" Award Recipients

Name	Location	Type
Alanx Products	Newark, DE	Ceramic/metal components for the mining industry
Altera	San Jose, CA	Programmable logic devices
Anaheim Marketing	Anaheim, CA	Management for food waste disposers; kitchen appliances
Aries Research	Fremont, CA	SPARC computer equipment
Arbor Technologies	Ann Arbor, MI	Filter devices for medical & laboratory processes
Brooklyn Chamber of Commerce/Downtown Brooklyn Development Association	Brooklyn, NY	Brooklyn Goes Global export promotion program
CA Botana	San Diego, CA	R&D firm for botanical skin care
Centrigram Communications	San Jose, CA	Voice-processing systems and software
Ceramco	Burlington, NJ	Dental porcelain and related products
Challenge Air Cargo	Miami, FL	All-cargo airline
D. J. Powers	Savannah, GA	Freight forwarder
Delphos	Washington, DC	Financial consulting firm
DLP	Grand Rapids, MI	Disposable medical products
Dawn Food Products	Jackson, MI	Mfr. and distributor for the bakery trade
Dynamo	Richland Hills, TX	Coin-operated amusement machines
Econocaribe Consolidators	Miami, FL	Non-vessel operating carrier and freight forwarder
Filtration Engineering	New Hope, MN	Osmosis filtration systems
Geo. S. Bush & Co.	Portland, OR	International freight forwarder/customs broker
Idaho Dept. of Commerce, Division of Intl. Business	Boise, ID	State agency
International Business Center SBDC	Dallas, TX	Export-promotion organization
Jim Walter International Sales	Tampa, FL	Full-service export trading company
Justice Brothers	Duarte, CA	Car care products
Lincoln Electric	Euclid, OH	Welding machines; industrial motors
Microwave Networks	Houston, TX	Microwave radios and auxiliary equipment
Mivco	Seabrook, TX	Export management for industrial applications
NationsBank Commercial	Tucker, GA	Asset-based lending management company
Osbon	Augusta, GA	Specialty medical devices
North Pacific Paper	Longview, WA	Newsprint
Penril Datability Networks	Gaithersburg, MD	Datacommunications, networking equipment
Plumley Companies	Paris, TN	Automotive parts
SynOptics Communications	Santa Clara, CA	Local area networks (LANs)
Valor Enterprises	Piqua, OH	Products for cellular and communication users
Worldwide Media Service	Jersey City, NJ	Exporter of books and magazines
Zippo Manufacturing	Bradford, PA	Cigarette lighters, writing instruments

The Top Reference Sources

World Trade
Freedom Communications, $24/year
P.O. Box 3000
Denville, NJ 07834

World Trade is the magazine for the people who run America's growing global companies. This monthly magazine shows how small and midsize U.S. firms are taking advantage of the latest international banking services, global technology, cargo transportation advances, and economic develpment trends to make themselves more globally competitive.

Cities for International Business

WORLD TRADE MAGAZINE publishes an annual ranking of the best cities for international business. The conclusions are based on a variety of scientific and qualitative criteria. The following table lists the top ten cities and how they ranked (with one being the highest and ten the lowest, with ties in some categories) in several key indicators. The final rank was determined by taking the average of the five areas

listed below with certain areas having more weight than others.

Recommended Resource

World Trade
Freedom Communications, $24/year
(714) 798-3500 (CA office)

Top Ten Cities for International Business

Cities	Population and Workforce	Trade-related Infrastucture/ Transportation	Foreign Interest/ Initiatives	Operating Costs	Quality of Life	Final Rank
Atlanta, GA	5	4	1	3	2	1
Miami, FL	7	3	1	2	4	2
Chicago, IL	5	1	4	5	2	3
Minneapolis, MN	2	6	4	5	1	4
Salt Lake City, UT	4	9	7	1	3	5
Denver, CO	1	8	5	4	4	6
Los Angeles, CA	7	2	6	6	3	7
San Francisco, CA	4	5	3	7	5	8
Phoenix, AZ	3	10	8	3	2	9
Baltimore, MD	6	7	2	5	4	10

Source: World Trade, Oct. 1994

Making International Contacts

Matchmaker Trade Delegations

Organized and led by Commerce Department personnel, Matchmaker trade delegations enable new-to-export and new-to-market firms to meet pre-screened prospects who are interested in their products or services in overseas markets. Matchmaker delegations usually target major markets in two countries and limit trips to a week or less. U.S. firms can interview a maximum number of prospective business partners with a minimum of time away from the office. Thorough briefings on market requirements and business practices and interpreters' services are provided. Delegation members pay their own expenses. For further information, call Export Promotion Services, International Trade Administration, (202) 482-4457.

Trade Fairs and Exhibitions

About 80 international worldwide events are selected annually for recruitment by the Commerce Department or by the private sector under the Commerce's certification program. Exhibitors receive pre- and post-event logistical and transportation support, design and management of the USA pavilion, and extensive overseas market promotional campaigns to attract appropriate business audiences. For further information on trade fairs and exhibitions, call the Trade Information Center, (800) 872-8723.

The ITA also publishes *The Export Promotion Calendar*, a quarterly publication listing trade shows, trade fairs, seminars, and other events by industry, with dates and contact numbers.

Export Regulations

EXPORT CONTROLS ARE ADMINISTERED by the Bureau of Export Administration (BXA) in the U.S. Department of Commerce, and are described in detail in the official publication *U.S. Export Administration Regulations (EAR)*. Whenever there is any doubt about how to comply with export regulations and licensing procedures, Department of Commerce officials or qualified professional consultants should be contacted for assistance.

The Department of Commerce controls exports for the following reasons:

- To restrict exports that would be detrimental to the national security of the United States;

- To advance the foreign policy of the United States, or to fulfill its declared international obligations;

- To protect the domestic economy from the excessive drain of materials that are in short supply and to reduce the serious inflationary impact of foreign demand.

Exports not controlled by the Department of Commerce are controlled by the following agencies:

- Department of State, Office of Defense Trade Controls (arms, ammunition, and implements of war, and related technical data);

- Department of Justice, Drug Enforcement Administration (exports of certain narcotics and dangerous drugs);

- U.S. Maritime Administration (certain water craft);

- Department of Agriculture (any tobacco seed and/or live tobacco plants);

- Department of the Interior (endangered fish and wildlife, migratory birds, and bald and golden eagles);

- Patent and Trademark Office (unclassified technical data contained in patent applications);

- Department of the Treasury, Office of Foreign Assets Control (certain business dealings involving U.S. persons and embargoed countries, and all exports to Libya).

In addition, exporters of food products should contact the Food and Drug Administration (FDA) Compliance Division, (202) 205-4726, to ensure that all foreign regulations, documents, and certification requirements are met.

Export Licenses

An export license is the government document that permits the export of designated goods to certain destinations. All Commerce Department export licenses fall into two broad categories. *General licenses* do not require prior Commerce Department approval before shipment. *Validated licenses* are given to a particular exporter for a specified commodity to specified destinations for a specific end use.

The majority of all exports leave the country under a general license authorization. A general license is a broad grant of authority by the government to all exporters for certain categories of products. Individual exporters do not need to apply for general licenses, since such authorization is already granted through *EAR*; they only need to know the authorization is available.

There are currently more than 20 different categories of general licenses. To qualify for a general license, an exporter must meet all the described provisions and not violate any of the prohibitions listed in Part 771.2 of *EAR*. Violations of the regulations carry both civil and criminal penalties.

The procedure for applying for a validated license is to submit a completed application to: U.S. Bureau of Export Administration, Room 2705, Washington, DC 20230. Application forms may be ordered by sending a self-addressed mailing label to "Forms Request" at this same U.S. Department of Commerce address.

For assistance in determining the proper license, exporters may contact the Exporter Counseling Division of the Department of Commerce, Herbert C. Hoover Building, Room 1099D, Washington, DC 20230, (202) 482-4811. The exporter may also check with the local Department of Commerce district office.

Contact Options

Bureau of Export Administration (BXA)
(202) 482-4811

BXA Western Regional Office
(714) 660-0144

Export Licensing Voice Information System (ELVIS)
(202) 482-4811
An automated attendant offers a range of licensing information and emergency handling procedures. Callers may order forms and publications or subscribe to the Office of Export Licensing (OEL) newsletter, called *OEL Insider*, which provides regulatory updates. Callers also will be given the option to speak to a consultant.

Export Regulations (cont'd)

Recommended Resource

A Basic Guide to Exporting
U.S. Government Printing Office, $9.50
(202) 512-1800

This comprehensive publication of the International Trade Administration helps businesses develop export strategies, find economic market research, ship overseas, complete export documentation, respond to overseas inquiries, and take advantage of available government export-assistance programs.

U.S. Export Administration Regulations
U.S. Government Printing Office, $88/year
(202) 512-1800

Import Regulations

Import regulations imposed by foreign governments vary from country to country. Exporters should be aware of the regulations that apply to their own operations and transactions. Many governments require such items as consular invoices, certificates of inspection, health certification, and various other documents.

Targeted Trade Barriers

TRADE BARRIERS CAN BE BROADLY DEFINED as government laws, regulations, policies, or practices that either protect domestic products from foreign competition or artificially stimulate exports of particular domestic products. While restrictive business practices sometimes have a similar effect, they are not usually regarded as trade barriers.

The most common foreign trade barriers are government-imposed measures and policies that restrict, prevent, or impede the international exchange of goods and services. These include:

- Import policies such as tariffs, quantitative restrictions, import licensing, and customs barriers;

- Testing, labeling, and certification with an unnecessarily restrictive application of standards;

- Export subsidies that offer export financing on preferential terms and displace U.S. exports in third-country markets;

- Lack of intellectual property protection;

- Service barriers that regulate international data flow and foreign data processing;

- Investment barriers;

- Other barriers.

The Office of the U.S. Trade Representative issues an annual report, called *Foreign Trade Barriers* ($21), on 45 countries describing the trade barriers that exist in each country and estimating the impact on U.S. exports. Some of the countries included in the report are Argentina, Brazil, Canada, China, Guatemala, India, Indonesia, Israel, Japan, Mexico, Nigeria, Singapore, Taiwan, Turkey, and Venezuela.

Foreign Trade Barriers may be directly ordered from the U.S. Government Printing Office (GPO), (202) 512-1800.

Other useful information may be obtained through the Trade Information Center, a one-stop information source on a multitude of federal export-assistance programs. This service connects the caller with international trade specialists on a toll-free line.

Trade Information Center
Department of Commerce, Room 7424
14th St., NW, and Constitution Ave.
Washington, DC 20230
(800) 872-8723

Import/Export Directories

American Export Register
Thomas Publishing, $120
5 Penn Plaza
New York, NY 10001
(212) 695-0500

This annual two-volume, 3,000-page directory features product listings in more than 4,200 categories. The reference also includes:

- Alphabetical listing of nearly 45,000 U.S. companies;

- Product listings in ten languages;

- Directory of import/export services (banks, cargo carriers, customs brokers, embassies, railroads).

Bergano's Register of International Importers, $95
Bergano Books
P.O. Box 190
Fairfield, CT 06430
(203) 254-2054

A comprehensive resource of 2,000 leading distributors, dealers, agents, and representatives in over 75 important international markets.

Directory of United States Importers
Directory of United States Exporters
Journal of Commerce Business Directories,
$399 each, $599 both
445 Marshall St.
Phillipsburg, NJ 08865
Attn: Directories, Jodi Corona
(800) 222-0356

World trade directories featuring numerical product listings and company profile listings.

The Newly Independent States

BISNIS

Business Information Service for the Newly Independent States (BISNIS) assists U.S. firms interested in doing business in the Newly Independent States (NIS) of the former Soviet Union. It maintains current information on prevailing trade regulations and legislation, economic and industrial market data, up-to-date lists of NIS government officials, potential business contacts, available financing, trade promotion activities, and other practical market and business reports. The Flashfax BISNIS Bank is an automated information bank of fast-breaking trade leads and market information provided immediately by fax, 24 hours a day, seven days a week.

Contact Option

Business Information Service for
the Newly Independent States (BISNIS)
U.S. Department of Commerce
International Trade Administration
Room 7413
Washington, DC 20230
(202) 482-4655
Flashfax: (202) 482-3145

International Price Indexes

THE U.S. EXPORT AND IMPORT PRICE indexes are general-purpose indexes that measure changes in price levels within the foreign trade sector. The all-export index provides a measure of price change for domestically produced U.S. products shipped to other countries. The all-import index measures price change of goods purchased from other countries by U.S. residents.

Import Price Indexes

	1984	1985	1986	1987	1988	1989	1990	1991	1992	1993	1994
ALL COMMODITIES	82.6	80.7	80.6	88.4	93.2	96.5	100.0	99.4	100.0	99.9	102.0
Non-petroleum	NA	76.9	88.3	89.7	96.8	98.5	100.0	101.3	102.6	103.3	106.2
Petroleum	118.8	112.8	59.9	80.0	67.0	80.4	100.0	84.5	81.8	73.4	70.8

Export Price Indexes

	1984	1985	1986	1987	1988	1989	1990	1991	1992	1993	1994
ALL COMMODITIES	89.6	88.0	87.1	90.4	96.9	99.3	100.0	100.5	101.0	101.5	103.9
Non-agricultural	NA	86.9	86.7	90.5	95.6	98.3	100.0	100.8	101.3	101.8	103.9
Agricultural	NA	92.5	85.6	87.0	103.3	106.2	100.0	98.6	98.9	100.1	105.0

Note: The average for the year 1990 is set to equal 100.

Source: Bureau of Labor Statistics

The Top Reference Sources

UNESCO Statistical Yearbook
UNIPUB, $86
Order #U-2997
(301) 459-7666

Member states of the United Nations Education, Scientific, and Cultural Organization report periodically on their laws, regulations, and statistics relating to educational, scientific, and cultural life. Statistics in this valuable yearbook include school enrollment ratios, educational expenditures, R&D expenditures, number of books, periodicals, and newspapers published, number of films imported, number of films produced, and radio and television broadcasting revenues and expenditures, among others.

Translation Services

THE TRANSLATION COMPANIES and language instruction services listed here all provide the following:

- Translation in all languages;

- All subjects (legal, technical, advertising, etc.);

- Interpreters (consecutive and simultaneous);

- Desktop publishing, typesetting, graphic arts;

- Film, video, and slide adaptations (narrative and voice-over).

Contact Options

Associations That Provide Referrals:

American Society of Interpreters
P.O. Box 9603
Washington, DC 20016
(703) 883-0611

American Translators Association
1800 Diagonal Rd., Suite 220
Alexandria, VA 33214
(703) 683-6100

Translation Companies:

Berlitz Translation Services
New York Center, 17th Floor
257 Park Ave. S.
New York, NY 10010
(212) 777-7878
    Has 29 translation centers located in 18 countries worldwide.

Inlingua
551 Fifth Ave., Room 720
New York, NY 10176
(212) 682-8585
    Offers services in over 250 offices worldwide.

The Language Lab
211 E. 43rd St.
New York, NY 10017
(212) 697-2020 or (800) 682-3126
    Also offers instruction services to corporations.

Berlitz International
293 Wall St.
Princeton, NJ 08540
(609) 924-8500 or (800) 257-9449
    Operates language centers in over 222 cities throughout the world, with training in all spoken languages.

Lingua Service Worldwide
216 E. 45th St., 17th Floor
New York, NY 10017
(800) 394-5327 or (212) 768-2728

Over-the-Phone Interpretation

AT&T Language Line offers 24-hour-a-day access to interpretations of over 140 languages, over the phone, within minutes. To reach an AT&T Language Line Services interpreter from the United States or Canada, call (800) 628-8486. The Language Line Service also provides software localization, translation and multinational document management services, and multilingual telephone marketing.

MCI does not offer a general interpretation service, but provides translators for customer-service calls in Spanish, Japanese, Vietnamese, Korean, German, French, Italian, Cantonese, Tagalog, Portuguese and Mandarin. Call (800) 888-0800.

Bilingual Business Cards

In some countries, Japan especially, exchanging business cards at any first meeting is considered a basic part of good business etiquette. As a matter of courtesy, it is best to carry business cards printed both in English and in the language of the country being visited. There are many companies in the United States that translate and print bilingual business cards, among them:

Advantage
All languages
(212) 213-6464

Inlingua
All languages
(713) 622-1516

Oriental Printing
Japanese, Chinese, Korean
(708) 439-4822

Paramount Process Printing
All languages
(212) 691-3700

Training for International Business

THE INCREASE IN INTERNATIONAL business opportunities has resulted in a need to train and prepare not only the global executive, but also the international regional director and the first-line supervisor. Overseas living requires cultural education and knowledge of the language, social, political, and economic institutions and business customs of a particular country. Corporate human resources departments are expanding to include programs which enhance the ability of the businessperson to cope and function in an alien environment and to facilitate the adjustment of spouses and children.

Experts point out that it is vital to prepare the international businessperson to deal with a new culture and thus reduce the incidence of failure in the overseas assignment. However, it is also critical to prepare the individual who has completed an extended assignment in a foreign land to return to the United States. Reassimilation into American culture after an extended absence or immersion in a radically different culture is an often neglected area of human resources and requires special attention and guidance.

The following are some current programs which focus on the needs of the international businessperson and his or her family:

Contact Options

The Business Council for International
Understanding Institute (BCIU)
The American University
3301 New Mexico Ave., NW, Suite 244
Washington, DC 20016
(202) 686-2771
Works with over 400 major international corporations and 30,000 families relocating in 162 nations.

The International Society for Intercultural Education, Training and Research (SIETAR International)
808 17th St., NW, Suite 200
Washington, DC 20006
(202) 466-7883
Provides information on programs of intercultural education, training, and research. Over 2,000 members contribute to a bimonthly newsletter and calendar of events, as well as a quarterly journal dealing with issues to promote intercultural understanding through nonpolitical avenues.

Intercultural Press
P.O. Box 700
Yarmouth, ME 04096
(207) 846-5168
Produces an extensive list of titles on cross-cultural interaction and offers consultation services for issues such as communication and supervision in overseas settings. Call for a catalogue.

Recommended Resources

Do's and Taboos Around the World
Edited by Roger E. Axtell
John Wiley & Sons, $12.95
(212) 850-6000

International Business Practices
U.S. Government Printing Office, $18
(202) 512-1800
Provides information about 117 countries including business organizations, exporting, regulatory agencies, foreign investment, and at least three useful contacts with phone numbers.

The International Businesswoman of the 1990s: A Guide to Success in the Global Marketplace
by Marlene L. Rossman
Praeger Publishers, $19.95
(203) 226-3571

The Multinational Executive Travel Companion
Suburban Publishing, $60
(203) 324-6439

Delphi offers a translation service that can handle documents in more than 100 languages. GO USING TRAN.

World Business Languages

World Countries and Suggested Business Languages

Country	Suggested Business Language(s)	Country	Suggested Business Language(s)
Afghanistan	English, Pushtu	Egypt	English, Arabic
Albania	Albanian	El Salvador	Spanish
Algeria	French, Arabic	Equatorial Guinea	Spanish
Andorra	French, Spanish	Ethiopia	English, Amharic
Angola	Portuguese	Fiji	English
Antigua and Barbuda	English	Finland	Finnish, Swedish
Argentina	Spanish	France	French
Australia	English	Gabon	French
Austria	German	Gambia	English
Bahamas	English	Germany	German
Bahrain	English, Arabic	Ghana	English
Bangladesh	English	Gibraltar	English, Spanish
Barbados	English	Greece	Greek
Belgium	French, Flemish	Grenada	English
Belize	English, Spanish	Guatemala	Spanish
Benin	French	Guinea	French
Bhutan	English	Guinea-Bissau	Portuguese
Bolivia	Spanish	Guyana	English
Botswana	English	Haiti	French, Kreyol
Brazil	Portuguese	Honduras	Spanish
Brunei	English	Hong Kong	English, Cantonese
Bulgaria	Bulgarian	Hungary	Hungarian
Burkina Faso (Upper Volta)	French	Iceland	Icelandic
Burma	English	India	English
Burundi	French	Indonesia	English
Cambodia	French, Khmer	Iran	English, Farsi
Cameroon	French, English	Iraq	English, Arabic
Canada	English, French	Irish Republic	English, Irish
Cape Verde	Portuguese	Israel	English, Hebrew
Central African Republic	French	Italy	Italian
Chad	French, Arabic	Ivory Coast	French
Chile	Spanish	Jamaica	English
China	English, Mandarin	Japan	English, Japanese
Colombia	Spanish	Jordan	English, Arabic
Comoros	French, Arabic	Kenya	English
Congo	French	Korea, North	English, Korean
Costa Rica	Spanish	Korea, South	English, Korean
Cuba	Spanish	Kuwait	English, Arabic
Cyprus	English	Laos	French
Czech Republic	Czech, Slovak	Lebanon	English, Arabic
Denmark	Danish	Lesotho	English
Djibouti	French, Arabic	Liberia	English
Dominica	English, French	Libya	Arabic, English
Dominican Republic	Spanish	Liechtenstein	German
Ecuador	Spanish	Luxembourg	French, German

World Business Languages (cont'd)

Country	Suggested Business Language(s)
Madagascar	French
Malaysia	English
Maldives	English
Mali	French
Malta	English, Maltese
Mauritania	French, Arabic
Mauritius	English, French
Mexico	Spanish
Monaco	French
Mongolia	Russian, Mongolian
Morocco	French, Spanish, Arabic
Mozambique	Portuguese
Namibia	Afrikaans, German, Eng.
Nauru	English
Nepal	English
Netherlands	English, Dutch
New Zealand	English
Nicaragua	Spanish
Niger	French
Nigeria	English
Norway	Norwegian
Oman	English, Arabic
Pakistan	English, Urdu
Panama	Spanish, English
Papua New Guinea	English
Paraguay	Spanish
Peru	Spanish
Philippines	English, Spanish
Poland	Polish
Portugal	Portuguese
Puerto Rico	English, Spanish
Qatar	English, Arabic
Romania	Romanian
Russia	Russian
Rwanda	French
St. Kitts & Nevis	English
St. Lucia	English, French
St. Vincent	English
San Marino	Italian
Sao Tome and Principe	Portuguese

Country	Suggested Business Language(s)
Saudi Arabia	English, Arabic
Senegal	French
Seychelles	English, French
Sierra Leone	English
Singapore	English
Solomon Islands	English
Somalia	English, Italian, Arabic
South Africa	English, Afrikaans, Xhosa
South Yemen	English, Arabic
Spain	Spanish
Sri Lanka	English
Sudan	English, Arabic
Suriname	Dutch, English
Swaziland	English
Sweden	Swedish
Switzerland	German, French, Italian
Syria	English, Arabic
Taiwan	English, Mandarin
Tanzania	English
Thailand	English, Thai
Tonga	English
Trinidad and Tobago	English
Tunisia	French, Arabic
Turkey	Turkish
Tuvalu	English
Uganda	English
United Arab Emirates	English, Arabic
United Kingdom	English
United States of America	English
Uruguay	Spanish
Vatican City	Italian
Venezuela	Spanish
Vietnam	French, Vietnamese
Western Samoa	English
Yemen	English, Arabic
Yugoslavia	Serbo-Croat
Zaire	French
Zambia	English
Zimbabwe	English

International Price Comparisons

Price Comparisons of Selected Items, by City (in U.S. Dollars)

Item	Amster-dam	Beijing	Berlin	Brussels	Dublin	Geneva	Hong Kong	London
Chocolate candy bar (150 g)	1.55	3.82	1.17	1.49	1.19	1.55	1.81	1.29
Carbonated soft drink (6 pack)	2.73	3.54	3.07	3.21	3.25	3.82	2.73	2.98
Bottled mineral water (1 liter)	0.57	1.64	0.94	0.69	0.66	0.54	0.70	0.56
Wine (750 ml)	6.80	23.72	5.14	7.69	11.12	8.89	15.61	8.16
Dry cleaning (man's suit–1 piece)	14.32	6.94	13.78	12.42	8.96	13.96	8.72	14.77
Woman's haircut–wash/dry	53.20	40.82	53.83	46.24	27.48	51.64	72.78	64.15
Toothpaste (100 ml)	2.08	4.38	2.13	2.20	1.95	2.26	1.15	1.89
Deodorant (155 ml)	2.33	9.06	2.28	3.42	2.06	4.05	4.44	2.03
Aspirin (20 units)	13.84	16.45	11.29	8.26	4.18	17.19	8.15	4.48
Blank video tape (1 unit)	8.29	5.14	6.71	4.61	5.57	9.30	5.06	5.79
Camera film (36 exposures)	29.51	10.45	20.17	23.29	15.44	26.89	13.11	15.49
Paperback book (1 unit)	13.37	9.62	14.77	12.06	8.63	11.29	14.25	9.61
Movie ticket (1 unit)	8.27	NA	8.45	7.80	6.13	10.68	6.46	9.56
Taxi ride (2 km)	5.46	1.54	7.50	5.33	5.86	7.12	1.62	5.46
Business lunch (for two)	56.64	44.32	79.37	56.90	40.94	72.38	62.33	63.69
Hotel (daily rate)	205.90	243.66	234.79	358.40	212.60	243.90	343.85	334.85

Item	Madrid	Moscow	Paris	Rome	São Paulo	Tokyo	Toronto	Vienna
Chocolate candy bar (150 g)	1.18	2.18	1.66	1.24	1.21	4.06	1.53	1.66
Carbonated soft drink (6 pack)	4.20	3.73	2.48	2.81	3.39	7.62	2.84	2.85
Bottled mineral water (1 liter)	0.33	0.96	0.35	0.33	0.44	1.73	0.83	0.89
Wine (750 ml)	7.75	20.63	5.00	9.12	19.33	16.20	7.13	9.35
Dry cleaning (man's suit–1 piece)	14.41	27.98	23.69	9.14	19.63	26.87	7.75	15.81
Woman's haircut–wash/dry	34.10	35.15	60.89	43.37	28.94	94.37	33.12	50.31
Toothpaste (100 ml)	2.51	3.87	2.40	2.51	1.35	7.40	1.31	2.52
Deodorant (155 ml)	2.71	7.83	2.49	4.51	4.50	15.35	1.86	4.21
Aspirin (20 units)	8.62	19.53	10.46	14.68	6.13	25.83	3.77	12.04
Blank video tape (1 unit)	4.67	14.21	8.31	4.98	9.45	8.02	5.11	13.32
Camera film (36 exposures)	20.71	26.36	30.77	14.02	33.69	14.76	16.25	17.30
Paperback book (1 unit)	9.96	10.51	12.23	9.60	8.88	15.62	7.39	14.16
Movie ticket (1 unit)	4.99	7.57	8.43	6.20	7.70	23.08	5.93	6.74
Taxi ride (2 km)	2.61	NA	3.98	6.01	0.96	6.02	3.86	4.42
Business lunch (for two)	36.33	72.00	80.79	59.83	75.83	45.45	36.75	91.58
Hotel (daily rate)	185.30	365.00	277.06	167.24	287.91	454.54	166.78	269.18

Note: Prices recorded between October 1994 and February 1995.

Source: Organization Resources Counselors

The Top Reference Sources

Export Profits
Dearborn Financial Publishing, $19.95
(312) 836-4400 or (800) 621-9621

This very thorough reference, written by international trade consultant Jack S. Wolf, is essential reading for managers of small- and mid-sized businesses who want to begin exporting.
With an extensive glossary, lists of resources, and sample documents, this book shows how to decide whether a business should export, find the right foreign markets for its products, choose distributors or agents, minimize currency risks, and cut through red tape.
Other topics discussed include pricing, shipping, finding a banker, property rights protection, and test marketing.

Carnets

THE ATA CARNET IS a standardized international customs document used to obtain duty-free temporary admission of certain goods into the countries that are signatories to the ATA Convention. Under the ATA Convention, commmercial and professional travelers may take commercial samples, tools of the trade, advertising material, and cinematographic, audiovisual, medical, scientific, or other professional equipment into member countries temporarily without paying customs duties and taxes, or posting a bond at the border of each country to be visited.

Countries participating in the ATA Carnet System include: Australia, Austria, Belgium, Bulgaria, Canada, Cyprus, Denmark, Finland, France, Germany, Gibraltar, Greece, Hong Kong, Hungary, Iceland, India (commercial samples only), Iran, Ireland, Israel, Italy, Ivory Coast, Japan, Luxembourg, Mauritius, Netherlands, New Zealand, Norway, Poland, Portugal, Romania, Senegal, Singapore, Sri Lanka (certain professional equipment not accepted), South Africa, South Korea, Spain, Sweden, Switzerland, Turkey, United Kingdom, and United States.

Since other countries are continuously added to the ATA Carnet system, travelers should contact the U.S. Council for International Business if the country to be visited is not included in this list. Applications for carnets should also be made through the U.S. Council. The fee depends on the value of the goods to be covered. A bond, letter of credit, or bank guaranty of over 40 percent of the value of the goods is also required to cover duties and taxes that would be due if goods imported into a foreign country by carnet were not re-exported and the duties were not paid by the carnet holder. The carnets generally are valid for 12 months.

Source: A Basic Guide to Exporting

Contact Option

U.S. Council for International Business
1212 Ave. of the Americas
New York, NY 10036
(212) 354-4480

PAL, SECAM, NTSC Conversion

PAL, SECAM, and NTSC refer to the different kinds of video systems around the world. For a videotape to play in a foreign country's system, it must be converted to the correct format. Check the local yellow pages under Video Production Services to find a local company that will convert U.S. tapes for viewing abroad and foreign tapes for viewing in the United States. Costs for this service vary according to the quality or definition required and the type of equipment used to make the conversions. Mid-range equipment conversions run from $40 to $70 for the first hour.

Formats Used

PAL
Western Europe (excluding France); also Australia, South Africa, and parts of Asia, including India, China

PAL-M
Brazil

PAL-N
Argentina

NTSC
North America

SECAM
France, former Eastern Bloc, and parts of the Middle East

Electric Current Conversions

Country	Cycles	Volts
Afghanistan	50/60	220/380
Algeria	50	127/220
	50	220/380
Andorra	50	110/130
	50	220/380
Angola	50	220/380
Antigua	60	110/220
Argentina	50	220/380
Australia	50	220/250
Austria	50	220/380
Bahamas	60	120/208
	60	120/240
Bahrain	50	230
Bangladesh	50	220/240
Barbados	50	110
Belgium (Brussels)	50	220/380
Belize	60	110/220
Benin	60	220
Bermuda	50	110/220
Bolivia	60	110/220
Botswana	50	230
Brazil		
(Belém)	60	127/220
(Brasília)	60	220/240
	60	220/380
(Recife)	60	127/220
(Rio de Janeiro)	60	127/220
(São Paulo)	60	115/230
Brunei	50	240
Bulgaria	50	220/380
Burkina Faso	50	220
Burma	50	230/250
Burundi	50	220
Cambodia	50	220
Cameroon	50	110/220
Canada	60	120/240 & 110
Central Afr. Rep.	50	220/380
Chad	50	220/380
Chile	50	220/380
China	50	220/380
	60	110/220
Colombia	60	110/120
Bogota	60	150/240
Congo	50	220
Costa Rica	60	120/240 & 110
Cuba	60	110/220
Curaçao	50	127/220
Cyprus	50	220/240
	50	240/415
Czech Republic	50	220/380

Country	Cycles	Volts
Denmark	50	220/380
Dominica	50	220/240
Dominican Rep.	60	110/220
Ecuador	60	120/208
	60	120/240
	60	110/220
	60	121/210
Egypt	50	110/220/380
El Salvador	60	110
Ethiopia	50	220/380
Finland	50	220/380
France	50	220/380
	50	110/115
	50	127/220
Gabon	50	220
Gambia	50	230/400, 200
Germany	50	220/380
Ghana	50	220/400
Great Britain	50	240 & 240/415
Greece	50	220, 220/380/127
Greenland	50	220/380
Grenada	50	220/240
Guatemala	60	120/240, 110
Guinea	50	220/380
Guyana	60	110
Haiti	60	110/220
Hawaii	60	120
Honduras	60	110/220
Hong Kong	50	220, 200/346
Hungary	50	220/380
Iceland	50	220/380/ 240
India	50	230/400/ 220
Indonesia	50	127/220
Iran	50	220/380
Iraq	50	220/380
Ireland	50	220/380
Israel	50	230/400/ 220
Italy	50	220/380
	50	127/220
Ivory Coast	50	220/380
Jamaica	50	110/220
Japan	50/60	100/200
Jordan	50	220/380
Kenya	50	240/415
Kiribati	50	240
Korea	60	110/220
Kuwait	50	240/415
Laos	50	220/380
Lebanon	50	110/190
	50	220/380

Electric Current Conversions (cont'd)

Country	Cycles	Volts
Lesotho	50	220
Liberia	60	110,120/240
		120/208
Libya	50	125/220
Liechtenstein	50	110/220
Luxembourg	50	120/208
	50	220/380
Madagascar	50	110/220
Malawi	50	230/400
Malaysia	50	230/240/415
Mali	50	220/380
Malta	50	240/415
Mauritania	50	220
Mauritius	50	230
Mexico	60	varies
Federal District	60	127/220
Monaco	50	220/380
	50	110/115
Morocco	50	115/200
	60	110/125
Mozambique	50	220/380
Namibia	50	220/240
Nauru	50	240
Nepal	50	220
Netherlands	50	220/380
New Zealand	50	230/400
Nicaragua	60	120/240/110
Niger	50	220/380
Nigeria	50	210/250
	50	230/415
Norway	50	220/230
Oman	50	220/240
Pakistan	50	220/230/400
Panama	60	110/120
Papua New Guinea	50	240/415
Paraguay	50	220
Peru	60	220
Philippines	60	110/220
	50	110/120
Poland	50	220/380
Portugal	50	220/380
	50	110/190
Puerto Rico	60	120/240
Qatar	50	220/240
Romania	50	220/380
Russia	50	127/220, 220
Rwanda	50	280/380
St. Kitts & Nevis	60	230
St. Lucia	50	220
St. Vincent	60	220/240

Country	Cycles	Volts
Saudi Arabia	60	110/120
Mecca	50	220
Senegal	50	110/220
Sierra Leone	50	220/400
Singapore	50	230/400
Solomon Islands	50	230/415
Somalia	50	200
South Africa	50	250
Spain	50	110/130
	50	220/380
Sri Lanka	50	230/400
Sudan	50	240/415
	60	127/220
Suriname	60	127/220
Swaziland	50	220
Sweden	50	220/380
Switzerland	50	110/220
	50	220/380
Syria	50	110/190
	50	220/380
Tahiti	60	220 & 110
Taiwan	60	110
Tanzania	50	230/400
Thailand	50	220/380
Togo	50	127/220
	50	220/380
Tonga	50	240
Trinidad & Tobago	60	115/220
	60	230/400
Tunisia	50	110/190
	50	220/380
Turkey	50	110/220
	50	220/380
Uganda	50	240/415
United Arab Emirates	50	220/240
Uruguay	50	220
U.S.	60	110
Venezuela	60	120/240
Caracas	50	120/208
Vietnam	50	120/127/220
	50	220/380
Virgir Islands	60	120/240
Yugoslavia	50	220/380
Zaire	50	220/380
Zambia	50	220/380
Zimbabwe	50	230

Note: Pay particular attention to cycles when using any electronic or computer equipment.

Currencies of the World

Country	Currency	Subcurrency
Afghanistan	afghani	100 puls
Algeria	dinar	100 centimes
Argentina	austral	100 centavos
Australia	dollar	100 cents
Austria	schilling	100 groschen
Bahamas	dollar	100 cents
Bahrain	dinar	1,000 fils
Barbados	dollar	100 cents
Belgium	franc	100 centimes
Belize	dollar	100 cents
Benin	franc	100 centimes
Bolivia	boliviano	100 centavos
Botswana	pula	100 thebe
Brazil	cruzeiro	100 centavos
Brunei	dollar	100 cents or sen
Bulgaria	lev	100 stotinki
Cameroon	franc	100 centimes
Canada	dollar	100 cents
Cayman Islands	dollar	100 cents
Central African Rep.	franc	100 centimes
Chad	franc	100 centimes
Chile	peso	100 centavos
China	yuan	10 fen
Colombia	peso	100 centavos
Congo	franc	100 centimes
Costa Rica	colón	100 centimos
Cuba	peso	100 centavos
Czechoslovakia	koruna	100 halers
Denmark	krone	100 ore
Djibouti	franc	100 centimes
Dominican Rep.	peso	100 centavos
Ecuador	sucre	100 centavos
Egypt	pound	100 piastres
El Salvador	colón	100 centavos
Ethiopia	birr	100 cents
Fiji	dollar	100 cents
Finland	markka	100 pennia
France	franc	100 centimes
Gabon	franc	100 centimes
Gambia	dalasi	100 bututs
Germany	deutsche mark	100 pfennige
Ghana	cedi	100 pesewas
Greece	drachma	100 lepta
Guatemala	quetzal	100 centavos
Guinea	franc	100 centimes
Guyana	dollar	100 cents
Haiti	gourde	100 centimes
Honduras	lempira	100 centavos
Hong Kong	dollar	100 cents
Hungary	forint	100 fillér

Country	Currency	Subcurrency
Iceland	krona	100 aurar
India	rupee	100 paise
Indonesia	rupiah	100 sen
Iraq	dinar	1,000 fils
Ireland	pound	100 pence
Israel	shekel	100 agorot
Italy	lira	100 centesimi
Ivory Coast	franc	100 centimes
Jamaica	dollar	100 cents
Japan	yen	
Jordan	dinar	1,000 fils
Kenya	shilling	100 cents
Kuwait	dinar	1,000 fils
Lebanon	pound	100 piastres
Luxembourg	franc	100 centimes
Malawi	kwacha	100 tambala
Malaysia	ringgit	100 sen
Maldives	rufiyaa	100 laari
Malta	lira or pound	100 cents
Mauritania	ouguiya	5 khoums
Mauritius	rupee	100 cents
Mexico	peso	100 centavos
Mongolia	tugrik	100 mongo
Morocco	dirham	100 centimes
Nepal	rupee	100 paisa
Netherlands	guilder	100 cents
New Zealand	dollar	100 cents
Nicaragua	cordoba	100 centavos
Niger	franc	100 centimes
Nigeria	naira	100 kobo
Norway	krone	100 ore
Oman	riyal-omani	1,000 baiza
Pakistan	rupee	100 paisa
Papua New Guinea	kina	100 toea
Paraguay	guarani	100 centimos
Peru	inti	
Philippines	peso	100 centavos
Poland	zloty	100 groszy
Portugal	escudo	100 centavos
Qatar	riyal	100 dirhams
Romania	leu	100 bani
Saudi Arabia	riyal	20 halali
Senegal	franc	100 centimes
Seychelles	rupee	100 cents
Sierra Leone	leone	100 cents
Singapore	dollar	100 cents
Solomon Islands	dollar	100 cents
Somalia	shilling	100 cents
South Africa	rand	100 cents
South Korea	won	100 chon

Currencies of the World (cont'd)

Country	Currency	Subcurrency
Spain	peseta	100 centimos
Sri Lanka	rupee	100 cents
Sudan	pound	100 piastres
Suriname	guilder	100 cents
Sweden	krona	100 ore
Switzerland	franc	100 centimes
Syria	pound	100 piastres
Taiwan	dollar	100 cents
Tanzania	shilling	100 cents
Thailand	baht	100 satang
Togo	franc	100 centimes
Trinidad & Tobago	dollar	100 cents
Tunisia	dinar	1,000 millimes
Turkey	lira	100 kurus
Uganda	shilling	100 cents

Country	Currency	Subcurrency
United Arab Emir.	dirham	1,000 fils
United Kingdom	pound	100 pence
United States	dollar	100 cents
Uruguay	peso	100 centesimos
Venezuela	bolivar	100 centimos
Vietnam	dong	100 xu
Western Samoa	tala	100 sene
Yugoslavia	dinar	100 paras
Zambia	kwacha	100 ngwee
Zimbabwe	dollar	100 cents

World Temperatures

Outside North America

Location	December–March (high/low)	June–August (high/low)
Amsterdam	40/32	69/53
Athens	58/44	90/72
Bali	90/74	94/76
Bangkok	89/70	90/75
Bogotá	67/48	64/50
Buenos Aires	87/62	57/40
Cairo	67/48	94/69
Caracas	77/57	78/63
Dublin	47/36	67/51
Guam	90/72	86/69
Hong Kong	68/57	87/59
Israel	57/41	90/65
Istanbul	48/38	80/64
Kathmandu	65/36	84/70
Lima	75/53	77/61
Lisbon	55/44	84/63

Location	December–March (high/low)	June–August (high/low)
London	44/35	70/52
Manila	87/70	90/75
Montevideo	84/72	77/70
Munich	36/23	73/53
Nairobi	77/54	69/51
New Delhi	71/43	96/80
Panama City	88/71	86/70
Paris	44/36	76/58
Quito	77/57	78/65
Rio de Janeiro	82/71	76/70
Rome	55/42	85/66
Santiago	86/70	78/69
Seoul	30/20	81/69
Singapore	88/74	87/73
Taiwan	70/61	90/72
Tokyo	47/32	81/69

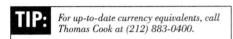

TIP: *For up-to-date currency equivalents, call Thomas Cook at (212) 883-0400.*

World Temperatures (cont'd)

North America

Location	December–March (high/low)	June–August (high/low)
Acapulco	87/70	89/75
Albuquerque	72/40	91/62
Austin	63/42	93/72
Bermuda	68/58	84/73
Boston	40/22	80/58
Cancún	87/70	89/75
Chicago	34/18	82/64
Dallas	58/37	92/72
Denver	43/17	85/57
Dominican Rep.	85/69	88/72
Honolulu	76/68	84/72
Jackson Hole, WY	36/11	80/52
Lake Tahoe	50/16	89/40
Las Vegas	65/34	103/71
Los Angeles	66/47	76/58
Mexico City	72/43	75/53

Location	December–March (high/low)	June–August (high/low)
Miami	76/59	88/75
Montreal	24/10	72/54
Nassau	77/67	88/76
New Orleans	65/48	90/76
New York	41/27	80/65
Palm Beach	79/43	95/73
Philadelphia	42/29	83/64
Port-au-Prince	86/68	70/73
St. Thomas	85/72	89/76
San Juan	82/72	87/76
Tucson	65/39	97/71
Vancouver	44/36	67/53
Washington, DC	45/29	85/64

Source: National Weather Service

The Top Reference Sources

The Economist Atlas of New Europe
Henry Holt, $75
(212) 886-9261

This revised edition of a bestselling reference provides a comprehensive, fully illustrated portrait of the world today. Included are up-to-date political and economic analyses, plus 70 pages of full-color political and geographical maps for every country in the world.

There are also 37 pages of thematic maps allowing comparisons between countries on a variety of subjects, from defense spending to foreign debt to environmental pollution.

MANUFACTURING

Industrial Buying Guides

RESEARCH SHOWS THAT 97 percent of all industrial purchases are initiated by the buyer, not the seller. And most purchases, either of a new product or plant facility, a new component or material, are made with the help of a buying guide. The best-known, most comprehensive, and most widely used industrial buying system is the *Thomas Register of Manufacturers*. More than $400 million in purchases of products or services are transacted each day through this system. The *Thomas Register* combines a products and services section, company directories, and a catalogue file section, in one multi-volume reference set. The location of a company's distributors, engineering or service offices, plants, and sales offices may be found in the company profiles section of this reference. Companies may advertise and/or distribute their catalogues in the *Thomas Register*.

Recommended Resources

Thomas Register of American Manufacturers
Thomas Publishing, $240
(212) 290-7277

Sweet's Catalogue
McGraw-Hill, free
(800) 442-2258
  Distributes manufacturers' catalogues for construction-related products.

MacRae's Blue Book
Business Research Publications, $165
(212) 673-4700
  National industrial directory listing manufacturers only.

U.S. Industrial Directory
Reed Reference Publishing, $195
(708) 574-7081
  Annual reference listing products and services for industrial manufacturing.

Standard & Poor's Register of Corporations, Directors and Executives
Standard & Poor's, $625
(212) 208-8786
  Descriptive listing of corporations, but not a buying guide.

Manufacturers' Sales Agencies

MANUFACTURERS' AGENTS ARE independent contractors who work on commission for more than one company. Most manufacturers who have turned to agents in recent years have done so after first working with a salaried sales force of their own. Companies switch for a variety of reasons, but often because they want to trim sales costs and fixed overhead. Start-up companies with little knowledge of what to expect from different territories, and with no sales benchmarks, also use agents rather than establish their own sales force. Ideally, the manufacturer's agent will represent other manufacturers' products which are compatible, but not competitive, with the company's own products. Experienced agents will be able to provide information on what to expect in various territories, when and how to advertise, and what a competitor's efforts are likely to be. Sales agencies are paid commissions only when they make a sale.

  The source of first resort for manufacturers in search of a sales agent or independent contractor is the *Directory of Manufacturers' Sales Agencies* ($92.50), the membership directory of the Manufacturers' Agents National Association. This reference of 9,000 member agents and agencies is organized in three sections: alphabetically by agency name, by state, and by product classification. Profiles of the agencies include the kinds of products sold, sales territories, names of key officials, warehousing facilities, size of sales staff, and location of branch offices.

Contact Option

Manufacturers' Agents National Association
P.O. Box 3467
Laguna Hills, CA 92654
(714) 859-4040
  MANA also publishes the monthly *Agency Sales Magazine* ($37.50/year), along with numerous special reports on making the agency decision, finding the right agent, negotiating the agreement, and so on.

Overseas Manufacturing

TO ASSIST U.S. MANUFACTURERS in the areas of trade and import/export, the International Trade Administration assigns country desk officers to every country in the world. These specialists collect information on a specific country's regulations, tariffs, business practices, and political and economic climate, and may provide selected industry sector analyses for that country as well. (*See also "Country Desk Officers" on page 361.*)

Contact Options

Hong Kong, Ireland, Canada, and Mexico are leading exporters of manufactured goods to the United States. For information on manufacturing, contact:

Hong Kong Government Industrial Promotion Office
680 Fifth Ave., 22nd Floor
New York, NY 10019
(212) 265-7232

Industrial Promotion Unit/Hong Kong
Economic & Trade Office
222 Kearny St., Suite 402
San Francisco, CA 94108
(415) 397-2215

Irish Development Office
345 Park Ave., 17th Floor
New York, NY 10154
(212) 750-4300

Investment Canada
P.O. Box 2800, Postal Station D
Ottawa, Ontario
Canada K1P 6A5
(613) 995-0465

Trade Commission of Mexico
375 Park Ave., Suite 1905
New York, NY 10152
(212) 826-2916

New Techniques and Consultants

The Manufacturing Technology Centers Program

The United States' long-dominant position in the world's marketplace is declining due to increasingly sophisticated foreign competition and swiftly changing technologies. While many small manufacturing firms have been able to maintain their competitive edge in smaller domestic markets and in special technology areas, they simply have not kept pace with the rapidly changing, computer-driven global marketplace of the past decade. To address this problem, the Omnibus Trade and Competitiveness Act established the Manufacturing Technology Centers (MTC) Program as a new initiative at the National Institute of Standards and Technology (NIST). The program, authorized by Congress in 1988, was created to improve U.S. industrial productivity and competitiveness in the growing international marketplace.

Each MTC's approach is unique, dictated by its location and the type of manufacturing in its client base. In general, the MTCs provide a wide range of services, including:

- Individual project engineering
- Training courses
- Demonstrations
- Assistance in selecting and using software and equipment
- Factory survey visits
- Technical training
- Introduction of modern manufacturing equipment.

Contact Option

Michael Baum
National Institute of Standards and Technology
Gaithersburg, MD 20899
(301) 975-2763

The Federal Laboratory Consortium

THE FEDERAL LABORATORY Consortium comprises over 700 member research laboratories and centers from 16 federal departments. If a company has a specific technology need or question, one of the more than 100,000 scientists or engineers who work in the federal laboratories may have the solution. The FLC provides a link between the individual laboratory members and the potential users of government-developed technologies. The federal laboratories contain technologies, facilities, and expertise in all areas of science and engineering and offer opportunities such as:

- Technical assistance
- Cooperative research projects
- Employee exchange
- Exclusive or non-exclusive licensing
- Visits to laboratories
- Printed documentation
- Sponsored research
- Use of unique laboratory facilities
- Workshops, seminars, briefings.

The FLC Locator is part of the FLC network that assists companies in locating the appropriate laboratory or individual scientist or technician to handle a company's specific request. Once the contact is made, the specific technology transfer arrangements are made between the laboratory and the business.

To take advantage of the Federal Laboratory Consortium network and access the federal laboratories, contact one of the FLC regional coordinators in your region, or the locator manager. The regional coordinator working with the FLC Locator will find the appropriate laboratory to meet specific requests.

FLC Laboratory Locator Network
DelaBarre & Associates
P.O. Box 545
Sequim, WA 98382
(206) 683-1005

Federal Laboratory Consortium Regional Contacts

Mid-Atlantic
Norma Vaught
ARL-Sensor, Signatures, Signal & Info Director
ATTN: AMSRL-CP-TT
2800 Powder Mill Rd.
Adelphi, MD 29783
(301) 394-2952

Mid-Continent
C. Dan Brand
HHS/PHS/FDA
National Center for Toxicological Research
3900 NCTK Rd.
Jefferson, AR 72079
(501) 543-7950

Midwest
Ted Schoenborn
HHS–National Institute for Occupational Safety & Health
4676 Columbia Pkwy., DPSE-R2
Cincinnati, OH 45226
(513) 841-4305

Northeast
Gary Conlon
Army Benet Laboratories
ATTN: SMCAR-CCB-T
Bldg. 115, Room 224
Watervliet, NY 12189
(518) 266-4946

Southeast
Eric Greene
HHS/PHS–Centers for Disease Control
Technology Transfer Office MS-E67
1600 Clifton Rd., NE
Atlanta, GA 30333
(404) 639-6268

Washington, DC
Dr. Beverly Berger
1850 M St., NW, Suite 800
Washington, DC 20036
(202) 331-4220

West
Geoffrey Phillips
Air Force Advanced Manufacturing Center
3237 Peacekeeper Way #13
McClellan AFB, CA 95652
(916) 643-1248

Industry Studies

OPTIONS FOR INDUSTRY RESEARCH, from market analyses to forecasts, to planning and strategy, include producing studies internally, or commissioning an outside firm to do customized research. Given the prohibitive cost of customized research, companies are turning more and more to commercially available off-the-shelf studies produced by market research firms.

The most comprehensive guide to published market research reports, studies, and surveys is the *Findex* directory. This reference contains descriptions of consumer and industrial studies and surveys, syndicated and multi-client studies, audits, and subscription research services, as well as published reports on general management and business topics. Individual reports may cover an entire industry, a specific segment of an industry, or an individual product or series of related products.

Recommended Resource

Findex
Cambridge Information Group
Attn: Marketing Department
7200 Wisconsin Ave., Suite 601
Bethesda, MD 20814
(800) 843-7751

Contact Options

Selected Market Research Firms:

Business Trend Analysts
2171 Jericho Tpke., Suite 200
Commack, NY 11725
(516) 462-5454

Leading Edge Reports
2171 Jerico Tpke., Suite 200
Commack, NY 11725
(800) 866-4648

The Fredonia Group
3570 Warrensville Center Rd.
Cleveland, OH 44122
(216) 921-6800

Frost & Sullivan
90 West St., Suite 1301
New York, NY 10006
(212) 233-1080

Euromonitor
60-61 Britton St.
London EC1M 5NA
England
[44]-(71)-251-8024

Find/SVP
625 Ave. of the Americas
New York, NY 10011
(212) 645-4500

The Top Reference Sources

Directory of Manufacturers' Sales Agencies
Manufacturers' Agents National Association,
$92.50
(714) 859-4040

This book offers the most efficient way to hire outside sales representatives. The directory includes informative articles on finding the best agents for your products, communication between agents, manufacturers, and customers, and agent marketing, among others. Membership listings are cross-referenced and organized geographically and by product classification.

Listings include agency name, address, telephone number, branch offices, warehousing facilities, number of field salespeople, territory covered, and complete descriptions of the types of products sold.

Environmental Issues

Hazardous Waste

In 1976 the United States Congress passed a law called the Resource Conservation and Recovery Act (RCRA). Under RCRA, the United States Environmental Protection Agency has developed specific requirements for handling hazardous waste. These requirements control hazardous waste from the moment it is generated until its ultimate disposal. Since 1980, the EPA has been refining the hazardous-waste program to further protect public health and the environment. As a result, the requirements were expanded to include small businesses that handle specified quantities of hazardous waste, and the number of wastes classified as hazardous has been increased.

Defining Hazardous Waste

A waste is a solid or liquid material that is no longer used. EPA defines waste as hazardous if it has certain properties that could pose dangers to human health and the environment after it is discarded. EPA considers a waste to be hazardous if it possesses certain characteristics (ignitability, corrosivity, reactivity, or toxicity) or if it is on a list of specific wastes determined by the EPA to be hazardous. RCRA regulations, found in the Code of Federal Regulations (CFR) Title 40, Part 261, present the listed hazardous wastes, describe hazardous-waste characteristics, and specify test methods for determining whether waste is hazardous.

Complete lists of wastes identified by the EPA as hazardous can also be obtained from the EPA's RCRA/Superfund Hotline at (800) 424-9346 or from the regional EPA offices and state hazardous-waste management agencies listed in this chapter.

In general, a business is likely to produce hazardous waste if it:

- Uses petroleum products;

- Uses dyes, paints, printing inks, thinners, solvents, or cleaning fluids;

- Uses pesticides or other related chemicals;

- Uses materials that dissolve metals, wood, paper, or clothing (acids and caustics);

- Uses flammable materials;

- Uses materials that burn or itch upon contact with skin;

- Uses materials that bubble or fume upon contact with water;

- Receives delivery of products accompanied by a shipping paper or label indicating that the product is hazardous.

Waste Production Threshold

The EPA considers small-quantity generators to be producers of more than 220 and less than 2,200 pounds (more than 100 and less than 1,000 kilograms) of hazardous waste in a calendar month. Small-quantity generators are subject to hazardous-waste requirements, and businesses should be aware that state agencies may have additional or more restrictive requirements. Producers of 1,000 kilograms or more of hazardous waste in any calendar month, or more than one kilogram of certain acutely hazardous wastes (waste that is fatal to humans in small doses) are subject to the more extensive regulations that apply to large-quantity generators.

A business that produces hazardous waste and is regulated under the Federal Hazardous Waste Requirements must:

- Obtain an EPA identification number for each site at which hazardous waste is generated. To obtain an EPA identification number, contact the EPA regional office or your state hazardous-waste management agency and ask for Form 8700-12.

- Properly handle waste on the company premises. A permit may be required if waste is stored, treated, or disposed of on site. Contact the regional EPA office, state agency, or RCRA/Superfund Hotline for information on permits, storing, and shipping of hazardous wastes.

Source: U.S. Environmental Protection Agency

Emergency Planning and Community Right-to-Know Act

Established as part of the Superfund Amendments passed by Congress in 1986, the Emergency Planning and Community Right-to-Know-Act (EPCRA) is intended to inform the public and community emergency-response services, such as fire departments, about the existence of certain toxic substances in area businesses. If toxic substances are being released into the air, land, or water while they are being manufactured, processed, or used in other ways, the EPCRA requires the business involved to file a "Form R" with the EPA. (A list of more than 300 toxic substances is available from the EPA.)

Manufacturers should be aware that failure to submit a Form R is a felony, and even an unintentional violation of this law is a civil offense. The EPA estimates that compliance costs for businesses total $147 million and acknowledges that small businesses are typically most burdened by these regulations.

For more information about environmental reporting laws, contact the EPCRA Hotline at (800) 535-0202 or your regional EPA office.

EPA Regional Offices

EPA Region 1

Connecticut, Maine, Massachusetts, New Hampshire, Rhode Island, Vermont
1 Congress St.
Boston, MA 02203
(617) 565-3420

EPA Region 2

New Jersey, New York, Puerto Rico, Virgin Islands
290 Broadway
New York, NY 10007
(212) 637-3000

EPA Region 3

Delaware, District of Columbia, Maryland, Pennsylvania, Virginia, West Virginia
841 Chestnut St.
Philadelphia, PA 19107
(215) 597-9800

EPA Region 4

Alabama, Florida, Georgia, Kentucky, Mississippi, North Carolina, South Carolina, Tennessee
345 Courtland St., NE
Atlanta, GA 30365
(404) 347-4727

EPA Region 5

Illinois, Indiana, Michigan, Minnesota, Ohio, Wisconsin
77 W. Jackson Blvd.
Chicago, IL 60604
(312) 353-2000

EPA Region 6

Arkansas, Louisiana, New Mexico, Oklahoma, Texas
1445 Ross Ave.
Dallas, TX 75202
(214) 665-6444

EPA Region 7

Iowa, Kansas, Missouri, Nebraska
726 Minnesota Ave.
Kansas City, KS 66101
(913) 551-7000

EPA Region 8

Colorado, Montana, North Dakota, South Dakota, Utah, Wyoming
999 18th St.
Denver, CO 80202
(303) 293-1603

EPA Region 9

Arizona, California, Hawaii, Nevada, Guam, Marianas
75 Hawthorne St.
San Francisco, CA 94105
(415) 744-1702

EPA Region 10

Alaska, Idaho, Oregon, Washington
1200 Sixth Ave.
Seattle, WA 98101
(206) 553-1200

The Top Reference Sources

Manufacturers' Alliance for Productivity and Innovation
1525 Wilson Blvd., Suite 900
Arlington, VA 72209
(703) 841-9000

This policy research organization is made up of over 500 member manufacturing companies in a broad range of industries. MAPI does research and analysis on economic, management, legal, and regulatory issues affecting the industrial sector. The organization produces some 75 subject-specific reports annually, and sponsors the Conference on Business and Economic Policies, an annual seminar series.

Waste Management

State Hazardous-Waste Management Agencies

Alabama
Land Division
Department of Environmental Management
(205) 271-7730

Alaska
Department of Environmental Conservation
Division of Environmental Quality
(907) 465-5260

Arizona
Waste Programs
Department of Environmental Quality
(602) 207-4202

Arkansas
Hazardous Waste Division
Department of Pollution Control and Ecology
(501) 570-2872

California
Department of Toxic Substances Control
Environmental Protection Agency
(800) 618-6942 or (916) 324-1781

Colorado
Hazardous Materials and Waste
Department of Health
(303) 692-3300

Connecticut
Waste Management Bureu
Department of Environmental Protection
(203) 424-3021

Delaware
Hazardous Waste Branch
Division of Air and Waste Management
(302) 739-3689

District of Columbia
Pesticides, Hazardous Waste and Underground
Storage Tanks Division
Department of Consumer and Regulatory Affairs
(202) 645-6080

Florida
Division of Waste Management (UST)
Department of Environmental Protection
(904) 488-0190

Georgia
Land Protection Branch
Industrial and Hazardous Waste
(404) 362-2537

Hawaii
Department of Health
Hazardous Waste Program
(808) 586-4225

Idaho
Permits and Enforcement Division of Environmental
Quality
Department of Health and Welfare
(208) 334-5898

Illinois
Division of Land Pollution Control
Environmental Protection Agency
(217) 782-6760

Indiana
Department of Environmental Management
(317) 232-3210

Iowa
Air Quality and Solid Waste Protection
Department of Natural Resources
(515) 281-8693

Kansas
Bureau of Waste Management
Department of Health and Environment
(913) 296-1600

Kentucky
Division of Waste Management
Department of Environmental Protection
Cabinet for Natural Resources and
Environmental Protection
(502) 564-6716

Louisiana
Office of Solid and Hazardous Waste
Department of Environmental Quality
(504) 765-0355

Maine
Bureau of Oil and Hazardous Materials Control
Department of Environmental Protection
(207) 287-2651

Maryland
Waste Management Administration
Department of the Environment
(410) 631-3000

Massachusetts
Division of Solid and Hazardous Waste
Bureau of Waste Prevention and Administration
(617) 292-5589

Waste Management (cont'd)

Michigan
Waste Management Division
Environmental Protection
Department of Natural Resources
(517) 373-2730

Minnesota
Solid and Hazardous Waste Division
Pollution Control Agency
(612) 297-8503

Mississippi
Division of Solid and Hazardous Waste Management
Office of Pollution Control
Department of Environmental Quality
(601) 961-5062

Missouri
Waste Management Program
Department of Natural Resources
(314) 751-5401

Montana
Solid and Hazardous Waste Bureau
Department of Health and Environmental Sciences
(406) 444-1430

Nebraska
Hazardous Waste Management Section
Resource Conservation Recovery Act
(402) 471-4217

Nevada
Bureau of Waste Management
Division of Environmental Protection
Department of Conservation and Natural Resources
(702) 687-4670

New Hampshire
Division of Public Health Services
Waste Management Division
Department of Environmental Services
(603) 271-2900

New Jersey
Hazardous Waste Regulations and Energy
Department of Environmental Protection
(609) 633-1418

New Mexico
Hazardous Waste Section
Health and Environment Department
(505) 827-4308

New York
Division of Solid and Hazardous Waste
Department of Environmental Conservation
(518) 457-6603

North Carolina
Solid and Hazardous Waste Management Branch
Division of Environment, Health and Natural Resources
(919) 733-2178

North Dakota
Division of Waste Management and Consolidated Laboratories
Department of Health
(701) 221-5166

Ohio
Division of Hazardous Waste Management
Environmental Protection Agency
(614) 644-2917

Oklahoma
Waste Management Service
Department of Health
(405) 271-5338

Oregon
Waste Management Cleanup
Department of Environmental Quality
(503) 229-5913

Pennsylvania
Bureau of Waste Management
Department of Environmental Resources
(717) 787-9870

Rhode Island
Solid Waste Management Program
Department of Environmental Management
(401) 277-2797

South Carolina
Bureau of Solid and Hazardous Waste Management
Department of Health and Environmental Control
(803) 896-4000

South Dakota
Office of Waste Management
Department of Environment and Natural Resources
(605) 773-3153

Waste Management (cont'd)

Tennessee
Division of Solid Waste Management
Department of Public Health
(615) 532-0780

Texas
Hazardous and Solid Waste Division
National Resources Conservation Commission
(512) 239-2334

Utah
Division of Solid and Hazardous Waste Management
Department of Environmental Quality
(801) 538-6170

Vermont
Waste Management Division
Agency of Environmental Conservation
(802) 241-3888

Virginia
Waste Management Division
Office of Environmental Quality
(804) 762-4000

Washington
Solid and Hazardous Waste and Toxics
Reduction Program
Department of Ecology
(206) 407-7014

West Virginia
Office of Waste Management
Bureau of Environment, Division of Environmental
Protection, Department of Natural Resources
(304) 558-5929

Wisconsin
Bureau of Solid and Hazardous Waste Management
Department of Natural Resources
(608) 266-1327

Wyoming
Solid and Hazardous Waste Division
Department of Environmental Quality
(307) 777-7752

Largest Waste Management Companies

Browning-Ferris Industries
P.O. Box 3151
Houston, TX 77253
(713) 870-8100

Chambers Development
10700 Frankstown Rd.
Pittsburgh, PA 15235
(412) 242-6237

Laidlaw
3221 N. Service Rd.
P.O. Box 5028
Burlington, Ontario L7R 3Y8
(905) 336-5151

WMX Technologies
3003 Butterfield Rd.
Oak Brook, IL 60521
(708) 218-1500

Western Waste Industries
21061 S. Western Ave.
Torrance, CA 90501
(310) 328-0900

Corporate Environmental Awards

National Corporate Environmental Awards

Sponsor	Award/Recipient(s) of 1994 Award	Telephone
American Marketing Association (c/o J. Ottman Consulting)	Edison Award for Environmental Achievement Gridcore Rayovac Reusable Alkaline Batteries 3M Scotch Brite Never-Rust Wool Soap Pads	(212) 255-3800
Composting Council	Hi Kellogg Award James Smith/University of Florida	(703) 739-2401
Council on Economic Priorities	Corporate Conscience Awards for Environmental Stewardship New England Electric System	(212) 420-1133
Direct Marketing Association	Robert Rodale Environmental Achievement Award Fingerhut National Wildlife Federation	(212) 768-7277
Ecological Society of America	Corporate Award Toyota Tapestry Program	(202) 833-8773
United Nations Environment Programme (1993 Awards)	Environmental Communications Award Patagonia/Lost Arrow Design Southern California Edison Coors Lake Michigan Federation Texas Department of Public Transportation Texas Water Commission Aveda/Time to Clear the Air Molson Beer Procter & Gamble/Pampers Ciba-Geigy Amway Recycle Minneapolis Neal Aspinall Shyam Madiraju/Leo Burnett	(801) 466-3600
Flexible Packaging Association	Green Globe Award Paramount Packaging	(202) 842-3880
Glass Packaging Institute	Clear Choice Award (Environmental Awareness) Veryfine Fruit Juices and Drinks	(202) 452-9450
Keep America Beautiful	Keep Your Recyclables at Play Lever Brothers	(203) 323-8987
National Arbor Day Foundation	Promise to the Earth CBS Broadcast Group Fox Network NBC	(402) 474-5655
National Recycling Coalition	Fred Schmitt Award for Outstanding Leadership Virco Manufacturing	(202) 625-6406
World Environment Center	Gold Medal Award S. C. Johnson & Son	(212) 683-4700

Environmental Hotlines

MANY CLEARINGHOUSES, HOTLINES, and electronic bulletin boards have been developed by the Environmental Protection Agency (EPA) to respond to legislative initiatives requiring the agency to provide outreach, communications, and technology transfer to businesses, individuals, and other organizations. Clearinghouses facilitate the exchange of critical information and are also useful as a central access point for hard-to-locate technical reports and documents. The following information clearinghouses and hotlines may be of particular interest to manufacturers:

Air and Radiation

Environmental Protection Agency Phone Numbers:

Aerometric Information Retrieval System Bulletin Board
(919) 541-5742

Air Risk Information Support Center Hotline
(919) 541-0888

Air/Superfund Coordination Program
(919) 541-5589

Control Technology Center Hotline
(919) 541-5285

Inspection, Control, and Compliance Technical Information Clearinghouse
(919) 541-4571

Small Business Assistance Program Support Center Hotline
(919) 541-0800

Pesticides and Toxic Substances

Toxic Substances Control Act Assistance Information Service
U.S. Environmental Protection Agency
Environmental Assistance Division, 7408
401 M St., SW
Washington, DC 20460
(202) 554-1404
Provides information on TSCA regulations to industry, labor, and trade organizations, environmental groups, and the public. Technical as well as general information is available.

Hazardous and Solid Waste

Emergency Planning and Community Right-to-Know Information Hotline
Booz, Allen & Hamilton
1725 Jefferson Davis Hwy.
Arlington, VA 22202
(800) 535-0202
Provides regulatory, policy, and technical assistance to federal agencies, local, and state governments, the public, and the regulated community in response to questions related to the Emergency Planning and Community Right-to-Know Act (Title III of SARA).

Solid Waste Information Clearinghouse and Hotline
P.O. Box 7219-20907
1100 Wayne Ave., #700
Silver Spring, MD 20910
(800) 67-SWICH
Developed and partially funded by the Solid Waste Association of North America and EPA, SWICH comprises a library system and an electronic bulletin board, and provides information on all aspects of solid waste management, including source reduction, recycling, composting, planning, education and training, legislation and regulation, waste combustion, collection, transfer, disposal, landfill gas, and special wastes.

Resource Conservation and Recovery Act/ Superfund/ Emergency Planning and Community Right-to-Know Act Hotline
Storage Tank Hotline (RCRA/SF/OUST)
1725 Jefferson Davis Hwy.
Arlington, VA 22202
(800) 424-9346
Provides information pertaining to federal EPA regulations, policy, and documents to federal agencies, local and state goernments, the public, and the regulated community in response to questions related to RCRA, underground storage tank issues, SF, Comprehensive Environmental Response Compensation and Liability Act (CERCLA), EPCRA, SARA Title III, and radiation site cleanup standards.

Hazardous Waste Ombudsman Program
U.S. Environmental Protection Agency
401 M St., SW, Room SE 301
Washington, DC 20460
(800) 262-7937
The hazardous-waste management program established under the RCRA is the most complex regulatory program developed by the EPA. It assists the public and regulated community in resolving problems concerning any program or requirement under the hazardous waste regulations. The Ombudsman Program, located at headquarters and in each regional office (see listing in this chapter), handles complaints from citizens and the regulated community, obtains facts, sorts information, and substantiates policy.

National Response Center
U.S. Coast Guard Headquarters
2100 Second St., SW, Room 2611
Washington, DC 20593
(202) 267-2675 or (800) 424-8802
Receives reports of oil, hazardous chemical, biological, and radiological releases. The NRC then

Environmental Hotlines (cont'd)

passes those reports to a predesignated federal on-scene coordinator who coordinates cleanup efforts with other responsible federal agencies.

Methods Information Communications
Exchange (MICE)
c/o Science Applications
7600-A Lewisburg Pike
Falls Church, VA 22043
(703) 821-4789
    Provides information on analytical test methods for the characterization of hazardous waste in support of the Resource Conservation and Recovery Act (RCRA).

Pollution Prevention

Stratospheric Ozone Information Hotline
Technical Resources
501 Third St., NW
Washington, DC 20001
(800) 296-1996
    Provides consultation on ozone protection regulations and requirements under Title VI of the Clean Air Act Amendments (CAAA) of 1990. Title VI covers the following key aspects of the production, use, and safe disposal of ozone-depleting chemicals: (1) production and phase-out controls; (2) servicing of motor vehicle air conditioners; (3) recycling and emission reduction; (4) technician and equipment certification; (5) approval of alternatives; (6) ban of nonessential uses; (7) product labeling; and (8) federal procurement.

Water

National Small Flows Clearinghouse
West Virginia University
P.O. Box 6064
Morgantown, WV 26506
(800) 624-8301
    Distributes publications and videotapes, performs literature searches, operates a toll-free hotline, produces free newsletters, and operates a computer bulletin board.

Small Business

Small Business Ombudsman Clearinghouse/Hotline
U.S. Environmental Protection Agency
Small Business Ombudsman, 1230C
401 M St., SW
Washington, DC 20460
(703) 305-5938
Fax: (703) 305-6462
    Apprises the trade associations representing small business interests of current regulatory developments.

Recommended Resource

Access EPA
U.S. Environmental Protection Agency, free
Public Information Center
(202) 260-2080
    A directory of U.S. Environmental Protection Agency and other public sector environmental information resources. First published in 1991, this annual directory provides information on documents, dockets, clearinghouses and hotlines, records, databases, models, EPA libraries, and state libraries. *Access EPA* is also available via the Internet, using Gopher, at gopher.epa.gov.

CompuServe features TRW Business Profiles, a wealth of general business and credit information on over 13 million companies.
GO TRWREPORT

Environmental Organizations

SELECTED INDUSTRY AND ASSOCIATION contacts for further information on recycling, waste management, and environmental issues include:

Aluminum Association
900 19th St., NW, Suite 300
Washington, DC 20006
(202) 862-5100

Aluminum Recycling Association
1000 16th St., NW, Suite 400
Washington, DC 20036
(202) 785-0951

American Forest and Paper Association
1111 19th St., NW, #700
Washington, DC 20036
(202) 463-2700

American Petroleum Institute
1220 L St., NW
Washington, DC 20005
(202) 682-8000

American Plastics Council
1275 K Street, NW, Suite 500
Washington, DC 20005
(202) 371-5319

American Public Works Association
1301 Pennsylvania Ave., NW, Suite 501
Washington, DC 20004
(202) 393-2792

Association of State and Territorial
Solid Waste Management Officials
444 N. Capitol St., NW, Suite 388
Washington, DC 20001
(202) 624-5828

Can Manufacturers Institute
1625 Massachusetts Ave., NW
Washington, DC 20036
(202) 232-4677

Council on Packaging in the Environment
1001 Connecticut Ave., NW
Washington, DC 20036
(202) 789-1310

Environmental Action Foundation
6930 Carroll Ave., #600
Tacoma Park, MD 20912
(301) 891-1100

Environmental Defense Fund
1875 Connecticut Ave., NW, #1016
Washington, DC 20009
(202) 387-3500

Glass Packaging Institute
1627 K St., NW, #800
Washington, DC 20006
(202) 887-4850

Institute of Clean Air Companies
1707 L St., NW, Suite 570
Washington, DC 20036
(202) 457-0911

Institute of Scrap Recycling Industries
1325 G St., NW, Suite 1000
Washington, DC 20005
(202) 737-1770

National Association for Plastic Container Recovery
100 N. Tryon St., #3770
Charlotte, NC 28202
(704) 358-8882

National Association of Chemical Recyclers
1200 G St., NW
Washington, DC 20005
(202) 434-8740

National Association of Counties
440 First St., NW
Washington, DC 20001
(202) 393-6226

National Association of Towns and Townships
1522 K St., NW, Suite 600
Washington, DC 20005
(202) 737-5200

National Governors Association
444 N. Capitol St., NW, Suite 267
Washington, DC 20001
(202) 624-5300

National League of Cities
1301 Pennsylvania Ave., NW
Washington, DC 20004
(202) 626-3000

National Recycling Coalition
1101 30th St., NW, Suite 305
Washington, DC 20007
(202) 625-6406

National Soft Drink Association
Solid Waste Management Dept.
1101 16th St., NW
Washington, DC 20036
(202) 463-6700

Environmental Organizations (cont'd)

National Solid Waste Management Association
4301 Connecticut Ave., NW, Suite 300
Washington, DC 20008
(202) 244-4700

National Tire Dealers and Retreaders Association
1250 I St., NW, Suite 400
Washington, DC 20005
(202) 789-2300

Plastics Recycling Institute
Rutgers, the State University of New Jersey
Center for Plastics Recycling Research
Bldg. 4109, Livingston Campus
New Brunswick, NJ 08903
(908) 932-3632

Polystyrene Packaging Council
1275 K St., NW, Suite 400
Washington, DC 20005
(202) 371-2487

Rubber Manufacturers Association
1400 K St., NW, Suite 900
Washington, DC 20005
(202) 682-4800

The Society of the Plastics Industry
1275 K St., NW, Suite 400
Washington, DC 20005
(202) 371-5200

Solid Waste Association of North America
P.O. Box 7219
Silver Spring, MD 20910
(301) 585-2898

Steel Recycling Institute
Foster Plaza X
680 Andersen Dr.
Pittsburgh, PA 15220
(800) 876-7274 or (412) 922-2772

Textile Fibers and By-Products Association
P.O. Box 550326
Charlotte, NC 28220
(404) 262-2477

U.S. Conference of Mayors
1620 I St., NW
Washington, DC 20006
(202) 293-7330

U.S. Department of Energy
Waste Material Management
1000 Independence Ave., SW
Washington, DC 20585
(202) 586-6750

The Vinyl Institute
65 Madison Ave.
Morristown, NJ 07960
(201) 898-6699

Source: List prepared in part by the Institute of Scrap Recycling Industries, Inc.

Labeling Regulations

FEBRUARY 11, 1993, marked the final ruling on Section 611 of the Clean Air Act, which requires labeling of products made with or containing class I and class II ozone-depleting substances (such as chlorofluorocarbons, or CFCs). It also requires that containers containing class I or class II substances be labeled.

An adhesive containing CFCs, for example, must be labeled as "containing" them. When that product is applied by a subsequent manufacturer in affixing a cushion to a seat, the seat must be labeled as a "product manufactured with" CFCs because the CFCs have been released. The subsequent sale of the seat to an automobile manufacturer, however, would not result in the labeling of a car based on that product.

All products made prior to May 15, 1993, are exempt from the labeling requirements if the manufacturer is able to show within 24 hours that its products were made before that date. Likewise, an importer, when so requested by the EPA, must be able to show that the products imported were manufactured before the deadline.

For additional information, including a complete list of class I and class II ozone-depleting chemicals, contact the Stratospheric Ozone Information Hotline at (800) 296-1996. To receive copies of the final rule and any follow-up notices regarding the labeling rule, see the Federal Register in a local university or government library.

Source: Environmental Protection Agency

Waste Exchanges

THE IDEA BEHIND WASTE EXCHANGE is that one company's waste or unwanted material may be another company's resource. It is estimated that by promoting the reuse and recycling of industrial materials through waste exchanges, the industry currently saves $27 million in raw material and disposal costs and the energy equivalent of more than 100,000 barrels of oil annually. With over 7 billion tons of industrial solid waste generated yearly, and only 6 million tons of waste currently on the exchange, there is an enormous potential for savings as more companies make use of waste exchanges.

Established in 1992, the National Materials Exchange Network is a partnership of industrial waste exchanges, supported in part by Congress and assisted by the Environmental Protection Agency, that increases recycling opportunities within industry. Materials listed on the Exchange include waste by-products, off-spec, overstock, obsolete, and damaged materials, used and virgin, solid and hazardous. Access to the National Materials Exchange Network is free with participation in your local exchange.

Contact Options

National Materials Exchange Network
For computer modem access: (509) 466-1019
Canada only: (509) 325-1724
Direct assistance: (509) 466-1532

Solid Waste Assistance Program
1100 Wayne Ave.
Silver Spring, MD 20910
(800) 677-9424

U.S. Waste Exchanges

Arizona Waste Exchange
4725 E. Sunrise Dr., Suite 215
Tucson, AZ 85718
(602) 299-7716

Arkansas Industrial Development Council
1 Capitol Hill
Little Rock, AR 72201
(501) 682-1370

B.A.R.T.E.R.
2512 Delaware St., S.E.
Minneapolis, MN 55414
(612) 627-6811

California Waste Exchange
P.O. Box 806
Sacramento, CA 95812
(926) 322-4742

CALMAX
8800 Cal Center Dr.
Sacramento, CA 95826
(916) 255-2369

Hawaii Materials Exchange
P.O. Box 1048
Paia, HI 96779
(808) 579-9109

IMEX
172 20th Ave.
Seattle, WA 98122
(206) 296-4899

Indiana Waste Exchange
P.O. Box 454
Carmel, IN 46032
(317) 574-6506

Industrial Materials Exchange Service
P.O. Box 19276
Springfield, IL 62794
(217) 782-0450

Intercontinental Waste Exchange
5200 Town Center Circle, Suite 303
Boca Raton, FL 33486
(800) 541-0400

Iowa Waste Reduction Center
75 BRC–University of Northern Iowa
Cedar Falls, IA 50614
(319) 273-2079

Kansas Materials Exchange
P.O. Box 152
Hutchinson, KS 67504
(316) 662-0551

Lousiana/Gulf Coast Exchange
1419 CEBA
Baton Rouge, LA 70803
(504) 388-4594

Missouri Environmental Improvement Authority
325 Jefferson St.
Jefferson City, MO 65101
(314) 751-4919

MISSTAP
P.O. Drawer CN
Mississippi State, MS 39762
(601) 325-8454

Waste Exchanges (cont'd)

Montana Industrial Waste Exchange
Montana Chamber of Commerce
P.O. Box 1730
Helena, MT 59624
(406) 442-2405

New Hampshire Waste Exchange
122 N. Main St.
Concord, NH 03301
(603) 224-5388

Northeast Industrial Waste Exchange
90 Presidential Plaza, Suite 122
Syracuse, NY 13202
(315) 422-6572

Pacific Materials Exchange
1522 N. Washington St., Suite 202
Spokane, WA 99201
(509) 325-0551

Portland Chemical Consortium
P.O. Box 751
Portland, OR 97207
(503) 725-4270

RENEW
Hope Castillo
P.O. Box 13087
Austin, TX 78711
(512) 463-7773

Rocky Mountain Materials Exchange
1445 Market St.
Denver, CO 80202
(303) 620-8093

SEMREX
171 W. Third St.
Winona, MN 55987
(507) 457-6460

South Carolina Waste Exchange
155 Wilton Hill Rd.
Columbia, SC 29212
(803) 755-3325

Wisconsin Bureau of Solid Waste Mgmt.
P.O. Box 7921
Madison, WI 53707
(608) 267-3763

Industrial Exchange Service Providers

Department of Environmental Protection
18 Riley Rd.
Frankfort, KY 40601
(502) 564-6761

Minnesota Technical Assistance Program
1313 Fifth St., Suite 307
Minneapolis, MN 55414
(612) 627-4555

Oklahoma Waste Exchange Program
P.O. Box 53551
Oklahoma City, OK 73152
(405) 271-5338

Canadian Waste Exchanges

Alberta Waste Materials Exchange
Bldg. #350
6815 Eighth St., NE
Calgary, AB T2E 7H7
(403) 297-7505

Bourse Québecoise des Matières Secondaires
14 Place du Commerce, Bureau 350
Le-des-Squeurs, Québec H3E 1T5
(514) 762-9012

British Columbia Waste Exchange
102 1525 W. Eighth Ave.
Vancouver, BC V6J 1T5
(604) 731-7222

Canadian Chemical Exchange
P.O. Box 1135
Ste-Adèle, AB J0R 1L0
(514) 229-6511

Canadian Waste Materials Exchange
2395 Speakman Dr.
Mississauga, ON L5K 1B3
(416) 822-4111

Manitoba Waste Exchange
1329 Niakwa Rd.
Winnipeg, MB R2J 3T4
(204) 257-3891

Ontario Waste Exchange
2395 Speakman Dr.
Mississauga, ON L5K 1B3
(416) 822-4111, ext. 512

Additional American Exchanges

Alabama Waste Materials Exchange
404 Wilson Dam Ave.
Sheffield, AL 35660
(205) 383-563

Hudson Valley Materials Exchange
P.O. Box 550, 1 Veterans Dr.
New Paltz, NY 12561
(914) 255-3749

New Jersey Materials Exchange
300 W. Commercial Ave.
Moonachie, NJ 07074
(800) 676-2754

Waste Exchanges (cont'd)

New Mexico Materials Exchange
Four Corners Recycling
P.O. Box 904
Farmington, NM 87499
(505) 325-2157

Olmsted County Materials Exchange
Olmsted County Public Works
2122 Campus Dr., SE
Rochester, MN 55904
(507) 285-8231

Vermont Business Materials Exchange
P.O. Box 630
Montpelier, VT 05601
(802) 223-3441

Recycling

MOST AUTHORITIES AGREE THAT recycling can realistically reduce the amount of municipal solid waste by approximately 25 percent. Recycling allows discarded materials to be diverted from the waste stream and begins with separation and collection of recyclable material at the source.

Easily Recycled Materials

- Aluminum: Today we recycle more than 65,000 aluminum beverage cans every minute.

- Iron and steel: In 1989, the U.S. scrap processing industry prepared 60 million tons for recycling, double the amount of paper, nonferrous metals (aluminum, copper, lead, zinc, etc.), glass, and plastics combined.

- Plastics: Currently, three principal types of plastics are being recycled:

  - PETE (polyethylene terephthalate) soft drink containers, especially the two-liter bottles, are the most common plastic containers manufactured—and discarded—today.

  - HDPE (high-density polyethylene) containers are used as milk and water jugs, base cups or bottoms of PET soft drink bottles, oil bottles, and detergent and other household cleaner bottles.

  - Polystyrene foam is used primarily to make fast-food carryout containers.

- Glass: The use of crushed glass, or cullet, in manufacturing offers economic advantages over virgin materials (sand, soda ash, limestone). Cullet melts at a lower temperature than the raw materials, so manufacturers can reduce energy usage as well as particulate emissions into the atmosphere. Today, 25 percent of any given glass container is made from recycled glass.

- Paper: Paper and paperboard constitute the largest proportion of municipal solid waste. More than 30 percent of all the paper and paperboard used in the United States today is being collected and used as either a component to make recycled paper and paperboard or as an export to foreign nations.

Source: Institute of Scrap Recycling Industries

The Top Reference Sources

American Demographics
Dow Jones, $62/12 issues
(800) 828-1133

Published monthly, this extremely informative magazine is must reading for businesses, especially their sales, marketing, and advertising departments.

Based primarily on census data, sample features include articles on aging, black suburbs, consumer confidence, influential Americans, market-driven companies, the real Hispanic market, the 1950s, and how market research can increase marketing efficiency.
    The editors do a great job of making a dry topic extremely interesting.

Recycled Content Mandates

TWELVE STATES NOW REQUIRE manufacturers to use recycled materials. Connecticut and California were the first states to enact these laws with mandates that responded to the glut of old newspapers in 1989. The following is a list of these 12 states and the amount of recycled materials that will be required in manufacturing:

- Arizona
  Newsprint: 50% by 2000.

- California
  Newsprint: 50% by 2000.
  Plastic containers: options similar to Oregon's; see below.
  Glass containers: 65% by 2005.

- Connecticut
  Newsprint: 50% by 2000.
  Phone books: 40% by 2001.

- Illinois
  Newsprint: 45% by 1997.

- Maryland
  Newsprint: 40% by 1998.
  Phone books: 40% by 2000.

- Missouri
  Newsprint: 50% by 2000.

- North Carolina
  Newsprint: 40% by 1997.

- Oregon
  Glass containers: 50% by 2000 (food/beverages).

- Rhode Island
  Newsprint: 40% by 2000.

- Texas
  Newsprint: 30% by 2000.

- West Virginia
  Newsprint: highest "practicable" content; advisory committee created to determine rate.

- Wisconsin
  Newsprint: 45% by 2001.

Source: National Solid Wastes Management Association

Recycling Symbols

IN 1990, THE SOCIETY OF THE Plastics Industry introduced the Plastic Container Material Code System to assist plastic recyclers in sorting plastic bottles by resin type. The PBI coding system, consisting of those now familiar chasing arrows, is intended to encourage comprehensive bottle recycling by providing the means to obtain the highest value from all plastic bottles.

The system is meant for voluntary use by bottle and container producers, to be imprinted onto the bottom surface of plastic containers. These consistent national identification marks are designed to be most convenient for those in the recycling industry who will sort containers, and is intended to avoid a complicated system that would require extensive worker training and possibly lead to missorting or confusion.

Recommended Resource

Recycled Plastic Products Source Book
American Plastics Council, free
(800) 243-5790
This terrific source book helps private sector and public sector buyers identify products made with recycled plastic. Organized by product category,

with a supplementary Gray Pages section of alphabetized company listings, this book provides a wealth of leads and information on recycled plastic products. A consumer edition of the source book is also available, and lists products that can be sold directly to the general public.

 1. Polyethylene terephthalate (PETE)

 2. High-Density Polyethylene (HDPE)

 3. Vinyl/Polyvinyl Chloride (V/PVC)

 4. Low-Density Polyethylene (LDPE)

 5. Polypropylene (PP)

 6. Polystyrene (PS)

 7. Other

Tax Incentives for Recycling

IN ADDITION TO THE specifics listed below, many states have tax credits that apply to new business in general, to business expansions, or to businesses locating in certain pre-designated areas. In all cases, consult with state commerce, economic development, or tax offices to learn the details of state law.

Arizona
Income tax credit of 10% of installed cost, up to lesser of 25% of total tax liability or $5,000.

Arkansas
30% tax credit on income/corporate taxes for purchase of equipment making products with at least 10% recycled content.

California
Banks and corporations may take a 40% tax credit for purchase of certain equipment to manufacture recycled products with minimum 50% secondary content and 10% post-consumer content. Development bonds for manufacturing products with recycled materials.

Colorado
Up to 20% tax credit for purchase of certain equipment to make products using post-consumer recycled materials. Special credits for plastic recycling.

Delaware
Corporate tax credits for investments and for job creation for use of minimum 25% secondary materials removed from in-state waste stream. Reductions in gross receipts tax also apply. Corporate tax credits also available for source reduction activities and for processors and collectors of recyclable materials.

Florida
Sales tax exemption on recycling machinery. Tax incentives to encourage affordable transportation of recycled goods from collection points to sites for processing and disposal.

Idaho
Tax credit for equipment used to manufacture products made from recycled paper, plastic, or glass.

Illinois
Sales tax exemption for manufacturing equipment.

Indiana
Property tax exemption for buildings, equipment, and land involved in converting waste into new products.

Iowa
Sales tax exemptions for recycling equipment.

Kansas
Tax abatement for equipment used to manufacture products made with at least 25% post-consumer material.

Kentucky
Property and income tax credits to encourage recycling industries.

Louisiana
Corporation and franchise tax credits for purchase of qualified recycling equipment; corporate and personal income tax credits for purchase of equipment to recycle CFCs used as refrigerants.

Maine
Corporate tax credits equal to 30% of cost of recycling equipment and machinery. Tax credits of up to $5.00 per ton of wood waste from lumber products used as fuel or to generate heat.

Maryland
Individual and corporate income credit for expenses incurred to convert a furnace to burn used oil or to buy and install equipment to recycle used Freon.

Minnesota
Sales tax exemptions for recycling equipment.

Montana
Tax credit of 25% on purchase of equipment to process recyclable materials; up to 5% off income taxes for purchase of business-related products made with recycled material.

New Jersey
Investment tax credit of 50% for recycling vehicles and machinery; 6% sales tax exemption on purchases of recycling equipment.

New Mexico
Tax credits on equipment to recycle or use recycled materials in a manufacturing process.

North Carolina
Industrial and corporate income tax credits and exemptions for equipment and facilities.

Oklahoma
Income tax credit of 15% on purchase of equipment and facilities to use recyclable materials in a product.

Tax Incentives for Recycling (cont'd)

Oregon
Individual and corporate income tax credits for capital investment in recycling equipment and facilities. Special credits for plastic recycling.

South Carolina
Scrap metal dealers defined as manufacturers for sales tax purposes and exempted from electricity and fuel sales taxes.

Texas
Sludge recycling corporations eligible for franchise tax exemptions.

Virginia
Individual and corporate income tax credits of 20% of the purchase price of machinery and equipment for processing recyclable materials. Manufacturing plants using recycled products are eligible for a 10% tax credit.

Washington
Motor vehicles are exempt from rate regulation when transporting recovered materials from collection to reprocessing facilities and manufacturers.

West Virginia
Disposal-tax waivers for commercial recyclers who reduce their solid waste by 50%.

Wisconsin
Sales tax exemptions for waste reduction and recycling equipment and facilities; business property tax exemptions for same equipment.

Source: Waste Age

Recommended Resources

PaperMatcher: A Directory of Paper Recycling Resources
American Forest & Paper Association, free
(800) 878-8878

American Recycling Market Directory, $175
(800) 267-0707

The Clean Air Act

ENACTED TO CORRECT SERIOUS air pollution problems in the United States, the Clean Air Act Amendments of 1990 contain some of the most important elements of environmental legislation in recent years.

The Environmental Protection Agency estimates the new Clean Air Act will remove 56 billion pounds of pollution from the air each year. In human terms, these measures will significantly reduce lung disease, cancer, and other serious health problems caused by air pollution.

Air quality improvements mandated by the Clean Air Act Amendments include:

• Greatly reduced emissions of toxic air pollution and acid rain-causing pollutants

• Attainment of air quality standards nationwide by the year 2010

• Cleaner cars, fuels, factories, and power plants

• Less damage to lakes, streams, parks, and forests

• Reduced emissions of greenhouse gases

• Less damage to the stratospheric ozone layer.

The regulatory requirements of the CAAA will exact profound changes in many U.S. industries. For example, the amendments significantly affect the electric utility industry and, consequently, the coal industry. Sulfur emissions controls in the CAAA are divided into two phases. Phase I controls set out specific 1995 sulfur dioxide emissions limits for power plants built before 1978 (about 110 power plants). Phase II controls, set for the year 2000, generally limit sulfur dioxide emissions to the same level as for post-1978 power plants: 1.2 pounds of sulfur dioxide per million Btu. To achieve these emissions levels, utilities will retrofit scrubbers, switch to low-sulfur coal, blend low-sulfur with high-sulfur coal, co-fire with natural gas, re-power with advanced technology boilers, or perhaps even close the plant. Plants may also trade emission allowance credits issued to them by the EPA.

The potential global climate change caused by so-called greenhouse gases is yet another environmental issue important to the coal industry. Carbon dioxide, which absorbs solar radiation and traps the sun's heat, has been steadily increasing in the earth's atmosphere. All fossil fuels emit carbon dioxide, but coal emits 80 percent more per unit of energy consumed than natural gas, and about 20 percent more carbon dioxide than fuel oil. Consequently, coal-fired power stations are prime candidates for controls on carbon dioxide emissions. While no actions affecting the coal industry are likely in the near future, the issue of global warming has far from disappeared.

The Clean Air Act (cont'd)

Passage of the CAAA also had a significant impact on the U.S. petroleum refining industry. The first oxygenated-gasoline season began in November of 1992, and mandates that motor gasoline sold during at least four winter months in 39 areas of the country classified as "moderate or serious carbon monoxide non-attainment areas" must have a minimum oxygen content of 2.7 percent by weight (2 percent in California). Beginning in January 1995, the nine worst ozone non-attainment areas with populations in excess of 250,000 had to begin using motor gasoline that meets mandated emissions and composition requirements. As a result of these and other mandates, U.S. refiners have had to closely examine their operations relative to the CAAA, committing considerable resources to plant additions and reconfigurations, product reformulations, and research and development to advance processing technologies.

The search for alternatives to CFC (chlorofluorocarbon) and HCFC (hydrofluorocarbon) refrigerants, as required by Title VI of the Clean Air Act, is one of the greatest challenges the air-conditioning and refrigeration industry has ever faced. On July 1, 1992, Section 608 of the Act prohibited intentional venting of CFCs and HCFCs during service, repair, or disposal of any air-conditioning or refrigeration equipment. There will be controls on the sale of refrigerants and the disposition of recovered refrigerants, as well as mandatory certification of recovery/recycling equipment, technicians, and the purity of refrigerant recovered, reclaimed, and resold. Section 612 (list of safe alternatives to CFCs and HCFCs) and Section 611 (labeling of products containing or manufactured with controlled substances) regulations are also under development.

Paper and pulp mills are affected, as the CAAA provides extensive changes to new and existing source-reduction requirements for ozone, carbon monoxide, and particulate matter. Paper companies will be required to demonstrate that they are in compliance with all existing air standards, or that the benefits of a mill outweigh the environmental and social costs of anti-pollution regulations.

Clean Air Act Amendments have created new markets in the United States for the general components industry, particularly valves and pipe fittings. Environmental and health concerns that are emerging abroad are also creating incipient markets for U.S. valve and pipe-fitting companies, which are global leaders in the pollution control and pollution abatement industry.

Industry Preparations

Large and small companies need to become aware of the many new clean-air requirements and deadlines for compliance. Industry needs to know about flexible options, pollution prevention incentives, programs that encourage technological innovation, and market-based programs that clean the air at a much lower cost. These programs include:

- *Early Reductions Program*: offers companies incentives to take early voluntary action to reduce emissions and, in so doing, receive a six-year deferral on new clean-air requirements.

- *Allowance Trading System*: enables utilities to buy and sell emission credits among themselves, provided that total emissions reductions are achieved.

- *Fuel Averaging Program*: enables oil companies to meet tight new reformulated fuel standards by averaging the oxygen content in different grades of gasoline.

Recommended Resource

The Clean Air Act Amendments
National Association of Manufacturers
Publications Coordinator
1331 Pennsylvania Ave., NW
Suite 1500, N. Tower
Washington, DC 20004
(800) 637-3005

Contact Options

Government Agencies:

Stratospheric Ozone Information Hotline
U.S. Environmental Protection Agency
(800) 296-1996

Clean Air Act Advisory Committee
U.S. Environmental Protection Agency
(202) 260-6379

State Air Quality Agencies:

Alabama
Department of Environmental Management
Air Division
(205) 271-7861

Alaska
Department of Environmental Conservation
Air Quality Management Section
(907) 465-5100

Arizona
Department of Environmental Quality
Office of Air Quality
(602) 207-2300

Arkansas
Department of Pollution Control and Ecology
Air Division
(501) 570-2161

The Clean Air Act (cont'd)

California
Environmental Protection Agency
Air Resources Board
(916) 445-4383

Colorado
Department of Health
Air Pollution Control Division
(303) 692-3100

Connecticut
Department of Environmental Protection
Bureau of Air Management/Planning and Standards
(203) 424-3027

Delaware
Division of Air and Hazardous Waste Management
Air Quality Management
(302) 739-4791

District of Columbia
Department of Consumer and Regulatory Affairs
Environmental Control Division
Air Quality Control and Monitoring Branch
(202) 404-1180

Florida
Department of Environmental Protection
Air Resources Management
(904) 488-0114

Georgia
Department of Natural Resources
Environmental Protection Division
Air Protection Branch
(404) 363-7000

Hawaii
Department of Health
Clean Air Branch
(808) 586-4200

Idaho
Division of Environmental Quality
Air Quality Bureau
(208) 334-5898

Illinois
Environmental Protection Agency
Division of Air Pollution
(217) 782-7326

Indiana
Department of Environmental Management
Office of Air Management
(317) 232-8384

Iowa
Department of Natural Resources
Air Quality Section
(515) 281-8852

Kansas
Department of Health and Environment
Bureau of Air and Waste Management
(913) 296-1593

Kentucky
Department of Environmental Protection
Division for Air Quality
(502) 564-3382

Louisiana
Department of Environmental Quality
Office of Air Quality and Radiation Protection
Air Quality Division
(504) 765-0219

Maine
Department of Environmental Protection
Bureau of Air Quality Control
(207) 287-2437

Maryland
Department of the Environment
Air and Radiation Management Administration
(410) 631-3255

Massachusetts
Department of Environmental Protection
Division of Air Quality Control
(617) 292-5630

Michigan
Department of Natural Resources
Air Quality Division
(517) 373-7023

Minnesota
Pollution Control Agency
Air Quality Division
(612) 296-7331

Mississippi
Department of Environmental Quality
Office of Pollution Control, Air Division
(601) 961-5171

Missouri
Department of Natural Resources
Division of Environmental Quality
Air Pollution Control Program
(314) 751-4817

Montana
Department of Health and Environmental Sciences
Division of Air Quality
(406) 444-3454

Nebraska
Department of Environmental Quality
Air Quality
(402) 471-2189

The Clean Air Act (cont'd)

Nevada
Division of Environmental Protection
Bureau of Air Quality
(702) 687-5065

New Hampshire
Air Resources Division
(603) 271-1370

New Jersey
Department of Environmental Protection
Division of Environmental Quality/
Air Quality Management
(609) 292-6710

New Mexico
Environmental Department
Air Quality Bureau
(505) 827-0070

New York
Department of Environmental Conservation
Division of Air Resources
(518) 457-7230

North Carolina
Department of Environment, Health, and
Natural Resources
Air Quality Section
(919) 733-3340

North Dakota
Department of Health
Division of Environmental Engineering
Air Quality Program
(701) 221-5188

Ohio
Environmental Protection Agency
Division of Air Pollution Control
(614) 644-2270

Oklahoma
State Department of Health
Air Quality Service
(405) 271-5220

Oregon
Department of Environmental Quality
Air Quality Control Division
(503) 229-5359

Pennsylvania
Department of Environmental Resources
Bureau of Air Quality Control
(717) 787-9702

Rhode Island
Department of Environmental Management
Division of Air Resources
(401) 277-2808

South Carolina
Department of Health and
Environmental Control
Bureau of Air Quality Control
(803) 734-4750

South Dakota
Department of Environment and Natural Resources
Point Source Control Program
(605) 773-3351

Tennessee
Department of Environment and Conservation
Division of Air Pollution Control
(615) 532-0554

Texas
Natural Resource Conservation Commission
Air Quality Office
(512) 239-1000

Utah
Department of Environmental Quality
Division of Air Quality
(801) 536-4000

Vermont
Agency of Natural Resources
Air Pollution Control Division
(802) 241-3840

Virginia
Office of Environmental Quality
Air Division
(804) 786-2378

Washington
Department of Ecology
Air Quality Program
(206) 407-6800

West Virginia
Division of Environmental Protection
Office of Air Quality
(304) 558-4022

Wisconsin
Department of Natural Resources
Bureau of Air Management
(608) 266-7718

Wyoming
Department of Environmental Quality
Air Quality Division
(307) 777-7391

The Worst Corporate Polluters

EVERY YEAR THE COUNCIL on Economic Priorities releases its list of America's top environmental offenders. The CEP is a non-profit research organization that analyzes the social and environmental records of corporations.

The CEP has listed the following companies as the greatest environmental offenders in 1995, and has offered them the following suggestions:

Exxon
Cooperate with organizations seeking to improve environmental policies and practices; release worldwide environmental data, as the majority of earnings are produced outside the U.S.; improve safety precautions at all chemical plants; substantially reduce toxic releases at Yellowstone refinery.

International Paper
Reduce overall toxic releases; improve compliance on air permit releases; commit to the complete phasing out of chlorine bleach; increase use of post-consumer fiber; replace clear cutting with selective harvesting.

MAXXAM
Develop an environmental policy, and report progress annually; cease timber harvesting in the Headwaters Forest; reduce emissions and deepwell injection at Mulberry, Florida, facility; reduce the releases of toxic chemicals by half.

The Southern Company
Reduce CO_2 emissions; investigate the potential of renewable resources (solar, wind, water).

Texaco
Disclose full study on the environmental impact of operations in Ecuador, and commit to thorough cleanup; establish a fund for the health screening and monitoring of Ecuadorian people living in affected communities; release information on safety procedures for workers and local communities near Texaco facilities; release worldwide environmental data, as substantial earnings are generated outside the U.S.

Union Carbide
Establish a timetable for Bhopal hospital, including plans to finance hospital upkeep and ensure long-term care for victims; reduce OSHA violations; interact and cooperate with employees and community groups to ensure worker and community safety; improve spill record; make available all ground water contamination data.

Westinghouse
Reduce toxic releases; improve compliance in correcting OSHA violations; develop corporate-wide environmental programs; develop procedures that ensure clients are promptly notified of problems with nuclear equipment; develop guidelines to make sure waste management facility placement does not discriminate against low-income or minority citizens.

Westvaco
Reduce toxic releases; disclose information about timber harvesting practices; employ selective cutting and phase out clear cutting; commit to completely phasing out chlorine bleach.

Source: Council on Economic Priorities

Contact Option

Council on Economic Priorities
30 Irving Pl.
New York, NY 10003
(212) 420-1133

Pollution Control Loan Program

THE SBA'S POLLUTION CONTROL Loan Program provides financial assistance to small businesses for the planning, design, or installation of a pollution control facility. Eligible businesses must be for-profit operations and must qualify as small according to the criteria set by the SBA's size standards; loans cannot be made to businesses involved in the creation or distribution of ideas or opinions, or those engaged in investment in rental real estate.

A pollution control loan can be used to finance the planning, design, or installation of a "pollution control facility." Such a facility is defined as:

• Real or personal property which is likely to help prevent, reduce, abate, or control noise, air, or

water pollution or contamination, by removing, altering, disposing of, or storing pollutants, contaminants, wastes, or heat.

• Real or personal property which will be used for the collection, storage, treatment, utilization, processing, or final disposal of solid or liquid waste.

• Any related recycling property when a local, state, or federal environmental regulatory agency says it will be useful for pollution control.

Contact Option

Small Business Answer Desk
(202) 205-7717, or (800) 827-5722 or
(202) 205-7701 for recorded information

Productivity

PRODUCTIVITY EXPRESSES the relationship between the quantity of goods and services produced—output—and the quantity of labor, capital, land, energy, and other resources that produced it—input.

Productivity is a key element in analyzing an economy. It demonstrates both the efficiency of industry and the wealth-generating capability of the economy.

The best-known measure of productivity relates output to the input of labor time: output per hour, or its reciprocal unit labor requirements. This kind of measure is used widely because labor productivity is relevant to most economic analyses, and because labor is the most easily measured input. Relating output to labor input provides a tool not only for analyzing productivity but also for examining labor costs, real income, and employment trends.

Trends in Productivity Growth

Productivity growth varies among individual industries. Large increases reflect many factors, including new technologies, advanced production methods, and increased output with economies of scale.

U.S. productivity growth has trailed that of other major industrial countries.

The absolute level of U.S. productivity, unlike its growth trend, is still ahead of that of other major industrial countries. Although the United States has the lowest rate of change in real domestic product per employed person among major industrialized countries, it still has the highest level of gross domestic product per employed person. The gap continues to shrink, however.

Productivity (cont'd)

Relative Levels in Real Gross Domestic Product per Employed Person, Selected Countries

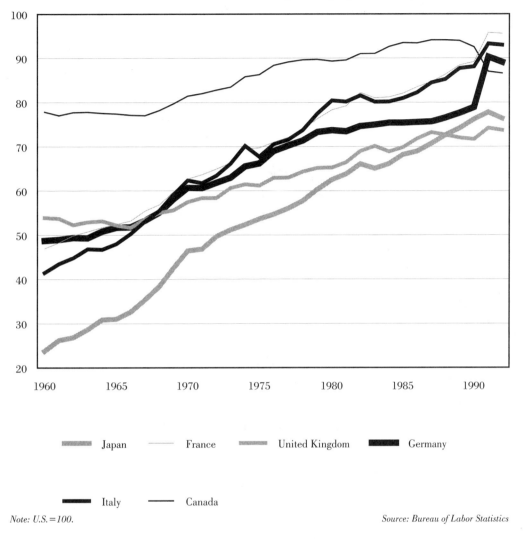

Japan — France — United Kingdom — Germany

Italy — Canada

Note: U.S.=100.   *Source: Bureau of Labor Statistics*

The Top Reference Sources

Who Knows What
Henry Holt, $27.50
(800) 488-5233

Written by Daniel Starer, this 1,239-page reference contains names of thousands of experts and
organizations for business information on any sub-

ject, from abrasives to yarn.
    Organized alphabetically, sections provide
resource information for individual industries,
states, and selected topics. A subject index is provided, along with an index of associations, periodicals, and companies.

Productivity (cont'd)

Trends in Real Gross Domestic Product per Employed Person, Selected Countries

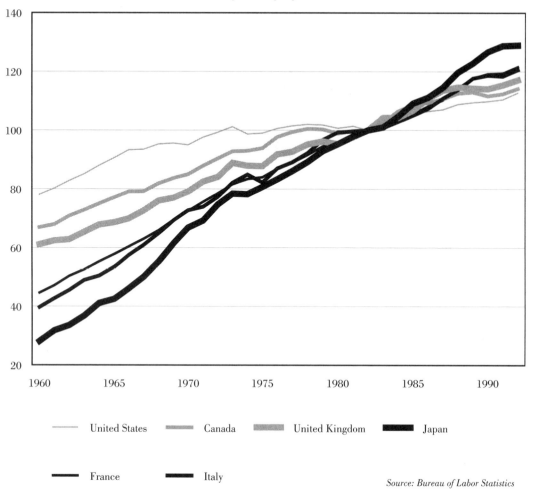

United States   Canada   United Kingdom   Japan

France   Italy

Source: Bureau of Labor Statistics

The Top Reference Sources

Lesko's Info Power
Information USA, $39.95
(800) 955-7693

Matthew Lesko's superb compilation of over 30,000 free and low-cost sources of information is an indispensable reference for use at home or at work.

Chapters provide information sources on consumer power, vacation and business travel, government financial help to individuals, investments and financial services, taxes, health and medicine, arts and humanities, housing and real estate, careers and workplace, law, science and technology, environment, patents, business and industry, and many more.

Research & Development

Corporate and Federal Spending on Industrial R&D Performance, 1992 ($ millions)

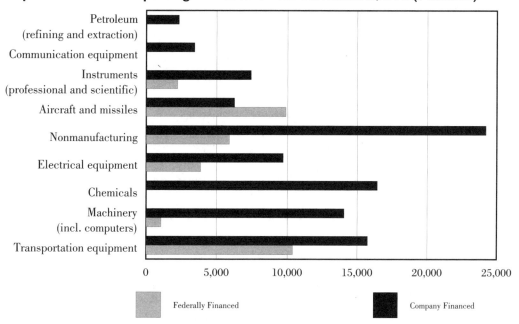

Percent of U.S. GDP Spent on Research and Development

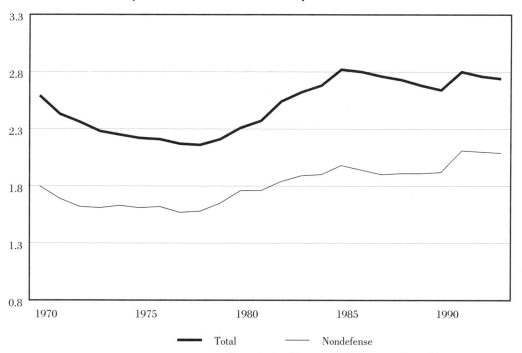

Source: National Patterns of R&D Resources, National Science Foundation

Industry Growth Rates

MODEST GROWTH IS PROJECTED for basic materials industries, including rubber, chemicals, plastic products, and wood products. High-tech sectors, such as computers and semiconductors, have favorable outlooks, especially when the growth rates of individual industries are compared. Motor vehicles and parts industries are recovering, with much of the strength coming from rising sales of light trucks.

The aerospace industry will continue to decline in shipments as a result of defense spending reductions and a leveling off in backlogs for large commercial aircraft; however, production levels for large commercial aircraft will still be at relatively high levels. Consumer durables should continue to improve.

Percent Change in Yearly Growth Rates for Selected Industries

Sector	1988-89	1989-90	1990-91	1991-92	1992-93	1993-94 (est.)
Construction	-1.3	-2.9	-9.2	7.3	3.0	1.9
Food and beverages	-1.9	1.0	1.4	1.0	1.3	1.0
Wood products	-1.1	-3.0	-5.9	4.9	0.2	2.3
Paper and allied products	1.7	0.2	0.0	1.0	0.5	3.0
Chemicals	1.1	3.6	-2.6	-0.6	-0.1	1.4
Rubber and plastic products	2.7	2.4	-1.5	1.2	3.6	4.7
Construction materials	-0.1	0.8	-8.0	3.3	0.4	0.8
Steel mill products	-2.6	-1.5	-7.8	8.4	5.0	2.5
Production machinery	4.7	-1.0	-8.1	-2.8	2.8	3.9
Metalworking equipment	7.4	-1.7	-9.7	0.1	7.4	5.7
Electrical equipment	-0.5	-2.5	-6.3	-1.2	2.0	3.8
Electronic components	4.3	3.4	8.8	13.4	13.1	11.1
Computers	-4.8	-1.3	-7.3	6.1	7.8	5.9
Telecommunications and navigation equipment	-4.7	5.5	-2.9	-2.9	-2.2	-2.6
Motor vehicles and parts	-0.8	-7.2	-6.6	4.9	9.6	6.4
Aerospace	2.6	6.4	0.1	-0.5	-11.0	-11.0
Instruments, controls, and medical equipment	-1.2	1.5	3.0	4.1	5.0	5.2
Durable consumer goods	0.3	-1.1	-3.3	4.6	4.0	3.3
Printing and publishing	-1.2	0.6	-4.0	-0.8	1.1	1.9

Source: U.S. Industrial Outlook, 1994

Ten Fastest-Growing Manufacturing Industries (% Change in Yearly Growth)

Industry	% Change 1993-94
Machine tools, metal-cutting types	12.8
Electronic components and accessories	11.1
Surgical appliances	10.0
Mobile homes	9.4
Automotive parts and accessories	7.7
Surgical and medical instruments	7.0
Lighting fixtures	6.6
Mattresses and bedsprings	6.4
Leather tanning and finishing	6.0
Analytical instruments	6.0

Source: U.S. Industrial Outlook, 1994

Ten Slowest-Growing Manufacturing Industries (% Change in Yearly Growth)

Industry	% Change 1993-94
Aircraft parts and equipment	-24.3
Aircraft engines and engine parts	-20.0
Aircraft	-11.3
Search and navigation equipment	-6.6
Ship building and repairing	-6.6
Space propulsion units and parts	-5.3
Personal leather goods	-5.2
Manifold business forms	-5.0
Phosphatic fertilizers	-4.8
Space vehicle equipment	-3.9

Source: U.S. Industrial Outlook, 1994

Industry Growth Rates (cont'd)

Forecast Growth Rates for Manufacturing Industries (Ranked by Compound Growth Rate)

Rank	Industry	(%) Growth Rate 1993-94	(%) Compound Annual Growth 1987-94
1	Fluid meters and counting devices	1.0	11.4
2	X-ray apparatus and tubes	5.0	11.3
3	Diagnostic substances	2.0	10.9
4	Electronic components and accessories	11.1	9.3
5	Motorcycles, bicycles, and parts	2.6	8.7
6	Surgical appliances and supplies	10.0	7.9
7	Space vehicle equipment	-3.9	7.6
8	Plastic plumbing fixtures	4.0	7.3
9	Electromedical equipment	0.2	7.1
10	Medicinals and botanicals	1.9	7.1
11	Surgical and medical instruments	7.0	6.1
12	Analytical instruments	6.0	6.0
13	Biological products, except diagnostic	1.9	5.9
14	Household audio and video equipment	2.0	5.6
15	Household vacuum cleaners	3.0	5.1
16	Mobile homes	9.4	5.0
17	Sporting and athletic goods	3.4	4.9
18	Ophthalmic goods	2.0	4.5
19	Synthetic rubber	3.0	4.1
20	Soap and other detergents	2.0	4.0
21	Dental equipment and supplies	3.5	3.8
22	Radio and TV communications equipment	2.2	3.7
23	Household appliances	4.1	3.3
24	Packaging machinery	3.9	3.3
25	Mattresses and bedsprings	6.4	3.3
26	Reconstituted wood products	4.0	3.3
27	Oil and gas field machinery	3.1	3.0
28	Electric housewares and fans	2.4	2.9
29	Optical instruments and lenses	4.0	2.9
30	Gypsum products	1.6	2.9
31	Measuring and controlling devices	2.0	2.9
32	Farm machinery and equipment	2.5	2.8
33	Special dies, tools, jigs, and fixtures	4.0	2.5
34	Process control instruments	5.0	2.5
35	Computers and peripherals	5.9	2.5
36	Screw machine products	6.0	2.4
37	Platemaking services	3.5	2.4
38	Industrial inorganic chemicals, except pigments	1.2	2.3
39	Steel mill products	2.5	2.3
40	Fabricated rubber products	3.0	2.3
41	Miscellaneous plastic products except bottles and plumbing	5.0	2.2
42	Upholstered household furniture	4.3	2.2
43	Ceramic wall and floor tile	3.0	2.2
44	Household laundry equipment	4.0	2.2
45	Plastic materials and resins	6.0	2.2
46	Automotive parts and accessories	7.7	2.1
47	Dolls, toys, and games	2.0	2.1
48	Book publishing	3.7	2.1
49	Household refrigerators and freezers	4.4	2.1
50	Agricultural chemicals	2.5	2.0

Source: U.S. Industrial Outlook, 1994

Government Industry Specialists

THESE U.S. GOVERNMENT SPECIALISTS, under the auspices of the Department of Commerce, will provide advice on industry analysis, trade promotion, and trade policy development:

Industry	Contact	Telephone
Aerospace	Sally Bath, Kim Farner, Ronald Green	(202) 482-4222
Apparel	Joanne Tucker	(202) 482-4058
Automotive parts	Mary Anne Slater	(202) 482-1420
Bicycles, motorcycles, boat building, sporting goods	John Vanderwolf	(202) 482-0348
CAD/CAM/CAE	Vera Swann	(202) 482-0396
Chemicals	Stuart Keitz	(202) 482-0128
Computer trends and industries	Joyce Watson	(202) 482-0574
Computers	Timothy Miles	(202) 482-2990
Construction	Patrick MacAuley	(202) 482-0132
Construction materials	Charles Pitcher	(202) 482-0132
Consumer electronics	Howard Fleming	(202) 482-5163
Dairy, bakery, candy and other products; bottled and canned drinks	William Janis	(202) 482-2250
Drugs and biotechnology	William Hurt	(202) 482-0128
Footwear, leather, and leather products	James Byron	(202) 482-4034
General industrial components	Richard Reise	(202) 482-3489
Household appliances	John Harris	(202) 482-1178
Household and office furniture	Donald Hodgen	(202) 482-3346
Industrial and analytical instruments	Marguerite Nealon	(202) 482-3411
Jewelry and musical instruments	John Harris	(202) 482-1178
Lawn and garden	John Vanderwolf	(202) 482-0348
Meat, poultry, fruits, vegetables, and spec. alcoholic beverages	William Janis	(202) 482-2250
Medical equipment/instruments	Matthew Edwards	(202) 482-0550
Medical, dental instruments, and supplies	Victoria Kader	(202) 482-4073
Metal industries	David Cammarota	(202) 482-5157
Metalworking equipment	Megan Pilaroscia	(202) 482-0609
Microelectronics	Margaret Donnelly	(202) 482-5466
Midrange portables	Jonathan Streeter	(202) 482-0480
Motor vehicles	Randy Miller	(202) 482-0669
Paper products	Gary Stanley	(202) 482-0132
Personal computers	R. Clay Woods	(202) 482-3013
Plastics and rubber	Ray Pratt	(202) 482-0128
Printing and publishing	Rose-Marie Bratland	(202) 482-0380
Production machinery	Edward Abrahams	(202) 482-0312
Semiconductor mfg. equipment	Michael Andrews	(202) 482-2795
Semiconductors	Robin Roark	(202) 482-3090
Semiconductors and related devices	Judee Mussehl-Aziz	(202) 482-0429
Software	Mary Smolenski	(202) 482-0551
Supercomputers	Sean Iverson	(202) 482-1987
Superconductors	Roger Chiarodo	(202) 482-0402
Telecommunications and navigation equipment	Alexis Kemper	(202) 482-1512
Telecommunications services	Dan Edwards	(202) 482-4331
Textiles	Basil Kiwan	(202) 482-4058
Textiles (artificial fibers)	Maria Corey	(202) 482-4058
Wood products	Barbara Wise	(202) 482-0375

Critical Technologies

THE DEPARTMENT OF COMMERCE defines a critical technology as one in which research has progressed far enough to indicate a high probability of technical success for new products and applications that might have substantial markets within approximately ten years.

Some critical technologies–usually self-contained products such as new medicines, or processes, such as X-ray lithography–have important, but focused, impacts. Others substantially affect the economy by advancing the technical infrastructure or by improving the quality and efficiency of the manufacturing process. Examples are components of a computer-integrated manufacturing system, such as robots or machining centers or the factory control system itself.

Critical technologies are also important because they will drive the next generation of research and development and spin-off applications. When an industry uses a new technology to design or improve a product, and successfully carries it to the marketplace, that new or improved product becomes the starting point for development of the next generation of products or services.

The Commerce Department has identified the following as critical technologies:

Materials
Advanced Materials
Superconductors

Electronics and Information Systems
Advanced Semiconductor Devices
Digital Imaging Technology
High-Density Data Storage
High-Performance Computing
Optoelectronics

Manufacturing Systems
Artificial Intelligence
Flexible Computer-Integrated Manufacturing
Sensor Technology

Life-Sciences Applications
Biotechnology
Medical Devices and Diagnostics

The Advanced Technology Program

MANAGED BY THE TECHNOLOGY Administration's National Institute of Standards and Technology, the Advanced Technology Program is an industry-driven, cooperative partnership between government and the private sector to advance the nation's competitive position. The purpose of the program, now in its third year, is to assist U.S. companies in creating and applying "generic technology" and research results to help commercialize new technology more quickly and improve manufacturing processes.

The ATP Awards are based on merit as determined through a full and open competition. In December 1992, twenty-one new awards were announced, two thirds of which were for small busi-

nesses. The projects cover a broad spectrum of technology areas, including machine tools, biotechnology, electronics, optics, materials engineering, lighting technology, and refrigeration.

Any business or industrial joint venture may apply for these grants.

Contact Option

Advanced Technology Program
Administration Bldg., Room A430
Rte. 270 & Quince Orchard Rd.
Gaithersburg, MD 20899
(301) 975-2636

CompuServe offers the D&B U.S. Business Locator, a searchable database of nearly 9 million companies, including company addresses, telephone numbers, SIC code, and number of employees. GO DYP.

The Advanced Technology Program (cont'd)

1994 ATP Awards

Company	Description	ATP Award ($ thou.)
Abnormal Situation Management Consortium, Honeywell Technology Center	Collaborative decision support for industrial process control	8,148
3M	Film technologies to replace paint on aircraft	6,126
Kopin	High-information-content display technology	6,097
BP Chemicals	Dual-purpose ceramic membranes	5,200
Consortium for Non-Contact Gauging, Ohio Aerospace Institute	Rapid agile metrology for manufacturing	4,267
Edison Industrial Systems Center	Die-casting technician's digital assistant	3,790
SI Diamond Technology	Diamond diode field emission display process technology development	3,465
Caterpillar	Engineered surfaces for rolling and sliding contacts	2,971
Intermagnetics General	Technologies for HTS components for magnetic resonance applications	2,852
CuraGen	Molecular recognition technology for precise design of protein-specific drugs	2,379
Texas Instruments	Single-chip receiver front-end with integrated filters	2,192
Integrated Surgical Systems	Computer-integrated revision total hip replacement surgery	2,051
Norton Diamond Film & Kennametal	Accelerated commercialization of diamond-coated round tools and wear parts	2,005
VivoRx	Treatment of diabetes by proliferated human islets in photocrosslinkable alginate capsules	2,000
GelTex Pharmaceuticals	Molecular recognition polymers as anti-infectives	2,000
AlliedSignal	Low-cost elastomeric composites with application to vehicle tires	2,000
Union Switch & Signal	Software technology for optimizing on-time performance in the transportation industry	2,000
Energy BioSystems	Process for biocatalytic desulfurization of crude oil	2,000
Progenitor	Application of gene therapy to treatment of cardiovascular diseases	1,996
Cargill	Development of improved functional properties in renewable-resource-based biodegradable plastics	1,994
Catalytica	Development of improved catalysts using nanometer-scale technology	1,994
Moldyn	Enhanced molecular dynamics simulation technology for biotechnology applications	1,988
Texas Instruments	Ultra-low k dielectric materials for high-performance interconnects	1,971
Large Scale Biology	Standardization of 2-D protein analysis using manufacturable gel media	1,902
Calimetrics	High-density and high-speed read-only optical data storage system	1,808
Solarex	Development of rapid thermal processing to produce low-cost solar cells	1,790
Displaytech	FLC/VLSI high-definition image generators	1,748
Laser Power	High-resolution multimedia laser projection display	1,695
Praxair	Advanced sorbents for reducing the cost of oxygen	1,220
Agracetus	Transgenic cotton fiber with polyester qualities via biopolymer genes	1,131
Crucible Compaction Metals Division	Rapid solidification powder metallurgy for high-nitrogen stainless steels	908

Producer Price Index

PRODUCER PRICE INDEXES measure average changes in prices received by domestic producers of commodities in all stages of processing. Most of the information used in calculating the indexes is obtained through the systematic sampling of nearly every industry in the manufacturing and mining sectors of the economy. Because producer price indexes are designed to measure only the change in prices received for the output of domestic industries, imports are not included. The stage-of-processing indexes organize products by class of buyer and degree of fabrication.

Within the stage-of-processing system, finished goods are commodities that will not undergo further processing and are ready for sale to the final individual or business consumer. Finished goods include unprocessed foods such as eggs and fresh vegetables, as well as processed foods such as bakery products and meats. Other finished consumer goods include durable goods such as automobiles, household furniture, and appliances, and nondurable goods such as apparel and home heating oil. Producer durable goods include heavy motor trucks, tractors, and machine tools.

Intermediate materials consist partly of commodities that have been processed but require further processing, such as flour, cotton yarn, steel mill products, and lumber. Nondurables in this category include diesel fuel, paper boxes, and fertilizers. Crude materials are products entering the market for the first time that have not been manufactured and that are not sold directly to consumers, such as grains and livestock. Raw cotton, crude petroleum, coal, hides and skins, and iron and steel scrap are examples of nonfood crude materials. The following chart shows that industrial prices have risen only incrementally in the last couple of years, mainly because of foreign competition and the recession.

Producer Price Indexes by Major Commodity Groups

Commodity	1980	1985	1990	1991	1992	1993	1994
All commodities	89.8	103.2	116.3	116.5	117.2	118.9	120.4
Farm products	102.9	95.1	112.2	105.7	103.6	107.0	119.1
Processed foods and feeds	95.9	103.5	121.9	121.9	122.1	124.0	125.5
Textile products and apparel	89.7	102.9	114.9	116.3	117.8	118.1	118.2
Hides, skins, and leather products	94.7	108.9	141.7	138.9	140.4	143.6	148.5
Fuels and related products and power	82.8	91.4	82.2	81.2	80.4	80.0	77.8
Chemicals and allied products	89.0	103.7	123.6	125.6	125.9	128.2	132.1
Rubber and plastic products	90.1	101.9	113.6	115.1	115.1	116.0	117.6
Lumber and wood products	101.5	106.6	129.7	132.1	146.6	174.0	180.1
Pulp, paper, and allied products	86.3	113.3	141.3	142.9	145.2	147.3	152.4
Metals and metal products	95.0	104.4	123.0	120.2	119.2	119.2	124.8
Machinery and equipment	86.0	107.2	120.7	123.0	123.4	124.0	125.1
Furniture and household durables	90.7	107.1	119.1	121.2	122.2	123.6	126.1
Nonmetallic mineral products	88.4	108.6	114.7	117.2	117.3	120.0	124.1
Transportation equipment	82.9	107.9	121.5	126.4	130.4	133.7	137.1
Miscellaneous products	93.6	109.4	134.2	140.8	145.3	145.5	141.8

Note: The average for the year 1982 is set to equal 100.   *Source: Department of Commerce, Bureau of Economic Analysis*

E-MAIL

Producer Price Indexes. Send e-mail to producer@almanac.yoyo.com. See p. xi for instructions.

A detailed table of producer price indexes for selceted commodities.

Purchasing Benchmarks

PURCHASING PERFORMANCE AND effectiveness has become one of the most closely watched economic indicators. The following chart is a comparison of select companies' total purchasing (dollars spent with vendors) as a percent of corporate sales in selected industries. For complete data on purchasing benchmarks, contact the Center for Advanced Purchasing Studies, an affiliate of the National Association of Purchasing Management, at (602) 752-2277.

Total Purchasing Dollars as a Percent of Sales, Selected Industries

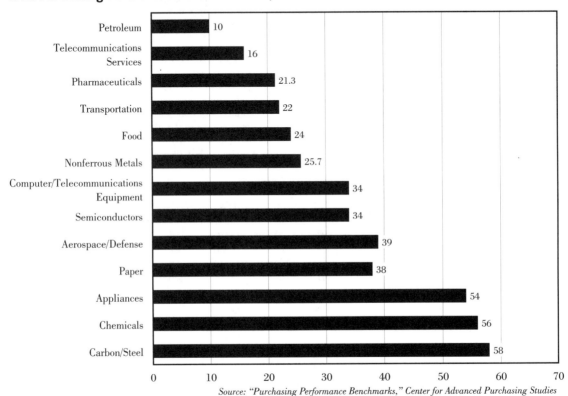

Source: "Purchasing Performance Benchmarks," Center for Advanced Purchasing Studies

Warehousing

A NATIONAL STUDY BY Tompkins Associates reveals a number of interesting trends and conditions:

- Warehousing is still a very labor-intensive industry with great room for productivity improvements.

- The average warehouse is approximately 50,000 square feet with an average clear height of 22 feet.

- The age of the average warehouse is 19 years. New construction is prohibitively expensive.

- Few warehouses have ventured beyond basic material handling and storage methods.

- The pressure to computerize the warehouse is great, but the level of understanding of need, benefit, and specific requirements is low. A total of 85 percent of warehouses responding in the Tompkins Associates survey maintain inventory data on computer and 68 percent have a computerized stock location system. And 33 percent of warehouses surveyed use bar codes.

Source: Tompkins Associates

Warehousing (cont'd)

The Public Warehouse Alternative

As warehousing costs continue to rise, public warehouses are more and more seen as a viable alternative. Jim McBride, president of Affiliated Warehouse Companies, estimates that public warehousing accounts for 16 percent of current warehousing needs. Criteria to be evaluated in selecting a public warehouse include:

- Financial stability
- Management depth
- Sanitation
- Facilities
- Rates
- Interest in the account
- Reputation
- Delivery capabilities
- Consolidations
- Ownership
- Similar accounts
- Building ownership
- Labor
- Security
- Data processing capabilities
- Contents insurance rate
- Legal liability insurance
- Taxes
- Location.

Source: Affiliated Warehouse Companies

Average Warehouse Rates in Major Cities as of Fourth Quarter, 1994

Market	Price/sq. ft. ($)	Rent/sq. ft./ yr. ($)
Atlanta	28.56	3.87
Baltimore	32.39	3.81
Boston	38.50	5.03
Chicago	35.72	5.22
Cincinnati	27.56	3.86
Cleveland	26.26	4.13
Columbus	30.60	3.56
Dallas	30.88	4.38
Denver	27.17	3.71
Detroit	31.80	5.01
Indianapolis	30.05	3.75
Los Angeles	36.83	4.63
Miami	39.21	4.52
Milwaukee	28.94	4.27
Minneapolis	32.71	5.79

Market	Price/sq. ft. ($)	Rent/sq. ft./ yr. ($)
New York	37.84	5.08
Norfolk	31.83	4.39
N. New Jersey	37.60	5.62
Philadelphia	33.28	4.03
Phoenix	28.81	3.69
Pittsburgh	30.12	3.92
Portland	30.48	4.65
Sacramento	31.42	3.69
St. Louis	25.32	3.74
San Antonio	21.95	3.12
San Diego	37.24	4.94
San Francisco	43.71	5.53
Seattle	42.05	5.26
Tampa	28.04	4.11
Washington, DC	36.05	5.25

Source: National Real Estate Index, published by Koll; Editorial Adviser, Ernst & Young

Prices and rents above represent Class A (i.e., space built or substantially renovated in the preceding ten years) warehouse/distribution space at the metropolitan level. Reported rents are effective gross (i.e., after concessions, if any). New York rates are for Nassau-Suffolk counties.

Contact Options

National Real Estate Index
1900 Powell St.
Emeryville, CA 94608
(800) 992-7257

Tompkins Associates
2809 Millbrook Rd., #200
Raleigh, NC 27604
(919) 876-3667

Tompkins Associates is an engineering-based consulting firm that specializes in distribution, warehousing, manufacturing, maintenance, organizational excellence, material handling, and facilities planning and layout.

TIP: *Robert Morris Associates and the American Institute of CPAs have developed a 32-page credit information package that could expedite the loan process for business borrowers. Call (215) 851-0585.*

Recommended Trade Journals

Adhesives Age
Argus Business
6151 Powers Ferry Rd., NW
Atlanta, GA 30339
(404) 955-2500

Advanced Material and Processes
ASM International
Materials Park, OH 44073
(216) 338-5151

American Printer
Maclean Hunter Publishing
29 N. Wacker Dr.
Chicago, IL 60606
(312) 726-2802

Appliance Manufacturer
5900 Harper Rd., Suite 105
Solon, OH 44139
(216) 349-3060

Automotive Industries
Chilton
Chilton Way
Radnor, PA 19089
(610) 964-4245

Automotive News
Crain Communications
1400 Woodbridge
Detroit, MI 48207
(313) 446-6000

Aviation Week and Space Technology
P.O. Box 503
Hightstown, NJ 08520
(800) 257-9402

Bakery Production and Marketing
Cahners Publishing
455 N. Cityfront Plaza Dr.
Chicago, IL 60611
(312) 222-2000

Beverage Industry
Stagnito Publishing
1935 Shermer Rd., Suite 100
Northbrook, IL 60062
(708) 205-5660

Chemical Engineering News
American Chemical Society
1155 16th St., NW
Washington, DC 20036
(202) 872-4600

Chilton's Food Engineering
Chilton
Chilton Way
Radnor, PA 19089
(610) 964-4445

Datamation
Cahners Publishing
275 Washington St.
Newton, MA 02158
(617) 964-3030

Designfax
29100 Aurora Rd., #200
Solon, OH 44139
(216) 248-1125

Distribution
Chilton
Chilton Way
Radnor, PA 19089
(610) 964-4386

Electronic Design
Penton Publishing
611 Rte. 46 W
Hasbrouck Heights, NJ 07604
(201) 393-6060

EDN (Electronic Design News)
Cahners Publishing
275 Washington St.
Newton, MA 02158
(617) 964-3030

Electronic Products
Harris Business Publishing
645 Stewart Ave.
Garden City, NY 11530
(516) 227-1300

Food Processing
Putnam Publishing
301 E. Erie St.
Chicago, IL 60611
(312) 644-2020

Industrial Engineering
Institute of Industrial Engineers
25 Technology Park
Norcross, GA 30092
(404) 449-0461

Industrial Maintenance and Plant Operation
Chilton
Chilton Way
Radnor, PA 19089
(610) 964-4041

Recommended Trade Journals (cont'd)

Industrial Products Bulletin
Gordon Publications
301 Gibraltar Dr.
Morris Plains, NJ 07950
(201) 361-9060

Instrumentation and Automation News
Chilton
Chilton Way
Radnor, PA 19089
(610) 964-4401

Industry Week
Penton Publishing
1100 Superior Ave.
Cleveland, OH 44114
(216) 696-7000

Iron Age
Chilton
191 S. Gary Ave.
Carol Stream, IL 60188
(708) 665-1000

Journal of Manufacturing Systems
Society of Manufacturing Engineers
P.O. Box 930
Dearborn, MI 48121
(313) 271-1500

Machine Design
Penton Publishing
1100 Superior Ave.
Cleveland, OH 44114
(216) 696-7000

Materials Handling Engineering
Penton Publishing
1100 Superior Ave.
Cleveland, OH 44114
(216) 696-7000

Mechanical Engineering
American Society of Mechanical Engineers
22 Law Dr.
Fairfield, NJ 07007
(800) 843-2763

Metal Fabricating News
Metal Fabricating Institute
P.O. Box 1178
Rockford, IL 61105
(815) 965-4031

Mining Engineering
Society of Mining Engineers
8307 Shaffer Pkwy.
Littleton, CO 80127
(303) 973-9550

Modern Materials Handling
Cahners Publishing
275 Washington St.
Newton, MA 02158
(617) 964-3030

Modern Plastics
P.O. Box 602
Hightstown, NJ 08520
(800) 257-9402

New Equipment Digest
Penton Publishing
1100 Superior Ave.
Cleveland, OH 44114
(216) 696-7000

Packaging
Cahners Publishing
1350 E. Touhy Ave.
P.O. Box 5080
Des Plaines, IL 60017
(708) 635-8800

Packaging Digest
Cahners Publishing
455 N. Cityfront Plaza Dr.
Chicago, IL 60611
(312) 222-2000

Paper Maker
Maclean Hunter Publishing
57 Executive Park S.
Atlanta, GA 30329
(404) 325-9153

Plant Engineering
Cahners Publishing
1350 E. Touhy Ave.
P.O. Box 5080
Des Plaines, IL 60017
(708) 635-8800

Prepared Foods
Cahners Publishing
455 N. Cityfront Plaza Dr.
Chicago, IL 60611
(312) 222-2000

Pulp and Paper
Miller Freeman Publications
600 Harrison St.
San Francisco, CA 94107
(415) 905-2200

Purchasing Magazine
Cahners Publishing
275 Washington St.
Newton, MA 02158
(216) 696-7000

Recommended Trade Journals (cont'd)

Quality Progress
ASQC
611 E. Wisconsin Ave.
Milwaukee, WI 53202
(414) 272-8575

Textile World
Maclean Hunter Publishing
4170 Ashford-Dunwoody Road, Suite 420
Atlanta, GA 30319
(404) 847-2770

Wood Technology
Miller Freeman Publications
600 Harrison St.
San Francisco, CA 94107
(415) 905-2200

Major Standards Developers

THE NATIONAL CENTER FOR Standards and Certification Information (NCSCI) is part of the National Institute of Standards and Technology, and provides information on national and voluntary standards, government regulations, and rules of certification for nonagricultural products. The Center serves as a referral service in the United States for information about standards and standards-related matters. It contributes to the Institute's goals of improving U.S. competitiveness in domestic and world markets by advancing the use of the nation's science and technology through providing up-to-date information on standards and certification programs. According to the Center, the following are among the major standards developers in the country:

Aerospace Industries Association
1250 I St., NW, Suite 1100
Washington, DC 20005
(202) 371-8400

American Association of Cereal Chemists
3340 Pilot Knob Rd.
St. Paul, MN 55121
(612) 454-7250

American Association of State Highway and
Transportation Officials
444 N. Capitol St., NW, Suite 249
Washington, DC 20001
(202) 624-5800

American Conference of Governmental
Industrial Hygienists
1330 Kemper Meadow Dr.
Cincinnati, OH 45240
(513) 742-2020

American National Standards Institute
11 W. 42nd St., 13th Floor
New York, NY 10036
(212) 642-4900

American Oil Chemists' Society
1608 Broadmoor Dr.
Champaign, IL 61821
(217) 359-2344

American Petroleum Institute
1220 L St., NW
Washington, DC 20005
(202) 682-8000

American Railway Engineering Association
50 F St., NW, Suite 7702
Washington, DC 20001
(202) 639-2190

American Society of Mechanical Engineers
345 E. 47th St.
New York, NY 10017
(212) 705-7722

American Society for Testing and Materials
1916 Race St.
Philadelphia, PA 19103
(215) 299-5585

Association of Official Analytical Chemists
2200 Wilson Blvd., Suite 400
Arlington, VA 22201
(703) 522-3032

Cosmetic, Toiletry and Fragrance Association
1101 17th St., NW, Suite 300
Washington, DC 20036
(202) 331-1770

Electronic Industries Association
c/o Global Engineering
1990 M St., NW, Suite 400
Washington, DC 20036
(800) 854-7179

Major Standards Developers (cont'd)

Institute of Electrical and Electronics Engineers
445 Hoes Ln.
P.O. Box 1331
Piscataway, NJ 08855
(800) 678-4333

National Fire Protection Association
1 Batterymarch Park
P.O. Box 9101
Quincy, MA 02269
(617) 770-3000

SAE International
400 Commonwealth Dr.
Warrendale, PA 15096
(412) 776-4841

Technical Association of the Pulp and
Paper Industry
15 Technology Pkwy. S.
P.O. Box 105113
Norcross, GA 30092
(404) 446-1400

U.S. Pharmacopeial Convention
12601 Twinbrook Pkwy.
Rockville, MD 20852
(301) 881-0666

Underwriters Laboratories
333 Pfingsten Rd.
Northbrook, IL 60062
(708) 272-8800

Contact Option

The National Center for Standards and
Certification Information
National Institute of Standards and Technology
Building 411, Room A163
Gaithersburg, MD 20899
(301) 975-4040

The Top Reference Sources

*The Directory of Industrial Design
in the United States*
Van Nostrand Reinhold, $49.95
(800) 842-3636

This directory is a comprehensive reference
to the field of industrial design. The information

presented allows readers to make discriminating
choices among consulting firms, design departments, schools, institutions, organizations, and
resources listed.

Detailed information is carried in the profiles;
product category and name entries are cross-
referenced with the profiles.

Major Industrial Design Awards

Industrial Design Excellence Awards

Presented each year by the Industrial Designers Society of America and sponsored by *Business Week* magazine, the IDEA is the nation's most coveted annual accolade for industrial design–from computers to packaging, toys to cars. A list of the most recent winners is included in this chapter.

IDEA/IDSA
1142 Walker Rd., Suite E
Great Falls, VA 22066
(703) 759-0100

I.D. Annual Design Review

I.D. (International Design) magazine presents this most comprehensive design award in categories such as consumer products, graphics, environments, furniture, equipment, packaging, surfaces, concepts, and student work.

I.D.
Design Review Editor
440 Park Ave. S.
New York, NY 10016
(212) 447-1400

Nesté Forma Finlandia Plastics Design

Prizes include a first prize of 300,000 Finnish Markka (about $70,000) in this popular international plastics design competition, sponsored by Nesté, one of Scandinavia's largest companies. Entries are considered in two categories: "Tomorrow's Challengers," for new, previously unpublished plastics product ideas; and "The World's Best Plastic Products," recognizing products that have been on the market for less than three years. The "working language" of the competition is English.

Nesté Forma Finlandia 3
P.O. Box 20
02151 Espoo, Finland
358-0-450-5044

International Design Competition, Osaka

This biennial competition sponsored by the Japan Design Foundation aims to question "the role of design in clarifying visions of the future of humankind in the 21st century" by inviting designers to enter imaginative works from a broad range of design fields. Each competition focuses on a singular theme, such as "wind," "air," or "terra." Prizes include a Grand Prize/Prime Minister's Prize of $35,000. Official languages for the award are Japanese and English.

International Design Competition, Osaka
Japan Design Foundation
3-1-800 Umeda 1-Chome
Kita-ku, Osaka 530
Japan
[81] (6) 346-2611

1994 IDEA Gold Award Winners

Automatch
Credit: Group Four Design, Avon, CT
Client: Macbeth, Newburg, NY

Backpack Personal Cooling System
Credit: Carlson Technology, Livonia, MI
Client: U.S. Army Natick Research, Development, Natick, MA

Flat Panel Display
Credit: ZIBA Design, Portland, OR;
Hewlett-Packard, Fort Collins, CO
Client: Hewlett-Packard, Fort Collins, CO

Kin-der-Link
Credit: Skools, New York, NY;
Autumn House, Granite Falls, NC;
Marshall Group, New Bern, NC
Client: Skools, New York, NY

Newton Message Pad 100
Credit: Apple Computer, Cupertino, CA
Client: Apple Computer, Cupertino, CA

PE 3000 Series Pallet Truck
Credit: Crown Design and Engineering, New Bremen, OH;
Fitch, Columbus, OH;
Design Central, Columbus, OH
Client: Crown Equipment, New Bremen, OH

PowerShot Staple Gun
Credit: Innovation & Development, Edgewater, NJ;
Work Tools, Chatsworth, CA;
Black & Decker , Towson, MD
Client: Black & Decker, Towson, MD

Rotary Cutter
Credit: Fiskars, Madison, WI
Client: Fiskars, Wausau, WI

The Measure of Man and Woman
Credit: Henry Dreyfuss Associates, New York, NY
Client: Henry Dreyfuss Associates, New York, NY

The Raynes Rail
Credit: Coco Raynes Associates, Boston, MA; New England Plastics, Woburn, MA;
Milgo Bufkin, Brooklyn, NY
Client: Massachusetts Eye and Ear Infirmary, Boston, MA

Major Industrial Design Awards (cont'd)

Tranquillity MP-r
Credit: Machen Montague/BOLT, Charlotte, NC;
Healthdyne Technologies, Marietta, GA
Client: Healthdyne Technologies, Marietta, GA

Transgenerational Design
Credit: James J Pirkl Design, Placitas, NM;
Van Nostrand Reinhold, New York, NY
Client: Van Nostrand Reinhold, New York, NY

U-Prog Mobil Workstation
Credit: Cleveland Institute of Art, Cleveland, OH
Client: Cleveland Institute of Art, Cleveland, OH

United States Holocaust Memorial Museum
Credit: Ralph Appelbaum Assoc., New York, NY;
Time Warner, New York, NY
Client: U.S. Holocaust Memorial Museum,
Washington, DC

Vision Date
Credit: Henry Dreyfuss Associates, New York, NY;
Polaroid, Cambridge, MA
Client: Polaroid, Cambridge, MA

VXR-12 Film Digitizer
Credit: Paradigm, Philadelphia, PA;
Vidar Systems, Herndon, VA
Client: Vidar Systems, Herndon, VA

Wieland Furniture Exhibit
Credit: Kane Design, San Francisco, CA
Client: Weiland Furniture, Grabill, IN

Zephyr Hammock
Credit: Gray Wolf Architects, Boston, MA;
Heliotrope, Providence, RI
Client: Heliotrope, Providence, RI

1994 I.D. Annual Design Review Winners (Best of Category)

Consumer Products
Philishave HS 190 Shaver, Philips Domestic Appliances and Personal Care, Groningen, Netherlands
Newton Message Pad 110 and Charging Station, Apple Computer, Cupertino, CA

Packaging
Paradice Ice Bag, Paradice, Eagan, MN
Program for The Tea Box at Takashimaya,
Takashimaya, New York, NY
Morningstar Binder, Morningstar, Chicago, IL

Environments
Aiding Awareness: Women's Stories, ARTSPACE,
New Haven, CT
U.S. Holocaust Memorial Museum, Washington, DC

Furniture
Surf Board Corner Unit, The Knoll Group,
New York, NY

Students
OHM Scooter, Achim Anscheidt, Joe Tan, students,
Art Center College of Design, Pasadena, CA

Recommended Resources

Deadlines
P.O. Box 3449
Alexandria, VA 22302
(703) 578-4918
 This monthly newsletter publishes announcements and deadline information for all national and international design competitions and award programs open to U.S. architects and designers.

Design Access
National Building Museum
401 F St., NW
Washington, DC 20001
(202) 272-5427
 Newly established by the National Endowment for the Arts and the National Building Museum, the Design Access database maintains information on all aspects of design, including industrial and product design, architecture, urban design and planning, graphic design, historic preservation, and landscape architecture.

The Top Reference Sources

Hoover's Handbook of American Business
The Reference Press, $39.95
(800) 486-8666

This annual reference book profiles 500 business enterprises based in the United States. The book should be of interest to anyone who invests in,

buys from, sells to, competes with, interviews with, or works for a large company in the U.S.
 The profiles include brief histories, names of officers and human resources contacts, headquarters address and telephone numbers, sales figures, income, markets, stock prices, products, affiliates and subsidiaries, key competitors, and rankings.

Patent Licensors

LICENSING IS THE PROCESS of transferring intellectual property (copyrights, patents, trademarks, trade secrets, business information, etc.) from one business, individual, or organization to another. The Licensing Executive Society, is a professional society of more than 3,200 members (scientists, engineers, lawyers, marketers, and licensing consultants), most of whom are engaged on behalf of their employers or clients in the transfer of intellectual property. These licensing professionals may provide a number of business services, including:

- Identifying potential markets and licenses;

- Evaluating and packaging licensable intellectual property;

- Funding research and development of intellectual property;

- Protecting the intellectual property to be licensed;

- Monitoring the flow of intellectual property and the payment of royalties;

- Determining what intellectual property rights should be licensed;

- Negotiating reasonable terms between the licensor (seller) and licensee (buyer) and drafting an appropriate license agreement which authorizes the use of intellectual property rights.

Source: Licensing Executive Society

Contact Options

The following consultants have been selected based on technical interests and the range of services provided. Each is a member of the Licensing Executive Society:

Denton Anderson
Sheldon & Mak
225 S. Lake Ave., Ninth Floor
Pasadena, CA 91101
(818) 796-4000
Medical technology, mechanical devices

James D. Donovan, President
Intercon Research Associates
6865 Lincoln Ave.
Lincolnwood, IL 60646
(708) 982-1101
Pharmaceutical, chemical, and medical

C. Richard Goodlet, Vice President
UC Industries
137 East Ave., P.O. Box 395
Tallmadge, OH 44278
(216) 633-1105
Plastics, building materials, specialized machinery

James E. Malackowski
IPC Group
101 N. Wacker Dr., Suite 1600
Chicago, IL 60606
(312) 641-0051
Automotive, electronics

William R. Mattson, Jr., President
The Mattson Jack Group
9 The Pines Court, Suite A
St. Louis, MO 63141
(314) 469-7600
Pharmaceuticals and health care

Jerry S. Oakes, CEO
Synergy Consultants
2915 LBJ Fwy., Suite 254
Dallas, TX 75234
(214) 243-1000
Software, manufacturing

Edward G. Tutle, President
Tutle International Technology Marketing
2601 Seabreeze Court
Orlando, FL 32805
(407) 423-8016
Manufacturing, communications technology

Terry N. Taschner, President & C.E.O.
BIEC International
3400 Bath Pike, Park Plaza
Bethlehem, PA 18017
(610) 694-0970
Steelmaking

Dominic Yen, Director
Yen Enterprises
1360 W. Ninth St., #210
Cleveland, OH 44113
(216) 621-5115
Industrial machinery, automotive products, chemicals

Manufacturing Apprenticeships

WHILE A NUMBER OF GOVERNMENT programs are now in place to make the school-to-work transition a more productive process for American workers and industry, a few U.S. companies may be said to be at the forefront of an industry-driven apprenticeship movement. Among them are:

Robert Bosch
38000 Hills Tech Dr.
Farmington Hills, MI 48331
(810) 553-9000

Corning
Human Resources Training Group
1 Riverfront Plaza, W2-H26
Corning, NY 14831
(607) 974-9000

Milford Fabricating
19200 Glendale Ave.
Detroit, MI 48223
(313) 272-8400

Remmele Engineering
10 Old Hwy. 8, SW
New Brighton, MN 55112
(612) 635-4189

Siemens
1301 Ave. of the Americas
New York, NY 10019
(212) 258-4046

Jobs for the Future

Jobs for the Future is a non-profit group that promotes workforce quality and helps to sponsor youth apprenticeship sites, along with state, school district, and industry support. The following programs are current and may be of particular interest to manufacturers:

Craftsmanship 2000
616 S. Boston
Tulsa, OK 74119
(918) 585-1201

Pennsylvania Youth Apprenticeship Program
Pennsylvania Department of Education
333 Market St., Tenth Floor
Harrisburg, PA 17126
(717) 787-5820

Cornell Youth and Work Program
Cornell University
Department of Human Development and Family Studies
Martha Van Rensselaer Hall, Room G62C
Ithaca, NY 14853
(607) 255-8394

Pickens County Youth Apprenticeship Initiative
School District of Pickens County
1348 Griffin Mill Rd.
Easley, SC 29640
(803) 855-8150

Roosevelt Renaissance 2000
Roosevelt High School
6941 N. Central St.
Portland, OR 97203
(503) 280-5138

Gwinnett County Youth Apprenticeship
Gwinnett County Public Schools
P.O. Box 343
Lawrenceville, GA 30246
(404) 822-6424

Manufacturing Technology Partnership Program
GASC Technology Center
G-5081 Torrey Rd.
Flint, MI 48507
(810) 760-1444

Illinois Work-Site Learning Experience Program
Illinois State Board of Education
100 N. First St.
Springfield, IL 62777
(217) 782-4620

Contact Options

CDS International
330 Seventh Ave.
New York, NY 10001
(212) 760-1400

Cushman Phillips
Phillips and Co.
19010 Rio Vista Dr.
Fairhope, AL 36532
(205) 928-3211

Jobs for the Future
1 Bowdoin Sq., 11th Floor
Boston, MA 02114
(617) 742-5995

U.S. Department of Labor
School to Work Office
400 Virginia Ave., SW, Room 210
Washington, DC 20024
(202) 401-6222

ISO 9000 Quality Standards

IN 1987, THE INCREASED FOCUS on global quality issues led the International Organization for Standardization, or ISO, headquartered in Geneva, Switzerland, to establish a series of international quality standards. Called the ISO 9000 Series of Standards, the series is not specific to any one industry, but when used with proper industry-specific standards, helps build a strong foundation for a quality system. The idea behind ISO is to promote standardization which will facilitate the international exchange of goods and services.

Currently, ISO 9000 certification is voluntary and not required or mandated in any country. However, the European community has recently required that quality systems of many suppliers of products related to health, safety, and the environment be formally registered, by a third party, according to the ISO 9000 Series standard. This action has made adoption of the ISO standards a virtual prerequisite for doing business in Europe. Countries in Asia, Africa, and South America are more and more considering adoption of these standards as a means to increased trade among themselves and the United States. Over 20,000 companies have been registered worldwide, and at least 52 nations are implementing the standards.

In the United States, the ISO 9000 Series of Standards was adopted verbatim as the ANSI/ASQC Q90 series of standards. The series comprises five individual, but related, international standards on quality management and quality assurance, known as ISO 9000, 9001, 9002, 9003, and 9004. For a company's quality system to become registered in one or more of these standards involves having an accredited, independent third party conduct an audit of the company's operations against the requirements of the ISO 9000 standards. Upon successful completion of this audit, the company will receive a registration certificate that identifies its quality system as being in compliance with ISO 9000 standards.

Accredited Registrars in the United States

ABS Quality Evaluations
16855 Northchase Dr.
Houston, TX 77060
(713) 873-9400

A.G.A. Quality
8501 E. Pleasant Valley Rd.
Cleveland, OH 44131
(216) 524-4990

American European Services (AES)
1054 31st St., NW, Suite 120
Washington, DC 20007
(202) 705-8590

American Association for Laboratory Accreditation
656 Quince Orchard Rd., #620
Gaithersburg, MD 20878
(301) 670-1377

American Society of Mechanical Engineers
United Engineering Center
345 E. 47th St.
New York, NY 10017
(212) 605-4796

AT&T Quality Registrar
650 Liberty Ave.
Union, NJ 07083
(908) 851-3058

AV Qualité
2900 Wilcrest, Suite 300
Houston, TX 77042
(713) 465-2850

Bellcore Quality Registration
6 Corporate Pl., Room 1-A230
Piscataway, NJ 08854
(908) 699-3739

Bureau Veritas Quality International
509 N. Main St.
Jamestown, NY 14701
(716) 484-9002

DLS Quality Technology Associates
108 Hallmore Dr.
Camillus, NY 13031
(315) 468-5811

DNV Industry
16340 Park Ten Pl., Suite 100
Houston, TX 77084
(713) 579-9003

Electronic Industries Quality Registry
2001 Pennsylvania Ave., NW
Washington, DC 20006
(202) 457-4970

Entela
3033 Madison Ave., SE
Grand Rapids, MI 49548
(800) 888-3787

Intertek
9900 Main St., Suite 500
Fairfax, VA 22031
(703) 476-9000

KEMA Registered Quality
4379 County Line Rd.
Chalfont, PA 18914
(215) 822-4258

ISO 9000 Quality Standards (cont'd)

KPMG Quality Registrar
150 John F. Kennedy Pkwy.
Short Hills, NJ 07878
(800) 716-5595

Lloyd's Register Quality Assurance
33-41 Newark St.
Hoboken, NJ 07030
(201) 963-1111

MET Laboratories
914 W. Patapsco Ave.
Baltimore, MD 21230
(410) 354-3300

National Quality Assurance
1146 Massachusetts Ave.
Boxborough, MA 01719
(508) 635-9256

Quality Systems Registrars
13873 Park Center Rd., Suite 217
Herndon, VA 22701
(703) 478-0241

SGS International Certification Services
Meadows Office Complex
301 Rte. 17N
Rutherford, NJ 07070
(800) 747-9047

Smithers Quality Assessments
425 W. Market St.
Akron, OH 44303
(216) 762-4231

Steel Related Industries Quality System Registars
2000 Corporate Dr., Suite 450
Wexford, PA 15090
(412) 935-2844

TRA Certification
700 E. Beardsley Ave.
P.O. Box 1081
Elkhart, IN 46515
(219) 264-0745

Tri-Tech Services
4700 Clairton Blvd.
Pittsburgh, PA 15236
(412) 884-2290

TUV America–Hartford Steam Boiler
5 Cherry Hill Dr.
Danvers, MA 01923
(508) 777-7999

TUV Rheinland of North America
12 Commerce Rd.
Newtown, CT 06470
(203) 426-0888

Underwriters Laboratories
1285 Walt Whitman Rd.
Melville, NY 11747
(516) 271-6200, ext. 284

Contact Options

American National Standards Institute (ANSI)
11 W. 42nd St.
New York, NY 10036
(212) 642-4900
   The American National Standards Institute an influential member of the ISO, is a nongovernment voluntary organization that provides a process for accrediting standards-writing bodies. The ISO 9000 Series is available from ANSI. (The ANSI/ASQC Q90 Series is identical to the ISO 9000 Series.)

American Society for Quality Control
P.O. Box 3005
Milwaukee, WI 53201
(800) 952-6587
   The American Society for Quality Control (ASQC) is an accredited standards-writing body. The ANSI/ASQC Q90 series is available from the customer service department of ASQC.

CEEM Information Services
P.O. Box 200
Fairfax Station, VA 22039
(800) 745-5565
   Publishes *Quality Systems Update* newsletter, ISO 9000 handbook, and a directory of registered companies.

National Institute of Standards and Technology
U.S. Department of Commerce
Rte. 270 and Quince Orchard Rd.
Administration Building, Room A537
Gaithersburg, MD 20899
(301) 975-2000

Consultants:

Booz, Allen & Hamilton
Safety and Environmental Group
8283 Greensboro Dr.
McLean, VA 22102
(703) 902-5000

Du Pont ISO 9000 Services
1007 Market St.
Wilmington, DE 19898
(800) 441-8040

Perry Johnson
3000 Town Center, Suite 2960
Southfield, MI 48075
(810) 356-4410

Malcolm Baldrige Quality Award

THE MALCOLM BALDRIGE NATIONAL Quality Award is widely acknowledged as having raised overall quality awareness and practice in U.S. manufacturing. According to David A. Garvin, Robert and Jane Cizik professor of business administration at the Harvard Business School, the award "has become the most important catalyst for transforming American business."

Established in 1987 by the Malcolm Baldrige National Quality Improvement Act, the award is administered by the Secretary of Commerce and the National Institute of Standards and Technology, with cooperation and financial support from the private sector. The Malcolm Baldrige National Quality Award is the highest level of national recognition for quality that a U.S. company can receive.

Officially, the Baldrige Award has three goals: to promote an understanding of quality excellence, to recognize the quality achievements of U.S. businesses, and to publicize successful quality strategies. Awards are presented to qualifying companies in manufacturing, service, and small business categories. A maximum of two awards per category may be given each year. Recipients of the award are allowed to publicize and advertise receipt of the award, in return for agreement to share their successful quality strategies with other U.S. organizations.

Applicants for the award are judged on these seven criteria:

- Leadership

- Information and analysis

- Strategic quality planning

- Human resource development and management

- Process management

- Business results

- Customer focus and satisfaction.

The information submitted in each of these criteria must demonstrate that the applicant's approaches could be replicated or adapted by other companies.

The award has achieved such high status that many large manufacturers encourage their supplier base to participate. And, since all applicants, win or lose, receive feedback from the award's board of examiners, many of these companies find the application process itself a worthwhile exercise. For others, the time and expense are not justified. Indeed, a report prepared by the Grant Thornton Survey of Manufacturers in 1993 reveals that mid-sized U.S. manufacturers may have become disenchanted with the Malcolm Baldrige Award. Sixty percent of companies responding in the Grant Thornton study agree that the award needs to address more substance (the quality, integrity, or innovativeness of a company's products) than form (the quality of a company's control procedures).

Number of Completed Applications/ Registrants Each Year

1988: 66
1989: 40
1990: 97
1991: 106
1992: 90
1993: 76
1994: 71

Previous Award Winners

1994

Service
AT&T Consumer Communications Services
GE Directories

Small Business
Wainwright Industries

1993

Manufacturing
Eastman Chemical, Kingsport, TN

Small Business
Ames Rubber, Hamburg, NJ

1992

Manufacturing
AT&T Network Systems Group, Morristown, NJ.
Texas Instruments, Dallas, TX

Service
AT&T Universal Card Services, Jacksonville, FL
The Ritz-Carlton Hotel, Atlanta, GA

Small Business
Granite Rock, Watsonville, CA

1991

Manufacturing
Solectron, San Jose, CA
Zytec, Eden Prairie, MN

Small Business
Marlow Industries, Dallas, TX

1990

Manufacturing
Cadillac Motor Car, Detroit, MI
IBM Rochester, Rochester, MN

Service
Federal Express, Memphis, TN

Small Business
Wallace, Houston, TX

Malcolm Baldrige Quality Award (cont'd)

1989

Manufacturing
Milliken & Company, Spartanburg, IL
Xerox Business Products and Systems, Stamford, CT

Malcolm Baldrige Award Application Fees

A nonrefundable Eligibility Determination Fee of $50 is required of all applicants. Additional fees for 1996 applicants covering all expenses associated with distribution of applications, review of applications, and development of feedback reports are $4,000 for Manufacturing and Service company categories and $1,200 for the Small Business category. Site visit review fees are established when the visits are scheduled.

Individual copies of the award criteria and application forms and instructions may be obtained free of charge from:

Malcolm Baldrige National Quality Award
National Institute of Standards and Technology
Rte. 270 and Quince Orchard Rd.
Administration Building, Room A537
Gaithersburg, MD 20899
(301) 975-2036

Multiple copies of the award criteria may be ordered in packets of ten (item number T999) for $29.95 per packet from:

American Society for Quality Control
Customer Service Department
P.O. Box 3066
Milwaukee, WI 53201
(800) 248-1946

Consultants for Malcolm Baldrige National Quality Award

The application for the Baldrige Award is sufficiently complicated that many companies rely on outside consultants for help in completing it. Here is a partial list, recommended by the Association of Management Consulting Firms:

Coopers & Lybrand
1251 Ave. of the Americas
New York, NY 10020
(212) 536-2000

K. W. Tunnell
900 E. Eighth Ave., Suite 106
King of Prussia, PA 19406
(610) 337-0820

Rath & Strong
92 Hayden Ave.
Lexington, MA 02173
(617) 861-1700

Robert E. Nolan
90 Hopmeadow St.
Simsbury, CT 06070
(203) 658-1941

Contact Options

Association of Management Consulting Firms
521 Fifth Ave., 35th Floor
New York, NY 10175
(212) 697-9693

Quality Benchmarking

BENCHMARKING, THE PROCESS of learning from the best practices of others, is increasing rapidly in the U.S. due to growing foreign competition, limited resources, and even the requirements of the Malcolm Baldrige National Award criteria. To assist firms, nonprofit organizations, and government agencies in the process of benchmarking, the American Productivity & Quality Center established an International Benchmarking Clearinghouse in 1992 as a source of information about "best practices" for a large number of organizational processes. The Clearinghouse provides standards of conduct, conducts in-depth secondary research, and collects and disseminates best practices through databases, case studies, publications, seminars, conferences, videos, and other media. The Clearinghouse also provides training and consulting.

Contact Options

International Benchmarking Clearinghouse
American Productivity & Quality Center
123 N. Post Oak Ln., #300
Houston, TX 77024
(713) 681-4020

International Quality and Productivity Center
P.O. Box 401
Little Falls, NJ 07424
(800) 882-8684

The IQPC has sponsored numerous workshops and seminars on benchmarking practices.

MARKETING

Ad Agencies Ranked

The 30 Hottest Agencies in the U.S., 1994

Rank	Agency	Headquarters	1994 Billings ($ thousands)	1993 Billings ($ thousands)	% Change
1	Foote, Cone & Belding	Chicago	2,760,349	2,564,915	7.6
2	J. Walter Thompson	New York	2,274,000	2,121,800	7.2
3	Leo Burnett	Chicago	2,226,340	2,106,403	5.7
4	Young & Rubicam	New York	2,187,685	2,070,685	5.7
5	D'Arcy Masius Benton & Bowles	New York	2,106,620	1,972,845	6.8
6	DDB Needham	New York	2,100,000	2,020,000	4.0
7	BBDO	New York	2,075,313	1,857,338	11.7
8	Grey	New York	2,015,700	1,885,700	6.9
9	Saatchi & Saatchi	New York	1,932,200	1,818,000	6.3
10	Ogilvy & Mather	New York	1,776,238	1,590,000	11.7
11	McCann-Erickson	New York	1,770,700	1,673,000	5.8
12	Lintas USA	New York	1,583,925	1,540,000	2.9
13	Bozell	New York	1,315,000	1,100,000	19.5
14	Bates USA	New York	1,248,309	1,260,000	-0.1
15	Wells Rich Greene/BDDP	New York	900,700	882,600	2.1
16	Chiat/Day	Venice, CA	895,000	847,000	5.7
17	N. W. Ayer & Partners	New York	861,238	800,998	7.5
18	Campbell Mithun Esty	Minneapolis	850,600	830,600	2.4
19	MVBMS/Euro RSCG	New York	708,000	588,500	20.3
20	Ketchum	Pittsburgh	600,600	617,000	-2.7
21	Lowe & Partners/SMS	New York	510,000	500,000	2.0
22	Ross Roy Communications	Bloomfield Hills, MI	508,000	540,000	-5.9
23	Temerlin McClain	Dallas	505,000	440,000	14.8
24	Hal Riney & Partners	San Francisco	475,000	400,000	18.8
25	Jordan, Case, McGrath & Taylor	New York	430,000	410,000	4.9
26	W. B. Doner & Co.	Southfield, MI	391,000	325,000	20.3
27	Earle Palmer Brown	Bethesda, MD	366,700	409,600	-10.5
28	Arnold Fortuna Lawner & Cabot	Boston	365,000	328,000	11.3
29	TBWA	New York	359,700	342,200	5.1
30	Avrett, Free & Ginsberg	New York	345,000	300,000	15.0

Source: Adweek, Feb. 27, 1995, © ASM Communications, Inc. Reprinted with permission

The Top Reference Sources

Guerrilla Marketing for the '90s
Houghton Mifflin, $9.95
(800) 352-5455

One in a series of marketing books by best-selling author Jay Conrad Levinson, this book provides

100 affordable marketing weapons for maximizing profits from your small business.

Levinson has created an approach to marketing that relies on low-cost, high-impact techniques for identifying, reaching, and keeping customers.

Ad Agencies Ranked (cont'd)

The Top 20 U.S.-Based Agencies Worldwide, 1994

Rank	Agency	Headquarters	1994 Billings ($ thousands)	1993 Billings ($ thousands)	% Change
1	McCann-Erickson	New York	7,177,544	6,594,159	8.8
2	Foote, Cone & Belding	Chicago	6,500,000	6,226,207	4.4
3	J. Walter Thompson	New York	6,133,000	5,811,800	5.5
4	BBDO Worldwide	New York	5,883,576	5,376,675	9.4
5	Young & Rubicam	New York	5,657,480	5,313,673	6.4
6	Ogilvy & Mather Worldwide	New York	5,302,582	4,749,884	11.6
7	Bates Worldwide	New York	5,048,216	4,673,491	8.0
8	Saatchi & Saatchi	New York	5,007,200	5,566,100	-10.0
9	Lintas: Worldwide	New York	5,006,000	4,700,000	5.5
10	Grey Advertising	New York	4,817,200	4,564,500	2.0
11	DDB Needham Worldwide	New York	4,700,000	4,670,000	0.6
12	D'Arcy Masius Benton & Bowles	New York	4,681,073	4,122,242	12.0
13	Leo Burnett	Chicago	4,591,982	4,223,482	8.7
14	The Lowe Group	New York/London	2,064,098	1,996,671	3.4
15	Bozell	New York	1,750,000	1,500,000	16.7
16	TBWA	New York	1,104,000	1,104,000	0.0
17	Campbell Mithun Esty	Minneapolis	1,000,700	968,900	3.3
18	Chiat/Day	Venice, CA	945,000	896,800	5.4
19	Wells Rich Greene/BDDP	New York	900,700	882,600	2.1
20	N. W. Ayer & Partners	New York	874,238	812,998	7.5

The 15 Largest Agency Holding Companies, 1994

Rank	Agency	Headquarters	1994 Billings ($ thousands)	1993 Billings ($ thousands)	% Change
1	WPP Group	London	20,127,000	19,710,000	2.1
2	Interpublic Group of Companies	New York	15,000,000	14,273,575	5.1
3	Omnicom Group	New York	14,000,000	13,440,651	4.2
4	Dentsu	Tokyo	11,149,000	11,149,374	0.0
5	Saatchi & Saatchi	London	10,000,000	10,809,600	-7.5
6	Young & Rubicam	New York	7,989,985	7,558,985	5.7
7	Publicis FCB	Chicago/Paris	7,040,293	6,764,207	4.1
8	Euro RSCG	Paris	6,154,937	6,211,790	-0.9
9	Hakuhodo	Tokyo	5,800,787	5,458,713	6.3
10	D'Arcy Masius Benton & Bowles	New York	5,338,538	4,770,054	11.9
11	Grey Advertising	New York	5,330,500	5,083,400	4.9
12	Leo Burnett	Chicago	4,591,982	4,223,482	8.7
13	Bozell Jacobs Kenyon & Eckhardt	New York	2,330,000	2,015,000	15.6
14	BDDP	Paris	2,030,608	2,060,342	-1.4
15	Chiat/Day	Venice, CA	896,800	855,400	4.8

Source: Adweek, Feb. 27, 1995, © ASM Communications, Inc. Reprinted with permission

Ad Agencies Ranked (cont'd)

The Top Ten Direct Response Agencies, 1994

Rank	Agency	Headquarters	1994 Billings ($ thousands)	1993 Billings ($ thousands)	% Change
1	Wunderman Cato Johnson Worldwide	New York	638,000	536,635	18.9
2	Rapp Collins Worldwide	New York	510,194	438,553	16.3
3	Ogilvy & Mather Direct	New York	413,000	440,000	-6.1
4	Bonner Slosberg Humphrey	Boston	333,502	305,154	9.3
5	Barry Blau & Partners	Fairfield, CT	261,604	204,259	28.1
6	Kobs & Draft	Chicago	259,800	201,230	16.3
7	Grey Direct	New York	184,300	161,000	14.5
8	Customer Development	Peoria, IL	171,915	150,580	14.2
9	Chapman Direct	New York	143,455	154,254	-7.0
10	Devon Direct Marketing & Advertising	Malvern, PA	139,100	130,000	6.0

Source: Adweek, Feb. 27, 1995, © ASM Communications, Inc. Reprinted with permission

The Top Reference Sources

SRDS Direct Mail List Rates and Data
Standard Rate and Data Service, $354/6 issues
(708) 375-5000

Virtually every mailing list available for rent to marketers is catalogued in this cumbersome volume.

This is a complete resource for direct-mail users that includes a subject/market classification index, title/list index, and a suppliers and services directory. Also included are mailing list brokers, compilers and managers, business lists, business co-ops and package insert programs, consumer lists, farm lists, consumer co-ops and package insert programs, and alternate delivery systems.

Major Ad Award Winners

Starch Awards

SINCE 1988, ROPER STARCH, a market research firm, has presented the Starch Award. The award is given to the print ads that achieved the highest recognition scores among consumers during the previous year. Winners are culled from more than 50,000 face-to-face interviews with consumers annually.

1990 Starch Winners

Agency	Category	Client/Product
Hakuhodo Advertising America	Electronic entertainment	Hitachi
Deutsch	Household materials	Oneida
Geer, DuBois	Automotive	Jaguar
Levine, Huntley, Vick & Beaver	Financial	Dreyfus
Tracy-Locke	Travel	Embassy Suites Hotels
Ogilvy & Mather	Beer, wine, and liquor	Seagram's Seven
DCA Advertising	Office equipment	Canon
Ad Group	Sportswear	Gitano
Saatchi & Saatchi	Computers	Hewlett-Packard
BBDO	Floor coverings	Armstrong
D'Arcy Masius Benton & Bowles	Food	Kraft Foods Cool Whip
Lawner Reingold Britton & Partners	Sporting goods, toys	Pinnacle Golf Balls
Revlon Professional Products (in-house)	Hair products	Revlon
Bozell	Lingerie	Vanity Fair
PR+	Sportswear	Zena

1991 Starch Winners

Agency	Category	Client/Product
Lintas USA	Hair products	Johnson's Baby Shampoo
TBWA Advertising	Beer, wine, and liquor	Absolut
Hakuhodo Advertising	Electronic entertainment	Hitachi
D'Arcy Masius Benton & Bowles	Food	Kraft Foods Cool Whip
BBDO	Floor coverings	Armstrong
Eisaman, Johns & Law Advertising	Women's toiletries	Giorgio Beverly Hills
Young & Rubicam	Automotive	Mercury
Bizell	Lingerie	Vanity Fair
Avrett, Free & Ginsberg	Tobacco products	Kent Cigarettes
Ogilvy & Mather	Financial	American Express
FCB/Leber Katz Partners	Bakery goods	Chips Ahoy
Waring & LaRosa	Sporting goods, toys	Fisher-Price
DDB Needham	Computers	NEC
Young & Rubicam	Insurance and real estate	MetLife
Carlson & Partners	Sportswear	Ralph Lauren

Source: Roper Starch

Major Ad Award Winners (cont'd)

1992 Starch Winners

Agency	Category	Client/Product
Bozell	Automotive	Chrysler
Ogilvy & Mather	Confectionery and snacks	Hershey
Saatchi & Saatchi	Soaps and detergents	Tide
BBDO	Floor coverings and fibers	Armstrong
George McWilliams Associates	Financial	TransAmerica
Severin Group (in-house)	Jewelry	Gucci
Guess Advertising (in-house)	Apparel	Guess
Greengage Associates	Resorts and travel	St. Croix, St. John, St. Thomas
Howard, Merrell & Partners	Pets and pet supplies	Defend
J. Walter Thompson	Cooking products	Miracle Whip
Lintas USA	Computer publications	OS/2-IBM
Walt Disney Home Video (in-house)	Pre-recorded records and tapes	Disney
Stein Robaire Helm	Computers, office equipment, and stationery	Day Runner
Falk Communications	Medical publications	Esgicplus
Brugnatelli & Partners	Medicines	Baby Orajel
Eisaman, Johns & Co.	Liquor	Kahlua
CRK Advertising (in-house)	Cosmetics and beauty aids	Calvin Klein/Obsession

1993 Starch Winners

Agency	Category	Client/Product
Merkley Newman Harty	Computers, office equipment, and stationery	WordPerfect
Wells Rich Greene	Travel, hotels, and resorts	ITT Sheraton
Campbell Mithun Esty	Insurance and real estate	The Travelers
Guess?	Apparel, footwear, and accessories	Guess Jeans
Young & Rubicam	Domestic passenger cars	Lincoln Mark VIII
Bozell North	Domestic sport utility vehicles and vans	Jeep Cherokee
Young & Rubicam	Food and food products	General Foods International Coffees
Ketchum Communications	Confectionery, snacks, and soft drinks	Orville Redenbacher's Original
Buena Vista Home Video	Electronic entertainment and supplies	Aladdin
J. Walter Thompson	Household equipment and supplies	Reynolds Plastic Wrap
William Douglas	Drugs and remedies	FemCare
Lowe & Partners/SMS	Business and consumer services	Hanson
Saatchi & Saatchi	Soaps, cleansers, and polishes	Comet
Merkley Newman Harty	Computers, office equipment, and stationery	WordPerfect
Wells Rich Greene	Travel, hotels, and resorts	ITT Sheraton

Source: Roper Starch

America Online features Hoover's profiles of 500 of the largest corporations in the United States. The profiles are set up in a searchable database. KEYWORD COMPANY.

Major Ad Award Winners (cont'd)

The Kelly Awards

The Magazine Publishers of America give the annual Kelly Award to the print ad that best demonstrates the ability to capture and hold the reader's attention.

Year	Agency	Client	Product/Campaign
1981	Ogilvy & Mather	Par Parfums	Paco Rabanne Cologne
1982	Ogilvy & Mather	International Paper	International Paper
1983	Doyle Dane Bernbach Group	Foodways National	Weight Watchers Frozen Foods
1984	Chiat/Day	Nike	Nike Apparel
1985	Ogilvy & Mather	American Express	Retail
1986	McKinney & Silver	North Carolina Travel & Tourism	Travel
1987	Ogilvy & Mather	American Express	"Green" Card
1988	TBWA	Carillon Importers	Absolut Vodka
1989	Wieden & Kennedy	Nike	Emotional Running
1990	TBWA	Carillon Importers	Absolut Vodka
1991	Wieden & Kennedy	Nike	Women's Fitness Campaign
1992	Wieden & Kennedy	Nike	Women's Fitness Campaign
1993	Carmichael Lynch	Schwinn Bicycles	Schwinn Bicycles

Source: Magazine Publishers of America

The EFFIE Awards

The EFFIE Award is presented annually by the New York City chapter of the American Marketing Association to advertisers and advertising agencies in recognition of those campaigns judged to be the most effective. Print, television, and radio campaigns are judged in over 30 categories.

Year	Agency	Client	Category	Product
1980	Ally & Gargano	Federal Express	Business products and services	Federal Express
	Advertising to Women	Gillette	Women's toiletries	Silkience Conditioner
1981	BBDO	G.E.	Household durables	G.E. products
	Doyle Dane Bernbach Group	Volkswagen	Automotive	Volkswagen Autos
1982	Doyle Dane Bernbach Group	Polaroid	Recreational products	Sun Camera
1983	Della Femina, Travisano & Partners	AAA	Automotive related	AAA, Auto Club
1984	SSC & B	Coca-Cola	Beverages: non-alcoholic	Diet Coke
	Ally & Gargano	Federal Express	Business products and services	Federal Express
1985	Chiat/Day	Apple Computer	Bus. computers: software	Apple Computer
1986	Chiat/Day	Pizza Hut	Restaurants	Pizza Hut
1987	Chiat/Day	NYNEX	Telecommunications services	Yellow Pages
1988	Jordan, Case, McGrath & Taylor	Quaker Oats	Breakfast food	Quaker Oatmeal
1989	Chiat/Day	NYNEX	Media: non-newspaper	Yellow Pages
1990	TBWA	Carillon Importers	Distilled spirits: non-wine	Absolut Vodka
1991	Northwoods	Senator Wellstone	Political	Senator Wellstone
1992	Hill Holiday Connors Cosmopoulos	Reebok	Fashion apparel	Blacktop Sneakers
1993	BBDO/Los Angeles	Apple Computer	Computers	Power Book intro.
1994	Boodby Berlin & Silverstein	Burrell Comm.	Inner-city drug campaign	Partnership for a Drug-Free America

Source: American Marketing Association, NY Chapter

Major Ad Award Winners (cont'd)

The Clio Awards

The Clio Awards for creative excellence in advertising are presented annually to agencies throughout the world. Previously awarded by product category, the new and improved Clios are now awarded in media categories only, as judged by a panel of advertising professionals.

1994 Television Hall of Fame Award Recipients

Advertiser	Title	Advertising Agency
Pepsi-Cola	Missing Link	BBDO
Ikea	Mobelfakta	Goldberg/Marchesano
Federal Express	You Got It	Ally & Gargano

Campaign Award Recipients

Advertiser	Product	Advertising Agency
Print—Local	Minneapolis Institute of Art	Martin Williams Doyle
Print—National	*Archive* magazine	Hermann Vaske
Radio—Local	Massachusetts State Lottery	Hill Holiday Connors Cosmopolous
Radio—Local	Spectrum Foods	Hoffman Lewis
Radio—Regional	Chevys Mexican Restaurant	Goodby Berlin and Silverstein

Source: Clio Awards

Contact Option

Clio Awards
276 Fifth Ave., Suite 401
New York, NY 10001
(212) 683-4300

AAAA A+ Creative Awards

The A+ Creative Awards, established by the American Association of Advertising Agencies, are awarded to advertising agencies rather than to a particular ad campaign. Each agency in the competition was asked to submit ten ads, in any combination of media, that ran for the first time the previous year.

Year	Agency	Location
1991	Carmichael Lynch	Minneapolis
1992	Cliff Freeman and Partners	New York
1993	Carmichael Lynch	Minneapolis
1994	Cliff Freeman and Partners	New York

Source: AAAA

The One Show Awards–Best in Show

The One Show Awards, gold, silver, and bronze, have been given each year since 1973 by The One Club for Art & Copy. The award is given to print, television, and radio ad campaigns in a variety of categories on the basis of effectiveness.

Best in Show

Year	Agency	Client
1990	Wieden & Kennedy, Portland, OR	Nike
1991	GGK, London	Electricity Association
1992	Saatchi & Saatchi, London	British Airways
1993	Streetsmart Advertising, New York	Coalition for the Homeless
1994	Hoffman Lewis, San Francisco	Prego

Source: One Club for Art & Copy

Major Ad Award Winners (cont'd)

1994 One Show Winners

Category	Agency	Client
Newspaper over 600 Lines: Single	Arnold Finnegan Martin/ Richmond	Play It Again Sports
Newspaper 600 Lines or Less: Single	Doyle Advertising and Design Group/Boston	Akva Spring Water
Newspapers 600 Lines or Less: Campaign	Doyle Advertising and Design Group/Boston	Akva Spring Water
Magazine Color 1 Page or Spread: Single	Cole & Weber/Portland	Dr. Martens/London Underground
Magazine Color 1 Page or Spread: Campaign	Doyle Advertising and Design Group/Boston	Akva Spring Water
	Cole & Weber/Portland	Dr. Martens/London Underground
	BSB/Hong Kong	Preparation H/Whitewall International
Magazine Less Than a Page B/W or Color	The Martin Agency/Richmond	Sturat Circle Pharmacy
Outdoor: Single	Abbott Mead Vickers BBDO/London	The Economist
Trade B/W 1 Page or Spread: Single	Martin/Williams, Minneapolis	Art Directors/Copywriters Club of Minnesota
	Cole & Weber/Portland, OR	The Oregonian
Trade Color 1 Page or Spread: Single	The Martin Agency/Richmond	FMC
Trade Any Size B/W or Color: Campaign	Wieden & Kennedy/Portland, OR	Oregon Film & Video
Collateral Direct Mail: Single	The Richards Group/Dallas	McQueeney Ties
Collateral Direct Mail: Campaign	The Richards Group/Dallas	McQueeney Ties
Collateral P.O.P.	The Richards Group/Dallas	McQueeney Ties
	The Richards Group/Dallas	Motel 6
Collateral Self-Promotion	Butler Shine & Stern/Sausalito	Butler Shine & Stern
Public Service/Political Newspaper or Magazine: Single	Young & Rubicam Adelaide/ Dulwich, South Australia	Royal Zoological Gardens
Public Service/Political Newspaper or Magazine: Campaign	EvansGroup/Salt Lake City	Humane Society of Utah
Public Service Outdoor and Posters: Single	Abbott Mead Vickers BBDO/London	RSPCA
	Doyle Advertising and Design Group/Boston	National Association of Atomic Veterans
Public Service Television: Campaign	Wells Rich Greene BDDP/New York	The Ad Council/DOT
Consumer Radio Single	McConnaughy Stein Schmidt Brown/Chicago	Zoo Station Teen Club
Consumer Radio Campaign	Hoffman/Lewis, San Francisco	Spectrum Foods/ Prego Restaurant
Consumer Television Over: 30 Single	Young & Rubicam/Toronto	Kodak Canada
	Wieden & Kennedy/Amsterdam	Nike Europe
Consumer Television :30/:25 Single	Kruskopf Olson/Minneapolis	Pet Food Warehouse
Consumer Television :30/:25 Campaign	Goodby Silverstein & Partners/San Francisco	Norwegian Cruise Line
Consumer Television Under $50,000 Budget	Larson & Berg/Chicago	ScrubYourPup, Chicago
College Competition	Portfolio Center/Atlanta	Anne Marie Floyd

Source: One Club for Art & Copy

Choosing an Ad Agency

ANY COMPANY THAT SPENDS more than $500,000 on advertising should seriously consider employing an agency to facilitate its advertising needs.

Adweek and Advertising Age are the two magazines that thoroughly cover the advertising industry. These sources, combined with the tips listed below, may help narrow the range of what you should be looking for and clarify how to evaluate what you've seen.

Finding the agency that is best suited to your company's needs can be a tricky business. Many agencies do a better job of selling themselves than the companies they represent, and the burden falls on the client to find a selection process that works.

Ten Questions to Ask Yourself Before Hiring an Ad Agency:

- Are we more interested in creativity or in short-term market share results?

- Does our agency need a media-buying capability or will we handle that separately?

- Do we want to pay our agency a flat fee or a percentage of our budget?

- Are we looking for a particular campaign or for a company?

- How important is it to have regular access to the head of the agency we choose?

- Which medium do we need our agency to handle?

- Do we need our agency to handle existing projects only or new product launches as well?

- Does it matter if our agency is conveniently located?

- Do we want a company with a particular philosophy or one that is willing to work with the philosophy of its clients?

- Whom do we want to be in charge?

Evaluate Each Agency by Asking the Following:

- Does it understand our company's objectives?

- Does it address our company's objectives?

- Does it have the necessary credentials and experience?

- Does it have a knowledge of our business?

- Does it have an interest in our business?

- Does it have a knowledge of our competitive situation?

- Does it present sound marketing strategies?

- Does it present clear, creative solutions?

- Does it have good internal resources?

- Does it have a strong account management team?

- Can we work together?

Source: Small Business Reports

Contact Options

The American Association of Advertising Agencies
666 Third Ave., 13th Floor
New York, NY 10017
(212) 682-2500
Industry Association

Selection Agencies:

Advertising Agency Register
155 E. 55th St., Suite 6A
New York, NY 10022
Leslie Winthrop
(212) 644-0790

Advertising Agency Search Service
30 E. Huron, Suite 1910
Chicago, IL 60611
Mary Jane Rumminger
(312) 649-1148

Bismark
30 Bismark Way
Dennis, MA 02638
William Weilbacher
(508) 385-6889

Dorward & Associates
150 Grand Ave., Suite 200
Oakland, CA 94612
Don Dorward
(510) 452-0587

EBJ Management Consultants
7229 S. Janmar Circle
Dallas, TX 75230
Eugene Jacobson
(214) 361-1427

Neal Gilliatt
1 Rockefeller Plaza, Suite 1510
New York, NY 10020
(212) 262-0660

Choosing an Ad Agency (cont'd)

Jones-Lundin Associates
625 N. Michigan Ave., Suite 500
Chicago, IL 60611

> Bob Lundin (Chicago)
> (312) 751-3470

> Kenneth Caffrey (New York)
> (212) 765-1986

> Jack McBride (California)
> (209) 577-1464

Robert Marker
10555 S.E. Terrapin Pl., #101
Tequesta, FL 33469
(407) 747-3237

Morgan, Anderson & Co.
136 W. 24th St.
New York, NY 10011
Lee Anne Morgan; Arthur Anderson
(212) 741-0777

New England Consulting Group
55 Green Farms Rd.
Westport, CT 06880
Gary Stibel
(203) 226-9200

Pile & Company
535 Boylston St.
Boston, MA 02116
"Skip" Pile
(617) 267-5000

Richard Roth Associates
73 Cross Ridge Rd.
Chappaqua, NY 10514
Richard Roth
(914) 238-9206

Wanamaker Associates
3060 Peachtree Rd., NW, Suite 1430
Atlanta, GA 30305
Ken Bowes
(404) 233-3029

Herb Zeltner
R.D. #1
North Salem, NY 10560
(914) 669-8530

Talent Agencies

MOST OF THE BIG TALENT NAMES are concentrated in a handful of top talent agencies.

Creative Artists Agency (CAA)
3310 West End Ave., Fifth Floor
Nashville, TN 37203
(615) 383-8787

International Creative Management (ICM)
40 W. 57th St.
New York, NY 10019
(212) 556-5600

The Gersh Agency
P.O. Box 25617
Beverly Hills, CA 90210
(310) 274-6611

Shapiro-Lichtman
8827 Beverly Blvd.
Los Angeles, CA 90048
(310) 859-8877

United Talent Agency
9560 Wilshire Blvd., Suite 500
Beverly Hills, CA 90212
(310) 273-6700

The William Morris Agency
1350 Ave. of the Americas
New York, NY 10019
(212) 586-5100

The Writers and Artists Agency
924 Westwood Blvd., Suite 900
Los Angeles, CA 90024
(310) 824-6300

Recommended Resource

Pacific Coast Studio Directory
Published by Jack and Harry Reitz, $13/issue
P.O. Box V
Pine Mountain, CA 93222
(805) 242-2722
    This is a triannual reference on the film and television industries.

Television Campaigns

Top 15 Television Campaigns of 1994

1994	1993	Brand	Ad Agency
1	3	Coca-Cola	Creative Artists Agency
2	5	Little Caesar's Pizza	Cliff Freeman & Partners
3	2	Pepsi	BBDO
4	1	McDonald's	Leo Burnett
5	–	Bud Light	DDB Needham
6	–	AT&T	FCB/Leber Katz; Ayer; Young & Rubicam; McCann
7	–	Miller Lite	Leo Burnett
8	13	Energizer	Chiat/Day
9	4	Nike	Wieden & Kennedy
10	8	Taster's Choice	McCann-Erickson
11	14	Pizza Hut	BBDO
12	5	Budweiser	DMB&B; DDB Needham
13	15	Burger King	Ammirati & Puris/Lintas
14	12	Ford	J. Walter Thompson; Wells Rich Greene
15	–	Diet Coke	Lowe & Partners/SMS

Source: Video Storyboard Tests

The Top Reference Sources

Zig Ziglar's Secrets of Closing the Sale
Berkley, $12
(800) 631-8571

This best-selling book is must reading for anyone who is serious about wanting to improve as a salesperson. Ziglar's inspiring work includes over 100 successful closings for every kind of persua-sion; more than 700 questions that will open your eyes to new possibilities you may have over-looked; how to paint word pictures and use your imagination to get results; plus tips from Amer-ica's 100 most successful salespeople.

This is one of the most important books on the topic—every salesperson should own a copy.

Newsletters. Send e-mail to newsletter@almanac.yoyo.com. See p. xi for instructions.

"Balancing Promotional Content with News" from the book Marketing with Newsletters by Elaine Floyd, owner of Newsletter Resources and author of the newsletter Newsletter News & Resources.

Leading National Advertisers

Rank	Advertiser	Ad Spending ($ millions)	Rank	Advertiser	Ad Spending ($ millions)
1	Procter & Gamble	2,397.5	51	Quaker Oats	246.5
2	Philip Morris	1,844.3	52	News	243.5
3	General Motors	1,539.2	53	Schering-Plough	233.1
4	Sears, Roebuck	1,310.7	54	Mazda Motor	228.0
5	PepsiCo	1,038.9	55	Tandy	223.1
6	Ford Motor	958.3	56	Federated Department Stores	223.0
7	AT&T	812.1	57	U.S. dairy farmers	215.1
8	Nestlé	793.7	58	S. C. Johnson & Son	209.9
9	Johnson & Johnson	762.5	59	General Electric	204.8
10	Chrysler	761.6	60	Mattel	201.1
11	Warner-Lambert	751.0	61	John A. Benckiser	199.2
12	Unilever	738.2	62	Clorox	198.3
13	McDonald's	736.6	63	Adolph Coors	197.8
14	Time Warner	695.1	64	ITT	196.2
15	Toyota Motor	690.4	65	Helene Curtis Industries	192.6
16	Walt Disney	675.7	66	Paramount Communications	185.3
17	Grand Metropolitan	652.9	67	ConAgra	183.2
18	Kellogg	627.1	68	Ciba-Geigy	182.7
19	Eastman Kodak	624.7	69	IBM	171.8
20	Sony	589.0	70	Citicorp	169.8
21	J. C. Penney	585.2	71	Broadway Stores	169.5
22	General Mills	569.2	72	Wendy's	168.3
23	K Mart	558.2	73	Gillette	167.2
24	Anheuser-Busch	520.5	74	Goodyear Tire & Rubber	163.1
25	American Home Products	501.6	75	Roll	160.1
26	RJR Nabisco	499.4	76	Philips	158.3
27	Nissan Motor	413.1	77	Campbell Soup	150.1
28	May Department Stores	403.6	78	Upjohn	146.5
29	Matsushita Electric Industrial	385.1	79	Bayer	145.3
30	Ralston Purina	372.8	80	Wrigley	144.9
31	Hershey Foods	366.3	81	American Stores	143.0
32	Honda Motor	354.4	82	American Brands	142.7
33	Coca-Cola	341.3	83	Marriott	132.6
34	Mars	337.6	84	AMR	131.3
35	American Express	324.8	85	CPC	129.4
36	H. J. Heinz	318.9	86	Apple Computer	129.1
37	Circuit City Stores	308.5	87	Seagram	126.8
38	U.S. government	304.4	88	Dr. Pepper/Seven-Up	125.5
39	Sara Lee	299.7	89	Dow Chemical	125.1
40	MCI Communications	297.4	90	Loews	124.5
41	Colgate-Palmolive	287.4	91	Visa	122.5
42	Nike	281.4	92	Kimberly-Clark	119.8
43	R. H. Macy	280.5	93	U.S. Shoe	118.8
44	Hasbro	277.3	94	Imasco	117.6
45	SmithKline Beecham	269.7	95	B.A.T. Industries	116.9
46	Dayton Hudson	266.7	96	Daimler-Benz AG	116.6
47	Sprint	264.8	97	Bally Manufacturing	115.1
48	Wal-Mart Stores	251.9	98	Pfizer	114.9
49	Bristol-Myers Squibb	250.2	99	Mitsubishi Motors	113.4
50	Levi Strauss	248.9	100	Delta Air Lines	113.1

Source: Ad Age, September 28, 1994

Music Permissions

A COMPANY SEEKING TO USE popular music or lyrics, either for commercial advertising or for an in-house corporate video, will have to get permission to do so.

Obtaining music permissions can be done simply and cheaply by purchasing music that comes with an automatic license for use, but the choice of music available will be significantly limited. On the other hand, obtaining permission to use protected music, which includes just about any song currently available in local music stores, can be costly and lead to extensive litigation since the copyright law protecting the use of current, popular music is very strict.

When choosing protected music, it is best to get a lawyer or an expert to help determine the appropriate legal procedures, and to keep the following information in mind.

To use music that is protected by copyright in any way, it is necessary to obtain permission from the copyright owners in writing. These include the music publisher who represents the composer and the lyricist, and the record company that owns the recording and represents the performer who made the recording.

A fee is generally charged by the copyright owners for permission, and the amount varies depending upon how it is used. Using a piece of protected music for a television or radio commercial is the most expensive. For a commercial in one state or city, the fees may be in the low thousands. For a national television commercial fees for one year can range from $40,000 to $200,000 each to the music publisher and the record company.

Once a piece of music has been chosen, a company may either use an already recorded piece of music by a known artist or obtain the rights to use the music and re-record it with other artists.

In the case of a performance by a known artist, for example, it may be necessary to pay various fees such as union new-use fees, which can increase costs. On the other hand, hiring unknowns to perform a hit song will still require obtaining permission from the music publisher, who then pays the original talent. Union fees may be incurred, depending upon the arrangements made with the talent.

If using protected music seems too expensive or too complicated, the alternative may be to use a stock music library or similar music service. These services provide hundreds of CDs containing appropriate background music recorded by professional musicians.

The cost of purchasing these CDs is nominal, averaging $20 per CD. Additional licensing fees are also nominal, depending upon use. A company may pay a blanket fee of several hundred dollars to cover the music used throughout a video, or what's called a "needle drop" fee for each use of a piece of music within a video. These fees generally range from $15 to $75 per needle drop.

Listed below are the telephone numbers and addresses of key rights organizations and several stock music libraries.

Contact Options

Barbara Zimmerman
BZ Rights and Permissions
125 W. 72nd St.
New York, NY 10023
(212) 580-0615
Rights Consultant

BMI
320 W. 57th St.
New York, NY 10019
(212) 586-2000
Trade Association

The American Society of Composers,
Authors and Publishers (ASCAP)
1 Lincoln Plaza
New York, NY 10023
(212) 621-6000
Trade Association

Music Libraries:

Associated Production Music
6255 Sunset Blvd., #820
Hollywood, CA 90026
(800) 543-4276

Chameleon Music Production Library
P.O. Box 243
Agawam, MA 01001
(413) 789-1917

Firstcom
13747 Montfort Dr., Suite 220
Dallas, TX 75240
(800) 858-8880

De Wolfe Music Library
25 W. 45th St., Eighth Floor
New York, NY 10036
(800) 221-6713 or (212) 382-0220

TRF Production Music Libraries
747 Chestnut Ridge Rd., Suite 301
Chestnut Ridge, NY 10977
(800) 899-6874

Green Marketing

GUIDELINES FOR THE USE of environmental marketing claims such as "recyclable," "biodegradable," "compostable," etc., have been established by the Federal Trade Commission, but the guides themselves are not enforceable regulations, nor do they have the force and effect of law. These guides specifically address the application of Section 5 of the Federal Trade Commission Act–which makes deceptive acts and practices in or affecting commerce unlawful–to environmental advertising and marketing practices. Guides for the Use of Environmental Marketing Claims provide the basis for voluntary compliance with such laws by members of industry, and are available from the EPA and the FTC.

Contact Option

Carol C. Weisner
Environmental Protection Specialist
Municipal & Industrial Solid Waste Division
U.S. Environmental Protection Agency
401 M St., SW (OS-301)
Washington, DC 20460
(202) 260-4489

FTC Environmental Marketing Guidelines

In 1992, the Federal Trade Commission issued its Guides for the Use of Environmental Marketing Claims, which are based on data from FTC investigations, hearings, and public input. While these guides are not legally enforceable, they provide guidance to marketers in conforming with legal requirements. The guides apply to advertising, labeling, and other forms of marketing to consumers, and do not preempt state or local laws or regulations.

The FTC guides specify that whenever marketers make objective environmental claims–explicit or implied–these must be substantiated by competent and reliable evidence. The guides outline four general concerns that apply to all environmental claims:

- Qualifications and disclosures should be clear and prominent to prevent deception.

- Environmental claims should make clear whether they apply to the product, the package, or a component of either. Claims need not be qualified with regard to minor, incidental components of the product or package.

- Environmental claims should not overstate the environmental attribute or benefit. Marketers should avoid implying a significant environmental benefit where the benefit is, in fact, negligible.

- A claim comparing the environmental attributes of one product with those of another product should make the basis for the comparison sufficiently clear and should be substantiated.

Certain environmental marketing claims are addressed specifically:

General Environmental Benefit Claims

In general, unqualified general environmental claims are difficult to interpret, and may have a wide range of meanings to consumers. Every express and material implied claim conveyed to consumers about an objective quality should be substantiated. Unless they can be substantiated, broad environmental claims should be avoided or qualified.

Degradable, Biodegradable, and Photodegradable

In general, unqualified claims of compostability should be substantiated by evidence that the product will completely break down and return to nature, that is, decompose into elements found in nature, within a reasonably short period of time after consumers dispose of it in the customary way. Such claims should be qualified to the extent necessary to avoid consumer deception about: (a) the product or package's ability to degrade in the environment where it is customarily disposed of; and (b) the extent and rate of degradation.

Compostable

In general, unqualified claims of compostability should be substantiated by evidence that all the materials in the product or package will break down into, or otherwise become a part of, usable compost (e.g., soil-conditioning material, mulch) in a safe and timely manner in an appropriate composting program or facility, or in a home compost pile or device. Compostable claims should be qualified to the extent necessary to avoid consumer deception: (1) if municipal composting facilities are not available to a substantial majority of consumers or communities where the product is sold; (2) if the claim misleads consumers about the environmental benefit provided when the product is disposed of in a landfill; or (3) if consumers misunderstand the claim to mean that the package can be safely composted in their home compost pile or device, when in fact it cannot.

Recyclable

In general, a product or package should not be marketed as recyclable unless it can be collected, separated, or otherwise recovered from the solid waste stream for use in the form of raw materials in the manufacture or assembly of a new product or package. Unqualified claims of recyclability may be made if the entire product or package, excluding incidental components, is recyclable.

Claims about products with both recyclable and non-recyclable components should be adequately qualified. If incidental components significantly limit the ability to recycle a product, the claim would

Green Marketing (cont'd)

be deceptive. If, because of its size or shape, a product is not accepted in recycling programs, it should not be marketed as recyclable. Qualification may be necessary to avoid consumer deception about the limited availability of recycling programs and collection sites if recycling collection sites are not available to a substantial majority of consumers or communities.

Recycled Content

In general, claims of recycled content should only be made for materials that have been recovered or diverted from the solid waste stream, either during the manufacturing process (pre-consumer) or after consumer use (post-consumer). An advertiser should be able to substantiate that pre-consumer content would otherwise have entered the solid waste stream. Distinctions made between pre- and post-consumer content should be substantiated. Unqualified claims may be made if the entire product or package, excluding minor, incidental components, is made from recycled material. Products or packages only partially made of recycled material should be qualified to indicate the amount, by weight, in the finished product or package.

Source Reduction

In general, an unqualified claim of refillableness should not be asserted unless a system is provided for: (1) the collection and return of the package for refill; or (2) the later refill of the package by consumers with product subsequently sold in another package. The claim should not be made if it is up to consumers to find ways to refill the package.

Ozone Safe and Ozone Friendly

In general, a product should not be advertised as "ozone safe," "ozone friendly," or as not containing CFCs if the product contains any ozone-depleting chemical. Claims about the reduction of a product's ozone-depletion potential may be made if adequately substantiated.

Source: FTC News, Summary of FTC Environmental Marketing Guidelines

Recommended Resource

For copies of the FTC Environmental Marketing Guidelines in their entirety, as well as the environmental assessment of these guidelines, and news releases on FTC cases in the green-marketing area, contact:

FTC Public Reference Branch
Room 130
Sixth St. and Pennsylvania Ave., NW
Washington, DC 20580
(202) 326-2222

Sources for Marketing Information

THE FOLLOWING ARE a few of the "Best 100 Sources for Marketing Information" as rated by *American Demographics' 1994 Directory:*

ACCRA (American Chamber of Commerce Research Association)
(703) 998-0072

American Business Information
(402) 593-4500

CACI Marketing Systems
(800) 292-2224

Donnelley Marketing
(203) 353-7223

Find/SVP
(212) 633-4510

Information Resources
(312) 726-1221

Mediamark Research (MRI)
(212) 599-0444

National Opinion Research Center
(312) 753-7500

Roper/Starch
(212) 599-0700

Licenses

Distribution of Licensed Product Sales by Property Type, U.S. and Canada ($ billions), 1994

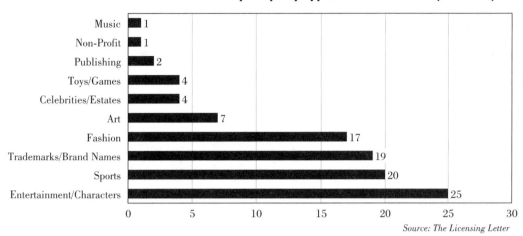

Music 1
Non-Profit 1
Publishing 2
Toys/Games 4
Celebrities/Estates 4
Art 7
Fashion 17
Trademarks/Brand Names 19
Sports 20
Entertainment/Characters 25

Source: The Licensing Letter

Recommended Resources

The Licensing Letter
EPM Communications, $295/12 issues
   An indispensable source of information on the
$91.1 billion licensing industry. Includes statistics,
new property tips, and exclusive industry surveys
and forecasts.

The Licensing Letter Sourcebook
EPM Communications, $295
   This annual directory is invaluable to anyone in–
or wanting to get into–the licensing community. It's
a comprehensive guide to more than 4,000 licensors,

licensing agents, licensees, trade associations, consultants, and other essential service providers. Also
included are details on properties owned and agents
used by licensors; properties represented by licensing agents; and licenses held and products manufactured by licensees.

Contact Option

EPM Communications
488 E. 18th St.
Brooklyn, NY 11226
(718) 469-9330

E-MAIL

eMarketing. Send e-mail to emarketing@almanac.yoyo.com. See p. xi for instructions.

A book from the editor of the Information Please Business Almanac on high-technology methods of marketing products, from the Internet
to database marketing to multimedia. The entire text of this book is available for free.

The Top Reference Sources

News Media Yellow Book
Monitor Publishing, $235/4 editions per year
104 Fifth Ave., Second Floor
New York, NY 10011
(212) 627-4140

Monitor's Yellow Book series includes several volumes containing names and phone numbers of

companies and key contact people in a given
industry.
   One of the best of Monitor's Yellow Book Reference series, the *News Media Yellow Book* is an
invaluable resource for anyone looking to establish solid media contacts and make informed public relations maneuvers.

Top Consumer Brands

FINANCIAL WORLD ANNUALLY EVALUATES major consumer brands, computing the value of the brand if it were to be sold. The following are the leading consumer brands by market value in each category.

Cash Value of Major Consumer Brands

Brand & Category	Company	Value ($ mil.)	1993 Sales ($ mil.)	One-Year Change (%)
Apparel & accessories				
Levi's	Levi Strauss	5,142	3,533	6
Beers				
Budweiser	Anheuser-Busch	9,724	5,960	-3
Champagnes and Wines				
Moet & Chandon	LVMH	385	472	-19
Soft drinks and juices				
Coca-Cola	Coca-Cola	35,950	9,687	9
Spirits				
Bacardi	Bacardi	7,163	1,505	16
Cosmetics & fashion				
Louis Vuitton	LVMH	3,117	912	25
Coffees				
Nescafé	Nescafé	11,549	5,710	7
Condiments & Spices				
Heinz	H.J. Heinz	3,325	1,691	8
Confectionery				
Nestlé	Nestlé	2,522	4,369	28
Prepared foods				
Kellogg's	Kellogg	9,372	5,477	-3
High-tech				
Kodak	Eastman Kodak	10,020	6,510	8
Household Products				
Tefal	SEB	456	508	0
Equipment				
GE	General Electric	5,710	7,450	7
Supplies				
Duracell	Duracell	2,693	1,742	26
Dental Care				
Colgate	Colgate-Palmolive	3,442	1,700	19
Hair Care				
Clairol	Bristol-Myers Squibb	766	930	-3
Medication				
Tylenol	Johnson & Johnson	1,976	1,023	1
Men's toiletries				
Gillette	Gillette	8,221	2,118	16
Miscellaneous				
Pampers	Procter & Gamble	5,732	4,141	-16
Moisturizers				
Oil of Olay	Procter & Gamble	788	700	14
Soaps				
Palmolive	Colgate-Palmolive	365	850	6
Tires				
Goodyear	Goodyear Tire & Rubber	2,866	6,905	12
Tobacco				
Marlboro	Philip Morris	33,045	9,782	-36
Toys & Games				
Nintendo	Nintendo	5,224	4,779	14

Source: Financial World, Aug. 2, 1994

Network and Cable TV Data

Advertising Volume in the United States ($ millions)

Year	Total Ad Volume	TV Ad Volume	% in TV
1983	75,850	16,759	22.1
1984	87,820	19,848	22.6
1985	94,750	21,022	22.2
1986	102,140	22,881	22.4
1987	109,650	23,904	21.8
1988	118,050	26,686	21.8
1989	123,930	26,891	21.7
1990	128,640	28,405	22.1
1991	126,400	27,402	21.7
1992	131,290	29,409	22.4
1993	138,080	30,584	22.1

Television Advertising Volume ($ millions)

Year	Network	Spot	Local	Total
1983	6,955	4,827	4,345	16,127
1984	8,318	5,488	5,084	18,890
1985	8,060	6,004	5,714	19,778
1986	8,342	6,570	6,514	21,426
1987	8,500	6,846	6,833	22,179
1988	9,172	7,147	7,270	23,589
1989	9,110	7,354	7,612	24,076
1990	9,902	7,788	7,856	25,546
1991	9,589	7,110	7,565	24,264
1992	10,249	7,551	8,079	25,879
1993	10,209	7,800	8,435	26,444

Sources: TVB 1993-94 & McCann-Erickson

Avg. Cost per :30 Commercial, 1994 ($ thou.)

Daytime (M–F 10 A.M.–4:30 P.M.)	14.4
Early News (M–F 6:30–7:30 P.M.)	49.3
Prime Time (M–S 8–11 P.M.)	123.6
Late Eve. (M–F 11:30 PM–1 A.M.)	24.1

Cost per TV Home Rating Point, 1994* ($)

Daytime (M–F 10 A.M.–4:30 P.M.)	3,445
Early News (M–F 6:30–7:30 P.M.)	5,803
Prime Time (M–S 8–11 P.M.)	10,338
Late Eve. (M–F 11:30 P.M.–1 A.M.)	8,792

average of 1st-4th quarter 1994   *Source: Marketer's Guide to Media*

Time Spent Viewing TV per Home per Day

Year	Average Viewing Time
1981	6 hours, 45 minutes
1983	7 hours, 2 minutes
1985	7 hours, 10 minutes
1989	7 hours, 1 minute
1990	6 hours, 53 minutes
1991	6 hours, 56 minutes
1992	7 hours, 4 minutes
1993	7 hours, 12 minutes
1994	7 hours, 15 minutes

Sources: TVB & Nielsen Media Research

Network and Cable TV Data (cont'd)

Network Commercial Activity by Commercial Length (% of total)

Year	:10	:15	:20	:30	:45	:60	:90+	Total
1981	0.9	0.1	–	94.2	3.2	1.5	0.1	100
1982	0.9	0.1	–	93.7	3.7	1.5	0.1	100
1983	0.9	0.2	–	93.8	2.9	1.8	0.4	100
1984	1.0	5.2	–	89.2	2.0	2.1	0.5	100
1985	1.3	10.1	0.8	83.5	1.7	2.2	0.4	100
1986	0.5	20.9	1.2	73.6	1.4	1.8	0.6	100
1987	0.2	30.9	1.0	65.1	0.9	1.5	0.4	100
1989	0.3	37.9	1.2	57.4	1.0	1.8	0.4	100
1990	0.1	35.4	1.4	60.1	1.0	1.7	0.3	100
1991	0.1	33.6	0.8	62.5	0.9	1.7	0.4	100
1992	0.1	31.9	0.9	63.1	1.0	1.7	1.3	100
1993	0.1	31.2	0.8	65.0	0.4	1.3	1.2	100

Sources: TVB & Arbitron, annual average

Commercial Television Stations

Year	Total	VHF	UHF
1981	756	519	237
1982	777	517	260
1983	813	519	294
1984	841	523	318
1985	883	520	363
1986	919	522	397
1987	968	524	444
1988	1,028	539	489
1989	1,061	545	516
1990	1,092	547	545
1991	1,099	547	552
1992	1,118	551	567
1993	1,137	552	585
1994	1,145	561	584

Sources: TVB & Television Digest

Growth of Cable TV Penetration by County Size (%)

Year	% of TV Homes with Cable	County Size "A"	County Size "B"	County Size "C"	County Size "D"
1969	5	1	3	14	9
1974	14	4	10	26	15
1979	23	8	19	35	22
1981	34	24	40	49	36
1983	42	31	50	58	43
1985	49	39	57	60	46
1986	48	41	55	57	43
1987	51	45	59	58	48
1988	56	48	61	61	48
1989	59	52	64	63	48
1990	61	58	67	66	51
1991	64	62	67	70	56
1992	65	64	69	72	58

Source: Nielsen

Network and Cable TV Data (cont'd)

TV Network Telephone Directory

Network	Telephone Number
A. C. Nielsen	(212) 708-7500
Arbitron	(212) 887-1300
Arts & Entertainment (A&E)	(212) 661-4500
Black Entertainment TV (BET)	(212) 697-5500
Cable News Network (CNN)	(212) 852-6900
Capital Cities/ABC	(212) 456-7777
CBS Network	(212) 975-4146
CNBC	(212) 664-6578
Comedy Central	(212) 767-8647
Country Music Television (CMT)	(212) 916-1000
Court TV	(212) 692-7859
The Discovery Channel (DSC)	(212) 751-2120
Entertainment Television (E!)	(212) 852-5100
ESPN Sales	(212) 916-9200
The Family Channel (FAM)	(212) 997-1710
Fox TV	(212) 452-5555
Group W Broadcasting	(212) 856-8000
The Learning Channel (TLC)	(212) 751-2120
Lifetime	(718) 424-7000
MTV/ VH-1/ Nickelodeon/ Nick at Night	(212) 258-8000
The Nashville Network (TNN)	(212) 916-1000
NBC Network	(212) 664-4444
Prevue	(800) 447-7388
Prime Network	(212) 664-3472
SportsChannel America (SCA)	(212) 664-7920
TBS	(212) 692-6900
Telemundo	(212) 492-5500
The Travel Channel	(212) 308-3055
Turner Broadcasting/Headline News	(212) 852-6600
Turner Network Television (TNT)	(212) 692-6900
Univision	(212) 455-5200
USA/SCI-FI	(212) 408-9100
The Weather Channel (TWC)	(212) 308-3055

Advertising Expenditures by Media, 1993

Category	Expenditures ($ millions)	% Change (1991-92)	Media as % of Total
Estimated unmeasured	89,728.8	3.1	65.0
Measured media	48,351.2	9.3	35.0
Local newspaper	11,774.8	18.7	8.5
Network TV	10,892.7	1.3	7.9
Spot TV	9,773.5	4.0	7.1
Magazine	7,590.5	6.8	5.5
Cable TV networks	2,329.0	46.4	1.7
Syndicated TV	1,620.1	25.9	1.2
National spot radio	1,131.6	3.6	0.8
National newspaper	1,034.4	7.3	0.7
Sunday magazine	925.1	-1.8	0.7
Outdoor	696.0	6.3	0.5
Network radio	583.6	6.3	0.4
TOTAL	138,080.0	5.2	100.0

Note: Measured media include above listed. Unmeasured include direct mail, promotion, co-op, couponing, catalogues, business and farm publications, and special events.

Source: AdAge/CMR, Robert J. Coen, McCann-Erickson

Radio Data

Radio Audience by Location of Listening (% all radio reach)

	Men 18+	Women 18+	Teens 12–17
At home	71.8	78.8	94.4
In car	85.2	76.8	78.8
Other	45.8	38.3	49.8

Source: RADAR®, copyright© by Statistical Research, Inc., Spring 1994

Radio Usage (average daily time spent listening)

By Age	Men (hr:min)	Women (hr:min)
18+	2:59	2:49
18-24	2:50	2:40
25-34	3:18	2:55
35-49	3:09	2:51
50+	2:39	2:46

Source: Calculated from RADAR®, copyright© by Statistical Research, Inc., Spring 1994

Profile of Daily Listeners of Radio Stations by Format

Format	% Male	% Female	Median Age	Median Income ($)	% 1+ Yrs. of College
TOTAL	47.97	52.03	41.88	35,696	40.83
Adult contemporary	42.08	57.92	37.39	42,293	48.57
All news	52.87	47.13	48.02	43,940	49.78
Album oriented rock	63.88	36.12	30.47	44,248	50.59
Black/R&B	41.27	58.73	34.01	30,356	38.06
Classic rock	60.70	39.30	32.31	38,281	47.83
Classical	56.55	43.45	48.27	42,085	62.49
Country	47.86	52.14	39.96	36,016	36.97
Easy listening	44.16	55.84	53.59	39,799	46.78
Educational	78.09	21.91	42.07*	42,409*	78.94*
Ethnic	43.37	56.63	37.45	54,446	53.22
Golden oldies	52.88	47.12	40.89	43,278	47.86
Jazz	55.82	44.18	40.29	40,908	47.97
MOR/nostalgia	44.37	55.63	58.90	34,107	39.22
New age	67.94	32.06	32.56	45,820	70.30
News/talk	55.59	44.41	50.64	43,784	49.43
Religious	37.18	62.82	41.80	35,345	42.71
Soft contemporary	43.88	56.12	41.88	40,423	46.14
Urban contemporary	46.32	53.68	34.34	25,500	30.56
Variety	46.58	53.42	41.65	43,218	54.29

*Number of cases too small for reliability

Source: Simmons, Study of Media Markets, 1994

Radio Data (cont'd)

Radio Network Telephone Directory

Station	Telephone Number
ABC Radio Network	(212) 456-1777
ActRadio	(800) 543-1101
American Urban Radio	(212) 714-1000
Arbitron	(212) 887-1300
Banner Radio	(212) 424-6160
Business Radio	(719) 528-7040
CBS Radio Network	(212) 975-4468
CBS Radio Reps	(212) 975-5354
CMN Radio Network	(212) 532-1900
Christal	(212) 424-6500
DNR	(212) 309-9000
Eastman	(212) 424-6400
Katz	(212) 424-6000
Katz & Powell	(212) 545-0600
Keystone Broadcasting System	(203) 364-2080
McGavern Guild	(212) 916-0500
MediaAmerica	(212) 302-1100
NBC Radio Networks	(212) 237-2500
Radio Advertising Bureau	(212) 254-4800
Radio Network Association	(212) 975-5333
Roslin	(212) 486-0720
Savalli Broadcast	(212) 239-3288
Torbet	(212) 309-9099
USA Radio Networks	(214) 484-2020
Wall St. Journal/Dow Jones	(212) 416-2380
Westwood One Entertainment/Source	(212) 641-2000

Source: Marketer's Guide to Media

The Top Reference Sources

Simmons Market Research Bureau
420 Lexington Ave.
New York, NY 10170
(212) 916-8958

Simmons Market Research Bureau is a leading supplier of syndicated consumer media and mar-keting studies. The studies available include: The Study of Media and Markets (SMM), Simmons Teenage Research Study (STARS), The Kids Study (6–14), and The Hispanic Study. The studies measure magazines, radio, television, cable, newspapers, outoor advertising, and the Yellow Pages.

Magazine Data

Adweek's Ten Hottest Small Magazines

Rank	Magazine	Revenue Up ($ millions)	Ad Pages Up (%)	Circulation Up (%)
1	Worth	5.7	23	53
2	Traditional Home	4.6	34	11
3	Men's Journal	6.1	47	82
4	Martha Stewart Living	7.6	76	27
5	Fitness	2.8	37	17
6	Elle Décor	4.7	54	6
7	Backpacker	3.2	35	18
8	Country Home	5.8	16	-3
9	Discover	3.2	16	-2
10	American Heritage	1.8	26	-1

Source: Adweek, Feb. 27, 1995, © ASM Communications, Inc. Reprinted with permission

Top Magazine Spending by Company

Rank	Company	Magazines	Media Total	% in Magazines
1	General Motors	389.9	1,380.6	28
2	Philip Morris	305.8	1,278.9	24
3	Ford Motor	239.3	908.0	26
4	Procter & Gamble	207.5	1,443.5	14
5	Roll International	151.5	157.0	96
6	Chrysler	145.4	724.1	20
7	Nestlé SA	144.7	472.1	31
8	Toyota Motor	128.7	517.9	25
9	Sony	121.7	327.7	37
10	Unilever PLC	90.0	390.7	23
11	Time Warner	87.3	456.9	19
12	Bradford Exchange	87.1	89.8	97
13	Bertelsmann AG	83.8	93.0	90
14	National Syndications	76.7	81.0	95
15	Benckiser, Joh A GMBH	70.1	120.7	58

Source: Adweek, Feb. 27, 1995, © ASM Communications, Inc. Reprinted with permission

Magazine Data (cont'd)

Top 50 Magazines in Paid Circulation

Rank	Magazine	Avg. Paid Circ., 1994	% Change vs. 1993
1	Parade	37,604,285	0.9
2	Modern Maturity	21,716,727	-2.3
3	USA Weekend	18,502,858	0.0
4	Reader's Digest	15,126,664	-5.8
5	TV Guide	14,037,062	-0.6
6	National Geographic	9,203,079	-2.0
7	Better Homes	7,613,661	0.2
8	Good Housekeeping	5,223,935	1.2
9	Ladies' Home Journal	5,048,081	-2.1
10	Family Circle	5,005,301	-2.1
11	Woman's Day	4,724,500	-2.8
12	McCall's	4,611,848	0.1
13	Time	4,063,146	-1.0
14	Prevention	3,427,803	6.4
15	People Weekly	3,424,858	-0.6
16	Redbook	3,401,775	1.7
17	Playboy	3,401,264	1.7
18	Sports Illustrated	3,252,641	-3.1
19	Newsweek	3,158,617	0.1
20	Cosmopolitan	2,527,928	-3.8
21	Southern Living	2,472,649	4.4
22	U.S. News	2,240,710	-1.8
23	Smithsonian	2,214,509	0.1
24	Glamour	2,181,316	-5.4
25	Field & Stream	2,004,087	-0.2
26	Money	1,982,123	-5.6
27	Seventeen	1,978,155	1.9
28	Ebony	1,937,095	0.3
29	YM	1,933,775	13.3
30	Country Living	1,932,840	-2.1
31	Parents	1,852,517	4.5
32	Popular Science	1,808,140	-0.4
33	Popular Mechanics	1,636,210	-1.3
34	Life	1,596,862	-1.7
35	Outdoor Life	1,503,257	0.0
36	Sunset	1,498,417	4.0
37	Golf Digest	1,465,494	0.3
38	Soap Opera Digest	1,422,958	-6.0
39	Penthouse	1,304,719	8.6
40	Mademoiselle	1,304,059	7.8
41	New Woman	1,301,859	-1.0
42	Teen	1,280,148	9.3
43	Golf	1,269,642	3.9
44	Men's Health	1,258,493	37.0
45	Cooking Light	1,248,939	11.5
46	Boys' Life	1,242,594	-1.8
47	Rolling Stone	1,221,417	-1.2
48	Consumer's Digest	1,208,643	-3.7
49	Self	1,201,395	-6.9
50	Bon Appétit	1,187,437	8.3

Top 50 Magazines in Ad Revenues

Rank	Magazine	1994 Rev. ($ mil.)	% Change vs. 1993
1	Parade	447.6	9.0
2	People Weekly	405.7	10.4
3	TV Guide	391.7	21.6
4	Sports Illustrated	385.3	27.6
5	Time	372.0	8.1
6	Newsweek	278.9	7.0
7	Business Week	233.8	7.5
8	U.S.A. News	221.1	9.4
9	Better Homes	221.0	17.1
10	Good Housekeeping	218.6	5.6
11	USA Weekend	218.1	19.4
12	Forbes	189.2	8.9
13	Family Circle	178.7	9.5
14	Woman's Day	167.3	14.3
15	Fortune	163.6	9.6
16	Cosmopolitan	148.0	5.1
17	Ladies' Home Journal	138.8	8.6
18	Reader's Digest	134.3	2.2
19	McCall's	114.4	11.6
20	Vogue	111.0	-1.0
21	NY Times Magazine	110.7	0.0
22	Money	104.2	5.8
23	Redbook	100.4	6.2
24	Glamour	98.3	-3.6
25	Southern Living	96.5	10.1
26	Rolling Stone	83.2	16.4
27	Golf Digest	82.8	-1.9
28	Car and Driver	82.4	36.8
29	New Yorker	77.4	9.7
30	Entertainment Weekly	70.0	43.4
31	Brides	69.8	16.9
32	Country Living	67.8	4.5
33	Parents	62.4	-8.4
34	Elle	60.1	11.3
35	Inc.	58.5	7.3
36	Golf	55.1	14.2
37	Harper's Bazaar	54.7	-4.6
38	Road & Track	54.2	35.2
39	Vanity Fair	53.5	-6.7
40	Modern Bride	53.4	5.6
41	Modern Maturity	53.2	2.0
42	Self	50.4	12.0
43	GQ	49.5	4.8
44	Sunset	49.4	-5.0
45	Travel	48.4	-5.4
46	House Beautiful	48.1	12.5
47	Seventeen	47.9	19.4
48	National Geographic	47.7	2.0
49	Playboy	45.9	-0.4
50	New York	43.2	-0.5

Source: Adweek, Feb. 27, 1995, © ASM Communications, Inc.
Reprinted with permission

Magazine Data (cont'd)

Magazine Ad Department Telephone Directory

Magazine Ad Departments	NY Telephone
American Health	(212) 366-8900
American Way	(212) 455-6200
Architectural Digest	(212) 880-8194
Automobile	(212) 332-0200
Barron's	(212) 808-7200
Better Homes & Gardens	(212) 557-6600
Black Enterprise	(212) 242-8000
Bon Appétit	(212) 880-8800
Boys' Life	(212) 532-0985
Business Week	(212) 512-2700
Cable Guide	(212) 683-6116
Chicago Tribune	(212) 682-3033
Colonial Homes	(212) 830-2900
Condé Nast Publications	(212) 880-8800
Cosmopolitan	(212) 649-3324
Country America	(212) 551-7022
Country Home	(212) 551-7028
Country Living	(212) 649-3192
Ebony	(212) 397-4500
Elle	(212) 767-5800
Endless Vacation	(212) 362-7654
Entertainment Weekly	(212) 522-5206
Esquire	(212) 649-4050
Family Circle	(212) 463-1000
Field & Stream	(212) 779-5450
Financial World	(212) 594-5030
Food & Wine	(212) 382-5600
Forbes	(212) 620-2200
Fortune	(212) 522-5203
GQ	(212) 880-8000
Glamour	(212) 880-8800
Golf Digest	(212) 789-3000
Golf Magazine	(212) 779-5000
Good Housekeeping	(212) 649-2557
Gourmet	(212) 880-2712
Harper's Bazaar	(212) 903-5000
Home	(212) 767-5519
Home Mechanix	(212) 779-5134
House Beautiful	(212) 903-5100
Inc.	(212) 326-2600
Inside Sports	(212) 687-1130
Insight	(800) 356-3588
Jet	(212) 397-4500
Kiplinger's Personal Finance	(212) 398-6320
Ladies' Home Journal	(212) 953-7070
Life	(212) 522-1212
Los Angeles Times Magazine	(800) 528-4637
Mademoiselle	(212) 880-7971
McCall's	(212) 463-1000
Metropolitan Home	(212) 767-5522
Modern Maturity	(212) 599-1880
Money	(212) 522-4829

Magazine Ad Departments	NY Telephone
Motor Trend	(212) 935-9150
National Enquirer	(212) 979-4810
National Geographic	(212) 974-1700
National Geographic Traveler	(212) 974-1700
Nation's Business	(212) 692-2215
Natural History	(212) 599-5555
New Choices	(212) 366-8800
New York	(212) 880-0700
New York Times Magazine	(212) 556-1633
The New Yorker	(212) 840-3800
Newsweek	(212) 445-4000
Omni	(212) 496-6100
Outdoor Life	(212) 779-5450
Parade	(212) 573-7000
Parenting	(212) 840-4200
Parents	(212) 878-8700
Penthouse	(212) 496-6100
People	(212) 522-1212
Playboy	(212) 261-5000
Popular Mechanics	(212) 649-3135
Popular Photography	(212) 767-6086
Popular Science	(212) 779-5000
Prevention	(212) 697-2040
Reader's Digest	(212) 953-0030
Redbook	(212) 649-3358
Rolling Stone	(212) 484-1616
Sassy	(212) 551-9500
Scientific American	(212) 754-0550
Scouting	(212) 532-0985
Self	(212) 880-8814
Seventeen	(212) 407-9700
Smithsonian	(212) 490-2510
Soap Opera Digest	(212) 332-0250
Southern Living	(212) 986-9010
Spin	(212) 633-8200
Sporting News	(212) 779-5600
Sports Afield	(212) 649-4300
Sports Illustrated	(212) 522-1212
Sunset	(212) 986-3810
Tennis	(212) 789-3000
Time	(212) 522-1212
Town & Country	(212) 903-5000
Travel & Leisure	(212) 382-5600
Travel Holiday	(212) 366-8700
TV Guide	(212) 852-7500
US	(212) 484-1616
U.S. News & World Report	(212) 830-1500
Vanity Fair	(212) 880-8194
Victoria	(212) 649-3700
Vogue	(212) 880-8405
Woman's Day	(212) 767-6000
Working Mother	(212) 551-9352

Source: Marketer's Guide to Media

Newspaper Data

Top 25 National Newspaper Advertisers

Rank	Advertiser	1993 Spending ($ millions)	% Change from 1992
1	AT&T	33.8	100.1
2	General Motors	28.3	-6.2
3	Ford Motor	23.2	39.2
4	Fidelity Investment	22.1	-25.8
5	Dreyfus	21.1	16.1
6	Toyota Motor	19.8	36.5
7	CML Group	13.4	158.9
8	Marriott	12.6	23.3
9	Merrill Lynch	12.5	6.8
10	Dow Jones	12.2	-16.7
11	Chrysler	9.4	-3.3
12	Charles Schwab	9.3	63.1
13	IBM	9.2	-48.9
14	Daimler-Benz	8.9	9.5
15	MCI Communications	8.7	255.4
16	Franklin Resources	8.5	0.1
17	American Express	8.0	2.7
18	Citicorp	7.8	214.0
19	Lehman Bros.	7.8	48.3
20	ITT	7.6	15.1
21	Spring	7.5	26.2
22	Damark	7.5	-49.0
23	Delta Air Lines	7.3	16.4
24	U.S. government	7.1	3.8
25	Xerox	7.1	59.7

Source: Advertising Age, September 8, 1994

The Top Reference Sources

Marketer's Guide to Media
Adweek, $110/2 editions per year
(800) 468-2395

This semiannual publication from the folks at
Adweek gives a terrific overview of the current

effectiveness of advertising. The statistics, facts,
and trends presented here are illuminating, and
the book is a useful telephone, address, and contact directory for the major media.

Newspaper Data (cont'd)

Newspaper Advertising Departments

Newspaper	Telephone
Albuquerque Journal/Tribune	(505) 823-3311
Arizona Republic/Phoenix Gazette	(602) 271-8498
Atlanta Journal-Constitution	(404) 577-5772
Baltimore Sun	(410) 332-6000
Boston Globe	(617) 929-2100
Boston Herald	(617) 426-3000
Buffalo News	(716) 849-3411
Charlotte Observer	(704) 358-5420
Chicago Sun-Times	(312) 321-2350
Chicago Tribune	(312) 222-4150
Christian Science Monitor	(617) 450-2652
Cincinnati Enquirer/Post	(513) 768-8220
Cleveland Plain Dealer	(216) 999-4360
Columbus Dispatch	(614) 461-5500
Dallas Morning News	(214) 977-8511
Denver Post	(303) 820-1434
(Denver) Rocky Mountain News	(303) 892-5411
Detroit Free Press/News	(313) 222-2700
Grand Rapids Press	(616) 459-1552
Greensboro News & Record	(910) 373-7150
Greenville News/Piedmont	(803) 298-4216
Hartford Courant	(203) 241-6221
Houston Chronicle	(713) 220-2680
Houston Post	(713) 840-5134
Indianapolis Star/News	(317) 633-1143
Kansas City Star	(816) 234-4150
Los Angeles Times	(213) 237-7291
Louisville Courier-Journal/Times	(502) 582-4711
Memphis Commercial Appeal	(901) 529-2251
Miami Herald	(305) 376-2820
Milwaukee Journal/Sentinel	(414) 224-2498
Minneapolis Star-Tribune	(612) 673-7777
Nashville Banner/Tennessean	(615) 259-8338
New Orleans Times-Picayune	(504) 826-3000
New York Daily News	(212) 210-2063
New York Newsday	(718) 343-9000
New York Times	(212) 556-8905
Newark Star Ledger	(201) 877-4072
Norfolk Ledger-Star/Virginia Pilot	(804) 446-2450
(Oklahoma City) Daily Oklahoman	(405) 475-3338
Orlando Sentinel	(407) 420-5191
Philadelphia Inquirer/News	(215) 854-2000
Pittsburgh Post Gazette	(412) 263-1333
Portland Oregonian	(503) 221-8334
Providence Journal/Bulletin	(401) 277-7060
Raleigh News & Observer	(919) 829-4646
Richmond Times-Dispatch	(804) 649-6251
Sacramento Bee	(916) 321-1476
(Salt Lake City) Tribune	(801) 237-2815
San Antonio Express/News	(210) 351-7482
San Diego Union/Tribune	(619) 293-1578
San Francisco Chronicle	(415) 777-7777
Seattle Times/Post-Intelligencer	(206) 464-2111
St. Louis Post-Dispatch	(314) 340-8500
St. Petersburg Times	(813) 893-8725
Tampa Tribune	(813) 259-7746
USA Today	(212) 715-5411
USA Weekend	(212) 715-2100
Wall Street Journal	(212) 808-6700
Washington Post	(202) 334-7642

Alternative Newspapers

WITH ORIGINS AMONG THE counterculture publications of the 1960s, alternative newspapers have come a long way. The Association of Alternative Newsweeklies counts 87 members and a collective readership of over 13 million–a distinct opportunity for the appropriate advertisers.

Contact Options

Association of Alternative Newsweeklies
Helene Seisel, Administrative Director
1201 E. Jefferson
Suite A-260
Phoenix, AZ 85034
(602) 229-8487
Call for membership roster, which includes addresses, telephone numbers, and staff information, as well as helpful circulation and demographic data.

Alternative Press Center
P.O. Box 33109
Baltimore, MD 21218
(410) 243-2471
Produces the quarterly Alternative Press Index, a selection of articles indexed by subject.

Alternative Newspapers (cont'd)

Alternative Newspapers

Newspaper	Telephone
Austin Chronicle	(512) 454-5766
Baltimore City Paper	(410) 523-2300
Boston Phoenix	(617) 536-5390
Chicago Reader	(312) 828-0350
City Pages (Minneapolis)	(612) 375-1015
Creative Loafing (Atlanta)	(800) 950-5623
Dallas Observer	(214) 757-9000
Fairfield/Westchester Weekly	(203) 226-4242
Houston Press	(713) 624-1400
Los Angeles Reader	(213) 965-7430
L.A. Weekly	(213) 465-4414
Metro (San Jose)	(408) 298-8000
Metro Times (Detroit)	(313) 961-4060
Miami New Times	(305) 372-0004
New York Press	(212) 941-1130
Philadelphia City Paper	(215) 735-8444
Phoenix New Times	(602) 271-0040
The Riverfront Times (St. Louis)	(314) 231-6666
Sacramento News & Review	(916) 737-1234
San Diego Reader	(619) 235-3000
San Francisco Bay Guardian	(415) 255-3100
SF Weekly	(415) 541-0700
Twin Cities Reader	(612) 321-7300
The Village Voice (New York)	(212) 475-3300
Washington City Paper	(202) 332-2100
Westword (Denver)	(303) 296-7744
Willamette Week (Portland)	(503) 243-2122

Note: All newspapers are over 70,000 circulation

College Newspaper Advertising

THE AVERAGE COLLEGE NEWSPAPER issue is read by 62 percent of the students in its market. If a company wants to reach that market by placing ads in college newspapers, it may be easier and more cost-efficient to contact one of the few existing college newspaper advertising syndicates.

These organizations will ship your company's copy to thousands of college newspapers and then collect tearsheets and monitor advertising performance. They can also match your company's specific needs to particular college newspapers, based on categories such as college enrollment, circulation, cost to attend, or college degrees offered.

It is not necessary to pay these syndicates for placing ads. They are commissioned by college newspapers to represent them to advertisers.

Contact Options

Newspaper Syndicates:

American Passage Media
1114 Ave. of the Americas, 14th Floor
New York, NY 10036
(212) 382-0560

Cass Communications
1800 Sherman Pl.
Evanston, IL 60201
(708) 475-8800

Outdoor Advertising

ACCORDING TO THE OUTDOOR Advertising Association of America, billboards and posters are the most cost-effective way of reaching the consumer.

The billboard, the most commonly used form of outdoor advertising, comes in two standard forms, the 30-sheet poster and the bulletin.

The 30-Sheet Poster

These are lithographed or silk-screened by a printer and shipped to an outdoor advertising company. They are then prepasted and applied in sections to the poster panel's face on location. Standard 30-sheet posters measure approximately 12 feet high by 24 feet wide.

The Bulletin

This can be hand-painted in an outdoor company's studio and erected in sections on location, painted directly at the location, or produced by computer. Most measure 14 feet high by 48 feet wide. The majority of painted bulletins in the United States are rotary panels, which can be dismantled and moved to a different location every 30–60 days. Permanent bulletins are placed at extremely high-traffic locations and remain at a fixed location for the duration of an advertiser's contract.

Other Types of Outdoor Advertising

- 8-sheet posters or junior panels
- Transit exteriors
- Painted walls
- Telephone kiosks
- Truck displays
- Taxi tops

- Transit/rail platforms
- Airport/bus terminal displays
- Transit clock platforms
- Bus shelter displays
- Shopping mall displays
- In-store clock and aisle displays.

In recent years, advertisers from various product categories have increased their use of outdoor advertising because of its relative cost-efficiency. Billboards are permitted in all states except Maine, Vermont, Hawaii, and Alaska. In fact, in 1991, the industry fared better than any other form of advertising. The chart on the next page reveals the top ten spending categories for the outdoor advertising industry.

The actual billboard design is generally developed by a company's ad agency, which then contacts one of the many outdoor companies operating throughout the country.

The cost of an outdoor ad will largely depend upon location. Unlike print advertising, which charges a space rate, billboard advertising sells by "showings." There are three types of showings, a 100, a 50, and a 25. A 50 showing, for example, is seen approximately 14 times a month by approximately 90 percent of the area's population. The billboard company will help distinguish the location that attracts the particular demographic population a company is trying to reach. The charts on the next page may provide a general sense of what costs to expect.

To visualize how a billboard will appear from 300 feet away, cut out the rectangular frame below or cut a frame that is 3 inches wide by 1 inch high, frame your artwork, and hold it at arm's length.

A billboard seen from 300 feet

Outdoor Advertising (cont'd)

Billboard Reach (% Frequency): Women

Characteristic	#100 Showing	#50 Showing	#25 Showing
AGE			
18–34	89.0	84.3	75.3
35–49	92.2	88.3	82.6
50 or older	84.3	76.4	66.4
EDUCATION			
Attended college or more	91.6	89.0	82.5
High school graduate	88.1	82.3	73.6
Other	81.7	70.4	58.8

Source: Simmons Market Research Bureau, 1994

Billboard Reach (% Frequency): Men

Characteristic	#100 Showing	#50 Showing	#25 Showing
AGE			
18–34	90.8	87.2	83.5
35–49	90.1	87.9	83.1
50 or older	86.8	82.7	76.4
EDUCATION			
Attended college or more	91.4	88.9	84.4
High school graduate	88.6	85.5	81.2
Other	85.5	80.2	73.4

Source: Simmons Market Research Bureau, 1994

Top Ten Outdoor Advertisers

Rank	Advertiser	1993 Outdoor Spending ($ millions)	1992 Outdoor Spending ($ millions)	% Change
1	Philip Morris	47.3	59.9	-21.1
2	Loews	27.7	26.4	4.9
3	BAT Industries	20.8	10.5	98.9
4	RJR Nabisco	19.6	29.6	-33.8
5	McDonald's	14.2	12.5	13.4
6	Anheuser-Busch	11.1	10.9	1.9
7	PepsiCo	7.9	3.8	106.7
8	Brown-Forman	6.3	4.5	38.8
9	American Brands	6.3	11.5	-45.6
10	Grand Metropolitan	5.7	5.9	-4.8

Source: Ad Age/Competitive Media Reporting

For a free booklet containing illustrations of the annual Obie Award–winning billboards, contact:

Outdoor Advertising Association of America
Marketing Division
12 E. 49th St., Floor 22
New York, NY 10017
(212) 688-3667

Contact Options

Several of the largest outdoor companies:

Ackerley Communications
3601 Sixth Ave. S.
Seattle, WA 98134
(206) 624-2888

Gannett Outdoor Group
666 Third Ave., Fourth Floor
New York, NY 10017
(212) 297-6400

Naegele Outdoor Advertising
1700 W. 78th St.
Richfield, MN 55423
(612) 869-1900

Patrick Media Group
338 N. Washington Ave.
Scranton, PA 18503
(717) 347-7100

3M National Advertising
6850 S. Harlem Ave.
Bedford Park, IL 60501
(708) 496-6500

Banners

MOST BANNERS ARE MADE of a vinyl- or acrylic-coated fabric. They average 3 feet by 5 feet in size but can be made 4 feet by 60 feet or even larger. The following is a partial listing of companies that provide stock banners carrying generic messages such as "Grand Opening" or "Clearance Sale." These companies will also custom-make banners to any specifications.

Contact Options

Banner Producers:

American Banner
6566 E. Skelly Dr.
Tulsa, OK 74145
(918) 621-4400

Best Buy Banner
6750-C Central Ave.
Riverside, CA 92504
(800) 624-1691

Davey Enterprises
44 Clinton St.
Newton, NJ 07860
(201) 579-5889

Eastern Banner Supply
2582 Spring Lake Rd.
Mooresville, IN 46158
(317) 831-6055

McCullough Manufacturing
27 Miller St.
Strasburg, PA 17579
(800) 423-8204

Blimps

CORPORATIONS LOOKING FOR an innovative way to advertise may now contact several companies that sell and/or lease small airships to advertisers who can't afford the likes of Goodyear Aerospace's 192-foot-long blimps.

The advantages of advertising on one of the new breed of airships that patrol the country's stadiums, golf courses, and race tracks are twofold. First, they are seen by the large crowds that attend sporting events. Second, because the airship companies request network coverage in exchange for providing aerial camera platforms, they are seen by the even larger audiences that watch the televised events. What's more, a poll conducted by Opinion Research revealed that consumer preference for a product rises by 19 percent after a blimp appearance.

Contact Options

Airship Advertising Brokers:

Airship
7380 Sand Lake Rd., Suite 350
Orlando, FL 32819
(407) 351-0011

Skyrider Airships
2840 Wilderness Pl., Suite E
Boulder, CO 80301
(303) 449-2190

The Top Reference Sources

Who's Who in Professional Speaking
National Speakers Association, $25 (free to meeting planners)
(602) 968-2552

This membership directory of the National Speakers Association contains the most recent information on more than 3,100 professional speakers. Listings include individual speakers, what topics they address, and how to get in touch with them. The directory is organized alphabetically and includes a geographic index.

Most speakers are happy to provide references and a tape to prospective clients.

Media-Buying Services

ONE WAY FOR A COMPANY TO save money on advertising costs is to use a media-buying service.

Many companies use an outside advertising agency and pay it a fee to design their ad campaign and place it in the media. That fee generally includes a fee of 15 percent of the cost of the ads which the ad agency charges to get the campaign placed in various media outlets. Since an accredited agency receives a 15 percent discount from the media, however, that 15 percent fee is generally profit for the advertising agency.

To reduce that 15 percent fee to a 5 percent fee, a company can hire an independent marketing consultant and art director and use a media-buying service. A freelance marketing consultant is paid a flat fee to help a company develop a marketing plan. The art director, also for a flat fee, will design the logo, ads, brochures, and everything else that needs designing. The media-buying service will then place all of the ads in the media for a charge of from 3 to 5 percent of the cost of the ads, amounting to a 10 percent savings for the client.

Contact Options

Western International Media
8544 Sunset Blvd.
Los Angeles, CA 90069
(310) 659-5711

Corinthian Media
600 Madison Ave., Tenth Floor
New York, NY 10022
(212) 371-5225

MBS International
104 Fifth Ave., Fifth Floor
New York, NY 10011
(212) 206-0600

DeWitt Media
460 Park Avenue S., Tenth Floor
New York, NY 10016
(212) 545-0120

Graphic Artists and Designers

FINDING THE RIGHT PHOTOGRAPHER, graphic designer, illustrator, or printer to design a brochure or package, or any other marketing tool is relatively simple.

Most art and office supply stores carry a substantial selection of graphic design portfolios. These books provide the names, addresses, and phone numbers of a varied assortment of working professionals. The catalogues are broken down by specialty and offer samples of each artist's work.

Recommended Resource

PrintBooks
PRINT, $79
(800) 222-2654

Contact Options

Designers and Design-Related Organizations:

American Center for Design
233 E. Ontario St., Suite 500
Chicago, IL 60611
(312) 787-2018 (in-state)
(800) 257-8657

American Institute of Graphic Arts
164 Fifth Ave.
New York, NY 10010
(212) 807-1990

Association of Professional Design Firms
685 High St., Suite 5
Worthington, OH 43085
(614) 888-3301

Graphic Artists Guild
11 W. 20th St.
New York, NY 10011
(212) 463-7730

Society of Environmental Graphic Designers
1 Story St.
Cambridge, MA 02138
(617) 868-3381

Society of Illustrators
128 E. 63rd St.
New York, NY 10021
(212) 838-2560

Society of Publication Designers
Lincoln Bldg.
60 E. 42nd St., # 721
New York, NY 10165
(212) 983-8585

University and College Designers Association
209 Commerce St.
Alexandria, VA 22314
(703) 548-1770

Graphic Artists and Designers (cont'd)

Art Directors Club
250 Park Ave. S.
New York, NY 10003
(212) 674-0500

Art Directors Club of Cincinnati
1021 Park Side
Cincinnati, OH 45202
(513) 241-4591

American Institute of Graphic Arts
9348 Civic Center Dr., Suite 450
Beverly Hills, CA 90210
(310) 364-1788 or (310) 246-5758

Creative Forum Nashville
P.O. Box 23512
Nashville, TN 37202
(615) 244-4220

Creative Club of Atlanta
P.O. Box 77244
Atlanta, GA 30309
(404) 881-9991

Dayton Advertising Club
P.O. Box 513
Dayton, OH 45409
(513) 436-9672

Graphic Arts Service
1612 Grand
Kansas City, MO 64108
(816) 421-3879

Western Art Directors Club
P.O. Box 996
Palo Alto, CA 94302
(415) 321-4196

Product Placement Firms

AFTER E.T. FOUND HIS HUMAN friend Elliot by following a trail of Reese's Pieces, sales of the candy leaped 66 percent in three months.

When Tom Cruise sported Ray-Ban sunglasses in *Top Gun*, sales of the company's aviator-style glasses jumped 40 percent in seven months.

The use of these brand-name products and many others on film and television is negotiated by companies called product placement firms. For a fee that can run as high as $50,000, these firms will provide their corporate clients with promotional consultation and placement of their products in television series, feature films, and even game shows. These deals enable corporations to market their products by using the entertainment industry, and allow filmmakers to cut production costs by getting free products and services in exchange for their placement.

Product placement firms are hired by corporate clients to review upcoming scripts and determine what products will be needed; whether they should be handled visually or simply mentioned in dialogue; and whether the film is aimed at the correct target audience for the product. They negotiate a deal beneficial for both the corporate client and the cost-conscious studio.

Contact Options

Product Placement Firms:

AIM Promotions
Kaufman Astoria Studios
34-12 36th St.
Astoria, NY 11106
(718) 729-9288

Ventura Media Group
11466 San Vicente Blvd.
Los Angeles, CA 90049
(310) 820-0607

Creative Entertainment Services
1015 N. Hollywood Way, Suite 101
Burbank, CA 91505
(818) 842-9119

Motion Picture Placement
9250 Wilshire Blvd., #412
Beverly Hills, CA 90212
(310) 858-1115

Rogers & Cowan
3701 W. Oak St.
Burbank, CA 91505
(818) 954-6944

UPP Entertainment Marketing
10865 Burbank Blvd.
N. Hollywood, CA 91601
(818) 508-8877

CompuServe's PR and Marketing Forum offers contacts and info for PR, marketing, and corporate communications. GO PRSIG.

Packaging

FOR A COMPANY NEEDING TO LOCATE professionals to design packaging, there are a number of alternatives. The Package Design Council publishes an annual membership directory that lists the names, addresses, and phone numbers of packaging professionals, broken down by design and industry specialty. The reference costs $125 and is published in January.

Also available is *Packaging Magazine*'s annual *Supplier Source Guide*, which provides an alphabetical listing of suppliers, associations, contract packagers, consultants, and design firms.

Recommended Resources

Package Design Council Membership Directory
Package Design Council International, $125
481 Carlisle Dr.
Herndon, VA 22070
(703) 318-7225

Packaging
Cahners Publishing
1350 E. Touhy Ave.
Des Plaines, IL 60017
(708) 635-8800

Packaging Award Winners

1994 Institute of Packaging Professionals AmeriStar Packaging Award Winners*

Category	Product	Designer
Food	Infant formula	Abbott Laboratories
Food	Vektor baking mix container	Pioneer/Sealright
Beverage	Juice cocktail bottle	Continental Pet Technologies
Beverage	Handy Can powdered soft drink package	Kraft General Foods
Medical device	Squeeze tray	Key Packaging
Other retail products	Sum Pak adhesive gel package	Polymeric Systems
Other retail products	Inkjet print cartridge package	Hewlett-Packard
Electronics	Cushion-Comb	Hexacomb
Regulated packaging	Child-resistant vapor barrier pouch	DowElanco
Industrial	Mono material packaging system	Rosemount
Graphics	Clear film pressure-sensitive labels	Spear

*Gold star winners

Source: Institute of Packaging Professionals

The Top Reference Sources

Who's Who and What's What in Packaging
Institute of Packaging Professionals, $125
(800) 432-4085

More than just the usual association membership directory, this is a terrific source of leads and information on all aspects of packaging–including lists of companies and their areas of packaging expertise, packaging and packaging-related professional organizations, educational institutions that offer packaging courses, and executive placement firms that specialize in packaging.

Celebrity Booking Services

IT MAY SEEM IMPOSSIBLE for a company to get Meryl Streep to appear at its annual convention or have Bill Cosby endorse its newest product at the local mall, but, in reality, many well-known celebrities are available for corporate appearances at a relatively reasonable cost.

A number of agencies are available whose job it is to book celebrities either to make a speech, perform, or simply appear at corporate conventions, publicity events, or charity benefits. These booking services cater to companies that believe that contact with major television, movie, music, and sports personalities will enhance their company's image. They rely on the fact that many celebrities are interested in getting alternative exposure and income.

These companies will contact a personality, present him or her with a company's proposal, and negotiate a deal, usually within a day or two.

Contact Options

Celebrity Booking Services or Providers of Agent Information:

Celebrity Service International
1780 Broadway, Suite 300
New York, NY 10019
(212) 245-1460

Washington Speakers Bureau
310 S. Henry St.
Alexandria, VA 22314
(703) 684-0555

Ingels
7080 Hollywood Blvd., Suite 1116
Hollywood, CA 90028
(213) 464-0800

Recommended Resources

Celebrity Service International Contact Book
Celebrity Service International, $50
(212) 245-1460

Cavalcade of Acts and Attractions
Amusement Business, $55
(615) 321-4250

Clipping Services

VERY OFTEN A COMPANY wants to monitor its own or a competitor's press coverage or needs to do subject research for a public relations campaign or a company presentation. The best solution may be to hire one of the several clipping services available across the country.

For a fee that averages $200 per month, these companies will read the country's major daily and weekly newspapers, magazines, and trade publications and monitor the wire services, radio, and network and cable television news broadcasts. They will clip all articles or transcribe or tape every broadcast that mentions any subject requested by their client company.

Clips may be received on a daily or weekly basis. Companies may find them useful when they need to know the exact words written or spoken by politicians, executives, or public figures either for background research or for a company briefing, press release, daily news update, or public relations campaign.

Most of these clipping services offer a range of services, including day-of-publication delivery, historical research, news clip analysis of public relations performance, advertising analysis of competitors, and foreign press monitoring.

Contact Options

Press Clipping Services:

Allen's Press Clipping Bureau
P.O. Box 2761
Los Angeles, CA 90051
(213) 628-4214

Bacon's Information
332 S. Michigan Ave., Suite 900
Chicago, IL 60604
(312) 922-2400

Burrelle's Information Services
75 E. Northfield Rd.
Livingston, NJ 07039
(201) 992-6600

Luce Press Clippings
420 Lexington Ave., Suite 203
New York, NY 10170
(212) 889-6711

Hiring a Copywriter

ANY TIME A COMPANY NEEDS TO disseminate information to the public, it's a good idea to hire a copywriter to ensure clean, effective, professional copy.

Herschell Gordon Lewis, author of *Direct Mail Copy That Sells*, suggests the following procedure for choosing a copywriter:

- Advertise for a copywriter listing enough specifics about the job to keep novices away.

- Ask for samples; then ask questions about the samples to validate authorship. If the candidate is boastful or seems more concerned with ego defense than with any admission of participation by others . . . beware.

- Conduct a convivial personal interview in which you lead the candidate to believe he or she actually has the job and the conversation is just a formality. Pay close attention to the degree of literacy. Look for two Achilles' heels (a) phony sincerity, and (b) contempt for whatever you're selling. Disqualify any candidate on either basis.

- Have the candidate take a timed writing test assignment. Pepper the instructions with weak words from the list below. If the writer regurgitates more than a couple of those words or uses platitudes and clichés, this person is not an original thinker.

- Give the top three candidates an actual, for-pay assignment. You'll find your writer.

A number of sources are available to help you find the writer that best suits your company's needs. The classified sections in *AdWeek* and *Advertising Age*, for example, are probably the best places to find the names of copywriters or place an advertisement.

Finally, it's always a good idea to check with a headhunter who specializes in advertising.

Recommended Resources

Dial-A-Writer
1501 Broadway, Suite 302
New York, NY 10036
(212) 398-1934

Dial-A-Writer connects more than 800 well-published, independent freelance writers with anyone needing a skilled professional.

The One Club for Art & Copy
32 E. 21st St.
New York, NY 10010
(212) 979-1900

The One Club boasts a membership of some 700 advertising art directors and copywriters and is another good referral source for professional writers.

Contact Options

Headhunters:

Baedar Chiu
9538 Brighton Way, Suite 306
Beverly Hills, CA 90210
(310) 274-0051

Greenberg & Associates
1133 Broadway, Suite 1204
New York, NY 10010
(212) 463-0020

Howsam & Weingarten
275 Madison Ave., Suite 1518
New York, NY 10016
(212) 682-5151

Sandy Wade
1 IBM Plaza, Suite 2901
Chicago, IL 60611
(312) 595-3200

The Watts Group
11601 Wilshire Blvd., Suite 500
Los Angeles, CA 90025
(310) 575-4882

Westerfield & Associates
15150 S. Florida Ave., #307
Lakeland, FL 33813
(813) 644-1216

Weak Words

administration	facilitate	product
affinity	features	purchase
amendment	fond	quality
approximately	formulate	replacement
attractive	humorous	requested
configuration	indeed	respond
constructed	merchant	rethink
contradictory	moderate	service
"Dear Friend"	needs (as a noun)	standards
define	pamphlet	utilize
dispatch	peruse	value
earn	prearranged	work

Working with the Press

WORKING WITH THE PRESS IS a sales process. And as in any other sales process, it is important for a company to establish clear goals and create on-going relationships with the press with which they are dealing. Here are several guidelines that should help:

1. Set your objectives
The key to successful interviews is to know what you want to accomplish before entering into a conversation with the press. Never enter into an interview process without knowing your objectives. If you get a spontaneous phone call from a reporter, the best way to handle it is to call the person back after you've had a chance to think about the key company objectives.

2. Know your key message
Find every opportunity during a conversation with a reporter to underline the company's key objectives.

3. Manage the conversation
Try to drive an interview rather than let it be driven for you. Answer questions by bringing them back to the points you want to emphasize. The goal is to communicate information rather than load the listener with data he or she may not understand.

4. Be responsive to your audience
Different types of press have different needs. Try to understand their needs, either by getting advice from your public relations firm beforehand, or by taking the first few minutes of your interview to chat with the interviewer to understand his or her concerns. Then, present your material as effectively as possible to meet those needs.

5. Respect deadlines
Press people are often under deadline pressure. Since the purpose of taking the time to do an interview is to develop a rapport, try to get an understanding of what deadline pressures the interviewer is under and be responsive to those pressures.

6. Remember the First Amendment
Every interview may not result in a story and every story that gets written may not be exactly the story the company wants to see published. Members of the press are entitled to freedom of the press. Remember that if you want something to be "off the record," you need to get agreement from the person you are speaking with before you are guaranteed anonymity.

Contact Option

Abigail Johnson
Roeder-Johnson
655 Skyway, Suite 130
San Carlos, CA 94070
(415) 802-1850

Publicity Services

BELOW ARE LISTED SEVERAL services that will, for a fee, take a company's press release or other publicity material and present it to media outlets:

Radio-TV Interview Report
Bradley Communications
135 E. Plumstead Ave.
Landsdowne, PA 19050
(610) 259-1070
　　This bimonthly magazine lists project pitches and is mailed to over 5,000 radio-TV talk show and TV news programming executives nationwide.

PR Newswire (PRN)
Harborside Financial Center
806 Plaza 3
Jersey City, NJ 07311
(800) 832-5522 or (212) 832-9400
　　This is a daily service that provides news releases and camera-ready photo transmissions to the world's largest media telecommunications network through satellite, fax, mail, and database.

News Broadcast Network
149 Madison Ave., #804
New York, NY 10016
(212) 889-0888
　　This is a daily radio feed servicing 2,000 news and talk radio stations and all AP and UPI audio-feed wire service subscribers.

Derus Media
500 N. Dearborn, #516
Chicago, IL 60610
(312) 644-4360
　　This is a monthly distributor of multimedia script and slide packages to radio and television outlets. They are the only firm to offer a full-service division for the Hispanic market.

Publicity Services (cont'd)

Metro Publicity Services
33 W. 34th St., Fourth Floor
New York, NY 10001
(212) 947-5100
This service mails to 7,000 newspapers monthly. It offers monthly theme sections 22 times a year featuring subject matter for targeted audiences.

Recommended Resources

Three newsletters list new columns, shows, and magazines, and what they are looking for. They also report on freelance project needs and provide names and addresses.

Bulldog Reporter
2115 Fourth St.
Berkeley, CA 94710
(800) 327-9893

Contacts
35-20 Broadway
Astoria, NY 11106
(718) 721-0508

Partyline
35 Sutton Pl.
New York, NY 10022
(212) 755-3487

Bacon's Media Directories
(Newspaper/Magazine, Radio/TV, Media Calendar, International Media)
Bacon's Information, $270 per edition
332 S. Michigan Ave., Suite 900
Chicago, IL 60604
(800) 621-0561 or (312) 922-2400

Burrelle's Media Directory
Burrelle's Media Information Systems
$200/2 updates per year
75 E. Northfield Rd.
Livingston, NJ 07039
(800) 631-1160

Marketer's Guide to Media
Adweek Directories, $110/2 editions per year
1515 Broadway
New York, NY 10036
(800) 468-2395

Power Media Selects
Broadcast Interview Source $166.50/year
2233 Wisconsin Ave., NW
Washington, DC 20007
(202) 333-4904

Selecting a Public Relations Firm

THOUGH THEY ARE OFTEN CONFUSED, public relations and advertising are not the same thing. A public relations firm is responsible for determining the way an organization is perceived by the public.

The first thing to consider when choosing a public relations firm is whether you want that firm to handle your company's entire public relations program or just its publicity. A firm that handles publicity sees to it that a company's products or services receive media coverage in the form of articles or radio and television broadcasts. When a firm handles public relations as a whole, its job is to help craft a company's image. Most PR firms do both. Here are some of the other ways they can help an organization:

• Provide an outside viewpoint or perspective;

• Increase an organization's overall visibility;

• Support a product or an overall marketing effort;

• Counsel in a crisis;

• Communicate with employees;

• Inform investors;

• Strengthen community relations;

• Act as a liaison with government agencies;

• Measure and evaluate existing public relations programs;

• Research public attitudes and behavior;

• Stage media events.

Once you have determined the specific communication needs of your organization, choosing the right public relations firm involves a certain amount of investigation. Begin by looking through the magazines in which you would like to have coverage; call the companies that are written about and find out which firm those companies employ.

When you have narrowed down your options, interview several firms. Don't assume that a large company is necessarily better equipped to handle your organization's needs. While advertising often requires a large staff of people to create and develop a campaign, public relations can usually be handled by a smaller team that is responsible for writing press releases and getting them out to an appropriate contact list.

Before deciding on a firm, consider the following questions:

• Does the firm have expertise in your company's field and understand your particular needs?

Selecting a Public Relations Firm (cont'd)

- Do you want greater awareness of your product nationally or in a targeted market?

- Do you want to pay your firm a flat fee, a retainer fee, a minimum monthly fee, or a project fee?

- What is your company's objective?

- How important is it to have regular access to the agency head and who is the backup?

- Which of the media do you need your agency to handle?

- How long will it take to learn about your account?

- What reporting/measurement methods are used?

- Must you have easy access to your firm's offices?

- Do you want a company with a particular philosophy or one that is willing to work with the philosophy of its clients?

- Whom do you want to be in charge?

If, after meeting with key people, you are still undecided, ask each firm to send a written proposal outlining how it would provide the public relations services your organization needs. When you have decided upon a firm, get references from other clients, and work out a reasonable budget so there are no surprises down the line.

Contact Option

Public Relations Society of America
33 Irving Pl.
New York, NY 10003
(212) 995-2230

Recommended Resource

O'Dwyer's Directory of Public Relations Firms
J. R. O'Dwyer, $125
271 Madison Ave.
New York, NY 10016
(212) 679-2471

Lists most existing public relations firms, noting their rank, specialties, number of employees, and clients.

Leading Public Relations Firms

Top 15 PR Firms by Net Fees

Agency	1993 Net Fees ($)	No. of Employees	% Change 1992-1993
Burson-Marsteller	192,491,000	1,739	-5.5
Shandwick	151,800,000	1,808	-8.6
Hill and Knowlton	146,767,000	1,281	-8.0
Omnicom PR Network	85,852,418	1,157	31.0
Fleishman-Hillard	69,518,000	703	18.5
Edelman PR Worldwide	63,351,064	745	5.9
Ketchum Public Relations	50,100,000	432	9.9
The Rowland Co.	38,000,000	391	-13.6
Robinson Lake/Sawyer Miller/Bozell	37,600,000	235	14.0
Manning, Selvage & Lee	31,321,000	290	-0.3
Ogilvy Adams & Rinehart	30,105,000	285	-16.7
Ruder Finn	27,162,219	256	0.3
GCI Group	26,397,716	353	-6.0
Cohn & Wolfe	14,093,000	117	-0.9
Financial Relations Board	12,485,452	141	21.6

Source: J.R. O'Dwyer Company

Leading Public Relations Firms (cont'd)

Leading PR Firms by Specialty

Agriculture

Firm	1993 Fee Income ($)
Gibbs & Soell	4,196,000
Shandwick	3,317,000
Fleishman-Hillard	3,036,000
Bader Rutter & Associates	2,616,745
Morgan & Myers	2,479,530

Beauty/Fashion

Firm	1993 Fee Income ($)
The Rowland Co.	5,000,000
Shandwick	4,362,000
Burson-Marsteller	2,887,000
Cairns & Associates	2,589,849
Fleishman-Hillard	2,564,000

Entertainment/Cultural

Firm	1993 Fee Income ($)
Shandwick	13,299,000
Ruder Finn	4,000,000
Dennis Davidson Associates	3,555,828
Edelman PR Worldwide	2,502,575
Manning, Selvage & Lee	2,092,000

Environmental

Firm	1993 Fee Income ($)
Burson-Marsteller	17,959,000
Ketchum Public Relations	15,300,000
Fleishman-Hillard	9,125,000
Shandwick	6,689,000
E. Bruce Harrison	6,550,991

Financial PR/Investor Relations

Firm	1993 Fee Income ($)
Burson-Marsteller	25,043,000
Fleishman-Hillard	17,973,000
Shandwick	15,363,000
Ogilvy Adams & Rinehart	13,600,000
Financial Relations Board	12,485,452

Foods & Beverages

Firm	1993 Fee Income ($)
Burson-Marsteller	34,687,000
Shandwick	19,219,000
Fleishman-Hillard	14,731,000
Ketchum Public Relations	13,100,000
Edelman PR Worldwide	10,535,078

Health Care

Firm	1993 Fee Income ($)
Burson-Marsteller	39,499,000
Edelman PR Worldwide	12,643,152
Porter/Novelli (Omnicom)	12,427,000
Shandwick	9,550,000
Ruder Finn	9,500,000

High Tech

Firm	1993 Fee Income ($)
Shandwick	29,975,000
Burson-Marsteller	13,494,000
Cunningham Communication	8,086,970
Fleishman-Hillard	8,086,000
Edelman PR Worldwide	7,282,527

Sports

Firm	1993 Fee Income ($)
Edelman PR Worldwide	3,803,287
Cohn & Wolfe	3,050,000
Burson-Marsteller	2,464,000
Manning, Selvage & Lee	2,239,000
Fleishman-Hillard	2,089,000

Travel

Firm	1993 Fee Income ($)
Shandwick	8,543,000
Burson-Marsteller	6,737,000
Fleishman-Hillard	4,953,000
Edelman PR Worldwide	4,166,007
M. Silver Associates	2,308,668

Source: O'Dwyer's Directory of PR Firms, 1994

Publicity. Send e-mail to publicity@almanac.yoyo.com. See p. xi for instructions.

"66 Ways to Make Your Business Newsworthy." Dozens of creative ideas for becoming worthy of media coverage and then getting into print or on the air, from Marcia Yudkin, Ph.D., author of Six Steps to Free Publicity (Plume Books).

VNR and Industrial Video

A VIDEO NEWS RELEASE IS basically a press release in video form–typically a 90-second video piece that is paid for by corporate sponsors and then distributed, via satellite or mail, to stations around the country to be included in local newscasts. They are, in effect, paid advertisements in a news format. When they are well made, it is almost impossible to distinguish them from a regular national news segment.

Presidential candidates use them for air time on local news channels. Fortune 500 companies create them to inform the public about their latest product research. And, in the last decade, a growing number of small companies have begun to use them as an effective public relations tool.

There are two basic categories of VNR: timely and "evergreen."

A timely VNR takes advantage of a newsworthy event to get across a company's ideas or products to the public. For example, 3M provided a high-tech coating for American luges in the 1988 Winter Olympics and produced a VNR featuring action race shots and experts applying the coating. The advantage of a timely VNR is that there's a good chance it will be picked up by stations that may be looking for news fillers. The disadvantage of a timely VNR is that it may become obsolete very quickly.

The "evergreen" VNR, on the other hand, is produced to have a longer shelf life; it typically deals with human interest stories that can be used by stations on a slow news day. Recent studies conducted by Nielsen Media Research, however, reveal that "evergreens" were preferred by 25 percent of all news producers, while just under 50 percent preferred timely pieces.

Most commonly, VNRs try to tie a company's new products and/or services to one of the following topics:

- Health tips
- Consumer affairs
- Community services
- Government issues
- New regulations
- Public service messages.

Creating an effective VNR can cost $20,000 or more including production, distribution, and follow-up costs.

The emphasis should be on the video's newsworthiness. Also effective are issue-oriented videos. The Insurance Institute for Highway Safety, for instance, transmitted a hard-hitting VNR on seatbelt safety by focusing on a car manufacturer whose seatbelts were not well designed.

A Medialink-Nielsen survey suggests the following rules to keep in mind when producing a video news release:

- Create a package containing a news-story-type release and a few minutes of background tape or B-Roll.
- Time your VNR to be approximately 90 seconds.
- Place audio signals on separate channels so that news producers may insert their own voice-overs on one sound channel with the natural sound of your VNR tape on the other.
- When distributing a VNR, always clearly identify it as a public relations service in the materials provided.

Nick Peters, Medialink vice-president, suggests the following "litmus test" when choosing a production firm to create your VNR:

- Ask your public relations firm or another that has had experience with VNRs to recommend a production company.
- Ask the production company whether it has done any VNRs before, and for whom. Ask what results it has had and how those results have been documented.
- Make sure the company has past experience in television news.
- Ask to see a demo reel.

For further information, contact Medialink, a major satellite distributor of VNRs and other video public relations services. Medialink has a variety of free reference books about VNR, as well as a listing of production companies nationwide.

Contact Options

Medialink Locations:

708 Third Ave., Ninth Floor
New York, NY 10017
(212) 682-8300

1401 New York Ave., Suite 520
Washington, DC 20005
(202) 628-3800

6430 Sunset Blvd., Suite 1205
Los Angeles, CA 90028
(213) 465-0111

The Time and Life Bldg.
541 N. Fairbanks Ct., Suite 2010
Chicago, IL 60611
(312) 222-9850

VNR and Industrial Video (cont'd)

For a price that most experts say averages $2,000 per minute, it is possible to create an in-house company video that uses sophisticated techniques like those of most television broadcasts.

Contact Options

Production Companies Specializing in VNR and Industrial Video:

Perri Pharris Productions
4590 MacArthur Blvd., Suite 620
Newport Beach, CA 92660
(714) 263-3737

Washington Independent Productions
400 N. Capitol St., NW, Suite 183
Washington, DC 20001
(202) 638-3400

Doug Manning Productions
300 W. Washington St., Suite 706
Chicago, IL 60606
(312) 782-2700

VNR-1
2311 C Roosevelt
Arlington, TX 76016
(817) 784-9920

Reality Productions
6161 Kingsberry
St. Louis, MO 63112
(314) 725-3838

Direct-Response Fulfillment Houses

APPROXIMATELY 80 PERCENT of the calls generated by commercials and infomercials occur within the first five minutes after the commercial has aired. These "call spikes" make setting up an in-house center for receiving telephone orders impractical and expensive.

"800" service bureaus that specialize in handling spot TV and half-hour infomercial-generated calls present the advertiser with an effective and relatively inexpensive resource for handling a high volume of calls.

In selecting an inbound call center or fulfillment house, the advertiser must determine if the number of lines and staff available at the times when specific ads are scheduled to run is sufficient to handle the expected number of calls. Advertisers should expect to pay the following costs:

- A one time setup fee that will include normal program setup and any unique programming or training that may be necessary.

- Call-processing fees based upon a negotiated per-call charge or actual usage, per minute, of on-phone conversation.

- A monthly minimum fee credited against call charges.

- Special transaction fees such as output, payment processing, etc.

Contact Options

Operator Centers with More Than 400 Workstations:

MATRIXX Marketing
2121 N. 117th Ave.
Omaha, NE 68164-3000
(402) 498-4000

West Telemarketing
9910 Maple St.
Omaha, NE 68134
(402) 571-7700

Operator Centers with 100–400 Workstations:

AT&T American Transtech
8000 Baymeadows Way
Jacksonville, FL 32256
(904) 636-1000

Neodata
833 W. South Boulder Rd.
Louisville, CO 80027
(303) 666-7000

Precision Response
1505 N.W. 167th St.
Miami, FL 33169
(305) 626-4600

The Product Line
2370 S. Trenton Way
Denver, CO 80231
(303) 671-8000

Sitel
5601 N. 103rd St.
Omaha, NE 68134
(402) 498-6810

Teletech
15355 Morrison St.
Sherman Oaks, CA 91403
(818) 501-5595

Infomercials

INFOMERCIALS ARE PROGRAM-LENGTH TV commercials that are devoted solely to one product. These programs are designed to heighten public awareness, develop brand-name identification, and create a consumer market for a product by providing potential customers with all the information they will need about the product.

On a per-minute comparison basis, infomercials are roughly one-fifth the cost of a 30-second commercial, but it is necessary to study the market carefully before buying air time. Some businesses have found that hiring a media-buying firm is more convenient and less expensive than buying air time directly. Media-buying firms purchase blocks of time in many areas of the country and allot these time blocks to their clients.

According to *Infomercial Marketing Report*, the top-grossing infomercials for 1994 were:

- Fitness Trends for the Nineties (American Telecast)

- Healthrider (Exerhealth)

- Psychic Friends Network (Inphomation)

- Powerwalk Plus (National Media)

- Gary Smalley (American Telecast).

Contact Options

American Telecast
16 Industrial Blvd.
Paoli, PA 19301
(610) 251-9933

Guthy-Renker
41550 Eclectic, Suite 200
Palm Desert, CA 92260
(619) 773-9022

National Infomercial Marketing Association
1201 New York Ave., NW, Suite 1000
Washington, DC 20005
(202) 962-8342

National Media
1700 Walnut St.
Philadelphia, PA 19103
(215) 772-5000

USA Direct
12701 Whitewater Dr.
Minnetonka, MN 55343
(612) 945-4391

Recommended Resources

Infomercial Marketing Report
11533 Thurston Circle
Los Angeles, CA 90049
(310) 472-5253

The Infomercial Producer Report
Television Time
178 Barsana Ave.
Austin, TX 78737
(512) 288-6400

The PLAY® (Program Length Advertisement of the Year) Awards are given by *Infomercial Marketing Report*.

The 1994 PLAY® Awards

Award	Title (Show)	Recipient
Most Innovative New Product	Proform Crosswalk	Proform Fitness/Tyee Productions
Most Innovative Use of an Infomercial	The Great Wall	Philips Consumer Electronics/Tyee Productions
Most Effective Home Fitness/Health Product Infomercial	The Gravity Edge	SLM/Tyee Productions
Most Effective Beauty Product Infomercial	The Thinking Man's Guide to Hair Restoration	Bosley Medical Institute/Tyee Productions
Most Effective Household Appliance/Consumer Electronics Infomercial	Jet Stream Oven 3000T	American Harvest/Stan Jacobs
Most Effective Entertainment Product Infomercial	The Great Wall	Philips Consumer Electronics/Tyee Productions
Most Effective Self-Help Infomercial	Hidden Keys to Loving Relationships	Steve Scott & Frank Kovacs
Most Effective Retail Campaign Infomercial	The Great Wall	Philips Consumer Electronics/Tyee Productions
Most Effective Campaign for an Established Product or Product Line	The Flying Lure III	Langer Technologies/Jim Caldwell

Source: Infomercial Marketing Report

Marketing with Audiotext

BECAUSE THE TELEPHONE is still the easiest and most reputable way to conduct business, audiotext, or interactive voice response (IVR), was developed to increase telemarketing efficiency. A caller uses the keypad on a touch-tone telephone to respond to prerecorded or digitally created instructions. This technology can be used to conduct surveys, dispense information, register applicants for prizes and drawings, and run promotions.

Contact Options

Call Interactive
2301 N. 117th Ave.
Omaha, NE 68164
(800) 428-2400

Intervoice
17811 Waterview Pkwy.
Dallas, TX 75252
(214) 669-3988

Network Telephone Services
6233 Variel Ave.
Woodland Hills, CA 91367
(800) 727-6874

Phone Programs
40 Elmont Rd.
Elmont, NY 11003
(516) 775-5410

The Product Line
2370 S. Trenton Way
Denver, CO 80231
(800) 343-4717

Scherers Communications
575 Scherers Ct.
Worthington, OH 43085
(800) 356-6161

Telecompute
1275 K St., NW
Washington, DC 20005
(800) 872-8642

Teleshare 900
227 N. University Ave., Suite 103
Provo, UT 84601
(801) 377-0600

Zycom Network Services
200 S. Los Robles, Suite 305
Pasadena, CA 91101
(800) 880-3061

Recommended Resource

eMarketing
Berkley Publishing Group, $14
(800) 223-0510

Bulletin Boards

BULLETIN BOARDS ARE online areas that can be accessed using a modem. There are hundreds of bulletin boards currently in place for people with an interest in business, from business owners and managers to accountants to individuals searching for new information about the business world.

Bulletin boards are also an excellent way for businesses to keep in touch with their customers. A customer who wants information or has questions can get almost immediate results by accessing different computer files on thousands of topics, including the most frequently asked questions. (*See also "Bulletin Boards" on page 595.*)

Contact Options

Aquila
4438 E. New York St., Suite 281
Aurora, IL 60504
(708) 820-0480

GW Associates
P.O. Box 6606
Holliston, MA 01746
(508) 429-6227

Mustang Software
P.O. Box 2264
Bakersfield, CA 93303
(805) 873-2500

Online Management Services
791 Del Ganado Rd.
San Rafael, CA 94903
(415) 257-4146

Marketing by Fax

BUSINESSES HAVE FOUND fax technology useful as a means to market their products. It allows them to provide information to their customers as soon as it is available, or at the moment a customer requests it. It can also cost less than post office mailings, will save costs in printing, and allows for easy last-minute changes in documentation.

There are three main ways to market by fax: fax on demand, database to fax, and fax broadcasting.

Fax on Demand

A fax-on-demand system involves a series of stored documents that customers can request by phone. These documents are stored in a computer. By entering a code number that is printed next to a product in a catalog or magazine, a customer can request the information he or she wishes to receive. The machine then sends the appropriate fax image to the caller automatically. The information and requests are handled quickly and cost-effectively, and the system can be set up in-house or through a service provider. Companies that find their customer representatives answering the same questions repeatedly have found fax on demand useful in that it responds to customers immediately, without putting them on hold. It also gives customer service representatives the time to handle more complicated requests.

Database to Fax

A database-to-fax system allows users to create customized documents based on multiple pieces of information. The caller requests blocks of information requested from a database, the computer assembles it into a document, and then faxes the document to the caller. This is useful in cases where information changes frequently or is stored in many pieces.

Fax Broadcasting

Much like a mass-mailing, a fax broadcasting system sends one or more documents to multiple locations automatically. Businesses have found fax broadcasting to be invaluable when sending newsletters, fast-breaking information, new price rates, and with public relations.

Contact Options

Service Providers:

Instant Information
5 Broad St.
Boston, MA 02109
(617) 523-7636
Fax demo: (617) 723-6522

The Kauffman Group
324 Windsor Dr.
Cherry Hill, NJ 08002
(609) 482-8288

Touch Tone Services
P.O. Box 2994
Renton, WA 98056
(206) 271-7200
Fax demo: (800) 791-1082

Hardware and Software Providers:

SpectraFax
3050 Horseshoe Dr., Suite 100
Naples, FL 33942
(813) 643-5060
Fax demo: (800) 333-1329

Ibex Technologies
550 Main St.
Placerville, CA 95667
(916) 621-4342
Fax demo: (800) 289-9998

Recommended Resource

eMarketing
Berkley Publishing Group, $14
(800) 223-0510

The Top Reference Sources

eMarketing
Berkley Publishing Group, $14
(800) 223-0510

The editor of the *Information Please Business Almanac* takes a fresh look at marketing with technology in *eMarketing*, a handbook for marketers in every variety of business, from the home-based business to the large corporation. The book includes information on fax technology, the Internet, bulletin boards, databases, multimedia, infomercials, and audiotext. It also features articles and interviews with experts in each of these fields, including Regis McKenna and Don Peppers.

Greeting Card Suppliers

Contact Options

Major Holiday Card Suppliers:

New England Art–Birchcraft
10 Railroad St.
Abington, MA 02351
(617) 878-5151

Century Engraving and Embossing
1500 W. Monroe
Chicago, IL 60607
(312) 666-8686

Handshake Greeting Cards
P.O. Box 9027
Columbus, GA 31908
(800) 634-2134

Masterpiece Studios
1735 James Dr.
North Mankato, MN 56002
(800) 333-4128

Gift Baskets, Gift Brokers, Flowers

Contact Options

Gift Brokers:

Dial-A-Gift
(800) 453-0428

800 Spirits
(800) 238-4373

The Peterson Nut Company
(800) 367-6887

Popcorn World
(800) 443-8226

Calyx & Corolla
(800) 800-7788

Phillips' Flower Shops
(800) 356-7257

Premium Sources

MANY COMPANIES PROVIDE catalogues with a wide range of personalized premium or specialty advertising items, ranging from key rings and mugs to calendars, pens, pads, and other office items.

Total industry sales in 1992 were $5.2 billion, up 30 percent since 1987.

Contact Options

Promotional Products Association
3125 Skyway Circle N.
Irving, TX 75038
(214) 252-0404

The association will provide free advice on developing a cost-efficient promotional plan and will provide a list of specialty advertising distributors by location. To find a local specialty advertising distributor, check the yellow pages under "Advertising Specialties."

Promotion and Marketing Association of America
257 Park Ave., S.
New York, NY 10010
(212) 420-1100
Trade Association

Promotional Product Sales by Large Distributors, by Category

Product	% Sales
Wearables	22.4
Writing instruments	14.0
Office accessories	9.3
Recognition awards	9.2
Glassware/ceramics	8.8
Calendars	8.2
Sporting goods/ leisure products	6.7
Buttons, badges, ribbons/ stickers, magnets	5.8
Automotive accessories	4.5

Source: Promotional Products Association International

Mailing Lists

DIRECT-MAIL MARKETERS RELY on mailing lists to target the particular geographical and demographical market they are trying to reach. It is possible to rent or purchase mailing lists that include the names, addresses, and telephone numbers of people in categories as specific as museum curators, tax shelter investors, or people who have recently moved.

Mailing lists are divided into two major categories:

- Compiled lists, which are derived from directories, associations, government data, yellow pages registration, and public records.

- Response lists, which comprise individuals who have taken a direct action such as making a purchase, subscribing to a publication, or joining an organization. In general, these lists are more accurate since they are compiled from less general sources.

Anyone can obtain either kind of list directly from a mailing list company, or they can hire a list broker. Mailing list companies all provide free catalogues of their available lists and generally charge between $50 and $100 per 1,000 names for one-time use of a list. Overall, it is a better idea to use a broker than rent a list directly. It is not necessary to pay a broker since the broker receives a commission directly from the list owner, and will investigate, select, and order the list that is most suitable for each individual client.

Recommended Resources

Standard Rate & Data Service
1700 W. Higgins Rd., Fifth Floor
Des Plaines, IL 60018
(718) 375-5000

This company publishes *Direct Mail List Rates and Data*, a directory of available mailing lists. The directory sells for $152 for a single issue, or $354 for a six-issue annual subscription.

Directory of Mailing List Companies
Todd Publications, $39.50
18 N. Greenbush Rd.
W. Nyack, NY 10994
(914) 358-6213

This book includes an alphabetical listing of the names, addresses, and telephone numbers of hundreds of mailing list brokers.

Contact Options

List Brokers:

Abelow Response
2 Dubon Ct.
Farmingdale, NY 17735
(516) 293-8550

AZ Marketing Services
31 River Rd.
Cos Cob, CT 06807
(203) 629-8088

Direct Media
200 Pemberwick Rd.
Greenwich, CT 06830
(203) 532-1000

The Kaplan Agency
1200 High Ridge Rd.
Stamford, CT 06905
(203) 968-8800

Kleid
530 Fifth Ave., 17th Floor
New York, NY 10036
(212) 819-3400

Leon Henry
455 Central Ave., Suite 315
Scarsdale, NY 10583
(914) 723-3176

Mal Dunn & Associates
2 Hardscrabble Rd.
Croton Falls, NY 10519
(914) 277-5558

Media Horizons
94 East Ave.
Norwalk, CT 06851
(203) 857-0770

Millard Group
10 Vose Farm Rd., P.O. Box 890
Peterborough, NH 03458
(603) 924-9262

Qualified Lists
1 American Ln.
Greenwich, CT 06831
(203) 552-6700

Package Inserts and Co-ops

WITH THE RISE OF POSTAL RATES over the last decade, the direct-mail industry has found increasing success in the use of alternative media such as package inserts, co-ops, and ride-alongs. These allow marketers to share the cost of direct-mail advertising by sending their material out together in one package.

Package inserts are advertisements in the form of postcards, flyers, folders, or envelopes (either from the company selling the product or from outsiders) placed in packages delivered to mail-order or retail buyers. The most popular format is a 5-by-8-inch one- or two-panel four-color advertisement.

The number of inserts enclosed will vary from four to eight. They are generally carried by an envelope or box that delivers an order sent by an established purveyor of mail-order merchandise, by a utility or credit card bill, or by a monthly bank statement. They can also be placed in an envelope containing photo-finishing, a package containing laundry or dry cleaning, a cereal box, a disposable-diaper carton, or anything else bought retail. The average cost to direct marketers of package inserts is between $45 and $55 per thousand.

When non-competing advertisements are mailed together to reduce costs and reach the same prospective customers, it's called a co-op mailing. These are generally carried in the same way or inserted in newspapers instead of being mailed.

When the mailing is run by a company with the primary purpose of mailing a catalogue or making an announcement, it's a ride-along. The spending on such mailings is now edging above the $30 million mark.

The most obvious advantage to using these alternative media is the low initial cost relative to the benefits, particularly after a successful format has been created.

Leon Henry's Ten Rules for the Most Effective Alternative Media Ad Placement

1. Choose the right distribution program

Look for demographics that are geared to your product or service, and try to ensure that the merchandise that your package insert accompanies will heighten the response to your offer.

2. Test at least ten programs at a time

Out of every ten programs tested, however, you will have an average of three losers. Experiment with new inserts to get an accurate measure of success.

3. Go with the maximum size

Different programs have different physical limitations. Go with the maximum size allowed by each program to prevent your insert from being lost in the shuffle.

4. Test with copy that you know works

Do not write new copy, create new graphics, or introduce a new offer when you first test your insert. Test what you already know works in direct mail or space advertising. If your program fails, you'll know it was the program and not your copy or offer that was at fault.

5. Be patient when evaluating a program

Inserts that accompany retail merchandise may take six months before they are fully distributed. Calculate a final cost-per-order you can be comfortable with, and as long as you come in under that number, you can consider your insert program a success.

6. Try to transform marginal performers into new profit-makers

By reducing printing costs, changing layout, or changing stock, color, or copy, you might be able to manipulate the cost of participation in a program and turn a marginal program into a real success.

7. Always key every insert package

Using a five- or six-digit code, mark every insert you send out with a key that will allow you to identify what package it was part of. It's better to pay the extra money to stop the press and change keys than it is to be unsure of your results.

8. Include an appropriate number of inserts

Unless you have at least 10,000 inserts in each program you test, your returns may not be statistically reliable. On the other hand, if the number of inserts you put in one program is too high, it will force you to wait too long a time until all of your inserts have been distributed and you can evaluate the results. You might break up a large number of inserts into several keys and evaluate them as you go along.

9. Choose a dependable broker

Many inserts miss the program they were intended for because of foul-ups in production or shipping. Your broker must make sure your materials are printed accurately, shipped to where they're supposed to go, received by the appropriate people, and inserted in the right program.

10. Always re-test favorable returns

If you don't, a competitor may jump in and pre-empt you from profiting from your success. On the other hand, you should maintain sizable reserves of pre-keyed inserts to take advantage of a new program or a competitor's failure to re-test promptly.

Contact Option

Leon Henry
455 Central Ave., Suite 315
Scarsdale, NY 10583
(914) 723-3176

Color Marketing

EFFECTIVE USE OF COLOR is the mission of The Color Marketing Group, an international non-profit association of 1,300 design and color professionals. The group forecasts color directions one to three years ahead in all industries, including consumer, contract, transportation, fashion, graphics, office, and health care. The Color Marketing Group provides a forum for the exchange of non-competitive information on all phases of color marketing, including color trends and combinations; styling and design; merchandising and sales; education and research.

Each year The Color Marketing Group selects emerging color preferences such as Ensign Blue, Plantation Shutter, and Canyon Rose for industry groups like exterior home, kitchen and bath, and retail.

Contact Option

The Color Marketing Group
5904 Richmond Hwy., #408
Alexandria, VA 22303
(703) 329-8500

Classic Marketing Books

BOOKS ABOUT MARKETING account for a large percentage of the greatest business books ever written. Here is an idiosyncratic list of some of the most useful books on the topic.

Direct Mail Copy That Sells
by Herschell Gordon Lewis
Prentice Hall, $12.95
(800) 947-7700

How to Write a Good Advertisement
by Victor O. Schwab
Wilshire Book Company, $20
(818) 765-8579

The Copy Workshop
by Bruce Bendinger
The Copy Workshop, $33
(312) 871-1179

Positioning
by Trout & Reis
McGraw-Hill, $24.95
(800) 882-8158

Tested Advertising Methods
by John Caples
Prentice Hall, $9.95
(800) 947-7700

The Top Reference Sources

1995 Mail Order Business Directory
B. Klein Publications, $85
(305) 752-1708

This directory is an essential tool for reaching the 9,500 most active mail order firms. This book also includes a very good summary of the mail order

market. Companies are listed by product categories, and all entries include company name, address, and telephone number.
   Foreign mail order companies are also included.

Typical Sales Rep Territories

No.	Regions
1	Eastern Massachusetts, Rhode Island, New Hampshire, Maine
2	Connecticut, western Massachusetts, Vermont
3	New York City, Long Island, Westchester County, New Jersey north of Trenton
4	Upstate New York
5	New Jersey, Trenton and south, Pennsylvania east of Harrisburg
6	Maryland, Delaware, District of Columbia, northern Virginia
7	Southern Virginia, North Carolina, South Carolina, eastern Tennessee
8	Georgia and Alabama
9	Florida
10	Western Pennsylvania to Harrisburg, West Virgina
11	Ohio north of Route 40
12	Ohio south of Route 40, Kentucky
13	Indiana except northwestern counties
14	Michigan and Toledo, Ohio
15	Illinois, north of Route 36 and Lake, Porter, and LaPorte counties of Indiana

No.	Regions
16	Wisconsin and northwestern Michigan (area northwest of Lake Michigan)
17	Minnesota; may include North and South Dakota and all or part of Iowa and Nebraska
18	Eastern Missouri, southern Illinois
19	Western Missouri, Kansas
20	Louisiana, Mississippi, Arkansas, western Tennessee
21	Texas and Oklahoma
22	Colorado, Utah; may include Montana, Idaho, Wyoming
23	California, Bakersfield and south; Arizona, southern Nevada, and New Mexico
24	California north of Bakersfield, part of Nevada
25	Washington and Oregon
26	Alaska
27	Hawaii and Guam
28	Puerto Rico and the Caribbean
29	Eastern Canada
30	Western Canada

Source: Manufacturers' Agents National Association

Trade Shows and Conventions

Convention Dates and Cities

American Booksellers Association Convention and Trade Exchange
American Booksellers Association   1996   Chicago   First weekend
(914) 591-2665   in June

American Chemical Society National Expo
American Chemical Society   1996   New Orleans   3/24 to 3/28
(202) 872-4485   Orlando   8/25 to 8/30

American Financial Services Association Expo
American Financial Services Association   1996   Reston, VA   5/6 to 5/8
(202) 296-5544

American Hospital Association
American Hospital Association   1996   Philadelphia   8/5 to 8/7
(312) 422-3000

American International Toy Fair
Toy Manufacturers of America   1996   New York   2/16 to 2/19
(212) 675-1141

Amusement and Music Operators Association
Smith, Bucklin and Associates   1996   New Orleans   NA
(312) 644-6610

Architectural Woodwork Institute Convention and Trade Show
Architectural Woodwork Institute   1996   Atlanta   9/22 to 9/24
(703) 222-1100

ASCD Annual Conference and Exhibit Show
Ass'n for Supervision and Curriculum Development   1996   New Orleans   3/16 to 3/19
(703) 549-9110

Associated General Contractors of America
Associated General Contractors of America   1996   San Antonio   2/29 to 3/5
(202) 393-2040

Association of Broadcasters Convention
National Association of Broadcasters   1996   Las Vegas   4/15 to 4/18
(202) 429-5300

ASTA's World Travel Congress
American Society of Travel Agents   1996   Bangkok,   10/6 to 10/12
(703) 739-2782   Thailand

The Builders Show
National Association of Home Builders   1996   Houston   1/26 to 1/27
(202) 822-0200

Building Owners & Managers Association Convention
Building Owners & Managers Association (BOMA)   1996   Boston   6/23 to 6/26
(202) 408-2662

Consumer Electronics Show
Electronic Industries Association   1996   Las Vegas   NA
(202) 457- 4900

Converting Machinery and Materials Conference & Expo
Blenheim Group   1997   Chicago   April
(201) 346-1400

Trade Shows and Conventions (cont'd)

COMDEX				
	The Interface Group (617) 449-6600	1996	Chicago	6/3 to 6/6
Frankfurt Book Fair				
	Ausstellungs-und-messe-GmbH (069) 2102-219	1996	Frankfurt	10/11 to 10/16
Insurance Accounting & Systems Association Conference				
	Insurance Accounting & Systems Association (919) 489-0991	1996	Las Vegas	6/2 to 6/5
International Craft Expo				
	Offinger Management (614) 452-4541	1996	Chicago	7/23 to 7/30
International Fashion Boutique Show				
	The Larkin Group (617) 964-5100	1996	New York	1/6 to 1/9 3/16 to 3/19 6/1 to 6/4 8/24 to 8/27 10/19 to 10/22
International Housewares Show				
	National Housewares Manufacturers Association (708) 292-4200	1996	Chicago	1/14 to 1/17
International Kids Fashion Show				
	The Larkin Group (212) 594-8556	1996	New York	1/14 to 1/16 3/17 to 3/20 8/4 to 8/7 10/20 to 10/23
Int'l Woodworking, Machinery and Furniture Supply Fair				
	Int'l Woodworking Fair (404) 246-0608	1996	Atlanta	8/22 to 8/25
The Licensing Show				
	International Licensing Industry Merchandising Association (212) 244-1944	1996	New York	6/25 to 6/27
Medical Group Management Association Conference				
	Medical Group Management Association (303) 799-1111	1995	Minneapolis	10/13 to 10/16
Nat'l Cable Television Association Annual Convention				
	Dobson & Associates (202) 463-7905	1996	L.A.	4/28 to 5/1
Nat'l Health Care and American Hospital Association Convention				
	American Health Care Association & American Hospital Association (202) 842-4444	1996	NA	NA
National Association of Realtors Annual Conference				
	National Association of Realtors (312) 329-8200	1996	San Francisco	11/14 to 11/18
National Business Aircraft Association Meeting and Convention				
	National Business Aircraft Association (202) 783-9000	1996	Orlando	11/19 to 11/21
National Education Association				
	CEPI (813) 530-0405	1996	Washington, DC	7/2 to 7/4

NA=Not available

Trade Shows and Conventions (cont'd)

Nat'l Environmental Health Association Educational Conference
    National Environmental Health Association   1996   Chicago   6/29 to 7/3
    (303) 756-9090

National Food Distributors Association Convention
    Smith, Bucklin and Associates   1996   Orlando   1/20 to 1/22
    (312) 644-6610   New Orleans   7/22 to 7/21

National Hardware Show
    Association of Expositions and Services   1996   Chicago   8/11 to 8/14
    (203) 840-4820

National Home Center Show
    Bldg./Remodeling Expo. Miller Freeman   1996   NA   NA
    (214) 239-3060

National Home Health Care Expositions
    SEMCO Productions   1996   Atlanta   11/13 to 11/17
    (404) 998-9800

National Merchandise Show
    Miller Freeman   1996   New York   9/7 to 9/10
    (212) 869-1300   (national)

Nat'l Office Products Association Convention and Exhibit
    National Office Products Association   1996   Chicago   8/26 to 8/29
    (703) 549-9040

National Restaurant, Hotel/Motel Show
    National Restaurant Association   1996   Chicago   5/18 to 5/22
    (312) 853-2525

National Stationery Show
    George Little Management   1996   New York   5/18 to 5/21
    (914) 421-3200

NATPE
    National Association of TV Programming Executives   1996   Las Vegas   1/22 to 1/25
    (310) 453-4440

New York International Gift Fair
    George Little Management   1996   New York   1/21 to 1/25
    (914) 421-3200

PACK Expo
    Packaging Machinery Manufacturing Institute   1996   Chicago   11/17 to 11/21
    (202) 347-3838

PC Expo in New York
    Blenheim Group   1996   New York   6/18 to 6/20
    (201) 346-1400   Oct. dates not
                                                              set

Premium and Incentive Show
    Miller Freeman   1996   New York   1st week in May
    (212) 869-1300   (Tues.–Thurs.)

SUPERCOMM
    E. J. Krause & Associates   1996   Dallas   6/24 to 6/27
    (301) 986-7800

NA=Not available

Trade Shows and Conventions (cont'd)

The Super Show
The Super Show (305) 893-8771	1996	Atlanta	2/4 to 2/7

Variety Merchandise Show
Miller Freeman (212) 869-1300	1996	New York	2/17 to 2/20

Recommended Resource

1994-95 Trade Show & Convention Guide
Amusement Business, $85
(615) 321-4250

Best Places to Start a Business

CHOOSING A LOCATION for a new business is critical to its success. *Entrepreneur Magazine* conducted a survey to determine the ideal locations for new businesses. Their results were based on the availability of an educated labor pool, labor costs, growth in personal income, and real estate costs. The following cities in four regional areas were ranked as ideal locations for the average new business.

Top Cities (By Region)

City	Decrease in Business Failures (%)	Growth in New Incorporations (%)
Atlanta, GA	15.9	9.7
Minneapolis/St. Paul, MN	44.1	8.5
Kansas City, MO	8.3	15.2
Columbus, OH	8.7	7.2
Phoenix, AZ	11.1	22.1
Seattle/Everett, WA	13.0	11.7
Cleveland, OH	20.4	7.2
St. Louis, MO	35.4	15.2
Chicago, IL	25.1	5.9
Tampa Bay/St. Petersburg, FL	12.9	2.3
Amarillo, TX	40.8	2.6
Springfield, IL	32.6	5.9
Canton, OH	20.3	7.2
Springfield, MO	23.3	15.2
Eugene/Springfield, OR	34.0	11.4
Tulsa, OK	19.2	8.7
Salem, OR	50.0	11.4
Knoxville, TN	26.6	4.1
Portland, OR	24.1	11.4
St. Cloud, MN	9.9	8.5
Medford, OR	35.8	11.4
Clarksville, TN/Hopkinsville, KY	29.5	4.1/ 8.4

Source: Reprinted with permission from Entrepreneur Magazine, Oct. 1994

Top Franchises

FRANCHISING IS A METHOD of distributing products or services as a result of an agreement between two parties. The franchisor is the parent company, whose owner desires to expand his or her operations without maintaining additional stores. The franchisee, in return for an initial fee or a continuing royalty payment based on sales, assumes the right to operate the franchise, maintaining the products, services, and quality of the original operation.

The franchisor benefits from the ability to more rapidly expand his or her operations, while the franchisee enters the retail world, bolstered by the established procedures, training, advice, and guidance of the parent company. The franchisor generally offers limited or expanded plan packages to the franchisee which may include support services such as: site selection, guidelines for decor and design, management training and consulting, employee training, advertising and merchandising support, and financial assistance.

The types of franchised businesses range from auto and truck dealerships to soft-drink bottlers, with a wide variety of establishments in between. While statistics can direct the entrepreneur to businesses displaying growth and financial opportunity, the International Franchise Association emphasizes that it is critical to consider financial growth and analyze the track record of any prospective franchisor. A pattern of rapid growth may indicate a lack of sound support systems, whereas a long, steady growth pattern suggests a solid foundation in business franchising.

According to IFA reports, the largest (in number of outlets) franchise chains are as follows:

Rank	Franchise Chains	Number of Outlets
1	McDonald's	14,298
2	Subway Sandwiches and Salads	10,041
3	KFC	8,187
4	Burger King	6,826
5	Tandy	6,600
6	Century 21 Real Estate	6,000
7	International Dairy Queen	5,348
8	Domino's Pizza	5,300
9	Jani-King	4,214
10	The ServiceMaster Company	4,181
11	Hardee's Food Systems	3,997
12	Wendy's	3,928
13	Snap-On Tools	3,657
14	Baskin-Robbins	3,511
15	Blockbuster Entertainment	3,473

Source: International Franchise Association, 1995

When contemplating a new business, the entrepreneur's first concern is how much money it will require and how to obtain that money. Sources for start-up capital include:

- Bank loans;

- Life insurance policies that may allow borrowing on the cash value of the policy while charging a lower interest rate than banks;

- Equipment suppliers who will allow a new business to pay for equipment on an installment plan or offer similar short-term credit;

- The Small Business Administration (see below for a description of its service);

- Private investors who are willing to commit money to a business in return for a percentage of the business's profits during a predetermined time period or during the life of the business. Limited partnerships are a form of private investing in which the partners are investors only and do not contribute to the management of the business;

- SBICs–Small Business Investment Companies that are licensed by the Small Business Administration to provide venture capital to small businesses. Venture capitalists are frequently prepared to wait for a considerable length of time for profits to begin and will charge a rate of 15 percent and higher on their investment. These investors will also require a higher percentage of ownership in the new company, as much as 51 percent. In addition to financing, they often provide marketing and product ideas and management consultation.

The Federal Trade Commission offers a free packet of information for individuals interested in franchises. It contains information regarding the pros and cons of franchising, and a detailed explanation of what information the franchisor is required to provide in fulfillment of the disclosure rule. Call (202) 326-3142.

Recommended Resources

Entrepreneur Magazine
Entrepreneur Group, $19.97/year
2392 Morse Ave.
Irvine, CA 92714
(714) 261-2325
Publishes an issue on franchises in January of each year.

Top Franchises (cont'd)

Success Magazine's Top Ten Franchises

Rank	Franchise	Product/Service	Phone Number
1	GNC Franchising	Retail	(800) 766-7099
2	Aaron's Rental Purchase	Retail	(404) 237-4016
3	Choice Hotels	Lodging	(301) 593-5600
4	Blimpie	Fast food	(800) 447-6258
5	Schlotzsky's Inc.	Restaurants	(512) 469-7500
6	Coldwell Banker Residential Affiliates	Real estate	(714) 367-1800
7	Rocky Mountain Chocolate Factory	Retail food	(303) 259-0554
8	Sonic	Restaurants	(405) 232-4334
9	Servpro Industries	Maintenance products and services	(615) 451-0200
10	Fuddrucker's	Restaurants	(508) 774-9115

Source: Success, Nov. 1994, © 1994 by Success Partners. Reprinted with permission

Entrepreneur Magazine's 16th Annual Franchise 500 issue (January 1995) was devoted exclusively to the top franchises in the United States. These companies were ranked using a formula which included the following objective criteria: length of time in business, number of years franchising, number of franchised units and company-owned operating units, start-up costs, growth rate, percentage of terminations, and financial stability of the company.

Entrepreneur Magazine's Top 50 Franchises

Rank	Name	Rank	Name
1	Subway	26	Super 8 Motels
2	McDonald's	27	Sonic Drive-In Restaurants
3	Burger King	28	Uniglobe Travel
4	Hardee's	29	The Medicine Shoppe
5	7-Eleven Convenience Stores	30	Popeye's Chicken & Biscuits
6	Dunkin' Donuts	31	Merry Maids
7	Mail Boxes Etc.	32	Play It Again Sports
8	Choice Hotels	33	Miracle Ear
9	Snap-On Tools	34	Long John Silver's Restaurants
10	Dairy Queen	35	Matco Tools
11	Baskin-Robbins USA	36	Fantastic Sam's
12	Jani-King	37	Servpro
13	Coverall North America	38	Sir Speedy Printing
14	Arby's	39	Blimpie
15	Chem-Dry Carpet Drapery & Upholstery Cleaning	40	Church's Chicken
16	Century 21 Real Estate	41	The Historical Research Center
17	ServiceMaster	42	Jiffy Lube
18	Coldwell Banker Residential Affiliates	43	ABC Seamless
19	Midas	44	Money Mailer
20	Re/Max	45	Minuteman Press
21	Electronic Realty Associates	46	O.P.E.N. Cleaning Systems
22	Holiday Inn Worldwide	47	Meineke Discount Mufflers
23	GNC Franchising	48	Great Clips
24	Tower Cleaning Systems	49	Ben Franklin Retail Stores/Ben Franklin Crafts
25	Jackson Hewitt Tax Service	50	Cost Cutters Family Hair Care

Source: Reprinted with permission from Entrepreneur Magazine, Jan. 1995

Top Franchises (cont'd)

As the accompanying tables illustrate, franchising is becoming an increasingly popular form of business in the United States. The International Franchise Association (IFA), the industry regulator, recently noted that over 30% of total retail sales in the U.S. were made by retail franchise businesses.

Domestic and International Franchising Summary: 1983 to 1991

Item	1983	1984	1985	1986	1987	1988	1989	1990	1991
DOMESTIC									
No. of franchises est. (thousands)	442	444	455	462	479	481	493	521	542
Company-owned (thousands)	86	87	86	88	89	94	95	97	100
Franchisee-owned (thousands)	355	357	369	374	390	387	398	424	442
Sales of prod. & svcs. ($ billions)	423	492	543	569	599	648	678	714	758
Company-owned ($ billions)	59	64	68	85	90	98	107	117	127
Franchisee-owned ($ billions)	364	428	475	484	509	550	570	597	631
Avg. sales per estab. ($ thousands)	958	1,108	1,193	1,231	1,251	1,348	1,376	1,369	1,399
Employment (thousands)	5,165	5,671	6,283	6,501	NA	NA	NA	NA	NA
INTERNATIONAL									
U.S.-operated foreign outlets	305	328	342	354	NA	374	NA	NA	NA
Foreign outlets (thousands)	26	27	30	32	NA	35	NA	NA	NA

Source: 1994 Statistical Abstract, Table No. 1291

Domestic Franchising by Number of Establishments (thousands): 1980 to 1991

Franchised Businesses	1980	1985	1987	1988	1989	1990	1991
TOTAL FRANCHISING	442.4	455.2	479.1	480.8	492.5	521.2	542.5
Auto and truck dealers	29.4	27.5	27.6	27.8	26.9	26.8	26.5
Restaurants (all types)	60.0	73.9	83.3	90.3	92.0	99.3	103.3
Gasoline service stations	158.5	124.6	115.9	113.2	111.5	107.5	107.0
Retailing (non-food)	35.2	45.1	47.9	46.2	50.0	54.4	57.0
Auto, truck rental services	7.3	11.2	10.0	9.5	9.8	10.7	11.1
Automotive products & services	40.2	36.5	39.3	34.7	36.2	39.2	42.2
Business aids & services							
Employment services	4.4	4.8	6.1	6.5	6.6	7.5	8.3
Tax preparation services	9.2	8.1	8.5	8.3	8.2	8.3	8.5
Accounting, credit, collection	2.4	2.1	2.0	1.7	1.7	1.8	1.9
Real estate	17.3	13.9	15.2	15.3	15.8	16.4	18.2
Printing & copying	2.8	4.5	5.6	5.9	6.3	6.8	7.4
Other business aids	4.8	16.4	19.4	17.9	19.5	23.6	25.3
Construction, home improvement, maint.	14.3	17.5	21.7	22.0	24.1	27.4	30.6
Convenience stores	15.6	15.1	16.3	17.2	17.6	17.2	17.3
Educational products & services	3.2	8.2	9.6	11.6	11.1	12.5	13.9
Equipment rental services	2.2	2.5	2.8	3.0	2.6	2.7	2.9
Food retailing	15.5	18.7	20.5	21.6	21.1	24.5	25.4
Hotels & motels	6.4	7.5	9.3	9.3	10.1	11.0	11.4
Laundry, dry-cleaning services	3.4	2.3	2.2	2.3	3.0	3.2	3.5
Recreation, entertainment, travel	4.6	7.8	8.2	8.8	9.8	10.9	11.6
Soft-drink bottlers	1.9	1.4	1.1	0.9	0.8	0.8	0.8
Miscellaneous	3.6	5.5	6.8	6.9	7.6	8.4	8.6

Source: 1994 Statistical Abstract, Table No. 1292

Top Franchises (cont'd)

Domestic Franchising by Sales ($ billions): 1980 to 1991

Franchised Businesses	1980	1985	1987	1988	1989	1990	1991
TOTAL FRANCHISING SALES	336.2	543.0	599.4	648.1	677.9	713.8	757.8
Auto and truck dealers	143.9	282.6	319.7	345.1	351.0	345.9	354.5
Restaurants (all types)	27.9	47.7	56.8	64.3	70.1	77.9	85.5
Gasoline service stations	94.5	100.8	89.2	101.9	109.4	128.6	143.2
Retailing (non-food)	10.5	20.6	25.4	23.3	26.7	29.3	31.4
Auto, truck rental services	3.1	5.7	6.5	6.6	6.9	7.5	8.0
Automotive products & services	7.1	10.7	12.3	11.4	12.5	13.9	15.5
Business aids & services	6.7	12.0	14.7	15.7	16.9	18.6	20.8
Employment services	1.6	2.7	3.7	4.7	5.0	5.7	6.4
Tax preparation services	0.3	0.4	0.5	0.6	0.7	0.7	0.7
Accounting, credit, collection	0.1	0.2	0.2	0.2	0.2	0.2	0.2
Real estate	3.6	4.6	5.6	5.9	6.2	6.8	7.7
Printing & copying	0.4	0.9	1.2	1.5	1.6	1.8	2.0
Other business aids	0.8	3.1	3.5	3.0	3.4	3.5	3.8
Construction, home improvement, maint.	1.5	4.1	5.2	5.3	5.8	6.5	7.1
Convenience stores	7.8	10.8	12.3	13.9	14.3	14.3	15.0
Educational products & services	0.3	0.8	1.0	1.7	1.7	2.0	2.3
Equipment rental services	0.4	0.7	0.7	0.7	0.7	0.7	0.8
Food retailing	7.4	10.1	11.1	10.2	10.0	11.7	12.2
Hotels & motels	9.5	14.8	17.7	19.7	21.6	23.8	26.0
Laundry, dry-cleaning services	0.3	0.3	0.3	0.3	0.4	0.4	0.5
Recreation, entertainment, travel	0.5	2.3	4.0	3.5	3.5	4.2	4.8
Soft-drink bottlers	14.4	18.3	20.9	22.7	24.6	26.2	28.0
Miscellaneous	0.4	0.9	1.5	1.7	2.0	2.3	2.6

Source: 1994 Statistical Abstract, Table No. 1292

Franchise Law

FRANCHISES ARE BECOMING INCREASINGLY popular with the aspiring small business owner. To protect the interests of the inexperienced entrepreneur, the Federal Trade Commission (FTC) requires every franchisor to provide an extensive disclosure document to prospective franchisees before they make any purchase. This statement must contain information about the following:

- Required fees;
- Basic investment;
- Bankruptcy;
- Litigation history of the company;
- Expected term of the franchise;
- Audited financial statement of the franchisor, including bankruptcy history;
- Earnings claims;
- List of directors, trustees, partners, and principal officers of the franchisor; history of the franchisor, its directors, and its key executives;
- Description of the franchise requirements, its directors and key executives and their business experience, and ongoing continuing expenses required of the franchisee to be paid to the franchisor;

- A list of individuals who are part of the franchisor or its affiliates and with whom the franchisee is required to do business;
- Celebrity involvement in the franchise and a list of royalties and/or commissions paid to such individuals by the franchisee, and statistical information about the rate of termination;
- Obligations of franchisee to purchase or lease from approved suppliers;
- Obligations of the franchisor to the franchisee, namely, types of assistance, and charges associated with these services;
- Conditions of renewal, extension, termination of franchise;
- The number, names, addresses, and phone numbers of franchisees;
- A copy of all agreements to be signed before the purchase of the franchise.

Franchise Law (cont'd)

On the federal level, the FTC allows the franchisors to distribute this information through a Uniform Franchise Offering Circular (UFOC). Fourteen individual states (California, Hawaii, Illinois, Indiana, Maryland, Michigan, Minnesota, New York, North Dakota, Rhode Island, South Dakota, Virginia, Washington, and Wisconsin) have disclosure laws similar to those required by the FTC. Write to the franchise division of the Department of Commerce of any of the state offices to request copies of the disclosure agreements of a specific company. While the forms vary from state to state, the essence of the reporting is the same. New York will send its report anywhere in the country:

New York State
Bureau of Investor and Protection Securities
120 Broadway
New York, NY 10271
(212) 416-8236

The next page provides a sample form for request of disclosure documents regarding any franchisor. Simply fill in the name of the franchise, complete the form, and send the request to the above address.

The franchisee must, in turn, sign a franchise agreement. There should be clear, concise statements regarding the following items:

- Franchise fee;

- Advertising fees;

- Royalty fees;

- Hidden costs such as equipment and supplies;

- Quotas;

- Franchise term;

- Assignment or permission to transfer franchise agreement to another individual;

- Termination rights of franchisor and franchisee;

- Competition.

The International Franchise Association (IFA) is the industry's regulatory agency. Members must maintain a satisfactory financial condition and are expected to comply with franchise law. The association continually updates its membership regarding changes in franchise law as well as methods of improving cooperative advertising, public relations, marketing, and field operations.

The IFA recommends that any individual considering a franchise should carefully discuss the disclosure materials and the history and reputation of both the company and its officers with both an accountant and an attorney. The organization also strongly suggests that the franchisee discuss the franchise with a number of other franchisees of the target organization.

Contact Option

International Franchise Association
1350 New York Ave., NW, Suite 900
Washington, DC 20005
(202) 628-8000

Recommended Resources

The Legal Guide for Starting and Running a Small Business
by Fred S. Steingold
Nolo Press, $22.95
(800) 992-6656 or (510) 549-1976

Nation's Business
Chamber of Commerce of the United States
$22/12 issues
(202) 463-5650

This outstanding publication includes four annual inserts specifically devoted to franchise trends, financing, seminars and expos, conversion, growth forecasts, and other related topics.

Franchise Disclosure

Many states require franchises doing business within the state to file complete background information, including financial facts about their companies. A potential investor should request disclosure of such information from the state office of the Bureau of Investor Protection. A sample Freedom-of-Information request form for New York State can be found on the next page.

The Top Reference Sources

Franchise Opportunities Guide
International Franchise Association, $15
(202) 628-8000

This reference provides a comprehensive listing of more than 2,000 franchises and contains answers to the most frequently asked questions about franchising. Special features include sources for legal advice and franchise consultants, and information on how to finance your franchise.

Franchise Law (cont'd)

FREEDOM OF INFORMATION REQUEST

I HEREBY APPLY TO INSPECT THE FOLLOWING RECORD:

NAME	REPRESENTING
MAILING ADDRESS	TELEPHONE NUMBER
SIGNATURE	DATE

FOR AGENCY USE ONLY

APPROVED _____

DENIED (for reason(s) checked below)

_____ Confidential disclosure
_____ Unwarranted invasion of personal privacy
_____ Record of which this agency is legal custodian cannot be found
_____ Record is not maintained by this agency
_____ Exempted by statute other than the Freedom of Information Act
_____ Request has been referred to department which has custody or control of original record
_____ Part of investigatory files
_____ Other (specify) _____

SIGNATURE	TITLE	DATE

NOTE: YOU HAVE THE RIGHT TO APPEAL A DENIAL OF THIS APPLICATION TO HEAD OF THIS AGENCY

NAME	BUSINESS ADDRESS

WHO MUST FULLY EXPLAIN HIS REASONS FOR WHICH DENIAL IN WRITING WITHIN SEVEN WORKING DAYS OF RECEIPT OF AN APPEAL.

I HEREBY APPEAL:

SIGNATURE	DATE

OFFICE MANAGEMENT

Auto Leasing

Number of Cars Leased for Business Use* (millions)

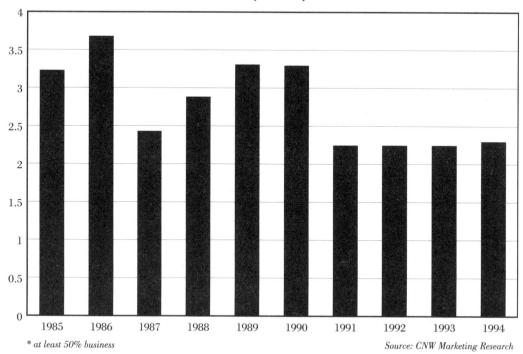

* at least 50% business

Source: CNW Marketing Research

E-MAIL   **Auto Theft and Damage.** Send e-mail to theft@almanac.yoyo.com. See p. xi for instructions.

Tables of auto registrations and thefts, average loss payment, and claim frequency, from the FBI and the Highway Loss Data Institute.

Electronic Surveillance

A FEW STORES SPECIALIZE in state-of-the-art electronic surveillance and security equipment. For prices that can run into the thousands, it is possible to purchase everything from hidden camera and alarm systems, to anti-bugging and wiretapping equipment, to telephone and fax scramblers, weapons detectors, and surveillance vehicles. Briefcases equipped with covert microphones and miniature cameras, and other specialized executive accessories, are also sold.

Contact Options

Electronic Surveillance Sources:

The Spy Store
164 Christopher St.
New York, NY 10014
(212) 366-6466

Communication Control Systems of New York
675 Third Ave.
New York, NY 10001
(212) 268-4779

Eavesdropping Detection Equipment
2480 Niagara Falls Blvd.
Tonawanda, NY 14150
(716) 691-3476
Attn: Bob

Sheffield Electronics
P.O. Box 377785
Chicago, IL 60637
(312) 643-4928

Security and Bodyguards

Contact Options

National Companies Providing Corporate Security:

Advance Security
2964 Peachtree Rd., NE, Suite 200
Atlanta, GA 30305
(800) 241-0267

Burns International Security Services
2 Campus Dr.
Parsippany, NJ 07054
(201) 397-2000

Guardsmark
22 S. Second St.
Memphis, TN 38103
(901) 522-6000

Orion Protective Services
1410 Gunston Rd.
Bel Air, MD 21015
(410) 515-7353

Pinkerton Security and Investigation Services
15910 Ventura Blvd., Suite 900
Encino, CA 91436
(818) 380-8800

Recommended Resources

The American Society for Industrial Security
1655 N. Fort Myer Dr., Suite 1200
Arlington, VA 22209
(703) 522-5800

The Security Industry Buyer's Guide 1996
The American Society for Industrial Security and
Phillips Publishing, $169
(800) 777-5006 or (301) 424-3338
   Lists all products and services available in the security industry alphabetically and by product and location.

   Also check the yellow pages under "Guard" and "Patrol Services."

Alarm Systems

Largest Security Installation Companies Based on Revenue, 1993

Rank	Name	Location	1993 Revenue ($)	No. of Accounts
1	ADT Security Systems	Parsippany, NJ	660,000,000	710,000
2	Honeywell	Minneapolis, MN	223,000,000	190,000
3	Wells Fargo Alarm Services	King of Prussia, PA	213,300,000	118,000
4	National Guardian	Greenwich, CT	191,000,000	215,000
5	Westinghouse Security Systems	Irving, TX	100,000,000	205,000
6	Brink's Home Security	Carrollton, TX	89,000,000	259,551
7	THORN Automated Systems	Westlake, OH	75,000,000	10,000
8	Rollins Protective Services	Atlanta, GA	65,000,000	113,942
9	ASH, USA	Culver City, CA	65,000,000	33,000
10	Westec Security	Newport Beach, CA	63,000,000	62,000
11	Winterfold/Winterfold Security	Irving, TX	60,000,000	2,000
12	The Alert Centre	Englewood, CO	58,000,000	157,000
13	Holmes Protection Group	New York, NY	54,000,000	30,000
14	SecurityLink	Oak Brook, IL	37,300,000	NA
15	Kastle Systems	Arlington, VA	35,500,000	48,000
16	Bay Alarm	Walnut Creek, CA	32,000,000	40,000
17	Network Multi-Family Security	Dallas, TX	28,000,000	160,000
18	Vector Security	Pittsburgh, PA	28,000,000	40,000
19	Guardian Alarm	Southfield, MI	26,000,000	58,000
20	AFA Protective Systems	Syosset, NY	25,200,000	11,400

Source: Security Distributing & Marketing, May 1994

The Top Reference Sources

Consumer Reports Travel Letter
Consumers Union, $37/year
(800) 272-0722

The *Travel Letter* is a monthly newsletter that helps track down the best travel values. It presents strategies for finding the best airfares, hotel rates, and car rental rates. Features include warnings about frauds and scams, ways to avoid hassles, and other timely guidance for travelers.

Comsumer Reports Books, a division of Consumers Union, publishes the *Travel Buying Guide*, an annual book that provides valuable information on/and evaluation of airfares, hotels, car rentals, and other items of interest to the traveler. It is available for $8.99.

The Strategies for Business area on America Online features "how-to" information, from starting a business to going public and much more.
KEYWORD BUSINESS KNOW HOW.

Corporate Charge Cards

EXPERTS ESTIMATE THAT COMPANIES spent a total of $120 billion on travel and entertainment (T&E) in 1992. What's more, T&E is the third largest controllable expense, after salaries and data processing, for most companies.

In an effort to serve this growing business as well as other corporate needs, major credit card companies currently provide their corporate clients with a wide range of services—from expense management, to disability insurance, to protection plans, to travel benefits and discounts, to billing options.

Below is a list of numbers to contact to obtain corporate credit cards. In general, the more cards a company orders for its employees, the lower the card's annual fee.

Contact Options

American Express Corporate Card
(800) 528-2122

Citibank Diner's Club Corporate Card
(800) 525-5289

Visa and MasterCard may be obtained through individual banks.

Office Machinery Buyers Guide

BUYERS LABORATORY, an independent provider of critical evaluations of office products and procedures, gives its "Line of the Year" and "Pick of the Year" awards to the manufacturers of copiers, printers, and facsimile machines that excelled in the company's extensive in-house testing.

Buyers Laboratory 1993 Awards

Device	Category	Company	Model
Copier	Line of the Year	Lanier Worldwide	All
Copier	Low-volume	Sharp	SF-2022
Copier	Mid-volume	Minolta	EP 5320 Pro Series
Copier	Mid-volume	Minolta	EP 5420 Pro Series
Copier	Technical achievement	Canon	CJ10, CJ7
Copier	Outstanding value	Océ	2400
Copier	Overall outstanding	Sharp	SD-3075
Page Printer	Overall outstanding	Hewlett-Packard	Laser Jet 4M
Page Printer	High-volume	Hewlett-Packard	Laser Jet 4SiMX
Page Printer	Outstanding value	Kyocera	ECOSYS a-SiFS-1500A
Dot-Matrix Printer	Outstanding value	Star Micronics	XR-1520 Multi-Font
Facsimile	High-volume plain paper	Canon	FAX-L785
Facsimile	High-volume plain paper value	JetFax	8000D
Facsimile	Mid-volume plain paper	Sharp	FO-5400
Facsimile	Low-volume thermal	Ricoh	FAX240

Source: Buyers Laboratory

The Top Reference Sources

Buyers Laboratory Test Reports for Office Equipment
Buyers Laboratory, $635/year
(201) 488-0404

Buyers Laboratory provides testing information to business consumers in much the same way as *Consumer Reports* provides information to the general public. Each test report is based on actual testing conducted by Buyers Laboratory test technicians. The Office Products subscription service provides reports on copiers, copier supplies, facsimile equipment, swivel chairs, file cabinets, typewriters, paper shredders, desks, printers, and postage meter machines, among others. A good source for critical, unbiased evaluations of business equipment.

Voice Mail

VOICE MAIL HAS PROGRESSED from prerecorded answering machine messages to sophisticated systems that use applications of computer-telephone integration. Current and future technological developments in this facet of telecommunications include interactive voice response and enhanced information services in combination with traditional office communications media such as facsimile and electronic messaging.

Contact Options

Companies Providing Voice Messaging Systems:

Digital Equipment
(800) 332- 4636, ext. 705

InterVoice
(214) 497-8862

MacroTel International
(407) 997-5500

Toshiba America Information Systems
(714) 583-3000

Voice Professionals
(800) 868-3684

Voice Technologies Group
(716) 689-6700

Voicetek
(508) 250-9393

The local phone company may also provide voice messaging systems.

Recommended Resources

Association of Telemessaging Services International
1150 S. Washington St., Suite 150
Alexandria, VA 22314
(703) 684-0016

Voice Processing, $39/year
131 W. First St.
Duluth, MN 55802
(800) 346-0085, ext. 477
This publication reports on the latest developments in computer-telephone integration and voice automation.

MCI's Tips on Preventing Toll Fraud

MCI COMMUNICATIONS HAS A LIST of recommendations for limiting your risk of toll fraud. These will sound familiar to those managing file servers and other network services, but make sure the PBX administrator knows them, too.

- Learn all the capabilities of your PBX, particularly any you may not be aware of now. The vendor who sells or services your equipment is the most logical source for this information.

- Delete all authorization codes that were programmed into your PBX for testing or initial servicing.

- Audit and change all active codes in your PBX frequently and de-activate those not authorized.

- Treat authorization codes as you would credit card numbers. Each code should be assigned individually and employees' codes kept confidential.

- Assign the longest possible authorization numbers your PBX can handle. And select codes at random; do not use telephone extension numbers, so-

cial security numbers, employee identification numbers, and the like.

- Be alert during PBX-related conversations to the possibility that the person on the other end may be an impersonator; it may be a thief trying to learn about your phone system in order to defraud you.

- Tailor access to your PBX to conform strictly with the needs of your company. Block access to international and long-distance domestic numbers that your company does not call.

- Use an unpublished number for the Remote Access Unit/Direct Inward System Access and program the PBX to wait at least five rings before responding to the call.

- Review carefully all billing information to identify unauthorized calling patterns.

- Avoid a steady tone as the prompt for inputting an authorization code. Instead, use a voice recording or no prompt, which will minimize your vulnerability to unauthorized activity.

Telecommunications Services

THERE ARE FOUR MAJOR CRITERIA a business must weigh when selecting telecommunications services. These are quality, service, reliability, and price. Some questions to ask a company are:

- Can you cut my telecommunications costs? How?
- Why should I choose your company?
- In what ways can your program for small business be tailored to my needs?
- What kinds of incentives do you offer?
- What kinds of guarantees do you offer?
- How do I change my local or long distance carrier?
- How long does it take to change carriers?
- Will changing long distance carriers disrupt my service?

In addition, businesses may ask for the following:

- An appointment to discuss specific requirements;
- Reimbursement of local telephone company charges for changing long distance carriers (called "PIC fees," usually $5.00 per telephone line);
- A list of the carrier's recurring "service" or "management" fees and installation charges (a standard "switched" service program should have no service or installation fees);
- Specifics on any minimum billing requirements (there is often a monthly "minimum usage requirement" associated with long distance programs. If a business does not meet this dollar

amount, it may be charged the difference. Some carriers require businesses to commit to an annual amount of spending and will charge severe penalties if these minimums are not met);

- A written statement of penalties for breaking a "Term Agreement" or changing carriers (one-, two-, and three-year agreements can be signed in exchange for significant price discounts. Otherwise, there should be no charge or penalty for changing long distance carriers);
- A local account representative who can make on-site visits;
- A 24-hour, toll-free number for all service issues;
- Information about a carrier's disaster-recovery and rerouting capabilities;
- Information about a carrier's fraud-protection policies.

Source: Sprint

Contact Options

AT&T
(800) 222-0400

MCI
(800) 888-0800

Sprint
(800) 877-2000

Tele-Trend Communications
(800) 848-1400

The Top Reference Sources

The Executive Desk Register of Publicly Held Corporations
Demand Research, $59.95
(614) 891-5600
73207.3434@compuserve.com or
dresearch@aol.com

The *Register* is a database that contains approximately 5,500 domestic corporations and financial

institutions. It is updated daily and published monthly on IBM PC diskettes.

The database includes executives in human resources, marketing, sales, manufacturing, and other areas, as well as computer and telecommunications companies. Portions of the database are released periodically as shareware.

Business & Office Supplies by Mail

BELOW IS A BRIEF LISTING OF SELECTED mail order business dealers. For a more complete listing, consult the *Mail Order Product Guide* or the *Mail Order Business Directory*.

Recommended Resources

Mail Order Product Guide
Todd Publications, $20
18 N. Greenbush Rd.
W. Nyack, NY 10994
(914) 358-6213

Mail Order Business Directory
B. Klein Publications, $85
P.O. Box 8503
Coral Springs, FL 33075
(305) 752-1708

Contact Options

Office Equipment:

Allied Business Machines
9281 Earl St.
La Mesa, CA 92041
(619) 461-6361

American Printing Equipment
42-25 Ninth St.
Long Island City, NY 11101
(718) 729-5779

Longacre Office Machines
20 E. 40th St.
New York, NY 10016
(212) 684-2471

Pitney Bowes
World Headquarters
Stamford, CT 06926
(203) 356-5000

Viking Office Products
24 Thompson Rd.
P.O. Box 1052
E. Windsor, CT 06088
(800) 421-1222

Office Supplies:

Adirondack Direct
31-01 Vernon Blvd.
Long Island City, NY 11106
(718) 932-4003

Charrette
P.O. Box 4010
Woburn, MA 01888
(617) 935-6000

City Office Supply
156 N. Jefferson St.
Chicago, IL 60661
(312) 559-0100

Modern Service Office Supply
19315 E. San Jose Ave.
City of Industry, CA 91748
(800) 672-6767

Staples
100 Pennsylvania Ave.
P.O. Box 9328
Framingham, MA 01701
(800) 333-3330

Wholesale Supply
P.O. Box 23437
Nashville, TN 37202
(800) 962-9162

Stationery:

Atlas Pen and Pencil
3040 N. 29th Ave.
P.O. Box 600
Hollywood, FL 33022
(305) 920-4444

Day Timers
1 Willow Lane
E. Texas, PA 18046
(610) 398-1151

Forms
P.O. Box 1109
La Jolla, CA 92038
(619) 454-5759

Standard Stationery
10 Furniture Row
Milford, CT 06460
(203) 874-1608

The Stationery House
1000 Florida Ave.
Hagerstown, MD 21740
(301) 739-4487

Office Furniture by Mail

Contact Options

Mail Order Furniture Companies:

A.T.D. American
135 Greenwood Ave.
Wyncote, PA 19095
(800) 523-2300

Business & Institutional Furniture
611 N. Broadway
Milwaukee, WI 53202
(414) 272-6080

Carl Manufacturing
P.O. Box 488
110 W. Washington St.
Lisbon, OH 44432
(216) 424-1421

Foster Manufacturing
414 N. 13th St.
Philadelphia, PA 19108
(215) 625-0500

National Business Furniture
222 E. Michigan St.
P.O. Box 92952
Milwaukee, WI 53202
(800) 558-1010

Office Furniture Center
135 Beaver St.
Waltham, MA 02154
(800) 343-4222

Standard Equipment
601 Concord Ave.
Williston Park, NY 11596
(800) 782-6866

Color Printing

A NUMBER OF COMPANIES will provide four-color brochures, catalogues, sales sheets, posters, and other computer-generated color graphics by mail order quickly and inexpensively.

Contact Options

Companies Specializing in Color Printing:

Color Impressions
1642 N. Besly Ct.
Chicago, IL 60622
(800) 626-1333

Multiprint
5555 W. Howard St.
Skokie, IL 60077
(800) 858-9999

Scangraphics
5300 Newport Dr.
Rolling Meadows, IL 60008
(708) 392-3980

Catalogue Sources

A WIDE RANGE OF BUSINESS-RELATED articles—from office furniture to stationery to heavy machinery—can be efficiently purchased by mail. These publications profile a wide variety of catalogues.

Recommended Resources

The Directory of Mail Order Catalogues
Grey House Publishing, $125
P.O. Box 1866
Pocket Knife Square
Lakeville, CT 06039
(203) 435-0868

Mail Order Business Directory
B. Klein Publications, $85
P.O. Box 8503
Coral Springs, FL 33075
(305) 752-1708

Airlines Ranked by Size

Domestic Airlines Ranked by Revenue, 1993

Sales Rank	Company	Location	1993 Revenue ($ thousands)	Load Factor (%)	No. of Major Airports Served
1	American	DFW Airport, TX	14,740,000	60.4	190
2	United	Chicago, IL	14,500,000	67.1	159
3	Delta	Atlanta, GA	12,294,800	61.3	190
4	Northwest	St. Paul, MN	8,648,900	66.7	139
5	USAir	Arlington, VA	7,100,000	59.2	213
6	Continental	Houston, TX	5,775,310	63.2	142
7	TWA	Mount Kisco, NY	2,873,800	63.5	110
8	Southwest	Dallas, TX	2,067,519	67.5	34
9	America West	Phoenix, AZ	1,300,000	65.3	44
10	Alaska Airlines	Seattle, WA	902,200	58.5	38
11	American Trans Air	Indianapolis, IN	467,900	67.9	19
12	Mesa	Farmingham, NM	353,640	50.6	55
13	Hawaiian Airlines	Honolulu, HI	297,100	74.5	14
14	Atlantic Southeast	Atlanta, GA	288,463	46.9	NA
15	Comair	Cincinnati, OH	237,133	47.0	68
16	Aloha Airlines	Honolulu, HI	213,964	60.9	5
17	Skywest	El Segundo, CA	146,800	46.0	42
18	Reno	Reno, NV	124,600	57.5	NA
19	Mesaba	Minneapolis, MN	124,331	45.4	52
20	Kiwi	Newark, NJ	100,000	56.3	9

Source: Business Travel News, May 30, 1994

The Top Reference Sources

FAA Statistical Handbook of Aviation, 1992
The National Technical Information Service, $27
(703) 487-4650

This report presents statistical information pertaining to the Federal Aviation Administration, the National Airspace System, airports, airport activity, U.S. Civil Air Carrier Fleet, U.S. Civil Air Carrier Operating Data, aircraft accidents, and aeronautical production. Also included are imports/exports, a listing of general aviation aircraft, and a glossary of terms.

Largest Transportation Companies

Rank	Company	1993 Sales ($ mil.)
1	United Parcel Service	17,782.4
2	AMR	15,816.0
3	UAL	14,511.0
4	Delta Air Lines	11,996.7
5	CSX	8,940.0
6	Northwest Airlines	8,648.9
7	Federal Express	7,808.0
8	Union Pacific	7,561.3
9	USAir Group	7,083.2
10	Continental Airlines	5,775.3
11	Ryder Systems*	5,303.6
12	Burlington Northern	4,699.0
13	Norfolk Southern	4,460.1
14	Consolidated Freightways	4,191.8
15	Roadway Services	4,155.9
16	Conrail	3,453.0
17	Trans World Airlines	3,157.4
18	Southern Pacific Rail*	2,918.6
19	Yellow	2,856.5
20	Santa Fe Pacific	2,726.4
21	American President	2,594.2
22	Southwest Airlines	2,296.7
23	Panhandle Eastern*	2,120.9
24	Airborne Freight	1,720.0
25	Carnival Cruise Lines	1,556.9
26	America West Airlines	1,325.4
27	Alaska Air Group	1,128.3
28	GATX*	1,086.9
29	Chicago & North Western Holdings	1,043.2
30	J. B. Hunt Transport	1,020.9
31	Arkansas Best	1,009.9
32	Alexander & Baldwin	966.3
33	Kansas City So. Industries	961.1
34	Unigroup	912.3
35	Penske Truck Leasing*	902.1
36	TNT Freightways*	898.9
37	BP Pipelines (Alaska)	857.3
38	Carolina Freight	845.3
39	Tejas Gas*	790.2
40	Landstar System	780.5
41	Air Express*	725.7
42	Mayflower Group	677.5
43	Greyhound Lines	666.5
44	Illinois Central	564.7
45	Colonial Pipeline	554.3
46	Exxon Pipeline	469.2
47	Arco Transportation Alaska	468.0
48	Amtran*	467.9
49	MNX	441.1
50	Harper Group*	429.9

*New to list in 1994

Source: Fortune, May 30, 1994

Special Meals on Airlines

Airline	Meals	Notice Required
American	Bland and soft, child, gluten free, Hindu, kosher, low cholesterol, Muslim, low calorie, lactose free, low carbohydrate, low sodium, ovo-lacto vegetarian, diabetic, non-dairy, fresh fruit bowl, heart-healthy, seafood platter	12 hours for kosher meal, 6 hours for others
Continental	Child, diabetic, fruit plate, Hindu, infant, kosher, low cholesterol/low fat, low sodium, Muslim, ovo-lacto vegetarian, seafood, vegetarian	6 hours
Delta	Asian vegetarian, baby, bland, child, diabetic, fruit plate, gluten free, Hindu, kosher, low calorie/low cholesterol, low sodium, ovo-lacto vegetarian, Muslim, cold seafood, hot seafood, toddler, vegetarian	12 hours for Asian, Hindu, kosher meals, 6 hours for others
Northwest	Baby, bland, child, diabetic, fruit, gluten free, Hindu, Japanese, kosher, low calorie, low carbohydrate, low sodium, Muslim, ovo-lacto vegetarian, seafood, soft diet, sulfite free, vegetarian	12 hours
TWA	Child, cold seafood, kosher, low calorie, low cholesterol/low fat, low sodium, low carbohydrate/low sugar, ovo-lacto vegetarian, vegetarian	24 hours
United	Bland, dietary (diabetic-hypoglycemic), child's platter, gluten free, high fiber, infant, low calorie/low carbohydrate, low protein, low purin, ovo-lacto vegetarian, chef's salad, fruit plate, Muslim, non-lactose, raw vegetarian, refugee meal, low sodium, boneless chicken, Asian vegetarian, kosher, Hindu, low fat-low cholesterol	6 hours
USAir	Asian vegetarian, baby, bland, child, diabetic, fruit plate, gluten-free, high fiber, high protein, Hindu, kosher, low calorie, low fat/low cholesterol, low protein, low purin, low sodium, Muslim, non-lactose, ovo-lacto vegetarian, vegetarian, seafood	6 hours

Top Travel Locations

THE FOLLOWING ARE the top domestic and international travel destinations, according to a 1994 Runzheimer survey of business travel policies and costs.

Top Ten Domestic Travel Destinations

Destination	Percent of Respondents*		
	1990	1992	1994
Chicago	61	71	45
New York City	53	57	37
Dallas	33	52	34
Los Angeles	38	57	32
Atlanta	37	50	31
Washington, DC	43	49	26
San Francisco	27	43	21
Boston	22	38	17
Denver	11	22	15
Houston	20	16	12

Percent of respondents who listed locations as a leading destination of their business travelers. Totals exceed 100 percent because of multiple answers.

Source: Runzheimer International, 1994

Top Five International Travel Destinations

Destination	Percent of Respondents 1994*
London	27
Tokyo	13
Paris	11
Hong Kong	10
Mexico City	9

Percent of respondents who listed location as the leading destination of their business travelers.

Source: Runzheimer International, 1994

The Business Traveler

THE MAGAZINE *FREQUENT FLYER* conducts a poll of its readers annually. Included in this survey are questions about choice of airlines, frequent flyer plans, inflight experience, car rental, choice of hotels, and other relevant topics.

The following chart shows their responses to the question "In how many frequent flyer programs are you enrolled?"

Number of Programs

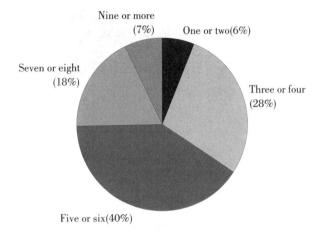

The following chart shows the responses to the question, "How many free tickets did you actually claim in the last twelve months?"

Frequent Flyer Tickets

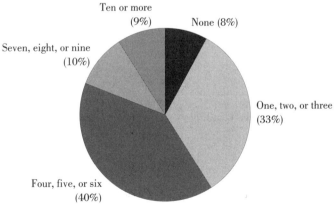

Source: Frequent Flyer, Dec. 1994

The Business Traveler (cont'd)

The following chart shows the responses to the question "How do you fly most frequently when traveling internationally?"

Ticket Type

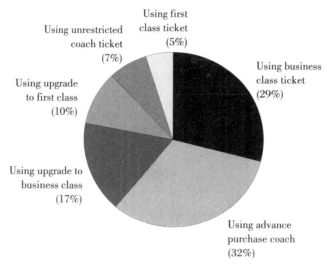

Using unrestricted coach ticket (7%)

Using first class ticket (5%)

Using business class ticket (29%)

Using upgrade to first class (10%)

Using upgrade to business class (17%)

Using advance purchase coach (32%)

Source: Frequent Flyer, Dec. 1994

Airline Quality Ratings

THE NATIONAL INSTITUTE for Aviation Research at Wichita State University produces an evaluation of the major U.S. airlines each year. Using data from the Department of Transportation, they give each airline an Airline Quality Rating. This rating is based on a variety of factors, including on-time percentage, load factor, number of accidents, frequent flier awards, mishandled baggage, fares, customer service, ticketing/boarding, financial stability, and average seat-mile cost.

The results for 1994 are summarized in the table to the right. The graphs on the next page show the airlines' scores on two key factors, denied boarding and baggage mishandling.

Airlines Ranked by Quality

Rank	Airline
1	Southwest
2	American
3	United
4	Delta
5	USAir
6	Northwest
7	TWA
8	America West
9	Continental

Source: National Institute for Aviation Research

Airline Quality Ratings (cont'd)

Denied Boarding (Involuntary, per 10,000 Passengers)

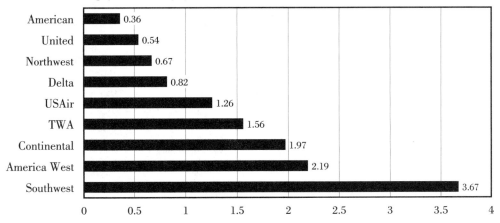

Mishandled Baggage (per 1,000 Passengers)

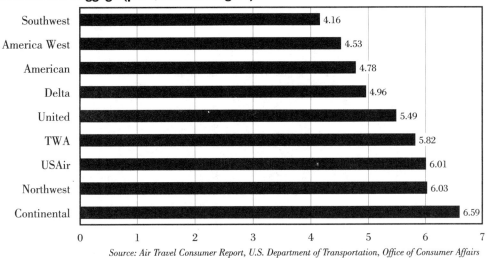

Source: Air Travel Consumer Report, U.S. Department of Transportation, Office of Consumer Affairs

Frequent Flyer Programs

InsideFlyer's Ratings of Frequent Flyer Programs

Grade	Program	Ease of Earning Awards		Service	Blackouts		Seat Availability		Hotel Partners
		Dom.	Int'l	All	Dom.	Int'l	Dom.	Int'l	All
B+	Northwest WorldPerks	B+	A	A-	B	A	A	C	B
B+	American AAdvantage	B+	C	C	A	C	A	C	A
B	USAir Frequent Traveler	B	B	B	A	C	A	C	A
B	United Mileage Plus	B+	C	A-	B	C	A	C	A
B	America West FlightFund	B	A	A-	B	B	A	C	B-
B	Alaska Mileage Plan	B	B	B-	B+	C	A-	C	B
B	Continental OnePass	B+	B	A-	C	D+	B	C	B
B-	Delta Frequent Flyer	B-	C-	A-	C	D	A	C	A
C+	TWA Frequent Flight Bonus	B	C	B	C	D	B	C	C
C	Southwest Company Club	C	N/A	A-	A	N/A	A+	N/A	F

Ratings: A = Best; F = Worst   *Source: InsideFlyer, 1994*

Frequent Flyer Programs (cont'd)

Airline, Hotel, Car Rental, Credit Card Partners

Airline	Car Rentals	Credit Cards	Hotels	Airlines
American AAdvantage	Avis Hertz Alamo	Citibank Visa or Master- Card MCI Long Distance	Forte Intercontinental Hilton Holiday Inn Marriott Red Lion Sheraton Wyndham	American Eagle Canadian Cathay Pacific Airways Hawaiian Japan Qantas Reno Air Singapore
Continental One Pass	Dollar National Thrifty Avis National (Inter- rent) Skycar	American Express Visa/MasterCard Marine Midland Diners Club	Aston Camino Real Canadian Pacific Doubletree Doubletree Club Marriott Melia Radisson Sheraton Sol	Aer Lingus Aerolineas Argentinas Air Canada Alitalia America West Austrian Airlines Brita Rocky Mountain BWIA Cayman Airways Continental Express Frontier GP Express Iberia Lan-Chile Malaysia Qantas SAS
Northwest WorldPerks	Hertz National Avis Alamo	MCI Long Distance First Bank WorldPerks (Visa)	Holiday Inn Hyatt Marriott New Ohtani Radisson Shangri-La Westin	Alaska Airlines America West (int'l) USAir (int'l) KLM Royal Dutch
TWA Frequent Flight Bonus Program	Avis Dollar	Bank of EAB Visa or MasterCard	Adam's Mark Doubletree Forte Marriott Radisson Ramada	Aerolineas Argentinas Air India Alaska Airlines Ladero Philippine Trans World Express
United Mileage Plus	Alamo Dollar Hertz National Avis Budget	United First Card (Visa) AT&T Long Distance	Hilton Holiday Inn Hyatt Intercontinental Radisson Shangri-La Ritz-Carlton Sheraton Westin	Air Canada Air France ALM Antillean Aloha Airlines Ansett British Midland Emirates Gulfstream Transportes Aeromar Lufthansa Scandinavian Trans Brazil TWA Express United Express
USAir Frequent Traveler Program	Alamo Hertz National	Nationsbank (Visa)	Hilton Hyatt Marriott Omni Radisson Renaissance Westin	Air France British Airways Northwest (int'l) Swissair Air New Zealand Sabena World KLM Alitalia ANA

Airline Directory

Airline	Phone
Aer Lingus	(800) 223-6537
AeroMexico	(800) 237-6639
Air Canada	(800) 776-3000
Air France	(800) 237-2747
Air India	(800) 442-4455
Alaska Airlines	(800) 426-0333
Alitalia	(800) 223-5730
All Nippon Airways	(800) 235-9262
Aloha Airlines	(800) 367-5250
America West Airlines	(800) 235-9292
American Airlines	(800) 433-7300
American Trans Air	(800) 225-2995
Austrian Airlines	(800) 843-0002
Avianca	(800) 284-2622
British Airways	(800) 247-9297
British Caledonian	(800) 543-7619
British Midland	(800) 788-0555
Canadian Airlines (int'l.)	(800) 426-7000
China Airlines	(800) 227-5118
Cathay Pacific Airways	(800) 233-2742
Continental Airlines	(800) 525-0280
Delta Airlines	(800) 221-1212
EVA Air	(800) 695-1188
Finnair	(800) 950-5000
Hawaiian Airlines	(800) 367-5320
Horizon Air	(800) 547-9308
Iberia Airlines	(800) 772-4642
Icelandair	(800) 223-5500
Japan Airlines	(800) 525-3663
Kiwi International Air Lines	(800) 538-5494

Airline	Phone
KLM Royal Dutch Airlines	(800) 374-7747
Korean Air	(800) 438-5000
Lufthansa German Airlines	(800) 645-3880
Markair	(800) 627-5247
Mesa Airlines	(800) 637-2247
Midwest Express	(800) 452-2022
Northwest Airlines (dom.)	(800) 225-2525
Northwest Airlines (int'l.)	(800) 447-4747
Olympic Airways	(800) 223-1226
Qantas Airways	(800) 227-4500
Reno Air	(800) 736-6247
Royal Jordanian	(800) 223-0470
Sabena Belgian World Airlines	(800) 873-3900
Scandinavian Airlines System	(800) 221-2350
Singapore Airlines	(800) 742-3333
Skywest	(800) 453-9417
Southwest Airlines	(800) 435-9792
Swissair	(800) 221-4750
TAP Air Portugal	(800) 221-7370
Thai Airways	(800) 426-5204
Tower Air	(800) 452-5531
Trans Brazil Airlines	(800) 872-3153
TWA (dom.)	(800) 221-2000
TWA (int'l)	(800) 892-4141
United Airlines	(800) 241-6522
USAir	(800) 428-4322
Varig Brazilian Airlines	(800) 468-2744
Virgin Atlantic	(800) 862-8621
Westair Airlines	(800) 253-9378

Airline Clubs

Domestic Airline Clubs: Fees and Services

Airline	Club	Phone	Annual Fee ($)	Enrollment Fee ($)	No. of Locations	Bar	Guests Permitted*
Alaska	The Board Room	(800) 654-5669	150	100	5	Free	2
America West	Phoenix Club	(602) 693-4072	100	50	2	Free	2
American	Admirals Club	(800) 237-7971	250	100	41	Cash	2
Continental	Presidents Club	(800) 322-2640	150	50	17†	NA	2
Delta	Crown Room	(404) 715-6615	150	NA	66	Free	2
Northwest	WorldClub	(800) 225-2525	150	50	26	Free	2
TWA	Ambassadors Club	(800) 527-1468	150	NA	19	NA	2
United	Red Carpet Club	(800) 241-6522	175	100	31	Cash	2
USAir	USAir Club	(800) 828-8522	150	50	26	Cash	2

* not including family members; they may enter at any time

† also affiliated with Air Canada

Paging at Major U.S. Airports

City	Airline	Phone
Atlanta	American	(404) 530-3170
	Continental	(404) 530-3530
	Delta	(404) 714-7250
	Northwest	(404) 530-3960
	TWA	(404) 530-2620
	United	(404) 765-1266
	USAir	(404) 530-3300
Baltimore	All	(410) 859-7111
Boston	All	(617) 561-1806
Chicago (O'Hare)	American	(312) 686-4477
	Continental	(312) 601-5305
	Delta	(312) 686-8635
	Northwest	(312) 686-5575
	TWA	(312) 686-2200
	United	(312) 601-3100
	USAir	(312) 686-7171
Chicago (Midway)	Continental	(312) 918-7676
	Delta	(312) 735-9041
	Northwest	(312) 471-4692
	TWA	(312) 471-8820
	USAir	(312) 735-3056
Cincinnati	All	(606) 283-3144
Cleveland	All	(216) 265-6030
Columbus	All	(614) 239-4083
Dallas	American	(214) 425-2477
	Continental	(214) 574-6673
	Delta	(214) 574-2247
	Northwest	(214) 574-6673
	TWA	(214) 574-6673
	United	(214) 574-6673
	USAir	(214) 574-6673
Denver	All	(303) 342-2300
Detroit	American	(313) 965-1000
	Continental	(313) 955-1797
	Delta	(313) 942-2643
	Northwest	(313) 942-4268
	TWA	(313) 942-3406
	United	(313) 942-4062
	USAir	(313) 942-2460
Houston	All	(713) 230-3000
Indianapolis	All	(317) 478-7243
Los Angeles	American	(310) 646-3533
	Continental	(310) 568-3131
	Delta	(310) 417-7335
	Northwest	(310) 646-7711
	TWA	(310) 646-2424
	United	(310) 646-3116
	USAir	(310) 646-2020

City	Airline	Phone
Miami	All	(305) 876-7000
Milwaukee	All	(414) 747-5245
Minneapolis	American	(612) 726-5843
	Continental	(612) 726-5818
	Delta	(612) 725-4931
	Northwest	(612) 726-3007
	TWA	(612) 726-5642
	United	(612) 726-5075
	USAir	(612) 726-5373
New York (JFK)	American	(718) 632-3100
	Delta	(718) 632-4180
	Northwest	(718) 244-5636
	TWA	(718) 244-2000
	United	(718) 632-0902
	USAir	(718) 553-5505
New York (La Guardia)	American	(718) 476-4156
	Continental	(718) 334-7132
	Delta	(718) 565-3940
	Northwest	(718) 476-7191
	TWA	(718) 803-6810
	United	(718) 476-4900
	USAir	(718) 533-2634
Norfolk	All	(804) 444-3040
Philadelphia	All	(215) 492-3222
Phoenix	All	(602) 273-3455
Pittsburgh	All	(412) 472-3525
Portland	All	(503) 335-1040
Sacramento	All	(916) 929-5411
St. Louis	All	(314) 426-8000
San Antonio	All	(210) 821-3411
San Diego	All	(619) 231-2294
Seattle	Continental	(206) 433-5545
	Delta	(206) 439-4324
	Northwest	(206) 433-3603
	TWA	(206) 433-5722
	United	(206) 433-4324
	USAir	(206) 433-7850
Tampa	All	(813) 870-8770
Wash., DC (Dulles)	All	(703) 661-8636
Wash., DC (Nat'l)	All	(703) 419-3972

TIP: *There are discount hotel reservations services for business travelers. They work on commissions from the hotels, so they do not charge the customer. Hotel Reservations Network, (800) 964-6835, and Quikbook, (800) 221-3531, are two such services.*

Busiest Airports

Airports Ranked by Number of Passengers, 1993

Rank	Name	City	No. of Passengers
1	O'Hare Int'l	Chicago	30,394,589
2	Dallas/Fort Worth Int'l	Dallas/Fort Worth	25,154,542
3	Los Angeles Int'l	Los Angeles	23,346,093
4	Hartsfield	Atlanta	23,143,454
5	San Francisco Int'l	San Francisco	15,497,824
6	Stapleton Int'l	Denver	15,322,837
7	Miami Int'l	Miami	14,030,586
8	John F. Kennedy Int'l	New York	13,016,655
9	Newark Int'l	Newark	12,817,855
10	Detroit Metro	Detroit	11,728,826
11	Phoenix Sky Harbor Int'l	Phoenix	11,549,889
12	Logan Int'l	Boston	11,388,184
13	Minneapolis/St. Paul Int'l	Minneapolis	11,028,723
14	Honolulu Int'l	Honolulu	10,880,076
15	McCarran Int'l	Las Vegas	10,720,746
16	Orlando Int'l	Orlando	10,246,596
17	Lambert-St. Louis Int'l	St. Louis	9,936,980
18	La Guardia	New York	9,656,182
19	Houston Intercontinental	Houston	9,517,842
20	Seattle-Tacoma Int'l	Seattle	9,224,990

Source: Federal Aviation Administration

Airline Service Contacts

Airline Service Contacts for the General Public

Airline	Contact	Phone
Alaska Airlines	Ms. Valerie Svilarich	(206) 431-7286
Aloha Airlines	Ms. Denise Yates	(808) 836-4115
America West Airlines	Ms. Susan Sampsell	(800) 235-9292, ext. 6019
American Airlines	Mr. George Goetz	(817) 967-2000
American Trans Air	Mr. Steve Simpson	(317) 243-4140
Continental Airlines	Ms. P. J. Robinette	(713) 987-6500
Delta Air Lines	Mr. Fred Elsberry	(404) 715-1450
Hawaiian Airlines	Ms. Crystal Ching	(808) 835-3424
Horizon Air	Ms. Sue Warner-Bean	(800) 523-1223, ext. 601
Markair	Ms. Penny Golden	(800) 544-0181
Midwest Express Airlines	Ms. Marie Johnson	(414) 747-4000
Northwest Airlines	Ms. Donna Shaw	(612) 726-2046
Southwest Airlines	Mr. Jim Ruppel	(214) 904-4223
Tower Air	Ms. Pam Buonincontri	(718) 553-4300
Trans World Airlines	Ms. Joyce Coleman	(314) 589-3600
United Airlines	Mr. Paul Tinebra	(708) 952-6796
USAir/USAir Shuttle	Ms. Deborah Thompson	(703) 892-7020 or (910) 661-0061
Westair Airlines	Mr. Robert Dynan	(209) 294-6915

Source: U.S. Department of Transportation

Best Times to Fly

Departure: Best Hour to Go

Airport	Best Hour	On-Time Percentage	Worst Hour	On-Time Percentage
Atlanta	7-8 A.M.	94.1	6-7 P.M.	73.2
Boston	6-7 A.M.	96.0	10-11 P.M.	72.9
Chicago	6-7 A.M.	93.3	7-8 P.M.	79.2
Cincinnati	10-11 A.M.	95.3	4-5 P.M.	75.6
Dallas	6-7 A.M.	94.8	2-4 P.M.	62.3
Denver	11 P.M.-6 A.M.	96.2	11 A.M.-NOON	69.9
Detroit	6-7 A.M.	95.1	8-9 P.M.	79.2
Houston	7-8 A.M.	94.8	9-10 P.M.	71.4
Los Angeles	6-7 A.M.	96.3	11 A.M.-NOON	64.5
Miami	7-8 A.M.	96.2	9-10 P.M.	68.2
Minneapolis	6-7 A.M.	93.2	10-11 P.M.	76.0
New York: Kennedy	10-11 A.M.	96.6	8-9 P.M.	61.5
New York: La Guardia	6-7 A.M.	93.6	3-4 P.M.	73.7
Philadelphia	7-8 A.M.	94.1	6-7 P.M.	73.9
Phoenix	7-8 A.M.	97.4	8-9 P.M.	57.2
Pittsburgh	7-8 A.M.	93.2	6-7 P.M.	34.6
St. Louis	6-7 A.M.	96.7	8-9 P.M.	68.7
San Diego	6-7 A.M.	92.8	5-6 P.M.	64.4
San Francisco	6-7 A.M.	97.3	NOON-1 P.M.	66.7
Seattle	8-9 A.M.	93.1	3-4 P.M.	72.2
Tampa	8-9 A.M.	95.0	1-2 P.M.	78.2
Washington (Dulles)	6-7 A.M.	96.5	4-5 P.M.	81.9

Arrival: Best Hour to Land

Airport	Best Hour	On-Time Percentage	Worst Hour	On-Time Percentage
Atlanta	7-9 A.M.	90.2	6-7 A.M.	53.3
Boston	9-10 A.M.	92.6	5-7 P.M.	67.2
Chicago	11 A.M.-NOON	91.2	10-11 P.M.	82.0
Cincinnati	9-10 A.M.	95.0	9-10 P.M.	73.3
Dallas	6-7 A.M.	100.0	5-6 P.M.	64.2
Denver	11 P.M-6 A.M.	90.6	10-11 P.M.	68.4
Detroit	7-8 A.M.	92.0	11 P.M-6 A.M.	76.1
Houston	6-8 A.M.	92.8	11 A.M.-NOON	67.2
Los Angeles	8-9 A.M.	92.6	11 A.M.-NOON	61.0
Miami	7-8 A.M.	100.0	7-8 P.M.	67.3
Minneapolis	6-7 A.M.	91.1	10-11 P.M.	77.1
New York: Kennedy	9-10 A.M.	100.0	6-7 P.M.	72.9
New York: La Guardia	7-8 A.M.	92.7	6-7 P.M.	74.1
Philadelphia	10-11 A.M.	91.8	6-7 P.M.	66.0
Phoenix	7-8 A.M.	97.1	4-5 P.M.	63.2
Pittsburgh	2-3 P.M	91.7	5-6 P.M.	48.7
St. Louis	6-7 A.M.	88.8	10-11 P.M.	61.9
San Diego	7-8 A.M.	97.1	7-8 P.M.	61.8
San Francisco	6-7 A.M.	92.9	11 A.M.-NOON	62.1
Seattle	7-8 A.M.	98.8	3-4 P.M.	66.3
Tampa	7-8 A.M.	97.6	6-7 P.M.	68.9
Washington (Dulles)	7-8 A.M.	98.0	7-8 P.M.	73.7

Source: Air Travel Consumer Report, U.S. Department of Transportation, Mar. 1995

Travel Agencies

Travel Agencies Ranked by U.S. Sales

Agency	1993 Sales ($ thou.)
American Express	4,300,000
Carlson	1,950,000
Thomas Cook	1,632,000
Rosenbluth	1,300,000
Maritz	915,000
USTravel	852,883
IVI	680,000
Omega World Travel	352,000
WorldTravel Partners	306,000
Wagonlit	282,000
Travel & Transport	273,000
Northwestern	237,950
VTS	228,535
Travel One	227,140
World Wide Travel Service	187,000

Agency	1993 Sales ($ thou.)
Associated Travel Services	178,900
Travel Incorporated	175,000
Corporate Travel Consultants	160,000
Total Travel Management	153,000
Arrington	143,200
Garber	141,967
McDonnell Douglas Travel	138,451
Supertravel	137,000
Morris	135,000
Worldtek	130,000

Source: Business Travel News, May 30, 1994

E-MAIL

Transportation from Airport. Send e-mail to transport@almanac.yoyo.com. See p. xi for instructions.
Tables of taxi fares from major domestic and international airports to the cities they serve.

The Top Reference Sources

Runzheimer International
Runzheimer Park
Rochester, Wisconsin 53167
(800) 558-1702

Runzheimer International is a management consulting firm that specializes in travel and living costs, serving over 2,000 businesses and gov-

ernment agencies worldwide. Areas of special knowledge include employee relocation, business driving programs, and travel management.

Runzheimer Reports on Travel Management, a monthly newsletter, contains information on airline ticket costs, city highlights, business travel price indexes, and other topics of interest to travel managers. A one-year subscription is $295.

Auto Rental Companies

Top Companies by Revenue

Company	1993 Revenue ($)	Telephone
Hertz	4,500,000	(800) 654-3131
Avis[1]	3,400,000	(800) 831-2847
Sears	2,200,000	(800) 527-0770
National[1,2]	2,000,000	(800) 328-4567
Alamo	1,100,000	(800) 327-9633
Enterprise[1,3]	1,100,000	(800) 325-8007
Dollar[1,4]	700,000	(800) 800-4000
Thrifty	425,300	(800) 367-2277
Agency[3]	300,000	NA
Carey[5]	197,000	(800) 585-9333
Value	140,000	(800) 822-1662
U-Save	80,000	(800) 438-2300
Airways	40,750	(708) 671-7070
Advantage[1]	40,000	(800) 777-5500
Payless[1]	40,000	(800) 952-9200
Practical[1]	20,000	(800) 233-1663

[1]Revenue estimated. [2]Revenue includes totals of National's overseas affiliate partners. [3]Primarily an insurance-replacement operator. [4]Revenue includes totals of Dollar's franchisee in Europe. [5]Primarily a limousine company.

Top Companies by Number of Locations

Company	No. of Locations
Hertz	5,400
Avis	4,800
National[1,2]	4,500
Sears	3,097
Enterprise[3]	1,700
Dollar[1,4]	1,087
Thrifty	1,039
U-Save	500
Agency[3]	475
Carey[5]	393
Payless	146
Alamo	140
Practical	115
Advantage	55
Value	47
Airways	46

Source: Business Travel News, May 30, 1994

Per Diems by City

THE PER DIEM TOTALS SHOWN BELOW represent average costs for the typical business traveler, and include breakfast, lunch, and dinner in business-class restaurants and single-rate lodging in business-class hotels and motels. Data is from the *Runzheimer Meal-Lodging Cost Index*, and was gathered between the second half of 1994 and the first quarter of 1995.

High-Priced Locations (Domestic)

Location	Total Cost per Diem ($)
New York, NY	289
Washington, DC	260
Honolulu, HI	246
Chicago, IL	229
Boston, MA	218

High-Priced Locations (International)

Location	Total Cost per Diem ($)
Tokyo, Japan	464
Hong Kong	433
Paris, France	342
London, England	337
Brussels, Belgium	322

Low-Priced Locations (Domestic)

Location	Total Cost per Diem ($)
Wheeling, WV	79
Johnson, TN	80
Macon, GA	82
Fort Smith, AR	84
Lincoln, NE	86

Low-Priced Locations (International)

Location	Total Cost per Diem ($)
Abidjan, Ivory Coast	85
London, Ontario, Canada	99
Panama City, Panama	109
Bordeaux, France	118
Guangzhou, China	121

Source: Runzheimer International

Largest Hotel Companies

Largest Hotel Companies by Number of Hotels, 1993

Rank	Name	No. of Hotels
1	Hospitality Franchise	3,783
2	Best Western	3,308
3	Choice	2,614
4	Holiday Inn	1,795
5	Marriott	783
6	Motel 6	769
7	Promus	509
8	Forte	460
9	Hospitality	368
10	ITT Sheraton	365
11	Carlson Hospitality	341
12	Hilton	220
13	Red Roof Inns	210
14	Journey's End	208
15	Knight Lodging	183
16	La Quinta	180
17	Budget Host	172
18	Renaissance	160
19	Hilton	159
20	Richfield	138
21	Hyatt	103
22	Doubletree	99
23	Budgetel	98
24	Inter-Continental	90
25	Motels of America	83

Source: Business Travel News, May 30, 1994

Largest Hotel Companies by Revenue, 1993

Rank	Name	1993 Revenue ($ thou.)
1	Best Western	4,840,000
2	ITT Sheraton	4,776,932
3	Marriott	4,688,000
4	Holiday Inn	4,600,000
5	Hospitality Franchise	3,278,988
6	Hyatt	2,500,000
7	Carlson	2,200,000
8	Choice	2,000,000
9	Inter-Continental	1,911,535
10	Hilton	1,393,500
11	Promus	1,251,855
12	Hyatt	1,190,000
13	Caesar's World	983,459
14	Hilton	894,100
15	Interstate	718,285
16	Doubletree	642,600
17	Richfield	625,000
18	Shangri-La	600,913
19	TCC	560,000
20	Canadian Pacific	544,000
21	Omni	440,000
22	Red Lion	440,000
23	Wyndham	367,000
24	Loews	330,567
25	Oakwood	300,000

Source: Business Travel News, May 30, 1994

The Top Reference Sources

America's Top Restaurants
Zagat Survey, $12.95
(212) 977-6000

This coat-pocket-sized book contains information on the top restaurants in 34 cities nationwide. Each entry includes the restaurant name, cuisine type, address, phone number, ratings on food, decor, and service, average meal price, and additional comments. The reviewers are volunteers.

The Zagat Survey also publishes 24 city/area restaurant guides as well as *America's Best Meal Deals* and *U.S. Hotel, Resort, and Spa Survey.*

U.S. Passport Agencies

Boston
Thomas P. O'Neill Federal Building
10 Causeway St., Room 247
Boston, MA 02222
(617) 565-6698*
(617) 565-6990

Chicago
Kluczynski Federal Building
230 S. Dearborn St., Suite 380
Chicago, IL 60604
(312) 353-7155*

Honolulu
New Federal Building
300 Ala Moana Blvd., Room C-106
Honolulu, HI 96850
(808) 541-1919*
(808) 541-1918

Houston
1919 Smith St., Suite 1100
Houston, TX 77002
(713) 653-3153*

Los Angeles
11000 Wilshire Blvd.
Room 13100, Federal Building
Los Angeles, CA 90024
(213) 575-7070

Miami
Federal Office Building
51 S.W. First Ave., 16th Floor
Miami, FL 33130
(305) 536-4681*

New Orleans
Postal Services Building
701 Loyola Ave.
Room T-12005
New Orleans, LA 70113
(504) 589-6728*
(504) 589-6161/68

New York City
Rockefeller Center
630 Fifth Ave., Room 270
New York, NY 10111
(212) 399-5290*

Philadelphia
Federal Building
600 Arch St., Room 4426
Philadelphia, PA 19106
(215) 597-7480*

San Francisco
525 Market St., Suite 200
San Francisco, CA 94105
(415) 744-4010*
(415) 744-4444

Seattle
Federal Building
915 Second Ave.
Room 992
Seattle, WA 98174
(206) 553-7941/42/43*
(206) 553-7945/46

Stamford
1 Landmark Square
Broad and Atlantic Sts.
Stamford, CT 06901
(203) 325-4401/02*
(203) 325-3530/38/39

Washington, DC
1111 19th St., NW
Washington, DC 20522
(202) 647-0518*

* *24-hour information line*

It also may be possible to apply at the local post office or another designated location. Check the government listings in the phone book under "Department of State" or "Passport Services."

The Best Restaurants

The Top Five Rated Restaurants in Selected U.S. Metro Areas, Ranked by the Zagat Survey

Restaurant	Type*
Atlanta	
Dining Rm., Ritz/Buck	NAm
Ciboulette	FB
Pano's and Paul's	Co
Chops	St
Hedgerose Heights	Co
Atlantic City	
White House	AR
Roberto's	I
Le Palais	Co
Tre Figlio	I
Capriccio	I
Baltimore	
Hampton's	NAm
Milton Inn	NAm
Prime Rib	St
M. Gettier	NF
Linwood's	NAm
Boston	
Olives	M
Aujourd'hui	NAm
Julien	FC
L'Espalier	NF
Jasper's	AR
Chicago	
Le Français	FC
Carlos'	FC
Ambria	NF
Jimmy's Place	As/NF
Tallgrass	NF
Cincinnati	
The Palace	AR
Maisonette	FC
Precinct	St
Orchids at Palm Court	AR
Barresi's	I
Cleveland	
Parker's	NAm
Johnny's Bar on Fulton	Co/I
Classics	Co
The Baricelli Inn	I
Hyde Park Grille	St
Columbus	
Rigsby's Cuisine Volatile	NAm/M
Handke's Cuisine	E/NAm
Carolyn's	NAm
Refectory Classic	NF
Restaurant Japan	J

Restaurant	Type*
Dallas	
The Riviera	M
Mansion on Turtle Creek	So
The French Room	FC
York Street	AT
Del Frisco's	St
Denver Area	
European Café (Boulder)	F/NAm
Piñons	NAm
Morton's of Chicago	St
Wildflower	A/I/F
Sweet Basil	E/NAm
Honolulu	
Roy's Restaurant	P
Maile Restaurant	Co
Le Mer Restaurant	FC
Hy's Steak House	St
Kua Aina Sandwich	H
Houston	
Chez Nous	FB
DeVille	AR
Rotisserie/Beef & Bird	AT
Ruggles Grill	NAm
La Réserve	NF/A
Kansas City	
Café Allegro	E
Venue	E
American Restaurant	E/NAm
Tatsu's	FC
Plaza III	St
Los Angeles	
Patina	Ca/F
Matsuhisa	J/Se
Shiro	As/F
Chinois on Main	E
Sushi Nozawa	J
Miami/Miami Beach	
Mark's Place	NAm
Chef Allen's	NAm
Grand Café	Co
The Fish Market	Se
Casa Larios	Cu
New Orleans	
Grill Room	NAm
La Provence	FC
Brigtsen's	Cr
Commander's Palace	Cr
Bayona	Cr/F

The Best Restaurants (cont'd)

Restaurant	Type*
New York City	
Bouley	NF
Aureole	NAm
Lespinasse	NF
La Grenouille	F
Peter Luger	St
Orange County, CA	
Pascal	FB
Gustaf Anders	Co
Antoine	NF
JW's	NF
The Ritz	Co
Orlando	
Dux	NAm
Le Coq Au Vin	FB
Hemingway's	Se
Park Plaza Gardens	Co
Arthur's 27	In
Palm Beach	
La Vieille Maison	FC
Gazebo Café	FB
Maxaluna Tuscan	I
Café Chardonnay	NAm
Café L'Europe	Co/F
Philadelphia	
Le Bec-Fin	FC
The Fountain	In
Evermay on the Delaware	NAm/F
The Green Hills Inn	A/F
Le Bar Lyonnais	FB
Phoenix/Scottsdale	
Vincent Guerithault	So
Yamakasa	J
Marquesa	Sp
Christopher's/The Bistro	NAm/NF
Palm Court	Co
Portland	
Genoa	I
Café Des Amis	FB
Winterborne	Se
Zefiro	M
Heathman Restaurant	No

Restaurant	Type*
Salt Lake City	
The New Yorker Club	Co
Café Mariposa	NAm/Co
Chez Betty	Co/E
Fresco Italian Café	I
The Riverhorse Café	NAm
San Diego	
WineSeller/Brasserie	I/NF
Mille Fleurs	Ca/F
El Bizcocho	FC
Marius	NF
Belgian Lion	B/F
San Francisco Bay Area	
Masa'a	NF
Erna's Elderberry House	Ca/F
Fleur de Lys	NF
Ritz-Carlton	NAm
Emile's	NF
Santa Fe	
SantaCafé	So
Old Mexico Grill	Mx
Pasqual's	So
Coyote Café	So
Pink Adobe	Co
Seattle	
The Herbfarm	A/No
Rover's	F/No
Shoalwater Restaurant	No
Saleh al Lago	I
Szmania	G/No
St. Louis	
Tony's	I
Café de France	FC
Fio's La Fourchette	FC
Zinnia	Ca/NAm
Giovanni's	I
Washington, DC	
Inn/Little Washington	NAm
Jean-Louis	NF
L'Auberge Chez François	FC
Le Lion d'Or	FC
Nicholas	NAm/Se

* A–American; AR–American Regional; As–Asian; AT–American Traditional; Ca–Californian; Co–Continental; Cr–Creole; Cu–Cuban; E–Eclectic; F–French; FB–French Bistro; FC–French Classic; G–German; H–Hamburgers and Sandwiches; In–International; I–Italian; J–Japanese; M–Mediterranean; Mx–Mexican; NAm–New American; NF–New French; No–Northwest; P–Pacific Rim; Se–Seafood; So–Southwestern; Sp–Spanish; St–Steakhouse

Source: Zagat Survey, America's Top Restaurants 1995

Guide to Audio-visual Rentals

WHEN YOU ARE TRAVELING to another city to give a presentation, your firm can save money by using a local company to provide multimedia equipment like televisions, slide projectors, or computers. This city-by-city listing highlights selected firms around the country.

Company	Telephone
Atlanta	
Atlanta Sound & Lighting	(404) 455-7695
Projexions Video Supply	(404) 872-6247
Total Audio Visual Services	(404) 875-7555
Baltimore	
American Audio-Video	(410) 837-1339
Audio Recording Services	(410) 643-4220
Chesapeake Audio/Visual Communications	(410) 796-0040
Crew Works	(410) 235-2037
Total Audio-Visual Systems	(410) 625-4700
Boston	
Immediate Connections	(617) 783-1599
Media 1	(617) 254-0770
Projection Video Services	(617) 254-6693
Audio Services	(617) 424-0065
Chicago	
Artistic Communication Center	(312) 280-0808
LeGrand Services	(708) 894-9389
Video Replay	(312) 822-0221
Williams Gerard Productions	(312) 467-5560
Cincinnati	
Cavalier Audio Visual Services	(513) 784-0055
CSI/Clarity Systems	(513) 784-1200
Visual Aids Electronics	(513) 684-0800
Cleveland	
CPS Meetings	(216) 771-7711
Colortone	(216) 581-5055
Eighth Day Sound	(216) 961-2900
Presentation Services	(216) 241-2777
Columbus	
Brite Lights	(614) 272-1404
Mills James Productions	(614) 777-9933
United States Audio-Visuals	(614) 461-8444
Dallas	
Bauer Audio Visual	(214) 630-6700
SAV Communications	(214) 423-5874
Brad Young Multi-Image	(214) 528-4888
Arapaho Audio Visual	(214) 458-1468
S Audio Visual	(214) 554-0481
Denver	
Colorado Visual Aids	(303) 733-9910
Ceavco Audio Visual Company	(303) 238-0443
Colorado Audio Visual	(303) 925-8508
Spectrum Audio-Visual	(303) 477-4456

Company	Telephone
Detroit	
Audio Visual Wholesalers	(612) 559-9666
Blumberg Communications	(612) 521-8225
Showtech Presentation Systems	(810) 547-8880
Gaithersburg, MD	
CPR Multimedia Solutions	(800) 825-4277
Houston	
A/V Texas	(713) 526-3687
Aves Audio Visual Systems	(713) 783-3440
Image in Action	(713) 932-9779
Photo & Sound	(713) 956-9566
Indianapolis	
Dodd Technologies	(317) 842-4905
Markey's Audio Visual	(317) 783-1155
United States Audio-Visuals	(317) 632-2527
Los Angeles	
Bauer/Southam Audio Video	(310) 815-8817
Jacobs Audio Visual Systems	(213) 882-8577
Studio Instrument Rental	(213) 848-3660
Video Equipment Rentals of Southern California	(818) 956-0212
Miami	
Blumberg Communications	(305) 594-3939
Metro Audio Visual	(305) 623-1300
Miami Audio Visual	(305) 757-5000
Southern Audio/Video & Business Rental	(305) 591-3888
Total Audiovisual	(407) 859-3399
Milwaukee	
Audio Visual of Milwaukee	(414) 258-1077
Midwest Visual Equipment	(414) 784-5880
Studio Gear	(414) 223-4884
United States Audio-Visuals	(414) 276-8688
Video Images	(414) 785-8998
Minneapolis	
Audio-Visual and Video Resources	(612) 456-9033
Twin City Audio-Visual Services	(612) 869-4501
New York	
Ace Audio Visual	(212) 685-3344
Bauer Audio Video	(212) 714-9648
Executive Audio-Visual Services	(212) 575-2500
Norfolk	
Craft-Work Sound	(804) 436-2577
Atlantic Audio Visual	(804) 422-5252

Guide to Audio-visual Rentals (cont'd)

Company	Telephone
Philadelphia	
Audio Visual Center	(215) 563-6872
Bauer Audio Video	(215) 625-0885
Visual Sound	(610) 544-8700
Phoenix	
A.V. Concepts	(602) 894-6642
Southwest Audio Visual	(602) 258-4911
Pittsburgh	
Pro-Com Systems	(412) 621-1950
Visual Aids Center of Pittsburgh	(412) 566-1800
Willowglen Productions	(412) 828-7777
Portland, OR	
Audio-Visual Rentals & Services	(503) 222-1664
Rose City Sound	(503) 238-6330
Sacramento	
Munday & Collins	(916) 451-6511
Pacific Crest Picture	(916) 652-4466
Photo & Sound	(916) 649-6999
St. Louis	
Audio-Visual Alternatives	(314) 773-9155
Audio-Visual Management	(314) 421-2862

Company	Telephone
San Francisco	
AVTS	(415) 882-7766
Concept Organization	(415) 495-6521
Projection Video Services	(415) 826-2244
Seattle	
Barr Audio Visual	(206) 763-7181
Pro-Image	(206) 284-5000
Tampa	
Advanced Visual Communications (AVCOM)	(813) 875-0888
Audio Visual Support Service	(813) 872-7914
Cypress Productions	(813) 289-6115
Vaughn Broadcast Rentals	(813) 887-3141
Washington, DC	
Chesapeake Audio/Video Communications	(301) 596-3900
Crew Works	(410) 235-2037

Convention and Visitors Bureaus

BELOW IS A LISTING of the names and phone numbers of the convention and visitors bureaus in 30 major cities. Any company in need of a trade show facilitator should contact the convention and visitors bureau in the city hosting the event. The telephone numbers of a variety of facilitators are available through the convention services department of each bureau.

Recommended Resource

International Association of Convention and Visitors Bureaus
2000 L St., NW, Suite 702
Washington, DC 20036
(202) 296-7888

City	Phone
Atlanta	(404) 222-6688
Baltimore	(410) 659-7300
Boston	(617) 536-4100
Chicago	(312) 567-8500
Cincinnati	(513) 621-6994
Cleveland	(800) 321-1004
Columbus	(614) 221-2489
Dallas	(214) 746-6677
Denver	(303) 892-1505
Detroit	(313) 567-1170
Houston	(713) 227-3180
Indianapolis	(317) 639-4282
Los Angeles	(213) 624-7300
Miami	(305) 539-3063
Milwaukee	(414) 273-3950

City	Phone
Minneapolis	(900) 860-0092
New York	(212) 397-8222
Norfolk	(804) 441-5266
Philadelphia	(215) 636-3300
Phoenix	(602) 254-6500
Pittsburgh	(412) 281-7711
Portland	(800) 962-3700
Sacramento	(916) 264-7777
St. Louis	(314) 421-1023
San Antonio	(800) 447-3372
San Diego	(619) 232-3101
San Francisco	(415) 974-6900
Seattle	(206) 461-5840
Tampa	(813) 223-2752
Washington, DC	(202) 789-7000

Convention Centers

Major Convention Centers in Selected Cities

City	Convention Center	Telephone
Atlanta	Georgia World Congress Center	(404) 223-4000
Baltimore	Baltimore Convention Center	(410) 659-7000
Boston	Hynes Convention Center	(617) 954-2000
Chicago	McCormick Place	(312) 791-7000
Cincinnati	Cincinnati Convention Center	(513) 352-3750
Cleveland	International Exposition (I-X) Center	(216) 676-6000
Columbus	Greater Columbus Convention Center	(614) 645-5000
Dallas	Dallas Convention Center	(214) 939-2700
Denver	Colorado Convention Center	(303) 640-8000
Detroit	Cobo Conference/Exhibition Center	(313) 224-1015
Houston	George R. Brown Convention Center	(713) 853-8000
Indianapolis	Indiana Convention Center & Hoosier Dome	(317) 262-3410
Los Angeles	Los Angeles Convention Center	(800) 448-7775
Miami	Miami Beach Convention Center	(305) 673-7311
Milwaukee	Mecca–Milwaukee Exposition & Convention Center	(414) 271-4000
Minneapolis	Minneapolis Convention Center	(612) 335-6000
New Orleans	Ernest N. Morial Convention Center	(504) 582-3000
New York	Jacob K. Javits Convention Center	(212) 216-2000
Norfolk	Norfolk Scope	(804) 441-2764
Philadelphia	Pennsylvania Convention Center	(215) 418-4700
Phoenix	Phoenix Civic Plaza	(602) 262-6225
Pittsburgh	David L. Lawrence Convention Center	(412) 565-6000
Portland, OR	Oregon Convention Center	(503) 235-7575
Sacramento	Sacramento Convention Center	(916) 264-5291
San Antonio	Henry B. Gonzalez Convention Center	(210) 299-8500
San Diego	San Diego Convention Center	(619) 525-5000
San Francisco	Moscone Convention Center	(415) 974-4000
Seattle	Washington State Convention and Trade Center	(206) 447-5000
St. Louis	Cervantes at America's Center	(314) 342-5036
Tampa	Tampa Convention Center	(800) 426-5630
Washington, DC	Washington Convention Center	(800) 368-9000

E-MAIL

Guerrilla Marketing Book. Send e-mail to guerrilla@almanac.yoyo.com. See p. xi for instructions.

The advertising section from The Guerrilla Marketing Handbook, written by Guerrilla Marketing guru Jay Conrad Levinson and Information Please Business Almanac editor Seth Godin. Learn the basics from the best!

Hotel & Resort Convention Centers

CONVENTION AND VISITORS BUREAUS are an invaluable aid to meeting planners and provide "one-stop shopping" for information on facilities, services, and suppliers available in a particular locale. *Meetings & Conventions* magazine annually awards the Gold Service Award to the CVBs rated on overall helpfulness by the magazine's voting readership.

Over the last 15 years *Meetings & Conventions* magazine has annually awarded the Gold Key Awards to those meeting properties that are judged to meet seven criteria deemed vital to a successful convention. These are meeting staff; meeting rooms; guest services; food and beverage service; reservations handling; A/V and other technical/support equipment; and–for resorts–recreational facilities.

1994 Gold Service Award Winners

Arizona
Phoenix and the Valley of the Sun Convention and Visitors Bureau
Scottsdale Chamber of Commerce
Metropolitan Tucson Convention and Visitors Bureau

California
Anaheim Convention and Visitors Bureau
Los Angeles Convention and Visitors Bureau
Palm Springs Desert Resorts Convention and Visitors Bureau
San Diego Convention and Visitors Bureau
San Francisco Convention and Visitors Bureau

Colorado
Denver Metro Convention and Visitors Bureau

District of Columbia
Washington D.C. Convention and Visitors Association

Florida
Greater Fort Lauderdale Convention and Visitors Bureau
Greater Miami and the Beaches Convention and Visitors Bureau
Orlando/Orange County Convention and Visitors Bureau
Palm Beach County Convention and Visitors Bureau

Georgia
Atlanta Convention and Visitors Bureau

Illinois
Chicago Convention and Tourism Bureau

Louisiana
Greater New Orleans Tourist and Convention Commission

Missouri
St. Louis Convention and Visitors Commission

Nevada
Las Vegas Convention and Visitors Authority
Reno-Sparks Convention and Visitors Authority

New Jersey
Greater Atlantic City Convention and Visitors Authority

New Mexico
Albuquerque Convention and Visitors Bureau

New York
New York Convention and Visitors Bureau

Ohio
Greater Cincinnati Convention and Visitors Bureau
Cleveland Convention and Visitors Bureau
Greater Columbus Convention and Visitors Bureau

Tennessee
Greater Lexington Convention and Visitors Bureau

Texas
Dallas Convention and Visitors Bureau
Fort Worth Convention and Visitors Bureau
Houston Convention and Visitors Bureau
Irving Convention and Visitors Bureau
San Antonio Convention and Visitors Bureau

Washington
Seattle-King County Convention and Visitors Bureau

Australia
Australian Tourism Commission

Bermuda
Bermuda Department of Tourism

Canada
Metropolitan Toronto Convention and Visitors Association

Hawaii
Hawaii Visitors Bureau

Hotel & Resort Convention Centers (cont'd)

Hong Kong
Hong Kong Tourist Association

Puerto Rico
San Juan-Puerto Rico Convention Center

Singapore
Singapore Convention Bureau

Gold Key Domestic Award Winners

Alabama
Marriott's Grand Hotel

Arizona
Arizona Biltmore
Hyatt Regency Scottsdale
Loews Ventana Canyon Resort
Marriott's Camelback Inn Resort, Golf Club & Spa
The Phoenician
The Pointe Hilton on South Mountain
The Pointe Hilton at Tapatio Cliffs
Scottsdale Conference Resort
Scottsdale Plaza Resort
Scottsdale Princess
Sheraton El Conquistador Resort and Country Club
Westin La Paloma
The Wigwam

California
Disneyland Hotel
Hotel Del Coronado
The Fairmont Hotel
La Costa Resort and Spa
La Quinta Resort and Club
Loews Coronado Bay Resort
Mark Hopkins Inter-Continental
Anaheim Marriott
Marriott's Desert Springs Resort and Spa
Marriott's Rancho Las Palmas Resort & Conference
Center
San Diego Marriott Hotel & Marina
Le Meridien San Diego
Parc Fifty-Five Hotel
Rancho Bernardo Inn
Resort at Squaw Creek
The Ritz-Carlton, Laguna Niguel
The Ritz-Carlton, Rancho Mirage
The Ritz-Carlton, San Francisco
Sheraton Grande Torrey Pines
Sheraton Harbor Island Resort
Sheraton Palace Hotel
Silverado Country Club & Resort
Stouffer Renaissance Esmeralda Resort
The Westin St. Francis

Colorado
The Broadmoor Resort & Country Club
Cheyenne Mountain Conference Center
Keystone Resort

District of Columbia
Washington Hilton and Towers
J. W. Marriott Hotel at National Place

Florida
The Boca Raton Resort & Club
Bonaventure Resort & Spa
The Breakers
Buena Vista Palace
Disney's Grand Floridian Beach Resort
Hilton at Walt Disney World
Fontainebleau Hilton Resort & Spa
Hyatt Regency Grand Cypress
Hyatt Regency Westshore
Innisbrook
Marriott's Harbor Beach Resort
Marriott's Orlando World Center
Marriott's Marco Island Resort & Golf Club
The Ocean Grand
The Peabody Orlando
PGA National Resort & Spa
The Registry Resort
The Ritz-Carlton, Amelia Island
The Ritz-Carlton, Naples
Saddlebrook Resort, Tampa
Sheraton Bal Harbour Beach Resort
South Seas Plantation Resort & Yacht Harbor
Villas of Grand Cypress
Walt Disney World Dolphin
Walt Disney World Swan

Georgia
The Ritz-Carlton, Buckhead
Stouffer Waverly Hotel

Illinois
Palmer House Hilton
Hyatt Regency Chicago
Chicago Marriott Downtown

Louisiana
Hotel Inter-Continental New Orleans
New Orleans Hilton Riverside

Maryland
Stouffer Harborplace Hotel

Massachusetts
Boston Marriott Copley Place

Michigan
Amway Grand Plaza Hotel

Missouri
Adam's Mark St. Louis

Nevada
Bally's Las Vegas Casino & Resort
Caesar's Palace
Las Vegas Hilton

Hotel & Resort Convention Centers (cont'd)

New York
Grand Hyatt New York
New York Marquis
The Plaza Hotel

North Carolina
The Grove Park Inn Resort
The Westin Resort, Hilton Head Island

Pennsylvania
The Hotel Hershey
The Hershey Lodge and Convention Center

Tennessee
Opryland Hotel
Sheraton Music City Hotel

Texas
Barton Creek Conference Resort

Loews Anatole Dallas
Marriott Rivercenter Hotel
Marriott Riverwalk Hotel
The Woodlands Executive Conference Center and Resort

Utah
Snowbird Ski & Summer Resort

Virginia
The Homestead
Westfields International Conference Center

West Virginia
The Greenbrier

The Top Reference Sources

Business Travel News
Corporate Travel
(212) 626-2466

These two publications provide valuable information for business travel managers. *Business Travel News* reports and analyzes breaking events and trends in the travel industry and redefines the jobs of business travel managers and purchasers.

Corporate Travel provides the "who's who and how" of travel management. It gives a practical approach to the duties of corporate travel services decision makers.

Both publications are free to qualified subscribers.

PERSONAL COMPUTING

Product Awards

EVERY YEAR *PC COMPUTING* selects noteworthy IBM PC compatible products in a variety of categories.

PC Computing MVP Awards, 1994

Category	Subcategory	Product	Phone
Systems	PCs	Dell Dimension XPS	(512) 338-4400
	Portables	Toshiba Portege 3600CT	(714) 583-3111
	Servers	ALR Evolution Q SMP	(714) 581-6770, ext. 3399
	Monitors	Nanao T2-20	(310) 325-5202, ext. 112
	Graphics/Video	Matrox Impression Plus	(514) 685-2630
	Monochrome Printers	HP LaserJet 4M Plus	(208) 396-6350
	Color Printers	Tektronix Phaser 220I	(503) 685-3150
	Desktop Storage	Western Digital AC31000	(714)932-6006
	Network Storage	MegaDrive MR-5	(310) 247-0006
	Multimedia Hardware	Proxima	(619) 457-5500
		Creative Solutions SoundBlaster AWE 32	(408) 428-6600, ext. 6416
		Zenith Portable CD-ROM	(708) 808-5000
	Input Devices	Visioneer PaperMax	(415) 812-6400
	Graphics Input Devices	HP ScanJet IIcx	(303) 350-4451
	Communication Hardware	U.S. Robotics V.34 modem	(708) 982-5230
Application Software	Application Suites	MS Office Professional 4.3	(206) 936-8674
	Word Processing	WordPerfect/Win 6.0a	(801) 228-5004
	Desktop Publishing	QuarkXpress 3.3	(303) 894-8888
	Document Management	Caere Pagekeeper	(408) 395-7000
	Spreadsheets	Microsoft Excel 5.0c	(503) 245-0905
	Database	Borland dBase v/Win 5.0	(408) 431-4705
	Finance/Accounting	Intuit Quicken CD 3.0	(415) 329-3569
	Management Applications	Austin-Hayne Employee Appraiser	(415) 610-6800
	Presentation Graphics	MS PowerPoint 4.0	(408) 986-1140
	Communications Software	DataStorm ProComm 2.0	(314) 443-3282
	PIMs	Arabesque Ecco 2.0 Professional	(206) 867-3757
System Software	Operating Systems	Microsoft Windows for Workgroups	(503) 245-0905
	Utilities	HP Dashboard 2.0	(408) 345-8889
	Application Development	Microsoft Visual Basic	(206) 637-9097
Network Software	Network OS	Novell Netware 4.02	(801) 429-7574
	Network Management	Intel Lan Desk 1.5	(503) 629-6536
	E-mail	Lotus cc:Mail 5.1	(415) 286-3990
	Groupware	DCA OpenWide	(404) 442-4830
	Online Services	NCSA Mosaic	(217) 244-3473
Multimedia/Graphics	Multimedia Authoring	Macromedia Director 4.0	(415) 252-2264
	Graphics Software	Shapeware Vision 3.0	(206) 521-4500
	CD-ROM Titles	Microsoft Bookshelf 1994	(206) 936-4200
	Innovation	The Web (Cern)	[44] (22) 767-5005
	Best Usability	Visioneer PaperMax	(415) 816-6400
	Best Product	Toshiba Portege 3600CT	(714) 583-3111

Source: PC Computing

Product Awards (cont'd)

Every year *MacUser* magazine gives the Eddy Awards, gold statuettes that honor the most innovative Macintosh products of the year.

MacUser Eddy Awards, 1994

Category	Product	Company
Hardware Product of the Year	Power Macintosh 6100/60	Apple Computer
Software Product of the Year	Code Warrior	Metrowerks
Breakthrough Technology of the Year	Quick Time VR	Apple Computer
Best New 3-D Modeling Software	Alias Sketch! 2.0	Alias Research
Best New Accelerator Product	Newer Technology Power Clip	New Technology
Best New Accounting Software	M.Y.O.B. 5.0	Best!Ware
Best New Animation Software	After Effects 2.0	Adobe Systems
Best New CAD Software	ArchiCAD 4.5	Graphisoft
Best New Edutainment Software	Cartoon History of the Universe	Putnam New Media
Best New Children's Software	Odell Down Under 1.1	MECC
Best New Color Printer	LaserMaster DisplayMaker	Professional LaserMaster
Best New Communications Software	Eudora 2.1	Qualcomm
Best New Connectivity Product	RunShare 1.0.2	RUN
Best New Data Management Tool	MapInfo 3.0	MapInfo
Best New Desktop Diversion	Star Trek: The Next Generation Screen Saver	Berkeley Systems
Best New Desktop Video Product	Avid Media Suite Pro 3.0	Avid
Best New Diagnostic Utility	MacTools Pro 4.0	Central Point (Symantec)
Best New Display Product	NEC MultiSync XE17	NEC
Best New Drawing Software	FreeHand 4.0	Altsys
Best New Game	SimCity 2000 1.1	Maxis
Best New Graphics/Publishing Utility	Cumulus PowerPro 2.0	Canto Software
Best New Imaging Software	Adobe Photoshop 3.0.1	Adobe Systems
Best New Input Device	Microfield Graphics Softboard Model 201	Microfield Graphics
Best New Integrated Application	ClarisWorks 3.0	Claris
Best New Monochrome Printer	Xanti Accel-a-Writer 8200	Xanti
Best New Multimedia Software	Digital Chisel 1.2	Pierian Spring
Best New Music Product	Vivace Coda	Music Technology
Best New Network Management Product	Skyline/Satellite 1.0	ag group
Best New Personal Organizational Tool	Claris Organizer 1.0	Claris
Best New Prepress Product	Colortron	Light Source
Best New Presentation Software	Microsoft PowerPoint 4.0	Microsoft
Best New Reference Software	Microsoft Bookshelf '94	Microsoft
Best New Scanner	Epson ES-1200C	Epson
Best New Special Effects Software	Typestry 2.1	Pixar
Best New Storage Product	Nakamichi MBR-7	Nakamichi
Best New System Enhancement	RAM Doubler 1.5	Connectix
Best New Visual Resource	TextureScape 1.5	Specular International
Best New Word Processing Tool	WordPerfect 3.1	WordPerfect (Novell)

Source: MacUser, 1994

Product Awards (cont'd)

Windows magazine chooses the top 100 Windows hardware products each year.

The Windows 100, 1994

Category	Product
Product of the Year	IBM ThinkPad 755C
CD-ROM Drives	Chinon 535 CD-ROM
	Mountain CD7
	NEC MultiSpin 4X Pro
	Plextor 4PLEX PX-43CH Internal
	Toshiba XM-3501
Desktop Systems	AcerPower Pentium Minitower
	American MultiSystems InfoGold P90
	Compaq Presario 520
	Everex Step SP/90 Mini Tower
	Gateway 2000 P5-90
	Hewlett-Packard Vectra XU 5/90C
	Intergraph TD-4
	Micron 4100 PCI Magnum
	Micron P90 Home PC
	NMC Expert-System+
	Robotech Cobra RS
	Silent Systems FE4
	Zeos Pantera 90
Diagnostic Tools	AllMicro Discovery Card
Graphics/Video Cards	ATI Graphics Pro Turbo
	Diamond Stealth 64 VRAM PCI 2MB
	Jazz Multimedia Jakarta/Projector/Port of Entry
	miroVideo DCI tv
	miroVideo 20TD live
	STB PowerGraph
Input Devices	Acecad Acecat II
	Alps Electric GlidePoint
	Kensington Thinking Mouse
	Logitech MouseMan Sensa
	Mind Path Remote Control IR50 F/X
	Wacom ArtPad
Modems	E-Tech Bullet 100E
	Hayes Optima 288 V.34/V.FC + FAX
	Microcom DeskPorte FAST External
	U.S. Robotics Sportster V.34
	U.S. Robotics WorldPort 14,400 Fax PCMCIA
Monitors	IBM 17P Multifrequency
	Mitsubishi Diamond Pro 21T
	Nanao FlexScan F340i-W
	Nanao FlexScan T2-17
	NEC MultiSync XE15
	Nokia Valuegraph 447L
	Panasonic PanaSync/Pro C-2192P
	Samsung SyncMaster 17GLs
	Sony Multiscan 15sf
	Sony Multiscan 20se
	ViewSonic 17
Networking	Coactive Connector
	Zenith CruiseLAN

Product Awards (cont'd)

Category	Product
Portable Computing	AcerNote 780cx
	AST Ascentia family
	AT&T Globalyst 200
	Canon NoteJet 11 486c
	Dell Latitude XP family
	Gateway 2000 Liberty DX2-50
	Hewlett-Packard OmniBook 600C
	IBM ThinkPad 755C
	NEC Versa M/75TC
	Texas Instruments TravelMate 4000M
	Toshiba Dynapad T200CS
	Toshiba T2450CT Satellite Pro
	Toshiba T4900CT
	Unlimited Systems Konexx Koupler Model 204
	Zenith Z-Player
	Zeos Meridian 400
	Zeos Meridian 800C
Printers	Apple LaserWriter 16/600 PS
	Canon BJC-600e
	Canon BJC-4000
	CoStar Label Writer XL Plus
	Epson Action Laser 1100
	Epson Stylus Color
	Hewlett-Packard Color LaserJet
	Hewlett-Packard DeskJet family
	Hewlett-Packard LaserJet 4 Plus
	Hewlett-Packard OfficeJet
	Lexmark Optra Lx
	Lexmark WinWriter family
	Tektronix Phaser 140
	Texas Instruments microLaser Powerpro
	Xerox 4900 Color Laser Printer
Projection Panels	Sharp QA-1500 LCD Projection Panel
Scanners	Agfa StudioScan II
	Canon IX-4015
	Hewlett-Packard ScanJet IIcx
	Hewlett-Packard ScanJet 3p
	UMAX PowerLook PS2400X
	Visioneer PaperPort
SCSI Adapters	AdvanSys AdvanSCSI Silver
	QLogic FastSCSI IQ PCI
Sound Cards	Creative Labs Sound Blaster AWE32
	Ensoniq Soundscape
	Mediatrix Audiotrix Pro
	Turtle Beach MultiSound Monterey
Storage	APS MobilStor 340
	APS MobilStor Tape 250
	Integral PocketFile 170
PCMCIA	Kingston Data Traveler
	Micro Solutions Backpack 250
Upgrade Chips	Intel OverDrive family

Source: Windows, May 1995

Industry Data

PC DATA COLLECTS DATA on the best-selling software products. Below are the top products as of February 1995:

Top-Selling Business Software (MS-DOS/OS/2)

Product	Company
MS-DOS 6.2	Microsoft
OS/2 Warp	IBM
QEMM	Quarterdeck
Norton Utilities	Symantec
70 Mil. Households Phone Bk.	American Business Info
Norton Antivirus	Symantec
Playboy Screensaver	Sony
QEMM Upgrade	Quarterdeck
11 Mil. Business Phone Bk.	American Business Info
Multimedia Stacker	Stac Electronics

Top-Selling Business Software (Windows)

Product	Company
UnInstaller	Micro Help
WordPerfect for Windows Upgrade	WordPerfect
Microsoft Windows 3.1	Microsoft
Microsoft Office Upgrade	Microsoft
Winfax Pro	Delrina
Corel Gallery (CD-ROM)	Corel
QuickBooks	Intuit
Microsoft Windows for Wkgrps Add-On	Microsoft
Microsoft Word Upgrade	Microsoft
Internet in a Box	Spry

Top-Selling Business Software (Macintosh)

Product	Company
Ram Doubler	Connectix
Norton Utilities	Symantec
Freehand Upgrade	Adobe
After Dark	Berkeley
QuickBooks	Intuit
Filemaker Pro	Claris
System 7.x	Apple
Adobe Photoshop Upgrade	Adobe
Quark XPress	Quark
Norton Utilities Upgrade	Symantec

Top-Selling Personal Productivity Software (MS-DOS/Windows)

Product	Company
TurboTax for Windows	Intuit
Quicken for Windows	Intuit
TurboTax Deluxe CD-ROM for Windows	Intuit
TaxCut for Windows	Block Fin.
Quicken CD-ROM Deluxe for Windows	Intuit
State TurboTax CA for Windows	Intuit
Print Shop Deluxe CD Ensemble	Brøderbund
Quicken Deluxe for Windows	Intuit
Print Shop Deluxe for Windows	Brøderbund
One Stop CD Shop (CD-ROM)	Softkey
Street Atlas USA (CD-ROM)	DeLorme
Quicken (MS-DOS)	Intuit
Quicken CD-ROM for Windows	Intuit
Family Treemaker Deluxe (CD-ROM)	Banner Blue
TaxCut (MS-DOS)	Block Fin.

Top-Selling Personal Productivity Software (Macintosh)

Product	Company
Macintax	Intuit
Quicken	Intuit
Macintax State CA	Intuit
Print Shop Deluxe	Brøderbund
TaxCut	Block Financial

Source: PC Data

The Upside 200

EACH YEAR, *UPSIDE* magazine selects the top 200 public technology companies on the basis of two criteria: the total dollars of value created, and the market peak at the close of the year compared to the previous year. Based on Standard Industry Classification (SIC) codes, their choice is determined according to those sectors most representative of nonmedical, high-technology businesses. The companies included in the sample must have reported public data in Compustat's database for both fiscal years 1993 and 1994.

Rank	Name	Value Created 1994 ($ mil.)	Market Value 1994 ($ mil.)	Sales Growth (%)
1	Microsoft	11,738.0	35,514	19
2	IBM	9,883.6	43,157	-3
3	Motorola	6,616.8	33,012	25
4	Hewlett-Packard	5,275.4	25,429	19
5	Oracle Systems	4,393.4	12,626	11
6	Compaq Computers	3,764.0	10,207	32
7	Ericsson North America	3,203.2	12,348	21
8	Micron Technology	2,558.8	4,496	75
9	Electronic Data Systems	2,400.7	10,258	-18
10	Air Touch Communications	2,093.1	14,373	5
11	3Com	1,825.5	3,402	-37
12	Tellabs	1,380.8	2,428	33
13	Computer Associates Int'l	1,324.4	7,846	7
14	LSI Logic	1,218.3	2,297	13
15	Lin Broadcasting	1,184.6	6,890	22
16	Apple Computer	1,132.4	4,662	15
17	Ameritech	1,093.3	22,222	6
18	Texas Instruments	1,033.0	6,936	12
19	EMC	1,030.3	4,309	39
20	Computer Sciences	902.5	2,594	17
21	Contel Cellular	855.8	2,492	30
22	Silicon Graphics	846.9	4,342	29
23	Stratacom	829.2	1,114	102
24	Autodesk	801.0	1,869	5
25	Intel	783.7	26,802	28
26	First Data	723.7	5,216	5
27	Tandem Computers	706.0	1,979	2
28	Informix	704.0	2,087	14
29	Dell Computer	696.9	1,603	9
30	Cisco Systems	695.7	9,052	78
31	Atmel	671.7	1,517	58
32	Andrew	669.7	1,335	27
33	Advanced Micro Devices	658.7	2,369	29
34	Northern Telecom	628.2	8,441	4
35	Amdahl	572.9	1,276	-9
36	DSC Communications	563.9	4,064	31
37	Brøderbund Software	560.4	917	33
38	Analog Devices	516.6	1,758	13
39	Peoplesoft	514.1	898	47
40	Sybase	477.8	2,686	50

The Upside 200 (cont'd)

Rank	Name	Value Created 1994 ($ mil.)	Market Value 1994 ($ mil.)	Sales Growth (%)
41	Automatic Data Processing	458.6	8,299	7
42	Sun Microsystems	454.0	3,428	2
43	Integrated Device Technologies	417.6	997	13
44	National Semiconductor	399.1	2,402	-1
45	ADC Telecommunications	398.1	1,394	17
46	Powersoft	395.3	901	109
47	Linear Technology	383.5	1,820	28
48	Compuware	373.8	1,618	45
49	Netmanage	372.6	788	88
50	Cadence Design Systems	370.6	850	6
51	General Datacomm Industries	349.8	579	0
52	Ceridian	347.0	1,205	3
53	Cypress Semiconductor	343.9	890	21
54	Adobe Systems	338.8	1,373	NA
55	HBO & Co.	335.8	1,090	15
56	Tektronix	325.4	1,051	0
57	Scientific-Atlanta	316.2	1,585	9
58	America Online	315.2	811	150
59	Microchip Technology	313.4	865	28
60	Maxim Integrated Products	307.9	1,012	36
61	Symbol Technologies	306.0	778	18
62	Cellular Communications	288.3	441	NA
63	Applied Materials	281.3	3,553	44
64	Intuit	270.3	1,271	77
65	Western Digital	269.5	752	21
66	Xilinx	263.1	1,369	19
67	Alliance Semiconductor	258.8	391	62
68	Network Equipment Technologies	258.6	424	-17
69	Total Systems Services	257.6	1,107	21
70	Microtouch Systems	251.5	300	55
71	Chipcom	242.5	824	11
72	LCI	241.4	792	20
73	Davidson & Associates	240.7	556	11
74	Vanguard Cellular Systems	240.0	1,489	20
75	Platinum Technology	234.7	464	23
76	Glenayre Technologies	227.1	951	15
77	Novellus Systems	223.1	800	54
78	Teradyne	218.6	1,219	19
79	Continuum	213.3	583	22
80	General Instrument	210.4	3,626	31
81	BMC Software	209.8	1,446	10
82	Legent	208.6	1,030	16
83	International Rectifier	207.4	494	14
84	Tencor Instruments	202.2	519	46
85	C-Cor Electronics	200.2	285	33
86	Adaptec	193.8	1,233	-12
87	United Video Satellite Group	193.1	422	14
88	Century Telephone Enterprises	192.4	1,576	14
89	Altera	186.2	867	34
90	Komag	182.3	592	-1

The Upside 200 (cont'd)

Rank	Name	Value Created 1994 ($ mil.)	Market Value 1994 ($ mil.)	Sales Growth (%)
91	Shared Medical Systems	179.2	751	4
92	Paging Network	176.9	1,721	18
93	Medic Computer Systems	172.6	329	27
94	Zenith Electronics	166.0	523	10
95	Network General	163.7	555	-18
96	Silicon Valley Group	162.8	388	29
97	Stratus Computer	159.3	920	8
98	Allen Systems Group	149.3	623	13
99	Sterling Software	148.8	756	13
100	American Management Systems	147.0	502	-11
101	Gateway 2000	144.8	1,565	39
102	McAfee Associates	142.8	230	50
103	California Microwave	142.6	439	34
104	Boston Technology	142.3	351	15
105	TSX	142.0	163	11
106	Sequent Computer Systems	136.1	614	16
107	Medstat Group	134.1	291	25
108	Electronics for Imaging	127.6	329	39
109	Wonderware	124.6	404	56
110	Three-Five Systems	124.5	281	80
111	Read-Rite	124.3	837	40
112	Proxima	123.1	176	51
113	In Focus Systems	122.5	296	40
114	Optical Data Systems	120.4	230	5
115	Sierra On-Line	120.0	260	-2
116	Alltel	117.2	5,659	19
117	Tekelec	115.7	143	14
118	Insilco	111.6	244	-28
119	FTP Software	111.2	717	48
120	Lam Research	109.9	876	72
121	Microtest	109.5	187	54
122	Standard Microsystems	109.4	390	-18
123	Colonial Data Technologies	107.6	151	92
124	Cellular Communication PR	107.4	333	78
125	Cabletron Systems	107.1	3,321	-6
126	Frame Technology	106.8	239	25
127	Commnet Cellular	102.5	340	67
128	U.S. Robotics	98.0	511	82
129	IMRS	96.8	282	27
130	International Cabletel	96.1	628	20
131	Micros Systems	95.7	294	35
132	Credence Systems	93.9	271	21
133	Planar Systems	93.2	233	30
134	Macromedia	93.0	277	19
135	Ionics	91.2	438	15
136	Digidesign	90.9	181	17
137	Harman International Industries	89.6	558	24
138	Cognos	88.8	235	5
139	Printronix	88.7	119	22
140	Photronics	87.9	195	63

The Upside 200 (cont'd)

Rank	Name	Value Created 1994 ($ mil.)	Market Value 1994 ($ mil.)	Sales Growth (%)
141	Caere	87.5	188	23
142	Fiserv	87.3	838	14
143	SyQuest Technology	84.6	200	7
144	Broadway & Seymour	83.5	177	23
145	Dynatech	82.8	299	3
146	Microdyne	82.5	150	31
147	Integrated Systems	82.1	172	10
148	OIS Optical Imaging Systems	80.9	181	63
149	Xylogics	80.8	123	17
150	Cambridge Technology Partners	79.8	295	15
151	Picturetel	79.5	367	30
152	Exabyte	79.4	458	22
153	Cellstar	79.3	420	79
154	Intersolv	79.3	267	8
155	Apertus Technologies	79.3	132	43
156	Digital Systems International	78.6	113	14
157	Sierra Semiconductor	77.7	157	9
158	Santa Cruz Operations	77.3	287	3
159	Keane	77.0	322	71
160	Exar	76.4	217	-2
161	Telco Systems	75.9	162	22
162	Health Management Systems	75.4	195	24
163	Interdigital Communications	74.3	296	62
164	Bisys Group	73.6	337	51
165	Spectrum Holobyte	72.9	272	69
166	Kent Electronics	71.8	257	-9
167	Mentor Graphics	71.5	743	-3
168	ALC Communications	70.0	1,048	19
169	Verifone	69.7	528	8
170	National Computer Systems	67.4	236	4
171	FSI International	66.9	164	16
172	Burr-Brown	66.7	129	10
173	Trident Microsystems	66.6	130	-12
174	Learning	66.6	178	36
175	Microcom	64.7	122	42
176	Incomnet	64.0	122	166
177	Acxiom	63.3	296	18
178	Genus	62.0	101	14
179	Boole & Babbage	61.7	193	11
180	Convex Computer	60.6	206	-18
181	Symmetricom	60.1	188	10
182	Mylex	59.5	159	2
183	FileNet	59.1	297	8
184	Franklin Electronic Publishers	58.6	159	14
185	Vicor	58.3	547	-4
186	Norand	57.8	261	15
187	Supertex	57.1	92	12
188	Electroglas	57.1	285	24
189	Kulicke & Soffa Industries	56.9	173	15
190	Altron	56.7	136	15

The Upside 200 (cont'd)

Rank	Name	Value Created 1994 ($ mil.)	Market Value 1994 ($ mil.)	Sales Growth (%)
191	Cellular Communications	56.1	522	NA
192	Siliconix	56.0	123	9
193	Zitel	55.3	81	-15
194	PSC	50.7	96	35
195	Safeguard Scientifics	49.0	164	-19
196	Computer Language Research	48.5	164	10
197	ATC Environmental	48.4	88	15
198	Pioneer Standard Electronics	48.3	235	-1
199	Telxon	48.0	214	18
200	Egghead	47.1	202	-48

Source: Upside, May 1995

Ordering by Mail

THE BEST PRICES, delivery, and support on computer hardware and software are often found from mail order dealers. Use a credit card to avoid delays.

Mail Order Supply Companies

Company	Phone
ACS	(800) 774-7014
APC	(800) 800-4272
APS Technologies	(800) 235-9125
Club Mac	(800) 258-2622
CompUSA Direct	(800) 266-7872
Computer Discount Warehouse	(800) 279-4239
Data Comm Warehouse	(800) 328-2261
Egghead	(800) 344-4323
First Source	(800) 439-9866
Insight Direct	(800) 998-8025
Macintosh Accessory Center	(800) 931-9711
Mac's Place	(800) 367-4222
MacMall	(800) 222-2808
Mac Zone	(800) 248-2088
Megahaus Hard Drives	(800) 473-0972
Micro Warehouse	(800) 367-7080

Company	Phone
Micro Systems Warehouse	(800) 660-3222
Midwest Micro	(800) 682-7248
NECX Direct	(800) 961-9208
Nevada Computer	(800) 982-2946
Pacific Coast Micro	(800) 581-6040
PC and Mac Connection	(800) 800-1111
PCs Compleat	(800) 598-4727
Sunshine Computers	(800) 854-7754
Tiger Direct	(800) 666-2562
U.S. Computer Supply	(800) 987-7877
USA Flex	(800) 766-1940
Worldwide Technologies	(800) 636-6792

Paris Anglophone. Send e-mail to paris@almanac.yoyo.com. See p. xi for instructions.

One hundred important phone numbers from Paris Anglophone, the most up-to-date, comprehensive directory of American, British, Irish, Canadian, and Australian businesses, organizations, services, and activities in France.

Shareware

SHAREWARE IS AN ALTERNATIVE method of software distribution. Instead of packaging the product and offering it for sale through dealers or mail order vendors, the author of the software posts a copy on various electronic bulletin boards (e.g. CompuServe) and allows users to try it for free. If the software does what it claims, and you find it useful, you're expected to send the requested fee directly to the author.

The only downsides of shareware are the lack of uniformity in technical support and the sometimes unpolished nature of the software.

Popular Windows Shareware Programs

Accesses (Utilities collection)
Almanac for Windows (Calendar)
ApiSpy (Windows development tool)
BackMenu and BigDesk (Program manager and desk space enlarger)
BizWiz Financial Calculator (Calculator)
CCIZip (File compression)
Chartist (Charts)
ClysBar (Program manager)
File Commander (File manager)
Folders (Program manager)
Hi, Finance! (Calculator)
KBS: People Management System (Address book/database)
M-B Analyst (Calculator)
Mega Edit (Text editor)
MGWalk (Heap utility)
MicroLink (Communications)
PixFolio (Image processor)
Plug-In for Program Manager (Program manager)
Scan for Windows (Viruses)
SideBar Lite (Program manager)
Time & Chaos (Personal information manaager)
WinBatch (Windows automator)
Windows Reminder (Personal information manager)
WindSock (Utility collection)
WinPoem (Database)
WinPost (Onscreen message memos)

Source: The Windows Shareware 500, John Hedtke, Ventana Press

Popular Mac Shareware Programs

DateKey (Date utility)
Disinfectant (Viruses)
11/22/63 EXTRA! (HyperCard stack)
FlashWrite II (Word processor)

Inigo Gets Out (HyperCard game)
Mariner (Spreadsheet)
MaxAppleZoom (Monitor enhancement)
NIH Image (Image processor)
PopChar (Key finder)
Programmer's Key (Interrupt switch)
StuffIt Lite (File compression)
To Do! (Scheduler)
ZTerm (Communications)

Source: The Mac Shareware 500, Ruffin Prevost and Rob Terrell, Ventana Press

Shareware Sources

The following are FTP sites, all of which have a variety of popular shareware programs:

- Mac.archive.umich.edu

- Wuarchive.wustl.edu

- Sunsite.unc.edu

- Oak.oakland.edu

- Ftp.rahul.net

- Garbo.uwasa.fi

- Ftp.apple.com

Recommended Resources

CWI
(800) 777-5636

Public Brand Software
(800) 426-3475

Shareware Express
(800) 346-2842

Ziffnet on CompuServe
(800) 848-8199

America Online
(800) 827-6364

Educorp
(800) 843-9497

Glossbrenner's Guide to Shareware for Small Businesses
Windcrest/McGraw Hill, $37.95
(800) 822-8138

Upgrading an Existing PC or Mac

AS PERSONAL COMPUTERS become more advanced, the chances that a company's PCs are "obsolete" increase. With the price of used computers plummeting, it usually makes more sense to upgrade than to replace an existing machine. Here are the ten most effective ways to get more out of a computer:

I. Buy more memory.

No computer has enough. Buy memory (SIMMs) from a reputable company like Techworks or the Chip Merchant. On some machines, the memory is easy to install. On others, see a dealer. Remember: Always buy as much as you can afford–the bigger memory chips are worth it.

2. Get a bigger screen.

Studies have shown that, depending on the task, a user's productivity can increase as much as 100% with a larger work area. The ideal screen size is 19 inches for most spreadsheet, graphics, and word processing users.

3. Install a bigger hard drive.

More complicated software (especially Windows or complex graphic modeling tools) uses lots of disk space. The price of hard disk storage has declined significantly. Look for a brand of drive with at least two years of history in the market, and a warranty of at least two years.

4. Install a better/faster printer.

Buy a PostScript printer (for more fonts and better graphics), or a printer with greater resolution (measured in dpi, or dots per inch). Owners of sophisticated printers should consider adding a color printer.

5. Get an accelerator board.

These boards work with (or replace) an existing computer chip to dramatically speed up the computer. Some accelerators can increase speed by as many as ten times (that means that an activity that took 60 seconds–like opening a large spreadsheet–now takes six). Daystar is the leader in the Mac market, while ATI is a leader in the PC market.

6. Buy a backup device.

No one likes to back up, but every competent user must. Tape drives or removable bulk storage make it less painful. Investigate digital audiotapes, cartridges, and Bernoulli or Syquest devices (available from many vendors) that make backup automatic and foolproof.

7. Take a training course.

Often the bottleneck isn't the computer, it's the user. Investigate courses that can help a user become even more expert at the software already in use.

8. Buy and use a macro program.

Macro programs remember keystrokes and make it easy to automate repetitive tasks. Type a return address with one keystroke, or reserve a function key to automatically open a file, print it out, update it, and save a backup. A popular tool for the Mac is Quickkeys, and there are several specialized ones available for the PC.

9. Get a very fast fax modem.

With prices falling every day, fax modems are an easy choice. Send a fax without printing the document and walking across the office to feed it into a busy machine. The built-in modem allows a user to access bulletin boards and gain free access to huge amounts of data. In addition, electronic mail will dramatically increase a user's ability to communicate with others.

10. Buy an Uninterruptible Power Supply.

A little box that resembles a surge suppressor, sometimes called a UPS, can automatically protect a computer from blackouts or power surges.

The Top Reference Sources

MacWEEK
Ziff Davis, Controlled
(609) 786-8230

InfoWorld
IDG, Controlled
(800) 227-8365

MacWEEK is the ultimate resource for the computer manager responsible for Macintoshes. Every week, the magazine offers fresh graphics, helpful advice, and the inside news on new technology.

MacWEEK is a controlled-circulation magazine, so you must qualify to get a subscription.

InfoWorld, whose circulation is also controlled, focuses on the issues facing managers who deal with computers. The reviews are among the best in the industry, and the news is usually more current and specific than you'll find anywhere else.

Used Computers

Contact Options

Used-Computer Brokers:

Boston Computer Exchange
P.O. Box 1177
Boston, MA 02103
(800) 262-6399

Rentex
337 Summer St.
Boston, MA 02210
(800) 545-2313

River Computer
14 Mill St.
Marlow, NH 03456
(800) 998-0090

Technical Support

Five Tips on Technical Support

1. Go to the bookstore and buy a third-party book. It is easier and faster than using the manual.

2. Several online services have technical support areas where you can post a message for the company that created your product. Post your message and look for an answer the next day.

3. Send a fax to tech support. Faxes are often given to the best adviser, and you're guaranteed not to spend time and money on the phone.

4. Turn off all TSRs, inits, and special software before calling. The tech support people usually won't help you until you prove that the problem is theirs.

5. If you have a modem, send your problem directly to the company's bulletin board.

Networking

NETWORKING PERSONAL COMPUTERS seems easy. For many businesses, however, it takes more time and money to establish a network than it does to purchase the computers in the first place.

There are several competing networking standards, including Ethernet, and Netware from Novell. For more information on each format, and to determine which is best for your organization, contact the Novell Netware hotline at (800) 638-9273. They publish a comprehensive buyer's guide and a general product guide to networking that is free on request.

Also available is an electronic faxback system that will automatically send information on a wide variety of topics to any fax machine. To access the system, dial (800) 638-9273 and press 1, then 1.

Recommended Resource

Novell
122 E. 1700 S.
Provo, UT 84606
(800) 638-9273

The Top Reference Sources

Ventana Press
P.O. Box 13964
Research Triangle Park, NC 27709
(919) 544-9404

This publisher's list is loaded with the best sort of computer help books—the truly useful kind. Ven-

tana features a number of titles especially for those in the desktop publishing mode. Call for a free catalogue.

Computer Conference Companies

ADmore Expositions
9701 Gravois Rd.
St. Louis, MO 63123
(314) 638-4050
Printing, Computer, Business Trade Shows

American Expositions
110 Greene St., Suite 703
New York, NY 10012
(212) 226-4141
Multimedia and Digital Video

Applied Computer Research (ACR)
P.O. Box 82266
Phoenix, AZ 85071
(800) 234-2227
Mainframe Computer Industry

Association Exposition & Services
1100 Summer St.
Stamford, CT 06905
(203) 325-5019
Telecommunications

Association for Computing Machinery (ACM)
1515 Broadway, 17th Floor
New York, NY 10036
(212) 869-7440
Technical Computer Science

Association for Information and Image
Management (AIIM)
1100 Wayne Ave., Suite 1100
Silver Spring, MD 20910
(301) 587-8202
Information and Image Management Users

Blenheim I. T. Events
Fort Lee Executive Park
One Executive Dr.
Fort Lee, NJ 07024
(800) 829-3976

Computer Security Institute (CSI)
600 Harrison St.
San Francisco, CA 94107
(415) 905-2626
Computer and Information Security

Computing Technology Industry Association (CTIA)
450 E. 22nd St.
Lombard, IL 60148
(708) 240-1818
Conferences for Computer Resellers

Concept Development
27292 Calle Arroyo, Suite A
Rancho Viejo, CA 92675
(714) 489-7575

Dataquest
1290 Ridder Park Dr.
San Jose, CA 95131
(408) 437-8000
Semiconductors, Computers & Peripherals, Software

Delphi Consulting Group
266 Beacon St.
Boston, MA 02116
(617) 247-1025
Imaging, Text Retrieval, Multimedia

Electronic Conventions Management
8110 Airport Blvd.
Los Angeles, CA 90045
(213) 215-3976
Electronics Trade Shows

EMAP International Exhibitions
12 Bedford Row
London, England WC1R 4DU UK
[44] (17) 404-484
Macintosh Trade Shows

Expocon Management Associates
363 Reef Rd., P.O. Box 915
Fairfield, CT 06430
(203) 256-4700
Electronics, Data Collection, Printing

Future Expositions
1975 Hamilton Ave., Suite 10
San Jose, CA 95125
(408) 369-7744
Home Office Technology

IDG World Expo
111 Speen St.
Framingham, MA 01701
(800) 225-4698
PC, Workstations, Software

InfoWorld Publishing
155 Bovet Rd., Suite 800
San Mateo, CA 94402
(800) 432-2478
New PC Products

Institute for International Research
708 Third Ave., Fourth Floor
New York, NY 10017
(212) 661-8740
Software Support

Computer Conference Companies (cont'd)

The Interface Group
300 First Ave.
Needham, MA 02194
(617) 449-6600

International Database Management Association
10675 Treena St., Suite 103
San Diego, CA 92131
(800) 767-7469
PC Trade Shows

Laptop Expositions
104 E. 40th St., Suite 802
New York, NY 10016
(212) 682-7968

Mecklermedia
20 Ketchum St.
Westport, CT 06880
(203) 226-6967
Multimedia and Online Conferences

Network World
P.O. Box 743485
Dallas, TX 75374
(214) 424-0565
E-Mail, Groupware, Networking, Security

Reed Exhibition Companies
P.O. Box 3833
Stamford, CT 06905
(203) 352-8459
Multimedia and CD-ROM Technology

Seybold Seminars
29160 Heathercliff Rd., Suite 200
Malibu, CA 90265
(310) 457-5850
Desktop Publishing Multimedia

Software Publishers Association (SPA)
1730 M St., NW, Suite 700
Washington, DC 20036
(202) 452-1600
PC Software

Ziff Institute
25 First St.
Cambridge, MA 02142
(617) 252-5119
Computer Training

The Top Reference Sources

The Macintosh Bible
Peachpit Press, $30
(800) 283-9444

The Macintosh Bible is a mammoth collection of tips, techniques, tricks, and advice. There should be a copy next to every Macintosh in the office.

Other books in the series include easy-to-use books on FileMaker, Excel, MacDraw, and a book called *What Do I Do Now?* that is ideal for novice users.

Computer Trade Shows

Spectrum '95

Tucson, AZ, Sept. 10-13, 1995
Focus: The future of print technologies
Sponsor: Graphic Communications Assoc.
100 Dangerfield Rd.
Alexandria, VA 22314
(703) 519-8160

Information Superhighway Summit

Santa Clara, CA, Sep. 11-14, 1995
Focus: Technology and how to build the
Information Superhighway
Sponsor: IDG World Expo
111 Speen St.
Framingham, MA 01701
(800) 225-4698

Multimedia Expo

San Francisco, CA, Sep. 11-14, 1995
Focus: Multimedia products and technologies
Sponsor: American Expositions
110 Greene St., Suite 703
New York, NY 10012
(212) 226-4141

WindowsWorld Dallas

Dallas, TX, Sept. 12-14, 1995
Focus: PC Windows applications
Sponsor: The Interface Group
300 First Ave.
Needham, MA 02194
(617) 449-6600

PC Expo Home

New York, NY, Sept. 28-Oct. 1, 1995
Focus: Small, home office, and home computing
Sponsor: Bruno Blenheim
Fort Lee Executive Park
1 Executive Dr.
Fort Lee, NJ 07024
(800) 829-3976

PC Expo

Chicago, IL, Oct. 3-5, 1995
Focus: PC and LAN products
Sponsor: Bruno Blenheim
Fort Lee Executive Park
1 Executive Dr.
Fort Lee, NJ 07024
(800) 829-3976

Eco Expo East

Boston, MA, Oct. 13-15, 1995
Focus: Environmental issues
Sponsor: National Marketplace for the Environment
14260 Ventura Blvd., Suite 201
Sherman Oaks, CA 91423
(818) 906-2700

Electronic Document Systems Global Conference & Exhibit

Minneapolis, MN, Nov. 5-10, 1995
Focus: Electronic document technologies and trends
Sponsor: Xplor
24238 Hawthorne Blvd.
Torrance, CA 90505
(310) 373-3633

Multimedia '95

San Francisco, CA, Nov. 6-9, 1995
Focus: Multimedia technology
Sponsor: ACM
1515 Broadway, 17th Floor
New York, NY 10036
(212) 626-0500

DB/Expo

New York, NY, Dec. 5-7, 1995
Focus: Database products and trends
Sponsor: Bruno Blenheim
Fort Lee Executive Park
One Executive Dr.
Fort Lee, NJ 07024
(800) 829-3976

Image World/Video Expo

Orlando, FL, Dec. 12-14, 1995
Focus: Video, graphics, multimedia, media, etc.
Sponsor: Knowledge Industry Publications
701 Westchester Ave.
White Plains, NY 10604
(914) 328-9157

Networks Expo

Boston, MA, Feb. 13-15, 1996
Focus: LAN, network products, and technology
Sponsor: Bruno Blenheim
Fort Lee Executive Park
1 Executive Dr.
Fort Lee, NJ 07024
(800) 829-3976

Computer Products and Services

Company	Phone	Tech Support	Fax
Abacus Accounting Systems	(403) 488-8100	same	(403) 488-8150
Abacus Software	(800) 451-4319	(616) 698-0330	(616) 698-0325
ABL Electronics	(800) 726-0610	same	(410) 584-2790
ABS-American Business Systems	(800) 356-4034	same	(508) 250-8027
Acculogic	(800) 234-7811	(714) 454-2441	(714) 756-9518
AceCad	(800) 676-4223	same	(408) 655-1919
Acer America	(800) 733-2237	same	(408) 922-2965
Acme Electric	(800) 325-5848	same	(716) 968-1420
Action Plus Software	(800) 766-7229	(801) 255-0600	(801) 255-0642
Acucobol	(800) 262-6585	(800) 399-7220	(619) 566-3071
Adaptec	(408) 945-8600	(408) 934-7240	(408) 262-2533
Addtron Technology	(800) 998-4638	(800) 998-4646	(510) 770-0171
ADI Systems	(800) 228-0530	same, ext. 335	(408) 944-0300
Adobe Systems	(800) 833-6687	same	(415) 235-0078
Advanced Gravis Computer Technology	(800) 663-8558	(604) 431-5020	(604) 434-7809
Advanced Logic Research	(800) 444-4257	same	(714) 581-9240
Advanced Matrix Technology	(800) 992-2264	same	(805) 484-5482
Advanced Media	(714) 965-7122	same	(714) 957-5977
Advantage Memory	(800) 245-5299	same	(714) 453-8158
Affinity	(800) 367-6771	(303) 442-4840	(303) 442-4999
Agfa	(800) 424-8973	same	(508) 657-8568
AimTech	(800) 289-2884	same	(603) 883-5582
Alacrity Systems	(800) 252-2748	(908) 813-2501	(908) 813-2490
Aladdin Systems	(408) 761-6200	same	(408) 761-6206
Aldus	(800) 333-2538	same	(206) 343-4240
Altec Lansing Multimedia	(800) 648-6663	same	(717) 296-2213
Altima Systems	(800) 356-9990	same	(510) 356-2408
Altsys	(214) 680-2060	(415) 252-9080	(214) 680-0537
American Power Conversion	(800) 800-4272	same	(401) 789-3710
AMP	(800) 522-6752	same	(717) 986-7575
Amrel Technology	(800) 882-6735	same	(818) 303-8538
Analog & Digital Peripherals	(513) 339-2241	same	(513) 339-0070
Analog Devices	(800) 262-5643	same	(617) 821-4273
Analog Technology	(818) 357-0098	same	(818) 303-4993
Andromeda Systems	(818) 709-7600	same	(818) 709-7407
Antec	(510) 770-1200	same	(510) 770-1288
Antex Electronics	(800) 338-4231	same	(310) 532-8509
Apple Computer	(800) 538-9696	(800) 767-2775	NA
Applied Micro Circuits	(619) 450-9333	same	(619) 450-9885
Appoint	(800) 448-1184	same	(510) 417-0614
Apricorn	(800) 458-5448	same	(619) 271-4888
Archive Software	(800) 821-8782	same	(407) 263-3555
Areal Technology	(408) 436-6800	(843) 436-6843	(408) 436-6844
Arnet	(800) 366-8844	same	(615) 834-5399
Artek Computer Systems	(510) 490-8402	NA	(510) 490-8405
Artisoft	(800) 846-9726	(602) 670-7000	(602) 670-7359
Asanté Technologies	(800) 662-9686	same	(408) 432-7511
askSam Systems	(800) 800-1997	(904) 584-6590	(904) 584-7481
ASP Computer Products	(800) 952-6277	same	(408) 732-0451
Aspen Imaging International	(800) 955-5555	same	(303) 665-2972

Computer Products and Services (cont'd)

Company	Phone	Tech Support	Fax
AST Research	(800) 876-4278	same	(714) 727-9355
Asymetrix	(800) 448-6543	(206) 637-1600	(206) 637-1504
ATI Technologies	(905) 882-2600	same	(905) 882-0546
Attachmate	(800) 426-6283	(800) 688-3270	(206) 747-9924
Austin Computer Systems	(800) 752-1577	same	(512) 719-8126
Autodesk	(800) 228-3601	NA	NA
Avance Logic	(510) 226-9555	same	(510) 226-8039
Award Software	(415) 968-4433	same	(415) 968-0274
Axelen (USA)	(206) 643-2781	NA	(206) 643-4478
Axis Communications	(617) 938-1188	same	(617) 938-6161
Baler Software	(800) 327-6108	(708) 506-1770	(708) 506-1808
Beame & Whiteside Software	(800) 463-6637	same	(919) 831-8990
Beaver Computer	(800) 827-4222	(800) 827-4888	(408) 452-1117
Behavior Tech Computer (U.S.A.)	(510) 657-3956	same	(510) 657-3965
Belkin Components	(800) 223-5546	same	(310) 898-1111
Bell & Howell	(800) 247-3724	same	(708) 675-5019
Berkeley Speech Technologies	(510) 841-5083	same	(510) 841-5093
Berkeley Systems	(510) 540-5535	same	(510) 540-5115
Best Data Products	(800) 632-2378	(818) 772-9600	(818) 773-9619
Best Power Technology	(800) 356-5794	same	(608) 565-2929
Bit 3 Computer	(612) 881-6955	same	(612) 881-9674
Bits Technical	(713) 735-9900	same	(713) 735-9999
Blue Sky Software	(800) 677-4946	same	(619) 459-6366
Boca Research	(407) 997-6227	(407) 241-8088	(407) 997-0918
Bold Data Technology	(510) 490-8296	same	(510) 490-9428
Borland	(800) 331-0877	same	(408) 461-9133
BOS National	(214) 956-7722	same	(214) 350-6688
Brier Technology	(404) 564-5699	same	(404) 381-2808
Brøderbund Software	(415) 382-4400	(415) 382-4700	(415) 382-4419
Brooks Power Systems	(800) 523-1551	same	(215) 244-0160
Brother International	(908) 356-8880	(908) 373-6256	(908) 469-5167
Brysis Data	(818) 810-0355	same	(818) 810-4555
Bureau of Electronic Publishing	(800) 828-4766	(201) 808-2780	(201) 808-2676
BusLogic	(408) 492-9090	(408) 654-0760	(408) 492-1542
Byte Brothers	(206) 271-9567	same	(206) 227-9702
C-Power Products	(800) 800-2797	NA	(214) 771-0462
CA Retail Solutions	(800) 668-3767	(905) 793-9302	(905) 793-9303
Cache Computers	(510) 226-9922	same	(510) 226-9911
Caere	(800) 535-7226	(800) 462-2373	(408) 354-2743
Calculus	(305) 481-2334	same	(305) 481-1866
Camintonn/Z-Ram	(714) 454-1500	same	(714) 830-4726
Campbell Services	(800) 345-6747	same	(810) 559-1034
Canon U.S.A.	(800) 848-4123	(800) 423-2366	(516) 354-5805
Cardiff Software	(800) 659-8755	(619) 931-4565	(619) 931-4550
CarNel Enterprises	(800) 962-1450	same	(714) 630-3180
Carroll Touch	(512) 244-3500	same	(512) 244-7040
Casio	(800) 962-2746	same	(201) 361-3819
CBIS	(404) 446-1332	same	(404) 446-9164
CD Technology	(408) 752-8500	same	(408) 752-8501
Central Point Software	(800) 445-4208	(800) 491-2764	(503) 690-8083
Centrepoint	(613) 235-7054	same	(613) 238-6549
Certified Management Software	(801) 534-1231	same	(801) 363-3653
CH Products	(800) 624-5804	(619) 598-2518	(619) 598-2524
Champion Business Systems	(800) 243-2626	same	(303) 792-0255
Chaplet Systems U.S.A.	(408) 732-7950	(408) 732-6159	(408) 732-6050

Computer Products and Services (cont'd)

Company	Phone	Tech Support	Fax
Cherry Electrical Products	(708) 662-9200	same	(708) 360-3566
Chicony America	(714) 380-0928	same	(714) 380-9204
Chinon America	(800) 441-0222	same	(310) 533-1727
Chipsoft	(602) 295-3110	same	(800) 756-1040
Chronocom	(418) 449-4378	same	(418) 449-1278
Chuck Atkinson Programs	(800) 826-5009	(800) 829-4005	(817) 560-8249
Cimmetry Systems	(800) 361-1904	same	(514) 735-6440
Cipher Data Products	(800) 424-7437	same	(619) 693-0491
Cirrus Logic	(510) 623-8300	same	(510) 226-2270
Citizen America	(800) 477-4683	(310) 453-0614	(310) 453-2814
Citrix Systems	(800) 437-7503	same	(305) 341-6880
Clarion Software	(800) 354-5444	(305) 785-4556	(305) 746-1650
Claris	(800) 325-2747	(408) 727-9054	(408) 987-3932
Clark Development	(800) 356-1686	(801) 261-1686	(801) 261-8987
Clary	(800) 442-5279	same, ext. 226	(818) 301-0049
CMG Technology	(800) 426-3832	same	(714) 455-1656
Codenoll Technology	(914) 965-6300	same	(914) 965-9811
Colorado Memory Systems	(303) 635-1500	same	(303) 667-0997
Command Communications	(800) 288-3491	(800) 288-6794	(303) 750-6437; 752-1903
Commax Technologies	(800) 526-6629	(408) 435-8272	(408) 435-5005
Commercial & Industrial Design	(714) 556-0888	same	(714) 556-0889
Compaq Computer	(800) 345-1518	(800) 652-6672	NA
CompSee	(800) 628-3888	same	(407) 723-2895
CompuAdd	(800) 999-9901	same	(512) 250-2629
CompuLan Technology	(800) 486-8810	same	(408) 954-8299
CompuRegister	(314) 365-2050	same	(314) 365-2080
Computer Aided Technology	(214) 350-0888	same	(214) 701-8885
Computer Associates International	(800) 225-5224	same	(516) 432-0614
Computer Dynamics Sales	(800) 627-1218	same	(803) 879-2030
Computer Friends	(800) 547-3303	(503) 626-2291	(503) 643-5379
Computer Law Systems	(800) 328-1913	same	(612) 942-3450
Computer Modules	(408) 496-1881	same	(408) 496-1886
Computer Peripherals	(800) 854-7600	(714) 454-2441	(805) 498-8360
Computone	(800) 241-3946	same	(404) 475-2707
CompuTrend Systems	(818) 333-5121	(800) 568-6388	(818) 369-6803
Comy Technology	(408) 437-1555	(800) 505-4295	(408) 456-0366
Concurrent Controls	(800) 487-2243	same	(415) 873-6091
Connect Tech	(519) 836-1291	same	(519) 836-4878
Connect-Air International	(800) 247-1978	same	(206) 813-5699
Conner Peripherals	(408) 456-3167	same	(408) 456-4501
Consumer Technology NW	(800) 356-3983	same	(503) 671-9066
Contact Software International	(800) 365-0606	NA	(214) 919-9750
Core International	(407) 997-6044	(407) 997-6033	(407) 997-6202
Corel Systems	(800) 836-7274	(800) 818-1848	(613) 728-9790
Corollary	(800) 338-4020	same	(714) 250-4043
Cougar Mountain Software	(800) 388-3038	(800) 727-0656	(208) 343-0267
CPU Products	(800) 882-1842	same	(316) 788-3800
Creative Labs	(800) 998-5227	(405) 742-6622	(405) 428-6611
Crystal Semiconductor	(512) 445-7222	(512) 445-3554	(512) 445-7581
CrystalGraphics	(408) 496-6175	same	(408) 496-6988

Computer Products and Services (cont'd)

Company	Phone	Tech Support	Fax
CTX International	(800) 289-2189	(800) 888-2012	(909) 595-6293
Cybex	(205) 430-4000	same	(205) 430-4030
CyCare Software Publishing	(800) 545-2488	(800) 548-2660	(602) 596-4466
CYMA Systems	(800) 292-2962	same	(602) 303-2969
DacEasy	(800) 222-8778	same	(214) 250-7905
Dallas Semiconductor	(214) 450-8170	(214) 450-3850	(214) 450-0470
Danpex	(408) 437-7557	same	(408) 437-7559
Dassault Automatismes	(212) 909-0550	same	(212) 909-0555
Data Access	(800) 451-3539	(305) 232-3142	(305) 238-0017
Data Entry Systems	(205) 430-3023	(205) 837-8715	(205) 430-0989
Data General	(800) 328-2436	(800) 344-3577	(508) 366-1319
Data I/O	(800) 247-5700	same	(206) 622-5596
Data Race	(800) 749-7223	(800) 940-7223	(512) 558-1929
Data Technology	(408) 942-4000	(408) 262-7700	(408) 942-4052
Databook	(716) 292-5720	(716) 292-5725	(716) 292-5737
Datacap	(914) 332-7515	same	(914) 332-7516
Datacap Systems	(215) 699-7051	same	(215) 699-6779
Datalux	(800) 328-2589	same	(703) 662-1682
Datasouth Computer	(800) 476-2120	same	(704) 523-9298
DataSym	(519) 758-5800	same	(519) 758-5600
Dataware	(800) 426-4844	same	(713) 432-1385
Daystar	(800) 962-2077	(404) 967-2077	(404) 967-3018
DD & TT Enterprise U.S.A.	(213) 780-0099	same	(213) 780-0419
Dell Computer	(800) 289-3355	(800) 624-9896	(800) 950-1329
DeLorme Mapping	(207) 865-4171	same	(207) 865-9291
Delrina Technology	(800) 268-6082	(416) 443-4390	(416) 441-0333
DeltaPoint	(800) 367-4334	(408) 375-4700	(408) 648-4020
Deltec Electronics	(800) 854-2658	same	(619) 291-2584
Deneba Software	(800) 622-6827	same	(305) 477-5794
Denistron	(310) 530-3530	same	(310) 534-8419
DesignCAD	(918) 825-4844	same	(918) 825-6359
Deskstation Technology	(913) 599-1900	(913) 599-0911	(913) 599-4024
DFM Systems	(800) 223-4791	same	(515) 244-4918
Diamond Computer Systems	(408) 325-7000	(408) 325-7100	(408) 730-5750
DigiBoard	(800) 344-4273	same	(612) 943-5398
Digicom Systems	(800) 833-8900	(408) 934-1601	(408) 262-1390
Digital Communications Associates	(800) 348-3221	(404) 740-0300	(404) 442-4364
Digital Equipment	(800) 332-4636	(800) 354-9000	(508) 493-8780
Digital Products	(800) 243-2333	same	(617) 647-4474
Digital Vision	(800) 346-0090	(617) 329-5400	(617) 329-6286
Digitalk	(800) 922-8255	same	(714) 513-3120
Digitan Systems	(408) 954-8270	same	(408) 954-9641
Discoversoft	(510) 769-2902	same	(510) 769-0149
Disctec	(407) 671-5500	same	(407) 671-6606
Distributed Processing Technology	(407) 830-5522	same	(407) 260-5366
Dolch Computer Systems	(800) 538-7506	same	(408) 263-6305
Dover Electronics Manufacturing	(800) 848-1198	same	(303) 776-1883
Dragon Systems	(800) 825-5897	(617) 965-7670	(617) 527-0372
Dubl-Click	(800) 266-9525	same	(818) 888-5405
Dycam	(818) 998-8008	(818) 407-3970	(818) 998-7951
Dynapro	(800) 667-0374	same	(604) 521-4629
DynaTek Automation Systems	(416) 636-3000	(800) 267-6007	(416) 636-3011
Eastman Kodak	(800) 242-2424	same	(716) 726-3585
Edimax Computer	(408) 496-1105	(408) 988-6092	(408) 980-1530
EFA of America	(408) 987-5400	same	(408) 987-5415

Computer Products and Services (cont'd)

Company	Phone	Tech Support	Fax
EFI Electronics	(800) 877-1174	same	(801) 977-0200
Electro Products	(800) 423-0646	same	(206) 859-9101
Electrohome Limited	(800) 265-2171	(716) 874-3630	(519) 749-3136
Electronic Arts	(800) 245-4525	same	(415) 571-7995
Electronic Frontier Foundation	(202) 347-5400	same	(202) 861-1258
Electronic Imagery	(800) 645-9657	same	(305) 968-7319
Elographics	(615) 482-4100	same	(615) 482-6617
Emigré	(916) 451-4344	same	(916) 451-4351
Empress Software	(301) 220-1919	same	(301) 220-1997
Emulex	(800) 854-7112	same	(714) 668-6819
Enable Software	(800) 888-0684	(518) 877-8236	(518) 877-5225; 877-3337 (sales fax)
Epson America	(800) 922-8911	NA	NA
Ergotron	(800) 888-8458	same	(612) 681-7715
ETC Computer	(510) 226-6250	same	(510) 226-6252
ETEQ Microsystems	(408) 432-8147	same	(408) 432-8146
Everex Systems	(800) 821-0806	(510) 498-4410	(510) 651-0728
Exabyte	(303) 442-4333	(800) 445-7736	(303) 417-7170
Exide Electronics	(800) 554-3448	same	(800) 753-9433
ExperVision	(800) 732-3897	(408) 428-9234	(408) 456-0823
Facit	(800) 879-3224	same	(603) 647-2724
Farallon Computing	(510) 814-5000	same	(510) 814-5023
FileNet	(714) 966-3400	(714) 966-9990	(714) 966-3490
Folex Film Systems	(800) 631-1150	same	(201) 575-4646
Folio	(800) 543-6546	same	(801) 344-3790
FontBank	(708) 328-7370	(305) 445-6304, ext. 1	(708) 328-7432
Fora	(800) 367-3672	NA	NA
Foresight Resources	(800) 231-8574	(816) 891-8418	(816) 891-8018
Franklin Quest Technologies	(800) 877-1814	same	(801) 978-1133
Free Computer Technology	(408) 945-1118	same	(408) 945-0604
Fuji Photo Film	(914) 789-8100	NA	NA
Fujitsu America	(800) 626-4686	(408) 894-3950	(408) 432-1318
Funk Software	(800) 828-4146	(617) 497-6339	(617) 547-1031
Future Domain	(800) 879-7599	(714) 253-0440	(714) 253-0913
FutureSoft Engineering	(713) 496-9400	same	(713) 496-1090
Futurus	(800) 327-8296	(404) 825-0379	(404) 392-9313
Gazelle Systems	(800) 786-3278	(801) 377-1288	(801) 373-6933
GEC Plessey Semiconductors	(408) 438-2900	same	(408) 438-5576
General Parametrics	(800) 223-0999	(510) 524-1060	(510) 524-9954
General Ribbon	(800) 423-5400	same	(818) 709-1209
Genesis Integrated Systems	(800) 325-6582	(612) 557-9226	(612) 544-4347
Genoa Systems	(800) 934-3662	(408) 432-8324	(408) 434-0997
Genovation	(714) 833-3355	same	(714) 833-0322
Glenco Engineering	(800) 562-2543	same	(708) 808-0313
GMC Technology	(909) 468-5686	same	(909) 595-0790
Golden Power Systems	(805) 582-4400	same	(805) 583-4411
Goldstar Technology	(800) 777-1192	same	(800) 448-4026
Graphic Enterprises of Ohio	(800) 321-9874	same	(800) 358-2230
Great Plains Software	(800) 456-0025	same	(701) 281-3752; 281-3171
Group 1 Software	(800) 368-5806	same	(301) 306-4373
GVC Technologies	(800) 289-4821	same	(201) 579-2702

Computer Products and Services (cont'd)

Company	Phone	Tech Support	Fax
Hayes Microcomputer Products	(800) 426-7704	NA	NA
Health Software	(216) 759-2103	same	(216) 759-7563
Hercules Computer Technology	(800) 532-0600	(510) 623-6050	(510) 623-1112
Hewlett-Packard	(800) 752-0900	same	N/A
Hitachi America	(800) 369-0422	(800) 241-6558, ex. 22	(404) 242-1414
Hooleon	(800) 937-1337	same	(602) 634-4620
Horizons Technology	(619) 292-8320	same	(619) 565-1175
HyperData	(909) 468-2955	same	(909) 468-2961
Hyundai Electronics America	(408) 473-9200	(800) 289-4986	(408) 943-9567
IBC/Integrated Business Computers	(800) 468-5847	NA	NA
IBM	(800) 426-3333	same	NA
In Focus Systems	(800) 327-7231	same	(503) 685-8631
Indiana Cash Drawer	(317) 398-6643	same	(317) 392-0958
Infomatic Power Systems	(310) 948-2217	same	(310) 948-5264
Intel	(800) 538-3373	(503) 264-7000	(503) 629-7580
Intellicom	(800) 992-2882	same	(818) 882-2404
International Keytech	(909) 598-6219	same	(909) 598-6379
International Power Machines	(800) 527-1208	same	(214) 494-2690
International Power Technology	(801) 224-4828	same	(801) 224-5872
Interphase	(214) 919-9000	same	(214) 919-9200
Intuit	(800) 624-8742	same	(415) 852-9370
Iomega	(800) 456-5522	same	(801) 778-3450
IPC America	(512) 339-3500	(800) 752-4171	(800) 752-4171
Iterated Systems	(800) 437-2285	same	(404) 840-0806
J-Mark Computer	(818) 814-9472	same	(818) 960-5937
JetFax	(800) 753-8329	same	(415) 326-6003
JMR Electronics	(818) 993-4801	same	(818) 993-9173
Joindata Systems	(818) 330-6553	same	(818) 330-6865
Jovian Logic	(510) 651-4823	same	(510) 651-1343
JVC Company of America	(201) 808-2100	same or (800) 252-5722	(201) 808-1370
Kalok	(408) 747-1315	same	(408) 747-1319
KAO Infosystems	(800) 274-5520	same	(508) 747-5521
KentMarsh	(800) 325-3587	(713) 522-8906	(713) 522-8965
Key Power	(310) 699-2438	same	(310) 699-0428
KeyTronic	(800) 262-6006	same	(509) 927-5224
KFC U.S.A.	(800) 253-2872	same	(800) 253-2872
Kingston Technology	(800) 845-2545	(800) 435-0640	(714) 435-2699
Knowledge Adventure	(800) 542-4240	same	(818) 542-4205
KnowledgePoint	(800) 727-1133	same	(707) 762-0802
Kofax Image Products	(714) 727-1733	same	(714) 727-3144
Koutech Systems	(310) 699-5340	same	(310) 699-0795
KYE International	(800) 456-7593	(909) 923-2417	(909) 923-1469
Kyocera Electronics	(800) 323-0470	same	(908) 560-8380
L.A. Computer	(310) 533-7177	same	(310) 533-6955
Labtec Enterprises	(206) 896-2000	same, ext. 105	(206) 896-2020
LaserTools	(510) 420-8777	same	(510) 420-1150
Leading Edge Products	(800) 874-3340	same	(508) 836-4504
Legacy Storage Systems	(800) 966-6442	same	(905) 475-1088
Linco Computer	(714) 990-2288	NA	NA
Link Technologies	(800) 448-5465	same	(510) 651-8808
Logical Operations	(800) 456-4677	same	(716) 288-7411
Logitech	(800) 231-7717	(510) 795-8100	(510) 792-8901
Longshine Electronics	(310) 903-0899	same	(310) 944-2201
Lotus Development	(800) 343-5414	same	(617) 225-1197
Lucas Deeco	(510) 471-4700	same	(510) 489-3500

Computer Products and Services (cont'd)

Company	Phone	Tech Support	Fax
M. Bryce & Associates	(813) 786-4567	same	(813) 786-4765
MA Laboratories	(408) 954-8188	same	(408) 954-0944
Mag InnoVision	(800) 827-3998	same	(714) 751-5522
Magic Solutions	(201) 587-1515	(201) 587-1517	(201) 587-8005
Mannesmann Tally	(800) 843-1347	same	(206) 251-5520
Manzanita Software Systems	(800) 447-5700	same	(916) 781-3814
MapInfo	(800) 327-8627	(800) 552-2511	(518) 275-6066
Mass Memory Systems	(407) 629-1081	same	(407) 628-3862
Mass Optical Storage Technologies	(714) 898-9400	same	(714) 373-9960
Matrix Digital Products	(800) 227-5723	same	(818) 566-1476
Matrox Electronic Systems	(800) 361-1408	(514) 685-0270	(514) 685-2853
Maxell of America	(800) 533-2836	same	(201) 796-8790
Maxoptix	(800) 848-3092	same	(408) 954-9711
Maxpeed	(415) 345-5447	same	(415) 345-6398
Maynard Electronics	(800) 821-8782	same	(407) 263-3555
Media Vision	(800) 845-5870	(800) 638-2807	(510) 770-9592
Megahertz	(800) 527-8677	(801) 320-7777	(801) 272-6077
Megatel Computer	(416) 245-2953	same	(416) 245-2953
Meridian Data	(800) 767-2537	(800) 755-8324	(408) 438-6816
Mextel	(800) 888-4146	same	(708) 595-4149
Micro Design International	(800) 228-0891	same	(407) 677-8365
Micro Direct International	(714) 251-1818	same	(714) 251-1877
Micro Palm Computers	(800) 832-0512	same	(603) 424-0330
Micro Solutions Computer Products	(815) 756-3411	same	(815) 756-2928
Micro Star Software	(800) 444-1343	(619) 931-4949	(619) 931-4950
Micro-Integration Bluelynx	(800) 642-5888	same	(301) 689-0808
Micrografx	(800) 733-3729	(214) 234-2694	(214) 234-2410
MicroMat Computer Systems	(800) 829-6227	same	(415) 897-3901
MicroNet Computer Systems	(714) 453-6100	(714) 453-6060	(714) 453-6061
Microprose	(410) 771-0440	(410) 771-1151	(410) 771-1174
Microrim	(800) 628-6990	(206) 649-9551	(206) 746-9350
MicroSlate	(514) 444-3680	same	(514) 444-3683
Microsoft	(800) 426-9400	same	(206) 883-8101
Microspeed	(800) 232-7888	same	(510) 490-1665
MicroStep	(818) 964-5048	same	(818) 336-5170
Microtest	(800) 526-9675	same	(602) 952-6401
MicroTouch Systems	(800) 866-6873	same	(508) 659-9100
Minuteman UPS	(800) 238-7272	same	(214) 446-9011
Mitsubishi Electronics America	(800) 843-2515	(800) 344-6352	(714) 236-6453
Monterey Electronics	(408) 437-5496	same	(408) 437-5499
Moses Computers	(408) 358-1550	same	(408) 356-9049
Mountain Network Solutions	(800) 458-0300	same	(408) 379-4302
Multi-Industry Technology	(800) 366-6481	same	(310) 802-9218
Multi-Tech Systems	(800) 328-9717	(800) 972-2439	(612) 785-9874
Mustang Software	(800) 999-9619	(805) 873-2550	(805) 395-0713
Mylex	(800) 776-9539	same	(510) 745-8016
Myriad	(510) 659-8782	same	(510) 659-8526
Nanao U.S.A.	(800) 800-5202	same	(201) 288-0729
National Instruments	(800) 433-3488	same	(512) 794-5794
National Semiconductor	(800) 272-9959	same	(800) 428-0065
NCL America	(408) 737-2496	same	(408) 730-1621
NCR	(800) 531-2222	same	(513) 445-4184
NEC Technologies	(800) 632-4636	(800) 388-8888	(508) 264-8673
Network Security Systems	(800) 755-7078	same	(619) 296-8039
New Media Graphics	(800) 288-2207	same	(508) 663-6678

Computer Products and Services (cont'd)

Company	Phone	Tech Support	Fax
Newer Technology	(800) 678-3726	same	(316) 685-9368
NewGen Systems	(800) 756-0556	(714) 436-5150	(714) 641-2800
Nikon	(800) 645-6687	same	(516) 547-0305
NMB Technologies	(800) 662-8321	(818) 341-3355	(818) 341-8207
Northgate Computer Systems	(800) 548-1993	same	(612) 943-6960
Novell	(800) 638-9273	same	(801) 429-3944
Now Software	(503) 274-2800	(503) 274-2815	(503) 274-0670
Ntergaid	(203) 380-1280	(203) 882-0838	(203) 882-0850
Numonics	(800) 247-4517	same	(215) 361-0167
nView	(800) 736-8439	(800) 775-7575	(804) 873-2153
Ocron	(800) 933-1399	(510) 252-0200	(510) 252-0202
Odyssey Development	(800) 992-4797	same	(303) 394-0096
Omnicomp Graphics	(713) 464-2990	same	(713) 827-7540
OnTrack Computer Systems	(800) 872-2599	same	(612) 937-5750
OPTi	(408) 980-8178	same	(408) 727-6917
Optibase	(800) 451-5101	same	(214) 386-2295
Optical Devices	(310) 320-9768	same	(310) 320-9357
Optima Technology	(714) 476-0515	same	(714) 476-0613
Orchid Technology	(800) 767-2443	(510) 683-0323	(510) 490-9312
Orientec of America	(818) 442-1818	same	(818) 442-8880
Output Technology	(509) 536-0468	same, ext. 491	(509) 533-1280
Overland Data	(800) 729-8725	same	(619) 571-0982
Pacific Data Products	(619) 552-0880	same	(619) 552-0889
Pacific Magnetics	(619) 474-8216	same	(619) 474-3979
Pacific Rim Systems	(800) 722-7461	same	(510) 782-1017
Panamax	(800) 472-5555	(415) 499-3900	(415) 472-5540
Panasonic Communications & Systems	(800) 742-8086	same	(201) 392-4792
Panduit	(800) 777-3300	same	(708) 532-1811
Parity Systems	(800) 514-4080	same	(408) 378-1022
Passport Designs	(415) 726-0280	(415) 726-3826	(415) 726-2254
Passport Software	(800) 969-7900	same	(708) 729-7909
Peachtree Software	(800) 554-8900	(404) 923-4318	(404) 564-5888
Pelikan	(615) 794-9000	same	(615) 794-4425
Perceptive Solutions	(800) 486-3278	same	(214) 953-1774
Percon	(800) 873-7266	same	(503) 344-1399
Peripheral Land	(800) 288-8754	same	(510) 683-9713
Phoenix Technologies	(800) 677-7300	NA	NA
Physician Micro Systems	(206) 441-8490	same	(206) 441-8915
Pinnacle Micro	(800) 553-7070	same	(714) 789-3150
Pioneer Communications of America	(800) 527-3766	same	(310) 952-2990
Pivar Computing Services	(800) 266-8378	same	(708) 459-6095
PKware	(414) 354-8699	same	(414) 352-3815
Plasmaco	(914) 883-6800	same	(914) 883-6867
PowerCom America	(800) 288-9807	same	(805) 962-0104
Practical Peripherals	(404) 840-9966	same	(805) 374-7216
Prima Storage Solutions	(408) 727-2600	same	(408) 727-2435
Primavera Systems	(800) 423-0245	(610) 668-3030	(215) 667-7894
Prime Portable Manufacturer	(800) 966-7237	(818) 444-7606	(818) 444-1027
Procom Technology	(800) 800-8600	same	(714) 549-0527
Procomp U.S.A.	(216) 234-6387	same	(216) 234-2233
Progen Technology	(714) 549-5818	same, ext. 108 or 111	(714) 549-8001
Progress Software	(800) 327-8445	same	(617) 275-4595
Prolink Computer	(213) 780-7978	same	(213) 780-7984
Prometheus Products	(800) 477-3473	(503) 692-9601	(503) 691-5197
Proxim	(800) 229-1630	same	(415) 964-5181

Computer Products and Services (cont'd)

Company	Phone	Tech Support	Fax
Proxima	(800) 447-7694	same	(619) 457-9647
PS Solutions	(214) 980-2632	same	(214) 783-6997
QMS	(800) 523-2696	same	NA
Qualitas	(800) 733-1377	(301) 907-7400	(301) 907-0905
Quantum	(800) 624-5545	(800) 826-8022	(408) 922-0735
Quantum Designs Computer	(310) 908-1029	same	(310) 908-1033
Quark	(800) 788-7835	(303) 894-8822	(303) 894-3398
QuaTech	(800) 553-1170	same	(216) 434-1409
Radiometrics Midwest	(708) 932-7262	same	(708) 932-7271
Radius	(800) 227-2795	(408) 541-5700	(408) 434-0770
Rainbow Technologies	(800) 852-8569	same	(714) 454-8557
Rancho Technology	(909) 987-3966	same	(909) 989-2365
RCI	(908) 874-4072	same	(908) 874-5274
RealWorld	(800) 678-6336	same	(603) 224-1955
Recognita of America	(800) 255-4627	same	(408) 241-6009
Red Wing Business Systems	(800) 732-9464	same	(612) 388-7950
Relialogic	(510) 770-3990	same	(510) 770-3994
Relisys	(408) 945-9000	same	(408) 945-0587
Reply	(800) 955-5295	same	(408) 942-4897
Rexon/Tecmar	(800) 422-2587	same	(216) 349-9176
Ricoh	(800) 955-3453	same	(408) 432-8372
Riso	(508) 777-7377	(508) 750-8497	(508) 777-2517
Rockwell	(800) 436-9988	(800) 854-8099	(714) 833-4391
Roland Digital Group	(213) 685-5141	same	(213) 722-0911
S-MOS Systems	(408) 954-0120	same	(408) 922-0238
Sampo of America	(404) 449-6220	same	(404) 447-1109
Sampson MIDI Source	(800) 726-6434	same	(214) 328-1092
Samsung Electronics America	(800) 624-8999, ext. 85	(310) 453-0614	(310) 453-2814
Samtron	(800) 726-8766	same	(310) 802-8820
Santa Cruz Operations (SCO)	(800) 726-8649	same	NA
SBT	(800) 944-1000	(415) 444-9700	(415) 444-9902
SCI Systems	(205) 882-4800	same	(205) 882-4305
Scitor	(415) 570-7700	same	(415) 462-4301
Seagate Technology	(800) 468-3472	(408) 438-8222	(408) 438-6172
Security Microsystems	(800) 345-7390	(718) 667-4720	(718) 667-0131
Shape Electronics	(800) 367-5811	same	(708) 620-0784
Sharp Electronics	(800) 237-4277	same	(201) 529-9695
Shiva	(617) 252-6300	(617) 270-8400	(800) 370-6917
Shuttle Computer International	(408) 945-1480	same	(408) 945-1481
Silicon Graphics	(800) 800-7441	same	(415) 961-0595
Silicon Star International	(510) 623-0500	same	(510) 623-1092
Silicon Systems	(800) 624-8999	same	(714) 573-6914
Smart Technologies	(403) 245-0333	same	(403) 245-0366
Softkey/Spinnaker	(800) 227-5609	(404) 428-0008	NA
SoftSolutions Technology	(801) 226-6000	(800) 861-2140	(801) 224-0920
Software Directions	(800) 346-7638	(201) 584-3882	(201) 584-7771
Software Products International	(800) 937-4774	same	(619) 450-1921
Software Publishing	(800) 282-6003	NA	NA
Software Toolworks, The	(800) 234-3088	(415) 883-5157	(415) 883-3303
Sola Electric	(800) 879-7652	same	(800) 626-6269
Soletek Computer Supply	(800) 437-1518	same, ext. 3017	(619) 457-2681
Sonera Technologies	(800) 932-6323	(908) 747-6886	(908) 747-4523
Sony of America	(800) 582-7669	same	(201) 930-7201
SourceMate Information Systems	(800) 877-8896	(415) 381-1793	(415) 381-6902
Sprite	(408) 773-8888	same	(408) 773-8892

Computer Products and Services (cont'd)

Company	Phone	Tech Support	Fax
SRW Computer Components	(800) 547-7766	same	(714) 259-8037
Stac Electronics	(800) 522-7822	(619) 929-3900	(619) 794-7578
Star Gate Technologies	(800) 782-7428	same	(216) 349-2056
Star Micronics	(800) 227-8274	same	(212) 286-9063
Statpower Technologies	(604) 420-1585	same	(604) 420-1591
STB Systems	(800) 234-4334	same	(214) 234-1306
Storage Technology	(800) 733-7381	same	(303) 673-5019
Summit Micro Design	(408) 739-6348	same	(408) 739-4643
Sun Microsystems	(800) 872-4786	same	(415) 969-9131
Suncom Technologies	(708) 647-4040	same	(708) 647-7827
SuperMac	(800) 541-7680	same	(408) 541-5008
SuperTime	(905) 764-3530	same	(905) 771-6170
Supra	(800) 727-8772	same	(503) 967-2401
Symantec	(800) 441-7234	same	(800) 554-4403
Symphony Laboratories	(408) 986-1701	same	(408) 986-1771
Synchronics	(800) 852-5852	(800) 852-8755	(901) 683-8303
Synergystex	(216) 225-3112	same	(216) 225-0419
Syntel Communications	(908) 651-0415	same	(908) 805-0596
SyQuest Technology	(800) 245-2278	same	(510) 226-4100
Sysgration U.S.A.	(415) 306-7860	NA	NA
Syspro Impact Software	(800) 369-8649	same	(714) 437-1407
Systems Plus	(800) 222-7701	(415) 969-7066	(415) 969-0118
Systems Strategies	(212) 279-8400	same	(212) 967-8368
Tandy	(817) 390-3011	(800) 843-7422	(817) 390-2774
Tatung Company of America	(800) 827-2850	same	(310) 637-8484
TDK Electronics	(516) 625-0100	• same	(516) 625-0651
Teac America	(213) 726-0303	(213) 727-7674	(213) 727-7656
Telemagic	(800) 835-6244	same	(619) 431-4006
Telex Communications	(612) 887-5531	(800) 331-2623	(612) 884-0043
Texas Instruments	(800) 527-3500	same	(512) 345-9509
Texas Microsystems	(800) 627-8700	same	(713) 933-1029
TextWare	(801) 645-9600	same	(801) 645-9610
THEOS Software	(510) 935-1118	same	(510) 935-1177
Thomas-Conrad	(800) 332-8683	(800) 334-4112	(512) 836-2840
TimeKeeping Systems	(216) 361-9995	same	(216) 361-0030
T/Maker	(415) 962-0195	same	(415) 962-0201
TMC Research	(408) 262-0888	same	(408) 262-1082
Toshiba America	(800) 334-3445	(800) 999-4273	(714) 583-3140
TOSOH U.S.A.	(800) 238-6764	same	(415) 888-2800
TouchStone Software	(800) 531-0450	same	(714) 960-1886
Trace Mountain	(408) 441-8040	(800) 468-7223	(408) 441-3420
Transition Engineering	(800) 325-2725	same	(612) 941-2322
Transitional Technology	(800) 437-4884	same	(714) 693-0225
Traveling Software	(800) 662-2652	(206) 483-8088	(206) 487-1284
Trident Microsystems	(415) 691-9211	same	(415) 691-9260
Tripp Lite Manufacturing	(312) 329-1777	same	(312) 329-9620
Triton Technologies	(800) 322-9440	same	(908) 855-9608
Truevision	(800) 344-8783	same	(317) 576-7700
Tseng Labs	(215) 968-0502	same	(215) 860-7713
Twelve Tone Systems	(800) 234-1171	(617) 924-6275	(617) 273-1494
Twinhead	(800) 545-8946	same	(408) 945-1080
US Robotics	(800) 342-5877	(800) 550-7800	(708) 676-7320
UDP Fonts	(800) 888-4413	same	(310) 782-1527
UDS Motorola	(800) 631-4869	(800) 221-4380	(205) 830-5657
Ultima Electronics	(510) 659-1580	same	(510) 440-1217

Computer Products and Services (cont'd)

Company	Phone	Tech Support	Fax
UltraStor	(714) 581-4100	(714) 581-4016	(714) 581-4102
Unlimited Systems	(619) 622-1400	(619) 622-1400	(619) 550-7330
Upsonic	(800) 877-6642	same	(714) 448-9555
US Logic/HM System	(800) 777-4875	(619) 467-1100	(619) 467-1011
Varta Batteries	(914) 592-2500	NA	NA
Corel Software	(800) 772-6735	same	(619) 673-7777
Verbatim	(704) 547-6500	same	(704) 547-6609
Videomedia	(408) 227-9977	same	(408) 227-6707
Videx	(503) 758-0521	same	(503) 752-5285
ViewSonic	(800) 888-8583	same	(909) 869-7958
Visionetics International	(310) 316-7940	same	(310) 316-7457
VLSI Technology	(602) 752-8574	(602) 752-6367	(602) 752-6000
Voyetra Technologies	(800) 233-9377	(914) 966-0600	(914) 738-6946
Wallaby Software	(201) 490-3100	(800) 638-4726	(201) 490-3101
WangDat	(216) 349-0600	same	(216) 349-0851
Wangtek	(800) 992-9916	same	(805) 522-1576
Western Telematic	(800) 854-7226	same	(714) 583-9514
Westrex	(617) 254-1200	same	(617) 254-6848
Wolfram Research	(800) 441-6284	(217) 398-6500	(217) 398-0747
WordPerfect	(800) 451-5151	NA	(801) 222-5077
WordStar	(800) 227-5609	(404) 428-0008	(415) 382-4952
XDB Systems	(800) 488-4948	(410) 312-9400	(410) 312-9500
Xing Technology	(805) 473-0145	same	(805) 473-0147
Xircom	(800) 775-0400	(805) 376-9200	(818) 878-7630
XyQuest	(410) 576-2040	same	(410) 576-1968
Y-E Data America	(708) 291-2340	(708) 855-0890	(708) 498-2430
Yamaha of America	(800) 543-7457	same	(408) 437-8791
Young Micro Systems	(310) 802-8899	same	(310) 802-8889
Z-Ram	(800) 368-4726	same	(714) 830-4726
Zedcor	(602) 881-8101	same	(800) 482-4511
Zenith Data Systems	(800) 582-0524	same	(800) 582-8194
Zoom Telephonics	(800) 631-3116	(617) 423-1076	(617) 423-9231
ZSoft	(404) 428-0008	same	(404) 427-1150
Zyxel Communications	(800) 255-4101	(714) 693-0808	(714) 693-8811

NA: Not available or not applicable   *Source: Computer Vendors Directory*

The Top Reference Sources

Before & After, $36/year
(916) 784-3880

Published bimonthly, *Before and After* is a four-color newsletter devoted to teaching amateur computer users to look like professionals in print.

Each issue has in-depth, step-by-step instructions on how to choose type, draw shadows, buttons, or logos, and use photos in articles. A consistently well-written, compellingly designed publication, *Before and After* is endlessly useful.

Specialized Computer Resources

Contact Options

Insurance:

Safeware
2929 N. High St.
Columbus, OH 43202
(800) 848-3469

The Computer Insurance Agency
6150 Old Millersport Rd., NE
Pleasantville, OH 43148
(800) 722-0385

Typefaces:

FontHaus
1375 Kings Hwy., E
Fairfield, CT 06430
(800) 942-9110

Monotype
150 S. Wacker Dr., Suite 2630
Chicago, IL 60606
(800) 666-6897

Off-Site Data Storage:

Iron Mountain
745 Atlantic Ave.
Boston, MA 02111
(617) 357-6966

Hard Disk Crash Recovery:

Drivesavers
400 Bel Marin Keys Blvd.
Novato, CA 94949
(415) 883-4232

Data Recovery Technology
5029 Stavan Creek Blvd.
Santa Clara, CA 95051
(408) 249-1986

Computer Peripheral Repair
11440 Okeechobee Rd., Suite 200
Royal Palm Beach, FL 33411
(800) 765-9292

Software Piracy:

Software Publishers of America
1730 M St., NW, Suite 700
Washington, DC 20036
(800) 388-7478

CD-ROM:

CD-ROM Professional
Magazine for CD-ROM Publishers
Pemberton Press
462 Danbury Rd.
Wilton, CT 06897
(203) 761-1466

Specialized Software Directories:

Redgate Communications
660 Beachland Blvd.
Vero Beach, FL 32963
(407) 231-6904

Electronic Mail

USING ELECTRONIC MAIL (E-MAIL), a business can instantly send a message to an employee or customer anywhere in the world. Unlike faxes, e-mail permits the recipient to edit the message and work with the data sent.

All electronic bulletin boards and information services provide their users with access to e-mail within the system. It is a straightforward and simple task to send mail to anyone on the same system. For this reason, many companies are asking their employees and customers to join one system or another.

Inter-bulletin board communication is handled through the Internet. Once an Internet address is known, most information systems (and some bulletin boards) permit users to send mail through the Internet. For example, to reach the editors of the *Information Please Business Almanac*, send mail from any service with Internet access to the Internet address: ALMANAC@SGP.COM.

Electronic Mail (cont'd)

Contact Options

Popular Electronic Mail Services:

America Online
(800) 827-6364

ATT Mail
(800) 367-7225

CompuServe
(800) 848-8990

Delphi
(800) 544-4005

eWorld
(800) 775-4556

GEnie
(800) 638-9636

MCI Mail
(800) 444-6245

Prodigy
(800) 776-3449

Recommended Resource

*The Electronic Mail Advantage: Applications
and Benefits*
Electronic Mail Association, $10
1655 N. Fort Myer Dr., Suite 850
Arlington, VA 22209
(703) 524-5550

Point and Click Internet
Peachpit Press, $12.95
(510) 548-4393

The Internet

MORE THAN 20 YEARS AGO, DARPA, a division of the Pentagon, created a network of computers being used by its researchers. These computers were located at universities and research facilities around the world. The purpose of the network was to permit researchers at one facility to contact others, and to exchange information as well.

Once the protocol for this network was established, the number of users and number of uses skyrocketed. With more than 5,000,000 people currently "on" the Internet, it has become the de facto standard for electronic mail.

In addition to a huge base of mail users, the Internet provides access to hundreds of millions of pieces of data. A quick search could find a state-of-the-art paper on the uses of silicon in biomedical engineering, or an article spoofing the latest State of the Union Address.

In general, a user can access the Internet only through a provider. The following is a list of Internet access providers:

Contact Options

ADVANCED NETWORK AND SERVICES (ANS) and ANS CORE
1875 Campus Commons Dr., Suite 220
Reston, VA 22091
(800) 456-8267
Net address: info@ans.net
Area served: U.S. and international
Services: Network connections

ALTERNET
3060 Williams Dr., Sixth Floor
Fairfax, VA 22031
(800) 488-6384 or
(703) 204-8000
Net address: alternet-info@uunet.uu.net
Area served: U.S.
Services: Network connections

AMERICA ONLINE
8619 Westwood Center Dr.
Vienna, VA 22182
(800) 827-6364
Net address: info@aol.com
Area served: U.S. and Canada
Services: Dial-up e-mail, other services

BARRNET
Bay Area Regional Research Network
Pine Hall, Room 115
Stanford, CA 94305
(415) 528-7070
Net address: gd.why@forsythe.stanford.edu
Area served: San Francisco Bay area,
northern California
Services: Network connections, national dial-up IP,
dial-up e-mail

TIP: *Many of the e-mail addresses in this list give automated responses to queries. A user who has an e-mail address simply sends mail to the appropriate address, and in a short time, a response with all pertinent information about the provider, including services and rates, is sent back to the user.*

The Internet (cont'd)

CERFNET
California Education and Research
Federation Network
P.O. Box 85608
San Diego, CA 92186
(800) 876-2373 or
(619) 455-3900
Net address: help@cerf.net
Area served: California and international
Services: Network connections, national dial-up IP,
dial-up e-mail

CICNET
Committee on Institutional Cooperation Network
ITI Building
2901 Hubbard Dr., Pod G
Ann Arbor, MI 48105
(313) 998-6103
Net address: info@cic.net
Area served: Continental U.S.
Services: Network connections

CLASS
Cooperative Agency for Library Systems
and Services
1415 Koll Circle, Suite 101
San Jose, CA 95112
(800) 488-4559 or
(408) 453-0444
Net address: class@class.org
Area served: U.S.
Services: Dial-up access for libraries in the U.S.

COLORADO SUPERNET
999 18th St., Suite 2640
Denver, CA 80202
(303) 296-8202
Net address: info@csn.net
Area served: Colorado
Services: Network connections, dial-up IP

COMMUNITY NEWS SERVICE
Internet Express
1155 Kelly Jonson Blvd.
Colorado Springs, CO 80920
(800) 592-1240 or
(719) 579-9120
Net address: service@usa.net
Area served: Colorado Springs (719 area code)
Services: Dial-up e-mail, other services

COMPUSERVE INFORMATION SYSTEM
5000 Arlington Center Boulevard
P.O. Box 20212
Columbus, OH 43220
(614) 457-0802 or
(800) 848-8990
Net address: postmaster@csi.compuserve.com
Area served: U.S. and international
Services: Dial-up e-mail, other services

EXPRESS ACCESS ONLINE
COMMUNICATIONS SERVICE
Digital Express Group
6006 Greenbelt Rd., Suite 228
Greenbelt, MD 20770
(301) 847-5000; 5050
Net address: info@ss1.digex.com
Area served: Northern VA; Baltimore, MD;
Washington, DC
(area codes 202, 310, 410, 703)
Services: Dial-up e-mail, other services

HALCYON
P.O. Box 40597
Bellevue, WA 98015
(206) 455-3505
Net address: info@remote.halcyon.com
Area served: Seattle, WA
Services: Dial-up e-mail

HOLONET
Information Access Technologies
46 Shattuck Sq., Suite 11
Berkeley, CA 94704
(510) 704-0160
Net address: info@holonet.mailer.net
Area served: U.S.
Services: Dial-up e-mail

INFOLAN
Infonet Service
2100 E. Grand Ave.
El Segundo, CA 90245
(310) 335-4548
Area served: International, including U.S., Europe,
Canada, Hong Kong, Japan, Singapore, and
Australia
Services: Dial-up IP, global dial, access to time-
shared host services for navigating and exchanging
mail over the Internet

INSTITUTE FOR GLOBAL COMMUNICATIONS
18 De Boom St.
San Francisco, CA 94107
(415) 442-0220
Net address: support@igc.apc.org
Area served: Worldwide
Services: Dial-up e-mail

JVNCNET
3 Independence Way
Princeton, NJ 08540
(609) 897-7300 or
(800) 358-4437
Net address: market@jvnc.net
Area served: U.S. and international
Services: Network connections, dial-up IP

The Internet (cont'd)

LOS NETTOS
University of Southern California
Information Sciences Institute
4676 Admiralty Way
Marina del Rey, CA 90292
(310) 822-1511
Net address: action@isi.edu
Area served: Los Angeles area, southern
California
Services: Network connections

MCI MAIL
1133 19th St., NW, Seventh Floor
Washington, DC 20036
(800) 444-6245 or
(202) 833-8484
Net address: 2671163@mcimail.com or
3248333@mcimail.com
Area served: U.S. and international
Services: Dial-up e-mail

MICHNET
4251 Plymouth Rd., Suite C
Ann Arbor, MI 48105
(313) 764-9430
Net address: info@merit.edu
Area served: Michigan
Services: Network connections, dial-up IP

MILWAUKEE INTERNET XCHANGE
Mix Communications
P.O. Box 17166
Milwaukee, WI 53217
(414) 351-1868
Net address: info@mixcom.com
Area served: Milwaukee, WI
Services: Dial-up e-mail

MRNET
Minnesota Regional Network
511 11th Avenue S., Box 212
Minneapolis, MN 55415
(612) 342-2570
Net address: info@mr.net
Area served: Minnesota
Services: Network connections

MSEN
320 Miller Ave.
Ann Arbor, MI 48103
(313) 998-4562
Net address: info@msen.com
Area served: U.S.
Services: Network connections, dial-up IP, dial-up
e-mail

NEARNET
New England Academic and Research Network
BBN Systems and Technologies
150 Cambridge Park Dr.
Cambridge, MA 02138
(617) 873-8730
Net address: ops@nic.near.net
Area served: Maine, Vermont, New Hampshire,
Connecticut, Massachusetts, Rhode Island
Services: Network connections, dial-up IP

NETCOM ONLINE COMMUNICATION
SERVICES
3031 Tisch Way
San Jose, CA 95117
(800) 501-8649 or
(408) 983-5950
Net address: info@netcom.com
Area served: California (area codes 213, 310, 408,
415, 510, 818)
Services: Dial-up e-mail, dial-up IP

NETILLINOIS
1840 Oak Ave.
Evanston, IL 60201
(708) 866-1825
Net address: info@illinois.net
Area served: Illinois
Services: Network connections

NEVADANET
P.O. Box 9060
Reno, NV 89507
(702) 784-6133
Net address: braddlee@nevada.edu
Area served: Nevada
Services: Network connections

NORTHWESTNET
Northwestern States Network
15400 S.E. 30th Pl., Suite 202
Bellview, WA 98007
(206) 562-3000
Net address: info@nwnet.net
Area served: Academic and research sites in
Alaska, Idaho, Montana North Dakota, Oregon,
Wyoming, and Washington
Services: Network connections

NYSERNET
New York State Education and Research Network
200 Elwood Davis Rd., Suite 103
Liverpool, NY 13088
(315) 453-2912
Net address: info@nysernet.org
Area served: New York state and international
Services: Network connections, dial-up e-mail,
dial-up IP

The Internet (cont'd)

OARNET
Ohio Academic Research Network
Ohio Supercomputer Center
2455 Northstar Rd.
Columbus, OH 43221
(800) 627-8101 or
(614) 728-8100
Net address: info@oar.net
Area served: Ohio
Services: Network connections

PANIX PUBLIC ACCESS UNIX
15 W. 18th St., Fifth Floor
New York, NY 10011
(212) 877-4854
Net address: staff@panix.com
Area served: New York, NY (area codes 212, 718)
Services: Dial-up e-mail

PERFORMANCE SYSTEMS
510 Huntmor Park Dr.
Herndon, VA 22070
(800) 827-7482 or
(703) 709-0300
Net address: all-info@psi.com
Area served: U.S. and international
Services: Network connections, dial-up e-mail,
dial-up IP

PORTAL COMMUNICATIONS
20863 Stevens Creek Blvd., Suite 200
Cupertino, CA 95014
(408) 973-9111
Net address: cs@cup.portal.com
info@portal.com
Area served: Northern California (area codes 408,
415)
Services: Dial-up e-mail

PREPNET
Pennsylvania Research and Economic Partnership
Network
305 S. Craig St., Second Floor
Pittsburgh, PA 15213
(412) 268-7870
Net address: nic@prep.net
Area served: Pennsylvania
Services: Network connections, dial-up IP

PSCNET
Pittsburgh Supercomputing Center Network
Pittsburgh Supercomputing Center
4400 Fifth Ave.
Pittsburgh, PA 15213
(412) 268-4960
Net address: pscnet-admin@psc.edu
Area served: Pennsylvania, Ohio, and West Virginia
Services: Network connections

RADIOMAIL
2600 Campus Dr., Suite 175
San Mateo, CA 94403
(800) 597-6245
Net address: info@radiomail.net
Area served: U.S.
Services: RadioMail

RISCNET
InteleCom Data Systems
11 Franklin Rd.
East Greenwich, RI 02818
(401) 885-6855
Net address: info@nic.risc.net
Area served: New England
Services: Network connections, dial-up IP, dial-up
e-mail

SESQUINET
Texas Sesquicentennial Network
Office of Networking and Computing Systems
Box 1892
Rice University
Houston, TX 77251
(713) 527-4988
Net address: farrell@rice.edu
Area served: Texas
Services: Network connections, dial-up IP

SPRINT NSFNET ICM
Sprint NSFNET International Connections Manager
12490 Sunrise Valley Dr.
Reston, VA 22096
(703) 904-2230
Net address: rcollet@icm1.icp.net
Area served: International
Services: International network connections to NSF-
NET; operates under cooperative agreement with
NSF and conforms to CCIRN guidelines

SPRINTLINK
Sprint
13221 Woodland Park Rd.
Herndon, VA 22071
(703) 904-2167
Net address: rdoyle@icm1.icp.net
Area served: U.S. and international
Services: Network connections, dial-up IP

SURANET
Southeastern Universities Research Association
Network
8400 Baltimore Blvd., Suite 101
College Park, MD 20740
(301) 982-4600
Net address: adman@sura.net
Area served: Alabama, Florida, Georgia, Kentucky,
Louisiana, Mississippi, North Carolina, South Caro-
lina, Tennessee, Virginia, and West Virginia
Services: Network connections

The Internet (cont'd)

THENET
Texas Higher Education Network
Computation Center
University of Texas
Austin, TX 78712
(512) 471-5046
Net address: tracy@utexas.edu
Area served: Texas
Services: Network connections

UUNET TECHNOLOGIES
3060 Williams Dr.
Fairfax, VA 22031
(800) 488-6384 or
(703) 204-8000
Net address: info@uunet.uu.net
Area served: U.S.
Services: Network connections, dial-up e-mail

VERNET
Virginia Education and Research Network
Academic Computing Center
Gilmer Hall
University of Virginia
Charlottesville, VA 22903
(804) 924-0616
Net address: net-info@ver.net
Area served: Virginia
Services: Network connections

WESTNET
Southwestern States Network
UCC
601 S. Howes, Sixth Floor S.
Colorado State University
Fort Collins, CO 80523
(303) 491-7260
Net address: pburns@yuma.acns.colostate.edu
Area served: Arizona, Colorado, New Mexico, Utah, Idaho, and Wyoming
Services: Network connections

WHOLE EARTH 'LECTRONIC LINK (WELL)
27 Gate Five Rd.
Sausalito, CA 94965
(415) 332-4335
Net address: info@well.sf.ca.us
Area served: San Francisco Bay area (area code 415)
Services: Dial-up e-mail, international access, UNIX, Usenet

WISCNET
Madison Academic Computing Center
1210 W. Dayton St.
Madison, WI 53706
(608) 262-4241
Net address: tad@cs.wisc.edu
Area served: Wisconsin
Services: Network connections

THE WORLD
Software Tool & Die
1330 Beacon St.
Brookline, MA 02146
(617) 739-0202
Net address: office@world.std.com
Area served: Boston (area code 617)
Services: Dial-up e-mail, other services

WVNET
West Virginia Network for Educational Telecomputing
837 Chestnut Ridge Rd.
Morgantown, WV 26505
(304) 293-5192
Net address: cc011041@wvnvms.wvnet.edu
Area served: West Virginia
Services: Network connections, dial-up IP

Internet Business Resources

THE FOLLOWING IS A sample of the hundreds of business resources available on the Internet. To find additional sources, do a keyword search for "business" in one of the major Internet browsers, such as Veronica, Archie, or Lycos.

Newsgroups

- alt.business
- alt.business.misc
- alt.business.multi-level
- misc.entrepreneurs
- misc.int-property
- misc.invest
- misc.invest.funds
- misc.invest.stocks

World Wide Web

Chicago Mercantile Exchange home page

- http://www.interaccess.com/users/wilbirk

Internet Business Resources (cont'd)

Personal Finance Center

- http://nearnet.gnn.com/gnn/meta/finance/index.html

Stock Quotes

- http://www.secapl.com

Home-Based Business

- http://telescope.com/telescope/homebb/

Global Business Directory

- http://maple.net/gbd/Overview.html

Business Information Sources on the Internet

- http://www.uic.edu/~doralyn/business/dedwards.html

Mailing List

Investment Club

- i-club-list@iti.cmhnet.org

Impact of Information Technology

A SURVEY OF SMALL and mid-sized businesses by National Small Business United and Arthur Andersen Enterprises found that 77 percent feel that information technology is important for the success of their business. The following graph shows the areas that these businesses felt were most strongly impacted by information technology:

Impact of Information Technology on Small and Mid-Sized Businesses (%)

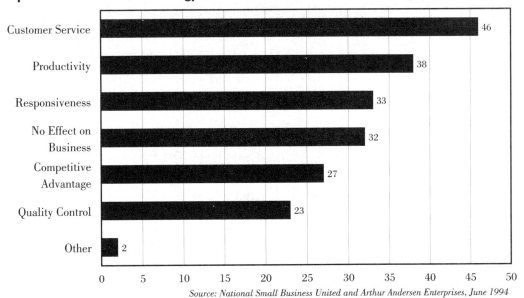

Source: National Small Business United and Arthur Andersen Enterprises, June 1994

> **TIP:** *There are literally hundreds of computer magazines. As the roster of titles changes almost daily, the best strategy is to start at your local newsstand. Consistent favorites are* MacUser, PCWorld, Boardwatch, InfoWorld *and* Computer Shopper.

Online Services

CompuServe

CompuServe is one of the oldest and largest online services. As the de facto standard, it offers a wide range of software and advice, allows users to send and receive electronic mail, and provides a wide range of non-computer-related information.

CompuServe offers a nationwide network of local phone numbers, which can be easily accessed by anyone with a computer and a modem. To obtain a local access number, call (800) 848-8199, 24 hours a day.

Once connected to CompuServe, the user can get detailed information on more than 1,000 topics, from wood carving to Amiga computers.

Divided into forums, the CompuServe service has segmented its users into nearly 1,000 special interest areas. This specialization allows the user to post a message directly to the people most interested in a topic. It's not unusual to post a question about a piece of software and receive more than a dozen answers within an hour.

In addition to forums and access to free files, CompuServe offers access to dozens of commercial services and databases. CompuServe will also monitor the wire services on request, clipping any stories that contain the keywords that the user has identified. The easiest way to use Compuserve is to use the forums to explore areas of interest.

CompuServe
500 Arlington Center Blvd.
P.O. Box 20212
Columbus, OH 43220
(800) 848-8199

Knight-Ridder Information

Knight-Ridder provides access to hundreds of research databases and publications. Corporations use it as a fast, easy way to search through the full text of thousands of publications.

By navigating through its occasionally difficult interface, a researcher can access all these sources in seconds.

Research-oriented services like Knight-Ridder and Nexis are quite expensive. Investigate subscription pricing as an alternative.

A 30-page list of Knight-Ridder publications can be requested by contacting Knight-Ridder directly.

Knight-Ridder
2440 El Camino Real
Mountain View, CA 94040
(800) 334-2564

Nexis

Nexis is a compendium of news. It features the full text of hundreds of magazines, ranging from *Time* to *Forbes* to obscure technical journals. It also contains every word that has passed through more than twenty news wires, including AP and the Xinhua News Agency.

Using Nexis, a business user can find every mention of a competitor or a topic over a given period of time. Far more efficient than a clipping service, Nexis allows users to perform complicated Boolean searches. For example, one could search for every instance of the word "wool" within three words of the phrase "cardigan sweaters." Within seconds, Nexis will find all relevant references. NOTE: Of all the services listed here, Nexis is far and away the most expensive.

Nexis
Mead Data Central
9393 Springboro Pike
Dayton, OH 45401
(800) 346-9759

Prodigy

Designed primarily for consumer use, Prodigy offers an excellent way to get basic information on a variety of sources. In addition, Prodigy's news and Wall Street services provide an extremely low-cost way to stay in touch with the world on a daily basis.

Prodigy
445 Hamilton Ave.
White Plains, NY 10601
(800) 776-3449

Dow Jones

Dow Jones News Retrieval is similar to Dialog and Nexis, in that it offers easy access to hundreds of publications. But Dow Jones focuses primarily on business, offering everything from *Barron's* to *Plastics World* online.

Dow Jones & Co.
P.O. Box 300
Princeton, NJ 08543
(609) 452-1511

Online Services (cont'd)

America Online

America Online (AOL) currently posts the largest membership of all electronic information services. It combines the friendly interface of Macintosh or Windows with a speedy and powerful information service. AOL provides user-friendly access to the Internet and the World Wide Web, as well as a large range of forums and information sources. AOL is highly recommended for first-time users of information services.

America Online
8619 Westwood Center Dr.
Vienna, VA 22182
(800) 827-6364 or (703) 448-8700

Other Online Services

Delphi
1030 Massachusetts Ave.
Cambridge, MA 02138
(800) 544-4005

eWorld
Apple Computer
20525 Mariani Ave., MS 36BC
Cupertino, CA 95014
(800) 775-4556

GEnie
General Electric
P.O. Box 6403
Rockville, MD 20849
(800) 638-9636

NewsNet
945 Haverford Rd.
Bryn Mawr, PA 19010
(800) 345-1301

Bulletin Boards

IT IS POSSIBLE to reach more than 70,000 bulletin boards around the world using a computer and a modem. These boards allow you to exchange software and data, find help on an awesome variety of topics, or just visit electronically with other computer users.

While there are a handful of large commercial bulletin boards, most are run by small businesses and individuals.

The typical bulletin board offers a large collection of shareware programs, frequently updated.

Many have specialties, which range from "adult" material to information on tropical fish. In addition, many give access to the Internet, allowing low-cost or free electronic mail around the world.

Recommended Resource

Boardwatch Magazine, $36/year
8500 W. Bowles Ave.
Littleton, CO 80123
(303) 973-6038

Selected Business-Oriented Bulletin Boards

Name	Phone	Baud Rate	Focus
The Ad Connection	(804) 978-3927	2400	Classified ads, shopping mall, and faxback services
American Business Research Net	(516) 754-9205	2400	Business services, files
American Home Business Network	(801) 273-5412	14400	For members of the American Home Business Association
The Bizopps Connection	(310) 677-7034	14400	Business, franchise, moneymaking opportunities
Bizynet	(619) 283-1721	14400	Full-feature business-oriented BBS
The Board Room BBS	(717) 393-2640	14400	Best of business shareware
The Business Center	(707) 451-0393	14400	Marketing of real estate, jobs, and foreign correspondence
Business Network Source	(201) 836-1844	14400	Business and minority business information
Business Online	(216) 332-2712	2400	For all interested in business
Business Opportunity BBS	(618) 423-2331	14400	Business opportunities, businesses for sale
The Bu$inessman's Special	(312) 736-5415	9600	Business files, online magazines, conferences
Career Connections	(415) 917-2125	14400	Career opportunities
Career Decisions BBS	(909) 864-8287	2400	Job ads, book reviews, recruiter directory, résumé service
Careers Online	(317) 873-6283	38400	Career placement for eng., mfg., computer professionals
City Senders BBS	(216) 734-1477	2400	Business and community advertising

Bulletin Boards (cont'd)

Name	Phone	Baud Rate	Focus
Cyberia	(717) 840-1444	57600	Small business section, many files
The "Delight the Customer" BBS	(616) 662-0393	14400	Networking, nationwide jobs database
DFG Financial BBS	(205) 745-0579	14411	Help for individuals and small businesses
The Digital X-Connect BBS	(214) 517-8315	14400	Job postings, résumés, job-related discussions
Edward Lowe Foundation	(616) 445-4342	28800	Small business and entrepreneur BBS
Electronic Publishers BBS	(503) 624-4966	14000	USA Today, closing stock quotes, etc.
Energy/Recycling BBS	(704) 547-3114	2400	Engineering, energy management, & waste recycling
Entrenet	(908) 647-2202	9600	Issues of interest to business owners
Evergreen BBS	(201) 398-2373	14400	Product sales and business opportunities
Executive Connection	(214) 306-3393	14400	Employment, careers, and business management
Fjob	(912) 757-3100	9600	Federal jobs
Free Financial Network	(212) 752-8660	14400	Largest financial BBS in the world
Home Business BBS	(512) 392-9489	19200	Dedicated to the home-based business entrepreneur
Ideas Online Business Net	(604) 324-3327	14400	Info on inventors, patentors, sales, marketing
Infonet International	(703) 591-5680	38400	International business-oriented network
Investors Online Data	(206) 285-5359	NA	Investment/stock market information
JoBBS	(404) 992-8937	NA	Job listings
Kimberely BBS	(612) 340-2489	9600	Economic data
Labor and Insurance Law BBS	(805) 495-9911	14400	Workers' compensation, labor, and insurance law issues
The Market BBS	(201) 467-3269	14400	Finance/investment and business-related topics
Marketing à la Carte	(508) 653-5151	14400	Marketing and business management
Max Ule	(212) 809-1160	9600	Online brokerage with competitive rates
The Meeting Works	(212) 737-6932	14400	For meeting and seminar planners
Moneyline Express	(718) 816-5502	2400	Home business ideas, consultation
Patent Hotline	(619) 723-4413	38400	Over 3,400 patents for sale or license
Pitstar BBS	(708) 687-4413	57600	Business/financial daily updated commodities quotes
Propnet	(202) 244-9291	14400	Doing business with the federal government
Sales Automation Success	(206) 392-8943	14400	How to use technology to improve sales and marketing
$ales Force	(817) 847-9255	14400	Database of resources of value to sales professionals
SBA Online	(800) 697-4636	9600	Small Business Administration
Search BBS	(206) 253-5213	2400	High-tech company profile database
Sleuth BBS	(818) 727-7639	14400	Full-feature business-oriented BBS
The Software Store	(516) 589-4984	9600	Professional business-related software
Stat Agline!	(604) 531-8818	2400	Agricultural market information, statistics
Strictly Business!	(614) 538-9250	2400	For entrepreneurs, managers, and business professionals
Successnet	(201) 653-6228	28800	Business-oriented BBS with online databases
Town Center Info Exchange	(410) 995-1809	14440	Business/community-oriented
The TQM BBS	(301) 585-1164	14400	Information in support of Total Quality Management
Trade Link	(604) 768-0988	14400	Promoting international trade
Traders' Connection	(317) 359-5199	14400	World's largest classified ad database, Wall Street Journal
Virtual Office Complex	(805) 339-0945	14400	Cyberspace office center
The Wall Street Connection	(808) 521-4356	14400	Investing, finance, and business
Wizinfo CBCS	(612) 721-8859	14400	Focus on small and home-based business
World Class Software BBS	(210) 656-7939	14400	Business software

Source: The "Delight the Customer" BBS

DOS Commands

DOS IS THE OPERATING SYSTEM used by more than 100 million computers around the world. Here are 28 common DOS commands, together with a brief description of their functions:

BACKUP	Archives data
BREAK	Turns cntrl–c on and off
CD	Change directory
CHKDSK	Checks a disk
CLS	Clear screen
COMP	Compares two files
COPY	Copy a file
DATE	Sets the date
DEL	Delete
DIR	Directory
DISKCOPY	Copy all files on a disk
FIND	Searches for text in a file
FORMAT	Wipes a disk and prepares for use
MD	Makes a directory
MEM	Describes memory status
MODE	Sets defaults
MORE	Pauses the printout of a text file
PATH	Accesses other subdirectories
PROMPT	Changes the C: prompt
REN	Rename
RESTORE	Opposite of backup
SYS	Makes a disk bootable
TIME	Sets the time
TYPE	Prints a text file to the screen
VER	Tells what version of DOS is running
VERIFY	Double-checks all disk writes
VOL	Tells a disk's volume
XCOPY	Copy and verify a file

The Hayes Command Set

VIRTUALLY ALL MODEMS for personal computers are Hayes-compatible modems. These modems can be controlled using an arcane code; speaker volume, auto answer, speed, and other features can be easily set once you know the proper code.

Code	Modem Operation
ATA	Answer phone immediately
ATDT	Tone dial the phone
ATH0	Hang up

Code	Modem Operation
ATL1	Make speaker soft
ATL3	Make speaker loud
ATM0	Turn monitor speaker (dial tone) off
ATDP	Pulse-dial the phone
ATS0=1	Auto answer on one ring
ATS8=4	Set the pause for a comma in the phone number to 4 seconds
ATZ	Reset the modem

Smileys

WHEN SENDING ELECTRONIC MAIL, users often want to express more emotion than the keyboard allows. These "smileys" can be more easily understood if you tilt your head to the left.

Smiley	Meaning
:-)	Your basic smiley
:)	Midget smiley
,-)	Winking happy smiley
(-:	Left-handed smiley
(:-)	Smiley big-face
(:-(	Very unhappy smiley
,-}	Wry and winking smiley
'-)	Winking smiley

Smiley	Meaning
:-#	My lips are sealed
:-*	Kiss
:-/	Skeptical smiley
:->	Sarcastic smiley
:-@	Screaming smiley
:-V	Shouting smiley
:-X	A big wet kiss!
:-\	Undecided smiley
:-]	Smiley blockhead
;-(	Crying smiley
>;->	A very lewd remark was just made

Source: The Smiley Dictionary

Program Templates

WordPerfect Commands

Key	Function
F1	Cancel
Alt F1	Thesaurus
Shift F1	Setup
Ctrl F1	Shell
F2	Search Forward
Alt F2	Replace
Shift F2	Search Backward
Ctrl F2	Spell
F3	Help
Alt F3	Reveal Codes
Shift F3	Switch
Ctrl F3	Screen
F4	Indent Right
Alt F4	Block
Shift F4	Indent Both Sides
Ctrl F4	Move
F5	List Files
Alt F5	Mark Text
Shift F5	Date/Outline
Ctrl F5	Text In/Out
F6	Bold
Alt F6	Flush Right
Shift F6	Center
Ctrl F6	Tab Align
F7	Exit
Alt F7	Columns/Table
Shift F7	Print
Ctrl F7	Footnote
F8	Underline
Alt F8	Style
Shift F8	Format
Ctrl F8	Font
F9	Merge R
Alt F9	Graphics
Shift F9	Merge Codes
Ctrl F9	Merge/Sort
F10	Save
Alt F10	Macro
Shift F10	Retrieve
Ctrl F10	Macro Define

XyWrite Commands

Key	Function
F1	Begin/End Text Define
Alt F1	Begin/End Column Define
Shift F1	—
Ctrl F1	—
F2	Make or Load Save/Gets
Alt F2	Display All Save/Gets
Shift F2	Append to a Save/Get
Ctrl F2	Display Save/Get on one key
F3	Release Define
Alt F3	Undelete
Shift F3	—
Ctrl F3	Open a Footnote or Header
F4	Define Line
Alt F4	Define Word
Shift F4	Define Paragraph
Ctrl F4	Define Sentence
F5	Clear Command Line
Alt F5	Delete Line
Shift F5	—
Ctrl F5	—
F6	Clear Command Line
Alt F6	Delete Define
Shift F6	—
Ctrl F6	—
F7	Copy Defined Block
Alt F7	—
Shift F7	—
Ctrl F7	—
F8	Move Defined Block
Alt F8	—
Shift F8	—
Ctrl F8	—
F9	Execute Command
Alt F9	Help
Shift F9	Show Page and Line Numbers
Ctrl F9	Normal or Expanded Display

TIP: *When buying a computer book, start from the back. Good computer books never have skimpy indexes. Look up a familiar technique and see if the explanation makes sense. Finally, don't be influenced by price. Sometimes the cheapest books are the best.*

MAPS

Atlanta

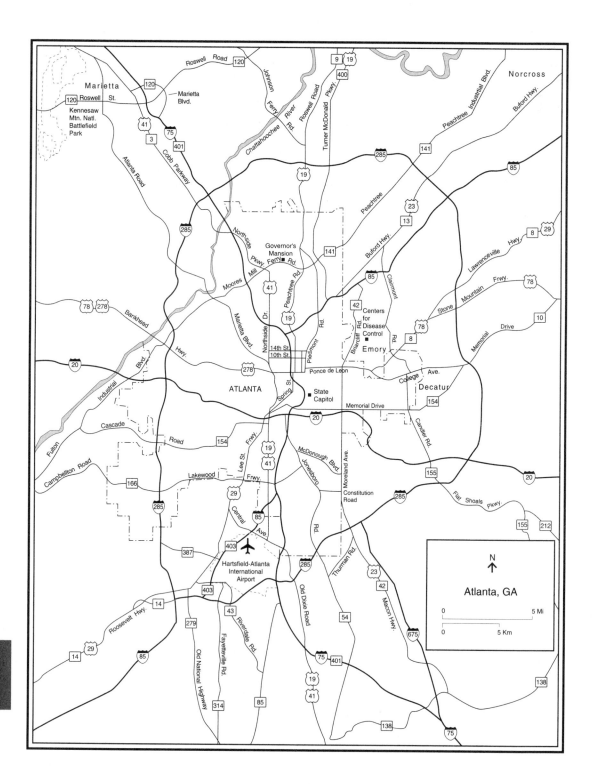

Boston

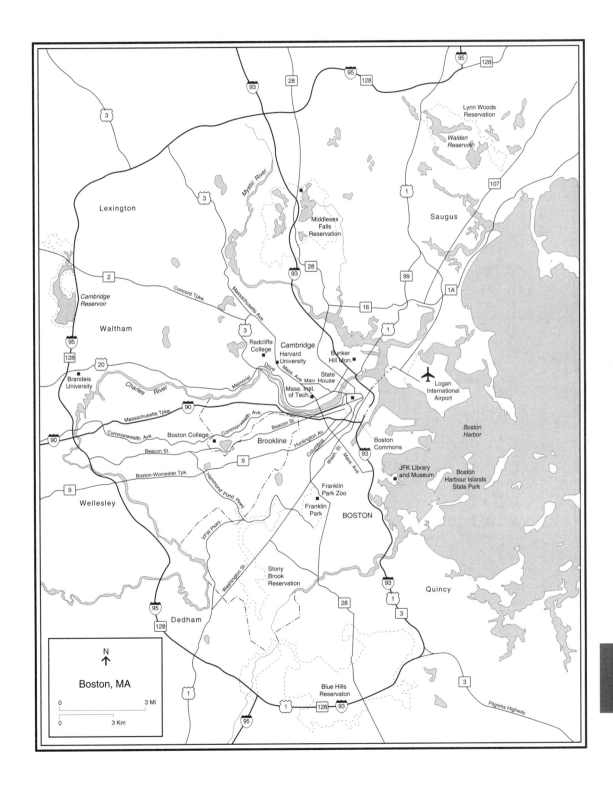

Lynn Woods
Reservation

Walden
Reservoir

Lexington

Middlesex
Falls
Reservation

Saugus

3

Cambridge
Reservoir

Concord Tpke.

Massachusetts Ave.

Waltham

Radcliffe
College

Cambridge

Harvard
University

Brandeis
University

Charles River

Memorial Drive

Mass. Ave. Main St.

Mass. Inst.
of Tech.

Bunker
Hill Mon.

State
House

Logan
International
Airport

Massachusetts Tpke.

Commonwealth Ave.

Boston College

Commonwealth Ave.

Beacon St.

Brookline

Huntington Av.

Columbus

Wash. St.

Mass. Ave.

Boston
Commons

Boston
Harbor

Beacon St.

Boston-Worcester Tpk.

Hammond Pond Pkwy.

JFK Library
and Museum

Boston
Harbour Islands
State Park

Wellesley

Franklin
Park Zoo

Franklin
Park

BOSTON

VFW Pkwy.

Washington St.

Stony
Brook
Reservation

Quincy

Dedham

Blue Hills
Reservaton

Pilgrims Highway

N

↑

Boston, MA

0 ——————————— 3 Mi

0 ——————————— 3 Km

Chicago

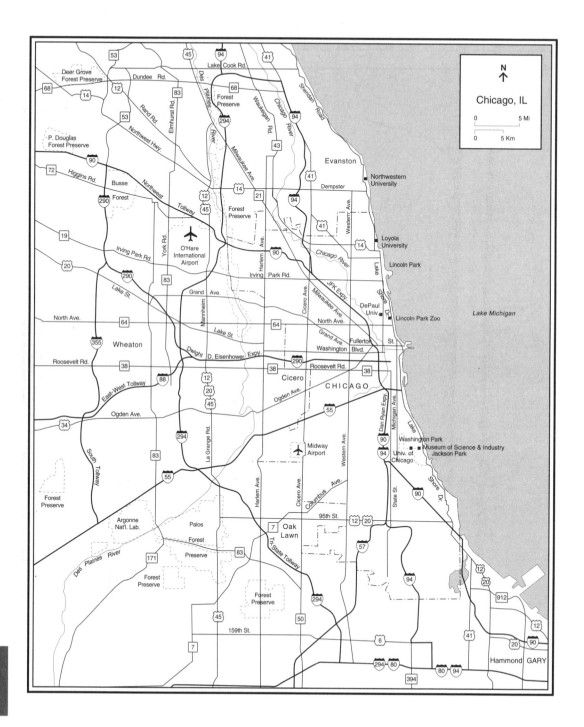

Cleveland

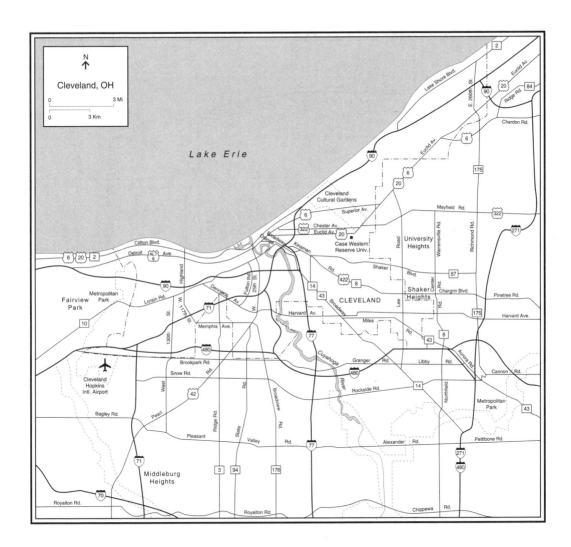

Columbus

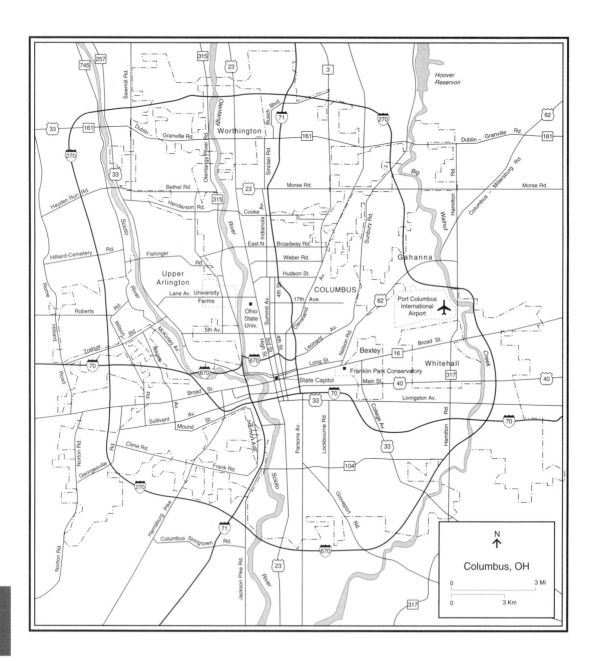

Hoover Reservoir

Worthington

Dublin - Granville Rd.

Morse Rd.

Upper Arlington

Gahanna

Ohio State Univ.

COLUMBUS

Port Columbus International Airport

Bexley

Whitehall

Franklin Park Conservatory

State Capitol

N

Columbus, OH

0   3 Mi

0   3 Km

Dallas–Fort Worth

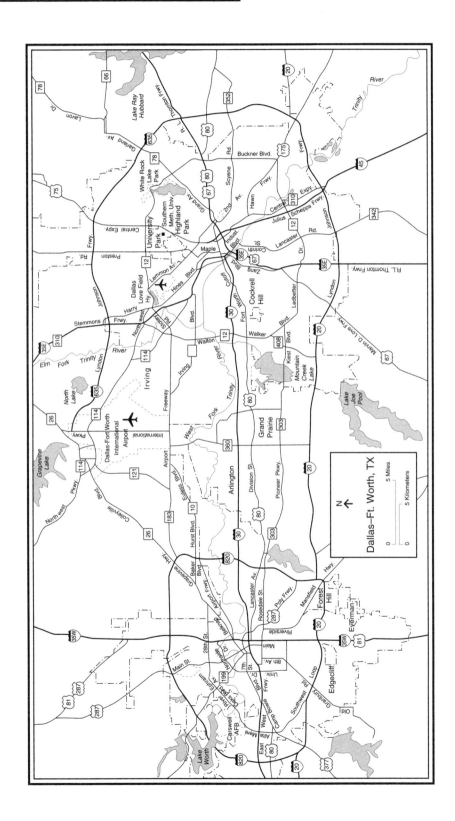

Denver

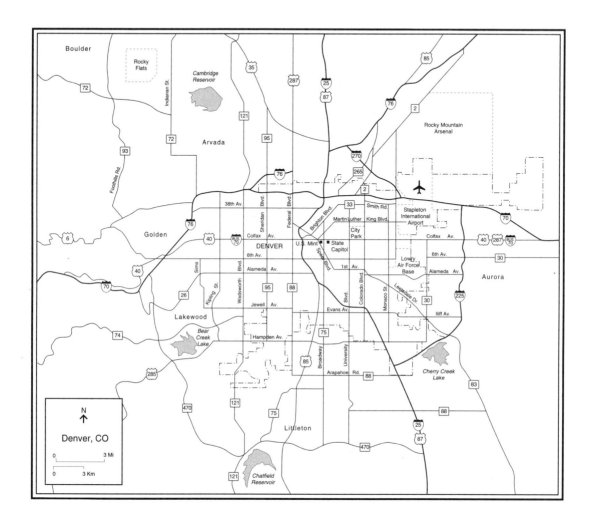

Boulder

Rocky Flats

Cambridge Reservoir

72

Indianan St.

35

121

287

25

87

85

76

2

Rocky Mountain Arsenal

72

Arvada

95

93

Foothills Rd.

76

270

265

38th Av.

Sheridan Blvd.

Federal Blvd.

2

Brighton Blvd.

33

Smith Rd.

Stapleton International Airport

76

Golden

40

BUS 70

Colfax Av.

DENVER

U.S. Mint

Martin Luther King Blvd.

City Park

State Capitol

Colfax Av.

40 287 BUS 70

6

6th Av.

1st Av.

Lowry Air Force Base

6th Av.

30

Aurora

40

Sims

Wadsworth Blvd.

95

88

Alameda Av.

Colorado Blvd.

Alameda Av.

70

26

Kipling St.

Speer Blvd.

Monaco St.

Leetsdale Dr.

30

225

Lakewood

Jewell Av.

Evans Av.

Iliff Av.

74

Bear Creek Lake

Hampden Av.

75

Cherry Creek Lake

83

285

85

Broadway

University

Arapahoe Rd.

88

470

121

75

Littleton

25

87

88

470

N
↑

Denver, CO

0   3 Mi

0   3 Km

121

Chatfield Reservoir

Detroit

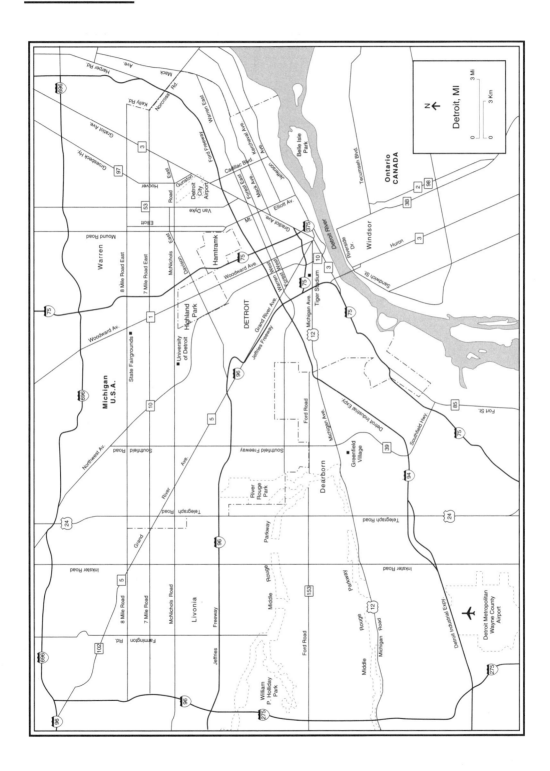

Honolulu

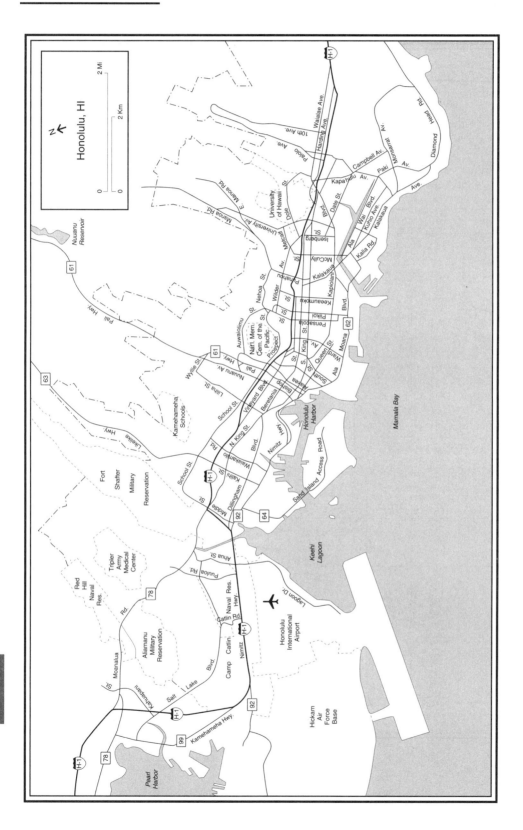

Houston

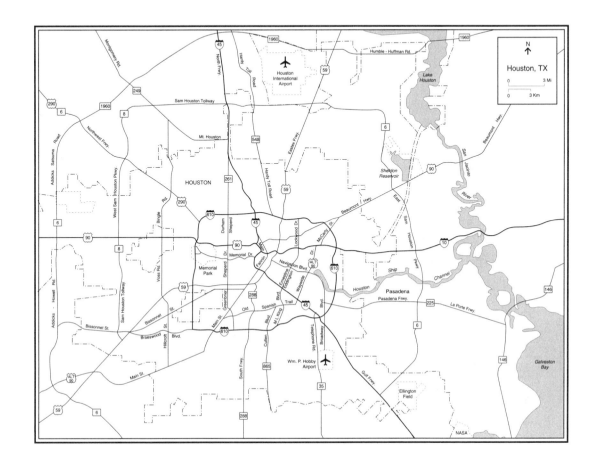

Indianapolis

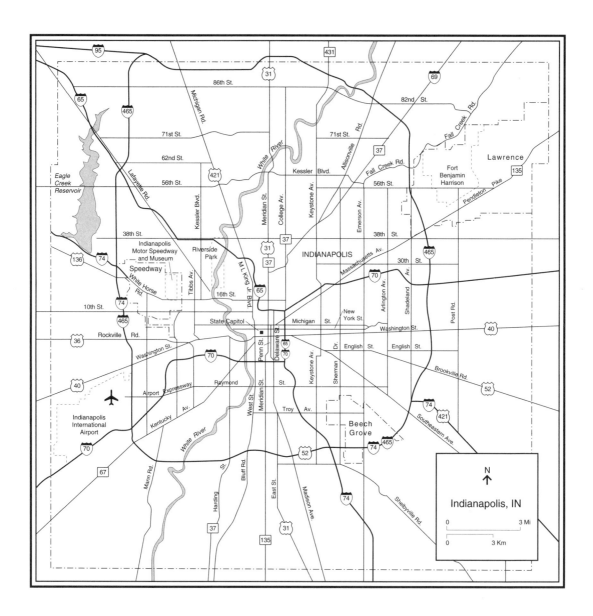

Kansas City

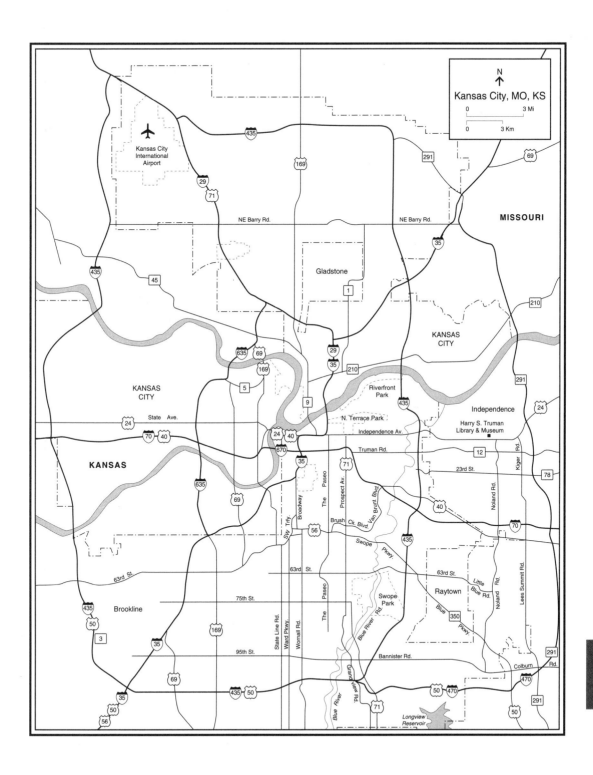

N

Kansas City, MO, KS

0   3 Mi

0   3 Km

Kansas City International Airport

435

169

291

69

29

71

NE Barry Rd.

NE Barry Rd.

35

MISSOURI

435

45

Gladstone

1

210

635 69

169

5

29

35

210

KANSAS CITY

291

9

Riverfront Park

435

Independence

24

KANSAS CITY

N. Terrace Park

24

State   Ave.

70 40

24 40

Independence Av.

Harry S. Truman Library & Museum

670

Truman Rd.

12

Kiger Rd.

KANSAS

35

71

23rd St.

78

635

69

The Paseo

Broadway

Prospect Av.

Van Brunt Blvd.

Brush   Ck. Blvd.

40

70

56

Swope   Pkwy.

435

SW. Trfy.

63rd   St.

63rd   St.

63rd St.

Little Blue Rd.

Noland Rd.

Lees Summit Rd.

Raytown

435

50

Brookline

75th St.

Swope Park

Blue River Rd.

350

Blue Pkwy.

3

169

The Paseo

35

95th St.

State Line Rd.

Ward Pkwy.

Womall Rd.

Bannister Rd.

291

Colburn   Rd.

470

69

35

435 50

Grand View Rd.

71

50 470

291

50

56

Blue River

Longview Reservoir

Los Angeles

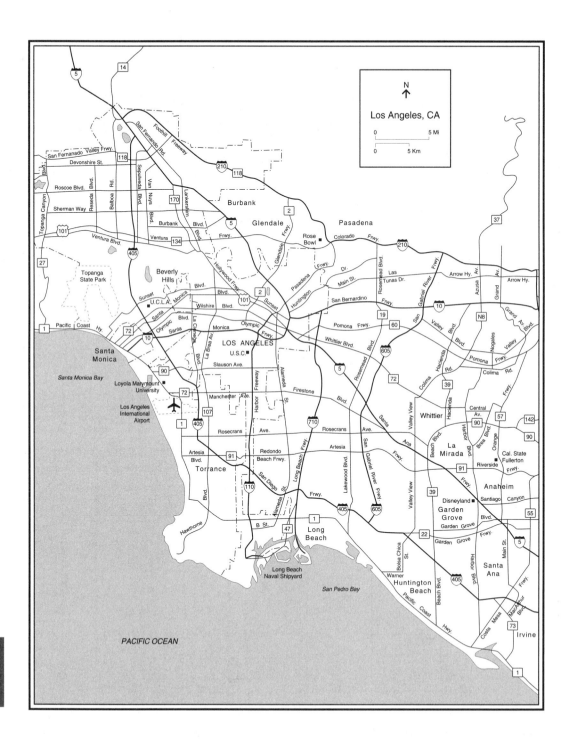

N
Los Angeles, CA

0   5 Mi

0   5 Km

San Fernanado Valley Frwy.

Devonshire St.

Roscoe Blvd.

Sherman Way

Topanga Canyon

Ventura Blvd.

San Fernando Rd.

Foothill Freeway

Sepulveda Blvd.

Van Nuys Blvd.

Lankershim

Balboa Rd.

Reseda Blvd.

Burbank

Burbank Blvd.

Glendale

Ventura

Pasadena

Rose Bowl

Colorado

Topanga State Park

Beverly Hills

U.C.L.A.

Sunset

Wilshire Blvd.

Santa Monica

Olympic

La Brea Av.

La Cienega Blvd.

Hollywood Frwy.

Glendale Frwy.

Pasadena Frwy.

Huntington

Main St.

San Bernardino Frwy.

Las Tunas Dr.

Rosemead Blvd.

San Gabriel River Frwy.

Arrow Hy.

Azusa Av.

Grand

Arrow Hy.

Pacific Coast Hy.

Santa Monica

Santa Monica Bay

Loyola Marymount University

Los Angeles International Airport

LOS ANGELES

U.S.C.

Slauson Ave.

Manchester Ave.

Harbor Freeway

Alameda St.

Firestone

Rosecrans Ave.

Artesia Blvd.

Torrance

Hawthorne Blvd.

Redondo Beach Frwy.

San Diego Frwy.

Alameda St.

B St.

Long Beach

Long Beach Naval Shipyard

San Pedro Bay

Olympic

Whittier Blvd.

Pomona Frwy.

Blvd.

Rosecrans Ave.

Artesia

San Gabriel River Frwy.

Lakewood Blvd.

Santa Ana Frwy.

Valley View

Valley

Blvd.

Hacienda Rd.

Colima

Colima Rd.

Whittier

Central Av.

Beach Blvd.

Harbor Blvd.

Brea Blvd.

Orange

La Mirada

Riverside

Cal. State Fullerton Frwy.

Nogales

Valley Blvd.

Pomona Frwy.

Grand Av. Blvd.

Disneyland

Santiago Canyon

Garden Grove

Garden Grove Blvd.

Anaheim

Garden Grove Frwy.

Santa Ana

Harbor Blvd.

Main St.

Bolsa Chica St.

Warner

Huntington Beach

Beach Blvd.

MacArthur Blvd.

Pacific Coast Hwy.

Costa Mesa Frwy.

Irvine

PACIFIC OCEAN

Miami

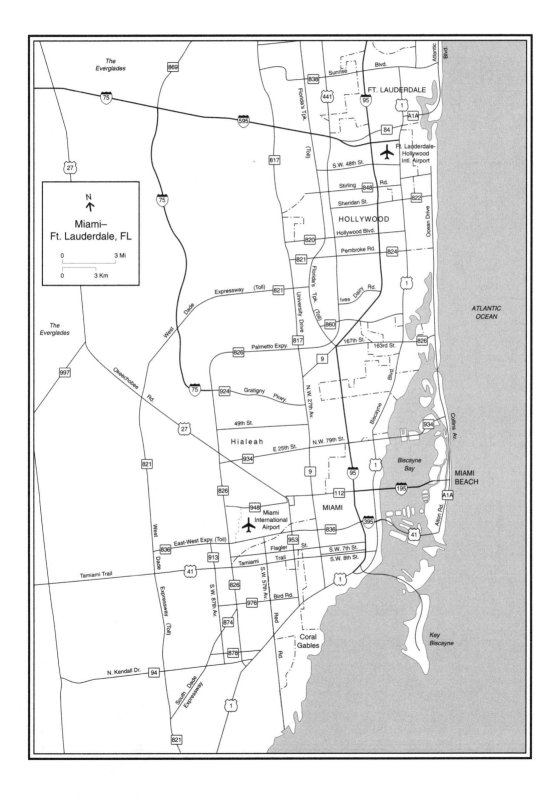

The Everglades

869

75

27

75

N

Miami–
Ft. Lauderdale, FL

0   3 Mi
0   3 Km

The Everglades

997

Okeechobee Rd

27

821

West Dade

Expressway (Toll)

Florida's Tpk.

(Toll)

838

Sunrise   Blvd.

441   95   FT. LAUDERDALE

1

A1A

84

Ft. Lauderdale-
Hollywood
Intl. Airport

S.W. 48th St.

Stirling   848   Rd.

Sheridan St.

HOLLYWOOD

Hollywood Blvd.

Pembroke Rd.   824

Ives   Dairy   Rd.

167th St.   163rd St.

Florida's Tpk. (Toll)

University Drive

595

817

820

821

821

817

860

826

9

826   924   Gratigny   Pkwy.

75

49th St.   N.W. 79th St.

Hialeah   E 25th St.

934

9

948   Miami
International
Airport

826

836   East-West Expy. (Toll)

913

Tamiami   Trail

41

Tamiami Trail

West Dade

Expressway (Toll)

South Dade Expressway

826   S.W. 57th Av.

976   Bird Rd.

874

878

94   N. Kendall Dr.

821

1

S.W. 87th Av.

Red   Rd.

Coral
Gables

953   Flagler   St.   S.W. 7th St.

S.W. 8th St.

1

MIAMI

836

395

41

112

195

9   95   1

934   E 25th St.

N.W. 27th Av.

Biscayne   Blvd.

822

Ocean Drive

Atlantic   Blvd.

ATLANTIC
OCEAN

1

826

934

Collins Av.

Biscayne
Bay

MIAMI
BEACH

A1A

Alton Rd.

Key
Biscayne

Minneapolis

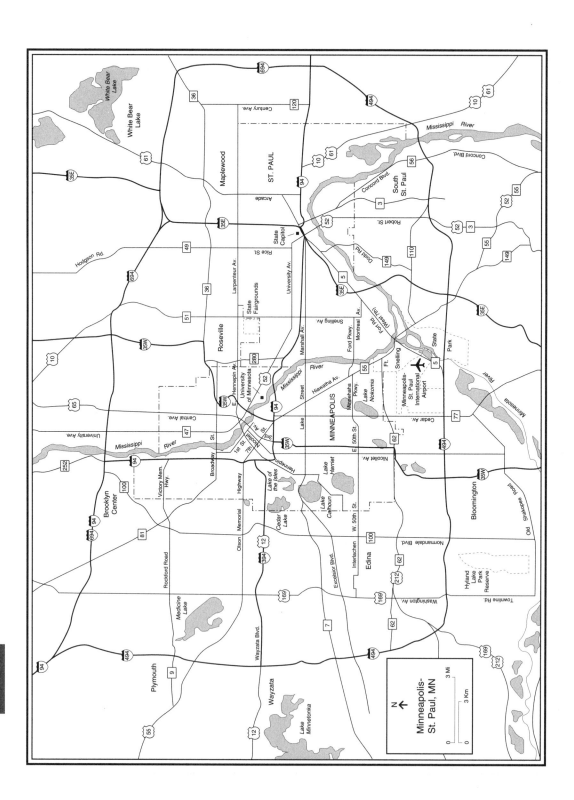

Minneapolis–
St. Paul, MN

New Orleans

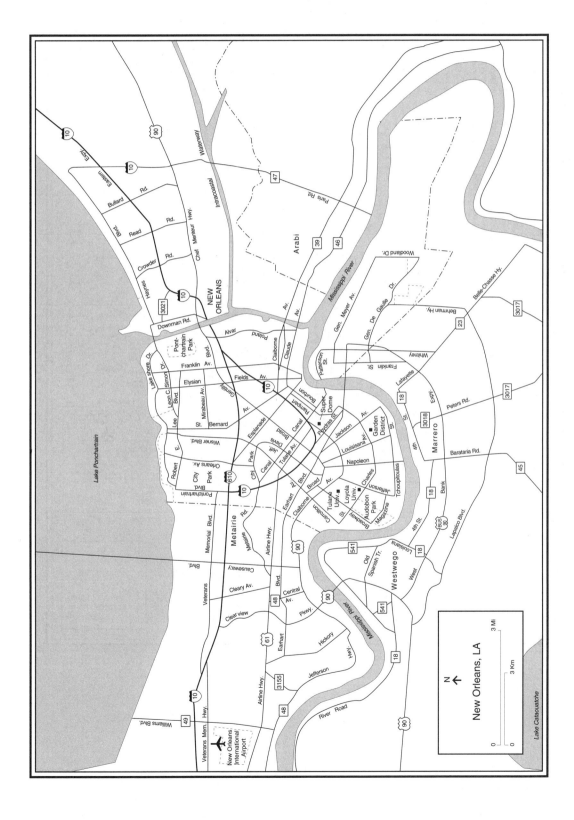

New Orleans, LA

New York

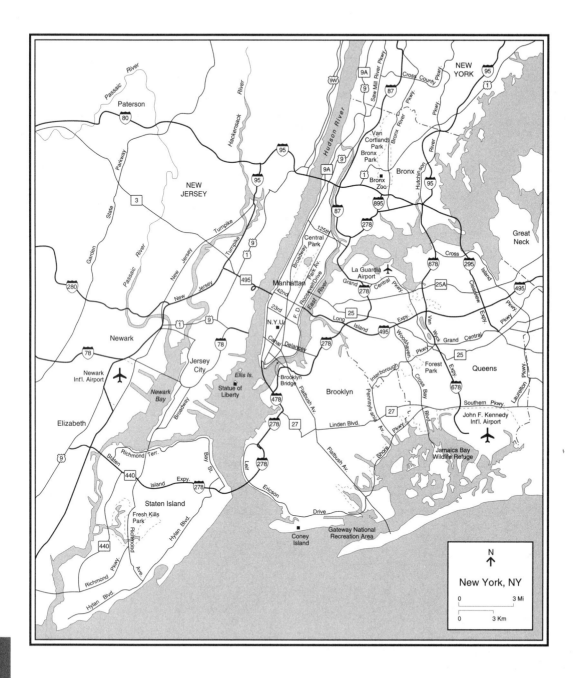

New York, NY

Philadelphia

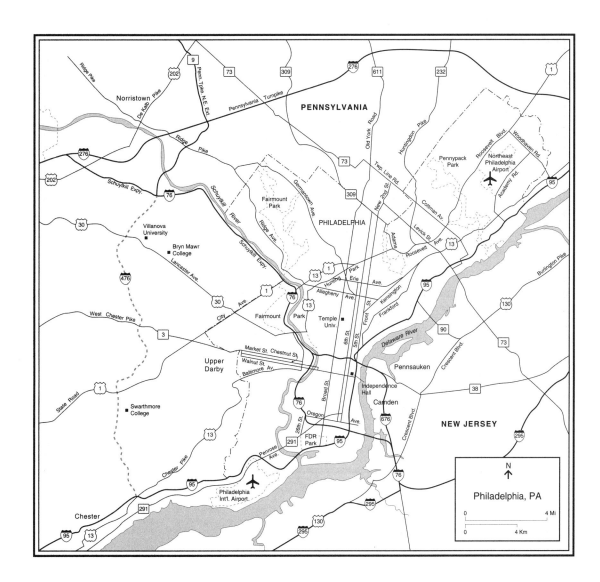

PENNSYLVANIA

PHILADELPHIA

NEW JERSEY

Ridge Pike

Norristown

Penn. Tpke. N.E. Ext.

Pennsylvania Turnpike

De Kalb Pike

Ridge Pike

Schuylkill Expy.

Schuylkill River

Schuylkill Expy.

Villanova University

Bryn Mawr College

Lancaster Ave.

West Chester Pike

State Road

Swarthmore College

Chester Pike

Chester

Fairmount Park

Germantown Ave.

Ridge Ave.

Fairmount Park

City Ave.

Market St. Chestnut St.

Walnut St.

Baltimore Av.

Upper Darby

Temple Univ.

Park Ave.

Huning Erie Ave.

Allegheny Ave.

Front St.

Kensington

Frankford

Broad St.

26th St.

Oregon Ave.

FDR Park

Penrose Ave.

Philadelphia Int'l. Airport

Old York Road

Twp. Line Rd.

New 2nd St.

Adams

Levick St.

Roosevelt Ave.

Huntingdon Pike

Cottman Av.

Pennypack Park

Northeast Philadelphia Airport

Roosevelt Blvd.

Woodhaven Rd.

Academy Rd.

Burlington Pike

Delaware River

Pennsauken

Independence Hall

Camden

Crescent Blvd.

Philadelphia, PA

N

0   4 Mi
0   4 Km

Phoenix

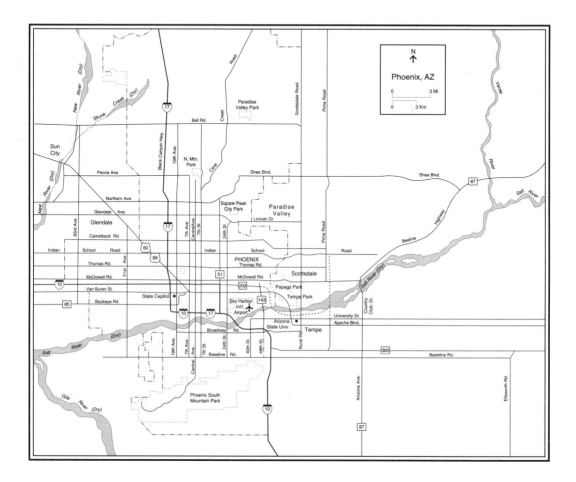

Pittsburgh

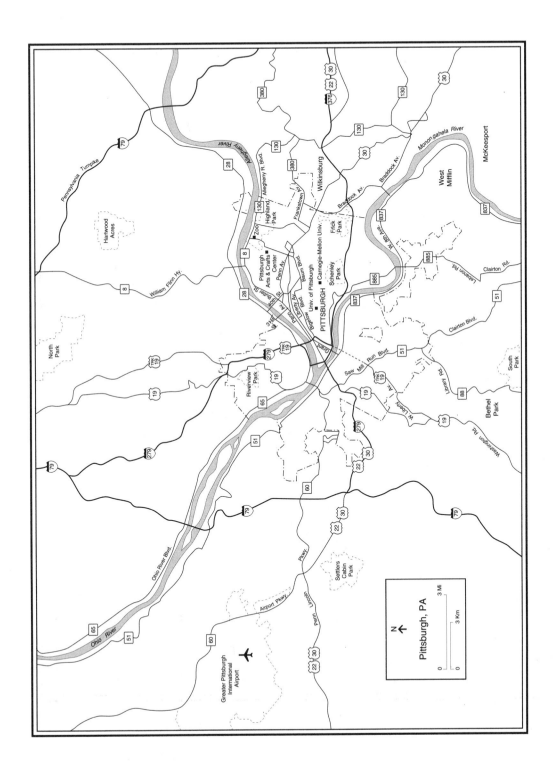

St. Louis

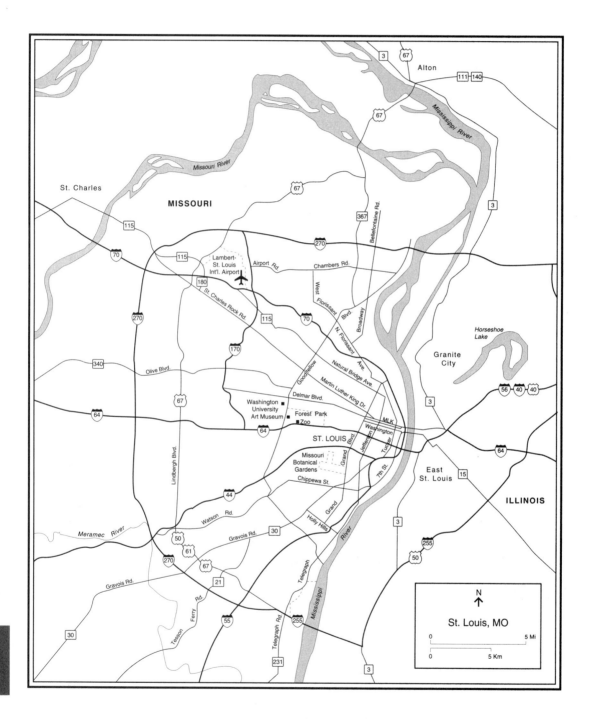

San Diego

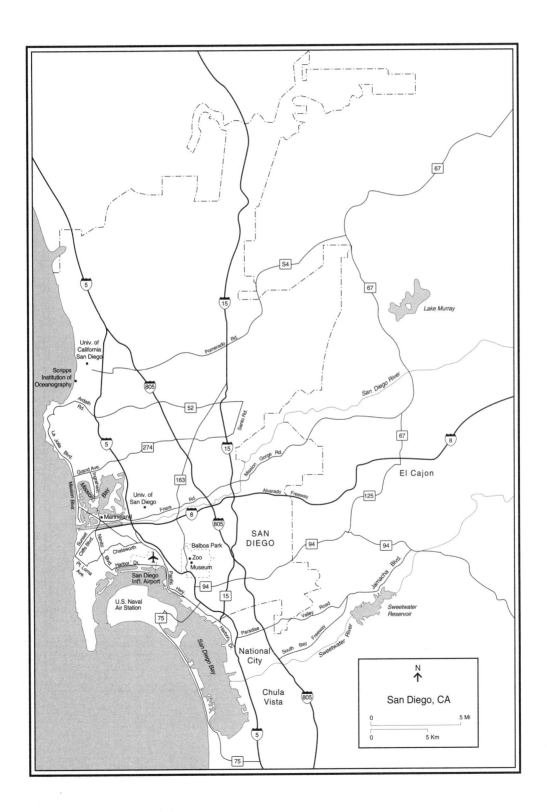

Univ. of California San Diego

Scripps Institution of Oceanography

Ardath Rd.

La Jolla Blvd.

Grand Ave.

Ingraham

Mission Bay

Mission Blvd.

Univ. of San Diego

Marineland

Friars Rd.

Sunset Cliffs Blvd.

Nimitz Blvd.

Chatsworth

Harbor Dr.

Pt. Loma Ave.

San Diego Int'l. Airport

Pacific Hwy.

Balboa Park

Zoo Museum

U.S. Naval Air Station

Harbor Dr.

San Diego Bay

National City

Paradise

Chula Vista

SAN DIEGO

Pomerado Rd.

San Diego River

Lake Murray

Santo Rd.

Mission Gorge Rd.

Alvarado Freeway

El Cajon

South Bay Freeway

Valley Road

Sweetwater River

Jamacha Blvd.

Sweetwater Reservoir

N

San Diego, CA

| 0 | 5 Mi |

| 0 | 5 Km |

5

15

S4

67

67

67

8

805

52

15

274

163

8

805

125

94

94

94

15

75

805

5

75

San Francisco

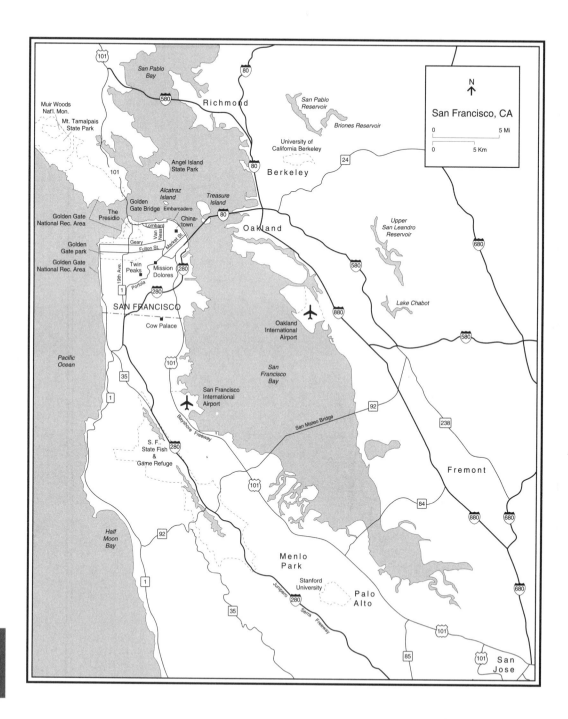

San Francisco, CA

N

0   5 Mi
0   5 Km

San Pablo Bay

101

80

580

Richmond

San Pablo Reservoir

Briones Reservoir

University of California Berkeley

Berkeley

24

Muir Woods Nat'l. Mon.

Mt. Tamalpais State Park

Angel Island State Park

101

Alcatraz Island

Treasure Island

Golden Gate Bridge

Embarcadero

China-town

80

Oakland

Upper San Leandro Reservoir

680

Golden Gate National Rec. Area

The Presidio

Lombard

Van Ness

Market St.

Geary

Fulton St.

Golden Gate park

Golden Gate National Rec. Area

19th Ave.

Twin Peaks

Mission Dolores

280

Portola

280

Lake Chabot

580

SAN FRANCISCO

Cow Palace

Oakland International Airport

880

Pacific Ocean

101

35

1

San Francisco Bay

580

San Francisco International Airport

92

San Mateo Bridge

238

Bayshore Freeway

280

S. F. State Fish & Game Refuge

101

Fremont

84

880

680

Half Moon Bay

92

Menlo Park

Stanford University

Palo Alto

680

1

35

Junipero Serra Freeway

280

85

101

San Jose

101

Seattle

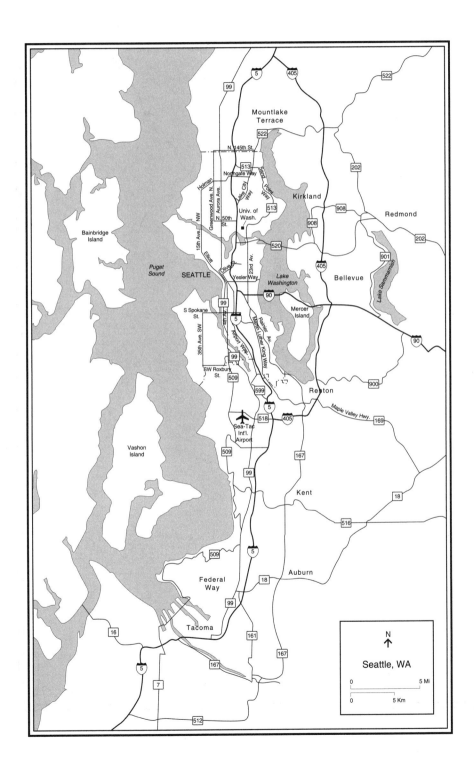

Mountlake
Terrace

N. 145th St.

Northgate Way

Kirkland

Univ. of
Wash.

Redmond

Bainbridge
Island

Puget
Sound

SEATTLE

Yesler Way

Lake
Washington

Bellevue

Lake Sammamish

Mercer
Island

S Spokane
St.

SW Roxbury
St.

Renton

Maple Valley Hwy.

Sea-Tac
Int'l.
Airport

Vashon
Island

Kent

Federal
Way

Auburn

Tacoma

N

Seattle, WA

0   5 Mi

0   5 Km

Washington, DC

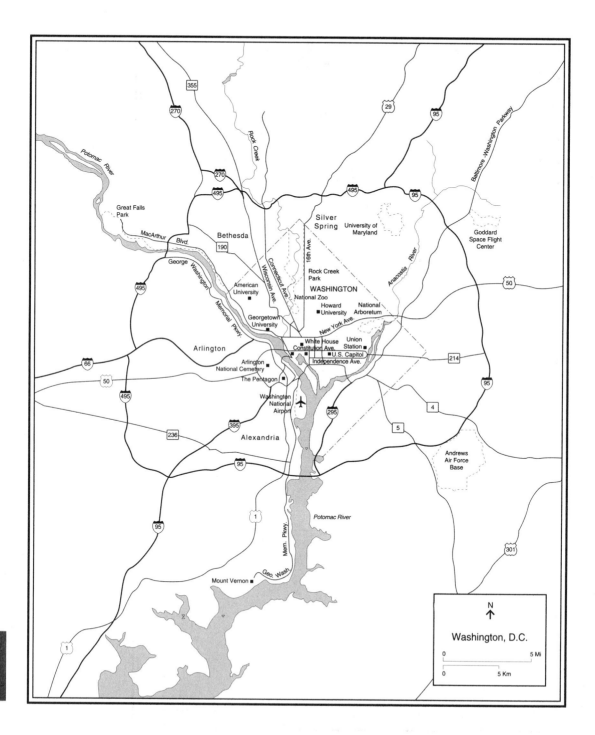

355

270

29

US 95

US 95

Potomac River

Rock Creek

Baltimore-Washington Parkway

270

495

495

US 95

Great Falls Park

Silver Spring

University of Maryland

Goddard Space Flight Center

MacArthur Blvd.

Bethesda

190

Connecticut Ave.

16th Ave.

Wisconsin Ave.

Rock Creek Park

US 50

George Washington Memorial Pkwy.

495

American University

WASHINGTON

National Zoo

Anacostia River

Georgetown University

Howard University

National Arboretum

Arlington

New York Ave.

White House

Union Station

214

66

Constitution Ave.

U.S. Capitol

Arlington National Cemetery

Independence Ave.

US 95

50

The Pentagon

495

Washington National Airport

295

4

236

395

5

Alexandria

Andrews Air Force Base

US 95

Potomac River

US 301

1

Mem. Pkwy.

US 95

Geo. Wash.

Mount Vernon

US 1

N

Washington, D.C.

0   5 Mi

0   5 Km

Africa

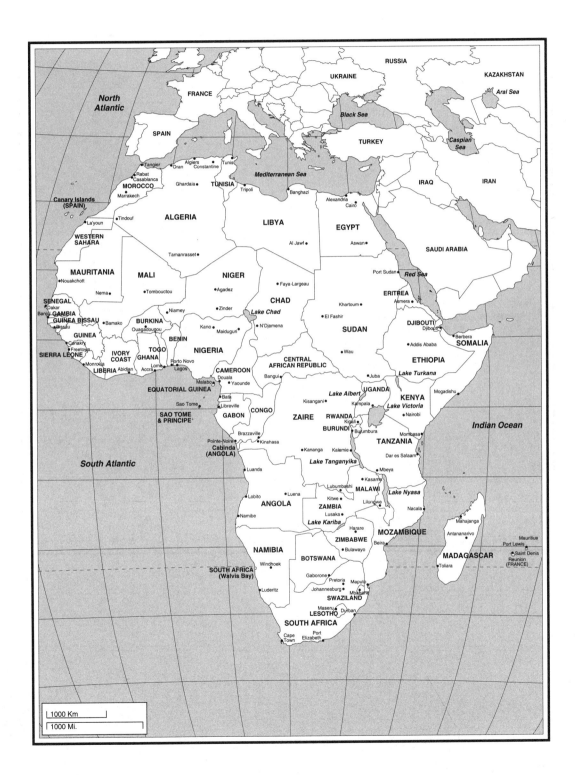

North
Atlantic

FRANCE

SPAIN

Tangier
Rabat
Casablanca
MOROCCO
Marrakech

Canary Islands
(SPAIN)

La'youn   Tindouf

WESTERN
SAHARA

MAURITANIA
Nouakchott

Nema

SENEGAL
Dakar
Banjul GAMBIA
GUINEA BISSAU
Bissau

GUINEA
Conakry
Freetown
SIERRA LEONE
Monrovia
LIBERIA   Abidjan

Algiers
Oran   Constantine
Tunis

TUNISIA

Ghardaia

ALGERIA

Tamanrasset

MALI

Tombouctou

Niamey
BURKINA
Ouagadougou

Bamako

IVORY
COAST   TOGO
GHANA   NIGERIA
Lome
Accra   Lagos
Porto Novo

BENIN

Kano

Zinder

NIGER
Agadez

Maiduguri

CHAD

Lake Chad

N'Djamena

Mediterranean Sea

Tripoli

Banghazi

LIBYA

Al Jawf

Alexandria
Cairo

EGYPT

Aswan

Faya-Largeau

Khartoum

El Fashir

SUDAN

Wau

RUSSIA

UKRAINE

Black Sea

TURKEY

IRAQ

KAZAKHSTAN

Aral Sea

Caspian
Sea

IRAN

SAUDI ARABIA

Port Sudan   Red Sea

ERITREA
Asmera

DJIBOUTI
Djibouti
Berbera

Addis Ababa   SOMALIA

ETHIOPIA

Lake Turkana

Mogadishu

CAMEROON
Douala
Malabo
Yaounde
Bata
EQUATORIAL GUINEA
Libreville
Sao Tome

SAO TOME
& PRINCIPE

GABON

Bangui

CENTRAL
AFRICAN REPUBLIC

Kisangani

Juba

Lake Albert   UGANDA
Kampala
Lake Victoria
Nairobi

KENYA

Indian Ocean

CONGO
Brazzaville
Pointe-Noire
Cabinda
(ANGOLA)

Kinshasa

ZAIRE
RWANDA
BURUNDI
Kigali
Bujumbura
Kananga
Kalemie

Luanda

South Atlantic

Lobito
Namibe

ANGOLA

Luena

Lubumbashi
Kitwe

ZAMBIA
Lusaka

Lake Kariba

NAMIBIA

Windhoek

SOUTH AFRICA
(Walvis Bay)

Luderitz

BOTSWANA

Gaborone

Mombasa

TANZANIA
Dar es Salaam

Lake Tanganyika

Mbeya

Kasama

MALAWI

Lake Nyasa

Lilongwe

Nacala

Mahajanga

Antananarivo

Mauritius
Port Lewis

Saint Denis
Reunion
(FRANCE)

MADAGASCAR

Toliara

Harare

ZIMBABWE
Bulawayo

Beira

MOZAMBIQUE

Pretoria
Johannesburg   Maputo
Mbabane
SWAZILAND
Maseru   Durban
LESOTHO
SOUTH AFRICA
Cape
Town   Port
Elizabeth

1000 Km

1000 Mi.

Asia

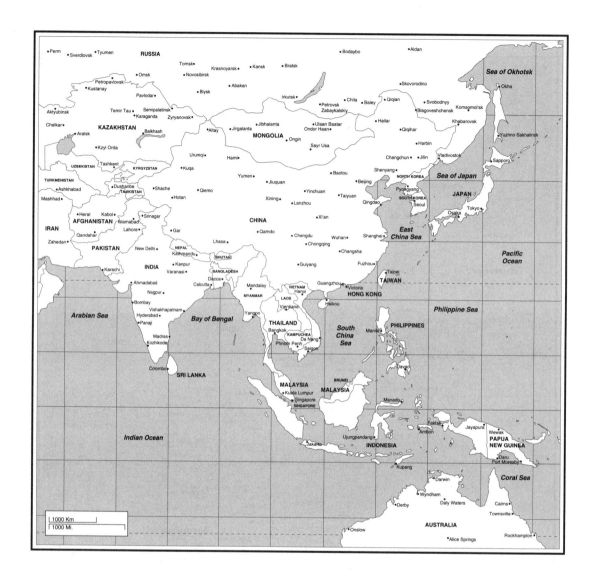

Australia

Arafura Sea

Darwin

Indian Ocean

Wyndham

Derby

Gulf of Carpentaria

Northern Territory

Cooktown

Cairns

Coral Sea

Mount Isa

Townsville

Mackay

Queensland

Alice Springs

Ayers Rock

Rockhampton

Western Australia

Charleville

Brisbane

South Australia

Geraldton

Bourke

Kalgoorlie

Broken Hill

Perth

Port Augusta

New South Wales

Adelaide

Newcastle

Sydney

Albany

Canberra

Victoria

Melbourne

Indian Ocean

Tasmania

Hobart

Australia

⊗ National Capital
Perth • City
——— International Boundary
——— State / Territory Boundary
Victoria State / Territory Name

0   Miles   500

Canada

RUSSIA

Arctic Ocean

Beaufort
Sea

GREENLAND
(DENMARK)

ICELAND

UNITED STATES

Baffin Bay

• Dawson

Victoria
Island

Pacific
Ocean

Yukon Territory

Great
Bear
Lake

Baffin
Island

• Whitehorse

Northwest Territories

Labrador Sea

Great Slave
Lake   • Yellowknife

British
Columbia

Lake
Athabasca

Hudson
Bay

Newfoundland

Alberta

Churchill

Saskatchewan

Manitoba

Edmonton •

St. John's

Victoria   •Vancouver

Quebec

• Calgary

• Saskatoon

Lake
Winnipeg

Ontario

P.E.I.
Sydney

Regina •

New
Brunswick

Winnipeg •

Quebec •   Fredericton •

Halifax
Nova Scotia

Thunder Bay •

Lake Superior

Montreal •

Canada

⊗ National Capital

Calgary •   City

─────── International Boundary

───── Provincial Boundary

Quebec   Province Name

0   Miles   500

Lake Huron
Ottawa ⊗

Lake Michigan

Toronto •   Lake Ontario

Atlantic
Ocean

UNITED STATES

Lake Erie

Europe

Mexico

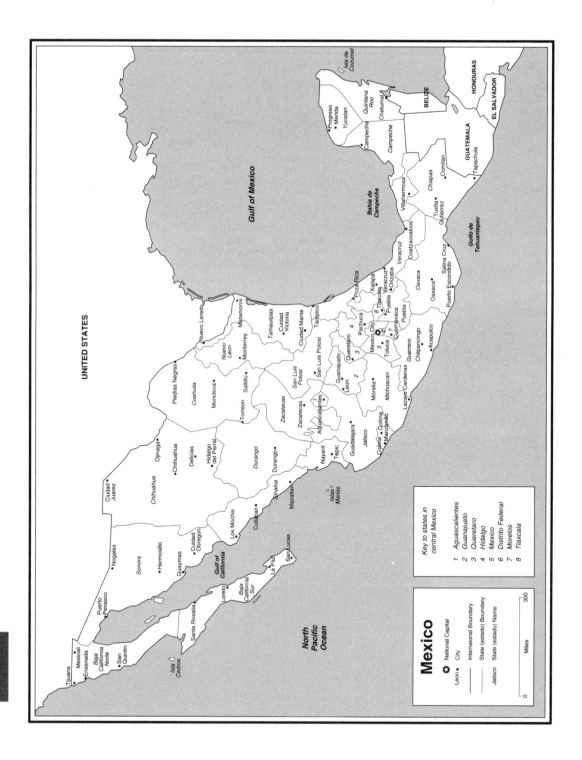

UNITED STATES

Gulf of Mexico

North
Pacific
Ocean

Gulf of
California

Bahia de
Campeche

Golfo de
Tehuantepec

BELIZE

HONDURAS

EL SALVADOR

GUATEMALA

Isla de
Cozumel

Quintana
Roo

Yucatan

Campeche

Chiapas

Chetumal

Progreso
Merida

Campeche

Villahermosa

Tuxtla
Gutierrez

Comitan

Tapachula

Veracruz

Coatzacoalcos

Oaxaca

Oaxaca

Salina Cruz

Puerto Escondido

Poza Rica

Xalapa
Tlacaba
Veracruz
Orizaba
Puebla
Cuernavaca

Pachuca

Mexico City
Toluca

Queretaro

Puebla

Acapulco

Chilpancingo

Guerrero

Lazaro Cardenas

Tamaulipas

Ciudad
Victoria

Ciudad Mante

Tampico

San Luis Potosi

San Luis Potosi

Nuevo Laredo

Matamoros

Nuevo
Leon

Monterrey

Reynosa

Guanajuato

Leon

Morelia

Michoacan

Zacatecas

Zacatecas

Aguascalientes

Piedras Negras

Coahuila

Monclova

Saltillo

Torreon

Durango

Durango

Sinaloa

Mazatlan

Colima
Colima
Manzanillo

Guadalajara

Jalisco

Nayarit

Tepic

Hidalgo
del Parral

Delicias

Chihuahua

Chihuahua

Ojinaga

Ciudad
Juarez

Los Mochis

Ciudad
Obregon

Culiacan

Islas
Marias

San Lucas

La Paz

Loreto

Baja
California
Sur

Santa Rosalia

Isla
Cedros

Guaymas

Hermosillo

Sonora

Nogales

Puerto
Penasco

San
Quintin

Ensenada

Mexicali

Tijuana

Baja
California
Norte

Mexico

⊕ National Capital

Leon • City

⎯⎯ International Boundary

⎯⎯ State (estado) Boundary

Jalisco State (estado) Name

Miles
0   300

Key to states in
central Mexico

1 Aguascalientes
2 Guanajuato
3 Queretaro
4 Hidalgo
5 Mexico
6 Distrito Federal
7 Morelos
8 Tlaxcala

Russia

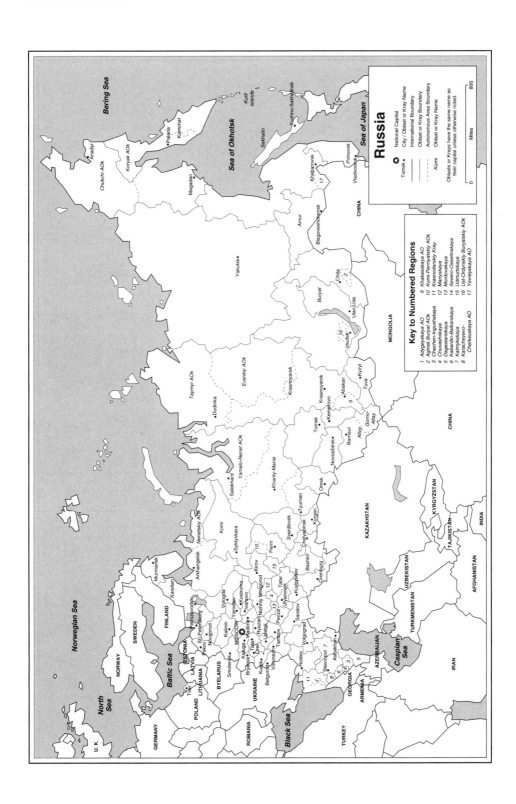

Russia

Tomsk •   National Capital
   City / Oblast or Kray Name
   International Boundary
   Oblast or Kray Boundary
   Autonomous Area Boundary
Komi   Oblast or Kray Name

Oblasts or Krays have the same name as
their capital unless otherwise noted.

0   Miles   800

Key to Numbered Regions

1 Adygeyskaya AO
2 Aginsk Buryat AOk
3 Chechen-Ingushskaya
4 Chuvashskaya
5 Dagestanskaya
6 Kabardin-Balkarskaya
7 Kalmykskaya
8 Karacheyevo-
   Cherkesskaya AO
9 Khakasskaya AO
10 Komi-Permyatskiy AOk
11 Krasnodarskiy Kray
12 Mariyskaya
13 Mordovskaya
14 Severo-Osetinskaya
15 Udmurtskaya
16 Ust-Ordynskiy Buryatskiy AOk
17 Yevreyskaya AO

South America

Caribbean Sea

North Atlantic Ocean

Barranquilla

Caracas

Cucuta • San Cristobal

Ciudad Guayana

Medellin

VENEZUELA

Georgetown
GUYANA

Paramaribo

SURINAME

FRENCH GUIANA (FRANCE)

Cayenne

Bogota

Boa Vista

Cali

COLOMBIA

Mitu

Macapa

Belem

Quito

ECUADOR

Guayaquil

Fonte Boa

Manaus

Santarem

Sao Luis

Fortaleza

Iquitos

Imperatriz

Teresina

Piura

PERU

BRAZIL

Natal

Trujillo

Rio Branco

Porto Velho

Porto Nacional

Recife

Lima

Aracaju

Ica

Cusco

BOLIVIA

Salvador

Arequipa

La Paz

Trinidad

Cuiaba

Brasilia

South Pacific Ocean

Cochabamba

Santa Cruz

Goiania

Arica

Sucre

Belo Horizonte

Vitória

CHILE

PARAGUAY

Rio de Janeiro

Antofagasta

Asuncion

Sao Paulo

San Miguel de Tucuman

Curitiba

Resistencia

Florianopolis

Cordoba

Porto Alegre

Mendoza

Rosario

Salto

Valparaiso

URUGUAY

Santiago

Buenos Aires

Montevideo

Concepcion

ARGENTINA

South Atlantic Ocean

Mar del Plata

Bahia Blanca

Valdivia

San Carlos de Bariloche

Comodoro Rivadavia

FALKLAND ISLANDS (U.K.)

500 Km

500 Mi.

SOUTH GEORGIA ISLAND (U.K.)

United States

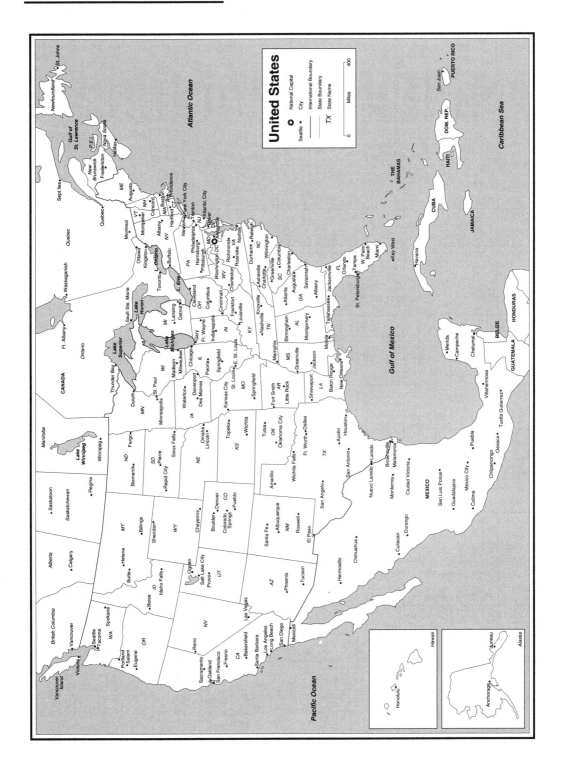

United States

⊛ National Capital
Seattle • City
—— International Boundary
—— State Boundary
TX State Name

0   400
|————————|
        Miles

Atlantic Ocean

Pacific Ocean

Gulf of Mexico

Caribbean Sea

CANADA

MEXICO

Hawaii

Alaska

MAPS

Mileage Table

	Atlanta	Baltimore	Boston	Chicago	Cincinnati	Cleveland	Columbus, OH	Dallas	Denver	Detroit	Houston	Indianapolis	Los Angeles	Miami	Milwaukee	Minneapolis	New York	Norfolk	Philadelphia	Phoenix	Pittsburgh	Portland, OR	Sacramento	St. Louis	San Antonio	San Diego	San Francisco	Seattle	Tampa	Washington, DC
Atlanta																														
Baltimore	576																													
Boston	945	368																												
Chicago	606	619	864																											
Cincinnati	374	428	750	264																										
Cleveland	555	313	561	314	221																									
Columbus, OH	569	411	767	354	110	147																								
Dallas	728	1213	1557	800	810	1019	1046																							
Denver	1204	1497	1761	898	1076	1209	1277	644																						
Detroit	596	407	630	233	229	94	209	984	1132																					
Houston	693	1243	1605	945	885	1105	1228	247	884	1091																				
Indianapolis	434	514	814	177	98	260	178	760	984	230	862																			
Los Angeles	1939	2321	2601	1739	1893	2045	2252	1230	846	1971	1385	1808																		
Miami	595	946	1258	1197	949	1081	1198	1118	1712	1147	953	1022	2334																	
Milwaukee	669	639	857	67	317	327	455	852	905	237	1004	237	1749	1259																
Minneapolis	906	933	1120	333	595	620	762	852	691	527	1057	501	1531	1501	296															
New York	761	185	184	730	583	417	567	1385	1626	500	1425	658	2460	1097	736	1017														
Norfolk	515	160	467	714	484	434	577	1209	1558	528	1206	580	2362	803	745	1042	296													
Philadelphia	665	89	281	675	505	361	473	1298	1563	452	1332	584	2392	1013	688	976	97	212												
Phoenix	1581	1992	2293	1436	1564	1732	1917	866	589	1666	1017	1485	368	1966	1456	1274	2141	2023	2068											
Pittsburgh	526	209	494	411	255	106	185	1064	1297	201	1129	323	2127	1013	201	724	333	329	266	1808										
Portland, OR	2165	2349	2528	1733	1968	2038	2439	1611	982	1946	1839	1870	833	2693	1711	1420	2436	2445	2397	1009	2140									
Sacramento	2085	2386	2627	1776	1970	2090	2200	1427	895	2006	1619	1877	373	2545	1772	1512	2505	2453	2448	646	2183	477								
St. Louis	483	735	1043	258	307	485	433	550	777	439	688	229	1586	1068	317	447	885	782	810	1258	551	1702	1673							
San Antonio	872	1404	1759	1041	1022	1239	1327	247	793	1213	191	984	1206	1140	1213	1097	1582	1378	1492	841	1273	1711	1459	785						
San Diego	1885	2287	2578	1718	1858	2019	2255	1167	837	1949	1308	1777	109	2260	1733	1528	2432	2322	2361	302	2099	933	481	1551	1126					
San Francisco	2131	2447	2693	1839	2029	2153	2457	1459	952	2071	1619	1937	337	2577	1838	1584	2569	2509	2510	649	2245	550	85	1728	1478	446				
Seattle	2175	2325	2485	1713	1956	2012	2460	1655	1015	1919	1889	1858	953	2717	1687	1393	2428	2368	2368	1105	2116	130	605	1703	1771	1050	678			
Tampa	406	843	1184	1012	773	928	999	926	1510	983	779	838	2150	205	1075	1305	716	919		1782	873	2490	2351	868	969	2079	2384	2513		
Washington, DC	546	30	398	609	409	309	407	1188	1482	405	1216	498	2302	920	632	928	214	141	118	1972	204	2341	2372	716	1377	2268	2433	2320	813	

REFERENCE

Glossary

Absolute net lease—Lease in which the tenant agrees to pay the landlord or owner a basic rent and also agrees to pay separately for all maintenance, operating, and other building expenses.

Abuse of process—The misuse of legal procedures for the benefit of an individual or business. For instance, suing someone simply in the hopes of frightening them into meeting one's demands.

Accounts payable—The amount of money owed to suppliers and vendors that is generally due within the next 30 days.

Accounts receivable—The amount of money due a business from its customers which is anticipated during the next 30 days.

Affidavit—A written statement certified by a notary public as to its authenticity.

Aggregate rent—Total dollar value of a lease.

Air rights—Space or air over a piece of property that legally belongs to, or is attached to, the property and can be transferred, sold, or rented. Frequently sold to permit a larger-than-zoned building on another property.

Amortize—Dividing a loan payment into a series of equal smaller payments to be made on a regular basis, thereby extending the payback over a longer period of time. A residential mortgage is generally amortized over a 30-year period, requiring monthly mortgage payments.

Annualized—Converting a monthly or daily figure to an annual basis.

Anticipatory breach—Notifying an individual or business that is part of a contract that another individual cannot meet the terms, thereby rendering the contract invalid.

Apparent authority—The situation in which a principal (individual or company) states or indicates that another individual or business may act on his or her behalf. The principal is then liable for the actions of the other individual, who is acting on his/her authority.

Arbitrage—Buying something in one market and selling it in another, profiting on the small differences between the two market prices.

Asset—Everything owned by a corporation that has value, including physical items, real estate, trademarks, and goodwill.

Assignment—Ability to transfer benefits and obligations of a contract or lease to another party.

Assumpsit—Reference to a contractual agreement made verbally or in writing with an individual or business that is not certified.

Assumption of risk—The situation that arises when an individual agrees to perform certain duties knowing that they could be potentially dangerous. Frequently, this claim is made in legal suits by the defendant, often an employer, in arguing that the plaintiff, often an employee, assumed the risk by agreeing to perform certain duties, such as on-the-job activities, despite the knowledge that they would be risky.

Attornment—Lease provision whereby the tenant agrees in advance to accept and pay rent or other required payments to a new landlord or legal owner.

Attorney-in-fact, subordination clause—Lease provision that permits the landlord to submit, on the tenant's behalf, without further approval, a certificate of subordination to a lender, trustee, or financing institution.

Bailor—An individual who delivers property to another individual who either owns the property or who holds it until it is claimed by the owner. Leaving your coat in a check room makes you a bailor.

Bait and switch pricing—An illegal sales tactic used by unscrupulous companies. Customers are lured into a store with advertising promises of low prices for an item. However, when the customer arrives at the store, the item is reported unavailable and an alternate, often higher-priced or lower-quality product, is recommended in its place.

Balance of trade—The difference between the amount of goods a country exports and imports. When the value of exports exceeds imports, the balance is positive. In the reverse, the balance is negative.

Balance sheet—An overview of a company's assets, liabilities, and owner's equity at a specific point in time.

Balloon payment—The term for the last payment on a loan if it is substantially larger than the previous series of payments. Generally, a balloon payment is negotiated when a large sum of money is anticipated before the payoff date, making such a payment possible.

Barter—An agreement between two individuals or firms where products or services of equal value are exchanged, with no cash changing hands.

Glossary (cont'd)

Basis—The original cost of an investment that must be reported to the IRS when it is sold, in order to calculate capital gains.

Basis point—The smallest measure used in quoting bond yields, .01%. When changes in bond yields are reported, the values are in basis points.

Bear market—A prolonged period of declining stock prices. Opposite of bull market.

Bearer bond—A type of bond that can be redeemed by whoever has possession. No proof of ownership is required. The opposite of a registered security.

Beta—A measure of a stock's volatility or changes in price, as compared with changes in other stocks. Stocks with a high beta are more likely to change dramatically.

Big Blue—Slang for International Business Machines (IBM).

Big Board—Slang for the New York Stock Exchange (NYSE).

Big Eight—Originally, the eight largest accounting firms in the U.S. Through mergers, they are now the Big Six: Arthur Andersen, Ernst & Young, Deloitte & Touche, KPMG Peat Marwick, Price Waterhouse, Coopers & Lybrand.

Binding letter of intent—Letter of intent that a court of law would uphold as the actual leasing of space, regardless of whether a lease document exists.

Black-Scholes model—A formula created by Fisher Black and Myron Scholes for evaluating stock option values.

Block trade—Buying or selling 10,000 or more shares of stock or $200,000 or more in bonds.

Blue sky laws—State laws governing the issuance and trading of securities established in order to prevent fraudulent transactions.

Board of directors—A group of advisors elected by stockholders to oversee the management of a public company. The Chief Executive Officer receives direction from the board.

Bond rating—A ranking system used to assess the financial solvency of bond issuers. The better the rating, the less the likelihood that the bond issuer will default.

Book value—The value of an asset or an entire business calculated by subtracting cumulative depreciation from the original purchase price.

Brainstorm—A group idea-generation technique. Ideas and problem-solving suggestions are offered by group members until no more are forthcoming. Then the group evaluates and considers each idea, looking for ways to combine and enhance ideas with those offered by other group members.

Brand—The name, symbol, packaging, and promotional theme surrounding a product that create an identity for that product, separate from the parent company's name and identity.

Brand extension—The addition of a new product to a family of similar products using the same brand name. Ivory Shampoo is a classic example.

Breach—The failure to perform certain duties as outlined in a contract, so that the contract is not fulfilled.

Break-even—The point at which revenues from a product exactly equal the cost to produce it. This calculation is frequently used to assess whether it is worth producing a product.

Break-even pricing—A pricing technique that provides for all costs to be covered but no profit realized.

Bridge loan—A short-term loan provided while longer-term financing is being finalized. Allows for business to proceed uninterrupted.

Bucket shop—A brokerage firm that accepts customer buy and sell orders, but does not immediately execute them as the SEC requires. Instead, the firm waits until the price has increased or decreased to the point of allowing the firm to buy or sell the stock and pocket the difference. In extreme cases, the firm just takes the money, with no intention of executing the order. Such practices are illegal.

Building standard workletter—Detailed specifications of the construction items that the developer will provide and use in building a tenant's office space. Available before a lease is executed, it should be included in the lease.

Bull market—A prolonged period of rising stock prices. Opposite of bear market.

Bylaws—The rules for running a company which are drafted when the business is incorporated. Items covered include the election of a board of directors, their responsibilities, and other committees to be established to assist in managing the company.

Call—The option to purchase shares of a stock at a specified price within a certain time frame. If a stock's price rises above the option price during the option period, there is an immediate financial advantage to making the purchase.

Glossary (cont'd)

Capital assets—Capital consists of property, inventory, cash on hand, accounts receivable, and other items of value owned by a company.

Capital expenditure—Money spent to purchase or repair a capital asset, such as a plant and machinery.

Capital gains/losses—The difference between an asset's purchase price and selling price. If the difference is positive, it is considered a capital gain and is taxable. If the difference is negative, it is a capital loss and can result in a tax reduction.

Capital stock—Stock sold by a corporation, rather than resold by an investor.

Capitalization—The amount of money used to start a company.

Carryforward—A tax benefit allowing a company to apply losses realized in a previous year to future years' revenue in order to reduce taxes.

Cartel—A group of businesses or countries that agree to work together to affect the pricing and availability of certain products that they produce. OPEC is a classic example.

Cash cow—Business that has had strong sales, generating revenue consistently. In most cases, cash cows are based on products with a strong brand name that generate repeat buying.

Cash discount—A discount offered to buyers who pay their bills within a specified time period. A prompt payment incentive.

Cash flow—The actual cash in and out of a corporation. Companies can secure paper profits but go bankrupt because of negative cash flow.

Channel of distribution—The means of getting a product into a customer's hands. This might include retail stores, direct salespeople, wholesalers, and distributors.

Chapter 11—A bankruptcy status that provides time for reorganizing a company in order to make it profitable and able to pay off its debts.

Chapter 7—A bankruptcy status that allows for liquidation of all of a company's assets in order to pay off creditors.

Churn—Unnecessary and excessive trading on a customer's brokerage account, thereby generating fee income for a broker without adding value to the investments. While this practice is illegal, it is also difficult to prove.

Class action—A suit filed by one or more individuals on behalf of a larger group of people who have been treated similarly by a situation. Once the suit has been filed and the court has approved its class action status, all people who may benefit from a ruling (the parties to the suit) must be notified.

Clifford Trust—A trust established for more than 10 years that allows the transfer of assets from one individual or organization to another and then back again when the trust expires. Before new regulations were established in 1986, these trusts were a popular means of transferring income-producing assets to children, who would be taxed at a lower tax rate. The assets were typically reclaimed when the child reached the age of 18.

Cognitive dissonance—A psychological state that occurs when an individual questions an action s/he has taken, such as a purchase s/he has made, and seeks reassurance that s/he has indeed made the right decision.

Cold call—A marketing technique that involves a salesperson placing a telephone call to a potential client without having had any previous contact.

Collateral—An item of value that is used to guarantee a loan. If the borrower fails to repay the loan, the lender keeps the asset pledged as collateral.

Commodity—Bulk goods, such as crops, food, and metals, that are traded on the commodities exchange. Such items are generally used as raw materials in other products.

Common areas—Portions of a building used by more than one tenant, such as hallways, elevators, and restrooms.

Common carrier—A business that specializes in providing transport of goods and services.

Common market—The group of European nations working cooperatively to establish a unified monetary and trading policy. Also called the European Economic Community (EEC).

Common stock—A class of stock that enables the owner to participate in management of the public corporation that has issued the stock, but which receives proceeds last in the case of bankruptcy.

Comparative advantage—The theory that if two countries specialize in manufacturing different products and each can sell its product at a relative price advantage, then trade between the countries results in more products at lower prices.

Compound interest—Interest that is earned on the original amount invested plus any additional interest earned.

Consideration—An item of value given from one individual or business to another in return for a promise or agreement to do something or sell

Glossary (cont'd)

something. In a contract, there must be consideration for both sides.

Constant dollar—A measurement tool used to gauge fluctuations in consumer purchasing power. The dollar in the base year is valued at $1, with its value being expressed over future years relative to the base year.

Consumer price index—The U.S. Department of Labor's measure of change in the U.S. cost of living. A survey is conducted monthly to gauge the cost of various consumer goods, such as food, housing, and transportation. Costs are tracked over time to monitor overall living expenses.

Contempt of court—An act that interferes with the ability of the court to conduct normal business, or which insults the court's authority.

Contest—A game of skill used to get consumers interested in a company's product. A prize is offered to the winner, who is selected based on criteria described in the contest guidelines.

Contingent agreement—Agreement between two parties in which lease, sale, purchase, or payment depends on a special condition usually involving a third party.

Contract—An agreement, signed by two individuals or businesses, outlining goods or services to be exchanged, and on what terms.

Convertible security—A security, such as a bond or preferred stock, that a stockholder can convert to common stock at any time.

Copyright—The legal right of artists, authors, and creative individuals to determine who can use works that they have created.

Corporate culture—The values, beliefs, and ways of doing business that affect the way employees act, think, and feel about their employer.

Corporation—A form of doing business that establishes a separate legal entity for transacting business, providing for limited liability on the part of the owners, easy transfer of ownership through the use of shares of stock, and continued existence following the death of the owner(s).

Cost per thousand (CPM)—The cost quoted in advertising to reach one thousand people using a promotional method. Allows comparison of various promotional methods by standardizing the way costs are reported.

Cost-plus contract—A type of contract negotiated that provides for full payment of all expenses incurred in fulfilling a contract, plus an additional percentage of the total costs as the profit margin. Cost-plus contracts are common in government work, where there are situations in

which there is no way to accurately gauge upfront what a product will actually cost to produce, such as in the development of new weapons technology.

Custodian—An individual or institution that has the responsibility for overseeing the financial management of a group of assets.

Debenture—An unsecured bond that has a maturity of 15 years or more.

Default judgment—A court's decision to grant a plaintiff's motion or request without a trial simply because the defendant failed to appear in court to provide any debate on the subject.

Deferred compensation—Salary and earnings to be received at some point in the future, rather than when they are earned. Deferring payment often hast ax advantages.

Deflation—A widespread decline in prices. The opposite of inflation.

Demographics—Characteristics of individuals, such as age, education level, and marital status, that are used to better target marketing efforts to appropriate groups of consumers.

Depreciation—An asset's decline in value due to usage or obsolescence.

Devaluation—Lowering a country's currency relative to the price of gold or to another country's currency.

Dilution—The decline in value of earnings per share and stock price when new shares are issued by a company.

Direct marketing—A marketing method that involves mailing brochures and promotional materials to a group of consumers believed to have a need for, or interest in, a company's product.

Discount rate—The rate used to calculate the time value of money; the value of future cash if it were to be received today.

Disposable income—Income available to consumers after expenses for food, clothing, shelter, and other debts have been covered. Also known as discretionary income.

Divestiture—The act of selling off an asset or business, typically because it is underperforming financially or no longer fits within a company's strategic plan.

Dividend—The distribution of a company's earnings to its shareholders.

Dividend yield—The amount of a company's annual dividend for one share of stock divided by the current price of one share.

Glossary (cont'd)

Dog—A product or service with minimal sales in a low-growth market. Generally, companies attempt to rid themselves of dogs, which can be a drain on cash flow.

Domicile—An individual's permanent address or where s/he consistently returns for periods of time, but does not necessarily reside.

Dow Jones Industrial Average—An index of 30 actively traded stocks of selected companies that is used to gauge overall price changes in the stock market.

Drawee—The individual or institution who has been instructed to pay another individual out of funds on deposit. Generally, when a check is written by an individual, the bank on which the check is drawn is the drawee.

Drawer—The individual or institution that has written the check or has requested that payment be made by the drawee.

Dumping—Selling large numbers of shares of a stock, despite the fact that such a large-scale sale may cause the share price to drop or the market to decline in response. Also used to define the act of selling goods at below cost to force competitors out of the market.

Dutch auction—A sale in which the price of an item is lowered until it reaches a price at which someone is willing to buy it.

Early adopters—The small group of consumers most likely to purchase new products immediately after they are made available on the market. The majority of consumers will wait for the reaction of the early adopters before making the decision of whether to purchase the product. Early adopters are most often mentioned with regard to the electronics market.

Earnings per share—A company's annual earnings divided by the total number of shares outstanding.

Easement—An agreement providing one individual or business with the right to use land owned by someone else. In the case of real estate transactions, long-term easements can affect the value of a property if they interfere with the potential usage of the land. One example of an easement is an agreement between a landowner and the telephone company to permit the installation of telephone poles on the land.

Economies of scale—The improvements in a company's operational efficiency as a result of savings from purchasing inventory in volume, the division of labor, and the learning curve.

80-20 rule—Business experience that indicates that 80% of a company's revenue will come from just 20% of its total customer base.

Elasticity of demand—A measure of the responsiveness of buyers to changes in a product's price. Demand is elastic if it increases due to price reductions or decreases due to price increases. Luxury items are generally more elastic, because consumers can wait for price changes before purchasing. Cigarette demand, on the other hand, is virtually inelastic.

Encumbrance—Any agreement involving the use of land that does not prohibit its sale, but which may reduce its value. An easement is one type of encumbrance. Other common encumbrances include liens and mortgages.

Equity—The value of common and preferred stock owned by stockholders.

Equity financing—Raising money by issuing stock, thereby offering part ownership in the company in return for an investment.

ERISA—The Employee Retirement Income Security Act, enacted in 1973 to set standards for how company pensions and retirement accounts are managed.

Escalator(s)—A clause in an agreement that increases prices or rents over time.

Escrow money—Assets held by a third party until the conditions of a contract are satisfied, at which time they are paid out.

ESOP—An Employee Stock Ownership Plan, a program to encourage employee investment in company stock.

Estoppel—A legal situation barring one individual or business from denying the existence of contracts or agreements when it is clear that a contract exists. Such situations can arise after one individual realizes that the terms of a signed contract is detrimental to his or her business and claims that the contract is invalid. An estoppel comes into play when the court recognizes that the contract exists and prevents the individual from trying to deny its existence as part of a legal suit.

Exchange rate—The price at which one country's currency can be converted to another currency.

Experience curve—The efficiency gains realized in production as more products are manufactured.

Fannie Mae—Federal National Mortgage Association. A publicly owned organization that purchases mortgages from banks and resells them on the open market to investors.

FASB—Financial Accounting Standards Board. A governing body established in 1973 to define and monitor the usage of generally accepted accounting principles.

Glossary (cont'd)

FDIC— Federal Deposit Insurance Corporation, the federal agency that guarantees deposits made by consumers in member banks.

Federal funds rate—The interest rate charged by Federal Reserve district banks for short-term, overnight loans to banks who cannot meet reserve cash requirements.

Federal Reserve Board—The governing body of the Federal Reserve System; seven presidential appointees who establish and oversee the U.S. money supply through its banking system.

Federal Reserve System—An organization established by the Federal Reserve Act of 1913 to regulate the U.S. banking system. Twelve regional Federal Reserve Banks and 24 branches oversee all of its member banks nationwide.

Fee—In real estate, property that is owned by an individual without any restrictions on its use.

FIFO—First In, First Out, a method of accounting for inventory that assumes that the first item to be produced was the first item sold. The opposite of LIFO.

Fixed cost—Production costs that do not vary, even when sales volumes change. Expenses such as rent, interest, and executive compensation are considered fixed costs.

Float—The time lag between when a check is deposited and when it clears.

Floor area ratio (F.A.R.)—Ratio between floor area and height.

Focus group—A non-scientific market research technique involving a group of 8 to 12 individuals who are brought together to provide feedback on such issues as new products, advertising campaigns, and a company's reputation.

Forward contract—An agreement to conduct business on a future date.

Franchise—The sale of the license and rights to establish and manage a business under a recognized name using set business practices. McDonald's, one of the most famous franchises, sells the rights to operate a restaurant within a specific geographic area provided all operating standards are maintained.

Franchisee—The individual or company that purchases the rights to operate a business from the owner or franchisor.

Franchisor—The owner of the rights to a business concept who sells them to the franchisee.

Fraudulent conveyance—The transfer of funds or property from one individual or business to another in order to avoid having to turn over such assets to creditors. A form of hiding assets.

Free on board (FOB)—Shipping arrangements that indicate exactly when the buyer assumes responsibility for the transport of a product. The location specified on an invoice as FOB Anywhere is the point to which the seller will assume responsibility for transport. Beyond that point, it is the buyer's responsibility.

Frequency—The calculation of how many times an advertisement has been seen by a specific population. An ad with a frequency of four, reaches each consumer four times. The higher the frequency, the better the chances that an ad will be noticed.

Full faith and credit—The requirement that legal judgments issued in one state be upheld and recognized by all other states.

Futures contract— An agreement made between traders on the floor of the commodity exchange regarding the purchase of commodities on a specific date in the future for an agreed-upon price.

GATT—General Agreement on Tariffs and Trade. A multinational trade agreement regarding trade issues and policies.

Generic—A non-branded product sold at prices generally below those of name-brand products.

Gold standard—A national monetary standard using gold as the basis.

Golden handcuffs—An employment contract between employer and employee that provides lucrative compensation and benefits during an employee's tenure with the firm. However, if the employee leaves, s/he is liable for repayment of the compensation and benefits received during his or her employment.

Golden parachute—A lucrative severance package negotiated for a top executive in the event of a takeover.

Goodwill—The intangible assets of a business that impact its overall value. Such assets might include company reputation, loyal customer base, brand recognition, and employee morale.

Greenmail—Repurchase of company stock from a potential acquirer in return for assurances that the acquirer will not pursue the takeover of the company. Generally, the purchase price of the stock is inflated by the acquirer.

Gross profit—The amount remaining after the cost to produce a product (cost of goods sold) is subtracted from the net sales.

Glossary (cont'd)

Gross rating point—A measure of the size of an audience watching a television program during a certain time period, reported in percentages of the total audience size.

Guaranty—An agreement to be responsible for the obligations of another individual or business.

Hedge—An investment tactic in which securities are purchased on both sides of a risk, so that any loss in one security is countered by gains in the other securities.

Holder in due course—An individual or business that accepts a check or form of payment in exchange for merchandise or property without noticing that the check is invalid. The individual accepting the check is the holder in due course and has the right to pursue full payment from the person who wrote the check.

Holding company—A company whose sole purpose is to hold stock in other companies, rather than creating a product or service itself.

Holdover rent—High rent that penalizes a tenant for staying beyond the term of a lease.

Horizontal market—A market with a wide range of customers–the market for sneakers, for example. As opposed to a vertical market, which might include people buying equipment for brain surgery.

In camera—The act of reviewing legal documents and motions in a judge's chambers, rather than in a public courtroom. In the case of sensitive information that could be publicly embarrassing or damaging to people involved in a suit, the information is often reviewed privately by a judge to decide whether it should become public through a court action.

Income statement—A summary of a company's revenue and expenses for a specified period of time, usually one year. This, and the balance sheet, make up a company's financial statements. Also known as a profit and loss statement.

Inelastic demand—A demand for products that remains relatively constant despite any changes in price. Basic needs for food and utilities, for instance, cannot be put off until prices drop.

Inflation—Widespread rise in prices that causes an overall increase in the cost of living.

Initial Public Offering—The first offering of a stock for sale to the public.

Injunction—A court order barring a defendant from doing something that would harm the plaintiff. If the defendant ignores the order, s/he may face fines, penalties, or formal charges.

Innovators—Consumers who are some of the first to try a new product.

Insider trading—Illegal trading of securities based on confidential information from internal company sources. Since such information would not be generally available to the public, the trader has an unfair advantage.

Intangible asset—Non-physical company assets such as patents, technical know-how, and trademarks.

Interest—Fees paid by a borrower to a lender for the use of the lender's money.

Internal rate of return (IRR)—The discount rate at which an investment has a net present value of $0.

Inventory turnover—The rate at which a firm's inventory is totally depleted over a period of time, usually a year. A company's average inventory divided by its annual sales will give you its inventory turnover.

Joint venture—An agreement between two or more groups to work together on a specific project.

Judgment debtor—An individual who owes an individual or business money following a legal judgment. The individual or business to whom the money is owed is the judgment creditor.

Junk bond—A bond with a rating of BB or worse that is considered to be more volatile than higher rated bonds. In return for the higher risk of default, the bonds promise higher yields.

Just-in-time purchasing—A purchasing method that schedules delivery of raw materials just at the point in the production when they are needed. Such arrangements reduce the cost of holding the inventory in-house and increase pressure on suppliers to create top quality materials.

Keogh plan—A pension program specifically for the self-employed.

Laches—The extended delay in processing a legal matter in which the defendant is placed at a disadvantage in proving his/her innocence because evidence no longer exists, witnesses are no longer living, or difficulties have occurred.

Laissez faire—The belief that government intervention in business should be minimal.

Latent defect—A problem or defect that cannot be discovered through normal examination and that is not noticed by the seller when turning the product or service over to the buyer. Such defects often become noticeable after a product or service has been delivered. Assets such as real estate, automobiles, and machinery most frequently have latent defects because it

Glossary (cont'd)

is difficult to check every possible source of future problems before the sale to the new owner.

Leading economic indicator—Twelve ratios tracked by the U.S. Department of Commerce as indications of economic activity.

Lease—A long-term rental agreement.

Lease term—Length of time a lease is in full force.

Lease year—Any period of 12 consecutive months, starting from the first day of a month.

Lessee—Tenant who pays rent in return for the right to use office space.

Lessor—Landlord who receives payment for renting out office space.

Letter of credit—A document provided by a bank on behalf of a customer guaranteeing that a debt will be paid up to a certain amount. Such letters are often necessary in international dealings.

Letter of intent—Good faith agreement signed by tenant and landlord prior to lease, setting forth major terms and conditions.

Letter of representation—Agreement between tenant and broker giving broker exclusive rights to locate and negotiate for office space.

Leveraged buyout—A purchase method that uses the existing assets of a company to finance its purchase by an outside investor.

Lien—A lender's claim to assets, usually as a guarantee against a loan.

LIFO—Last In, First Out. An accounting method for valuing inventory that assumes that the last or most recently produced item is the next item to be sold.

Limited partnership—A form of a partnership composed of a general manager responsible for the day-to-day management of the business and several limited partners who invest money but who have limited involvement in the management of the firm and, hence, limited liability for its financial obligations.

Line of credit—An agreement between a lender and borrower allowing the borrower to draw on a pool of money up to an established limit.

Liquid—Easily converted into cash.

Liquidated damages—The amount of money one individual or business agrees to pay another in the event that they breach a contract signed by both parties. Liquidated damages are calculated as part of the contract, so that both parties know at the outset what it will cost them if they are responsible for a breach of contract.

Load—The sales charge paid by an investor for the privilege of buying shares in a mutual fund.

Loss leader—Products sold at a loss as a means of drawing customers into a store. For example, Toys 'R' Us toy store sells childrens' diapers at an extreme discount in order to draw parents into the store on a regular basis, hoping that once they are in the store, they will buy something else.

M1—The amount of U.S. currency in circulation at any given point in time, plus consumer bank deposits.

M2—M1 plus overnight European transactions, savings, and money market mutual fund transactions.

M3—A broad measure of the money supply, including M1, M2, and time deposits over $100,000 in value.

Manufacturer's agent—An independent salesperson representing a manufacturing firm or firms on a non-exclusive basis. Such arrangements reduce the need for manufacturers to keep large sales forces on staff.

Margin—Money borrowed from a brokerage house in order to purchase more securities.

Marginal cost—The cost of producing one more unit of a product or service beyond the planned quantity.

Marginal revenue—The change in total revenues for a firm from the sale of one more product.

Market rent—Current rental rates for similar kinds of office space.

Market share—The percentage of total industry sales that one company is responsible for. For instance, XYZ Co. has $10 million in sales in the widget industry, which has a total of $100 million in sales from all companies in the industry. So, XYZ has a 10% market share.

Marketing mix—The tools used to market a product or service, including the price, channels of distribution, promotional methods, and the product features.

Markup—The difference between the cost to produce a product and its selling price.

Material—Information relevant to a particular matter that may affect the outcome of a legal suit.

Mean—The average of a set of numbers. Calculated by adding several numbers together, counting how many numbers are being added, and then dividing by that number.

Median—The middle point in a series of numbers where half the numbers are higher and half are lower. For example, 3 is the median between 1 and 5.

Glossary (cont'd)

Mitigation of damages—The legal requirement that an individual who has been negatively affected by the action of another and who has been repaid for that action must make every effort not to hold the other responsible for any self-inflicted aggravation to the situation.

Mode—The number appearing most frequently in a series of numbers. For instance in the series 1,2,5,2,7,2,8, 2 is the mode, appearing more frequently than any of the other numbers.

Monetarism—The economic perspective that the federal money supply has great impact on the growth of the economy and should be handled carefully.

Monetary policy—Decisions made by the Federal Reserve Board regarding the amount of money in circulation at a given point. By supplying more credit to the banking system or withdrawing credit, the Federal Reserve Board can affect the growth of the economy.

Money market—The market for safe, short-term investments.

Monopoly—A market with one firm in control of the manufacture and supply of a product. Until the advent of Federal Express, the Postal Service was a monopoly.

Monopsony—A market with just one buyer for a product or service and many sellers.

Mortgage—A loan to purchase real estate, with the property used as collateral to guarantee the loan.

Mortgage REIT—A real estate investment trust that invests in real estate mortgages. Instead of investing in one or two properties, investors can buy shares in an REIT, which owns many different types of properties.

Multinational—A company with branch offices in many countries.

Mutual fund—A diversified portfolio of investments purchased in shares through brokers.

Naked option—The situation in which an investor has purchased a put or call, but does not own any shares. If the share price rises, there is the potential for great gains, without having to invest large sums of money to actually purchase shares. However, if the price drops and the investor has to replace the shares "borrowed" for the transaction, the cash outlay can be huge.

Nationalization—Action by the government to acquire ownership in a company or industry.

Negotiable—Investments that can be easily transferred to another form.

Negotiable instrument—A document, promising to pay an amount of money to another individual or business, that can be transferred to someone else and still be valid. A check is the most common form of a negotiable instrument.

Net present value—Today's discounted value of a string of cash inflows in the future.

Net sales—Gross sales minus such costs as cash discounts, shipping charges, and inventory returns.

Net worth—An individual's or business's total asset value minus all obligations.

No par—Stocks issued without a specific face value.

Non-callable—Securities that issuers cannot redeem before the date of maturity.

Non-conforming use—Changes in zoning requirements that occur after a structure has been built and is in use and that now make the structure noncompliant. A non-conforming use permits continued use of the structure, but requires that any future changes to it be approved by the zoning board.

Offering circular—Brief marketing materials describing a new stock issue.

Oligopoly—A market in which there are several firms, none of which is dominant enough to control the entire market through its actions.

Operating income—Income generated from day-to-day operations of a firm.

Opinion—A written evaluation of the accuracy of a firm's financial statements provided by the firm's certified public accounting firm.

Opportunity cost—The cost of giving up one opportunity in order to invest in another. For instance, the opportunity cost of eating a hot fudge sundae is the brownie you could have had instead.

Option—The purchased right to buy or sell securities at a set price for a specified period of time. Key executives often receive options to purchase company stock at an advantageous price as part of their compensation package.

Original equipment manufacturer (OEM)—A manufacturer that supplies its product to other firms who sell it as part of their product line, often under a different brand name.

Over the counter (OTC)—The market for securities that are not bought and sold over the major exchanges. Penny stocks are one example of securities that are only available over the counter.

Overdraft—A situation in which the amount of money deposited in an account does not adequately cover the obligations on the account.

Glossary (cont'd)

Overreaching—The advantage that one business acquires when it cheats or defrauds another business. Any agreements or contracts that arise from overreaching are invalid.

Owner's equity—The total value of a company's shares of stock minus obligations.

Paper—Short-term obligations issued for terms of 2 to 270 days. Such investments are targeted to investors with large amounts of cash available on a short-term basis.

Par value—The value of a security printed on the certificate.

Parking—Investing funds temporarily in short-term, safe havens while longer-term investment options are considered.

Partial breach—A minor breach of contract that does not affect an agreement to a major extent. As a result, the contract is maintained. An example of a partial breach would be if a business is a day late in delivering some materials necessary for a contract. If a one day delay has no material affect on the ability of the other business to hold up its part of the bargain, then it is only a partial breach.

Partnership—A firm owned by two or more people who are jointly liable for the assets and obligations of the firm.

Patent—A legal claim to a new process or device that provides protection from theft by other companies or individuals for 17 years. Patents must be registered in order to be protected.

Penny stock—A stock with an initial offering price of less than one dollar, available through over-the-counter markets and considered a high risk investment.

Pension fund—An investment fund established by a corporation or organization to manage retirement benefits and investments for its employees.

PERT—Program Evaluation and Review Technique, a scheduling method that graphically shows when certain project tasks must be completed before other activities can begin.

Piercing the corporate veil—The process of suing individuals involved in the management of a corporation. Since corporations generally shield individuals from liability, such action can only be taken if it can be proven that there is a good reason to disregard the corporate entity.

Point-of-purchase promotion—A piece of marketing literature that is placed in a store where a customer is likely to be making a purchase decision about a product.

Poison pill—A resolution passed by a company's board of directors that makes it difficult or impossible to stage an unfriendly takeover.

Ponzi scheme—A pyramid marketing program in which the proceeds from new investors are used to pay off existing investors. The last wave of investors is left with nothing.

Portfolio—Several securities owned by one individual or institution. A variety of securities reduces investment risk, so a diversified portfolio is the goal.

Position—The amount of money an individual has invested in a particular security; a company's stake.

Positioning—The way a company wants to be perceived by its public. The position is supported by investments in advertising, direct marketing, and public relations.

Power of acceptance—An individual's right and ability to accept or reject the terms of a contract.

Power of attorney—Appointing an individual to make important decisions for another individual.

Preferred stock—A class of stock that receives its dividends before common stock. Common stock dividends cannot be paid until and unless preferred stockholders have been paid.

Premium—The additional amount a stock is worth relative to other stocks. When one stock is selling at a higher price than another it is said to be selling at a premium of X%.

Pre-paid expense—Paying for an expense in advance, usually for tax or accounting reasons.

Price-earnings ratio (P/E ratio)—Current share price divided by a stock's earnings per share. Stocks in similar industries often have similar P/E ratios. Any differences reflect investor anticipation of the company's prospects.

Prime rate—The interest rate banks offer to their best commercial customers.

Principal—The base amount of money borrowed as part of a loan on which interest will be charged.

Private placement—Offering securities directly to private investors, rather than through a public offering.

Privileged communication—Discussions that take place between an attorney and his/her client that may not be forcibly divulged in court proceedings.

Product life cycle—The stages through which a product progresses in the marketplace. This

Glossary (cont'd)

normally includes introduction, acceptance, growth, and maturity.

Product portfolio—All the products a company has to sell.

Profit margin—The selling price of an item less all variable costs.

Profit-sharing plan—A plan that provides for the division of a portion of the company's profits, part of which are generally deposited into a tax-deferred account. The funds are paid out when the employee retires or leaves the company.

Program trading—Computerized buying and selling of stocks, bonds, and commodities.

Progressive tax—A type of tax that takes a larger proportion of income from those with higher incomes.

Promotion—Marketing tactics that communicate product and company information to the public through such vehicles as newsletters, advertisements, sweepstakes, and brochures.

Proprietorship—A type of business that is controlled and managed by one person.

Prospecting—The marketing practice of seeking out and classifying potential clients in terms of their likelihood to buy.

Prospectus—A summary of the registration statement for a security that has been filed with the SEC.

Protectionism—Government policy of establishing barriers to entry for foreign products, making domestic products more desirable. Such barriers protect domestic firms and products by making foreign products more expensive.

Proxy—Written authorization to act on behalf of someone else in a specific capacity, such as with stock voting rights.

Public relations—Activities on behalf of a company or organization that increase the company's exposure in the community through media coverage, sponsorships, and community involvement.

Put—An option to sell a specific stock for a specified price within a set time frame.

Pyramid—An illegal investment practice that involves soliciting investors by promising them high returns, but then using their invested funds to pay earlier investors, rather than actually investing those funds in securities.

Quantum meruit—The right to sue for payment resulting from an implied or existing contract. When individuals or businesses provide goods or services through an implied contract but are not paid, they can sue the other party in quantum meruit in order to be paid.

Question mark—A classification of a product line that is in a high growth market, but which isn't yet performing as well as anticipated. Such ventures can either yield great returns by acquiring a large share of the growing market, or they can lose money by falling behind.

Quick ratio—A measure of liquidity calculated by subtracting inventory values from current assets and dividing that figure by current liabilities.

Raider—An investor who aims to take control of a company by purchasing a majority stake in the firm.

Real estate—Land and property, including any building and structures on a parcel of land.

Real estate investment trust (REIT)—A real estate investment trust that invests in a variety of real estate properties. Instead of investing in one or two properties, investors can buy shares in a REIT, which owns many different types of properties, and reduce their risk.

Real income—Income adjusted for inflation, which is considered to be a truer measure of purchasing power than income itself.

Receiver—A court-appointed individual who is responsible for managing the day-to-day affairs of a company involved in bankruptcy proceedings. The receiver does not own the company and is not liable for the company's obligations, but simply keeps the company running until a determination is made on the bankruptcy claim.

Recession—Several months of decline in business activity.

Recoupment—A discount or reduction negotiated by a buyer or defendant in a legal matter.

Red herring—A preliminary prospectus issued before SEC approval for a security sale. Identified by the red band across the first page.

Registration statement—A document prepared prior to the public offering of securities, detailing the financial situation of the company, its history and background, and the qualifications of the business managers.

Regression analysis—A statistical tool used to look at past events and determine cause and effect.

Regressive tax—A type of tax that takes a larger proportion of income from those with lower incomes.

Re-insurance—The practice of spreading the risk of insuring someone across several insurance companies, in return for a portion of the pre-

Glossary (cont'd)

mium payment. Lloyd's of London is a re-insurance marketplace.

Release—A document that certifies that an individual or business has given up a claim to something.

Rent abatement—Reducing rent by omitting payments for a number of months to induce tenants to lease office space.

Replacement cost—The cost of replacing an asset with the same asset if the original were to break or malfunction.

Reserve requirement—The percentage of funds the Federal Reserve Board requires that member banks maintain on deposit at all times.

Retained earnings—Earnings that are left after dividends are paid out.

Retention—The number of units retained by an investment banker during the process of underwriting a securities sale, minus the units set aside for institutional sales.

Return on equity (ROE)—The return investors receive on their investment in a security, expressed as a percentage.

Royalty—Payment made to the owner of an asset in return for its use in generating income. Such payments are made to patent holders who grant permission to use the patent, as well as to authors, who are paid royalties based on book sales.

Sale and leaseback—The sale of an asset which is immediately leased from the new owner. Such a transaction helps to increase short-term cash flow for the seller, and can provide tax advantages.

Sallie Mae—Student Loan Marketing Association. A government-funded agency that guarantees student loans, purchasing them from financial institutions and selling them on the secondary market.

Scrip—A document issued by a corporation to represent a fractional share of stock. Scrip may be collected and presented for full shares.

Sector—Stocks from one particular industry. Stocks from firms in the automotive industry are in the automotive sector, for instance. Brokerage firms may specialize in tracking particular sectors.

Securities and Exchange Commission (SEC)—The government agency responsible for monitoring the issuance and sale of securities.

Security interest—The right to collateral in return for granting some form of financing. A creditor has a security interest in assets that have been pledged as collateral on a loan.

Segment—A grouping of customers within a market with similarities in their purchasing needs or preferences.

Self-liquidating premium—A premium paid in part or in full by the buyer. Includes gimmicks offered on the side of cereal boxes.

Senior debt—Debt that must be paid before subordinated debt, such as common stock, can be paid. This is a consideration in bankruptcy situations.

Service of process—The action of delivering or communicating information on a legal proceeding to the plaintiff or defendant in a suit.

Settlement—Completing a transaction by paying all obligations.

Seven sisters—The seven major international oil companies: British Petroleum, Chevron, Exxon, Gulf, Mobil, Shell, and Texaco.

Shakeout—The shutdown or closing of several firms in an industry, leaving only a few dominant players.

Share—One unit of stock in a corporation.

Shark repellent—Provisions established by a corporation to discourage unwanted takeover attempts by making it more expensive and difficult to purchase the company.

Short hedge—Hedges taken to lessen or eliminate the financial loss occurring from falling share prices.

Short position—A stock purchase procedure that involves "borrowing" shares of stock through a broker, selling them, and repurchasing them when the price has dropped. The buyer never actually takes possession of the shares and can make a profit if the shares are repurchased for less than what they were "borrowed" for. However, if the stock price rises, the buyer must pay to buy back the shares, thereby losing money.

Shrinkage—Losses experienced from worker and customer shoplifting.

Simple interest—Interest earned only on the initial capital investment. Unlike compound interest, which continues to accrue on both the capital and the earned interest, simple interest only applies to the capital.

Simulation—The process of creating an investment model in order to adjust certain variables to see their effect on investments. This type of learning can help brokers make decisions regarding where to place their clients' money.

Sixteenth—Reference to one sixteenth of a point change in the price of stocks, bonds, and options.

Glossary (cont'd)

Small-capitalization stock—Shares of stock issued by small firms with little equity or stock outstanding.

Smokestack industry—Basic manufacturing industries that have experienced minimal growth during the past decades.

Sovereign risk—Risk that lenders assume when making loans to foreign governments due to the fact that a change in the national power structure could cause the country to default on its commitments.

Specialist—A member of the securities exchange responsible for executing securities trades on a particular stock.

Spinoff—Separating a corporate division from the parent company and establishing it as its own independent operating unit.

Split—Increasing the number of shares outstanding without increasing the shareowner's equity, causing a drop in the share price proportional to the number of new shares.

Sponsor—A trader, generally an institution or brokerage firm, whose large scale purchases influence the purchases of other traders. The demand for a stock can be significantly affected by the actions of a sponsor.

Spread—The difference between yields of various maturities. For instance, the spread between a 3-month CD of 3% and a 5-year CD of 6% is 3 percentage points.

Stagflation—The economic condition of slowed economic growth and rising unemployment coupled with rising prices.

Standard deviation—A statistical measure used to assess variability.

Standard Metropolitan Statistical Area (SMSA)—A geographical area consisting of at least 50,000 residents. Used in marketing to determine potential sales and advertising costs for an area.

Star—A business or product line with growth potential–a market leader in a fast-growing market. Stars can become a cash cow or a question mark, depending on their performance.

Stock—Units of ownership in a publicly-held company.

Stock dividend—A dividend paid in shares of stock instead of cash.

Stock option—The opportunity to purchase shares of stock at a specified price and within a specified time period.

Stop order—An order given to a broker to buy or sell a security when it reaches a certain price.

Straight-life annuity—A series of payments that continues only while the recipient is alive.

Straight-line depreciation—A method of depreciating an asset by reducing its value in equal amounts each year.

Strategic business unit (SBU)—An organizational unit within a company that is typically focused on selling to one market segment or specializing in one type of product.

Strategic plan—A long-term road map for a company, spelling out its financial and operational objectives for the next 3-5 years.

Strip—The practice of dividing a bond into a series of lesser-valued zero-coupon bonds.

Strong dollar—When the foreign exchange rate results in the U.S. dollar being able to purchase foreign goods more cheaply.

Subordinated debenture—Debt which is paid out after preferred stock and bonds.

Supply-side economics—Economic policy that supports reduction in taxes as a means of improving the long-term growth of the economy.

Sweepstakes—A type of contest that encourages participants to purchase a product in order to be considered for free prizes. A lottery, which is illegal, requires a payment for a game of chance. A sweepstakes offers an alternative means of entry, eliminating the cost to play.

Syndicate—A group of individuals who have formed a joint venture to undertake a project they would have been unable to complete individually.

Synergy—A theory that states that businesses or groups merged into a large organization will be more productive and successful than the businesses were individually; the whole is greater than the sum of its parts.

Takeover—The action of assuming control of a business, usually by a raider.

Tangible asset—Physical assets, such as land, buildings, and machinery, that can be sold separately from the business entity.

Target market—A group of consumers or businesses believed to have a need for a company's products that the company attempts to communicate with through advertising.

Tariff—A tax levied on imported products that makes them more expensive, and hence less desirable, than domestic products.

Tax haven—A geographic location that charges little or no taxes on businesses in the area.

Technical correction—An unexplained drop in stock prices after several days of increases.

Glossary (cont'd)

10-K—An annual report filed with the SEC on behalf of any company that has stock issued, providing information on revenues and income.

Tenancy—Possession or occupancy of real estate by title, under a lease, or on payment of rent, with or without a written lease.

Tenant—Individual or entity paying rent to use or occupy property owned by another.

Tender offer—An offer made by one company seeking to buy another company by purchasing its shares of stock at a price above the current market price.

Term-to-maturity—The amount of time that will elapse before an obligation becomes due.

Time value of money—A dollar received today is worth more than a dollar received at some point in the future, considering the fact that rising prices will mean that a dollar will buy even less in the future.

Tombstone—A form of advertisement announcing the issuance of a security by a particular firm or group of firms.

Tout—To promote a firm or security to a group of clients by praising it.

Trade deficit—The difference between the amount of exports and imports a country has. When there are more imports than exports, a trade deficit exists for the country receiving the imports.

Trade secrets—Secret ideas, processes, or ways of doing business that give a firm an advantage but which are not patented. Businesses try to protect such information from being given to the competition.

Trade surplus—When a country's exports exceed its imports.

Trademark—A registered symbol, theme, mark, or identification related to a person or company. Only that company can use or grant the use of a trademarked item.

Transfer pricing—The cost to sell a company's product to another division or department internally. Since there is no need for markup and external distribution costs with an internal sale, the transfer price is typically less than the retail price.

Trend—A series of occurrences that indicate a pattern.

Triple witching hour—The hour before the market closes on a day when both stock options and futures expire.

Trust—A relationship established that gives one individual, the trustee, responsibility for the management and care of assets on behalf of another individual, the beneficiary.

Undercapitalized—A situation in which a business does not have the necessary funds to transact normal business.

Undervalued—When a share is trading at a price lower than its market value.

Underwrite—The process of purchasing securities from the issuer in order to sell them back to the public.

Unfriendly takeover—The acquisition of a business under protest from the current managers and/or owners.

Unrealized loss—A loss that has occurred on paper through a drop in price but which has not yet been realized because the security has not yet been sold.

Value-added tax—A tax levied at each stage in the production cycle, when another feature is added to the functioning of the product.

Variable cost—Production costs involving raw materials, labor, and utilities that vary according to the production quantity.

Venture capital—Capital provided by a pool of investors for use by firms just starting or expanding, in return for an equity position in the venture.

Voting rights—The opportunity to vote on issues of importance to the company. Owners of common stock acquire voting rights.

Warrant—A type of security that gives the owner the right to purchase a certain number of shares of stock at a price slightly higher than the market price at issuance. The warrant is usually good for several years, however, providing time for the stock price to appreciate.

Wasting asset—An asset that declines in value.

Workout—The process of renegotiating a loan package.

Yield curve—A graph showing the various bond maturities and corresponding yields. When the shorter-term bond rates are higher than the longer-term rates, the yield curve is negative. And when the shorter-term bond rates are lower than the longer-term rates, the curve is positive.

Weights and Measures

Linear Measure

12 inches (in) = 1 foot (ft)
3 feet = 1 yard (yd)
5 1/2 yards = 1 rod (rd), pole, or perch (16 1/2 ft)
40 rods = 1 furlong (fur) = 220 yds = 660 ft
8 furlongs = 1 statute mile (mi) = 1,760 yds = 5,280 ft
3 land miles = 1 league
5,280 feet = 1 statute or land mile
6,076.11549 feet = 1 international nautical mile

Area Measure

144 square inches = 1 sq ft
9 square feet = 1 sq yd = 1,296 sq in
30 1/4 square yards = 1 sq rd = 272 1/4 sq ft
160 square rods = 1 acre = 4,840 sq yds = 43,560 sq ft
640 acres = 1 sq mi
1 mile square = 1 section (of land)
6 miles square = 1 township = 36 sections = 36 sq mi

Cubic Measure

1,728 cubic inches = 1 cu ft
27 cubic feet = 1 cu yd

Liquid Measure

2 pints = 1 quart (qt) (= 57.75 cu in.)
4 quarts = 1 gallon (gal) (= 231 cu in.) = 8 pts

Apothecaries' Fluid Measure

60 minims (min.) = 1 fluid dram (fl dr)
8 fluid drams = 1 fluid ounce (fl oz)
16 fluid ounces = 1 pt
2 pints = 1 qt
4 quarts = 1 gal

Dry Measure

2 pints = 1 qt (= 67.20 cu in.)
8 quarts = 1 peck (pk) (= 537.60 cu in.) = 16 pts
4 pecks = 1 bushel (bu) (= 2,150.42 cu in.) = 32 qts

Avoirdupois Weight

27 11/32 grains = 1 dram (dr)
16 drams = 1 oz = 437 1/2 grains
16 ounces = 1 lb = 256 drams = 7,000 grains
100 pounds = 1 hundredweight (cwt)1
20 hundredweights = 1 ton(tn) = 2,000 lbs 1

Units of Circular Measure

Minute (') = 60 seconds
Degree (°) = 60 minutes
Right angle = 90 degrees
Straight angle = 180 degrees
Circle = 360 degrees

Troy Weight

24 grains = 1 pennyweight (dwt)
20 pennyweights = 1 ounce troy (oz t)
12 ounces troy = 1 pound (lb t)

Metric and U.S. Equivalents

1 angstrom (light wave measurement) = 0.1 millimicron
1 angstrom = 0.0000001 millimeter
1 angstrom = 0.0000004 inch
1 cable's length = 120 fathoms
1 cable's length = 720 feet
1 cable's length = 219.45 meters
1 centimeter = 0.39 inch
1 chain (Gunter's or surveyor's) = 66 feet
1 chain (Gunter's or surveyor's) = 20.11 meters
1 decimeter = 3.93 inches
1 dekameter = 32.80 feet
1 fathom = 6 feet
1 fathom = 1.82 meters
1 foot = 0.30 meter
1 furlong = 10 chains (surveyor's)
1 furlong = 660 feet
1 furlong = 220 yards
1 furlong = 1/8 statute mile
1 furlong = 201.16 meters
1 inch = 2.54 centimeters
1 kilometer = 0.62 mile
1 league (land) = 3 statute miles
1 league (land) = 4.82 kilometers
1 link (Gunter's or surveyor's) = 7.92inches
1 link (Gunter's or surveyor's) = 0.201168 meter
1 meter = 39.37 inches
1 meter = 1.09 yards
1 micron = 0.00 millimeter
1 micron = 0.00003937 inch
1 mil = 0.00 inch
1 mil = 0.02 millimeter
1 mile (statute or land) = 5,280 feet
1 mile (statute or land) = 1.60 kilometers
1 mile (nautical international) = 1.85 kilometers
1 mile (nautical international) = 1.15 statute miles
1 mile (nautical international) = 0.99 U.S. nautical miles
1 millimeter = 0.03937 inch
1 millimicron = 0.00 micron
1 millimicron = 0.00000003937 inch
1 nanometer = 0.00 micrometer
1 nanometer = 0.00000003937 inch
1 point (typography) = 0.013837 inch
1 point (typography) = 1/72 inch
1 point (typography) = 0.35 millimeter
1 yard = 0.91 meter

Areas or Surfaces

1 acre = 43,560 square feet
1 acre = 4,840 square yards
1 acre = 0.40 hectare
1 hectare = 2.47 acres

Weights and Measures (cont'd)

1 square centimeter = 0.15 square inch
1 square decimeter = 15.5 square inches
1 square foot = 929.03 square centimeters
1 square inch = 6.45 square centimeters
1 square kilometer = 0.38 square mile
1 square kilometer = 247.10 acres
1 square meter = 1.19 square yards
1 square meter = 10.76 square feet
1 square mile = 258.99 hectares
1 square millimeter = 0.00 square inch
1 square rod, square pole or square perch = 25.29 square meters
1 square yard = 0.83 square meters

Capacities or Volumes

1 cord (firewood) = 128 cubic feet
1 cubic centimeter = 0.06 cubic inch
1 cubic decimeter = 61.02 cubic inches
1 cubic foot = 7.48 gallons
1 cubic foot = 28.31 cubic decimeters
1 cubic inch = 0.55 fluid ounce
1 cubic inch = 4.43 fluid drams
1 cubic inch = 16.38 cubic centimeters
1 cubic meter = 1.30 cubic yards
1 cubic yard = 0.76 cubic meter
1 cup, measuring = 8 fluid ounces
1 cubic inch = 1/2 liquid pint
1 dram, fluid or liquid (U.S.) = 1/8 fluid ounce
1 dram, fluid or liquid (U.S.) = 0.22 cubic inch
1 dram, fluid or liquid (U.S.) = 3.69 milliliters
1 dram, fluid or liquid (U.S.) = 1.04 British fluid drams
1 dekaliter = 2.64 gallons
1 dekaliter = 1.13 pecks
1 gallon (U.S.) = 231 cubic inches
1 gallon (U.S.) = 3.78 liters
1 gallon (U.S.) = 0.83 British gallon
1 gallon (U.S.) = 128 U.S. fluid ounces
1 gallon (British Imperial) = 277.42 cubic inches
1 gallon (British Imperial) = 1.20 U.S. gallons
1 gallon (British Imperial) = 4.54 liters
1 gallon (British Imperial) = 160 British fluid ounces
1 liter = 1.05 liquid quarts
1 liter = 0.90 dry quart
1 milliliter = 0.27 fluid dram
1 ounce, fluid or liquid (U.S.) = 1.80 cubic inch
1 ounce, fluid or liquid (U.S.) = 29.57 milliliters
1 ounce, fluid or liquid (U.S.) = 1.04 British fluid ounces
1 peck = 8.81 liters
1 pint, dry = 0.55 liter
1 pint, liquid = 0.47 liter
1 quart, dry (U.S.) = 1.10 liters
1 quart, liquid (U.S.) = 0.94 liter
1 quart (British) = 1.03 U.S. dry quarts
1 quart (British) = 1.20 U.S. liquid quarts
1 tablespoon, measuring = 3 teaspoons
1 tablespoon, measuring = 4 fluid drams
1 tablespoon, measuring = 1/2 fluid ounce

1 teaspoon, measuring = 1/3 tablespoon
1 teaspoon, measuring = 1 1/3 fluid drams
1 assay ton = 29.16 grams
1 carat = 200 milligrams
1 carat = 3.08 grains
1 dram, apothecaries' = 60 grains
1 dram, apothecaries' = 3.88 grams
1 gram = 15.43 grains
1 kilogram = 2.20 pounds
1 microgram (μg) = 0.000001 gram
1 milligram = 0.01 grain
1 ounce, avoirdupois = 437.5 grains
1 ounce, avoirdupois = 0.91 troy or apothecaries' ounce
1 ounce, avoirdupois = 28.35 grams
1 pennyweight = 1.55 grams
1 point = 0.01 carat
1 point = 2 milligrams
1 ton = 2,240 pounds
1 ton, gross = 1.12 net tons
1 ton, gross = 1.01 metric tons
1 ton, metric = 2,204.62 pounds
1 ton, metric = 0.98 gross ton

Miscellaneous Units of Measure

Acre–An area of 43,560 square feet. Originally, the area a yoke of oxen could plow in one day.

Agate–Originally a measurement of type size (5 1/2 points). Now equal to 1/12 inch. Used in printing for measuring column length.

Ampere–Unit of electrical current.

Astronomical Unit (A.U.)–93,000,000 miles, the average distance of the earth from the sun.

Bale–A large bundle of goods (hay, cotton).

Board Foot (fbm)–144 cubic inches (12 in. x 12 in. x 1 in.). Used for lumber.

Bolt–40 yards. Used for measuring cloth.

Btu–British thermal unit. Amount of heat needed to increase the temperature of one pound of water by one degree Fahrenheit (252 calories).

Carat (c)–200 milligrams or 3.08 grains troy (precious stones). See also Karat.

Chain (ch)–A chain 66 feet or one-tenth of a furlong in length, divided into 100 parts called links. One mile is equal to 80 chains. Cubit – 18 inches or 45.72 cm.

Decibel–Unit of relative loudness. One decibel is the smallest amount of change detectable by the human ear.

Freight, Ton (also called Measurement Ton) – 40 cubic feet of merchandise (cargo freight).

Great Gross–12 gross or 1,728 pieces.

Weights and Measures (cont'd)

Gross–12 dozen or 144 pieces.

Hand–4 inches or 10.16 cm. Derived from the width of the hand. Used for measuring the height of horses at withers.

Hertz–Modern unit for measurement of electromagnetic wave frequencies (equivalent to "cycles per second").

Horsepower–The power needed to lift 33,000 pounds a distance of one foot in one minute. Used mostly for measuring power of engines.

Karat (kt)–A measure of the purity of gold, indicating how many parts out of 24 are pure. For example – 18 karat gold is 3/4 pure. See also, carat.

Knot–The rate of speed of one nautical mile per hour.

League–Usually estimated at 3 miles in English-speaking countries.

Light-Year–5,880,000,000,000 miles, the distance light travels in a vacuum in a year at the rate of 186,281.7 miles (299.79 kilometers) per second. (If an astronomical unit were represented by one inch, a light-year would be represented by about one mile.) Used for measurements in interstellar space.

Magnum–Two-quart bottle. Used for measuring wine.

Ohm–Unit of electrical resistance. A circuit in which a potential difference of one volt produces a current of one ampere has a resistance of one ohm.

Parsec–Approximately 3.26 light-years or 19.2 million miles. Used for measuring interstellar distances.

Pi (π)–3.14159+. The ratio of the circumference of a circle to its diameter. The value is usually rounded to 3.1416

Pica–1/6 inch or 12 points. Used in printing for measuring column width, etc.

Point–0.013837 (approximately 1/72) inch or 1/12 pica.

Quire–25 sheets of paper.

Ream– 500 sheets of paper.

Roentgen–International unit of radiation exposure produced by X-rays.

Score–20 units.

Sound, speed of–1,088 ft per second at 32°F at sea level.

Span–9 inches or 22.86 cm.

Square–100 square feet. Used in building.

Therm–100,000 Btu's.

Tun–252 gallons, but often larger. Used for measuring wine and other liquids.

Watt–Unit of power. The power used by a current of one ampere across a potential difference of one volt equals one watt.

Public Library Reference Contacts

THE LIBRARIES LISTED BELOW are delighted to answer almost any question by phone. Librarians are usually able to find the answer to a question in just a few minutes—longer searches may require a personal visit. The Brooklyn Business Library is an excellent source for business information, and the Honolulu library is great for after-hours research.

City	Phone
Atlanta	(404) 730-1700
Baltimore	(410) 396-5430
Boston	(617) 536-5400
Brooklyn Business Library	(718) 722-3333
Buffalo	(716) 858-8900
Chicago	(312) 747-4090
Cincinnati	(513) 369-6900
Cleveland	(216) 623-2800
Columbus	(614) 645-2800
Dallas	(214) 670-1400
Denver	(303) 640-6200
Detroit	(313) 833-1000
Hartford	(203) 293-6000
Honolulu	(808) 586-3704
Houston	(713) 236-1313
Indianapolis	(317) 269-1700
Jacksonville	(904) 630-2665
Los Angeles	(310) 645-6082
Memphis	(901) 725-8895
Miami	(305) 375-2665

City	Phone
Milwaukee	(414) 286-3020
Minneapolis	(612) 372-6500
Nashville	(615) 862-5800
New Orleans	(504) 596-2550
New York City	(212) 340-0849
Norfolk	(804) 441-2887
Orlando	(407) 425-4694
Philadelphia	(215) 686-5322
Phoenix	(602) 262-4636
Pittsburgh	(412) 622-3114
Portland, OR	(503) 248-5402
St. Louis	(314) 241-2288
Salt Lake City	(801) 943-4636
San Antonio	(512) 299-7790
San Diego	(916) 264-2770
San Francisco	(415) 557-4400
Seattle	(206) 386-4100
Tampa	(813) 273-3634
Washington, DC	(202) 727-1101

Industry Newsletters

Advertising

Ad Business Report
Executive Communications
411 Lafayette St., Suite 3
New York, NY 10003
(212) 254-1823

AD/PR Agency Report
Pen & Inc.
P.O. Box 5350
Woodland Hills, CA 91364
(818) 222-6262

Briefings
National Business Services
1120 Wheeler Way
Langhorne, PA 19047
(215) 752-4200

Broadcast Investor Charts
Paul Kagan Associates
126 Clock Tower Pl.
Carmel, CA 93923
(408) 624-1536

Broadcast Stats
Paul Kagan Associates
126 Clock Tower Pl.
Carmel, CA 93923
(408) 624-1536

Bulldog Reporter
Infocom
1250 45th St., Suite 200
Emeryville, CA 94608
(510) 596-9300

Channels
PR Publishing
P.O. Box 600
Exeter, NH 03833
(603) 778-0514

Directory MarketPlace
Todd Publications
18 N. Greenbush Rd.
West Nyack, NY 10994
(914) 358-6213

Interactive Video News
Phillips Business Information
1201 Seven Locks Rd.
Potomac, MD 20854
(301) 340-2100

Levin's Public Relations Report
Levin Public Relations & Marketing
30 Glenn St.
White Plains, NY 10603
(914) 993-0900

Media Industry Newsletter
Phillips Publishing
305 Madison Ave., Suite 4417
New York, NY 10165
(212) 983-5170

Media Matters
Media Dynamics
18 E. 41st St., Suite 1806
New York, NY 10017
(212) 683-7895

The Multinational PR Report
Pigafetta Press
P.O. Box 39244
Washington, DC 20016
(202) 244-2580

The Nido Qubein Letter
Creative Services
P.O. Box 6008
High Point, NC 27262
(910) 889-3010

On Achieving Excellence
Tom Peters Group
555 Hamilton Ave., Suite 300
Palo Alto, CA 94301
(800) 367-4310

Partyline, The PR Media Newsletter
Partyline Publishing
35 Sutton Pl.
New York, NY 10022
(212) 755-3487

PR Marcom Jobs West
Rachel PR Services
1650 S. Pacific Coast Hwy., Suite 200C
Rodondo Beach, CA 90277
(310) 792-1313

PR Reporter
PR Publishing
P.O. Box 600
Exeter, NH 03833
(603) 778-0514

The Pricing Advisor
3277 Roswell Rd., Suite 620
Atlanta, GA 30305
(404) 509-9933

Industry Newsletters (cont'd)

Professional Selling
Bureau of Business Practice
24 Rope Ferry Rd.
Waterford, CT 06386
(800) 876-9105

Public Relations News
Phillips Business Information
1201 Seven Locks Rd.
Potomac, MD 20854
(800) 777-5006

Publisher's Multinational Direct
Direct International
1501 Third Ave.
New York, NY 10028
(212) 861-4188

Radio Business Report
P.O. Box 782
Springfield, VA 22150
(703) 719-9500

Television & Radio Newsletter
Restivo Communications
107 S. West St., Suite 199
Alexandria, VA 22314
(703) 793-5226

Tested Copy
Roper Starch Worldwide
566 E. Boston Post Rd.
Mamaroneck, NY 10543
(914) 698-0800

Air Travel

Airline Newsletter
Roadcap Aviation Publications
1030 S. Green Bay
Lake Forest, IL 60045
(708) 234-4730

Airport Highlights
Airport Council International–North America
1775 K St., NW, Suite 500
Washington, DC 20006
(202) 293-8500

Aviation Daily
McGraw-Hill
1200 G St., Suite 200
Washington, DC 20005
(202) 383-2369

The Business Flyer
Holcon
P.O. Box 276
Newton Centre, MA 02159
(203) 782-2155 or
(800) 359-3774

Automobiles

Automotive Parts International
International Trade Services
P.O. Box 5950
Bethesda, MD 20824
(202) 857-8454

Automotive Week
Automotive Week Publishing
P.O. Box 3495
Wayne, NJ 07474
(201) 694-7792; 6076

Car Rental/Leasing Insider
United Communications Group
11300 Rockville Pike, Suite 1100
Rockville, MD 20852
(301) 816-8950

Banking

Bank Bailout Litigation News
Buraff Publications
747 Dresher, Suite 500
Horsham, PA 19044
(215) 784-0860

Bank Mergers & Acquisitions
SNL Securities LP
P.O. Box 2124
Charlottesville, VA 22902
(804) 977-1600

Bank Securities Monthly
SNL Securities LP
P.O. Box 2124
Charlottesville, VA 22902
(804) 977-1600

EximBank Letter
International Business Affairs
4938 Hampden Ln., #346
Bethesda, MD 20814
(301) 907-8647

Business Law

Antitrust FOIA Log
Washington Regulatory Reporting Assocs.
P.O. Box 356
Basye, VA 22810
(703) 856-2216

Bankruptcy Alert
Clark Boardman Callaghan
155 Pfingsten Rd.
Deerfield, IL 60015
(800) 323-1336

Industry Newsletters (cont'd)

Bankruptcy Law Letter
Warren, Gorham & Lamont
31 St. James Ave.
Boston, MA 02116
(800) 950-1205

BNA's Bankruptcy Law Reporter
Bureau of National Affairs
1231 25th St., NW
Washington, DC 20037
(202) 452-4200

BNA's Corporate Counsel Weekly
Bureau of National Affairs
1231 25th St., NW
Washington, DC 20037
(202) 452-4200

BNA's Patent, Trademark & Copyright Journal
Bureau of National Affairs
1231 25th St., NW
Washington, DC 20037
(202) 452-4200

Cable TV and New Media Law & Finance
Leader Publications
345 Park Ave S.
New York, NY 10010
(212) 779-9200

Commodities Litigation Reporter
Andrews Publications
P.O. Box 1000
Westtown, PA 19395
(610) 399-6600

Corporate Control Alert
American Lawyer Media LP
600 3rd Ave., 2nd Floor
New York, NY 10016
(212) 973-2800

Environmental Compliance and Litigation
Leader Publications
345 Park Ave. S.
New York, NY 10010
(212) 779-9200

FTC: Watch-FTC Freedom Of Information Log
Washington Regulatory Reporting Assocs.
P.O. Box 356
Bayse, VA 22810
(703) 856-2216 or
(703) 856-8331

Futures Law Letter
Commodities Law Press Associates
40 Broad St., Suite 2000
New York, NY 10004
(212) 612-9545

Liability Reporter
Americans for Effective Law Enforcement
5519 N. Cumberland Ave., Suite 1008
Chicago, IL 60656
(312) 763-2800

Licensing Law and Business Report
Clark Boardman Callaghan
155 Pfingsten Rd.
Deerfield, IL 60015
(800) 221-9428

Manager's Legal Bulletin
Alexander Hamilton Institute
70 Hilltop Rd.
Ramsay, NJ 07446
(201) 825-3377

National Bankruptcy Litigation Reporter
Andrews Publications
P.O. Box 1000
Westtown, PA 19395
(610) 399-6600

Product Safety Letter
Washington Business Information
1117 N. 19th St., Suite 200
Arlington, VA 22209
(703) 247-3423

Product Safety News
Institute for Product Safety
P.O. Box 1931
Durham, NC 27702
(919) 489-2357

Securities Regulation & Law Report
Bureau of National Affairs
1231 25th St., NW
Washington, DC 20037
(202) 452-4200

Worker's Compensation Law Bulletin
Quinlan Publishing Company
23 Drydock Ave.
Boston, MA 02110
(800) 229-2084

You & The Law
National Institute of Business Management
P.O. Box 25348
Alexandria, VA 22313
(800) 543-2055

Cellular Phones

Wireless Telecom Investor
Paul Kagan Associates
126 Clock Tower Pl.
Carmel, CA 93923
(408) 624-1536

Industry Newsletters (cont'd)

Collectibles

Car Collecting & Investing
Insightful Investor
175 Great Neck Rd., Suite 307
Great Neck, NY 11021
(516) 466-7788

Connoisseur's Guide to California Wines
P.O. Box V
Alameda, CA 94501
(510) 865-3150

Jukebox Collector Newsletter
2545 S.E. 60th Ct.
Des Moines, IA 50317
(515) 265-8324

The Photograph Collector
Photographic Arts Center
163 Amsterdam Ave., Suite 201
New York, NY 10023
(212) 838-8640

The Print Collector's Newsletter
119 E. 79th St.
New York, NY 10021
(212) 988-5959

The Rosen Numismatic Advisory
Numismatic Counseling
P.O. Box 38
Plainview, NY 11803
(516) 433-5800

The Wine Investor/Buyer's Guide
Wine Investor
3284 Barham Blvd., Suite 201
Los Angeles, CA 90068
(213) 876-7590

The Wine Investor-Executive Edition
3284 Barham Blvd., Suite 201
Los Angeles, CA 90068
(213) 876-7590

Colleges

Administrator: The Management Newsletter
for Higher Education
Magna Publications
2718 Dryden Dr.
Madison, WI 53704
(608) 246-3580

MBA Newsletter
79 Verbena Ave.
Floral Park, NY 11001
(516) 488-2010

Communications

Communications Daily
Warren Publishing
2115 Ward Ct., NW
Washington, DC 20037
(202) 872-9200

Communications Industries Report
International Communications Industries
Association
3150 Spring St.
Fairfax, VA 22031
(703) 273-7200

Communications Product Reports
Phillips Decisionpoint Resources
P.O. Box 5062
1111 Marlkress Rd.
Cherry Hill, NJ 08003
(609) 424-1100

Current News on File
Facts on File
460 Park Ave. S.
New York, NY 10016
(212) 683-2244

Disaster Trends Update
QW Communications
P.O. Box 6591
Concord, NH 03303
(603) 648-2629

Computers

Computer Industry Report
International Data
P.O. Box 573
Oxon Hill, MD 20750
(800) 217-9828

Computer Price Guide
Computer Merchants
22 Saw Mill River Rd.
Hawthorne, NY 10532
(914) 592-1060

Electronic Services Update
Link Resources
79 5th Ave.
New York, NY 10003
(212) 627-1500

Infoperspectives
Technology News of America
110 Greene St.
New York, NY 10012
(212) 334-9750

Industry Newsletters (cont'd)

Information Industry Alert
Industry News Service
P.O. Box 457
Wilton, CT 06897
(203) 762-3206

Information Industry Bulletin
Digital Information Group
P.O. Box 110235
Stamford, CT 06911
(203) 348-2751

ISDN News
Phillips Business Information
1201 Seven Locks Rd.
Potomac, MD 20854
(301) 340-2100

National Report on Computers & Health
United Communications Group
11300 Rockville Pike, Suite 1000
Rockville, MD 20852
(301) 816-8950

Packaged Software Reports
Phillips Decisionpoint Resources
P.O. Box 5062
1111 Marlkress Rd.
Cherry Hill, NJ 08003
(609) 424-1100

Software Digest
National Software Testing Laboratories
Plymouth Corporate Center, Box 1000
Plymouth Meeting, PA 19462
(215) 941-9600

Software Industry Bulletin
Digital Information Group
P.O. Box 110235
Stamford, CT 06901
(203) 348-2751

Software-Industry Report
Millin Publishing Group
714 Church St.
Arlington, VA 22314
(703) 739-8500

Word Processing: Quality Clinic
Bureau of Business Practice
24 Rope Ferry Rd.
Waterford, CT 06386
(203) 442-4365

Construction

Construction Market Data
4126 Pleasantdale Rd.
Atlanta, GA 30340
(404) 447-6633

Economic Development–from the State Capitals
Wakeman/Walworth
300 N. Washington St.
Alexandria, VA 22314
(703) 549-8606

Consulting

Management Consultant International
Lafferty Publications
420 Lexington Ave., Suite 1745
New York, NY 10170
(212) 557-6729

The Professional Consultant
123 N.W. 2nd Ave., Suite 405
Portland, OR 97209
(503) 224-8834

Consumer Trends

Consumer Trends
International Credit Association
P.O. Box 419057
St Louis, MO 63141
(314) 991-3030

Shopper Report
Consumer Network
3624 Market St.
Philadelphia, PA 19104
(215) 386-5890

Credit

Credit Risk Management Report
Phillips Business Information
1201 Seven Locks Rd.
Potomac, MD 20854
(301) 340-2100

Dangerous Substances

Job Safety and Health
Bureau of National Affairs
1231 25th St., NW
Washington, DC 20037
(202) 452-4200

Economic Indicators

Blue Chip Economic Indicators
Capitol Publications
1101 King St., Suite 444
Alexandria, VA 22314
(703) 683-4100

Charting the Economy
P.O. Box 829
New Haven, CT 06504
(203) 666-8664

Industry Newsletters (cont'd)

Economic Education Bulletin
American Institute for Economic Research
P.O. Box 1000
Great Barrington, MA 01230
(413) 528-1216

Inside the Economy
Statistical Indicator Associates
P.O. Box 187
North Egremont, MA 01252
(413) 528-3280

Electronic Mail

Electronic Messaging News
Phillips Business Information
1201 Seven Locks Rd.
Potomac, MD 20854
(301) 340-2100

EMMS–Electronic Mail &Message Systems
Telecom Reports
65 Bleecker St., 5th Floor
New York, NY 10012
(202) 842-0520

ISDN Newsletter
Information Gatekeepers
214 Harvard Ave.
Boston, MA 02134
(617) 232-3111 or
(800) 323-1088

Electronics

Henderson Electronic Market Forecast
Henderson Ventures
101 1st St., #444
Los Altos, CA 94022
(415) 961-2900

Environment

Business & the Environment
Cutter Information
37 Broadway
Arlington, MA 02174
(617) 648-8700

Environment Report
Trends Publishing
1079 National Press Building
Washington, DC 20045
(202) 393-0031

Environment Reporter
Bureau of National Affairs
1231 25th St., NW
Washington, DC 20037
(202) 452-4200

Environmental Manager's Compliance Advisor
Business & Legal Reports
39 Academy St.
Madison, CT 06443
(203) 245-7448

Facsimile

Fax Reporter
Buyers Laboratory
20 Railroad Ave.
Hackensack , NJ 07601
(201) 488-0404

Faxpaper
Hartford Courant
285 Broad St.
Hartford, CT 06115
(203) 241-6200

Finance

Accounting & Tax Highlights
Warren Gorham & Lamont
31 St. James Ave.
Boston, MA 02116
(800) 950-1216

The Advisory Letter for Concerned Investors
Franklin Research and Development
711 Atlantic Ave., Fourth Floor
Boston, MA 02111
(617) 423-6655

Blue Chip Financial Forecasts
Capitol Publications
1101 King St., Suite 444
Alexandria, VA 22314
(703) 683-4100

Bond Week
Institutional Investor
488 Madison Ave., 16th Floor
New York, NY 10022
(212) 224-3233

Buy Low–Sell High
Securities Investment Management
1224 Vallecita Dr.
Santa Fe, NM 87501
(505) 989-9224

Commodity Price Charts
Futures Magazine
P.O. Box 6
219 Parkade
Cedar Falls, IA 50613
(319) 277-6341

Industry Newsletters (cont'd)

The CPA Letter
American Institute of CPAs
1211 Ave. of the Americas
New York, NY 10036
(212) 596-6200

Financial Market Trends
Organization for Economic
Cooperation and Development
2001 L St., NW, Suite 650
Washington, DC 20036
(202) 785-6323

Futures Market Service
Knight-Ridder Financial Publishing
135 S. LaSalle St., Dept. 2212
Chicago, IL 60674
(800) 621-5271

GOOD MONEY Newsletter
Good Money Publications
P.O. Box 363
Worcester, VT 05682
(800) 535-3551

*IBC's Quarterly Report on
Money Fund Performance*
P.O. Box 9104
290 Eliot St.
Ashland, MA 01721
(508) 881-2800 or
(800) 343-5413

Investment Guide
American Investment Services
Division St.
Great Barrington, MA 02130
(413) 528-1216

IRS Practice Alert
Warren Gorham & Lamont
31 St. James Ave.
Boston, MA 02116
(800) 922-0066

The Jacobs Report on Asset Protection Strategies
Research Press
4500 W. 72nd Terrace
Shawnee Mission, KS 66208
(913) 362-9667

Long Term Investing
Concept Publishing
P.O. Box 203
York, NY 14592
(716) 243-3148

Making Ends Meet
Pascit Publications
P.O. Box 1125
Traverse City, MI 49685
(616) 929-7227

Marketing Timing Report
P.O. Box 225
Tucson, AZ 85702
(602) 795-9552

Marple's Business Newsletter
Newsletter Publishing
117 W. Mercer St., Suite 200
Seattle, WA 98119
(206) 281-9609

Mutual Fund Investing
Phillips Publishing
7811 Montross Rd.
Potomac, MD 20854
(301) 340-2100

O.T.C. Growth Stock Watch
O.T.C. Research
1040 Great Plain Ave.
Needham, MA 02192
(617) 444-6100

Penny Stocks Newsletter
31731 Outer Highway 10
Redlands, CA 92373
(909) 794-0313

Platinum Perspective
Henry Gammage & Co.
2846 Redding Rd.
Atlanta, GA 30319
(404) 261-7744

Real Estate Tax Ideas
Warren Gorham & Lamont
31 St. James Ave.
Boston, MA 02116
(617) 423-2026 or
(800) 950-1205

The Review of Securities & Commodities Regulation
Standard & Poor's
25 Broadway
New York, NY 10004
(212) 208-8650

SEC Today
Washington Service Bureau
655 15th St., NW, Suite 270
Washington, DC 20005
(202) 508-0600

Securities Week
McGraw-Hill
1221 Avenue of the Americas
New York, NY 10020
(212) 512-2000

Industry Newsletters (cont'd)

The Small Business Tax Review
A/N Group
17 Scott Dr.
Melville, NY 11747
(516) 549-4090

The Tax Adviser
Harborside Financial Center
201 Plaza III
Jersey City, NJ 07311
(201) 938-3447

Tax Haven Reporter
Thomas P. Azzara
P.O. Box CB 11552
Nassau, Bahamas
(809) 327-7359

Tax Management Compensation Planning Journal
Tax Management Estates, Gifts, and Trusts Journal
Tax Management Financial Planning Journal
Tax Management Foreign Income Portfolios
Tax Management International Journal
Tax Management Real Estate Journal
Tax Management Washington Tax Review
Tax Management
1231 23rd St., NW
Washington, DC 20037
(202) 833-7240

Taxwise Money
Agora
824 E. Baltimore St.
Baltimore, MD 21202
(410) 234-0691

Technical Trends
P.O. Box 792
Wilton, CT 06897
(203) 762-0229 or
(800) 736-0229

General Business

Association's Report
Galloway Publications
2940 N.W. Circle Blvd.
Corvallis, OR 97330
(503) 754-7464

The Bruce Report
Bruce Consulting Group
2865 Broderick
San Francisco, CA 94123
(415) 346-7230

Business & Acquisition Newsletter
Newsletters International
2600 S. Gessner Rd.
Houston, TX 77063
(713) 783-0100

Business Ideas
Dan Newman
1051 Bloomfield Ave.
Clifton, NJ 07012
(201) 778-6677

Business Newsletter
Business Newsletter
537 E. Vine St.
Owatonna, MN 55060
(507) 455-3220

The Business Publisher
JK Publishing
P.O. Box 71020
Milwaukee, WI 53211
(414) 332-1625

Forecaster
Forecaster Pub
19623 Ventura Blvd.
Tarzana, CA 91356
(818) 345-4421

Global Report
Center for War/Peace Studies
218 E. 18th St.
New York, NY 10003
(212) 475-1077

Homebased Business News Report
1151 N.E. Todd George Rd.
Lee's Summit, MO 64086
(816) 525-4484

Industry Forecast
Jerome Levy Economic Institute of Bard College
P.O. Box 26
223 N. Greeley Ave.
Chappaqua, NY 10514
(914) 238-3665

The Main Report Business & Executive Letter
Main Report Publications
P.O. Box 1046
47 Birmingham Dr.
Christchurch, New Zealand 8000
[64] 3-338-6068

The Outlook–from the State Capitals
Wakeman/Walworth
300 N. Washington St., Suite 204
Alexandria, VA 22314
(703) 549-8606

The TJFR Business News Reporter
TJFR Publishing
545 N. Maple Ave.
Ridgewood, NJ 07450
(201) 444-6061

Industry Newsletters (cont'd)

Working Smart
National Institute of Business Management
P.O. Box 25287
Alexandria, VA 22313
(800) 543-2049

The Yellow Sheet
Communications Management
13523 Barrett Parkway Dr., Suite 221
Ballwin, MO 63021
(314) 882-0555

Gold and Precious Metals

The Powell Gold Industry Guide
Reserve Research
P.O. Box 4135, Station A
Portland, ME 04101
(207) 774-4971

Precious Metals Data Base
Moneypower
P.O. Box 22644
Minneapolis, MN 55422
(612) 537-8096

Graphics

Board Report for Graphic Artists
P.O. Box 300789
Denver, CO 80203
(717) 774-5413

Plus Business
Metro Creative Graphics
33 W. 34th St.
New York, NY 10001
(212) 947-5100

Health

Benefits Today
Bureau of National Affairs
1231 25th St., NW
Washington, DC 20037
(202) 452-4200

Employee Health & Fitness
American Health Consultants
P.O. Box 740056
Atlanta, GA 30374
(404) 262-7436

The Executive Report on Managed Care
American Business Publishing
3100 Hwy. 138
P.O. Box 1442
Wall Township, NJ 07719
(908) 681-1133

OSHA Compliance Advisor (OCA)
Business & Legal Reports
39 Academy St.
Madison, CT 06443
(203) 245-7448

*OSHA Compliance Advisor
(with Encyclopedia) (OCB)*
Business & Legal Reports
39 Academy St.
Madison, CT 06443
(203) 245-7448

Safety Compliance Letter
Bureau of Business Practice
24 Rope Ferry Rd.
Waterford, CT 06386
(203) 442-4365

Human Resources

Coursetrends
Learning Resources Network
1554 Hayes Dr.
Manhattan, KS 66502
(913) 539-5376

Creative Training Techniques
Lakewood Publications
50 S. Ninth St.
Minneapolis, MN 55402
(612) 333-0471

Discipline and Grievances
Bureau of Business Practice
24 Rope Ferry Rd.
Waterford, CT 06386
(203) 442-4365

EEOC Compliance Manual
Bureau of National Affairs
1231 25th St., NW
Washington, DC 20037
(202) 452-4200

Employee Benefit Notes
Employee Benefit Research Institute
2121 K St., NW, Suite 600
Washington, DC 20037
(202) 659-0670

Employee Benefits Cases
Bureau of National Affairs
1231 25th St., NW
Washington, DC 20037
(202) 452-4200

Employee Relations and Human Resources Bulletin
Bureau of Business Practice
24 Rope Ferry Rd.
Waterford, CT 06386
(800) 243-0876

Industry Newsletters (cont'd)

Employee Security Connection
National Security Institute
57 E. Main St., Suite 217
Westbourough, 01581
(508) 366-5800

Employers' Health Benefits Management Letter
American Business Publishing
3100 Hwy. 138
P.O. Box 1442
Wall Township, NJ 07719
(908) 681-1133

Equal Employment Compliance Update
Clark Boardman Callaghan
155 Pfingsten Rd.
Deerfield, IL 60015
(708) 948-7000 or
(800) 323-1336

Fair Employment Practices
Bureau of National Affairs
1231 25th St., NW
Washington, DC 20037
(202) 452-4200

Government Employee Relations Report
Bureau of National Affairs
1231 25th St., NW
Washington, DC 20047
(202) 452-4200

Hiring & Firing
Carswell
2075 Kennedy Rd.
Scarborough, Ontario, Canada MIT 3V4
(416) 609-3800

Individual Employment Rights
Bureau of National Affairs
1231 25th St., NW
Washington, DC 20037
(202) 452-4200

Job Finder
Western Governmental Research Association
10900 Los Alamitos Blvd., Suite 201
Los Alamitos, CA 90720
(310) 795-6694

The Office Professional
Professional Training Associates
210 Commerce Blvd.
Round Rock, TX 78664
(512) 255-6006

The Personnel Alert
Alexander Hamilton Institute
70 Hilltop Rd.
Ramsey, NJ 07446
(201) 825-3377

Personnel Management
Bureau of National Affairs
1231 25th St., NW
Washington, DC 20037
(202) 452-4200

Personnel Update
Dartnell
4660 N. Ravenswood Ave.
Chicago, IL 60640
(312) 561-4000

PPF Survey (Personnel Policies Forum)
Bureau of National Affairs
1231 25th St., NW
Washington, DC 20037
(202) 452-4200

Recruitment and Retention
Magna Publications
2718 Dryden Dr.
Madison, WI 53704
(608) 246-3580

Training & Development Alert
Advanced Personnel Systems
P.O. Box 1438
Roseville, CA 95678
(916) 781-2900; 2901

Wages and Hours
Bureau of National Affairs
1231 25th St., NW
Washington, DC 20037
(202) 452-4200

What To Do About Personnel Problems In (your state)
Business & Legal Reports
39 Academy St.
Madison, CT 06443
(203) 245-7448

What's Ahead in Human Resources
Remy Publishing
350 W. Hubbard
Chicago, IL 60610
(312) 464-0300

International

Business Asia
Economists Intelligence Unit
111 W. 57th St.
New York, NY 10019
(212) 554-0600

East-West Technology Digest
Welt Publishing
1413 K St., NW, Suite 1400
Washington, DC 20005
(202) 371-0555

Industry Newsletters (cont'd)

Government Business Reports Worldwide
P.O. Box 5997
Washington, DC 20016
(202) 244-7050

The Harriman Institute Forum
Harriman Institute, Columbia University
420 W. 118th St., 12th Floor
New York, NY 10027
(212) 854-6218

Inside U.S. Trade
Inside Washington Publishers
P.O. Box 7167, Ben Franklin Station
Washington, DC 20044
(703) 416-8500

International Information Report
Washington Researchers Publishing
P.O. Box 19005
Washington, DC 20036
(202) 333-3533

International Money & Politics
Sound Money Investors
531 Versailles Dr., Suite 110
Maitland, FL 32751
(407) 629-9229

International Trade Reporter Current Reports
Bureau of National Affairs
1231 25th St., NW
Washington, DC 20037
(202) 452-4200

Japan Financial Market Report
Japan Market Research
609 Columbus Ave.
New York, NY 10024
(212) 496-6760

Major Trends
250 W. Coventry Ct.
Milwaukee, WI 53217
(414) 352-8460

Market Europe
W-Two Publications
202 The Commons, Suite 401
Ithaca, NY 14850
(607) 277-0934

Near East Report
Near East Research
440 1st St., NW, Suite 607
Washington, DC 20001
(202) 639-5254

Random Lengths Export Market Report
Random Lengths Publications
P.O. Box 867
Eugene, OR 97440
(503) 686-9925

Washington Export Letter
International Business Affairs
4938 Hampden Ln., Suite 346
Bethesda, MD 20814
(301) 907-8647

Washington Tariff & Trade Letter
Gilston Communications Group
P.O. Box 467
Washington, DC 20044
(301) 570-4544

Literacy

Report on Literacy Programs
Business Publishers
951 Pershing Dr.
Silver Spring, MD 20910
(301) 587-6300

Management

Academy of Management News
Administration 3-17
Northeast Louisiana University
Monroe, LA 71209
(318) 342-1210

Administration & Management
National Technical Information Service
U.S. Department of Commerce
5285 Port Royal Rd.
Springfield, VA 22161
(703) 487-4630

Applied Management Newsletter
National Association for Management
5920 E. Central, Suite 205
Wichita, KS 67208
(316) 688-0763

Collective Bargaining Negotiations and Contracts
Bureau of National Affairs
1231 25th St., NW
Washington, DC 20037
(202) 452-4200

*Employee Policy for the Private and Public
Sector—from the State Capitals*
Wakeman/Walworth
300 N. Washington St.
Alexandria, VA 22314
(703) 549-8606

Industry Newsletters (cont'd)

Employee Relations Weekly
Bureau of National Affairs
1231 25th St., NW
Washington, DC 20037
(202) 452-4200

The Entrepreneurial Manager's Newsletter
Center for Entrepreneurial Management
180 Varick St., Penthouse
New York, NY 10014
(212) 633-0060

From Nine To Five
Dartnell
4660 N. Ravenswood Ave.
Chicago, IL 60640
(312) 561-4000

Labor Notes
Labor Education & Research Project
7435 Michigan Ave.
Detroit, MI 48210
(313) 842-6262

Labor Relations
Bureau of National Affairs
1231 25th St., NW
Washington, DC 20037
(202) 452-4200

Labor Relations Reporter
Bureau of National Affairs
1231 25th St., NW
Washington, DC 20037
(202) 452-4200

Management Letter
Bureau of Business Practice
515 Main St.
Yalesville, CT 06492
(800) 876-9105

Management Matters
Infoteam
P.O. Box 15640
Plantation, FL 33318
(305) 473-9560

OSHA Compliance Advisor
Business & Legal Reports
39 Academy St.
Madison, CT 06443
(203) 245-7448

Small Business Confidential
Fleet Street Publications
IBC House, Vickers Dr.
Brooklands Industrial Park
Weybridge, Surrey, England KT13 0XS
[44] (171) 453-2208

Smart Workplace Practices
Employers of America
520 S. Pierce, Suite 224
Mason City, IA 50401
(515) 424-3187

Union Labor Report
Bureau of National Affairs
1231 25th St., NW
Washington, DC 20037
(202) 452-4200

Update: The Executive's Purchasing Advisor
Buyers Laboratory
20 Railroad Ave.
Hackensack, NJ 07601
(201) 488-0404

Manufacturing

American Industry
Publications for Industry
21 Russell Woods Rd.
Great Neck, NY 11021
(516) 487-0990

Industrial Purchasing Agent
Publications for Industry
21 Russell Woods Rd.
Great Neck, NY 11021
(516) 487-0990

Inside R&D
Technical Insights
P.O. Box 1304
Fort Lee, NJ 07024
(201) 568-4744

Quality Management
Bureau of Business Practice
515 Main St.
Yalesville, CT 06492
(800) 876-9105

Marketing

American Marketplace
Business Publishers
951 Pershing Dr.
Silver Spring, MD 20910
(301) 587-6300

Business Mailers Review
1813 Shepherd St., NW
Washington, DC 20011
(202) 723-3397

Frohlinger's Marketing Report
Marketing Strategist Communications
7 Coppell Dr.
Tenafly, NJ 07670
(800) 962-7538

Industry Newsletters (cont'd)

The Information Report
Washington Researchers Publishing
P.O. Box 19005
Washington, DC 20036
(202) 333-3533

Infomercial Marketing Report
11533 Thurston Cir.
Los Angeles, CA 90049
(310) 472-5253

Jack O'Dwyer's Newsletter
J.R. O'Dwyer
271 Madison Ave.
New York, NY 10016
(212) 679-2471

John Naisbitt's Trend Letter
The Global Network
1101 30th St., NW, Suite 130
Washington, DC 20007
(202) 337-5960

Marketing Breakthroughs
World Business Publications
4th Floor, Britannia House
960 High Rd.
London, N12 9RY England
[44] (81) 446-5141

The Marketing Pulse
Unlimited Positive Communications
11 N. Chestnut St.
New Paltz, NY 12561
(914) 255-2222

Sales and Marketing Executive Report
Dartnell
4660 N. Ravenswood Ave.
Chicago, IL 60640
(312) 561-4000

Marketing to Women
About Women
33 Broad St.
Boston, MA 02109
(617) 723-4337

Professional Telephone Selling
Bureau of Business Practice
515 Main St.
Yalesville, CA 06492
(800) 876-9105

Public Pulse
Roper Organization
205 E. 42nd St.
New York, NY 10017
(212) 599-0700

Sales and Marketing Executive Report
Dartnell
4660 N. Ravenswood Ave.
Chicago, IL 60640
(312) 561-4000

School Marketing Newsletter
School Market Research Institute
P.O. Box 10
1721 Saybrook Rd.
Haddam, CT 06438
(203) 345-4018

The SpeciaList's MarketPulse
SpeciaLists
1200 Harbor Blvd., 9th Floor
Weehawken, NJ 07087
(201) 865-5800

Telephone Selling Report
Business By Phone
13254 Stevens St.
Omaha, NE 68137
(402) 895-9399

Miscellaneous

Andrew Harper's Hideaway Report
Harper Associates
P.O. Box 50
Sun Valley, ID 83353
(208) 622-3183

Antitrust & Trade Regulation Report
Bureau of National Affairs
1231 25th St., NW
Washington, DC 20037
(202) 452-4200

Bottom Line Personal
Boardroom Reports
P.O. Box 2614
Greenwich, CT 06836
(203) 625-5900

Business Information Alert
Alert Publications
401 W. Fullerton Pkwy.
Chicago, IL 60614
(312) 525-7594

Buyouts Newsletter
Securities Data Publishing
40 W. 57th St., 11th Floor
New York, NY 10019
(212) 765-5311

Drugs In The Workplace
Business Research Publications
65 Bleecker St., 5th Floor
New York, NY 10012
(800) 822-6338

Industry Newsletters (cont'd)

Hazardous Materials Transportation
Washington Business Information
1117 N. 19th St., Suite 200
Arlington, VA 22209
(703) 247-3424

Innovator's Digest
Infoteam
P.O. Box 15640
Plantation, FL 33318
(305) 473-9560

The Licensing Journal
Kent Communications
P.O. Box 1169
Stamford, CT 06904
(203) 358-0848

Metals Week
McGraw-Hill
1221 Ave. of the Americas
New York, NY 10020
(212) 512-2823

National Right To Work Newsletter
8001 Braddock Rd.
Springfield, VA 22160
(703) 321-9820

The Newsletter On Newsletters
Newsletter Clearinghouse
P.O. Box 311
44 W. Market St.
Rhinebeck, NY 12572
(914) 876-2081

Nutshell—A Digest of Employee Benefit Publications
Country Press
P.O. Box 5880
Snowmass Village, CO 81615
(303) 923-3210

The Ontario Worker's Compensation Review
Carswell
2075 Kennedy Rd.
Scarborough, Ont. Canada M1T 3V4
(416) 609-3800

The PresentFutures Report
PresentFutures Group
101 Park Washington Ct.
Falls Church, VA 22046
(703) 538-6181

Safety Management
Bureau of Business Practice
515 Main St.
Yalesville, CA 06492
(800) 876-9105

Taxation & Revenue Policies—from the State Capitals
Wakeman/Walworth
300 N. Washington St.
Alexandria, VA 22314
(703) 549-8606

Travel Expense Management
American Business Publishing
P.O. Box 1442
3100 Hwy. 138
Wall Township, NJ 07719
(908) 681-1133

Networking

Linc: Linking Issue Networks for Cooperation
Issue Action Publications
207 Loudoun St., SE
Leesburg, VA 22075
(703) 777-8450

Public Speaking

The Executive Speechwriter Newsletter
Words Ink
Emerson Falls Business Park
St. Johnsbury, VT 05819
(802) 748-4472

Speechwriter's Newsletter
Ragan Communications
212 W. Superior St., Suite 200
Chicago,, IL 60610
(312) 335-0037

Publishing

Publishing Trends & Trendsetters
Oxbridge Communications
150 Fifth Ave.
New York, NY 10011
(212) 741-0231

Real Estate

Digest of State Land Sales Regulations
Land Development Institute
1401 16th St., NW
Washington, DC 20036
(202) 232-2144

Housing Market Report
CD Publications
8204 Fenton St., 2nd Floor
Silver Spring, MD 20910
(301) 588-6380

Managing Housing Letter
CD Publications
8204 Fenton St., 2nd Floor
Silver Spring, MD 20910
(301) 588-6380

Industry Newsletters (cont'd)

People & Profits
Lee Resources
P.O. Box 16711
Greenville, SC 29606
(803) 232-5264

Professional Apartment Management
Brownstone Publishers
149 5th Ave., 16th Floor
New York, NY 10010
(212) 473-8200

Real Estate Digest
Infocom
1250 45th St., Suite 200
Emeryville, CA 94608
(510) 596-9300

Real Estate Insider
Alexander Communications
215 Park Ave. S., Suite 1301
New York, NY 10003
(212) 228-0246

Real Estate Law Report
Warren Gorham & Lamont
31 St. James Ave.
Boston, MA 02116
(800) 950-1205

The Real Estate Tax Digest
Matthew Bender & Co.
1275 Broadway
Albany, NY 12204
(800) 833-9844

Span
Shiefman and Associates
33300 Five Mile Rd., Suite 202
Livonia, MI 48154
(313) 422-6100

Trade Dimensions
263 Tresser Blvd., 5th Floor
Stamford, CT 06901
(203) 977-7600

Reference

Business Information From Your Public Library
Administrator's Digest
P.O. Box 993
South San Francisco, CA 94080
(415) 573-5474

Census and You
Superintendent of Documents
P.O. Box 371954
Pittsburgh, PA 15250
(202) 512-1800

Current News on File
Facts on File
460 Park Ave. S.
New York, NY 10016
(212) 683-2244

Research Recommendations
National Institute of Business Management
P.O. Box 25287
Alexandria, VA 22313
(800) 543-2051

The SIMBA Report on Directory Publishing
SIMBA Information
P.O. Box 7430
Wilton, CT 06897
(203) 834-0033

Sales

Executive Compensation Report
DP Publications
P.O. Box 7188
Fairfax Station, VA 22039
(703) 425-1322

Professional Selling
Bureau of Business Practice
515 Main St.
Yalesville, CT 06492
(800) 876-9105

Rep World
Albee-Campbell
806 Penn Ave., Box 2087
Sinking Spring, PA 19608
(610) 678-3361

Research Alert
EPM Communications
488 E. 18th St.
Brooklyn, NY 11226
(718) 469-9330

Sales Leads
Sales Leads Publishing
705 Park Ave.
Lake Park, FL 33403
(407) 845-0133

Sales Manager's Bulletin
Bureau of Business Practice
515 Main St.
Yalesville, CT 06492
(800) 876-9105

Salesman's Insider
Modell Associates
P.O. Box 4111
Stanford, CA 94309
(408) 270-4526

Industry Newsletters (cont'd)

Salesmanship
Dartnell
4660 N. Ravenswood Ave.
Chicago, IL 60640
(312) 561-4000

Selling to Seniors
CD Publications
8204 Fenton St., 2nd Floor
Silver Spring, MD 20910
(301) 588-6380

Small Business

Bootstrappin' Entrepreneur Bulletin
8726 S. Sepulveda Blvd., Suite B261-BAP
Los Angeles, CA 90045
(310) 568-9861

SBANE Enterprise
Smaller Business Association of
New England
204 2nd Ave.
Waltham, MA 02154
(617) 890-9070

Venture Capital

Venture Capital Journal
Securities Data Publishing
40 W. 57th St., 11th Floor
New York, NY 10019
(212) 765-5311

Source: Almanac research and Hudson's Subscription Newsletter Directory

Recommended Resource

Hudson's Subscription Newsletter Directory
Hudson's, $140
(914) 876-2081

The Business Almanac 2000

The following is a list of the 2,000 largest companies in the United States. The list was compiled by comparing data from a number of publicly available sources.

Name	Address	Phone
3COM	5400 Bayfront Plaza, Santa Clara, CA 95052	(408) 764-5000
3M	3M Ctr., St. Paul, MN 55144	(612) 733-1110
20th Century Industries	6301 Owensmouth Ave., Suite 700, Woodland Hills, CA 91367	(818) 704-3700
2002 Target Term Trust	1285 Ave. of the Americas, New York, NY 10019	(212) 713-2000
A. G. Edwards	1 N. Jefferson Ave., St. Louis, MO 63103	(314) 289-3000
A. H. Belo	400 S. Record St., Dallas, TX 75202	(214) 977-6606
A. L. Pharma	1 Executive Dr., P.O. Box 1399, Fort Lee, NJ 07024	(201) 947-7774
A. O. Smith	P.O. Box 23972, Milwaukee, WI 53223	(414) 359-4000
A. Schulman	3550 W. Market St., Akron, OH 44333	(216) 666-3751
A.M. Castle & Co.	3400 N. Wolf Rd., Franklin Park, IL 60131	(708) 455-7111
AAR	1111 Nicholas Blvd., Elk Grove Village, IL 60007	(708) 439-3939
Abbey Healthcare Group	3560 Hyland Ave., Costa Mesa, CA 92626	(714) 957-2000
Abbott Laboratories	1 Abbott Park Rd., Abbott Park, IL 60064	(708) 937-6100
Abex	Liberty Ln., Hampton, NH 03842	(603) 926-5911
Acclaim Entertainment	71 Audrey Ave., Oyster Bay, NY 11771	(516) 624-8888
Acme Metals	13500 S. Perry Ave., Riverdale, IL 60627	(708) 849-2500
Acordia	120 Monument Circle, Indianapolis, IN 46204	(317) 488-6666
The Actava Group	4900 Georgia-Pacific Ctr., Atlanta, GA 30303	(404) 658-9000
Acuson	1220 Charleston Rd., Mountain View, CA 94043	(415) 969-9112
ACX Technologies	16000 Table Mountain Pkwy., Golden, CO 80403	(303) 271-7000
Adams Resources & Energy	6910 Fannin, Houston, TX 77030	(713) 797-9966
Adaptec	691 S. Milpitas Blvd., Milpitas, CA 95035	(408) 945-8600
ADC Telecommunications	4900 W. 78th St., Minneapolis, MN 55435	(612) 938-8080
Adelphia Communications	5 W. Third St., P.O. Box 472, Coudersport, PA 16915	(814) 274-9830
Adobe Systems	1585 Charleston Rd., Mountain View, CA 94043	(415) 961-4400
Adolph Coors	Golden, CO 80401	(303) 279-6565
Advanced Marketing Services	5880 Oberlin Dr., Suite 400, San Diego, CA 92121	(619) 457-2500
Advanced Micro Devices	1 AMD Pl., P.O. Box 3453, Sunnyvale, CA 94088	(408) 732-2400
Advanced Technology Laboratories	22100 Bothell Everett Hwy., SE, Bothell, WA 98012	(206) 487-7000
ADVANTA	300 Welsh Rd., Horsham, PA 19044	(215) 657-4000
ADVO	1 Univac Ln., P.O. Box 755, Windsor, CT 06095	(203) 285-6100
The AES Corp.	1001 N. 19th St., Arlington, VA 22209	(703) 522-1315
Aetna Life and Casualty	151 Farmington Ave., Hartford, CT 06156	(203) 273-0123
Affiliated Computer Services	2828 N. Haskell Ave., Dallas, TX 75204	(214) 841-6111
AFLAC	1932 Wynnton Rd., Columbus, GA 31999	(706) 323-3431
AGCO	4830 River Green Pkwy., Duluth, GA 30136	(404) 813-9200
Air & Water Technologies	P.O. Box 1500, Somerville, NJ 08876	(908) 685-4600
Air Express	120 Tokeneke Rd., P.O. Box 1231, Darien, CT 06820	(203) 655-7900
Air Products and Chemicals	7201 Hamilton Blvd., Allentown, PA 18195	(610) 481-4911
Airborne Freight	3101 Western Ave., P.O. Box 662, Seattle, WA 98111	(206) 285-4600
Airgas	100 Matsonford Rd., Radnor, PA 19087	(610) 687-5253
AirTouch Communications	1 California St., San Francisco, CA 94111	(415) 658-2000
AK Steel Holding	703 Curtis St., Middletown, OH 45043	(513) 425-5000
Alaska Air Group	19300 Pacific Hwy. S., Seattle, WA 98188	(206) 431-7040
Albany	1373 Broadway, Albany, NY 12204	(518) 445-2200
Albemarle	451 Florida Blvd, Baton Rouge, LA 70801	(504) 388-8011
Alberto-Culver	2525 Armitage Ave., Melrose Park, IL 60160	(708) 450-3000
Albertson's	250 ParkCenter Blvd., Boise, ID 83726	(208) 385-6200
ALC Communications	30300 Telegraph Rd., Bingham Farms, MI 48025	(810) 647-4060
Alco Standard	825 Duportail Rd., Wayne, PA 19087	(610) 296-8000

The Business Almanac 2000 (cont'd)

Name	Address	Phone
Alcoa	425 Sixth Ave., Pittsburgh, PA 15219	(412) 553-3042
Alex. Brown	135 E. Baltimore St., Baltimore, MD 21202	(410) 727-1700
Alexander & Alexander Services	1185 Ave. of the Americas, New York, NY 10036	(212) 840-8500
Alexander & Baldwin	822 Bishop St., P.O. Box 3440, Honolulu, HI 96801	(808) 525-6611
Alfa	2108 E. South Blvd., Montgomery, AL 36116	(205) 288-3900
Alleghany	Park Ave. Plaza, New York, NY 10055	(212) 752-1356
Allegheny Ludlum	1000 Six PPG Pl., Pittsburgh, PA 15222	(412) 394-2800
Allegheny Power System	12 E. 49th St., New York, NY 10017	(212) 752-2121
Allen Group	25101 Chagrin Blvd., Suite 350, Beachwood, OH 44122	(216) 765-5818
Allergan	2525 Dupont Dr., P.O. Box 19534, Irvine, CA 92715	(714) 752-4500
Alliance Entertainment	110 E. 59th St., New York, NY 10022	(212) 935-6662
Alliant Techsystems	600 Second St., NE, Hopkins, MN 55343	(612) 931-6000
ALLIED Group Insurance	701 Fifth Ave., Des Moines, IA 50391	(515) 280-4211
Allied Holdings	160 Clairemont Ave., Suite 510, Decatur, GA 30030	(404) 373-4285
AlliedSignal	101 Columbia Rd., P.O. Box 2245, Morristown, NJ 07962	(201) 455-2000
Allmerica Property & Casualty	440 Lincoln St., Worcester, MA 01653	(508) 855-1000
Allou Health & Beauty Care	50 Emjay Blvd., Brentwood, NY 11717	(516) 273-4000
The Allstate Corp.	Allstate Plaza, Northbrook, IL 60062	(708) 402-5000
ALLTEL	1 Allied Dr., Little Rock, AR 72202	(501) 661-8000
Alltrista	301 S. High St., P.O. Box 5004, Muncie, IN 47307	(317) 281-5000
Allwaste	5151 San Felipe, Suite 1600, Houston, TX 77056	(713) 623-8777
Alumax	5655 Peachtree Pkwy., Norcross, GA 30092	(404) 246-6600
ALZA	950 Page Mill Rd., Palo Alto, CA 94303	(415) 494-5000
AMBAC	1 State St. Plaza, New York, NY 10004	(212) 668-0340
AMC Entertainment	106 W. 14th St., P.O. Box 419615, Kansas City, MO 64141	(816) 221-4000
Amcast Industrial	7887 Washington Village Dr., Dayton, OH 45459	(513) 291-7000
Amdahl	1250 E. Arques Ave., Sunnyvale, CA 94088	(408) 746-6000
Amerada Hess	1185 Ave. of the Americas, New York, NY 10036	(212) 997-8500
AMERCO	1325 Airmotive Way, Suite 100, Reno, NV 89502	(702) 688-6300
America West Airlines	4000 Sky Harbor Blvd., Phoenix, AZ 85034	(602) 693-0800
American Annuity Group	580 Walnut, Cincinnati, OH 45202	(513) 333-5300
American Bankers Insurance Group	11222 Quail Roost Dr., Miami, FL 33157	(305) 253-2244
American Brands	1700 E. Putnam Ave., Old Greenwich, CT 06870	(203) 698-5000
American Building Maintenance Industries	50 Fremont St., Suite 2600, San Francisco, CA 94105	(415) 597-4500
American Business Products	2100 River Edge Pkwy., Atlanta, GA 30328	(404) 953-8300
American Colloid	1500 W. Shure Dr., Suite 500, Arlington Heights, IL 60004	(708) 392-4600
American Electric Power	1 Riverside Plaza, Columbus, OH 43215	(614) 223-1000
American Express	World Financial Ctr., New York, NY 10285	(212) 640-2000
American Freightways	2200 Forward Dr., Harrison, AR 72601	(501) 741-9000
American General	2929 Allen Pkwy., Houston, TX 77019	(713) 522-1111
American Greetings	1 American Rd., Cleveland, OH 44144	(216) 252-7300
American Heritage Life	1776 American Heritage Life Blvd., Jacksonville, FL 32224	(904) 992-1776
American Home Products	5 Giralda Farms, Madison, NJ 07940	(201) 660-5000
American International Group	70 Pine St., New York, NY 10270	(212) 770-7000
American Maize Products	250 Harbor Plaza Dr., Stamford, CT 06904	(203) 356-9000
American Management Systems	4050 Legato Rd., Fairfax, VA 22033	(703) 267-8000
American Media	600 S. E. Coast Ave., Lantana, FL 33462	(407) 586-1111
American Medical Holdings	14001 N. Dallas Pkwy., Dallas, TX 75240	(214) 789-2200
American Medical Response	67 Batterymarch St., Boston, MA 02110	(617) 261-1600
American National Insurance	1 Moody Plaza, Galveston, TX 77550	(409) 763-4661

The Business Almanac 2000 (cont'd)

Name	Address	Phone
American Power Conversion	132 Fairgrounds Rd., West Kingston, RI 02892	(401) 789-5735
American Premier Underwriters	1 E. Fourth St., 14th Floor, Cincinnati, OH 45202	(513) 579-6600
American President Companies	1111 Broadway, Oakland, CA 94607	(510) 272-8000
American Publishing	111-115 S. Emma St., West Frankfort, IL 62896	(618) 937-6411
American Re-insurance	555 College Rd. E., Princeton, NJ 08543	(609) 243-4200
American Stores	709 E. S. Temple, Salt Lake City, UT 84102	(801) 539-0112
American Water Works	1025 Laurel Oak Rd., Voorhees, NJ 08043	(609) 346-8200
AmeriData Technologies	700 Canal St., Stamford, CT 06902	(203) 357-1464
Ameritech	30 S. Wacker Dr., Chicago, IL 60606	(312) 750-5000
Ameron	245 S. Los Robles Ave., Pasadena, CA 91101	(818) 683-4000
AMETEK	Station Sq., Paoli, PA 19301	(610) 647-2121
Amgen	1840 Dehavilland Dr., Thousand Oaks, CA 91320	(805) 447-1000
Amoco	200 E. Randolph Dr., Chicago, IL 60601	(312) 856-6111
AMP	470 Friendship Rd., Harrisburg, PA 17112	(717) 564-0100
Amphenol	358 Hall Ave., P.O. Box 5030, Wallingford, CT 06492	(203) 265-8900
AMR	4333 Amon Carter Blvd., Fort Worth, TX 76155	(817) 963-1234
AMSCO	2 Chatham Ctr., 112 Washington Pl., Pittsburgh, PA 15219	(412) 338-6500
AmSouth Bancorporation	1900 Fifth Ave. N., Birmingham, AL 35203	(205) 320-7151
Amtran	7337 W. Washington St., Indianapolis, IN 46231	(317) 247-4000
Anacomp	11550 N. Meridian St., Indianapolis, IN 46240	(317) 844-9666
Anadarko Petroleum	17001 Northchase Dr., Houston, TX 77060	(713) 875-1101
Analog Devices	3 Technology Way, Norwood, MA 02062	(617) 329-4700
Andrew	10500 W. 153rd St., Orland Park, IL 60462	(708) 349-3300
Angelica	424 S. Woods Mill Rd., Chesterfield, MO 63017	(314) 854-3800
Anheuser-Busch Companies	1 Busch Pl., St. Louis, MO 63118	(314) 577-2000
Ann Taylor Stores	142 W. 57th St., New York, NY 10019	(212) 541-3300
Antec	2850 W. Golf Rd., Rolling Meadows, IL 60008	(708) 439-4444
Anthony Industries	4900 S. Eastern Ave., Los Angeles, CA 90040	(213) 724-2800
Aon	123 N. Wacker Dr., Chicago, IL 60606	(312) 701-3000
Apache	2000 Post Oak Blvd., Suite 100, Houston, TX 77056	(713) 296-6000
Apogee Enterprises	7900 Xerxes Ave. S., Minneapolis, MN 55431	(612) 835-1874
Apple Computer	1 Infinite Loop, Cupertino, CA 95014	(408) 996-1010
Applied Magnetics	75 Robin Hill Rd., Goleta, CA 93117	(805) 683-5353
Applied Materials	3050 Bowers Ave., Santa Clara, CA 95054	(408) 727-5555
Applied Power	13000 W. Silver Spring Dr., Butler, WI 53007	(414) 781-6600
APS Holding	3000 Pawnee St., Houston, TX 77054	(713) 741-2470
AptarGroup	475 W. Terra Cotta Ave., Crystal Lake, IL 60014	(815) 477-0424
Aquila Gas Pipeline	100 N.E. Loop, Suite 1000, San Antonio, TX 78216	(210) 342-0685
Arbor Drugs	3331 W. Big Beaver Rd., Troy, MI 48084	(810) 643-9420
Arcadian Partners	6750 Poplar Ave., Suite 600, Memphis, TN 38138	(901) 758-5200
Archer Daniels Midland	4666 Faries Pkwy., Decatur, IL 62525	(217) 424-5200
ARCO Chemical	3801 W. Chester Pike, Newtown Square, PA 19073	(610) 359-2000
Arctco	600 Brooks Ave. S., Thief River Falls, MN 56701	(218) 681-8558
Arden Group	2020 S. Central Ave., Compton, CA 90220	(310) 638-2842
Argonaut Group	1800 Ave. of the Stars, Los Angeles, CA 90067	(310) 553-0561
Armco	1 Oxford Ctr., 15th Floor, 301 Grant St., Pittsburgh, PA 15219	(412) 255-9800
Armstrong World Industries	313 W. Liberty St., Lancaster, PA 17603	(717) 397-0611
Arnold Industries	625 S. Fifth Ave., Lebanon, PA 17042	(717) 274-2521
Arrow Electronics	25 Hub Dr., Melville, NY 11747	(516) 391-1300
Arthur J. Gallagher & Co.	2 Pierce Pl., Itasca, IL 60143	(708) 773-3800

The Business Almanac 2000 (cont'd)

Name	Address	Phone
Arvin Industries	1 Noblitt Plaza, P.O. Box 3000, Columbus, IN 47202	(812) 379-3000
ASARCO	180 Maiden Ln., New York, NY 10038	(212) 510-2000
Ashland	1000 Ashland Dr., Russell, KY 41169	(606) 329-3333
Ashland Coal	2205 Fifth St. Rd., Huntington, WV 25701	(304) 526-3333
Associated Banc-Corp	112 N. Adams St., Green Bay, WI 54301	(414) 433-3166
AST Research	16215 Alton Pkwy., P.O. Box 19658, Irvine, CA 92713	(714) 727-4141
Astoria Financial	1 Astoria Federal Plaza, Lake Success, NY 11042	(516) 327-3000
Astrum	40-301 Fisher Island Dr., Fisher Island, FL 33109	(305) 532-2426
AT&T	32 Ave. of the Americas, New York, NY 10013	(212) 387-5400
AT&T Capital	44 Whippany Rd., Morristown, NJ 07962	(201) 397-3000
Atlanta Gas Light	303 Peachtree St., NE, Atlanta, GA 30308	(404) 584-4000
Atlantic Energy	1199 Black Horse Pike, Pleasantville, NJ 08232	(609) 645-4500
Atlantic Richfield	515 S. Flower St., Los Angeles, CA 90071	(213) 486-3511
Atlantic Southeast Airlines	100 Hartsfield Ctr., Suite 800, Atlanta, GA 30354	(404) 530-3838
Atmel	2125 O'Nel Dr., San Jose, CA 95131	(408) 441-0311
Atmos Energy	5430 LBJ Fwy., Dallas, TX 75240	(214) 934-9227
Audiovox	150 Marcus Blvd., Hauppauge, NY 11788	(516) 231-7750
Augat	89 Forbes Blvd., P.O. Box 448, Mansfield, MA 02048	(508) 543-4300
Autodesk	111 McInnis Pkwy., San Raphael, CA 94903	(415) 507-5000
Automatic Data Processing	1 ADP Blvd., Roseland, NJ 07068	(201) 994-5000
Automotive Industries Holding	4508 IDS Ctr., Minneapolis, MN 55402	(612) 332-6828
AutoZone	3030 Poplar Ave., Memphis, TN 38111	(901) 325-4600
Avery Dennison	150 N. Orange Grove Blvd., Pasadena, CA 91103	(818) 304-2000
Aviall	2055 Diplomat Dr., Dallas, TX 75234	(214) 956-5000
Avnet	80 Cutter Mill Rd., Great Neck, NY 11021	(516) 466-7000
Avon Products	9 W. 57th St., New York, NY 10019	(212) 546-6015
Avondale Industries	5100 River Rd., Avondale, LA 70094	(504) 436-2121
Aztar	2390 E. Camelback Rd., Phoenix, AZ 85016	(602) 381-4100
B M C West	P.O. Box 8008, Boise, ID 83707	(208) 387-4300
The B.F.Goodrich Co.	3925 Embassy Pkwy., Akron, OH 44333	(216) 374-3985
Baker Hughes	3900 Essex Ln., Houston, TX 77027	(713) 439-8600
Baldor Electric	5711 R. S. Boreham, Jr. St., Fort Smith, AR 72902	(501) 646-4711
Ball	345 S. High St., P.O. Box 2407, Muncie, IN 47307	(317) 747-6100
Bally Entertainment	8700 W. Bryn Mawr Ave., Chicago, IL 60631	(312) 399-1300
Ballys Grand	3645 Las Vegas Blvd. S., Las Vegas, NV 89109	(702) 739-4900
Baltimore Gas and Electric	39 W. Lexington St., Baltimore, MD 21202	(410) 783-5920
Banc One	100 E. Broad St., Columbus, OH 43271	(614) 248-5944
Bancorp Hawaii	130 Merchant St., Honolulu, HI 96813	(808) 537-8111
BancTec	4435 Spring Valley Rd., Dallas, TX 75244	(214) 450-7700
Bandag	2905 N. Hwy. 61, Muscatine, IA 52761	(319) 262-1400
Bank of Boston	100 Federal St., Boston, MA 02110	(617) 434-2200
Bank of New York	48 Wall St., New York, NY 10286	(212) 495-1784
Bank South	55 Marietta St., NW, Atlanta, GA 30303	(404) 529-4111
BankAmerica	Bank of America Ctr., San Francisco, CA 94104	(415) 622-3530
Bankers Life Holdings	222 Merchandise Mart Plaza, Chicago, IL 60654	(312) 396-6000
Bankers Trust New York	280 Park Ave., New York, NY 10017	(212) 250-2500
Banponce	209 Munoz Rivera Ave., Hato Rey, PR 00918	(809) 765-9800
Banta	P.O. Box 8003, Menasha, WI 54952	(414) 751-7777
Barnes & Noble	122 Fifth Ave., New York, NY 10011	(212) 633-3300
Barnes Group	123 Main St., P.O. Box 489, Bristol, CT 06011	(203) 583-7070

The Business Almanac 2000 (cont'd)

Name	Address	Phone
Barnett Banks	50 N. Laura St., Jacksonville, FL 32202	(904) 791-7720
Bassett Industries	P.O. Box 626, Bassett, VA 24055	(703) 629-6000
Battle Mountain Gold	333 Clay St., 42nd Floor, Houston, TX 77002	(713) 650-6400
Bausch & Lomb	1 Chase Sq., Rochester, NY 14604	(716) 338-6000
Baxter	1 Baxter Pkwy., Deerfield, IL 60015	(708) 948-2000
Bay State Gas	300 Friberg Pkwy., Westborough, MA 01581	(508) 836-7000
BayBanks	175 Federal St., Boston, MA 02110	(617) 482-1040
BE Aerospace	1400 Corporate Ctr. Way, Wellington, FL 33414	(407) 791-5000
The Bear Stearns Companies	245 Park Ave., New York, NY 10167	(212) 272-2000
Bearings	3600 Euclid Ave., Cleveland, OH 44115	(216) 881-2838
Beazer Homes USA	5775 Peachtree-Dunwoody Rd., Suite C 550, Atlanta, GA 30342	(404) 250-3420
Beckman Instruments	2500 Harbor Blvd., Fullerton, CA 92634	(714) 871-4848
Becton, Dickinson and Co.	1 Becton Dr., Franklin Lakes, NJ 07417	(201) 847-6800
Bed Bath & Beyond	715 Morris Ave., Springfield, NJ 07081	(201) 379-1520
Belden	7701 Forsyth Blvd., Suite 800, St. Louis, MO 63105	(314) 854-8000
Bell Atlantic	1717 Arch St., Philadelphia, PA 19103	(215) 963-6000
Bell Industries	11812 San Vicente Blvd., Los Angeles, CA 90049	(310) 826-2355
Bell Microproducts	1941 Ringwood Ave., San Jose, CA 95131	(408) 451-9400
BellSouth	1155 Peachtree St., NE, Atlanta, GA 30309	(404) 249-2000
Bemis	222 S. Ninth St., Suite 2300, Minneapolis, MN 55402	(612) 376-3000
Ben Franklin Retail Stores	500 E. North Ave., Carol Stream, IL 60188	(708) 462-6100
Beneficial	301 N. Walnut St., Wilmington, DE 19801	(302) 425-2500
Bergen Brunswig	4000 Metropolitan Dr., Orange, CA 92668	(714) 385-4000
Berkshire Hathaway	1440 Kiewit Plaza, Omaha, NE 68131	(402) 346-1400
Berlitz	293 Wall St., Princeton, NJ 08540	(609) 924-8500
Best Buy	7075 Flying Cloud Dr., Eden Prairie, MN 55344	(612) 947-2000
Best Products	1400 Best Plaza, Richmond, VA 23227	(804) 261-2000
Bethlehem Steel	1170 Eighth Ave., Bethlehem, PA 18016	(610) 694-2424
Betz Laboratories	4636 Somerton Rd., Trevose, PA 19053	(215) 355-3300
Beverly Enterprises	1200 S. Waldron Rd., Suite 155, Fort Smith, AR 72903	(501) 452-6712
BHC Communications	767 Fifth Ave., New York, NY 10153	(212) 421-0200
BIC	500 BIC Dr., Milford, CT 06460	(203) 783-2000
Big B	2600 Morgan Rd., SE, Birmingham, AL 35023	(205) 424-3421
Bindley Western Industries	4212 W. 71st St., Indianapolis, IN 46268	(317) 298-9900
Bio-Rad Laboratories	1000 Alfred Nobel Dr., Hercules, CA 94547	(510) 724-7000
Biomet	Airport Industrial Park, Warshaw, IN 46581	(219) 267-6639
Birmingham Steel	1000 Urban Ctr. Pkwy., Birmingham, AL 35242	(205) 970-1200
BJ Services	5500 N.W. Central Dr., Houston, TX 77092	(713) 462-4239
The Black & Decker Corp.	701 E. Joppa Rd., Towson, MD 21286	(410) 716-3900
Blair	220 Hickory St., Warren, PA 16366	(814) 723-3600
Block Drug	257 Cornelison Ave., Jersey City, NJ 07302	(201) 434-3000
Blount	4520 Executive Park Dr., Montgomery, AL 36116	(205) 244-4000
BMC Software	2101 City W. Blvd., Houston, TX 77042	(713) 918-8800
Boatman's Banking	200 W. Capitol Ave., Little Rock, AR 72201	(501) 378-1521
Boatmen's Bancshares	800 Market St., St. Louis, MO 63101	(314) 466-6000
Bob Evans Farms	3776 S. High St., Columbus, OH 43207	(614) 491-2225
The Boeing Co.	7755 E. Marginal Way S., Seattle, WA 98108	(206) 655-2121
Boise Cascade	1111 W. Jefferson St., Boise, ID 83702	(208) 384-6161
The Bombay Co.	550 Bailey Ave., Suite 700, Fort Worth, TX 76107	(817) 347-8200
The Bon-Ton Stores	2801 E. Market St., York, PA 17402	(717) 757-7660

The Business Almanac 2000 (cont'd)

Name	Address	Phone
Borden	180 E. Broad St., Columbus, OH 43215	(614) 225-4000
Borden Chemicals and Plastics	P.O. Box 427, Geismar, LA 70734	(504) 673-6121
Borg-Warner Automotive	200 S. Michigan Ave., Chicago, IL 60604	(312) 322-8500
Borland	100 Borland Way, Scotts Valley, CA 95066	(408) 431-1000
Boston Edison	800 Boylston St., Boston, MA 02199	(617) 424-2000
Boston Scientific	1 Boston Scientific Pl., Natick, MA 01760	(508) 650-8000
Bowater	55 E. Camperdown Way, Greenville, SC 29602	(803) 271-7733
Bowne & Co.	345 Hudson St., New York, NY 10014	(212) 924-5500
Boyd Gaming	2950 S. Industrial Rd., Las Vegas, NV 89109	(702) 792-7200
Brad Ragan	4404-G Stuart Andrew Blvd., Charlotte, NC 28217	(704) 521-2100
Bradlees	1385 Hancock St., Quincy, MA 02169	(617) 380-8000
Breed Technologies	5300 Old Tampa Hwy., Lakeland, FL 33811	(813) 284-6000
Briggs & Stratton	12301 W. Wirth St., Wauwatosa, WI 53222	(414) 259-5333
Brinker	6820 LBJ Fwy., Dallas, TX 75240	(214) 980-9917
Bristol-Myers Squibb	345 Park Ave., New York, NY 10154	(212) 546-4000
Broadway Stores	3880 N. Mission Rd., Los Angeles, CA 90031	(213) 227-2000
Brooke Group	100 S.E. Second St., 32nd Floor, Miami, FL 33131	(305) 579-8000
Brooklyn Bancorp	211 Montague St., Brooklyn, NY 11201	(718) 780-0400
Brooklyn Union Gas	1 MetroTech Ctr., Brooklyn, NY 11201	(718) 403-2000
Brown Group	8300 Maryland Ave., St. Louis, MO 63105	(314) 854-4000
Brown-Forman	850 Dixie Hwy., Louisville, KY 40210	(502) 585-1100
Browning-Ferris Industries	757 N. Eldridge, P.O. Box 3151, Houston, TX 77253	(713) 870-8100
Bruno's	800 Lakeshore Pkwy., Birmingham, AL 35211	(205) 940-9400
Brunswick	1 N. Field Ct., Lake Forest, IL 60045	(708) 735-4700
Brush Wellman	17876 St. Clair Ave., Cleveland, OH 44110	(216) 486-4200
Buffets	10260 Viking Dr., Suite 100, Eden Prairie, MN 55344	(612) 942-9760
Builders Transport	2029 W. DeKalb St., Camden, SC 29020	(803) 432-1400
Burlington Coat Factory Warehouse	1830 Route 130, Burlington, NJ 08016	(609) 387-7800
Burlington Industries	3330 W. Friendly Ave., Greensboro, NC 27410	(910) 379-2000
Burlington Northern	777 Main St., Fort Worth, TX 76102	(817) 333-2000
Burlington Resources	5051 Westheimer, Suite 1400, Houston, TX 77056	(713) 624-9000
Bush Boake Allen	7 Mercedes Dr., Montvale, NJ 07645	(201) 391-9870
Butler	110 Summit Ave., Montvale, NJ 07645	(201) 573-8000
Butler Manufacturing	BMA Tower, Penn Valley Park, Kansas City, MO 64141	(816) 968-3000
Buttrey Food and Drug Stores	601 Sixth St., SW, Great Falls, MT 59403	(406) 761-3401
BW/IP	200 Oceangate Blvd., Suite 900, Long Beach, CA 90802	(310) 435-3700
CCH	4025 W. Peterson, Chicago, IL 60646	(312) 583-8500
C Tec	105 Carnegie Ctr., Princeton, NJ 08540	(609) 734-3700
C. R. Bard	730 Central Ave., Murray Hill, NJ 07974	(908) 277-8000
Cabletron Systems	35 Industrial Way, Rochester, NH 03867	(603) 332-9400
Cablevision Systems	1 Media Crossways, Woodbury, NY 11797	(516) 364-8450
Cabot	75 State St., Boston, MA 02109	(617) 345-0100
Cabot Oil & Gas	15375 Memorial Dr., Houston, TX 77079	(713) 589-4600
Cadence Design Systems	555 River Oaks Pkwy., San Jose, CA 95134	(408) 943-1234
Cadmus Communications	6620 W. Broad St., Suite 500, Richmond, VA 23230	(804) 287-5680
Caesars World	1801 Century Park E., Los Angeles, CA 90067	(310) 552-2711
Cagle's	2000 Hills Ave., NW, Atlanta, GA 30318	(404) 355-2820
The Caldor Corp.	20 Glover Ave., Norwalk, CT 06856	(203) 846-1641
Calgon Carbon	400 Calgon Carbon Dr., Pittsburgh, PA 15205	(412) 787-6700
California Federal Bank	5700 Wilshire Blvd., Los Angeles, CA 90036	(213) 932-4200

The Business Almanac 2000 (cont'd)

Name	Address	Phone
California Microwave	985 Almanor Ave., Sunnyvale, CA 94086	(408) 732-4000
Callaway Golf	2285 Rutherford Rd., Carlsbad, CA 92008	(619) 931-1771
CalMat	3200 San Fernando Rd., Los Angeles, CA 90065	(213) 258-2777
Cambrex	1 Meadowlands Plaza, East Rutherford, NJ 07073	(201) 804-3000
Camco	7030 Ardmore, Houston, TX 77054	(713) 747-4000
Cameron Ashley	11100 Plano Rd., Dallas, TX 75238	(214) 340-1996
Campbell Soup	Campbell Pl., Camden, NJ 08103	(609) 342-4800
Canandaigua Wine	116 Buffalo St., Canandaigua, NY 14424	(716) 394-7900
Capital Cities/ABC	77 W. 66th St., New York, NY 10023	(212) 456-7777
Capital One Financial	2980 Fairview Park Dr., Falls Church, VA 22042	(804) 967-1000
Capitol American Financial	1001 Lakeside Ave., Cleveland, OH 44114	(216) 696-6400
Capstead Mortgage	2711 N. Haskell Ave., Suite 900, Dallas, TX 75204	(214) 874-2323
Carauster Industries	3100 Washington St., Austell, GA 30001	(404) 948-3101
Cardinal Health	655 Metro Pl. S., Dublin, OH 43017	(614) 761-8700
Career Horizons	177 Crossways Park Dr., Woodbury, NY 11797	(516) 496-2300
Caremark	2215 Sanders Rd., Suite 400, Northbrook, IL 60062	(708) 559-4700
Carl Karcher Enterprises	1200 N. Harbor Blvd., Anaheim, CA 92801	(714) 774-5796
Carlisle Companies	250 S. Clinton St., Suite 201, Syracuse, NY 13202	(315) 474-2500
Carlisle Plastics	1314 N. Third St., Suite 30, Phoenix, AZ 85004	(602) 407-2100
Carmike Cinemas	1301 First Ave., Columbus, GA 31901	(706) 576-3400
Carnival	3655 N.W. 87th Ave., Miami, FL 33178	(305) 599-2600
Carolina Freight	North Carolina Hwy. 150 E., Cherryville, NC 28021	(704) 435-6811
Carolina Power & Light	411 Fayetteville St., Raleigh, NC 27601	(919) 546-6111
Carpenter Technology	101 W. Bern St., Reading, PA 19612	(610) 208-2000
Carr-Gottstein Foods	6411 A St., Anchorage, AK 99518	(907) 561-1944
Carson Pirie Scott & Co.	331 W. Wisconsin Ave., Milwaukee, WI 53203	(414) 347-4141
Carter-Wallace	1345 Ave. of the Americas, New York, NY 10105	(212) 339-5000
Case	700 State St., Racine, WI 53404	(414) 636-6011
Casey's General Stores	1 Convenience Blvd., Ankeny, IA 50021	(515) 965-6100
Cash America	1600 W. Seventh St., Fort Worth, TX 76102	(817) 335-1100
Castle Energy	100 Matsonford Rd., Suite 250, Radnor, PA 19087	(610) 995-9400
Caterpillar	100 N.E. Adams St., Peoria, IL 61629	(309) 675-1000
Catherines Stores	3742 Lamar Ave., Memphis, TN 38118	(901) 363-3900
The Cato Corp.	8100 Denmark Rd., Charlotte, NC 28273	(704) 554-8510
CBI Industries	800 Jorie Blvd., Oak Brook, IL 60521	(708) 572-7000
CBS	51 W. 52nd St., New York, NY 10019	(212) 975-4321
CCB Financial	111 Corcoran St., Durham, NC 27701	(919) 683-7500
CCP Insurance	11825 N. Pennsylvania St., Carmel, IN 46032	(317) 573-6900
CDI	1717 Arch St., 35th Floor, Philadelphia, PA 19103	(215) 569-2200
CDW Computer Centers	1020 E. Lake Cook Rd., Buffalo Grove, IL 60089	(708) 465-6000
CellStar	1730 Briercroft Dr., Carrollton, TX 75006	(214) 323-0600
Centennial Cellular	50 Locust Ave., New Canaan, CT 06840	(203) 972-2000
Centerior Energy	6200 Oak Tree Blvd., Independence, OH 44131	(216) 447-3100
Centex Construction Products	3333 Lee Pkwy., Dallas, TX 75219	(214) 559-6500
Central and South West	1616 Woodall Rodgers Fwy., Dallas, TX 75202	(214) 777-1000
Central Fidelity Banks	1021 E. Cary St., Richmond, VA 23219	(804) 782-4000
Central Garden & Pet	3697 Mt. Diablo Blvd., Suite 310, Lafayette, CA 94549	(510) 283-4573
Central Hudson Gas & Electric	284 South Ave., Poughkeepsie, NY 12601	(914) 452-2000
Central Louisiana Electric	2030 Donahue Ferry Rd., Pineville, LA 71360	(318) 484-7400
Central Maine Power	83 Edison Dr., Augusta, ME 04336	(207) 623-3521

The Business Almanac 2000 (cont'd)

Name	Address	Phone
Central Newspapers	135 N. Pennsylvania St., Indianapolis, IN 46204	(317) 231-9200
Central Tractor Farm & Country	3915 Delaware Ave., Des Moines, IA 50316	(515) 266-3101
Central Vermont Public Service	77 Grove St., Rutland, VT 05701	(802) 773-2711
Centura Banks	134 N. Church St., P.O. Box 1220, Rocky Mount, NC 27802	(919) 977-4400
Century Telephone Enterprises	100 Century Park Dr., Monroe, LA 71203	(318) 388-9500
Ceridian	8100 34th Ave. S., Minneapolis, MN 55425	(612) 853-8100
Chambers Development	10700 Frankstown Rd., Pittsburgh, PA 15235	(412) 242-6237
Champion	1 Champion Plaza, Stamford, CT 06921	(203) 358-7000
Champion Enterprises	2701 University Dr., Suite 320, Auburn Hills, MI 48326	(810) 340-9090
Chaparral Steel	300 Ward Rd., Midlothian, TX 76065	(214) 775-8241
The Charles Schwab Corp.	101 Montgomery St., San Francisco, CA 94104	(415) 627-7000
Charming Shoppes	450 Winks Ln., Bensalem, PA 19020	(215) 245-9100
Charter Medical	3414 Peachtree Rd., NE, Atlanta, GA 30326	(404) 841-9200
Charter One Financial	1215 Superior Ave., Cleveland, OH 44114	(216) 589-8320
Chase Brass Industries	State Route 15, Montpelier, OH 43543	(419) 485-3193
The Chase Manhattan Corp.	1 Chase Manhattan Plaza, New York, NY 10081	(212) 552-2222
Chemed	255 E. Fifth St., Cincinnati, OH 45202	(513) 762-6900
Chemical Banking	270 Park Ave., New York, NY 10017	(212) 270-6000
The Cherry Corp.	3600 Sunset Ave., Waukegan, IL 60087	(708) 662-9200
Chesapeake	1021 E. Cary St., P.O. Box 2350, Richmond, VA 23218	(804) 697-1000
Chevron	225 Bush St., San Francisco, CA 94104	(415) 894-7700
Chic by H.I.S.	1372 Broadway, New York, NY 10018	(212) 302-6400
Chicago & North Western Transporation	165 N. Canal St., Chicago, IL 60606	(312) 559-7000
Chipcom	118 Turnpike Rd., Southborough, MA 01772	(508) 460-8900
Chiquita Brands	250 E. Fifth St., Cincinnati, OH 45202	(513) 784-8011
Chiron	4560 Horton St., Emeryville, CA 94608	(510) 655-8730
Chock Full O'Nuts	370 Lexington Ave., New York, NY 10017	(212) 532-0300
Chrysler	12000 Chrysler Dr., Highland Park, MI 48288	(313) 956-5741
The Chubb Corp.	15 Mountain View Rd., P.O. Box 1615, Warren, NJ 07061	(908) 903-2000
Church & Dwight	469 N. Harrison St., Princeton, NJ 08543	(609) 683-5900
CIGNA	1 Liberty Pl., Philadelphia, PA 19192	(215) 761-1000
CILCORP	300 Hamilton Blvd., Suite 300, Peoria, IL 61602	(309) 675-8810
Cincinnati Bell	201 E. Fourth St., P.O. Box 2301, Cincinnati, OH 45201	(513) 397-9900
Cincinnati Financial	6200 S. Gilmore Rd., Fairfield, OH 45014	(513) 870-2000
Cincinnati Milacron	4701 Marburg Ave., Cincinnati, OH 45209	(513) 841-8100
CINergy	139 E. Fourth St., Cincinnati, OH 45202	(513) 381-2000
Cintas	6800 Cintas Blvd., Mason, OH 45040	(513) 459-1200
CIPSCO	607 E. Adams St., Springfield, IL 62739	(217) 523-3600
Circuit City Stores	9950 Mayland Dr., Richmond, VA 23233	(804) 527-4000
Circus Circus Enterprises	2880 Las Vegas Blvd. S., Las Vegas, NV 89109	(702) 734-0410
Cirrus Logic	3100 W. Warren Ave., Fremont, CA 94538	(510) 623-8300
Cisco Systems	170 W. Tasman Dr., San Jose, CA 95134	(408) 526-4000
Citicorp	399 Park Ave., New York, NY 10043	(800) 285-3000
Citizens Bancorp	14401 Sweitzer Ln., Laurel, MD 20707	(301) 206-6080
Citizens Utilities	High Ridge Park, P.O. Box 3801, Stamford, CT 06905	(203) 329-8800
Claire's Stores	3 S.W. 129th Ave., Pembroke Pines, FL 33027	(305) 433-3900
CLARCOR	2323 Sixth St., P.O. Box 7007, Rockford, IL 61125	(815) 962-8867
Clark Equipment	100 N. Michigan St., South Bend, IN 46601	(219) 239-0100
Clayton Homes	623 Market St., Knoxville, TN 37902	(615) 970-7200
Cleveland-Cliffs	1100 Superior Ave., Cleveland, OH 44114	(216) 694-5700

The Business Almanac 2000 (cont'd)

Name	Address	Phone
The Clorox Co.	1221 Broadway, Oakland, CA 94612	(510) 271-7000
The Clothestime	5325 E. Hunter Ave., Anaheim, CA 92807	(714) 779-5881
Club Med	40 W. 57th St., New York, NY 10019	(212) 977-2100
CML Group	524 Main St., Acton, MA 01720	(508) 264-4155
CMS Energy	330 Town Ctr. Dr., Dearborn, MI 48126	(313) 436-9200
CNA Financial	CNA Plaza, Chicago, IL 60685	(312) 822-5000
Coachmen Industries	601 E. Beardsley Ave., Elkhart, IN 46514	(219) 262-0123
Coast Savings Financial	1000 Wilshire Blvd., Los Angeles, CA 90017	(213) 362-2000
The Coastal Corp.	9 Greenway Plaza, Houston, TX 77046	(713) 877-1400
Coca-Cola Bottling Consolidated	1900 Rexford Rd., Charlotte, NC 28211	(704) 551-4400
The Coca-Cola Co.	1 Coca-Cola Plaza, NW, Atlanta, GA 30313	(404) 676-2121
Coca-Cola Enterprises	Coca-Cola Plaza, NW, Atlanta, GA 30313	(404) 676-2100
Cold Metal Products	8526 South Ave., Youngstown, OH 44514	(216) 758-1194
Cole National	5915 Landerbrook Dr., Mayfield Heights, OH 44124	(216) 449-4100
Coleman	1526 Cole Blvd., Suite 300, Golden, CO 80401	(303) 202-2400
Colgate-Palmolive	300 Park Ave., New York, NY 10022	(212) 310-2000
Collective Bancorp	716 W. White Horse Pike, Cologne, NJ 08213	(609) 625-1110
Collins & Aikman Group	701 McCullough Dr., Charlotte, NC 28262	(704) 548-2350
Coltec Industries	430 Park Ave., New York, NY 10022	(212) 940-0400
Columbia Gas System	20 Montchanin Rd., Wilmington, DE 19807	(302) 429-5000
Columbia/HCA Healthcare	201 W. Main St., Louisville, KY 40202	(502) 572-2000
Comair Holdings	P.O. Box 75021, Cincinnati, OH 45275	(606) 525-2550
Comcast	1500 Market St., Philadelphia, PA 19102	(215) 665-1700
Comdata Holdings	5301 Maryland Way, Brentwood, TN 37027	(615) 370-7000
Comdisco	6111 N. River Rd., Rosemont, IL 60018	(708) 698-3000
Comerica	P.O. Box 75000, Detroit, MI 48275	(313) 222-4000
Commerce Bancshares	1000 Walnut St., Kansas City, MO 64106	(816) 234-2000
Commerce Group	211 Main St., Webster, MA 01570	(508) 949-4480
Commercial Federal	2120 S. 72nd St., Omaha, NE 68124	(402) 554-9200
Commercial Intertech	1775 Logan Ave., Youngstown, OH 44505	(216) 746-8011
Commercial Metals	7800 Stemmons Fwy., Dallas, TX 75247	(214) 689-4300
Commonwealth Energy System	1 Main St., P.O. Box 9150, Cambridge, MA 02142	(617) 225-4000
Community Health Systems	3707 FM 1960 W., Suite 500, Houston, TX 77068	(713) 537-5230
Community Psychiatric Centers	6600 W. Charleston Blvd., Suite 118, Las Vegas, NV 89102	(702) 259-3600
Compaq Computer	20555 State Hwy. 249, Houston, TX 77070	(713) 370-0670
Compass Bancshares	15 S. 20th St., Birmingham, AL 35233	(205) 933-3000
CompuCom Systems	10100 N. Central Expwy., Dallas, TX 75231	(214) 265-3600
CompUSA	14951 N. Dallas Pkwy., Dallas, TX 75240	(214) 383-4000
Computer Associates,	1 Computer Associates Plaza, Islandia, NY 11788	(516) 342-5224
Computer Sciences	2100 E. Grand Ave., El Segundo, CA 90245	(310) 615-0311
Computer Task Group	800 Delaware Ave., Buffalo, NY 14209	(716) 882-8000
Computervision	100 Crosby Dr., Bedford, MA 01730	(617) 275-1800
Compuware	31440 Northwestern Hwy., Farmington Hills, MI 48334	(810) 737-7300
COMSAT	6560 Rock Spring Dr., Bethesda, MD 20817	(301) 214-3000
ConAgra	1 ConAgra Dr., Omaha, NE 68102	(402) 595-4000
Cone Mills	1201 Maple St., Greensboro, NC 27405	(910) 379-6220
Connecticut Energy	855 Main St., Bridgeport, CT 06604	(203) 579-1732
Connecticut Natural Gas	100 Columbus Blvd., Hartford, CT 06144	(203) 727-3000
Conner Peripherals	3081 Zanker Rd., San Jose, CA 95134	(408) 456-4500
Conrail	2001 Market St., Philadelphia, PA 19101	(215) 209-4000

The Business Almanac 2000 (cont'd)

Name	Address	Phone
Conseco	11825 N. Pennsylvania St., Carmel, IN 46032	(317) 573-6100
Consolidated Edison of New York	4 Irving Pl., New York, NY 10003	(212) 460-4600
Consolidated Freightways	3240 Hillview Ave., Palo Alto, CA 94304	(415) 494-2900
Consolidated Natural Gas	625 Liberty Ave., Pittsburgh, PA 15222	(412) 227-1000
Consolidated Papers	231 First Ave. N., Wisconsin Rapids, WI 54495	(715) 422-3111
Consolidated Stores	300 Phillipi Rd., P.O. Box 28512, Columbus, OH 43228	(614) 278-6800
Contel Cellular	245 Perimeter Ctr. Pkwy., Atlanta, GA 30346	(404) 804-3400
Continental Airlines Holdings	2929 Allen Pkwy., Suite 2010, Houston, TX 77019	(713) 834-5000
Continental Can	1 Aerial Way, Syosset, NY 11791	(516) 822-4940
The Continental Corp.	180 Maiden Ln., New York, NY 10038	(212) 440-3000
Continental Homes Holding	7001 N. Scottsdale Rd., Scottsdale, AZ 85253	(602) 483-0006
Continental Medical Systems	600 Wilson Ln., P.O. Box 715, Mechanicsburg, PA 17055	(717) 790-8300
The Continuum Co.	9500 Arboretum Blvd., Austin, TX 78759	(512) 345-5700
Control Data Systems	4201 Lexington Ave. N., Arden Hills, MN 55126	(612) 482-2401
Converse	1 Fordham Rd. , North Reading, MA 01864	(508) 664-1100
Cooper Industries	First City Tower, 1001 Fannin St., Suite 4000, Houston, TX 77210	(713) 739-5400
Cooper Tire & Rubber	Lima and Western Aves., Findlay, OH 45840	(419) 423-1321
Coram Healthcare	1125 17th St., Suite 1500, Denver, CO 80202	(303) 292-4973
Cordis	14201 N.W. 60th Ave., Miami Lakes, FL 33014	(305) 824-2000
CoreStates Financial	P.O. Box 7618, Philadelphia, PA 19101	(215) 973-3827
Corning	1 Riverfront Plaza, Corning, NY 14831	(607) 974-9000
Corporate Express	325 Interlocken Pkwy., Broomfield, CO 80021	(303) 373-2800
Countrywide Credit Industries	155 N. Lake Ave., Pasadena, CA 91109	(818) 304-8400
Coventry	53 Century Blvd., Suite 250, Nashville, TN 37214	(615) 391-2440
CPC	International Plaza, Englewood Cliffs, NJ 07632	(201) 894-4000
CPI	1706 Washington Ave., St. Louis, MO 63103	(314) 231-1575
Cracker Barrel Old Country Store	305 Hartmann Dr., Lebanon, TN 37087	(615) 444-5533
Crane	100 First Stamford Pl., Stamford, CT 06902	(203) 363-7300
Crawford & Co. Risk Management Services	5620 Glenridge Dr., NE, Atlanta, GA 30342	(404) 256-0830
Cray Research	655-A Lone Oak Dr., Eagan, MN 55121	(612) 683-7100
Crestar Financial	919 E. Main St., Richmond, VA 23219	(804) 782-5000
Crompton & Knowles	1 Station Pl., Stamford, CT 06902	(203) 353-5400
Crown Books	3300 75th Ave., Landover, MD 20785	(301) 731-1200
Crown Central Petroleum	1 N. Charles St., Baltimore, MD 21201	(410) 539-7400
Crown Cork & Seal	9300 Ashton Rd., Philadelphia, PA 19136	(215) 698-5100
CSF Holdings	1221 Brickell Ave., 16th Floor, Miami, FL 33131	(305) 577-0400
CSX	901 E. Cary St., Richmond, VA 23219	(804) 782-1400
CTS	905 West Blvd. N., Elkhart, IN 46514	(219) 293-7511
Cubic	9333 Balboa Ave., San Diego, CA 92123	(619) 277-6780
CUC	707 Summer St., Stamford, CT 06901	(203) 324-9261
Culbro	387 Park Ave. S., New York, NY 10016	(212) 561-8700
Cullen/Frost Bankers	100 W. Houston St., San Antonio, TX 78205	(210) 220-4011
Culp	101 S. Main St., High Point, NC 27261	(910) 889-5161
Cummins Engine	500 Jackson St., P.O. Box 3005, Columbus, IN 47202	(812) 377-5000
Cygne Designs	1372 Broadway, New York, NY 10018	(212) 354-6474
Cypress Semiconductor	3901 N. First St., San Jose, CA 95134	(408) 943-2600
Cyprus Amax Minerals	9100 E. Mineral Circle, Englewood, CO 80112	(303) 643-5000
Cyrk	3 Pond Rd., Gloucester, MA 01930	(508) 283-5800
Cytec Industries	5 Garret Mountain Plaza, W. Patterson, NJ 07424	(201) 357-3100
D.R. Horton	1901 Ascension Blvd., Suite 100, Arlington, TX 76006	(817) 856-8200

The Business Almanac 2000 (cont'd)

Name	Address	Phone
Dairy Mart Convenience Stores	1 Vision Dr., Enfield, CT 06082	(203) 741-4444
Daisytek	500 N. Central Expwy., Plano, TX 75074	(214) 881-4700
DAKA	55 Ferncroft Rd., Danvers, MA 01923	(508) 774-9115
DAMARK	7101 Winnetka Ave. N., Brooklyn Park, MN 55428	(612) 531-0066
Dames & Moore	911 Wilshire Blvd., Suite 700, Los Angeles, CA 90017	(213) 683-1560
Dana	4500 Dorr St., P.O. Box 1000, Toledo, OH 43697	(419) 535-4500
Danaher	1250 24th St., NW, Suite 800, Washington, DC 20037	(202) 828-0850
Darling	251 O'Connor Ridge Blvd., Irving, TX 75038	(214) 717-0300
Data General	4400 Computer Dr., Westboro, MA 01580	(508) 898-5000
Dauphin Deposit	213 Market St., Harrisburg, PA 17101	(717) 255-2121
Dayton Hudson	777 Nicollet Mall, Minneapolis, MN 55402	(612) 370-6948
Dean Foods	3600 N. River Rd., Franklin Park, IL 60131	(708) 678-1680
Dean Witter Reynolds	2 World Trade Ctr., New York, NY 10048	(212) 392-2222
DeBartolo Realty	7620 Market St., Youngstown, OH 44513	(216) 758-7292
Deere & Co.	John Deere Rd., Moline, IL 61265	(309) 765-8000
DEKALB Genetics	3100 Sycamore Rd., DeKalb, IL 60115	(815) 758-3461
Del Webb	2231 E. Camelback Rd., Phoenix, AZ 85016	(602) 808-8000
Delchamps	305 Delchamps Dr., Mobile, AL 36602	(205) 433-0431
Dell Computer	9505 Arboretum Blvd., Austin, TX 78759	(512) 338-4400
Delmarva Power & Light	800 King St., P.O. Box 231, Wilmington, DE 19899	(302) 429-3011
Delphi Financial Group	1105 N. Market St., Suite 1230, Wilmington, DE 19801	(302) 478-5142
Delta Air Lines	Hartsfield Atlanta International Airport, Atlanta, GA 30320	(404) 715-2600
Delta Woodside Industries	233 N. Main St., Suite 200, Greenville, SC 29601	(803) 232-8301
Deluxe	1080 W. County Rd. F, St. Paul, MN 55126	(612) 483-7111
DENTSPLY	570 W. College Ave., York, PA 17405	(717) 845-7511
Deposit Guaranty	P.O. Box 1200, Jackson, MS 39215	(601) 354-8564
Designs	1244 Boylston St., Chestnut Hill, MA 01267	(617) 739-6722
Destec Energy	2500 CityWest Blvd., Suite 150, Houston, TX 77042	(713) 735-4000
Detroit Diesel	13400 Outer Dr. W., Detroit, MI 48239	(313) 592-5000
The Detroit Edison Co.	2000 Second Ave., Detroit, MI 48226	(313) 237-8000
The Dexter Corp.	1 Elm St., Windsor Locks, CT 06096	(203) 627-9051
Diagnostek	4500 Alexander Blvd., NE, Albuquerque, NM 87107	(505) 345-8080
The Dial Corp.	Dial Tower, Phoenix, AZ 85077	(602) 207-4000
Diamond Shamrock	9830 Colonnade Blvd., San Antonio, TX 78230	(210) 641-6800
The Diana Corp.	8200 W. Brown Deer Rd., Suite 200, Milwaukee, WI 53223	(414) 355-0037
Diebold	5995 Mayfair Rd., North Canton, OH 44720	(216) 489-4000
Digital Equipment	111 Powdermill Rd., Maynard, MA 01754	(508) 493-5111
Dillard Department Stores	1600 Cantrell Rd., Little Rock, AR 72201	(501) 376-5200
Dime BanCorp	589 Fifth Ave., New York, NY 10017	(212) 326-6170
Dimon	512 Bridge St., Danville, VA 24543	(804) 792-7511
The Walt Disney Co.	500 S. Buena Vista St., Burbank, CA 91521	(818) 560-1000
Dixie Yarns	1100 S. Watkins St., Chattanooga, TN 37404	(615) 698-2501
Dole Food	31355 Oak Crest Dr., Westlake Village, CA 91361	(818) 879-6600
Dollar General	104 Woodmont Blvd., Suite 500, Nashville, TN 37205	(615) 783-2000
Dominion Resources	901 E. Byrd St., Richmond, VA 23219	(804) 775-5700
Donaldson	1400 W. 94th St., Minneapolis, MN 55431	(612) 887-3131
Donnelly	414 E. 40th St., Holland, MI 49423	(616) 786-7000
Doskocil Companies	2601 N.W. Expwy., Suite 1000, Oklahoma City, OK 73112	(405) 879-5500
Douglas & Lomason	24600 Hollywood Ct., Farmington Hills, MI 48335	(810) 478-7800
Dover	280 Park Ave., New York, NY 10017	(212) 922-1640

The Business Almanac 2000 (cont'd)

Name	Address	Phone
The Dow Chemical Co.	2030 Dow Ctr., Midland, MI 48674	(517) 636-1000
Dow Jones & Co.	200 Liberty St., New York, NY 10281	(212) 416-2000
Downey Financial	3501 Jamboree Rd., Newport Beach, CA 92660	(714) 854-3100
DPL	1065 Woodman Dr., Dayton, OH 45432	(513) 224-6000
DQE	301 Grant St., Pittsburgh, PA 15279	(412) 393-6000
Dr. Pepper/Seven-Up Companies	8144 Walnut Hill Ln., Dallas, TX 75231	(214) 360-7000
Dravo	3600 Oliver Plaza, Pittsburgh, PA 15222	(412) 566-3000
Dress Barn	30 Dunnigan Dr., Suffern, NY 10901	(914) 369-4500
Dresser Industries	2001 Ross Ave., Dallas, TX 75201	(214) 740-6000
Dreyer's Grand Ice Cream	5929 College Ave., Oakland, CA 94618	(510) 652-8187
Drug Emporium	155 Hidden Ravines Dr., Powell, OH 43065	(614) 548-7080
DSC Communications	1000 Coit Rd., Plano, TX 75075	(214) 519-3000
E. I. Du Pont de Nemours and Co.	1007 Market St., Wilmington, DE 19898	(302) 774-1000
Duckwall-ALCO Stores	401 Cottage St., Abilene, KS 67410	(913) 263-3350
Duke Power	422 S. Church St., Charlotte, NC 28242	(704) 594-0887
The Dun & Bradstreet Corp.	200 Nyala Farms, Westport, CT 06880	(203) 834-4200
Duplex Products	1947 Bethany Rd., P.O. Box 1947, Sycamore, IL 60178	(815) 895-2101
Duracell	Berkshire Industrial Park, Bethel, CT 06801	(203) 796-4000
The Duriron Co.	3100 Research Blvd., Dayton, OH 45420	(513) 476-6100
Duty Free	63 Copps Hill Rd., Ridgefield, CT 06877	(203) 431-6057
Dynatech	3 New England Executive Park, Burlington, MA 01803	(617) 272-6100
E-Systems	6250 LBJ Fwy., P.O. Box 66028, Dallas, TX 75266	(214) 661-1000
E-Z Serve	2550 N. Loop W., Houston, TX 77092	(713) 684-4300
The E. W. Scripps Co.	1105 N. Market St., Wilmington, DE 19890	(302) 478-4141
Eagle Food Centers	Rte. 67 & Knoxville Rd., Milan, IL 61264	(309) 787-7730
Eagle Hardware & Garden	101 Andover Park E., Suite 200, Tukwila, WA 98188	(206) 431-5740
Eastern Enterprises	9 Riverside Rd., Weston, MA 02193	(617) 647-2300
Eastern Utilities Associates	1 Liberty Sq., Boston, MA 02109	(617) 357-9590
Eastex Energy	1000 Louisiana, Houston, TX 77002	(713) 650-6255
Eastman Chemical	100 N. Eastman Rd., Kingsport, TN 37660	(615) 229-2000
Eastman Kodak	343 State St., Rochester, NY 14650	(716) 724-4000
Eaton	Eaton Ctr., Cleveland, OH 44114	(216) 523-5000
Echlin	100 Double Beach Rd., Branford, CT 06405	(203) 481-5751
Eckerd	8333 Bryan Dairy Rd., Largo, FL 34647	(813) 399-6000
Ecolab	370 N. Wabasha St., St. Paul, MN 55102	(612) 293-2233
Edison Brothers Stores	501 N. Broadway, St. Louis, MO 63102	(314) 331-6000
Edisto Resources	2121 San Jacinto St., 26th Floor, Dallas, TX 75201	(214) 880-0243
EG&G	45 William St., Wellesley, MA 02181	(617) 237-5100
Egghead	22011 S.E. 51st St., Issaquah, WA 98027	(206) 391-0800
Ekco Group	98 Spit Brook Rd., Suite 102, Nashua, NH 03062	(603) 888-1212
El Paso Electric	303 N. Oregon St., El Paso, TX 79901	(915) 543-5711
El Paso Natural Gas	100 N. Stanton St., El Paso, TX 79901	(915) 541-2600
Elco Industries	1111 Samuelson Rd., Rockford, IL 61125	(815) 397-5151
Electronic Arts	1450 Fashion Island Blvd., San Mateo, CA 94404	(415) 571-7171
Electronic Data Systems	5400 Legacy Dr., Plano, TX 75024	(214) 604-6000
Elek Tek	7350 N. Linder Ave., Skokie, IL 60077	(708) 677-7660
Eli Lilly and Co.	Lilly Corporate Ctr., Indianapolis, IN 46285	(317) 276-2000
Eljer Industries	17120 Dallas Pkwy., Suite 205, Dallas, TX 75248	(214) 407-2600
EMC	171 South St., Hopkinton, MA 01748	(508) 435-1000
Emerson Electric	8000 W. Florissant Ave., St. Louis, MO 63136	(314) 553-2000

The Business Almanac 2000 (cont'd)

Name	Address	Phone
Emerson Radio	9 Entin Rd., Parsipany, NJ 07054	(201) 884-5800
Emphesys Financial Group	1100 Employers Blvd., Green Bay, WI 54344	(414) 336-1100
Employee Benefit Plans	435 Ford Ave., Suite 500, Minneapolis, MN 55426	(612) 546-4353
Energen	2101 Sixth Ave. N., Birmingham, AL 35203	(205) 326-2700
Energy Service	1445 Ross Ave., Suite 2700, Dallas, TX 75202	(214) 922-1500
Energy Ventures	5 Post Oak Park, Suite 1760, Houston, TX 77027	(713) 297-8400
Engelhard	101 Wood Ave., Iselin, NJ 08830	(908) 205-5000
Engle Homes	123 N.W. 13th St., Boca Raton, FL 33432	(407) 391-4012
ENRON	1400 Smith St., Houston, TX 77002	(713) 853-6161
ENSERCH	300 S. St. Paul St., Dallas, TX 75201	(214) 651-8700
Entergy	639 Loyola Ave., New Orleans, LA 70113	(504) 529-5262
EnviroSource	5 High Ridge Park, Stamford, CT 06904	(203) 322-8333
EOTT Energy Partners	1330 Post Oak Blvd., Houston, TX 77056	(713) 993-5200
Equifax	1600 Peachtree St., NW, Atlanta, GA 30309	(404) 885-8000
The Equitable Companies	787 Seventh Ave., New York, NY 10019	(212) 554-1234
Equitable of Iowa Companies	604 Locust St., Des Moines, IA 50309	(515) 245-6911
Equitable Resources	420 Blvd. of the Allies, Pittsburgh, PA 15219	(412) 261-3000
ERLY Industries	10990 Wilshire Blvd., Suite 1800, Los Angeles, CA 90024	(213) 879-1480
Ernst Home Center	1511 Sixth Ave., Seattle, WA 98101	(206) 621-6700
ESCO Electronics	8100 W. Florissant Ave., St. Louis, MO 63136	(314) 553-7777
Esterline Technologies	10800 N.E. Eighth St., Bellevue, WA 98004	(206) 453-9400
Ethan Allen Interiors	Ethan Allen Dr., Danbury, CT 06811	(203) 743-8000
Ethyl	330 S. Fourth St., P.O. Box 2189, Richmond, VA 23217	(804) 788-5000
Exabyte	1685 38th St., Boulder, CO 80301	(303) 442-4333
Excel Industries	1120 N. Main St., Elkhart, IN 46514	(219) 264-2131
EXECUTONE Information Systems	478 Wheelers Farm Rd., Milford, CT 06460	(203) 876-7600
Exide	1400 N. Woodward Ave., Bloomfield Hills, MI 48304	(810) 258-0080
Exide Electronics Group	8521 Six Forks Rd., Raleigh, NC 27615	(919) 872-3020
Expeditors International of Washington	19119 16th Ave. S., Seattle, WA 98188	(206) 246-3711
Exxon	225 E. John W. Carpenter Fwy., Irving, TX 75062	(214) 444-1000
F & M Distributors	25800 Sherwood Rd., Warren, MI 48091	(810) 758-1400
Fabri-Centers of America	5555 Darrow Rd., Hudson, OH 44236	(216) 656-2600
Fairchild	P. O. Box 10803, 300 W. Service Rd., Chantilly, VA 22021	(703) 478-5800
Falcon Building Products	2 N. Riverside Plaza, Chicago, IL 60606	(312) 906-9700
Family Dollar Stores	10401 Old Monroe Rd., Matthews, NC 28105	(704) 847-6961
Farah	8889 Gateway W., El Paso, TX 79925	(915) 593-4444
Fay's	7245 Henry Clay Blvd., Liverpool, NY 13088	(315) 451-8000
Fedders	Westgate Corporate Ctr., 505 Martinsville Rd., Liberty Corner, NJ 07938	(908) 604-8686
Federal Express	2005 Corporate Ave., Memphis, TN 38132	(901) 369-3600
Federal Home Loan Mortgage	8200 Jones Branch Dr., McLean, VA 22102	(703) 903-2000
Federal National Mortgage Association	3900 Wisconsin Ave., NW, Washington, DC 20016	(202) 752-7000
Federal Paper Board	75 Chestnut Ridge Rd., Montvale, NJ 07645	(201) 391-1776
Federal Signal	1415 W. 22nd St., Oak Brook, IL 60521	(708) 954-2000
Federal-Mogul	26555 Northwestern Hwy., Southfield, MI 48034	(810) 354-7700
Federated Department Stores	7 W. Seventh St., Cincinnati, OH 45202	(513) 579-7000
Ferrellgas Partners	1 Liberty Plaza, Liberty, MO 64068	(816) 792-1600
Ferro	1000 Lakeside Ave, Cleveland, OH 44114	(216) 641-8580
FFP Partners	2801 Glenda Ave., Fort Worth, TX 76117	(817) 838-4700
FHP	9900 Talbert Ave., P.O. Box 8000, Fountain Valley, CA 92708	(714) 963-7233
Fibreboard	2121 N. California Blvd., Walnut Creek, CA 94596	(510) 274-0700

The Business Almanac 2000 (cont'd)

Name	Address	Phone
Fidelity National Financial	2100 S.E. Main St., Suite 400, Irvine, CA 92714	(714) 852-9770
Fieldcrest Cannon	326 E. Stadium Dr., Eden, NC 27288	(910) 627-3000
Fifth Third Bancorp	38 Fountain Sq. Plaza, Cincinnati, OH 45263	(513) 579-5300
Figgie	4420 Sherwin Rd., Willoughby, OH 44094	(216) 953-2700
Filene's Basement	40 Walnut St., Wellesley, MA 02181	(617) 348-7000
FINA	8350 N. Central Expwy., Dallas, TX 75206	(214) 750-2400
Fingerhut Companies	4400 Baker Rd., Minnetonka, MN 55343	(612) 932-3100
Finova Group	1850 N. Central Ave., Phoenix, AZ 85004	(602) 207-6900
First American	First American Ctr., Nashville, TN 37237	(615) 748-2000
The First American Financial Corp.	114 E. Fifth St., Santa Ana, CA 92701	(714) 558-3211
First Bancorporation of Ohio	800 First National Tower, Akron, OH 44308	(216) 384-8000
First Bank System	601 Second Ave. S., Minneapolis, MN 55402	(612) 973-1111
First Brands	83 Wooster Heights Rd., Danbury, CT 06813	(203) 731-2300
First Chicago	1 First National Plaza, Chicago, IL 60670	(312) 732-4000
First Citizens BancShares	239 Fayetteville St., Raleigh, NC 27601	(919) 755-7000
First Colony	901 E. Byrd St., Suite 1350, Richmond, VA 23219	(804) 775-0300
First Commerce	210 Baronne St., P.O. Box 60279, New Orleans, LA 70160	(504) 561-1371
First Commercial	400 W. Capitol Ave., Little Rock, AR 72201	(501) 371-7000
First Data	11718 Nicholas St., Omaha, NE 68154	(402) 222-2000
First Empire State	1 M&T Plaza, Buffalo, NY 14240	(716) 842-5445
First Fidelity Bancorporation	550 Broad St., Newark, NJ 07102	(201) 565-3200
First Financial	1305 Main St., Stevens Point, WI 54481	(715) 341-0400
First Financial Management	3 Corporate Sq., Suite 700, Atlanta, GA 30329	(404) 321-0120
First Hawaiian	1132 Bishop St., Honolulu, HI 96813	(808) 525-7000
First Interstate Bancorp	633 W. Fifth St., Los Angeles, CA 90071	(213) 614-3001
First Mississippi	700 North St., Jackson, MS 39202	(601) 948-7550
First of America Bank	211 S. Rose St., Kalamazoo, MI 49007	(616) 376-9000
First Security	79 S. Main St., P.O. Box 30006, Salt Lake City, UT 84130	(801) 246-5706
First Tennessee National	165 Madison Ave., Memphis, TN 38103	(901) 523-4444
First Union	1 First Union Ctr., Charlotte, NC 28288	(704) 374-6565
First USA	2001 Bryan Tower, Dallas, TX 75201	(214) 746-8400
First Virginia Banks	6400 Arlington Blvd., Falls Church, VA 22042	(703) 241-4000
Firstar	777 E. Wisconsin Ave., Milwaukee, WI 53202	(414) 765-4316
FirstFed Financial	401 Wilshire Blvd., Santa Monica, CA 90401	(310) 319-6000
FirstFed Michigan	1001 Woodward Ave., Detroit, MI 48226	(313) 965-1400
FirsTier Financial	17th and Farnam, Omaha, NE 68102	(402) 348-6000
FIserv	255 FIserv Dr., Brookfield, WI 53045	(414) 879-5000
Fisher Scientific	Liberty Ln., Hampton, NH 03842	(603) 929-2650
Flagstar Companies	203 E. Main St., Spartansburg, SC 29319	(803) 597-8000
Fleet Financial Group	50 Kennedy Plaza, Providence, RI 02903	(401) 278-5800
Fleet Mortgage Group	1333 Main St., Columbia, SC 29201	(803) 929-7900
Fleetwood Enterprises	3125 Myers St., P.O. Box 7638, Riverside, CA 92513	(909) 351-3500
Fleming Companies	6301 Waterford Blvd., Oklahoma City, OK 73118	(405) 840-7200
FlightSafety	La Guardia Airport, Flushing, NY 11371	(718) 565-4100
Florida East Coast Industries	1650 Prudential Dr., Jacksonville, FL 32207	(904) 396-6600
Florida Progress	1 Progress Plaza, St. Petersburg, FL 33701	(813) 824-6400
Florida Rock Industries	155 E. 21st St., Jacksonville, FL 32206	(904) 355-1781
The Florsheim Shoe Co.	130 S. Canal St., Chicago, IL 60606	(312) 559-2500
Flowers Industries	P.O. Box 1338, Thomasville, GA 31799	(912) 226-9110
Fluor	3333 Michelson Dr., Irvine, CA 92730	(714) 975-2000

The Business Almanac 2000 (cont'd)

Name	Address	Phone
FMC	200 E. Randolph Dr., Chicago, IL 60601	(312) 861-6000
Foamex	1000 Columbia Ave., Linwood, PA 19061	(610) 859-3000
Food Lion	2110 Executive Dr., Salisbury, NC 28145	(704) 633-8250
Foodarama Supermarkets	303 W. Main St., Freehold, NJ 07728	(908) 462-4700
Foodmaker	9330 Balboa Ave., San Diego, CA 92123	(619) 571-2121
Ford Motor	The American Road, Dearborn, MI 48121	(313) 322-3000
Foremost of America	5600 Beach Tree Ln., Caledonia, MI 49316	(616) 942-3000
Forest City Enterprises	10800 Brookpark Rd., Cleveland, OH 44130	(216) 267-1200
Forest Laboratories	909 Third Ave., New York, NY 10022	(212) 421-7850
Forstmann & Co.	1185 Ave. of the Americas, New York, NY 10036	(212) 642-6900
Foster Wheeler	Perryville Corporate Park, Clinton, NJ 08809	(908) 730-4000
Foundation Health	3400 Data Dr., Rancho Cordova, CA 95670	(916) 631-5000
Fourth Financial	100 N. Broadway, Wichita, KS 67202	(316) 261-4444
FoxMeyer	1220 Senlac Dr., Carrollton, TX 75006	(214) 446-4800
FPL Group	700 Universe Blvd., Juno Beach, FL 33408	(305) 552-3552
Franklin Electric	400 E. Spring St., Bluffton, IN 46714	(219) 824-2900
Franklin Quest	2200 W. Parkway Blvd., Salt Lake City, UT 84119	(801) 975-1776
Franklin Resources	777 Mariners Island Blvd., San Mateo, CA 94404	(415) 312-2000
Fred Meyer	3800 S.E. 22nd Ave., Portland, OR 97202	(503) 232-8844
Fred's	4300 New Getwell Rd., Memphis, TN 38118	(901) 365-8880
Freeport-McMoRan Copper & Gold	1615 Poydras St., New Orleans, LA 70112	(504) 582-4000
Fremont General	2020 Santa Monica Blvd., Santa Monica, CA 90404	(310) 315-5500
Fresenius USA	2637 Shadelands Dr., Walnut Creek, CA 94598	(510) 295-0200
Fretter	12501 E. Grand River Rd., Brighton, MI 48116	(810) 220-5000
Fritz Companies	706 Mission St., San Francisco, CA 94103	(415) 904-8360
Frontier	180 S. Clinton Ave., Rochester, NY 14646	(716) 777-1000
Frozen Food Express Industries	318 Cadiz St., Dallas, TX 75207	(214) 630-8090
Fruehauf Trailer	P.O. Box 94913, Indianapolis, IN 46244	(317) 630-3000
Fruit of the Loom	233 S. Wacker Dr., Chicago, IL 60606	(312) 876-1724
Fund American Enterprises Holdings	The 1820 House, Norwich, VT 05055	(802) 649-3633
Furon	29982 Ivy Glenn Dr., Laguna Niguel, CA 92677	(714) 831-5350
The Future Now	8044 Montgomery Rd., Suite 601, Cincinnati, OH 45236	(513) 792-4500
G&K Services	505 Waterford Park, Suite 455, Minneapolis, MN 55441	(612) 546-7440
Galey & Lord	980 Ave. of the Americas, New York, NY 10018	(212) 465-3000
Gander Mountain	P.O. Box 128, Hwy. W, Wilmot, WI 53192	(414) 862-2331
Gannett	1100 Wilson Blvd., Arlington, VA 22234	(703) 284-6000
The Gap	1 Harrison, San Francisco, CA 94105	(415) 952-4400
Gateway 2000	610 Gateway Dr., P.O. Box 2000, North Sioux City, SD 57049	(605) 232-2000
GATX	500 W. Monroe St., Chicago, IL 60661	(312) 621-6200
Gaylord Container	500 Lake Cook Rd., Suite 400, Deerfield, IL 60015	(708) 405-5500
Gaylord Entertainment	1 Gaylord Dr., Nashville, TN 37214	(615) 316-6000
GBC Technologies	444 Kelley Dr., Berlin, NJ 08009	(609) 767-2500
GC Companies	27 Boylston St., Chestnut Hill, MA 02167	(617) 278-5600
GEICO	GEICO Plaza, Washington, DC 20076	(301) 986-3000
GenCorp	175 Ghent Rd., Fairlawn, OH 44333	(216) 869-4200
Genentech	460 Point San Bruno Blvd., S. San Francisco, CA 94080	(415) 225-1000
General Binding	1 GBC Plaza, Northbrook, IL 60062	(708) 272-3700
General Dynamics	3190 Fairview Park Dr., Falls Church, VA 22042	(703) 876-3000
General Electric	3135 Easton Tpke., Fairfield, CT 06431	(203) 373-2211
General Host	1 Station Pl., Stamford, CT 06902	(203) 357-9900

The Business Almanac 2000 (cont'd)

Name	Address	Phone
General Instrument	181 W. Madison St., Chicago, IL 60602	(312) 541-5000
General Mills	1 General Mills Blvd., Minneapolis, MN 55426	(612) 540-2311
General Motors	3044 W. Grand Blvd., Detroit, MI 48202	(313) 556-5000
General Nutrition Companies	921 Penn Ave., Pittsburgh, PA 15222	(412) 288-4600
General Public Utilities	100 Interpace Pkwy., Parsippany, NJ 07054	(201) 263-6500
General Re	695 E. Main St., Stamford, CT 06901	(203) 328-5000
General Signal	High Ridge Park, Stamford, CT 06904	(203) 329-4100
Genesco	Genesco Park, Nashville, TN 37217	(615) 367-7000
Genesis Health Ventures	148 W. State St., Kennett Sq., PA 19348	(610) 444-6350
Geneva Steel	10 S. Geneva Rd., Vineyard, UT 84058	(801) 227-9000
GENICOM	14800 Conference Ctr. Dr., Suite 400, Chantilly, VA 22021	(703) 802-9200
The Genlyte Group	100 Lighting Way, Secaucus, NJ 07096	(201) 864-3000
Genovese Drug Stores	80 Marcus Dr., Melville, NY 11747	(516) 420-1900
Genuine Parts	2999 Circle 75 Pkwy., Atlanta, GA 30339	(404) 953-1700
Genzyme	1 Kendall Sq., Cambridge, MA 02139	(617) 252-7500
The Geon Co.	6100 Oak Tree Blvd., Independence, OH 44131	(216) 447-6000
Georgia Gulf	400 Perimeter Ctr. Terrace, Atlanta, GA 30346	(404) 395-4500
Georgia-Pacific	133 Peachtree St., NE, Atlanta, GA 30303	(404) 652-4000
Gerber Scientific	83 Gerber Road W., South Windsor, CT 06074	(203) 644-1551
Getty Petroleum	125 Jericho Tpke., Jericho, NY 11753	(516) 338-6000
Giant Food	6300 Sheriff Rd., Landover, MD 20785	(301) 341-4100
Giant Industries	23733 N. Scottsdale Rd., Scottsdale, AZ 85255	(602) 585-8888
Gibson Greetings	2100 Section Rd., Cincinnati, OH 45237	(513) 841-6600
Giddings & Lewis	142 Doty St., P.O. Box 590, Fond du Lac, WI 54936	(414) 921-9400
Gilbert Associates	P.O. Box 1498, Reading, PA 19603	(610) 775-5900
The Gillette Co.	Prudential Tower Building, Boston, MA 02199	(617) 421-7000
Glendale Federal Bank	700 N. Brand Blvd., Glendale, CA 91203	(818) 500-2000
Global Marine	777 N. Eldridge Rd., Houston, TX 77079	(713) 596-5100
Golden Poultry	244 Perimeter Ctr. Pkwy., NE, Atlanta, GA 30346	(404) 393-5000
Golden West Financial	1901 Harrison St., Oakland, CA 94612	(510) 446-3420
The Good Guys	7000 Marina Blvd., Brisbane, CA 94005	(415) 615-5000
Goody's Family Clothing	400 Goody's Ln., Knoxville, TN 37922	(615) 966-2000
The Goodyear Tire & Rubber Co.	1144 E. Market St., Akron, OH 44316	(216) 796-2121
Gottschalks	7 River Park Pl. E., Fresno, CA 93720	(209) 434-8000
Goulds Pumps	240 Fall St., Seneca Falls, NY 13148	(315) 568-2811
Government Tech Services	4100 Lafayette Ctr. Dr., Chantilly, VA 22021	(703) 502-2000
Graco	4050 Olson Memorial Hwy., Golden Valley, MN 55422	(612) 623-6000
GranCare	1 Ravina Dr., Suite 1240, Atlanta, GA 30346	(404) 393-0199
Grand Casinos	13705 First Ave. N., Plymouth, MN 55441	(612) 449-9092
Granite Construction	585 W. Beach St., Watsonville, CA 95076	(408) 724-1011
Graphic Industries	2155 Monroe Dr., NE, Atlanta, GA 30324	(404) 874-3327
The Great Atlantic & Pacific Tea Co.	2 Paragon Dr., Montvale, NJ 07645	(201) 573-9700
Great Lakes Chemical	P.O. Box 2200, West Lafayette, IN 47906	(317) 497-6100
Great Western Financial	9200 Oakdale Ave., Chatsworth, CA 91311	(818) 775-3411
Green Tree Financial	345 St. Peter St., St. Paul, MN 55102	(612) 293-3400
The Greenbrier Cos.	1 Centerpointe Dr., Suite 200, Lake Oswego, OR 97035	(503) 684-7000
Greenfield Industries	470 Old Evans Rd., Augusta, GA 30809	(706) 863-7708
Grey Advertising	777 Third Ave., New York, NY 10017	(212) 546-2000
Greyhound Lines	15110 N. Dallas Pkwy., Dallas, TX 75248	(214) 789-7000
Grossman's	200 Union St., Braintree, MA 02184	(617) 848-0100

The Business Almanac 2000 (cont'd)

Name	Address	Phone
Ground Round Restaurants	35 Braintree Hill Office Park, Braintree, MA 02184	(617) 380-3100
Group Technologies	10901 Malcolm McKinley Dr., Tampa, FL 33612	(813) 972-6000
Grow Group	200 Park Ave., New York, NY 10166	(212) 599-4400
GTE	1 Stamford Forum, Stamford, CT 06904	(203) 965-2000
GTECH	55 Technology Way, West Greenwich, RI 02817	(401) 392-1000
Guaranty National	P. O. Box 3329, Englewood, CO 80155	(303) 754-8400
Guidant	307 E. McCarty St., Indianapolis, IN 46225	(317) 276-8734
Guilford Mills	4925 W. Market St., Greensboro, NC 27407	(910) 316-4000
Guy F. Atkinson of California	1001 Bayhill Dr., Second Floor, San Bruno, CA 94066	(415) 876-1000
H&R Block	4410 Main St., Kansas City, MO 64111	(816) 753-6900
H. B. Fuller	2400 Energy Park Dr., St. Paul, MN 55108	(612) 645-3401
H. F. Ahmanson and Co.	4900 Rivergrade Rd., Irwindale, CA 91706	(818) 960-6311
H. J. Heinz	600 Grant St., Pittsburgh, PA 15219	(412) 456-5700
Hadco	12A Manor Pkwy., Salem, NH 03079	(603) 898-8000
Hadson	P.O. Box 569550, Dallas, TX 75356	(214) 640-6800
Haemonetics	400 Wood Rd., Braintree, MA 02184	(617) 848-7100
Haggar	6113 Lemmon Ave., Dallas, TX 75209	(214) 352-8481
Hahn Automotive Warehouse	415 W. Main St., Rochester, NY 14608	(716) 235-1595
Halliburton	3600 Lincoln Plaza, Dallas, TX 75201	(214) 978-2600
Hancock Fabrics	3406 W. Main St., P.O. Box 2400, Tupelo, MS 38803	(601) 842-2834
Handleman	500 Kirts Blvd., Troy, MI 48084	(810) 362-4400
Handy & Harman	250 Park Ave., New York, NY 10177	(212) 661-2400
Hannaford Bros.	145 Pleasant Hill Rd., Scarborough, ME 04074	(207) 883-2911
Hanover Direct	1500 Harbor Blvd., Weehawken, NJ 07087	(201) 863-7300
Harcourt General	27 Boylston St., Chestnut Hill, MA 02167	(617) 232-8200
Harley-Davidson	3700 W. Juneau Ave., Milwaukee, WI 53208	(414) 342-4680
Harleysville Group	355 Maple Ave., Harleysville, PA 19438	(215) 256-5000
Harman International Industries	1101 Pennsylvania Ave., NW, Washington, DC 20004	(202) 393-1101
Harnischfeger Industries	13400 Bishops Ln., Brookfield, WI 53005	(414) 671-4400
The Harper Group	260 Townsend St., San Francisco, CA 94107	(415) 978-0600
Harris	1025 W. NASA Blvd., Melbourne, FL 32919	(407) 727-9100
Harsco	350 Poplar Church Rd., Camp Hill, PA 17001	(717) 763-7064
Harte-Hanks Communications	P.O. Box 269, San Antonio, TX 78291	(210) 829-9000
The Hartford Steam Boiler Inspection and Insurance Company	1 State St., Hartford, CT 06102	(203) 722-1866
Hartmarx	101 N. Wacker Dr., Chicago, IL 60606	(312) 372-6300
Harvard Industries	2502 N. Rocky Point Dr., Suite 960, Tampa, FL 33607	(813) 288-5000
Hasbro	1027 Newport Ave., Pawtucket, RI 02861	(401) 431-8697
Haverty Furniture Companies	866 W. Peachtree St., NW, Atlanta, GA 30308	(404) 881-1911
Hawaiian Electric Industries	900 Richards St., Honolulu, HI 96813	(808) 543-5662
Hayes Wheels	38481 Huron River Dr., Romulus, MI 48174	(313) 941-2000
HBO & Co.	301 Perimeter Ctr. N., Atlanta, GA 30346	(404) 393-6000
HCA Hospital Corp. of America	1 Park Plaza, Nashville, TN 37203	(615) 327-9551
Health Care and Retirement	1 Seagate, Toledo, OH 43666	(419) 247-5000
Health Management Associates	5811 Pelican Bay Blvd., Naples, FL 33963	(813) 598-3131
Health Systems	21600 Oxnard St., Woodland Hills, CA 91367	(818) 719-6978
Healthsource	2 College Park Dr., Hooksett, NH 03106	(603) 268-7000
Healthsouth	2 Perimeter Park S., Birmingham, AL 35243	(205) 967-7116
Healthtrust–The Hospital Co.	4525 Harding Rd., Nashville, TN 37205	(615) 383-4444
Hechinger	3500 Pennsy Dr., Landover, MD 20785	(301) 341-1000
Heilig-Meyers	2235 Staples Mill Rd., Richmond, VA 23230	(804) 359-9171

The Business Almanac 2000 (cont'd)

Name	Address	Phone
Helene Curtis Industries	325 N. Wells St., Chicago, IL 60610	(312) 661-0222
Helmerich & Payne	Utica at 21st St., Tulsa, OK 74114	(918) 742-5531
Herbalife	9800 La Cienega Blvd., Inglewood, CA 90301	(310) 410-9600
Hercules	1313 N. Market St., Wilmington, DE 19894	(302) 594-5000
Heritage Media	13355 Noel Rd., Suite 1500, Dallas, TX 75240	(214) 702-7380
Herman Miller	855 E. Main Ave., Zeeland, MI 49464	(616) 654-3000
Hershey Foods	100 Crystal A Dr., Hershey, PA 17033	(717) 534-6799
Hewlett-Packard	3000 Hanover St., Palo Alto, CA 94304	(415) 857-1501
Hexcel	5794 W. Las Positas Blvd., Pleasonton, CA 94588	(510) 847-9500
Hi-Lo Automotive	2575 W. Bellfort, Houston, TX 77054	(713) 663-6700
Hibernia National Bank	313 Carondelet St., New Orleans, LA 70137	(504) 533-3333
Hillenbrand Industries	700 State Route 46 E., Batesville, IN 47006	(812) 934-7000
The Hillhaven Corp.	1148 Broadway Plaza, Tacoma, WA 98402	(206) 572-4901
Hills Stores	15 Dan Rd., Canton, MA 02021	(617) 821-1000
Hilton Hotels	9336 Civic Ctr. Dr., Beverly Hills, CA 90210	(310) 278-4321
Holly	100 Crescent Court, Suite 1600, Dallas, TX 75201	(214) 871-3555
Hollywood Casino	13455 Noel Rd., LB 48, Dallas, TX 75240	(214) 392-7777
The Home Depot	2727 Paces Ferry Rd., Atlanta, GA 30339	(404) 433-8211
Home Holdings	59 Maiden Ln., New York, NY 10038	(212) 530-6600
Home Shopping Network	2501 118th Ave. N., St. Petersburg, FL 33716	(813) 572-8585
Homedco Group	17650 Newhope St., Fountain Valley, CA 92708	(714) 755-5600
Homestake Mining	650 California St., San Francisco, CA 94108	(415) 981-8150
HON Industries	414 E. Third St., P.O. Box 1109, Muscatine, IA 52761	(319) 264-7400
Honeywell	Honeywell Plaza, Minneapolis, MN 55408	(612) 951-1000
Hooper Holmes	170 Mt. Airy Rd., Basking Ridge, NJ 07920	(908) 766-5000
Horace Mann Educators	1 Horace Mann Plaza, Springfield, IL 62715	(217) 789-2500
Horizon Healthcare	6001 Indian School Rd., NE, Albuquerque, NM 87110	(505) 881-4961
Hormel Foods	1 Hormel Pl., Austin, MN 55912	(507) 437-5611
Hospitality Franchise Systems	339 Jefferson Rd., Parsippany, NJ 07054	(201) 428-9700
Host Marriott	10400 Fernwood Rd., Bethesda, MD 20817	(301) 380-9000
Houghton Mifflin	222 Berkeley St., Boston, MA 02116	(617) 351-5000
House of Fabrics	13400 Riverside Dr., Sherman Oaks, CA 91423	(818) 995-7000
Household	2700 Sanders Rd., Prospect Heights, IL 60070	(708) 564-5000
Houston Industries	4400 Post Oak Pkwy., Houston, TX 77027	(713) 629-3000
Hovnanian Enterprises	10 Hwy. 35, P.O. Box 500, Red Bank, NJ 07701	(908) 747-7800
Howell	1111 Fanin St., Houston, TX 77002	(713) 658-4000
Hubbell	584 Derby Milford Rd., Orange, CT 06477	(203) 799-4100
Hudson Foods	1225 Hudson Rd., Rogers, AR 72756	(501) 636-1100
Huffy	7701 Byers Rd., Miamisburg, OH 45342	(513) 866-6251
Hughes Supply	20 N. Orange Ave., Suite 200, Orlando, FL 32801	(407) 841-4755
Humana	500 W. Main St., Louisville, KY 40202	(502) 580-1000
Hunt Manufacturing	230 S. Broad St., Philadelphia, PA 19102	(215) 732-7700
Huntington Bancshares	Huntington Ctr., Columbus, OH 43287	(614) 476-8300
Hutchinson Technology	40 W. Highland Park, Hutchinson, MN 55350	(612) 587-3797
IBM	Old Orchard Rd., Armonk, NY 10504	(914) 765-1900
IBP	IBP Ave., P.O. Box 515, Dakota City, NE 68731	(402) 494-2061
ICF Kaiser	9300 Lee Hwy., Fairfax, VA 22031	(703) 934-3600
Idaho Power	1221 W. Idaho St., Boise, ID 83702	(208) 383-2200
IDEX	630 Dundee Rd., Suite 400, Northbrook, IL 60062	(708) 498-7070
IES Industries	200 First St., SE, Cedar Rapids, IA 52401	(319) 398-4411

The Business Almanac 2000 (cont'd)

Name	Address	Phone
Illinois Central	455 N. Cityfront Plaza Dr., Chicago, IL 60611	(312) 755-7500
Illinois Tool Works	3600 W. Lake Ave., Glenview, IL 60025	(708) 724-7500
Illinova	500 S. 27th St., P.O. Box 511, Decatur, IL 62525	(217) 424-6600
IMC Global	2100 Sanders Rd., Northbrook, IL 60062	(708) 272-9200
Imo Industries	1009 Lenox Dr., Bldg. 4 W., Lawrenceville, NJ 08648	(609) 896-7600
Imperial Holly	1 Imperial Sq., Suite 200, Sugar Land, TX 77487	(713) 491-9181
Inacom	10810 Farnam Dr., Omaha, NE 68154	(402) 392-3900
Independent Insurance Group	1 Independent Dr., Jacksonville, FL 32276	(904) 358-5151
Indiana Energy	1630 N. Meridian St., Indianapolis, IN 46202	(317) 926-3351
INDRESCO	2121 San Jacinto St., Dallas, TX 75201	(214) 953-4500
Infinity Broadcasting	600 Madison Ave., New York, NY 10022	(212) 750-6400
Information Resources	150 N. Clinton St., Chicago, IL 60661	(312) 726-1221
Informix	4100 Bohannon Dr., Menlo Park, CA 94025	(415) 926-6300
Ingersoll-Rand	200 Chestnut Ridge Rd., Woodcliff Lake, NJ 07675	(201) 573-0123
Ingles Markets	P.O. Box 6676, Asheville, NC 28816	(704) 669-2941
Inland Steel Industries	30 W. Monroe St., Chicago, IL 60603	(312) 346-0300
Inmac	2465 Augustine Dr., Santa Clara, CA 95052	(408) 727-1970
Inphynet Medical Management	1200 S. Pine Island Rd., Fort Lauderdale, FL 33324	(305) 475-1300
Insilco	425 Metro Pl. N., Dublin, OH 43017	(614) 792-0468
Insteel Industries	1373 Boggs Dr., Mt. Airy, NC 27030	(910) 786-2141
Instrument Systems	100 Jericho Quadrangle, Jericho, NY 11753	(516) 938-5544
Integon	500 W. Fifth St., P.O. Box 3199, Winston-Salem, NC 27102	(910) 770-2000
Integra Financial	4 PPG Pl., Pittsburgh, PA 15222	(412) 644-7669
Integrated Device Technology	2975 Stender Way, Santa Clara, CA 95054	(408) 727-6116
Integrated Health Services	10065 Red Run Blvd., Owings Mill, MD 21117	(410) 998-8400
Intel	2200 Mission College Blvd., Santa Clara, CA 95052	(408) 765-8080
Intelligent Electronics	411 Eagleview Blvd., Exton, PA 19341	(610) 458-5500
Inter-Regional Financial Group	60 S. Sixth St., Minneapolis, MN 55402	(612) 371-7750
INTERCO	101 S. Hanley Rd., St. Louis, MO 63105	(314) 863-1100
Interface	Orchard Hill Rd., P.O. Box 1503, LaGrange, GA 30241	(706) 882-1891
Intergraph	Huntsville, AL 35894	(205) 730-2000
Interim Services	2050 Spectrum Blvd., Fort Lauderdale, FL 33309	(305) 938-7600
The Interlake Corp.	550 Warrenville Rd., Lisle, IL 60532	(708) 852-8800
Intermet	2859 Paces Ferry Rd., Atlanta, GA 30339	(404) 431-6000
International Dairy Queen	7505 Metro Blvd., Minneapolis, MN 55439	(612) 830-0200
International Flavors & Fragrances	521 W. 57th St., New York, NY 10019	(212) 765-5500
International Game Technology	5270 Neil Rd., Reno, NV 89510	(702) 686-1200
International Jensen	25 Tri-State International Office Ctr., Lincolnshire, IL 60069	(708) 317-3700
International Multifoods	33 S. Sixth St., P.O. Box 2942, Minneapolis, MN 55402	(612) 340-3300
International Paper	2 Manhattanville Rd., Purchase, NY 10577	(914) 397-1500
International Recovery	700 S. Royal Poinciana Blvd., Miami Springs, FL 33166	(305) 884-2001
International Rectifier	233 Kansas St., El Segundo, CA 90245	(310) 322-3331
International Shipholding	650 Poydras St., Suite 1700, New Orleans, LA 70130	(504) 529-5461
International Specialty Products	818 Washington St., Wilmington, DE 19801	(302) 429-8554
International Technology	23456 Hawthorne Blvd., Torrance, CA 90505	(310) 378-9933
The Interpublic Group of Companies	1271 Ave. of the Americas, New York, NY 10020	(212) 399-8000
Interstate Bakeries	12 E. Armour Blvd., Kansas City, MO 64141	(816) 561-6600
Interstate Power	1000 Main St., P.O. Box 769, Dubuque, IA 52004	(319) 582-5421
Intertrans	125 E. John W. Carpenter Fwy., Irving, TX 75062	(214) 830-8888
Intuit	155 Linfield Ave., Menlo Park, CA 94025	(415) 322-0573

The Business Almanac 2000 (cont'd)

Name	Address	Phone
Invacare	899 Cleveland St., P.O. Box 4028, Elyria, OH 44036	(216) 329-6000
Iowa-Illinois Gas and Electric	206 E. Second St., Davenport, IA 52801	(319) 326-7111
IPALCO Enterprises	25 Monument Circle, Indianapolis, IN 46204	(317) 261-8261
Itel	2 N. Riverside Plaza, Chicago, IL 60606	(312) 902-1515
ITT	1330 Ave. of the Americas, New York, NY 10019	(212) 258-1000
IVAX	8800 N.W. 36th St., Miami, FL 33178	(305) 590-2200
J&L Specialty Steel	1 PPG Pl., Pittsburgh, PA 15222	(412) 338-1600
J. B. Hunt Transport Services	615 J.B. Hunt Corporate Dr., Lowell, AR 72745	(501) 820-0000
J. Baker	555 Turnpike St., Canton, MA 02021	(617) 828-9300
J. C. Penney	6501 Legacy Dr., Plano, TX 75024	(214) 431-1000
The J. M. Smucker Co.	Strawberry Ln., Orrville, OH 44667	(216) 682-3000
J. P. Morgan & Co.	60 Wall St., New York, NY 10260	(212) 483-2323
Jabil Circuit	10800 Roosevelt Blvd., St. Petersburg, FL 33716	(813) 577-9749
Jacobs Engineering Group	251 S. Lake Ave., Pasadena, CA 91101	(818) 449-2171
Jacobson Stores	3333 Sargent Rd., Jackson, MI 49201	(517) 764-6400
James River of Virginia	120 Tredegar St., Richmond, VA 23219	(804) 644-5411
Jan Bell Marketing	13801 N.W. 14th St., Sunrise, FL 33323	(305) 846-8000
Jason	411 E. Wisconsin Ave., Milwaukee, WI 53202	(414) 277-9300
Jefferies Group	11100 Santa Monica Blvd., Los Angeles, CA 90025	(310) 445-1199
Jefferson Smurfit	8182 Maryland Ave., St. Louis, MO 63105	(314) 746-1100
Jefferson-Pilot	100 N. Greene St., Greensboro, NC 27401	(910) 691-3441
Jenny Craig	445 Marine View Ave., Suite 300, Del Mar, CA 92014	(619) 259-7000
John Alden Financial	7300 Corporate Ctr. Dr., Miami, FL 33126	(305) 715-3767
John Fluke Manufacturing	6920 Seaway Blvd., Everett, WA 98203	(206) 347-6100
John H. Harland	2939 Miller Rd., Decatur, GA 30035	(404) 981-9460
John Wiley & Sons	605 Third Ave., New York, NY 10158	(212) 850-6000
Johnson & Johnson	1 Johnson & Johnson Plaza, New Brunswick, NJ 08933	(908) 524-0400
Johnson Controls	5757 N. Green Bay Ave., Milwaukee, WI 53201	(414) 228-1200
Johnson Worldwide Associates	1326 Willow Rd., Sturtevant, WI 53177	(414) 884-1500
Johnstown America Industries	980 N. Michigan Ave., Suite 1000, Chicago, IL 60611	(312) 280-8844
Jones Apparel Group	250 Rittenhouse Circle, Bristol, PA 19007	(215) 785-4000
Jostens	5501 Norman Ctr. Dr., Minneapolis, MN 55437	(612) 830-3300
JP Foodservice	9830 Patuxent Woods Dr., Columbia, MD 21046	(410) 312-7100
Justin Industries	2821 W. Seventh St., P.O. Box 425, Fort Worth, TX 76101	(817) 336-5125
K Mart	3100 W. Big Beaver Rd., Troy, MI 48084	(810) 643-1000
Kaiser Aluminum	5847 San Felipe, Suite 2600, Houston, TX 77057	(713) 267-3777
Kaman	Blue Hills Ave., Bloomfield, CT 06002	(203) 243-7100
Kansas City Power & Light	1201 Walnut St., Kansas City, MO 64106	(816) 556-2200
Kansas City Southern Industries	114 W. 11th St., Kansas City, MO 64105	(816) 556-0303
Kasler Holding	27400 E. Fifth St., Highland, CA 92346	(909) 884-4811
Kaufman and Broad Home	10877 Wilshire Blvd., Los Angeles, CA 90024	(310) 443-8000
KCS Energy	379 Thornall St., Edison, NJ 08837	(908) 632-1770
Keane	10 City Sq., Boston, MA 02129	(617) 241-9200
Kellogg	1 Kellogg Sq., Battle Creek, MI 49016	(616) 961-2000
Kellwood	600 Kellwood Pkwy., Chesterfield, MO 63017	(314) 576-3100
Kelly Services	999 W. Big Beaver Rd., Troy, MI 48084	(810) 362-4444
Kemet	2835 Kemet Way, Simpsonville, SC 29681	(803) 963-6300
Kemper	1 Kemper Dr., Long Grove, IL 60049	(708) 320-4700
Kenetech	500 Sansome St., Suite 800, San Francisco, CA 94111	(415) 398-3825
Kennametal	P.O. Box 231, Latrobe, PA 15650	(412) 539-5000

The Business Almanac 2000 (cont'd)

Name	Address	Phone
Kent Electronics	7433 Harwin Dr., Houston, TX 77036	(713) 780-7770
Kerr-McGee	Kerr-McGee Ctr., Oklahoma City, OK 73125	(405) 270-1313
KeyCorp	127 Public Sq., Cleveland, OH 44114	(216) 689-3000
Keystone	9600 W. Gulf Bank Dr., Houston, TX 77040	(713) 466-1176
Keystone Consolidated Industries	5430 LBJ Fwy., Suite 1740, Dallas, TX 75240	(214) 458-0028
Kimball	1600 Royal St., Jasper, IN 47549	(812) 482-1600
Kimberly-Clark	P.O. Box 619100, Dallas, TX 75261	(214) 830-1200
Kindercare Learning Centers	2400 Presidents Dr., Montgomery, AL 36116	(334) 277-5090
Kinetic Concepts	8023 Vantage Dr., San Antonio, TX 78230	(210) 524-9000
King World Productions	1700 Broadway, 35th Floor, New York, NY 10019	(212) 315-4000
Kirby	1775 St. James Pl., Suite 300, Houston, TX 77056	(713) 629-9370
KLA Instruments	160 Rio Robles, San Jose, CA 95134	(408) 434-4200
KN Energy	370 Van Gordon St., Lakewood, CO 80228	(303) 989-1740
Knight-Ridder	1 Herald Plaza, Miami, FL 33132	(305) 376-3800
Kohl's	N54 W13600 Woodale Dr., Menomenee, WI 53051	(414) 783-5800
Komag	275 S. Hillview Dr., Milpitas, CA 95035	(408) 946-2300
Kroger	1014 Vine St., Cincinnati, OH 45202	(513) 762-4000
The Krystal Co.	1 Union Sq., Chattanooga, TN 37402	(615) 757-1550
KU Energy	1 Quality St., Lexington, KY 40507	(606) 255-2100
Kuhlman	1 Skidaway Village Walk, Suite 201, Savannah, GA 31411	(912) 598-7809
Kysor Industrial	1 Madison Ave., Cadillac, MI 49601	(616) 779-2200
L. B. Foster	415 Holiday Dr., Pittsburgh, PA 15220	(412) 928-3400
L.A. Gear	2850 Ocean Park Blvd., Santa Monica, CA 90405	(310) 452-4327
La Quinta Inns	112 E. Pecan St., San Antonio, TX 78205	(210) 302-6000
La-Z-Boy	1284 N. Telegraph Rd., Monroe, MI 48162	(313) 241-4414
Laclede Gas	720 Olive St., St. Louis, MO 63101	(314) 342-0500
Laclede Steel	1 Metropolitan Sq., St. Louis, MO 63102	(314) 425-1400
LADD Furniture	1 Plaza Ctr., P.O. Box HP-3, High Point, NC 27261	(910) 889-0333
Lafarge	11130 Sunrise Valley Dr., Reston, VA 22091	(703) 264-3600
Lakehead Pipe Line Partners	21 W. Superior St., Suite 400, Duluth, MN 55802	(218) 725-0100
Lam Research	4650 Cushing Pkwy., Fremont, CA 94538	(510) 659-0200
Lamson & Sessions	25701 Science Park Dr., Beachwood, OH 44122	(216) 464-3400
Lancaster Colony	37 W. Broad St., Columbus, OH 43215	(614) 224-7141
Lance	8600 South Blvd., Charlotte, NC 28232	(704) 554-1421
Lands' End	Lands' End Ln., Dodgeville, WI 53595	(608) 935-9341
Landstar Systems	1000 Bridgeport Ave., Shelton, CT 06484	(203) 925-2900
Lawyers Title	6630 W. Broad St., Richmond, VA 23230	(804) 281-6700
LCI	4650 Lakehurst Ct., Dublin, OH 43017	(614) 798-6862
LDDS Communications	515 E. Amite St., Jackson, MS 39201	(601) 360-8600
Lear Seating	21557 Telegraph Rd., Southfield, MI 48034	(810) 746-1500
Leaseway Transportation	3700 Park E. Dr., Beachwood, OH 44122	(216) 765-5500
Lechters	1 Cape May St., Harrison, NJ 07029	(201) 481-1100
Lee Enterprises	215 N. Main St., Davenport, IA 52801	(319) 383-2100
LEGENT	575 Herndon Pkwy., Herndon, VA 22070	(703) 708-3000
Legg Mason	111 S. Calvert St., Baltimore, MD 21202	(410) 539-0000
Leggett & Platt	1 Leggett Rd., Carthage, MO 64836	(417) 358-8131
Lehman Brothers Holdings	3 World Financial Ctr., New York, NY 10285	(212) 526-7000
Lennar	700 N.W. 107th Ave., Miami, FL 33172	(305) 559-4000
Leslie Fay Companies	1400 Broadway, New York, NY 10018	(212) 221-4000
Leucadia National	315 Park Ave. S., New York, NY 10010	(212) 460-1900

The Business Almanac 2000 (cont'd)

Name	Address	Phone
Levitz Furniture	6111 Broken Sound Pkwy., NW, Boca Raton, FL 33487	(407) 994-6006
LG&E Energy	220 W. Main St., Louisville, KY 40202	(502) 627-2000
Libbey	420 Madison Ave., Toledo, OH 43604	(419) 727-2100
The Liberty Corp.	2000 Wade Hampton Blvd., Greenville, SC 29602	(803) 268-8436
Life Partners Group	7887 E. Belleview Ave., Englewood, CO 80111	(303) 779-1111
Life Re	969 High Ridge Rd., Stamford, CT 06905	(203) 321-3000
Life Technologies	8717 Grovemont Circle, Gaithersburg, MD 20877	(301) 840-8000
Lilly Industries	733 S. West St., Indianapolis, IN 46225	(317) 687-6700
The Limited	2 Limited Pkwy., Columbus, OH 43216	(614) 479-7000
LIN Broadcasting	5400 Carillon Point, Kirkland, WA 98033	(206) 828-1902
Lincoln National	1300 S. Clinton St., Fort Wayne, IN 46802	(219) 455-2000
Litton Industries	2140 Burbank Blvd., Woodland Hills, CA 91367	(818) 598-5000
Liuski	10 Hub Dr., Melville, NY 11747	(516) 454-8220
Living Centers of America	15415 Katy Fwy., Suite 800, Houston, TX 77094	(713) 578-4700
Liz Claiborne	1441 Broadway, New York, NY 10018	(212) 354-4900
Lockheed	4500 Park Granada Blvd., Calabasas, CA 91399	(818) 876-2000
Loctite	10 Columbus Blvd., Hartford, CT 06106	(203) 520-5000
Loews	667 Madison Ave., New York, NY 10021	(212) 545-2000
Logicon	3701 Skypark Dr., Torrance, CA 90505	(310) 373-0220
Lomas Financial	1600 Viceroy Dr., Dallas, TX 75235	(214) 879-4000
Lone Star Industries	300 First Stamford Pl., Stamford, CT 06912	(203) 969-8600
Lone Star Technologies	5501 LBJ Fwy., Suite 1200, Dallas, TX 75240	(214) 386-3981
Long Island Lighting	175 E. Old Country Rd., Hicksville, NY 11801	(516) 755-6650
The Long Island Savings Bank	201 Old Country Rd., Melville, NY 11747	(516) 547-2000
Longs Drug Stores	141 N. Civic Dr., P.O. Box 5222, Walnut Creek, CA 94596	(510) 937-1170
Longview Fibre	End of Fibre Way, Longview, WA 98632	(206) 425-1550
Loral	600 Third Ave., New York, NY 10016	(212) 697-1105
Lotus Development	55 Cambridge Pkwy., Cambridge, MA 02142	(617) 577-8500
The Louisiana Land and Exploration Co.	909 Poydras St., New Orleans, LA 70112	(504) 566-6500
Louisiana-Pacific	111 S.W. Fifth Ave., Portland, OR 97204	(503) 221-0800
Lowe's Companies	State Hwy. 268 E., North Wilkesboro, NC 28659	(910) 651-4000
LSB Industries	16 S. Pennsylvania Ave., Oklahoma City, OK 73107	(405) 235-4546
LSI Logic	1551 McCarthy Blvd., Milpitas, CA 95035	(408) 433-8000
The LTV Corp.	25 W. Prospect Ave., Cleveland, OH 44115	(216) 622-5000
The Lubrizol Corp.	29400 Lakeland Blvd., Wickliffe, OH 44092	(216) 943-4200
Luby's Cafeterias	2211 Northeast Loop 410, San Antonio, TX 78265	(210) 654-9000
Lukens	50 S. First Ave., Coatesville, PA 19320	(215) 383-2000
Lyondell Petrochemical	1221 McKinney Ave., Suite 1600, Houston, TX 77010	(713) 652-7200
M. A. Hanna	200 Public Sq., Cleveland, OH 44114	(216) 589-4000
M. K. Rail	1200 Reedsdale St., Pittsburgh, PA 15233	(412) 237-2250
M. S. Carriers	3171 Directors Row, Memphis, TN 38116	(901) 332-2500
M.D.C. Holdings	3600 S. Yosemite St., Suite 900, Denver, CO 80237	(303) 773-1100
M/A-COM	100 Chelmsford St., Lowell, MA 01853	(508) 442-5000
M/I Schottenstein Homes	41 S. High St., Suite 2410, Columbus, OH 43215	(614) 221-5700
Mac Frugal's Bargains	2430 E. Del Amo Blvd., Dominguez, CA 90220	(310) 537-9220
Madison Gas and Electric	133 S. Blair St., P.O. Box 1231, Madison, WI 53701	(608) 252-7923
Magma Copper	7400 N. Oracle Rd., Suite 200, Tucson, AZ 85704	(602) 575-5600
Magna Group	1401 S. Brentwood Blvd., St. Louis, MO 63144	(314) 963-2500
MagneTek	26 Century Blvd.; P.O. Box 290159, Nashville, TN 37229	(615) 316-5100
Mallinckrodt Group	7733 Forsyth Blvd., St. Louis, MO 63105	(314) 854-5200

The Business Almanac 2000 (cont'd)

Name	Address	Phone
The Manitowoc Co.	700 E. Magnolia Ave., Suite B, Manitowoc, WI 54220	(414) 684-4410
Manor Care	10750 Columbia Pike, Silver Spring, MD 20901	(301) 681-9400
Manpower	5301 N. Ironwood Rd., Milwaukee, WI 53217	(414) 961-1000
Manville	717 17th St., Denver, CO 80202	(303) 978-2000
MAPCO	1800 S. Baltimore Ave., Tulsa, OK 74119	(918) 581-1800
The Marcus Corp.	250 E. Wisconsin Ave., Milwaukee, WI 53202	(414) 272-6020
Marion Merrell Dow	9300 Ward Pkwy., P.O. Box 8480, Kansas City, MO 64114	(816) 966-4000
Mark IV Industries	501 John James Audubon Pkwy., Amherst, NY 14228	(716) 689-4972
Mark VII Risk Management	10100 N.W. Executive Hills Blvd., Kansas City, MO 64153	(816) 891-0500
Markel	4551 Cox Rd., Glen Allen, VA 23060	(804) 747-0136
Marquette Electronics	8200 W. Tower Ave., Milwaukee, WI 53223	(414) 355-5000
Marriott	10400 Fernwood Rd., Bethesda, MD 20817	(301) 380-3000
Marsh & McLennan Companies	1166 Ave. of the Americas, New York, NY 10036	(212) 345-5000
Marsh Supermarkets	9800 Crosspoint Blvd., Indianapolis, IN 46256	(317) 594-2100
Marshall & Ilsley	770 N. Water St., Milwaukee, WI 53202	(414) 765-7801
Marshall Industries	9320 Telstar Ave., El Monte, CA 91731	(818) 307-6000
Martin Marietta	6801 Rockledge Dr., Bethesda, MD 20817	(301) 897-6000
Martin Marietta Materials	2710 Wycliff Rd., Raleigh, NC 27607	(919) 781-4550
Marvel Entertainment Group	387 Park Ave. S., New York, NY 10016	(212) 696-0808
Masco	21001 Van Born Rd., Taylor, MI 48180	(313) 274-7400
Mascotech	21001 Van Born Rd., Taylor, MI 48180	(313) 274-7405
Masland	50 Spring Rd., Carlisle, PA 17013	(717) 249-1866
MasTec	8600 N.W. 36th St., Eighth Floor, Miami, FL 33166	(305) 599-1800
Matlack Systems	1 Rollins Plaza, Wilmington, DE 19803	(302) 426-2700
Mattel	333 Continental Blvd., El Segundo, CA 90245	(310) 252-2000
Maxicare Health Plans	1149 S. Broadway St., Los Angeles, CA 90015	(213) 765-2000
Maxtor	211 River Oaks Pkwy., San Jose, CA 95134	(408) 432-1700
Maxus Energy	717 N. Harwood St., Dallas, TX 75201	(214) 953-2000
MAXXAM	5847 San Felipe, Suite 2600, Houston, TX 77057	(713) 975-7600
May Department Stores	611 Olive St., St. Louis, MO 63101	(314) 342-6300
Maybelline	3030 Jackson Ave., Memphis, TN 38112	(901) 324-0310
Mayflower Transit	9998 N. Michigan Rd., Carmel, IN 46032	(317) 875-1000
Maytag	403 W. Fourth St. N., Newton, IA 50208	(515) 792-8000
MBIA	113 King St., Armonk, NY 10504	(914) 273-4545
MBNA	400 Christiana Rd., Newark, DE 19713	(302) 453-9930
McClatchy Newspapers	2100 Q St., Sacramento, CA 95816	(916) 321-1846
McCormick & Co.	18 Loveton Circle, Sparks, MD 21152	(410) 771-7301
McDermott	1450 Poydras St., New Orleans, LA 70112	(504) 587-5400
McDonald's	McDonald's Plaza, Oak Brook, IL 60521	(708) 575-3000
McDonnell Douglas	J. S. McDonnell Blvd. & Airport Rd., St. Louis, MO 63134	(314) 232-0232
McGraw-Hill	1221 Ave. of the Americas, New York, NY 10020	(212) 512-2000
MCI Communications	1801 Pennsylvania Ave., NW, Washington, DC 20006	(202) 872-1600
McKesson	1 Post St., San Francisco, CA 94104	(415) 983-8300
MCN	500 Griswold St., Detroit, MI 48226	(313) 256-5500
McWhorter Technologies	400 E. Cottage Pl., Carpentersville, IL 60110	(708) 428-2657
MDU Resources Group	400 N. Fourth St., Bismarck, ND 58501	(701) 222-7900
The Mead Corp.	Courthouse Plaza Northeast, Dayton, OH 45463	(513) 495-6323
Measurex	1 Results Way, Cupertino, CA 95014	(408) 255-1500
Medaphis	2700 Cumberland Pkwy., Atlanta, GA 30339	(404) 319-3300
Media General	333 E. Grace St., Richmond, VA 23219	(804) 649-6000

The Business Almanac 2000 (cont'd)

Name	Address	Phone
Medtronic	7000 Central Ave., NE, Minneapolis, MN 55432	(612) 574-4000
Medusa Cement	3008 Monticello Blvd., Cleveland Heights, OH 44118	(216) 371-4000
Mellon Bank	1 Mellon Bank Ctr., Pittsburgh, PA 15258	(412) 234-5000
Melville	1 Theall Rd., Rye, NY 10580	(914) 925-4000
Men's Wearhouse	5803 Glenmont, Houston, TX 77081	(713) 295-7200
Mentor Graphics	8005 S.W. Boeckman Rd., Wilsonville, OR 97070	(503) 685-7000
Mercantile Bancorporation	P.O. Box 524, St. Louis, MO 63166	(314) 425-2525
Mercantile Bankshares	2 Hopkins Plaza, Baltimore, MD 21201	(410) 237-5900
Mercantile Stores	9450 Seward Rd., Fairfield, OH 45014	(513) 881-8000
Merck & Co.	1 Merck Dr., P.O. Box 100, Whitehouse Station, NJ 08889	(908) 423-1000
Mercury Finance	40 Skokie Blvd., Suite 200, Northbrook, IL 60062	(708) 564-3720
Mercury General	4484 Wilshire Blvd., Los Angeles, CA 90010	(213) 937-1060
Meredith	1716 Locust St., Des Moines, IA 50309	(515) 284-3000
Meridian Bancorp	35 N. Sixth St., Reading, PA 19601	(610) 655-2000
Merisel	200 Continental Blvd., El Segundo, CA 90245	(310) 615-3080
Merrill	1 Merrill Circle, St. Paul, MN 55108	(612) 646-4501
Merrill Lynch & Co.	World Financial Ctr., New York, NY 10281	(212) 449-1000
Merry-Go-Round Enterprises	3300 Fashion Way, Joppa, MD 21085	(410) 538-1000
Mesa	2001 Ross Avenue, Dallas, TX 75201	(214) 969-2200
Mesa Airlines	2325 E. 30th St., Farmington, NM 87401	(505) 327-0271
Mestek	260 N. Elm St., Westfield, MA 01085	(413) 568-9571
Methode Electronics	7447 W. Wilson Ave., Chicago, IL 60656	(708) 867-9600
MFS Communications	3555 Farnam St., Suite 200, Omaha, NE 68131	(402) 271-2890
MGIC Investment	250 E. Kilbourn Ave., Milwaukee, WI 53202	(414) 347-6480
MGM Grand	3799 Las Vegas Blvd. S., Las Vegas, NV 89109	(702) 891-3333
Michael Baker	420 Rouser Rd., Bldg. 3, Coraopolis, PA 15108	(412) 269-6300
Michael Foods	5353 Wayzata Blvd., Minneapolis, MN 55416	(612) 546-1500
Michaels Stores	5931 Campus Circle Dr., Irving, TX 75063	(214) 714-7000
Michigan National	2777 Inkster Rd., Farmington Hills, MI 48334	(810) 473-3000
Micro Warehouse	535 Connecticut Ave., South Norwalk, CT 06854	(203) 899-4000
MicroAge	2308 S. 55th St., Tempe, AZ 85282	(602) 968-3168
Micron Technology	2805 E. Columbia Rd., Boise, ID 83706	(208) 368-4000
Micropolis	21211 Nordhoff St., Chatsworth, CA 91311	(818) 709-3300
Microsoft	1 Microsoft Way, Redmond, WA 98052	(206) 882-8080
Mid Atlantic Medical Services	4 Taft Court, Rockville, MD 20850	(301) 294-5140
The Midland Co.	537 E. Pete Rose Way, Cincinnati, OH 45202	(513) 721-3777
Midlantic	499 Thornall St., Edison, NJ 08837	(908) 321-8000
Midwest Resources	666 Grand Ave., P.O. Box 9244, Des Moines, IA 50306	(515) 242-4300
Mikasa	20633 S. Fordyce Ave., Long Beach, CA 90810	(310) 886-3700
Millipore	80 Ashby Rd., Bedford, MA 01730	(617) 275-9200
Mine Safety Appliances	121 Gamma Dr., Pittsburgh, PA 15238	(412) 967-3000
Minerals Technologies	405 Lexington Ave., New York, NY 10174	(212) 878-1800
Minnesota Power & Light	30 W. Superior St., Duluth, MN 55802	(218) 722-2641
Mirage Resorts	3400 Las Vegas Blvd. S., Las Vegas, NV 89109	(702) 791-7111
Mississippi Chemical	Hwy. 49 E., Yazoo City, MS 39194	(601) 746-4131
Mitchell Energy & Development	2001 Timberloch Pl., The Woodlands, TX 77380	(713) 377-5500
Mobil	3225 Gallows Rd., Fairfax, VA 22037	(703) 846-3000
Modine Manufacturing	1500 DeKoven Ave., Racine, WI 53403	(414) 636-1200
Mohawk Industries	1755 The Exchange, Atlanta, GA 30339	(404) 951-6000
Molex	2222 Wellington Court, Lisle, IL 60532	(708) 969-4550

The Business Almanac 2000 (cont'd)

Name	Address	Phone
The Money Store	2840 Morris Ave., Union, NJ 07083	(908) 686-2000
Monk-Austin	1200 W. Marlboro Rd., Farmville, NC 27828	(919) 753-8000
Monsanto	800 N. Lindbergh Blvd., St. Louis, MO 63167	(314) 694-1000
The Montana Power Co.	40 E. Broadway, Butte, MT 59701	(406) 723-5421
Moog	Seneca St. & Jamison Rd., East Aurora, NY 14052	(716) 652-2000
Moore Medical	389 John Downey Dr., New Britain, CT 06050	(203) 826-3600
Morgan Products	25 Tri-State International, Lincolnshire, IL 60069	(708) 317-2400
Morgan Stanley Group	1251 Ave. of the Americas, New York, NY 10020	(212) 703-4000
Morningstar Group	5956 Sherry Ln., Suite 1800, Dallas, TX 75225	(214) 360-4700
Morrison Knudsen	Morrison Knudsen Plaza, Boise, ID 83729	(208) 386-5000
Morrison Restaurants	4721 Morrison Dr., Mobile, AL 36609	(205) 344-3000
Morton	100 N. Riverside Plaza, Chicago, IL 60606	(312) 807-2000
Mosinee Paper	1244 Kronenwetter Dr., Mosinee, WI 54455	(715) 693-4470
Motorola	1303 E. Algonquin Rd., Schaumburg, IL 60196	(708) 576-5000
Mueller Industries	2959 N. Rock Rd., Wichita, KS 67226	(316) 636-6300
The Multicare Companies	411 Hackensack Ave., Hackensack, NJ 07601	(201) 488-8818
Multimedia	305 S. Main St., Greenville, SC 29601	(803) 298-4373
Murphy Oil	200 Peach St., P.O. Box 7000, El Dorado, AR 71731	(501) 862-6411
Musicland Stores	10400 Yellow Circle Dr., Minnetonka, MN 55343	(612) 931-8000
Myers Industries	1293 S. Main St., Akron, OH 44301	(216) 253-5592
Mylan Laboratories	130 Seventh St, Pittsburgh, PA 15222	(412) 232-0100
Nabors Industries	515 W. Greens Rd., Suite 1200, Houston, TX 77067	(713) 874-0035
NAC Re	1 Greenwich Plaza, Greenwich, CT 06836	(203) 622-5200
NACCO Industries	5875 Landerbrook Dr., Mayfield Heights, OH 44124	(216) 449-9600
Nalco Chemical	1 Nalco Ctr., Naperville, IL 60563	(708) 305-1000
Nash Finch	7600 France Ave. S., Minneapolis, MN 55435	(612) 832-0534
Nashua	44 Franklin St., P.O. Box 2002, Nashua, NH 03061	(603) 880-2323
National Auto Credit	30000 Aurora Rd., Solon, OH 44139	(216) 349-1000
National Beverage	1 N. University Dr., Fort Lauderdale, FL 33324	(305) 581-0922
National City	1900 E. Ninth St., Cleveland, OH 44114	(216) 575-2000
National Commerce Bancorporation	1 Commerce Sq., Memphis, TN 38150	(901) 523-3242
National Computer Systems	11000 Prairie Lakes Dr., Minneapolis, MN 55344	(612) 829-3000
National Convenience Stores	100 Waugh Dr., Houston, TX 77007	(713) 863-2200
National Education	18400 Von Karman Ave., Irvine, CA 92715	(714) 474-9400
National Fuel Gas	30 Rockefeller Plaza, New York, NY 10112	(212) 541-7533
National Gypsum	2001 Rexford Rd., Charlotte, NC 28211	(704) 365-7300
National Health Laboratories	4225 Executive Sq., Suite 800, La Jolla, CA 92037	(619) 550-0600
National Healthcare	100 Vine St., Murfreesboro, TN 37130	(615) 890-2020
National Medical Enterprises	2700 Colorado Ave., Santa Monica, CA 90404	(310) 998-8000
National Re	777 Long Ridge Rd., Stamford, CT 06902	(203) 329-7700
National Sanitary Supply	255 E. Fifth St., Cincinnati, OH 45202	(513) 762-6500
National Semiconductor	2900 Semiconductor Dr., Santa Clara, CA 95052	(408) 721-5000
National Service Industries	1420 Peachtree St., NE, Atlanta, GA 30309	(404) 853-1000
National Steel	4100 Edison Lakes Pkwy., Mishawaka, IN 46545	(219) 273-7000
National Western Life Insurance	850 E. Anderson Ln., Austin, TX 78752	(512) 836-1010
NationsBank	NationsBank Corporate Ctr., Charlotte, NC 28255	(704) 386-5000
Nautica Enterprises	40 W. 57th St., Third Floor, New York, NY 10019	(212) 541-5990
Navistar	455 N. Cityfront Plaza Dr., Chicago, IL 60611	(312) 836-2000
NBD Bancorp	611 Woodward Ave., Detroit, MI 48226	(313) 225-1000
NCH	2727 Chemsearch Blvd., Irving, TX 75062	(214) 438-0211

The Business Almanac 2000 (cont'd)

Name	Address	Phone
The Neiman Marcus Group	27 Boylston St., P.O. Box 9187, Chestnut Hill, MA 02167	(617) 232-0760
Nellcor	4280 Hacienda Dr., Pleasanton, CA 94588	(510) 463-4000
Network Equipment Technologies	800 Saginaw Dr., Redwood City, CA 94063	(415) 366-4400
Network Systems	7600 Boone Ave. N., Minneapolis, MN 55428	(612) 424-4888
Nevada Power	6226 W. Sahara Ave., Las Vegas, NV 89102	(702) 367-5000
New Age Media Fund	100 E. Pratt St., Baltimore, MD 21202	(410) 547-2000
New England Business Service	500 Main St., Groton, MA 01471	(508) 448-6111
New England Electric System	25 Research Dr., Westborough, MA 01582	(508) 366-9011
New England Investment Companies	399 Boylston St., Boston, MA 02116	(617) 578-3500
New Jersey Resources	1415 Wycoff Rd., Wall, NJ 07719	(908) 938-1480
New World Communications Group	3200 Windy Hill Rd, Atlanta, GA 30339	(404) 955-0045
New York State Electric & Gas	P.O. Box 3287, Ithaca, NY 14852	(607) 347-4131
New York Times	229 W. 43rd St., New York, NY 10036	(212) 556-1234
Newell	29 E. Stephenson St., Freeport, IL 61032	(815) 235-4171
Newmont Gold	1700 Lincoln St., Denver, CO 80203	(303) 863-7414
Niagara Mohawk Power	300 Erie Blvd. W., Syracuse, NY 13202	(315) 474-1511
NICOR	P.O. Box 3014, Naperville, IL 60566	(708) 305-9500
NIKE	1 Bowerman Dr., Beaverton, OR 97005	(503) 671-6453
Nine West Group	9 W. Broad St, Stamford, CT 06902	(203) 324-7567
NIPSCO Industries	5265 Hohman Ave., Hammond, IN 46320	(219) 853-5200
NL Industries	16825 Northchase Dr., Suite 1200, Houston, TX 77060	(713) 423-3300
Noble Affiliates	110 W. Broadway, Ardmore, OK 73401	(405) 223-4110
Noble Drilling	10370 Richmond Ave., Suite 400, Houston, TX 77042	(713) 974-3131
Noland	2700 Warwick Blvd., Newport News, VA 23607	(804) 928-9000
NorAm Energy	P.O. Box 2628, Houston, TX 77252	(713) 654-5699
Nordson	28601 Clemens Rd., Westlake, OH 44145	(216) 892-1580
Nordstrom	1501 Fifth Ave., Seattle, WA 98101	(206) 628-2111
Norfolk Southern	3 Commercial Pl., Norfolk, VA 23510	(804) 629-2680
Norrell	3535 Piedmont Rd., NE, Atlanta, GA 30305	(404) 240-3000
Norstan	6900 Wedgwood Rd., Suite 150, Maple Grove, MN 55311	(612) 420-1100
Nortek	50 Kennedy Plaza, Providence, RI 02903	(401) 751-1600
North American Mortgage	3883 Airway Dr., Santa Rosa, CA 95403	(707) 523-5000
Northeast Federal	50 State House Sq., Hartford, CT 06103	(203) 280-1000
Northeast Utilities	P.O. Box 270, Hartford, CT 06141	(203) 665-5000
Northern States Power	414 Nicollet Mall, Minneapolis, MN 55401	(612) 330-5500
Northern Trust	50 S. La Salle St., Chicago, IL 60675	(312) 630-6000
Northrop Grumman	1840 Century Park E., Los Angeles, CA 90067	(310) 553-6262
Northwest Airlines	5101 Northwest Dr., St. Paul, MN 55111	(612) 726-2111
Northwest Natural Gas	220 N.W. Second Ave., Portland, OR 97209	(503) 226-4211
Northwestern Steel and Wire	121 Wallace St., Sterling, IL 61081	(815) 625-2500
Norwest	Sixth and Marquette, Minneapolis, MN 55479	(612) 667-1234
NovaCare	1016 W. Ninth Ave., King of Prussia, PA 19406	(610) 992-7200
Novell	122 E. 1700 S., Provo, UT 84606	(801) 429-7000
NPC	720 W. 20th St., Pittsburg, KS 66762	(316) 231-3390
NS Group	Ninth & Lowell Sts., Newport, KY 41072	(606) 292-6809
Nucor	2100 Rexford Rd., Charlotte, NC 28211	(704) 366-7000
NUI	550 Rte. 202-206, P.O. Box 760, Bedminster, NJ 07921	(908) 781-0500
NVR	7601 Lewinsville Rd., Suite 300, McLean, VA 22102	(703) 761-2000
NYNEX	1095 Ave. of the Americas, New York, NY 10036	(212) 395-2121
O'Sullivan	1944 Valley Ave., P.O. Box 3510, Winchester, VA 22604	(703) 667-6666

The Business Almanac 2000 (cont'd)

Name	Address	Phone
O'Sullivan Industries Holdings	1900 Gulf St., Lamar, MO 64759	(417) 682-3322
Oak Industries	1000 Winter St., Waltham, MA 02154	(617) 890-0400
Oakwood Homes	2225 S. Holden Rd., Greensboro, NC 27417	(910) 855-2400
Occidental Petroleum	10889 Wilshire Blvd., Los Angeles, CA 90024	(310) 208-8800
Oceaneering	16001 Park Ten Pl., Suite 600, Houston, TX 77084	(713) 578-8868
Octel Communications	1001 Murphy Ranch Rd., Milpitas, CA 95035	(408) 321-2000
Office Depot	2200 Old Germantown Rd., Delray Beach, FL 33445	(407) 278-4800
Office Max	3605 Warrensville Ctr. Rd., Shaker Heights, OH 44122	(216) 921-6900
Ogden	2 Pennsylvania Plaza, New York, NY 10121	(212) 868-6100
Ohio Casualty	136 N. Third St., Hamilton, OH 45025	(513) 867-3000
Ohio Edison	76 S. Main St., Akron, OH 44308	(216) 384-5100
OHM	16406 U.S. Rte. 224 E., Findlay, OH 45840	(419) 423-3529
Oklahoma Gas and Electric	101 N. Robinson, Oklahoma City, OK 73101	(405) 553-3000
Old Dominion Freight Line	1730 Westchester Dr., High Point, NC 27260	(910) 889-5000
Old Kent Financial	1 Vandenberg Ctr., Grand Rapids, MI 49503	(616) 771-5000
Old National Bancorp	420 Main St., Evansville, IN 47708	(812) 464-1434
Old Republic	307 N. Michigan Ave., Chicago, IL 60601	(312) 346-8100
Olin	120 Long Ridge Rd., Stamford, CT 06904	(203) 356-2000
Olsten	175 Broad Hollow Rd., Melville, NY 11747	(516) 844-7800
Olympic Steel	5080 Richmond Rd., Cleveland, OH 44146	(216) 292-3800
OM Group	3800 Terminal Tower, Cleveland, OH 44113	(216) 781-0083
OMI	90 Park Ave., New York, NY 10016	(212) 986-1960
Omnicare	255 E. Fifth St., Cincinnati, OH 45202	(513) 762-6666
Omnicom Group	437 Madison Ave., New York, NY 10022	(212) 415-3600
ONBAN	101 S. Salina St., P.O. Box 4983, Syracuse, NY 13221	(315) 424-4400
One Price Clothing Stores	P.O. Box 2487, Spartanburg, SC 29304	(803) 433-8888
One Valley Bancorp of West Virginia	P.O. Box 1793, Charleston, WV 25326	(304) 348-7000
Oneida	Kenwood Ave., Oneida, NY 13421	(315) 361-3636
ONEOK	100 W. Fifth St., P.O. Box 871, Tulsa, OK 74102	(918) 588-7000
Oracle Systems	500 Oracle Pkwy., Redwood Shores, CA 94065	(415) 506-7000
Orange & Rockland Utilities	1 Blue Hill Plaza, Pearl River, NY 10965	(914) 352-6000
Orchard Supply Hardware Stores	6450 Via Del Oro, San Jose, CA 95119	(408) 281-3500
Oregon Steel Mills	1000 S.W. Broadway, Suite 2200, Portland, OR 97205	(503) 223-9228
Orion Capital	600 Fifth Ave., New York, NY 10020	(212) 332-8080
OrNda Health	3401 W. End Ave., Suite 700, Nashville, TN 37203	(615) 383-8599
Oryx Energy	13155 Noel Rd., Dallas, TX 75240	(214) 715-4000
Oshkosh B'Gosh	112 Otter Ave., P.O. Box 300, Oshkosh, WI 54902	(414) 231-8800
Oshkosh Truck	2307 Oregon St., Oshkosh, WI 54901	(414) 235-9151
Oshman's Sporting Goods	2302 Maxwell Ln., Houston, TX 77023	(713) 928-3171
Otter Tail Power	215 S. Cascade St., P.O. Box 496, Fergus Falls, MN 56538	(218) 739-8200
Outback Steakhouse	550 N. Reo St., Suite 204, Tampa, FL 33609	(813) 282-1225
Outboard Marine	100 Sea-Horse Dr., Waukegan, IL 60085	(708) 689-6200
Overseas Shipholding Group	1114 Ave. of the Americas, New York, NY 10036	(212) 869-1222
Owens & Minor	4800 Cox Rd., Glen Allen, VA 23060	(804) 747-9794
Owens-Corning Fiberglas	Fiberglas Tower, Toledo, OH 43659	(419) 248-8000
Oxford Health Plans	800 Connecticut Ave., Norwalk, CT 06854	(203) 852-1442
Oxford Industries	222 Piedmont Ave., NE, Atlanta, GA 30308	(404) 659-2424
P. H. Glatfelter	228 S. Main St., Spring Grove, PA 17362	(717) 225-4711
PACCAR	777 106th Ave., NE, Bellevue, WA 98004	(206) 455-7400
Pacific Enterprises	633 W. Fifth St., Suite 5400, Los Angeles, CA 90071	(213) 895-5000

The Business Almanac 2000 (cont'd)

Name	Address	Phone
Pacific Gas and Electric	77 Beale St., P.O. Box 770000, San Francisco, CA 94177	(415) 973-7000
Pacific Physician Services	1826 Orange Tree Ln., Redlands, CA 92374	(909) 825-4401
Pacific Scientific	620 Newport Ctr. Dr., Newport Beach, CA 92660	(714) 720-1714
Pacific Telecom	805 Broadway, P.O. Box 9901, Vancouver, WA 98668	(206) 696-0983
Pacific Telesis Group	130 Kearny St., San Francisco, CA 94108	(415) 394-3000
PacifiCare Health Systems	5995 Plaza Dr., Cypress, CA 90630	(714) 952-1121
PacifiCorp	700 N.E. Multnomah, Portland, OR 97232	(503) 731-2000
Paging Network	4965 Preston Park Blvd., Plano, TX 75093	(214) 985-4100
Pall	2200 Northern Blvd., East Hills, NY 11548	(516) 484-5400
Pamida	8800 F St., Omaha, NE 68127	(402) 339-2400
Panhandle Eastern	P.O. Box 1642, Houston, TX 77251	(713) 627-5400
Paragon Trade Brands	505 S. 336th St., Federal Way, WA 98003	(206) 924-4509
Parametric Technology	128 Technology Dr., Waltham, MA 02154	(617) 398-5000
Park Electrochemical	5 Dakota Dr., Lake Success, NY 11042	(516) 354-4100
Parker & Parsley Petroleum	303 W. Wall, Suite 101, Midland, TX 79701	(915) 683-4768
Parker Hannifin	17325 Euclid Ave., Cleveland, OH 44112	(216) 531-3000
Patrick Industries	1800 S. 14th St., P.O. Box 638, Elkhart, IN 46515	(219) 294-7511
Patterson Dental	1100 E. 80th St., Minneapolis, MN 55420	(612) 686-1600
Paul Revere	18 Chestnut St., Worcester, MA 01608	(508) 799-4441
Paychex	911 Panorama Trail S., Rochester, NY 14625	(716) 385-6666
Payless Cashways	2300 Main, P.O. Box 419466, Kansas City, MO 64141	(816) 234-6000
PECO Energy	2301 Market St., P.O. Box 8699, Philadelphia, PA 19101	(215) 841-4000
Pegasus Gold	9 N. Post St., Suite 400, Spokane, WA 99201	(509) 624-4653
PennCorp Financial Group	745 Fifth Ave., New York, NY 10151	(212) 832-0700
Pennsylvania Enterprises	39 Public Sq., Wilkes-Barre, PA 18711	(717) 829-8843
Pennsylvania Power & Light	2 N. Ninth St., Allentown, PA 18101	(610) 774-5151
Pennzoil	700 Milam St., Houston, TX 77002	(713) 546-4000
Pentair	1500 County Rd., Suite B2 W., St. Paul, MN 55113	(612) 636-7920
People's Bank	850 Main St., Bridgeport, CT 06604	(203) 338-7171
Peoples Energy	130 E. Randolph Dr., Chicago, IL 60601	(312) 240-4000
The Pep Boys	3111 W. Allegheny Ave., Philadelphia, PA 19132	(215) 229-9000
PepsiCo	700 Anderson Hill Rd., Purchase, NY 10577	(914) 253-2000
Performance Food Group	25 Century Blvd., Suite 509, Nashville, TN 37214	(615) 391-0112
Perini	73 Mt. Wayte Ave., P.O. Box 9160, Framingham, MA 01701	(508) 628-2000
The Perkin-Elmer Corp.	761 Main Ave., Norwalk, CT 06859	(203) 762-1000
Perrigo	515 Eastern Ave., Allegan, MI 49010	(616) 673-8451
Perry Drug Stores	5400 Perry Dr., P.O. Box 436021, Pontiac, MI 48343	(810) 334-1300
Pet	400 S. Fourth St., St. Louis, MO 63102	(314) 622-7700
Petrie Stores	70 Enterprise Ave., Secaucus, NJ 07094	(201) 866-3600
Petroleum Heat and Power	2187 Atlantic St., Stamford, CT 06902	(203) 325-5400
Petrolite	369 Marshall Ave., St. Louis, MO 63119	(314) 961-3500
PETsMART	10000 N. 31st Ave., C-100, Phoenix, AZ 85051	(602) 944-7070
Pfizer	235 E. 42nd St., New York, NY 10017	(212) 573-2323
Phelps Dodge	2600 N. Central Ave., Phoenix, AZ 85004	(602) 234-8100
PHH	11333 McCormick Rd., Hunt Valley, MD 21031	(410) 771-3600
Philip Morris Companies	120 Park Ave., New York, NY 10017	(212) 880-5000
Phillips Petroleum	Phillips Bldg., Bartlesville, OK 74004	(918) 661-6600
Phillips-Van Heusen	1290 Ave. of the Americas, New York, NY 10104	(212) 541-5200
Physician of America	5835 Blue Lagoon Dr., Miami, FL 33126	(305) 267-6633
Physicians Health Services	120 Hawley Ln., Trumbull, CT 06611	(203) 381-6400

The Business Almanac 2000 (cont'd)

Name	Address	Phone
Piccadilly Cafeterias	3232 Sherwood Forest Blvd., Baton Rouge, LA 70816	(504) 293-9440
PictureTel	222 Rosewood Dr., Danvers, MA 01923	(508) 762-5000
Piedmont Natural Gas	1915 Rexford Rd., Charlotte, NC 28211	(704) 364-3120
Pier 1 Imports	301 Commerce St., Suite 600, Fort Worth, TX 76102	(817) 878-8000
Pilgrim's Pride	110 S. Texas St., Pittsburg, TX 75686	(903) 855-1000
Pillowtex	4111 Mint Way, Dallas, TX 75237	(214) 333-3225
Pinkerton's	15910 Ventura Blvd., Suite 900, Encino, CA 91436	(818) 380-8800
Pinnacle West Capital	400 E. Van Buren St., Suite 700, Phoenix, AZ 85004	(602) 379-2500
Pioneer Financial Services	304 N. Main St., Rockford, IL 61101	(815) 987-5000
Pioneer Hi-Bred	400 Locust St., Des Moines, IA 50309	(515) 248-4800
Pioneer-Standard Electronics	4800 E. 131st St., Cleveland, OH 44105	(216) 587-3600
Piper Jaffray Companies	222 S. Ninth St., Minneapolis, MN 55402	(612) 342-6000
Pitney Bowes	1 Elmcroft Rd., Stamford, CT 06926	(203) 356-5000
Pitt-Des Moines	3400 Grand Ave., Pittsburgh, PA 15225	(412) 331-3000
Pittston Minerals Group	100 First Stamford Pl., Stamford, CT 06902	(203) 978-5200
Pittway	200 S. Wacker Dr., Suite 700, Chicago, IL 60606	(312) 831-1070
Plains Resources	1600 Smith St., Houston, TX 77002	(713) 654-1414
Playboy Enterprises	680 N. Lake Shore Dr., Chicago, IL 60611	(312) 751-8000
Playtex Products	300 Nyala Farms, Westport, CT 06880	(203) 341-4000
Plexus	55 Jewelers Park Dr., Neenah, WI 54956	(414) 722-3451
Plum Creek Timber	999 Third Ave., Suite 2300, Seattle, WA 98104	(206) 467-3600
Ply-Gem Industries	777 Third Ave., New York, NY 10017	(212) 832-1550
PNC Bank	Fifth Ave. and Wood St., Pittsburgh, PA 15265	(412) 762-2000
Polaris Industries	1225 Hwy. 169 N., Minneapolis, MN 55441	(612) 542-0500
Polaroid	549 Technology Sq., Cambridge, MA 02139	(617) 386-2000
Policy Management Systems	1 PMS Ctr., Blythewood, SC 29016	(803) 735-4000
Pool Energy Services	10375 Richmond Ave., Houston, TX 77042	(713) 954-3000
Pope & Talbot	1500 S.W. First Ave., Portland, OR 97201	(503) 228-9161
Portland General	121 S.W. Salmon St., Portland, OR 97204	(503) 464-8820
Potlatch	1 Maritime Plaza, San Francisco, CA 94111	(415) 576-8800
Potomac Electric Power	1900 Pennsylvania Ave., NW, Washington, DC 20068	(202) 872-2456
PPG Industries	1 PPG Pl., Pittsburgh, PA 15272	(412) 434-3131
Pratt & Lambert United	75 Tonawanda St., Buffalo, NY 14207	(716) 873-6000
Pratt Hotel	13455 Noel Rd., LB 48, Dallas, TX 75240	(214) 386-9777
Praxair	39 Old Ridgebury Rd., Danbury, CT 06810	(203) 794-3000
Precision Castparts	4600 S.E. Harney Dr., Portland, OR 97206	(503) 777-3881
Premark	1717 Deerfield Rd., Deerfield, IL 60015	(708) 405-6000
Premier Bancorp	451 Florida St., Baton Rouge, LA 70801	(504) 332-4011
Premier Industrial	4500 Euclid Ave., Cleveland, OH 44103	(216) 391-8300
The Presley Companies	19 Corporate Plaza, Newport Beach, CA 92660	(714) 640-6400
Price/CostCo	10809 120th Ave., NE, Kirkland, WA 98033	(206) 803-8100
Primark	1000 Winter St., Suite 4300N, Waltham, MA 02154	(617) 466-6611
The Procter & Gamble Co.	1 Procter & Gamble Plaza, Cincinnati, OH 45202	(513) 983-1100
Proffitt's	115 N. Calderwood, Alcoa, TN 37701	(615) 983-7000
Progressive	6300 Wilson Mills Rd., Mayfield Village, OH 44143	(216) 461-5000
Promus Companies	1023 Cherry Rd., Memphis, TN 38117	(901) 762-8600
Protective Life	2801 Hwy. 280 S., Birmingham, AL 35223	(205) 879-9230
Provident Bancorp	1 E. Fourth St., Cincinnati, OH 45202	(513) 579-2000
Provident Life and Accident Insurance	1 Fountain Sq., Chattanooga, TN 37402	(615) 755-1011
Providian	400 W. Market St., Louisville, KY 40202	(502) 560-2000

The Business Almanac 2000 (cont'd)

Name	Address	Phone
Public Service Company of Colorado	1225 17th St., Denver, CO 80202	(303) 571-7511
Public Service Company of New Mexico	Alvarado Sq., Albuquerque, NM 87158	(505) 848-2700
Public Service Company of North Carolina	400 Cox Rd., P.O. Box 1398, Gastonia, NC 28053	(704) 864-6731
Public Service Enterprise Group	80 Park Plaza, P.O. Box 1171, Newark, NJ 07101	(201) 430-7000
Puget Sound Power & Light	411 108th Ave., NE, Bellevue, WA 98004	(206) 454-6363
Pulitzer Publishing	900 N. Tucker Blvd., St. Louis, MO 63101	(314) 340-8000
Pulte	33 Bloomfield Hills Pkwy., Bloomfield Hills, MI 48304	(810) 647-2750
Puritan-Bennett	9401 Indian Creek Pkwy., Overland Park, KS 66210	(913) 661-0444
QMS	1 Magnum Pass, Mobile, AL 36618	(334) 633-4300
The Quaker Oats Co.	321 N. Clark St., Chicago, IL 60610	(312) 222-7111
Quaker State	225 Elm St., Oil City, PA 16301	(814) 676-7676
QUALCOMM	6455 Lusk Blvd., San Diego, CA 92121	(619) 587-1121
Quality Food Centers	10112 N.E. Tenth St., Bellevue, WA 98004	(206) 455-3761
Quanex	1900 W. Loop S., Suite 1500, Houston, TX 77027	(713) 961-4600
Quantum	500 McCarthy Blvd., Milpitas, CA 95035	(408) 894-4000
Questar	180 E. First S., Salt Lake City, UT 84111	(801) 534-5000
The Quick & Reilly Group	230 S. County Road, Palm Beach, FL 33480	(407) 655-8000
Quorum Health Group	155 Franklin Rd., Suite 401, Brentwood, TN 37027	(615) 371-7979
R. P. Scherer	2075 W. Big Beaver Rd., Troy, MI 48084	(810) 649-0900
R. R. Donnelley & Sons	77 W. Wacker Dr., Chicago, IL 60601	(312) 326-8000
Radius	1710 Fortune Dr., San Jose, CA 95131	(408) 434-1010
Ralcorp	901 Chouteau Ave., St. Louis, MO 63102	(314) 982-5900
Ralston Continental Baking Group	Checkerboard Sq., St. Louis, MO 63164	(314) 982-1000
Raychem	300 Constitution Dr., Menlo Park, CA 94025	(415) 361-3333
Raymond James Financial	880 Carillon Pkwy., St. Petersburg, FL 33716	(813) 573-3800
Rayonier	1177 Summer St., Stamford, CT 06905	(203) 348-7000
Raytheon	141 Spring St., Lexington, MA 01273	(617) 862-6600
Read-Rite	345 Los Coches St., Milpitas, CA 95035	(408) 262-6700
The Reader's Digest Association	Reader's Digest Rd., Pleasantville, NY 10570	(914) 238-1000
Redman Industries	2550 Walnut Hill Ln., Dallas, TX 75229	(214) 353-3600
Reebok	100 Technology Ctr. Dr., Stoughton, MA 02072	(617) 341-5000
Regal-Beloit	200 State St., Beloit, WI 53511	(608) 364-8800
Regions Financial	417 N. 20th St., P.O. Box 10247, Birmingham, AL 35202	(205) 326-7100
Regis	7201 Metro Blvd., Minneapolis, MN 55439	(612) 947-7777
Reinsurance Group of America	660 Mason Ridge Ctr. Dr., St. Louis, MO 63141	(314) 453-7300
Reliance Group Holdings	55 E. 52nd St., New York, NY 10055	(212) 909-1100
Reliance Steel and Aluminum	2550 E. 25th St., Los Angeles, CA 90058	(213) 582-2272
Reliastar Financial	20 Washington Ave. S., Minneapolis, MN 55401	(612) 372-5432
Republic New York	452 Fifth Ave., New York, NY 10018	(212) 525-6100
Resorts	1133 Boardwalk, Atlantic City, NJ 08401	(609) 344-6000
Revco D.S.	1925 Enterprise Pkwy., Twinsburg, OH 44087	(216) 425-9811
REX Stores	2875 Needmore Rd., Dayton, OH 45414	(513) 276-3931
Rexel	150 Alhambra Circle, Suite 900, Coral Gables, FL 33134	(305) 466-8000
Rexene	5005 LBJ Fwy., Dallas, TX 75244	(214) 450-9000
Reynolds and Reynolds	115 S. Ludlow St., Dayton, OH 45402	(513) 443-2000
Reynolds Metals	6601 W. Broad St., Richmond, VA 23230	(804) 281-2000
Rhodes	4370 Peachtree Rd., NE, Atlanta, GA 30319	(404) 264-4600
Rhone-Poulenc Rorer	500 Arcola Rd, Collegeville, PA 19426	(610) 454-8000
Richfood Holdings	P.O. Box 26967, Richmond, VA 23261	(804) 746-6000
Riggs National	1503 Pennsylvania Ave., NW, Washington, DC 20005	(202) 835-6000

The Business Almanac 2000 (cont'd)

Name	Address	Phone
RightChoice Managed Care	1831 Chestnut St., St. Louis, MO 63103	(314) 923-4444
Riser Foods	5300 Richmond Rd., Bedford Heights, OH 44146	(216) 292-7000
Rite Aid	30 Hunter Ln., Camp Hill, PA 17011	(717) 761-2633
The Rival Co.	800 E. 101st Terr., Kansas City, MO 64131	(816) 943-4100
Riverwood	3350 Cumberland Circle, Atlanta, GA 30339	(404) 644-3000
RJR Nabisco	1301 Ave. of the Americas, New York, NY 10019	(212) 258-5600
Roadmaster Industries	7315 E. Peakview Ave., Englewood, CO 80111	(303) 290-8150
Roadway Services	1077 Gorge Blvd., P.O. Box 88, Akron, OH 44309	(216) 384-8184
Roberd's	1100 E. Central Ave., West Carrollton, OH 45449	(513) 859-5127
Robert Half	2884 Sand Hill Rd., Suite 200, Menlo Park, CA 94025	(415) 854-9700
Robertson-Ceco	222 Berkeley St., Boston, MA 02116	(617) 424-5500
Rochester Community Savings Bank	40 Franklin St., Rochester, NY 14604	(716) 258-3000
Rochester Gas and Electric	89 E. Ave., Rochester, NY 14649	(716) 546-2700
Rock-Tenn	504 Thrasher St., Norcross, GA 30071	(404) 448-2193
Rockwell	2201 Seal Beach Blvd., Seal Beach, CA 90740	(310) 797-3311
Rohm and Haas	100 Independence Mall W., Philadelphia, PA 19106	(215) 592-3000
Rohr	850 Lagoon Dr., Chula Vista, CA 91910	(619) 691-4111
Rollins	2170 Piedmont Rd., NE, Atlanta, GA 30324	(404) 888-2000
Roosevelt Financial Group	900 Roosevelt Pkwy., Chesterfield, MO 63017	(314) 532-6200
Rose's Stores	218 S. Garnett St., Henderson, NC 27536	(919) 430-2600
Ross Stores	8333 Central Ave., Newark, CA 94560	(510) 505-4400
Rouge Steel	3001 Miller Rd., Dearborn, MI 48121	(313) 390-6877
The Rouse Co.	10275 Little Patuxent Pkwy., Columbia, MD 21044	(410) 992-6000
Rowan Companies	2800 Post Oak Blvd., Houston, TX 77056	(713) 621-7800
Roy F. Weston	1 Weston Way, West Chester, PA 19380	(610) 701-3000
Royal Appliance Mfg.	650 Alpha Dr., Cleveland, OH 44143	(216) 449-6150
Royal Caribbean Cruises	1050 Caribbean Way, Miami, FL 33132	(305) 539-6000
RPM	2628 Pearl Rd., P.O. Box 777, Medina, OH 44258	(216) 273-5090
Rubbermaid	1147 Akron Rd., Wooster, OH 44691	(216) 264-6464
Ruddick	2000 Two First Union Ctr., Charlotte, NC 28282	(704) 372-5404
Russ Berrie & Co.	111 Bauer Dr., Oakland, NJ 07436	(201) 337-9000
Russell	1 Lee St., Alexander City, AL 35010	(205) 329-4000
Rust	100 Corporate Pkwy., Birmingham, AL 35242	(205) 995-7878
Ryan's Family Steak Houses	405 Lancaster Ave., P.O. Box 100, Greer, SC 29652	(803) 879-1000
Ryder System	3600 N.W. 82nd Ave., Miami, FL 33166	(305) 593-3726
Rykoff-Sexton	761 Terminal St., Los Angeles, CA 90021	(213) 622-4131
The Ryland Group	11000 Broken Land Pkwy., Columbia, MD 21044	(410) 715-7000
SAFECO	SAFECO Plaza, Seattle, WA 98185	(206) 545-5000
Safeguard Scientifics	435 Devon Park Dr., Wayne, PA 19087	(610) 293-0600
Safety-Kleen	1000 N. Randall Rd., Elgin, IL 60123	(708) 697-8460
Safeway	Fourth and Jackson Sts., Oakland, CA 94660	(510) 891-3000
Sahara Gaming	2535 Las Vegas Blvd. S., Las Vegas, NV 89109	(702) 737-2111
Salant	1114 Ave. of the Americas, New York, NY 10036	(212) 221-7500
Salomon	7 World Trade Ctr., New York, NY 10048	(212) 783-7000
San Diego Gas & Electric	101 Ash St., San Diego, CA 92101	(619) 696-2000
Santa Fe Energy Resources	1616 S. Voss, Suite 1000, Houston, TX 77057	(713) 783-2401
Santa Fe Pacific	1700 E. Golf Rd., Shaumburg, IL 60173	(708) 995-6000
Santa Fe Pacific Gold	6200 Uptown Blvd., NE, Suite 400, Albuquerque, NM 87110	(505) 880-5300
Sara Lee	3 First National Plaza, Chicago, IL 60602	(312) 726-2600
Savannah Foods & Industries	P.O. Box 339, Savannah, GA 31402	(912) 234-1261

The Business Almanac 2000 (cont'd)

Name	Address	Phone
Sbarro	763 Larkfield Rd., Commack, NY 11725	(516) 864-0200
SBC Communications	175 E. Houston, San Antonio, TX 78205	(210) 821-4105
SCANA	1426 Main St., Columbia, SC 29201	(803) 748-3000
SCEcorp	2244 Walnut Grove Ave., Rosemead, CA 91770	(818) 302-2222
Schering-Plough	1 Giralda Farms, Madison, NJ 07940	(201) 822-7000
Schlumberger	277 Park Ave., New York, NY 10172	(212) 350-9400
Schnitzer Steel Industries	3200 N.W. Yeon Ave., Portland, OR 97210	(503) 224-9900
Scholastic	555 Broadway, New York, NY 10012	(212) 343-6100
Schult Homes	221 U.S. 20 W., Middlebury, IN 46540	(219) 825-5881
Schultz Sav-O Stores	2215 Union Ave., Sheboygan, WI 53081	(414) 457-4433
Scientific-Atlanta	1 Technology Pkwy. S., Atlanta, GA 30092	(404) 903-5000
SCOR U.S.	110 William St., New York, NY 10038	(212) 978-8200
Scotsman Industries	775 Corporate Woods Pkwy., Vernon Hills, IL 60061	(708) 215-4500
Scott Paper	Scott Plaza, Philadelphia, PA 19113	(610) 522-5000
The Scotts Co.	14111 Scottslawn Rd., Marysville, OH 43041	(513) 644-0011
Seaboard	9000 W. 67th St., Shawnee Mission, KS 66202	(913) 676-8800
Seagate Technology	920 Disc Dr., Scotts Valley, CA 95066	(408) 438-6550
Seagull Energy	1001 Fannin St., Suite 1700, Houston, TX 77002	(713) 951-4700
Sealed Air	Park 80 E., Saddle Brook, NJ 07662	(201) 791-7600
Sealright	7101 College Blvd., Overland Park, KS 66210	(913) 344-9000
Sears, Roebuck and Co.	Sears Tower, Chicago, IL 60684	(312) 875-2500
Seaway Food Town	1020 Ford St., Maumee, OH 43537	(419) 893-9401
Security-Connecticut	20 Security Dr., Avon, CT 06001	(203) 677-8621
SEI	680 E. Swedesford Rd., Wayne, PA 19087	(610) 254-1000
Selective Insurance Group	40 Wantage Ave., Branchville, NJ 07890	(201) 948-3000
Seneca Foods	1162 Pittsford-Victor Rd., Pittsford, NY 14534	(716) 385-9500
Sensormatic Electronics	500 N.W. 12th Ave., Deerfield Beach, FL 33442	(305) 420-2000
Sequa	200 Park Ave., New York, NY 10166	(212) 986-5500
Sequent Computer Systems	15450 S.W. Koll Pkwy., Beaverton, OR 97006	(503) 626-5700
Service	1929 Allen Pkwy., Houston, TX 77019	(713) 522-5141
Service Merchandise	7100 Service Merchandise Dr., Brentwood, TN 37027	(615) 660-6000
ServiceMaster	1 ServiceMaster Way, Downers Grove, IL 60515	(708) 271-1300
SFFed	88 Kearny St., San Francisco, CA 94108	(415) 955-5800
Shared Medical Systems	51 Valley Stream Pkwy., Malvern, PA 19355	(610) 219-6300
Shaw Industries	616 E. Walnut Ave., Dalton, GA 30720	(706) 278-3812
Shawmut National	777 Main St., Hartford, CT 06115	(203) 728-2000
Shelter Components	27217 Country Rd. 6, Elkhart, IN 46514	(219) 262-4541
The Sherwin-Williams Co.	101 Prospect Ave., NW, Cleveland, OH 44115	(216) 566-2000
Shiloh Industries	402 Ninth Ave., Mansfield, OH 44905	(419) 525-2315
Shoney's	1727 Elm Hill Pike, Nashville, TN 37210	(615) 391-5201
ShopKo Stores	700 Pilgrim Way, P.O. Box 19060, Green Bay, WI 54307	(414) 497-2211
Shorewood Packaging	55 Engineers Ln., Farmingdale, NY 11735	(516) 694-2900
ShowBiz Pizza Time	4441 W. Airport Fwy., Irving, TX 75015	(214) 258-8507
Showboat	2800 Fremont St., Las Vegas, NV 89104	(702) 385-9123
Sierra Health Services	2724 N. Tenaya Way, Las Vegas, NV 89128	(702) 242-7000
Sierra Pacific Resources	6100 Neil Rd., Reno, NV 89511	(702) 689-5400
Sigma-Aldrich	3050 Spruce St., St. Louis, MO 63103	(314) 771-5765
Signet Banking	7 N. Eighth St., Richmond, VA 23219	(804) 747-2000
Silicon Graphics	2011 N. Shoreline Blvd., Mountain View, CA 94043	(415) 960-1980
Silicon Valley Group	2240 Ringwood Ave., San Jose, CA 95131	(408) 434-0500

The Business Almanac 2000 (cont'd)

Name	Address	Phone
Simon Property Group	115 W. Washington St., Indianapolis, IN 46204	(317) 636-1600
Simpson Industries	47603 Halyard Dr., Plymouth, MI 48170	(810) 540-6200
Sithe Energies	450 Lexington Ave., New York, NY 10017	(212) 450-9000
Sizzler	12655 W. Jefferson Blvd., Los Angeles, CA 90066	(310) 827-2300
Skyline	2520 By-Pass Rd., P.O. Box 743, Elkhart, IN 46515	(219) 294-6521
SLM	43 W. 23rd St., New York, NY 10010	(212) 675-0070
Smart & Final	4700 S. Boyle Ave., Los Angeles, CA 90058	(213) 589-1054
Smith	16740 Hardy St., Houston, TX 77032	(713) 443-3370
Smith Corona	65 Locust Ave., New Canaan, CT 06840	(203) 972-1471
Smith's Food & Drug Centers	1550 S. Redwood Rd., Salt Lake City, UT 84104	(801) 974-1400
Smithfield Foods	501 N. Church St., Smithfield, VA 23430	(804) 357-4321
Snap-On	2801 80th St., Kenosha, WI 53141	(414) 656-5200
Snyder Oil	777 Main St., Fort Worth, TX 76102	(817) 338-4043
Software Spectrum	2140 Merritt Dr., Garland, TX 75041	(214) 840-6600
Solectron	847 Gibraltar Dr., Milpitas, CA 95035	(408) 957-8500
Sonat	AmSouth-Sonat Tower, Birmingham, AL 35203	(205) 325-3800
Sonat Offshore Drilling	4 Greenway Plaza, Houston, TX 77046	(713) 871-7500
Sonoco Products	N. Second St., Hartsville, SC 29550	(803) 383-7000
Sotheby's Holdings	1334 York Ave., New York, NY 10021	(212) 606-7000
South Jersey Industries	1 S. Jersey Plaza, Rte. 54, Folsom, NJ 08037	(609) 561-9000
Southdown	1200 Smith St., Suite 2400, Houston, TX 77002	(713) 650-6200
Southeastern Michigan Gas Enterprise	405 Water St., P.O. Box 5026, Port Huron, MI 48061	(810) 987-2200
Southern California Edison	2244 Walnut Grove Ave., Rosemead, CA 91770	(818) 302-1212
The Southern Co.	64 Perimeter Ctr. E., Atlanta, GA 30346	(404) 393-0650
Southern Electronics	4916 N. Royal Atlanta Dr., Atlanta, GA 30085	(404) 491-8962
Southern Indiana Gas and Electric	20 N.W. Fourth St., Evansville, IN 47741	(812) 424-6411
Southern National	500 N. Chestnut St., Lumberton, NC 28358	(910) 671-2000
Southern New England Telecommunications	227 Church St., New Haven, CT 06510	(203) 771-5200
Southern Pacific Rail	1 Market Plaza, San Francisco, CA 94105	(415) 541-1000
Southern Union Exploration	504 Lavaca St., Eighth Floor, Austin, TX 78701	(512) 477-5981
The Southland Corp.	2711 N. Haskell Ave., Dallas, TX 75204	(214) 828-7011
SouthTrust	420 N. 20th St., Birmingham, AL 35203	(205) 254-5000
Southwest Airlines	P.O. Box 36611, Dallas, TX 75235	(214) 904-4000
Southwest Gas	5241 Spring Mountain Rd., Las Vegas, NV 89102	(702) 876-7237
Southwestern Life	500 N. Akard St., Dallas, TX 75201	(214) 954-7111
Southwestern Public Service	Tyler at Sixth, Amarillo, TX 79101	(806) 378-2121
Sovereign Bancorp	1130 Berkshire Blvd., Wyomissing, PA 19610	(610) 320-8400
SpaceLabs Medical	15220 N.E. 40th St., Redmond, WA 98052	(206) 882-3700
Spain Fund	1345 Ave. of the Americas, New York, NY 10105	(212) 969-1000
SPARTECH	7733 Forsyth, Suite 1450, Clayton, MO 63105	(314) 721-4242
Specialty Equipment	6581 Revlon Dr., Belvidere, IL 61008	(815) 544-5111
Spelling Entertainment Group	5700 Wilshire Blvd., Los Angeles, CA 90036	(213) 965-5700
Spiegel	3500 Lacey Rd., Downers Grove, IL 60515	(708) 986-8800
Sportmart	7233 W. Dempster St., Niles, IL 60714	(708) 966-1700
Sports & Recreation	4701 W. Hillsborough Ave., Tampa, FL 33614	(813) 886-9688
The Sports Authority	3383 N. State Rd. 7, Fort Lauderdale, FL 33319	(305) 735-1701
Spreckels Industries	4234 Hacienda Dr., Pleasanton, CA 94588	(510) 460-0840
Springs Industries	205 N. White St., P.O. Box 70, Fort Mill, SC 29715	(803) 547-1500
Sprint	2330 Shawnee Mission Pkwy., Westwood, KS 66205	(913) 624-3000
SPS Technologies	101 Greenwood Ave., Suite 470, Jenkintown, PA 19046	(215) 517-2000

The Business Almanac 2000 (cont'd)

Name	Address	Phone
SPS Transaction Services	2500 Lake Cook Rd., Riverwoods, IL 60015	(708) 405-3700
SPX	700 Terrace Point Dr., Muskegon, MI 49443	(616) 724-5000
St. Jude Medical	1 Lillehei Plaza, St. Paul, MN 55117	(612) 483-2000
St. Paul Bancorp	6700 W. North Ave., Chicago, IL 60635	(312) 622-5000
The St. Paul Companies	385 Washington St., St. Paul, MN 55102	(612) 221-7911
Staff Builders	1981 Marcus Ave., Lake Success, NY 11042	(516) 358-1000
Standard Commercial	2201 Miller Rd., Wilson, NC 27893	(919) 291-5507
Standard Federal Bank	2600 W. Big Beaver Rd., Troy, MI 48084	(810) 643-9600
Standard Microsystems	80 Arkay Dr., Hauppauge, NY 11788	(516) 273-3100
Standard Motor Products	37-18 Northern Blvd., Long Island City, NY 11101	(718) 392-0200
Standard Pacific	1565 W. MacArthur Blvd., Costa Mesa, CA 92626	(714) 668-4300
The Standard Products Co.	2130 W. 110th St., Cleveland, OH 44102	(216) 281-8300
The Standard Register Co.	600 Albany St., Dayton, OH 45408	(513) 443-1000
Standex	6 Manor Pkwy., Salem, NH 03079	(603) 893-9701
Stanhome	333 Western Ave., Westfield, MA 01085	(413) 562-3631
The Stanley Works	1000 Stanley Dr., New Britain, CT 06053	(203) 225-5111
Stant	425 Commerce Dr., Richmond, IN 47374	(317) 962-6655
Staples	100 Pennsylvania Ave., Framingham, MA 01701	(508) 370-8500
Star Banc	425 Walnut St., Cincinnati, OH 45202	(513) 632-4000
Starbucks	2401 Utah Ave. S., Seattle, WA 98134	(206) 447-1575
Starter	370 James St., New Haven, CT 06513	(203) 781-4000
State Street Boston	225 Franklin St., Boston, MA 02110	(617) 786-3000
Station Casinos	2411 W. Sahara Ave., Las Vegas, NV 89102	(702) 367-2411
Steel Technologies	15415 Shelbyville Rd., Louisville, KY 40245	(502) 245-2110
Stein Mart	1200 Gulf Life Dr., Jacksonville, FL 32207	(904) 346-1500
Stepan	22 W. Frontage Rd., Northfield, IL 60093	(708) 446-7500
Sterling Chemicals	1200 Smith St., Suite 1900, Houston, TX 77002	(713) 650-3700
Sterling Electronics	4201 S.W. Fwy., Houston, TX 77027	(713) 627-9800
Sterling Software	8080 N. Central Expwy., Dallas, TX 75206	(214) 891-8600
Stewart & Stevenson Services	2707 N. Loop W., Houston, TX 77008	(713) 868-7700
Stewart Enterprises	110 Veterans Memorial Blvd., Metairie, LA 70005	(504) 837-5880
Stewart Information Services	1980 Post Oak Blvd., Houston, TX 77056	(713) 625-8100
Stolt Neilsen	8 Sound Shore Dr., Greenwich, CT 06836	(203) 625-3608
Stone & Webster	250 W. 34th St., New York, NY 10119	(212) 290-7500
Stone Container	150 N. Michigan Ave., Chicago, IL 60601	(312) 346-6600
Storage Technology	2270 S. 88th St., Louisville, CO 80028	(303) 673-5151
Stratus Computer	55 Fairbanks Blvd., Marlborough, MA 01752	(508) 460-2000
Strawbridge & Clothier	801 Market St., Philadelphia, PA 19107	(215) 629-6000
The Stride Rite Corp.	5 Cambridge Ctr., Cambridge, MA 02142	(617) 491-8800
Stryker	2725 Fairfield Rd., Kalamazoo, MI 49002	(616) 385-2600
The Student Loan Corp.	99 Garnsey Rd., Pittsford, NY 14534	(716) 248-7187
Student Loan Marketing Association	1050 Thomas Jefferson St., NW, Washington, DC 20007	(202) 333-8000
Sudbury	30100 Chagrin Blvd., Suite 203, Cleveland, OH 44124	(216) 464-7026
The Summit Bancorporation	1 Main St., Chatham, NJ 07928	(201) 701-2666
Sun	1801 Market St., Philadelphia, PA 19103	(215) 977-3000
Sun Distributors	1 Logan Sq., Philadelphia, PA 19103	(215) 665-3650
Sun Healthcare Group	5131 Masthead St., NE, Albuquerque, NM 87109	(505) 821-3355
Sun Microsystems	2550 Garcia Ave., Mountain View, CA 94043	(415) 960-1300
Sun Television and Appliances	1583 Alum Creek Dr., Columbus, OH 43209	(614) 445-8401
SunAmerica	1 SunAmerica Ctr., Los Angeles, CA 90067	(310) 772-6000

The Business Almanac 2000 (cont'd)

Name	Address	Phone
Sunbeam-Oster	200 E. Las Olas Blvd., Suite 2100, Fort Lauderdale, FL 33301	(305) 767-2100
Sundstrand	4949 Harrison Ave., Rockford, IL 61125	(815) 226-6000
SunGard Data Systems	1285 Drummers Ln., Wayne, PA 19087	(610) 341-8700
Sunrise Medical	2382 Faraday Ave., Suite 200, Carlsbad, CA 92008	(619) 930-1500
SunTrust Banks	25 Park Pl., NE, Atlanta, GA 30303	(404) 588-7711
Super Food Services	3233 Newmark Dr., Miamisburg, OH 45342	(513) 439-7500
Super Rite	3900 Industrial Rd., Harrisburg, PA 17110	(717) 232-6821
Superior Industries	7800 Woodley Ave., Van Nuys, CA 91406	(818) 781-4973
SUPERVALU	11840 Valley View Rd., Eden Prairie, MN 55344	(612) 828-4000
Surgical Care Affiliates	102 Woodmont Blvd., Suite 610, Nashville, TN 37205	(615) 385-3541
Swift Transportation	5601 W. Mohave, Phoenix, AZ 85043	(602) 269-9700
Sybase	6475 Christie Ave., Emeryville, CA 94608	(510) 596-3500
Sybron	411 E. Wisconsin Ave., Milwaukee, WI 53202	(414) 274-6600
Symantec	10201 Torre Ave., Cupertino, CA 95014	(408) 253-9600
Symbol Technologies	116 Wilbur Pl., Bohemia, NY 11716	(516) 563-2400
Syms	Syms Way, Secaucus, NJ 07094	(201) 902-9600
SynOptics Communications	4401 Great America Pkwy., Santa Clara, CA 95054	(408) 988-2400
Synovus Financial	901 Front Ave., Suite 301, Columbus, GA 31901	(706) 649-2311
SyQuest Technology	47071 Bayside Pkwy., Fremont, CA 94538	(510) 226-4000
Sysco	1390 Enclave Pkwy., Houston, TX 77077	(713) 584-1390
System Software Associates	500 W. Madison St., 32nd Floor, Chicago, IL 60661	(312) 641-2900
T2 Medical	1121 Alderman Dr., Alpharetta, GA 30202	(404) 442-2160
The Talbots	175 Beal St., Hingham, MA 02043	(617) 749-7600
Talley Industries	2702 N. 44th St., Phoenix, AZ 85008	(602) 957-7711
Tambrands	777 Westchester Ave., White Plains, NY 10604	(914) 696-6000
Tandem Computers	19333 Vallco Pkwy., Cupertino, CA 95014	(408) 285-6000
Tandy	1800 One Tandy Ctr., Fort Worth, TX 76102	(817) 390-3700
Tandycrafts	1400 Everman Pkwy., Fort Worth, TX 76140	(817) 551-9600
TBC	4770 Hickory Hill Rd., Memphis, TN 38115	(901) 363-8030
TCF Financial	801 Marquette Ave., Suite 302, Minneapolis, MN 55402	(612) 661-6500
Tech Data	5350 Tech Data Dr., Clearwater, FL 34620	(813) 539-7429
TECO Energy	702 N. Franklin St., Tampa, FL 33602	(813) 228-4111
Tecumseh Products	100 E. Patterson St., Tecumseh, MI 49286	(517) 423-8411
Tejas Gas	1301 McKinney St., Suite 700, Houston, TX 77010	(713) 658-0509
Tejas Power	200 WestLake Park Blvd., Houston, TX 77079	(713) 597-6200
Tektronix	26600 S.W. Pkwy., P.O. Box 1000, Wilsonville, OR 97070	(503) 627-7111
Tele-Communications	5619 DTC Pkwy., Englewood, CO 80111	(303) 267-5500
Teledyne	1901 Ave. of the Stars, Los Angeles, CA 90067	(310) 277-3311
Teleflex	630 W. Germantown Pike, Plymouth Meeting, PA 19462	(610) 834-6301
Telephone and Data Systems	30 N. LaSalle St., Suite 4000, Chicago, IL 60602	(312) 630-1900
Tellabs	4951 Indiana Ave., Lisle, IL 60532	(708) 969-8800
Telxon	3330 W. Market St., P. O. Box 5582, Akron, OH 44334	(216) 867-3700
Temple-Inland	303 S. Temple Dr., Diboll, TX 75941	(409) 829-2211
Tennant	701 N. Lilac Dr., P.O. Box 1452, Minneapolis, MN 55440	(612) 540-1200
Tenneco	Tenneco Bldg., P.O. Box 2511, Houston, TX 77252	(713) 757-2131
Teradyne	321 Harrison Ave., Boston, MA 02118	(617) 482-2700
Terex	500 Post Rd. E., Westport, CT 06880	(203) 222-7170
Terra Industries	600 Fourth St., P.O. Box 6000, Sioux City, IA 51102	(712) 277-1340
Terra Nitrogen	5100 E. Skelly Dr., Suite 800, Tulsa, OK 74135	(918) 660-0050
Tesoro Petroleum	8700 Tesoro Dr., San Antonio, TX 78217	(210) 828-8484

The Business Almanac 2000 (cont'd)

Name	Address	Phone
Texaco	2000 Westchester Ave., White Plains, NY 10650	(914) 253-4000
Texas Industries	7610 Stemmons Fwy., Dallas, TX 75247	(214) 647-6700
Texas Instruments	13500 N. Central Expwy., Dallas, TX 75243	(214) 995-2011
Texas Utilities	1601 Bryan St., Dallas, TX 75201	(214) 812-4600
Texfi Industries	5400 Glenwood Ave., Suite 215, Raleigh, NC 27612	(919) 783-4736
Textron	40 Westminster St., Providence, RI 02903	(401) 421-2800
Thermadyne Holdings	101 S. Hanley Rd., Suite 300, St. Louis, MO 63105	(314) 721-5573
Thermo Cardiosystems	81 Wyman St., Waltham, MA 02254	(617) 622-1000
Thermo Instrument Systems	504 Airport Rd., Santa Fe, NM 87504	(505) 438-3171
Thiokol	2475 Washington Blvd., Ogden, UT 84401	(801) 629-2000
Thomas & Betts	1555 Lynnfield Rd., Memphis, TN 38119	(901) 682-7766
Thomas Industries	4360 Brownsboro Rd., Suite 300, Louisville, KY 40207	(502) 893-4600
Thomas Nelson	Nelson Pl. at Elm Hill Pike, Nashville, TN 37214	(615) 889-9000
Thomaston Mills	115 E. Main St., Thomaston, GA 30286	(706) 647-7131
Thor Industries	419 W. Pike St., Jackson Center, OH 45334	(513) 596-6849
Thorn Apple Valley	18700 W. Ten Mile Rd., Southfield, MI 48075	(810) 552-0700
Tidewater	1440 Canal St., New Orleans, LA 70112	(504) 568-1010
Tiffany & Co.	727 Fifth Ave., New York, NY 10022	(212) 755-8000
TIG Holdings	65 E. 55th St, New York, NY 10022	(212) 446-2700
Timberland	11 Merrill Industrial Dr., Hampton, NH 03842	(603) 926-1600
Time Warner	75 Rockefeller Plaza, New York, NY 10019	(212) 484-8000
The Times Mirror Co.	Times Mirror Sq., Los Angeles, CA 90053	(213) 237-3700
The Timken Co.	1835 Dueber Ave., SW, Canton, OH 44706	(216) 438-3000
Titan Wheel	2701 Spruce St., Quincy, IL 62301	(217) 228-6011
TJ	380 E. ParkCenter Blvd., Boise, ID 83706	(208) 345-8500
The TJX Companies	770 Cochituate Rd., Framingham, MA 01701	(508) 390-1000
TNP Enterprises	4100 International Plaza, Fort Worth, TX 76109	(817) 731-0099
TNT Freightways	9700 Higgins Rd., Suite 570, Rosemont, IL 60018	(708) 696-0200
Toll Brothers	3103 Philmont Ave., Huntingdon Valley, PA 19006	(215) 938-8000
Tootsie Roll Industries	7401 S. Cicero Ave., Chicago, IL 60629	(312) 838-3400
The Topps Co.	1 Whitehall St., New York, NY 10004	(212) 376-0300
Tops Appliance City	45 Brunswick Ave., Edison, NJ 08818	(908) 248-2850
Torchmark	2001 Third Ave. S., Birmingham, AL 35233	(205) 325-4200
The Toro Co.	8111 Lyndale Ave. S., Bloomington, MN 55420	(612) 888-8801
Tosco	72 Cummings Point Rd., Stamford, CT 06902	(203) 977-1000
Tower Air	JFK International, Hangar 17, Jamaica, NY 11430	(718) 553-4300
Town & Country	25 Union St., Chelsea, MA 02150	(617) 884-8500
TPI Enterprises	777 S. Flagler Dr., West Palm Beach, FL 33401	(407) 835-8888
Tracor	6500 Tracor Ln., Austin, TX 78725	(512) 926-2800
Tractor Supply	320 Plus Park Blvd., Nashville, TN 37217	(615) 366-4600
Trans World Entertainment	38 Corporate Circle, Albany, NY 12203	(518) 452-1242
Transamerica	600 Montgomery St., San Francisco, CA 94111	(415) 983-4000
Transatlantic Holdings	80 Pine St., New York, NY 10005	(212) 770-2000
Transco Energy	2800 Post Oak Blvd., Houston, TX 77056	(713) 439-2000
TransTexas Gas	363 N. Sam Houston Pkwy. E., Houston, TX 77060	(713) 447-3111
The Travelers	65 E. 55th St., New York, NY 10022	(212) 891-8900
Treadco	1000 S. 21st St., Fort Smith, AR 72901	(501) 785-6000
Tredegar Industries	1100 Boulders Pkwy., Richmond, VA 23225	(804) 330-1000
Triangle Pacific	16803 Dallas Pkwy., Dallas, TX 75248	(214) 931-3000
Triarc Cos.	900 Third Ave., New York, NY 10022	(212) 230-3000

The Business Almanac 2000 (cont'd)

Name	Address	Phone
Tribune	435 N. Michigan Ave., Chicago, IL 60611	(312) 222-9100
Trident NGL Holding	10200 Grogan's Mill Rd., The Woodlands, TX 77380	(713) 367-7600
TriMas	315 E. Eisenhower Pkwy., Ann Arbor, MI 48108	(313) 747-7025
Trinity Industries	2525 Stemmons Fwy., Dallas, TX 75207	(214) 631-4420
TRINOVA	3000 Strayer, Maumee, OH 43537	(419) 867-2200
Truck Components	302 Peoples Ave., Rockford, IL 61104	(815) 964-3301
True North Communications	101 E. Erie St., Chicago, IL 60611	(312) 751-7000
Trustmark	248 E. Capitol St., Jackson, MS 39205	(601) 354-5111
TRW	1900 Richmond Rd., Cleveland, OH 44124	(216) 291-7000
Tucson Electric Power	220 W. Sixth St., Tucson, AZ 85701	(602) 571-4000
Tultex	101 Commonwealth Blvd., Martinsville, VA 24115	(703) 632-2961
Turner	375 Hudson St., New York, NY 10014	(212) 229-6000
Turner Broadcasting System	100 International Blvd., Atlanta, GA 30303	(404) 827-1700
Tyco	1 Tyco Park, Exeter, NH 03833	(603) 778-9700
Tyco Toys	6000 Midlantic Dr., Mt. Laurel, NJ 08054	(609) 234-7400
Tyler	3200 San Jacinto Tower, Dallas, TX 75201	(214) 754-7800
Tyson Foods	2210 W. Oaklawn Dr., Springdale, AR 72764	(501) 290-4000
U.S. Bancorp	111 S.W. Fifth Ave., Portland, OR 97204	(503) 275-6111
U.S. Can	900 Commerce Dr., Suite 302, Oak Brook, IL 60521	(708) 571-2500
U.S. Healthcare	980 Jolly Rd., P.O. Box 1109, Blue Bell, PA 19422	(215) 628-4800
U.S. Home	1800 W. Loop S., Houston, TX 77027	(713) 877-2311
U.S. Trust	114 W. 47th St., New York, NY 10036	(212) 852-1000
U.S. Xpress Enterprises	2931 S. Market St., Chattanooga, TN 37410	(615) 697-7377
UAL	1200 E. Algonquin Rd., Elk Grove Township, IL 60007	(708) 952-4000
UDC Homes	4812 S. Mill Ave., Tempe, AZ 85282	(602) 820-4488
UGI	P.O. Box 858, Valley Forge, PA 19482	(610) 337-1000
UJB Financial	301 Carnegie Ctr., P.O. Box 2066, Princeton, NJ 08543	(609) 987-3200
Ultramar	2 Pickwick Plaza, Suite 300, Greenwich, CT 06830	(203) 622-7000
UMB Financial	928 Grand Ave., Kansas City, MO 64106	(816) 860-7000
UNC	175 Admiral Cochrane Dr., Annapolis, MD 21401	(410) 266-7333
Uni-Marts	477 E. Beaver Ave., State College, PA 16801	(814) 234-6000
The Unicom Corp.	1 First National Plaza, 37th Floor, Chicago, IL 60690	(312) 394-4321
Unifi	7201 W. Friendly Rd., Greensboro, NC 27410	(910) 294-4410
UniFirst	68 Jonspin Rd., Wilmington, MA 01887	(508) 658-8888
Union Bank	350 California St., San Francisco, CA 94104	(415) 705-7350
Union Camp	1600 Valley Rd., Wayne, NJ 07470	(201) 628-2000
Union Carbide	39 Old Ridgebury Rd., Danbury, CT 06817	(203) 794-2000
Union Electric	1901 Chouteau Ave., St. Louis, MO 63103	(314) 621-3222
Union Pacific	Eighth and Eaton Aves., Bethlehem, PA 18018	(610) 861-3200
Union Planters National Bank	6200 Poplar Ave., Memphis, TN 38119	(901) 383-6000
Union Texas Petroleum Holdings	1330 Post Oak Blvd., Houston, TX 77056	(713) 623-6544
Unisys	Township Line & Union Meeting Rds., Blue Bell, PA 19424	(215) 542-4011
United Asset Management	1 International Pl., Boston, MA 02110	(617) 330-8900
United Carolina Bancshares	127 W. Webster St., Whiteville, NC 28472	(910) 642-5131
United Cities Gas	5300 Maryland Way, Brentwood, TN 37027	(615) 373-5310
United Companies Financial	4041 Essen Ln., Baton Rouge, LA 70809	(504) 924-6007
United HealthCare	9900 Bren Rd. E., Minnetonka, MN 55343	(612) 936-1300
The United Illuminating Co.	157 Church St., New Haven, CT 06506	(203) 499-2000
United Insurance Companies	4001 McEwen Dr., Suite 200, Dallas, TX 75244	(214) 960-8497
United Retail Group	365 W. Passaic St., Rochelle Park, NJ 07662	(201) 845-0880

The Business Almanac 2000 (cont'd)

Name	Address	Phone
United States Cellular	8410 W. Bryn Mawr, Suite 700, Chicago, IL 60631	(312) 399-8900
The United States Shoe Corp.	1 Eastwood Dr., Cincinnati, OH 45227	(513) 527-7000
United States Surgical	150 Glover Ave., Norwalk, CT 06856	(203) 845-1000
United Stationers	2200 E. Golf Rd., Des Plaines, IL 60016	(708) 699-5000
United Technologies	United Technologies Bldg., Hartford, CT 06101	(203) 728-7000
United Water Resources	200 Old Hook Rd., Harrington Park, NJ 07640	(201) 784-9434
United Wisconsin Services	401 W. Michigan St., Milwaukee, WI 53203	(414) 226-6900
Unitrin	1 E. Wacker Dr., Chicago, IL 60601	(312) 661-4600
Univar	6100 Carillon Point, Kirkland, WA 98033	(206) 889-3400
Universal	1501 Hamilton St., Richmond, VA 23260	(804) 359-9311
Universal Foods	433 E. Michigan St., Milwaukee, WI 53202	(414) 271-6755
Universal Forest Products	2801 E. Beltline, NE, Grand Rapids, MI 49505	(616) 364-6161
Universal Health Services	367 S. Gulph Rd., King of Prussia, PA 19406	(610) 768-3300
Unocal	1201 W. Fifth St., P.O. Box 7600, Los Angeles, CA 90017	(213) 977-7600
UNR Industries	332 S. Michigan Ave., Chicago, IL 60604	(312) 341-1234
UNUM	2211 Congress St., Portland, ME 04122	(207) 770-2211
The Upjohn Co.	7000 Portage Rd., Kalamazoo, MI 49001	(616) 323-4000
US Robotics	8100 N. McCormick Blvd., Skokie, IL 60076	(708) 982-5010
US West	7800 E. Orchard Rd., Englewood, CO 80111	(303) 793-6500
USAir Group	2345 Crystal Dr., Arlington, VA 22227	(703) 418-5306
USF&G	100 Light St., Baltimore, MD 21202	(410) 547-3000
USG	125 S. Franklin St., Chicago, IL 60606	(312) 606-4000
USLIFE	125 Maiden Ln., New York, NY 10038	(212) 709-6000
UST	100 W. Putnam Ave., Greenwich, CT 06830	(203) 661-1100
USX - Delhi Group	600 Grant St., Pittsburgh, PA 15219	(412) 433-1121
UtiliCorp United	911 Main, Kansas City, MO 64105	(816) 421-6600
V. F.	1047 N. Park Rd., Wyomissing, PA 19610	(610) 378-1151
Valassis Communications	36111 Schoolcraft Rd., Livonia, MI 48150	(313) 591-3000
Valero Energy	530 McCullough Ave., San Antonio, TX 78215	(210) 246-2000
Valhi	5430 LBJ Fwy., Suite 1700, Dallas, TX 75240	(214) 233-1700
Valley National Bancorp	1445 Valley Rd., Wayne, NJ 07470	(201) 305-8800
Valmont Industries	Valley, NE 68064	(402) 359-2201
The Valspar Corp.	1101 Third St. S., Minneapolis, MN 55415	(612) 332-7371
Value City Department Stores	3241 Westerville Rd., Columbus, OH 43224	(614) 471-4722
Value Health	22 Waterville Rd., Avon, CT 06001	(203) 678-3400
Varian Associates	3050 Hansen Way, Palo Alto, CA 94304	(415) 493-4000
Varity	672 Delaware Ave., Buffalo, NY 14209	(716) 888-8000
Varlen	55 E. Shuman Blvd., Suite 500, Naperville, IL 60566	(708) 420-0400
Vastar Resources	15375 Memorial Dr., Houston, TX 77079	(713) 584-6000
Vencor	400 W. Market St., Louisville, KY 40202	(502) 569-7300
Venture Stores	2001 E. Terra Ln., P.O. Box 110, O'Fallon, MO 63366	(314) 281-5500
VeriFone	3 Lagoon Dr., Suite 400, Redwood City, CA 90465	(415) 591-6500
Viacom	1515 Broadway, New York, NY 10036	(212) 258-6000
VICORP Restaurants	400 W. 48th Ave., P.O. Box 16601, Denver, CO 80216	(303) 296-2121
The Vigoro Corp.	225 N. Michigan Ave., Chicago, IL 60601	(312) 819-2020
Viking Office Products	13809 S. Figueroa St., Los Angeles, CA 90061	(213) 321-4493
Vishay Intertechnology	63 Lincoln Hwy., Malvern, PA 19355	(610) 644-1300
Vivra	400 Primrose, Suite 200, Burlingame, CA 94010	(415) 348-8200
VLSI Technology	1109 McKay Dr., San Jose, CA 95131	(408) 434-3000
Volt Information Sciences	1133 Sixth Ave., 19th Floor, New York, NY 10036	(212) 704-2400

The Business Almanac 2000 (cont'd)

Name	Address	Phone
The Vons Companies	618 Michillinda Ave., Arcadia, CA 91007	(818) 821-7000
Vulcan Materials	1 Metroplex Dr., Birmingham, AL 35209	(205) 877-3000
VWR	1310 Goshen Pkwy., West Chester, PA 19380	(610) 431-1700
W. H. Brady	727 W. Glendale Ave., Milwaukee, WI 53201	(414) 332-8100
W. R. Berkley	165 Mason St., P.O. Box 2518, Greenwich, CT 06836	(203) 629-2880
W. R. Grace & Co.	1 Town Ctr. Rd., Boca Raton, FL 33486	(407) 362-2000
W. W. Grainger	5500 W. Howard St., Skokie, IL 60077	(708) 982-9000
Waban	1 Mercer Rd., P.O. Box 9600, Natick, MA 01760	(508) 651-6500
Wabash National	1000 Sagamore Pkwy. S., Lafayette, IN 47905	(317) 448-1591
Wachovia	301 N. Main St., Winston-Salem, NC 27150	(910) 770-5000
The Wackenhut Corp.	1500 San Remo Ave., Coral Gables, FL 33146	(305) 666-5656
Wainoco Oil	1200 Smith St., Suite 2100, Houston, TX 77002	(713) 658-9900
Wal-Mart Stores	702 S.W. Eighth St., Bentonville, AR 72716	(501) 273-4000
Walbro	6242 Garfield St., Cass City, MI 48726	(517) 872-2131
Walgreen	200 Wilmot Rd., Deerfield, IL 60015	(708) 940-2500
Wallace Computer Services	4600 W. Roosevelt Rd., Hillside, IL 60162	(312) 626-2000
Wang Laboratories	1 Industrial Ave., Lowell, MA 01851	(508) 459-5000
The Warnaco Group	90 Park Ave., New York, NY 10016	(212) 661-1300
Warner-Lambert	201 Tabor Rd., Morris Plains, NJ 07950	(201) 540-2000
Washington Energy	815 Mercer St., Seattle, WA 98109	(206) 622-6767
Washington Federal	425 Pike St., Seattle, WA 98101	(206) 624-7930
Washington Gas Light	1100 H St., NW, Washington, DC 20080	(703) 750-4440
Washington Mutual	1201 Third Ave., Seattle, WA 98101	(206) 461-2000
Washington National	300 Tower Pkwy., Lincolnshire, IL 60069	(708) 793-3000
The Washington Post Co.	1150 15th St., NW, Washington, DC 20071	(202) 334-6000
The Washington Water Power Co.	1411 E. Mission Ave., Spokane, WA 99202	(509) 489-0500
Watkins-Johnson	3333 Hillview Ave., Palo Alto, CA 94304	(415) 493-4141
Watsco	2665 S. Bayshore Dr., Coconut Grove, FL 33133	(305) 858-0828
Watts Industries	815 Chestnut St., North Andover, MA 01845	(508) 688-1811
Wausau Paper Mills	1 Clark's Island, Wausau, WI 54402	(715) 845-5266
WCI Steel	1040 Pine Ave., SE, Warren, OH 44483	(216) 841-8000
Weathersford	1360 Post Oak Blvd., Suite 1000, Houston, TX 77056	(713) 439-9400
Weirton Steel	400 Three Springs Dr., Weirton, WV 26062	(304) 797-2000
Weis Markets	1000 S. Second St., Sunbury, PA 17801	(717) 286-4571
Wellman	1040 Broad St., Suite 302, Shrewsbury, NJ 07702	(908) 542-7300
WellPoint Health Networks	21555 Oxnard St., Woodland Hills, CA 91367	(818) 703-4000
Wells Fargo & Co.	420 Montgomery St., San Francisco, CA 94104	(415) 477-1000
Wendy's	4288 W. Dublin-Granville Rd., Dublin, OH 43017	(614) 764-3100
Werner Enterprises	Interstate 80 & Hwy. 50, Omaha, NE 68137	(402) 895-6640
West	101 Gordon Ave., Lionville, PA 19341	(610) 594-2900
West One Bancorp	101 S. Capitol Blvd., Boise, ID 83702	(208) 383-7000
Western Atlas	360 N. Crescent Dr., Beverly Hills, CA 90210	(310) 888-2500
Western Beef	47-05 Metropolitan Ave., Ridgewood, NY 11385	(718) 821-0011
The Western Co. of North America	515 Post Oak Blvd., Suite 1200, Houston, TX 77027	(713) 629-2600
Western Digital	8105 Irvine Ctr. Dr., Irvine, CA 92718	(714) 932-5000
Western Gas Resources	12200 N. Pecos St., Denver, CO 80234	(303) 452-5603
Western National	5555 San Felipe Rd., Houston, TX 77056	(713) 888-7800
Western Publishing Group	444 Madison Ave., New York, NY 10022	(212) 688-4500
Western Resources	818 Kansas Ave., Topeka, KS 66612	(913) 575-6300
Western Waste Industries	21061 S. Western Ave., Torrance, CA 90510	(310) 328-0900

The Business Almanac 2000 (cont'd)

Name	Address	Phone
Westinghouse Electric	11 Stanwix St., Pittsburgh, PA 15222	(412) 244-2000
Westmoreland Coal	200 S. Broad St., Philadelphia, PA 19102	(215) 545-2500
WestPoint Stevens	400 W. Tenth St., West Point, GA 31833	(706) 645-4000
Westvaco	299 Park Ave., New York, NY 10171	(212) 688-5000
Weyerhaeuser	33663 Weyerhaeuser Way S., Federal Way, WA 98477	(206) 924-2345
Wheelabrator Technologies	Liberty Ln., Hampton, NH 03842	(603) 929-3000
Whirlpool	2000 M-63, Benton Harbor, MI 49022	(616) 923-5000
Whitman	3501 Algonquin Rd., Rolling Meadows, IL 60008	(708) 818-5000
Whole Foods Market	1705 Capital of Texas Hwy., Austin, TX 78746	(512) 328-7541
WHX	110 E. 59th St., New York, NY 10022	(212) 355-5200
Wickes Lumber	706 N. Deer Path Dr., Vernon Hills, IL 60061	(708) 367-3400
WICOR	626 E. Wisconsin Ave., Milwaukee, WI 53201	(414) 291-7026
Willamette Industries	1300 S.W. Fifth Ave., Suite 3800, Portland, OR 97201	(503) 227-5581
The Williams Companies	1 Willliams Ctr., Tulsa, OK 74172	(918) 588-2000
Williams-Sonoma	100 N. Point St., San Francisco, CA 94133	(415) 421-7900
Wilmington Trust	1100 N. Market St., Wilmington, DE 19890	(302) 651-1000
Winn-Dixie Stores	5050 Edgewood Court, Jacksonville, FL 32254	(904) 783-5000
Winnebago Industries	P.O. Box 152, Forest City, IA 50436	(515) 582-3535
WinsLoew Furniture	2665 S. Bayshore Dr., Suite 800, Miami, FL 33133	(305) 858-2200
Wisconsin Electric	333 W. Everett St., Milwaukee, WI 53203	(414) 221-2345
Witco	1 American Ln., Greenwich, CT 06831	(203) 552-2000
WLR Foods	P.O. Box 7000, Broadway, VA 22815	(703) 896-7001
Wm. Wrigley Jr.	410 N. Michigan Ave., Chicago, IL 60611	(312) 644-2121
WMS Industries	3401 N. California Ave., Chicago, IL 60618	(312) 961-1000
WMX Technologies	3003 Butterfield Rd., Oak Brook, IL 60521	(708) 572-8800
Wolohan Lumber	1740 Midland Rd., Saginaw, MI 48603	(517) 793-4532
Wolverine Tube	2100 Market St., Decatur, AL 35601	(205) 353-1310
Wolverine World Wide	9341 Courtland Dr., Rockford, MI 49351	(616) 866-5500
Woolworth	233 Broadway, New York, NY 10279	(212) 553-2000
Worthington Industries	1205 Dearborn Dr., Columbus, OH 43085	(614) 438-3210
WPL Holdings	222 W. Washington Ave., Madison, WI 53703	(608) 252-3311
WPS Resources	700 N. Adams St., P.O. Box 19001, Green Bay, WI 54307	(414) 433-1445
WTD Industries	10260 S.W. Greenburg Rd., Portland, OR 97223	(503) 246-3440
Wyle Electronics	15370 Barranca Pkwy., Irvine, CA 92718	(714) 753-9953
Wyman-Gordon	244 Worcester St., P.O. Box 8001, Grafton, MA 01536	(508) 839-4441
Wynn's	500 N. State College Blvd., Orange, CA 92668	(714) 938-3700
Xerox	800 Long Ridge Rd., Stamford, CT 06904	(203) 968-3000
Xilinx	2100 Logic Dr., San Jose, CA 95124	(408) 559-7778
XTRA	60 State St., Boston, MA 02109	(617) 367-5000
Yankee Energy System	599 Research Pkwy., Meridan, CT 06450	(203) 639-4000
Yellow	10777 Barkley Ave., Overland Park, KS 66207	(913) 967-4300
York	631 S. Richland Ave., York, PA 17403	(717) 771-7890
Younkers	Seventh and Walnut Sts., Des Moines, IA 50397	(515) 244-1112
Zale	901 W. Walnut Hill Ln., Irving, TX 75038	(214) 580-4000
Zeigler Coal Holding	50 Jerome Ln., Fairview Heights, IL 62208	(618) 394-2400
Zenith Electronics	1000 Milwaukee Ave., Glenview, IL 60025	(708) 391-7000
Zenith National Insurance	21255 Califa St., Woodland Hills, CA 91367	(818) 713-1000
ZEOS	1301 Industrial Blvd., Minneapolis, MN 55413	(612) 623-9614
Zions Bancorporation	1380 Kennecott Bldg., Salt Lake City, UT 84133	(801) 524-4787
Zurn Industries	1 Zurn Pl., Erie, PA 16505	(814) 452-2111

INDEX

Sidebar Navigation

Business Law & Government

Communications

Corporate Administration

Finance

Human Resources

International

Manufacturing

Marketing

Office Management

Personal Computing

Maps

Reference

Business Law & Government

Pages 1 to 52

Includes:
Contracts
Intellectual Property
Working with the SBA
Federal Information Center
Finding a Lawyer
Regulatory Agencies
Alternate Dispute Resolution
Political Action Committees
OSHA
Members of Congress
U.S. Lawyers with Foreign Offices

Communications

Pages 53 to 82

Includes:
Postal Abbreviations
Shipping
UPS
FEDEX
USPS
Postal Answer Line
World Time Chart
International Dialing
Phone Cards on Other Systems
Time Zones
Area Codes

Corporate Administration

Pages 83 to 154

Includes:
Supporters of the Arts & Chari
Corporate Social Responsibilit
Demographics
Annual Reports
The Fortune 500
The Inc. 500
The Forbes 400
Business Plan Outline
Construction Starts
Mortgage Tables
BOMA Standards
Lease Negotiation Tips

Manufacturing

Pages 415 to 464

Includes:
Industrial Buying Guides
Sales Agencies
The Federal Laboratory Consortium
Research & Development
EPA Regional Offices
Recycling
New Techniques
Environmental Issues
Productivity
Warehousing
Design Awards
Quality Standards

Marketing

Pages 465 to 526

Includes:
Ad Agencies
Magazines
The Top Brands
College Newspaper Advertising
Infomercials
Product Placement Firms
Public Relations
Direct Marketing
Premium and Novelty Sources
The Sales Hall of Fame
Mailing Lists
Franchising
Trade Shows

The Almanac is divided into twelve chapters, each focusing on a different area of business. The first page of each chapter lists the topics covered. There is also an index at the end of the book.